Morley Library
184 Phelps Street
Painesville, OH 44077
(440) 352-3383
www.morleylibrary.org

WORLDMARK
ENCYCLOPEDIA
of Religious Practices

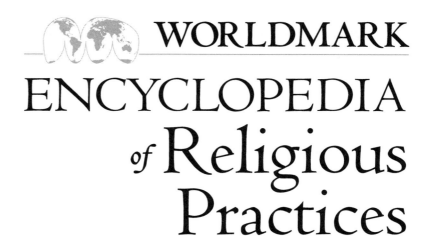

WORLDMARK
ENCYCLOPEDIA
of Religious
Practices

Volume 2
COUNTRIES
A–L

Thomas Riggs, Editor

Detroit • New York • San Francisco • San Diego • New Haven, Conn. • Waterville, Maine • London • Munich

Worldmark Encyclopedia of Religious Practices, Volume 2

Thomas Riggs

Product Managers
Carol DeKane Nagel, Bonnie Hawkwood

Project Editors
Michael L. LaBlanc, Thomas Carson, Jason M. Everett, Bernard Grunow

Editorial
Mary Rose Bonk, Andrew Clapps, Sara Constantakis, Angela Doolin, Anne Marie Hacht, Gillian Leonard, Stephanie Macomber, Ellen McGeagh, Ira Mark Milne, Rebecca Parks, Mark E. Rzeszutek, Jennifer York Stock.

Rights Acqusition and Management
Peg Ashlevitz, Jacqueline Key, Susan J. Rudolph

Manufacturing
Wendy Blurton

Imaging and Multimedia
Lezlie Light, Dan Newell, Christine O'Bryan

Product Design
Kate Scheible

LIBRARY OF CONGRESS CATALOGING-IN-PUBLICATION DATA

Worldmark encyclopedia of religious practices / Thomas Riggs, editor in chief.
   p. cm.
     Includes bibliographical refrences and index.
     ISBN 0-7876-6611-4 (set hardcover : alk. paper)—
     ISBN 0-7876-6612-2 (vol 1 : alk paper)—;
     ISBN 0-7876-6613-0 (vol 2 : alk. paper)—;
     ISBN 0-7876-6614-9 (vol 3 : alk. paper)
     1. Religions. I. Riggs, Thomas, 1963-

BL80.3.W67 2006
200.9—dc22

2005027456

This title is also available as an e-book.
ISBN 0-7876-9390-1

Contact your Thomson Gale representative for ordering information.

Printed in the United States of America
10 9 8 7 6 5 4 3 2 1

Contents

CONTENTS

VOLUME 3: COUNTRY ENTRIES
M–Z

CONTENTS

Editor's Preface

In 2001 Thomson Gale had a simple but ambitious goal: to produce an encyclopedia outlining the contemporary religious practices of every country in the world—from the very largest, such as China, India, Brazil, and Russia, to the smallest, such as Tuvalu, Andorra, and Antigua and Barbuda. Because this information has not been readily available in books or other sources in libraries, as well as on the Internet, the project required years of planning and hard work by a large group of people: our distinguished board of 10 advisers, the 245 scholars and other subject specialists commissioned to write essays or to review the text of their colleagues, and the editorial staff of Thomson Gale. The result was this publication, the *Worldmark Encyclopedia of Religious Practices.* It joins an already existing series of Worldmark encyclopedias, including the *Worldmark Encyclopedia of the Nations* and the *Worldmark Encyclopedia of Cultures and Daily Life.*

Organization

The *Worldmark Encyclopedia of Religious Practices* has three volumes. Volume 1 includes essays on the history, beliefs, and contemporary practices of 13 major faith groups—African Traditional Religions, Bahá'í, Buddhism, Christianity, Confucianism, Hinduism, Islam, Jainism, Judaism, Shinto, Sikhism, Taoism, and Zoroastrianism—and 28 of their subgroups, such as Anglicanism, Reform Judaism, Mahayana Buddhism, and Vaishnavism. These essay topics, selected by our advisory board, represent not only the world's largest religious groups but also smaller faiths that have had significant historical, cultural, or theological impact. Because of space limitations, we could not include essays on all groups worthy of discussion. Each essay in volume 1 is organized with the same subject headings—for example, "Moral Code of Conduct" and "Sacred Symbols"—allowing easy comparison of a topic from one religion or subgroup to another. Printed at the top

of each essay in volume 1 is a population map displaying the group's distribution throughout the world.

By discussing broadly various religions and subgroups, volume 1 provides the background or context for more fully understanding the information in volumes 2 and 3. These subsequent volumes together contain 193 essays, each focusing on the contemporary religious practices of a particular country. Organizing the topic of religious practices by country assumes that geographical and, in particular, political boundaries—because in varying degrees they mark off areas of unique history, culture, and influence—encourage distinctive ways in which a religion is practiced, despite shared beliefs held by all members of a religion.

The essays in volumes 2 and 3 follow a standard format: statistical information, an overview of the country, one or more sections on major religions, a discussion of other religions, and a bibliography. The statistical information includes the country's total population and a breakdown by percentage of the major religious groups. The "Country Overview" section contains an "Introduction," providing a geographical or historical summary of the country needed to understand religious activities in the area, and a subsection on "Religious Tolerance," discussing such topics as freedom of worship, religious discrimination, ecumenical movements, and the relationship between church and state.

Every country essay then proceeds with a major religion section on each religion whose followers make up 25 percent or more of the country's population. In some countries just one religion, such as Christianity, Islam, or Buddhism, has at least this percentage of followers, but in other countries two or three religions each have more than 25 percent, thus resulting in the essay including two or three major religion sections. Exceptions to the rule were made for a small number of essays, most notably for China, where Buddhism, at 8 percent of the population, and Christianity, at 6.5 percent, were given their own sections. China's population, however, is immense, and Buddhism's 8 percent, for example, represents 103 million people, more than the entire population of most countries. In some essays the major religion section is on a religious subgroup; this occurs when a subgroup, such as Roman Catholicism, dominates the country or when the country, such as Sweden, has had a historically important state church.

Each major religion section is broken down into the following 18 subsections, which describe the religion's distinctive qualities in that country. "Date of origin," for example, refers to the year not when the religion was founded but when it was introduced into the country. "Major Theologians and Authors" discusses significant religious writers from the country. "Mode of Dress" details any clothing or styles distinctive to adherents in the country. Because each major religion section is divided into the same 18 subject headings, religions can be easily compared from one country to another.

1. Date of Origin
2. Number of Followers
3. History
4. Early and Modern Leaders
5. Major Theologians and Authors
6. Houses of Worship and Holy Places
7. What is Sacred?
8. Holidays and Festivals
9. Mode of Dress
10. Dietary Practices
11. Rituals (outlining such practices as worship services, prayer, and pilgrimages)
12. Rites of Passage
13. Membership (discussing ways of encouraging new members)
14. Social Justice (in relation to poverty, education, and human rights)
15. Social Aspects (focusing on marriage and family)
16. Political Impact
17. Controversial Issues
18. Cultural Impact (in the arts, such as literature, painting, music, dance, and architecture)

Each country essay ends with a summary of other religions—those that make up less than 25 percent of the population—and a bibliography, which recommends other books and articles for further reading.

Acknowledgments

I would like to express my appreciation to the encyclopedia's editorial staff. Among those in-house at Thomson Gale are Bonnie Whitaker, who helped identify the need for the book and develop its main outline; Bernard Grunow, who calmly guided the early in-house steps; Thomas Carson, whose wisdom and background in religious studies kept the encyclopedia on the right path; Rita Runchock, whose editorial judgment proved essential at various stages of the project; Carol Nagel, who in the final months provided editorial focus, in the process finding solutions to lingering problems; and Michael LaBlanc, whose good humor, common sense, and fine editorial skills helped bring the project to a needed and gentle ending.

I am also grateful to Stephen Meyer, the associate editor, who was involved from the very beginning of the project, helping develop the book's editorial plan, contacting scholars to write essays and working with them on their revisions, and involving himself in other tasks too numerous to list; Mariko Fujinaka, an assistant editor, whose day-to-day organizational skills made all our lives easier; Erin Brown, our other assistant editor, who was involved in photo selection, contacting and corresponding with peer reviewers, and many other areas; Joyce Meyer, who translated a number of essays from French into English; Robert Rauch, the senior line editor, who helped create the editing guidelines and oversee the other line editors; and the line editors themselves—Lee Esbenshade, Laura Gabler, Natalie Goldstein, Anne Healey, Elizabeth Henry, and Janet Moredock—who were asked to ensure that the text, even when containing challenging or esoteric information, be accessible to a wide range of readers.

Finally, I would like to thank the advisers and contributors. Much of the information in the essays cannot be readily found in any other source, and without the involvement of our advisers and contributors, this encyclopedia, of course, could not have been produced.

Thomas J. Riggs

Comments

Although great effort has gone into this work, we would appreciate any suggestions for future editions of the *Worldmark Encyclopedia of Religious Practices.* Please send comments to the following address:

Editor
Worldmark Encyclopedia of Religious Practices
Thomson Gale
27500 Drake Road
Farmington Hills, Michigan 48331

Introduction

While religion is universal throughout human culture, its variations are so extensive that authorities do not always agree on a definition. Scholars have identified more than 50 characteristics of religion, from belief in gods or God to sophisticated ideas about a philosophical worldview. Some authorities regard religion as a particular kind of human experience, as a special way of living together, or as offering answers to certain vexing questions, such as why there is something rather than nothing or whether there is a larger purpose for evil. Religion is sometimes held to be bound up with what a particular group chooses as sacred, whether that be an object (totem), a being (God), a text (scripture), or a fundamental law of nature. Some believers hold that religion is beyond comprehension by the human mind, with study of it reserved for specially gifted people, a view that makes religion an esoteric, or secret, activity. On the other hand, many languages have no specific word to identify the human sensibility we call "religion." In these cases, acts of piety are simply considered natural or ordinary, so that there is no need to identify a distinctive experience.

In addition, how are innovations in religion under the pressures of modern life to be understood? For example, is the cooking and eating of a wild boar by a contemporary urban Melanesian a religious rite, even if it is not accompanied by the ceremony and ideology that traditionally attended such an act? Is a pious attitude sufficient for the act to be called religious? Further, if ideas are modern, are they less religious than views established long ago? What, for example, is to be made of the belief held by some Muslims that the best community existed at the time of the Prophet Muhammad, that the Islamic community today is somehow "less Muslim" than it was then? Or how is one to understand ancient gods? Osiris, for example, was once widely worshipped in Egypt but has few, if any, followers today. Does this mean that the most powerful beings humans once identified with and worshipped can "die"? And is a rule dating from biblical times still applicable today, or can "timeless" revelations be modified in the light of new discoveries? Despite the fact that there seem to be thousands of new religions, is it possible to say that a new religion is "better" than an old one? These and other issues surrounding contemporary religion are staggering in their complexity.

In spite of the difficulties in defining religion, it is essential to understand the phenomenon, for it touches almost every facet of life, from themes in popular culture, to perceptions of well-being, to motivations for global terrorism. Even those who reject religion, who blame it for human problems, or who regard it as a relic of the past should understand contemporary religion. It is also important that people understand the history of religion, including its power and its spread. Consider Christianity, for example, which began as an obscure movement in a tiny place outside Jerusalem some 2,000 years ago but which spread to Byzantium and Rome, centers of the then-known world, where it was adopted as the state religion. It later spread throughout Europe and followed European movement into the New World, and it has since spread to virtually every part of the earth. In the late twentieth century, reform movements from countries outside its traditional home, as with the doctrines of the Korean evangelist Sun Myung Moon, began to return to the heartland of Christianity with a revitalized vision. Thus, there are Christians from the so-called Third World who are now challenging Western nations to become "religious" once again. Such dynamism cannot be ignored by those who wish to understand the forces that motivate societies today.

The *Worldmark Encyclopedia of Religious Practices* focuses on contemporary expressions of world religion. It accepts the fact that there are international communities of faith, along with numerous branches within them, and that these define the world of religion today.

Volume 1 contains articles on the following 13 major religious groups: African indigenous beliefs, the Bahá'í faith, Buddhism, Christianity, Confucianism, Hinduism, Islam, Jainism, Judaism, Shinto, Sikhism, Taoism, and Zoroastrianism. In addition, there are separate articles on a number of major branches within these groups—for example, in Buddhism, on the Mahayana, Theravada, and Tibetan traditions.

This organization may seem misleading, for it does not indicate that religious ideas interact with one another or that similar perceptions are found in several religions. In addition, there is far more variety within each of these religions and subgroups than this approach suggests. Such matters are dealt with in Volumes 2 and 3 of the encyclopedia, where the diversity of religious practices in the various countries of the world is discussed. Still, the organization of Volume 1 is useful in showing that the subject is not limitless. It is possible to sketch the main dimensions of religious practice according to the traditions with which believers identify, an approach that scholarship has come to accept.

Common Elements in Religious Practice

Given the religious diversity found throughout the world, how can one hope to gain adequate knowledge of the subject? Are there basic ways of approaching the study of religion? It is often said that religion insists on a certain kind of reality, something that is larger than the individual or the immediate community. Such a reality is usually defined as a force or person of greater "power," something beyond human creation. What results from human interaction with this power may be called "religious." It may not be possible to prove such a reality, or to "know" it, conclusively. Nonbelievers, for example, do not accept its existence or share in the relationship. What is possible, however, is to document how people act when they are acting religiously. Thus, what appears to be crucial in understanding religion is practice—that is, activity related to the experience of a greater power.

Consider prayer, for example. Although there are considerable variations in how people pray, normally it is possible to tell the difference between believers at prayer and believers acting in an "ordinary" way. In prayer there are certain ways of moving, stances adopted, demeanors assumed, and words uttered—all of which appear to indicate a direct relationship between the believer and the greater power. Prayer brings believ-

ers into communication with the transforming agent, or higher power, that is the basis of their religion and their world.

Every religion has a system that establishes how that religion is experienced (as, for example, in prayer), giving a structure to its activities and providing an intellectual basis for the believer's perception of reality. Students of religion have an number of terms for such systems, including "philosophy," "theology," "beliefs," "values," and "doctrines." In some religions these systems are spelled out in an elaborate manner, as, for example, in the doctrine of the Trinity (Father, Son, and Holy Spirit) in Christianity. They may be part of a larger system of teaching and learning, as with Dianetics in the Church of Scientology. In some religions, however, there is less emphasis on theory than on acts, with reference made to basic beliefs only when queries are raised or when disagreements arise. This can be seen, for example, among Japanese shamans who perform healing rituals but who seldom talk about the spirit world they are encountering.

It is important to note that many religious practices arose from ancient rituals related to major life passages—for example, rites for girls and boys when they reach puberty. Some practices, such as those surrounding birth, marriage, and death, are as old as humankind. For many believers there is something reassuring about religion's connection with the stages and cycles of life, and people may actively participate in such rites even when they are not sure about the meaning of what they are doing.

Although every religion has distinctive practices, several common features are discussed here.

RITUALS Throughout life, rituals are used to express meaning. There are formal words used when greeting someone of an official rank, for example; gifts for people on special occasions; and the shaking of a hand when it is offered. It is possible for a person to ignore these practices, but there may be repercussions in doing so. By providing a grounding for life, rituals, rites, and ceremonies take on critical importance.

One of the most important ways of expressing religious feeling is through rituals. Believers, for example, use rituals to interact with their conception of the source of life. The indigenous people of the Plains tradition in North America smoke a pipe as a means of sending their prayers to the Spirit World, and Tibetan Buddhists chant in meditation to encounter the

Thunderbolt reality that lies beyond ordinary perception. In conveying their concerns and feelings to their sacred entities, believers do not see themselves as "using" rituals to manipulate the situation. Rather, they believe that such acts are a way of communicating with the object of their religious sensibilities.

For those who hold that communication with the gods or God is the purpose of religion, worship is a basic ritual, and in most religions worship is demanded of the faithful. Even in Buddhism, where the basis of religion is not worship, loving adoration of the Buddha is ordinarily a crucial part of the believer's rituals. In addition, most religions have developed rites that chart the growth of a person from birth to death and beyond, thus providing activities called rites of passage. These rites move a person through various levels of privilege and responsibilities. In some religions the performance of rites and ceremonies is considered so critical that they can be carried out only by specially endowed people, usually called priests, who operate as mediators between divine power and the individual believer.

The practices and rituals of any religion are directly affected by its conception of the spiritual world, that is, by its system of beliefs. When theism (belief in God) is a central tenant, the resulting religious practices in one way or another invoke the deity in its rituals. Further, how people conceive of the gods or God directly shapes practices. Christians speak of God's love as revealed through Jesus Christ and hold that God offers spiritual fulfillment and personal redemption through the doctrines reflected in the Trinity. As a result, Christians have developed rituals that embrace this belief, such as the commemorations and celebrations of Easter or the rituals of baptism. Jews, on the other hand, stress the worship of "the God of our Fathers, the God of Abraham, Isaac and Jacob," emphasizing the importance of a spiritual lineage with God. For Jews this lineage is demonstrated through the reading of the laws of God as set forth in the Hebrew Scriptures. By contrast, Hinduism has embraced many names for the diversity of spiritual reality, and Hindus observe a great number of rituals to express this exuberance of deities. On the other hand, those religions that do not involve belief in gods, including those of certain indigenous peoples, have quite different rituals. For example, in the past, Inuit shamans and medicine people maintained a vigorous religious life that involved spirits of the "other" world. They performed ceremonies honoring and submitting to these spirits, although they did not "worship" them in the sense commonly understood in Western religious rituals.

CELEBRATIONS AND OBSERVANCES Festive occasions bring people together and foster a sense of belonging, reflecting the deep-seated need within humans to move beyond the everyday. People celebrate birthdays, couples toast each other on a wedding anniversary, and victories on battlefields give rise to ceremonies of remembrance and introspection. Likewise, religions pause throughout the year to celebrate those events that make them unique, the result being an array of religious holidays and festivities. From the wandering Hindu sannyasi (mendicant), whose presence is regarded as beneficial, to the reaction of an infant upon first seeing Santa Claus, celebrations bond people to their religious families.

Many religions also celebrate their founding. Such celebrations look to a defining time in the past and rejoice at its continuing influence. For believers such a celebration brings with it a sense of liberation and freedom. Sometimes such observances, along with their accompanying feasts and festivals, are criticized for the waywardness they encourage or for their expense on the public purse. Critics, for example, often single out Christmas decorations and gift giving as reflections of such extravagance. Despite this, they are treasured by people for the benefits they bestow.

SCRIPTURE Authoritative religious teachings are those sources of inspiration that embody a tradition's wisdom. They take on a hallowed character that puts them beyond normal human creativity. For believers such teachings are not exhausted through reading, for they can become the source of theology, meditation, or even healing, to say nothing of their use to provoke division and militancy. The teachings also reveal the standards by which the believer is to live. In most religions there is a written document, or scripture, that conveys this material. The oldest is thought to be the Rig Veda, which includes materials that may date from before the beginning of writing—that is, to around 4000 B.C.E. Scripture is sometimes held to be timeless, as, for example, with the Koran—thewords were delivered by the Prophet Muhammad but the message is believed to date to the very establishment of humans upon the earth.

Because writing is relatively recent in human history, religion has not always relied on a written text. Even some literate peoples have never assigned true authority to written forms, preferring instead the immediacy of the oral version. Devout Muslims, for example, pointing to the oral origins of the Koran, regard the oral version of "pure Arabic" as the only authoritative version. Others, like the Quakers, hoping to ward off dogma and worrying that a text might become frozen into literalism, have refused to accept anything but a flexible interpretation. Further, in certain religious contexts, such as ritual activity, there remains a preference for oral versions among some groups—for example, Buddhists—even though they have written texts. In place of a written canon some religions have sacred stories that are passed on orally from one authoritative speaker to another. The stories may take on the character of scripture, with people referring to them as the basis for their actions. In such traditions the authorities have the freedom of recasting the stories according to the audience and the spiritual need of the moment.

One of the most important uses of scripture is to provide the language of religious rites, with believers using its passages as a means of communicating with the living object of their faith. In this case the text becomes a vehicle of communication at another, perhaps deeper spiritual level than when it is simply used to affirm a specific doctrine. At this level scripture fosters a state of spiritual being and unites those focused upon it in ways that few other writings can. This is why it is difficult to disassociate scripture from the ritual life and personal piety of the group. The use of a scriptural text in scholarship outside the religious tradition is sometimes said to distort its original purpose, provoking criticism from believers that outsiders are trying to interpret what are essentially sacred sources.

Not all scriptures are conceived of as written by God. The Analects of Confucius, for example, are regarded as inspired writings that give details on a properly ordered life, but they are held up not as the word of God but rather as spiritually superior insights from a master. In addition, many practitioners of New Age beliefs argue that true religion is syncretic or eclectic, that people may pick and choose which scriptures or parts thereof are most meaningful and then make up their own authoritative text. Such individualism seems to violate the traditional sense of a sacred text as the focus of group loyalty. Thus, not only can scripture undergo transformation within the life of a tradition itself but its traditional meaning has been challenged in the contemporary world.

THEOLOGY In many religions it is particularly important to describe the intellectual basis of the faith. Throughout history great minds have wrestled with the problems of explaining the reality behind one or another religion, their efforts producing an interpretation of God and related terminology that is called "theology." As with activities like prayer or sacrifice, the theologies of the various religions show considerable diversity, and despite the attempt to use words and phrases that can be understood by ordinary people, the subject is sometimes difficult. Further, in some religions certain ideas are not discussed in a systematic way, even though they involve important doctrines of the tradition. Ideas surrounding death and life after death are examples.

Theology has been of particular importance in Western religions, especially in Christianity. In the Christian tradition theology is a highly organized profession, with the various churches exercising vigorous control over the ideas perpetrated in their names. At least in Western culture, theology has a long history separate from both philosophy and science, and it often involves intellectual activity at a sophisticated level. When theology addresses doctrine, it attempts to explain the principal ideas of a religion in a way that both adherents and interested observers can understand. It also develops ways of dealing with puzzles that are created by its own system of thought. For example, in Judaism, Christianity, and Islam, which as monotheistic religions embrace the doctrine of God as all-powerful and all-good, the existence of evil in the world is a problem. For the ordinary believer some of these complications may be beyond solution, and believers sometimes simply embrace such difficulties as part of the weakness of the human mind in trying to comprehend what is beyond the everyday.

ETHICS Every religion serves as the foundation for a system of ethics, or standards of moral behavior. For some religions adherence to such standards is regarded as the very basis of the believer's relationship with God, as, for example, with the Torah, or teachings, in Judaism. For others ethics promotes well-being and a healthy society. In the Confucian tradition, for example, devotees believe that the successful person is one who is neighborly and giving. In effect, that person's key moral goal in life is to express *ren* (or *jen*). Such a person is held to be dedicated to human relationships and consequently subjects all personal acts to the rule of moral conduct. Acting out that value in life is religion. Confucius thus summed up the standard for human relationships in the

Analects as "Never do to others what you would not like them to do to you," which is strikingly similar to the biblical adage "Do unto others as you would have others do into you" (Matt. 7:12). Islam also asserts that God has established the true way and that living according to the Shari'ah, or religious law, is the most basic responsibility of the Muslim.

Most religions share the concern that their moral values be expressed concretely in people's lives. There is, for example, an almost universal interest among religions in helping the poor and in providing education for children. Religion affirms that there are certain principles that should be enshrined in society, since the values they represent are the foundation of a beneficial community life. It is for this reason that religions advocate such qualities as honesty and truthfulness and oppose greed and materialism. Likewise, everywhere religion thrives there is concern for the uniqueness and sanctity of human life. Agreements on matters such as these suggest deeper patterns that transcend religious boundaries.

Ethical questions also arise in the relationship between religion and science. There was a time when science, seen as objective and free of "beliefs," was held to be a type of knowledge unfettered by religious convictions. Few people would agree with this view now, however, for modern science itself has come to be seen as the result of particular cultural assumptions. Science has developed in certain ways because of complex influences from the culture in which it has grown, with one of these influences being religion. The freedom to pursue research regardless of the consequences, for example, reflects an aggressive individualism that could not have developed without belief in the individual's responsibility for knowledge, a view derived from religion.

Scientists are themselves human, of course, and they respond to various religious sensibilities. Because science is a human activity, scientists are not "outside" culture or totally "objective," especially when they deal with human problems. Thus, science sometimes comes into conflict with a deeper sense of what is right. Issues like human cloning, for example, are debated by all people, and scientists must sometimes arbitrate between their religious feelings and values and what is scientifically possible. Further, questions have been raised about the legitimacy of any science that operates without social and cultural oversight—that is, outside a solidly-based ethics.

It has been argued that, since different religions promote different standards of moral behavior, ethics should not be grounded in religious belief. Further, some people have pointed to new problems, such as the international scourge of HIV/AIDS, faced by humans today as evidence that religion cannot handle modern ethical problems. Others have claimed that some of the problems of the modern world are legacies of religion itself.

Such critics usually advocate a system of secular ethics. Religious believers, however, argue that in a secular system people are not schooled in and do not internalize the age-old patterns that have undergirded human civilization. Believers maintain, for example, that secular ethics seems not to provide an educational grounding in matters of respect and dutifulness, which have traditionally been provided by religion as the foundation for relationships among people. Moreover, believers point out that charges of inadequacy against religious ethics are unfair, since the world is littered with failed attempts to shape a secular moral sensibility. The rise and fall of Marxism is a notable example. The history of such attempts gives little comfort to those making the secular argument, and the result has been a renewed attempt to reaffirm religious value as a foundation of modern life.

Thus, although the modern world poses many difficulties for believers in every culture, religious groups maintain that their perspective is essential for civilization. Most believers argue that religious tradition addresses issues in a more positive way than does any other approach. Using the tools of promotion and advertising, religions have entered into competition with other forces as they challenge individuals and societies to live according to a better plan. Seen from this perspective, religion has taken on a business hue, with the various traditions competing for followers in the marketplace of contemporary life.

OBSERVANCE AND EXPLANATION OF DEATH Most religions deal with death by providing rituals of condolence and assurances that life goes on, even if in a different way and on another level. Some religions claim to hold keys to eternal life as part of their mandate, while others claim to provide the means by which a person can face the next phase of life. Even those religions that do not maintain a belief in life after death provide means for a sense of closure and acceptance at the ending of life.

Most cultures accept the idea that death falls within the compass of religion. As in other matters, there is a wide variety of approaches. Indigenous peoples anticipate living on in an ancestral world, sometimes characterized by festivities that provide endless moments of delight before some part of a person once again takes on bodily form in this world. Hindus believe in a form of transmigration: with the death of the body in this world a movement into a transitory state from which a person, depending on his or her karma, ultimately exits in another form. Buddhists hope to achieve nirvana, a state that is not material. Western religions, on the other hand, are based on a strong sense of linear time, and although they hold that death is the end of earthly life, they believe that at least a spiritual element lives on. Such religions hold that following death there occur various events, including judgment, purification, and, ultimately for believers, a glorious life in a paradise, or heaven.

Geographic Variations in Religious Practice

In the contemporary world there is great diversity within religious groups, and religious practices often vary by country or region. Consider meditation, for example. As practiced across India in early Hinduism, meditation seems to have been associated with mendicants, those who left their families and homes, took vows, and became wandering holy men. When the practice was adopted by Buddhism, which spread from India to China, it seems initially to have been restricted to monks. In Zen Buddhism, which took root in Japan, meditation eventually took on much broader forms, for the possibility of instant awareness had the effect of weakening the commitment to a monastic life and made the benefits of meditation available to the lay population.

Volumes 2 and 3 of this encyclopedia, containing essays on the contemporary religious practices of individual countries, reveal that religions have frequently been influenced by and vary according to political and geographical boundaries. For example, people do not celebrate Christmas in the same way in Sweden, Uganda, and China. This "mixture" of forms is, however, a contentious issue, for postcolonial critics argue that contemporary political boundaries sometimes reflect the historical presence of imperialism, not the "natural" configuration of an ethnic or religious group. It is also true that religion seldom is restrained by national borders, as is seen by the spread of fundamentalism. Nonetheless, whatever its limitations, the view that political bound-

aries play a critical role in shaping religious life is commonly accepted, even as it makes analysis more difficult.

Trends in Contemporary Religion

One important trend in the contemporary world is the growth of local religious groups made up of small but highly engaged memberships. These groups, whose practices are especially diverse, claim to redefine traditional views, and they sometimes challenge tradition over the "proper" way to practice religion. The numbers of such groups are staggering, with perhaps thousands having sprung up throughout the world in the past quarter century alone.

Contemporary religion is also characterized by its close relation to politics. As religion has come to play an increasing role in political life, nearly every major government in the world now faces pressure from groups that form political movements clothed in religious mantles and that raise ethical questions over public policy. Further, the rise of radical religious groups like al-Qaeda or the Tamil Tigers of Sri Lanka has sometimes made religion a prime force in political events. All of this demonstrates that religion has not retreated, even in the face of the widespread embrace of secularism by governments. Even in countries that might be conceived as firmly advanced in secularism, such as France, the official banning of a religious symbol like the *hijab* can raise a storm of protest, signaling that religious sensitivities are far from quiescent. Indeed, many governments in Muslim countries have quietly abandoned their secular stance, with one eye toward the rising tide of religious revivalism.

Obviously not even Western democratic governments are free from religious influence. This is a striking change compared with, say, Europe during the sixteenth-century Protestant Reformation, when whole countries and peoples became Protestant or Roman Catholic at the conversion of a ruler and stroke of a pen. Today it tends to be the other way around, with the religious values of the people having a direct impact on the government. Religious issues, moreover, are receiving more and more attention in the media. Whereas newspapers, for example, once were restrained in their reporting of religious issues, such matters are now front-page news. At the same time powerful religious organizations like the Roman Catholic Church are no longer free from scrutiny by the public press.

Another feature of contemporary religion is the changing role of women. Holding everything from volunteer to executive positions, women are more important than ever before in religious organizations. While some organizations have been slow to revise their official policies on the role of women, women themselves often have developed their own ways of circumventing the system. Their influence in religion has also changed many people's views about the relationship between the sexes, despite the view of women in traditional theology.

Along with this challenge from women, religious groups have also faced greater demands from the laity. Many laypeople have come to insist that their understanding of tradition is just as valid as that of the professional religionist, something that has consequences for everything from ritual activity to doctrine and organization. Prominent in this movement is the use of the Internet and other modern technology to promote alternative religious views. Whereas a traditional religious organization tends to adopt this technology only to serve its existing structures and approaches, lay leaders often use it as a means for developing new ideas and ways of interacting, which further alienates them from the traditional centers of authority.

The practice of religion without the trappings of wealth and privilege, what is called "antiformalism," is another contemporary idea of global significance. Although it is difficult to see the outlines of the movement clearly, one noticeable feature is the rejection of elaborate settings for worship. In Christianity, for example, architecture has historically played a major role, with basilicas, monasteries, and other religious and educational edifices being central to the life of the Church. The trend in Christianity away from embodying tradition in ornate, expensive buildings may have important ramifications for all religions, as this movement can be seen as part of a broader challenge to established religious understanding and practice.

Hand in hand with these movements are those associated with fundamentalism. A complex phenomenon that arose in American Christianity in the early twentieth century, variations of this movement have spread to most major religions and countries around the world. Fundamentalism involves a militant return to first principles, even as its very existence requires the presence of modernity, with which it clashes. It is not a return to traditional views, for most fundamentalists see such views as hopelessly entwined with political and secular issues. Instead, for fundamentalists religion is primary. Resisting the concept of compromise, fundamentalism affirms a direct and literal interpretation of what is seen as essential in religion. While it is claimed that the roots of fundamentalism connect it to ancient religious founders, there is no mistaking the modern tone and strident individualism of the movement, regardless of the religion in which it occurs.

An Invitation to Explore

These, then, are some of the ways in which people have fashioned responses to their religious sensibilities. It is this material that is summarized, or, perhaps better, sketched in the *Worldmark Encyclopedia of Religious Practices*. The essays in the encyclopedia attempt to describe the rich detail of religious activity in an accessible way. Given the wealth to be found in contemporary religion, however, it is not possible in the essays to do more than provide a sampling, supplemented by suggestions for further reading in the bibliographies. In fact, given limitations of time and space and of human understanding, it is impossible ever to fully describe contemporary religious practices. While acknowledging these limitations, we invite you to engage in studying this cultural wealth with us.

Earle H. Waugh

Advisory Board

EARLE H. WAUGH, CHAIR
Professor of Religious Studies
University of Alberta
Edmonton, Canada

STEPHEN D. CROCCO
James Lennox Librarian
Princeton Theological Seminary
Princeton, New Jersey

JAY DOLAN
Professor Emeritus of History
University of Notre Dame
Notre Dame, Indiana

GARY EBERSOLE
Professor of History and Religious
  Studies
Director, Center for Religious
  Studies
University of Missouri
Kansas City, Missouri

NORMAN GIRARDOT
University Distinguished Professor of
  Religion
Lehigh University
Bethlehem, Pennsylvania

GERRIE TER HAAR
Professor of Religion, Human
  Rights, and Social Change
Institute of Social Studies
The Hague, The Netherlands

VALERIE J. HOFFMAN
Associate Professor of Religion
University of Illinois
Urbana, Illinois

VASUDHA NARAYANAN
Former President, American
  Academy of Religion
Professor of Religion
University of Florida
Gainesville, Florida

GRANT WACKER
Professor of Church History
The Divinity School
Duke University
Durham, North Carolina

BERNARD WASSERSTEIN
Harriet and Ulrich E. Meyer
  Professor of Modern European
  Jewish History
University of Chicago
Chicago, Illinois

Notes on Contributors

ABELA, ANTHONY M. Contributor and peer reviewer. Associate professor of sociology and social policy, University of Malta; principal investigator, European Values Study, Malta; and member, European Values Steering Committee, Tilburg, The Netherlands. Author of *Transmitting Values in European Malta*, 1991, *Changing Youth Culture*, 1992, *Shifting Family Values*, 1994, *Secularized Sexuality: Youth Values in a City-Island*, 1998, *Women and Men in the Maltese Islands: A Comparative European Perspective*, 2000, *Youth Participation in Voluntary Organizations*, 2001, and *Women's Welfare in Society*, 2002. Essay: Malta.

AGUILAR, MARIO I. Contributor and peer reviewer. Dean, Faculty of Divinity, Saint Mary's College, University of Saint Andrews, Scotland. Author of *Being Oromo in Kenya*, 1998, *The Rwanda Genocide and the Call to Deepen Christianity in Africa*, 1998, and *Current Issues on Theology and Religion in Latin America and Africa*, 2002. Editor of *The Politics of Age and Gerontocracy in Africa: Ethnographies of the Past and Memories of the Present*, 1998. Essays: Rwanda, Uganda.

AKERS, DEBORAH S. Contributor. Assistant professor of anthropology, Miami University, Oxford, Ohio. Author, with Abubaker Bagader, of *They Die Strangers: Selected Works by Abdel-Wali*, 2001, *Whispers from the Heart: Short Stories from Saudi Arabia*, 2003, and *Oranges in the Sun: Short Stories from the Persian Gulf*, 2004. Essays: Qatar, Saudi Arabia.

AKINADE, AKINTUNDE E. Contributor. Associate professor of world religions, High Point University, North Carolina. Coeditor of *The Agitated Mind of God: The Theology of Kosuke Koyama*, 1996. Essay: Gambia.

AMAYA, BENJAMÍN. Contributor. Assistant professor of anthropology and sociology, University College of Cape Breton, Nova Scotia, Canada. Author of *Violencia y culturas juveniles en El Salvador*, 2002. Author of book reviews for the scholarly journals *Anthropologie et Société* and *Culture*. Essay: El Salvador.

ANDERSON, LEONA. Contributor and peer reviewer. Professor of religious studies, University of Regina, Saskatchewan, Canada. Author of *The Vasantotsava: The Spring Festivals of India: Texts and Contexts*, 1993. Producer of the video documentaries *The Kumbh Mela*, 1991, and *The Ganesh Festival: Ten Days in the Presence of God*, 1999. Essay: India.

ANDERSON, PAUL N. Contributor. Professor of biblical and Quaker studies and chair, Department of Religious Studies, George Fox University, Newberg, Oregon. Author of *The Christology of the Fourth Gospel: Its Unity and Disunity in the Light of John 6*, 1997, and *Navigating the Living Waters of the Gospel of John: On Wading with Children and Swimming with Elephants*, 2000. Editor of *Evangelical Friend*, 1990–94, and *Quaker Religious Thought*, since 2000. Contributor to such journals as *Semeia*, *Horizons in Biblical Theology*, *Review of Biblical Literature*, *Journal of Biblical Literature*, *Critical Review of Books in Religion*, *Princeton Seminary Bulletin*, and *Pastoral Theology*, as well as to various Friends journals and collections. Author of the *Meet the Friends* series, 2003. Essay: Religious Society of Friends (Quakers).

ANDREEVA, LARISSA A. Contributor. Senior research fellow, Department of Cultural Anthropology, Center for Civilizational and Regional Studies, Russian Academy of Sciences, Moscow. Author of the monographs, in Russian, *Religion and Power in Russia*, 2001, and *Vicarius Christi on the Royal Throne: The Christian Civilization Model of Power Sacralization*, 2002. Essays: Belarus, Russia.

APRAHAMIAN, SIMA. Contributor. Research associate and lecturer, Simone de Beauvoir Institute, Concordia University, Quebec, Canada. Author of articles on Armenia and Lebanon in numerous scholarly journals and edited volumes. Essay: Armenia.

ARENS, WILLIAM. Contributor and peer reviewer. Professor of anthropology and dean of International Academic Programs, State University of New York, Stony Brook. Author of *On the Frontier of Change*, 1979, *The Man-Eating Myth*, 1979, and *The Original Sin*, 1986. Editor of *A Century of Change in Eastern Africa*, 1976. Coeditor of *Creativity of Power*,

1989. Author of numerous articles and essays in scholarly journals and other publications. Essay: Tanzania.

ARMSTRONG, CHARLES. Peer reviewer. Associate professor of history, Columbia University, New York, New York. Author of *Korean Society: Civil Society, Democracy, and the State,* 2002, and *The North Korean Revolution, 1945–1950,* 2003. Contributor to journals, including *Journal of Asian Studies, Critical Asian Studies,* and *Acta Koreana.*

AZEVEDO, MARIO J. Contributor and peer reviewer. Chair and Frank Porter Graham Professor, Department of African-American and African Studies, University of North Carolina, Charlotte. Author of *The Returning Hunter,* 1978, *Roots of Violence: A History of War in Chad,* 1998, and *Tragedy and Triumph: Mozambique Refugees in Southern Africa,* 2002. Coauthor of *Chad: A Nation in Search of Its Future,* 1998, and *A Historical Dictionary of Mozambique,* 2003. Editor of *Cameroon and Chad in Historical and Contemporary Perspectives,* 1988, *Africana Studies: A Survey of Africa and the African Diaspora,* 1998, and *Kenya: The Land, the People, and the Nation,* 1993. Author of articles in numerous scholarly journals, including *African Studies Review, African Affairs, Current History, Journal of Negro History,* and *Science and Medicine.* Essays: Central African Republic, Chad, Kenya, Lesotho, Mozambique, Nigeria.

BAKER, DONALD L. Contributor and peer reviewer. Professor of Asian studies, as well as director, Centre for Korean Research, University of British Columbia, Vancouver, Canada. Coeditor of *Sourcebook of Korean Civilization,* 1996. Author of numerous journal articles and book chapters on the history of Korean religion and traditional science. Essay: North Korea.

BALISKY, E. PAUL. Contributor. Lecturer, Ethiopian Graduate School of Theology, Addis Ababa. Director, Serving in Mission (SIM) Ethiopia, 1999–2003. Author of articles for the 14th International Conference of Ethiopian Studies, 2000, and the online *Dictionary of African Christian Biography.* Essay: Ethiopia.

BARBOSA DA SILVA, ANTÓNIO. Peer reviewer. Professor of systematic theology, philosophy of religion, ethics, and health care ethics, Misjonshøgskolen, Stavanger, Norway. Author of *The Phenomenology of Religion as a Philosophical Problem with Particular Reference to Mircea Eliade's Phenomenological Approach,* 1982, and *Is There a New Imbalance in Jewish-Christian Relations?* Author, in Norwegian, of *Hva er religionsfenomenologi?* Author of numerous articles.

BARCLAY, HAROLD B. Contributor and peer reviewer. Professor emeritus of anthropology, University of Alberta, Edmonton, Canada. Author of *Buurri al Lamaab, a Suburban Village in the Sudan,* 1964, *The Role of the Horse in Man's Culture,* 1980, *Culture, the Human Way,* 1986, and *People without Government: An Anthropology of Anarchy,* 1990. Author of the chapters "Egypt: Struggling with Secularization" and "Sudan: On the Frontier of Islam" in *Religions and Societies, Asia and the Middle East,* edited by Carlo Caldarola, 1982. Essays: The Sudan, Tunisia.

BAREJA-STARZYNSKA, AGATA. Contributor. Assistant professor, Department of Inner Asia, Institute of Oriental Studies, University of Warsaw, Poland. Author of "The History of Ancient Tibet according to the 17th Century Mongolian Chronicle 'Erdeni-yin tobci' by Sagang Secen," in *Proceedings of the 5th International Seminar on Tibetan Studies in Narita, Japan, 1989,* edited by S. Ihara and Z. Yamaguchi, 1992, and "The Essentials of Buddhism in the 'Ciqula kereglegci,' the 16th Century Mongolian Buddhist Treatise," in *Proceedings of the International Seminar on Buddhism 'Aspects of Buddhism' in Liw, Poland, 1994,* edited by A. Bareja-Starzynska and M. Mejor, 1997. Essay: Mongolia.

BARLOW, PHILIP L. Peer reviewer. Professor of theological studies, Hanover College, Indiana. Author of *Mormons and the Bible: The Place of the Latter-Day Saints in American Religion,* 1991. Coauthor of *New Historical Atlas of Religion in America,* 2000. Editor of *A Thoughtful Faith: Essays on Belief by Mormon Scholars,* 1986, and *Religion and Public Life in the Midwest: Microcosm and Mosaic,* 2004.

BEBBINGTON, DAVID. Peer reviewer. Professor of history, University of Stirling, Scotland. Author of *Evangelicalism in Modern Britain: A History from the 1730s to the 1980s,* 1989, and *Holiness in Nineteenth-Century England,* 1998. Editor of *The Baptists in Scotland: A History,* 1988, and *The Gospel in the World: International Baptist Studies,* 2002. Coeditor of *Evangelicalism: Comparative Studies of Popular Protestantism in North America, the British Isles and Beyond, 1700–1990,* 1994, and *Modern Christianity and Cultural Aspirations,* 2003.

BERNAL, VICTORIA. Contributor. Associate professor of anthropology, University of California, Irvine. Author of *Cultivating Workers: Peasants and Capitalism in a Sudanese Village,* 1991. Author of articles in such scholarly journals as *American Ethnologist, American Anthropologist, Comparative Studies in Society and History, Cultural Anthropology, African Studies Review,* and *Political and Legal Anthropology Review.* Essay: Eritrea.

BERRY, MOULOUK. Contributor. Assistant professor of Arabic, as well as director of the Arab and Chaldean American Writers Series and the Quranic Forum, University of Michigan-Dearborn. Essay: Lebanon.

BESNIER, NIKO. Peer reviewer. Visiting professor, Department of Anthropology, University of California, Los Angeles. Author of *Literacy, Emotion, and Authority: Reading and*

Writing on a Polynesian Atoll, 1995, and *Tuvaluan: A Polynesian Language of the Central Pacific*, 2000. Contributor to numerous journals in anthropology and linguistics, including *American Ethnologist*, *American Anthropologist*, *Anthropological Quarterly*, *Ethnos*, *Social Anthropology*, *Journal of Anthropological Research*, *Annual Review of Anthropology*, *Language*, and *Language in Society*, as well as many edited volumes.

BLUMHOFER, EDITH. Contributor. Professor of history, as well as director, Institute for the Study of American Evangelicals, Wheaton College, Illinois. Author of *The Assemblies of God: A Chapter in the Story of American Pentecostalism*, 1989, *Aimee Semple McPherson: Everybody's Sister*, 1993, and *Restoring the Faith: The Assemblies of God, Pentecostalism, and American Culture*, 1993. Coeditor of *Modern Christian Revivals*, 1993, and *Pentecostal Currents in American Protestantism*, 1999. Essay: Pentecostalism.

BOELDERL, ARTUR R. Contributor. Assistant professor of philosophy, Private Catholic University of Linz, Austria. Author of *Alchimie, Postmoderne und der arme Hölderlin: Drei Studien zur Philosophischen Hermetik*, 1995, and *Literarische Hermetik: Die Ethik zwischen Hermeneutik, Psychoanalyse und Dekonstruktion*, 1997. Coeditor of several volumes, including *Rituale: Zugänge zu einem Phänomen*, 1999, and *Die Sprachen der Religion*, 2003. Essay: Austria.

BONK, JONATHAN J. Peer reviewer. Executive director, Overseas Ministries Study Center, New Haven, Connecticut, as well as editor, *International Bulletin of Missionary Research*, and project director, *Dictionary of African Christian Biography*. Author of *An Annotated and Classified Bibliography of English Literature Pertaining to the Ethiopian Orthodox Church*, 1984, *The World at War, the Church at Peace: A Biblical Perspective*, 1988, *The Theory and Practice of Missionary Identification, 1860–1920*, 1989, *Missions and Money: Affluence as a Western Missionary Problem*, 1991, and *Between Past and Future: Evangelical Mission Entering the Twenty-First Century*, 2003.

BOOLELL, SHAKUNTALA. Contributor. Senior lecturer in French, Department of Humanities and Social Sciences, University of Mauritius. Author of *La femme enveloppée et autres nouvelles de Maurice*, 1996, and *De l'ombre à la lumière: Sur les traces de l'Indo-Mauricienne*, 1998. Coauthor of *Fonction et représentation de la Mauricienne dans le discours littéraire*, 2000. Essay: Mauritius.

BOROWIK, IRENA. Peer reviewer. Professor of religion and post-Communist transformation, Institute of Religious Studies, Jagiellonian University, Kraków, Poland. Author, in Polish, of *Charyzma a codziennosc: Studium wplywu religii na zycie codzienne*, 1990, *Procesy instytucjonalizacji i prywatyzacji religii w powojennej Polsce*, 1997, and *Odbudowywanie pamieci: Przemiany religijne w Srodkowo-wschodniej Europie po upadku komun izm'*, 2000. Coauthor, with Tadeusz Doktór, in Polish, of *Religijny i*

moralny pluralizm w Polsce, 2001. Editor of *State Relations in Central and Eastern Europe after the Collapse of Communism*, 1999, and *Religions, Churches and the Scientific Studies of Religion: Poland and Ukraine*, 2003. Coeditor, with Miklos Tomka, of *Religion and Social Change in Post-Communist Europe*, 2001. Coeditor and contributor to *The Future of Religion*, 1995, and *New Religious Phenomena in Central and Eastern Europe*, 1997.

BOYARIN, DANIEL. Peer reviewer. Hermann P. and Sophia Taubman Professor of Talmudic Culture, Department of Near Eastern Studies and Rhetoric, University of California, Berkeley. Author of *Carnal Israel: Reading Sex in Talmudic Culture*, 1995, *A Radical Jew: Paul and the Politics of Identity*, 1997, *Unheroic Conduct: The Rise of Heterosexuality and the Invention of the Jewish Man*, 1997, *Dying for God: Martyrdom and the Making of Christianity and Judaism*, 1999, and *Border Lines: The Partition of Judaeo-Christianity*, 2004. Coauthor, with Jonathan Boyarin, of *Powers of Diaspora: Two Essays on the Relevance of Jewish Culture*, 2002. Coeditor, with Jonathan Boyarin, of *Jews and Other Differences: The New Jewish Cultural Studies*, 1997, and, with Daniel Itzkovitz and Ann Pellegrini, of *Queer Theory and the Jewish Question*, 2003.

BRATT, JAMES D. Peer reviewer. Professor of history, as well as director of the Calvin Center for Christian Scholarship, Calvin College, Grand Rapids, Michigan. Author of *Dutch Calvinism in Modern America: A History of a Conservative Subculture*, 1984. Coauthor of *Gathered at the River: Grand Rapids, Michigan, and Its People of Faith*, 1993. Editor of *Viewpoints: Exploring the Reformed Vision*, 1992, and *Abraham Kuyper: A Centennial Reader*, 1998.

BRINKMAN, INGE. Contributor. Research fellow, Ghent University, Belgium. Author of *Kikuyu Gender Norms and Narratives*, 1996, as well as various articles in such scholarly journals as *Journal of African History*, *Africa*, *Journal of South African Studies*, and *Historische Anthropoligie*. Editor of *Singing in the Bush: MPLA Songs during the War for Independence in South-East Angola (1966–1975)*, 2001. Coeditor of *Grandmother's Footsteps: Oral Tradition and South-East Angolan Narratives on the Colonial Encounter*, 1999. Essay: Angola.

BROWERS, MICHAELLE. Contributor. Assistant professor of political science, Wake Forest University, Winston-Salem, North Carolina. Coeditor of *An Islamic Reformation?*, 2003. Essay: Syria.

BUCHENAU, KLAUS. Contributor. Research assistant, Eastern European Institute, Free University of Berlin. Author of two monographs, as well as various articles on religion in the former Yugoslavia. Essay: Bosnia and Herzegovina.

BUCKSER, ANDREW. Contributor. Associate professor of anthropology, Purdue University, Lafayette, Indiana. Author of *Communities of Faith: Sectarianism, Identity, and Social Change on a Danish Island*, 1996, and *After the Rescue: Jewish Identity and Community in Contemporary Denmark*, 2003. Coeditor of *The Anthropology of Religious Conversion*, 2003. Essay: Denmark.

CAHN, PETER S. Contributor. Assistant professor of anthropology, University of Oklahoma, Norman. Author of *All Religions Are Good in Tzintzuntzan: Evangelicals in Catholic Mexico*, 2003, and a chapter in *Chronicling Cultures: Long-Term Field Research in Anthropology*, 2002. Essay: Brazil.

CALKOWSKI, MARCIA. Contributor and peer reviewer. Associate professor and head, Department of Anthropology, University of Regina, Saskatchewan, Canada. Author of articles in edited volumes and journals, including *Canadian Review of Sociology and Anthropology, Anthropologica, American Ethnologist, Journal of Asian Studies, Tibetan Review,* and *Culture.* Essays: Myanmar, Thailand, Tibetan Buddhism.

CAMPBELL, SIRI. Contributor. Journalist. Author of *Inside Monaco*, 2000, and contributor to numerous television organizations and travel shows, including the Discovery Channel, BBC *Travel Show*, NBC *Today Show*, CBS *News*, and Denmark 2. Essay: Monaco.

CAMPO, JUAN E. Peer reviewer. Associate professor, Religious Studies Department, University of California, Santa Barbara. Author of *The Other Sides of Paradise: Explorations into the Religious Meanings of Domestic Space in Islam*, 1991. Contributor to *Merriam-Webster's Encyclopedia of World Religions*, 1999, and to journals, including *Traditional Dwellings and Settlements Review, Contention, Annals of the American Academy of Political and Social Science,* and *Muslim World.*

CAREY, PATRICK. Peer reviewer. Professor of theology, Marquette University, Milwaukee, Wisconsin. Author of *An Immigrant Bishop: John England's Adaptation of Irish Catholicism to American Republicanism*, 1982, *People, Priests and Prelates: Ecclesiastical Democracy and the Tensions of Trusteeism*, 1987, *The Roman Catholics*, 1993, and *The Roman Catholics in America*, 1996. Editor of *American Catholic Religious Thought*, 1987, and *The Early Works of Orestes A. Brownson*, 2000. Coeditor of *Theological Education in the Catholic Tradition: Contemporary Challenges*, 1997, and *Biographical Dictionary of Christian Theologians*, 2002.

CASEBOLT, JAMES. Contributor. Associate professor of psychology, Ohio University Eastern Campus, Saint Clairsville. Contributor to the edited volume *Measures of Religiosity*, 1999, and to various journals, including *AURCO Journal.* Essay: Unitarianism and Universalism.

CATE, SANDRA. Contributor. Lecturer, Department of Anthropology, San Jose State University, California. Author of *Making Merit, Making Art: A Thai Temple in Wimbledon*, 2003. Coeditor of *Converging Interests: Travelers, Traders, and Tourists in South East Asia*, 1999. Essay: Laos.

CAULKINS, D. DOUGLAS. Contributor. Earl D. Strong Professor of Social Studies, Department of Anthropology, Grinnell College, Iowa. Formerly a visiting researcher at the Institute for Social Research, Oslo, Norway, and at the universities of Trondheim, Norway; Bergen, Norway; Stirling, Scotland; and Durham, England. Author of numerous articles in journals, including *Cross-Cultural Research, Journal of Anthropological Research, Field Methods,* and *Practicing Anthropology.* Essay: Norway.

CHAKANZA, J.C. Contributor. Associate professor and head, Department of Theology and Religious Studies, Chancellor College, Zomba, Malawi. Author of *Voices of Preachers in Protest: The Ministry of Two Malawian Prophets: Elliot Kamwana and Wilfrid Gudu*, 1998, *Religion in Malawi: An Annotated Bibliography*, 1998, *Islam in Malawi Week*, 1999, and *Wisdom of the People: 2000 Chinyanja Proverbs*, 2001. Author of articles in various journals, including *Lamp.* Essay: Malawi.

CHEVANNES, BARRY. Contributor. Professor of social anthropology and dean of the Faculty of Social Sciences, University of the West Indies at Mona, Kingston, Jamaica. Author of *Rastafari: Roots and Ideology*, 1994, and *Learning to Be a Man: Culture, Socialisation and Gender in Five Caribbean Communities*, 2001. Editor of *Rastafari and Other African-Caribbean Worldviews*, 1995. Essay: Jamaica.

CHEYEKA, AUSTIN. Contributor. Lecturer in religious studies, University of Zambia, Lusaka. Author of articles in various scholarly journals, including *African Ecclesial Review (AFER)* and *African Christian Studies.* Essay: Zambia.

CHILTON, TUTII. Contributor. Assistant professor of social science, Palau Community College, Republic of Palau. Essay: Palau.

CHOKSY, JAMSHEED. Peer reviewer. Professor of central Eurasian studies, professor of history, and adjunct professor of religious studies, Indiana University, Bloomington. Author of *Purity and Pollution in Zoroastrianism: Triumph over Evil*, 1989, *Conflict and Cooperation: Zoroastrian Subalterns and Muslim Elites in Medieval Iranian Society*, 1997, and *Evil, Good, and Gender: Facets of the Feminine in Zoroastrian Religious History*, 2002. Contributor to *Women in Iran from the Rise of Islam to 1800*, edited by G. Nashat and L. Beck, 2003, *Jamshid Soroush Soroushian Memorial Volume*, edited by C. Cereti and F.J. Vajifdar, 2003, and the periodicals *Indo-Iranian Journal, Iranian Studies, Iranica Antiqua, Journal of the American Oriental Society, Journal of*

Ritual Studies, Journal of the Royal Asiatic Society of Great Britain and Ireland, and *Studia Iranica,* among others.

CINNAMON, JOHN. Contributor. Assistant professor of anthropology, Miami University, Hamilton, Ohio. Author of various articles on religion and political ecology in Gabon. Essays: Comoros, Equatorial Guinea, Gabon, São Tomé and Príncipe.

CLAYER, NATHALIE. Contributor and peer reviewer. Researcher, Centre Nationale de la Recherche Scientifique (CNRS), Paris. Author of *L'Albanie: Pays des derviches,* 1990, and *Mystiques, etat et société: Les halvetis dans l'aire balkanique de la fin du XVe siècle à nos jours,* 1994. Coeditor, *Le nouvel Islam balkanique: Les musulmans, acteurs du post-communisme,* 2001. Essay: Albania.

COLE, JUAN R. Peer reviewer. Professor of modern Middle East and South Asian history, Department of History, University of Michigan, Ann Arbor. Author of *Roots of North Indian Shi'ism in Iran and Iraq: Religion and State in Awadh, 1722–1859,* 1988, *Colonialism and Revolution in the Middle East: Social and Cultural Origins of Egypt's 'Urabi' Movement,* 1993, *Modernity and the Millennium: The Genesis of the Baha'i Faith in the Nineteenth-Century Middle East,* 1998, and *Sacred Space and Holy War: The Politics, Culture and History of Shi'ite Islam,* 2002. Translator of *Miracles and Metaphors,* by Mirza Abu'l-Fadl Gulpaygani, 1982, *Letters and Essays 1886–1913,* by Mirza Abu'l-Fadl Gulpaygani, 1985, *Spirit Brides,* by Kahlil Gibran, 1993, *The Vision,* by Kahlil Gibran, 1998, and *Broken Wings: A Novel,* by Kahlil Gibran, 1998. Contributor to and coeditor of *From Iran East and West: Studies in Babi and Baha'i History,* 1984. Coeditor of *Shi'ism and Social Protest,* 1986. Editor of *Comparing Muslim Societies,* 1992, and *Religion in Iran: From Zoroaster to Baha'u'llah,* by Alessandro Bausani, 2000. Author of articles in numerous journals and books.

COLEMAN, SIMON. Contributor. Reader in anthropology, University of Durham, England. Author of *The Globalisation of Charismatic Christianity: Spreading the Gospel of Prosperity,* 2000. Coauthor of *Pilgrimage: Past and Present in the World Religions,* 1995. Coeditor of *Tourism: Between Place and Performance,* 2002, *Religion, Identity, and Change: Perspectives on Global Transformations,* 2003, *Pilgrim Voices: Narrative and Authorship in Christian Pilgrimage,* 2003, *The Cultures of Creationism: Antievolution in English-Speaking Countries,* 2003, and *Reframing Pilgrimage: Cultures in Motion,* 2004. Essay: Sweden.

COLLINGE, WILLIAM J. Contributor. Knott Professor of Theology and professor of philosophy, Mount Saint Mary's College, Emmitsburg, Maryland. Author of *A Historical Dictionary of Catholicism,* 1997, and *The A to Z of Catholicism,* 2001, as well as articles in various journals, including

Horizons, Living Light, Faith and Philosophy, and *Augustinian Studies.* Essay: Roman Catholicism.

COSENTINO, DONALD. Contributor and peer reviewer. Professor of world arts and cultures, University of California, Los Angeles, as well as editor of *African Arts,* since 1988. Author of *Defiant Maids and Stubborn Farmers: Tradition and Invention in Mende Story Performance,* 1982, and *Vodou Things: The Art of Pierrot Barra and Marie Cassaise,* 1998. Editor of *Sacred Arts of Haitian Vodou,* 1995. Author of articles in numerous journals, magazines, and catalogs, from *Aperture* to *Playboy.* Essay: Haiti.

COWE, S. PETER. Peer reviewer. Narekatsi Professor of Armenian Studies, University of California, Los Angeles. Author of *The Armenian Version of Daniel,* 1992, and *Catalogue of the Armenian Manuscripts in the Cambridge University Library,* 1994. Editor of *Mxit'ar Sasnec'i's Theological Discourses,* 1993, and *Ani: World Architectural Heritage of a Medieval Armenian Capital,* 2001. Coeditor of *Modern Armenian Drama: An Anthology,* 2001. Translator of *Commentary on the Divine Liturgy,* by Xosrov Anjewac'I, 1991.

CROCCO, STEPHEN D. Adviser. James Lennox Librarian, Princeton Theological Seminary, Princeton, New Jersey. Editor, *The Essential Paul Ramsey: A Collection,* 1994.

DAIBER, KARL-FRITZ. Contributor. Professor emeritus, College of Protestant Theology, University of Marburg, Germany. Author of *Praktische Theologie als Handlungswissenschaft,* 1977, *Diakonie und Kirchliche Identitaet,* 1988, *Religion unter den Bedingungen der Moderne—Die Situation in der Bundesrepublik Deutschland,* 1995, and *Religion in Kirche und Gesellschaft: Theologische und Soziologische Studien zur Präsenz von Religion in der Gegenwärtigen Kultur,* 1997. Coeditor of *Religion in den Gegenwartsströmungen der Deutschen Soziologie,* 1983. Essay: Germany.

DAMATTA, ROBERTO. Peer reviewer. Professor emeritus, Department of Anthropology, University of Notre Dame, Indiana. Author of *Carnivals, Rogues and Heroes: An Interpretation of the Brazilian Dilemma* and *A Divided World: Apinayé Social Structure.* Contributor to *Revisão do paraíso: Os brasileiros e o estado em 500 anos de história,* edited by Mary Del Priori, 2000, and *Brazil 2001: A Revisionary History of Brazilian Literature and Culture,* 2001. Coauthor and coeditor of *The Brazilian Puzzle* and coauthor of *Aguias, burros e borboletas: Um estudo antropologico do jogo do bicho,* 1999.

DARROW, WILLIAM. Contributor. Jackson Professor of Religion, Williams College, Williamstown, Massachusetts. Author of articles in various edited volumes and journals, including *Journal of the American Academy of Religion, Harvard Theological Review,* and *History of Religions.* Essay: Zoroastrianism.

DAVIS, MARTHA ELLEN. Contributor. Affiliate associate professor of anthropology and music, University of Florida, Gainesville. Member, Dominican Academy of Sciences, and researcher, Museo del Hombre Dominicana, Santo Domingo, Dominican Republic. Author of *Afro-Dominican Religious Brotherhoods: Structure, Ritual, and Music*, 1976, *Cries from Purgatory: A Study of the Dominican "Salve,"* 1981, and *The Other Science: Dominican Vodú as Folk Religion and Medicine*, 1987. Essay: Dominican Republic.

DIAGNE, SOULEYMANE BACHIR. Contributor. Professor of philosophy, Northwestern University, Evanston, Illinois. Author of *Boole: 1815–1864: L'oiseau de nuit en plein jour*, 1989, *Reconstruire le sens: Textes et enjeux de prospectives africaines*, 2000, *Islam et société ouverte: La fidélité et le mouvement dans la philosophie de Muhammad Iqbal*, 2001, and *100 mots pour dire l'Islam*, 2002. Coauthor of *The Cultural Question in Africa*, 1996. Essay: Senegal.

DIALLO, GARBA. Contributor. Director of international programs, International People's College, Elsinore, Denmark. Author of *Mauritania, the Other Apartheid*, 1993, *Indigenous Learning Forms in West Africa: The Case of Mauritania*, 1994, *Entrance to Hell—The Concentration Camp (Goree) That Lasted for 400 Years*, 1996, and *Mauritania—Neither Arab nor African*, 2001, as well as articles in journals, including *Global Ecology* and *Kontakt*. Editor of *Educators' Contribution to the Peace Process in the Middle East*, 1998. Essay: Mauritania.

DOLAN, JAY. Adviser. Professor emeritus of history, University of Notre Dame, Indiana. Author of *The Immigrant Church: New York's Irish and German Catholics, 1815-1865*, 1975, *Catholic Revivalism: The American Experience, 1830-1900*, 1978, *The American Catholic Experience: A History from Colonial Time to the Present*, 1985, and *In Search of an American Catholicism: A History of Religion and Culture in Tension*, 2002. Coauthor of *The American Catholic Parish: A History from 1850 to the Present*, 1987, and *Transforming Parish Ministry: The Changing Roles of Catholic Clergy, Laity, and Women Religious in the United States, 1930-1980*, 1989.

DOUGLAS, IAN T. Contributor. Professor of mission and world Christianity, as well as director of Anglican, global, and ecumenical studies, Episcopal Divinity School, Cambridge, Massachusetts. Author of *Fling Out the Banner: The National Church Ideal and the Foreign Mission of the Episcopal Church*, 1993. Editor of *Waging Reconciliation: God's Mission in a Time of Globalization and Crisis*, 2002. Coeditor of *Beyond Colonial Anglicanism: The Anglican Communion in the Twenty-First Century*, 2001. Essay: Anglicanism.

EBERSOLE, GARY. Adviser, contributor, and peer reviewer. Professor of history and religious studies, as well as director of the Center for Religious Studies, University of Missouri-

Kansas City. Author of *Ritual Poetry and the Politics of Death in Early Japan*, 1989, and *Captured by Texts: Puritan to Postmodern Images of Indian Captivity*, 1995. Author of articles in numerous journals, including *History of Religions, Religion, Journal of Religion, Journal of Japanese Studies*, and *Momumenta Nipponica*. Essays: Japan, Shinto.

EDGECOMBE-HOWELL, OLIVIA. Contributor. Head, University Centre, University of the West Indies, Basseterre, St. Kitts. Essay: Saint Kitts and Nevis.

EL-ASWAD, EL-SAYED. Contributor. Professor of anthropology and chair, Department of Sociology, Tanta University, Egypt, as well as adjunct professor, Wayne State University, Detroit, Michigan. Author of books in Arabic and English, including *Religion and Folk Cosmology: Scenarios of the Visible and Invisible in Rural Egypt*, 2002, and *Symbolic Anthropology*, 2002. Author of articles in journals, including *AAA Anthropology Newsletter* and *Anthropos*. Essay: United Arab Emirates.

EL-HASSAN, KHALID. Contributor. Research assistant professor and program coordinator, African Studies Resource Center, University of Kansas, Lawrence. Author of articles and book reviews in edited volumes and journals, including *Horizons, Journal of International Programs for the University of Kansas*, and *African Studies Quarterly*. Essay: Bahrain.

ELOLIA, SAMUEL K. Contributor. Associate professor of Christian doctrine and missiology, Emmanuel School of Religion, Johnson City, Tennessee. Author of articles in several edited volumes. Essays: Burundi, Djibouti.

ESPOSITO, JOHN L. Contributor. Professor, School of Foreign Service and Theology, Georgetown University, Washington, D.C. Author of *Islam and Politics*, 1998, and coauthor of *Islam and Democracy*, 1996. Editor of *Islam and Development: Religion and Sociopolitical Change*, 1980, *Voices of Resurgent Islam*, 1983, *Islam in Asia: Religion, Politics, and Society*, 1987, *The Iranian Revolution: Its Global Impact*, 1990, and *The Islamic World: Past and Present*, 2004. Coeditor of *Islam, Gender, and Social Change*, 1998, *Muslims on the Americanization Path?*, 2000, *Religion and Global Order*, 2000, *Islam and Secularism in the Middle East*, 2001, *Daughters of Abraham: Feminist Thought in Judaism, Christianity, and Islam*, 2001, *Iran at the Crossroads*, 2001, *Muslims and the West: Encounter and Dialogue*, 2001, *Religion and Immigration: Christian, Jewish, and Muslim Experiences in the United States*, 2003, and *Turkish Islam and the Secular State: The Gülen Movement*, 2003. Essay: Islam.

ESTGEN, ALOYSE. Contributor. Member, Centre Luxembourgeois de Documentation et d'êtudes MÇdiÇvales, and former instructor of medieval history.

Author of numerous articles, as well as coeditor of *Les Actes de Jean l'Aveugle*, 1997. Essay: Luxembourg.

ESTGEN, PAUL. Contributor. Sociologist, SESOPI-Centre Intercommunautaire, Luxembourg. Contributor to *Les valeurs au Luxembourg: Portrait d'une société au tournant du 3e millénaire*, 2002. Essay: Luxembourg.

FERNEA, ELIZABETH. Peer reviewer. Professor emeritus of English and Middle Eastern studies, University of Texas, Austin. Author of *Guests of the Sheik: An Ethnography of an Iraqi Village*, 1965, *A View of the Nile*, 1970, *A Street in Marrakech*, 1975, and *In Search of Islamic Feminism*, 1998. Coauthor, with Robert A. Fernea, of *The Arab World: Personal Encounters*, 1985, *Nubian Ethnographies*, 1991, and *The Arab World: Forty Years of Change*, 1997. Editor of *Women and the Family in the Middle East: New Voices of Change*,1985, *Children of the Muslim Middle East*, 1995, and *Remembering Childhood in the Middle East: Memoirs from a Century of Change*, 2001. Coeditor of *Middle Eastern Muslim Women Speak*, 1977, and *The Struggle for Peace: Israelis and Palestinians*, 1992. Ethnographer and consultant for the film *Some Women of Marrakech*, 1976. Producer of numerous documentaries, including *A Veiled Revolution, Women and Religion in Egypt*, 1982, *The Price of Change*, 1982, *Women under Siege*, 1982, *The Struggle for Peace: Israelis and Palestinians*, 1991, *The Road to Peace: Israelis and Palestinians*, 1995, and *Living with the Past: Historic Cairo*, 2001.

FINE-DARE, KATHLEEN. Peer reviewer. Professor of anthropology and women's studies, Fort Lewis College, Durango, Colorado. Author of *Cotocollao: Ideología, historia, y acción en un barrio de Quito*, 1991, and *Grave Injustice: The American Indian Repatriation Movement and NAGPRA*, 2002. Contributor to journals, including *Radical History Review* and *Anthropological Quarterly*.

FLAKE, KATHLEEN. Contributor. Assistant professor of American religious history, Graduate Department of Religion and Divinity School, Vanderbilt University, Nashville, Tennessee. Author of *The Politics of American Religious History: The Seating of Senator Reed Smoot, Mormon Apostle*, 2004. Essay: The Church of Jesus Christ of Latter-day Saints.

FOHR, SHERRY. Contributor. Assistant professor of world religions, Wofford College, Spartanburg, South Carolina, and board member, Southeastern Commission for the Study of Religions. Essay: Jainism.

GALINIER-PALLEROLA, JEAN-FRANÇOIS. Contributor. Member, Department of Theology, Institut Catholique de Toulouse, France. Author of *La religion populaire en Andorre*, 1990, and of articles in *Bulletin de Littérature Ecclésiastique*. Essay: Andorra.

GATTAMORTA, LORENZA. Contributor. Research associate of the sociology of culture, University of Bologna, Forli, Italy. Author of *La memoria delle parole: Luzi tra Eliot e Dante*, 2002. Author of articles in numerous journals, including *Strumenti Critici, Lingua e Stile, Ideazione,* and *Sociologia e Politiche Sociali*. Essay: San Marino.

GAUSSET, QUENTIN. Contributor. Associate professor, University of Copenhagen, Denmark. Author of articles in numerous journals, including *Africa, Journal of the Royal Anthropological Institute, Cahiers d'Études Africaines, Social Sciences and Medicine,* and *Anthropos*. Essay: Cameroon.

GEFFEN, RELA MINTZ. Contributor. President, Baltimore Hebrew University, and editor of the journal *Contemporary Jewry*. Coauthor of *The Conservative Movement in Judaism: Dilemmas and Opportunities*, 2000. Editor of *Celebration and Renewal: Rites of Passage in Judaism*, 1993. Coeditor of *A Double Bond: The Constitutional Documents of American Jewry*, 1992, and *Freedom and Responsibility: Exploring the Challenges of Jewish Continuity*, 1998. Essay: Conservative Judaism.

GHANNAM, FARHA. Contributor. Visiting assistant professor of anthropology, Swarthmore College, Pennsylvania. Author of *Remaking the Modern: Space, Relocation, and the Politics of Identity in a Global Cairo*, 2002. Author of articles in various journals, including *Visual Anthropology, City and Society,* and *Middle East Report*. Essay: Egypt.

GIBBS, PHILIP. Contributor and peer reviewer. Faculty member, Melanesian Institute, Soroka, Papua New Guinea. Author of *The Word in the Third World*, 1996. Author of articles in journals, including *Point 24* and *Studia Missionalia*. Essay: Papua New Guinea.

GIBSON, KEAN. Contributor. Senior lecturer in linguistics, University of the West Indies, Cave Hill, Barbados. Author of *Comfa Religion and Creole Language in a Caribbean Community*, 2001, and *The Cycle of Racial Oppression in Guyana*, 2003. Author of articles in numerous journals, including *Lingua, American Speech, International Folklore Review, Mankind Quarterly, Lore and Language,* and *Journal of Caribbean Studies*. Essay: Guyana.

GILL, ANTHONY. Contributor. Associate professor of political science, University of Washington, Seattle. Author of *Rendering unto Caesar: The Catholic Church and State in Latin America*, 1998, and of articles in numerous journals, including *American Journal of Political Science, Rationality and Society, Politics and Society,* and *Journal of Church and State*. Essays: Argentina, Chile, Uruguay.

GIRARDOT, NORMAN. Adviser and peer reviewer. University Distinguished Professor, Department of Religious Studies,

Lehigh University, Bethlehem, Pennsylvania. Author of *Myth and Meaning in Early Taoism*, 1983, and *The Victorian Translation of China*, 2002. Editor of the section on China in the *HarperCollins Dictionary of Religion*, edited by Jonathan Z. Smith and William Scott Green, 1995. Coeditor of *Imagination and Meaning: The Scholarly and Literary Worlds of Mircea Eliade*, 1982, and *Daoism and Ecology*, 2001. Cotranslator of *Taoist Meditation*, 1993. Contributor to books, including *Self-Taught Artists of the 20th Century: An American Anthology*, edited by Elsa Longhauser, 1998, and *Changing Religious Worlds, the Meaning and End of Mircea Eliade*, edited by Bryan Rennie, 2001, and to journals such as the *Journal of the American Academy of Religion*.

GOLDSMITH, MICHAEL. Contributor and peer reviewer. Senior lecturer in anthropology, University of Waikato, Hamilton, New Zealand. Coauthor of *The Accidental Missionary: Tales of Elekana*, 2002. Coeditor of *Other Sites: Social Anthropology and the Politics of Interpretation*, 1992. Author of numerous book chapters and encyclopedia entries, as well as of articles in various journals, including *Journal of Pacific History*, *Journal of Pacific Studies*, and *Ethnologies Comparées*. Essay: Tuvalu.

GOOREN, HENRI. Contributor. Researcher, IIMO Utrecht University, The Netherlands. Coeditor of *Under Pressure: Essays on Development Research*, 1997. Author of chapters in books, as well as of articles in various journals, including *Journal for the Scientific Study of Religion* and *Dialogue*. Essay: Nicaragua.

GOOSEN, GIDEON. Contributor. Associate professor of theology, Australian Catholic University, Sydney. Author of *Religion in Australian Culture: An Anthropological View*, 1997, *Australian Theologies: Themes and Methodologies into the Third Millennium*, 2000, and *Bringing Churches Together: A Popular Introduction to Ecumenism*, 2001. Author of articles in numerous journals, including *Theological Studies*, *Compass*, *Australasian Catholic Record*, *Word in Life*, *St. Mark's Review*, and *Peace and Change*. Essay: Australia.

GOTHÓNI, RENÉ. Peer reviewer. Professor of comparative religion, University of Helsinki, Finland. Author of several books, including *Paradise within Reach: Monasticism and Pilgrimage on Mt. Athos*, 1993, and *Attitudes and Interpretations in Comparative Religion*, 2000.

GRANT, BRUCE. Peer reviewer. Associate professor of anthropology, Swarthmore College, Pennsylvania. Author of *In the Soviet House of Culture: A Century of Perestroikas*, 1995, and editor of and author of the foreword and afterword to *The Social Organization of the Gilyak*, by Lev Shternberg, 1999. Contributor to *Paranoia within Reason: A Casebook on Conspiracy as Explanation*, edited by George Marcus, 1999, and to journals, including *American Ethnologist*.

GREEN, KATHRYN L. Contributor. Independent scholar. Contributor to various publications on African and Middle Eastern history. Essay: Mali.

GROELSEMA, ROBERT. Contributor. Civil society analyst, U.S. Agency for International Development. Author of articles on African politics, culture, and current events for encyclopedias and other publications, as well as regular articles on Guinea and the Seychelles in *Africa Contemporary Record*. Essays: Republic of the Congo, Ghana, Guinea, Seychelles, Sierra Leone.

HAAR, GERRIE TER. Adviser. Professor of religion, human rights, and social change, Institute of Social Studies, The Hague, The Netherlands. General Editor, Religion in Contemporary Africa (series), as well as author of *Faith of Our Fathers: Studies on Religious Education in Sub-Saharan Africa*, 1990, *Spirit of Africa: The Healing Ministry of Archbishop Milingo of Zambia*, 1992, *African Traditional Religions in Religious Education*, 1992, *Halfway to Paradise: African Christians in Europe*, 1998, and *Worlds of Power: Religious Thought and Political Practice in Africa*, 2004.

HALE, JOE. Peer reviewer. General secretary, 1976–2001, then emeritus, World Methodist Council.

HAMM, THOMAS D. Peer reviewer. Professor of history and archivist and curator of the Friends Collection and College Archives, Earlham College, Richmond, Indiana. Author of *God's Government Begun: The Society for Universal Inquiry and Reform, 1842–1846*, 1995, *The Transformation of American Quakerism: Orthodox Friends, 1800–1907*, 1998, and *The Quakers in America*, 2003.

HEITZENRATER, RICHARD P. Contributor. William Kellon Quick Professor of Church History and Wesley Studies, Duke University, Durham, North Carolina. Author of *Mirror and Memory: Reflections on Early Methodism*, 1989, and of several books about John Wesley, including *John Wesley As Seen by Contemporaries and Biographers*, 1984, *Wesley and the People Called Methodists*, 1995, and *The Elusive Mr. Wesley*, 2003. Editor of *Diary of an Oxford Methodist, Benjamin Ingham, 1733–1734*, 1985, *The Poor and the People Called Methodists, 1729–1999*, 2002, and other volumes. Essay: Methodism.

HERMANSEN, MARCIA. Peer reviewer. Professor of theology, Loyola University Chicago, Illinois. Author of *The Conclusive Argument from God*, including a translation from the Arabic of *Hujjat Allah al-Baligha*, by Shah Wali Allah, 1996. Coeditor of *Encyclopedia of Islam and the Muslim World*, 2003. Contributor to books, including *Women and Revolution in Iran*, edited by G. Nashat, 1983, *God Experience or Origin*, 1985, *Muslims of America*, edited by Yvonne Haddad, 1991, *Muslim Communities in America*, edited by Yvonne Haddad, 1994, *New*

Trends and Developments in the World of Islam, edited by Peter Clarke, 1997, and *Teaching Islam*, edited by Brannon Wheeler, 2002. Contributor to numerous journals, including *Studies in Islam, Journal of Near Eastern Studies, Arabica, Islamic Quarterly, Studies in Religion*, and *Muslim Education Quarterly*.

HEZEL, FRANCIS. Peer reviewer. Director, Micronesian Seminar, Kolonia, Pohnpei, Federated States of Micronesia. Author of *The First Taint of Civilization: A History of the Caroline and Marshall Islands in Pre-Colonial Days, 1521–1885*, 1983, *From Conquest to Colonization: Spain in the Mariana Islands, 1690 to 1740*, 1989, *The Catholic Church in Micronesia*, 1991, *Strangers in Their Own Land*, 1995, and *The New Shape of Old Island Cultures: A Half Century of Social Change in Micronesia*, 2001.

HILL, JACK A. Contributor. Assistant professor of religion, Texas Christian University, Fort Worth. Author of *I-Sight: The World of Rastafari: An Interpretive Sociological Account of Rastafarian Ethics*, 1995, and *Seeds of Transformation: Discerning the Ethics of a New Generation*, 1998. Author of numerous articles in scholarly journals, including *Annual of the Society of Christian Ethics, Journal of Religious Thought, Journal of Beliefs and Values, Journal for the Study of Religion*, and *Pacific Journal of Theology and Missiology*. Essays: Fiji, Federated States of Micronesia.

HILLERBRAND, HANS. Peer reviewer. Professor of religion and history, Duke University, Durham, North Carolina. Author of numerous books, including *The Reformation: A Narrative History Related by Contemporary Observers and Participants*, 1964, *Christendom Divided: The Protestant Reformation*, 1971, *The World of the Reformation*, 1973, *Anabaptist Bibliography, 1520–1630*, 1991, and *Historical Dictionary of the Reformation and Counter-Reformation*, 1999. Editor of many books, including *Protestant Reformation*, 1968, *Oxford Encyclopedia of the Reformation*, 1996, and *Encyclopedia of Protestantism*, 2003. Contributor to numerous journals.

HJELM, TITUS. Contributor. Researcher, Department of Comparative Religion, University of Helsinki, Finland. Author of Finnish high school philosophy textbooks, as well as various articles on satanism and new religious movements in Finnish and English anthologies. Essay: Finland.

HOFFMAN, VALERIE. Adviser and contributor. Associate professor of religion, University of Illinois, Urbana-Champaign. Author of *Sufism, Mystics, and Saints in Modern Egypt*, 1995. Author of numerous articles in scholarly journals, including *International Journal of Middle East Studies, Journal of American Academy of Religion, Muslim World, Religion, Religion and the Arts*, and *Mystics Quarterly*, as well as for *Encyclopedia of Modern Islam, The Encyclopedia of the Qur'an, Holy People: An Encyclopedia, HarperCollins Dictionary of Religion*, and *The Dictionary of Feminist Theologies*. Essay: Oman.

HOLLAND, CLIFTON L. Contributor. Director of PROLADES (Latin American Socio-Religious Studies Program), San José, Costa Rica, and editor of *Mesoamerica*, a monthly news journal published by the Institute of Central American Studies (ICAS), San José. Author of *Religious Dimension in Hispanic Los Angeles: A Protestant Case Study*, 1974, as well as numerous published research reports, documents, and magazine articles. Editor of *World Christianity: Central American and the Caribbean*, 1981. Essays: Belize, Costa Rica, Mexico, Paraguay, Portugal, Spain, Suriname.

HOLMBERG, DAVID H. Contributor. Professor of anthropology and Asian studies, as well as chair of the Anthropology Department, Cornell University, Ithaca, New York. Author of *Order in Paradox: Myth, Ritual, and Exchange among Nepal's Tamang*, 1989, as well as articles in numerous journals, including *Journal of Asian Studies, Signs, American Ethnologist, Journal of Ritual Studies*, and *Himalayan Research Bulletin*. Essay: Nepal.

HOLT, JOHN C. Contributor and peer reviewer. William R. Kenan Professor of the Humanities and Religion, as well as chair of the Religion Department, Bowdoin College, Brunswick, Maine. Author of *Discipline: The Canonical Buddhism of the Vinayapitaka*, 1981, *Buddha in the Crown: Avalokitesvara in the Buddhist Traditions of Sri Lanka*, 1991, *The Religious World of Kirti Sri: Buddhism, Art, and Politics in Late Medieval Sri Lanka*, 1996, and *The Buddhist Visnu: Religious Assimilation, Politics, and Culture*, 2004. Essay: Sri Lanka.

HUDEPOHL, KATHRYN A. Contributor. Assistant professor of modern language and intercultural studies, Western Kentucky University, Bowling Green. Essay: Saint Lucia.

HURLEY, SCOTT. Contributor. Visiting assistant professor of religion, Department of Religion and Philosophy, Luther College, Decorah, Iowa. Coauthor of "Some Thoughts on the Theory of Religious Capital in a Global Era: The Tzu Chi Movement and the Praxis of Charity," in *The Annual Bulletin of the Japan Academy for Foreign Trade*, 2003, and "The Lotus of Capital: Tzu Chi Foundation and the Praxis of Charity," in *Kokushikan Journal of Asia*, 21, 2003. Essay: Taiwan.

HUSSAINMIYA, B.A. Contributor. Senior lecturer in history, University of Brunei Darussalam. Author of *Orang Rejimen: The Malays of the Ceylon Rifle Regiment*, 1990, and *Sultan Omar Ali Saifuddin and Britain: The Making of Brunei Darussalam*, 1995. Essay: Brunei.

ISAAK, PAUL JOHN. Contributor. Head, Department of Religion, University of Namibia, Windhoek. Author of *Religion and Society: A Namibian Perspective*, 1997. Editor of *The Evangelical Lutheran Church in the Republic of Namibia in the 21st Century*, 2000. Author of articles in numerous journals, including *Black Theology: An International Journal, African Theological Journal, African Bible Commentary, Journal of Religion and Theology in Namibia, Panorama, Journal of Constructive Theology, Southern Africa,* and *Ecumenical Review.* Essay: Namibia.

ISKENDEROVA, MAYA. Contributor. Doctoral candidate, Institute of History, Azerbaijan Academy of Sciences, Baku. Essay: Azerbaijan.

JACKSON, ROGER. Peer reviewer. Professor of religion and director of Asian studies, Carleton College, Northfield, Minnesota. Author of *Is Enlightenment Possible?*, 1993, and *Tantric Treasures*, 2004. Coauthor of *The Wheel of Time: Kalachakra in Context*, 1985. Coeditor of *Tibetan Literature: Studies in Genre*, 1996, and *Buddhist Theology*, 1999. Author of numerous articles and reviews.

JACOBS, CLAUDE. Contributor. Associate professor of behavioral science, University of Michigan-Dearborn. Coauthor of *The Spiritual Churches of New Orleans: Origins, Beliefs, and Rituals of an African-American Religion*, 1991. Author of articles in numerous journals. Essay: Panama.

JAFFEE, MARTIN. Peer reviewer. Professor, Henry M. Jackson School of International Studies, University of Washington, Seattle. Author of *Mishnah's Theology of Tithing: A Study of Tractate Maaserot*, 1981, *The Talmud of the Land of Israel: A Preliminary Translation and Explanation*, Vol. 7, 1987, *The Talmud of Babylonia: An American Translation*, 1987, *Early Judaism: Religious Worlds of the First Judaic Millennium*, 1997, and *Torah in the Mouth: Writing and Oral Tradition in Palestinian Judaism*, 2001. Coauthor of *Jews, Christians, Muslims: A Comparative Introduction to Monotheistic Religions*, 1998. Coeditor of *Innovation and Religious Traditions: Essays in the Interpretation of Religious Change*, 1992, and *Readings in Judaism, Christianity, and Islam*, 1998. Contributor to numerous books and journals.

JAHANBAKHSH, FOROUGH. Contributor. Assistant professor of religious studies, Queen's University, Kingston, Ontario, Canada. Author of *Islam, Democracy and Religious Modernism in Iran (1953–2000)*, 2001. Author of articles in journals, including *Brown Journal of World Affairs, ISIM Newsletter,* and *Historical Reflection.* Essays: Iran, Shiism.

JAKSIC, IVAN. Peer reviewer. Professor of history, University of Notre Dame, Indiana. Author of *Academic Rebels in Chile: The Role of Philosophy in Higher Education and Politics*, 1989, and *Andres Bello: Scholarship and Nation Building in Nineteenth-Century Latin America*, 2001. Editor of *Selected Writings of Andres Bello*, 1998, and *The Political Power of the Word: Press and Oratory in Nineteenth-Century Latin America*, 2002. Coeditor of *Filosofia e identidad cultural en America Latina*, 1988, *The Struggle for Democracy in Chile, 1982–1990*, 1991, and *Sarmiento: Author of a Nation*, 1994.

JOCHIM, CHRISTIAN. Contributor. Professor of comparative religious studies, as well as director, Center for Asian Studies, and chair of the Humanities Department, San Jose State University, California. Author of *Chinese Religions: A Cultural Perspective*, 1986. Author of articles in various journals, including *Journal of Chinese Religions, Modern China,* and *Philosophy East and West.* Essay: Confucianism.

JOHNSON, MICHELLE C. Contributor. Assistant professor of anthropology, Bucknell University, Lewisburg, Pennsylvania. Author of chapters in *Female Circumcision in Africa: Culture, Controversy, and Change*, 2000, and *A World of Babies: Imagined Child-Care Guides for Seven Societies*, 2000. Essay: Guinea-Bissau.

JOHNSON, RHONDA. Contributor. Assistant professor and head of access services, Hostos Community College Library, Bronx, New York. Researcher for *Encyclopedia of the United Nations and International Agreements*, by Edmund Jan Osmanczyk, 2003. Essay: Saint Kitts and Nevis.

JONES, STEVEN. Contributor. Associate director, Center on Religion and Democracy, as well as lecturer, Department of Sociology, University of Virginia, Charlottesville. Author of various articles on religion and democracy, including essays on Alexis de Tocqueville, the Nation of Islam, and the intersection of religion and globalization. Essays: Baptist Tradition, Honduras.

KAPLAN, DANA EVAN. Contributor. Visiting research fellow, University of Miami, Coral Gables, Florida. Author of *American Reform Judaism*, 2003, and coauthor of *Platforms and Prayer Books*, 2002. Editor of *Conflicting Visions: Contemporary Debates in American Reform Judaism*, 2001, and *Cambridge Companion to American Judaism*, 2004. Essay: Reform Judaism.

KAUFMAN, PETER IVER. Peer reviewer. Professor of religious studies, University of North Carolina, Chapel Hill. Author of several books, including *Augustinian Piety and Catholic Reform: Augustine, Colet, and Erasmus*, 1982, *The "Polytyque Churche": Religion and Early Tudor Political Culture, 1485–1516*, 1986, and *Prayer, Despair, and Drama: Elizabethan Introspection*, 1996.

KERKHOFS, JAN. Contributor and peer reviewer. Professor emeritus, Kotholieke Universiteit, Leuven, Belgium, and founder, European Values Study. Author of many books in Dutch, as well as *Europe without Priests*, 1995, and *A Horizon of Kindly Light*, 1999, both in English. Essay: Belgium.

KHAN, AISHA. Contributor. Associate professor, Department of Anthropology, New York University, New York. Author of articles and essays, including "Juthaa in Trinidad: Food, Pollution, and Hierarchy in a Caribbean

Diaspora Community," in *American Ethnologist*, 1994, "'Rurality' and 'Racial' Landscapes in Trinidad," in *Knowing Your Place: Rural Identity and Cultural Hierarchy*, edited by Barbara Ching and Gerald Creed, 1997, and "Journey to the Center of the Earth: The Caribbean as Master Symbol," in *Cultural Anthropology*, 2001. Essay: Trinidad and Tobago.

KHAZANOV, ANATOLY M. Contributor. Ernest Gellner Professor of Anthropology, University of Wisconsin, Madison. Author and editor of many books, including *Nomads and the Outside World*, 1984, *Soviet Nationality Policy during Perestroika*, 1991, and *After the USSR: Ethnicity, Nationalism and Politics in the Commonwealth of Independent States*, 1995. Essay: Kazakhstan.

KHODJIBAEV, KARIM. Contributor. Voice of America radio broadcaster. Author of *U.N. Special Report of Tajikistan*, 1994, as well as a series of radio features on American democracy, 1995, and articles in journals, including *Central Asia Monitor*. Essay: Tajikistan.

KIMMERLING, BARUCH. Contributor. George S. Wise Professor of Sociology, Hebrew University of Jerusalem, Israel. Author of numerous books and articles, including *Zionism and Territory*, 1983, *The Interrupted System: Israeli Civilians in War and Routines*, 1985, *The Invention and Decline of Israeliness: State, Society and the Military*, 2001, and *Immigrants, Settlers and Natives: Israel between Multiculturalism and Kulturkampf*, 2003. Coauthor of *The Palestinians: A History*, 2003. Essay: Israel.

KINNARD, JACOB. Contributor and peer reviewer. Assistant professor of religion, College of William and Mary, Williamsburg, Virginia. Author of *Imagining Wisdom: Seeing and Knowing in the Art of Indian Buddhism*, 1999. Coeditor of *Constituting Communities: Theravada Buddhism and the Religious Cultures in South and Southeast Asia*, 2003. Essay: Buddhism.

KIRKLAND, J. RUSSELL. Contributor. Associate professor of religion, University of Georgia, Athens. Author of *Taoism: An Enduring Tradition*, 2004, as well as articles in numerous journals, including *History of Religions* and *Journal of the American Academy of Religion*. Essay: Taoism.

KIVILU, SABAKINU. Contributor. Professor and president, Institut de Recherche et d'Études Historiques du Présent, University of Kinshasa, Democratic Republic of the Congo. Contributor to *Démocratie et paix en République Démocratique du Congo*, 2000, *Élites et démocratie en République Démocratique du Congo*, 2002, *Les consequences de la guerre de la République Démocratique du Congo en Afrique Centrale*, 2003, as well as to journals, including *Journal of African Studies*, 1999, and *Laurent Monnier*, 2000. Essay: Democratic Republic of the Congo.

KNOWLTON, DAVID. Contributor. Associate professor, Behavioral Science Department, Utah Valley State College, Orem, Utah. Essays: Bolivia, Colombia, Ecuador.

KNYSH, ALEXANDER. Peer reviewer. Professor of Islamic studies, as well as chairman, Department of Near Eastern Studies, University of Michigan, Ann Arbor. Author of *Ibn al-'Arabi in the Later Islamic Tradition: The Making of a Polemical Image in Medieval Islam*, 1998, and *Islamic Mysticism: A Short History*, 2000. Author, in Russian, of *Ibn al-'Arabi: The Meccan Revelations: Selected Translations of Ibn al-'Arabi's Early Works and a Chapter from al-Futuhat al-makkiya*, 1995. Contributor to books, including *History of Islamic Philosophy*, edited by S.H. Nasr and O. Leaman, 1996, *Hadhrami Traders, Scholars, and Statesman in the Indian Ocean, 1750s–1960s*, edited by U. Freitag and W. Clarence-Smith, 1997, *Companion to Arabic Literature*, 1998, and *Cambridge History of Arabic Literature: The Literature of al-Andalus*, edited by M.R. Menocal, R. Sheindlin, and M. Sells, 2000. Contributor to numerous journals.

KOLB, ROBERT. Contributor and peer reviewer. Missions Professor of Systematic Theology, Concordia Seminary, Saint Louis, Missouri. Author of *The Christian Faith: A Lutheran Exposition*, 1993, *Speaking the Gospel Today: A Theology for Evangelism*, 1995, *Luther's Heirs Define His Legacy: Studies on Lutheran Confessionalization*, 1996, and *Martin Luther as Prophet, Teacher, Hero: Images of the Reformer, 1520–1620*, 1999. Coeditor of *The Book of Concord: The Confessions of the Evangelical Lutheran Church*, 2000, and other books. Essay: Lutheranism.

KOLLAR, NATHAN R. Contributor. Professor of religious studies, Saint John Fisher College, Rochester, New York; senior lecturer, Department of Education and Human Development, University of Rochester, New York; and chair, Center for Interfaith Studies and Dialogue, Nazareth College, Rochester, New York. Author of *Death and Other Living Things*, 1973, and *Songs of Suffering*, 1982, as well as numerous articles in edited volumes and journals. Editor of *Options in Roman Catholicism: An Introduction*, 1983. Essay: Canada.

KRINDATCH, ALEXEI. Contributor. Research associate, Center for Geopolitical Studies, Institute of Geography, Russian Academy of Sciences, Moscow, and research associate, Institute for the Study of American Religion, University of California, Santa Barbara. Author of *Geography of Religions in Russia*, 1996, as well as articles in numerous journals, including *Osteuropa*, *Journal for the Scientific Study of Religion*, and *Religion, State, and Society*. Essays: Lithuania, Moldova.

KRÜGGELER, MICHAEL. Contributor. Project manager, Schweizerisches Pastoralsoziologisches Institut (SPI), Saint Gall, Switzerland. Author of *Individualisierung und Freiheit: Eine Praktisch-Theologische Studie zur Religion in der Schweiz*, 1999, and coauthor of *Solidarität und Religion: Was Bewegt Menschen in Solidaritätgruppen?*, 2002. Coeditor of *Religion und Moral: Entkoppelt oder Verknüpft?*, 2001. Essay: Liechtenstein.

KUBURIĆ, ZORICA. Contributor. Professor of the sociology of religion, Faculty of Philosophy, University of Novi Sad, Serbia and Montenegro, and president, Center for Empirical Researches of Religion, Novi Sad. Author of *Religion, Family, and Youth*, 1996, *Faith, Freedom, and Religious Institutions in Yugoslavia*, 2002, *Faith and Freedom: Religious Institutions in Yugoslavia*, 2002, and *Religion and Mental Health*, 2003. Editor of *Religion, Religious Education and Tolerance*, 2002. Essay: Serbia and Montenegro.

KVASNIĆKOVÁ, ADELA. Contributor. Lecturer in sociology, Comenius University, Bratislava, Slovakia. Author of an essay in the edited volume *Slovakia in the 90s*, 2003. Essay: Slovakia.

LAMB, CONNIE. Contributor. Middle East librarian, Brigham Young University, Provo, Utah. Coeditor of *Agricultural and Animal Sciences Journals and Serials: An Analytical Guide*, 1986, and *Jewish American Fiction Writers: An Annotated Bibliography*, 1991. Essay: Jordan.

LANG, KAREN C. Peer reviewer. Associate professor of religious studies, University of Virginia, Charlottesville. Author of *Four Illusions: Candrakirti's Advice to Travelers on the Bodhisattva Path*, 2002. Contributor to *Buddhist-Christian Studies*, 1982, *Feminist Studies in Religion*, 1986, and *Off with Her Head! The Denial of Women's Identity in Myth, Religion, and Culture*, edited by Howard Eilberg-Schwartz and Wendy Doniger, 1995.

LEFFERTS, LEEDOM. Contributor. Professor of anthropology, as well as director of the Asian Studies Department, Drew University, Madison, New Jersey. Cocurator of and coauthor of the catalog for *Textiles and the Tai Experience in Southeast Asia*, an exhibition at the Textile Museum, Washington, D.C., 1992. Author of numerous articles on textiles, social organization, and women's roles in Lao and Thai Theravada Buddhism and on Lao and Thai material culture. Essay: Laos.

LEGRAND, MICHEL. Contributor. Sociologist, SESOPI-Centre Intercommunautaire, Luxembourg. Editor of *Les valeurs au Luxembourg: Portrait d'une société au tournant du 3e millénaire*, 2002. Essay: Luxembourg.

LEHTSAAR, TÕNU. Contributor. Professor of practical theology, as well as vice rector for academic affairs, University of Tartu, Estonia. Author of *Religious Experiencing: A Psychological Study of Religious Experiences in the Lifelong Perspective*, 2000. Essay: Estonia.

LEUSTEAN, LUCIAN N. Contributor. Graduate research student, Interfaculty Institute of Central and Eastern Europe, University of Fribourg, Switzerland. Author of a book chapter, as well as articles in such journals as *Romania, Journal for the Study of Religions and Ideologies*, and *Romanian Military Thinking*. Essay: Romania.

LITTLEWOOD, ROLAND. Peer reviewer. Professor of psychiatry and anthropology, Department of Anthropology, University College, London. Author of *The Butterfly and the Serpent: Essays in Psychiatry, Race and Religion*, 1988, *Pathology and Identity: The Work of Mother Earth in Trinidad*, 1993, *Religion, Agency, Restitution: The Wilde Lectures in Natural Religion*, 1999, and *Pathologies of the West: An Anthropology of Mental Illness in Europe and America*, 2002. Coauthor, with Maurice Lipsedge, of *Aliens and Alienists: Ethnic Minorities and Psychiatry*, 1982, and, with Simon Dein, of *Cultural Psychiatry and Medical Anthropology*, 2000. Coeditor, with Jafar Kareem, of *Intercultural Therapy*, 1999. Contributor to numerous books and journals.

LOBBAN, JR., RICHARD. Contributor. Professor of anthropology and African studies, as well as director of the program in African and Afro-American studies, Rhode Island College, Providence, and vice president of the Rhode Island Black Heritage Society, Providence. Author of *Cape Verde: Crioulo Colony to Independent Nation*, 1995, *Cape Verde Islands*, 2001, and *Historical Dictionary of Ancient and Medieval Nubia*, 2004. Coauthor of *Cape Verdeans in Rhode Island*, 1990, and *Historical Dictionary of the Republic of Cape Verde*, 1995. Essay: Cape Verde.

LOVELL, NADIA. Contributor. Lecturer, University of Linkoping, Sweden. Author of *Locality and Belonging*, 1998, and *Cord of Blood: Possession and the Making of Voodoo*, 2002. Contributor to various journals, including *Ethnos*. Essay: Togo.

MAKRIDES, VASILIOS. Contributor and peer reviewer. Professor and chair of religious studies, Faculty of Philosophy, University of Erfurt, Germany. Author of *Die Religiöse Kritik am Kopernikanischen Weltbild in Griechenland zwischen 1794 und 1821: Aspekte Griechisch-Orthodoxer Apologetik Angesichts Naturwissenschaftlicher Fortschritte*, 1995, as well as numerous other books and articles in German, Greek, English, French, and Italian. Essays: Cyprus, Greece.

MALIK, SAADIA. Contributor. Independent researcher. Author of "Displacement as Discourse" in *Ìrìnkèrindò: A Journal of African Migration*. Essay: Bahrain.

MANN, GURINDER SINGH. Peer reviewer. Professor of Sikh and Punjab studies, University of California, Santa Barbara. Author of *The Goindval Pothis*, 1996, *The Making of Sikh Scripture*,

2001, *Sikhism*, 2004, and all Sikhism-related entries in *Merriam-Webster's Encyclopedia of World Religions*, 1999.

MANSURNOOR, IIK A. Contributor. Associate professor of history, University of Brunei Darussalam. Author of *Islam in an Indonesian World: Ulama of Madura*, 1990, as well as chapters in books and articles in numerous journals, including *Islamic Quarterly*, *Islamic Studies*, *Journal of Al-Islam*, *Oxford Journal of Islamic Studies*, *Prajna Vihara*, and *Islamic Culture*. Essay: Kuwait.

MARINOV, MARIO. Contributor. Assistant professor of sociology, South-West University "Neofit Rilski," Blagoevgrad, Bulgaria, and adjunct assistant professor, Sofia University "Saint Kliment Ohridski," Bulgaria. Author of articles in various publications, including the journal *Sociologicheski Problemi*. Essay: Bulgaria.

MARSTON, JOHN. Contributor. Professor and researcher, Centro de Estudios de Asia y África, El Colegio de México, Mexico City. Author of *Cambodia 1991–94: Hierarchy, Neutrality, and Etiquettes of Discourse*, 1997, as well as articles in numerous edited volumes and such journals as *Estudios de Asia y África*, *Southeast Asian Affairs*, and *Crossroads: An Interdisciplinary Journal of Southeast Asia*. Essay: Cambodia.

M'BAYO, TAMBA. Contributor. Ph.D. candidate, African history, Michigan State University, East Lansing. Author of articles and book reviews for journals, including *H-West-Africa* and *Historian*. Essays: Benin, Côte d'Ivoire.

MCCLYMOND, MICHAEL J. Contributor. Clarence Louis and Helen Irene Steber Professor of Theological Studies, Saint Louis University, Missouri. Author of *Encounters with God: An Approach to the Theology of Jonathan Edwards*, 1998, and *Familiar Stranger: An Approach to Jesus of Nazareth*, 2004. Editor of *Embodying the Spirit: New Perspectives on North American Revivalism*, 2004. Coeditor of *The Rivers of Paradise: Moses, Buddha, Confucius, Jesus, and Muhammed as Religious Founders*, 2001, and *Dimensions of North American Revivalism*, 2002. Essay: Christianity.

MCKIM, DONALD K. Contributor. Academic and reference editor, Westminster John Knox Press, Louisville, Kentucky. Author of numerous books, including *What Christians Believe about the Bible*, 1985, *Ramism in William Perkins' Theology*, 1987, *Theological Turning Points*, 1988, *The Bible in Theology and Preaching*, 1994, *Westminster Dictionary of Theological Terms*, 1996, *Introducing the Reformed Faith*, 2001, *Presbyterian Beliefs: A Brief Introduction*, 2003, and *Presbyterian Questions, Presbyterian Answers: Exploring Christian Faith*, 2003. Editor of numerous books, including *The Authoritative Word: Essays on the Nature of Scripture*, 1983, *Readings in Calvin's Theology*, 1984, *How Karl Barth Changed My Mind*, 1986, *God Never Forgets: Faith, Hope, and Alzheimer's Disease*, 1997, *Historical Handbook of Major Biblical Interpreters*, 1998, and

The Cambridge Companion to Martin Luther, 2003. Essays: Protestantism, Reformed Christianity.

MEADOW, MARY JO. Contributor. Professor emeritus, Minnesota State University, Mankato, and founder, Resources for Ecumenical Spirituality, Forest Lake, Minnesota. Author of *Other People*, 1984, *Gentling the Heart: Buddhist Loving-Kindness Practice for Christians*, 1994, and *Through a Glass Darkly: A Spiritual Psychology of Faith*, 1996. Coauthor of *Psychology of Religion: Religion in Individual Lives*, 1984, and *Purifying the Heart: Buddhist Insight Meditation for Christians*, 1994. Coeditor of *A Time to Weep, a Time to Sing: Faith Journeys of Women Scholars of Religion*, 1985. Essay: Theravada Buddhism.

MENDES-FLOHR, PAUL. Contributor. Professor of modern Jewish thought, Divinity School, University of Chicago, Illinois, and director, Franz Rosenzweig Research Center in German-Jewish Literature and Cultural History, Hebrew University of Jerusalem, Israel. Essay: Judaism.

MICALLEF, ROBERTA. Contributor. Assistant professor of language and literature, University of Utah, Salt Lake City. Coauthor of *Islam in Turkic Central Asia*, 1997, as well as articles in numerous edited volumes and journals. Essay: Uzbekistan.

MIŠOVIC, JÁN. Contributor. Researcher, Institute of Sociology of the Academy of Science of the Czech Republic, Prague. Author of articles in various edited volumes in Czech and English, including *New Religious Phenomena in Central and Eastern Europe*, 1997, and *Church-State Relations in Central and Eastern Europe*, 1999. Essay: Czech Republic.

MOFFIC, EVAN. Contributor. Rabbinic student, Jewish Institute of Religion, Hebrew Union College, Cincinnati, Ohio. Author of articles in *CCAR Journal*. Essay: Reform Judaism.

MOLNAR, ANDREA. Contributor. Associate professor of anthropology, Northern Illinois University, DeKalb. Author of *Grandchildren of the Ga'e Ancestors: Social Organization and Cosmology among the Hoga Sara of Flores*, 2000, as well as essays in various edited volumes and articles in journals, including *Anthropos* and *Antropologi Indonesia*. Essay: East Timor.

MOLNÁR, ATTILA KAROLY. Contributor. Assistant professor, Eötvös University and Pázmány Péter Catholic University, Budapest, Hungary. Author of the monographs *The "Protestant Ethic" in Hungary*, 1994, *Notes from the Chaotic Prison*, 1999, and *Edmund Burke*, 2000. Essay: Hungary.

MOSAAD, MOHAMED. Contributor. Anthropologist and director, Religion and Society Studies Center, Cairo, Egypt. Author of a biography of the Prophet Muhammad, 2000, and of *Islam and Postmodernity: The New Islamic Discourse in Egypt*, 2004. Author of articles in various publications, including the newspaper *Al Qahira* and the magazine *Ar-Risala* magazine. Essays: Algeria, Iraq.

MULLIN, ROBERT BRUCE. Peer reviewer. Subdean of academic affairs and the Society for the Promotion of Religion and Learning, professor of history and world mission, and professor of modern Anglican studies, General Theological Seminary of the Episcopal Church, New York, New York. Author of *Episcopal Vision/American Reality: High Church Theology and Social Thought in Evangelical America*, 1986, *Miracles and the Modern Religious Imagination*, 1996, and *The Puritan as Yankee: A Life of Horace Bushnell*, 2002. Coauthor of *The Scientific Theist: A Life of Francis Ellingwood Abbot*, 1987, and coeditor of *Reimagining Denominationalism: Interpretive Essays*, 1994.

MUZOREWA, GWINYAI H. Contributor. Professor and chair, Religion Department, Lincoln University, Pennsylvania. Author of *The Origin and Development of African Theology*, 1987, *An African Theology of Mission*, 1990, and *Mwari: The Great Being God: God Is God*, 2001. Essay: Zimbabwe.

NADEAU, KATHLEEN M. Contributor. Assistant professor of anthropology, California State University, San Bernardino. Author of articles in various journals, including *Philippine Quarterly of Culture and Society*, *East Asian Pastoral Review*, and *Journal for the Scientific Study of Religion*. Essay: Philippines.

NARAYANAN, VASUDHA. Adviser and contributor. Professor of religion, University of Florida, Gainesville, and former president, American Academy of Religion. Author of *The Way and the Goal: Expressions of Devotion in the Early Srivaisnava Tradition*, 1987, and *The Vernacular Veda: Revelation, Recitation, and Ritual*, 1994. Coauthor of *The Tamil Veda: Pillan's Interpretation of the Tiruvaymoli*, 1989. Coeditor of *Monastic Life in the Christian and Hindu Traditions: A Comparative Study*, 1990. Author of articles in various journals, including *Journal of the American Academy of Religion*, *Journal of Vaishnava Studies*, and *Daedalus: Journal of the American Academy of Arts and Sciences*. Essays: Hinduism, Vaishnavism.

NDLOVU, HEBRON. Contributor. Senior lecturer in theology and religious studies, as well as dean of the Faculty of Humanities, University of Swaziland, Kwaluseni. Author of *Phenomenology in Religion*, 1997, as well as articles in edited volumes and various journals, including *UNISWA Research Journal*, *Theologia Viatorum*, *ATISCA Bulletin*, and *Journal of Black Theology in South Africa*. Essay: Swaziland.

NELSON, JOHN K. Peer reviewer. Associate professor of theology and religious studies, University of San Francisco, California. Author of *A Year in the Life of a Shinto Shrine*, 1996,

and *Enduring Identities: The Guise of Shinto in Contemporary Japan*, 2000.

NEUMAIER, EVA. Contributor. Professor emeritus, University of Alberta, Edmonton, Canada. Author of several volumes, some under the name Eva Dargyay, including *The Rise of Esoteric Buddhism in Tibet*, 1979, *Tibetan Village Communities: Structure and Change*, 1982, and *The Sovereign All-Creating Mind—the Motherly Buddha: A Translation of the Kun-byed rgyal po'i mdo*, 1992. Coauthor of *Ladakh: Innenansicht eines Landes*, 1980, and coeditor of *Gender, Genre, and Religion: Feminist Reflections*, 1995. Essay: Mahayana Buddhism.

NEUSNER, JACOB. Peer reviewer. Research professor of theology and senior fellow, Institute of Advanced Theology, Bard College, Annandale-on-Hudson, New York. Author of more than 900 books and articles. Editor of the *Encyclopedia of Judaism*, 1999, editorial board chairman of *Review of Rabbinic Judaism*, and editor in chief of the Brill Reference Library of Judaism.

NKOMAZANA, FIDELIS. Contributor. Senior lecturer and head, Department of Theology and Religious Studies, University of Botswana, Gaborone. Author of *A New Approach to Religious Education in Botswana*, 1999, as well as articles in various edited volumes and journals, including *PULA: Botswana Journal of African Studies*, *Scriptura*, *Journal of Religion and Theology in Namibia*, and *Religion and Theology*. Essay: Botswana.

NORDBECK, ELIZABETH C. Contributor. Moses Brown Professor of Ecclesiastical History, Andover Newton Theological School, Wolfeboro, New Hampshire. Author of *Thunder on the Right: Understanding Conservative Christianity*, 1990, and coeditor of *Living Theological Heritage of the United Church of Christ*, 1999. Essay: United Church of Christ.

NUMBERS, RONALD. Peer reviewer. Hilldale and William Coleman Professor of the History of Science and Medicine, University of Wisconsin, Madison. Author of numerous books, including *The Creationists*, 1992, and *Darwinism Comes to America*, 1998. Coeditor of *God and Nature: Historical Essays on the Encounter between Christianity and Science*, 1986, *Caring and Curing: Health and Medicine in the Western Religious Traditions*, 1986, *Disseminating Darwinism: The Role of Place, Race, Religion, and Gender*, 1999, and *When Science and Christianity Meet*, 2003. Contributor to numerous books and journals.

OLADIPO, CALEB. Contributor and peer reviewer. Assistant professor, Baylor University, Waco, Texas, and director of the Baylor in West Africa Program. Author of *Development of the Doctrine of the Holy Spirit in the Yoruba (African) Indigenous Christian Movement*, 1996, as well as articles in numerous edited volumes and journals, including *International Christian Digest*,

Chicago Studies, Interpretation: A Journal of Bible and Theology, and *Journal of Church-State Studies.* Essays: Somalia, South Africa.

OLDSTONE-MOORE, JENNIFER. Peer reviewer. Associate professor, Department of Religion, Wittenberg University, Springfield, Ohio. Author of *Confucianism: Origins, Beliefs, Practices, Holy Texts, Sacred Places,* 2002, and *Taoism: Origins, Beliefs, Practices, Holy Texts, Sacred Places,* 2003. Contributor to *World Religions: The Illustrated Guide,* edited by Michael Coogan, 1998, *China: Empire and Civilization,* edited by Edward Shaughnessy, 2000, and to journals and encyclopedias.

OLSON, ERNEST. Contributor. Associate professor of anthropology and religion, as well as chair of the sociology/anthropology major, Wells College, Aurora, New York. Author of articles in various journals, including *Journal of Ritual Studies.* Essay: Tonga.

OLUPONA, JACOB K. Contributor. Director, African and African-American Studies, University of California, Davis. Author of *Religion, Kingship and Rituals in a Nigerian Community,* 1991, editor of *African Traditional Religions in Contemporary Society,* 1991, and coeditor of *Religious Pluralism in Africa: Essays in Honor of John Mbiti,* 1993. Essay: African Traditional Religions.

OTTENHEIMER, MARTIN. Peer reviewer. Professor of anthropology, Kansas State University, Manhattan. Author of *Marriage in Domoni: Husbands and Wives in an Indian Ocean Community,* 1985, and *Forbidden Relatives,* 1996. Coauthor of *Historical Dictionary of the Comoro Islands,* 1994. Contributor to books, including *The Encyclopedia of Vernacular Architecture of the World,* 1997, and *The Encyclopedia of Sub-Saharan Africa,* 1997. Contributor to numerous journals, including *Journal of Cognition and Culture, Choice, Czech Sociological Review,* and *American Anthropologist.*

PAPONNET-CANTAT, CHRISTIANE. Contributor. Professor and chair, Department of Anthropology, University of New Brunswick, Fredericton, Canada. Author of articles in various French-, Spanish-, and English-language journals, including *Agalter, Anthropologica, Canadian Review of Sociology and Anthropology, Ciencias Agrarias, Culture, Egalité, Extension Rural,* and *Journal of Clinical Engineering.* Essay: France.

PATTERSON, MARY. Contributor. Senior lecturer in anthropology, University of Melbourne, Australia. Author of book chapters on the arts, sorcery, and witchcraft in Oceania, as well as articles in various scholarly journals, including *Anthropological Forum, Oceania,* and *Australian Journal of Anthropology.* Essay: Vanuatu.

PENTON, M. JAMES. Contributor. Professor emeritus, University of Lethbridge, Alberta, Canada. Author of

Jehovah's Witnesses in Canada: Champions of Freedom of Speech and Worship, 1976, and *Apocalypse Delayed: The Story of Jehovah's Witnesses,* 1997, as well as articles in various edited volumes and journals, including *Journal of Church and State.* Essay: Jehovah's Witnesses.

PETERSON, WILLIAM. Contributor. Associate professor, California State University, San Bernardino. Author of *Theatre and the Politics of Culture in Contemporary Singapore,* 2001. Author of numerous articles on theater and politics in Singapore, Maori theater, Australian theater, Indonesian dance, and American performance art for journals, including *Contemporary Dramatists, Theatre Research International, Asian Theatre Journal, Australasian Drama Studies, Theatre Journal, Journal of Dramatic Theory and Criticism, High Performance,* and *Theatre Insight.* Essay: Singapore.

PÉTURSSON, PÉTUR. Contributor. Professor of theology, University of Iceland, Reykjavík. Author of numerous books and articles on modern Icelandic church history, new religious movements, and Christian themes in film, art, and literature. Essay: Iceland.

PHUNTSHO, KARMA. Contributor. Scholar of Buddhism and Bhutan studies, as well as a trained Tibetan Buddhist. Author of various articles on Buddhism, Bhutan, and Tibetan studies and of a book on Buddhist epistemology. Essay: Bhutan.

POLLAK-ELTZ, ANGELINA. Contributor. Professor, Universdad Católica A. Bello, Caracas, Venezuela. Author of numerous books, including *Umbanda en Venezuela,* 1989, *Los santos populares en Venezuela,* 1989, *La religiosidad popular en Venezuela,* 1993, *Religiones Afroamericanos,* 1994, *Trommel und Trance: Afroamerikanische Religionen,* 1995, *El pentecostalismo en Venezuela,* 2000, and *La medicina tradicional en Venezuela,* 2001. Essay: Venezuela.

POLLOCK, NANCY J. Contributor. Acting director of development studies, Victoria University, Wellington, New Zealand. Author of *These Roots Remain: Food Habits in Islands of the Central and Eastern Pacific since Western Contact,* 1992. Coeditor of *Social Aspects of Obesity,* 1995. Essays: Fiji, Marshall Islands, and Nauru.

POTOCNIK, VINKO. Contributor. Associate professor, Faculty of Theology, University of Ljubljana, Slovenia. Contributor to *Mate-Toth,* 2001, as well as to numerous journals. Essay: Slovenia.

PRANDI, CARLO. Contributor and peer reviewer. Professor of the sociology of religion, University of Parma, Italy. Author of *I dinamismi del sacro fra storia e sociologia,* 1990, *La*

tradizione religiosa, 2000, and *La religione populare fra tradizione e modernita*, 2002. Essay: Italy.

RAUSCH, MARGARET JEAN. Contributor and peer reviewer. Assistant professor of religious studies, University of Kansas, Lawrence. Author of various scholarly articles on the social and spiritual role of women in Morocco. Coauthor of *Modern Literary Arabic*, 1981. Essay: Morocco.

REINSCHMIDT, MICHAEL C. Contributor. Lecturer, Department of Anthropology, California State University, Chico, and research associate, UCLA Fowler Museum of Cultural History, Los Angeles, California. Author of articles in various edited volumes and for conferences. Coeditor of *Strengthened Abilities: Assessing the Vision of Tosan Ahn Chang-Ho*, 1998. Essay: South Korea.

ROBBINS, JOEL. Peer reviewer. Associate professor, Department of Anthropology, University of California, San Diego. Coeditor of *Money and Modernity: State and Local Currencies in Contemporary Melanesia*, 1999. Coeditor of a special issue of the journal *Anthropology and Humanism*, 1997. Author of articles in journals, including *Ethnology*, *Social Analysis*, *Anthropological Quarterly*, and *Anthropology and Humanism*.

ROBERTS, ALLEN F. Peer reviewer. Director, James S. Coleman Center for African Studies, University of California, Los Angeles. Curator and contributor to exhibition catalogs, including *The Rising of a New Moon*, 1985, *Animals in African Art*, 1995, and, with Mary Nooter Roberts, *Memory: Luba Art and the Making of History*, 1996, and *A Sense of Wonder*, 1997.

ROEBER, A. GREGG. Contributor. Professor of early modern history and religious studies and head of the History Department, Penn State University, University Park, Pennsylvania, and member of the Orthodox Theological Society of America. Author of *Faithful Magistrates and Republican Lawyers: Creators of Virginia Legal Culture, 1680–1810*, 1981, and *Palatines, Liberty, and Property: German Lutherans and Colonial British North America*, 1993, as well as articles in edited volumes and in such journals as *Lutheran Forum* and *William and Mary Quarterly*. Essay: Eastern Orthodoxy.

SALAMONE, FRANK A. Contributor. Professor of sociology and anthropology, Iona College, New Rochelle, New York. Author of *Gods and Goods in Africa: Persistence and Change in Ethnic and Religious Identity in Yauri Emirate, North-Western State, Nigeria*, 1974, *The Hausa People, a Bibliography*, 1983, *Who Speaks for Yanomami?*, 1996, *The Yanomami and Their Interpreters: Fierce People or Fierce Interpreters?*, 1997, *Italians in Rochester, New York, 1900–1940*, 2000, and *Popular Culture in the Fifties*, 2001, as well as numerous articles for journals, including *American*

Anthropologist, *African Studies Review*, *Popular Culture*, and *Eastern Anthropologist*. Essays: Liberia, Niger, Vatican City.

SAMSON, C. MATHEWS. Contributor. Visiting lecturer, Department of Anthropology, University of Oklahoma, Norman. Author of articles in various journals, including "Texts and Context: Social Context and the Content of Liturgical Texts in Nicaragua and El Salvador," in *Human Mosaic*, 1991, and "The Martyrdom of Manuel Saquic: Constructing Maya Protestantism in the Face of War in Contemporary Guatemala," in *La Fait Missionaire*, 2003. Essay: Guatemala.

SANDS, CANON KIRKLEY C. Contributor. Lecturer, School of Social Sciences, College of The Bahamas, Nassau, and associate priest, Holy Trinity Church, Nassau. Author of *The Christian Church and the Penal Code: A Christian Response to Crime in The Bahamas*, 1983, and contributor to *Bahamas: Independence and Beyond*, 2003, *Cultural Perspectives*, 2003, and *Junkanoo and Religion: Christianity and Cultural Identity in The Bahamas*, 2003. Essay: The Bahamas.

SARNA, JONATHAN. Peer reviewer. Joseph H. and Belle R. Braun Professor of American Jewish History, Department of Near Eastern and Judaic Studies, Brandeis University, Waltham, Massachusetts. Author of *Jacksonian Jew: The Two Worlds of Mordecai Noah*, 1981, *JPS: The Americanization of Jewish Culture*, 1989, and *American Judaism: A History*, 2004. Coauthor of *American Synagogue History: A Bibliography and State-of-the-Field Survey*, 1988, *The Jews of Cincinnati*, 1989, *Yahadut Amerika: American Jewry: An Annotated Bibliography of Publications in Hebrew*, 1991, *The Jews of Boston*, 1995, and *Religion and State in the American Jewish Experience*, 1997. Editor of *Jews in New Haven*, 1978, *People Walk on Their Heads: Moses Weinberger's Jews and Judaism in New York*, 1982, *Observing America's Jews*, by Marshall Sklare, 1993, *The American Jewish Experience: A Reader*, 2nd edition, 1997, and *Minority Faiths and the American Protestant Mainstream*, 1997. Coeditor of *Jews and the Founding of the Republic*, 1985, *Yehude Artsot Ha-Berit*, 1992, *Ethnic Diversity and Civic Identity: Patterns of Conflict and Cohesion in Cincinnati since 1820*, 1992, *A Double Bond: The Constitutional Documents of American Jewry*, 1992, *Abba Hillel Silver and American Zionism*, 1997, and *Woman and American Judaism: Historical Perspectives*, 2001. Contributor to numerous journals.

SAUL, MAHIR. Contributor. Associate professor of anthropology, University of Illinois, Urbana. Coauthor of *West African Challenge to Empire: Culture and History in the Volta-Bani Anticolonial War*, 2001. Author of articles in numerous journals, including *American Anthropologist*, *American Ethnologist*, *Journal of the Royal Anthropological Institute*, *Africa*, and *International Journal of African Historical Studies*. Essay: Burkina Faso.

SCHOEPFLIN, RENNIE. Peer reviewer. Professor of history, La Sierra University, Riverside, California. Author of *Christian Science on Trial: Religious Healing in America*, 2003.

SHANKLAND, DAVID. Contributor. Senior lecturer in social anthropology, University of Bristol, England. Author of *Islam and Society in Turkey*, 1999, and *The Alevis in Turkey: The Emergence of a Secular Islamic Tradition*, 2003. Editor of *The Turkish Republic at Seventy-Five Years: Progress, Development, Change*, 1999. Essay: Turkey.

SHIPPS, JAN. Peer reviewer. Professor emeritus of religious studies and history, Indiana University–Purdue University, Indianapolis. Author of *Mormonism: The Story of a New Religious Tradition*, 1985, and *Sojourner in the Promised Land: Forty Years among the Mormons*, 2000. Editor of *Religion and Public Life in the Mountain West: Sacred Landscapes in Tension*, 2004. Coeditor of *The Journals of William E. McLellin, 1831–1836*, 1994.

SIDKY, HOMAYUN. Contributor. Associate professor of anthropology, Miami University, Oxford, Ohio. Author of *Irrigation and State Formation in Hunza: The Anthropology of a Hydraulic Kingdom*, 1997, *Witchcraft, Lycanthropy, Drugs, and Disease: An Anthropological Study of the European Witch-Hunts*, 1997, *Bitan: Oracles and Healers in the Karakorams*, 2000, *The Greek Kingdom of Cactria: From Alexander to Eurcratides the Great*, 2000, *Halfway to the Mountain: The Jirels of Eastern Nepal*, 2000, *A Critique of Postmodern Anthropology—In Defense of Disciplinary Origins and Traditions*, 2003, and *Perspectives on Culture: A Critical Introduction to Theory in Cultural Anthropology*, 2003. Essays: Afghanistan, Pakistan, Turkmenistan.

SIMONTON, MICHAEL J. Contributor. Lecturer in anthropology, Northern Kentucky University, Highland Heights, and adjunct professor, Wilmington College of Ohio. Essays: Antigua and Barbuda, Ireland.

SINGH, PASHAURA. Contributor. Assistant professor of Sikh studies, University of Michigan, Ann Arbor. Author of *The Guru Granth Sahib: Canon, Meaning and Authority*, 2000, and *The Bhagats of the Guru Granth Sahib: Sikh Self-Definition and the Bhagat Bani*, 2003. Coeditor of *The Transmission of Sikh Heritage in the Diaspora*, 1996, and *Sikh Identity: Continuity and Change*, 1999. Author of articles in numerous journals, including *Journal of American Academy of Religion*, *Journal of American Oriental Society*, *Religious Studies Review*, and *Studies in Religion/Sciences Religieuses*. Essay: Sikhism.

SOTIRIU, ELENI. Contributor. Instructor in sociology and social anthropology, University of Erfurt, Germany. Author of various articles in Greek and English on women's issues and Orthodox Christianity. Essays: Cyprus, Greece.

SPINDLER, MARC. Contributor and peer reviewer. Professor emeritus of missiology and ecumenics, University of Leiden and University of Utrecht, The Netherlands, and research associate, Centre d'Étude d'Afrique Noire, Institut d'Études Politiques de Bordeaux, France. Author of *La mission, combat pour le salut du monde*, 1967, and *Pour une théologie de l'espace*, 1968. Coeditor of *Missiology: An Ecumenical Introduction: Texts and Contexts of Global Christianity*, 1995, *Cultures of Madagascar: Ebb and Flow of Influences*, 1995, *Chrétiens d'outre-mer en Europe: Un autre visage de l'immigration*, 2000, *Dictionnaire oecuménique de missiologie*, 2001, and *Les relations églises-états; en situation post-coloniale*, 2003. Essay: Madagascar.

STENHOUSE, JOHN. Contributor. Lecturer in history, University of Otago, Dunedin, New Zealand. Coeditor of *Science and Theology: Questions at the Interface*, 1994, *God and Government: The New Zealand Experience*, 1999, and *Disseminating Darwinism: The Role of Place, Race, Religion, and Gender*, 1999. Contributor to journals, including *Journal of the History of Biology*, *Journal of Religious History*, *Journal of Law and Religion*, *New Zealand Journal of History*, and *British Journal for the History of Science*. Essay: New Zealand.

ST JOHN, RONALD BRUCE. Contributor and peer reviewer. Author and independent scholar. Author of numerous books, including *Qaddafi's World Design: Libyan Foreign Policy, 1969–1987*, 1987, *Boundaries, Trade, and Seaports: Power Politics in the Atacama Desert*, 1992, *The Foreign Policy of Peru*, 1992, *Historical Dictionary of Libya*, 1998, *The Land Boundaries of Indochina: Cambodia, Laos, and Vietnam*, 1998, and *Libya and the United States: Two Centuries of Strife*, 2002. Author of articles in numerous journals, including *Asian Affairs: An American Review*, *Asian Survey*, *Contemporary Southeast Asia*, and *Asian Affairs: Journal of the Royal Society for Asian Affairs*. Essays: Libya, Vietnam.

STILLMAN, NORMAN. Peer reviewer. Professor and Schusterman/Josey Chair in Judaic History, Department of History, University of Oklahoma, Norman. Author of *The Jews of Arab Lands*, 1979, *The Language and Culture of the Jews of Sefrou*, 1988, *The Jews of Arab Lands in Modern Times*, 1991, and *Sephardi Religious Responses to Modernity*, 1995. Coauthor, with Yedida K. Stillman, of *Samuel Romanell's Travail in an Arab Land*, 1989, and, with Yedida K. Stillman, of *From Iberia to Diaspora: Studies in Sephardic History and Culture*, 1998. Editor of *Arab Dress: A Short History*, by Yedida K. Stillman, 2000.

STOCKMAN, ROBERT. Contributor. Director, Institute for Bahá'í Studies, Wilmette, Illinois. Author of *The Bahá'í Faith in America*, Vol. 1, *Origins, 1892–1900*, 1985, *The Bahá'í Faith in America*, Vol. 2, *Early Expansion, 1900–1912*, 1995, and *Thornton Chase: First American Bahá'í*, 2002, as well as articles in various edited volumes and journals, including *World Order*, *Religion*, *The Bahá'í Studies Review*, *Iranian Studies*, *Bahá'í News*, and *Theosophical History*. Essay: Bahá'í Faith.

STOFFELS, HIJME C. Contributor. Professor of the sociology of religion, Faculty of Theology, Vrije Universiteit, Amsterdam, The Netherlands; member of the steering committee of the International Society for the Study of Reformed Communities and of the steering committee of the Hollenweger Center for the Study of Pentecostal and Charismatic Movements, Amsterdam. Author of *Walking in the Light: Values, Beliefs, and Social Positions of Dutch Evangelicals,* 1990. Coeditor of *Reformed Vitality: Continuity and Change in the Face of Modernity,* 1998, and *Reformed Encounters with Modernity: Perspectives from Three Continents,* 2001. Essay: The Netherlands.

STOLZ, JÖRG. Contributor and peer reviewer. Professor of the sociology of religion, University of Lausanne, Switzerland, and director of the Observatoire des Religions en Suisse (ORS). Author of *Soziologie der Fremdenfeindlichkeit: Theoretische und Empirische Analysen,* 2000, and of numerous articles on the sociology of religion and on migration. Essay: Switzerland.

STRAUGHN-WILLIAMS, MARITZA. Contributor. Assistant professor of anthropology and African-American studies, Colby College, Waterville, Maine. Essays: Barbados, Dominica.

SUÁREZ, MARGARITA. Contributor. Assistant professor, Department of Religion and Philosophy, Meredith College, Raleigh, North Carolina. Author of "Across the Kitchen Table: Cuban Women Pastors and Theology," in *Gender, Ethnicity and Religion: Views from the Other Side,* edited by Rosemary Radford Ruether, 2002, and "Cubana/os," in *Handbook on Latino/a Theologies,* edited by Edwin David Aponte and Miguel A. de la Torre, 2005. Essay: Cuba.

SUSANTO, BUDI. Contributor. Director, Realino Study Institute, Sanata Dharma University, Yogyakarta, Indonesia. Author of *People (Trick) Theater: Politics of the Past in Present Day Java,* 2000. Contributor to *Indonesian Heritage,* Vol. 9, *Religion and Ritual,* 1998. Essay: Indonesia.

SYNAN, VINSON. Peer reviewer. Professor and dean, Regent University Divinity School, Virginia Beach, Virginia. Author of *The Twentieth-Century Pentecostal Explosion: The Exciting Growth of Pentecostal Churches and Charismatic Renewal Movements,* 1987, *The Spirit Said "Grow,"* 1992, *The Holiness-Pentecostal Tradition: Charismatic Movements in the Twentieth Century,* 1997, *Oldtime Power: A Centennial History of the International Pentecostal Holiness Church,* 1998, *In the Latter Days: The Outpouring of the Holy Spirit in the Twentieth Century,* 2001, *Century of the Holy Spirit: 100 Years of Pentecostal and Charismatic Renewal,* 2001, and *Voices of Pentecost: Testimonies of Lives Touched by the Holy Spirit,* 2003.

TABYSHALIEVA, ANARA. Contributor. Chair, Institute for Regional Studies, Bethesda, Maryland. Author of articles on Kyrgyzstan and Central Asia in various edited volumes and journals, including *Anthropology and Archaeology of Eurasia, Nordic Newsletter of Asian Studies,* and *OSCE Yearbook.* Essay: Kyrgyzstan.

TAIVANS, LEONS. Contributor. Professor of religion, University of Latvia, Riga. Author, in Russian, of *Po Latgalyi,* 1988, and *Vostochnaya misteriya: Politiya v relifioznom soznanii indoneziycev,* 2001. Author, in Latvian, of *Teologijas vesture I. Primkristigo laikmets, AD 1–313,* 1995, as well as numerous articles in edited volumes and journals, including *Religion in Eastern Europe.* Essay: Latvia.

TAYLOR, CHRIS. Peer reviewer. Associate professor of anthropology, University of Alabama, Birmingham. Author of *Milk, Honey, and Money: Changing Concepts in Rwandan Healing,* 1992, and *Sacrifice as Terror: The Rwandan Genocide of 1994,* 1999. Contributor to *Culture and AIDS: The Human Factor,* edited by D. Feldman, 1990, *Anthropological Approaches to the Study of Ethnomedicine,* edited by M. Nichter, 1992, *Encyclopedia of Cultures and Daily Life,* 1997, *Annihilating Difference: The Anthropology of Genocide,* edited by Alex Hinton and Nancy Scheper-Hughes, 2002, and *Anthropology and Chaos Theory,* edited by Mark Mosko and Fred H. Damon, 2004. Contributor to numerous journals, including *Social Science and Medicine, Medical Anthropology, Political and Legal Anthropology Review,* and *Anthropos.*

TEAIWA, KATERINA. Contributor. Assistant professor, Center for Pacific Islands Studies, School of Hawaiian, Asian and Pacific Studies, University of Hawaii at Manoa, Honolulu. Member of the editorial board of *Contemporary Pacific: A Journal of Island Affairs.* Essay: Kiribati.

TITUS, NOEL. Contributor. Principal and professor of church history, Codrington College, St. John, Barbados. Author of *The Church and Slavery in the English-Speaking Caribbean,* 1983, *The Development of Methodism in Barbados, 1823–1883,* 1994, and *Conflicts and Contradictions,* 1998, as well as articles in various journals, including *Howard Journal of Religion, Journal of Negro History, Anglican and Episcopal History,* and *Mission Studies.* Essays: Grenada, Saint Vincent and the Grenadines.

TRANQUILLE, DANIELLE. Contributor. Lecturer, University of Mauritius, Reduit. Coauthor of *Anthologie de la littérature Mauricienne d'expression française,* 2000. Coeditor of *Rencontres: Translation Studies,* 2000. Essay: Mauritius.

TROMPF, GARRY W. Contributor. Professor of the history of ideas, University of Sydney, Australia. Author or coauthor of numerous books, including *Melanesian Religion,* 1991, *Payback: The Logic of Retribution in Melanesian Religions,* 1994, and *The Religions of Oceania,* 1995. Editor of various books, including *Cargo Cults and Millenarian Movements: Transoceanic*

Comparisons of New Religious Movements, 1990. Essay: Solomon Islands.

TUITE, KEVIN. Contributor. Professor of anthropology, Université de Montréal, Québec, Canada. Author of *Kartvelian Morphosyntax: Number Agreement and Morphosyntactic Orientation in the South Caucasian Languages,* 1988, as well as articles in various journals, including *Anthropos, Historiographia Linguistica, Lingua, Anthropological Linguistics, Journal of Indo-European Studies,* and *Cosmos.* Editor of *Anthology of Georgian Folk Poetry,* 1994. Essay: Georgia.

UDDIN, SUFIA MENDEZ. Contributor. Assistant professor of religion, University of Vermont, Burlington. Author of articles in various edited volumes and journals, including *Journal for Islamic Studies.* Essay: Bangladesh.

UHL, FLORIAN. Contributor. Professor of philosophy and head of the Philosophy Department, Private Catholic University of Linz, Austria, and president, Austrian Society for the Philosophy of Religion (ÖGRph), Linz. Editor of *Roger Bacon in der Diskussion,* 2001, and *Roger Bacon in der Diskussion II,* 2002. Coeditor of *Rituale: Zugänge zu einem Phänomen,* 1999, *Zwischen Verzückung und Verzweiflung: Dimenensionen religiöser Erfahrung,* 2001, and *Die Sprachen der Religion,* 2003. Author of articles in various edited volumes and journals. Essay: Austria.

UNDERBERG, NATALIE M. Contributor. Visiting assistant professor of folklore, University of Central Florida, Orlando. Author of articles in edited volumes and journals, including *Folklore Forum,* 1997. Essay: Peru.

URBAN, HUGH B. Contributor and peer reviewer. Associate professor, Department of Comparative Studies, Ohio State University, Columbus. Author of *The Economics of Ecstasy: Tantra, Secrecy and Power in Colonial Bengal,* 2001, and *Tantra: Sex, Secrecy, Politics and Power in the Study of Religion,* 2003. Essay: Saivism.

VA'A, UNASA L.F. Contributor. Senior lecturer in Samoan language and culture and anthropology, National University of Samoa, Apia. Author of *Saili Matagi: Samoan Migrants in Australia,* 2001, as well as articles in various edited volumes and journals. Essay: Samoa.

VALK, PILLE. Contributor. Docent of religious education, Faculty of Theology, Tartu University, Estonia. Author of *Uhest heledast laigust Eesti kooli ajaloos 1918.1940,* 1997, and *Eesti kooli religiooniõpetuse kontseptsioon,* 2002. Author of articles in various journals, including *Panorama* and *International Journal of Practical Theology.* Essay: Estonia.

VAN BEMMELEN, PETER M. Contributor. Professor of theology, Andrews University, Berrien Springs, Michigan. Author of articles in various edited volumes, including *Adventist Missions Facing the 21st Century: A Reader,* 1990, *Women in Ministry: Biblical and Historical Perspectives,* 1998, and *Handbook of Seventh-day Adventist Theology,* 2000. Essay: Seventh-day Adventist Church.

VAN DOORN-HARDER, NELLY. Contributor and peer reviewer. Associate professor of world religions, Valparaiso University, Indiana. Author of *Contemporary Coptic Nuns,* 1995, and *Between Desert and City: The Coptic Orthodox Church Today,* 1997, as well as numerous articles about the Copts and Islam. Essay: Coptic Christianity.

VAN ROMPAY, LUCAS. Peer reviewer. Professor of Eastern Christianity, as well as director of the Center for Late Ancient Studies, Duke University, Durham, North Carolina. Coeditor of *After Chalcedon: Studies in Theology and Church History Offered to Professor Albert Van Roey for His Seventieth Birthday,* 1985, *Studies in Hebrew and Aramaic Syntax: Presented to Professor J. Hoftijzer on the Occasion of His Sixty-Fifth Birthday,* 1991, and *The Book of Genesis in Jewish and Oriental Christian Interpretation: A Collection of Essays,* 1997. Editor and translator of *Fragments syriaques du commentaire des psaumes,* by Théodore de Mopsueste, 1982, and *Le commentaire sur Genèse-Exode 9,32 du manuscrit (olim) Diayrbakir 22,* 1986.

VICTOR, ISAAC HENRY. Contributor. Research fellow, Milan V. Dimic Institute for Comparative Literary and Cultural Studies, as well as visiting professor, University of Alberta, Edmonton, Canada. Author of articles in numerous journals, including *Sri Lanka Journal for South Asian Studies, Indian Church History Review,* and *Vidyajyoti.* Essay: Maldives.

VOAS, DAVID. Contributor. Simon Research Fellow, Centre for Census and Survey Research, University of Manchester, England, and lecturer in sociology, University of Sheffield, England. Author of *The Alternative Bible,* 1993, and *The Bad News Bible,* 1994, as well as articles in various journals, including *Transactions of the Institute of British Geographers, American Sociological Review,* and *British Journal of Sociology.* Essay: United Kingdom.

VOM BRUCK, GABRIELE. Contributor. Lecturer in the anthropology of the Middle East, University of Edinburgh, Scotland. Author of articles in various journals, including *Journal of Material Culture, Die Welt der Islams, History and Anthropology,* and *Annales, Histoire, Sciences Sociales.* Essay: Yemen.

WACKER, GRANT. Adviser. Professor of church history, The Divinity School, Duke University, Durham, North Carolina. Author of *Augustus H. Strong and the Dilemma of Historical Consciousness,* 1985, *Religion in Nineteenth Century America,* 2000 (expanded in *Religion in American life: A Short History*, 2003), and *Heaven Below: Early Pentecostals and American Culture*, 2001. Coeditor of *Pentecostal Currents in American Protestantism*, 1999, *Portraits of a Generation: Early Pentecostal Leaders*, 2002, and *The Foreign Missionary Enterprise at Home: Explorations in North American Cultural History*, 2003.

WALKER, RANDI. Peer reviewer. Associate professor of church history, Pacific School of Religion, Berkeley, California. Author of *Protestantism in the Sangre de Cristos 1850–1920*, 1991, and *Emma Newman: A Frontier Woman Minister*, 2000. Contributor to *Religion and Modern New Mexico*, edited by Ferenc M. Szasz and Richard W. Etulain, 1997, *Religion and American Culture*, 1998, and *The Evolution of a UCC Style: Essays on the History and Ecclesiology of the United Church of Christ*, 2004. Contributor to journals, including *Prism*.

WASSERSTEIN, BERNARD. Adviser. Harriet and Ulrich E. Meyer Professor of Modern European Jewish History, University of Chicago, Illinois. Author of *The British in Palestine: The Mandatory Government and the Arab-Jewish Conflict*, 1978, *Britain and the Jews of Europe, 1939-1945*, 1979, *The Secret Lives of Trebitsch Lincoln*, 1988, *Herbert Samuel: A Political Life*, 1992, *Vanishing Diaspora: The Jews in Europe since 1945*, 1996, *Secret War in Shanghai*, 1999, *Divided Jerusalem: The Struggle for the Holy City*, 2001, and *Israelis and Palestinians: Why Do They Fight? Can They Stop?*, 2003. Editor of two volumes of the letters of the Zionist leader Chaim Weizmann, as well as coeditor of *The Jews in Modern France*, 1985.

WAUGH, EARLE H. Chair of advisory board, contributor, and peer reviewer. Professor of religious studies, University of Alberta, Edmonton, Canada. Author of *Peace As Seen in the Qur'an*, 1986, and *The Munshidin of Egypt: Their World and Their Song*, 1989. Coeditor of *The Muslim Community in North America*, 1983, *Muslim Families in North America*, 1991, and *The Shaping of an American Islamic Discourse: A Memorial to Fazlur Rahman*, 1999. Essay: Sunnism.

WELLMAN, JAMES K., JR. Contributor. Assistant professor of Western Christianity and comparative religion, University of Washington, Seattle. Author of *The Gold Coast Church and the Ghetto: Christ and Culture in Mainline Protestantism*, 1999. Coeditor of *The Power of Religious Publics: Staking Claims in American Society*, 1999. Author of articles in various journals, including *Review of Religious Research* and *Journal of Presbyterian History*. Essay: World Evangelicalism.

WHITE, DAVID. Peer reviewer. Professor, Department of Religious Studies, University of California, Santa Barbara. Author of *Myths of the Dog-Man*, 1991, *The Alchemical Body: Siddha Traditions in Medieval India*, 1996, and *Kiss of the Yogini: "Tantric Sex" in Its South Asian Contexts*, 2003. Editor and

author of the introductory essay, *Tantra in Practice*, 2000. Translator of *The Making of Terrorism*, by Michel Wieviorka, 1993, and cotranslator of *Ashes of Immortality: Widow-Burning in India*, by Catherine Weinberger-Thomas, 1999. Contributor to journals, including *Numen* and *History of Religions*.

WILLEMSEN, HEINZ. Contributor. Ph.D. candidate, Ruhr Universität, Bochum, Germany. Author of articles in various edited volumes and journals, including *Osteuropa*, *Südosteuropa*, and *Jahrbücher für Geschichte und Kultur Südosteruopas*. Essay: Macedonia.

WILLIAMS, PETER. Contributor and peer reviewer. Distinguished professor of comparative religion and American studies, Miami University, Oxford, Ohio. Author of *Houses of God: Region, Religion, and Architecture in the United States*, 1997, *America's Religions: Traditions and Cultures*, 1998, and *Popular Religion in America: Symbolic Change and the Modernization Process in Historical Perspective*, 2002. Essay: United States.

WOLDEMIKAEL, TEKLE. Contributor. Associate professor and chair, Department of Sociology and Anthropology, University of Redlands, California. Author of *Becoming Black American: Haitians and American Institutions in Evanston, Illinois*, 1989, as well as articles in various journals, including *African Studies Review*. Essay: Eritrea.

WU, SILAS. Contributor. Professor emeritus of Chinese and Japanese history, Boston College, Massachusetts, and associate, Fairbank Center for East Asian Research, Harvard University, Cambridge, Massachusetts. Author of *Communication and Imperial Control in China: Evolution of the Palace Memorial System, 1693–1735*, 1970, *Passage to Power: K'ang-hsi and His Heir Apparent, 1661–1722*, 1979, and *Dora Yu and Christian Revival in 20th Century China*, 2002, as well as articles in numerous journals, including *Harvard Journal of Asiatic Studies*, *American Historical Review*, *Tong Pao*, and *Academia Sinica*. Essay: China.

YOUSIF, AHMAD. Contributor. Associate professor, Institute of Islamic Studies, University of Brunei Darussalam. Author of *Muslims in Canada: A Question of Identity*, 1993, and *Religious Freedom, Minorities and Islam: An Inquiry into the Malaysian Experience*, 1998, as well as articles in various edited volumes and journals, including *Journal of Religious Studies and Theology*, *ISIM Newsletter*, and *Studies in Contemporary Islam*. Essay: Malaysia.

YURASH, ANDRIJ. Contributor. Assistant professor, Ivan Franko L'viv National University, Ukraine. Author, in Russian, of *Religious Organizations of Contemporary Ukraine*, 1997, as well as articles in various edited volumes and journals in

Ukraine, Poland, Russia, Germany, The Netherlands, England, and the United States. Essays: Eastern Catholic Churches, Ukraine.

ZALECKI, PAWEL. Contributor. Assistant professor of sociology, Nicolaus Copernicus University, Toruń, Poland. Author, in Polish, of *Religious Community as a Primary Group*, 1997, and *Between Triumphs and the Feeling of Danger: The Roman Catholic Church in Contemporary Poland in the Eyes of Its Representatives*, 2001. Coeditor, in Polish, of *Cultural Tools of Rule*, 2002. Essay: Poland.

ZOHAR, ZION. Contributor. Associate director, Institute for Judaic and Near Eastern Studies, Florida International University, Miami. Author of *Song of My People: A High Holy Day Machzor*, 1995, as well as articles in various edited volumes and journals, including *Jewish Studies*. Essay: Orthodox Judaism.

ZRINŠČAK, SINIŠA. Contributor. Associate professor of comparative social policy, Department of Social Work, Faculty of Law, University of Zagreb, Croatia, and vice president, International Study of Religion in Central and Eastern Europe Association (ISORECEA). Author, in Croatian, of *Sociology of Religion: The Croatian Experience*, 1999, as well as numerous articles in edited volumes and journals. Essay: Croatia.

Chronology

c. 1800 B.C.E.   Zarathustra, founder of Zoroastrianism, is born in Persia (modern-day Iran).

c. 1500 B.C.E.   Vishnu, the supreme deity of Vaishnava Hinduism, appears in the Vedas, the earliest sacred compositions in India.

c. 587 B.C.E.   Babylonian armies destroy the Temple in Jerusalem. The occupation of Palestine initiates the Jewish Diaspora.

c. 565 B.C.E.   Siddhartha Gautama, founder of Buddhism, is born in a small village on the border of modern-day Nepal and India.

c. 551 B.C.E.   Master Kong, or Confucius, is born in China.

c. 550 B.C.E.   Lord Mahavira, an ascetic living in Bihar, India, first sets forth the doctrines and practices of Jainism.

c. 550 B.C.E.   Rudra-Shiva is described as the lord and creator of the universe in the Upanishads, the final portion of the Hindu Vedas, laying the foundation of Shaivism.

c. 550 B.C.E.   The Achaemenian dynasty, the first empire to adopt Zoroastrianism as a state religion, originates in Persia.

c. 525 B.C.E.   In Varanasi, India, the Buddha introduces the Four Noble Truths to the public. These fundamental beliefs soon came to form the core of Theravada Buddhist teachings.

500 B.C.E.   Vishnu is featured in two popular Indian epics, the *Mahabharata* and the *Ramayana*. By portraying Vishnu as the supreme being who alone can grant salva-

tion, the epics help establish Vaishnavism as a distinct system of faith and practices within Hinduism.

c. 285 B.C.E.   Scholars in China complete the *Tao-te Ching*, or *Lao-tzu*, a written record of the oral tradition of the southern land of Ch'u and the earliest foundation of Taoism.

c. 250 B.C.E.   The emperor Ashoka, of the Mauryan dynasty, converts to Buddhism and soon begins propagating Buddhist precepts throughout India.

c. 247 B.C.E.   Venerable Mahinda, son of the Indian emperor Ashoka, carries Theravada Buddhism to Sri Lanka.

c. 30 C.E.   Roman authorities in Palestine execute Jesus of Nazareth.

c. 48 C.E.   The evangelist Saint Mark introduces Christianity to Egypt, laying the foundation of the Coptic Orthodox Church.

95 C.E.   A letter of Clement asserts the authority of the Christian church in Rome over the church in Corinth, laying the foundation of the Roman Catholic papacy.

c. 135 C.E.   Simeon Bar Kokhba, the leader of a Jewish revolt against occupying Roman forces, is killed in battle. Jews are subsequently banished from Jerusalem, while the Land of Israel becomes a non-Jewish state.

175 C.E.   The emperor Han Xiaoling orders that stelae inscribed with sacred texts of Confucianism be erected at the Chinese national university.

c. 200 C.E.   The Indian monk Nagarjuna sets forth the fundamental precepts of Mahayana Buddhism.

c. 200 c.e. The Pashupata tradition, the earliest known Shaivite branch of Hinduism, originates in India.

c. 313 c.e. Emperor Constantine revokes the ban on Christianity in the Roman Empire.

325 c.e. Constantine calls the first ecumenical council of Christian bishops at Nicaea, leading to the formation of the Eastern Orthodox Church.

c. 400 c.e. The Shvetambara branch of Jainism establishes its principal doctrines at the Council of Valabhi, creating a permanent rift with the Digambara branch.

406 c.e. Lu Hsiu-ching, a scholar and sage who collected diverse Chinese scriptures and religious teachings to create a coherent Taoist tradition, is born.

431 c.e. The Council of Chalcedon accepts Pope Leo I's solution to the question of Jesus' divinity and humanity, solidifying the authority of the papacy over Christian churches.

c. 525 c.e. Bodhidharma, a disciple of Mahayana Buddhism, founds Ch'an, or Zen, Buddhism in China.

c. 610 c.e. On what is known in Muslim tradition as the Night of Power, Muhammad ibn Abdullah, a Meccan businessman and the founder of Islam, receives his first revelation from Allah.

617 c.e. King Songtsen Gampo, responsible for laying the foundation of Buddhism in Tibet, is born.

c. 622 c.e. Muhammad forms the first Muslim community in the northern Arabian city of Yathrib, later renamed Medinat al-Nabi (modern-day Medina), or "City of the Prophet."

632 c.e. Sunni Islam originates following the death of the Prophet Muhammad.

c. 650 c.e. Followers of Zoroastrianism flee Persia in the wake of the Muslim invasion, resettling in the Gujarat region of India.

c. 656 c.e. Ali, son-in-law of the Prophet Muhammad, becomes the fourth caliph of Islam. He is recognized as the first imam of Shiism.

680 c.e. Hussein, son of Ali and the third imam of Shiism, is martyred at the hands of the Umayyads in the Battle of Karbala.

c. 712 c.e. The *Kojiki* ("Record of Ancient Matters"), a narrative that contains the earliest known written record of Shinto mythology, practices, and beliefs, appears in Japan.

859 c.e. The Yoshida Shrine, one of the oldest and most revered holy structures in the Shinto tradition, is established in Kyoto, Japan.

1054 c.e. Cardinal Humbert of Rome excommunicates the patriarch of Constantinople, precipitating what is known as the Great Schism between Roman Catholicism and Eastern Orthodoxy.

1182 c.e. The Maronite Church declares unity with the Roman Catholic Church, establishing the Uniate, or Eastern Catholic, tradition.

c. 1200 c.e. Jagachandrasuri founds Tapa Gaccha (austere practices) branch of Jainism.

c. 1209 c.e. Saint Francis of Assisi forms the order of Franciscan friars, founded on principles of "holy poverty."

1435 c.e. Yoshida Kanetomo, a Japanese scholar and the founder of Yoshida Shinto, is born. His vigorous defense of purist principles helped define Shinto culture in Japan for centuries.

1463 c.e. Guru Nanak, the founder of Sikhism, is born to an upper-caste Hindu family in the village of Talwandi, India (modern-day Nankana Sahib, Pakistan).

1517 c.e. Martin Luther nails his "Ninety-five Theses," an attack on Roman Catholic practices, to a church door, thus planting the seeds of the Protestant Reformation.

1523 c.e. After public debate the canton of Zurich, Switzerland, moves to adopt the theological doctrines of Ulrich Zwingli, one of the founders of the Reformed movement in Christianity.

c. 1530 c.e. King Henry VIII of England severs ties with the Roman Catholic Church, laying the foundation for the creation of the national Church of England, or Anglican Church.

1536 c.e. John Calvin publishes *Institutes of the Christian Religion,* outlining the theology that would prove pivotal to the development of Reformed Christianity.

1565 c.e. The Minor Reformed Church, the first organized body founded on Unitarian theology, is established in Poland.

c. 1580 c.e. The Congregationalist Church, one of four groups making up the modern-day United Church of Christ, is formed in England in reaction to the liberal doctrines of the Anglican Church.

1596 c.e. The Brest Union Council leads to the formation of national Uniate churches in Ukraine and Belarus.

1606 c.e. Guru Arjan becomes the first Sikh martyr after his execution by the Mughal emperor Jahangir.

1609 c.e. John Smyth, a dissenting pastor and the founder of the Baptist tradition, rebaptizes himself in an act of protest against the Church of England.

1652 c.e. George Fox, an English preacher, founds the Religious Society of Friends (Quakers).

1656 c.e. "Dragon Gate" Taoism, widely regarded as the foundation of modern-day "Northern Taoism," is established at the White Cloud Abbey in Beijing by disciples of the Taoist sage Wu Shou-yang.

1666 c.e. Philipp Jakob Spener becomes the pastor of the Lutheran Church in Frankfurt. The founder of the movement known as Pietism, Spener preached a Christian faith based on the individual's personal devotion to Jesus Christ, a belief that lies at the core of modern-day evangelicalism.

1699 c.e. Guru Gobind Singh creates the Khalsa Panth, or "pure path," based on strict Sikh principles.

1729 c.e. John Wesley forms a religious society with fellow students in Lincoln College, Oxford, thus laying the foundation of the Methodist Church.

1741 c.e. George de Benneville, the founder of Universalism in England, emigrates to the United States, where he soon begins preaching Universalist theology.

1746 c.e. The American pastor Jonathan Edwards writes *A Treatise concerning Religious Affections,* which describes the principal characteristics of the evangelical experience.

1775 c.e. Anglicans in the United States break from the Church of England to form the Protestant Episcopal Church.

1776 c.e. At the Philadelphia Yearly Meeting members of the Religious Society of Friends move to prohibit American Quakers from owning slaves.

1795 c.e. The term "orthodox" is first used by Jewish reformers to disparage those who refuse to adapt their faith to modern society. Almost immediately the term comes to represent Jewish groups who adhere to traditional beliefs and practices.

1801 c.e. Israel Jacobson, a seminal figure in Reform Judaism, forms the first Reform prayer chapel in Westphalia, Germany.

1824 c.e. American Reform Judaism originates in Charleston, South Carolina.

1830 c.e. Joseph Smith founds the Church of Jesus Christ of Latter-day Saints, or Mormon Church.

1831 c.e. William Miller, a farmer in upstate New York, publishes the pamphlet *Evidences from Scripture and History of the Second Coming of Christ about the Year 1843, And of His Personal Reign of One Thousand Years.* Some of Miller's disciples would later found the Seventh-day Adventist movement.

1836 c.e. The rabbi Samson Raphael Hirsch publishes *Nineteen Letters,* in which he elucidates the central tenets of modern Orthodox, or Neo-Orthodox, Judaism.

1844 c.e. 'Alí-Muhammad of Shiraz, an Iranian merchant and the founder of the Bábiacute; movement, declares himself to be the "hidden Imam" of the Shiites, laying the foundation for the Bahá'í faith.

1845 C.E. American Baptists split into Northern and Southern conventions, with the Southern Baptist Convention eventually becoming the largest Protestant group in North America.

1850 C.E. Brigham Young becomes the governor of the Utah Territory, and the headquarters of the Church of Jesus Christ of Latter-day Saints is relocated in Salt Lake City.

1863 C.E. The Bábí leader Mírzá Husayn-'Alí of Núr, or Bahá'u'lláh, launches his public ministry, declaring himself the divine messenger of the Bahá'í faith.

1870 C.E. The doctrine of papal infallibility is established at the First Vatican Council.

1879 C.E. Charles Taze Russell, founder of the Bible Students (renamed Jehovah's Witnesses in 1931), establishes the journal *Zion's Watch Tower and Herald of Christ's Presence* in order to propagate his beliefs.

1881 C.E. The World Methodist Council is formed.

1886 C.E. With the establishment of the Jewish Theological Seminary in New York City, Conservative Judaism is founded in the United States.

1901 C.E. Charles Fox Parham, an evangelist living in eastern Kansas, preaches that speaking in tongues is evidence of baptism with the Holy Spirit, launching the Pentecostal revival in Christianity.

1913 C.E. Solomon Schechter founds the United Synagogue of America, a confederation of Conservative congregations in the United States and Canada.

1917 C.E. The Bolsheviks come to power in Russia, establishing a Communist government and pursuing a policy of forced atheism.

1918 C.E. The Sunday School Movement helps launch a major revival of Coptic Christianity in Egypt.

1921 C.E. The Chinese scholar Liang Shuming publishes *Eastern and Western Cultures and Their Philosophies,* a modern defense of traditional Confucian principles.

1928 C.E. Hasan al-Banna, an Egyptian schoolteacher, founds the Ikhwan al-Muslimin, or Muslim Brotherhood, in reaction to European colonial domination in the Middle East.

1947 C.E. British territory in the Indian subcontinent is partitioned along religious lines into two independent nations—India, with a majority of Hindus, and Pakistan, becoming the first modern state founded on Sunni Muslim principles.

1947 C.E. Shoghi Effendi authorizes representation of the Bahá'í' faith, under the name Bahá'í International Community, at the United Nations.

1948 C.E. The modern Jewish state of Israel is founded.

1957 C.E. Four American groups—the Congregational Church, Christian Churches, German Reformed Church, and German Evangelical Church—join to form the United Church of Christ.

1959 C.E. In the wake of China's occupation of Tibet, the 14th Dalai Lama, Tibet's head of state and the spiritual leader of Tibetan Buddhism, is forced into exile.

1962 C.E. Pope John XXIII convenes the Second Vatican Council to reform and modernize the Roman Catholic Church.

1966 C.E. The Chinese Communist Party under Chairman Mao begins the Cultural Revolution, suppressing all religious activity in the world's most populous country and lasting until 1976.

1977 C.E. The Universal Church of the Kingdom of God is founded in Brazil, reflecting the growth of evangelical churches in Latin America.

1979 C.E. The Islamic Revolution, lead by Ayatollah Ruhollah Khomeini, overthrows the Shah of Iran and establishes an Islamic republic.

1991 C.E. The Union of Soviet Socialist Republics, composed of Russia and other Eastern European and Asian countries, dissolves, resulting in greater religious freedom in the area.

1994 C.E. In Memphis, Tennessee, white and black Pentecostal churches of the United States, long divided along racial lines, formally unify to create the Pentecostal/Charismatic Churches of North America.

2003 C.E. The Right Reverend V. Gene Robinson is consecrated in the United States as bishop of the Episcopal Diocese of New Hampshire, becoming the first openly gay, noncelibate bishop in the Anglican Communion.

List of Holy Days

2005

DECEMBER 2005

1 THURSDAY

New Moon

4 SUNDAY

Advent begins (Christian)

15 THURSDAY

Full Moon

21 WEDNESDAY

Winter Solstice

25 SUNDAY

Christmas (Christian)

26 MONDAY

Chanukah begins (Jewish)

31 SATURDAY

New Moon

Oharae, or Great
Purification (Shinto)

Begin Maidhyaiya, mid-
year/winter feast
(Zoroastrian)

2006

JANUARY 2006

1 SUNDAY

Oshogatsu, or New Year
(Shinto)

2 MONDAY

Chanukah ends (Jewish)

4 WEDNESDAY

End Maidhyaiya, mid-
year/winter feast
(Zoroastrian)

5 THURSDAY

Parkash (Birthday) Guru
Gobind Singh (Sikh)

6 FRIDAY

Epiphany (Christian)

10 TUESDAY

Id-al-Adha begins
(Muslim)

12 THURSDAY

Id-al-Adha ends (Muslim)

14 SATURDAY

Full Moon

New Year (Mahayanan)

15 SUNDAY

Seijin no hi, or *Coming of Age
Day* (Shinto)

20 FRIDAY

Id al-Ghadir (Shi'a)

27 FRIDAY

Tse Gutor (Tibetan
Buddhist)

29 SUNDAY

New Moon

New Year (Tibetan
Buddhist, Confucian)

31 TUESDAY

Muharram, New Year
(Muslim)

FEBRUARY 2006

1 WEDNESDAY

Begin Mönlam Chenmo,
the great prayer ceremo-
ny (Tibetan Buddhist)

2 THURSDAY

Setsubun no hi, Change
of Seasons, (Shinto)

9 THURSDAY

Ashura (Shi'a Muslim)

13 MONDAY

Full Moon

Tu Bi-Shevat (Jewish)

20 MONDAY

End Mönlam Chenmo,
the great prayer ceremo-
ny (Tibetan Buddhist)

26 SUNDAY

Maha Shivaratri (Saivism)

28 TUESDAY

New Moon

MARCH 2006

1 WEDNESDAY

Ash Wednesday, begin-
ning of Lent (Christian)

2 THURSDAY

Annual Fast begins
(Bahá'í)

3 FRIDAY

Hina matsuri Doll
Festival, or Girls' Day
(Shinto)

14 TUESDAY

Full Moon

Holi (Hindu, Vaishnava)

15 WEDNESDAY

Holi (Hindu, Vaishnava)

16 THURSDAY

Begin
Hamaspathmaêdaya,
feast of All Souls
(Zoroastrian)

20 MONDAY

Annual Fast ends (Bahá'í)

End Hamaspathmaêdaya,
feast of All Souls
(Zoroastrian)

21 TUESDAY

Spring Equinox

Naw-Rúz, or New Year
(Bahá'í, Zoroastrian)

29 WEDNESDAY

New Moon

APRIL 2006

5 WEDNESDAY

Qing Ming festival
(Confucian)

6 THURSDAY

Ram Navami (Hindu,
Vaishnava)

9 SUNDAY

Palm Sunday
(Christianity)

11 TUESDAY

Mawlid-al-Nabi
(Muslim)

13 THURSDAY

Full Moon

New Year (Theravadan)

Passover begins (Jewish)

14 FRIDAY

Good Friday (Christian)

Vaisakhi, Birth
Anniversary of Khalsa,
(Sikh)

16 SUNDAY

Easter (Christianity)

20 THURSDAY

Passover ends (Jewish)

21 FRIDAY

Ridván festival holy day
(Bahá'í)

25 TUESDAY

Yom Hashoah, or
Holocaust Memorial
Day (Jewish)

27 THURSDAY

New Moon

29 SATURDAY

Ridván festival holy day (Bahá'í)

30 SUNDAY

Begin Maidhyõizarêmaya, mid-spring feast (Zoroastrian)

MAY 2006

2 TUESDAY

Ridván festival holy day (Bahá'í)

3 WEDNESDAY

Yom Ha'atzmaut, or Israel Independence Day: (Jewish)

4 THURSDAY

End Maidhyõizarêmaya, mid-spring feast (Zoroastrian)

5 FRIDAY

Tango no sekku, Boys' Day (Shinto)

13 SATURDAY

Full Moon

Vesak, Buddha's Birthday (Buddhist)

23 TUESDAY

Declaration of the Báb (Bahá'í)

27 SATURDAY

New Moon

29 MONDAY

Ascension of Bahá'u'lláh (Bahá'í)

JUNE 2006

2 FRIDAY

Shavuot (Jewish)

3 SATURDAY

Shavuot (Jewish)

4 SUNDAY

Pentecost, or Whitsunday (Christian)

11 SUNDAY

Full Moon

16 FRIDAY

Guru Arjan, martyrdom day (Sikh)

25 SUNDAY

New Moon

29 THURSDAY

Begin Maidhyõishêma, mid-summer feast (Zoroastrian)

30 FRIDAY

Oharae, or Great Purification (Shinto)

JULY 2006

3 MONDAY

End Maidhyõishêma, mid-summer feast (Zoroastrian)

9 SUNDAY

Martyrdom of the Báb (Bahá'í)

11 TUESDAY

Full Moon

Asalha Puja (Buddhist)

21 FRIDAY

Summer Solstice

25 TUESDAY

New Moon

AUGUST 2006

3 THURSDAY

Tishah be-Av (Jewish)

9 WEDNESDAY

Full Moon

13 SUNDAY

Obon, Festival of the Dead begins (Shinto)

16 WEDNESDAY

Obon, Festival of the Dead ends (Shinto)

Krishna Janmashthami (Hindu, Vaishnava)

23 WEDNESDAY

New Moon

27 SUNDAY

Ganesh Chaturthi (Hindu)

SEPTEMBER 2006

7 THURSDAY

Full Moon

12 TUESDAY

Begin Paitishaya, feast of bringing in the harvest (Zoroastrian)

16 SATURDAY

End Paitishaya, feast of bringing in the harvest (Zoroastrian)

21 THURSDAY

Autumn Equinox

22 FRIDAY

New Moon

Begin Ulambana, or Ancestor Day, (Mahayana)

23 SATURDAY

Rosh Hashana, New Year (Jewish)

Begin Navaratri (Hindu, Vaishnava)

24 SUNDAY

Rosh Hashana, New Year (Jewish)

Begin Ramadan (Muslim)

28 THURSDAY

Master Kong Birthday (Confucian)

OCTOBER 2006

1 SUNDAY

End Navaratri (Hindu, Vaishnava)

2 MONDAY

Yom Kippur (Jewish)

6 FRIDAY

End Ulambana, or Ancestor Day, (Mahayana)

7 SATURDAY

Full Moon

Begin Sukkot (Jewish)

12 THURSDAY

Begin Ayathrima, bringing home the herds (Zoroastrian)

13 FRIDAY

End Sukkot (Jewish)

14 SATURDAY

Shemini Atzeret (Jewish)

15 SUNDAY

Simchat Torah (Jewish)

16 MONDAY

End Ayathrima, bringing home the herds (Zoroastrian)

20 FRIDAY

Birth of the Báb (Bahá'í)

21 SATURDAY

Dipavali, Festival of Lights (Hindu, Vaishnava, Jain, Sikh)

22 SUNDAY

New Moon

24 TUESDAY

End Ramadan Id al-Fitr (Muslim)

NOVEMBER 2006

5 SUNDAY

Full Moon

Parkash (Birthday) of Guru Nanak (Sikh)

12 SUNDAY

Birth of Bahá'u'lláh (Bahá'í)

15 WEDNESDAY

Shichi-go-san, children's rite of passage, (Shinto)

20 MONDAY

New Moon

23 THURSDAY

Niiname-sai, harvest festival (Shinto)

24 FRIDAY

Niiname-sai, harvest festival (Shinto)

Guru Tegh Bahadur, martyrdom day (Sikh)

26 SUNDAY

'Abdu'l-Bahá, Day of the Covenant (Bahá'í)

28 TUESDAY

Ascension of 'Abdu'l-Bahá (Bahá'í)

DECEMBER 2006

3 SUNDAY

Advent begins (Christian)

5 TUESDAY

Full Moon

16 SATURDAY

Chanukah begins (Jewish)

20 WEDNESDAY

New Moon

21 THURSDAY

Winter Solstice

23 SATURDAY

Chanukah ends (Jewish)

25 MONDAY

Christmas (Christian)

31 SUNDAY

Id-al-Adha begins (Muslim)

Oharae, or Great Purification (Shinto)

Begin Maidhyaiya, mid-year/winter feast (Zoroastrian)

2007

JANUARY 2007

1 MONDAY

Oshogatsu, or New Year (Shinto)

2 TUESDAY

Id-al-Adha ends (Muslim)

3 WEDNESDAY

Full Moon

New Year (Mahayanan)

4 THURSDAY

End Maidhyaiya, mid-year/winter feast (Zoroastrian)

5 FRIDAY

Parkash (Birthday) Guru Gobind Singh (Sikh)

6 SATURDAY

Epiphany (Christian)

10 WEDNESDAY

Id al-Ghadir (Shi'a)

15 MONDAY

Seijin no hi, or Coming of Age Day (Shinto)

19 FRIDAY

New Moon

20 SATURDAY

Muharram, New Year (Muslim)

29 MONDAY

Ashura (Shi'a Muslim)

FEBRUARY 2007

2 FRIDAY

Full Moon

Setsubun no hi, Change of Seasons, (Shinto)

3 SATURDAY

Tu Bi-Shevat (Jewish)

16 FRIDAY

Maha Shivaratri (Saivism)

Tse Gutor (Tibetan Buddhist)

17 SATURDAY

New Moon

18 SUNDAY

New Year (Tibetan Buddhist, Confucian)

21 WEDNESDAY

Ash Wednesday, beginning of Lent (Christian)

Begin Mönlam Chenmo, the great prayer ceremony (Tibetan Buddhist)

MARCH 2007

2 FRIDAY

Annual Fast begins (Bahá'í)

3 SATURDAY

Full Moon

Hina matsuri, Doll Festival, or Girls' Day (Shinto)

Holi (Hindu, Vaishnava)

4 SUNDAY

Holi (Hindu, Vaishnava)

12 MONDAY

End Mönlam Chenmo, the great prayer ceremony (Tibetan Buddhist)

16 FRIDAY

Begin Hamaspathmaêdaya, feast of All Souls (Zoroastrian)

19 MONDAY

New Moon

20 TUESDAY

Annual Fast ends (Bahá'í)

End Hamaspathmaêdaya, feast of All Souls (Zoroastrian)

21 WEDNESDAY

Spring Equinox

Naw-Rúz, or New Year (Bahá'í, Zoroastrian)

27 TUESDAY

Ram Navami (Hindu, Vaishnava)

31 SATURDAY

Mawlid-al-Nabi (Muslim)

APRIL 2007

1 SUNDAY

Palm Sunday (Christian)

2 MONDAY

Full Moon

3 TUESDAY

New Year (Theravadan)

Passover begins (Jewish)

5 THURSDAY

Qing Ming festival (Confucian)

6 FRIDAY

Good Friday (Christian)

8 SUNDAY

Easter (Christian)

10 TUESDAY

Passover ends (Jewish)

14 SATURDAY

Vaisakhi, Birth Anniversary of Khalsa, (Sikh)

15 SUNDAY

Yom Hashoah, or Holocaust Memorial Day (Jewish)

17 TUESDAY

New Moon

21 SATURDAY

Ridván festival holy day (Bahá'í)

23 MONDAY

Yom Ha'atzmaut, or Israel Independence Day: (Jewish)

29 SUNDAY

Ridván festival holy day (Bahá'í)

30 MONDAY

Begin Maidhyõizarêmaya, mid-spring feast (Zoroastrian)

MAY 2007

2 WEDNESDAY

Full Moon

Vesak, Buddha's Birthday (Buddhist)

Ridván festival holy day (Bahá'í)

4 FRIDAY

End Maidhyõizarêmaya, mid-spring feast (Zoroastrian)

5 SATURDAY

Tango no sekku, Boys' Day (Shinto)

16 WEDNESDAY

New Moon

23 WEDNESDAY

Declaration of the Báb (Bahá'í)

Shavuot (Jewish)

24 THURSDAY

Shavuot (Jewish)

27 SUNDAY

Pentecost, or Whitsunday (Christian)

29 TUESDAY

Ascension of Bahá'u'lláh (Bahá'í)

JUNE 2007

1 FRIDAY

Full Moon

15 FRIDAY

New Moon

16 SATURDAY

Guru Arjan, martyrdom day (Sikh)

29 FRIDAY

Begin Maidhyõishêma, mid-summer feast (Zoroastrian)

30 SATURDAY

Full Moon

Oharae, or Great Purification (Shinto)

JULY 2007

3 TUESDAY

End Maidhyõishêma, mid-summer feast (Zoroastrian)

9 MONDAY

Martyrdom of the Báb (Bahá'í)

14 SATURDAY

New Moon

21 SATURDAY

Summer Solstice

24 TUESDAY

Tishah be-Av (Jewish)

30 MONDAY

Full Moon

Asalha Puja (Buddhist)

AUGUST 2007

5 SUNDAY

Ganesh Chaturthi (Hindu)

12 SUNDAY

New Moon

13 MONDAY

Obon, Festival of the Dead begins (Shinto)

16 THURSDAY

Obon, Festival of the Dead ends (Shinto)

28 TUESDAY

Full Moon

SEPTEMBER 2007

4 TUESDAY

Krishna Janmashthami (Hindu, Vaishnava)

11 TUESDAY

New Moon

Begin Ulambana, or Ancestor Day, (Mahayana)

12 WEDNESDAY

Begin Paitishaya, feast of bringing in the harvest (Zoroastrian)

13 THURSDAY

Begin Ramadan (Muslim)

Rosh Hashana, New Year (Jewish)

14 FRIDAY

Rosh Hashana, New Year (Jewish)

16 SUNDAY

End Paitishaya, feast of bringing in the harvest (Zoroastrian)

21 FRIDAY

Autumn Equinox

22 SATURDAY

Yom Kippur (Jewish)

25 TUESDAY

End Ulambana, or Ancestor Day, (Mahayana)

26 WEDNESDAY

Full Moon

27 THURSDAY

Begin Sukkot (Jewish)

28 FRIDAY

Master Kong Birthday (Confucian)

OCTOBER 2007

3 WEDNESDAY

End Sukkot (Jewish)

4 THURSDAY

Shemini Atzeret (Jewish)

5 FRIDAY

Simchat Torah (Jewish)

11 THURSDAY

New Moon

12 FRIDAY

Begin Ayathrima, bringing home the herds (Zoroastrian)

Navaratri (Hindu, Vaishnava)

13 SATURDAY

End Ramadan, Id-al-Fitr (Muslim)

16 TUESDAY

End Ayathrima, bringing home the herds (Zoroastrian)

20 SATURDAY

Birth of the Báb (Bahá'í)

Navaratri (Hindu, Vaishnava)

26 FRIDAY

Full Moon

NOVEMBER 2007

9 FRIDAY

New Moon

Dipavali, Festival of Lights (Hindu, Vaishnava, Jain, Sikh)

12 MONDAY

Birth of Bahá'u'lláh (Bahá'í)

15 THURSDAY

Shichi-go-san, children's rite of passage, (Shinto)

23 FRIDAY

Niiname-sai, harvest festival (Shinto)

24 SATURDAY

Full Moon

Niiname-sai, harvest festival (Shinto)

Parkash (Birthday) of Guru Nanak (Sikh)

Guru Tegh Bahadur, martyrdom day (Sikh)

26 MONDAY

'Abdu'l-Bahá, Day of the Covenant (Bahá'í)

28 WEDNESDAY

Ascension of 'Abdu'l-Bahá (Bahá'í)

DECEMBER 2007

2 SUNDAY

Advent begins (Christian)

5 WEDNESDAY

Chanukah begins (Jewish)

9 SUNDAY

New Moon

12 WEDNESDAY

Chanukah ends (Jewish)

20 THURSDAY

Id-al-Adha begins (Muslim)

21 FRIDAY

Winter Solstice

22 SATURDAY

Id-al-Adha ends (Muslim)

24 MONDAY

Full Moon

25 TUESDAY

Christmas (Christian)

30 SUNDAY

Id al-Ghadir (Shi'a)

31 MONDAY

Oharae, or Great Purification (Shinto)

Begin Maidhyaiya, mid-year/winter feast (Zoroastrian)

2008

JANUARY 2008

1 TUESDAY

Oshogatsu, or NewYear (Shinto)

4 FRIDAY

End Maidhyaiya, mid-year/winter feast (Zoroastrian)

5 SATURDAY

Parkash (Birthday) Guru Gobind Singh (Sikh)

6 SUNDAY

Epiphany (Christian)

8 TUESDAY

New Moon

10 THURSDAY

Muharram, New Year (Muslim)

15 TUESDAY

Seijin no hi, or *Coming of Age Day (Shinto)*

19 SATURDAY

Ashura (Shi'a Muslim)

22 TUESDAY

Full Moon

New Year (Mahayanan)

Tu Bi-Shevat (Jewish)

FEBRUARY 2008

2 SATURDAY

Setsubun no hi, Change of Seasons, (Shinto)

5 TUESDAY

Tse Gutor (Tibetan Buddhist)

6 WEDNESDAY

Ash Wednesday, beginning of Lent (Christian)

7 THURSDAY

New Moon

New Year (Tibetan Buddhist, Confucian)

10 SUNDAY

Begin Mönlam Chenmo, the great prayer ceremony (Tibetan Buddhist)

21 THURSDAY

Full Moon

29 FRIDAY

End Mönlam Chenmo, the great prayer ceremony (Tibetan Buddhist)

MARCH 2008

2 SUNDAY

Annual Fast begins (Bahá'í)

3 MONDAY

Hina matsuri, Doll Festival, or Girls' Day (Shinto)

6 THURSDAY

Maha Shivaratri (Saivism)

7 FRIDAY

New Moon

16 SUNDAY

Palm Sunday (Christian)

Begin amaspathmaêdaya, feast of All Souls (Zoroastrian)

20 THURSDAY

Mawlid-al-Nabi (Muslim)

Annual Fast ends (Bahá'í)

End Hamaspathmaêdaya, feast of All Souls (Zoroastrian)

21 FRIDAY

Full Moon

Spring Equinox

Naw-Rúz, or New Year (Bahá'í, Zoroastrian)

Good Friday (Christian)

Holi (Hindu, Vaishnava)

22 SATURDAY

Holi (Hindu, Vaishnava)

23 SUNDAY

Easter (Christian)

APRIL 2008

5 SATURDAY

Qing Ming festival (Confucian)

6 SUNDAY

New Moon

14 MONDAY

Ram Navami (Hindu, Vaishnava)

Vaisakhi, Birth Anniversary of Khalsa, (Sikh)

20 SUNDAY

Full Moon

New Year (Theravadan)

Passover begins (Jewish)

21 MONDAY

Ridván festival holy day (Bahá'í)

27 SUNDAY

Passover ends (Jewish)

29 TUESDAY

Ridván festival holy day (Bahá'í)

30 WEDNESDAY

Begin Maidhyôizarêmaya, mid-spring feast (Zoroastrian)

MAY 2008

1 THURSDAY

Yom Hashoah, or Holocaust Memorial Day (Jewish)

2 FRIDAY

Ridván festival holy day (Bahá'í)

4 SUNDAY

End Maidhyôizarêmaya, mid-spring feast (Zoroastrian)

5 MONDAY

New Moon

Tango no sekku, Boys' Day (Shinto)

10 SATURDAY

Yom Ha'atzmaut, or Israel Independence Day: (Jewish)

11 SUNDAY

Pentecost, or Whitsunday (Christian)

20 TUESDAY

Full Moon

Vesak, Buddha's Birthday (Buddhist)

23 FRIDAY

Declaration of the Báb (Bahá'í)

29 THURSDAY

Ascension of Bahá'u'lláh (Bahá'í)

JUNE 2008

3 TUESDAY

New Moon

9 MONDAY

Shavuot (Jewish)

10 TUESDAY

Shavuot (Jewish)

16 MONDAY

Guru Arjan, martyrdom day (Sikh)

18 WEDNESDAY

Full Moon

29 SUNDAY

Begin Maidhyôishêma, mid-summer feast (Zoroastrian)

30 MONDAY

Oharae, or Great Purification (Shinto)

JULY 2008

3 THURSDAY

New Moon

End Maidhyôishêma, mid-summer feast (Zoroastrian)

9 WEDNESDAY

Martyrdom of the Báb (Bahá'í)

18 FRIDAY

Full Moon

Asalha Puja (Buddhist)

21 MONDAY

Summer Solstice

AUGUST 2008

1 FRIDAY

New Moon

10 SUNDAY

Tishah be-Av (Jewish)

13 WEDNESDAY

Obon, Festival of the Dead begins (Shinto)

16 SATURDAY

Full Moon

Obon, Festival of the Dead ends (Shinto)

24 SUNDAY

Krishna Janmashthami (Hindu, Vaishnava)

30 SATURDAY

New Moon

31 SUNDAY

Begin Ulambana, or Ancestor Day, (Mahayana)

SEPTEMBER 2008

2 TUESDAY

Begin Ramadan (Muslim)

3 WEDNESDAY

Ganesh Chaturthi (Hindu)

12 FRIDAY

Begin Paitishaya, feast of bringing in the harvest (Zoroastrian)

14 SUNDAY

End Ulambana, or Ancestor Day, (Mahayana)

15 MONDAY

Full Moon

16 TUESDAY

End Paitishaya, feast of bringing in the harvest (Zoroastrian)

21 SUNDAY

Autumn Equinox

28 SUNDAY

Master Kong Birthday (Confucian)

29 MONDAY

New Moon

30 TUESDAY

Rosh Hashana, New Year (Jewish)

Navaratri (Hindu, Vaishnava)

OCTOBER 2008

1 WEDNESDAY

Rosh Hashana, New Year (Jewish)

2 THURSDAY

End Ramadan, Id-al-Fitr (Muslim)

8 WEDNESDAY

Navaratri (Hindu, Vaishnava)

9 THURSDAY

Yom Kippur (Jewish)

12 SUNDAY

Begin Ayathrima, bringing home the herds (Zoroastrian)

14 TUESDAY

Full Moon

Begin Sukkot (Jewish)

16 THURSDAY

End Ayathrima, bringing home the herds (Zoroastrian)

20 MONDAY

Birth of the Báb (Bahá'í)

End Sukkot (Jewish)

21 TUESDAY

Shemini Atzeret (Jewish)

22 WEDNESDAY

Simchat Torah (Jewish)

28 TUESDAY

New Moon

Dipavali, Festival of Lights (Hindu, Vaishnava, Jain, Sikh)

NOVEMBER 2008

12 WEDNESDAY

Birth of Bahá'u'lláh (Bahá'í)

13 THURSDAY

Full Moon

Parkash (Birthday) of Guru Nanak (Sikh)

15 SATURDAY

Shichi-go-san, children's rite of passage, (Shinto)

23 SUNDAY

Niiname-sai, harvest festival (Shinto)

24 MONDAY

Niiname-sai, harvest festival (Shinto)

Guru Tegh Bahadur, martyrdom day (Sikh)

26 WEDNESDAY

'Abdu'l-Bahá, Day of the Covenant (Bahá'í)

27 THURSDAY

New Moon

28 FRIDAY

Ascension of 'Abdu'l-Bahá (Bahá'í)

30 SUNDAY

Advent begins (Christian)

DECEMBER 2008

9 TUESDAY

Id-al-Adha begins (Muslim)

11 THURSDAY

Id-al-Adha ends (Muslim)

12 FRIDAY

Full Moon

19 FRIDAY

Id al-Ghadir (Shi'a)

21 SUNDAY

Winter Solstice

22 MONDAY

Chanukah begins (Jewish)

25 THURSDAY

Christmas (Christian)

27 SATURDAY

New Moon

29 MONDAY

Muharram, New Year (Muslim)

Chanukah ends (Jewish)

31 WEDNESDAY

Oharae, or Great Purification (Shinto)

Begin Maidhyaiya, midyear/winter feast (Zoroastrian)

2009

JANUARY 2009

1 THURSDAY

Oshogatsu, or New Year (Shinto)

4 SUNDAY

End Maidhyaiya, midyear/winter feast (Zoroastrian)

5 MONDAY

Parkash (Birthday) Guru Gobind Singh (Sikh)

6 TUESDAY

Epiphany (Christian)

7 WEDNESDAY

Ashura (Shi'a Muslim)

11 SUNDAY

Full Moon

New Year (Mahayanan)

15 THURSDAY

Seijin no hi, or *Coming of Age Day (Shinto)*

24 SATURDAY

Tse Gutor (Tibetan Buddhist)

26 MONDAY

New Moon

New Year (Tibetan Buddhist, Confucian)

29 THURSDAY

Begin Mönlam Chenmo, the great prayer ceremony (Tibetan Buddhist)

FEBRUARY 2009

2 MONDAY

Setsubun no hi, Change of Seasons, (Shinto)

9 MONDAY

Full Moon

Tu Bi-Shevat (Jewish)

17 TUESDAY

End Mönlam Chenmo, the great prayer ceremony (Tibetan Buddhist)

23 MONDAY

Maha Shivaratri (Saivism)

25 WEDNESDAY

New Moon

Ash Wednesday, beginning of Lent (Christian)

MARCH 2009

2 MONDAY

Annual Fast begins (Bahá'í)

3 TUESDAY

Hina matsuri Doll Festival, or Girls' Day (Shinto)

9 MONDAY

Mawlid-al-Nabi (Muslim)

11 WEDNESDAY

Full Moon

Holi (Hindu, Vaishnava)

16 MONDAY

Begin Hamaspathmaêdaya, feast of All Souls (Zoroastrian)

20 FRIDAY

Annual Fast ends (Bahá'í)

End Hamaspathmaêdaya, feast of All Souls (Zoroastrian)

21 SATURDAY

Spring Equinox

Naw-Rúz, or New Year (Bahá'í, Zoroastrian)

26 THURSDAY

New Moon

APRIL 2009

3 FRIDAY

Ram Navami (Hindu, Vaishnava)

5 SUNDAY

Palm Sunday (Christian)

Qing Ming festival (Confucian)

9 THURSDAY

Full Moon

New Year (Theravadan)

Passover begins (Jewish)

10 FRIDAY

Good Friday (Christian)

12 SUNDAY

Easter (Christian)

14 TUESDAY

Vaisakhi, Birth Anniversary of Khalsa, (Sikh)

16 THURSDAY

Passover ends (Jewish)

21 TUESDAY

Ridván festival holy day (Bahá'í)

Yom Hashoah, or Holocaust Memorial Day (Jewish)

25 SATURDAY

New Moon

29 WEDNESDAY

Ridván festival holy day (Bahá'í)

Yom Ha'atzmaut, or Israel Independence Day: (Jewish)

30 THURSDAY

Begin Maidhyõizarêmaya, mid-spring feast (Zoroastrian)

MAY 2009

2 SATURDAY

Ridván festival holy day (Bahá'í)

4 MONDAY

End Maidhyõizarêmaya, mid-spring feast (Zoroastrian)

5 TUESDAY

Tango no sekku, Boys' Day (Shinto)

9 SATURDAY

Full Moon

Vesak, Buddha's Birthday (Buddhist)

23 SATURDAY

Declaration of the Báb (Bahá'í)

24 SUNDAY

New Moon

29 FRIDAY

Ascension of Bahá'u'lláh (Bahá'í)

Shavuot (Jewish)

30 SATURDAY

Shavuot (Jewish)

31 SUNDAY

Pentecost, or Whitsunday (Christian)

JUNE 2009

7 SUNDAY

Full Moon

16 TUESDAY

Guru Arjan, martyrdom day (Sikh)

22 MONDAY

New Moon

29 MONDAY

Begin Maidhyõishêma, mid-summer' feast (Zoroastrian)

30 TUESDAY

Oharae, or Great Purification (Shinto)

JULY 2009

3 FRIDAY

End Maidhyõishêma, mid-summer feast (Zoroastrian)

7 TUESDAY

Full Moon

Asalha Puja (Buddhist)

9 THURSDAY

Martyrdom of the Báb (Bahá'í)

21 TUESDAY

Summer Solstice

22 WEDNESDAY

New Moon

30 THURSDAY

Tishah be-Av (Jewish)

AUGUST 2009

6 THURSDAY

Full Moon

13 THURSDAY

Obon, Festival of the Dead begins (Shinto)

14 FRIDAY

Krishna Janmashthami (Hindu, Vaishnava)

16 SUNDAY

Obon, Festival of the Dead begins (Shinto)

20 THURSDAY

New Moon

22 SATURDAY

Begin Ramadan (Muslim)

23 SUNDAY

Ganesh Chaturthi (Hindu)

SEPTEMBER 2009

4 FRIDAY

Full Moon

12 SATURDAY

Begin Paitishaya, feast of bringing in the harvest (Zoroastrian)

16 WEDNESDAY

End Paitishaya, feast of bringing in the harvest (Zoroastrian)

19 SATURDAY

New Moon

Rosh Hashana, New Year (Jewish)

Begin Ulambana, or Ancestor Day, (Mahayana)

Navaratri (Hindu, Vaishnava)

20 SUNDAY

Rosh Hashana, New Year (Jewish)

21 MONDAY

Autumn Equinox

End Ramadan, Id-al-Fitr (Muslim)

27 SUNDAY

Navaratri (Hindu, Vaishnava)

28 MONDAY

Master Kong Birthday (Confucian)

Yom Kippur (Jewish)

OCTOBER 2009

3 SATURDAY

Begin Sukkot (Jewish)

Ulambana, or Ancestor Day, (Mahayana)

4 SUNDAY

Full Moon

9 FRIDAY

End Sukkot (Jewish)

10 SATURDAY

Shemini Atzeret (Jewish)

11 SUNDAY

Simchat Torah (Jewish)

12 MONDAY

Begin Ayathrima, bringing home the herds (Zoroastrian)

16 FRIDAY

End Ayathrima, bringing home the herds (Zoroastrian)

17 SATURDAY

Dipavali, Festival of Lights (Hindu, Vaishnava, Jain, Sikh)

18 SUNDAY

New Moon

20 TUESDAY

Birth of the Báb (Bahá'í)

NOVEMBER 2009

2 MONDAY

Full Moon

Parkash (Birthday) of Guru Nanak (Sikh)

12 THURSDAY

Birth of Bahá'u'lláh (Bahá'í)

15 SUNDAY

Shichi-go-san, children's rite of passage, (Shinto)

16 MONDAY

New Moon

23 MONDAY

Niiname-sai, harvest festival (Shinto)

24 TUESDAY

Niiname-sai, harvest festival (Shinto)

Guru Tegh Bahadur, martyrdom day (Sikh)

26 THURSDAY

'Abdu'l-Bahá, Day of the Covenant (Bahá'í)

28 SATURDAY

Ascension of 'Abdu'l-Bahá (Bahá'í)

Id-al-Adha begins (Muslim)

30 MONDAY

Id-al-Adha ends (Muslim)

DECEMBER 2009

2 WEDNESDAY

Full Moon

8 TUESDAY

Id al-Ghadir (Shi'a)

12 SATURDAY

Chanukah begins (Jewish)

16 WEDNESDAY

New Moon

18 FRIDAY

Muharram, New Year (Muslim)

19 SATURDAY

Chanukah ends (Jewish)

21 MONDAY

Winter Solstice

25 FRIDAY

Christmas (Christian)

27 SUNDAY

Ashura (Shi'a Muslim)

31 THURSDAY

Full Moon

Oharae, or Great Purification (Shinto)

Begin Maidhyaiya, mid-year/winter feast (Zoroastrian)

Practices and Beliefs

Worldmark Encyclopedia of Religious Practices

Religion	Year founded	Prominent leaders	Place of origin	Primary texts	Number of followers
African Traditional Religions	200,000–100,000 B.C.E.	priests and priestesses, sacred kings and queens, prophets and prophetesses, and seers	Africa	• myths and oral narratives	84.5 million
Anglicanism	sixteenth century C.E.	King Henry VIII (1491–1547) Thomas Cranmer (1489–1556) William Tyndale (c. 1492–1536)	England	• Bible • Book of Common Prayer	84.5 million
Bahá'í Faith	1863 C.E.	'Alí-Muhammad, or the Báb (1819–50) Bahá'u'lláh (1817–92) 'Abdu'l-Bahá (1844–1921) Shoghi Effendi Rabbani (1897–1957)	Iran	• writings of Bahá'u'lláh, the Báb, and of 'Abdu'l-Bahá	6.5 million
Baptist Tradition	1690 C.E.	John Smyth (died in 1612) William Carey (1761–1834) Martin Luther King, Jr. (1929–68)	England	• Bible	117 million
Buddhism	fifth century B.C.E.	Siddhartha Gautama, or the Buddha (sixth century B.C.E.) Bodhidharma (sixth century C.E.) Padmasambhava (eighth century C.E.)	northern India	• *Tipitaka* ("three baskets") • Additional books, such as the Lotus Sutra and the Prajnaparamita (Perfection of Wisdom) texts	390 million
Christianity	first century C.E.	Peter (died c. 64) Paul (died c. 64) Ignatius of Antioch (c. 35–c. 107) Constantine I (died 337) Saint Augustine (354–430) Saint Patrick (c. 390–c. 460) Pope Gregory I (reigned 590–604) Francis of Assisi (c. 1181–1226) Pope Innocent III (reigned 1198–1216) Martin Luther (1483–1546) Ulrich Zwingli (1484–1531) John Calvin (1509–64)	Palestine	• Bible	2.21 billion
Confucianism	c. 1050–256 B.C.E.	Confucius, or Master Kong (551–479 B.C.E.) Mencius, or Master Meng (c. 391–308 B.C.E.) Dong Zhongshu (c. 176–104 B.C.E.) Zhu Xi (1130–1200 C.E.) Wang Yangming (1472–1529 C.E.) Ngo Thi Nham (1746–1803 C.E.) Motoda Nagazane (1818–91 C.E.)	China	• *Yijing* (Book of Changes) • *Shujing* (Book of Documents) • *Shijing* (Book of Odes) • *Liji* (Book of Rites) • *Zhouli* (Rites of Zhou) • *Yili* (Book of Etiquette and Ritual) • *Lun yu* (Analects) • *Xiaojing* (Scripture of Filiality) • the Chinese dictionary *Erya* • *Mengzi* (Master Meng) • *Chunqiu* (Spring and Autumn Annals)	6.5 million
Conservative Judaism	1886 C.E.	Solomon Schechter (1847–1915) Cyrus Adler (1863–1940) Louis Ginzberg (1872–1953) Mordecai Kaplan (1881–1983)	United States	• Tanakh (Hebrew Bible) • Talmud (Oral Torah)	1.56 million

[continued]

Worldmark Encyclopedia of Religious Practices [CONTINUED]

Religion	Year founded	Prominent leaders	Place of origin	Primary texts	Number of followers
Coptic Christianity	48 C.E.	Saint Mark the Evangelist (first century) Athanasius (c. 293–373) Patriarch Cyril I (reigned 412–44)	Egypt	• Bible • Liturgy of Saint Basil, the Liturgy of Saint Gregory of Nazianzus, and the ancient liturgy of Saint Mark, also known as the Liturgy of Saint Cyril • *Katamaros*, a study of the stages of Christ's life • *Agbiya,* the book of the hours, contains the Psalms, prayers, and Gospels for the seven daily prayers • in addition, Copts use a psalmody, a book of doxologies (praise), and the *Synaxarium,* a book that commemorates Coptic saints	7.8 million
Eastern Catholic Churches	twelfth century C.E.	Patriarch Jeremias II al-Amshitti (early thirteenth century) Saint Josaphat Kuntsevych (died in 1623) Patriarch Abraham Pierre I (eighteenth century)	Lebanon and Armenia	• Bible • Euchologions, the Books of Needs, the Anthologions, the Festal Anthologies, the Floral and the Lenten Triodions, Oktoechos, Horologions, Typikons, Menologions, Menaions, the Books of Akathistos, and the Books of Commemoration	13 million
Eastern Orthodox Christianity	325 C.E.	Constantine I (died in 337) Saint Basil the Great (329–79) Saint John Chrysostom (347–407)	eastern half of the Roman Empire (now Turkey, Greece, Bulgaria, Romania, and Serbia)	• Septuagint Greek version of the Old Testament • Greek New Testament	227.5 million
Hinduism	before 3000 B.C.E.	Shankara (eighth century C.E.) Ramanuja (c. 1017–1137 C.E.) Madhva (c. 1199–1278 C.E.) Ram Mohan Roy (1772–1833 C.E.) Dayananda Sarasvati (1824–83 C.E.) Ramakrishna (1836–86 C.E.)	India	• Vedas • *Ramayana* ("Story of Rama") • *Mahabharata* ("Great Sons of Bharata") • *Puranas* ("Ancient Lore") • *Dharma Sastra*s	910 million
Islam	622 C.E.	Prophet Muhammad (570–632) **Four Rightly Guide Caliphs:** Abu Bakr (reigned 632–34) Umar (reigned 634–44) Uthman (reigned 644–56) Ali (reigned 656–61)	Mecca and Medina (now in Saudi Arabia)	• Koran	1.3 billion
Jainism	c. 550 B.C.E.	Lord Mahavira (sixth century B.C.E.)	India	• **Shvetambara tradition:** • 45 texts organized into five groups: • Angas ("Limbs") • Upanga ("Supplementary Limbs") • Chedasutras ("Delineating Scriptures") • Mulasutras ("Root Scriptures") • Prakirnaka ("Miscellaneous")	6.5 million

[continued]

Worldmark Encyclopedia of Religious Practices [CONTINUED]

Religion	Year founded	Prominent leaders	Place of origin	Primary texts	Number of followers
				• **Digambara tradition:** • it is believed that the original canon has been lost • Shatakanda Agama Kashayaprabhrita • others	
Jehovah's Witnesses	1879 C.E.	Charles Taze Russell (1852–1916) Joseph Franklin Rutherford (1869–1942)	United States	• Bible	15.6 million
Judaism	c. eighteenth century B.C.E.	Abraham (eighteenth century B.C.E.) Isaac Jacob Moses (fourteenth–thirteenth centuries B.C.E.) Joshua (twelfth century B.C.E.) Samuel (eleventh century B.C.E.) David (eleventh–tenth centuries B.C.E.) Solomon (tenth century B.C.E.) Elijah (ninth century B.C.E.) Isaiah (eighth century B.C.E.) Rabbi Johanan ben Zakkai (died c. 80 C.E.)	Mesopotamia	• Tanakh (Hebrew Bible), divided into three parts: the Torah (also called the Pentateuch), the Prophets (Nevi'im), and the Writings (Ketuvim or Hagiographa) • Talmud (Oral Torah)	16.25 million
Lutheranism	1517 C.E.	Martin Luther (1483–1546) Philipp Melanchthon (1497–1560) Johannes Bugenhagen (1485–1558)	Germany	• Bible	65 million
Mahayana Buddhism	c. 200 C.E.	Nagarjuna (born in 150) Tenzin Gyatso, the 14th Dalai Lama (born in 1935)	India	• Perfection of Wisdom Sutras • Bible	208 million 76 million
Methodism	1729 C.E.	John Wesley (1703–91)	England	• Bible	12.35 million
The Church of Jesus Christ of Latter-day Saints	1830 C.E.	Joseph Smith (1805–44) Brigham Young (1801–77)	Fayette, New York, U.S.A.	• Book of Mormon • Pearl of Great Price • Doctrine and Covenants	
Orthodox Judaism	nineteenth century C.E.	**Hasidic community:** Rabbi Israel ben Eliezer, also called the Baal Shem Tov (c. 1700–60), **non-Hasidic Haredi community:** Rabbi Elijah ben Shlomo Zalman, known as the Vilna Gaon (1720–97) **Modern Orthodox community:** Rabbi Samson Raphael Hirsch (1808–88)	Europe	• Tanakh (Hebrew Bible) • Talmud (Oral Torah)	2.6 million
Pentecostalism	1901 C.E.	Charles Fox Parham (1873–1929) William J. Seymour (1870–1922)	Kansas, U.S.A.	• Bible	552.5 million

[continued]

Worldmark Encyclopedia of Religious Practices [CONTINUED]

Religion	Year founded	Prominent leaders	Place of origin	Primary texts	Number of followers
Protestantism	1517 C.E.	Martin Luther (1483–1546) John Calvin (1509–64) Ulrich Zwingli (1484–1531) Menno Simons (1496–1561)	Germany	• Bible	377 million
Reformed Christianity	sixteenth century C.E.	John Calvin (1509–64) Ulrich Zwingli (1484–1531)	Switzerland	• Bible	77.35 million
Reform Judaism	early nineteenth century C.E.	Israel Jacobson (1768–1828) Rabbi Isaac Mayer Wise (1819–1900)	western and central Europe	• Tanakh (Hebrew Bible) • Talmud (Oral Torah)	3.9 million
Religious Society of Friends (Quakers)	1652 C.E.	George Fox (1624–91) William Penn (1644–1718)	England	• Bible	390,000
Roman Catholicism	first century C.E.	Peter (died c. 64) Saint Ignatius of Loyola (1491–1556) Pope Pius IX (reigned 1846–78) Pope John XXIII (reigned 1958–63) Pope John Paul II (reigned 1978–2005)	Rome	• Bible, with 46 books in the Old Testament—the 39 from the Hebrew canon as well as 7 deutercanonical books	1.105 billion
Seventh-day Adventist Church	1863 C.E.	Ellen Gould White (1827–1915) James Springer White (1821–81) Joseph Bates (1792–1872)	United States	• Bible	13 million
Shaivism	second century C.E.	Lakulisha (c. second century) Basava (died in 1167) Sathya Sai Baba (born in 1926)	South Asia	• Upanishads • Shaivite Puranas • individual Shaivite groups have various other texts	208 million
Shiism	632 C.E.	Prophet Muhammad (570–632) Ali (c. 600–661) Husayn (626–80) Ja'far al-Sadiq (702–65)	Medina (now in Saudi Arabia)	• Koran	143 million
Shinto	c. 500 C.E.	Yamazaki Ansai (1618–82) Keichū (1640–1701) Motoori Norinaga (1730–1801)	Japan	• none sacred to all Shinto worshippers	117 million
Sikhism	c. 1499 C.E.	Guru Nanak (1469–1539) Guru Gobind Singh (1666–1708)	the Punjab (now in India and Pakistan)	• Adi Granth (Original Book) • Dasam Granth (Book of the 10th Guru) • Works of Bhai Gurdas and Bhai Nand Lal Goya • *janam-sakhi*s (birth narratives) • *rahit-nama*s (manuals of code of conduct) • *gur-bilas* (pleasure of the Guru) literature	19.5 million
Sunnism	632 C.E.	Prophet Muhammad (570–632) **Four Rightly Guided Caliphs:** Abu Bakr (reigned 632–34) Umar (reigned 634–44) Uthman (reigned 644–56) Ali (reigned 656–61)	Medina (now in Saudi Arabia)	• Koran	975 million

[continued]

Worldmark Encyclopedia of Religious Practices [CONTINUED]

Religion	Year founded	Prominent leaders	Place of origin	Primary texts	Number of followers
Taoism	c. 450–500 C.E.	Lu Hsiu-ching (406–77) T'ao Hung-ching (456–536) Ssu-ma Ch'eng-chen (646–735)	China	• *Tao-tsang*	65 million
Theravada Buddhism	fifth century B.C.E.	Mahasi Sayadaw (1904–82 C.E.) Ajahn Chah (1918–92 C.E.)	India	• *Tipitika*	123.5 million
Tibetan Buddhism	seventh and eighth centuries C.E.	Santaraksita (eighth century) Padmasambhava (eighth century) Tenzin Gyatso, the 14th Dalai Lama (born in 1935)	Tibet	• *Kanjur* • *Tenjur*	195,000
Unitarianism and Universalism	1565 C.E. (Unitarianism) and 1723 C.E. (Universalism)	Ferenc Dávid (1510–79) Faustus Socinus (1539–1604)	Poland and Transylvania (now in Romania) (Unitarianism) England (Universalism)	• Bible • many congregations include the sacred writings of all religions in worship	325,000
United Church of Christ	1957 C.E.	**Congregational:** John Winthrop (1588–1649) Jonathan Edwards (1703–58) **Reformed:** John Williamson Nevin (1803–86) **German Evangelical:** Reinhold Niebuhr (1892–1971)	United States	• Bible	1.3 million
Vaishnavism	c. 500 B.C.E.	Ramanuja (c. 1017–1137 C.E.) Madhvacarya (1296–1386 C.E.) Chaitanya (1485–1533 C.E.) Ghanshyam, or Swaminarayan (born in 1781 C.E.)	India	• Vedas • *Ramayana* • *Mahabharata* • Vaishnava Puranas	617.5 million
World Evangelicalism	seventeenth century C.E.	Philipp Jakob Spener (1635–1705) Charles Grandison Finney (1792–1875) Aimee Semple McPherson (1890–1944) Billy Graham (born in 1918)	Germany	• Bible	780 million
Zoroastrianism	second millennium B.C.E.	Tansar, or Tosar (died in 240 C.E.) Kirdīr, or Kartir (third century C.E.) K.R. Cama (1831–1909 C.E.)	Central Asia or eastern Iran	• Avesta, containing the *Yasna, Yasht*s, and *Vendidad*	149,500

Quotations on Beliefs

I. God or gods

"Acts of God are like riddles."

African Traditional Religions
African proverb

"To every discerning and illuminated heart it is evident that God, the unknowable Essence, the Divine Being, is immensely exalted beyond every human attribute, such as corporeal existence, ascent and descent, egress and regress. Far be it from His glory that human tongue should adequately recount His praise, or that human heart comprehend His fathomless mystery."

Bahá'í Faith
Bahá'u'lláh

"God then is infinite and incomprehensible and all that is comprehensible about Him is His infinity and incomprehensibility. . . . For when you speak of Him as good, and just, and wise, and so forth, you do not tell God's nature but only the qualities of His nature."

Christianity
John of Damascus

"Heaven/God [Tian] bestows one's inner nature; the Way [Tao] consists in following one's inner nature; the Teaching [Jiao] derives from cultivating the Way."

Confucianism
Doctrine of the Mean 1

"You are the supreme being, the supreme abode, the supreme purifier, the eternal one, the divine being. You are the Primordial deity without birth."

Hinduism
Bhagavad Gita 10:22

"Say: He is Allah, the One and Only; Allah, the Eternal, Absolute. He begetteth not, nor is He begotten; And there is none like unto Him."

Islam
Koran 112

"Hear, O Israel! The Lord our God, the Lord is one. You shall love the Lord your God with all your heart and with all your soul and with all your might."

Judaism
Deuteronomy 6:4-6

"Generally speaking, 'kami' denotes . . . all kinds of beings—including not only human beings but also such objects as birds, beasts, trees, grass, seas, mountains, and so forth—any being whatsoever which possesses some eminent quality out of the ordinary and awe-inspiring."

Shinto
Motoori Norinaga

"My Master is the One. He is the One, brother, and He alone exists."

Sikhism
Guru Nanak, Adi Granth, p. 150

"Then as holy I have recognized Thee, Ahura Mazda, when I saw Thee at first at the birth of life, when Thou didst appoint rewards for acts and words, bad for the bad, a good recompense for the good, by Thy innate virtue, at the final turning point of creation."

Zoroastrianism
Yasna 43:5

II. Prayer

"The prayer of the chicken hawk does not get him the chicken."

African Traditional Religions
Swahili proverb

"The state of prayer is the best of conditions, for man is then associating with God. Prayer verily bestoweth life, particularly when offered in private and at times, such as midnight, when freed from daily cares."

Bahá'í Faith
'Abdu'l-Bahá

"Sitting cross-legged,
They should wish that all beings
Have firm and strong roots of goodness
And attain the state of immovability.
Cultivating concentration,
They should wish that all beings
Conquer their minds by concentration
Ultimately, with no reminder.
When practicing contemplation,
They should wish that all beings
See truth as it is
And be forever free of oppression and contention."

Buddhism
Garland Sutra (Gandavyuha) 11

"When you are praying, do not use meaningless repetition, as the Gentiles do, for they suppose that they will be heard for their many words. Therefore do not be like them; for your Father knows what you need, before you ask Him."

Christianity
Matthew 6:7

"Knowing in what to abide, one can settle the mind; with settled mind, one can achieve quiet; in quietude, one can reach a state of calm; in calmness, one can contemplate; in contemplation, one can attain the goal."

Confucianism
Great Learning 1

"Lead me from unreality to reality; lead me from darkness to light; lead me from death to immortality. Om Peace, Peace, Peace."

Hinduism
Brihadaranyaka Upanishad 1:3:28

"Recite what is sent of the Book by inspiration to thee, and establish regular Prayer: for Prayer restrains from shameful and unjust deeds; and remembrance of Allah is the greatest [thing in life] without doubt. And Allah knows the [deeds] that ye do."

Islam
Koran 29:45

"Homage to the Jinas.
Homage to the perfected souls.
Homage to the renouncer-leaders.
Homage to the renouncer-teachers.
Homage to all renouncers."

Jainism
Namaskar Mantra

"What then is left for us to do except to pray for the ability to pray, to bewail our ignorance of living in His presence? And even if such prayer is tainted with vanity, His mercy accepts and redeems our feeble efforts. It is the continuity of trying to pray, the unspoken loyalty to our duty to pray, that lends strength to our fragile worship; and it is the holiness of the community that bestows meaning upon our individual acts of worship. These are three pillars on which our prayer rises to God: our own loyalty, the holiness of Israel, and the mercy of God."

Judaism
Abraham Joshu Heschel

"When [the Shinto priest] pronounces the ritual prayers,
the heavenly deities will push open the heavenly rock door,
and pushing with an awesome pushing,
through the myriad layers of heavenly clouds,
will hear and receive [these prayers]."

Shinto
From ninth-century norito (prayer)

"Nanak prays: the divine Name may be magnified;
May peace and prosperity come to one and all by your grace, O Lord!"

Sikhism
Ardas prayer

"Those Beings, male and female, whom Ahura Mazda knows the best for worship according to truth, we worship them all."

Zoroastrianism
Yenghe Hatam prayer

III. Duty toward other people

"A lone traveler is swept away by a stream."

African Traditional Religions
Tonga proverb

"Be generous in prosperity, and thankful in adversity. Be worthy of the trust of thy neighbor, and look upon him with a bright and friendly face. Be a treasure to the poor, an admonisher to the rich, an answerer of the cry of the needy. . . . Be unjust to no man, and show all meekness to all men. Be as a lamp unto them that walk in darkness, a joy to the sorrowful, a sea for the thirsty, a haven for the distressed, an upholder and defender of the victim of oppression. Let integrity and uprightness distinguish all thine acts. Be a home for the stranger, a balm to the suffering, a tower of strength for the fugitive. Be eyes to the blind, and a guiding light unto the feet of the erring. Be an ornament to the countenance of truth, a crown to the brow of fidelity, a pillar of the temple of righteousness, a breath of life to the body of mankind, an ensign of the hosts of justice, a luminary above the horizon of virtue, a dew to the soil of the human heart, an ark on the ocean of knowledge, a sun in the heaven of bounty, a gem on the diadem of wisdom, a shining light in the firmament of thy generation, a fruit upon the tree of humility."

Bah·á'í Faith
Bahá'u'lláh

"Hatred is never quelled by hatred in this world. It is quelled by love. This is an eternal truth."

Buddhism
Dhammapada 1:5

"You shall love your neighbor as yourself."

Christianity
Mark 12:31

"The duties of universal obligation are five . . . those between ruler and subject, father and child, husband and wife, older and younger siblings, and two friends."

Confucianism
Doctrine of the Mean 20

"Lack of enmity to all beings in thought, word, and deed; compassion and generous giving—these are the marks of the eternal faith; this is the eternal duty."

Hinduism
Mahabharata

"It is not righteousness that ye turn your faces towards east or west; but it is righteousness to believe in Allah and the Last Day, and the Angels, and the Book, and the Messengers; to spend of your substance, out of love for Him, for your kin, for orphans, for the needy, for the wayfarer, for those who ask, and for the ransom of slaves; to be steadfast in prayer, and practice regular charity; to fulfill the contracts which ye have made; and to be firm and patient, in pain (or suffering) and adversity, and throughout all periods of panic. Such are the people of truth, the Allah-fearing."

Islam
Koran 2:177

"The observer of vows should cultivate friendliness towards all living beings, delight in the distinction and honor of others, [show] compassion for miserable, lowly creatures and equanimity towards the vainglorious."

Jainism
Tattvartha Sutra

"Love your fellow as yourself: I am the Lord."

Judaism
Leviticus 19:18

"The hearts of all you encounter shall be as a mirror to you, reflecting the face you have presented to them."

Shinto
Kurozumi Munetada

"One should live on what one has earned through hard work and share with others the fruit of one's exertion." Guru Nanak

Sikhism
Adi Granth, p. 1,245

"The sage does not accumulate [for himself].
The more that he expends for others, the more does he possess of his own;
the more that he gives to others, the more does he have himself."

Taoism
Tao te ching 81

"I pledge myself to the well-thought thought, I pledge myself to the well-spoken word, I pledge myself to the well-acted act."

Zoroastrianism
Yasna 12:8

IV. Poverty and wealth

"The lack of money does not necessarily mean that one is poor."

> *African Traditional Religions*
> *African proverb*

"O CHILDREN OF DUST!
Tell the rich of the midnight sighing of the poor, lest heedlessness lead them into the path of destruction, and deprive them of the Tree of Wealth. To give and to be generous are attributes of Mine; well is it with him that adorneth himself with My virtues."

> *Bahá'í Faith*
> *Bahá.'u.'lláh*

"Goodwill, and wisdom, a mind trained by method
The highest conduct based on good morals
This makes humans pure, not rank or wealth."

> *Buddhism*
> *Samyutta Nikaya*

"For I was hungry, and you gave me something to eat; I was thirsty, and you gave me drink; I was a stranger, and you invited me in; naked, and you clothed me; I was sick, and you visited me; I was in prison, and you came to me."

> *Christianity*
> *Matthew 25:35-36*

"Facilitate their cultivation of fields, lighten their tax burden, and the common people can be made wealthy."

> *Confucianism*
> *Master Meng [Mencius] VII:2:23*

"This body—it is for the service of others."

> *Hinduism*
> *Anonymous*

"Alms are for the poor and the needy, and those employed to administer the [funds]; for those whose hearts have been [recently] reconciled [to Truth]; for those in bondage and in debt; in the cause of Allah and for the wayfarer: [thus is it] ordained by Allah, and Allah is full of knowledge and wisdom."

> *Islam*
> *Koran 9:60*

"Speak up for the dumb,
For the rights of all the unfortunate.
Speak up, judge righteously,
Champion the poor and the needy."

> *Judaism*
> *Proverbs 31:8*

"True service is the service of poor people; I am not inclined to serve others of higher social status; charity will bear fruit, in this and the next world if given to such worthy and poor people."

Sikhism
Guru Gobind Singh, Adi Granth, p. 1,223

"There is no guilt greater than to sanction ambition;
no calamity greater than to be discontented with one's lot;
no fault greater than the wish to be getting.
Therefore the sufficiency of contentment is an enduring and unchanging sufficiency."

Taoism
Tao te ching 46

"As the Master, so is the Judge to be chosen in accord with truth. Establish the power of acts arising from a life lived with good purpose, for Mazda and for the lord whom they made pastor for the poor."

Zoroastrianism
Ahuna Vairya prayer

V. Women

"And among the teachings of Bahá'u'lláh is the equality of women and men. The world of humanity has two wings—one is women and the other men. Not until both wings are equally developed can the bird fly."

Bahá'í Faith
'Abdu'l-Bahá

"Whoever has such a vehicle, whether it is a woman or a man, by means of that vehicle shall come to nirvana."

Buddhism
Samyutta Nikaya

"The knot of Eve's disobedience was loosed by the obedience of Mary. For what the virgin Eve had bound fast through unbelief, this did the virgin Mary set free through faith."

Christianity
Saint Irenaeus

"To be a woman, one must develop as a person; to do this, strive to establish one's purity and chastity. With purity, one remains undefiled; with chastity, one keeps one's virtue."

Confucianism
Analects for Women 2:1a

"If any do deeds of righteousness—be they male or female—and have faith, they will enter Heaven, and not the least injustice will be done to them."

Islam
Koran 4:124

"Jewish feminism focuses on three issues: attaining complete religious involvement for Jewish women; giving Jewish expression to women's experiences and self-understanding; and highlighting the imagery, language, rituals already present within the tradition that center around the feminine and the women. These efforts involve changing or eliminating aspects of Jewish law, customs, and teachings that prevent or discourage women from developing positions of equality to men within Judaism as well as bringing new interpretations to bear on the tradition."

Judaism
Susannah Heschel

"Woman is the foundation of the faith."

Shinto
Nakayama Miki

"Blessed are they, both men and women, who endlessly praise their Lord. Blessed are they in the True One's court; there shall their faces shine."

Sikhism
Guru Nanak, Adi Granth, p. 473

"The valley spirit dies not, aye the same;
The female mystery thus do we name.
Its gate, from which at first they issued forth,
Is called the root from which grew heaven and earth.
Long and unbroken does its power remain,
Used gently, and without the touch of pain."

Taoism
Tao te ching 6

"We call upon you the Waters, and you the milk cows, and you the mothers, giving milk, nourishing the poor, possessed of all kinds of sustenance; who are the best, the most beautiful. Down we call you, O good ones, to be grateful for and pleased by shares of the long-armed offering, you living mothers."

Zoroastrianism
Yasna 38:5

VI. Death

"The elephant has fallen."

African Traditional Religions
Yoruba metaphor for the death of an elderly person

"O SON OF THE SUPREME!
I have made death a messenger of joy to thee. Wherefore dost thou grieve?"

Bahá'í Faith
Bahá'u'lláh

"[D]eath, which we want nothing to do with, is unavoidable. This is why it is important that during our lifetime we become familiar with the idea of death, so that it will not be a real shock to us at the moment it comes. We do not meditate regularly on death in order to die more quickly; on the contrary, like everyone, we wish to live a long time. However, since death is inevitable, we believe that if we begin to prepare for it at an earlier point in time, on the day of our death it will be easier to accept it."

Buddhism
Dalai Lama

"Death has been swallowed up in victory. Where, O death, is your victory? Where, O death, is your sting? . . . Thanks be to God! He gives us the victory through our Lord Jesus Christ."

Christianity
1 Corinthians 15:54-55

"If one is not yet able to serve living persons, how can one serve spirits of the dead? If one does not yet understand life, how can one understand death?"

Confucianism
Analects of Confucius 11:12

"Just as one casts away old clothes and gets new ones, so too, after casting away worn-out bodies, the soul gets new ones."

Hinduism
Bhagavad Gita 2:22

"Every soul shall have a taste of death: And only on the Day of Judgment shall you be paid your full recompense. Only he who is saved far from the Fire and admitted to the Garden will have attained the object [of Life]: For the life of this world is but goods and chattels of deception."

Islam
Koran 3:185

"The physical body with all its sense organs, its health and youth, strength, radiance, good fortune and beauty—all resemble the rainbow which vanishes within seconds. They are impermanent."

Jainism
Acharya Kundakunda

"By the sweat of your brow
Shall you get bread to eat,
Until you return to the ground—
For from it you were taken.
For dust you are,
And to dust you shall return."

Judaism
Genesis 3:19

"Death proceeds from life, and life is the beginning of death. The [Ise] Shrine official informed me that this was handed down as the reason for the taboos surrounding both birth and death."

Shinto
Muju Ichien

"To whom should one complain, O Nanak, when death carries the mortal away without one's consent?"

Sikhism
Guru Nanak, Adi Granth, p. 1,412

"Death and life are not within our power, so we must be content with death. In this world we are like a foreign traveler and our body is just like a hired shell which we are in. From it man goes to his original abode. There should be no deep mourning for that. Everybody dies; others go before us, and we have to follow. Thus to be mournful is a sinful act."

Zoroastrianism
Dastur Erachji Sohrabji Meherjirana

Populations

African Traditional Religions 79,913,910

Anglicanism 79,913,910

Baha'I 6,147,224

Baptist Tradition 110,650,029

Buddhism 368,833,430

Christianity .2,090,056,103

Church of Jesus Christ of Latter-day Saints . .11,679,725

Confucianism 6,147,224

Conservative Judaism 1,475,334

Coptic Christianity 7,376,669

Eastern Catholicism 12,294,448

Eastern Orthodox Christianity 215,152,834

Evangelicalism .737,666,860

Hinduism 860,611,337

Islam 1,229,444,767

Jainism 6,147,224

Jehovah'S Witnesses 14,753,337

Judaism 15,368,060

Lutheranism 61,472,238

Mahayana Buddhism 196,711,163

Methodism 71,922,519

Orthodox Judaism 2,458,890

Pentecostalism .522,514,026

Protestantism 356,538,982

Reform Judaism .3,688,334

Reformed Christianity 73,151,964

Religious Society of Friends 368,833

Roman Catholicism 1,045,028,052

Seventh-day Adventist 12,294,448

Shaivism 196,711,163

Shiism 135,238,924

Shinto 110,650,029

Sikhism 18,441,671

Sunnism 922,083,575

Taoism 61,472,238

Theravada Buddhism 116,797,253

Tibetan Buddhism .184,417

Unitarianism 307,361

United Church of Christ 1,229,445

Vaishnavism 583,986,264

Zoroastrianism 141,386

Combined populations exceed total world population since some people qualify as members more than one religious group. A Buddhist, for example, may also practice Confucianism. Likewise, a Methodist might also be counted as a Christian, a Protestant, an Evangelical, and a Pentecostal, depending on their beliefs.

Glossary

10 paramitas (Buddhism) 10 perfections of the bod-hisattva: (1) *dana* (generosity), (2) *sila* (morality), (3) *ksanti* (patience and forbearance), (4) *virya* (vigor, the endless and boundless energy that bodhisattvas employ when helping others), (5) *dhyana* (meditation), (6) *prajna* (wisdom), (7) *upaya* (skillful means), (8) conviction, (9) strength, and (10) knowledge

Abaluhya (African Traditional Religions) an ethnic group in Kenya

Achaemenian dynasty (Zoroastrianism) dynasty that ruled Iran from 550 to 330 B.C.E.

acharya (Hinduism) a formal head of a monastery, sect, or subcommunity

acharya (Jainism) head of a subsect or smaller group of renouncers

Adi Granth (Sikhism) Original Book; the primary Sikh scripture

Advent (Christianity) period of four weeks, beginning four Sundays before Christmas, sometimes observed with fasting and prayer

afrinagan (Zoroastrianism) Zoroastrian ceremony involving the distribution of blessings

Aggadah (Judaism) nonlegal, narrative portions of the Talmud and Mishna, which include history, folklore, and other subjects

ahimsa (Jainism) nonviolence

Ahura Mazda (Zoroastrianism) supreme deity of Zoroastrianism; likely an honorific title meaning "Wise Lord" rather than a proper name

Akal Purakh (Sikhism) Timeless One; God

al-hajj / al-hajji (Islam) pilgrim; prefix added to a name to indicate that the person has made the hajj

Allah (Islam) God

Amaterasu (Shinto) the sun goddess

Amesha Spentas (Zoroastrianism) the six entities that aid Ahura Mazda, sometimes with an additional figure, Spenta Mainyu, to compose the divine heptad (group of seven)

amrit (Sikhism) divine nectar; sweetened water used in the initiation ceremony of the Khalsa

anagarika (Buddhism) ascetic layperson

anekant (Jainism) doctrine of the multiplicity of truth

Anglicanism (Christianity) Church of England, which originated in King Henry VIII's break with Rome in 1534, and those churches that developed from it, including the Episcopal Church in the United States; with a wide spectrum of doctrines and practices, it is sometimes called Episcopalianism

Angra Mainyu (Zoroastrianism) primordial evil spirit, twin of Spenta Mainyu

Apocrypha (Christianity) books of the Old Testament included in the Septuagint (Greek translation used by early Christians) and Catholic (including the Latin Vulgate) versions of the Bible but not in Protestant or modern Jewish editions

arahitogami (Shinto) a *kami* in human form

arhat (Buddhism) worthy one

aryika (Jainism) a Digambara nun who wears white clothing

asha (Zoroastrianism) truth; righteousness

Ashkenazim (Judaism) Jews whose ancestors in the Middle Ages lived in Germany (Ashkenaz in Hebrew) and the surrounding countries

ashrama (Hinduism) one of the four stages of life

atashkadeh (Zoroastrianism) "place of fire"; fire temple; more narrowly, the enclosed chamber in a fire temple that contains a fire continuously fed by the priests

atman (Hinduism) the human soul

Atonement (Christianity) doctrine that the death of Jesus is the basis for human salvation

Avestan (Zoroastrianism) ancient East Iranian language

Ayurveda (Hinduism) "knowledge of a long life"; a Hindu healing system

Ba Kongo (African Traditional Religions) a group of Bantu-speaking peoples who largely reside in Congo (Brazzaville), Democratic Republic of the Congo (Kinshasa), and Angola

Ba Thonga (African Traditional Religions) a group of Bantu-speaking peoples who live in the southern African countries of Mozambique, Zimbabwe, Swaziland, and South Africa

babalawo (African Traditional Religions) a divination specialist in Yoruba culture

Babi (Bahá'í) a follower of Ali-Muhammad of Shiraz (1819–50), who took the title of the Bab (Arabic: "gate")

Baganda (African Traditional Religions) the largest ethnic group in Uganda

Baha (Bahá'í) glory, splendor, or light; the greatest name of God; the root word in Bahaullah, the title of the founder of the Bahá'í faith, and in Bahá'í

Bambara (African Traditional Religions) an ethnic group in Mali

Bantu (African Traditional Religions) a large group of languages spoken in central, eastern, and southern Africa

baptism (Christianity) sacrament practiced by Christians in which the sprinkling, pouring of, or immersion in water is a sign of admission into the faith community

bar mitzvah (son of commandment) (Judaism) initiation ceremony for boys at age 13, when they are held to be responsible for their actions and hence are obliged to observe all of the commandments of the Torah; bat mitzah, a similar ceremony for girls at age 12, is observed by some Jews

barashnum (Zoroastrianism) Zoroastrian purification ceremony used primarily by priests to prepare for their ordination

Bhagavad Gita (Hinduism) one of the most sacred texts of the Hindus; a book of 18 chapters from the epic the *Mahabharata*

bhakti (Hinduism) devotion; the practice of devotion to God

bhikkhu (Buddhism) monk

bhikkhuni (Buddhism) female monk

bodhi (Buddhism) enlightenment; awakening

bodhisattva (Buddhism) an enlightened being who works for the welfare of all those still caught in samsara

Brahma (Hinduism) a minor deity; the creator god

brahmacharya (Jainism) chastity in marriage or celibacy

Brahman (Hinduism) the upper, or priestly, caste

Brahman (Hinduism) the term used in the Upanishads to refer to the supreme being

Brit Milah (Judaism) circumcision of a male infant or adult convert as a sign of acceptance of the covenant

caliph (Islam) successor; deputy to the Prophet Muhammad

caste (Hinduism) a social group (frequently one that a person is born into) in Hindu society

casuistry (Christianity) type of moral reasoning based on the examination of specific cases

catechesis (Christianity) formal instruction in the faith

"Celestial Masters" tradition (T'ien-shih) (Taoism) Taoist tradition of late Han times, with which several later traditions, especially Cheng-i, claimed affiliation

Ch'an (Zen in Japan) (Buddhism) a school of Mahayana Buddhism

ch'i (Taoism) life-energy

ch'i-kung (qigong) (Taoism) the skill of attracting vital energy

Ch'ing dynasty (Taoism) dynasty that ruled China from 1644 to 1911; also called the Manchu dynasty

Ch'ing-wei (Taoism) "Clarified Tenuity"; a Taoism subtradition the emerged in the tenth century; it involves a system of therapeutic rituals

ch'uan-ch'i (Taoism) type of traditional Chinese literary tale

Ch'üan-chen (Taoism) "Integrating the Perfections"; practice that originated in the eleventh century and continued in modern "Dragon Gate" Taoism; sometimes called "Northern Taoism"

chai (Taoism) type of Taoist liturgy that originated in the Ling-pao tradition in the fifth century

charismatics (Christianity) major expression of Christianity that includes those who affirm the gifts of the Holy Spirit but who are not affiliated with Pentecostal denominations

chen (Taoism) perfection or realization; ultimate spiritual integration

Cheng-i (Taoism) "Orthodox Unity"; Taoist tradition that emerged during the conquest period (approximately the twelfth through fourteenth centuries) and became a part of "Southern Taoism"

chen-jen (Taoism) perfected ones; a term used both for angelic beings and for the human ideal of fully perfected or realized persons

chiao (Taoism) extended Taoist liturgy; a sequence of events over several days that renews the local community by reintegrating it with the heavenly order

Chin dynasty (Taoism) dynasty that ruled China from 266 to 420 C.E.

ching (Taoism) vital essence

Ching-ming (Taoism) "Pure Illumination"; a Taoism sub-tradition that emerged during the Ming dynasty; it was absorbed into the "Dragon Gate" tradition

chin-tan (Taoism) "Golden Elixir"; a set of ideas about spiritual refinement through meditation

chrismation (Christianity) anointing with oil

Chuang-tzu (Taoism) classical text compiled c. 430 to 130 B.C.E.

classical China (Taoism) the period before 221 B.C.E.

conciliar (Christianity) governance through councils of bishops

confirmation (Christianity) sacrament marking membership in a church

congregationalism (Christianity) self-governance by a local congregation

Conservative Judaism (Judaism) largest denomination of American Judaism, with affiliated congregations in South America and Israel; advocating moderate modifications of Halakhah, it occupies a middle ground between Reform and Orthodox Judaism

cosmogony (African Traditional Religions) a theory about the creation of the universe

cosmology (African Traditional Religions) an explanation of the nature of the universe

daeva (Zoroastrianism) demon

Dagara (African Traditional Religions) an ethnic group of the Niger region of western Africa

dakhma (Zoroastrianism) "tower of silence"; a tower in which a corpse is traditionally exposed

dan (Sikhism) charity; a person's relation with society

dana (Buddhism) proper giving; generosity

dar-i Mihr (Zoroastrianism) "the court of Mithra"; the room in a fire temple where the *yasna* is performed

Dashalakshanaparvan (Jainism) yearly Digambara festival during which the Tattvartha Sutra is read and that ends in atonement

dastur (Zoroastrianism) "master"; honorific title for a Zoroastrian priest

dawa (Islam) call to Islam; propagation of the faith

de (Confucianism) virtue; potential goodness conferred on a person by *Tian* (Heaven)

deva (Buddhism) deity; divine being; divine

deva (Hinduism) a divine being

Devi (Hinduism) in the Sanskrit literary tradition, the name for the Goddess

dharma (Hinduism) duty, or acting with a sense of what is righteous; sometimes used to mean "religion" and "ethics"

dharma (Pali, dhamma) (Buddhism) the teachings of the Buddha

Dharma Sastra (Hinduism) any of a set of treatises on the nature of righteousness, moral duty, and law

dhimmi (Islam) protected person, specifically a Jew or Christian

Diaspora (Judaism) communities of Jews dispersed outside the Land of Israel, traditionally referred to as the Exile

Digambara (Jainism) wearing the sky; sect of Jainism, largely based in southern India, in which full monks do not wear any clothing

diksha (Jainism) rite of initiation for a monk or a nun

divination (African Traditional Religions) any of various methods of accessing sacred knowledge of the deities; it often involves interpreting signs

"Dragon Gate" tradition (Lung-men) (Taoism) Taoist tradition that originated in the seventeenth century, incorporating Ch'üan-chen and Ching-ming; the dominant form of Taoism in mainland China today

dua (Islam) personal prayer

duhkha (Pali, dukkha) (Buddhism) suffering; unsatisfactoriness

Durga (Hinduism) a manifestation of the Goddess (represented as a warrior)

Edo (African Traditional Religions) an ethnic group of southern Nigeria

Eightfold Path (marga; Pali, magga) (Buddhism) a systematic and practical way to realize the truth and eliminate suffering, traditionally divided into three distinct phases that should be progressively mastered

Epiphany (Christianity) January 6, a celebration of the coming of the Magi and, in Orthodoxy, of the baptism of Jesus

eschatology (Christianity) doctrine concerning the end of the world, including the Second Coming of Christ, God's judgment, heaven, and hell

Eucharist (Communion; Lord's Supper) (Christianity) sacrament practiced by Christians in which bread and wine become (in Roman Catholicism and Orthodoxy) or stand for (in Protestantism) the body and blood of Christ

evangelicalism (Christianity) movement that emphasizes the authority of the Scriptures, salvation by faith, and individual experience over ritual

extreme unction (Christianity) sacrament; blessing of the sick

Fang (African Traditional Religions) an ethnic group of west-central Africa

fasli (Zoroastrianism) seasonal calendar that places New Year's Day in March; compare with *qadimi*

fast of Ramadan (Islam) fast during ninth month; fourth pillar

fatwa (Islam) legal opinion or judgment of a mufti, a specialist in Islamic law

Five Pillars of Islam (Islam) fundamental observances

Five Scriptures (Confucianism) *Wujing;* Confucianism's most sacred texts

Fon (African Traditional Religions) an ethnic group of Benin

Four Books (Confucianism) *Sishu;* central texts of Confucian philosophy and education

frashkard (Zoroastrianism) the renewal of the world at the end of history

Fukko Shintō (Shinto) the "pure Shinto" of the scholar Motoori Norinaga

Gāthā (Zoroastrianism) one of the 17 hymns traditionally ascribed to Zoroaster

gūji (Shinto) Shinto head priest

Gahambar (Zoroastrianism) one of six five-day Zoroastrian festivals

Ganesha (Hinduism) a popular Hindu god; a son of the goddess Parvati, he is depicted with an elephant head

Gathic (Zoroastrianism) older Avestan dialect

getig (Zoroastrianism) form; physical world

ghusl (Islam) ritual cleansing before worship

Goddess (Hinduism) a powerful, usually gracious, deity in female form sometimes seen as a manifestation of Parvati, the wife of Shiva; she is called any number of names, including Shakti, Durga, Kali, or Devi

gon-gūji (Shinto) Shinto assistant head priest

goryō (Shinto) haunting spirit of a wronged individual

gotra (Hinduism) a clan group

grace (Christianity) unmerited gift from God for human salvation

granthi (Sikhism) reader of scripture and leader of rituals in the *gurdwara*

gurdwara (Sikhism) door of the Guru; house of worship

Gurmukh (Sikhism) a person oriented toward the Guru

guru (Hinduism) a charismatic teacher

Guru (Sikhism) spiritual preceptor, either a person or the mystical "voice" of Akal Purakh

Guru Granth, or Guru Granth Sahib (Sikhism) the Adi Granth, or scripture, functioning as Guru

Guru Panth (Sikhism) the Sikh Panth, or community, functioning as Guru

Hachiman (Shinto) a Shinto-Buddhist deity popular with samurai

hadith (Islam) tradition; reports of Muhammad's sayings and deeds

Haggadah (Judaism) book used at the Passover seder, containing the liturgical recitation of the Passover story and instructions on conducting the ceremonial meal

hajj (Islam) pilgrimage to Mecca; fifth pillar

Halakhah (Judaism) legal portions of the Talmud as later elaborated in rabbinic literature; in an extended sense it denotes the ritual and legal prescriptions governing the traditional Jewish way of life

halal (Islam) meat slaughtered in a religious manner

Han dynasty (Taoism) dynasty that ruled China from 206 B.C.E. to 221 C.E.

Hand of the Cause of God (Bahá'í) one of 50 individuals appointed by Bahaullah, Abdul-Baha, or Shoghi Effendi whose duties included encouraging Bahá'ís and their institutions, advising them about the development of the Bahá'í community worldwide, and informing the head of the faith about conditions and developments in local Bahá'í communities

haoma (Zoroastrianism) sacred drink, now pressed from ephedra and pomegranate twigs

haoxue (Confucianism) love of (moral) learning

harae (Shinto) purification rites

Hasidism (Judaism) revivalist mystical movement that originated in Poland in the eighteenth century

hijab (Islam) Muslim dress for women, today often referring to a headscarf

hijra (hegira) (Islam) migration of early Muslims from Mecca to Medina

himorogi (Shinto) sacred space demarcated by a rope (*shimenawa*) or other marker

hitogami (Shinto) a living *kami* in human form

honji-suijaku (Shinto) Buddhist philosophy of the assimilation of Buddhas and *kami*

Hsiang-erh (Taoism) "Just Thinking"; text that is couched as a commentary on the *Lao-tzu*

hsin (Taoism) heart/mind

hsing (Taoism) inner nature; internal spiritual realities

hsiu chen (Taoism) cultivating reality; term by which Taoists frequently refer to religious practice

hsiu tao (Taoism) cultivating Tao; nearly synonymous with *hsiu chen*

hsiu-lien (Taoism) cultivation and refinement; an enduring Taoist term for self cultivation

hukam (Sikhism) divine order

huququllah (Bahá'í) "right of God"; a 19-percent tithe that Bahá'ís pay on their income after essential expenses

Ifa (African Traditional Religions) a form of divination that originated in West Africa

Igbo (African Traditional Religions) an ethnic group of Nigeria

imam (Islam) Shiite prayer leader; also used as the title for Muhammad's successors as leader of the Muslim community, consisting of male descendants through his cousin and son-in-law Ali

Inner Alchemy (Taoism) *nei-tan*; a generic term used for various related models of meditative self-cultivation

ishnan (Sikhism) purity

Islam (Islam) submission to the will of God; peace

iwasaka (Shinto) sacred stone circles

janam-sakhi (Sikhism) birth narrative; a hagiographical biography

jashan (Zoroastrianism) festival

jati (Hinduism) birth group

jihad (Islam) strive, struggle; a holy war

Jina (Jainism) victor or conqueror; periodic founder or reviver of the Jain religion; also called a Tirthankara (ford or bridge builder)

jingzuo (Confucianism) "quiet sitting"; meditation

jiva (Jainism) soul; every soul is endowed with perfect energy, perfect bliss, perfect perception, and perfect knowledge

jizya (Islam) poll, or head, tax paid by Jews and Christians

juma (Islam) Friday congregational prayer

Jurchen (Taoism) Manchurian tribe; founders of the Chin dynasty (1115–1234)

Kaaba (Islam) sacred structure in Mecca; according to tradition, built by Abraham and Ismail

Kabbalah (Judaism) mystical reading of the Scriptures that arose in France and Spain during the twelfth century, culminating with the composition in the late thirteenth century of the *Zohar* ("Book of Splendor"), which, especially as interpreted by Isaac Luria (1534–72), exercised a decisive influence on late medieval and early modern Jewish spiritual life

kagura (Shinto) Shinto ritual dances

Kaguru (African Traditional Religions) an ethnic group in Tanzania

kami (Shinto) Shinto deity or deities

kannushi (Shinto) lower-ranking Shinto priest

karah prashad (Sikhism) sanctified food, prepared in a large iron dish, or *karahi*

karma (Buddhism) law of cause and effect; act; deed

karma (Hinduism) literally "action"; the system of rewards and punishments attached to various actions

karma (Jainism) microscopic particles that float in the universe, stick to souls according the quality of their actions, and manifest a like result before becoming detached from them

karma (Sikhism) influence of a person's past actions on his future lives

kasruth (Judaism) rules and regulations for food and its preparation, often known by the Yiddish "kosher"

katha (Sikhism) a discourse on scripture in a *gurdwara*; homily

Kaur (Sikhism) female surname meaning Princess

kegare (Shinto) bodily or spiritual pollution

Khalsa (Sikhism) order of "pure" Sikhs, established by Guru Gobind Singh in 1699

ki (Shinto) vital spirit or energy

kirpan (Sikhism) sword

kirtan (Sikhism) devotional singing

Kojiki (Shinto) eighth-century Japanese mythological text

kokoro (Shinto) heart-mind

kokugaku (Shinto) Japanese nativist school of scholarship

Koran (Quran) (Islam) revelation; Muslim scripture

Krishna (Hinduism) a manifestation of the supreme being; one of the most popular Hindu deities, he is considered by many Hindus to be an incarnation of the god Vishnu

kuan (Taoism) Taoist abbeys or temples

kundalini (Hinduism) the power that is said to lie dormant at the base of a person's spine and that can be awakened in the search for enlightenment

kusti (Zoroastrianism) sacred cord worn around the torso by Zoroastrians and tied and untied during prayer

Lakshmi (Hinduism) a goddess; wife of the god Vishnu

langar (Sikhism) community dining

Lao-tzu (Taoism) the supposed author of the *Tao te ching*; also another name for the *Tao te ching*

Legalism (Taoism) Chinese school of philosophy that advocated a system of government based on a strict code of laws; prominent in the fifth through third centuries B.C.E.

Lent (Christianity) period of 40 days from Ash Wednesday to Easter, often marked by fasting and prayer

li (Confucianism) cosmic ordering principle

li (Confucianism) norms for the interaction of humans with each other and with higher forces (a different Chinese character from the other *li*, meaning "principle," above)

liangzhi (Confucianism) innate moral knowledge

libationers (Taoism) *chi-chiu*; men and women officiants in the early "Celestial Masters" organization

lien-shih (Taoism) refined master or mistress; an honorific term that was the highest Taoist title in T'ang times

Ling-pao (Taoism) "Numinous Treasure"; a set of Taoist revelations produced in the fourth century C.E.

Lixue (Confucianism) "study of principle"; Neo-Confucian philosophical movement

Lupupa (African Traditional Religions) a subgroup of the Basongye, an ethnic group of Democratic Republic of the Congo (Kinshasa)

madrasah (Islam) Islamic religious school

Magi (Zoroastrianism) priestly group that was initially active in western Iran under the Medes

Mahabharata (Hinduism) "Great Epic of India" or the "Great Sons of Bharata"; one of the two Hindu epics

Mahavira Jayanti (Jainism) celebration of the birth of Lord Mahavira, the 24th and last Jina of the current period, by Shvetambaras and Digambaras in March–April

Mahayana (sometimes called Northern Buddhism) (Buddhism) one of two major schools of Buddhism practiced mainly in China, Japan, Korea, and Tibet; evolved from the Mahasanghika (Great Assembly)

Man'yōshū (Shinto) eighth-century Japanese poetry anthology

mandala (Hinduism) a geometric design that represents sacredness, divine beings, or sacred knowledge or experience in an abstract form

manifestation of God (Bahá'í) an individual recognized in Bahá'í authoritative writings as a source of divine revelation and usually as the founder of a religion

mantra (Hinduism) a phrase or string of words, with or without meaning, recited repeatedly during meditation

Manyika (African Traditional Religions) an ethnic group of the southern African countries of Zimbabwe and Mozambique

marebito (Shinto) wandering spirits of the dead

Masai (African Traditional Religions) a nomadic people who inhabit Tanzania and Kenya

masjid (Islam) place for ritual prostration; mosque

matrimony (Christianity) sacrament; the joining of a man and woman in marriage

matsuri (Shinto) Shinto festivals

meng-wei (Taoism) covenant

Messiah (Christianity) the "anointed one," Jesus

Midrash (Judaism) commentary on the Scriptures, both Halakhic (legal) and Aggadic (narrative), originally in the form of sermons or lectures

mihrab (Islam) niche in mosque indicating the direction of Mecca

miko (Shinto) female medium or shaman

millet (Islam) protected religious community

minbar (Islam) raised platform in mosque; pulpit

ming (Taoism) destiny; the realities of a person's external life

Ming dynasty (Taoism) dynasty that ruled China from 1368 to 1644

Mishnah (Judaism) collection of the Oral Torah, or commentary on the Torah, first compiled in the second and third centuries C.E.

moksha (Hinduism) liberation from the cycle of birth and death

moksha (Jainism) nirvana; enlightenment achieved when practitioners purify themselves of all karma so that they will not be reborn

Mongols (Taoism) originally nomadic people who established the Yüan dynasty in China in the thirteenth century

muhapatti (Jainism) mouth guard worn by some renouncers to avoid harming insects and air beings

muni (Jainism) a Digambara monk who wears no clothing

Murtipujak (Jainism) a Shvetambara subsect that worships by means of images

Mwari (African Traditional Religions) a creator god worshiped in the southern African countries of Zimbabwe and Botswana

nam (Sikhism) the divine name

Namaskar Mantra (Jainism) the preeminent mantra that all Jains know and recite

negi (Shinto) senior Shinto priest

neisheng waiwang (Confucianism) "sage within and king without"; phrase used to describe one who is both a spiritual seeker and a social leader

nei-tan (Taoism) "Inner Alchemy"; the practice of spiritual refinement through meditation

Nei-yeh (Taoism) "Inner Cultivation"; an early Taoist text, likely a prototype for the well-known text *Tao te ching*

Neo-Confucianism (Taoism) Confucian teachings that were turned into a sociopolitical orthodoxy in China in the twelfth century

nigoda (Jainism) microscopic being

Nihon shoki (Shinto) eighth-century chronicle of Japanese history

Nineteen Day Feast (Bahá'í) a special meeting of the Bahá'í community held once every Bahá'í month, with devotional, business, and social portions

nirvana (Buddhism) the absolute elimination of karma; the absence of all states (the Sanskrit word literally means "to blow out, to extinguish")

norito (Shinto) Shinto liturgical prayers

Northern Sung dynasty (Taoism) dynasty that ruled China until 1126; part of the Sung dynasty

"Northern Taoism" (Taoism) modern term for Taoist traditions (Ch'üan-chen and Lung-men) that stress self-cultivation

odu (African Traditional Religions) poetic oral narratives memorized by *Ifa* diviners and recited during divination

Olódùmarè (African Traditional Religions) the Supreme Being in the religion of the Yoruba people

oni (Shinto) demon

opele (African Traditional Religions) a divining chain used in *Ifa* divination

ordination (Christianity) sacrament, in which a person is invested with religious authority or takes holy orders

orisa (African Traditional Religions) in the Yoruba religious tradition, the pantheon of deities

Orthodox Judaism (Judaism) traditional Judaism, characterized by strict observance of laws and rituals (the Halakhah)

Orthodoxy (Christianity) one of the main branches of Christianity, with a lineage that derives from the first-century apostolic churches; historically centered in Constantinople (Istanbul), it includes a number of autonomous national churches

Pahlavi (Zoroastrianism) middle Persian language of the Sasanian period; also the name of an Iranian dynasty (twentieth century)

pancha sila (Buddhism) five ethical precepts; the basic ethical guidelines for the layperson

panth (Sikhism) path

parahom (Zoroastrianism) sacred drink prepared during the *yasna*; a mixture of *haoma* and milk

Parsi (Zoroastrianism) member of a Zoroastrian group living mainly in western India and centered around Mumbai (Bombay)

Parvati (Hinduism) a goddess; the wife of the god Shiva

Paryushan (Jainism) yearly Shvetambara festival during which the Kalpa Sutra is read and that ends in atonement

Passover (Pesach) (Judaism) festival marking the deliverance of the Israelites from Egyptian bondage

pati (Sikhism) the core of a person, including self-respect

Pentecost (Christianity) seventh Sunday after Easter, commemorating the descent of the Holy Spirit on the apostles

Pentecostalism (Christianity) movement that emphasizes grace, expressive worship, evangelism, and spiritual gifts such as speaking in tongues and healing

People of the Book (Islam) Jews and Christians, who Muslims believe received divine revelations in the Torah and Gospels, respectively

Petrine primacy (Christianity) view that, as the successor to Peter, the bishop of Rome (pope) is supreme

prajna (Buddhism) wisdom

presbyterianism (Christianity) governance by a presbytery, an assembly of local clergy and lay representatives

Prophets (Nevi'im) (Judaism) second of the three parts of the Tanakh, made up of the books of 7 major and 12 minor prophets

Protestantism (Christianity) one of the main branches of Christianity, originating in the sixteenth-century

Reformation; rejecting the authority of the pope, it emphasized the role of grace and the authority of the Scriptures

puja (Jainism) rite of worship

puja (Buddhism) honor; worship

puja (Hinduism) religious rituals performed in the home

Purana (Hinduism) "Ancient Lore"; any of a set of sacred texts known as the old narratives

Purvas (Jainism) oldest scriptures of Jainism, now lost

qadimi (Zoroastrianism) "old" Zoroastrian calendar, which has New Year's Day in late July; compare with *fasli*

qi (Confucianism) matter-energy; life force pervading the cosmos

qiblih (Bahá'í) "point of adoration"; the location toward which Bahá'ís face when saying their obligatory prayer

rahit (Sikhism) code

Ramayana (Hinduism) "Story of Rama"; one of the two Hindu epics

raspi (Zoroastrianism) assistant priest, who feeds the fire during the *yasna*

reconciliation (Christianity) sacrament; the confession of and absolution from sin

Reconstructionist Judaism (Judaism) movement founded in the United States in the early twentieth century by Mordecai M. Kaplan (1881–1983) that holds Judaism to be not only a religion but also a dynamic "civilization" embracing art, music, literature, culture, and folkways

Reform Judaism (Judaism) movement originating in early nineteenth-century Germany that adapted the rituals and liturgy of Judaism to accommodate modern social, political, and cultural developments; sometimes called Liberal Judaism

ren (Confucianism) humaneness; benevolence

renyu (Confucianism) human desires

renzheng (Confucianism) humane government

riba (Islam) usury

Roman Catholicism (Christianity) one of the main branches of Christianity, tracing its origins to the apostle Peter; centered in Rome, it tends to be uniform in organization, doctrines, and rituals

Rosh Hashanah (Judaism) Jewish New Year; also known as the Day of Judgment, it is a time of penitence

sacrament (Christianity) any rite thought to have originated with or to have been sanctioned by Jesus as a sign of grace

sacramental (Christianity) devotional action or object

sadaqah (Islam) almsgiving for the poor, for thanksgiving, or to ward off danger

sadre (Zoroastrianism) sacred shirt; a thin, white, cotton garment worn that is worn under clothes and should never be removed

salat (Islam) prayer or worship; second pillar

sallekhana (Jainism) ritual fasting until death

salvation (Christianity) deliverance from sin and its consequences

samadhi (Hinduism) the final state of absorption into, and union with, the divine

samsara (Buddhism) the cyclical nature of the cosmos; rebirth

samsara (Hinduism) continuing rebirths; the cycle of life and death

samsara (Jainism) the cycle of reincarnation

samudaya (Buddhism) arising (of suffering); the second noble Truth

sanatana dharma (Hinduism) "eternal dharma"; in the *Dharma Sastra*s, virtues common to all human beings; also, a word used to denote Hinduism in general after the nineteenth century

sangat (Sikhism) holy fellowship; a congregation

sangha (Buddhism) community of monks

Sanhedrin (Judaism) supreme religious body of ancient Judaism, disbanded by the Romans early in the fifth century C.E.

sansar (Sikhism) rebirth; transmigration

Sanskrit (Hinduism) a classical language and part of the Indo-European language family; the language of ancient India

Sasanian dynasty (Zoroastrianism) dynasty that ruled Iran from 224 to 651 C.E.

sati (Jainism) virtuous woman; a chaste wife or a nun

Sephardim (Judaism) Jews of Spain and Portugal and their descendants, most of whom, in the wake of expulsion in 1492, settled in the Ottoman Empire and in North Africa; in the early seventeenth century small groups of descendants of Jews who had remained on the Iberian Penin

shabad (Sikhism) the divine word

Shabuoth (Feast of Weeks) (Judaism) originally a harvest festival, now observed in commemoration of the giving of the Torah to the Israelites

shahadah (Islam) declaration of faith; first pillar

shakti (Hinduism) energy or power, frequently used for the power of the Goddess; also a name for a manifestation of the Goddess

shan (Taoism) goodness

Shang-ch'ing (Taoism) "Supreme Clarity"; a tradition involving visualization meditation

Shariah (Islam) Islamic law

shen (Taoism) spirit; spiritual consciousness

shen-hsien (Taoism) spiritual transcendence

Shiite (Islam) member of second-largest Muslim sect, believing in the hereditary succession of Ali, the cousin and son-in-law of Muhammad, to lead the community

shinjin goitsu (Shinto) the essential identity of *kami* and humans

shintai (Shinto) the "body" of a *kami*, the object into which it descends following a ritual summons

Shiva (Hinduism) "the auspicious one"; a term for the supreme being; one of the most important deities in the Hindu tradition

shramana (Buddhism) wanderer

Shvetambara (Jainism) wearing white; sect of Jainism, largely based in northwestern India, in which monks and nuns wear white clothing

sikh (Sikhism) learner

Sikh Panth (Sikhism) the Sikh community

Sikh Rahit Maryada (Sikhism) Sikh Code of Conduct

sila (Buddhism) ethics; morality

Singh (Sikhism) male surname meaning Lion

smriti (Hinduism) "remembered"; a set of sacred compositions that includes the two epics, the *Puranas*, and the *Dharma Sastras*

"Southern Taoism" (Taoism) modern term for the Chengi Taoist tradition that survives mainly in Taiwan and along China's southeast coast; it stresses public liturgies such as *chiao* rather than self-cultivation

Spenta Mainyu (Zoroastrianism) primordial good spirit, twin of Angra Mainyu

sruti (Hinduism) "that which is heard"; a set of sacred compositions more popularly known as the Vedas

Sthanakwasi (Jainism) Shvetambara aniconic subsect

Sufi (Islam) mystic

Sung dynasty (Taoism) dynasty that ruled China from 960 to 1279

sunnah (Islam) example of Muhammad

Sunni (Islam) member of largest Muslim sect, holding that the successor (caliph) to Muhammad as leader of the community should be elected

surah (Islam) chapter of the Koran

svastika (Jainism) well-being; symbol representing the four realms into which souls are reincarnated, the three jewels, the abode of enlightened beings, and the enlightened beings themselves

swami (Hinduism) "master"; a charismatic teacher

T'ai-ch'ing (Taoism) "Great Clarity"; a tradition involving ritual alchemy

t'ai-p'ing (Taoism) grand tranquillity; a classical Chinese term for peace and harmony throughout the world; the most common Taoist political ideal

T'ai-p'ing ching (Taoism) "Scripture of Grand Tranquillity," an important early Taoist text

T'ang dynasty (Taoism) dynasty that ruled China from 618 to 907 C.E.

t'ien-shih (Taoism) celestial master; historical title for certain eminent Taoists, especially figures related to Chang Tao-ling

Talmud (Judaism) also known as the Gemara, a running commentary on the Mishnah written by rabbis (called *amoraim*, or "explainers") from the third to the fifth centuries C.E. in Palestine and Babylonia; the

Tamil (Hinduism) a classical language of southern India that is still spoken

Tanakh (Judaism) anagram for Jewish Scriptures, comprising the Torah, Prophets, and Writings

Tantra (Hinduism) literally "loom" or "to stretch"; generic name given to varied philosophies and rituals that frequently involve mantras, meditation on mandalas, or forms of yoga, leading to a liberating knowledge and experience

Tao (Taoism) classical Chinese term for any school's ideals and practices; among Taoists a term generally used to suggest the highest dimensions of reality, which can be attained by practitioners of traditional spiritual practices

tao (also dao) (Confucianism) "the way"; the Confucian life path

Tao te ching (Taoism) classical Taoist text; also known as the *Lao-tzu*

Tao-chiao (Taoism) the teachings of the Tao; the Taoist's name for their religion

Taoism (Taoism) *Tao-chiao*; a Chinese religious tradition that emphasizes personal transformation and integration with the unseen forces of the universe

tao-shih (Taoism) Taoist priest or priestess; a person recognized by the Taoist community as having mastered a specific body of sacred knowledge and the proper skills and dedication necessary to put that knowledge into effect for the sake of the community

Tao-tsang (Taoism) today's library of Taoist literature

tap (tapas, tapasya) (Jainism) austerities performed to purify the soul of karma

tattva (Jainism) any of the nine realities that characterize the universe and that include souls (*jivas*), matter (*ajiva*), matter coming in contact with souls (*ashrava*), the binding of karma and the soul (*bandha*), beneficial karma (*punya*), harmful karma (*papa*), inhibiting the influx of karma (*samvara*), purifying the soul of karma (*nirjara*), and liberation (*moksha*, or *nirvana*)

Tattvartha Sutra (Jainism) the only Jain scripture shared by both Shvetambaras and Digambaras, composed by Umasvati in c. 300 C.E.

tawhid (Islam) oneness, or unity, of God; monotheism

Terapanthi (Jainism) Shvetambara aniconic subsect that has only one *acharya*

Theravada (sometimes called Southern Buddhism) (Buddhism) one of two major schools of Buddhism practiced mainly in Cambodia, Laos, Myanmar [Burma], Sri Lanka, and Thailand; evolved from the Sthavira (Elders)

Three Bonds (Confucianism) obedience of subject to ruler, child to parent, and wife to husband

three jewels (Jainism) right faith, right understanding, and right conduct

Three Refuges, or Triple Gem (Buddhism) the Buddha, the dharma, and the sangha; the taking of the Three Refuges is a basic rite of passage in Buddhism

Tian (Confucianism) "Heaven"; entity believed to represent cosmic and moral order

tianli (Confucianism) ultimate, Heaven-rooted cosmic ordering principle permeating all phenomena

tianming (Confucianism) Mandate of Heaven

Torah (Pentatuch or Law) (Judaism) first division of the Tanakh, constituting the five books of Moses

torii (Shinto) gate marking the entrance to the grounds of a Shinto shrine

Trinity (Christianity) God as consisting of three persons—the Father, Son, and Holy Spirit

tripitaka (Pali, tipitaka) (Buddhism) three baskets, or three sets; the Tripitaka (Pali, Tipitaka), a collection of the Buddha's teachings—the Vinaya (Discipline), the Dharma (Doctrine), and the Abhidharma (Pali, Abhidhamma; Advanced Doctrine—forms the basis of the Buddhist canon

ubasoku, or hijiri (Shinto) mountain ascetics and holy men

ulama (Islam) religious leader or scholar

ummah (Islam) the transnational community of followers of Islam

Uniate (Christianity) any group observing Eastern rites but recognizing the authority of the pope

Universal House of Justice (Bahá'í) the supreme governing body of the worldwide Bahá'í community

upadesa (Hinduism) the sacred teaching

Upanishad (Hinduism) any of the Hindu sacred texts composed in about the sixth century B.C.E.; generally considered to be the "last" and philosophically the most important part of the Vedas

upaya (Buddhism) the concept of skillful means

Vaishnava (Hinduism) a member of a group of people devoted to Vishnu; also used to describe an object or an institution devoted to Vishnu

Vajrayana, or Tantra (Buddhism) a school of Mahayana Buddhism

vak (Sikhism) divine command

varna (Hinduism) literally "color"; the social class into which a person is born

varna-ashrama dharma (Hinduism) the behavior recommended for each class and each stage of life

Veda (Hinduism) literally "knowledge"; any of a set of compositions dating from the second millennium B.C.E. that is the highest scriptural authority for many educated Hindus

Vedanta (Hinduism) a philosophical school within Hinduism

Vishnu (Hinduism) literally "all-pervasive"; a term for the supreme being; one of the most important deities in the Hindu tradition; his incarnations include Rama and Krishna

wai-tan (Taoism) alchemy; a process of self-perfection involving the preparation of spiritualized substances called *tan* (elixirs)

wali (Islam) friend of God; Sufi saint

Wheel of the Dharma (Buddhism) visual symbol representing the Buddha's preaching his first sermon and also, with its eight spokes, Buddhism's Eightfold Path Yogacara, or Consciousness-Only school of Buddhism

Writings (Ketuvim or Hagiographa) (Judaism) third division of the Tanakh, including the Psalms and other works said to have be written under holy guidance

wu-wei (Taoism) nonaction; in the *Tao te ching*, a behavioral ideal of trusting the world's natural processes instead of one's own activity

wudu (Islam) ablution before worship

xin (Confucianism) heart-mind; human organ of moral evaluation

xing (Confucianism) inner human nature

Xinxue (Confucianism) "study of mind"; Neo-Confucian philosophical movement

ya Baha ul-abha (Bahá'í) "O Glory of the Most Glorious"; a form of the greatest name of God

Yasht (Zoroastrianism) one of a group of hymns to Iranian deities

yasna (Zoroastrianism) main Zoroastrian ritual; also the name of the main liturgical text, which is recited during the ritual

yazata (Zoroastrianism) any of a number of Zoroastrian divinities, the two most important of which are Mithra and the river goddess Anahita

yi (Confucianism) rightness; to act justly

yoga (Hinduism) physical and mental discipline by which one "yokes" one's spirit to a god; more generally, any path that leads to final emancipation

Yom Kippur (Day of Atonement) (Judaism) end of 10 days of penitence that begin with Rosh Hashana; the most holy of Jewish days

Yoruba (African Traditional Religions) an ethnic group residing in Nigeria and parts of Benin and Togo

yuga (Hinduism) in Hindu cosmology, any of four ages into which each cycle of time is divided

yuitsu genpon sōgen shintō (Shinto) "unique original essence Shinto"

zakat (Islam) purification; tithe or almsgiving; third pillar

zaotar (Zoroastrianism) priest

Zardushti (Zoroastrianism) name for the Zoroastrian tradition in Iran

Zoroaster (Zoroastrianism) founder of the Zoroastrian tradition; his Iranian name is Zarathustra

Zoroastrianism (Zoroastrianism) religion of pre-Islamic Iran; now represented by two communities, Parsi (Indian) and Zardushti (Iranian)

zot (Zoroastrianism) chief priest who performs the *yasna*

Zulu (African Traditional Religions) a large ethnic group in South Africa

Afghanistan

POPULATION 27,755,775

MUSLIM 99 percent

OTHER 1 percent

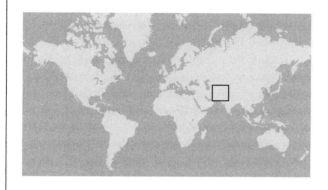

Country Overview

INTRODUCTION Afghanistan, since 2001 officially known as the Transitional Islamic State of Afghanistan, is a mountainous, landlocked country that lies in the heart of the Eurasian continent. It borders Iran to the west, Turkmenistan to the northwest, Tajikistan and Uzbekistan to the north, China to the northeast, and Pakistan to the east and south. Located at the crossroads of trade routes connecting south-central Asia to northern Europe and the Mediterranean region, Afghanistan has experienced incessant waves of invaders, migrants, and traders, creating an ethnically and linguistically diverse cultural mosaic. Despite a violent and turbulent past, Afghanistan has also been a place of great cultural efflorescence, because of its unique geographical location.

In ancient times Afghanistan was the center of Zoroastrianism, a Persian religion founded by the prophet Zoroaster (c. 628–c. 551 B.C.E.). Buddhism, first introduced in Afghanistan from India during the third century B.C.E., reached its apogee during the first and second centuries C.E., after which it spread to China and Southeast Asia. Between the eleventh and thirteenth centuries, Afghanistan became an important center for the development of Sufi Islam. Afghanistan emerged as an autonomous state after gaining independence from the British in 1919, which lasted until 1992, when factional fighting plunged the country into a protracted civil war that destroyed its state apparatus. The chaos of the civil war enabled the Taliban, a force contrived by the Pakistani military intelligence, to wrest control of the country beginning in 1994. Nation-building resumed in 2001 after the defeat of the Taliban.

Nearly all the inhabitants of Afghanistan are Muslim. According to estimates, approximately 84 percent, including the Taliban, follow the orthodox Sunni Hanafi school of Islam. Hanafi Sunnism has been heavily influenced by the radicalized and puritanical precepts of the Deobandi *madrasahs* (religious schools) in Pakistan. A significant number of Sunnis in Afghanistan adhere to mystical Islam and are members of Sufi brotherhoods, which emphasize personal spirituality and the idea of oneness with the divine. Many Sufis went underground during the Taliban regime, reemerging in the post-Taliban period. The remaining 15 percent of the Muslim population are Shias, differing from Sunnis through their belief in a divinely appointed leadership, or imamate. They belong to the largest branch of Shiism, the Twelvers—so called because they recognize 12

A worshipper stands outside of the shrine of Hazrati-i-Ali (Caliph Ali) in Mazar-i-Sharif. The shrine is one of the most famous and widely revered sacred places in Afghanistan. © RIC ERGENBRIGHT/CORBIS.

successive imams, or divinely inspired leaders, beginning with the Caliph Ali, the Prophet Muhammad's cousin and son-in-law.

RELIGIOUS TOLERANCE The rule of the Taliban (1994–2001) was marked by a historically unprecedented period of religious persecution, including the mass murder of religious and ethnic minorities, gross human rights abuses, and the ill treatment of women. Incarcerations, the severing of limbs, public beatings, and staged public executions by stoning in sports stadiums became routine measures by which the Taliban's Ministry of Fostering Virtue and Suppressing Vice enforced its eccentric interpretation of the Koran and Islamic law.

After the fall of the Taliban, the interim government of Afghanistan announced that it would pursue a policy of religious tolerance and provisionally adopted the constitution of 1964 as the legal basis for religious freedom until a new constitution could be drafted. Is-

lamic ultraconservatives within the government, however, strongly opposed this move, and the extent of religious freedom varies from region to region within the country, depending on the political faction in control.

Major Religion

SUNNI ISLAM

DATE OF ORIGIN 650 C.E.
NUMBER OF FOLLOWERS 27.5 million

HISTORY Islam arrived in Afghanistan as early as 650 C.E. Within the next two hundred years the people inhabiting contemporary Afghanistan, Pakistan, and northern India were converted to Sunnism. This branch of Islam became firmly entrenched in the region by the Ghaznavids (962–1186 C.E.), a Turkish dynasty that had forged the first great Islamic empire in Afghanistan by the middle of the tenth century and launched numerous military campaigns into India. A monarchical system dates back to 1747 with the reign of the Pashtun Ahmad Shah Durrani.

While Islam has been present in Afghanistan for many centuries, the rise of Afghanistan as an Islamic state occurred in the nineteenth century during the reign of Abdul Rahman Khan (1880–1901), who constructed an Islamic state, emphasized the primacy of Shariah (Islamic law) over the Pushtunwali tribal code, and inducted the religious leadership, or the ulama, into the state bureaucracy. Throughout its existence in the subsequent century, Afghanistan remained an Islamic state governed by Shariah, the basis of which is the Koran and the hadith (traditions of the Prophet Mohammad).

Islam has generally served as a unifying force that, despite sectarian variations, has overridden the many ethnic, cultural, and linguistic differences among the Afghans. Muslim identity served as the basis of the popular opposition to the Soviet invasion in 1979, but not of the Pan-Afghan constituency in the period following the Soviet withdrawal, when factionalism, ethnic polarization, and sectarian rivalries plunged the country into a bloody and debilitating civil war, leaving the already war-torn nation in ruins. By 2001 the antimodernist Pashtun Taliban from the puritanical Deobandi religious schools of Pakistan had captured 90 percent of Afghanistan. The Taliban renamed the country the Islamic Emirate of Afghanistan, signifying an effort to create a purely Islamic polity, patterned after the one established by Muhammad in Medina, rather than a modern nation-state. The Taliban's rivals, the Northern Alliance, which controlled the remaining 10 percent of the country, referred to their own regime as the Islamic State of Afghanistan. Following the expulsion of the Taliban in 2001 by the U.S.-led coalition, the country became known as the Transitional Islamic State of Afghanistan.

Nearly all the inhabitants of Afghanistan are Muslim. At the start of the twenty-first century, a census had not been conducted for several decades, and, therefore, there was no reliable data on Afghanistan's religious demography. According to estimates, approximately 84 percent, including the Taliban, follow the orthodox Sunni Hanafi school of jurisprudence. Hanafi Sunnism has been heavily influenced by the radicalized and puritanical precepts of the Deobandi *madrasah*s (religious schools) in Pakistan. A significant number of Sunnis in Afghanistan adhere to mystical Islam and are members of Sufi brotherhoods. Sufism, with its emphasis on personal spirituality and the idea of oneness with the divine, has been very influential in cities, towns, and rural areas, and it gives Islam in Afghanistan its own distinctive flavor. Many Sufis went underground during the Taliban regime, reemerging in the post-Taliban period. The remaining 15 percent of the Muslim population are Shias, differing from Sunnis through their belief in a divinely appointed leadership, or imamate. They belong to the largest branch of Shiism, the Twelvers, because they recognize 12 successive imams, or divinely inspired leaders, beginning with the Caliph Ali, the Prophet Muhammad's cousin and son-in-law.

EARLY AND MODERN LEADERS Key figures in Afghanistan's history include Ahmad Shah Durrani (1724–73), founder of the Durrani dynasty; Abdul Rahman Khan, founder of the modern Afghan state; Amanullah Khan (reigned 1919–29), who won independence from the British; Habibullah II (a non-Pashtun commoner popularly known as *Bacha-i-Saqao*, "son of the water carrier"), who briefly seized Amanullah's throne; Nadir Shah (reigned 1929–33), who defeated Habibullah II and assumed the title of king; Zahir Shah (reigned 1933–73), son of Nadir Shah, who introduced a constitutional monarchy in 1964, opening the door to democracy and the formation of political parties; and Mohammad Daud, King Zahir's cousin, who overthrew the monarchy, initiated the Republic of

Afghanistan, and assumed the office of president in 1973. Nur Mohammad Taraki, Hafizullah Amin, Babrak Karmal, and Mohammad Najibullah, key members of the Communist party, ousted Daud in 1978. Some of the major figures in the jihad, or holy war, against the Communist regime and the invading Soviet army included Sibghatullah Mojaddedi of the Afghan National Liberation Front; Burhanuddin Rabbani and Ahmad Shah Massud of the Islamic Society Party; and Gulbuddin Hekmatyar of the Islamic Party.

The spiritual leader of the Taliban, Mullah Omar, emerged as the head of the Taliban movement in 1994. Following the collapse of his regime in 2001, his whereabouts became unknown. Hamid Karzai, a Pashtun tribal leader from Kandahar and clansman of Zahir Shah, was elected head of the transitional administration of Afghanistan in 2002 and became the principal post-Taliban political figure.

MAJOR THEOLOGIANS AND AUTHORS A number of noted Afghan authors were Sufi philosophers whose writings encapsulate Sufi mysticism, which has played a significant role in Afghanistan and Central Asia in general. These philosopher-poets include Abdullah Ansari of Herat (eleventh century); Sanayi of Ghazni (twelfth century), who wrote the first mystical poetry in Dari; Rumi of Balkh (thirteenth century), the founder of the Mevlavi or Mawlawi order of dervishes, whose *Mathnawi*, comprising more than 25,000 verses, is believed to be among the greatest works of poetry written in Persian; and Maulana Nuruddin Jami of Herat (fifteenth century), who is regarded as the last great Persian mystical poet. A key figure during the nineteenth century was Sayed Jamaludin Afghani, a modernist reformer whose writings had international impact on the Pan-Islamic movement. Significant twentieth-century Afghan writers, whose poetry as well as historical and philosophical treatises appeared prior to the Soviet invasion, include Ahmad Kohzad, Said Qassim Rishtya, Abdul Rahman Pazhwak, Salauddin Seljuki, Ravan Fharhadi, Osman Sidky, Abdul Hal Habibi, Khalilullah Khalili, Abdul Rauf Benawa, Gul Pacha Ulfat, Sayyid Shamsuddin Majruh, and Zia Qarizada.

HOUSES OF WORSHIP AND HOLY PLACES Among the famous mosques in Afghanistan are the Id Gah Mosque and Shah-Do-Shamshira Mosque in Kabul, the Masjid-i-Jami in Herat, the Mosque of Ali in Mazar-i-Sharif, and the mosque of Kandahar, where the Khairqa-i-Moubarak, the cloak of the Prophet Muhammad, is enshrined. Although the worship of saints and shrines is tacitly forbidden in Islam, Afghans attribute magical powers to these local sites. Pilgrims converge upon these places in annual festivals, seeking miraculous cures and supernatural assistance. Amulets called *tawiz* that purportedly can cure diseases are dispensed at these shrines.

WHAT IS SACRED? Afghans consider the Koran both a sacred text and a sacred object that is thought to possess miraculous powers. The graves of Sufi saints, religious martyrs, and *malang* (wandering mendicants), as well as places where holy relics are kept, called *ziarats* (shrines), are considered sacred. The shrine of Hazrati-i-Ali (Caliph Ali) in Mazar-i-Sharif is one of the most famous and widely revered sacred places in Afghanistan. The shrine of Khairqa-i-Moubarak in Kandahar is another such place. When the Taliban captured Kandahar in 1994, its leader, Mullah Omar, took out the cloak of the Prophet Mohammad and held it before the gathered crowd as a way to unite the different Taliban factions and to legitimize his position as commander of the faithful.

HOLIDAYS AND FESTIVALS Afghans celebrate the main Muslim religious festivals, such as Id-i-Qurban, Id-i-Ramazan, and Id-i-Mawlud. The Tenth of Moharram, Martyr's Day, is observed by the Shia to commemorate the death of Hussain, the grandson of the Prophet Muhammad. Sunni Afghans also consider this a solemn occasion. Nauroz, New Year's celebration, which falls on the first day of spring and the first day of the Afghan solar calendar, is traditionally a time of great festivities. After the Taliban came to power, its leaders adopted the Islamic lunar calendar in 1998 and banned Nauroz as an anti-Islamic practice. After the Taliban regime was defeated, Nauroz was reinstated.

MODE OF DRESS There is variation in the mode of dress throughout Afghanistan. Typically, however, men wear loose cotton trousers, long-tailed shirts that extend over the trousers, and a wide waist sash. Sleeveless vests are worn over the shirts. Men wear skullcaps, or *kulah*, over which turbans, or *lungi*, are tied. Sandals, or *chapli*, and leather shoes called *paizar* are used for footwear. Typical Afghan attire for women includes a long dress (*peran*) over trousers (*tumban*) and a shawl, or *chador*, covering the head. Women in villages seldom wear the head-to-toe *burqa* veil, called *chadari*. In urban areas arti-

cles of European clothing, such as jackets, jeans, dresses, shoes, and boots, are commonly worn as well. Although the *chadari* is a traditional item of clothing, most educated urban women did not wear the *chadari* until the Taliban came to power and imposed a strict compulsory religious dress code upon everyone. Men were compelled to shed all articles of European clothing and wear the Pakistani *shalwar-kameez* (baggy trousers and long shirt), as well as cover their heads with a cap or turban.

DIETARY PRACTICES Afghans follow the dietary codes of Islam. For example, the consumption of alcohol and pork is forbidden. Some urban dwellers educated in the West or in the former Soviet Union consumed alcohol that was once available in the exclusive restaurants in Kabul until the fall of the Communist regime in 1992. While some Afghans may violate the prohibition on alcohol, even those living in Europe and the United States strictly observe the prohibition on pork. Also, despite Islamic interdictions, some Afghans use drugs, such as *chars* (marihuana), *taryak* (opium), and heroin. The Taliban derived much of its revenue from the production of opium until 2000, when a temporary ban was imposed on growing poppy.

RITUALS Afghans follow the obligatory codified rituals of Sunni Islam, known as the Five Pillars of Islam, which include *shahadah* (profession of the faith), *salat* (prayer five times a day), *zakat* (alms to the poor), *ruza* (fasting during the month of Ramadan), and hajj (pilgrimage to Mecca). In general there are no Islamic rituals that are distinctive to Afghanistan, aside from the observances associated with religious shrines, such as the shrine of Hazrati-i-Ali and the shrine of Khairqa-i-Moubarak, as well as homage to such saints as Sayed Mehdi Atesh Nafas or Miali Sahib. These practices, however, fall outside orthodox Sunni Islam, and they are at odds with the puritanical Deobandi tenets of the Taliban and other Islamic extremists.

RITES OF PASSAGE Rites of passage associated with birth, circumcision, marriage, and death differ in certain respects regionally and in terms of ethnic identity. Certain general similarities, however, do exist throughout Afghanistan. Parents and relatives rejoice at the birth of a child by beating drums, firing guns into the air, and giving alms to the poor. On the third day the child is named, and a mullah whispers "Allahu Akbar" into the child's ear, indicating its entrance into Muslim society.

Between the ages of ten and twelve boys are circumcised, signifying their passage into manhood. This is based upon the *sunnah*, examples set by the actions of the Prophet Muhammad during his lifetime. Traditionally, on the appointed day selected by the family, relatives gather to witness the circumcision. The family then celebrates the occasion by holding a feast that is accompanied by music and dancing. Comparable puberty rites generally do not exist for girls.

Traditionally Afghan marriages are arranged. Lengthy arrangements include everything from the initial agreement between the families of the bride and groom to the actual wedding ceremony, which is usually several days long. A religious judge, or *qazi* (*qadi*), validates the union, issues the *nikanamah* (marriage certificate), and recites Koranic marriage injunctions during the wedding ceremony.

Afghans follow Islamic burial rites. A mullah oversees the preparation of the body and says a prayer for the dead, or the *duwa-i jenaza*. Afghans follow a 40-day mourning period, marked by various observances, such as relatives gathering at the gravesite on the 14th day after burial. Mourning culminates on the 40th day, or *ruz-i-chel*, with a *qari* (reciter) performing *khatmi* Koran, reciting the Koran from start to finish.

MEMBERSHIP With the collapse of the Taliban regime in Afghanistan in 2001, most of its followers were driven to Pakistan, although some defected to the new Afghan regime, and an unknown number went underground inside Afghanistan. After that time, the largest drive for new followers to the brand of Deobandi Islam practiced by the Taliban took place across the border in Pakistan. Taliban operatives in Afghanistan began actively recruiting new members from among Pakistani and Afghan students in the country's religious seminaries in a bid to retake southern Afghanistan. Leaders called for a jihad against the forces that dislodged them from power in 2001.

SOCIAL JUSTICE Before the Soviet invasion and subsequent civil war, Afghanistan was one of the most moderate and peaceful societies in the Islamic world. No systematic efforts to impose compliance of religious duties existed, and there was considerable tolerance with respect to other sects and other religions. Afghans took great pride in their cultural heritage, both Islamic and pre-Islamic. The Soviet invasion and the events that followed resulted in the politicization of Islam. The Koran

upholds the right of every person to life, sustenance, work, justice, freedom of religious expression, property, protection of body and offspring, honor and dignity for women and men, and freedom for everyone to practice his or her talents and skills among other members of the community. In Afghanistan, however, these injunctions have been interpreted variably.

The Taliban adopted an uncompromising literal interpretation of Shariah as a divine compulsory system of rules and punishments applicable to all spheres of public and private life. Taliban officials implemented punishments stipulated in Shariah called *hudud*, which include stoning to death for adultery and amputation of arms for theft. Social justice meant establishing a pure Islamic state by the rigorous implementation of Shariah. Claiming that it was to be acting in the name of social justice by fulfilling its Islamic obligation to protect the honor and dignity of women, the Taliban imposed extremely repressive measures against females, which has been viewed as gender apartheid in the West. Whether the post-Taliban government of Afghanistan will be able to establish legislation to protect the poor, women, and ethnic and religious minorities will depend upon how its leaders are able to deal with the Islamic fundamentalists and ultraconservatives inside the government vying for a strict Islamic state.

SOCIAL ASPECTS As Muslims, Afghan men are permitted to marry Muslim women as well as People of the Book (Jews and Christians). Marriage, however, with non-Muslims who are not People of the Book, including Hindus, Buddhists, and atheists, is forbidden. Afghan Muslim women are permitted to marry only Muslim men. Within the family the male head of the household has the obligation, as stipulated by Islam, to provide for his family's material needs, while the female head of the household is responsible for taking charge of domestic affairs and the care and upbringing of children.

POLITICAL IMPACT Religion has had a tremendous political impact upon Afghanistan. Resistance groups following the Soviet invasion were referred to as the mujahideen—those who undertake jihad, or struggle, in defense of the faith. In fighting their Cold War by proxy in the battlefields of Afghanistan, the United States and its allies in this effort, Pakistan and Saudi Arabia, sent large sums of money and shipments of arms that led to the aggrandizement of foreign-backed Islamic groups at the expense of moderate Afghan nationalists. With the fragile state structure undermined as a result of over two decades of outside intervention, the withdrawal of the Soviets and the collapse of the Communist regime in Kabul transformed Afghanistan into a stateless territory. The Taliban movement, a Pakistani-contrived force of Pashtun religious extremists recruited from the tribal areas of Pakistan, was able to take advantage of the circumstances, seizing Kabul in 1996 and imposing a policy of repression and ethnic cleansing in the pretext of stabilizing the country. Under the Taliban, Afghanistan became the training ground for international terrorist groups, such as Osama bin Ladin's al-Qaeda, which perpetrated the attacks on the United States on 11 September 2001, sparking another war, this time against the Americans.

CONTROVERSIAL ISSUES Although the Western media has focused on human rights issues and the treatment of women in Afghanistan, both of which remain a problem in the post-Taliban period, the larger issue is political Islam, which represents the main obstacle to peace and security in Afghanistan. At war with modernity and all things Western and aspiring toward an Islamic state based on the strictest interpretation of Shariah, Islamists and their backers in Pakistan and the Middle East are opposed to efforts that would establish a stable democratic government.

CULTURAL IMPACT In some ways Islam pervades every aspect of Afghan life. Afghans, however, were never puritanical in their appreciation of art, music, and poetry. Thus, even though Islam forbids the depiction of the human form, painting and drawing were taught in schools. During the time of King Zahir's reign in the mid-twentieth century, there was active government patronage of the local artistic traditions, drama, and Afghan music. Promising students were sent overseas on government scholarships for training as actors, playwrights, musicians, and painters. There was also great interest by many in Afghanistan's cultural heritage, including its Greek and Buddhist archeological monuments and treasures. Many Afghans were shocked and outraged over the looting and destruction of the collection in the Kabul Museum and the destruction of the colossal Buddhas in Bamiyan by the Taliban.

It was during the time of the Taliban that religious restrictions were imposed upon aspects of life that were traditionally outside the scrutiny of, or restriction by, religious authorities. The Taliban banned cassettes, movies, television, dancing, singing, playing drums, flying kites, photography, and drawing images of humans or animals. When many of these restrictions were lifted in early post-Taliban Afghanistan, ardent fundamentalists in the government expressed their desire for a return to Taliban codes regulating the arts and artistic expression.

Other Religions

Historically Afghanistan did not experience sectarian conflicts until the war against the Soviets and the politicization of Islam, which brought these divisions to the forefront. Before the Soviet invasion there were sizable communities of non-Muslims in Afghanistan, including some 25,000 Hindus and 15,000 Sikhs, as well as a small Jewish community of about 2,000. Mostly engaged in commerce in the cities, these groups maintained their own cultural identities, openly practiced their respective faiths, and managed their own distinctive temples and houses of worship. Many of the Hindus and Sikhs left the country as a result of the disorder caused by the civil war during the early part of the 1990s and especially because of mistreatment by the Taliban. The post-Taliban period has witnessed the return of many of the Hindus and Sikhs. Only a handful of Jews remain.

Homayun Sidky

See Also Vol. 1: *Islam, Shia Islam, Sunni Islam, Zoroastrianism*

Bibliography

Amnesty International. *Afghanistan: Grave Abuses in the Name of Religion.* ASA 11/012/1996, November 1996.

Bureau of Democracy, Human Rights, and Labor. *International Religious Freedom Report: Afghanistan.* Washington, D.C., 2002.

Dupree, Louis. *Afghanistan.* Princeton, N.J.: Princeton University Press, 1973.

Marsden, Peter. *The Taliban: War and Religion in Afghanistan.* London: Zed Books, 2002.

Nyrop, Richard F., and Donald M. Seekins, eds. *Afghanistan: A Country Study.* Washington, D.C.: American University, 1986.

Roy, Olivier. *Afghanistan: From Holy War to Civil War.* Princeton, N.J.: Darwin Press, 1995.

Albania

POPULATION 3,544,841

MUSLIM between 60 and 80 percent

ORTHODOX CHRISTIAN between 15 and 20 percent

ROMAN CATHOLIC between 10 and 15 percent

OTHER less than 5 percent

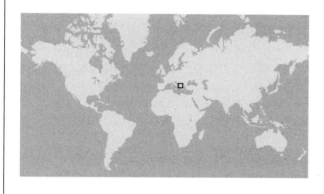

Country Overview

INTRODUCTION Albania is a small mountainous country on the western fringe of the Balkan Peninsula. It borders the Adriatic Sea to the west, Serbia and Montenegro to the north, Macedonia to the east, and Greece to the southeast. Its regions were Christianized during the first centuries of the Common Era. Situated between Rome and Constantinople, Albania embraced Catholicism more strongly in its northern regions and Orthodoxy more strongly in the south.

During Ottoman domination, from the fifteenth century to 1913, large portions of the Albanian population converted to Islam. With the collapse of the Ottoman Empire, the European Great Powers recognized an Albanian principality in 1913, but the country did not acquire full independence until after World War I, in 1920. Albania emerged as the only European country with a Muslim majority.

Religion during the Ottoman period became a determining factor for social and political identity, and it remained so in the twentieth century, even though a nation-building process attempted to unify Albania, despite its internal differences. Having endured an Italian occupation (1939–43), followed by a short German occupation (1943–44), the country recovered its independence and became a socialist republic. During the Communist era Albania was a satellite of Yugoslavia (1945–48), the Soviet Union (1948–61), and China (1961–78) before becoming completely isolated from the rest of the world. In 1991–92 a democratic system of government was established. Since then there have been important social changes, notably because of extensive internal and external migration spawned by extreme poverty, especially in the overpopulated countryside.

RELIGIOUS TOLERANCE Since the foundation of Albania in 1913, the country has never declared an official state religion. With the Communist takeover in 1944, repressive antireligion measures were adopted. These campaigns continued to grow until religion was banned during the so-called Cultural and Ideological Revolution of 1967. With an amendment to the Albanian constitution in 1976, Albania became the only officially atheistic country in the world. In November 1990 religious freedom was granted once again, although reli-

Albanian worshippers enter a tekke. *In Albania, Muslims worship in mosques and in* tekkes, *places belonging to dervish orders where Islamic prayers are performed along with the special rituals of the order.* © SETBOUN/CORBIS.

gions considered "traditional" (Islam, Orthodoxy, Catholicism) enjoyed higher status, both symbolically and politically, than did other religious groups (including Protestants).

Major Religion

SUNNI ISLAM

DATE OF ORIGIN 1385 C.E.
NUMBER OF FOLLOWERS Between 2.1 and 2.8 million

HISTORY During Ottoman rule the Hanafi rite of Sunni Islam (one of the four Islamic juridical schools) spread throughout Albania. The Catholic north experienced significant Islamization during the seventeenth century, while the Orthodox south saw widespread conversion in the eighteenth and nineteenth centuries. These conversions, especially among Catholics, continued until the end of Ottoman domination, in 1912–13. Several mystical brotherhoods, most notably the Halvetiyye and the Bektashiyye dervish orders, also spread among Albanian Muslims. The strongly syncretistic and heterodox doctrine of the Bektashiyye order enabled Albanian nationalists to portray Bektashism as another

Islam, distinct and separate from the Sunni Islam "of the Turks." As such, the image of the Bektashiyye order served as an important tool in the crystallization of Albanian nationalism, particularly in southern Albania, in the last decades of Ottoman domination. With the advent of an independent Albania, Islam was organized along national lines, and the Islamic community, like other religious communities, became subject to political power.

In the interwar period, in the face of opposition from a traditionalist trend that was strong in Shkodra and in central Albania, a reformist group tried to "modernize" Islam and its institutions. The reformists also fought against the decline of Sunni Islam among elites educated in the West and against the Bektashis, whose brotherhood developed into a religious community with de facto independence from the Sunni Islamic community. (By a decree of the Communists, Bektashi independence from the Muslim Sunni community became official in 1944.) Since the restoration of religious freedom in 1990, Islam in Albania has been defined by a convergence of both national and foreign influences. Because of the formation of various groups, the official Islamic community no longer has a monopoly.

EARLY AND MODERN LEADERS Since 1920 the Albanian Islamic community has been headed successively by Vehbi Dibra (1920–29), Behxhet Shapati (1919–42), Hafiz Sherif Langu (1942–45), Hafiz Musa Ali (1945–54), Hafiz Sulejman Myrtaj (1954–66), Esat Myftiju (1966–67), and Hafiz Sabri Koçi (beginning in 1990). In the interwar period Salih Vuçitern, the general secretary of the Vakfs (pious foundations), played an important role in the reform process. Salih Nijazi Dede, who was the last Bektashi head in the Ottoman Empire, led the Albanian Bektashi community from 1930 until his assassination in 1941. Ahmet Myftar Dede led the Bektashis from 1948 until 1958; beginning in 1990 Dede Reshat Bardhi has occupied this position.

Until contemporary times the main Albanian political leaders were Muslims, although they identified themselves as national leaders. This distinction also applied to most of the Albanian presidents of the twentieth century, including Ahmed Zogu (before 1939), Enver Hoxha (1944–85), Ramiz Alia (1985–92), and Sali Berisha (1992–97).

MAJOR THEOLOGIANS AND AUTHORS A number of Islamic judges (*kadi*s) of the Ottoman Empire were born in the region that is now southern Albania. Among them Abdurrahman Nesib became *shaikh-ül-islam,* the highest religious authority of the Ottoman Empire, in 1911–12. In independent Albania the leading theologians were Hafiz Ali Korça (1873–1956), a commentator on the Koran; Hafiz Ibrahim Dalliu (1878–1952); Shaykh Qazim Hoxha (1883–1959), a member of a dervish order who belonged to the dominant theological school of Shkodra; and Baba Ali Tomori (died in 1947), the most active Bektashi leader in the interwar period. After World War II the main Albanian theologians remained in exile: Baba Rexhebi and Imam Vehbi Ismaili in the United States and Vehbi Sulejman Gavoçi and Nasruddin Albani in Arab countries.

HOUSES OF WORSHIP AND HOLY PLACES In Albania, Muslims worship in mosques and in *tekke*s, places belonging to dervish orders where Islamic prayers are performed along with the special rituals of the order. During the antireligion campaigns of 1967, all Albanian mosques and *tekke*s were destroyed or appropriated and transformed for use as museums, sports halls, or warehouses or for other nonreligious purposes. Since the end of 1990, however, with help from Albanians and donations from foreign Islamic entrepreneurs, several hundred mosques have been rebuilt, especially in northern and central Albania. Only a few *tekke*s have been rebuilt or reopened, but many *türbe*s (tombs of Muslim saints), often linked with *tekke*s, have been restored.

WHAT IS SACRED? For Albanian Muslims the Koran is not only the most sacred text of Islam but also a means of protection, and they keep a copy on hand in their homes, offices, and even automobiles. Otherwise, there is nothing uniquely sacred to Muslims in Albania.

HOLIDAYS AND FESTIVALS Albania Muslims observe the usual Islamic feasts, most notably the Bayram of Ramadan and the Bayram of the Sacrifice (also known as the Small and Big Bayrams). These two days are national public holidays, as is the Day of Ashure, the 11th day of the lunar month of Muharrem, which is celebrated by the Bektashis and members of others mystical brotherhoods in remembrance of the martyrdom of Husein, grandson of the Prophet Muhammad. Between the 20th and the 25th of August, Bektashis also make a pilgrimage to the tomb of Abbas Ali, the supposed half brother of Husein, atop Mount Tomor in southern Albania.

MODE OF DRESS Most Muslim men and women in Albania wear Western-style clothing. Only a few wear Islamic dress. For women this means an overcoat and a headscarf. For some men it means ample garments, rather than the Western dress of a shirt and trousers, along with a beard to show their Islamic identity.

Imams of the older generation traditionally wore berets. Since the reestablishment of religious freedom, high clerics have begun again to wear special dress. Muftis and sheikhs, for example, wear a robe with full sleeves and long skirts, as well as specific headdresses.

DIETARY PRACTICES Fasting during Ramadan is increasingly widespread among Albanian Muslims, although it is hardly universal. Further, it is not uncommon for Muslims to eat pork, which is prohibited, and the prohibition against alcohol is rarely respected.

The Bektashis maintain their own fasting practices. Although they may eat during the first 10 days of the lunar month of Muharrem, they refrain from drinking anything, even water. On the 11th day Bektashis eat *ashure,* a meal of cereals and dried fruits.

RITUALS Attendance is not regular at the worship services held five times each day, but it is higher for the Friday prayers. A religious wedding is not common among the secular Muslims of Albania, and some young people who are nominally Muslim even prefer to go to a Christian, especially Protestant, church for such an occasion. Funerals also are highly secular, and many tombs do not show any sign of Islamic influence.

The mystical Islamic orders have their own rituals, called *ziqir* (Arabic *zikr*), during which names of God and formulas are unflaggingly repeated. Such rituals are now performed in only a few places. More common are the cults of saints and the pilgrimages to saints' tombs, especially those of Sari Saltik in Kruja and Dervishe Hatixhe in Tirana. On special occasions people go to the tombs, either individually or in groups; perform prayers; leave money, food, cloth, or other gifts; and sometimes offer a sacrifice, such as a sheep.

RITES OF PASSAGE Important rites of passage for Albanian Muslims include funerals and circumcision for boys. Those who enter Muslim brotherhoods participate in rites of initiation.

MEMBERSHIP Since 1990, as religious indifference has remained widespread and a movement toward Christianity has developed, the main activity of Islamic leaders, as well as missionaries from outside, has been to win back the heart of the Muslim population and to counter Christian proselytism. Especially among young city dwellers and migrants, conversion to Protestantism, Catholicism, or Orthodoxy is common.

Within Islam different versions, including Wahhabism and Shiism, compete for followers not only by providing religious services but also by offering humanitarian, economic, and educational services such as courses in English and computer literacy. The Bektashis tend to monopolize mystical Islam, but new Sufi groups have also tried to extend their networks.

SOCIAL JUSTICE All Islamic groups in Albania are active in humanitarian and educational programs. These include sponsoring orphans, supporting widows, distributing food, and improving water supplies in rural areas.

SOCIAL ASPECTS Albanian attitudes toward marriage and the family reflect the convergence of Islamic tradition and Albanian customary law, whereby the family—often the extended family—is the basic unit of social and economical life. Any threats to this unit, including celibacy and divorce, are strongly discouraged. Such attitudes remain prevalent throughout Albania, except among a small, secularized urban fringe.

POLITICAL IMPACT The political impact of Islam in Albania in the twentieth century was more indirect than direct. Sunni Islam tended to be considered the religion of the majority and Bektashism an alternative form that was seen as an "Albanian Islam," one that diminished the influence of the Sunnis.

Between 1992 and 1997 Islam was used by the president, Sali Berisha, to reinforce his power. By making Albania a member of the Organization of the International Islamic Conference, he secured funds to sustain the secret police and other internal networks. The president's opportunistic use of Islam for political gain provoked much public outcry.

CONTROVERSIAL ISSUES Religious Islamic leaders in Albania hold the same position as their colleagues throughout the Muslim world on such questions as birth control, divorce, and abortion. Divorce, which was forbidden by the Communist authorities, has become more common since 1990. Muslim religious leaders expect women to play a central role in the re-Islamization of Albanian society by raising their children to be good Muslims.

CULTURAL IMPACT During the Ottoman period the influence of Islam on Albanian culture was pervasive, as is evident in the architecture of the towns as well as in the music (especially in northern and central Albania) and literature of the era. Muslim writers of this period included Nezim Frakull (died in 1760), Hasan Zyko Kamberi (died at the beginning of the nineteenth century), and Muhamet Kyçyku (died in 1844). In the twentieth century, however, the Westernization of Albanian culture reduced, and even supplanted, the influence of Islam.

Other Religions

Orthodoxy and Roman Catholicism are the two dominant non-Islamic religions in Albania. During the Ottoman period Albanian Orthodox were linked to the Patriarchate of Constantinople. In the United States in 1908, under the leadership of Fan Noli, a priest ordained by the Russian Orthodox Church, the Albanian Orthodox Church made its first attempt to break from Constantinople and thereby establish itself as an autocephalous, or independent, body. In 1922 the autocephaly was officially proclaimed within the framework of the new Albanian state, and in 1924 Noli became the prime minister of a short-lived government. He was forced to leave the country in 1925 after Ahmed Zog's comeback, and Constantinople did not recognize the independence of Albanian Orthodoxy until 1937. In 1991 the Patriarchate of Istanbul appointed a Greek, Anastas Janullatos, as exarch of the Albanian Orthodox Church, and the following year he became archbishop. Some people criticized the appointment as Greek interference in Albanian affairs and as threatening the independence of the Albanian church.

Concentrated mainly in southern and central Albania, the country's Orthodox population comprises not only Albanians but Aroumanians, also called Vlahs; Greeks, who are recognized as an ethnic minority; and even small groups of Slavs, with Macedonians in the southeast and Serbs and Montenegrins in the north. In the 1990s there was a wave of conversions among Albanian migrants to Greece. Since 1990 the church has built and rebuilt many churches throughout the country.

Catholicism in Albania is confined to the northwest, in the city of Shkodra and the surrounding area. In some places Catholicism has long been mingled with local customs, or "the law of the mountains," and influences of the Serbian Orthodox Church—for example, in the celebrating of a family's patron—can also be found. Unlike the other religious communities in Albania, Catholicism did not acquire a purely national structure, instead remaining close to the Vatican. Nonetheless, Catholics clerics played a significant role in the cultural and intellectual scene during the interwar period. Generally being strongly anti-Communist, Catholics suffered particular tension with government authorities after World War II. With the fall of the Communist regime, Catholicism came to be seen by some as the religion most compatible with a European identity, and it began to attract many young city dwellers and intellectuals as well as Albanian migrants in Italy.

Protestant missionary activity in Albania began in the nineteenth century. While early missionaries played a key role in establishing an Albanian literature and in the development of an Albanian national identity, they did not attract many followers. Indeed, at the beginning of the 1940s, the Protestant community numbered only a few hundred people. After World War II, however, Protestantism often came to be seen as an embodiment of the American and European model. In addition, Protestants became more adept at presenting their religion as an appealing alternative to traditional forms of Christianity. Following the collapse of the Communist regime, Protestant missionary activity experienced a large-scale resurgence, this time with greater success, and since then Protestantism and other small proselytizing groups have gained membership.

Nathalie Clayer

See Also Vol. 1: *Christianity, Islam, Roman Catholicism, Sunni Islam*

Bibliography

Bartl, Peter. "Religionsgemeinschaften und Kirchen." In *Albania: Handbook.* Göttingen: Vandenhoeck and Ruprecht, 1993.

Bougarel, Xavier, and Nathalie Clayer. *Le Nouvel Islam balkanique: Les Musulmans acteurs du post-communisme 1990–2000.* Paris: Maisonneuve et Larose, 2001.

Clayer, Nathalie. "God in the 'Land of the Mercedes': The Religious Communities in Albania since 1990." In *Religion et nation chez les Albanais: XIXe–XXe siècles.* Istanbul: Isis, 2003.

———. "Islam, State and Society in Post-Communist Albania." In *Muslim Identity and the Balkan State.* Edited by Hugh Poulton and Suha Taji-Farouki. London: Hurst, 1997.

Elsie, Robert. *A Dictionary of Albanian Religion, Mythology, and Folk Culture.* London: Hurst, 2001.

Popovic, Alexandre. *L'islam balkanique: Les Musulmans du sud-est européen dans la période post-ottomane.* Berlin-Wiesbaden: Otto Harrassowitz, 1986.

Sinishta, Gjon. *The Fulfilled Promise: A Documentary Account of Religious Persecution in Albania.* Santa Clara, Calif.: Albanian Catholic Information Center, 1976.

Stutzman, Linford. "To Win the Hearts and Minds: Evangelical Mission Activity in Albania as a Global Culture War." *Journal of Ecumenical Studies* 33, no. 1 (winter 1996): 44–58.

Trix, Frances. "The Resurfacing of Islam in Albania." *East European Quarterly* 28, no. 4 (1995): 533–49.

Algeria

POPULATION 32,277,942

MUSLIM 97 percent

CHRISTIAN AND JEWISH 1 percent

ATHEIST 2 percent

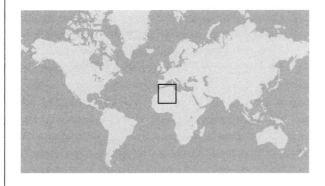

Country Overview

INTRODUCTION The People's Democratic Republic of Algeria lies in North Africa. It is bordered on the east by Tunisia and Libya; on the south by Niger, Mali, and Mauritania; on the west by Western Sahara and Morocco; and on the north by the Mediterranean Sea. It is the second largest country in Africa and the eleventh largest in the world. There is a narrow coastal area in the north, which is fairly fertile, and a vast desert in the south. The two parts are separated by mountain ranges, including the Atlas.

From 1100 B.C.E. the Phoenicians established colonies in the region. The Romans ruled from 200 B.C.E. to about 670 C.E., when the area was conquered by Arabs. Christianity, which had arrived with the Romans, declined after the Arab conquest. From the eighth to the eleventh centuries the region was fragmented into kingdoms ruled by Berbers, who took Shiite Islam as their creed. From the eleventh to the thirteen centuries, two empires, the Almoravid and the Almohad, successively ruled northwestern Africa, part of the Maghreb. These empires followed Sunni Islam. The Almohad court especially was known for its cultivation of learning, and it was there that Ibn Rushd (Averroës) wrote his commentaries on Aristotle. Virtually all Muslims in Algeria today adhere to the Malikite school, one of the four main branches of Sunni Islam.

With the fall of Granada to Christians in 1492, Moors took refuge in Algeria. By 1510 the Spanish had established control over Algerian ports. Muslims called on the Ottomans to liberate them, and by 1519 the Ottomans had conquered most of Algeria. The French captured Algeria beginning in 1830, and Christianity was reintroduced. Algerians who resisted the French were brutally suppressed. Nationalist and Islamic movements developed, however, culminating in a military revolution under the Front Libération Nationale (FLN; National Liberation Front) from 1954 to 1962, when Algeria became independent.

By the 1980s there were violent protests against government policies, and in 1990 the Front Islamique du Salut (FIS; Islamic Salvation Front) won provincial and municipal elections. In 1992, after the FIS had won the first round of parliamentary elections, a group of civilian and military leaders forced the president to resign, canceled the elections, and declared a state of emergency. The new president was assassinated, as Algeria faced civil war between Islamic militants and government forces. Since then, although hardline governments have maintained control, violence has continued.

RELIGIOUS TOLERANCE With independence in 1962, Islam became the state religion of Algeria. The government monopolized the building of mosques and supervised the activities that took place within them. Religious property was confiscated and put under state control, and the government also took charge of religious education. By the 1970s and 1980s, however, a movement that viewed Islam as a holistic faith embracing all aspects of life, both public and private, had begun to spread on university campuses. Although it initially enjoyed the tolerance of the government, the movement began to have political aspirations. Compensating for the government's failure, Islamists offered comprehensive social programs that included tutoring sessions, schooling, business development, and assistance for needy families and even such services as neighborhood beautification and garbage pickup.

It was from this movement that the Front Islamique du Salut (FIS; Islamic Salvation Front) developed. The FIS stood for municipal elections in 1990 and won nearly 56 percent of the seats. In December 1991 the FIS won the first round of parliamentary elections, which resulted in the cancellation of the results. When subsequent governments tried to suppress the Islamists, Algeria fell into a fierce civil war between Islamic extremists, the government army, and government militias. In the conflict members of the Christian minority were attacked by the extremists.

Under Algerian law both Christians and Jews have maintained the right to practice their religions. Muslims may not convert, however. Atheists, generally regarded as a relic of French rule, are tolerated but resented. One of the results of the rising Islamism has been an increase in criticism of non-Muslims, along with sporadic cases of discrimination and violence.

Major Religion

ISLAM

DATE OF ORIGIN c. 670 C.E.
NUMBER OF FOLLOWERS 31.3 million

HISTORY Islam entered Algeria with Arab conquerors in around 670 C.E. By the eleventh century the native

A woman walks in front of a mosque as Muslim men bow in prayer. Women generally wear the hijab, *a long dress with a head covering.*
© ANTOINE GYORI/CORBIS SYGMA.

Berbers had become Islamized and partly Arabized. In 705 northwestern Africa, part of the Maghreb, came under the Umayyad caliphate as the *wilayah* (province) of Ifriqiyah, thus separating it from Egypt, from which it had formerly been administered. The Berbers, however, protested against what they saw as unjust Arab rule, taking Shiite Islam as the basis of their rebellion.

The Kharijites, a sect of Shiite Islam, used the revolutionary potential of their beliefs in the struggle against Umayyad rule. Kharijite doctrine rejected the idea that the Arabs had a monopoly on the political leadership of Muslims, stressed piety and learning as the main qualifications for leadership of the Muslim community, and sanctioned rebellion against the head when he acted unjustly. Shiite Berber kingdoms prevailed from the eighth to the eleventh centuries, culminating in the Fatimid empire, beginning in the ninth century, that grounded its ideology in the Ismaili movement, an extremist branch of Shiism.

From the eleventh to the thirteenth centuries Sunni Islam returned to the region through two successive empires, the Almoravid and the Almohad, which united the fragmented Maghreb under Berber rule. The Malikite school prevailed in the Maghreb, with its jurists providing religious legitimacy for political authority, supervising the administration of justice and the work of provincial governors, and acting as advisers to the rulers.

Although Malikite jurists resisted the Sufi mystical tendencies that reached northwestern Africa from Spain, the influence of Sufism and of Sufi saints spread throughout the Maghreb from the twelfth century onward. This was especially true in the countryside, where Sufi leaders allied themselves with tribal chiefs and contributed toward the establishment of order and stability by using their moral authority to uphold religious norms and to arbitrate conflicts. With the French occupation that began in 1830, Emir Abdel Qadir took Sufi and traditional Islam into a new direction by using the concept of *jihad* (struggle) as the basis for an ideology of anticolonization.

After World War I, Abdel Hamid Ben Badis, who had been influenced by the reform ideas of Muhammad Abduh and Rashid Rida of Al-Azhar University in Cairo, introduced a new reform movement, through which he tried to reconcile Islamic tradition with modernity. His efforts resulted into the foundation of a so-called high tradition in Islam that distanced itself from the mysticism of the Sufis. Ben Badis promoted his views through writings and his educational endeavors.

After independence in 1962, the Algerian government adopted and also monopolized a moderate and somewhat socialist form of Islam that was conciliatory with its policies. An Islamic revival took place in the 1970s, however, and by the 1980s the movement was advocating a more orthodox form of Islam and was challenging the legitimacy and authority of the state. The clashes between Islamists and the state since the early 1990s have resulted in the emergence of a violent and militant Islam in Algeria that has sought military victory over the state and led to a fierce civil war.

EARLY AND MODERN LEADERS Emir Abdel Qadir, one of the most important national heroes of Algeria, is often considered the founder of the Algerian state. In 1832, at the age of 25, he led a jihad against the French occupation, starting from his capital in Tlemcen in western Algeria. The emir, who was known as a cunning political leader, a resourceful warrior, and a devout Sufi, gained the support of Algerian tribes to build a Muslim state that by 1839 controlled more than two-thirds of the country. His government maintained an army and a bureaucracy, collected taxes, supported education, undertook public works, and established agricultural and manufacturing cooperatives. After fierce battles Abdel Qadir signed a treaty with the French in 1837, by which his state was recognized. The French army provoked the emir in 1839, however, by violating the treaty and extending its occupation into new territories. Military confrontations began again, but the emir suffered a series of defeats by a force that included a third of the entire French army. In 1847 Abdel Qadir surrendered to the French, who took him as a prisoner to France. In 1852 Napoleon III freed Abdel Qadir, who reached Damascus in 1855 and remained there until his death in 1883, devoting himself to scholarly pursuits and charity and declining all invitations to return to public life. In 1860, however, Abdel Qadir intervened to save the lives of an estimated 12,000 Christians, including the French consul and staff, during riots against the Christian minority.

Ferhat Abbas (1899–1985) advocated a popular, and frequently social, version of Islam that mobilized the Algerian people in the struggle for independence. Educated as a pharmacist, he abandoned assimilation as an alternative to self-determination, and in 1943 he presented the French administration with the "Manifesto of the Algerian People," signed by 56 Algerian nationalist and international leaders. The manifesto demanded an Algerian constitution that would guarantee immediate political participation and legal equality for Muslims. It called for agrarian reform, recognition of Arabic as an official language on equal terms with French, a full range of civil liberties, and the liberation of political prisoners of all parties. The negative reaction of the French administration resulted in Abbas's demand for an independent Algerian state in federation with France. In 1956 he joined the Front Libération Nationale (FLN; National Liberation Front), based in Cairo, which waged a war of independence against the French. From 1958 to 1961 he headed the FLN government in exile. After independence in 1962, Abbas quarreled with the more radical NLF leadership, and he was held under house arrest from 1964 to 1965. He then retired from public life.

MAJOR THEOLOGIANS AND AUTHORS Abdel Hamid Ben Badis (1889–1940) pursued an education in theology in Algeria, Tunisia, and Egypt. After World War I he began his work in Algeria, seeking to distance himself from politics in favor of involvement in educational and journalistic activities that focused on cultural, social, and religious matters. In 1931, with other scholars, he founded the Muslim Scholars Society, and he promoted the Islamic Conference of 1936 that gathered together the various nationalist forces of Algeria. Ben Badis become known especially as an Islamic reformist. By 1945 his work had resulted in the opening of some 150 schools enrolling more than 40,000 students, about a third of the number enrolled in French schools at the time. In 1919 he and his colleagues opened the first school for girls in Algeria. He established a number of newspapers to help spread the message of reform Islam and to preserve Arabic, which under French occupation was considered a foreign language.

Malik Ben Nabbi (1905–1973) was one of the most prominent Arab intellectuals and philosophers of modern Algeria. He grounded his thought in the views both of the historian Ibn Khaldun (1332–1406) and of modern Western philosophers and used psychology and sociology to analyze Arab and Islamic society and culture. In his writings he emphasized his conviction that until Arabs creatively restored and rebuilt their civilization they would have no chance for progress. The products of civilization could be imported, he taught, but civilization itself had to be created locally. To achieve cultural independence, there must be Islamic intellectual and scientific alternatives to Western ideas. Ben Nabbi promoted the idea of the "availability to be colonized" as the root of colonization. Like Ibn Khaldun, he also saw civilizations as going through cycles of birth, flourishing, decay, and death, and he advocated that people learn the causes of the different phases and their characteristics.

HOUSES OF WORSHIP AND HOLY PLACES As in the rest of the Islamic world, the house of worship in Algeria is the mosque, which frequently, however, has a North African character to its architecture. Algeria also is known for its many *zawiyah*s. Constructed around a shrine to a saint, these consist of a prayer hall, a place for lectures, and a number of small, humble rooms for students, the needy, or wayfarers. They also serve as places for people who want a retreat from the noise of daily life. It is estimated that Algeria has about 5,000 *zawiyah*s, most of them located in the countryside.

WHAT IS SACRED? Among Algerian Muslims, as in Islam elsewhere, only God is held to be sacred. Especially in the countryside, however, believers may hold the shrines of saints, usually Sufi, as sacred places, at which their prayers will be blessed.

HOLIDAYS AND FESTIVALS Muslims in Algeria join believers throughout the Islamic world in celebrating Id al-Fitr, the feast that breaks the Ramadan fast, and Id al-Adha, which marks the end of the pilgrimage to Mecca. Among other celebrations is the birthday of the Prophet Muhammad. In addition, Algerian Muslims commemorate the birthdays of some Sufi saints. In Oran (Wahran) in western Algeria, for instance, some 5,000 people annually celebrate the birthday of the saint Sayyid al-Hassani in a festival called al-Waada.

MODE OF DRESS Both men and women are expected to dress modestly in Algeria. Women generally wear the *hijab,* a long dress with a head covering. In the larger cities women are more relaxed about the wearing of a veil. Clerics usually wear loose white garments, with their heads covered by a hat.

DIETARY PRACTICES As in the rest of the Islamic world, Muslims in Algeria are instructed to eat only food that is *halal,* or religiously sanctioned. Thus, the eating of pork and the consumption of alcohol are forbidden.

RITUALS Muslims in Algeria observe the rituals of believers elsewhere in the Islamic world. These include the *salat,* or prayer, that is performed five times each day. Those who are able make the hajj, or pilgrimage to Mecca, at least once during their lifetimes.

RITES OF PASSAGE As with other Muslims, it is the tradition of Algerians to say the *azan,* or call to prayer, in the ear of a baby at the time of birth. In the baby's seventh day there is sometimes a celebration in which a lamb is sacrificed to feed the family, friends, and the poor. Male babies are circumcised. Marriages and burials are other important rites of passage, but there is nothing distinctive about their observance in Algeria.

MEMBERSHIP Because almost all of the population of Algeria is Muslim, there is no proselytization. Efforts to recruit believers to various Islamic political groups and ideologies is not uncommon, however. This is especially true in contemporary Algeria, in which Islam has become highly politicized and in which there are clashes between Islamic groups and the government.

SOCIAL JUSTICE Islam has long played a role in ideas about social justice in Algeria. Before independence in

1961, most Algerian nationalists at least partly grounded their claims for social justice in Islamic teachings like those of Abdel Hamid Ben Badis and Ferhat Abbas. After independence Houari Boumedienne, president of Algeria from 1965 until his death in 1978, sought to reconcile Islam and socialism, pointing out, for example, that the Prophet Muhammad "made his living from his own work" and that Islam "prohibited that a sector of society would live in the hell of poverty while another sector is living in the paradise of wealth." Islamists later stressed a commitment to social welfare projects. It was in this way that Islamists gained popular support, especially in times of economic crises, which helped them in their political struggles.

SOCIAL ASPECTS Marriage in Algeria is more a family than a personal affair. The tradition of strong family life still dominates most areas of the country. A trend toward the smaller nuclear family, however, has affected the structure of the traditional extended family, both in urban and in rural areas. Although the nuclear family is more pronounced in cities, it is fast becoming the prevalent family structure in Algeria.

An Islamic marriage in Algeria, as elsewhere, is a civil contract rather than a sacrament. As a consequence, representatives of the bride's interests negotiate a marriage agreement with representatives of the bridegroom. Divorce is discouraged, but it is allowed.

POLITICAL IMPACT Throughout history Islam has played a predominant role in the political life of Algeria. From the eighth to the eleventh centuries, Shiite Islam became the ideology of the Berbers in rebellion against the Sunni caliphate. Beginning in the eleventh century, in a shift away from the earlier Shiite kingdoms, both the Almoravids and the Almohads based their rule in Sunni Islam. The Almohads emphasized the importance of following the Koran and the *sunnah* (example of Muhammad) rather than submitting to the ideas of one or another of the schools of *fiqh* (law), such as the Malikite. In modern Algerian history both military and political Islam have been adopted to fight the French occupation, to legitimize the state, and finally to challenge the government and frame a new basis for social and political reform.

CONTROVERSIAL ISSUES Algerian scholars have long maintained their objection to the popular Islam preached by Sufi sheikhs. They have argued that, instead of spreading modern views, the Sufi sheikhs hold on to traditional and mysterious forms of Islam that contradict enlightenment and that work only for their own material benefit.

The role of Islam in civil life, including the position of Shariah (religious law) within the civil legal code, is a source of controversy in Algeria. While both Islamists and the government admit the significance of Islam in everyday life in Algeria, they take different positions on the extent to which Islam should determine the country's regulations and laws.

CULTURAL IMPACT *Raï* (way of seeing, aim, or thought), a style of music that originated in the urban centers of Algeria and Morocco in the early 1970s, became popular among young people who sought to modernize traditional Islamic values and attitudes. Incorporating a number of influences, including Western instruments, *raï* is a danceable music that is characterized by simple lyrics in local dialects. Among Berbers women are the primary source for organized musical activities. Each village has its "professional" poet, who improvises as she sings and is accompanied by a female chorus, which also plays small drums. An example might be a song composed for a bride and performed at the wedding feast.

Like those elsewhere in North Africa and in Spain, mosques in Algeria are characterized by a square minaret. The Almohads took pride in the construction of mosques and, because of its symbolic significance, paid particular attention to the minaret. The great mosque of Masurah, in Tlemcen, is perhaps the best known in Algeria. Built between 1303 and 1336, it has stone columns and a square minaret with a simple base, pairs of windows with large arches, and richly ornamented top sections.

Other Religions

There are a few thousand Roman Catholics living in Algeria. Most are foreigners or Algerians who have married French or Italians and then converted. In addition, there is a small Protestant community.

Jewish settlements in Algeria can be traced to the first centuries C.E. Many Sephardic Jews migrated from Spain to Algeria in the fourteenth century. The Jewish population that remains appears to have stabilized at roughly a thousand people.

Mohamed Mosaad

See Also Vol. 1: *Islam, Sunni Islam*

Bibliography

Al Barazi, Tammam. *Algeria under the Rule of Military.* Cairo: Madbouli, 2002.

Al Rasi, George. *The Algerian Islam from Emir Abdel Qadir to the Emirs of Groups.* Beirut: Dar Al Jadid, 1997.

Bekkar, Rabia. "Taking Up Space in Tlemcen: The Islamist Occupation of Urban Algeria." *Middle East Report* 179 (November–December 1992): 11–15.

Cheriet, Boutheina. "Islamism and Feminism: Algeria's 'Rites of Passage' to Democracy." In *State and Society in Algeria.* Edited by John P. Entelis and Phillip C. Naylor. Boulder, Colo.: Westview Press, 1992.

Deeb, Mary-Jane. "Islam and the State: The Continuity of the Political Discourse of Islamic Movements in Algeria from 1832 to 1992." Paper delivered at the "Islam and Nationhood" conference at Yale University, November 1992.

Entelis, John P., and Lisa J. Arone. "Algeria in Turmoil: Islam, Democracy, and the State." *Middle East Policy* 1, no. 2 (1992): 23–35.

Fudail, Abdel Qadir, and Mohamed Ramadan. *The Imam of Algeria: Abdel Hamid Ben Badis.* Algiers: Dar Al Umma, 1998.

Hermida, Alfred. "Death in Algiers." *Africa Report* 37, no. 5 (September–October 1992): 49–53.

Hourani, Albert. *A History of the Arab Peoples.* New York: Warner Books, 1992.

Kapil, Arun. "Algeria's Elections Show Islamist Strength." *Middle East Report* 165 (September–October 1990): 31–36.

Lapidus, Ira M. *A History of Islamic Societies.* Cambridge: Cambridge University Press, 1988.

Mandron, Guy. "The Algerian Confrontation." *Jane's Intelligence Review* 4, no. 7 (July 1992): 321–24.

Mortimer, Robert A. "Islam and Multiparty Politics in Algeria." *Middle East Journal* 45, no. 4 (autumn 1991): 575–93.

Ruedy, John. *Modern Algeria: The Origins and Development of a Nation.* Bloomington: Indiana University Press, 1992.

Stone, Martin. *The Agony of Algeria.* London: C. Hurst, 1997.

Talbott, John. *The War without a Name: France in Algeria, 1954–1962.* New York: Knopf, 1980.

Willis, Michael. *The Islamist Challenge in Algeria: A Political History.* New York: New York University Press, 1999.

Andorra

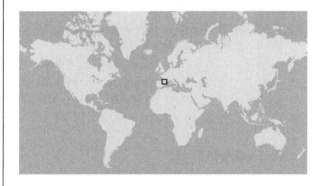

governmental authority resides in the elected General Council and its cabinet.

RELIGIOUS TOLERANCE Until 1993 Catholicism was the official religion in Andorra, and freedom of worship was only tolerated. The Andorran people and the coprinces have since worked toward changing this situation. The constitution of 1993 respects civil rights, religious freedom, and separation of power between governmental branches, all the while recognizing the preeminence of Catholicism.

Major Religion

ROMAN CATHOLICISM

DATE OF ORIGIN Sixth century C.E.
NUMBER OF FOLLOWERS 41,000

HISTORY Andorra is part of the Urgell diocese in Catalonia, whose first known bishop was Saint Just (sixth century). It is probable that the people of Andorra were already converted to Christianity at that time. The first official mention of the original six parishes of Andorra dates back to the ninth century. In 843 the bishop of Urgell was granted sovereignty over Andorra, and this deeply affected the development of Andorran Catholicism. In the thirteenth century the count of Foix (France), also holding ruling power in Andorra, came into conflict with the bishop of Urgell. An agreement concerning control of the lands, known as the Paréages, was signed in 1278 under the aegis of Père II, king of

Country Overview

INTRODUCTION The Principality of Andorra, a small country of 181 square miles (468 square kilometers), is situated between France and Spain on the south side of the Pyrenees Mountains. Its geographical location and the Catalan language unite Andorrans with the people of the Iberian Peninsula. Historically the majority of Andorrans have been Roman Catholic. Since the 1960s Andorran citizens have represented a minority of the population, while Spanish, Portuguese, and French immigrants have made up the majority.

Andorra has been a parliamentary coprincipality since 1993. Two coprinces, the Catholic bishop of Urgell, Spain, and the president of the French Republic, collectively fulfill the function of head of state, although

Aragon and count of Barcelona. The Paréages partitioned control over of Andorra between the bishop of Urgell and the count of Foix (the rights of latter were subsequently inherited by the president of the French Republic).

Until the middle of the nineteenth century, the clergy strictly supervised the population and managed to impose an almost unanimous church attendance. The Catholic Church in Andorra exerted strong control over shaping the moral values of families and communities. Despite the fact that Andorrans married late and their marriages were arranged by families, the number of illegitimate births and pregnancies was low. During this period religious life in Andorra was not intellectual and consisted mainly of communal religious practices and rituals marking important stages of life.

During the nineteenth and twentieth centuries Andorra suffered the repercussions of political events in France and Spain, weakening the position of the Catholic Church in the principality. The abolition of the tithe given to the church and the progressive establishment of universal suffrage led to confrontations between conservatives, partisans of the bishop, and progressives. France, followed by the Spanish state and the Andorran government, thwarted the influence of the episcopal co-prince by proposing nondenominational education.

Until 1993 all of Andorra was nominally Catholic according to the parish registers that serve as a record of births, marriages, and deaths. At the start of the twenty-first century, only half of the Andorran population could be considered Catholic according to baptismal and marriage records.

EARLY AND MODERN LEADERS Saint Just, the first known bishop of Urgell (died 531), has been venerated as a martyr since the eleventh century. He is honored in the chapel of the Cathedral of La Seu d'Urgell.

Joan Marti i Alanis, the bishop of Urgell from 1977 to 2003, played an important role in the democratic evolution of Andorran political institutions and in the change of church attitude toward greater tolerance.

MAJOR THEOLOGIANS AND AUTHORS In 1748 lawyer Antoni Fiter i Rossell drafted rules and statutes that were published in *Le Manual Digest de les Valls d'Andorra.* Twenty years later Rev. Antoni Puig revised Rossell's work in *Le Politar Andorra,* published in 1768. These two

books formed the basis of ancient Andorran political institutions, including the status of the Catholic Church. According to the *Manual Digest,* "The crown of the Andorran Valley is the Roman Catholic religion."

HOUSES OF WORSHIP AND HOLY PLACES Each of the original six parishes of Andorra has a parish church in its principal town. A seventh parish, Escaldes-Engordany, was established in 1978. All parishes have secondary chapels to serve each village. The Marian sanctuary of Meritxell in the Canillo parish attracts pilgrims from all over the country and constitutes Andorra's major spiritual center. In 1972 Nostra Senyora de Meritxell burned down. A new sanctuary was designed by the Catalan architect R. Bofill, and it was inaugurated in 1976. Nostra Senyora de Meritxell has come to represent the country's recent prosperity and its entry into the modern world.

WHAT IS SACRED? Andorrans show strong devotion to the Virgin Mary, especially as represented by Nostra Senyora de Meritxell, patron saint of Andorra since 1823. Andorrans attribute the absence of invasion and heresy since the Paréages (1278) to her, and there are numerous popular hymns sung in her honor. According to legend, a shepherd discovered the famous Romanesque statue of Nostra Senyora de Meritxell at the foot of wild rose bush, miraculously in bloom in the middle of winter. The statue, solemnly crowned in 1921, was the object of pilgrimages until it disappeared with its precious crown during the fire in 1972. A copy of the statue occupies a place of honor in the new sanctuary and receives daily homage with flowers and candles.

HOLIDAYS AND FESTIVALS The Andorran national holiday, on 8 September, celebrates the birth of the Virgin Mary. On this day Andorrans make pilgrimages to the sanctuary at Meritxell, where they hold evening vigils, participate in torch-lit processions, and gather for a solemn mass in the morning.

Throughout Andorra young people who are not married organize local festivities. In Ordino each spring residents choose a girl who is beautiful and modest to honor the Virgin Mary, but the religious significance of this feast has diminished.

MODE OF DRESS Catholics in Andorra do not dress any differently from non-Catholics, even for religious holidays. Andorrans typically wear European style clothing. During village festivals that honor the patron saint of the parish, some Andorrans wear traditional Catalan clothing.

DIETARY PRACTICES In 1803 Bishop Antoni Dueño y Cisneros obtained for Andorrans the right to eat meat on Fridays, except those Fridays from Ash Wednesday to Easter, when the faithful would have a meatless meal at noon and a snack in the evening. Families who would like the privilege of eating meat on Fridays would purchase from their parish priest a papal bull that would exempt them from abstaining from meat. In contemporary times meatless meals are not obligatory except on Lenten Fridays and Ash Wednesday. Many families still eat fish on Fridays, more for nutritional than for religious reasons.

RITUALS Sunday Mass in Andorra is similar to that in other Catholic countries, although participation is relatively weak, especially in urban parishes. Each parish organizes an annual festival for a local patron saint. Religious holidays are important occasions for ritual observance in Andorra, and most Andorrans participate in *aplechs*, joyous gatherings with meals and popular dances.

RITES OF PASSAGE The sacraments of the Catholic Church, including baptism, first Communion, confirmation, reconciliation, marriage, ordination of priests, and anointing of the sick, make up the rites of passage in Andorra. Couples usually live together before having a church wedding.

MEMBERSHIP Without government support, Catholicism in Andorra has retreated into a defensive position, losing much of its missionary zeal. Among the various educational systems in the principality, only the Catholic schools (21 percent of the students) and the Spanish schools (18 percent) offer full religious instruction; Andorran public schools (22 percent) offer such instruction only in elementary school, while the French coprince schools (39 percent) offer none. The parishes provide catechism only for children in the primary grades.

SOCIAL JUSTICE There are two Catholic educational institutions that offer social services. AINA in Canillo organizes summer camps and weekend events for young volunteers who deliver Christian-inspired service to oth-

ers. The Andorran division of Caritas has developed charitable activities in Andorra and in developing countries.

SOCIAL ASPECTS The Catholic Church has had to accept that the principality has created civil marriage and instituted divorce. Catholic morality and Andorran legislation forbid abortion and euthanasia.

POLITICAL IMPACT Although reduced, the political influence of the bishop of Urgell is exercised in the principality through multiple channels, and Catholic priests are paid by the civil authorities. Andorrans have not allowed new religious communities to settle in their country, with the exception of small charitable congregations. On the other hand, Opus Dei, the conservative political and religious Catholic organization founded in Spain in 1928, is well established.

The Catholic religion is a component of the Andorran identity. The national hymn proclaims the Nostra Senyora de Meritxell mother of the country and glorifies the Catholic faith, loyalty to the coprinces, and political neutrality.

CONTROVERSIAL ISSUES There is little conflict between the government of Andorra and the Catholic Church, but unresolved issues remain. One is the possible introduction of religious instruction to secondary school students in the Andorran school system. Another is the proposed secularization of the still extensive church property. The church argues that civil authorities cannot levy taxes on church property.

CULTURAL IMPACT Romanesque chapels and baroque altars are testimony to the artistic contribution of Catholicism within the culture of Andorra. With the exception of the new sanctuary in Meritxell, contemporary religious art is less inspiring.

Other Religions

Members of other religions in Andorra are found primarily among the expatriate populations, such as Anglicans and evangelicals among the British and Muslims among the North Africans. There are also small groups of Jehovah's Witnesses, as well as some members of the Unification Church.

Jean-François Galinier-Pallerola

See Also Vol. I: *Roman Catholicism*

Bibliography

"Andorra Romanica." In *Fundacio Enciclopedia Catalana.* Andorra-la-Vella: Govern d'Andorra, 1989.

Armengol Vila, Lidia. *Approach to the History of Andorra.* Andorra-la-Vella: Institut d'Estudis Andorrans, 1989.

Badia Batalia, Francesc. *Assaig sobre el barroc andorra.* Andorra-la-Vella: Ed Andorra, 1991.

Degage, Alain, and Antoni Duro. "Que sais-je?" In *L'Andorre.* Paris: P.U.F., 1998.

Fiter, Ricard, ed. *Les llegendes d'Andorra.* Andorra-la-Vella: Ed Andorra, 1966.

Galinier-Pallerola, Jean-François. *La religion populaire en Andorre.* Toulouse: Presses Universitaires du Mirail, 1990.

Morgan, Brian. *Andorra: The Country in Between.* Nottingham, England: Ray Palmer, 1964.

Palau i Marti, Montserrat. *Andorra: Historia, institucions, costums.* Andorra-la-Vella: Ed Andorra, 1987.

Taylor, Barry, comp. *Andorra.* Oxford: Clio Press, 1993.

Viader, Roland. *L'Andorre du IXème au XIVème siècle, montagne, féodalité, communautés.* Toulouse: Presses Universitaires du Mirail, 2003.

Angola

POPULATION 10,593,171

AFRICAN INDIGENOUS BELIEFS 47
percent

ROMAN CATHOLIC 38 percent

PROTESTANT 15 percent

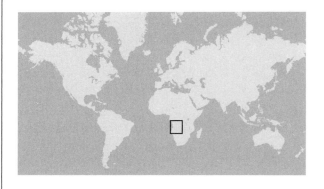

Country Overview

INTRODUCTION The Republic of Angola lies on the southwestern coast of Africa. It is bordered by Zaire on the north and east, Zambia on the southeast, Namibia on the south, and the Atlantic Ocean on the west. Also part of the country is Cabinda, a small enclave to the north along the Atlantic coast, which is separated from the rest of Angola by Zaire.

In precolonial times the region was inhabited by people with various political and religious traditions, some of which continue to be important. There was contact between the area and Portugal from the end of the fifteenth century, but formal Portuguese colonial rule was established only at the end of the nineteenth

century. At the same time missionaries of various denominations sought to convert the people to Christianity. Most denominations focused their activities in a particular ethnic-linguistic region.

Beginning in 1961 nationalist movements led a war for the liberation of Angola from Portuguese rule. The most important of these were the Movimento Popular de Libertação de Angola (MPLA; Popular Liberation Movement of Angola), which was Marxist in its outlook; the Frente Nacional de Libertação de Angola (FNLA; National Front for the Liberation of Angola); and the União Nacional para a Independência Total de Angola (UNITA; National Union for the Total Independence of Angola), which later gained support from the West. After a coup in Portugal in 1974, the anticolonial war ended, and on 11 November 1975 Angola was declared independent. A civil war then broke out, principally between MPLA, the government party, and the rebel UNITA. The war ended only in 2002.

The growth of Christianity in Angola during the twentieth century was spectacular. Elements of African traditions have been incorporated into church services, and traditional religious specialists, such as diviners and healers, often integrate Christian elements into their practices. For many Angolans there has come to be little contradiction between a Christian faith and various aspects of African indigenous religions. In addition, the number of Christian denominations has grown rapidly, especially within the Pentecostal sphere. Today there are more than 400 Christian denominations in Angola.

The role of Christian churches in Angolan society has been extremely important. During the colonial period churches provided many of the basic educational and health services, and since independence their functions have increased. In many respects the state does not function, and churches often assume responsibilities far beyond the religious. In the wake of extreme poverty and hunger, for example, many Angolans depend on churches for survival. Churches have also played a crucial role in the Angolan peace process, and they represent the most important pressure group in the Angolan political landscape. Most political leaders are products of Western Christian missions, which affects their outlook on the world.

RELIGIOUS TOLERANCE During the colonial period the Portuguese, who were Roman Catholic, saw the influence of the Protestant churches as a threat. The Catholic Church was regarded with less suspicion. After independence the government frequently came in conflict with religious leaders. The constitution provided for freedom of religion, and there existed freedom of worship. Yet the MPLA government also declared Angola to be a secular state and decreed that educational services could no longer be organized by churches. Since the move toward a more liberal political system at the end of the 1990s, relations between the government and the established churches have eased considerably, although incidents that trouble the relationship have continued to occur. Churches must be registered with the government.

Among Christians in Angola there are a number of ecumenical movements, including Comité Intereclesial para a Paz em Angola (COIEPA; Interdenominational Committee for Peace in Angola), Concelho de Igrejas Cristãs em Angola (CICA; Council of Christian Churches in Angola), and Aliança Evangélica de Angola (AEA; Evangelical Alliance of Angola). On 2 June 1991 the ecumenical movements, along with many churches, organized a massive prayer for peace that was held in Luanda's football (soccer) stadium.

Major Religions

AFRICAN INDIGENOUS BELIEFS

ROMAN CATHOLICISM

AFRICAN INDIGENOUS BELIEFS

DATE OF ORIGIN No specific date
NUMBER OF FOLLOWERS 5 million

A healer leads a church service at an Angolan asylum. Traditional healers are sought after to address the problems that are believed to be caused by witches and evil spirits. © BACI/CORBIS.

HISTORY Angola's indigenous religious traditions have changed throughout the centuries. The rapid spread of Christianity beginning at the end of the nineteenth century has led to the disappearance of many traditional beliefs. Thus, belief in a variety of spiritual entities, such as mermaids and water spirits, is on the decline. Furthermore, many rituals involving reverence for ancestors have disappeared, and certain religious institutions, such as secret societies that in the past often functioned as police forces, no longer exist. Yet other concepts and practices, such as witchcraft and magic, are becoming more important. These are sometimes reinterpreted within a Christian context, but traditional healers are also much sought after to address the problems that witches and evil spirits are believed to cause and to assist in obtaining protective magic. Some of the indigenous religions recognize a Supreme Being, held to be the creator of the universe, who has control of spirits and ancestors.

The proportion of Angola's population that follows indigenous beliefs is often estimated to be 47 percent. The number of people who, if asked, would state that their only religious adherence is "African religion" is probably much lower, however.

EARLY AND MODERN LEADERS Over the course of Angola's history, religious specialists, such as healers and diviners, have often been of paramount importance. In general, they derive their power from ancestral spirits. The role of the *kimbanda* (healer) has not diminished, and in rural as well as urban areas people of all backgrounds visit *kimbanda*s for analysis of their problems. Many healers have integrated modern techniques and new elements into their practices. Some healers have a profound knowledge of herbs, and in many cases their treatments have important therapeutic consequences. Their role in healing war traumas, for example, has hitherto hardly been recognized. Religious powers often were traditionally attributed to political leaders, and this remains the case today.

MAJOR THEOLOGIANS AND AUTHORS The indigenous religions of Angola do not have a formal written theological tradition.

HOUSES OF WORSHIP AND HOLY PLACES One characteristic of most African religions, including those of Angola, is that places of worship and sacred places may shift. Thus, the Kongo *minkisi* (empowered statuettes) can be regarded as portable shrines. Places in nature that impress people through their particularity, such as a formation of rocks or a waterfall, may come to have a special ritual meaning. Mbanza Kongo, the old capital of the Kongo kingdom, has had enormous religious significance throughout its history, and it is held by many people to be a holy place.

WHAT IS SACRED? As such, plants and animals are not regarded as holy in Angola. Yet it is believed that the forces of nature may be used by spirits, witches, and powerful people to further their plans, be they for evil or for good. Examples include the idea that a witch can change into a crocodile, that seeing an owl may be a bad omen, and that a leopard is associated with political power. Some species of trees play a role in religious ceremonies, and some plants are of special religious importance because they are used in herbal potions. Water may be blessed by religious specialists so as to be used for protective magic.

HOLIDAYS AND FESTIVALS Holidays and festivals among Angolan traditional religions did not follow a fixed calendar but rather were celebrated each year during the same season. There were a number of harvest festivals. Initiation schools usually concluded with a performance by masked dancers in a festival that often attracted people from other villages. During colonial times many festivals became less frequent, and with civil war in the late twentieth century most disappeared altogether.

MODE OF DRESS Religious specialists in Angola may dress in special clothes, wearing attire made from animal skin, wood, and other materials that are associated with tradition rather than modernity. In the past masked dancers wore elaborate costumes, novices wore a special outfit during initiation ceremonies, and political leaders wore leopard skins to mark their religious and political powers. Except for initiation ceremonies, these practices are no longer followed.

DIETARY PRACTICES In many Angolan traditional religions there were food taboos. For example, women might not be allowed to eat certain species of fish, novices could not eat salt during their initiation school, and healers were prohibited from eating roasted meat. In most communities such rules are no longer observed. Rules that accompany magical potions often do include food taboos, however.

RITUALS Two factors have brought about the decline of traditional rituals in Angola. Under the influence of Christian churches, a number of practices from the African indigenous tradition have disappeared. In addition, because of civil war many religious practices and religio-cultural institutions have been discontinued. On the other hand, the violence and the suffering of the people during the late twentieth century increased the need for means to deal with social problems. Especially in the war zones, people attempted to find new ways to address their critical situation. Thus, malign spirits were exorcized in newly established churches, children wore amulets to prevent them from being forced into the army, and soldiers tried to follow rules thought to make a magic potion work against bullets. Many of these procedures were connected with the strict observance of rules and rituals.

RITES OF PASSAGE In many Angolan cultures initiation from childhood into adulthood traditionally received special ritual attention. Boys and girls often lived for a considerable time in seclusion, during which circumcision was performed on boys and, in some societies, labial enlargement on girls. The novices learned various dances and were taught about their culture in moral, religious, and historical terms. In some Angolan communities these rites of passage are still observed, although in abbreviated form, and circumcision is sometimes done in a hospital. Initiation into further age-grade groups, which formerly moved people into the ranks of the elderly, have probably now become entirely obsolete.

Other steps in life, such as marriage and the birth of a child, were also regarded in many communities as crucial transformative moments in the life of a person. They were often marked by elaborate rites, sometimes with clear religious references. Some of these elements, such as music and dancing, have been incorporated into Christian marriage ceremonies.

In many Angolan societies the funeral is an extremely important event, with mourning rituals often regarded as essential for the peace of the soul of the deceased. In the civil war there was often no opportunity to carry out the appropriate rituals for the dead. Although people sought alternative forms of mourning, war victims were sometimes left unburied. Apart from the personal trauma this caused, many people feared that restless spirits would further disrupt social life. Even if rituals for ancestral spirits are no longer practiced, on the whole people are respectful concerning ancestors.

MEMBERSHIP Children learn their religion mainly at home, from observation, admonition, participation in religious activities, and initiation ceremonies. Some traditional healers use placards to attract customers, although their fame is usually spread by word of mouth. Healers sometimes house apprentices, who are "called" to become healers through dreams, disease, or other signs.

SOCIAL JUSTICE Angolan traditional religions include proper retribution and compensation for wrongs, sanctioned by established norms and trials. Accusations of witchcraft have traditionally been used as a means of social control. Although such accusations have wrecked many families, they also function as a popular means of protesting unbridled greed and the egotism of the political leadership. In this sense accusations of witchcraft are an attempt to arrive at a more equal society.

SOCIAL ASPECTS In traditional African religions marriage is seen as a necessary step in people's lives. In most Angolan communities marriage was not just an affair of two people but involved the entire families. Usually

both the girl and the boy had some say in the matter, although the role of fathers and uncles especially was considerable in the choice of a spouse. Fertility in women was, and is, highly valued. If a woman remains childless, help may be sought from religious specialists. Because of the war, there are many female-headed households, and in Angola, unlike other African countries, polygamous marriages are hardly on the decline.

POLITICAL IMPACT Traditional healers and diviners were largely disregarded by the government of the newly independent Angola. Although the role of religious practitioners in the community often increased during the civil war, the MPLA government refused to recognize their function and at times hindered them in the execution of their profession. In areas under the control of UNITA, the function of healers and diviners seems to have been acknowledged to a far greater extent. There were widespread accusations, however, that UNITA abused the influence of healers and diviners so as to intimidate civilians under their control and that charges of witchcraft were used to eliminate political opponents.

CONTROVERSIAL ISSUES Indigenous African religions do not have an explicit theology, and so they do not take a formal, dogmatic stance on social issues. Religious specialists in Angola, however, sometimes express their personal opinions on such issues as abortion, divorce, feminism, homosexuality, and AIDS. These are often condemned as imports from the West and foreign to African traditions, although religious specialists assist people faced with problems. Today contraception is mostly an affair of the medical services, although the practice is not accepted by some. In the past female healers often had knowledge of herbs that would produce an abortion. Today abortion is legal only under restricted circumstances, as when the life of the woman is endangered. Some healers promise their clients that they are able to cure AIDS.

CULTURAL IMPACT African art objects, such as masks and statuettes, usually have a religious significance. Traditionally they were used during religious ceremonies. Masked dancers performed mostly in the festivals that closed initiation schools. The Kongo *minkisi* (statuettes) were often considered to contain spiritual power that could be used for good or evil. The well-known Kongo nail figures belong this group of statuettes. Music played an important role during many religious ceremonies, and dancing, drumming, and singing form an important legacy in many Angolan communities.

ROMAN CATHOLICISM

DATE OF ORIGIN 1491 C.E.; reestablished 1881
NUMBER OF FOLLOWERS 4 million

HISTORY Roman Catholicism was first introduced to what is now Angola at the end of the fifteenth century by Portuguese travelers. In 1518 a son of the Kongo king was ordained the first Angolan bishop. The Antonian movement, led by Dona Beatriz Kimpa Vita, started at the end of the seventeenth century. Proclaiming that Jesus and Mary had been black, it aimed at ending the civil war in the region and reestablishing the Kongo kingdom. Because it was seen as a threat by the Catholic clergy, Dona Beatriz was burned at the stake in 1706.

By the end of the nineteenth century only remnants of this early Christianity could be found, and beginning in the 1880s the Roman Catholic Church was established anew in Angola. French Spiritans (Congregation of the Holy Ghost) were especially important in this process. Benedictines, Capuchins, Redemptorists, and others later joined in the Catholic missionary activities. When Portugal became a republic in 1910, a number of laws were introduced that restricted the power of the Catholic Church. Because the role of the church in colonial society, as well as in Portugal, was so important, however, anticlerical legislation never became extreme. Under the regime of António Salazar, from 1932 to 1968, Catholicism developed into a near state religion. Especially among the lower clergy, there were many critics of Portuguese colonial rule, but the church leadership did not take a stance against colonialism.

After the independence of Angola in 1975, the Catholic Church continued to grow despite the government's anticlerical outlook. The visit of Pope John Paul II in 1992 was a major event. There has been a increase in the importance of the Legion of Mary, a lay organization that emphasizes discipline and rigor. Although there are no firm figures on the number of Roman Catholics in Angola, estimates range from 38 to 68 percent of the population. Thus, there may be as few as 4 million or as many as 7.2 million Angolan Catholics.

EARLY AND MODERN LEADERS Angolan nationalism was generally associated with Protestantism rather than Roman Catholicism. Still, such important Catholic leaders as Bishop Manuel Das Neves and Father Joaquim Pinto de Andrade became widely known when they were arrested at the beginning of the 1960s on suspicion of leading nationalist activities against the colonial state. In 1983, after independence, Alexandre de Nascimento was ordained the first Angolan cardinal. Dom Zacarias Kamuenho, archbishop of Lubango since 1997 and president of COIEPA, won the Andrey Sakharov Prize for Peace in 2001 for his role in the Angolan peace process.

MAJOR THEOLOGIANS AND AUTHORS There have not been any notable Roman Catholic theologians or authors from Angola. Many Angolans, Roman Catholics included, hardly have access to books apart from the Bible and hymnbooks.

HOUSES OF WORSHIP AND HOLY PLACES As in other countries, the Roman Catholic Church in Angola is organized in dioceses and parishes. Catholic churches can be found in many areas of the country, although in the former war zones all infrastructure, including churches, has been destroyed. Luanda, the nation's capital, is the seat of the archbishop. The remnants of the cathedral in Mbanza Kongo (Nkulumbimbi), built in the sixeenth century, are of special historical importance. There are no specifically holy places in Angola.

WHAT IS SACRED? Roman Catholics in Angola observe the sacraments and honor the saints and the Virgin Mary, but there are no specifically Angolan saints. As with Catholics throughout the world, the cross is sacred and plays an important role in many ceremonies, being kissed, for example, at Easter. Cemeteries are sacred, but there are no particular plants, animals, or relics that are held to be sacred.

HOLIDAYS AND FESTIVALS Angolan Roman Catholics observe the important holidays of the church year. There are two holidays that are of especial importance. One is All Soul's Day, on 2 November, on which Catholics remember the dead and in Angola perhaps related to African practices of ancestor worship. The other is Fátima's Day (13 May), honoring the appearance of the Virgin Mary to children in the Portuguese village in 1917.

Although largely a secular festival, the Luandan carnival has long been a focal point of religious and political struggles. Formerly the carnival was a pre-Lenten festival. After independence the government changed the date to 27 March, the day on which South Africans withdrew from Angola in 1976. The move was seen as a strategy to create a ceremonial environment separate from the church.

MODE OF DRESS There are no specific dress codes for Roman Catholics in Angola. The standards are decency and cleanliness, and Catholics are asked to wear their best on Sundays and holy days. Clergy wear robes, usually white, with bright red belts and caps.

DIETARY PRACTICES The Roman Catholic Church in Angola does not require its members to observe any dietary restrictions not practiced by Roman Catholics in other countries. Some Catholics fast on Fridays during Lent, especially on Good Friday, but because many of the poorer families often face periods of hunger, the church does not require its members to observe this. Special days of fasting and prayer have occasionally been organized to further the peace process.

RITUALS Roman Catholics in Angola observe all major Roman Catholic rituals, including baptism and the Eucharist.

RITES OF PASSAGE In Angola most Roman Catholic children, and sometimes adults, are baptized with water, a ceremony that tends to take place during the Easter period. At a later stage they may become active members through the ceremony of confirmation. Marriage is a festive occasion in the church. The church also plays an important role in funerals. The funerary rites, called *óbito*, sometimes take place over several days, and many church members may participate in the mourning.

MEMBERSHIP The Roman Catholic Church has continued to grow in Angola. In former war areas this can be explained by missionary activities. In areas where the church has already become established, people know it as an important channel for experiencing their religious convictions and for establishing a social network. In addition, apart from worship services Catholic churches organize various activities, including choirs, football (soccer) matches, Bible classes, and educational projects. The Catholic Church uses a number of methods to spread its message, including videos and music cassettes, and there are a bookshop and a Catholic radio station.

SOCIAL JUSTICE The Roman Catholic Church in Angola plays a role in many spheres of life. The Angolan branch of Caritas has been prominent among the many nongovernmental organizations active in the country. It has distributed enormous amounts of medicine, clothes, blankets, and other supplies, mainly to displaced citizens. Apart from general relief programs Caritas also has developed programs for preventing and treating diseases, such as sleeping sickness, and for aiding specific groups, such as victims of land mines, orphans, and displaced persons. In addition, Caritas has had a large role in the area of education.

Backed by the international Catholic community, the church leadership in Angola has frequently spoken out against human rights abuses, especially criticizing violations of the country's laws on religious freedom. The Conference of Bishops and the Movimento pro Pace (Movement for Peace) have been important in the peace process.

SOCIAL ASPECTS Because of the war in Angola, the number of orphans and widows is disproportionately high. Members of some families have been forced to live separately from one another for long periods of time. People often live temporarily with relatives. Although the Roman Catholic Church does not sanction divorce, divorce rates are considerable, and many households are headed by women.

POLITICAL IMPACT At the time of independence in Angola, the Roman Catholic Church was seen as having supported the Portuguese colonial government. Thus, the measures of the MPLA government after independence to curb the power of the Christian churches were enforced with more vigor in the case of Catholics than of Protestants. Catholics have at times strongly criticized the MPLA government. This has come not only from church members and the lower clergy but also from the Catholic leadership in Angola, which in public letters and statements has been relatively open in its criticism of the government. In the 1990s relations between the Catholic Church and the government eased, however.

In areas held by UNITA, the Catholic Church had initially been discriminated against. Beginning in the second half of the 1980s, however, Catholic priests were allowed to work among the people in those regions.

CONTROVERSIAL ISSUES While on the whole the Roman Catholic Church has not been known for its liberal point of view concerning AIDS, on a local level the church in Angola has developed initiatives to prevent the disease and to assist people with HIV. In general, homosexuality is frowned upon, but the stance depends largely on the individual church leader.

Women often play a large role in the Catholic Church community. Many church choirs are led by women, and women may read from the Bible during the service or lead a prayer. As elsewhere, however, the Angolan church does not allow women to enter the clergy.

CULTURAL IMPACT Civil war and the political climate in Angola have not been conducive to the development of a strong religious artistic tradition among Roman Catholics. Angolan churches, however, have an outstanding reputation for their choirs. The Universidade Católica, based in Luanda, was established in 1997.

The Catholic radio station, Rádio Ecclésia, broadcast during colonial times, but at independence it was closed down by the government. It was reestablished in 1997. Although the Angolan government did not dare close down the station again, its staff was subject to frequent harassment and threats. In 2001 Rádio Ecclésia was briefly closed after the state-owned journal *Jornal de Angola* accused the station of supporting UNITA.

Other Religions

It was estimated in 1998 that 15 percent of the population of Angola was Protestant. The figure was probably much higher, however. In addition, there has been rapid growth among Protestant denominations, particularly Pentecostals. Further, Protestants have played a far more significant role in Angola's history than their relatively small numbers would suggest.

Older Protestant denominations in Angola include the Baptist Missionary Society (first active in 1878), American Board of Commissioners for Foreign Missions (1881), Methodist Episcopal Church (1885), Congregational Foreign Missionary Society (1886), Christian Mission in Many Lands (1889; also known as Plymouth Brethren), Philafrican Mission (1901), and Seventh-day Adventists (1925). There also are two important African Independent Churches (AICs): Kimbanguism (1921; later Igreja de Jesus Cristo Sobre a Terra, or IJCST), originally led by Simon Kimbangu in what was then the Belgian Congo (now Zaire); and Tokoism (1949; later Igreja do Nosso Senhor Jesus

Cristo no Mundo), led by the Angolan Simão Toko. Of the Pentecostal movements Igreja Universal do Reino de Deus, Igreja Evangélica Pentecostal em Angola, and Assembleia de Deus Pentecostal de Angola each claims more than a million members, although these numbers are exaggerated. The Pentecostal groups Igreja Mana and Igreja Nova Apostólica have around 250,000 and 100,000 members, respectively.

The Protestant missionaries who went to Angola at the end of the nineteenth century came mostly from the United Kingdom and the United States. Because they saw spreading the gospel in the local languages as their prime task, they made remarkable efforts at Bible translations, linguistic studies, and education in the vernacular. Bishop William Taylor (Methodist), Héli Chatelain (Philafrican), Lawrence W. Henderson, and other early-twentieth-century missionaries published material in the areas of linguistics, ethnography, and Angolan history. Because of the focus on the vernacular, most of the missionary societies restricted their activities to one language group. The Portuguese decree of 1921 that stipulated all education and religious services be given in Portuguese hit the Protestant missions particularly hard.

The partition of Angola by missionaries into spheres of influence later had consequences for Angolan nationalism. Thus, the leadership of the FNLA consisted mainly of a northern Baptist network. Methodists, along with Catholics, from the central region became the core of MPLA. Congregationalists were important among the southern elite, prominent in the leadership of UNITA. During the war for independence, Protestant churches were singled out for repression and persecution, and some of the churches saw their infrastructure completely destroyed. After independence many of the older missionary denominations changed their names, signifying a greater independence of the Western mother churches. Their leadership also came to consist predominantly of Angolans. As with the Catholic Church, many leaders of Protestant churches have been crucial in bringing peace and democratization to Angola. A Methodist bishop, Emílio de Carvalho, who was ordained in 1972, gained national and international renown for his work in the peace process, as well as in the church-led Africa University of Zimbabwe.

During the colonial period Protestant missions were often built in the rural areas of Angola, while the Roman Catholic Church tended to focus on towns. After independence many areas became uninhabitable because of the civil war. With the restoration of peace in Angola, many Protestant denominations have aspired to set up stations in rural areas that were formerly too dangerous to travel into. In the poorer parts of Luanda, Protestant churches are often only temporary buildings, with few or no facilities.

Several of the Protestant denominations in Angola have dress codes and dietary rules for their members. For women the use of makeup and the wearing of jewelry, miniskirts, and trousers is sometimes restricted. In some churches members must cover their heads and take off their shoes before entering church. In most Protestant churches the use of alcohol and tobacco is discouraged or even forbidden. Kimbanguists are not allowed to eat pork, and their members are not allowed to sleep or wash naked. Many Protestant denominations explicitly condemn satanism, witchcraft, and the use of harmful magic.

In AICs, as well as in the Pentecostal movement in Angola, baptism is central to religious life. In some denominations, such as the Kimbanguist Church, this takes the form of baptism with the Holy Spirit (which involves speaking in tongues). Some of the stricter Protestant denominations strongly condemn traditional religious practices. Rituals of healing and exorcism may be performed in other churches, however, and especially in Pentecostal churches confession takes a central position. On the whole church services are more expressive in Angola than, for example, in Europe, and elements of African culture, such as dancing and drumming, may be incorporated.

As with the Roman Catholic Church, the role of Protestant churches in Angola reaches far beyond the purely religious sphere. Many Protestant churches organize basic education programs, adult literacy classes, various other courses, and leisure activities. Not only is the Bible often the only book available to Angolans, but its importance is reinforced by the traditional stress that Protestant missionaries laid on independent Bible reading. Protestant organizations distribute goods to citizens in need of food, clothing, and other basic commodities and also sometimes provide shelter. Much of the basic health care in Angola depends on churches rather than on state services. The churches often play an important role in social projects—for example, in giving assistance to street children and displaced people and in supplying such items as sewing machines and bicycles to collectives that operate in poor areas.

Protestant churches have opened several schools for higher education in Angola. One of the best known is the school in Dondi, founded in 1957 by the United Church of Canada and the United Church of Christ. As is the case with Catholicism, art with a strong religious expression did not find a fertile climate in the context of war and the secular, socialist policies of independent Angola. Some Protestant choirs, especially the Baptist Coro Central Evangélico de Luanda, are internationally renowned, however.

Inge Brinkman

See Also Vol. I: *African Indigenous Beliefs, Protestantism, Roman Catholicism*

Bibliography

Birmingham, David. *Frontline Nationalism in Angola and Mozambique.* London: James Currey, 1993.

Grenfell, F. James. *História da Igreja Baptista em Angola, 1879–1975.* Queluz, Portugal: Baptist Missionary Society, 1998.

Henderson, Lawrence W. *The Church in Angola: A River of Many Currents.* Cleveland: Pilgrim Press, 1992.

Morier-Genoud, Éric. "Religion in Angola." 1 June 2004. www2.unil.ch/lefaitmissionnaire/old_pages/angola.html.

Péclard, Didier. "Religion and Politics in Angola: The Church, the Colonial State and the Emergence of Angolan Nationalism, 1940–1961." *Journal of Religion in Africa* 28, no. 2 (1998): 162–86.

Santos, Eduardo dos. *Religiões em Angola.* Lisbon: Junta de Investigações do Ultramar, 1969.

Schubert, B. *Der Krieg und die Kirchen: Macht, Ohnmacht und Hoffnung in Angola, 1961–1991.* Lucerne: Edition Exodus, 1997.

Thornton, John. "Mbanza Kongo/São Salvador: Kongo's Holy City." In *Africa's Urban Past.* Edited by David Anderson and Richard Rathbone. Oxford: James Currey, 2000.

Viegas, Fátima. *Angola e as religiões.* Luanda: Edição Patrocinada, 1999.

Antigua and Barbuda

POPULATION 71,500

ANGLICAN 45 percent

MORAVIAN 12 percent

METHODIST 9.1 percent

SEVENTH-DAY ADVENTIST 8.8 percent

ROMAN CATHOLIC 8 percent

JEHOVAH'S WITNESSES 1.45 percent

RASTAFARIAN 0.8 percent

OTHER 14.85 percent

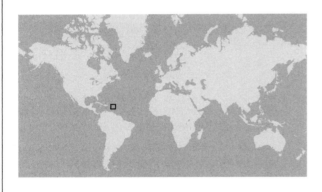

Country Overview

INTRODUCTION Antigua and Barbuda is an island nation in the northern Caribbean Sea with a total land area of just 171 square miles (442 square kilometers). It is made up of two inhabited islands, Antigua and Barbuda, as well as a small, uninhabited rock island named Redonda (with an area of 0.5 square miles). Part of the chain of Leeward Islands in the West Indies, Antigua and Barbuda lies 250 miles east of Puerto Rico. The islands Antigua (the largest of the Leeward Islands) and Barbuda (primarily a nature preserve) are now important tourist destinations.

Religion is a powerful force in the Caribbean, and the tension in Antigua and Barbuda between its two main religious traditions, Christianity and West African beliefs (especially Dahomean and Yoruba), has formed the basis for the country's major social and economic divisions. As on other islands of the Caribbean, these differences have been resolved in part by a *syncretism* (combining) between the beliefs of the European Protestant elite (especially Anglican and the Moravian churches, which have widespread influence) and those of the African peasantry and urban workers.

Christopher Columbus was the first European to arrive on Antigua in 1493. He named it after Santa Maria de la Antigua, a cathedral in Seville, Spain. Slaves were freed in 1834. Although Antigua and Barbuda attained independence as a parliamentary democracy on 1 November 1981, the head of state is still Queen Elizabeth II.

RELIGIOUS TOLERANCE Antigua and Barbuda is seen as tolerant of religious differences, and its constitution guarantees freedom of religion. Although most Antiguans describe themselves as "Protestant," nearly half specify that they are Anglican, the result of a major wave of Anglican proselytizing between 1919 and 1940. Some of this Anglican membership is nominal, as many Antiguans are syncretists who combine Anglicanism (and the other Protestant denominations) with West

African beliefs. Also common in Antigua and Barbuda is Obeah, the institutionalized magic of the West Indies. Although Obeah is illegal, authorities normally ignore its practice.

Major Religion

ANGLICANISM

DATE OF ORIGIN 1632 C.E.
NUMBER OF FOLLOWERS 32,175

HISTORY The Anglican Church arrived in Antigua with the first English colonists in 1632, when Sir Thomas Warner led a group of free English and indentured servants from Saint Christopher (Saint Kitt's). After successfully defending themselves against raids from Caribs and the French, the settlers quickly established parishes and vestries (church councils). Barbuda was colonized by settlers from Antigua in 1661.

African slaves were first brought to Antigua in 1671 to work on the sugar plantations. Free Antiguans could be married by Anglican priests, but mixed-race consensual unions could not be formalized. It was illegal for ministers to perform marriages for the slave population until a uniform marriage code was adopted with the abolition of slavery in 1834. Most of the present population is descended from African slaves.

In 1962 the church authority in the British Virgin Islands was transferred from the bishop of Antigua to the Episcopal Church in the United States. In 1969 Curacao (in the Netherlands Antilles) was transferred from the diocese of Antigua to that of Venezuela. In 1979 the celebration of the Eucharist was revised, and an agreement was reached that would approve the ordination of women.

EARLY AND MODERN LEADERS The diocese of Barbados, of which Antigua was a part, was formed in 1824 with William Coleridge as bishop. The diocese of Antigua and Guyana was established in 1842. The province of the West Indies was not created until 1883; its first archbishop was named in 1895. The two archbishops who have come from Antigua are Edward Hutson in the 1920s and O.U. Lindsay in the 1990s. The current archbishop, Rev. Drexel Wellington Gomez, Lord Archbishop of the West Indies in Nassau, Bahamas, assumed control of the nation's church in 1998.

The twin spires of the Cathedral Church of St. John the Divine rise above the city of St. John's in Antigua. © BRUCE ADAMS; EYE UBIQUITOUS/CORBIS.

MAJOR THEOLOGIANS AND AUTHORS The theological schools of the Caribbean are located on other islands, primarily Barbados, Jamaica, and the Bahamas. These schools tend to be ecumenical in nature. In 1913 the Rev. J. B. Ellis, formerly warden of Jamaica Church Theological College, wrote a book entitled *The Diocese of Jamaica,* which includes information on Anglicanism in Antigua.

HOUSES OF WORSHIP AND HOLY PLACES The Cathedral Church of St. John the Divine, located in the capital city of St. John's, is large and impressive, particularly its twin spires. Two previous churches were located on the same site. The first was a wooden structure built in 1681, but it was replaced by a brick structure in 1720. The current stone cathedral was consecrated in 1848. Other churches include St. Paul's (Falmouth), St. Phillip's (Newfield), St. Peter's (Parham), and St. George's (Fitches Creek).

WHAT IS SACRED? Anglicans in Antigua and Barbuda view the sacred in the same manner as Anglicans in other parts of the world.

HOLIDAYS AND FESTIVALS In Antigua and Barbuda the standard Christian holidays of Christmas, Ash

Wednesday, Good Friday, Easter, Pentecost, and All Souls are observed by Anglicans. There is nothing distinctive about how these holidays are celebrated.

MODE OF DRESS Anglicanism in Antigua and Barbuda does not require a particular mode of dress for the laity. Nuns are now rare in the Anglican church, and those who remain no longer wear a habit. Priests tend to wear cooler, more relaxed clothing compared with their counterparts in colder climates.

DIETARY PRACTICES Anglicanism prescribes no special dietary practices in Antigua and Barbuda.

RITUALS There is nothing particularly distinctive about the way Antiguans observe Anglican rituals, such as Matins, Holy Eucharist, and Vespers (called Evensong or Evening Prayer after the tradition of the modern American Episcopal church). This has been especially true since the 1960s, when the Antiguan church came under the authority of the Episcopal Church in the United States.

RITES OF PASSAGE Anglicans in Antigua and Barbuda recognize the same rites of passage, such as First Communion and confirmation, as do Anglicans elsewhere the world.

MEMBERSHIP Although in the spirit of ecumenism Anglican membership is open to all, it is obtained through baptism and confirmation. Some Anglicans counted on the census are sycretists, combining both Christian and traditional West African beliefs and practices.

SOCIAL JUSTICE In the late eighteenth century Beilby Porteus, the bishop of London, formed the Incorporated Society for the Conversion, Religious Instruction and Education of the Negroes as a means of bringing Christianity to slaves. In 1799 the Society for the Propagation of the Gospel sent a catechist to Antigua. The first bishops in the Caribbean, Christopher Lipscombe and William Coleridge, attempted to counter the discriminatory practices they found among ministers serving the black population.

The Anglican Church has established several universities throughout the province of the West Indies. Not the least of these was Codrington College, which, although on Barbados, has a strong Antiguan connec-

tion, as it was founded by Christopher Codrington of Antigua. Its ecumenical training also draws Methodist, Moravian, and African Methodist Episcopal students.

SOCIAL ASPECTS Marriage is encouraged by the church. As elsewhere in the Caribbean, some women, including Anglicans, are thought to pursue economic security by having children with more than one man.

POLITICAL IMPACT In England during the mid-seventeenth century, the Puritan rule of Oliver Cromwell caused many Anglicans to go to the Caribbean by choice or as exiles. The restoration of the English monarchy in 1660 returned England to Anglicanism, which subsequently became the religion of English territories, including Antigua, and also their governing hierarchy.

CONTROVERSIAL ISSUES Positions in the community traditionally held by the clergy are being assumed today by psychiatric, social, and welfare workers, undermining the authority of the clergy. To counteract this trend, modern theological training in the Caribbean is attempting to balance spiritual and pastoral concerns.

CULTURAL IMPACT Although much popular culture today is influenced by Rastafarianism, Anglicanism remains a cultural force in the country. The double spires on St. John's Cathedral, for example, are considered a local architectural accomplishment. The Cathedral Cultural Centre (at St. John's Cathedral) has held important cultural events, including the debut of *The Sweetest Mango* (2001), the first full-length feature film produced in Antigua and Barbuda.

Other Religions

The Moravian Church, also known as the United Brethren, arrived in the Caribbean in 1731 when Anthony Ullrich, a slave from the Danish West Indies, traveled to Denmark and Germany to recruit missionaries for the black population of the Caribbean. By 1756 the missionaries had arrived on Antigua, but unlike what occurred in other parts of the Caribbean, they did not become planters. This led to better relations between the missionaries and the slaves, whose membership in the Moravian Church had reached 11,000 by 1799.

Members of the Moravian Church are expected to keep a journal of their spiritual development, which is to be completed and read by a minister at their funeral. Communion is restricted to the faithful. There are 11 Moravian churches on Antigua, and most appear to be larger and more impressive than those of the other denominations.

Methodism came to Antigua in 1760 when Nathaniel Gilbert and two of his slaves returned from hearing John Wesley speak in England. By 1774 Methodists in Antigua, who were primarily black, became affiliated with the antislavery movement. The Methodist Church in the Caribbean and the Americas, with its headquarters in Antigua, became independent in 1967.

The Seventh-day Adventists in Antigua and Barbuda are part of the North Caribbean Conference of Seventh-day Adventists, Inc. They number nearly 5,500, or more than 8 percent of the population. They maintain eight churches, a home, a manse, and the Antigua Seventh-day Adventist School in St. Johns. A prominent local member of the religion is Governor General Sir James Carlisle, appointed by Queen Elizabeth.

The Catholic diocese of St. John's-Basseterre, Parish of Antigua, has seven churches: Holy Family Cathedral, St. Anthony's, St. Martin de Porre's, Villa Chapel, Our Lady of Perpetual Help, Good Shepard, and Our Lady of Mt. Carmel. The church operates a primary school in St. John's.

The Jewish presence in Antigua and Barbuda is negligible. There may have been a small number of Sephardic Jews in the seventeenth and eighteenth centuries, notably the Gideon Abudiente family, which traveled back and forth between Antigua and the island of Nevis. In 1694 the Leeward Island Council and Assembly passed an act against Jew's trading in commodities and slaves. Although the law was repealed in 1701, most Jews left Antigua and Barbuda to join congregations in the British colonies of North America.

Islam has been in Antigua since 1955, when Ahmadiya missionaries arrived from Pakistan. Its presence remains small on the islands.

Michael J. Simonton

See Also Vol. 1: *Anglicanism/Episcopalianism, Christianity*

Bibliography

Antigua and Barbuda: 1834 to 1984—From Bondage to Freedom. St. John's, Antigua: National Emancipation Committee for Ministry of Economic Development, Tourism, and Energy, 1984.

Gaspar, Barry. *Bondmen and Rebels: A Study of Master-Slave Relations in Antigua.* Baltimore: Johns Hopkins University Press, 1985.

O'Marde, Dorbrene E., ed. *A Decade of Development, 1981–1991.* St. John's, Antigua: I. Archibald and Associates, 1991.

Argentina

POPULATION 37,812,817

ROMAN CATHOLIC 88.0 percent

PROTESTANT 7.0 percent

MUSLIM 2.0 percent

JEWISH 1.5 percent

OTHER OR NONAFFILIATED 1.5 percent

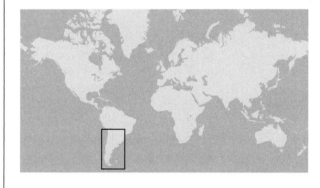

Country Overview

INTRODUCTION The Argentine Republic is, by area, the eighth largest country in the world. Extending almost 2,400 miles from north to south, with the Andes Mountains forming its western border, the country occupies most of South America's southern cone, an area of widely varying climate and geography. Argentina is bordered by Bolivia and Paraguay to the north; Brazil, Uruguay, and the Atlantic Ocean to the east; and Chile to the south and west.

Demographically Argentina is one of the most "European" of the Latin American nations, its population

made up mostly of people of Spanish, Italian, and German ancestry. At the time of European settlement, the indigenous population was relatively small, and it remains only a tiny fraction of the total population. Its ethnic composition has given Argentina a strong Catholic flavor. Eighty-eight percent of the population consider themselves to be Catholic, though active participation in Catholicism occurs at a much lower rate, with only about 25 percent of declared Catholics attending Mass regularly. Roman Catholicism remains the nation's official religion and receives substantial financial support from the government.

Since the return to democracy in 1983 and the corresponding relaxation in regulations inhibiting non-Catholic religious proselytizing, evangelical Protestants and other Christian groups—such as the Mormons—have established an increasingly significant presence in the country. Argentina's Jewish community is the largest in Latin America, though it accounts for only 1 to 2 percent of the nation's population. The public visibility of the Jewish community has led to numerous acts of anti-Semitism, including the 1994 bombing of a Jewish cultural center and frequent desecrations of grave sites. Argentina's Muslim population has increased tenfold since the 1970s, and Muslims now outnumber Jews as the largest non-Christian minority. Indigenous religious practice is almost nonexistent today, given the absence of any sizable native population.

RELIGIOUS TOLERANCE The strong links between the Catholic Church and the state, including two military regimes, created an environment hostile to the promotion of religious freedom and toleration throughout

A roadside shrine dedicated to María Antonia Delinda Correa. Pilgrims often leave containers of water at these shrines to commemorate the saint who died of thirst. © FRANK LANE PICTURE AGENCY/CORBIS.

much of the twentieth century. During the most recent dictatorship (1976–83), the government repeatedly harassed religious minorities and progressive Catholics. With the return to democracy in the mid-1980s, the situation of religious freedom improved noticeably. A constitutional requirement that the Argentine president be Catholic was abolished in 1994, indicating a growing legal toleration of religious minorities. In contemporary Argentina the government pursues a general policy of religious freedom. During the abbreviated presidency of Fernando de la Rua (1999–2001), an effort was made to provide non-Catholic religions with a legal status equivalent to that of the Catholic Church and to promote religious pluralism. These efforts were ended in 2002 as the government's attention turned to solving severe economic problems and ending political instability. Anti-Semitism remains a problem, and there have been reports of anti-Islamic activities since September 2001.

Major Religion

ROMAN CATHOLICISM

DATE OF ORIGIN 1539 C.E.

NUMBER OF FOLLOWERS 33.3 million

HISTORY Catholicism arrived in Argentina with Spanish colonizers in 1539. Unlike the Mesoamerican and Andean regions of Spanish colonial America, the Argentine territory was sparsely populated by indigenous tribes, most of which were nomadic. While some missionizing of the natives occurred (carried out largely by Jesuits), the Catholic clergy primarily served European settlers during the colonial era. After Argentina gained full independence from Spain in 1816, the church struggled to gain autonomy from the government, requesting an end to the *patronato*, wherein the nation's secular rulers were granted authority to appoint bishops and approve papal decrees. With many monarchist bishops and clergy fleeing the country, the church lacked sufficient leadership and largely acquiesced to the will of political leaders. During this time the government took control of many church properties and services—marriage, for example. Nonetheless, Catholicism retained many privileges, including state funding for its activities. A de facto arrangement between the Vatican and Liberal governments during the mid-nineteenth century allowed Rome greater leeway in choosing the Catholic leadership in Argentina, though the Argentine president retained a seldom-used veto over appointments.

An influx of non-Spanish immigrants during the late 1800s led to an increase in the number of Protestants in Argentina. More important, Italian and German immigrants brought with them socialist and communist ideologies. Fearing the influence of these secular ideologies, the Catholic Church began intensive efforts to engage the citizenry in church organizations. The clergy promoted Catholic Action, a broad organization of mainly youth and worker groups. Conflict during the administration of Juan Perón (1946–55) led many church officials to become closer to the more authoritarian elements in Argentine society in an effort to protect Catholicism's historic privileges. Discredited following their complicity with two brutal dictatorships, contemporary Catholic leaders have found themselves in competition with an increasing Protestant population and have sought to strengthen their connection to lay Catholics by opening up to a number of different pastoral trends, including charismatic Catholicism. A severe shortage of priests and seminarians has made the task of "re-evangelizing" the population difficult, however.

EARLY AND MODERN LEADERS Distinguished leadership has been largely absent from the Argentine Catholic Church, primarily due to the close connection between church and state. The monk and lawyer Gregorio Funes (1749–1829), rector of the University of Cordova, played an influential role in the independence movement and, in 1819, helped prepare the new nation's constitution. During the remainder of the nineteenth century, however, the de facto veto power the Argentine president held over Vatican appointments led to a series of relatively weak prelates, who were mostly interested in preserving the status quo. Faced with an increasing socialist threat in the late 1800s and early 1900s, the Catholic episcopacy as a whole agreed to promote Catholic Action, but no single prelate was associated strongly with this movement.

During the latter half of the twentieth century, Catholic bishops retained a strong tie to state officials, most notably those in the military who were anti-Peronist, and received substantial institutional support from the state. Enrique Angel Angelelli (1923–76) and Carlos Ponce de León (1914–77) emerged during the 1960s and 1970s as the two bishops most critical of the church's preference for the status quo, but their efforts to change the course of the church ended prematurely when both died under suspicious circumstances. Perhaps the most prominent recent Catholic leader has been the retired archbishop Stanislao Karlic (born in 1926), who during the 1990s sought to distance the Argentine church from its former pro-authoritarian stance and asked forgiveness for clerical abuses committed under the most recent dictatorship.

MAJOR THEOLOGIANS AND AUTHORS Argentina has not produced any major Catholic theologians or authors of note. The most notable theologian to emerge from Argentina has been José Míguez Bonino, an ordained Methodist minister who has written extensively on progressive Christian ethics.

HOUSES OF WORSHIP AND HOLY PLACES The central plaza of each Argentine town includes the local Catholic cathedral as well as the city hall. The most famous cathedral is the Basilica of Luján, just to the west of Buenos Aires. Legend has it that a platoon of soldiers transporting a statue of the Virgin Mary from Brazil to Chile had to stop at the site and leave the statue when their oxen would not move forward. Many took this as a sign that the town of Luján was specifically blessed by the Virgin. In the western province of San Juan is the shrine of the Difunta Correa. This spot is dedicated to María Antonia Delinda Correa, who died crossing the desert in pursuit of her husband, a soldier in the Desert War, in 1835. Her newborn son was miraculously found alive and breastfeeding upon the deceased (*difunta*) woman. Small roadside shrines in her honor are common throughout Argentina and are frequently used to mark the sites of fatal traffic accidents. Pilgrims often leave containers of water at these shrines to commemorate the saint who died of thirst.

WHAT IS SACRED? As in many Latin American Catholic societies, the Virgin Mary remains a central focus of worship for Argentine Catholics. The patroness of Argentina is the Virgin of Luján. Taxi drivers frequently travel with small statues of the Virgin Mary or Saint Andrew in their cabs. Crucifixes are commonplace in government offices and private homes. Unique to Argentina is the cult of San La Muerte, or the Saint of Good Death. It is believed that the cult originated in the mid-1700s with Jesuit missionaries who spoke of a good death. Local residents interpreted the message of salvation to be specifically related to a saintly figure. Many devoted Catholics carry an image of San La Muerte when receiving a priestly blessing.

HOLIDAYS AND FESTIVALS Argentine Catholics celebrate all holidays common to Roman Catholicism, including Christmas and Easter. Local towns also celebrate the various days devoted to their particular patron saints. On the Virgin of Luján's Day (8 May), thousands of pilgrims trek the 45 miles from Buenos Aires to the Basilica of Luján over the course of two days.

MODE OF DRESS Argentine Catholics exhibit no distinctive everyday mode of dress. Dress typically follows western European and North American fashions. During local religious festivals some individuals will dress in the traditional gaucho (cowboy) style with a wool poncho and a flat, wide-brimmed hat.

DIETARY PRACTICES No significant dietary restrictions are required of Catholics in Argentina beyond those required of Catholics in any other country.

RITUALS Catholic rituals in Argentina are similar to those of Catholic societies elsewhere. Argentina recognizes civil marriage, but most marriages involve a religious ceremony.

RITES OF PASSAGE As in other Catholic nations, baptism, First Communion, religious marriages, and funeral services are widely observed.

MEMBERSHIP Although nearly 90 percent of all Argentines declare themselves Catholic, the number in regular religious attendance is significantly lower. The 1995 World Values Survey estimates that only one in four Catholics attends Mass on a weekly basis in Argentina. Efforts to actively reengage the population in the Catholic Church have included opening up to alternative pastoral movements, such as charismatic Catholicism, as well as greater recognition of such "folk practices" as the pilgrimage to the Basilica of Luján.

SOCIAL JUSTICE The Argentine church retains an image as one of the most conservative among Catholic churches in Latin America. Attempts to involve factory workers in the church during the early 1900s were more defensive efforts against the advance of socialist labor unions than they were an awakening to issues of social justice. Argentine church leaders were slow to adopt many of the reforms of the Second Vatican Council (1962–65). Liberation theology and Christian base communities, prominent in Brazil and Chile, never took hold in Argentina. Nonetheless, small pockets of Catholic progressivism did exist in the country. The most notable Catholic progressive was Enrique Angel Angelelli, a bishop in the La Rioja province who was outspoken about the plight of the poor and rural working class. Such progressive clergy were not well received by the military government in the late 1970s, and several, including Bishop Angelelli, died or disappeared under highly suspicious circumstances.

SOCIAL ASPECTS While Argentina, along with neighboring Uruguay, resembles a secular European nation, Catholicism nonetheless influences Argentine society, particularly the upper and middle classes. While divorce is legal, abortion is not, due to the influence of the Catholic hierarchy and conservative Catholic groups such as Opus Dei.

POLITICAL IMPACT Unlike its counterparts in neighboring Chile and Brazil, the Argentine Catholic Church has, until recently, rejected the more progressive trends in Latin American Catholicism and is noted as one of the region's most politically conservative churches. This conservatism, though it had originated in a preference for strong church-state relations during the colonial era, was exacerbated during the rule of Juan Perón (1946–55). Initially the Catholic Church forged a strong relationship with the populist president. Perón's attempt to consolidate social power through state control of most social institutions and groups, however, conflicted with the church's own activities in civil society. Perón's government frequently harassed Catholic Action groups, which sought to organize Catholic youth and workers. The conflict came to a head in 1955, when the president legalized divorce and prostitution. Catholic bishops became ardent supporters of the military coup that toppled Perón that same year.

As Perón's supporters continued to cause social unrest in the following decades, church leaders actively sided with two anti-Perónist dictatorships, which lasted from 1966 to 1973 and from 1976 to 1983, respectively. During the latter, more brutal dictatorship, priests were known to be present at torture sessions, and appeals by the citizenry for church leaders to criticize the government were largely ignored. Since the collapse of the last dictatorship, the Catholic Church has attempted to repair the tarnished image gained from its support for both dictatorships and to distance itself from politics. Slightly more progressive members of the clergy were allowed to assume leadership roles during the 1990s, though the church still receives substantial funding from the government and is not as outspoken on political matters as other churches in the region.

CONTROVERSIAL ISSUES As in most Catholic nations, abortion and contraception remain highly controversial in Argentina. The use of contraceptives is common, though abortion remains illegal. Divorce has been widely accepted by most Argentines and thus is not a major controversial issue. A constitutional law requiring the president to be Catholic was overturned in 1994. The complicit role of many within the Catholic hierarchy during the most recent military regime was of major concern for many citizens in the 1980s and early '90s. Since that time the Catholic episcopacy has acknowledged its role and has asked forgiveness from the citizenry.

CULTURAL IMPACT The Catholic Church exerted a great influence on art and architecture in Argentina during the colonial period. Religious themes predominated in painting and sculpture, much of it produced by Europeans, and church architecture also reflected European ideas. The influence of Catholicism on the arts declined following independence. In contemporary Argentina the Catholic Church per se has had minimal impact on the arts community. While Catholicism remains an important part of Argentine life, contemporary culture is more secular than religious.

Other Religions

Argentina was opened to non-Catholic religions relatively early in its postcolonial history. Liberal governments during the mid-nineteenth century were interested in increasing trade with northern Europe and the United States and, therefore, permitted Protestants the free exercise of their religion. The free expression of religion granted to Protestants, however, extended in practice only to ethnic enclaves, primarily the British, Germans, and Scandinavians. Argentine Protestantism has thus historically been correlated with ethnic identities and, until recently, failed to spill over into—and indigenize itself in—that portion of the Argentine population that is of Spanish origin.

The missionizing that did occur in Argentina during the nineteenth and early twentieth century was limited. In large part, foreign missionaries did not consider Argentina a ripe mission field, as it was perceived to have been already Christianized by the Catholic Church. With the closing of the Asian mission fields during the mid-twentieth century because of war, missionary organizations began turning their attention to Latin America. In Argentina, however, collaboration between the Catholic Church and various governments meant severe restrictions on non-Catholic proselytizing religions. Although President Juan Perón began to warm to Protestant missionizing in 1954 and '55, largely in reaction to his conflict with the Catholic episcopacy, the political turbulence of that era and the military coup that ended his government made it difficult for Protestants to gain any significant foothold. Subsequent military regimes acquiesced to the Catholic Church's demands to limit missionary activity in the country. The military went so far as to physically expel Jehovah's Witnesses from the country in the late 1970s. Non-Catholic groups that were somewhat established in the country, such as the Mormons, took heed of these actions and retained a low public profile. Since greater religious freedom began to be promoted in the mid-1980s, the rate of Protestant expansion has increased dramatically. The Protestant community's annual growth rate is approximately 1.9 percent (compared to total population growth of 1.3 percent per annum) and is largely attributable to the expansion of Pentecostal and evangelical denominations.

Judaism is also an important minority religion in Argentina. Although it comprises only about 1.5 percent of the population, the Argentine Jewish community is the largest in Latin America and the fifth largest in the world. Its origins can be traced primarily to Russian immigration in the latter half of the nineteenth century, and the Jews were once frequently referred to as "Rusos." Argentina's open-door policy encouraging immigration and the country's general prosperity made it an attractive destination for Jews facing persecution in Russia and eastern Europe prior to World War I. Fear that the Russian Revolution of 1917 would spread to

Argentina led to a wave of anti-Semitism between World War I and World War II. Anti-Semitism was exacerbated by the fascist elements within Peronism and the military governments that followed Juan Perón's administrations. Argentina also became home to several Nazi war criminals. Despite the return of democracy and a culture increasingly tolerant of religious pluralism, anti-Semitism persists in the country. In 1994 nearly 100 people were killed in the bombing of a Jewish community center. Although Islamic extremists were suspected in the bombing, the perpetrators were never apprehended.

Argentina's Islamic population has increased tenfold since the 1970s, and it is widely believed that Muslims now outnumber Jews. While this increase was due largely to immigration from the Middle East and North Africa after 1970, a high birthrate and a sizable number of conversions in recent years have contributed to the growth. The country's Muslim population is the largest in Latin America, numbering between 720,000 and 900,000.

Anthony Gill

See Also Vol. 1: *Christianity, Roman Catholicism*

Bibliography

Farrell, Gerardo T. *Iglesia y pueblo en Argentina: Historia de 500 años de evangelización.* 4th ed. Buenos Aires: Editora Patria Grande, 1992.

Gill, Anthony. *Rendering unto Caesar: The Catholic Church and the State in Latin America.* Chicago: University of Chicago Press, 1998.

Ivereigh, Austen. *Catholicism and Politics in Argentina, 1810–1916.* New York: St. Martin's Press, 1995.

Mecham, J. Lloyd. *Church and State in Latin America: A History of Politico-Ecclesiastical Relations.* Rev. ed. Chapel Hill: University of North Carolina Press, 1966.

Mignone, Emilio F. *Witness to the Truth: The Complicity of Church and Dictatorship in Argentina.* Translated by Phillip Berryman. Maryknoll, N.Y.: Orbis Books, 1988.

Sigmund, Paul E., ed. *Religious Freedom and Evangelization in Latin America: The Challenge of Religious Pluralism.* Maryknoll, N.Y.: Orbis Books, 1999.

Armenia

POPULATION 3,330,099

ARMENIAN APOSTOLIC 94 percent

OTHER CHRISTIAN 4 percent

OTHER 2 percent

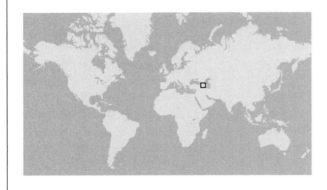

Country Overview

INTRODUCTION The Republic of Armenia is a small country located in southwestern Asia. South of the Caucasus Mountains, it is bordered by Georgia and Azerbaijan to the north and east, Iran to the south, and Turkey to the west. The historical Armenia was situated in a complex of volcanic and earthquake-prone mountain ranges known as the Armenian Highlands, a region 10 times the size of the modern country. According to tradition, in 301 C.E. Armenia became the first nation to adopt Christianity as its state religion.

Located between major empires of the East and the West, Armenia has endured a history marked by periods of both independence and foreign domination. It has been invaded by numerous powers, including Assyrians, Babylonians, Iranians, Romans, Arabs, Seljuks, Mongols, and Ottoman Turks. Despite attempts by many of the invaders to force religious conversion on the Armenians, the unique character of the country's Christian culture has remained intact.

After seven decades of repressive Soviet rule, an independent Armenia was established on 21 September 1991. In the post-Soviet era Christian identity has become an ethnic marker both for local Armenians and for the estimated 5 million living in the worldwide diaspora. More than 90 percent of the population identifies with the Armenian Apostolic Church, an Orthodox community whose supreme spiritual and administrative center (catholicate) is located at the cathedral and monastery of Ejmiadzin, west of the capital of Yerevan. Some sections of the Armenian diaspora are under the jurisdiction of the Catholicate of the Great House of Cilicia, which once resided in the medieval capital of Sis (now Kozan, Turkey) but which today is located in Antelias, Lebanon. There are also two patriarchates, one in Istanbul and another in Jerusalem.

RELIGIOUS TOLERANCE The constitution of Armenia guarantees freedom of religious practice, but there is some popular resistance to groups such as Jehovah's Witnesses. There are also restrictions on the funding of religious organizations. By law foreign funding is not allowed, although some newer religious groups—for example, the Church of Jesus Christ of Latter-day Saints—are supported by sources outside Armenia.

Major Religion

ARMENIAN APOSTOLIC CHURCH

DATE OF ORIGIN 40–60 C.E.
NUMBER OF FOLLOWERS 3.1 million

HISTORY According to tradition, Armenia was Christianized by two apostles, Thaddaeus and Bartholomew. From 35 to 43 C.E., Thaddaeus worked to establish the first Christian church in Armenia. His efforts were continued by Bartholomew from 44 to 60. Christianity grew in Armenia, leading to its official adoption as the state religion in 301. This development is credited to Gregory the Illuminator and to the virgin saints Hripsime and Gayane and their followers, known collectively as the Hripsimeank, who fled persecution in Rome.

Mesrop Mashtots, an army general who became a priest and dedicated himself to scholarship under the patronage of Catholicos Sahak Partev, created the Armenian alphabet early in the fifth century. The Old and New Testaments were among the first works translated and written in the new alphabet, and the fifth century marked the beginning of the country's literary heritage and the golden age of the church. An early major resistance movement in defense of the Armenian faith culminated in the Battle of Avarayr in 451. After the martyrdom of Vardan Mamikonian and of the priest Ghevond Yeretz and his followers, known collectively as the Ghevondeank, the resistance ended in 484 when the Treaty of Nvarsag was signed with Iran.

Accepting the Council of Ephesus (421), the Armenians rejected the Christology of Nestorius as undermining the unity of Christ's Godhead and manhood. They later appropriated the doctrine of Saint Cyril of Alexandria and rejected the Christology of the Council of Chalcedon (451) as a form of Nestorianism. In 1860, under the Ottoman Empire, Armenians initiated church reforms and established a national assembly with two councils, one religious and the other civil. The two sees, in continuity with the Ottoman Empire, the Armenian Patriarchate of Constantinople and the Catholicate of Cilicia, retain this administrative structure.

Over centuries of Ottoman hegemony, Armenian Christians were able to live as an autonomous *millet,* or community. At the end of nineteenth century, however, this autonomy was brutally disrupted. Armenians were subjected to pogroms in 1895–96 and then again in 1909. Beginning in 1915 Turkish authorities imposed

A woman prays at the lance with which Christ was pierced during the Crucifixion. The lance is located in Ejmiadzin, the site of the state church and the location of one of the two modern sees of the Armenian Apostolic Church. © DEAN CONGER/CORBIS.

systematic genocide and deportation on the country's Armenian population. The practice of religion was discouraged under Soviet rule, beginning in 1920, and churches were neglected and many monasteries closed. After the fall of the Soviet Union and the establishment of an independent Armenia, people once again began to identify themselves with the national church. In 2001 Armenians everywhere celebrated 1,700 years of Christianity as the state religion.

EARLY AND MODERN LEADERS Gregory the Illuminator established Christianity as the state religion in 301. The priest Ghevond and his associates were religious leaders who stood with Vartan Mamikonian in the resistance movement against Iran in 451. Other important historical leaders included Nerses the Gracious, who, as catholicos, in the twelfth century revived the church and initiated social programs, and Grigor Tatewatsi, a notable theologian of the fourteenth century. Garegin II was elected catholicos of the see of Ejmiadzin in 1999. Aram I became catholicos of the see of Cilicia in 1995.

MAJOR THEOLOGIANS AND AUTHORS Yeznik Koghbatsi, an archbishop of Bagrevand and a student of Catholicos Sahak Partev and of Mesrop Mashtots, was a fifth-century theologian of the Armenian Church. His well-known work *Yeghtz Aghantotz* ("Refutation of the Sects") is a treatise against various heresies. Two women of the eighth century, Sahakdukht and Khosrovidukht, are renowned for their expressive hymns.

Considered the father of Armenian spirituality, Gregory of Nareg (died c. 1003) is among the country's most beloved religious scholars and poets. He is best known for *The Book of Lamentation,* a masterpiece consisting of 95 sections. Among modern Armenian theologians, Catholicos Garegin I (1931–99) was particularly noteworthy as a scholar and reformer.

HOUSES OF WORSHIP AND HOLY PLACES Armenian ecclesiastical architecture has been considered to be a precursor of the European Gothic style, which flourished in the twelfth and thirteenth centuries. Churches in Armenia vary in shape and may be rectangular, round, or built in the shape of a cross, and some have four apses. The interiors vary according to the presence or absence of an altar canopy, niches, and galleries. An altar that faces east, toward the sunrise, is common to all Armenian churches. Some churches and monasteries in Armenia are built into the rugged mountainsides.

Among the most noteworthy sacred places is Ejmiadzin, the site of Gregory the Illuminator's vision that led to the establishment of the state church and the location of one of the two modern sees of the Armenian Apostolic Church. There also is a holy shrine in Antelias, Lebanon, that is dedicated to the victims of the 1915 genocide. Outside Armenia itself, some sacred sites of the church are found in the western part of historical Armenia, now in eastern Turkey. They include ancient monasteries and churches, many of which are in ruins.

WHAT IS SACRED? Among the most important of Armenian church relics are the remains of Gregory the Illuminator, the manuscripts of Gregory of Nareg's *Book of Lamentation,* and ancient illuminated manuscripts that are housed in the Matenadaran institute in Yerevan.

Reverence for the so-called Tree of Life, historically a poplar, continues in Armenian folklore. Devotees tie small parts of their clothes to trees near monasteries and pilgrimage sites in hopes of having their prayers answered.

HOLIDAYS AND FESTIVALS The Armenian Apostolic Church marks a number of sacred holidays. Among the most important are Christmas and Theophany (Christ's Nativity and Baptism), celebrated on 6 January; Christ's Presentation in the Temple, in February; Easter, according to the Gregorian calendar, followed by the Feasts of Ascension and Pentecost; the Feast of Transfiguration, also celebrated as the Day of Roses, in July; the Dormition of the Mother of God, also a first fruit festival for grapes, in August; and the Exaltation of the Holy Cross, in September. Most of the holidays are preceded by a period of fasting. A memorial Monday, with special services for the dead, follows each of the holidays. The church recognizes Nahatakats, or Martyr's Day, on 24 April as a memorial day for the victims of the 1915 Armenian genocide.

Armenian Christians also celebrate saint's days, often related to the history of the church and its early leaders. Saints honored for their roles in the conversion of Armenia to Christianity include Thaddaeus and Bartholomew, the martyred Hripsime and her followers, and Sandukht, another early martyr, as well as the confessor Saint Gregory the Illuminator. Other notable saints include the translators Sahak and Mesrop, and such martyrs as Vartan Mamikonian and Ghevond and his fellow priests.

MODE OF DRESS Religious personnel, including clerks, deacons, married parish priests, celibate priests, bishops, and archbishops, wear vestments that vary according to rank. Most are associated with the liturgy. Called "garments of salvation," these include a long white robe, a stole, a girdle that symbolizes encirclement by the grace of God, arm cuffs, a high collar, and a radiant cape worn as a symbol of the faith. During each celebration of the liturgy, the priest is ceremonially vested and given a crown.

DIETARY PRACTICES Except for Lent, when no meat of any kind, including fish, is permitted, Armenians do not follow dietary restrictions. The feast for some major holidays, however, is preceded by a period of strict fasting, usually three to five days, during which only water is consumed.

RITUALS Contemporary rituals of the Armenian Apostolic Church are based on ancient traditions. The liturgy, celebrated mainly on Sundays, is chanted. A liturgy may end with a memorial service. The sign of the cross, made from left to right, is performed before a prayer. The principal prayer is the Our Father. Armenians also express their devotion and make requests by lighting candles and offering gifts of incense before sacred icons.

Weddings are celebratory. Special hymns are sung, and the couple are crowned and proclaimed Ashkhen and Trdat, a king and queen of ancient Armenia, for the day. During the ceremony the priest asks three times if the bride will obey the groom and if the groom will be responsible for the bride. This questioning has been criticized but has continued to be practiced.

During funerals final rites are given to the deceased, and it is asked that the person be returned to the earth. Memorial services are held 3, 7, and 40 days after the burial, and there also are annual memorials.

Some rituals are specific to certain holidays, as when sunrise and evening vigils are held during Lent. Blessings of water are performed at Theophany and Transfiguration, of basil at the Exaltation of the Holy Cross, and of grapes at Dormition.

RITES OF PASSAGE Armenians combine baptism with confirmation. Through baptism the person, usually a child, is accepted as a Christian. Infant baptism also is practiced.

Religious personnel observe elaborate and strictly regulated rites for ordaining each rank of priest. Distinguished by Armenian music and text, the rites bear resemblance to the Coptic and Orthodox traditions.

MEMBERSHIP Membership in the Armenian Apostolic Church is open to all, and the church communicates its message through the mass media. In the aftermath of Soviet rule, the church has developed religious education programs aimed at Armenian youth and the general public. In 2001, the year that marked 1,700 years of Christianity as the state religion, the church published tour guides, particularly aimed at Armenians of the diaspora, encouraging pilgrims to visit sacred historical sites.

SOCIAL JUSTICE Since its early history the Armenian Apostolic Church has championed social justice, establishing orphanages, hospitals, and shelters for the needy and providing secular and religious education for Armenians throughout the diaspora. These efforts have been particularly concerted in the post-Soviet era, as the advent of Armenian independence has been accompanied by a protracted economic crisis.

SOCIAL ASPECTS In general, marriage and family issues in Armenia are governed by civil laws, and the church concerns itself with these matters only symbolically, as, for example, through the wedding ceremony. In Lebanon, however, the church does have authority in civil matters and family law, including mediation and divorce.

POLITICAL IMPACT Although Armenia is a secular state, centuries of religious persecution and pressure to convert to other faiths have helped make Christianity an integral facet of ethnic identity. In addition, despite the official separation of church and state, the Armenian Apostolic Church plays a key role in politics, with some political leaders identifying with the church. Further, it is widely believed that some candidates for the catholicate during the contemporary period have been elected partly through the influence of high-ranking government officials. A controversy surrounding the election in 1999 of Catholicos Garegin II led the country's president to attest that the government had not taken a formal position on any candidate.

CONTROVERSIAL ISSUES The Armenian Apostolic Church refrains from making public statements about such issues as birth control and abortion, leaving these matters to the state. Although the church maintains its own guidelines concerning family matters, including a list of conditions under which divorce is approved, these are handled under civil law.

CULTURAL IMPACT The Armenian Apostolic Church has long been considered the guardian of Armenian culture and its heritage. During the 600 years of Ottoman domination and during other periods when Armenia was denied its sovereignty, the church preserved the Armenian language, musical heritage, literary production, architectural heritage, and values. Mkhitar Sebastatsi, a priest who converted to Roman Catholicism and in 1701 founded a new religious order that later moved to the island of San Lazzaro in Venice, did much to promote Armenian education and publishing and to advance its culture.

Other Religions

In addition to the Armenian Apostolic Church, there are a number of smaller religious communities in Armenia. A small percentage belongs to the Armenian Catholic Church, a Uniate communion that gives allegiance to Rome but follows Eastern rites. The Mkhitar-ist monastic order is included among Armenian Catholics. Along with Greek Orthodox, Catholics are concentrated in the northern region of Armenia. Other faiths include Pentecostal, the Armenian Evangelical Church, Baptist, charismatic, Jehovah's Witness, Seventh-day Adventist, and Mormon. In addition, there are Yezidis, Jews, Muslims, Bahais, Hare Krishnas, and pagan groups in Armenia.

The Yezidis, a Kurdish group whose practices include elements derived from Zoroastrianism, are largely concentrated in agricultural areas around Mount Aragats, northwest of Yerevan. Most religious minorities, however, including Jews, Mormons, and Bahais, live in Yerevan. Muslims in Yerevan include Kurds, Iranians, and other temporary visitors from neighboring Muslim countries. A small Muslim Kurdish community is established in the Abovian region, and there are also Muslims of Azeribaijani descent living along the eastern and northern borders.

Sima Aprahamian

See Also Vol. 1: *Christianity, Eastern Orthodoxy*

Bibliography

Dowling, Theodore Edward. *The Armenian Church.* 1910. Reprint, New York: AMS Press, 1970.

Fortescue, Edward Francis Knottesford. *The Armenian Church.* 1872. Reprint, New York: AMS Press, 1970.

Hovannisian, Richard G., ed. *Remembrance and Denial.* Detroit: Wayne State University Press, 1998.

Karekin I, Catholicos of Armenia. *The Council of Chalcedon and the Armenian Church.* 2nd ed. New York: Armenian Church Prelacy, 1975.

Kasparian, Vartan. *Garments of Salvation.* N.p.: YACE, 1981.

Kiwlēsērean, Babgēn. *The Armenian Church.* Translated by Terenig Vartabed Poladian. New York: AMS Press, 1970.

Lang, David Marshall, and Christopher J. Walker. *The Armenians.* London: Minority Rights Group, 1987.

Ōrmanean, Maghakìa. *The Church of Armenia.* 2nd English ed. London: Mowbray, 1955.

Samuelian, Thomas J., ed.. *Classical Armenian Culture: Influences and Creativity.* Chico, Calif.: Scholars Press, 1982.

Samuelian, Thomas J., and Michael E. Stone, eds. *Medieval Armenian Culture.* Chico, Calif.: Scholars Press, 1984.

Saraydarian, Torkom. *The Symbolism of the Ecclesiastical Vestments and Vessels of the Armenian Apostolic Church.* Van Nuys, Calif.: Armenian Church, 1967.

Thierry, Jean-Michel. *Armenian Art: Principal Sites by Patrick Donabédian with the Assistance of Jean-Michel and Nicole Thierry.* Translated by Célestine Dars. New York: H.N. Abrams, 1989.

Walker, Christopher J. *Armenia: The Survival of a Nation.* 2nd ed. New York: St. Martin's Press, 1990.

Australia

POPULATION 18,972,350

ROMAN CATHOLIC 26.7 percent

ANGLICAN 20.7 percent

UNITING CHURCH IN AUSTRALIA
  6.7 percent

PRESBYTERIAN 3.4 percent

OTHER CHRISTIAN 8.5 percent

MUSLIM, BUDDHIST, HINDU,
  JEWISH 4.4 percent

OTHER 29.6 percent

Country Overview

INTRODUCTION Australia is a vast, dry continent, slightly smaller in size than the United States. It lies in the Southern Hemisphere between the Indian Ocean and Pacific Ocean. Australia is separated by seas from several island nations, including Indonesia to the northwest, Papua New Guinea to the northeast, and New Zealand to the southeast.

Australia was originally inhabited by Aborigines and Torres Strait Islanders (inclusively referred to as Indigenous Australians), whose origins go back 40,000 years or more. At the time of European settlement in 1788, there were an estimated 600 language groups (and between 300,000 and a million people). In the eighteenth century the British government founded a penal settlement in Australia because of overcrowding in the prisons in England. The colony grew quickly as a permanent settlement in the nineteenth century. The British convicts and settlers took their Catholic (Irish) and Anglican (English) religions into a land of many indigenous religions, or "spiritualities." The British also took to Australia other Christian churches, such as Methodism, Congregationalism, and Presbyterianism. Jews were on the first fleet in 1788, and their numbers have remained small and steady.

The camel drivers who arrived from northern India and Afghanistan in the 1850s were probably the first Muslims to settle in Australia. Confucianism and Buddhism arrived with the Chinese gold miners in the midnineteenth century, though in small numbers.

Additional colonies had been established on the Australian continent in the nineteenth century, and these were united into a federation, called the Commonwealth of Australia, on 1 January 1901. It was only after World War II that the general population increased rapidly (with a large wave of immigrants) and that Roman Catholicism in particular grew faster than Anglicanism. As a result of migration from the Catholic countries of southern Europe and South America, and from Asian countries such as Vietnam, Roman Catholicism overtook Anglicanism as the largest denomination

A Catholic Archbishop listens as an Aborigine plays the didgeridoo. Only belatedly have Roman Catholic churches realized the importance of indigenous culture and the need for enculturation. © TIM GRAHAM/CORBIS SYGMA.

in the 1986 census. Muslims from the Middle East also dramatically increased their numbers in Australia. By the 2001 census, however, Christianity accounted for 68 percent of the population, and other world religions, such as Buddhism, Islam, Judaism, Hinduism, and Sikhism, remained numerically small (less than five percent). Although Roman Catholicism has become the largest religion, attendance has declined.

Among Christians there have been two distinctive organizational developments. The first was the founding of the Australian Church by the Presbyterian preacher and theologian Charles Strong (1844–1942). The second development, in 1977, was the uniting of three Christian churches (Congregationalist, Methodist, and Presbyterian) to form the Uniting Church in Australia.

According to the 2001 census, Indigenous Australians constituted about 1.5 percent of the total Australian population, with roughly one-third being traditional tribal and two-thirds being either urban or semiurban. In addition, during the 200 years since settlement, miscegenation has occurred, as well as marriages between

people from European and Asian cultures. This has led to some indigenous groups moving away from what might be called traditional tribal cultures.

There has also been an increase in the number of "no religion" responses in the national census. This may be attributed to growing secularism, disaffection with institutional religion, and an unwillingness on the part of some immigrants to disclose their religion.

RELIGIOUS TOLERANCE Anglicanism was never the official state religion of the colony, but it tended to be seen as such in practice. The Church Act of 1836 was an effort to treat religions equally by providing financial aid to all religions. Sectarianism, however, was never far away. When the churches refused to give up their rights to run their own religious schools, the government withdrew financial funding in the 1870s, declaring that education should be "free, secular, and compulsory."

Although in Australia all Christian denominations came to be treated equally, the settlers and governments did not recognize indigenous religion, so Indigenous Australians were condemned as having no religion. Attempts were made to proselytize to the indigenous peoples; when these failed, efforts were redirected into trying to assimilate them to European lifestyle and thinking as a first step toward conversion. Over time some indigenous people have become Christians, but they have been obliged to do so in a European way. Only since the 1990s have the Christian churches been actively promoting inculturation (attempting to express themselves in the idiom of a particular culture).

The strong sectarianism among Christian denominations in the eighteenth and nineteenth centuries eased in the twentieth century. The National Council of Churches in Australia has, as its main aim, the promotion of ecumenism. Even given the small percentage of Muslims in Australia, the rise of militant Islamic groups worldwide has given impetus to interfaith dialogue. The intolerance of small extreme anti-Islamic and anti-Jewish groups has also become more apparent through occasional attacks on mosques and synagogues.

Major Religion

ROMAN CATHOLICISM

DATE OF ORIGIN 1788 C.E.
NUMBER OF FOLLOWERS 5 million

HISTORY The Australian Catholic community began as a group of laypeople. From 1788 to 1820 the church functioned as a community without the permanent presence of a Catholic priest. The building of churches began shortly after the appointment of John Therry, and thereafter it followed the pattern of the institutional church in many other countries, where a church building, presbytery, convent, and church school were erected when possible. The Roman Catholic Church in Australia was mostly Irish in its membership and clergy. The government was favorably disposed to churches, because it saw them as moral policemen who could help control the unruly populace in the port city of Sydney.

The relationship between the state and the Catholic Church deteriorated among differences over a national system of education, and eventually funding was withdrawn in the 1870s (not to be reintroduced until the 1960s). Roman Catholics retained their schools, and the church hierarchy started a recruiting campaign for religious orders from overseas. During the latter half of the nineteenth century, hundreds of religious sisters and brothers arrived from Ireland and England to teach in Catholic schools or to nurse in Catholic hospitals.

The origin of monasticism in Australia represents an unexpected development in Australian history, as it came from a Spanish, not an Irish, source. In 1846 the Spanish bishop Rosendo Salvado (1814–1900) founded the Benedictine monastery at New Norcia, north of Perth, Western Australia. The goal was to create among indigenous peoples a Christian, largely self-sufficient village based on agriculture and the European Benedictine vision. The attempt to turn Aborigines into habit-wearing Benedictine monks failed, however, and their efforts were redirected to educate, "civilize," and evangelize the local peoples.

With the First Vatican Council in 1870, Australian Roman Catholicism, which had been mostly Irish in orientation, took a pronounced turn toward Rome. Bishops were often appointed from the small pool of clergy chosen to study in Rome. Such bishops were characterized by a strong loyalty to the Vatican. One exception was Archbishop Daniel Mannix of Melbourne, who made a name for himself as the champion of the Irish cause in Australia.

The Second Vatican Council (1962–65) introduced turmoil into Roman Catholicism in Australia. As a result, Catholicism was divided into conservatives, moderates, and progressives. The conservative group was characterized by the rise of groups such as Opus Dei, Neo-Catechumenate, and Focolare.

The relationship between Roman Catholicism and indigenous peoples has a checkered history in Australia. Attempts at evangelization and conversion were largely unsuccessful, yet in spite of that the missionaries continued the difficult work of instructing, teaching, nursing, looking after orphans and lepers, and pastoral caring in general. A lack of any knowledge of anthropology and an expectation that Aborigines would quickly become "civilized" were impediments under which the missionaries unconsciously labored. Unfortunately, in the twentieth century many churches were also implicated in the Stolen Generation saga, whereby indigenous children were forcibly removed from their parents and brought up in institutions. Only belatedly have churches realized the importance of indigenous culture and the need for inculturation.

EARLY AND MODERN LEADERS Bishop John Bede Polding was an outstanding Catholic leader in the early nineteenth century, notable for his understanding of Aboriginal culture and his ecumenical spirit. John Plunkett, who became attorney general of the colony in the early nineteenth century, was a layman noted for his involvement in church matters and for his fair-mindedness.

Two outstanding women were Caroline Chisholm, noted for her work among migrant women in the 1840s and for her ecumenical outlook, and Blessed Mary MacKillop, who in 1866 founded the teaching order of the Josephite sisters, a native Australian congregation of nuns. Father Julian Tennison Woods played a leadership role in helping MacKillop found her congregation. Archbishop Daniel Mannix (served from 1917 to 1963) was noteworthy for his ability to think differently and for his outspokenness on behalf of Irish Catholics. The Pallotine priest and anthropologist Ernest A. Worms (1891–1963) showed a sensitivity and understanding of Aboriginal customs, which was unusual for missionaries at the time.

MAJOR THEOLOGIANS AND AUTHORS David Coffey was one of Australia's leading systematic theologians, who, in the 1980s, attracted the attention of the Congregation of the Defence of the Faith through his writings, which challenged a fundamentalist and naive understanding of the meaning of the Resurrection. Other prominent theologians who wrote in the latter part of the twentieth century and into the present century are Gerald O'Collins, John Thornhill, Denis Edwards, and Tony Kelly.

Notable scripture scholars include William Dalton, Francis Moloney, Brendan Byrne, and Elaine Wainwright (all active in the late twentieth and early twenty-first centuries). Frank Sheed provided leadership in reviving theology in the English-speaking world in the 1940s and '50s. Since the 1990s Pauline Allen and Robert C. Hill have made substantial contributions in patristics (the study of early theologians).

HOUSES OF WORSHIP AND HOLY PLACES The chapel of the Sisters of Saint Joseph in North Sydney is where Blessed Mary MacKillop, founder of the Josephite sisters, is buried. It has become a place of pilgrimage for many Australians; on 8 August every year, thousands of people celebrate the feast of Blessed Mary MacKillop at her shrine. These pilgrims are mainly of Chinese, Vietnamese, and southern European backgrounds.

WHAT IS SACRED? Catholics of European origin left their sacred sites behind when they migrated to Australia. What is sacred for them now are their churches and religious rites.

There is also much popular Catholicism, especially among immigrants from Italy, Spain, and South and Central American countries, where a statue or relic becomes the sacred object. Among the Anglo-Celtic part of Catholicism, some traditional devotions persist, such as those connected to an excessive Mariology (which becomes Mariolatry, with a statue of Mary being a sacred object).

HOLIDAYS AND FESTIVALS The Catholic feast days in Australia are those of the normal liturgical calendar. The Feast of the Assumption is a holy day of obligation for Catholics in Australia but is celebrated simply with attendance at Mass. Christmas is celebrated with the usual midnight Mass, European-style cribs, Christmas trees, and imitation snow—though, with the growing consciousness of inculturation, Australian-produced hymns are now making an appearance. At Easter, ecumenical dawn services are also becoming more prominent, as are interdenominational youth rallies on Easter Sunday, organized by a group called Fusion.

In Australia traditional Catholic festivals such as Corpus Christi have all but disappeared, as have religious processions. Different cultural groups within Catholicism in Australia, such as Italians or Vietnamese, continue to celebrate their particular saint's days and religious festivals, but these are not celebrated in the broader Catholic Church. An underlying reason for this is the fact that many immigrants to Australia have moved from a culture in which religion is public to one in which religion is a private matter.

MODE OF DRESS In general Australians tend to dress informally even when going to church. Some Roman Catholic men of European origin continue to wear business suits and ties when attending Sunday Mass, but this is the exception. Among the religious orders and congregations, most wear neat but casual clothes, with or without a religious symbol, although the more conservative tend to wear the old religious habits.

DIETARY PRACTICES In Australia there are no dietary practices that distinguish Roman Catholics from others. Even the old custom of eating fish on Fridays has virtually disappeared. In Australia, as elsewhere, dietary practices are influenced by the ethnic origins of the community or parish.

RITUALS Among the Aborigines and Torres Strait Islanders some inculturation is taking place. Indigenous Australians now use a smoking ceremony as the penitential rite in the Catholic Mass. In this traditional ceremony, wood is placed in a pile and set alight. Participants then walk in a circular fashion through the smoke a number of times, during which clapsticks are used and chants are sung. The ceremony purifies the participants. It was used for the beatification Mass for Blessed Mary MacKillop celebrated by Pope John Paul II in 1995. Sometimes the Eucharist is celebrated sitting on the ground, which traditionally emphasized Indigenous Australian's relationship to the earth and their outdoor lifestyle.

On Bathurst Island the children role-play each Station of the Cross and take part in body painting, traditional songs, and dancing. At Santa Teresa on Ash Wednesday the bark of a local tree is cooked and made into powder for the ashes. At Daly River on Good Friday people are rubbed with red ocher as a sign of new life before they kiss the feet of Jesus on the cross. Distinctive Eucharistic prayers for Aborigines have also been written.

Among other Australian Catholics, with the establishment of the post–Vatican II pattern of the Saturday vigil and the Sunday and weekday celebration of the Eucharist, the traditional service called Benediction has mostly disappeared. Prayer forms, pre– and post–Vatican II, offer a wide range of devotional practices, reflecting the cultures of immigrants from Ireland, England, Europe, the Middle East, South and Central America, and Southeast Asia.

Australia does not have centers of pilgrimages as found in older Catholic countries. Church leaders in 2000 undertook an ecumenical pilgrimage to Uluru (Ayers Rock), which is an Aboriginal sacred site. This was an isolated incident, although many make the trip as part of a secular pilgrimage.

There is a growing number of young Catholics who choose to have secular weddings. The annual blessing of the fleet by a priest is an ongoing ritual in fishing communities of Italian origin in Australia.

RITES OF PASSAGE There are no Catholic rites of passage that are distinctive to Australia. Of course Australians have the sacraments, many of which mark important stages in life, like Catholics worldwide.

MEMBERSHIP Membership has continued to increase, according to the national census, but regular Sunday church attendance is down to about 18 percent. Membership continues to be by way of infant baptism. The phenomenon of nominal church membership is a problem for the institution. Although many Australians do not attend church, they may well practice alternative forms of spirituality in small groups. The church tries to increase its membership through missions, agencies such as the National Catholic Enquiry Centre, and a program known as the Rite of Christian Initiation of Adults.

SOCIAL JUSTICE The Roman Catholic bishops have set up a Bishop's Committee for Justice, Development, and Peace, which oversees the Australian Catholic Social Justice Council and Caritas Australia nationally. They occasionally produce statements and booklets on justice topics. Every year Social Justice Sunday is marked with a special statement on social justice (e.g., ecology, refugees, or racism). The bishop's conference is also active in lobbying the government on social justice issues such as taxation of the poor, health care, unemployment, ref-

ugees, and migrants. Individual parishes also may have social justice groups.

Patrick Dodson was the first Aboriginal Australian to be ordained a Catholic priest (in 1975), but he left the priesthood in the 1980s. The former chair of the Council for Aboriginal Reconciliation, he has been a strong and persistent voice for indigenous justice. The Catholic organization Saint Vincent de Paul Society is the largest welfare agency in Australia.

SOCIAL ASPECTS The Roman Catholic community in Australia used to be comprised of Irish men and women from generally poor socioeconomic backgrounds who were uneducated and who belonged to the Labour Party. This is no longer the case. Large families have given way to those with less than two children, on average. The divorce rate among Catholics is the same as for the general population (about one in three). Despite the Roman Catholic Church's position against birth control, most Australian Catholic couples practice it. Social aspects are influenced by the ethnic origins of a community.

POLITICAL IMPACT The church's political alliances have changed over the last 200 years. After federation in 1901, with the establishment of political parties the Roman Catholic Church aligned itself with the Irish/Labour party, but this Irish-Catholic-Labour nexus became increasingly less valid in the second half of the twentieth century. After the Spanish Civil War (1936–39), and with the rise of Communism in Europe, anti-Communist feeling grew in Australia and led to a layman, B.A. Santamaria, starting a vigorous and secretive campaign ("the Movement") to rid the trade unions of Communists. This movement led to some polarization in the Catholic Church between the left and right wings, among bishops as well as laity. Some bishops with sympathies toward workers distanced themselves from any Catholic movement that would be seen as too rigid and extreme. Others, especially Catholic women, were content with the older, traditional pieties of the Sacred Heart, Mary Queen of Peace, or Saint Therese of Lisieux.

A number of previous prime ministers (Scullin, Curtin, Chifley, and Keating) were influenced by their Catholic working-class backgrounds. The Catholic Church worked toward changes in certain items of the General Sales Tax (GST), enacted in 2000, softening the impact of the tax on those at the lower end of the socioeconomic scale. Political efforts are often made in cooperation with other churches (e.g., the National Council of Churches in Australia) and other agencies.

Bishops no longer try to tell their flock how to vote, although they might mention the importance of Catholic values. When a Catholic congregation of nuns, the Sisters of Charity, agreed to operate a safe needle clinic for drug addicts in Sydney with the consent of the local archbishop, the Roman Curia intervened and forbade them. The clinic opened instead under supervision of the Uniting Church in Australia.

CONTROVERSIAL ISSUES For Roman Catholics in Australia the Third Rite of Reconciliation (a ritual in which a group receives forgiveness for their sins) has been a controversial issue. It became popular in Australia, but the Vatican judged that that it should be discontinued, since the rules for its use were receiving too liberal an interpretation, and private, individual confession is to be preferred to general absolution in most cases.

The ordination of women continues to be an issue, as does the role of priests and lay ministries in the face of an increased shortage of priests. The practice by some bishops of inviting celibate males from other cultures and countries to train for the priesthood is rejected by many as exploitative and unjust to both the local church and the individual candidate. Other issues relate to reproduction, sexual ethics (e.g., homosexuality, oral sex, in vitro fertilization, and the use of condoms to avoid HIV), and bioethical issues (such as euthanasia and stem-cell research).

Native title (the ownership of the land by the indigenous people) is another controversial issue in Australia, and Catholics, among others, have been strongly supportive of the principles involved. Indigenous Australians are trying to reclaim parts of the land that they maintain belonged to their clan or people. Frank Brennan, a Jesuit priest and lawyer, has been involved in championing issues of justice and land rights on behalf of the indigenous people.

CULTURAL IMPACT The musicians in religious orders—who are mainly nuns—have been the greatest influence on music in Australia. They have taught music to children of all creeds before and after school and on Saturdays. In religious music there have been outstanding composers, such as Dom Stephen Moreno, Christopher Wilcox, Richard Connolly, and Colin Smith.

In art probably the greatest contribution to Australian culture is the Blake Prize for Religious Art, which was founded in 1951 by a Jesuit priest, Michael Scott, and is sponsored by Australian Catholic University. It sought to get away from the "kitsch" art of the nineteenth century and to interest artists in religious themes. Though it has not healed the divorce between the church and the artist, it has stimulated the creation of individual works of authentic religious art. There have been many Catholic painters in Australia, including John Coburn, Justin O'Brien, and John Ogburn. Sculptor Tom Bass is noted for his statues, created during the liturgical revival of the 1950s.

The influence of Roman Catholicism on literature in Australia has often taken the form of a rejection of formal constraints and the "re-visioning" of Catholic doctrine from perspectives of the individual. Australia has a history of revolt against authority in its artists and writers. Key Australian writers influenced, positively or negatively, by Catholicism include Christopher Brennan, James McAuley, Francis Webb, Vincent Buckley, Les Murray, Thomas Keneally, and Morris West. Germain Greer and Anne Summers, who both represent a more strident strand of feminism, were both products of convent schools.

Other Religions

The Anglican Church in Australia (originally known as the Church of England in Australia) had humble origins. It was the establishment of a penal settlement, not religion, that motivated British colonization in Australia. In 1787 the British government instructed the first governor of the colony to require convicts to attend Anglican worship services. Thus, other than the government officials, the convicts were the bulk of the congregation. Rev. Richard Johnson, an Evangelical, was the first chaplain (appointed in 1786), and William Broughton was the first bishop (appointed in 1836).

Like the Church of England, the Anglican Church of Australia is based on *The Book of Common Prayer* and the Thirty-nine Articles, but it has also produced *The Australian Hymn Book* (1977), *An Australian Prayer Book* (1978), and *A Prayer Book for Australia* (1995). In 1981 it officially terminated all legal ties with the Church of England and changed its name to the Anglican Church of Australia. Nevertheless, the church has not been noted for adapting itself to local conditions and culture, and it has had to contend with its image as the church of the British, of the ruling group, and of the privileged. As a percentage of the Australian population, Anglicans slipped from 54.7 percent in 1881 to 20.7 percent in 2001.

The Anglican Church of Australia has two main theological strands: the Evangelical (Protestant, or Low Church) tradition and the Tractarian (Catholic, or High Church) tradition. The former has stronger ties to the Reformation and is individualistic, while the latter emphasizes the church, episcopacy, and community. The Evangelical tradition is strong in the dioceses of Sydney and Armidale, while the other Anglican dioceses in Australia tend toward the Tractarian tradition. There is, however, a wide diversity of styles, beliefs, and patterns of "being Church" among Anglicans in Australia.

The dioceses of Sydney and Armidale refuse to ordain women, although the worldwide Anglican communion allows it. The Sydney diocese has considered introducing lay presidency of the Eucharist. It accepts only one source of revelation—the Bible—and has run a campaign to recruit more Bible-Christians, as they call their faithful.

Toward the end of the twentieth century Pentecostalism, Buddhism, and neo-paganism were the fastest-growing religions in Australia. The Assembly of God churches in Australia have strong links with their North American churches and emphasize healing and financial giving.

Other revivalists groups, such as Fusion, are Pentecostal in worship style. Some run radio stations. These churches often have revivalist preachers from the United States or elsewhere, such as Billy Graham, his son Franklin Graham, Leighton Ford, Greg Laurie, and Bill Hybels, who have all traveled to Australia. They run crusades for weeks on end. One characteristic of these churches is that they tend to emphasize spiritual salvation and a person's relationship with Jesus, with no interest in trying to address social justice issues.

An important Christian historical figure was Rev. Alan Walker (1911–2003), who was a Methodist minister at the Central Methodist Mission and who was well known for his concern for social justice (including opposing the Vietnam War). Another personage was the Anglican bishop Ernest Burgmann (1855–1967), who was noted for his social justice and who identified with the struggles of working-class people during the Depression of the 1930s and the postwar period. Rev.

John Flynn, superintendent of the Australian Inland Mission, was an outstanding Christian who devoted himself to attending to the sick in the outback of Australia. He established the Flying Doctor Service, which covers huge tracts of outback Australia by plane. Also worthy of mention is Rev. Dorothy MacMahon of the Uniting Church in Australia, who has regular divorce rituals.

Among the Greek Orthodox community in Australia, a noteworthy ritual is the Blessing of the Waters on the Feast of Theophany (6 January). Also known as the Baptism of Christ, it is when the Greek Orthodox archbishop of Sydney throws a crucifix into the sea off the coast near Sydney, and swimmers dive in to retrieve it. The winner is rewarded with the crucifix and a blessing from the archbishop.

Judaism has been in Australia since 1788 and is well established, with schools and synagogues. Some individual Jews have played significant roles in civic life. The number of Australians who practice Islam, Hinduism, and Sikhism has increased significantly since the Second World War. Buddhism also grew during this period, especially during the 1970s, when "boat people" arrived before and after the fall of Vietnam to Communism. Muslims, Hindus, Sikhs, and Buddhists tend to live in cities and within certain neighborhoods. Because of cultural differences between these groups and the dominant Anglo-Celtic culture, they have not been fully accepted by mainstream society. They have all built places of worship, and Muslims have built a number of Islamic schools.

A new phenomenon in Australia is that of paganism or neo-paganism. It is a new-age movement characterized by a general religious eclecticism, which makes it difficult to define or describe. It often has a feminine bent, seen especially in goddess worship. It is connected to environmentalism or earth-based worship; it often involves ecological activism, antiestablishment thinking, the culture of acceptance, and loose doctrinal content; and it proclaims and promotes the value of self-empowerment. Structurally neo-paganism has no hierarchy or charismatic leaders. Some see its popularity as a sign that many Australians do not find much spiritual nourishment within the language, rituals, and rules of the institutional churches. In the 2001 census more than ten thousand people called themselves pagans, and more than eight thousand claimed to be witches.

Neo-pagans have no tangible place of worship but simply meet in small groups, covens, homes, or public spaces. They use dance, candles, incense, flowers, mediation, and prayers. Neo-pagans recognize some sort of power, force, energy, or "chi." The dominant pagan group in Australia is Wicca, which was first established in the United Kingdom. Other groups include Pagan Awareness Network, Celtic Pagan, Chaos Magician, Druids, Runesters, Shaman, and Goddess Worshipers.

In the past most missionaries thought the indigenous people were in need of being civilized, and attempted to force Christianity upon them. Nevertheless, some individuals did show anthropological sensitivity. The Presbyterian pastor John Matthew (1849–1929) was noted for his work in anthropology among the Aborigines, and in the nineteenth century the London Missionary Society preacher Lancelot Threlkeld was appointed to do missionary work among the Aborigines in the Lake Macquarie area of New South Wales. This led to his translation of the Gospel of Luke into the local Aboriginal language.

Only about one-third of Australia's Aboriginal population are traditional Aborigines, while the others are urban or semi-urban. In its traditional form Aboriginal spirituality is an expression of life's meaning through an aesthetic, metaphorical frame of mind, as opposed to the Western rational, utilitarian approach to forming meaning. There is no tension between the culture and religion. Stories about a mythological past called *alcheringa* (also called "the Dreaming") portray humans as participants in a cosmic drama. *Alcheringa* informs all institutions in Aboriginal society; the stories are constantly lived out through storytelling, rituals, songs, art, and celebrations. In the northern parts of Australia there are tribal Aborigines who continue to practice their sacred ceremonies, such as corroborees, rites of initiation, renewal ceremonies, burials, and ceremonies associated with the visitation of sacred sites.

Gideon Goosen

See Also Vol. 1: *Anglicanism/Episcopalianism, Christianity, Pentecostalism, Roman Catholicism*

Bibliography

Bentley, Peter. *The Uniting Church in Australia.* Canberra: Australian Government Service, 1996.

Campion, Edmund. *Australian Catholics.* Melbourne: Viking, 1987.

Duncan, Bruce. *Crusade or Conspiracy? Catholics and the Anti-Communist Struggle in Australia.* Sydney: University of New South Wales Press, 2001.

Goosen, G. *Australian Theologies: Themes and Methodologies into the Third Millennium.* Strathfield: St. Pauls Publications, 2000.

Habel, Norm, ed. *Rainbow Spirit Theology: Towards Australian Aboriginal Theology.* Blackburn: HarperCollins, 1997.

Hughes, Philip, ed. *Australian Religious Communities: A Multimedia Exploration.* Kew: Christian Research Association, 2000. CD-ROM.

Kaye, Bruce. *Anglicanism in Australia: A History.* Melbourne: Melbourne University Press, 2002.

Molony, John. *History of Australia: The Story of 200 Years.* Ringwood: Viking, 1987.

———. *The Roman Mould of the Australian Catholic Church.* Melbourne: Melbourne University Press, 1969.

O'Farrell, Patrick. *The Catholic Church and Community: An Australian History.* 3rd rev. ed. Sydney: University of New South Wales Press, 1992.

———. *The Irish in Australia: 1788 to Present.* 3rd ed. Sydney: University of New South Wales Press, 2000.

Tacey, David. *The Spirituality Revolution: The Emergence of Contemporary Spirituality.* Sydney: HarperCollins, 2003.

Turner, Naomi. *Catholics in Australia: A Social History.* Melbourne: CollinsDove, 1992.

Wilson, Bruce. *Can God Survive in Australia?* Sydney: Albatross Books, 1983.

Austria

POPULATION 8.2 million

ROMAN CATHOLIC 73.6 percent

PROTESTANT 4.7 percent

MUSLIM 4.2 percent

JEWISH 0.1 percent

NONRELIGIOUS 12.0 percent

NOT INDICATED 2.0 percent

OTHER 3.4 percent

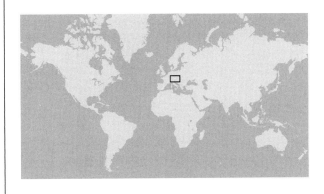

Country Overview

INTRODUCTION Austria covers a total area of 32,368 square miles and shares borders with the Czech Republic, Germany, Hungary, Italy, Liechtenstein, Slovakia, Slovenia, and Switzerland. In the west and south it is mountainous, and the eastern and northern margins are mostly flat.

With roughly 6 million Roman Catholics, Austria is a Catholic stronghold in the center of Europe. Reduced from a powerful (Austro-Hungarian) empire before World War I to a small republic by the end of World War II, the permanently neutral country has a religious landscape that has developed alongside those of other European countries in the postwar period. While the Catholic Church continues to play a formidable role in political and social affairs, the general trend of secularization, prominent even among Catholics, has eroded the church's influence in Austria. Further, notwithstanding the Roman Catholic Counter-Reformation of the sixteenth and seventeenth centuries, the multinational heritage and religious heterogeneity of this same Habsburg Empire has determined the country's traditional secular climate of religious tolerance, a national characteristic that developed in the late eighteenth century and has been observed for the most part ever since.

RELIGIOUS TOLERANCE The Austrian constitution provides for freedom of religion, and in general there have been no violations of this right. There are 13 officially recognized religions. The status of religious organizations is governed by the 1874 Law on the Recognition of Churches and by the 1998 Law on the Status of Religious Confessional Communities, which established three legal categories: (1) officially recognized religious societies, (2) religious confessional communities, and (3) associations. Once a religious confessional community is officially recognized by the government, it has juridical standing and is granted state subsidies for religious teachers at both public and private schools.

On the holiday of Corpus Christi, the lakes of Upper Austria are the sites of colorful flower boat processions. The origins of this tradition date back to the early seventeenth century. © K.M. WESTERMANN/CORBIS.

Fourteen Christian churches have been engaged in an interreligious dialogue within the Ecumenical Council of Austrian Churches (established in 1958), and the Austrian Roman Catholic Church traditionally has been keen on maintaining a good atmosphere between the Christian, Jewish, and Islamic communities. While there are generally amicable relations among the various religious groups in Austria, some nonrecognized minor religious groups (most prominently Jehovah's Witnesses and the Church of Scientology) have sporadically expressed discontent with the legal status granted them and have reported a tendency of societal mistrust and discrimination against their followers.

Major Religion

ROMAN CATHOLICISM

DATE OF ORIGIN 172/173 C.E.
NUMBER OF FOLLOWERS 6 million

HISTORY Since 172/173 C.E., the date of the so-called Rain Miracle of Carnuntum (in which a Roman army was released from thirst by a rainfall that was said to have been brought about by a prayer), Christianity has been the most influential religion in the region.

In the time of Emperor Augustus (reigned 27 B.C.E.–14 C.E.) the Romans took possession of the land south of the Danube. Under Emperor Diocletian the persecution of Christians led to the murder of the Roman soldier Florianus in 304. On the spot where he was buried (in what is now Upper Austria) stands the monastery of Saint Florian, a house of Augustinian canons. From about 453 to 482 Saint Severinus made efforts to evangelize the region of Noricum along the Danube and became widely known for his preaching and prophesying.

Following the decline of the Roman Empire (395 C.E.), various peoples came into and through the region that is now Austria. In about the year 650 the Croats were the first to be converted to Christianity by Roman priests. The Bajuvari (Bavarians), a German people from the west, spread themselves north of the Enns in the Danube district (now Upper Austria). Saint Rupert, Bishop of Worms, baptized the Bavarian duke Theodo at Ratisbon (Regensburg) and founded the monastery of Saint Peter in Salzburg (c. 700), which has remained continually active since its founding. Nonnberg, the Benedictine cloister for women in Salzburg, was founded by Saint Rupert's niece Ehrentraut and is the world's oldest continually active nunnery. In 798 Charlemagne raised the episcopal see of Salzburg to an archbishopric. At the turn of the first millennium the early Babenberg rulers (Leopold I and Henry I) moved their abode from Melk to Vienna. One of their successors, Henry II "Jasomirgott" (1141–77), became the first duke of Austria. In 1282 the Catholic Habsburg dynasty took over Austria, which they would govern until 1918.

During the Reformation period the overwhelming majority of the German-speaking population in the Habsburg dominions converted to Protestantism, mainly Lutheranism. In the principality of the Tirol, however, the majority remained Catholic, with a strong minority following Anabaptist convictions. The Counter-Reformation of the sixteenth and seventeenth centuries brought Catholicism into uncontested dominance in Austria, often through violent measures, such as expulsions of those not willing to reconvert to Catholicism. The last expulsion was in 1837, when the small Protestant community of the Zillertal was forced into exile. The Counter-Reformation was less successful in only a few areas, including those now covered by the federal provinces of Carinthia and Burgenland, where Protestant percentages remain somewhat higher than the national average. In the Habsburg Empire the relationship between the Austrian imperial state and the Roman Catholic Church was close. The Empire's stance toward other religious communities was, however, generally tolerant, a remnant of the enlightened absolutism of the late eighteenth century.

After the fall of the Austro-Hungarian Empire in 1918, and during the interwar period, there evolved a form of "political Catholicism" whose antiliberal and antisocialist views amounted to support of the authoritarian "Christian corporate state" under Chancellor Engelbert Dollfuss. Following the *Anschluss* (annexation) of Austria to Hitler's Germany in 1938, the Roman Catholic Church first sought to accommodate itself with the Nazis, but then it began to assume an oppositional stance (though without offensively confronting the Nazi regime). In postwar Austria the Roman Catholic Church has largely abstained from interfering with world politics and has adopted a policy of "equidistance" toward all political parties.

EARLY AND MODERN LEADERS Among the most important Catholic historical leaders in Austria was Virgilius (c. 700–784), bishop of Salzburg; missionary of the Alpine Slavs, he is called the "Apostle of Carinthia." Gebhard (c. 1010–88), archbishop of Salzburg, founded the episcopal see Gurk in Carinthia, and Eberhard II (c. 1170–1246), archbishop of Salzburg, founded the episcopal see Graz-Seckau in Styria. Nikolaus Seyringer (1360–1425), rector of the University of Vienna and abbot of Melk, was responsible for the thorough reorganization of the Benedictine monasteries known as "Melker Reform."

Melchior Klesl (1552–1630), bishop and the first cardinal of Vienna, was the leader of the Counter-Reformation in Austria. Abraham a Sancta Clara (Johann Ulrich Megerle, 1640–1709) was legendary for

his literary, rhetorical, and homiletic skills, which influenced even German romantic authors such as Schiller and Jean Paul. Saint Klemens Maria Hofbauer (1751–1820), called the "Apostle of Vienna," was head of the Viennese romanticism circle. He was canonized in 1909. Josef Othmar von Rauscher (1797–1875), the archbishop and cardinal of Vienna, initiated the concordat with Rome in 1855.

Ignaz Seipel (1876–1932), prelate, served as chancellor (1922–24 and 1926–29). Theodor Innitzer (1875–1955), cardinal of Vienna, served as minister for social administration (1929/30) under Chancellor Johann Schober; Innitzer was later a supporter of the "Christian corporate state" and a proponent of the concordat of 1933. Franz König (born in 1905), cardinal of Vienna (1956–85), was one of the leading figures of the Second Vatican Council.

MAJOR THEOLOGIANS AND AUTHORS Franz Stephan Rautenstrauch (1734–85) advocated reforming theology by reinforcing the disciplines with the highest practical relevance. Anton Günther (1784–1863) set forth his original idea of a modern Christian philosophy, which was critical of what he recognized as secular modern philosophy's pantheism. Franz Joseph Freindaller (1753–1825) founded and edited a theological journal called *Theologisch-praktische Monathschrift* (1802–21; Theological-Practical Monthly), which since 1848 has appeared as *Theologisch-praktische Quartalschrift* (Theological-Practical Quarterly) and is the second-oldest theological quarterly in German. Carl Werner (1821–88) was the first to do proper research in the philosophy and theology of the Middle Ages and had an essential influence on scholars in medieval studies.

Other important theologians of the nineteenth and early twentieth centuries include Leopold Fonk (the founder and long-term rector of the Papal Bible Institute in Rome), Hermann Zschokke, Franz Xaver Pölzl, and Theodor Innitzer. Cardinal Franz König and Ferdinand Klostermann (1907–82) were among the masterminds of the Second Vatican Council. The most prominent theologian of the council, Karl Rahner (1904–84), was a professor of dogmatic theology at the Jesuit Faculty of Innsbruck. Christoph Schönborn (born in 1945) contributed to the actual "Catechism of the Catholic Church" (1992) as its chief editorial secretary.

HOUSES OF WORSHIP AND HOLY PLACES Among the most important Catholic churches and monasteries in Austria are Saint Stephen's Cathedral in Vienna; the Benedictine monasteries Saint Peter's Abbey (in Salzburg) and Kremsmünster; Klosterneuburg, the Augustinian Canon's monastery near Vienna; and the Cistercian monasteries Heiligenkreuz (which, founded in 1133, is the second-oldest Cistercian abbey in existence) and Wilhering.

The basilica of Mariazell dates to 1157, when a Benedictine monk is said to have built a cell for his beloved statue of the Madonna (called Magna Mater Austriae). It is Austria's best-known place of pilgrimage. The Benedictine abbey of Melk is one of Europe's great jewels of baroque architecture, as is the library of the Benedictine monastery at Admont, whose hall represents the world's most spacious monastic library.

In the town of Saint Wolfgang on the Wolfgangsee, there is a church that was allegedly founded by the saint of the same name (c. 924–94), the bishop of Regensburg. It became a highly popular place for pilgrims, surpassed in the fifteenth and sixteenth centuries only by Rome, Einsiedeln, and Aachen.

Heiligenblut in Carinthia is a town whose name (meaning "holy blood") derives from a legend about a Danish nobleman who, on his way back from Constantinople, carried with him a vial supposedly containing a few drops of Christ's blood, now kept in a reliquary in the Gothic parish church.

WHAT IS SACRED? Catholics in Austria do not diverge from other Catholics in what they consider sacred, but they have always emphasized the worship of the Holy Cross and the Trinity, as well as the Immaculata (the Virgin Mary), a practice that culminated in Holy Roman Emperor Ferdinand III dedicating Austria to the Virgin Mary in 1647.

HOLIDAYS AND FESTIVALS In Austria most of the traditional holidays of Catholicism are also official national holidays. On Corpus Christi the lakes of Upper Austria are the sites of colorful flower boat processions, the origins of which date back to the early seventeenth century. They involve the participation of many people, worshipers as well as tourists. The same holiday is also hugely celebrated in the Tyrolean village of Villnöss, where it lasts for three days.

MODE OF DRESS There are no particular dress codes for Catholics in Austria, but followers in nonurban areas often wear traditional rural clothes (*tracht,* which vary from region to region) on special holidays.

DIETARY PRACTICES No special dietary practices belong to Austrian Catholics. There is, however, a wide tradition of developing special vegetarian Lenten dishes to comply with the respective dietary prescriptions of the holiday.

RITUALS Most Austrian Catholic rituals are Christian reinterpretations of formerly pagan habits and popular beliefs. In addition to the boat processions on Corpus Christi, Austrian Catholics make a unique pilgrimage over four Carinthian mountains, called the Vier-Berge-Lauf (a ritual mentioned as early as 1612). This traditionally starts the night before Dreinagelfreitag (three-nails Friday), the second Friday after Easter, and it lasts for almost 24 hours.

RITES OF PASSAGE Austrian Catholics observe the traditional Catholic rites of passage, including christening, first Communion, confirmation, wedding, and extreme unction (rites for the sick). In Austria the godfather or godmother plays an important role; as the spiritual father or mother, he or she is responsible for the godchild's religious education and welfare.

MEMBERSHIP In response to a significant decrease in membership in Austria during the last decades of the twentieth century, the Catholic Church has redoubled its efforts to recruit new (or regain former) members. It has been most successful when it has taken open, nonpartisan political action on social welfare and when it has criticized government measures that are biased against the unemployed, the sick, the poor, and other marginalized groups. Many Austrians support these activities by continuing to pay the official "church tax" (about one percent of their annual income), while remaining detached from religious parish life (a common stance of the *Taufscheinkatholiken,* or "baptismal certificate Catholics"). A number of Austrians also sponsor Christian institutions without themselves being members of one of the major Christian confessions.

SOCIAL JUSTICE As the Austrian state has increasingly denied responsibility for the poor, Christian organizations have come to take charge of basic aspects of social welfare and human rights. The Catholic Church in Austria espouses the so-called preferential option for the poor, an eminent principle of Catholic social teaching that entails respecting the poor and acknowledging the special needs they have in society.

SOCIAL ASPECTS Although Catholic doctrine identifies marriage and children as two of the most important aspects of life, young Austrian Catholics have been increasingly less committed to these institutions. As a result, divorce rates have risen, while birth rates have sunk.

POLITICAL IMPACT If there is any considerable political impact of the Roman Catholic Church in Austria, it is most prominent where the church takes concrete measures toward improving social welfare and where it acts as a major nongovernmental organization.

The separation between church and state has been keenly observed in postwar Austria, and Catholic views influence political decisions only indirectly. Since the 1970s ideological tensions between the left and the church have been eased, largely through the common efforts of socialist chancellor Bruno Kreisky and the cardinal of Vienna, Franz König. Support for traditional Christian values has been set forth not only by the Austrian People's Party (Österreichische Volkspartei, or ÖVP)—which calls itself a Christian party—but also by other parties, including the Social Democrats (Sozialdemokratische Partei Österreichs) and the Greens, in critique of ÖVP policies.

CONTROVERSIAL ISSUES The few controversial issues that are discussed among Austrian Catholics with varying intensity include abortion, which was legalized in Austria in the early 1970s. Another issue is homosexuality among the clergy; this controversy is embedded in a broader debate about the church's moral stance toward homosexuality, a stance that is widely considered hypocritical.

There has also been controversy about the hierarchical structures within the church, particularly concerning Rome's appointment of bishops (sometimes without the consent of, or against the express wish of, the representatives and people of the local diocese) and the participation and ecclesiastical status of women.

CULTURAL IMPACT For centuries the Roman Catholic Church has significantly influenced Austrian artists. Austrian composers such as Haydn, Mozart, Schubert, Liszt, and Bruckner have achieved some of the greatest masterpieces of classical (and particularly of church) music.

Many highlights of Austrian literature, from Frau Ava's poem "Life of Christ" (c. 1120) to Franz Grillparzer, Nikolaus Lenau, and Adalbert Stifter in the nineteenth century, owe much to the Catholic convictions of their creators. The same is true of art, from the Gothic painters/sculptors Hans von Judenburg and the Master of Grosslobming, to the eighteenth-century painters Martin Johann "Kremser" Schmidt and Franz Anton Maulbertsch, to the nineteenth-century painter Josef Führich. Architects who have worked in the spirit and realm of Catholicism include Johann Bernhard Fischer von Erlach and Jakob Prandtauer in the baroque/rococo eras as well as Friedrich von Schmidt in the nineteenth century.

The positive reference to Christianity prevailed with some twentieth-century writers and artists, such as Paula von Preradović (who wrote the lyrics of Austria's postwar national anthem), Paula Grogger, Herbert Boeckl, and Fritz Wotruba. In the late twentieth century the tendency had, however, largely given way to criticism of Christian doctrine and its Roman Catholic representatives. The concrete poetry and experimental texts of the Vienna Group and of Ernst Jandl; the poems of Christine Lavant; the novels of Thomas Bernhard, Peter Handke, Franz Innerhofer, and Josef Winkler; and the paintings of Arnulf Rainer, Hermann Nitsch, and Günter Brus all portray and treat Catholic views and habits in a controversial, even provocative, manner.

Other Religions

Officially recognized religions in Austria (other than Catholic) are the Old Catholic Church, the Protestant (Lutheran and Calvinist) Church, the Greek Oriental Church (Orthodox, including the Serbian, Romanian, Russian, and Bulgarian Orthodox Churches), the Armenian Apostolic Church, the New Apostolic Church, the Syrian Orthodox Church, Judaism, Islam, Buddhism, the Church of Jesus Christ of Latterday Saints, the Methodist Church, and the Coptic Church.

Muslims make up the largest group among these, a fact that is partly a result of Austria's official policy in the 1970s and early 1980s to actively invite foreign workers (most notably from Turkey and the former Yugoslavia) to come into the country. The wars in the former Yugoslavia in the 1990s sent to Austria another wave of immigrants, most of whom were followers of Islam or Serbian Orthodoxy.

Until 1933–38 Austria's Jewish population had been much larger and had an immense influence on Austrian culture and society, providing the intellectual ferment of an entire epoch (most notably in Vienna at the turn of the twentieth century). Having been forced into emigration or almost entirely killed by the Nazi regime, the Jewish community has never regained its former strength and impact, much to the detriment of Austria's achievements and international reputation in terms of science and art.

Florian Uhl and Artur R. Boelderl

See Also Vol. 1: *Christianity, Roman Catholicism*

Bibliography

Austria—A Country Study. Library of Congress. 18 Dec. 2003. http://lcweb2.loc.gov/frd/cs/attoc.html.

Brook-Shepherd, Gordon. *The Austrians: A Thousand-Year Odyssey*. New York: Carroll and Graf, 1997.

"International Religious Freedom Report 2002—Austria." Bureau of Democracy, Human Rights, and Labor. 7 Oct. 2002. U.S. Department of State. 18 Dec. 2003. www.state.gov/g/drl/rls/irf/2002/13920.htm.

Kann, Robert A. *A History of the Habsburg Empire, 1526–1918*. Berkeley: University of California Press, 1975.

Klostermann, Ferdinand, and Erika Weinzierl, eds. *Kirche in Österreich, 1918–1968*. 2 vols. Vienna: Herold, 1966–67.

Leeb, Rudolf, Maximilian Liebmann, Georg Scheibelreiter, and Peter G. Tropper. *Geschichte des Christentums in Österreich: Von der Spätantike bis zur Gegenwart*. Vienna: Ueberreuter, 2003.

Liebmann, Maximilian. *Theodor Innitzer und der Anschluss: Österreichs Kirche 1938*. Graz: Styria, 1988.

Wodka, Josef. *Kirche in Österreich: Wegweiser durch ihre Geschichte*. Vienna: Herder, 1959.

Azerbaijan

POPULATION 7,798,497

MUSLIM 86 percent

OTHER 14 percent

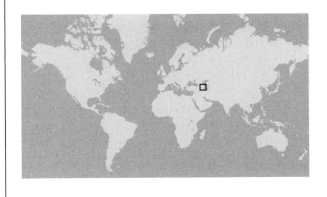

Country Overview

INTRODUCTION The Republic of Azerbaijan, bordered on the east by the Caspian Sea, was until 1991 a part of the former Soviet Union. To the north is Russia, to the northwest is Georgia, to the west is Armenia, and to the south is Iran. Geopolitically Azerbaijan is located at the junction of Europe and Asia, East and West, thus forming a crossing point for nations, cultures, and religions. This has resulted in a great diversity of religions in the country.

Historically the territory of Azerbaijan stretched across the eastern Caucasus and northwestern Iran. In the nineteenth century Azerbaijan was divided between Russia and Iran by the treaties of Gulistan (1813) and Turkmenchay (1828), which established "Southern Azerbaijan" as part of Iran and passed "Northern Azer-

baijan" (now the Republic of Azerbaijan) to Russia. Twenty percent of the present territory of the Republic of Azerbaijan is occupied by Armenian military forces.

Prehistoric fire cults played an important role in the religious history of Azerbaijan; fire worship in Azerbaijan and the Caucasus was enabled by natural fire spouts present across the landscape. The name of the country was possibly derived from the Persian words *azer,* meaning "fire," and *baigan,* meaning "place," and Azerbaijanis most commonly identify themselves as "Azeris." Zoroastrianism played a central role in the formation of Azerbaijani culture.

Christianity arrived in the area of Azerbaijan in the first century C.E. By the fourth century (313) the country was Christianized. Islam, which is dominant in Azerbaijan, was the religion of foreign invaders. By the seventh century Arab conquests had resulted in the conversion to Islam and had also introduced vigorous policies of cultural and religious assimilation.

RELIGIOUS TOLERANCE While Shia Islam is the dominant religion of Azerbaijan, Shiites are tolerant of (and indeed are strongly influenced by) animism and Zoroastrianism, and religious authority functions independently of the state. To promote religious freedom, President Heydar Aliyev in 2001 established the State Committee of the Azerbaijan Republic for Work with Religious Associations of Azerbaijan. The committee officially recognized for the first time many religious groups, including Islam, Christianity, Judaism, Jehovah's Witnesses, and others. While not all religious adherents are actively faithful, many attend a variety of religious services

An Azerbaijani woman visits the grave of a loved one. Muslim tradition forbids women to visit the cemetery for 40 days after a funeral; it is thought that they could worry the soul of the deceased. © DAVID TURNLEY/CORBIS.

to exercise the spiritual freedom they were denied under Soviet rule.

Major Religion

ISLAM

DATE OF ORIGIN 667 C.E.
NUMBER OF FOLLOWERS 6.7 million

HISTORY Unlike Christianity, Arabic Islam spread through conquest rather than missionary activity. In the seventh century the fall of Sassanian Iran and the subsequent acceptance of Arab vassalage by Javanshir, the king of Aran (northern Azerbaijan), were factors in the spread of Islam to Azerbaijan. Azerbaijanis resisted Arab conquest. In 816 Babek, a follower of the Khurrami religious movement, an anti-Islamic sect, led 300,000 adherents to take up arms against the Arabs in what became known as Babek's Revolt (816–838). They based their struggle on Zoroastrian doctrine: to fight evil for the final victory of Mazda, the Supreme God.

The revolt failed, however, and from the first half of the seventh century to the beginning of the eighth, Islam moved into the most accessible, flat regions of both Zoroastrian southern Azerbaijan and Christian

Aran. In the resulting encounters, both sides drew from new cultural traditions, and Azerbaijan gradually evolved into a broader and more world-oriented Muslim culture.

Today the majority of Azerbaijanis identify with Shiism above Sunnism, but in practice most Muslims in Azerbaijan do not see themselves as defined or constrained by these categories. Indeed, one might better describe Islam in Azerbaijan as a pervasive social consciousness.

EARLY AND MODERN LEADERS In the Middle Ages, the era of the Muslim Renaissance in Azerbaijan, there were a number of notable Islamic leaders, especially Sufis (Muslim mystics). Ahmad al-Bardiji (844–914) was one of the first Sufi leaders. Other renowned representatives of Sufism were Sheikh Baba Kukhi Bakuvi (948–1050), Sheikh Safieddin Ardabili (1252–1334), Sheikh Sadraddin Musa (1334–92), Naimi Tabrizi (1339–1402), and Sheikh Ibrahim (1447–60), whose many followers accepted the Shiite trend of Islam. *Pir* (which means both a saint and a holy place) is another name for the spiritual Azerbaijan Sufi teachers. Sufi traditions were prohibited after the Soviet occupation of Azerbaijan. In modern Azerbaijan Sufi-style practices have become the major form of religious practice.

Prominent contemporary leaders include Sheikhülislam (a term meaning "leader of Islam") Allahshükür Pashazadeh, chairman of Caucasian Muslim's Ecclesiastical Board; Haji Cabir, rector of Baku Islam University; and Rafik Aliev, chairman of the State Committee of the Azerbaijan Republic for Work with Religious Associations.

MAJOR THEOLOGIANS AND AUTHORS Azerbaijan's Islamic authors of the Middle Ages include Sheikh Nizami Ganjevi (1141–1204) from Ganja, who wrote the well-known, five-poem *Khamsa;* Sirajaddin Urmavi (1198–1283); and Imammeddin Nasimi (1369–1417), a Sufi poet and theologian. Muhammad Fizuli (1494–1556), Aghahusein Khalkhali, and Sadraddin Shirvani (seventeenth century) were also well-known Islamic theologians.

HOUSES OF WORSHIP AND HOLY PLACES The most common house of worship in Azerbaijan is the mosque. Compared with many other Muslim countries, Azerbaijan has fewer rules concerning the use of mosques and other temple spaces. The less formal temple spaces are called *pirs*. Muslims work to maintain these shrines to local saints. Many historians believe that *pirs* were first established by followers of indigenous forms of animism practiced long before Islam, Christianity, or Zoroastrianism.

WHAT IS SACRED? Despite the Soviet campaign to eradicate religion and, particularly, Islamic traditions in Azerbaijan, many indigenous traditions connected to flora and fauna survived and remain popular. The "stone plant" (*Celtic caucasica*) and elm tree (*Ulmus densa*) are considered to have magical effects, and people support this magic with prayers from the Koran. Azeris make amulets engraved with Muslim prayers to ward off the evil eye. Butterflies, especially moths, have been considered sacred for millennia. They are perceived as carrying the spirits of Muslim ancestors; it is a great sin to kill them. Because the prophet Muhammad was said to be fond of cats, they are highly regarded. Doves are perceived as untouchable creatures—heralds of angels—whose murder can bring damnation. Spiders are also highly revered, following a belief that a spider once helped Muhammad escape his enemies.

HOLIDAYS AND FESTIVALS The most popular festival and one of the most ancient holidays is Novruz (meaning "new day"), the Great Feast. Although Novruz (21 March) was forbidden during the Soviet reign, Azeris were able to preserve the festival's traditions. People prepare to celebrate it 40 days after the beginning of winter, and they consider Novruz to be the New Year. They buy new clothes, visit relatives and friends, and clean houses and yards. The main symbols of Novruz are *samani* (fresh green shoots of wheat) and fire. People build community fires throughout their neighborhoods.

Novruz is popularly considered to be the birthday of Zoroaster, one of the prophets respected by Islam. On the other hand, Novruz is deeply connected with Islamic traditions. The very day of Novruz is sacred, as on that day the prophet Muhammad pulled down the idols in Kaaba, the main Muslim temple in Mecca. Special prayers from the Koran, such as "Hamd" and "Annas," are recited during the festival.

Kurban Bayram (meaning "sacrifice festival") is an Islamic holiday that takes place on the 10th day of the 12th month of the lunar calendar, 70 days after Ramadan. Its origin is in the Koranic stories of Abraham, who agreed to sacrifice his only son, Ismail, to God. Instead, God sent Abraham a lamb as an offering from Paradise.

This holiday is also called "the sacrifice for Ismail." Azeris believe that Kurban is a universal holiday, as it ended human sacrifices. There are two other Muslim celebrations in Azerbaijan: Ramadan (the Muslim fasting period) and Mukharram (Shiite mourning rituals for Hussein, the grandson of Muhammad).

MODE OF DRESS During the Soviet period Azerbaijanis were discouraged from wearing distinctive national dress. Today men and women wear Western-style clothing. Some traditional features remain, however, in headdress. The most popular type of female head covering is the *kalaghai* (or *chargat*), a square, thin, silk kerchief. Headdress is important when attending mosques and in the dressing of Muslim officials. Muslim men wear a knitted skullcap resembling the Uzbek *akarchin*. Azerbaijan clergy wear white clothes.

DIETARY PRACTICES Rice is almost sacred; it is considered "saint's food." It is used in a wide number of dishes called *plov*, which are components of all Muslim celebrations. It is believed that if a person dreams of the deceased, he or she should cook *plov* and recite "Ya Sin" (*surah* 36) from the Koran (considered spiritual food for all living and dead souls). Mutton is the most widely consumed meat, especially during Kurban. Traditional foods take on a religious character when consumed in tandem with religious celebrations.

RITUALS One of the most prominent Muslim customs is *nazir*, a personal pledge, given in a holy place, to make a sacrifice on the occasion of childbirth either by giving money or by offering a sheep. Women without children often visit local *pirs* and pledge to observe *nazir* if a child is born to them. Childbirth is regarded as a period of spiritual mystery, and strong precautions against the evil eye are taken within the first 40 days of the child's life; special prayers are recited from the Koran in the morning and late afternoon.

Name-giving ceremonies differ throughout Azerbaijan. In the Qazax region (west Azerbaijan) parents give their child two names as a measure of protection against evil spirits; the second name is sometimes held in secret for the child's entire life and even after death. Many claim that this also has roots in Avestan and Zoroastrian traditions.

There are several marriage ceremonies, from engagement to wedding. A matchmaker comes to the home of the potential bride, and if the family agrees to the match, they serve sweet tea, and the bride puts on her wedding ring. It is obligatory for a couple to visit the mosque before and after the wedding.

Muslim tradition forbids women to visit the cemetery for 40 days after a funeral; it is thought that they could worry the soul of the deceased. Every Thursday for 40 days and on the anniversary of the death, people visit the grave and hold a special meal called *ehsan* (funeral repast).

RITES OF PASSAGE There are no religious rites of passage in Azerbaijan. Nonetheless, the Koran is studied by girls and boys from 5 to 12 years old. The ages from 5 to 12 are generally recognized as important among Azerbaijani Muslim families wishing to continue the ecclesiastical education of their children.

MEMBERSHIP There are no significant efforts by Muslims in Azerbaijan to convert people from other faiths.

SOCIAL JUSTICE Most Azerbaijanis consider Islam their moral guide. Muslim believers try to help fight poverty, which has become more widespread since the collapse of the Soviet Union. Azerbaijani Muslims believe they can receive forgiveness for the long years of Soviet godlessness if they are able to help each other in this difficult period. Islamic institutions actively work against poverty, but there are no specific Muslim programs dedicated to this cause. Muslim-based human rights programs deal mainly with matters of religious tolerance and interrelations.

SOCIAL ASPECTS Marriage is considered both a social and a religious obligation for Azeris. The choice of a future husband or wife has rigid regulations. Traditionally a future husband should be provided with home and work (by the wife's relatives); a wife should be a virgin and educated. These regulations are distinct from those of many other Muslim countries, as they are not so much a matter of social concern but rather associated with moral self-esteem for both Azerbaijan men and women. Notably, too, this criterion is not applied for mixed marriages.

Family is sacred and based on the respect for seniority. Right conduct of parents is especially emphasized. Women's responsibilities have traditionally been confined to domestic and educational activities, and men have been in charge of the material prosperity of the family. Family relationships in Azerbaijan have been changing, however, and women have increasingly begun to move beyond the household to the workplace and social spheres.

POLITICAL IMPACT In 1990s, in the political chaos that followed the collapse of the Soviet Union, Islam reemerged as an important source of social and spiritual cohesion. Azerbaijan is now a secular state, and the constitution defines the country as a "sovereign democratic republic." There are many political parties, New Azerbaijan being the most dominant. Religious parties do not have representatives in the parliament (Milli Majlis), but Islam influences national cultural and educational policies.

CONTROVERSIAL ISSUES The Azerbaijan constitution and daily life itself have been considerably influenced by Western social values. But unlike in large cities, where such events as the birth of a child and abortions are regulated, rural areas have their own ethnic and cultural practices, and there is no regulation of divorce, abortion, and birth.

Nevertheless, because women are more religiously active than men and are considered the carriers of Muslim values, they tend to adhere to Islamic norms of conduct. They seldom seek abortions, preferring to give birth to a child (thus having many children). While a divorced woman can marry again, she is expected not to have a lover between marriages, as this would be detrimental to her reputation and could make it impossible for her to marry again.

CULTURAL IMPACT Islam is a central theme celebrated in mugham, a highly developed musical style in Azerbaijani classical music. It is also prominent in medieval miniature graphic arts, in ornamental painting, in classical and modern poetry, and in contemporary prose. Important works by such authors as Nizami Ganjavi (an Azerbaijani poet, philosopher, and thinker who lived in the twelfth century) looked to unite the religious experiences of Islam with wider conceptions of global unity. Azerbaijani poetry bloomed in the medieval period with the works of Muslims such as Fizuli and Nasimi.

The Tabriz Islamic school of miniature painting (or *Mutter Schule,* as it was called by the German scientist Philipp Walter Schulz) deeply influenced arts all across Asia. These miniatures are held in London.

Other Religions

The magi of Atropatena (the ancient name of the region) influenced the development of Zoroastrianism, the world's first monotheistic religion. It in turn played a central role in the formation of Azerbaijani culture. It has been perceived as an indigenous religion by Azeris.

The Zoroastrian religious practices of modern-day Muslim Azeris follow from Zoroaster's significant role in Islam as one of the respected prophets and from his importance in Azerbaijan's history. According to Zoroastrian tradition in Azerbaijan and to Arab historians, the Holy Avesta (the sacred book of Zoroastrianism) was written in the caves of the Apsheron Peninsula on the Caspian shores.

The main temple of fire worshipers in Surakhani (around Baku) serves as a museum as well as a place of worship for Azeris and foreigners, who gradually began to pilgrimage to Baku after the fall of the Soviet Union. Muslims visit the temple on Novruz (21 March, considered to be the birthday of Zoroaster) and during the month of Ramadan. Descendants of the magi, who have continued to live in Mughan (a region in Azerbaijan), combine Koranic prayers with their centuries-old mystical practices.

Christianity arrived in Aran (northern Azerbaijan) in the first century C.E., and by 313 the area had been Christianized. In the fifth century the Nestorian faith was adopted and practiced in Kish (modern-day Sheki, in northwestern Azerbaijan) and in monastic settlements. In the eighth century Arab emirs started ruling the area, and Armenians, with the help of Arabs, subordinated the Albanian Church, then dominant, to the church of Armenia.

The monk Mekhitar Gosh (1130–1213) from Ganja was renowned for his Law Code (1184), a guide for Christian social conduct. It was written at the request of Katholicos Stepannos III (1155–95), the head of the Albanian Church. After the spread of Islam, the Law Code helped Albanian Christians maintain their religious practice, beginning in the early twelfth century.

The Albanian Church maintained its independence both in matters of faith and in the election of its head until 1836, when the Russian tsar, Nicholas I, dissolved the church. Many Albanian churches (functioning and in ruins) are still scattered throughout present-day Azerbaijan. The remaining Christian Azeris have struggled for the Albanian Church's status to be restored. Jesus is respected among Muslim Azeris; he is considered equal to the prophet Adam, making Christianity and churches the subject of special respect. Muslim Azeris visit churches (even church ruins, which they call *pirs*) on special Muslim occasions.

Maya Iskenderova

See Also Vol. I: *Islam, Shia Islam, Sunni Islam, Zoroastrianism*

Bibliography

Ernst, Herzfeld. *The Persian Empire.* Wiesbaden: F. Steiner, 1968.

Dragadze, Tamara. "Islam in Azerbaijan: The Position of Women." In *Muslim Women's Choices: Religious Belief and Social Reality.* Edited by Camillia Fawzi El-Solh and Judy Mabro. Oxford: Berg, 1994.

Swietochowski, Tadeusz. "Azerbaijan: The Hidden Faces of Islam." *World Policy Journal* 19, no.3 (2002): 69–76.

———. "Islam and the Growth of National Identity in Soviet Azerbaijan." In *Muslim Communities Reemerge: Historical Perspectives on Nationality, Politics, and Opposition in the Former Soviet Union and Yugoslavia.* Edited by Andreas Kappeler et al. Durham, N.C.: Duke University Press, 1994.

The Bahamas

POPULATION 303,611

BAPTIST 35.4 percent

ANGLICAN 15.2 percent

ROMAN CATHOLIC 13.5 percent

PENTECOSTAL 12.9 percent

METHODIST 4.3 percent

SEVENTH-DAY ADVENTIST 3.6
percent

NO RELIGIOUS AFFILIATION 2.9
percent

OTHER 12.2 percent

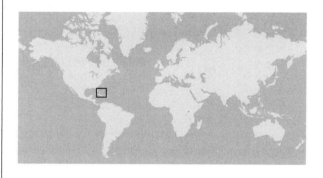

Country Overview

INTRODUCTION The Commonwealth of The Bahamas, an archipelago in the North Atlantic Ocean, lies north of Cuba and southeast of Florida. In 1492 C.E. Christopher Columbus made his historic landfall in The Bahamas. At that time the islands were inhabited by Native Americans whom anthropologists have variously identi-

fied as Lucayan, Taino Lucayan, and Arawak. With Columbus's arrival, Spain claimed the islands, but Spaniards never settled there. Within three decades of Iberian contact the Lucayan population had been taken from the islands and exterminated (as a result of harsh forced labor and European-borne diseases), and the islands remained uninhabited until 1648, when a group of English adventurers sailed from Bermuda to the island of Segatoo (now called Eleuthera).

Thereafter, the population of The Bahamas increased steadily. Immigrants included whites and free blacks from Bermuda, slaves imported from West Africa, white and black loyalists (who fled the United States at the end of the American Revolution) and their slaves, Black Seminoles (people of mixed Creek Indian and black ancestry) from Florida, and blacks liberated from slavery. The religious background of the white settlers was predominantly Anglican; a minority were Presbyterian and Methodist.

The Bahamas remained under British rule until 1973, when the archipelago became a sovereign nation within the Commonwealth. Today the majority of Bahamians are Christians, the largest percentage of whom are Baptists. Among the non-Christians are Muslims, Rastafarians, Jews, and Baha'is.

RELIGIOUS TOLERANCE Under The Bahamas Independence Order of 1973, all Bahamians are granted freedom of thought and religion. Christianity is taught in all schools, but a student may be exempted from these lessons. All church-sponsored schools receive annual grants from The Bahamas government. Church-state partnership is further evidenced by the fact that various churches administer—with state sponsorship—homes for children and the elderly.

Ecumenical activities in The Bahamas normally take place under the auspices of the Bahamas Christian Council. Its aims are to promote understanding and trust between the various churches, to engage in unified service efforts, and to witness for the Christian community in The Bahamas on matters of social or common concern. Membership in the council is open to every autonomous body of Christians.

Major Religion

BAPTIST CHURCHES

DATE OF ORIGIN 1790 C.E.
NUMBER OF FOLLOWERS 107,000

HISTORY In 1790 C.E. two freed slaves from the United States, Prince Williams and Sharper Morris, built Bethel Baptist Chapel on the Bahamian island of New Providence. Thereafter they traveled throughout The Bahamas, evangelizing slaves and establishing Baptist communities.

In 1833, at the request of the Bethel Baptist community, the Baptist Missionary Society (BMS) sent the missionary Joseph Burton from Jamaica to New Providence. Later that year Burton was joined by another BMS missionary, Kilner Pearson. In 1835 they built Zion Baptist Chapel, the first of the Baptist communities that now constitute the Zion Baptist Convention.

There are Baptist communities throughout The Bahamas. They are variously grouped into autonomous associations, conventions, unions, fellowships, and consortiums. In 1935 several of these bodies united to form the Bahamas Baptist Missionary and Educational Convention. In the 1960s and 1970s the Baptist communities supported the Progressive Liberal Party in its nonviolent struggle for The Bahamas to attain full adult suffrage (1962), a new constitution (1964), majority rule (1967), and political independence (1973).

EARLY AND MODERN LEADERS Rev. Harcourt W. Brown (1910–79), pastor of Bethel Baptist Church, was vocal during The Bahamas' social and political struggles of the 1960s. Under Brown, Bethel Baptist Church became a center for spiritual nurture and the distribution

On San Salvador Island in the Bahamas, a cross stands on the beach overlooking the sea. © FARRELL GREHAN/CORBIS.

of food and clothing. Brown was among a delegation of eight members of the Progressive Liberal Party who successfully pleaded The Bahamas' case for majority rule at the United Nations in 1965. Rev. Reuben E. Cooper (1913–80) was pastor of the Mission Baptist Church from 1940 to 1980. During the 1960s and '70s his concern for the poor led him to become involved in the Bahamas Christian Council, of which he served as chairman and then president.

Rev. Charles W. Saunders (born in 1930) has had a distinguished career as a public servant and as a Baptist pastor. He taught in many schools throughout The Bahamas and held administrative positions in the Ministry of Education. During his presidency (1981–97) of the Bahamas National Baptist Missionary and Educational Convention, the Bahamas Baptist Community College was established and the Baptist Bookstore was opened. Rev. William Thompson (born in 1943) succeeded Saunders as head of the convention in 1997 and was appointed president of the Bahamas Christian Council in 2004.

MAJOR THEOLOGIANS AND AUTHORS Rev. Philip A. Rahming (born in 1933), an educator, author, and Baptist pastor, served as president of the Bahamas Christian Council during the 1970s and '80s. In 2000 he was a member of a delegation of theologians sent by the Baptist World Alliance to the Vatican to discuss relations between Baptists and the Catholic Church. Rahming has written several books, including a biography (1986) of Martin Luther King, Jr.

HOUSES OF WORSHIP AND HOLY PLACES Bethel Baptist Church, in New Providence, is regarded as the mother church of the Baptist community in The Bahamas; the church that stands today was built in 1866 after the original building was destroyed by a hurricane. Saint John's Native Baptist Church, Zion Baptist Church, and Salem Baptist Church are other important churches.

WHAT IS SACRED? Like Baptists worldwide, Bahamian Baptists are careful to avoid anything that may even appear to be idolatrous, and therefore they have no sacred objects.

HOLIDAYS AND FESTIVALS There are no holidays or festivals distinct to Bahamian Baptists.

MODE OF DRESS Baptists in The Bahamas wear the same Western styles of dress as other Bahamians.

DIETARY PRACTICES Apart from an official ban on the consumption of alcohol and other intoxicants, Baptist churches in The Bahamas do not restrict the dietary practices of their members. The strict avoidance of alcohol consumption is not practiced by all members of the Bahamian Baptist community, neither laity nor clergy. When alcohol is consumed, it is normally done privately.

RITUALS Baptist worship is centered on the ministry of the Word, which emphasizes dynamic preaching and deemphasizes ritual. Bahamian Baptists celebrate the Lord's Supper once a month. On this occasion, grape juice is used instead of wine. Prayer is usually offered extemporaneously (praying "from the heart" rather than reading prayers from a book). There are Baptist weddings in The Bahamas, but there is nothing specifically Baptist about them; weddings are performed in accordance with the Marriage Act of The Bahamas.

RITES OF PASSAGE Like all Baptists, members in The Bahamas practice believer's baptism, which takes place when a candidate says that he or she believes. There is no particular age attached to this, although the voluntary nature of it precludes infant baptism. In The Bahamas baptism, in the form of triple immersion, usually takes place in the sea, but some Baptist church buildings have a baptismal pool.

MEMBERSHIP Attempts to increase membership in the Baptist faith in The Bahamas include an annual crusade sponsored by the Bahamas National Baptist Missionary and Educational Convention (which takes place in January) and revivals organized by individual Baptist churches. It is common for Bahamian Baptists to invite non-Baptists to attend their worship services.

SOCIAL JUSTICE Bahamian Baptists began their involvement in education in 1943, with the formation of the Jordan Memorial School (renamed Jordan Prince Williams School in 1961). Baptists also run the Charles W. Saunders Baptist School and the Bahamas Baptist Community College. There are often preschools attached to Baptist churches, particularly in New Providence.

SOCIAL ASPECTS Baptists in The Bahamas regard marriage and the family as institutions created by God, and they tend to frown on divorce and remarriage. The Baptists have been particularly vocal about this when divorced and remarried persons have sought public office. Many Baptist ministers urge Bahamian husbands and fathers to imitate the roles of husbands and fathers in biblical times.

POLITICAL IMPACT Baptists in The Bahamas first became involved in the politics of the islands when they joined the Methodists and Presbyterians in successfully agitating for the disestablishment and disendowment of the Anglican Church in 1869. The Baptists made their most significant impact on the Bahamian political scene in 1960s and the 1970s during the struggles for universal suffrage, constitutional reform, majority rule, and political independence. It is common for Baptist ministers in The Bahamas to put their pulpits at the disposal of politicians whose party they support, but many Baptists have been making efforts to discontinue this practice.

CONTROVERSIAL ISSUES There are two controversial issues on which Baptists in The Bahamas are not prepared to compromise: homosexuality and a proposed expansion of organized gambling. Both of these issues have implications for The Bahamas' major industry, tourism, especially regarding the arrival of "gay cruise ships" into Bahamian ports (an issue that arose in 1996) and the expansion of hotel construction throughout the archipelago. In both instances Baptists and other Christians are at odds with The Bahamas government.

CULTURAL IMPACT The Baptists' greatest artistic contribution to Bahamian culture is in the area of music, especially black spirituals, gospel music, rhyming spirituals, and a cappella singing. Rhyming spirituals, which originated in The Bahamas among Bahamians of African descent, recount a story in verse with two or more singers, one of whom is the rhyme or lead singer, and the other of whom is the bass singer. These types of music have, in turn, influenced Bahamian popular music.

Other Religions

The Anglican presence in The Bahamas dates back to 1648 C.E., when the English first arrived on the islands. In 1729 the Anglican Church was legally established and endowed as the Church of England in The Bahamas. With its establishment, the church was placed under the jurisdiction of the Bishop of London. The initial purpose of the church was to minister to the English colonists and to assist the government with the formation of a Christian society.

The latter purpose greatly affected the African diaspora in the islands, because Bahamian slave owners were mandated to see to the moral and religious instruction of their slaves with a view to making them members of the church. This action was further intensified in 1824, when the British Parliament established two bishoprics in the Anglophone Caribbean, one in Barbados and the other in Jamaica. Integral to the purpose of these two dioceses was preparing slaves in the British West Indies for emancipation in 1834 and for their full integration into civil society. In 1861 The Bahamas (along with the Turks and Caicos Islands) became a diocese separate from Jamaica.

In 1866 a devastating hurricane brought economic depression to The Bahamas. Church properties throughout the archipelago sustained damage. Because it was the state church, the Anglican Church had its properties repaired at the expense of the state. The Baptists, Methodists, and Presbyterians deemed this unfair and thus successfully agitated for the disestablishment and disendowment of the Church of England in The Bahamas in 1869. The first Bahamian-born bishop of the di-

ocese, Michael H. Eldon, was appointed in 1972. He was succeeded in 1996 by another Bahamian, Drexel W. Gomez, who was also elected archbishop of the province of the West Indies in 1998.

The Anglican Church in The Bahamas has maintained its historic partnership with the state in providing education for the nation's children. With state sponsorship, the Anglican Church also administers a home for children and a home for teenage boys.

The Methodists and the Presbyterians arrived in The Bahamas in early nineteenth century around the same time as the Baptists. Religious pluralism continued apace with the arrivals of Roman Catholics in 1858, Brethren in 1877, African Methodist Episcopalians in the 1880s, Seventh-day Adventists in 1893, Pentecostals in 1910, the Salvation Army in 1931, the Greek Orthodox Church in 1932, and the Assemblies of God in 1935. Since the early twentieth century there has also been a small Jewish population in The Bahamas.

Religious groups that arrived during the second half of the twentieth century include Lutherans, Muslims, Rastafarians, Baha'is, Latter-day Saints (Mormons), Christian Scientists, and Jehovah's Witnesses. Hinduism is practiced by members of the Guyanese and Indian populations, who were among the immigrants to The Bahamas in the second half of the twentieth century.

Like the Anglican Church, other churches in The Bahamas now operate schools with the sponsorship of the state. In addition, the Methodists, the Catholic Church, and the Brethren administer children's homes, and the Seventh-day Adventists run a home for the elderly. All of these homes are sponsored by the state.

Canon Kirkley C. Sands

See Also Vol. 1: *Christianity, Baptist Tradition; Anglican; Roman Catholicism*

Bibliography

Churton, Edward T. *The Island Missionary of The Bahamas.* London: J. Masters and Co., 1888.

Glinton-Meicholas, Patricia. *From The Void To The Wonderful.* Nassau, The Bahamas: Guanima Press, 1995.

Hervey, G. Winfred. *The Story of Baptist Missions in Foreign Lands.* St. Louis: Chancy R. Barns, 1885.

Myers, John Brown, ed. *The Centenary Volume of The Baptist Missionary Society, 1792–1892.* Second ed. London: Baptist Missionary Society, 1892.

Taggart, Norman W. *The Irish in World Methodism.* London: Epworth Press, 1986.

Williams, Colbert. *The Methodist Contribution to Education in The Bahamas.* Gloucester: A. Sutton, 1982.

Bahrain

POPULATION 656,397

MUSLIM 85 percent

OTHER 15 percent

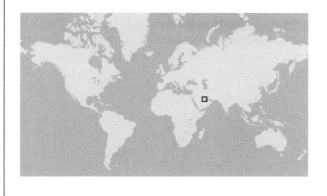

Persian, and Urdu are also spoken. Foreigners, including Christians, Buddhists, and Hindus, along with a tiny congregation of indigenous Jews, make up 15 percent of the population.

RELIGIOUS TOLERANCE Although the Sunni government in Bahrain allows some religious freedom, it discriminates against Shiites, banning them from the armed forces, the police, the Ministry of the Interior, and other positions. They allow foreign Christians and the Jewish community to practice their religious rituals. Despite being discriminated against, the Shiite sect enjoys more religious freedom in Bahrain than in Saudi Arabia.

Country Overview

INTRODUCTION The Kingdom of Bahrain (the official name since 2002) is an archipelago of more than 36 islands in the Persian Gulf east of Saudi Arabia. It is a Muslim country represented by both Sunni and Shiite sects, and the background of its culture and society is religion. Islamic beliefs pervade the sociopolitical life of the people. Unlike in neighboring countries, where Sunnis predominate, Shiite Muslims make up more than two-thirds of Bahrain's population. Even so, Sunni Islam is the belief held by those in the government, military, and corporate sectors. The country has been controlled by the Al-Khalifa dynasty for the past two centuries.

The country's official language is Arabic, and the word "Bahrain" in Arabic means "two seas." English,

Major Religion

ISLAM

DATE OF ORIGIN Seventh century C.E.
NUMBER OF FOLLOWERS 557,937

HISTORY The people of Bahrain embraced Islam peacefully in 629 C.E. after the Prophet Mohammed sent a messenger calling them to the faith. The country soon became a launching post for the spread of the new religion. Bahrainis, skilled in navigation, played an important role in spreading Islam from Arabia to Persia and the Indus Valley region. Bahrain was the base for Islamic eastern conquests during the period of the Rightly Guided Caliphs (632–61) and also during the reign of the Umayyads (661–750). The Umayyad Dynasty hated Bahrainis for their loyalty to Imam Ali, the fourth

Shiite Muslim Bahraini men cut themselves to demonstrate their love for the third imam, Husayn. Husayn, the grandson of Islam's prophet Muhammad, was beheaded in 680 C.E. AP/WIDE WORLD PHOTOS.

EARLY AND MODERN LEADERS The imamate represents the religious leadership for Shiites in Bahrain. Ali was the first imam, and his descendants, beginning with his sons Hasan and Husayn, continued the line through twelve imams.

The mullahs represent the Shiite clergy in Bahrain. They can be sayyids, which means they are direct descendants of Imam Husayn, or a sharif, which indicates a direct descendant of Imam Hasan. Within Shiism in Bahrain, especially among the Twelvers, mullahs possess strong political and religious authority. Some contemporary Shiite political leaders are the sheikh Abdul Amir Aljamri, Abdul Wahab Hussain, Hassan Almushaimea, and Shaikh Issa Qassim, a cleric and the former head of the Shiite religious party. Sunni political leaders include Hassan Sultan and Haji Hassan Jasrallah.

MAJOR THEOLOGIANS AND AUTHORS In addition to the Koran and the "Narrations of the Prophet Mohammed," Shiites in Bahrain follow the commentaries of holy descendants of Muhammad's household (*Ahl Al Bayt*). Some of these teachings are found in "Peak of Eloquence" (*Nahj Al Balagha*) by Imam Ali and *As-Sahifa Al Sajjadyya* by Imam Ali bin Al Husayn.

An important author in Bahrain history is Sheikh Maitham Al Bahrani (died in 1299), who wrote on Muslim theology and philosophy. The mosque and tomb of Sheikh Maitham are on the outskirts of Manama, Bahrain's capital. Sunni Muslims in Bahrain follow the school established by Ahmad ibn Hanbal (780–855), which emphasizes the Prophet's sayings (hadith) as a source of Muslim law.

HOUSES OF WORSHIP AND HOLY PLACES The most important religious place in Bahrain is the mosque (*mesjid*), where congregational prayers, as well as prayers and rites associated with religious observances, take place. Compared with Shiite mosques, Sunni mosques are bigger and distinguishable by their tall minarets, from which the call to prayer is transmitted. Shiite mosques are characterized by their flat green domes. Al Khamis Mosque near Manama is thought to be one of the oldest mosques in the Gulf. According to local tradition, it was built during the reign of the eighth Umayyad caliph, Umar bin Abd Al Aziz (reigned 717–20).

Another important place of worship is the *maqamat,* which varies in size and structure. It houses *dhikrs,* or remembrance ceremonies, and other activities of Shiite associations. Additional holy places for Shiites in Bahrain

caliph of Islam. After the assassination of Ali in 661, religious schism emerged in Bahrain with the movement Shiah Ali (Partisans of Ali), marking the beginning of the Shiite branch of Islam. Nineteen years after Ali's death, his son Husayn was killed during a battle with troops supporting the Umayyad caliph. Bahrain then became a center for the Shiite sect.

The dominant Shiite sect in Bahrain has been the Twelver, or *Ithna-Ashari,* which follows the teachings of the twelve imams, descendants from Muhammad's household specially designated to hold supreme authority in the Muslim community according to Shiite doctrine. They believe in seven pillars of faith, which detail the acts necessary to demonstrate and reinforce faith. The first five of these pillars are shared with Sunni Muslims. They also believe in the imamate (the office of an imam), which is the distinctive institution of Shiism in general.

The significant Sunni sects in Bahrain have been Wahhabis, the Muslim Brotherhood, and Sufis.

are the shrines of imams in Iraq and Iran. The pilgrimage to Mecca is considered a religious obligation for both Muslim sects in Bahrain.

WHAT IS SACRED? The Koran, the Prophet Mohammed, his descendants, and the mosque are all considered sacred. The Koran and the mosque are sacred objects, to be touched or entered only when a person is in a state of ritual purity, which can be reached by ritual cleansing.

HOLIDAYS AND FESTIVALS The most important religious festivals in Bahrain are Id Al Adha, a sacrificial festival held on the tenth day of the pilgrimage month (Dhu al-Hijja), and Id al-Fitr, the festival of breaking the fast, which celebrates the end of the fasting month (Ramadan). Each festival lasts three or four days, during which time Bahrainis put on their best clothes and visit, congratulate, and bestow gifts on one other. Celebrations also take place, although less extensively, on the Prophet's birthday. In addition, there are celebrations that are intimately associated with Shiite Muslims: the observance of the month of martyrdom (Muharram) and pilgrimages to the shrines of the twelve imams and their descendants. The Muharram observances commemorate the death of the third imam, Husayn, and are intensely religious. Shiites in Bahrain hold passion plays at this time.

MODE OF DRESS There is no official dress code for men or women, and styles vary from Western attire to modern and traditional indigenous clothing. Most Bahrainis believe that obligatory Islamic dress for women consists of loose clothing that covers the body entirely from the neck to the wrists and ankles. Men are likely to dress in Western-style clothing or wear the national gown, called the *thob.* Some men, however, especially older ones, prefer to wear a loose, ankle-length overgarment known as a *bisht.* The Shiite clergy (mullahs) wear a white turban and an aba, a loose, sleeveless brown cloak that is open in front. A sayyid, who is a clergyman descended from Muhammad, wears a black turban and a black aba.

DIETARY PRACTICES Muslims in Bahrain follow Islamic dietary rules, which include bans on the consumption of pork and alcoholic beverages. Unlike in Saudi Arabia, alcohol is available, particularly in the three-star hotels and above, for foreigners.

RITUALS Religious rituals are the same within the two Muslim sects, with some exceptions. Muslims in Bahrain pray five times daily. Among the Sunnis there are five daily calls (*azthan*) for prayers, whereas Shiites have only three: morning, noon, and evening. Each time of prayer has its fixed number of prostrations. Both Sunnis and Shiites respect the direction toward Mecca, the *Qibla.* Whereas Sunnis touch the prayer mat or carpet during prostrations, Shiites touch a piece of flat, lightly baked clay (*mohrah*), brought from Karbala in Iraq, where the holy shrine of the third imam, Husayn, is located. In Bahrain both Sunnis and Shiites use rosaries, *tasbih* or *sibha,* a practice that originated in India. The Shiite sect prefers that the 99 beads in the rosary be made of the sacred clay from Karbala.

In commemoration of the martyrdom of Husayn, processions are held in the Shiite towns and villages of Bahrain. Ritual mourning (*taaziya*) is performed by groups of five to twenty people each. There is great rivalry among groups for the best performance of the *taaziya* passion plays.

RITES OF PASSAGE In Bahrain children receive their names on the seventh day after birth. This rite is celebrated by recitations from the Koran and by slaughtering an animal. Male circumcision, which occurs between the ages of three and six, is undertaken as a religious obligation. Marriage, the most important Islamic rite of passage in Bahrain, involves decorating the bride's house with colored electric bulbs and painted peacocks, a bird of great importance in Shiite decoration. There is a procession from the groom's home to the bride's home, as well as a celebration. At a funeral special prayers are recited over the corpse after it has been washed. The body is then placed in a coffin and transported in a procession to the cemetery. In the grave it is placed on its right side facing Mecca.

MEMBERSHIP Islam is promoted in Bahrain in various ways. Both Sunnis and Shiites raise their children on the basis of their religious beliefs and values. Children are encouraged to do their prayers, and the public school curriculum includes lessons in religion, ensuring that citizens understand their religion and practice it properly. Just before each of the five daily prayers, a public call to prayer is chanted. In addition, national television broadcasts call for prayers, Koran recitations, and religious programs.

SOCIAL JUSTICE Shiites in Bahrain are banned from working in the armed forces, the Ministry of the Interior, the police, customs, and other public-sector bodies. They feel additionally threatened because of the government's policy of granting citizenship to foreign Sunnis from other Gulf countries, as well as to Syrians, Yemenis, Pakistanis, and others recruited into the armed forces and the police.

Within the Shiite sect in Bahrain, a great number of female saints are found, and women occupy a prominent place in the Shiite passion history. The roles of the mourners in the passion legends have been taken over by women.

SOCIAL ASPECTS Marriage and procreation are considered to be religious obligations and are highly valued in Bahraini society. Monogamy is preferable, but polygamy is acceptable when all wives can be treated equally. Concerning divorce and inheritance, Shiite practice in Bahrain is more favorable to women than Sunni practice. This has been explained by the high esteem in which Fatima, the wife of Ali and the daughter of the Prophet, was held.

POLITICAL IMPACT Shiites in Bahrain have struggled against the minority rule of the Sunnis, culminating in the uprising of 1994–97, which pushed for democracy, social justice, and reinstatement of the parliament that was dissolved in 1975. The government's dismissal of the political unrest as Iranian-sponsored terrorism has enjoyed the support of Arab states in the region, particularly Saudi Arabia. The new prince (emir), installed in 1999, has pushed economic and political reforms and has worked to improve relations with the Shiite community.

Ras Ruman mosque in Manama has become known as a place from which political demonstrations start.

CONTROVERSIAL ISSUES Two distinctive and frequently disputed issues in Bahrain are *mutah* (temporary marriage) and *taqiyyah* (religious dissimulation). The *mutah*, is a marital relationship based on a fixed-term contract that is subject to renewal. It differs from permanent marriage in that the *mutah* does not require divorce to terminate the union. It can be for a period as short as an evening or as long as a lifetime. It is supported by the Shiites but condemned by the Sunnis. The Sunnis also consider the *Taqiyyah*, cowardly and irreligious. It allows one to hide or disavow one's religion or its practices to escape the danger of death from those opposed to the faith. Persecution of Shiite imams during the Umayyad and Abbasid caliphates reinforced the need for *taqiyyah* by the Shiites. In addition Sunnis in Bahrain, particularly the Wahhabis, are opposed to any form of idolatry, including the adoration and worship of imams, martyrs, and saints. This is a particularly controversial issue, since Shiites permit the veneration of important religious personages.

CULTURAL IMPACT Traditional Bahraini culture reflects its Islamic, mercantile, and Arab Bedouin roots. Traditional performing arts include ceremonial dances accompanied by drums, readings of the Koran, and storytelling. Mosques, palaces, and other official buildings are decorated with floral and geometric designs and with Arabic calligraphy.

Other Religions

Most of the country's Christians, Hindus, and Buddhists are foreigners. Roman Catholic and Protestant churches exist, as does an Indian Orthodox church, completed in 2003 in Salmaniya. The Jewish community consists of four families, who have a cemetery and a synagogue in Bahrain and are considered to be close to the ruling family.

Khalid El-Hassan and Saadia Malik

See Also Vol. I: *Islam, Shia Islam, Sunni Islam*

Bibliography

Al Khalifa, Hamad bin Isa. *First Light: Modern Bahrain and Its Heritage.* New York: Kegan Paul International, 1994; distributed by Columbia University Press.

Cole, Juan. "Rival Empires of Trade in Imami Shi'ism in Eastern Arabia, 1300–1800." *International Journal of Middle East Studies* 19 (1987): 177–204.

Guazzone, L. *The Islamist Dilemma: The Political Role of Islamist Movements in the Contemporary Arab World.* Dryden, N.Y.: Ithaca Press, 1995.

Haddad, Yvonne Y., and John L. Esposito, eds. *Islam, Gender, and Social Change.* New York: Oxford University Press, 1998.

Hansen, Henny H. *Investigations in a Shia Village in Bahrain.* Copenhagen: National Museum of Denmark, 1968.

Human Rights Watch/Middle East. *Routine Abuse, Routine Denial, Civil Rights and the Political Crisis in Bahrain.* New York: Human Rights Watch, 1997.

U.S. Department of State, Bureau of Near Eastern Affairs. *Background Note, Bahrain.* Washington, D.C.: U.S. Department of State, 2002.

Bangladesh

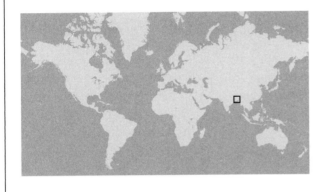

Country Overview

INTRODUCTION Located in South Asia, the People's Republic of Bangladesh is bordered to the west, north, and east by India and to the southeast by Myanmar (Burma). It spreads across a low-lying delta region where three great rivers—the Meghna, Brahmaputra, and Ganges—meet and flow into the Bay of Bengal. Because politically and culturally Bangladesh was once part of the greater region of Bengal (along with parts of the present-day Indian states Assam and West Bengal), there are many cultural values shared among ethnic Bengalis in India and Bangladesh.

Bangladesh has one of the largest Muslim populations in the world. Most are Sunni. Although its inhabitants are primarily Muslim, Bangladesh has a diverse cultural past and present, reflected in the ruins of ancient Hindu temples, as well as Buddhist monasteries and stupas, found throughout the country. More than 60 ethnic groups—including Chakmas, Santals, Marmas, Tripuras, Garos, and Biharis—make up the non-Bengali population.

Muslims ruled Bengal from the thirteenth century until the middle of the eighteenth century, when the British took over administration of the area. The Muslim rulers were preceded by Buddhist and Hindu dynasties, such as the Palas and the Senas. Christian missionaries, predominantly Danish and English Baptists in West Bengal and Portuguese Catholics in southern Bengal, arrived as early as the seventeenth century.

RELIGIOUS TOLERANCE When Bangladesh gained independence in 1971, the country was founded on the four principles of democracy, socialism, nationalism, and secularism. Religious tolerance, or respect for diverse interpretations of religious traditions, was to be promoted, and religious minorities were protected by the constitution. National holidays included major Muslim holidays and those of Christian, Hindu, and Buddhist traditions. After independence, religion played little part in national politics, and religiously oriented political parties were banned from politics under the country's first president and prime minister, Sheikh Mujib (Mujibur Rahman, 1920–75). Beginning with Sheikh Mujib's successor, Ziaur Rahman (1936–81), in response to religious nationalism and Islamism, religiously oriented political parties were again legalized, and in 1988 Islam became the state religion (though other faiths were allowed practice in "peace and harmo-

A passenger train carries Muslims returning from the Tablighi Jama'at gathering in Tungi, Bangladesh. The event is a time for spiritual renewal and an opportunity to organize mosque tours. AP/WIDE WORLD PHOTOS.

ny"). The major political parties, the Bangladesh National Party (BNP) and the Awami League, have voiced their support for tolerance of all religious communities.

Major Religion

ISLAM

DATE OF ORIGIN Thirteenth century C.E.
NUMBER OF FOLLOWERS 117 million

HISTORY In 1204 the Bengal region was conquered by Muhammad Bakhtiyar, a Turkish Muslim. With capitals at Gaur, Pandua, Dhaka, and Lakhnauti, Turkish Muslims governed Bengal (under the Delhi sultanate) until 1342. The area was subsequently controlled by the independent Ilyas Shahi and Husayn Shahi dynasties, which included Abyssinian (*Habshi*), Arab, and Afghan rulers. By 1612 the Mughals, a Muslim dynasty that

spread across India, had gained control of Bengal. The Mughals ruled Bengal until the British took over its administration, an event attributed in great part to Robert Clive's defeat of the Nawab of Bengal at the Battle of Plassey in 1757. Bengal thus became part of British India.

In the Bengal region Islam was spread by Sufis (Muslim mystics) and itinerant holy men and not by the patronage of Muslim rulers. As elsewhere in the Muslim world, Sufis were interested in Islamic philosophy and values. Evidence of their great impact on the culture of Bengal can be found in the preserved literature of the Sufis, the shrines (*mazars*) dedicated to the Sufi saints, and the continued appeal of Sufism in Bangladesh. None of the many Muslim rulers of Bengal were interested in converting the indigenous people to Islam. In fact, they were tolerant of the diverse religious practices of people in their territory, often patronizing the arts and literature of the various communities.

In 1905 the British divided Bengal, viewed as too large to govern, into two states, East Bengal and West Bengal, with the majority of Muslims living on the eastern side. In 1947 British India was partitioned into the newly independent nations of India, with a Hindu majority, and Pakistan, dominated by Muslims. East Bengal became a province of Pakistan, although a thousand miles of Indian territory, as well as differences in language and culture, separated it from the rest of Pakistan to the west.

Not long after independence, with the hope of promoting unification of Pakistan through a common cultural identity, Pakistan's central government, dominated by West Pakistan, established Urdu as the national language. In East Pakistan, where Bengali was the common language, this policy was interpreted as cultural imperialism on the part of the central government. Bengalis took great offense to what they perceived as an attempt to "de-Banglacize" their culture and to replace it with cultural elements of West Pakistan. West Pakistanis, however, saw their own culture as more authentically Islamic and associated Bengali culture with Hinduism. In response, Muslims in East Pakistan began to assert a Bengali identity, which they shared with their Hindu neighbors, and many Bengali Muslim politicians no longer believed that having a common religious identity with West Pakistan was enough. In 1952 the Language Movement, advocating Bengali as the language of East Pakistan, began, which led to agitation for independence from Pakistan in the name of linguistic nationalism. In 1971 East Pakistan became the independent state of Bangladesh.

EARLY AND MODERN LEADERS Sheikh Mujib, also known as Bangabandu (Friend of Bengal), was one of South Asia's most charismatic leaders. From the moment Muhammad Ali Jinnah declared Urdu the national language (because he saw it as an Islamic language and thus appropriate for the new Muslim country), Sheikh Mujib was driven to change the direction in which Pakistan was headed. In 1949 Ataur Rahman, Maulana Bashani, Shamsul Huq, and Sheikh Mujib together founded a new political party called the Awami Muslim League (People's Muslim League), later renamed the Awami League, which party leaders hoped would demonstrate their representation of all people of Bengal, not just Muslims. The Awami League emphasized the cultural distinctiveness of East Bengal and sought to protect it. Sheikh Mujib spent much of his political career

in prison for his outspokenness, which impassioned and united both the Bengali people and the non-Muslim ethnic minorities. After the independence of Bangladesh, he became the first president of this secular nation, though his time in office was controversial and repressive.

After Sheikh Mujib was assassinated in 1975, Ziaur Rahman (1936–81), a decorated major general, became chief martial law administrator, and in 1977 he was elected president. Opposed to the secular status of the newly independent country, he proclaimed Islam as the religion of Bangladesh. In 1979 Ziaur Rahman formed a new political party, the Bangladesh National Party (BNP), which emphasized Islam as the religion of the people, thus distinguishing them from the Bengalis of India. In 1981 Ziaur Rahman was assassinated.

Muslim leadership in Bangladesh takes different forms. The ulama (religious scholars) provide guidance to the people, but they also offer legal and religious opinions on all matters concerning Muslims, including foreign and domestic policy. In a less formal way there are the pirs (Sufi masters and teachers), who are revered among many Bangladeshi Muslims. Pirs provide guidance and offer advice to those who seek it on personal and professional matters. Pir Atroshi was the spiritual guide for the former president Hussain Ershad (ruled 1982–90), who was known to consult frequently with the pir. Other pirs have run for political office and endorsed candidates.

MAJOR THEOLOGIANS AND AUTHORS Girish Chandra Sen (1835–1910), a Hindu born in Dhaka, was a teacher when he was introduced to the Brahma Samaj, a Hindu reform movement that incorporated teachings from traditions represented in India at the time, including Islam and Christianity. Educated in Persian, Sen studied Islam and published many books on the religion, including the first full-text translation and commentary of the Koran in Bengali. In recognition of his achievement and contribution to Bengali Islamic culture, Bengali Muslims bestowed on him the title maulana, typically reserved for learned scholars of Islam.

Muhammad Naimuddin (c. 1840–1908), born in Tangail, was a scholar of Islam and a prolific writer of books on Islam in Bengali. In 1871 he wrote Jabdatal Masayel (Essence of the Issues), one of the first prose works in Bengali on Islamic practice. Naimuddin was the second to write a commentary of the Koran in Bengali.

Muhammad Akram Khan (1868–1968) was born in Calcutta and moved to Dhaka in East Pakistan during the partition. Khan was the provincial leader of the Muslim league and so was a proponent for the creation of Pakistan. A journalist, politician, and scholar, he wrote a biography of the prophet Muhammad and a Bengali commentary of the Koran. Although he favored the creation of a Muslim nation, he was a modernist, believing the Koran should be interpreted according to the needs of a changing society.

HOUSES OF WORSHIP AND HOLY PLACES In Bangladesh, as elsewhere in the Islamic world, the house of worship is called the mosque (*masjid*). Bangladesh has a national mosque, built in Dhaka in 1967, that is known as Baitul Mukarram. It is also home to the Islamic Foundation. Its architectural style replicates the Kaaba in Mecca. Tara Masjid (Star Mosque), also in Dhaka, is an eighteenth-century mosque that features porcelain stars on its domes and interior ceilings. The largest mosque in Bangladesh, aside from the contemporary national mosque, is the seventeenth century Mughal mosque in Khulna called Sait Gumbad (seven-domed).

In addition to mosques, other holy places include the many Sufi *mazar*s, or shrines, that dot the landscape. The most famous and commonly visited shrines are those of the saints Shah Jalal in Sylhet, Khan Jahan Ali in Khulna, and Bayezid Bistami in Chittagong. There are many more that are frequently visited, especially on Thursday evenings for *dhikr* (remembrance of Allah), a Sufi practice in which a short religious phrase is repeated again and again, and on Fridays after congregational prayers.

WHAT IS SACRED? Most sacred in Bangladesh, as elsewhere in the Islamic world, are the Koran and Muhammad. This is reflected in the importance and meaning attached to Koranic recitation and the celebration of the Prophet's birth. The sacredness of the Koran is also seen in its use as an amulet to avert danger.

In Bangladesh the many shrines of Sufi saints are regarded as sacred sites. These shrines are destinations for lesser pilgrimages known in Islam as *ziyara*.

HOLIDAYS AND FESTIVALS Thursday is the last day of the six-day work week. On Friday men go to the mosque for congregational prayers. In Bangladesh it is not customary for women to attend Friday prayers, though there is no Islamic legal injunction prohibiting their participation.

In Bangladesh other important Islamic holidays include the celebration of the Prophet's birthday, known as *Mawlid al-nabi*, and the '*urs* (death anniversaries) of the many saints. One of the largest '*urs* celebrations takes place at Maijbandar near the city of Chittagong. Another major annual event in Bangladesh is the Tablighi Jama'at gathering in Tungi. It is considered one of the largest gatherings of people in the world. The event is a time for spiritual renewal and an opportunity to organize mosque tours. The Tablighi Jama'at is a pietistic movement of the early 1900s founded by the Indian Muslim Muhammad Ilyas Shah (d. 1944), who wanted to revive and reform religious observance among Muslims. As the organization expanded, their mission came to include conversion. Participants devote time to traveling from community to community to inspire others to strict observance of ritual life.

MODE OF DRESS Muslim women typically wear the sari, which is the customary dress for women of Bangladesh. A more observant Muslim woman, especially outside a major city, uses the end of the sari, called the *achol*, to cover her head. Traditionally women begin to wear the sari at marriage. When in public women from conservative and Islamist backgrounds also wear the burka (a long overcoat and veil) over the sari. To attend prayers in a mosque, men often choose to wear *pajamas* (cotton trousers) with a *panjabi* (knee-length shirt).

DIETARY PRACTICES There are no Islamic dietary practices distinctive to Bangladesh.

RITUALS Muslims in Bangladesh perform the same rituals as Muslims elsewhere.

RITES OF PASSAGE Muslims choose Koranic and biblical names for their children, but Persian names associated with rulers are also quite common. The marriage ceremony has many features distinctive to Bangladesh, including the *panchini*, when the ring is given to the bride by a parent or guardian, as well as a *gay holud* (symbolic bathing in turmeric water) for the bride and then a *gay holud* for the groom. After a feast arranged by the bride's family, the groom's family organizes a *bou bhat*, which is a feast held primarily for the groom's family.

MEMBERSHIP The Tablighi Jama'at is a worldwide Muslim pietistic movement active in Bangladesh. Participants travel the country advocating the observance of Islamic rituals and make great efforts to convert others to Islam. The Islamist political party Jam'at-i-Islami, also active in this way, supports government policy that is informed by Islamic values. Sufis welcome membership in their orders to both men and women.

SOCIAL JUSTICE Social justice is an important element in Islam. In Bangladesh it is reflected in the platforms of such religious political parties as the Jam'at-i-Islami, which argue that Muslims are obligated to care for the poor and needy.

In a country as impoverished as Bangladesh, efforts toward social justice take on particular importance, and throughout Bangladesh there are international and local nongovernmental organizations (NGOs) pursuing the issue. Many of these organizations, however, find themselves in conflict with Islamist groups over the meaning of social justice. Islamist groups such as the Jam'at-i-Islami, for example, believe the roles of men and women are different yet complementary. A woman is expected to remain at home and take care of her husband and family. It is the husband's responsibility to provide for the family financially. In contrast, NGOs work to make women self-reliant and financially independent.

SOCIAL ASPECTS Traditionally in Bangladesh, when a woman marries, she moves in with her husband's family and joins the other women of the household in caring for the men and children. Increasingly, however, women are forced to work outside the home, and there are now a large number of female-headed households in Bangladesh. For impoverished Bangladeshi women, the conservative social values of Islamists pose great obstacles to their social mobility and means of livelihood.

POLITICAL IMPACT Several Islamist parties have formed a coalition with the ruling BNP. The BNP may be described as a conservative party that identifies strongly with religious heritage, while Islamist parties would like to see the institution of some kind of Islamic government. Although Islamist parties are not popular in Bangladesh, their coalition with the BNP grants them significant power.

CONTROVERSIAL ISSUES Nongovernmental organizations (NGOs), as well as the poor people and women they represent and work with, are overwhelmingly opposed to fundamentalist oriented policies, as these would likely hinder access to better jobs and other means of generating income for women. Another controversial issue has been Sufi saints (*pirs*) and the many practices associated with their veneration, which have come under attack from some Islamist groups, though many Bangladeshis venerate saints and acknowledge their power.

CULTURAL IMPACT Islam has had a tremendous impact on Bengali architecture, music, art, and literature for centuries. Throughout Bangladesh, Mughal and Sultan rulers built mosques and mausoleums in traditional Islamic architectural style. These buildings feature domes, minarets, and arches typically associated with Islam while incorporating local and easily available materials of brick and stone.

Notable in Bangladesh and neighboring West Bengal, India, are the Bauls, a wandering community famed for their beautiful and captivating musical tradition. The Bauls are not only Bengali troubadours but also a religious sect inspired by Sufi and indigenous traditions of Bengal. Some Baul communities today identify themselves with Islam, and their music is a form of Islamic devotion, while others are associated with Hinduism.

Sufism has greatly influenced culture in Bangladesh and continues to do so today. One of the celebrated Sufi brotherhoods in Bangladesh is the Maijbhandari *tariqa*, known throughout Bangladesh for its devotional music. Much of it is performed in Bengali using Bengali instruments, such as the *mandira*, a percussive instrument made of two metal bowls.

The extent of Sufi influence goes back to the rise of Islam in Bengal and is found in the literature of the past several centuries. Themes and stories from the Arab and Persian world were adopted and expressed through Bengali artistic forms, and many have been written down and preserved. This early *puthi* literature includes biographies of the prophet Muhammad, Sufi themes of separation and union with God as expressed in the love stories of Laila and Majnun and of Yusuf and Zulaikha, and more philosophical texts, creation stories, and elegies of the Shi'a martyr Hussain.

Other Religions

Buddhists, Hindus, and Christians have lived in the region for centuries. Most Buddhists are from the Chakma, Mro, and Marma ethnic groups. Buddhism flourished under the patronage of the Mauryan emperor Asoka in the third century B.C.E., and the archeological ruins of Buddhist monasteries are found throughout Bangladesh. One of the oldest ruins, of a monastery from the seventh or eighth century C.E., is located in Mainamati near Comilla. In eastern Bengal, Buddhism continued to exist under the Pala kings from the eighth to twelfth centuries, but patronage disappeared with the rise of the Senas, who venerated the Hindu god Vishnu. Today there are fewer than one million Buddhists in Bangladesh, the majority living in the region of the Chittagong Hill Tracts. The most celebrated holiday among the Buddhists is Buddha Purnima (Full Moon Day), which is a commemoration of the Buddha's birth, death, and enlightenment.

The popularity of Vaisnavism, a branch of Hinduism devoted to Vishnu, dates back to the Mauryan period (fourth to second century B.C.E.). In Bangladesh bhakti, or devotion, to Krishna (an incarnation of Vishnu) and Radha (a lover of Krishna) can be attributed in large part to the teachings of Krishna Chaitanya Mahaprabhu (1486–1533). Even more popular than Vaisnavism among the Hindus of Bangladesh is the worship of the goddess (known variously as Kali, Durga, or Uma). In the old sections of Dhaka, where many Hindus live, there are *mandir*s (temples) dedicated to the goddess.

Among Hindus in Bangladesh, the major festival is Durga Puja, held every fall for nine consecutive days. It celebrates a time when the goddess, in the form of Durga, rode her lion and slew a buffalo demon. *Pandals*, temporary shelters for the goddess (who arrives on the sixth night), are ritually installed by a priest. The most important days of the festival are the seventh through the tenth. During this period Hindus visit a *pandal* to see the goddess. On the final day of the festival, an image of the deity is thrown into the Buriganga River. The celebration of Durga Puja is not nearly as grand an affair as it once was (or as the one held at the same time in Kolkata, India). There is growing fear among Bangladeshi Hindus that the celebration invites persecution from Muslim fundamentalists.

Most Christians in Bangladesh are Roman Catholic and from the Garo and Lushai ethnic groups. Portuguese traders, who arrived as early as the sixteenth century, introduced Catholicism to the region. Protestant missionaries arrived in the late 1700s and had more of an impact in the western part of Bengal (now mostly in West Bengal, India).

Sufia Mendez Uddin

See Also Vol. 1: *Hinduism, Islam*

Bibliography

Ahmed, Rafiuddin. *The Bengal Muslims 1871–1906: A Quest for Identity.* 2nd ed. Oxford: Oxford University Press, 1996.

———, ed. *Understanding the Bengal Muslims: Interpretive Essays.* Oxford: Oxford University Press, 2001.

Eaton, Richard M. *The Rise of Islam and the Bengal Frontier.* Berkeley: University of California Press, 1993.

Jahan, Rounaq. *Bangladesh: Promise and Performance.* Dhaka: The University Press Limited, 2000.

Openshaw, Jeanne. *Seeking Bauls of Bengal.* Cambridge: Cambridge University Press, 2002.

Salomon, Carol. "Baul Songs." In *Religions of India in Practice.* Edited by Donald S. Lopez, Jr., 187–208. Princeton, N.J.: Princeton University Press, 1995.

Seabrook, Jeremy. *Freedom Unfinished: Fundamentalism and Popular Resistance in Bangladesh Today.* London: Zed Press, 2001.

Stewart, Tony K. "In Search of Equivalence: Conceiving Muslim-Hindu Encounter through Translation Theory." *History of Religions*, vol. 40 (2001): 260–287.

Barbados

POPULATION 276,607

ANGLICAN 33 percent

PENTECOSTAL 12.7 percent

METHODIST 5.9 percent

SEVENTH-DAY ADVENTIST 4.5
  percent

ROMAN CATHOLIC 4.4 percent

OTHER 16.7 percent

NOT STATED 22.8 percent

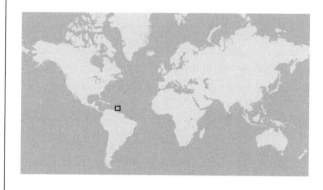

Country Overview

INTRODUCTION When the British first arrived on the small Caribbean island of Barbados in 1625, they found the land uninhabited. They quickly developed a plantation system dominated by a small white plantocracy that required the importation of a large number of slaves during the seventeenth and eighteenth centuries. Since slaves were considered property, very little was done to minister to their religious needs until Sunday schools

were established in 1808 to give religious instruction to slave children. It was not until 1825, however, that the Anglican Church (Church of England), which had developed close ties with the state from as early as 1685, began a full outreach program to educate and evangelize the slaves.

On the other hand, Quakers, Moravians, and Methodists preached a doctrine of equality from the very beginning of their ministries in Barbados, which eventually led to the ejection of the Quakers and the persecution of the Methodists. Despite the efforts of the Methodist and Moravian churches, the majority of the Barbadian population remained loyal to the Anglican Church. During the 1930s, however, the Anglican Church began to lose ground, a process that accelerated after the country's independence in 1966. Since then Anglicans have been joined by other Christian sects, among them Pentecostal churches, the Sons of God Apostolic Spiritual Baptist Church, and the Rastafarian movement.

RELIGIOUS TOLERANCE In Barbados the primary religion has historically been the Anglican Church. So great was Anglican influence that white Barbadians were originally required to say morning and evening prayers and to attend Sunday services. Free worship was not allowed until 1652, when, after a compromise was reached between the Cromwellians and the Royalists, the English Parliament gave white Barbadians the right to express their religious beliefs freely. The Anglican Church nevertheless remained the official religion of the state until 1969, when the legislature repealed the Anglican Church Act of 1911. The constitution allows freedom of religious belief and practice and permits religious communities the right to establish and maintain schools at their own expense.

Major Religion

ANGLICAN CHURCH

DATE OF ORIGIN 1626 C.E.
NUMBER OF FOLLOWERS 91,300

HISTORY Barbados, like other colonies in the Caribbean, did not have a bishop until the seventeenth century, and the majority of the clergy were sent from England. In 1629 Sir William Tufton, the governor of Barbados, established parishes and constructed several churches and chapels. He also instituted a vestry system responsible for maintaining church buildings and attending to the welfare of the poor. By 1645 Governor William Bell had added more parishes and instituted a system of sanctions against Barbadians who did not attend to their religious duties and who exhibited what was considered lewd and wanton behavior. The relationship between the state and the Church of England was such that state and church were one.

The slaves imported to Barbados were not allowed to join the Anglican Church. Because the church was identified with the landowning ruling class, it is not surprising that many of the slaves chose to join other denominations when they were emancipated in 1833. Despite the lack of concern for the welfare of the predominantly black population, in the early 1800s the bishop of London recommended the establishment of Sunday schools to instruct slave children. With the arrival of William Hart Coleridge, the first bishop of Barbados and the Leeward Islands, the church became better organized.

The Anglican Church has remained by far the wealthiest of the denominations, and its bishop is the chief spokesperson for all religious matters. Nevertheless, its influence began to decline in 1944 when a bill was introduced in the legislature to disendow the church. Since then the legislature has passed the Partial Suspension Act (1955), which furthered the end of the church-state relationship; abolished the vestry system (1959); and repealed the Anglican Church Act of 1911 (1969).

EARLY AND MODERN LEADERS Sir William Tufton, who was credited with establishing the first parishes in

A priest leads parishioners through Sunday Mass in an Anglican church in Barbados. The primary religion in Barbados has historically been the Anglican Church. © TONY ARRUZA/CORBIS.

Barbados in 1629, and Governor William Bell, who established additional parishes in 1645, were early leaders. A Reverend Harte established the first Sunday school in 1808. It was Bishop William Hart Coleridge, however, who was credited with being the organizing hand behind the Anglican Church in Barbados. He was responsible for the construction of churches and chapels and of school buildings. Contemporary church leaders have included Bishop John Holder, who has maintained tremendous influence even though church and state have become separate.

MAJOR THEOLOGIANS AND AUTHORS The bishops of the Anglican Church in Barbados have been trained theologians who have interpreted and dictated church doctrine. Bishop William Hart Coleridge is considered to have been the most influential theologian, setting the pace for the church in Barbados. Bishop Thomas Parry, who succeeded Coleridge in 1842, consolidated the work of his predecessor by expanding the work of the church and furthering the educational system. Important contemporary priests have included H.S. Pudor, Oswald Jones, Iver Jones, and Ossie Haynes.

HOUSES OF WORSHIP AND HOLY PLACES There are some 50 Anglican churches in Barbados. Notable among them are the Sharon Chapel, constructed in 1799; Saint Michael's Cathedral, rebuilt in 1784–86;

and Saint George's, reconstructed in 1784. Saint George's is well known for its beautiful altar painting of the Resurrection. Saint John's is renowned for its unique structure, appearing to be carved out of solid rock, and also for its pulpit carved of wood. In addition, Saint Joseph's and Saint Philip's have distinct Gothic features, while Saint Peter's and Saint Paul's were built in the Georgian style.

WHAT IS SACRED? Like Anglicans elsewhere, believers in Barbados hold a number of activities and objects to be sacred. Foremost among sacred activities is the Eucharist, which is offered daily during Mass and on Sundays during High Mass. Among sacred symbols, perhaps the most important is the cross.

HOLIDAYS AND FESTIVALS Christmas and Easter are both national and religious holidays in Barbados. Other important religious holidays include Ash Wednesday, Good Friday, and the feast of Pentecost, or Whitmonday. At the end of the growing season, parishioners take a portion of their harvest to local churches as thanksgiving for their bounty. Foods such as yams, potatoes, fruits, and even fish are blessed by the priests and later distributed to the poor.

MODE OF DRESS Although the Anglican Church in Barbados is viewed as the church for upward social mobility, its members no longer wear black or white to Mass, and children are no longer required to be formally attired. Priests have become more liberal in their daily attire, but they continue to wear the traditional vestments during Mass.

DIETARY PRACTICES The dietary practices of the Anglican Church in Barbados closely resemble those of the Catholic Church. For example, members are encouraged to fast during Lent by abstaining from meat.

RITUALS There are no indigenous rituals celebrated by the Anglican Church in Barbados. Morning and evening prayers are observed during daily Mass and again on Sundays during High Mass, and the stations of the cross are observed during Lent.

Marriages are a village and community event, with people coming together to celebrate the occasion with food, music, and dancing. The same is true of funerals, when villagers visit the home of the deceased to console the family and to take food to help during the time of bereavement. Many families commemorate the life of the deceased over nine nights by offering prayers, singing hymns, and giving a fete.

RITES OF PASSAGE The Anglican Church in Barbados does not observe any particular rites of passage. Children are confirmed at an early age, so a first Communion is not observed.

MEMBERSHIP Not until the late twentieth century did the Anglican Church in Barbados make an effort to revise its doctrines to reflect changing times and declining membership. Since the 1960s some Anglicans have shifted their loyalties to other denominations. The church has responded by making more of an effort to reach out to its membership. Even though the Anglican Church does not own radio or television stations in Barbados, it broadcasts religious programs and services. The church has also developed a website to provide information locally and internationally.

SOCIAL JUSTICE Although this was not always the case, the Anglican Church of Barbados has come to promote human rights and social justice for all. Over time the church came to be in the forefront of educational development on the island. The Anglican Church runs some 40 primary schools as well as 2 secondary schools and a preparatory school. Codrington College, which is an Anglican school, is part of the University of the West Indies, and the campus at Cave Hill prepares Barbadians for the clergy. The church has also established homes for handicapped children and for the aged. It provides relief for the poor and encourages its members to contribute their time and money to poor relief.

SOCIAL ASPECTS The European colonizers of Barbados reserved marriage as a privilege for whites only. The sentiment was shared and upheld by the church until the nineteenth century, when it began to make a concerted effort to encourage marriage among the black population. The church has had little success, however, with the majority of Barbadians remaining in common-law unions. Nevertheless, the Anglican Church performs 95 percent of all the marriages that take place on the island.

POLITICAL IMPACT Because the Anglican Church was long the established religion of Barbados, it has influenced the political life of the island. Even after the Anglican Church Act of 1969 was passed to disestablish the relationship between church and state, the bishop of Barbados continued to conduct prayers at the opening of the legislature and remained the moral and social conscience of the island. The Ecclesiastical Ministry within the government is responsible for all issues pertaining to the church.

CONTROVERSIAL ISSUES The Anglican Church of Barbados permits abortion only in the case of rape. The church supports the state's family-planning policies and believes that the issue is a matter of individual choice. It is only since the 1980s that the church has permitted divorce.

CULTURAL IMPACT Because the Anglican Church in Barbados has been responsible for the early education of the majority of the Barbadian population, it has had a significant influence on the development of many of the writers, artists, and musicians on the island. In conjunction with other churches, the Anglican Church has sponsored various art festivals.

Other Religions

By the mid-1940s a significant number of Pentecostal churches had arrived from the United States and become a part of Barbadian life. The churches are a blend of American religious and Barbadian cultural beliefs. Even though Barbadian society has become more secular, membership in these churches has continued to grow. Gospel music also has become popular, pointing to the tremendous influence of the black American church on the Barbadian cultural experience.

The numbers of Afrocentric religions have increased steadily since the 1960s. The Sons of God Apostolic Spiritual Baptist Church, led by Bishop Granville Williams, has preached a kind of African Christianity that many Barbadians find attractive. It is a religion that believes in spirit possession and that sometimes leads to dancing, singing, and shouting. Although it does not support the ordination of women, the church believes that women have a special place because of their virtuousness. Consequently, women may become mother reverends and deaconesses, positions equal to those of men in spiritual knowledge.

Maritza Straughn-Williams

See Also Vol. 1: *Christianity, Anglicanism*

Bibliography

Barrow, Christine. "Living in Sin: Church and Common-Law Union in Barbados." *Journal of Caribbean History* 29, no. 2: 47–69.

Blackman, Woodie. *Methodism: 200 Years in Barbados.* Bridgetown, Barbados: Caribbean Contact, 1988.

Campbell, P.F. *The Church in Barbados in the Seventeenth Century.* Saint Ann's Garrison, Barbados: Barbados Museum and Historical Society, 1982.

Dann, Graham. *The Quality of Life in Barbados.* London: Macmillan, 1984.

Dann, M.S. *Everyday Life in Barbados: A Sociological Perspective.* Leiden: Royal Institute of Linguistic Anthropology, Department of Caribbean Studies, 1976.

Forde, G. Addenton. *Folk Beliefs of Barbados.* Barbados: National Cultural Foundation, 1988.

Fraser, Henry S. *Treasures of Barbados.* London and Basingstoke: Macmillan Education, 1990.

Holder, John. "Religious Trends in Barbados during the Last Sixty Years." *Journal of the Barbados Museum and Historical Society* 62 (1994): 58–65.

Lewis, Kingsley. *The Moravian Mission in Barbados, 1816–1886.* Frankfurt am Main: Verlag Peter Lang, 1985.

Lewis, Linden. "Exploring the Folk Culture of Barbados through the Medium of the Folk Tale." *Caribbean Studies* 23, nos. 3–4 (1988): 85–93.

Pearce, Clifford. "The Quaker Property in Barbados." *Journal of the Barbados Museum and Historical Society* 35, no. 4 (1976): 287–99.

Belarus

POPULATION 10,335,382

BELARUSAN ORTHODOX 35 percent

ROMAN CATHOLIC 7 percent

PROTESTANT 5 percent

BYZANTINE RITE CATHOLIC 3.5 percent

OTHER 2 percent

NONRELIGIOUS 47.5 percent

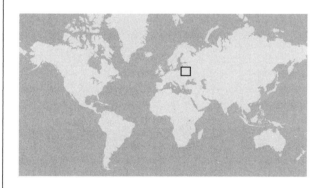

Country Overview

INTRODUCTION The Republic of Belarus is an eastern European country that gained its independence in 1991 after the disintegration of the Soviet Union. Poland lies to the west, Lithuania and Latvia to the north, Russia to the east, and Ukraine to the south. Poland and Russia in particular have had profound effects on Belarusan history. During the second half of the twentieth century Belarus became heavily industrialized, although its flatlands continue to support a significant agricultural

economy. The population is overwhelmingly Belarusan, an East Slavic people.

The land that is now Belarus came under the control of Kievan Rus in the ninth century C.E., under which Eastern Orthodoxy was introduced. When Lithuania and Poland formed a union in the fourteenth century, Belarusan lands came under their jurisdiction, and Roman Catholicism gained a strong footing, particularly among landowners. The Byzantine rite of Catholicism, the Uniate faith, later developed. By the late eighteenth century Belarus had passed to Russian control as Belorussia (White Russia). After World War I the Belarusan territory was disputed between Poland and Russia. The Soviet Union established a Belorussian republic and on the eve of World War II incorporated the former Polish areas into it.

The principal religion in Belarus is Eastern Orthodoxy. Its main body is the Belarusan Orthodox Church, an exarchate (branch) of the Moscow Patriarchate of the Russian Orthodox Church. The Belarusan church has only limited autonomy, with the Russian church further extending its authority by appointing bishops directly rather than through the exarchate.

RELIGIOUS TOLERANCE Belarus is a secular country, with all religious faiths independent of the state. In October 2002, however, the parliament adopted the law On Freedom of Confessions and Religious Organizations, whose preamble declares the determining role of the Orthodox Church in the emergence and development of the Belarusan people's spiritual, cultural, and state traditions. Thus, there is a clear trend toward giving Orthodoxy a privileged status in comparison with other religions. The Belarusan president, Alyaksandr Lukashenko, for example, has described himself as an "Orthodox atheist."

Those of other faiths dislike the 2002 law, which imposes limitations on the registration of religious communities, with only those at least 20 years old and with at least 20 members being eligible for registration. There also are restrictions on worship services, and liturgies performed in the open are equated with mass actions, which require the permission of government authorities. According to the law, foreign priests cannot work in the country for more than one year, although about two-thirds of Roman Catholic priests in Belarus are Polish nationals.

Major Religion

BELARUSAN ORTHODOX CHURCH

DATE OF ORIGIN Tenth century C.E.
NUMBER OF FOLLOWERS 3.6 million

HISTORY The religious history of Belarus is closely related to the influence of the various political forces that have governed its territory. Orthodoxy was introduced beginning in the tenth century C.E. In 992, when Belarus was a part of Kievan Rus, the ancient Russian state with its capital at Kiev, an episcopal see was created in Polotsk. Up to the mid-fifteenth century the Belarusan Orthodox Church was governed by the metropolitan see at Kiev, but it later came under the jurisdiction of the metropolitan see of Lithuania-Novgorod, one of the successors to Kiev.

Roman Catholicism also established a presence in Belarus during that time, and in 1596, when Belarus was a part of the union of Poland and Lithuania, the Byzantine rite of the Roman Catholic Church was introduced. In exchange for recognition of the pope's authority and of the principal Catholic dogmas, the Uniates, as they became known, were permitted to preserve the ritual aspects of the Orthodox service. In time 80 percent of the population came to profess the Uniate version of Christianity. In 1839, however, Nicholas I, the Russian tsar, issued a decree prohibiting the Byzantine rite of the Catholic Church, and in the late nineteenth century, when the territory of Belarus had passed to Russia, the restoration of the Orthodox Church began. Roman Catholicism also suffered oppression from Russian author-

A women kisses an icon in a Belarusan Orthodox Church in Minsk, Belarus. As in the Russian Orthodox Church, icons play an important role in the worship of Belarusan Orthodox churchgoers. © REUTERS NEWMEDIA INC./CORBIS.

ities, with cathedrals and monasteries closed and believers forced to embrace Orthodoxy.

After World War I the western part of Belarus was joined with Poland, where Orthodox parishes were governed by the Autocephalous (Independent) Orthodox Church of Poland. In the eastern part, which became a Soviet republic, the communist authorities launched a campaign of oppression against the Orthodox Church, as against all religions. In the 1930s the Orthodox clergy of Belarus, as well as clerics of other confessions, were subject to reprisals. Numerous churches were closed, and priests were charged with anticommunist activities and executed or exiled. The Orthodox Church bodies were exterminated by the early 1930s.

During World War II, when the Germans occupied the territory of Belarus, an attempt was made to restore the Orthodox Church. Episcopal sees were created, and churches were reopened. The German occupation authorities considered the Orthodox Church a tool of their influence, however, and the attempt to revive the church ended with the defeat of German troops. After the Belarusan territories were united within the Soviet Union, the Orthodox Church, under the Moscow Patriarchate, was restored. The 1960s witnessed another campaign against religion, with many churches closed and the number of parishes drastically reduced.

A religious renaissance began in 1988, when the 1,000th anniversary of the christening of Kievan Rus was celebrated. Episcopal sees were restored, and churches and religious educational institutions were reopened. In 1990 the Belarusan Orthodox Church became an exarchate of the Moscow Patriarchate. This arrangement continued after Belarus achieved independence in 1991. The church is governed on behalf of the Moscow patriarch by his vicar, who serves as the exarch of all Belarusans. In addition to its episcopal sees and churches, the Belarusan Orthodox Church has monasteries and convents under its jurisdiction.

EARLY AND MODERN LEADERS Among the most influential persons in the Belarusan Orthodox Church was Kirill, bishop of Turov (c.1130–82), a religious thinker and authoritative figure of the medieval Church. Evfrosiniya of Polotsk (c. 1110–73) was a princess and later a nun who founded the Spaso-Evfrosiniev monastery, copied church books, performed a pilgrimage to Constantinople and Jerusalem, died during her travels, and was later canonized. Sofiya of Slutsk (1585–1612) was a duchess whose activities made Slutsk the religious center of Belarus; she protected the Orthodox from the imposition of union with the Roman Catholic Church, for which she was canonized. Iosif Semashko (1798–1868), metropolitan of Lvov and Wilno, was a Uniate bishop who later embraced Orthodoxy and who, in 1839, played the key role in the restoration of Orthodoxy in Belarus.

The most eminent contemporary leaders of the Belarusan Orthodox Church include Filaret (born in 1935), an experienced church diplomat and politician and the exarch of Belarus; Maksim (born in 1928), archbishop of Mogilev and Mstislavl and an opponent of ecumenism; and Feodosii (born in 1956), bishop of Polotsk and Gluboksk, who is known as a conservative cleric. All of these leaders advocate religious and political unity with Russia.

MAJOR THEOLOGIANS AND AUTHORS The most renowned theological figure in Belarus was Kirill, bishop of Turov, who left a rich epistolary heritage. In his view the genuine sense and purpose of human activity was to achieve salvation. An advocate of the monastic way of life, he considered laymen to be sinners. He believed that humility was the principal virtue and the only reliable path toward salvation and that the essence of a monk's service to God was the development of humility.

During the period when Belarus was a part of the Russian Empire, the most eminent religious writer was Michail Osipovich Koyalovich (1828–91). Born into a noble family, he became a professor of theology and a philosopher who advocated the religious and ethnic unity of Russians and Belarusans.

HOUSES OF WORSHIP AND HOLY PLACES The most revered churches and holy places of the Belarusan Orthodox Church include the Sofiya cathedral in Polotsk, built in the eleventh century; the temple complex of the Belchitsa monastery in Polotsk, constructed in the twelfth century; and the Spaso-Evfrosiniev convent in Polotsk, also built in the twelfth century. The Saint Spirit cathedral in Minsk, the capital of Belarus, was built in the seventeenth century as a Roman Catholic church, but in the nineteenth century it was transformed into an Orthodox church. Relics of Sofiya, the duchess of Slutsk, and of the martyr Saint Varvara and the icon of the Minsk Virgin are preserved there.

WHAT IS SACRED? The dogmas and beliefs of the Belarusan Orthodox Church do not differ from those of the Russian Orthodox Church. Thus, both the Scriptures and the writings of church fathers serve as guides. As with other Orthodox churches, the decisions of those councils held before 1054, the date of the schism with Roman Catholicism, are recognized. Saints and relics are worshiped, and icons play an important role in worship.

HOLIDAYS AND FESTIVALS Among the principal holidays in Belarus, the most important is Easter. Christmas is both a religious holiday and a state festival. The overwhelming majority of Belarusans celebrating such holidays as Easter and Christmas, however, observe them merely as cultural events. Although they designate themselves as Orthodox Christians, most Belarusans do not observe the fasts before Easter and Christmas and do not attend worship services on these days.

MODE OF DRESS The garments of the Belarusan Orthodox clergy are the same as those worn in the Russian Orthodox Church. The dress of the clergy, especially of the supreme hierarchs, is luxurious. Monks and nuns, however, wear modest black garments. There are no dress restrictions for laypersons, but women traditionally go to church with their heads covered. Women also are discouraged from using makeup and from wearing short skirts, pants, and garments of bright colors in church.

DIETARY PRACTICES The Easter, Christmas, Saint Peter's Day, and Assumption holidays are preceded by fasts, when believers refrain from consuming meat, milk, eggs, and sometimes even fish, as well as any food made of them. The strictest fast is the seven weeks of Lent before Easter. In addition, all Wednesdays and Fridays, except those of Easter week, are days of fasting. The Belarusan Orthodox clergy may exempt sick and elderly persons, travelers, and certain others from fasting.

RITUALS The rituals of the Belarusan Orthodox worship service are sophisticated and solemn. The services are long, and believers stand during them. The language of the service is Church Slavonic, which is not intelligible to most believers. Sermons, however, are given in both Russian and Belarusan. Only clerics are entitled to perform the services and administer the sacraments.

RITES OF PASSAGE Baptism, or christening, is usually done in childhood and is administered by a priest in church. This marks the most important rite of passage, for every Belarusan who has been baptized is considered to be an Orthodox Christian.

MEMBERSHIP Members of the Belarusan exarchate of the Russian Orthodox Church are divided into laypersons and clergy. The laity includes everyone who has been christened and who goes to church for confession and for Communion at least once a year. Polls have shown that at least 3.5 million Belarusan citizens consider themselves Orthodox. Only 3 to 5 percent of the population observes church discipline, however, so that the number of active believers is no more than 300,000–500,000. As in Russia, most of those who call themselves Orthodox in Belarus are ignorant of the main dogmas of the church, do not take part in church life, and do not observe religious rituals. Evangelizing and mission work by the church is weak, especially in comparison to that of Protestants.

SOCIAL JUSTICE Being a component of the Russian church, the Belarusan Orthodox Church is guided by the parent body's "Fundamentals of the Social Conception of the Russian Orthodox Church" (2000). This document proclaims that the church shall protect the poor and advocates a just distribution of the products of labor, warning society against too strong a striving for material wealth. According to the document, a person's property status cannot in itself be treated as a sign of his being welcomed or not welcomed by God. A number of church organizations render humanitarian aid to orphans, to the elderly and disabled, and to others in need.

SOCIAL ASPECTS The Belarusan Orthodox Church emphasizes traditional social values. The role of the woman as mother, wife, and housekeeper is strongly encouraged. It is taught that participation in the workforce should not have a negative impact on the woman's role in the family. A religious marriage is regarded by the church as the only true marriage. The church discourages premarital and extramarital relations and condemns divorce. Abortions are discouraged. The church insists on the religious upbringing and education of children. Only heterosexual marriage is recognized, with homosexual relations strongly condemned.

POLITICAL IMPACT The political role of the Orthodox Church in contemporary Belarus is determined primarily by the state authoritie's attempts to use the church as an institution to influence people's views. On the other hand, the fact that the Belarusan church is completely dependent on the Moscow Patriarchate determines the pro-Russian orientation of the clergy. This is a source of dissatisfaction on the part of much of the population, which would like a more independent policy for Belarus.

CONTROVERSIAL ISSUES The Belarusan Orthodox Church emphasizes the social role of the family and strongly opposes feminist views. Orthodox ideology opposes any attempt to belittle the social importance of motherhood and fatherhood for the sake of success in the workplace, and it condemns women's neglect of their roles as mothers and wives. There is no open conflict between the views of the church and of the people generally.

CULTURAL IMPACT The adoption of Orthodoxy by the Belarusan people was a strong impetus to the development of architecture and painting. The oldest Orthodox buildings, from the eleventh and twelfth centuries, are found in Polotsk, Vitebsk, and Grodno. There was an original school of highly artistic fresco painting, done on cathedral walls, in Polotsk from the eleventh to thirteenth centuries. After Christianity was embraced by the Belarusans, literacy began to spread rapidly, with books written and copied at monasteries. Orthodoxy also influenced literature in the form of the lives of various saints, for example, of Evfrosiniya of Polotsk. At the same time, however, because Belarus was a possession of Poland and Russia for long periods, its culture has been subject to the influences of its neighbors.

Other Religions

The Roman Catholic Church is the second largest confession in Belarus. There are several Catholic convents and two seminaries in the country. Catholic churches in Belarus run many Sunday schools. The Catholic Church is active in the field of charitable work, with its episcopal sees running branches of Caritas.

Protestantism appeared in Belarus in the second half of the sixteenth century, and today there are a number of Protestant confessions found in the country, mostly in the Minsk and Brest oblasts. Protestant groups have shown dynamic growth, even though the Belarusan political climate is anything but favorable to them. Many Protestant faiths have criticized the 2002 law on religions, pointing out that it creates obstacles to those groups that are not privileged.

Religious minorities with long historical roots in Belarus but with insignificant numbers include the Byzantine rite of the Roman Catholic Church, the Old Ritualist sects of Orthodoxy, Islam, and Buddhism. The Byzantine rite of the Roman Catholic Church, or Uniate faith, is today found in western Belarus, which experienced a strong Polish influence. Although it was the dominant religion in Belarus in the seventeenth and eighteenth centuries, Uniates were persecuted under Russian rule, and in 1839 believers were forced to embrace Orthodoxy. After World War I, when western Belarus was occupied by Poland, there was a renaissance of the Uniate church, but it was later discouraged by Soviet authorities. There was some revival of the Bzyantine

rite in the 1980s, but the Uniate church lacks a significant social basis or influence in Belarus.

The Old Ritualist sects appeared in Belarus in the second half of the seventeenth century when Orthodox dissenters fled Russia to avoid persecution by the authorities. These believers rejected Patriarch Nikon's ritual innovations.

Islam is the religion of the Tatar population, whose ancestors went to Belarus in the fourteenth century. The mosque in the village of Davbuchishki, built in the sixteenth century, is among the most ancient in Europe. Since the late 1980s the Tatar's religious, social, and cultural activity has strengthened. In 1994 an independent muftiate was formed in Belarus. Most of the Tatars follow the Sunni version of Islam.

Jews also settled in Belarus in the fourteenth century, and by the sixteenth century they had developed educational institutions. In the eighteenth century Hasidism, a Jewish mystical teaching, spread in Belarus. During the Soviet period the role of religion in the lives of Jews was greatly weakened, with schools, synagogues, and prayer houses closed. A revival of Jewish religious activity began in the late 1980s. Jewish beliefs and rites in Belarus differ little from those in other countries. Some Jews in Belarus are Orthodox, while others, particularly the young and intellectuals, adhere to Reform Judaism.

Newer religious groups of foreign origin can also be found in Belarus. These include the Society of Krishna's Consciousness and Bahai communities. They are very small, however.

Larissa A. Andreeva

See Also Vol. I: *Christianity, Eastern Rite Churches, Roman Catholicism, Russian Orthodoxy*

Bibliography

Kozhokin, Evgenij Mikhajlovich, ed. *Belorussiya: Put' k novym gorizontam.* Moscow: Izdatel'stvo Rossijskogo Instituta Strategicheskikh Issledovanij, 1996.

Narbut, A.N. *Genealogiya Belorussii.* Pts. I and 2. Moscow: Knizhnaja Palata, 1995.

Rigsby, J. "Standing Room Only: Christian Resurgence in Belarus." *Christian Century* III (July 17–August 3, 1994): 709–711.

Belgium

POPULATION 10,274,595

ROMAN CATHOLIC 85.6 percent

MUSLIM 3 percent

ANGLICAN AND OTHER PROTESTANT 1.7 percent

ORTHODOX CHRISTIAN 0.3 percent

JEWISH 0.1 percent

NONAFFILIATED AND OTHER 9.3 percent

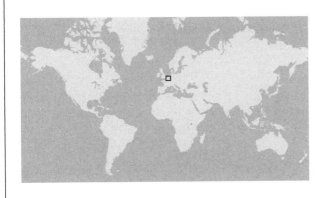

Country Overview

INTRODUCTION The Kingdom of Belgium is a small European state bordered on the northeast by the Netherlands, on the east by Germany and Luxembourg, on the south and west by France, and on the northwest by the North Sea. It has been predominantly Roman Catholic since the eighth century.

The country is divided into three regions: Flanders (5.9 million inhabitants), Wallonia (3.3 million inhabi-

tants), and Brussels (960,000 inhabitants). It is also divided into three communities: Dutch-speaking Flanders, the French-speaking community in Wallonia and Brussels, and the German-speaking community in Wallonia near the German border.

During the sixteenth century, at the time of the Protestant Reformation, Luther and Calvin had a substantial following in some villages and particularly in the major cities, such as Ghent and Antwerp. The Spanish emperors, as the landlords of the Low Lands, suppressed this "revolt," and most Protestants emigrated to the Netherlands. The emigrants included about 40 percent of the population of Antwerp, at the time the most important city of northern Europe. In the course of the nineteenth century some Belgians, mostly from the small educated class and influenced by the French Enlightenment, became "freethinkers." A small percentage of them joined the anticlerical Freemasons. In the same century religious practice began declining, mainly among the workers in Wallonia and in the major Flemish cities, though most people were still baptized and buried as Catholics. After World War II the number of practicing members of all faiths declined further. The main institutions, such as the schools, hospitals, and trade unions, however, remained under the control of Catholics, a situation unique among European countries. Although the vast majority of elder Belgians are baptized Catholics, few actually practice their faith, particularly those who are less than 50 years old.

Until 1999 the Christian People's Party (CVP; founded in 1945) was the most important political party, with numerous prime ministers coming from its ranks. Since World War I Belgium's kings—including

Crowds form to watch the Holy Blood Procession in Brugge. © JOHN VAN HASSELT/CORBIS SYGMA.

Bauduin (1930–93), who served as the country's monarch from 1951 to 1993—have been Catholic.

RELIGIOUS TOLERANCE The Belgian constitution, one of the most liberal at the time of its acceptance (1970) and a model for many other countries, guarantees the freedoms of religion and worship. Notwithstanding the fact that few Belgians are not Catholic, the ecumenical movement has been active and, from its beginning, has been supported by the bishops. Cardinal Désiré Joseph Mercier (1851–1926) started the well-known "dialogues of Mechlin" with the Anglicans, and several dioceses continue to have links with Anglican dioceses in England. Benedictine monks set up the abbey of Chevetogne for promoting dialogue with the Orthodox Church, and they publish the review *Irénikon,* which covers the Catholic-Orthodox dialogue as well as those with other faiths. In addition, the Catholic University of Louvain, the most influential institution of its kind in the country, promotes ecumenism with special courses.

The separation of church and state is not complete in Belgium. According to a concordat with Napoleon,

as compensation for the secularization of church property, Roman Catholic ministers (and, later, leaders of Anglicanism, Protestantism, Orthodoxy, Judaism, Islam, and non-Christian humanism) are subsidized by the Ministry of Justice. Parish priests are given free lodging, and the parish churches are supported by a complex system of *fabriques d'Église,* state institutions that maintain parochial properties. The membership of each *fabrique d'Église* includes the parish priest and representatives of the local commune.

Major Religion

ROMAN CATHOLICISM

DATE OF ORIGIN Fourth century C.E.
NUMBER OF FOLLOWERS 8.8 million

HISTORY Except for the Reformation period and the upheavals and persecution that occurred during the French Revolution, no major event affected Catholicism in Belgium until the nineteenth century. The centralizing policy of Austrian emperor Joseph II (1741–90), by which he tried to control church life, had no lasting effect. From 1878 to 1884 the so-called School War, which was brought about by the actions of an anticlerical government, closed Catholic schools and resulted in a rebellion by the population.

After World War II all the schools, universities, and hospitals came to be substantially subsidized by the state. Meanwhile, the process of secularization continued and, as in neighboring countries, sped up. Ecclesiastical authorities met the growing number of Muslim immigrants with tolerance, as well as with initiatives for dialogue, though the arrival of Muslims led to polarization in the general population. Similar initiatives have promoted dialogue with Belgian Jewish communities.

Also since World War II there has been a "de-pillarization" of Catholic institutions in Belgium. Previously Belgian society—even sports clubs and theater groups—was organized according to membership in religious-ideological "pillars." People were supported by, but also imprisoned within, their respective pillars. Although pillarization has not completely disappeared, it has been seriously weakened, and tolerance has come to prevail.

Since 1962 the Catholic Church has been divided into eight dioceses: Liège, Brugge, Ghent, Tournai, Antwerp, Namur, Hasselt, and the archdiocese of Mechlin-Brussels. Belgium has only one bishop's conference, which meets regularly according to the two main language groups.

EARLY AND MODERN LEADERS The major center for theological study in Belgium is still the Catholic University of Louvain, which was founded in 1425. Highly influential during the Second Vatican Council (1962–65) were a number of Louvain professors and Belgian bishops and theologians, including professor G. Philips (1898–1972); scriptures scholar Lucien Cerfaux (1883–1968); Gustave Thils (1909–2000), a professor of dogmatics; Albert Descamps (1916–80), who later served as rector of the Catholic University of Louvain; Charles Moeller (1912–86); theologian Philippe Delhaye (1912–86); canon lawyer Willy Onclin (1905–89); and bishops Cardinal Léon-Joseph Suenens (1904–91), Emile De Smedt (1909–95), André-Marie Charue (1898–1977), and J. Heuschen (1915–2002).

MAJOR THEOLOGIANS AND AUTHORS Louvain scholar Cornelius Jansenius (1585–1638), a Dutchman who later became bishop of Ieper (Ypres), originated the reform movement known as Jansenism, which developed a rather narrow interpretation of Catholicism after Jansenius's death. Church historian Roger Aubert has gained influence throughout Europe with his *History of the Church* (1981) and his work on Pius IX. Cardinal Godfried Danneels (born in 1933), of Mechlin-Brussels, is well known even outside Belgium for his writings and his television programs.

HOUSES OF WORSHIP AND HOLY PLACES A particular feature of popular religiosity in Belgium is the traditional devotion to Mary, the mother of Jesus Christ. Thousands of statues of Mary are found on street corners in the cities and in the countryside. Huge medieval cathedrals attract the faithful as well as tourists in Antwerp, Brugge, Ghent, Brussels, and Tournai, as does the national basilica of Koekelberg in Brussels.

WHAT IS SACRED? Devotion in Belgium is characterized by soberness and common sense. Whereas in the past fields, stables, horses, and cars were blessed, this tradition of rural times is disappearing. No holy oaks or animals are revered. Even the cult of relics is absent in many areas. People pray to a selection of saints, particularly Mary but also Saint Rita; Saint Antony; Saint

Thérèse of Lisieux; Saint Jan Berchmans; Saint Lutgardis, the patron of the Flemings; and, in Wallonia, Brother Mutien-Marie.

HOLIDAYS AND FESTIVALS Christmas and Easter are considered the most important feast days in Belgium. Other main holidays commemorate the assumptions of Jesus and Mary. For many, both believers and nonbelievers, All Saints Day is of central importance. Many people take flowers to the cemeteries on this day to commemorate their deceased. All of these holidays are officially recognized by the state. In some cities crowds form for processions, including the Holy Blood procession in Brugge and the septennial procession, in honor of Mary (the Virga Jesse, a title taken from the Old Testament), in Hasselt.

MODE OF DRESS In the past Belgian priests and religious orders colored the streets with their typical black cassocks and a great variety of habits, but even the black "clergyman" with the clerical, or Roman, collar has disappeared. Some sisters still wear the veil. Within the monasteries monks and sisters continue to wear their particular frocks.

DIETARY PRACTICES Before the Second Vatican Council most practicing Catholics observed the Lenten customs of not eating meat on Wednesdays and Fridays and of having only one substantial meal a day. These customs have completely disappeared and have been replaced by campaigns by which gifts are gathered for the country's poor (at Advent) and for aid to developing countries (at Lent).

RITUALS Sunday, or Saturday night, service is still the most important Catholic ritual in Belgium, particularly in the countryside. It was traditionally obligatory, and nonobservance was considered a mortal sin. This way of thinking has totally disappeared. Whereas, in 1950, 50 percent of the population went to church about every weekend, in 1998 only 11 percent did so. According to the European Values Study, an ongoing research program that began collecting data on the basic beliefs and attitudes of Europeans in 1981, more people in Belgium declare that they pray regularly than declare that they attend the weekly Eucharist.

RITES OF PASSAGE Since the 1960s participation in the Catholic rites of passage has declined. Resisting this trend are church funerals, mainly because other, secular funeral rites do not exist. Nevertheless, according to the European Values Study, when respondents in Belgium were asked if they personally think it is important to hold religious services for special events, 67 percent answered positively for birth; 68 percent, for marriage; and 72 percent, for death. According to the latest figures published by the Bishop's Conference, between 1967 and 1998 weekly church attendance declined in Belgium from 42.9 to 11.2 percent of the Catholic population; baptisms, from 93.6 to 64.7 percent; church weddings, from 86.1 to 49.2 percent; and church funerals, from 84.3 to 76.6 percent.

MEMBERSHIP Particularly since World War II the number of priests and religious has declined continuously. For the sisters this decline had already started before the war. In 1997, the latest year for which figures were available, Belgium had 4,183 male religious clergy, 70 percent of whom were in Flanders. Only 2 percent of the monks were under the age of 30, while 62 percent were more than 65 years old. Entrances into missionary congregations have disappeared almost totally, though Belgium has been for several centuries one of the most active missionary countries in Europe. Many young lay missionaries have switched to development work, as in Broederlijk Delen (Fraternal Sharing). In the past often more than 30 new candidates a year entered each of the religious orders, but the number of candidates has declined to one or two—or none. The diocesan clergy, with 4,938 priests in 2000, has faced a similar trend, with hardly two new seminarians a year per diocese, even though each diocese includes, on average, more than a million baptized Catholics. As a consequence, parishes have been merged, priests have been placed in charge of several parishes, and laypeople have presided over Sunday celebrations in the absence of priests.

In 1961 Belgium had 44,669 religious sisters; in 1982, 29,721; and in 2001, only 14,966. Their average age has risen above 70. The apostolic consequences have been enormous, for the sisters had been running a great number of schools and hospitals and had a great influence on their pupils. Facing the decline in church attendance and the increase in the numbers of "convinced atheists" (more than 8.5 percent of the population) and agnostics, church leaders have begun searching for new models of evangelization.

In the past the country had important daily newspapers with a "Christian climate"; all except for one in Wallonia have disappeared, as have the Christian monthlies. Christian literature has dwindled as well. Still influential are the weekly publications *Kerk en Leven* (Church and Life) in Flanders and *Dimanche* (Sunday) in Wallonia and the French-speaking part of Brussels. To fill the void *Tertio*, a high-quality weekly, began publication in Flanders. The national television and radio channels offer Catholics Sunday masses and religious programs, in addition to programs for Protestants, Jews, and nonbelievers. Brussels has a Catholic radio station, Radio Spes, and the Catholic Church in Flanders has a website.

The Catholic lay movements continue to support the church with their meetings and publications. After the Second Vatican Council new movements started. These include Focolare; Marriage Encounter; Family Groupings; Friends of Taizé, which originated in France; Christians for Socialism; the Sant' Egidio Community; Communities of Christian Life; Franciscan Brotherhoods; and the charismatic movement. The majority of the youth movements, such as Chiro and scouting, are still officially Catholic but with few signs indicating this affiliation. Meanwhile, the Catholic Action movements have lost their impact, for they have been too closely linked to the church hierarchy. A more recent phenomenon has been the appearance of "base communities," where Catholics disillusioned with the official church or alienated from the parishes have sought refuge. In the base communities they may experiment with new forms of liturgy and catechetics.

SOCIAL JUSTICE Since the nineteenth century Belgium has been a leader in its concern for the working classes. In almost all the parishes lay sections of Saint Vincent de Paul were set up to help the poor. Later the Christian trade unions supported religious organizations for workers and their spouses and children. In 1925 Cardinal Joseph Cardijn (1882–1967) launched the international Young Christian Workers movement. Similarly, an impressive network of Christian "mutualities" has been organized in Belgium, with local centers for taking care of the sick, the disabled, and the poor. It is the most important such network in the country. Since the nineteenth century the Boerenbond (Christian Farmers League) has promoted the protection and development of rural areas. Christian businessmen launched their own organizations—VKW (Verbond Kristelijke Werkgevers) in Flanders and ADIC (Association des Dirigeants Chrétiens) in Wallonia and Brussels. UNIZO

(Unie van Zelfstandige Ondernemers), a parallel organization with a female branch, sees to the defense of the middle class, especially merchants. The impact of Christianity on these mainly professional organizations remains present, even though it is decreasing.

Since the Second Vatican Council, Commissions Justice et Paix (Justice and Peace Commissions) have studied the main social problems in both linguistic parts of Belgium. Brussels houses the European secretariat of Justice and Peace, as well as the CIDSE (International Cooperation for Development and Solidarity) center, which coordinates all the national Lenten charitable campaigns. The international headquarters of Pax Christi, a global peace movement, are located in Brussels. Also in Brussels a team of Jesuits runs the OCIPE Catholic European Study and Information Center (OCIPE), which, together with COMECE, the secretariat of the bishop's conferences of the European Union, publishes the monthly *Euro Infos* in four languages. The Dominican order set up Espaces in Brussels in 1992 to promote concern for the religious dimension of the European Union. In 1989 the Catholic University of Louvain established the European Centre for Ethics, which deals particularly with business ethics and bioethics and publishes the quarterly *Ethical Perspectives.*

SOCIAL ASPECTS In the past, social life and life in the church were wholly intertwined in Belgium. The liturgical feasts ordered the year. In the parish the priest was a member of the small core of influential people that also included the doctor and the schoolteacher. He was in charge of the observance of ethical standards. This world has disappeared. In the European Values Study, when people were asked whether the church provided answers to the moral problems of the individual, to the problems of family life, or to the social problems facing Belgium, the percentage of respondents who answered negatively was, respectively, 63.7 percent, 67 percent, and 72 percent. A majority, 52 percent, also responded negatively when asked whether the church provides for people's spiritual needs.

POLITICAL IMPACT In the past strong links existed between the Catholic hierarchy and the Catholic Party, later called the Christian People's Party (CVP; renamed Christian Democrats and Flemish Party [CD&V] in 1999). As such, for many decades a monsignor was a member of the Upper House (Senate). Sometimes bishops publicly forbade voting for certain parties, such as the Flemish nationalist party. This ecclesiastical interference brought about heavy tensions between the clerical and anticlerical segments of society, but this changed completely after the Second Vatican Council. Only on ethical questions—abortion, euthanasia, and racism, for example—that are important to all the parties does the episcopate publish statements.

CONTROVERSIAL ISSUES Although there is still some debate about bioethical matters, discussions have become focused upon attitudes concerning divorce (many parish priests have allowed remarried divorcees to receive Communion), homosexuality (of priests as well as laypersons), the blessing of gay marriages, and, more particularly, the ordination of women in the diaconate and the priesthood, as well as the ordination of married men. In the latter area tensions between the Flemish interdiocesan pastoral council and the bishops have signaled a deeper uneasiness in the minds of the faithful, who want a leadership that allows more participation and is more accepting of the role of "the sense of the faithful" in decision making. Debates have arisen concerning the future of parishes as workable pastoral units. Even some church leaders dream about networks of "base communities."

CULTURAL IMPACT Flanders, in particular, with its great tradition of musicians, architects, and painters—including such "primitives" as Jan van Eyck in the fifteenth century and the Renaissance genius Peter Paul Rubens (1577–1640)—still offers many symbols of a long dialogue between Christianity and culture. The unique Davidsfonds, an organization with branches in most communes in Flanders, presents lectures, colloquia, and publications throughout Belgium. Many church buildings host exhibitions, concerts, and choirs. Although in the past a Christian literature flourished in Belgium, this tradition now seems completely lost.

Other Religions

Protestant churches in Belgium have about 175,000 members. Since the sixteenth century Calvinism has remained rooted in a small number of villages. The majority of Protestants (mainly Dutch merchants), however, entered in the nineteenth century or later. In 1978 the main Protestant denominations set up the United Protestant Church of Belgium.

Since the Second Vatican Council ecumenical relations have greatly improved at both the national and local level. The Anglican community, with about 11,000 members, is concentrated in the main cities and looks after British immigrants. The approximately 31,000 Orthodox Christians in Belgium are mainly descendants of Russian refugees, though some Catholics converted to Orthodoxy. Together with their Dutch coreligionists, they constitute an Orthodox diocese with a metropolitan see in Brussels. In 2003, for the first time, a Flemish Orthodox priest, Father Athenagoras, was ordained a bishop of the Orthodox Church, which belongs to the Patriarchate of Constantinople. Relations between Orthodox Christians and the Roman Catholic Church have been excellent.

After World War II an increasing number of Muslims, mostly from Morocco and Turkey, migrated to Belgium. They were needed as an unskilled labor force in the coal mines and steel factories. More than 300,000 Muslims live in Belgium, where they have become more and more concentrated in such cities as Antwerp and Brussels. They have set up a national council that has been accepted as a partner in dealings with the government, which recognizes Islam as a religion (having been the first in Europe to do so, in 1974) and supports its schoolteachers and community leaders. Most Muslims in the country celebrate the holy month of Ramadan. They have one important mosque in Brussels; elsewhere they meet in simple houses that have been adapted for the purpose. Some of the imams belong to the fundamentalist wing of Islam, while others seek a more open and tolerant "European Islam." Dutch and Flemish Catholics have launched, together with some Muslims, a periodical called *Begrip* (Understanding), which promotes interreligious dialogue.

From the Middle Ages onward Jews have been present in Belgium, particularly in Antwerp. During the Nazi occupation many were taken to German extermination camps, though many others were hidden by Belgian families and convents. Belgium's Jewish community totals about 10,300 members, who live mainly in Antwerp and Brussels. In general, relations with Roman Catholics have been warm and open. There are synagogues in Antwerp and Brussels.

Jan Kerkhofs

See Also Vol. 1: *Christianity, Reformed Christianity, Roman Catholicism*

Bibliography

Aubert, Roger. *150 ans de vie des Églises.* Brussels: P. Legrain, 1980.

————. *Christian Centuries: Church in a Secularised Society.* Mahwah, N.J.: Paulist Press, 1978.

Bright, James Franck. *Joseph II.* University Press of the Pacific, 2003.

Cook, Bernard A. *Belgium: A History.* Vol. 50 of *Studies in Modern European History.* New York: Peter Lang Publishing, 2004.

Dobbelaere, Karel. *Het "volk-Gods" de mist in? Over de kerk in België.* Louvain: Acco, 1988.

Kerkhofs, Jan, ed. *De Kerk in Vlaanderen: pastoraal-sociologische studie van het leven en de structuur der Kerk.* Tielt: Lannoo, 1962.

Moreau, Édouard de. *Histoire de l'église en Belgique.* 6 vols. Brussels: l'Édition Universelle, 1947–48.

Orcibal, Jean. *Jansénius d'Ypres (1585–1638).* Paris: Etudes Augustiniennes, 1989.

Suenens, Léon-Joseph. *Ways of the Spirit: The Spirituality of Cardinal Suenens.* Nashville: Darton Longman Todd, 1976.

Witte, Els, Jan Craeybeckx, and Alain Meynen. *Political History of Belgium from 1830 Onwards.* Amsterdam: Vu. Univ. Pr. Amsterdam, 2001.

Belize

POPULATION 262,999

ROMAN CATHOLICISM 49.6 percent

PROTESTANTISM 27.0 percent

OTHER 14.0 percent

NONRELIGIOUS 9.4 percent

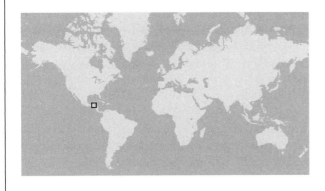

Country Overview

INTRODUCTION Belize, known as British Honduras until 1973, is located on the Caribbean coast of the Yucatán Peninsula. It is bordered by Mexico to the north and Guatemala to the west and south.

During the 1700s British colonists and their African slaves went to Belize from other British-controlled Caribbean islands for agricultural development and to exploit the forests for lumber and dyes. Belize achieved its independence from Britain in 1981 and became part of the British Commonwealth of Nations. Its government is a parliamentary democracy with a prime minister. Nevertheless, Guatemala has continued to insist that part of southern Belize belongs to the Republic of Gua-

temala, and maps of that country have historically included Belize as part of its national territory.

Because of its British influence, Belize is the only country in Central America where English is the national language. Protestantism was the dominant religion until the 1930s. As a result of the large-scale immigration of Spanish-speaking peoples from Mexico, Guatemala, and El Salvador during the nineteenth and twentieth centuries, the size of the Spanish-speaking Catholic population had increased to about half of the nation's total population by the year 2000.

Belizeans are of multiracial descent. About half of the population is of mixed Mayan and Spanish descent (Mestizo); a quarter are of African and Afro-European (West Indian Creole) ancestry; about 10 percent are of Mayan Indian descent; and about 6 percent are Afro-Amerindian (Black Carib or Garifuna). The rest of the population includes European, East Indian (descendants of immigrants from India), Chinese, Middle Eastern, and North American groups (American and Canadian citizens). The European population includes many Swiss-German Mennonites who arrived in the 1950s and '60s by way of Canada and Mexico. The sizeable community of East Indians is traditionally Hindu; their ancestors went to Belize in the 1880s to work on the sugar plantations as indentured servants. There are also small communities of Jews and Arabs (mainly Lebanese Christians) in Belize.

RELIGIOUS TOLERANCE Since the mid-nineteenth century freedom of religion has existed in Belize, and the constitution of 1981 provides for freedom of religion. The government generally respects this right in practice. Religion in Belize historically has been associated with ethnicity and region; Protestant groups have dominated in Belize City, and the Roman Catholic Church has been dominant among the Amerindian and Garifuna populations in the rest of the country.

Among the older religions in Belize, relations are generally friendly. Some religious groups work together on social service projects; such ecumenical efforts are usually coordinated by the Belize Council of Churches or nondenominational service organizations.

Major Religions

ROMAN CATHOLICISM
PROTESTANTISM

ROMAN CATHOLICISM

DATE OF ORIGIN 1851 C.E.
NUMBER OF FOLLOWERS 130,000

HISTORY Roman Catholicism was first taken to the colony of British Honduras (now Belize) in the late 1840s by Mayan refugees from Mexico, who were nominal adherents to the religion. In 1848 the Mayans had revolted against the Mexican government and the large landowners who had oppressed them since the Spanish conquest. The resulting Caste War forced many Indians to flee south to British Honduras. This migration led to the growth of Roman Catholicism in the northern region of the colony.

The first two Jesuit priests in British Honduras arrived in 1851; they had been sent by the apostolic vicar of Jamaica to preach the Gospel and convert the natives. The Catholic Church gained strength in the colony as a result not only of the missionary zeal of the Jesuits (mainly Europeans) but also of their readiness to work in the remote villages of the interior. There they found a greater responsiveness among the Spanish-speaking Indians and Mestizos than they had among the English-speaking Creoles (largely Protestants) in the coastal settlements.

The growth of the Catholic Church in British Honduras during the late nineteenth century led Pope Leo XIII to create the Vicariate of Belize in 1893. The vicariate was administered by the American Society of Jesus (Jesuits) from Missouri. In 1956 a bishopric was created in Belize, but the Missouri Jesuits maintained their control of church affairs.

The Catholic Church was the dominant religion of Belize during most of the twentieth century. It reached its high point (65 percent) in 1970; it began slowly declining thereafter, largely because of the growth of Protestant groups among the Indian and Mestizo populations. By 2000 the Catholic population in Belize had fallen to 50 percent.

EARLY AND MODERN LEADERS David F. Hickey, S.J., became the first bishop of the Diocese of Belize in 1956. The first Belizean-born bishop, O.P. Martin, was appointed in 1984.

MAJOR THEOLOGIANS AND AUTHORS Belize has not produced any significant Roman Catholic theologians or authors.

HOUSES OF WORSHIP AND HOLY PLACES The Cathedral of the Most Holy Redeemer was the first Roman Catholic temple built in Belize (1853). The first wooden structure was destroyed by a fire in 1856, and it was rebuilt in 1857–58. The cathedral is headquarters for the Diocese of Belize City and Belmopan (the capital).

WHAT IS SACRED? In many Catholic churches throughout Belize there are statues of Mary, Jesus, the apostles, and other saints. These are revered and maintained by the faithful and used for special occasions, such as the processions during Easter Week, Christmas, and saint's days.

HOLIDAYS AND FESTIVALS For Catholics in Belize the most important religious holidays are Lent (the 40 days before Easter) and Holy Week (the final week of Lent). Christmas is more of a family holiday than a religious one, although there are special activities, such as pageants and parades.

MODE OF DRESS There is no special dress code for Catholics in Belize.

DIETARY PRACTICES Belizean Catholics observe the same dietary practices as Catholics worldwide.

RITUALS All the traditional rituals of the Catholic Church are practiced in Belize, but many poor Catholics often do not have the resources to pay for formal religious ceremonies, such as weddings and funerals.

RITES OF PASSAGE In Belize Catholic ritual marks the important transitions in life: baptism, confirmation, marriage, and last rites. Many poor couples, however, cannot afford a formal church wedding and forego this ritual for a civil ceremony or decide to live together without the benefit of a ceremony.

MEMBERSHIP For many Belizeans affiliation with the Catholic Church has been more of a social obligation than a moral and spiritual commitment. Historically Catholicism has been more identified with the Mestizo, Mayan, and Garifuna communities than with the Creole population or other ethnic minorities, but since the 1970s many Creoles have converted to Catholicism. Although the Catholic clergy has attempted to evangelize non-Catholics in Belize, most of the increase in Catholic affiliates since the 1950s has been a result of the immigration of Catholics from nearby Spanish-speaking countries, mainly Mexico and Guatemala.

SOCIAL JUSTICE Catholic religious devotion in Belize is a sphere of activity traditionally dominated by women and children, and this trend has been strengthened by the role of church-run public schools, which are administered by the Catholic Church in partnership with the government. Many non-Catholic children have been influenced by the positive examples of their Catholic teachers and consequently have become Catholics along with other family members.

Liberation theology (a progressive Catholic political and social movement that originated in Latin America during the 1960s) has not had much influence in Belize. The polarization between the conservative and liberal-progressive wings of the Catholic Church, common in other Latin American countries, was not as strong in Belize. This was a result of various circumstances. For example, Belize is mainly an English-speaking country, and most liberation theology literature was originally written in Spanish. Further, most Belizeans share a common cultural heritage with other English-speaking Caribbean nations, where the Catholic Church is a minority religion. Another factor is that some elements of liberation theology have been closely identified with Marxism and Marxist-inspired liberation movements that have sought the violent overthrow of the established government, usually in areas where right-wing dictatorships seriously restricted civil liberties. This was not the case in Belize.

SOCIAL ASPECTS Since the 1960s a large gap has emerged in Belize between the moral and ethical teachings of the Catholic Church and the practices of the Catholic population, resulting in an overall disintegration of traditional family values. For example, there has been an increase in the number of couples opting for a civil rather than a religious wedding, the divorce rate has risen, and the number of children born to single mothers has grown.

POLITICAL IMPACT Catholic social thought has continued to influence political life in Belize, mainly through primary and secondary schools run by the church. Of particular importance has been the Jesuit-administered Saint John's College (a secondary school), which in the 1940s educated many leaders of the nationalistic movement. These Catholic leaders, along with others, sought independence from Great Britain and formed the People's United Party (PUP), which was the party in power when Belize finally achieved independence in 1981.

Most Catholics do not vote as a bloc on important issues in Belize, but politicians have tended not to support positions that contradict Catholic social doctrine because they fear a backlash from conservative Catholic voters.

Although no political party or social movement in Belize has been based on religious affiliation, Roman Catholics have had close ties to the PUP, which dominated Belizean politics from the 1950s until 1984. Nevertheless, the leadership of the United Democratic Party (UDP) has included many Roman Catholics, some of whom who held key government positions when the UDP was in power (1984–89 and 1993–98). Beginning in 1998 the Belizean government was once again controlled by the PUP.

CONTROVERSIAL ISSUES The growth of Protestant denominations and non-Protestant Christian groups at the local level—where many of these groups are openly hostile to the Catholic Church—is seen as threatening to the social cohesion of some ethnic communities, especially in Mayan and Garifuna villages and Mestizo towns that traditionally have been Catholic.

During the 1990s a growing number of Catholics in Belize were unhappy with the church's official policy on issues such as birth control, divorce, remarriage, abortion, the role of women in the church, obligatory celibacy for priests and nuns, the absolute authority of the pope and bishops, and the lack of lay participation in decision making.

CULTURAL IMPACT Catholicism has had a significant influence on many aspects of Belizean life, especially among the Mestizos, Mayans, and Garifunas, where Catholic religious symbols are dominant but are mixed with indigenous cultural elements. The result has been a syncretism of religious values and a blending of art forms such as music, dance, and handcrafts.

PROTESTANTISM

DATE OF ORIGIN c. 1770 C.E.
NUMBER OF FOLLOWERS 71,000

HISTORY Beginning in the 1770s Anglican chaplains were sent to the Colony of British Honduras (now Belize) by the Society for the Propagation of the Gospel in Foreign Parts. Their goal was to attend to the spiritual needs of the British colonists and the military garrison concentrated in Belize City. In 1824 the colony became part of the Anglican Diocese of Jamaica. Until the 1860s the Anglican Church, financed by the colonial government, dominated the religious life of the colonists. The Diocese of British Honduras was created in 1891. The size of the Anglican community in Belize has fluctuated over the years, mainly because of natural population growth and migration.

During the early 1800s groups of "nonconformists," or "dissenters" (meaning non-Anglicans), began arriving in British Honduras, leading to an erosion of Anglican influence. These included Baptist and Methodist missionaries from England and Presbyterians from Scotland. The British Wesleyan Methodist Missionary Society sent missionaries to Belize in the 1820s. Early Methodist missionary endeavors in Belize were plagued by sickness, storms, staff shortages, and membership growth and decline.

The London Baptist Missionary Society began work in Belize City in 1822, not to serve the spiritual needs of the English colonists (as had been the case with the Anglicans) but to Christianize their slaves and the "freedmen" (former slaves). During the 1880s the Jamaican Baptist Missionary Society took responsibility for Baptist work in Belize. In 1961 the Conservative Baptist Home Mission Society (from the United States) began to work with the Belize Baptist Mission. In the

late 1970s several Southern Baptist missionaries arrived in Belize to begin work in the interior and to assist Baptist work in Belize City.

The Seventh-day Adventist Church entered Belize in the early 1900s, extending the work it had begun in Honduras in 1887. The Adventist Mission in British Honduras was officially organized in 1922.

In 1931 the Church of the Nazarene entered Belize. During the 1960s work began among East Indians, Garifuna, Kekchí, and Mopan-Maya. The Nazarenes started a program of Theological Education by Extension (decentralized theological education in which the teachers go to the students rather than having the students go to a central location where the teachers live) throughout Belize in several languages, including English, Spanish, and various Indian dialects.

In the 1950s numerous Anabaptist-Mennonite groups began arriving in Belize from Mexico, Canada, and the United States. By 1978 there were at least 15 Mennonite agricultural colonies in the country, mainly composed of Old Colony Mennonites (Reinlaenders) and Kleinegemeinde Mennonites ("The Little Brotherhood"), both of whom speak Low German (the dialects spoken in parts of northern Germany). After Hurricane Hattie devastated parts of Belize in 1961, a number of Mennonite agencies, including the Beachy-Amish and the Eastern Mennonite Board of Missions and Charities, arrived to offer disaster relief. By 1978 the Belize Evangelical Mennonite Church had been organized with five congregations among Creoles, Mestizos, Mayans, and Garifuna.

Other non-Pentecostal Protestant groups in Belize include the Gospel Missionary Union, the National Presbyterian Church of Mexico, numerous independent Churches of Christ, the Wesleyan Church, and dozens of independent churches. Although few Pentecostal churches existed in Belize in 1960, since that time the Pentecostal movement has experience substantial growth throughout the country. By 2000 there were about a dozen Pentecostal denominations, with approximately 4,780 members.

EARLY AND MODERN LEADERS Several of the early British and American missionaries made significant contributions to the work of their respective denominations in Belize. These included Joseph Bourne (served 1822–34), Alexander Henderson (1834–79), and Robert Cleghorn (1889–1939) for the British and Jamaican

Baptists; James Edney (1832–50), Richard Fletcher (1855–80), and James William Lord (1881–1911) for the Wesleyan Methodists; Gordon and Joyce Lee (1955–1980s) for the Gospel Missionary Union; the N.T. Dellingers (1961–1980s) for the Conservative Baptists; and Paul and Ella Martin (1964–1980s) for the Mennonites.

MAJOR THEOLOGIANS AND AUTHORS Belize has not produced any significant native Protestant theologians or authors. The English missionary Robert Cleghorn, who served in Belize (1889–1939) with the Belize Baptist Mission, wrote *A Brief History of Baptist Missionary Work in British Honduras, 1822–1939* (1939), a highly descriptive account of missionary work in Belize.

HOUSES OF WORSHIP AND HOLY PLACES Protestant places of worship in Belize include churches, mission stations, and preaching points (locations where occasional preaching takes place in outlying areas). There are no known "holy places" among Protestants. Anglicans have a special reverence for Saint John's Cathedral in Belize City; built in 1817, it is considered the oldest Protestant church building in the country, as well as the oldest Protestant church in Central America.

WHAT IS SACRED? Anglicans often revere and maintain statues of Mary, Jesus, the apostles, and other Christian saints; these are used for special occasions. No other Protestant groups in Belize have any use for such statues.

HOLIDAYS AND FESTIVALS There are no Protestant holidays or festivals that are unique to Belize.

MODE OF DRESS There are no special modes of dress among Protestants in Belize, except for the Mennonites. Most of the Old Colony Mennonites continue to wear garments like those that were worn in the nineteenth century by their German and Swiss ancestors.

DIETARY PRACTICES The Adventists are vegetarians and produce a variety of health-food products. Otherwise, there are no special dietary restrictions among Protestants in Belize.

RITUALS Most Protestant groups in Belize place strong emphasis on the rituals of repentance and conversion for young people and adults, followed by the adult believ-er's baptism. Pentecostal groups add the rituals of glossolalia (speaking in tongues) and faith healing as important ceremonies in the life of their congregations; "dancing in the Spirit" is only practiced by some Pentecostals.

RITES OF PASSAGE There are no special rites of passage among Protestants in Belize, but baptism—for infants among Anglicans and Methodists and for adults among most other Protestant groups—is important as an official initiation into the Christian faith.

MEMBERSHIP Except for the Adventists and the Pentecostals, who have aggressive programs of evangelism (preaching the Gospel in every possible location), most Protestant groups in Belize have not experienced significant growth in the past 20 years. Mennonite membership is restricted largely to their isolated agricultural colonies and to the biological growth of their families.

SOCIAL JUSTICE In the nineteenth century it was clear that the very existence of the colony depended upon slave labor, even though the Abolition Act of 1807 had made it illegal for British subjects to engage in the slave trade. Most of the early Baptist and Methodist missionaries, as well as some of the Anglican chaplains, argued against the slave trade and condemned its abuses during the early nineteenth century. These abolitionist evangelicals eventually achieved a significant following among freed slaves and poor immigrants.

SOCIAL ASPECTS The Protestant population in Belize has maintained stronger marriage and family ties than has the nominal Catholic population. Most Protestants are affiliated with conservative evangelical congregations that promote strong family values based on New Testament teachings.

POLITICAL IMPACT Since the early colonial era Protestant churches in Belize have been heavily involved in the operation of public and private schools (which have been subsidized by the government). This has given the Anglicans, Methodists, Baptists, and Adventists a distinct advantage in the nation's socialization process and in maintaining their own social strength within Belizean society. Until the 1930s these English-speaking Protestant groups dominated the political and social life of the nation.

CONTROVERSIAL ISSUES There have been conflicts between the older denominations (Anglicans, Methodists, and Baptists) and the newer ones, especially those that arrived after the Second World War (mainly Pentecostal groups). The relationship between the Seventh-day Adventist Church and other Protestant groups has often been tense because of some of the Adventist's unique beliefs and practices (such as Saturday worship and vegetarianism). Tensions also increased between Protestant denominations and the Catholic Church—a result of a decline since the 1930s in Protestantism's social strength and an increase in that of Catholicism.

Because of their unique denominational histories, Belizean Protestants vary greatly in their views on issues such as birth control, divorce, abortion, homosexuality, and the role of women in the church and society. The Old Colony Mennonites and the Adventists represent the most conservative views on these issues, whereas the Anglicans, Methodists, and Presbyterians profess more liberal views. The viewpoints of people in other Protestant denominations tend to fall between these two extremes.

CULTURAL IMPACT Historically Protestantism has had a strong influence on many aspects of Belizean life, including music, art, and literature, mainly through the socialization process in their churches and private schools and particularly among the Afro-American Creole population. Protestant churches and schools teach a "Protestant worldview" that is notably different from a "Roman Catholic worldview." This difference is derived from the distinctive history, theology, organizational structure, and social fabric of Protestantism, which originated in Europe and was taken to Belize via the British West Indies before 1930. Since then the older Belizean Protestant culture has been strongly influenced by Protestants from North America, mainly the Mennonites and Pentecostals, who imported their own styles of morality, worship, music, literature, and art forms.

Other Religions

Non-Protestant Christian groups in Belize include Jehovah's Witnesses, Mormons, Christadelphians, Unity School of Christianity, and the Children of God (disciples of cult leader David Berg [1919–94]).

Non-Christian religions include the Bahai faith, Hinduism, Islam, and Judaism among the immigrant population; animistic religions among the Mayan Indians; Garifuna religion among the Black Caribs (Afro-Amerindians); and Myalism-Obeah, Rastafarianism, and Black Muslim religions among the Creoles (who are concentrated in Belize District).

The East Indians in Belize are traditionally Hindus, and the Lebanese are traditionally Maronite Christians. Many of the Mayans are nominal Catholics who maintain native Amerindian religious practices, such as shamanism (a religion involving a spiritual guide and healer) and witchcraft. The Afro-Amerindian people known as Garifunas or Black Caribs were deported by the British from the Caribbean island of Saint Vincent in 1797 to the Bay Islands of Honduras; eventually they settled along the Caribbean coast of Central America, from Belize in the north to Nicaragua in the south. Most Garifunas are marginal Christians (some claim to be Catholics, whereas others have been influenced by Protestants) who largely maintain their unique cultural and religious (animistic) practices, in which spirit-possession is a strong component of normal village life. Most West Indian Creoles are English-speaking and Protestant, but some continue to practice Myalism, a syncretistic Afro-Caribbean religion that was dominant among their slave ancestors in the British colonies; Obeah is the practice of "black magic," or witchcraft associated with Myalism.

Clifton L. Holland

See Also Vol. 1: *Christianity, Roman Catholicism*

Bibliography

Brierly, Peter, ed. *World Churches Handbook.* London: Christian Research, 1997.

Cleghorn, Robert. *A Brief History of Baptist Missionary Work in British Honduras, 1822–1939.* London: The Kingsgate Press, 1939.

Holland, Clifton L., ed. *World Christianity: Central America and the Caribbean.* Monrovia, Calif.: MARC-World Vision, 1981.

PROLADES-RITA official website. 23 August 2004. http://www.prolades.com.

Benin

POPULATION 6,787,625

VODUN 57 percent

ROMAN CATHOLIC 21 percent

MUSLIM 15 percent

PROTESTANT 4 percent

INDEPENDENT 3 percent

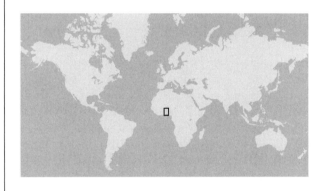

Country Overview

INTRODUCTION Set in western Africa along the Gulf of Guinea, the Republic of Benin is a small, narrow country between Togo to the west and Nigeria to the east. To the north is Burkina Faso and Niger. Until 1975 Benin was called Dahomey, a name derived from the former kingdom of Dahomey, which dominated the slave trade between the interior and the Atlantic coast from the early eighteenth to the late nineteenth century. Among the largest ethnic groups represented in Benin are the Fon, Aja, and Gun. The population also contains groups of Yoruba- and Ewe-speaking peoples.

Traditionally Dahomeans have practiced Vodun, a religion involving the worship of hundreds of deities (*vodun*) who play an intermediary role between the Supreme Being (Mawu) and humans. Beginning in the sixteenth century slaves transported from Dahomey took the religion with them to the New World, where a derogatory and sensationalized form, voodoo, captured the Western imagination. Vodun remains the dominant religion of contemporary Benin.

Islam had trickled into the northern part of what became Benin well before the colonial period. Traders and clerics brought Islam with them and lived under the auspices of non-Islamic leaders who hoped to profit from the wider Islamic trade network. In 1815 the Fulani Jihad of Sokoto (present-day northern Nigeria), led by Uthman dan Fodio (1754–1817), extended the influence of Islam in the region.

Portuguese missionaries, first arriving in the seventeenth century, introduced Christianity to Dahomey as they tried to convert one Dahomean king after another to Roman Catholicism. In the early twentieth century, after Dahomey became a French colony, Catholicism began to gain some measure of popularity with the establishment of mission schools, where the local elite sent their children to get a Western education. Most in the educated class became functionaries of the colonial administration and provided the political leadership when decolonization got underway after World War II. In 1958 Dahomey gained administrative autonomy within a French community of West African states. The country gained independence from France on I August 1960.

People rejoice at a festival during Benin's National Voodoo Day. Celebrated since 1996, National Voodoo Day occurs each January 10 and attracts thousands of believers and spectators. AP/WIDE WORLD PHOTOS.

Major Religion

VODUN

DATE OF ORIGIN 1400 C.E.
NUMBER OF FOLLOWERS 3.9 million

HISTORY Vodun is rooted in ancient beliefs and practices that originated in the southern part of Benin along the Atlantic coast. Situated between a rain forest and savannah, the area was a meeting place for the Fon, Ewe, and Gun cultures, among others. From the early sixteenth century onward, this part of West Africa gradually became an important conduit of the Atlantic slave trade. Passing through the region en route to slave ships moored on the coast, captives from different West African societies—including some who were new to Vodun—drew upon Vodun spirituality, which they then transported to the New World.

Successive kingdoms, among them Allada and, beginning around the 1720s, Dahomey, controlled this part of West Africa. Two deities, Mawu (male) and Lisa (female), came to symbolize the political control over religious life the Dahomean monarchy achieved under King Tegbesu (reigned 1740–74). By joining the two deities the monarchy asserted that power and authority derived from a male-female pairing. All throughout the colonial period, despite the growing presence of Christianity, Vodun continued to play an important political and sociocultural role in the lives of Dahomeans, and its elements became enshrined in Christian practices.

In the postcolonial era Vodun came under attack during the rule (1972–91) of Marxist dictator Mathieu Kérékou (born in 1933). Ironically, Kérékou maintained a close relationship with the leading Vodun priests, whose influence he perceived as a political threat. After Nicéphore Soglo (born in 1935) was elected president in 1991, Vodun was reinstated as a national religion. Kérékou returned to power with a victory in the 1996 presidential election, and he used a Christian discourse to distance himself from the previous military regime, which he associated with Vodun and occult forces. He publicly identified himself with Christianity, the constitution, and democracy, while denouncing Soglo and the opposition as well as the military regime of the past. Nevertheless, Vodun regained its traditional sociocultural status and was recognized in 1996 as an official religion alongside Christianity and Islam.

RELIGIOUS TOLERANCE The military government of President Mathieu Kérékou, who held power from 1972 to 1991, pursued a Marxist-Leninist ideology and antireligious campaigns and witch-hunts, undermining the influence of Vodun. After the restoration of democratic politics in 1990, however, Vodun rapidly regained its traditional vitality. From May to June 1991 a national symposium, which brought various Vodun leaders together, sought to gain legal recognition for the religion. Two years later Ouidah 92, an international Vodun festival organized and held in Benin, attracted thousands of national and international participants, especially people of African descent from the Americas. Pope John Paul II's visit to Benin in 1993 and his much-publicized meeting with Vodun leaders reflected the atmosphere of tolerance the government intended to promote.

The 1990 constitution guarantees freedom of worship as long as the state's secular status is respected. Persons who wish to form a religious group, however, must register with the Ministry of Interior. It is rare for the government to refuse permission to register.

EARLY AND MODERN LEADERS According to oral tradition, Kpojito (Reign Mate) Hwanjile—who served the kings Tegbesu, Kplinga, and Agonglo from 1740 to 1797—introduced several deities to Abomey (the residence of the kings of Dahomey). From Aja lands along the coast, she is believed to have brought the twin deities Mawu and Lisa, creators of the world to whom all other gods were subordinate. The highest-ranking woman in the kingdom, Hwanjile single-handedly took control of religious life in Dahomey by the mid-eighteenth century.

Although spirit mediums and various forms of divination existed in Dahomey before the eighteenth century, the system of divination known among Yoruba-speaking peoples as Fá, or Ifa, was, according to tradition, introduced in Abomey during the reign of Tegbesu's predecessor, Agaja (1716–40). King Tegbesu, however, was the first king initiated in Fá, which gave him access to his *kpoli*, a sacred object that he could use to learn the details of his destiny.

Sossa Guedehoungue was considered the country's chief priest by most Vodun believers until his death in 2001. Daagbo Hounon Houna (born in 1923) of Ouidah, the heartland of Vodun, had contested Guedehoungue's position, claiming that his own family's successive accessions to the priesthood date back to 1452. After Guedehoungue's death, Daagbo Hounon Houna became Benin's chief priest of Vodun.

MAJOR THEOLOGIANS AND AUTHORS The term Vodun first appeared in print in a *Doctrina Christiana* of 1658, which the ambassador of the king of Allada presented to the court of Spain. The study translated the word *Vodun* as "god" or "sacred." Some scholarly controversy continues over the etymology of the word, and different scholars insist that the correct spelling is *Vodun, Vodoun,* or the French *Vaudou.* They reject *voodoo,* the corrupted version of the word that was sensationalized and trivialized by colonial authorities and Hollywood moviemakers and in Western media representations.

Bernard Maupoil, a French colonial official who served in Dahomey from 1934 to 1936, wrote a detailed study of divination and Dahomean religion based on the memoirs of Gedegbe, one of the chief diviners of King Behanzin (reigned 1889–94). During the 1930s American anthropologist Melville J. Herskovits also relied on a local informant, René Aho, a grandson of King Glele (reigned 1858–89), as a source for his

ethnographic study of Dahomey, in which Vodun was covered in great detail.

HOUSES OF WORSHIP AND HOLY PLACES As in other traditional religions of West Africa, Vodun holds that the Supreme Being or Creator designates shrines where sacrifices are to be performed to protect believers against misfortunes, illness, and evil forces. These shrines may take different forms, such as altars, mud huts, groves of trees, and rocks. Any place where ancestral spirits converge and receive libations from the living becomes a sacred space. Apart from being the focal point of worship, the shrine is important because it serves as the unifying center of a localized unit, such as a family, clan, or lineage. Members identify with the deity of a particular shrine because they share common experiences of initiation and worship. Each member is bound to the shrine on both an emotional and spiritual level. Only rarely do important ceremonies take place away from the shrine of the deity or deities that the local group worships.

WHAT IS SACRED? All the elements of the universe bear spiritual relevance to Vodun because they are the creation of the Supreme Being. There is, therefore, a deity of the earth, a deity of the sky, a deity of the sea, and a deity representing the ancestors. Some pantheons include pythons and trees as deities. Masks, wooden statues and statuettes, dancing-wands, clay pots, calabashes, kola nuts, palm oil, and seashells are all revered items associated with Vodun rituals and ceremonies. Some items—masks and wooden statues, for example—take on added sacredness when they represent a deity.

HOLIDAYS AND FESTIVALS Since 1996 Benin has celebrated National Vodun Day on January 10, giving the religion an official status alongside Christianity and Islam. The celebrations on National Vodun Day involve, among other things, paying homage to the gods and ancestors through prayers led by the chief priest of Vodun. Colorful costume parades also take place in Ouidah, a coastal town well known for its Vodun tradition; there slaves once boarded ships destined for the New World. Other ceremonies, such as the homage paid to the sea at the end of each year, usually attract thousands of believers and spectators.

MODE OF DRESS Vodun does not prescribe any specific dress for its followers. It is not strange, therefore, to see Vodun practitioners in Muslim attire (typical of people from the north) or in French suits (signifying the European influence in the south). Traditionalists are more likely to prefer African costumes to Western clothing. At a funeral service for a Vodun believer, the colors most commonly worn by those in attendance are black, red, and white. Special ceremonies may require costumes for initiates, dancers, and priests, and these vary from clan to clan.

DIETARY PRACTICES There are no rules about what Vodun believers should eat. Diet is dictated mostly by economic necessity rather than spiritual considerations. Thus, the rural poor consume bush meat (apes and monkeys) more frequently than those who make their living as merchants, bankers, and government functionaries in Cotonou or Porto Novo.

RITUALS Vodun rituals in Benin range from the mundane to the highly elaborate, depending on the occasion. Rituals generally are emotional experiences that are intended to elicit specific responses from the gods. To this end a connection between the natural world of things and the spiritual realm has to be made through the use of herbs, wine, perfumes, pastes of blood and ashes, animals, and mixtures of leaves and bark, among other things. These objects by themselves are believed to be dwellings of gods. A ritual can be an act as simple as dropping some wine on the ground as a libation for an ancestor before a meal. Alternatively, it can involve covering the entire body with pastes in order to transform the worshiper into a living Vodun sculpture. In any case Vodun thrives on ceremonies and rituals that are performed to appease the gods so that they will prevent misfortune, illness, and malevolence.

Some Vodun rituals involve intense dancing to a pulsating drumbeat that is aimed at inducing a hypnotic trance. The dances are in honor of the gods or ancestors. The audience, including family members of the dancers and other Vodun adherents, generally watches in complete silence.

At a funeral of a Vodun adherent, a ritual is performed to extricate the Vodun spirit from the deceased, leaving the dead to continue the afterlife journey. There are two reasons for this ritual. Spirits are guardians of the living, not the dead, and they serve only as an intermediary between humans and the Creator, to whom the dead is simply returned. The Vodun spirit of the deceased is recalled and reserved for someone who will inherit it.

RITES OF PASSAGE Three rites of initiation typical of the Fon of southern Benin are central to Vodun. The first rite—the most important one, which everyone must go through—introduces the child to the family community, including the deceased members and guardian spirits. This rite is performed in the living room of a representative of an ancestor. A divine healer reveals the child's *joto*, the Vodun or protective force that will direct the child's existence. The second rite marks late adolescence and takes place when boys and girls reach about the age of twenty. At this time youthful freedom must be surrendered to the will of the Supreme Being in order to gain more strength. A divine healer thus offers a sacrifice to clear the initiate's path of obstacles and misfortune. The last initiation rite, performed in adulthood, is reserved for men. It gives the initiate access to the Fá divination system.

MEMBERSHIP Vodun is an organized religion that recognizes four categories of membership. The chief priest, or *voduno*, represents the highest category, followed by his assistant, the *xunso*, or "carrier." Then there is the believer, or *vodunsi*, and the Legbáno, who incarnates the Legbá, the messenger of Vodun. The position of chief priest is hereditary, though in precolonial and colonial times a chief priest had to be confirmed by the king. Priestesses are as much revered as their male counterparts. Chief priests and chief priestesses wield tremendous influence over their followers. The families of candidates for initiation bring them to the chief priest, who performs rites giving social recognition to initiates as active participants in Vodun ceremonies. Both women and men can become active members of Vodun. While members may pass on their membership to relatives, outsiders attracted to the power of a particular deity can become members only after going through the proper initiation ceremonies.

SOCIAL JUSTICE Vodun emphasizes good behavior and meaningful moral choices geared toward keeping the peace in society. Because Vodun does not preclude dialogue with other religions, its practitioners tolerate nonbelievers. Social cohesion is central to Vodun, and its significance is not limited to the community of believers. Rather, peaceful coexistence with others in the wider community is an essential element of Vodun's ethos.

Vodun rests on a strong sense of attachment to family—both living and dead members—which forms the basis of wider social relations within the community. Underlying most social relations are expectations of mutual respect between family members and different families, clans, and generations. The young are expected to respect elders because of their age and wisdom. Elders in turn advise and guide the young because they are vulnerable to the caprices of life. Girls and women are expected to obey their fathers and husbands because the latter are the heads of family. Laziness is abhorred because the gods do not support those who do not consciously make an effort to improve their lot. Labor is, therefore, a spiritual undertaking. Initiates of Vodun, for example, may be asked to cultivate the farm of a chief priest without any material compensation.

SOCIAL ASPECTS Each family, clan, or lineage has its special Vodun spirit, which provides meaning for its existence. It is difficult, therefore, to divorce everyday life from spiritual life. The family, the first unit of social organization, is a bloodline community united by an ancestor. The family owes its spirit great loyalty and must honor the prohibitions prescribed in sacred practices. Traditionally marriage was considered a union of lineages rather than of two individuals, and procreation was the avowed purpose of marriage. In the past marriages were arranged by heads of lineages, with at least the tacit consent of the would-be husband and wife. Nowadays individuals are more likely to choose their spouses, though both families involved must give their consent before the marriage can be finalized.

POLITICAL IMPACT As in precolonial and colonial times, Vodun continues to have great impact on politics in Benin. The influence of chief priests among believers has been an important reason for politicians to seek their support. President Mathieu Kérékou, who viewed Vodun as detrimental to his Marxist-Leninist ideology, banned the religion in 1972. Vodun was reinstated as a national religion only after a national conference held in 1990 returned the country to multiparty politics. In 1996 President Nicéphore Soglo declared that January 10 was National Vodun Day, thereby giving the religion official recognition. State-run television now features coverage of National Vodun Day.

CONTROVERSIAL ISSUES Although since the 1990s violent confrontations over religious issues have been rare in Benin, Vodun continues to be viewed as a challenge to Christian evangelization, especially with the growing influence of Pentecostalism in the country. Moreover, President Kérékou has used pro-Christian rhetoric to denounce political opposition and the previous military regime, raising concerns about the constitution's guarantee of freedom of religious expression.

National and international activists against female circumcision have accused Vodun adherents of encouraging the practice. Most Vodun believers say that the practice is not part of Vodun and that the accusations constitute a smear campaign by other religious groups, especially Christians, to discredit the religion.

CULTURAL IMPACT Among artistic forms of expression in Benin, woodcarving has been the one most influenced by Vodun. Statues and statuettes of the gods and human forms, or *gbo*, that are believed to protect households and their owners are common in shrines and homes. Some statues are carved specifically for sale to European tourists, however. Brass casting is another highly developed art form that is used for religious expression. It is common to see carvings that glorify various gods in both public and private spaces.

Vodun's influence on contemporary music has been exemplified by the music of internationally known Beninese songwriter and performer Angélique Kidjo (born in 1960). Kidjo combines traditional beats and pop music and uses lyrics that draw upon the spiritual influences of Vodun. She also celebrates the connections between Benin and Brazil, where the descendants of African slaves have kept alive their African heritage.

Other Religions

Vodun has coexisted with Islam since precolonial times and with Christianity since the colonial era. In present-day Benin, Muslims are represented most heavily in the northern and southeastern parts of the country. Almost all Muslims belong to the Sunni branch of Islam. In recent decades the Ahmadiyya movement, a heterodox sect that originated in India in the late nineteenth century, has sought to extend its influence in Benin by opening a number of centers. Christianity is more common in southern Benin, especially in Cotonou, the economic capital of the country. Many people who nominally identify themselves as Christians and Muslims also participate in Vodun.

As in most of sub-Saharan Africa, the Malikite school, one of four Sunni branches, predominates in Benin. Shiism never made much headway across the Sahara. The Tijaniyya and Qadiriyya Sufi orders also have followings in Benin. Islam most probably spread into the northern part of Benin by trade routes linked to such Sudanic empires as Ghana, Mali, and Songhay, bringing Muslim traders and clerics. They settled among non-Muslims, attempting at first to convert the local leadership. Islam advanced slowly until the colonial period, when more people began to convert, in part as a reaction against French rule. Today most Muslims in Benin belong to the Fulani, Bariba, and Dend ethnic groups, which are found predominantly in the northern part of the country. Despite their Islamic faith many Muslims in Benin are known to consult Vodun priests and visit Vodun shrines, practices that are also common among the country's Christians.

Although European activities along the coast of Benin began as early as the sixteenth century, it was not until the following century that the first significant step was taken to introduce Christianity in the kingdom of Allada. In 1685 King Toxonu sent an envoy to Philip VI of Spain and Louis XIV of France asking them to send missionaries to his kingdom. Capuchin missionaries working in Sierra Leone were then asked to send missionaries to the kingdom of Allada. The subsequent arrival of nine missionaries had little impact on converting the local people to Christianity, however. Attempts by priests of the Orders of Saint Thomas and Saint Augustine during the same period met a similar fate. In 1689 Portuguese Roman Catholic priests established a chapel in Ouidah. It was not until the 1860s, however, that missionary activities in the interior began in earnest with the efforts of the Society of African Missions of Lyon.

During the eighteenth century two Portuguese priests sent to convert the king of Dahomey, Agonglo, to Roman Catholicism failed to accomplish their mission because Agonglo was assassinated before converting. It is not clear whether the king was killed because his followers feared that he was going to make Christianity the state religion. In any case Christianity did not gain much of a following because powerful persons in Abomey feared that it might pose a threat to Vodun.

After Dahomey was incorporated into French West Africa in 1904, Roman Catholicism slowly began to win more converts through the establishment of mission schools. Although the number of converts was relatively small and mostly confined to the southern part of Benin, the mission-educated elite began to develop a separate identity. While some members of the elite, like their European mentors, condemned Vodun as a pagan practice, the majority continued to practice Vodun, seeing no conflict between the Christian concept of God and the Vodun Mawu, the Supreme Being. Although a seminary was opened in Dahomey in 1913, it was not until 1928 that the first African priest was ordained.

Christians in Benin are predominantly Roman Catholic and represent about a fifth of the country's population. The Catholic Church in Benin comprises two archdioceses and eight dioceses. Other Christian groups in Benin include Aladura (independent African churches), Assemblies of God, Baptists, Jehovah's Witnesses, Pentecostals, Methodists, Seventh-day Adventists, and the Church of Jesus Christ of Latter-day Saints. Aladura churches have proliferated in Benin since the early 1990s. These churches, which broke away from mainstream congregations during the early twentieth century, have their origin among the Yoruba. Generally, evangelical and Pentecostal churches in Benin have been more directly involved in politics than the Catholic Church has. After Mathieu Kérékou returned to the presidency in 1996 and declared himself a born-again Christian, he invited to Benin German evangelist Reinhard Bonnke, whose tent meetings in Cotonou attracted thousands of Christians and curious onlookers.

Tamba M'bayo

See Also Vol. I: *African Indigenous Beliefs, Islam, Roman Catholicism*

Bibliography

Akinjogbin, I.A. *Dahomey and its Neighbors: 1708–1818.* Cambridge: Cambridge University Press, 1967.

Bay, Edna G. *Wives of Leopard: Gender, Politics, and Culture in the Kingdom of Dahomey.* Charlottesville, Va., and London: University of Virginia Press, 1998.

Decalo, Samuel. *Historical Dictionary of Benin.* 3rd ed. Lanham, Md.: Scarecrow Press, 1995.

Eades, J.S., and Chris Allen, comps. *Benin.* Oxford and Santa Barbara, Calif.: ABC-CLIO, 1996.

Falcon, Paul. "Religion du vodun." *Études dahoméenes* 18–19 (1970): 1–211.

Herskovits, Melville J. *Dahomey: An Ancient West African Kingdom.* 2 vols. Evanston, Ill.: Northwestern University Press, 1967.

Law, Robin. "Dahomey and the Slave Trade: Reflections on the Historiography of the Rise of Dahomey." *Journal of African History* 27, no. 2 (1986): 237–67.

Manning, Patrick. *Slavery, Colonialism, and Economic Growth in Dahomey, 1640–1960.* Cambridge and New York: Cambridge University Press, 1982.

Sulikowski, Ulrike. "Eating the Flesh, Eating the Soul: Reflections on Politics, Sorcery, and Vodun in Contemporary Benin." In *L'invention religieuse en Afrique: Histoire et religion en Afrique noire.* Edited by Jean-Pierre Chrétien, 379–92. Paris: A.C.C.T.; Karthala, 1993.

Bhutan

POPULATION 692,000

NYINGMAPA BUDDHIST 45 percent

DRUKPA KAGYUDPA BUDDHIST 40 percent

HINDU 14 percent

OTHER 1 percent

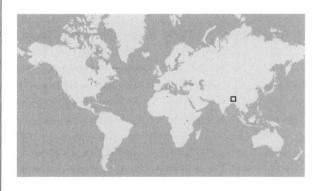

Country Overview

INTRODUCTION The Kingdom of Bhutan, sandwiched between India and China, is the only independent Buddhist state in the Himalayas. Roughly the size of Switzerland, it has a population estimated to be less than 700,000 and is composed of three major ethnic groups speaking about 19 different languages. Well known for its policy of isolation and conservation, Bhutan today is celebrated for its thriving Buddhist culture and for its ethnolinguistic and ecological diversity.

The Indian saint Padmasambhava, who remains the most important spiritual figure in Bhutan, first brought Buddhism from the south in the eighth century. In the following centuries Buddhism came from the north through Tibetan missionaries, who disseminated Buddhist teachings across the country and firmly established it as the faith of the land. In the nineteenth and twentieth centuries immigrants from Nepal brought Hinduism to the southern districts of Bhutan. Since the 1960s there has also been some restricted Christian missionary work in the south.

Before the mid-seventeenth century Bhutan was divided into many fiefdoms ruled by local warlords and chieftains. In the seventeenth century the present nation of Bhutan was created through the leadership of Zhabdrung Ngawang Namgyal, a Buddhist hierarch who came into exile from southern Tibet. Zhabdrung's plan to establish a hereditary religious line was not realized, and the new nation came to be ruled by a theocratic government of changing regency. Most of the early regents were monks, but as more and more laypersons vying for power held the regency, the country was beset by anarchy. The theocratic-regent system was replaced by a monarchy in 1907, when Sir Ugyen Wangchuk became the first king. His great-grandson Jigme Singye Wangchuk became the fourth king in 1972.

In the last half of the twentieth century Bhutan stepped out of its historic isolation, establishing diplomatic relations and building roads, schools, hospitals, post offices, and banks. It saw the introduction of television and the Internet, democratization of the political system, and judicial reform—all having immense impact on the simple Buddhist way of living. Gross National Happiness—a concept developed from King Jigme Singye Wangchuk's remark that Gross National Happiness is more important than Gross National Product—

A Bhutanese man stands among prayer flags on a hill overlooking Bhutan's capital city, Thimphu. Religious objects such as prayer flags are attributed much sanctity and are treated with respect. AP/WIDE WORLD PHOTOS.

today forms the main objective of the country's plans and policies, integrating economic development with spiritual edification. A constitution for the country was being developed at the beginning of the twenty-first century, leaving most Bhutanese wondering what role religion would play in shaping this last Mahayana Buddhist state.

RELIGIOUS TOLERANCE Bhutan's main religious traditions are the Drukpa Kagyud and Nyingma schools of Tibetan Buddhism. Although Drukpa Kagyud is the state religion, the Nyingma school dominates central and eastern Bhutan. As they are close in philosophy and practice, most people view them as the same or of equal significance. Thus, there has been little sectarian tension, much less communal conflict, among the country's Buddhist communities.

Most Bhutanese Buddhists, however, have strong reservations about other religious traditions. Some Christian missionary work has been condemned for using material incentives to proselytize and has even be-

come a serious subject of debate in the National Assembly, the nation's highest legislative body. In the 1980s and 1990s there were political conflicts between the Nepali minority and the Bhutanese government, resulting in an exodus of a large number of ethnic Nepali. This ethnic conflict was also partly a religious struggle between Bhutanese Buddhists and Nepali Hindus.

Major Religion

TIBETAN BUDDHISM

DATE OF ORIGIN Seventh century C.E.
NUMBER OF FOLLOWERS 600,000

HISTORY In Bhutan the first phase of the spread of Buddhism occurred between the seventh and seventeenth centuries. Two Buddhist temples, Jampa Lhakhang in Bumthang and Kyerchu Lhakhang in Paro, are believed to have been built by the Tibetan emperor

Srongtsen Gampo in the seventh century. The proper advent of Buddhism to Bhutan, however, was the arrival of the Indian master Padmasambhava at the court of a local ruler in Bumthang in the middle of the eighth century. Although there are no historical records of change brought by his mission, oral traditions have it that people took lay Buddhist vows and gave up animal sacrifices.

During the centuries after Padmasambhava's journeys to Bhutan, Buddhist savants from Tibet, including Myos Lhanangpa, Longchenpa, Barawa Gyaltshen Palzang, and Phajo Drukgom Zhigpo, poured into the region. The Nyingma tradition of Tibetan Buddhism spread widely in what are now the central and eastern parts of Bhutan and produced such religious figures as Padma Lingpa (1450–1521), perhaps the most famous Bhutanese master in history. Other sects, such as Lhapa, Barawa, Nenying, Sakya, Drukpa, and Karma Kagyud, spread mainly in central and western Bhutan. Thus, during this period Bhutan saw the arrival and propagation of several schools of Tibetan Buddhism and a gradual conversion of the people. Historians also believe that it was at about this time that Bhutan came to be known as Drukyul (Land of the Thunder Dragon), after the Drukpa Kagyud school.

A second phase of Buddhism in Bhutan dates from 1616, the year Zhabdrung Ngawang Namgyal escaped from Tibet and began his temporal and spiritual unification of Bhutan. Under his supervision the Drukpa Kagyud school of the Tibetan Kagyud tradition was promulgated in the country, and the Zhung Dratshang, or the central ecclesiastical body, was established. All other schools except the Nyingmapa declined after the Drukpa domination of the Bhutanese valleys. During the following centuries the Drukpa Kagyud tradition spread across the entire country through the establishment of numerous branches of the central ecclesiastical body.

For centuries Buddhism influenced all aspects of Bhutanese life, at both the individual and state level. It became the guiding light for an individual's daily life, as well as for the country's development policies, legal system, social service, and traditional etiquette. From the construction of the earliest temples in the seventh century to the writing of the modern constitution, Buddhism has played a vital role in Bhutanese history and forms an integral part of Bhutanese identity.

EARLY AND MODERN LEADERS The first and foremost religious figure in Bhutanese Buddhism was Padmasambhava, who lived in the eighth century and who surpasses even the Buddha as an object of worship and prayer. The two most important religious sites in Bhutan, and hundreds of others, are dedicated to this master, and devotion, prayers, and offerings to him form the rudiments of Bhutanese Buddhism.

The second most respected historical figure is Zhabdrung Ngawang Namgyal (1594–1651?), under whom the country was unified and a theocratic system of government was founded. Zhabdrung established some of the most important religious institutions and traditions in Bhutan. For example, he created the post of the Je Khenpo (chief abbot of the Drukpa Kagyud school in Bhutan). The Zhabdrung reincarnate (the series of people who are considered his reincarnation) is the other chief hierarch of the Drukpa Kagyud school. The 70th Je Khenpo, Trulku Jigme Choedra (appointed in 1996), is a well-respected and active religious leader.

A major saint of Bhutanese origin is Padma Lingpa (1450–1521), who is widely revered in the Himalayan region as a prominent *terton,* or discoverer of religious treasures buried for posterity by Padmasambhava and his disciples. Like Zhabdrung, Padma Lingpa has had a profound influence on Bhutanese society through his family lineage and through the religious institutions he founded.

MAJOR THEOLOGIANS AND AUTHORS Until the middle of the twentieth century Bhutan produced more prominent historians than religious thinkers and philosophers. The most notable religious scholar of the twentieth century was the Je Khenpo Gedun Rinchen, who composed 11 volumes on Buddhist philosophy, mysticism, grammar, and history. Today, however, Bhutan is witnessing an active generation of Buddhist scholarship. Contemporary Bhutanese religious authors such as Khenpo Tsewang Sonam and Lopon Thegchog are popular even among Tibetan scholars.

HOUSES OF WORSHIP AND HOLY PLACES The two oldest places of worship in Bhutan are Jampa Lhakhang in Bumthang and Kyerchu Lhakhang in Paro, thought to have been built by the Tibetan emperor Srongtsen Gampo in the seventh century. Kurje Lhakhang, where Padmasambhava is believed to have left an imprint of his body on the wall of a cave, is revered. Another sacred place is Taktsang (Tiger's Lair) monastery, which hangs precariously on a cliff in Paro; Padmasambhava is believed to have visited there on a tigress's back. In addition, all Bhutanese districts have forts known as *dzongs*, which house district religious headquarters, and every village has a temple where people gather for religious ceremonies. Every family home also contains a chapel, or *choesham*, where most of the family rituals and ceremonies take place. Hundreds of *gompas* (hermitages) and *chotens* (monuments containing religious relics) dot the Bhutanese landscape.

WHAT IS SACRED? Most Bhutanese are devout Buddhists and therefore treat all kinds of sentient life as sacred. Killing of animals is a religious violation and is thus viewed as a social taboo in many districts. There are a number of valleys and mountains, particularly those associated with Padmasambhava, that are considered sacred and powerful landscapes and that attract pilgrims. Monasteries and religious objects, including Buddhist scriptures, statues, and prayer flags, are attributed much sanctity and are treated with respect.

HOLIDAYS AND FESTIVALS In Bhutan there are about a half dozen national holidays associated with the Buddha and other Buddhist figures. There are also anniversaries to mark the birthday of the king and to commemorate the founding (17 December 1907) of the monarchy. Major religious festivals, mostly known as *tshechu* or *drubchoe*, are observed in the monasteries with colorful religious mask dances performed by monks and folk dances performed by girls.

The most festive occasions, however, are the local village festivals held to propitiate local deities or to celebrate good harvests, among other reasons. During these festivals dances are performed in the temple courtyard during the day, and parties are held in the mornings and evenings.

MODE OF DRESS Bhutanese men wear a long-sleeved robe known as a *gho*, which, pulled up to the knees, is then tied at the waist with a sash. Women wear a long dress called a *kira*, held by silver hooks on the shoulder and tied with a sash at the waist. A short jacket is worn on top of the *kira*. These garments, worn originally by the Buddhist Bhutanese in the north, has become the national dress and is worn by most Bhutanese. There are, however, a small number of tribal people who continue to wear their unique costumes in the far northern, southern, and eastern parts of the country. Most men

and women keep fairly short hair. It is believed that this tradition derives from the shaving of the hair during Padmasambhava's ordination of Bhutanese men and women as lay Buddhists. Monks and lay priests wear red robes similar to those of Tibetan Buddhist clergies.

DIETARY PRACTICES Although nonviolence and compassion are fundamental to Bhutanese Buddhism, and most people are strongly opposed to taking life, meat is a common part of the Bhutanese diet. This is because much meat eating does not involve killing, as people eat the meat of dead animals from their herds. Since the 1990s a controversial regulation banning the sale of meat during holy months has been enforced. Rice, wheat, maize, and buckwheat are the main staple foods, and Bhutanese are known for their consumption of chilies. Bhutan's best-known dishes are *phagsha pah*, a pork dish, and *ema datshi*, chili with cheese.

Most Bhutanese chew *doma*, the betel nut with slaked lime wrapped in pan (betel leaf). Legend has it that the pre-Buddhist Bhutanese were wild cannibals and that when Padmasambhava tamed them he had to substitute cannibalism with the habit of eating *doma*, the three parts of which are said to symbolize parts of the human body: the leaf stands for the tongue, the lime for the brain, and the betel nut for the heart.

Although intoxicating drinks form one of the primary Buddhist prohibitions, alcohol, in the form of locally brewed spirits and ciders, is popular in Bhutanese societies, and festivities are marked by drinking. Religious influence, however, has led many to give up alcohol, meat, eggs, and fish and also to observe fasts during holy days and weeks.

RITUALS Bhutanese Buddhists perform a wide variety of rituals throughout the year. These may be ceremonies known as *choga* (performances of religious rites with monastic music) or simply the recitation of prayers and scriptures. Ritual services for the sick are common and diverse, and funeral rituals are long (lasting for 21 days or more) and economically cumbersome.

A popular family ritual is the *lochoe*, which is the annual supplication to the family's tutelary deities. There is no formal Buddhist marriage ritual, and Bhutanese generally do not have a wedding ceremony.

RITES OF PASSAGE There are no formal rites of passage in Bhutanese Buddhism or in Buddhism in general.

A person first becomes a Buddhist by taking refuge in the Three Jewels: the Buddha, the dharma (his teachings), and the sangha (the spiritual community). This is done in early childhood before a lama, who cuts the tip of the person's hair and gives him or her a new name. Bhutanese Buddhists use names received from a lama in this manner and do not share family names. The practice of taking refuge and naming is often repeated several times in a person's lifetime as a ritual of blessing. Many tantric practices in Bhutanese Buddhism require specific preliminary procedures such as *wang* (empowerment), *lung* (scriptural authorization), and *thri* (quintessential instructions). Most of the major religious ceremonies in the country are connected to these preliminary rites.

MEMBERSHIP It is through taking refuge in the Three Jewels—accepting the Buddha as the teacher, the dharma as the path, and the sangha as the companions on the path—that one truly becomes a Buddhist. Most Bhutanese, however, consider themselves to be Buddhists by birth. People who do not believe in *le jumday* (karma, or the law of cause and effect) or who subscribe to theism are sometimes viewed as heretics.

SOCIAL JUSTICE Buddhism adopts an egalitarian approach to social issues. A person's status is determined not by birth, caste, color, or race but by his or her moral and spiritual qualities. Because it is believed that there is no inherent self and that everyone is equal in being an assembly of psychosomatic components, there is no innate difference in people's status. It is the quality of the physical and spiritual components that determines the personality and that differentiates one person from another.

Bhutanese Buddhists also believe that all sentient beings are endowed with the Buddha nature and that all beings have been a person's mother in the course of the innumerable rebirths he or she has had in this cycle of existence. Both of these beliefs help nurture a sense of equality and equanimity toward all persons. Perhaps because of these religious influences, Bhutan has greater social, racial, and sexual equality than its neighbors.

The strongest and most vivid impact of Buddhism on Bhutanese society is perhaps seen in the application of the two principles *le jumday*, the law of cause and effect, and *tha damtshig*, a popular Bhutanese code of moral rectitude (which has a variety of referents, including honesty, fidelity, integrity, gratitude, and loyalty). These concepts dictate the Bhutanese way of life, and since the 1980s they have also taken on strong political overtones. The government has also worked on incorporating into its judicial system and its plan for decentralization the values of Buddhist *vinaya* (monastic rules), which uses a democratic style of decision-making through consensus.

SOCIAL ASPECTS Although the spirit of Buddhism pervades all facets and all levels of Bhutanese life, there are no formal Buddhist rites and rituals pertaining to family life and marriage. Religious influences are, however, evident in Bhutanese family life. Bhutanese are well known for their laxity and openness in sexual affairs, and most indulge in sexual promiscuity, perhaps because of the influence of tantric figures such as the "crazy saint" Drukpa Kunley (1455–1529). The fact that both polygynous and polyandrous relations remain common may be explained by the same influences.

POLITICAL IMPACT Since its foundation in the seventeenth century, Bhutan has professed a political system of *choesrid zungjug*: the union of religious and temporal power. Because theocratic leaders, including monks and religious kings, ruled Bhutan for ages, religion has played a vital role in governing the country.

The resonance of religious influence persists in political idioms such as Tsawa Sum (a concept borrowed from Buddhism to refer to the trio of the king, country, and people) and Gross National Happiness, the overall goal of the country's development policies. The latter concept has been promoted by the king, Jigme Singye Wangchuk, as a means of maximizing both spiritual happiness and economic development.

There have been controversies about which sects should be supported by the state. One of the key issues of debate surrounding the drafting of a constitution is whether or not Bhutan should in fact have a secular government. The adoption of a secular system would end the historical status of Buddhism, and of the Drukpa Kagyud school in particular, as the state religion. Most Bhutanese, however, attribute the sovereignty, peace, and prosperity of their country to its close association with Buddhism and pray for its longevity, as can be seen in the last two lines of the national anthem: "May dharma, the teaching of the Buddha, flourish / May the sun of happiness and peace shine on the people."

CONTROVERSIAL ISSUES The status of the Drukpa Kagyud school as the state religion, and the prerogatives and benefits to which it is entitled, have been issues of persistent questioning and disquiet. The Nyingmapas in central and eastern Bhutan have often accused the state school of a vicious policy of monopolizing the religious domain. They allege that the Drukpa Kagyud school has used coercion to extend its authority and jurisdiction in areas originally dominated by Nyingmapas, and they have even launched antigovernment campaigns in the far eastern districts.

A related issue that has been much debated is the visits of renowned Tibetan lamas from India and elsewhere. Because these lamas often own property given as offerings, and because they compete with local religious figures, some Bhutanese are concerned about the socioeconomic effect they have on Bhutanese society.

Another controversial issue, though one that is more political than religious, concerns the dispute between the ruling family and the line of Zhabdrung reincarnates. The last Zhabdrung candidate went into exile to India and lived in Manali, where thousands of Bhutanese pilgrims visited him until his death in 2003.

CULTURAL IMPACT In Bhutan Buddhism is almost the only theme in art forms such as painting and sculpture, though much of what can be classified as folk craft, comprising architecture, metalwork, weaving, carving, and bamboo work, has little to do with religion. Folk songs evoke both religious and worldly subjects, while monastic hymns and music are of a purely religious nature. Performing arts are more or less bifurcated into profane folk dances and sacred religious dances. The growing number of new songs, dances, and dramas, which are set in modern Western styles and reflect contemporary Bhutanese life, do not usually touch on spiritual themes.

Most traditional Bhutanese literature focuses on religion or is heavily laden with religious content. Even writings on nonreligious topics such as language, history, biography, and folktales could not escape the influence of religion. Today, however, there is an emerging class of literati who are trained in the West or receive a Western-style education and who write in English, although there are also a large number of traditional virtuosi who write in classical Tibetan and take their inspiration from Buddhism.

Other Religions

Hinduism is the only other religion that a visitor to Bhutan may notice. The followers of Hinduism are mostly of Nepali ethnic origin and are concentrated mainly in the southern districts. As in India and Nepal, Hindu communities are divided into four major, and hundreds of minor, castes. The Brahmans, as the highest caste, transmit the religion through family lines and religious schools known as *patshalas*. Religious training is done in Sanskrit, the language of such Hindu scriptures as the Vedas and the Upanishads and of the epics *Ramayana* and *Mahabharata*. In the 1970s and 1980s the government, in an endeavor to promote cultural and religious harmony, supported some of these Sanskrit *patshalas* and also encouraged scholars to write on the similarities between the Buddhist and Hindu religions.

Bhutanese Hindus believe in the trinity of Brahma, Vishnu, and Shiva and observe dozens of religious festivals in a calendar year. The two most important occasions are the Dashain and the Tihar, both falling in October. During Dashain the goddess Kali is worshiped, and hundreds of animals are slaughtered as sacrificial offerings. This practice of animal sacrifice is perhaps the most contentious religious issue for southern Hindus and northern Buddhists. In contrast, Tihar, or Deepavali, which is celebrated with lights and fanfare, is a veneration of the goddess Lakshmi, and even some Buddhist Bhutanese take part in it. Such religious affinity is strengthened by the fact that Lakshmi, along with other gods, appears in both the Hindu and Bhutanese Buddhist pantheon.

Among both Buddhist communities in the north and Hindu communities in the south, there is a growing number of Christian neophytes. The first Christian missionaries arrived in Bhutan as early as the seventeenth century. Active missionary work started only in the 1960s, but Christian movements, facing the opposition of staunch Buddhists, have not succeeded in Bhutan as they have in other parts of the Himalayas. Most Bhutanese shun Christian missionary work as proselytization of the poor and ignorant through economic and material incentives. A small, fledgling movement, Christianity has no known public place of worship or formal organization in Bhutan.

Prior to the arrival of Buddhism, most Bhutanese followed folk beliefs that involved pagan and shamanistic practices. Some of these archaic religious customs—

akin to, and often associated with, Bon, the pre-Buddhist religion of Tibet—are extant in remote valleys. In addition, a wide range of folk beliefs and rituals are prevalent throughout Bhutan and sometimes play even more important roles than the institutionalized religions. Shamans, oracles, fortune-tellers, and astrologers form crucial components of Bhutanese society and are consulted on such occasions as birth, illness, and death as often as are Buddhist and Hindu clerics. They are trusted even more than the clerics on matters such as the construction of a new house, the beginning of a journey or a business, and the tracing of lost items. Although most of their practices have been assimilated into the greater Buddhist system, much of what they do evokes a local and folk religious culture reminiscent of pre-Buddhist Bhutan.

Karma Phuntsho

See Also Vol. 1: *Buddhism, Hinduism, Tibetan Buddhism*

Bibliography

Ardussi, John. "Bhutan before the British: A Historical Study." Ph.D. diss., Australian National University, 1977.

Aris, Michael. *Bhutan: The Early History of a Himalayan Kingdom.* Warminster, England: Aris and Phillips, 1980.

Gedun Rinchen. *dPal ldan 'brug pa'i 'dul zhing lho phyogs nag mo'i ljongs kyi chos 'byung blo gsal rna ba'i rgyan.* Thimphu, Bhutan: Tango Monastery, n.d.

Mynak Tulku. "Religion and Rituals." In *Bhutan: Mountain Fortress of the Gods.* Edited by Christian Schicklgruber and Françoise Pommaret, 137–57. London: Serindia Publications, 1997.

Olschak, Blanche C. *Ancient Bhutan: A Study on Early Buddhism in the Himalayas.* Zurich: Schweizerische Stiftung für Alpine Forschung, 1979.

Bolivia

POPULATION 8,445,134

ROMAN CATHOLIC 79.3 percent

PROTESTANT 10.1 percent

NONRELIGIOUS 9.4 percent

OTHER 1.2 percent

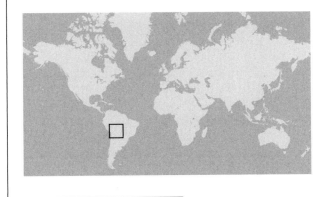

Country Overview

INTRODUCTION The Republic of Bolivia, located in South America, is a remote and landlocked country. It is bordered by Brazil to the northeast, as well as by Peru, Chile, Argentina, and Paraguay. Once a part of the Inca empire (twelfth to sixteenth centuries C.E.), Bolivia has about one-third of its territory in the high Andes mountains, while about two-thirds lie in the tropical lowlands of the Amazon drainage. Its population has the highest percentage of Indians of any nation in Latin America. Despite more than 500 years of Spanish control, indigenous languages continue to be widely spoken there. A strong and vital Indian movement developed in Bolivia

during the twentieth century, causing a rethinking of the relationship of ethnicity to Bolivian life.

The highlands were the site of major pre-Columbian populations that formed the Inca province of Kollasuyo, and the population centers of the colonial period were also in the highlands. Upon arriving in what is now Bolivia in the early sixteenth century C.E., the Spanish began to impose Roman Catholicism. The effort involved the secular system of governance as well as the various Catholic orders. Before the Jesuits' expulsion from Latin America at the end of the eighteenth century, they had formed missions in the lowlands, especially in the contemporary department of Santa Cruz, for the Tupi Guaraní peoples. As a result of the colonial period, Bolivia developed a varied Catholic society that today includes much indigenous religion, particularly in matters related to agriculture and rural life; a syncretic popular Catholicism; and changing formal, institutional worship.

In 1825 the province was liberated from Spain, and the new nation took the name of Bolivia in honor of the revolutionary leader Simó Bolívar. At the end of the nineteenth century Protestant denominations entered Bolivia with the blessing of the country's liberal, anticlerical governments. Initially, the Protestant groups built schools and hospitals and initiated development projects. During the last third of the twentieth century Protestant churches—especially Pentecostal churches—garnered substantial numbers of converts. Other religions, such as Mennonites, also entered Bolivia in the twentieth century, giving the country an even more complex religious system.

Two Bolivian Indians pay tribute to the Virgin of Copacabana at a pilgrimage site overlooking the shores of Lake Titicaca. © REUTERS NEWMEDIA INC./CORBIS.

RELIGIOUS TOLERANCE Bolivia's constitution guarantees the public exercise of any religion, although it also recognizes the Catholic Church as the official religion. During the last third of the twentieth century non-Catholic religions developed a significant public presence, both in practice and in law. Nevertheless, the Catholic Church maintains an important public role as a symbol of the nation and as a mediator among Bolivia's political and social groups.

Major Religion

ROMAN CATHOLICISM

DATE OF ORIGIN Early sixteenth century C.E.
NUMBER OF FOLLOWERS 6.7 million

HISTORY In the early sixteenth century C.E. Catholicism arrived in the area that is now Bolivia; it was brought there by the Spanish conquistadors and missionaries from the various Catholic orders. Given the region's importance as a mining center, Pope Julius III created the bishopric of La Plata in 1555. During the colonial period the Catholic Church was one of the pillars of the province's society. It played a strong social role by pro-

viding a sacred canopy for colonial rule, and it increasingly dominated indigenous communities and religion. As a result, it was a wealthy and important religious and financial institution.

The *patronato real* (the understanding that the Spanish king, rather than the Vatican, maintained the right to name bishops) gave the Spanish crown and subsequent colonial governments substantial control over the church as a critical civil institution. Images of Catholic saints, the Virgin Mary, and Jesus (and the mythologies and practices surrounding them) became identified with certain regions and thus were important in the formation of local, regional, and subsequently national identities.

Nevertheless, in the nineteenth century the Vatican engaged in a struggle to Romanize the Latin American Church, in which a major focus lay in reclaiming the *patronato* from the colonial governments. At the same time, Bolivian liberal political leaders and movements challenged the church's dominant place in society. This led to a reconfiguration of the church's relationship to the state and society in the nineteenth and twentieth centuries. For instance, the church lost its exclusive right to public practice and its control over social institutions such as education and matrimony. Significant religious pluralism developed within Bolivia, eroding membership in the Catholic Church. Another issue for the church was its relationship with Bolivia's indigenous peoples, among whom it saw a particularly large loss of membership. The church reacted by becoming strongly concerned about issues of social justice and the relationship of Catholicism to Indian culture and society.

In the 1960s Bolivia's bishops formed the Bolivian Episcopal Conference, which has been important in nationally coordinating church affairs, engaging Latin American bishops in general, and providing the institutional church with a strong national identity. By the end of the twentieth century the church had become a critical element of Bolivia's political life as well as an ecumenical force.

EARLY AND MODERN LEADERS When the government gave up its right to mediate in church affairs (1961), the country's bishops, organized in the Bolivian Episcopal Conference, were able to speak more openly about issues in Bolivian society. Cardinal Julio Terrazas Sandoval (born in 1936) has served a number of terms as president of the Episcopal Conference.

MAJOR THEOLOGIANS AND AUTHORS Catholic intellectuals in Bolivia have been strongly influenced by broader Latin American movements such as liberation theology and by the church's relationship to Bolivia's indigenous peoples and societies. This has led to a break with the scholasticism of the past and a focus on inculturation (the understanding that the Christian gospel can be located within indigenous cultures rather than imposed on them) and what is called Indian theology and the Indian pastoral.

Some of Bolivia's best religious thinkers, following the example of many colonial religious writers, have dedicated themselves to the study of Bolivian society and history. Among them is Xavier Albó (born in 1934), a Jesuit and an anthropologist known for bringing his religious training and commitment to understanding the culture, society, and political reality of Bolivians. He is the author of numerous works that examine Bolivia's indigenous peoples anthropologically, politically, and in terms of the changing relationship between the Catholic Church and Bolivia's Indians.

HOUSES OF WORSHIP AND HOLY PLACES Catholicism in Bolivia maintains a full hierarchy of religious buildings, from cathedrals to local neighborhoods and community chapels. In addition, it has several pilgrimage sites, such as those of the Virgin of Copacabana on the shores of Lake Titicaca and of the Virgin of Urqhupiña in the valleys of Cochabamba. Because of Catholicism's syncretic relationship with indigenous religiosity, Bolivia's high mountains, as well as other features of the landscape, are invested with holiness and attract the devotion of many people, sometimes under Catholic terms and sometimes without them.

WHAT IS SACRED? Official Catholicism in Bolivia follows the standards of the church, holding sacred the Holy Trinity, the Virgin Mary, saints, and popular holy figures. Popular Catholicism follows indigenous practice by recognizing sanctity in the landscape—particularly the high, snow-clad mountains. The earth itself is often associated with the Virgin Mary. Syncretic popular religion also acknowledges a holiness in certain animals, such as the condor and the puma. In addition, numerous images, such as that of the Virgin of Copacabana (the patroness of the nation), are invested with enormous significance.

HOLIDAYS AND FESTIVALS Bolivian Catholics celebrate the Catholic calendar of holy days. In addition,

each community, town, city, and region has patron saints. Each saint's day initiates a period of ritual activity, both inside the church and in the streets—where there are processions, pilgrimages, and performances by dance troupes. The national holiday is 6 August, the day after the feast day of the patroness of Bolivia, the Virgin of Copacabana.

MODE OF DRESS Dress in Bolivia is less a religious marker than a distinguishing characteristic of ethnicity and class. Indigenous people tend to dress in regionally specific or community-specific style; this is truer for women than for men.

DIETARY PRACTICES Catholics in Bolivia are not required to observe any dietary practices not practiced by Catholics worldwide, although popular Catholicism emphasizes the importance of shared food as part of ritual. Fasting during Lent is voluntarily observed by a minority of Bolivian Catholics.

RITUALS Catholics in Bolivia celebrate formal Catholic rituals. Nevertheless, feast days (with performances by dance troupes) occupy an important place in the religious calendar. Their prominence is a result both of the weight of historical Catholicism in Bolivia and of indigenous religion's influence on Catholicism. Feast days have been losing their connection with the church, becoming increasingly seen as "folkloric." They continue, however, to manifest an important moral and spiritual aesthetic, and they play a critical role in mobilizing social groups and resources.

Popular Catholicism in Bolivia also focuses on rites such as the *ch'alla*, the blessing and baptism of a home or vehicle. This involves spraying beer or wine on the house or vehicle; in some cases, the object will first be sprinkled with holy water. These rituals for cars, along with the blessing of money and of miniatures of commodities people would like to obtain, often center on the pilgrimage sites of Urqupiña and Copacabana. People travel to these sites from throughout Bolivia and from neighboring countries to worship incarnations of the Virgin Mary, who is associated with the indigenous Pachamama, or Earthmother (Lady of Space and Time). It is thought that prayers to the Virgin can bring blessings of fertility (both sexual and agricultural) and economic fortune into the worshiper's life.

RITES OF PASSAGE Bolivians follow the standard Catholic rites of passage. Additionally, they celebrate a first haircut when a child is about three years of age. Called the *mururaña* or *rutucha*, this rite is considered important for the appropriate growth of the child, and it invests him or her with a social identity and a social network, as well as providing the child with the beginnings of a capital fund (which includes animals and cash).

Bolivian popular religiosity emphasizes the importance of godparents and the relationships among co-godparents. This notion is extended to provide sponsorship for all kinds of events, such as graduations and football tournaments.

MEMBERSHIP The Catholic Church in Bolivia has been strongly concerned about defending its membership against the inroads of non-Catholic religion, especially among indigenous peoples. As a result, it has developed a new commitment to missionize its people. This has included the formation of Catholic renewal efforts, such as establishing lay catechists in rural communities and renewing parish life and devotion in the cities. In addition, the church has strengthened its missionary commitment to indigenous societies in the lowlands of Bolivia. Nevertheless, the Catholic Church has ceased to refer to most Protestant denominations as "sects" and instead has encouraged ecumenical dialogue.

SOCIAL JUSTICE The Catholic Church is actively involved as a mediator and moral force in Bolivian political life. Because Bolivia is the poorest country in the American continental mainland, Bolivia's Catholic hierarchy is concerned about addressing the problem of widespread poverty. They also emphasize respect for and acceptance of Bolivia's indigenous peoples and their culture.

SOCIAL ASPECTS While the church in Bolivia maintains and promotes formal Catholic doctrine on marriage and the family, it exists in a secular state where divorce and abortion are practiced. The church crititicizes certain widespread Bolivian social customs, such as the *sirwinakuy* (often called trial marriage, although ethnographers prefer to emphasize its nature as a sequence of events over time rather than a single moment of ritual). The church encourages couples to marry formally rather than practice *sirwinakuy*. The church also expresses its disapproval about the growth of an open gay community in Bolivia and the increasing public acceptance of homosexuality.

POLITICAL IMPACT In the nineteenth century the struggle in Bolivia between liberals and conservatives over, among other things, the relationship of the church to society was occasionally violent. The contest to define the church's place in society continued into the twentieth century. During the dictatorships of the mid- to late-twentieth century, the left-leaning church and its clergy were subject to political repression. By the end of the twentieth century, however, the church had become a respected mediator between Bolivia's often fractious political groups.

CONTROVERSIAL ISSUES The most controversial issues affecting the Bolivian Catholic Church involve the church's role in struggles over poverty, social movements, and neoliberalism. Bolivia finds itself caught between the demands of foreign powers (such as the United States and international lending institutions) and the mobilization of grassroots movements (such as labor unions and Indian rights groups). The church is an important voice for social justice at the same time that it attempts to mediate among the forces in conflict.

CULTURAL IMPACT Catholicism continues to have an impact on Bolivian culture. In colonial times much of the art in Bolivia was religious art. During the seventeenth and eighteenth centuries the Potosí school of painters and sculptors (led by the mestizo painter Melchor Pérez de Holguín) prepared art for the religious buildings constructed in Bolivia. In style they followed many of the canons of the Spanish Baroque.

Even though there is a formal separation between state and religion, the church and Catholic culture continue to be represented widely in Bolivia's arts. Catholic images remain important means by which the nation and its regions are represented. For example, although secular images of the nation abound, it is not uncommon for the image of the Virgin of Copacabana or the Virgin of Urqupiña to be used to signify the Bolivian people and state.

Other Religions

The most important religion besides Catholicism in Bolivia consists of a myriad of indigenous religious practices. Much of this has been *syncretized* (combined) with Catholicism and has become a font of popular Catholic religiosity. Nevertheless, identifiably indigenous religion continues to exist in Bolivia and has been undergoing something of a revitalization. Urban Indian leaders have resurrected and created forms of Indian religiosity, which have been spreading to regional towns and communities. One example of this is the celebration of the Aymará new year, the *machakmara*, when people, with music and offerings, ritually await the first rays of the sun on the morning of the southern hemisphere's winter solstice.

In addition to creating such ritual forms, the revitalization has been forming an Aymará priesthood from the seers and healers of rural communities and their urban counterparts. Shamans, known in Quechua as *yachaj*, play important divination, healing, mediating, and advice-dispensing roles, often in collaboration with Catholic practitioners. The Qollahuaya (also spelled Kallawaya) healers from midwestern Bolivia have been renowned throughout the entire Andean region for centuries. The roles of healing, misfortune management, ancestor worship, and dealing with death and the dead are key features of Andean religious practice.

Andean indigenous religion emphasizes the relationship between people and the landscape. Certain features of the land are sacred and are seen as living beings with which people maintain a relationship. These landforms, called *huacas* (in the case of the mountains they are called *achachilas* or *apus*), require service and regular feeding through offerings called *mesas* (tables, or masses). The offerings contain various items depending on the nature of the ritual need. They might include llama fat and wool, coca leaves, molded sugar representations of many things, or seeds.

In addition, indigenous religiosity emphasizes rituals that integrate people into larger groups, such as rites of passage (including those mentioned above as part of Catholic practices) and religious *fiestas* (feasts). Important to this is the use of the coca leaf as something sacred; people share coca among themselves as well as with the earth in ritual. When a person receives the coca, he or she often blows on it with a prayer, offering it to the earth shrines. Because of their importance in ritual and social life, coca leaves are believed to connect people and the cosmos.

In Bolivia during the last third of the twentieth century, there was a rapid and socially significant growth of Pentecostalism and of Protestantism in general. Since the 1960s there has been a massive surge of religious change. Evangelicals and Pentecostals are increasingly prominent and publicly represented. Protestants, among

them the Methodists, Baptists, and Seventh-day Adventists, have historically been important in pioneering and providing public education to a broad range of Bolivian people. This has given each of these religious groups an important place in the social history and contemporary reality of the country.

Bolivia also has an important area of Mennonite colonies in its tropical lowlands. Mennonites in Canada had experienced pressure to assimilate to secular, English-speaking culture. After World War I many migrated to Mexico and Paraguay; beginning in the 1950s these Mennonites began establishing colonies in Bolivia. Mennonites in Bolivia adhere to various degrees of strictness in separation between themselves and the outer society and have various relationships with transnational Mennonite movements. They produce agroindustrial products for local consumption and export, but despite their importance in the Bolivian economy, the Mennonites are an ethnic enclave religiously separated from the mainstream religious population.

Since the 1970s Bolivia has seen impressive growth in the Church of Jesus Christ of Latter-day Saints, leading to its strong presence in the nation's cities. Mormons have built prominent chapels in every Bolivian city, and in Cochabamba a Mormon temple (a building restricted to faithful Latter-day Saints for rituals sealing the living and the dead together) attracts pilgrims from throughout Bolivia and from neighboring countries.

The country has a significant population of Bahais, focused in the department of Oruro. It also has a small but socially significant Jewish population and a small number of Muslims. Secularity, or not identifying with religion, is also an important social option in contemporary Bolivia.

David Knowlton

See Also Vol. I: *Christianity, Roman Catholicism*

Bibliography

Abercrombie, Thomas A. *Pathways of Memory and Power: Ethnography and History among an Andean People.* Madison: University of Wisconsin Press, 1998.

Bastien, Joseph W. *Mountain of the Condor: Metaphor and Ritual in an Andean Ayllu.* Prospect Heights, Ill.: Waveland Press, 1985.

Bastien, Joseph W., and Eleanor Forfang Stauffer. *Healers of the Andes: Kallawaya Herbalists and their Medicinal Plants.* Salt Lake City: University of Utah Press, 1988.

Bauer, Brian S., and Charles Stanish. *Ritual and Pilgrimage in the Ancient Andes: The Islands of the Sun and Moon.* Austin: University of Texas Press, 2001.

Block, David. *Mission Culture on the Upper Amazon: Native Tradition, Jesuit Enterprise, and Secular Policy in Moxos, 1660–1880.* Lincoln: University of Nebraska Press, 1994.

MacCormack, Sabine. "From the Sun of the Incas to the Virgin of Copacabana." *Representations* 8 (1984): 30–60.

———. *Religion in the Andes.* Princeton, N.J.: Princeton University Press, 1991.

Salles-Reese, Verónica. *From Viracocha to the Virgin of Copacabana: Representation of the Sacred at Lake Titicaca.* Austin: University of Texas Press, 1997.

Stoll, David. *Fishers of Men or Founders of Empire? The Wycliffe Bible Translators in Latin America.* Cambridge, Mass.: Cultural Survival, 1982.

Taussig, Michael. *The Devil and Commodity Fetishism in South America.* Chapel Hill: University of North Carolina Press, 1980.

Bosnia and Herzegovina

POPULATION 3,964,388

MUSLIM 40 percent

ORTHODOX CHRISTIAN 31 percent

ROMAN CATHOLIC 15 percent

PROTESTANT 4 percent

OTHER 10 percent

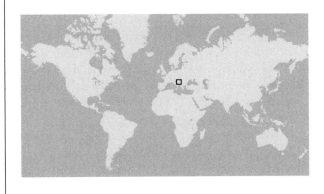

Country Overview

INTRODUCTION Bosnia and Herzegovina is a largely mountainous country located in the west-central part of the Balkan Peninsula. The population consists of three principal ethnic-religious groups—Bosnians (Muslim), Serbs (Orthodox Christian), and Croats (Roman Catholic). From 1918 to the early 1990s Bosnia and Herzegovina was a part of Yugoslavia. Following a declaration of independence in 1992, the country suffered fierce warfare. In 1995 a peace agreement was reached that established two divisions within the country—a Bosnian-Croat federation in the central and western areas and Republika Srpska (Serb Republic) in the north and east.

There has been no census since the 1992–95 war, as a result of which the ethnic and religious makeup of contemporary Bosnia and Herzegovina can only be estimated.

The religious makeup of Bosnia and Herzegovina is a product of its history. Until the Ottoman conquest of the fifteenth century, the country was formally considered to be Roman Catholic, with Orthodoxy found only in Herzegovina in the south. Neither Western nor Eastern Christianity managed to penetrate Bosnia and Herzegovina deeply, however, and from the end of the twelfth century sources indicate the existence of a specifically Bosnian church. This situation, among other factors, facilitated conversions to Islam in the early Ottoman period. In addition, Turkish rule guaranteed a special legal status to Orthodox Christianity, which helped it spread. The numbers of Catholics, on the other hand, were reduced by flight and by conversion to both Islam and Orthodoxy, although a considerable number survived Ottoman rule without a formal hierarchy. Those who remained developed strong local characteristics under the leadership of the Franciscan order. After the Reconquista of Spain and Portugal, Sephardic Jews settled in such urban centers as Skopje and Salonika, and they are first mentioned in Sarajevo, the national capital, in the second half of the sixteenth century.

RELIGIOUS TOLERANCE Since the nineteenth century religious adherence in Bosnia and Herzegovina has been a marker of national identity. Orthodoxy is equated with Serbian nationality and Catholicism with Croatian, while Islam is one of the main pillars of the Bosnian self. This fact made possible the use and misuse of religious

Bosnian Muslims gather in front of a reconstructed mosque. In Bosnia and Herzegovina during the twentieth century, ethnic cleansing was always connected to the destruction of the enemy's sacred buildings. AP/WIDE WORLD PHOTOS.

symbols in the war of the 1990s, and it continues to be an important obstacle to religious tolerance.

The constitution of Bosnia and Herzegovina, negotiated in the 1995 peace agreement, provides for freedom of religion. The same is true for the constitution of Republika Srpska, the Serb-dominated political entity within the state. As a matter of fact, however, many regions of the country have been ethnically cleansed, and in these areas religious freedom is enjoyed only by the ethnic majority, with severe restrictions for minorities.

Major Religions

SUNNI ISLAM

SERBIAN ORTHODOX CHURCH

SUNNI ISLAM

DATE OF ORIGIN Fifteenth–sixteenth century C.E.
NUMBER OF FOLLOWERS 1.6 million

HISTORY After the Ottoman conquest of 1463, it took almost 150 years for a majority of the population of Bosnia and Herzegovina to become Muslim. In contrast to popular assumptions among Serbs and Croats, Islamicization was a mainly nonviolent process. The Ottoman state granted self-administration to the non-Muslim People of the Book, as Christians and Jews were called, even though they were subject to some social and economic discrimination. Thus, most Christians who converted did so for opportunistic motives, and folk Islam retained many traits of the Christian folk religion.

In 1878 Bosnia and Herzegovina was annexed by Austria-Hungary, which was ruled by the Habsburg dynasty, a royal family that furnished rulers for many European countries and the Holy Roman Empire. They were strongly identified with Roman Catholicism, and Islam lost its privileged status, causing some 65,000 Muslims to leave the region by the end of World War I. Even before the Habsburg conquest Muslims had lost their status as the majority, giving way to the Orthodox Serbs. In communist Yugoslavia religion as such was repressed, but from the 1960s Muslims were recognized as a separate nation. Numerically they once again overtook the Serbs. Many Serbs were unwilling to accept Muslim emancipation or dominance, however, and when the Bosnian Muslims and Croats voted for independence from Yugoslavia in 1992, the political leadership in Serbia supported a violent partition of Bosnia and Herzegovina. In the following year the government of Croatia took the same position. Thus, Muslims became the main victims of ethnic cleansing in the 1992–95 war. In 1993 the legislature in Sarajevo decided to replace the national name Musliman, with its religious and national ambiguity, with Bošnjak, stressing the transformation of the Bosnian Muslim community into a political and sovereign nation.

EARLY AND MODERN LEADERS From the middle of the eighteenth century Bosnia's Muslim elite, though part of the Ottoman establishment, began to show its reserve toward the central rulers. Husejn-kapetan, from Gradačac, is often seen as a leading figure of the movement for autonomy, but his revolt in the 1830s failed. During the Habsburg period Mehmed-beg Kapetanović tried to fend off the claims of both Serb and Croats nationalists who argued that the Muslims of Bosnia were actually Serbs or Croats. In the first Yugoslav state, between World Wars I and II, Mehmed Spaho, who maneuvered between Serb and Croat nationalists, was influential in managing to retain benefits for Muslim landowners.

From the 1960s communist functionaries such as Atif Purivatra were successful in strengthening the Muslim position by advocating the establishment of a secular Muslim nation. On the other hand, a minority of religious intellectuals, including Alija Izetbegović wanted to strengthen the Islamic identity of Bosnia's Muslims. In 1990 he founded the Party of Democratic Action, whose religious nationalism determined Muslim politics throughout the decade.

MAJOR THEOLOGIANS AND AUTHORS Between 1914 and 1931 Džemaludin Čaušević, the *reis-ul-ulema*, or leader of the Muslim community, fought against traditionalism and tried to win over his coreligionists for a secular Yugoslav state. He had read the great Muslim modernists and reformers Jamal al-Din al-Afghani and Muhammad Abduh, and he had visited the Turkey of Kemal Atatürk. Čaušević's main opponents were a group of antimodernist clergymen educated in interwar Cairo. These religious leaders managed to influence such Muslim laymen as Alija Izetbegović, who advocated Islamic nationalism.

HOUSES OF WORSHIP AND HOLY PLACES As elsewhere, the Muslim house of worship in Bosnia and Herzegovina is the mosque. In addition, Bosnian folk Islam is centered around graves (*turbes*) belonging to Muslim martyrs (*šehits*) or to pious men called *evlijas* for their extraordinary powers to prophesy or to perform miracles. Ajvatovica, near Prusac, is a national pilgrimage center that dates to a pre-Islamic water cult, but Islamic authorities stress that Ajvatovica has no great theological significance.

WHAT IS SACRED? While orthodox Islam does not recognize saints, folk Islam in Bosnia and Herzegovina often does so, with *šehits* and *evlijas* seen as mediators between man and God. Popular notions about *šehits* are less specific than in other parts of the Muslim world, and the term can mean any Muslim who has been innocently killed or who has suffered a violent or tragic death. While many local *hodžas* (Islamic teachers) support the cults of saints, educated religious functionaries

do not approve of the practice, considering it to be a Christian or even pre-Christian influence.

HOLIDAYS AND FESTIVALS In the Bosnian-Croat federation there are five official holidays. None, however, is religious, although workers are entitled to four religious holidays each year. The Muslim New Year, which is rarely celebrated, is primarily a holiday of devout urban families.

The Bosnian festival of *mevlud*, which commemorates the birthday of the Prophet Muhammad, is celebrated mainly in private homes. There is no standard manner of celebration, although the festivities usually include Islamic recitations, songs, and poems honoring the birth of Muhammad, as well as a large meal. Households may also decide to hold a *mevlud* for other reasons, for example, the birth of a baby or in connection with moving into a new house. There sometimes are separate *mevlud*s for men and women, but unlike the practice in Turkey there are no formal differences between the festivities. Since the fall of communism purist theologians and laypeople have increasingly criticized the practice of *mevlud*.

MODE OF DRESS Until the end of the nineteenth century, dress in Bosnia and Herzegovina was as much a marker of social and regional identity as of religious affiliation. It then became Westernized and unified, although some features became markers of national identity. Today elderly Muslim peasant women often wear wide, baggy trousers called *dimije* or a long skirt and a headscarf, but they may dress in a modern style when they go into town. Women wear a headscarf during religious services and the reading of the Koran, and since the 1980s this accessory has spread into everyday urban life. The headscarf, together with a skirt and long-sleeved blouse, has come to constitute a new, Arab-influenced Muslim style. Except for white prayer caps during religious ceremonies, Muslim men generally dress in a Western style. A cap called a *fes* is worn by some members of the older generation and by religious functionaries.

DIETARY PRACTICES As with dress, dietary practices in Bosnia and Herzegovina are a means of national differentiation, and differences in cooking and eating have sometimes been considered an obstacle to intermarriage. On the other hand, fasting and the prohibition of alcohol are not as strictly observed as in other Muslim countries. It is common for men to drink alcohol, and during the socialist decades many men abandoned the habit of fasting, thus conferring this practice mainly on their wives. The prohibition against eating pork is observed by a great majority of Muslims.

RITUALS According to the Hanafi school of Sunni Islam, to which Bosnian Muslims belong, there are seven categories of ritual action. They range from *farz*, practices that God has commanded and that all believers must therefore perform, to *haram*, that which is forbidden. In many Bosnian villages this system is simplified into two broad categories, distinguishing, on the one hand, between what is *propisano* (prescribed, according to the law) and *obavezno* (obligatory) and, on the other, what is *lijep* (beautiful) and of *dobra volja* (goodwill).

The most elaborate rituals for Bosnian Muslims are those for marriage and death. The marriage ceremony, which takes place in the bridegroom's house, is lead by a *hodža*. When the bride arrives, her mother-in-law places a loaf of bread under her right arm and the Koran under her left, thus symbolizing the key roles of a wife—giving birth to the next generation and maintaining the household's moral and religious values. The marriage ceremony is considered complete only after the two families have acknowledged their new relationship by a ritual exchange of gifts.

Besides the obligatory funeral rites prescribed by the Shariah (Islamic law), Bosnian women hold domestic commemorations called *tevhid*. While this Arabic term means "praise of God," Bosnian folk Islam understands *tevhid* not as a prayer for the soul of the dead but as a "gift" to the person. Many religious functionaries are opposed to women's *tevhids*, which may have evolved under dervish influence, and would prefer that they take place only in a mosque and under the leadership of a *hodža*.

RITES OF PASSAGE The timing of Bosnian rites of passage differ for men and women. For example, while in rural areas a boy (*momak*) becomes a man (*čovjek*) by marriage, the situation for a women is different. A girl (*cura*) becomes a bride (*mlada*) by marriage, but only after she has given birth to a child is she considered a woman (*žena*). This is reinforced by the fact that in many cases a civic marriage is contracted only after the birth of the first child.

MEMBERSHIP The Islamic community in Bosnia and Herzegovina pursues internal mission work but not external growth. It tries to enhance the level of piety and observance among people of Muslim background who abandoned religious practices during the communist decades and among Bosnian youth. Islam uses means such as television and the Internet, and there are optional classes in religious education in state schools.

SOCIAL JUSTICE For a Muslim helping the poor is *tewab*, that is, an act pleasing to God, and Bosnians, who use the Turkish form *sevap*, follow this practice. During the war of the 1990s and its aftermath numerous charitable organizations from the Muslim world appeared in Bosnia and Herzegovina, not only to underline this attitude and express pan-Islamic solidarity but also to strengthen their respective countries' influence among Bosnian Muslims.

In the folk culture, however, there also exists the opposite tendency. People sometimes see the success, especially material success, of a household to be a result of its devoutness and ascribe poverty to a "weak faith."

SOCIAL ASPECTS Bosnian Islam is characterized by a relative degree of equality between the sexes, although this has somewhat abated since the 1990s, and by its negative stance toward intermarriage with Christians. As with other Muslims, Bosnians formerly observed the institution of milk kinship, in which people who were breast-fed by the same wet nurse called each other sister or brother "through milk" (*po mlijeku*). Marriage among milk kin was considered as serious a taboo as marrying a blood relative. Unlike Arab Muslim societies, however, Bosnian milk kinship was rarely needed to manage interfamily relations, since polygamy was seldom practiced in Bosnia and marriages between cousins were taboo.

POLITICAL IMPACT In everyday life as well as in politics, Islamic symbols serve Bosnians as an expression of collective identity and as a means of self-definition against Orthodox Serbs and Catholic Croats. On the other hand, the impact of Islam as a guideline for political and social action has lessened. Although in the 1990s there were episodes of Islamism, sometimes supported by organizations from Iran and from Arab countries, since then the influence of radical religious groups seems to have declined.

CONTROVERSIAL ISSUES In 1993 Alija Izetbegović's Party of Democratic Action forcibly took control of Bosnian Islamic religious institutions, ousted the pro-Yugoslav *reis-ul-ulema* Jakub Selimoski, and installed Mustafa Cerić, a nationalist Islamist. The once unified Islamic community of Yugoslavia was thus split, and Bosnia and Herzegovina was left with a controversy about the relationship between official Islam, the Bošnjak nation, and party politics.

CULTURAL IMPACT Until the nineteenth century Islam had a great impact on Bosnian architecture and music, even outside the sacred sphere. In the twentieth century socialism marginalized these influences, but in the early 1990s religious songs called *ilahija*s played an important role in mass mobilization. In the following war many masterpieces of Islamic architecture were destroyed. In contemporary Bosnia and Herzegovina the imprint of Islam has again been felt in several fields of culture, with the *reis-ul-ulema,* Mustafa Cerič, charging that the religious impact should be even more intense. Although this has led to a rise in Muslim cultural consciousness, contemporary artists and intellectuals tend to pursue their own individual paths.

SERBIAN ORTHODOX CHURCH

DATE OF ORIGIN Thirteenth century C.E. (Herzegovina) and fifteenth century C.E. (Bosnia)
NUMBER OF FOLLOWERS 1.2 million

HISTORY At the beginning of the thirteenth century, the medieval Serbian empire expanded southwest, and in 1219 an Orthodox bishopric of Hum (later Herzegovina) was created. In Bosnia proper Orthodox Church institutions were mostly established only after the Ottoman conquest in 1463. In the sixteenth and seventeenth centuries the Orthodox population grew rapidly because of the conversion of Roman Catholics and from the settlement of Orthodox Serbs and Vlachs from Serbia. In 1557 the Serbian medieval Patriarchate of Peć was reestablished and expanded into Bosnia proper. Because of the cooperation of the Peć patriarch with foreign powers during the Austro-Turkish wars of the seventeenth and eighteenth centuries, the Serb hierarchy lost its credibility with the Ottoman rulers, and in 1766 the patriarchate was abolished.

The patriarch of Constantinople then reintegrated Bosnia and Herzegovina into his jurisdiction, and until the 1878 Habsburg annexation Greek bishops administered the Bosnian bishoprics in a corrupt manner. The Habsburg administrators worked out an agreement with the patriarch of Constantinople that gave Vienna the right to nominate bishops, but the church as a whole became increasingly inclined toward unification with Serbia. When the Habsburg empire collapsed in 1918, the four bishoprics of Bosnia and Herzegovina were united with the Serbian Orthodox Church. During World War II, when Bosnia and Herzegovina became a part of Croatia, Serbian Orthodoxy was severely persecuted. In the 1992–95 war the Orthodox Church in Bosnia and Herzegovina mainly supported the Bosnian Serb leadership of Radovan Karadžić.

EARLY AND MODERN LEADERS During the nineteenth and twentieth centuries Bosnian Serb leaders were torn between Serb nationalism and allegiance to Yugoslavia. Many Orthodox, such as Vaso Pelagić, agitated against Habsburg rule and for the Serbian national cause. In 1918 Vojislav Šola, the leading Serb politician at the time, presented a joint memorandum of Bosnian Serbs and Croats in favor of the creation of Yugoslavia. The Montenegro-born Radovan Karadžić, who was the leader of the Bosnian Serbs in the 1992–95 war, came to be considered one of the principal Serbian war criminals.

MAJOR THEOLOGIANS AND AUTHORS Bosnia and Herzegovina has proven a much better field for political activists than for theologians. Between 1941 and 1994 there was not a single Orthodox seminary in the country. Atanasije Jevtić, a Serbia-born theologian with expertise in patristics, was bishop of the Zahum-Herzegovina diocese from 1992 to 1999. He is one of the main exponents of anti-Westernism among contemporary Serbian Orthodox.

HOUSES OF WORSHIP AND HOLY PLACES In Bosnia and Herzegovina sacred buildings serve as markers of ethnic as well as religious presence. For this reason ethnic cleansing during the twentieth century was always connected to the destruction of the enemy's sacred buildings. Orthodox churches and chapels, however, suffered less damage during the 1992–95 war than did Muslim mosques and Catholic churches. Church construction frequently causes political conflict.

WHAT IS SACRED? Orthodoxy reveres saints, and in contemporary Bosnia and Herzegovina the saints are pronouncedly Serbian in character. There were differences between the arsenal of saints in medieval Serbia and Bosnia, and in early Ottoman times some prominent personalities of Islamic mysticism were transformed into Orthodox saints. The immigration of Serbs and Vlachs from Serbia caused a shift, however, with the church coming to stress the cults of the medieval Serbian rulers, most of whom had been canonized by the Serbian Orthodox Church. Saint Sava, the founder in 1219 of the first autocephalous, or independent, Serbian archbishopric, is by far the most revered saint.

HOLIDAYS AND FESTIVALS In contrast to the Bosnian-Croat federation, Republika Srpska gives an official status to religious holidays, all of which follow the Orthodox calendar. Christmas is celebrated on 6–8 January, the Orthodox New Year on 14–15 January, Epiphany on 19 January, Saint Sava's Day on 27 January, and Saint Vitus's Day on 28 June. The other holidays are Good Friday and Easter.

A specific feature of Serbian Orthodoxy is the *slava*, the festival of a household patron. As with *mevlud* among Muslims, this festival regulates social relationships. A household invites relatives, friends, and neighbors and expects to be invited in return. Other important holidays are dedicated to Saint Elias and Saint George, both of whom formerly appeared in a modified form among Bosnian Muslims.

MODE OF DRESS In modern Bosnia and Herzegovina the Orthodox population can hardly be distinguished by dress. In church some women wear a headscarf, but there is no obligation to do so. The *šajkača*, a soldier's cap with a double brim introduced from Serbia, is considered a symbol of Serbdom.

DIETARY PRACTICES Except for fasting, Orthodoxy in Bosnia and Herzegovina has no specific dietary prescriptions. Among the faithful even fasting is not always observed. The plum brandy *šljivovica* is a popular alcoholic drink among Bosnian Serbs.

RITUALS The Holy Liturgy, including confession and the Eucharist, are the central rituals of Orthodoxy in Bosnia and Herzegovina. Many people go to church only irregularly, however, and from a social standpoint the most significant rituals are baptism, weddings, *slavas*, and funerals. Before the war of the 1990s, Bosnian Serbs sometimes frequented Muslim faith healers if no one else could help them. Since the war an increasing number of Orthodox have turned to spiritist movements and to other rituals of non-Orthodox origin.

RITES OF PASSAGE Baptisms, weddings, and funerals are important rites of passage among Bosnian Orthodox, although they are observed in traditional ways. Orthodox funerals, however, have turned into occasions for showing off the family's social status, and some graveyards have come to be dominated by pompous gravestones of nouveaux riches who died young.

MEMBERSHIP While theologically church membership is constituted by baptism, in the popular view Serbs as such are an Orthodox people. Thus, the fear of proselytism by others, long an element of Serbian religious history, is increased by the anxiety that, in converting from Orthodoxy to another faith, a Serb loses his national identity. Today various Protestant denominations have come to be the center of Orthodox criticism on this point, and the Orthodox Church has joined with other traditional faiths in attempting to legislate restrictions against missionary organizations from outside the country.

SOCIAL JUSTICE Orthodoxy identifies with the Serbian people, who in many areas have been poor for centuries. Bosnian Orthodox priests share the lifestyles of the faithful and thus have a close understanding of their social needs. On the oppression of non-Serbs by Serbs, however, Orthodoxy sometimes remains silent. According to the long tradition of idealizing national rulers, the people appreciate Bosnian Serb politicians more for enhancing national territory than for alleviating social needs.

SOCIAL ASPECTS In rural areas of Bosnia and Herzegovina there formerly was a strong tradition among Serbs of wives being subordinate to their husbands and of sons to their fathers. Although these role models were revived in the national discourse of the 1990s, they were not necessarily transformed into practice. In socialist Yugoslavia the Serb population was generally more tolerant toward religious intermarriage than were Catholics and Muslims, but intermarriage today is extremely rare. As with Muslims, Bosnian Serbs formerly observed the institution of milk kinship, whereby those sharing the same wet nurse were held to be related, but marriage taboos were not as strict.

POLITICAL IMPACT While the Bosnian-Croat federation has no official religion, Republika Srpska treats Orthodoxy almost as a state religion. Orthodox religious instruction is obligatory for Serb pupils, and attempts to turn it into a voluntary subject have been prevented by the Orthodox hierarchy. There are signs, however, that the church has lost some influence. Under pressures from the international community and the Bosnian-Croat federation, for example, the government of Republika Srpska has significantly reduced its material support for the Orthodox Church. Orthodox bishops from Bosnia and Herzegovina occupy key positions in Serbia and in the diaspora, thus giving a specifically conservative and national note to Serbian Orthodoxy as a whole.

CONTROVERSIAL ISSUES The main controversies in Orthodoxy in Bosnia and Herzegovina revolve around the stance toward Western civilization in general and toward ecumenism in particular. Pro-Western and ecumenical currents seems to be weaker in Bosnia and Herzegovina than in Serbia, for example. Such matters as birth control, abortion, and divorce are more often discussed in the context of the Serbs' demographic survival than as religious or moral questions.

CULTURAL IMPACT In general the cultural impact of Orthodoxy in Republika Srpska is even greater than in Serbia itself. In Bosnia and Herzegovina, Orthodoxy is perceived as the distinctive and most important quality of Serbian identity, and various types of officially promoted culture are impregnated with Orthodox music and iconography. Unlike Orthodoxy in Habsburg-influenced Croatia and in Vojvodina, in northern Serbia, church architecture and painting in Bosnia and Herzegovina do not have baroque features. Rather, as in Serbia, Serbo-Byzantine and neo-Byzantine models dominate.

Other Religions

The number of Roman Catholics in Bosnia and Herzegovina has decreased during the twentieth century. For one thing, about half of the Catholic Croat population has left the country since 1992. Catholicism in Bosnia and Herzegovina is heterogeneous, the main division being between Franciscans and the secular clergy introduced during the Habsburg period. At the same time there is a division among Franciscans in Bosnia and in Herzegovina that dates to 1852, when Herzegovinian Franciscans split from Bosnian Franciscans and developed in a more nationalist and antiliberal direction. The Franciscan-led church in Bosnia and Herzegovina, used to being a minority organization in a non-Catholic environment, was prone to subordination and compromise. The Franciscans found ways to coexist with Habsburg authorities, with the Serb-dominated Kingdom of Yugoslavia, with the Ustasha fascist dictatorship during World War II, and with communist rulers after 1945, and they have continued to coexist since the war of the 1990s.

In 1882, however, the Vatican appointed the Zagreb theologian Josip Stadler as archbishop of Sarajevo. As with many other Catholic clergymen from Croatia, Stadler saw the Franciscan dominance in Bosnia and Herzegovina as an anomaly conditioned by Ottoman rule, and he strove to replace the order by regular clergy subordinated to himself. While Stadler justified his policies as a means of normalization and modernization and saw intervention in political matters as a prerogative of the church, the Franciscans felt that he did not appreciate their historical role in keeping the Catholic faith during centuries of Islamic domination. Thus, since the end of the 19th century, both views have been present in the Catholic Church in Bosnia and Herzegovina, with the secular clergy stressing the dangers of living in a non-Catholic environment.

In Ottoman times Western Catholic travelers to Bosnia and Herzegovina often described the Franciscans as backward and uneducated and as despotic supervisors of their parishioners' personal lives. Bosnian Croat authors, however, have portrayed them as the only transmitters of Western civilization into the country. Concerning religious practices, the Franciscans have fought folk religion more vigorously than the Orthodox or Muslim clergy, largely because they were urged to do so by inspectors from Rome, and these policies have not been without results. Among Catholics, for example, the institution of milk kinship was less frequent than among Muslims or Orthodox. In prewar Bosnia and Herzegovina Catholics turned less frequently than did Orthodox to Muslim faith healers. And Catholics are at least as hostile as are Muslims toward intermarriage. Nevertheless, Bosnian Catholics continue to share common practices with Muslims and with Orthodox Christians, including, in some parts of the country, the *slava* celebration.

Protestants constitute only a small part of the population of Bosnia and Herzegovina. Although their missionary activity has been limited, it has grown. The Methodist Church, Seventh-day Adventists, Jehovah's Witnesses, and Church of Jesus Christ of Latter-day Saints (Mormons) are present in the country. There also are followers of Krishna Consciousness.

The Jewish community in Bosnia and Herzegovina is also small in numbers. Before 1941 there were Jewish communities in several towns, but they were almost completely extinguished during the Nazi occupation. The Jewish religious organization was reestablished after 1945, but in the 1990s war and its aftermath the community lost about two-thirds of its members by emigration. As one of the traditional faiths, it is represented in the Interreligious Council of Bosnia and Herzegovina, founded in 1997 by representatives of the Muslim, Orthodox, and Catholic communities.

Klaus Buchenau

See Also Vol. I: *Christianity, Eastern Orthodoxy, Islam, Roman Catholicism, Sunni Islam*

Bibliography

Bax, Mart. *Medjugorje: Religion, Politics and Violence in Rural Bosnia.* Amsterdam: VU, 1995.

Bougarel, Xavier. "Islam in the Post-Communist Balkans: Understanding a Decade of Changes." In *Religionen und Kulturen in Südosteuropa: Nebeneinander und Miteinander von Muslimen und Christen.* Edited by Johannes Kandel, Ernst Pulsfort, and Holm Sundhaussen. Berlin: Friedrich-Ebert-Stiftung, 2002.

Bringa, Tone. *Being Muslim the Bosnian Way.* Princeton, N.J.: Princeton University Press, 1995.

Lovrenović, Ivan. *Hrvati Bosanski: Esej o agoniji jedne Evropsko-Orijentalne mikrokulture.* Zagreb: Durieux, 2002.

Perica, Vjekoslav. *Balkan Idols: Religion and Nationalism in Yugoslav States.* Oxford: Oxford University Press, 2002.

Botswana

POPULATION 1,591,232

AFRICAN INDIGENOUS BELIEFS,
  65 percent

CHRISTIAN 34.18 percent

OTHER 0.82 percent

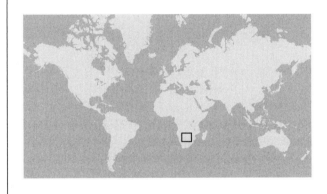

Country Overview

INTRODUCTION The Republic of Botswana is a semiarid, sparsely populated country in southern Africa. It is bordered by South Africa on the southeast and south, Namibia on the west, Zambia on the north, and Zimbabwe on the northeast. As Bechuanaland, it became a British protectorate in 1885. In 1966 the country gained its independence. Since then Botswana has become one of Africa's most stable democracies, with one of the continent's fastest growing economies. There has been rapid urbanization, including the newly built capital, Gaborone.

Botswana has some 14 ethnic groups that largely follow either indigenous religions or Christianity. European missionaries introduced Christianity in around 1843. In precolonial times religion was pivotal to all spheres of community life, but since independence no particular religion has been associated with the government.

RELIGIOUS TOLERANCE The constitution of Botswana protects the rights of religious freedom, expression, and assembly. Forced religious instruction or participation in religious ceremonies or the taking of oaths that run counter to a person's beliefs are prohibited. A multireligious curriculum is taught to all children in the public schools. There are no reports of religious prisoners or of the denial of migration rights on religious grounds.

Indigenous religions, which dominated the life of Botswana for centuries, have accommodated new faiths, even when they have offered serious challenges to tradition. Today different religions in Botswana live together in peace.

Major Religions

AFRICAN INDIGENOUS BELIEFS
CHRISTIANITY

AFRICAN INDIGENOUS BELIEFS

DATE OF ORIGIN Early C.E.
NUMBER OF FOLLOWERS 1 million

HISTORY The indigenous religions found in Botswana are believed to have existed for 2,000 years, since the

A diviner wears rattles around his ankles. Along with beaded necklaces and bracelets, this indicates that the person is associated with the sangoma *cult in Botswana.* © PETER JOHNSON/CORBIS.

people of the area came to live in settled communities. The beliefs evolved over the years, and the Batswana have countless stories and myths. One of the best-known creation myths involves Matsieng, God's messenger and the great tribal ancestor whose rock footprints are found about 25 miles from Gaborone.

Over time the indigenous religions of the Batswana have been weakened, but not completely eroded, by modernity. Particularly in rural areas a large majority still follows traditional practices and beliefs. Although young people may tend to prefer modern ways of life, in a crisis they revert to the ways of their forefathers or mix the traditional with the modern. Some unemployed youth, and some Batswana in general, resort to indigenous rituals of purification or carry protective charms. Although urbanization has had an impact, the religious sacrifice of animals is still allowed in towns.

EARLY AND MODERN LEADERS Traditional Batswana religious leaders, including kings, healers, prophets, doctors, and rainmakers, are looked upon as representatives of *badimo* (ancestors) and hence possess immense authority. Their pronouncements are believed to come from the *badimo*, and they act as mediators between *badimo* and humans. As priests, they are ordained to serve in religious functions, including sacrifices, prayers, and cere-

monies. They also give advice, perform judicial and political functions, and manage shrines. A community takes its problems to the priest, who in turn approaches ancestors through prayer, dreams, and sacrifices.

King Sechele I of the Bakwena, from the late 1830s to 1892, and King Sekgoma I of the Bangwato, from 1835 to 1872, were prominent religious leaders in their time. Sekgoma was a staunch defender of indigenous beliefs and practices, and he resisted the missionaries' destruction of traditional institutions. Among medium-priests Ntogwa became a well-known leader in the 1970s of the Mwali rainmaking community in the northeast. His rise invigorated the community, and through his leadership old oracles and practices were revived and new ones created.

MAJOR THEOLOGIANS AND AUTHORS In the past all who wrote on the religious beliefs and practices of the Batswana were outsiders. The reports of nineteenth-century explorers, travelers, and traders like Petrus Borcheds provided the first accounts. The writings of missionaries also sometimes give useful information. Influenced by their Eurocentric colonial attitudes, however, such men as Robert Moffat presented traditional religions as a morass of bizarre beliefs and practices. Moffat, for example, referred to *badimo* as "demons." Yet not all missionaries shared this view. David Livingstone, as well as such modern writers as Isaac Schapera, Gabriel M. Setiloane, and James Amanze, provide a more objective assessment. Leslie Nthoi is one of the leading contemporary scholars on indigenous religions in Botswana.

HOUSES OF WORSHIP AND HOLY PLACES Individuals or families and the community designate various places as holy or as sites for worship. Certain parts of a forest or specific trees, rivers or pools of water, mountains, caves, cemeteries, and other sites believed to be the abodes of ancestors are regarded as holy. The houses of such leaders as rainmakers are also held to be holy.

WHAT IS SACRED? Followers of indigenous beliefs in Botswana hold certain objects, animals, relationships, and sites to be sacred. These include divining bones (*ditaolas*), used for diagnosing the causes of diseases or calamities; the drums used in songs and dances to inspire the spirits of *badimo*; various animals or animal products, such as the leopard skin worn by a king during his coronation; domestic animals that represent ancestral spirits; and animals that are ethnic symbols, or totems. Deliberately harming a totem animal is taboo (*moila*) and is believed to result in harm to the whole clan. Some tribes have named themselves after their totem animal. The totem for the Batlhaping, for example, is the *tlhapi* (fish). Strings and charms are tied around the neck, arms, and legs or kept in pockets or bags, on rooftops, or in holes dug at the gates of compounds or in fields and under trees.

In general, the ground that harbors *badimo* is regarded as sacred. Hence, when people eat, they throw food down for the *badimo*. Relationships between children and elders are also held to be sacred.

HOLIDAYS AND FESTIVALS Indigenous holidays and festivals in Botswana are observed within tribal domains. For example, at the command of the medium-priest Ntogwa, in the 1970s Friday became a religious holiday among the Mwali in the northeast. Referred to as Nsi, it was a time for worship, prayer, and ritual performances, with no one allowed to engage in any economic activity. Lack of rain was attributed to disrespect for Nsi. In one village enforcement of these practices led to conflict between the Mwali and some Christian churches, especially Seventh-day Adventists, who insisted on Saturday as the day of worship and rest.

MODE OF DRESS Special dress is associated with indigenous religious figures in Botswana. For example, a *sangoma*, a diviner whose ancestral spirit delivers messages through his or her mouth as a sign that the person has been called to the office, wears beaded necklaces and bracelets and sagging ankle rattles. The bracelets are not to be removed during the person's lifetime, for they represent bondage and submission to the *sangoma* cult. A leopard skin on the shoulder is a sign of seniority. During the Mwali rainmaking dance, women dress in black skirts, for black is believed to symbolize rainy clouds, coolness, and goodness. Most herbal *dingaka* (singular *ngaka*; "traditional doctor," or "herbalist") wear plain black clothes and leather hats with feathers. Traditionalists insist on garments made of animal skins.

DIETARY PRACTICES Indigenous religions and cultures in Botswana have a wide range of dietary practices and restrictions that apply to women, children, the community, and religious mediators. Certain foods, for example, are believed to interfere with the safety of childbirth. Foods such as eggs and certain animal meats, including the kidneys and male reproductive organs, are

not to be eaten by pregnant women or children. Meat from totem animals is not to be eaten or touched. Once a year a *sangoma* drinks an animal's blood and eats its inner parts (heart, liver, and intestines). Together with the drinking of beer made of sorghum, these are believed to contribute to the health of the *sangoma*.

RITUALS In Batswana indigenous religions there are social, political, and economic rituals, all of which serve for purification or protection. Traditionally all rituals were performed by priests and medicine men under the authorization of the king.

Social rituals are mainly associated with the rites of passage of childbirth, puberty, marriage, death, and burial. Pregnancy and birth are marked by rituals that ensure the safety of the fetus and mother and that strengthen the bond of the newborn with the mother, family, and *badimo*. These may involve shaving the baby's hair and burning the dried umbilical cord, which is then mixed with charms and applied to the baby's fontanel. When a woman gives birth before her due date or miscarries, this is believed to pollute the environment, and it becomes necessary to perform purification rituals. Puberty is marked by the initiation rituals conducted during *bogwera* (for boys) and *bojale* (for girls). A dead body is ritually washed, the hair shaved, and the grave prepared before burial. At times protective rituals are conducted against sorcery, witchcraft, and other destructive elements. Purification and protective rituals may be carried out when a new home or village is established or for a new marriage.

Political and economic rituals include the installation of a king and the preparation of warriors and their weapons before battle. Economic activities such as hunting, ploughing, and harvesting may also be preceded by rituals. Rainmaking rituals are conducted on a seasonal basis.

RITES OF PASSAGE Virtually every ethnic group in Botswana observes rites of passage for pregnancy, birth, puberty, marriage, status installation, and death. These rites, which emphasize the role of the community and affirm the identity of the individual, are occasions for festivity. They mark a change in the status of an individual and involve separation, ritual cleansing, and entry into a new stage of life. Thus, children become adults, young women and men marry and have children, and at death the old become *badimo* and continue to assist family members. During puberty rites young people became adults by being taught treasured secrets, including historical landmarks, key beliefs, values, myths, and symbols of their community, as well as a new language understood only by initiates. At puberty young people are also taught to care for the community. Marriage is presented as an obligatory rite of passage for all, and old age is seen as a period of experience, wisdom, and respect.

Throughout history there have been changes in the rituals associated with rites of passage, as well as occasional revivals of earlier practices. Today simpler ceremonies may be used as a way of giving at least some measure of instruction.

MEMBERSHIP Membership in an indigenous religion is automatic, for a person is born into a community and religion. Religious instruction is passed by word of mouth and through myths, proverbs, sayings, songs, and rituals.

SOCIAL JUSTICE Traditional Batswana society insisted on social justice, which contributed to stability and harmonious relationships among the people. At all levels of society, leaders such as family heads, the *kgosi* (king), who presided over the *kgotla* (traditionally the highest policymaking and legal institution), and designated community leaders were responsible for justice. *Badimo* were believed to empower the leaders and to deal with injustice and its perpetrators.

Ideas of justice and fairness were handed down by *badimo* and conveyed and reinforced through family and tribal education. Thus, an offence against human beings was an offence against the *badimo*. In addition to murder, crimes included adultery, incest, seduction, rape, unkindness to parents, lying, theft, and swearing falsely, all of which were punishable acts.

SOCIAL ASPECTS In traditional Batswana society the status of men, women, and children was defined by religion. Men and women had clearly defined roles, with women expected to be subordinate and submissive to their brothers, uncles, and husbands. Although women could not take leadership in the family or community, they could become *sangoma*s and *dingaka*, and they were free to plough their own fields. Children were expected to obey elders, while elders were responsible for the proper growth of children.

The modern family is governed by civil law, although those who choose to marry according to tradi-

tional codes are governed by customary law, which is a mixture of religious and social customs and laws. Although the Batswana traditionally practiced polygamy, it was forbidden by missionaries and by some chiefs. Polygamy is still permitted under customary, but not under civil, law. Mainly as the result of labor migration, a new kin grouping has emerged, with a dramatic increase in the number of unmarried mothers. A 1970 law allowed unmarried mothers to sue the fathers of their children without the assistance of male relatives.

POLITICAL IMPACT In precolonial Botswana there was a close identity between the religious and political spheres and a strong sense of common purpose. Religious authorities were often political authorities. Such relationships were not free of conflict, however, for rulers sometimes attempted to control reverence for royal ancestors, rainmaking ceremonies, male circumcision camps, and other matters. But Batswana rulers were not priest-kings or god-kings, and they worked through *dingaka*.

CONTROVERSIAL ISSUES The attitude of indigenous religions toward HIV/AIDS is highly controversial. Adherents hold that the disease results from the wrath of *badimo* and is punishment for failing to maintain the traditional culture. Punishing those who engage in sex outside marriage and conducting sacrifices to please the *badimo* are believed to be effective ways of dealing with the problem.

CULTURAL IMPACT Music is an important aspect of Batswana culture and religion that has survived the onslaught of Western influence. In traditional settings music and singing are always accompanied by dancing and clapping. The Batswana sing everywhere, with music an integral part of both everyday activities and such ceremonies as weddings and funerals. Children are taught traditional music and dancing in the home and in school. Institutions of higher learning have their own dance troupes and choirs, some of which have performed overseas. During holidays groups perform to entertain the public. The emotional tunes and styles of Batswana music have also been incorporated into Christian churches. Batswana dancers, who wear traditional costumes of skins and beaded jewelry, move exuberantly and energetically.

CHRISTIANITY

DATE OF ORIGIN 1843 C.E.
NUMBER OF FOLLOWERS 543,900

HISTORY Christianity was introduced to Botswana by European missionaries, notably the Scottish Congregationalist Robert Moffat and his son-in-law David Livingstone, both of whom were agents of the London Missionary Society. Moffat began work among the Batlhaping, on the South African side of the border, in the 1820s. In 1841 he was joined by Livingstone, who opened the northern territories to missionary activity. The conversion of King Sechele I of the Bakwena in 1846 and of King Khama III of the Bangwato in 1859 marked important developments. Because of Khama's influence especially, Christianity spread to other peoples and parts of Botswana. Later German Lutheranism and the Dutch Reformed Church were introduced, as Methodism had been earlier.

These formed the so-called tribal state churches, allegiance to which was disrupted by the missions of the Anglican, Seventh-day Adventist, and Roman Catholic churches in the early and mid-twentieth century. Anglicanism was first established in Botswana in 1912 through the influence of Lena Rauwe after her marriage to King Sechele II. The fastest growing groups in Botswana, African Initiated Churches (AICs) and Pentecostals, were introduced by migrant laborers and others returning from South Africa in the 1960s. Through their healing and protection practices and incorporation of African cultural values, they have expanded rapidly, while membership in the mission churches has declined.

EARLY AND MODERN LEADERS The first and the leading Christian missionaries in Botswana were Robert Moffat and David Livingstone. In the twentieth century Arthur Kretchma played a leading role in the establishment of the Seventh-day Adventist Church, and Walter Makhulu has been the most influential Anglican bishop. Sam Makgaola and William Scheffers were among those who played a crucial role in the early growth and spread of Pentecostalism. In 1982 Boniface Setlalekgosi became the first Motswana Roman Catholic bishop. In African Initiated Churches (AICs), Christinah M. Nku of Saint John Apostolic Faith Mission of Botswana, Barnabas E. Lekganyane of the Zion Christian Church, and Israel Motswasele of the Spiritual Healing Church have been influential. A number of women, such as Ma Boamamuri S. Molotsi, have founded churches.

MAJOR THEOLOGIANS AND AUTHORS There are a number of contemporary theologians and authors on Christianity in Botswana. They include James Amanze, who has written on such topics as church history and ecumenical theology, as well as on traditional religions; Musa Shomanah, a New Testament scholar who has published works on gender issues and HIV/AIDS; Fidelis Nkomazana, who has written on church history and religious education and on traditional religions; Obed Kealotswe, who has focused on developing theologies, including those of new religious movements; and Joseph Gaie, who has written on medical, political, and business ethics.

HOUSES OF WORSHIP AND HOLY PLACES Mission churches in Botswana are typical of those in Europe and the United States. Most African Initiated Churches (AICs), however, meet in simple shelters made of poles and roofed with corrugated iron or thatched with grass. It is a cultural practice to hold a public meeting in an open space, and some churches meet under a special tree.

WHAT IS SACRED? For all Christians in Botswana, the Bible is treated as a sacred book. Roman Catholics venerate European saints. Some church uniforms are believed to be sacred. In the Zion Christian Church, for instance, the male uniform is not to be touched by women.

The AICs have other religious objects, including the holy stick used for healing and exorcizing evil spirits and for blessing *sewachô* (holy water). The water, which contains cow dung and the ashes of the *motswere* tree, is sometimes taken by the sick or ritually splashed on the face to remove bad luck. Most members of AICs tie green strings around their necks, wrists, waists, or ankles for protection and fortification.

HOLIDAYS AND FESTIVALS Among other holidays, Christians in Botswana celebrate Christmas, Good Friday, Easter Sunday, and Ascension Day. The holidays are celebrated nationally, but in different ways. African Initiated Churches (AICs), for example, hold conferences and night vigils that may last for days. During holidays most people, including non-Christians, return to their ancestral villages for family reunions. The Roman Catholic Church observes some saints' days, although no African saints are celebrated.

MODE OF DRESS In Botswana even the poor put on their best clothes to attend church. In some churches women are expected not to wear pants, and they must cover their heads. In both mission churches and African Initiated Churches (AICs), the clergy wear special garments. In missionary churches especially a minister is seen as unfit without his sacred garments, which are a symbol of authority and of his role as a mediator between God and the people. In Pentecostal churches ministers wear expensive suits and ties.

In some churches members wear a uniform. Men in the Zion Christian Church, for example, wear a khaki suit, a badge with either a dove or a cross, white or khaki boots, and a khaki or gray cap. Members of Mokgatio wa Bomme, the women's fellowship, wear a gray or green dress, a green or blue jersey, and black tennis shoes both for church services and in their own meetings. In other AICs, such as the Head Mountain of God Apostolic Church in Zion, the uniform is generally white, with belts of different colors indicating the status of the wearer. The garments are believed to be so powerful that they sanctify all who come into contact with them, and they are also said to scare witches. Members of women's fellowship groups in missionary churches also wear uniforms.

DIETARY PRACTICES Seventh-day Adventists in Botswana follow the Levitical rules on clean and unclean foods and for medical reasons discourage high-cholesterol foods. Many African Initiated Churches (AICs) also have food taboos based on Old Testament regulations, although their practices are motivated by religion rather than health. Certain animals not known in the biblical world, such as the *mopane* worm, have posed questions as to whether or not they are clean. The AICs and Pentecostals oppose the consumption of alcohol for reasons of both religion and health.

RITUALS Baptism and the Lord's Supper (Communion) are commonly practiced by Christians throughout Botswana. In some cases Christian rituals have been adapted to local customs. The Roman Catholic Church, for example, uses Tswana and indigenous music in the Mass. Some traditional African religious and medical practices, notably respect for patriarchal ancestors, have been assimilated within Christian beliefs.

RITES OF PASSAGE Such Christian rites of passage as consecration, confirmation, baptism, marriage, ordination, and burial are observed in Botswana. Many of these rites have been adapted to include elements of indigenous African practices. Traditional rites of adolescent initiation for males have been retained in a few places, although circumcision is now done in hospitals.

Some evangelicals, especially Pentecostals and certain African Initiated Churches (AICs), have taken a hostile approach toward indigenous religions. They forbid members to participate in traditional initiation rites, and in Pentecostal churches those who disobey are "disfellowshipped."

MEMBERSHIP Membership in Christian churches in Botswana is open to anyone who satisfies the criteria set by a particular church. Protestants, especially Pentecostals, may insist on an individual conversion before granting membership. For Roman Catholics group membership is allowed. In African Initiated Churches (AICs) an experience of healing usually leads to membership. There is little or no proselytizing.

SOCIAL JUSTICE Although at times Christianity operated as a vehicle for the spread of colonialism in Botswana, thus reinforcing divisions within communities, such missionaries as David Livingstone played a leading role in addressing issues of social injustice. They condemned acts of brutality toward women and children by Afrikaners and protested the killing of innocent persons, forced labor, and the attempts of aggressors to take Batswana land. In modern times various churches, especially under the leadership of the Botswana Christian Council, have continued to promote social justice, protesting corruption and representing the voiceless and underprivileged. Churches have spoken in favor of the empowerment of women and against the abuse of women and children and also have established educational and medical services.

SOCIAL ASPECTS For Christians in Botswana the family forms the basic unit of society, and every member is expected to carry out his or her responsibilities. Children, who are held to be a gift from God, are to be protected, cared for, and loved. For most Christians marriage is a mutual, exclusive, and lifelong union that cannot be terminated. The majority of Christians belong to extended families, but nuclear families have become more popular, and single parenthood and families headed by a single parent also have increased. While in theory women have equal rights with men, there are certain cultural barriers that marginalize them even within the church.

A Christian marriage in Botswana continues to be characterized by the traditional practices of family negotiations (*patlo*) and the payment of bride wealth or exchange of goods (*bogadi*) and by traditional dances, songs, and rejoicing. Christianity, however, has strongly opposed other traditional practices, such as widow inheritance (*seantlo*)—or levirate marriage, by which the wife of a deceased man is given to a brother, who henceforth acts as her husband and provider—and polygamy (*nyalo ya lefufa*).

POLITICAL IMPACT Although Botswana is not officially a Christian country, Christianity is seen as having contributed in various ways to the process of national integration and unity. Christians have been encouraged to take political positions and have played a leading role in various national issues. Through such bodies as the Botswana Christian Council, the church acts as a voice to the nation. The widening gap between rich and poor; the relocation of the Basarwa (the so-called Bushmen) from the Central Kgalagadi Game Reserve; the increase in instability, crime, and corruption; and rights of homosexuals are some of the problems the Botswana Christian Council has addressed.

CONTROVERSIAL ISSUES In some churches in Botswana, such as the Roman Catholic, Anglican, and Dutch Reformed, women cannot be ordained as priests or ministers. Other churches, however, ordain women and celebrate their leadership. The African Initiated Churches (AICs) are particularly notable for their gender-inclusive practices.

The scourge of HIV/AIDS has left Christians with widely varying views on how to respond. Many churches oppose safe-sex education and the use of condoms, which are promoted by the government, and instead advocate sexual abstinence and fidelity. On the extreme are those Christians who see HIV/AIDS as punishment from God.

CULTURAL IMPACT The introduction of Christianity in Botswana contributed to the weakening of indigenous cultural and religious institutions and practices, including kingship (*bogosi*), rainmaking rites, traditional medicine (*bongaka*), polygamy, the role of ancestors (*badimo*), and initiation schools. Except for the erection of buildings by some mainline churches in the Western style, Christianity has had little effect in architecture and on the arts in general. On the other hand, traditional prac-

tices and artistic styles, including singing, dancing, hand clapping, and drumming and the playing of other instruments, have influenced the church, especially African Initiated Churches (AICs), whose members have remained Christianized Africans. Music in the AICs and in Pentecostal churches is happy, full of feeling, and infectious, with church choirs, gospel concerts, and music festivals popular.

Other Religions

Islam was first introduced to Botswana by Indian traders in 1882. Today Islamic schools serve as a point of contact with the community and as a source of growth. Hinduism was taken to Botswana by expatriates in 1890. The Bahai faith was introduced by a Canadian family in 1967. Buddhism and Sikhism, the latter introduced by expatriates, have been present in Botswana since 1974. These communities, which range in size from a few hundred to about 3,000, are found in the major towns.

Fidelis Nkomazana

See Also Vol. 1: *African Indigenous Beliefs, Christianity*

Bibliography

Amanze, James. *African Traditional Religion and Culture in Botswana*. Gaborone: Pula Press, 2002.

Botswana Handbook of Churches. Gaborone: Pula Press, 1998.

Campbell, John. *Travels in South Africa Undertaken at the Request of the Missionary Society*. London: Black and Parry, 1815.

Chirenje, Mutero J. *A History of Northern Botswana, 1850–1910*. London: Associated University Presses, 1977.

Hepburn, J.D. *Twenty Years in Khama's Country*. Edited by C.H. Lyall. London: Hodder and Stoughton, 1895.

Lichtenstein, Henry. *Travels in Southern Africa in the Years 1803–1806*. Translated by Anne Plumtree. Cape Town: Van Riebeck Society, 1928.

Livingstone, David. *Missionary Travels and Researches in South Africa*. London: John Murray, 1857.

Mackenzie, John. *Ten Years North of the Orange River*. Edinburgh: Hodder and Stoughton, 1871.

Mbiti, John S. *Introduction to African Religion*. 2nd rev. ed. London: Heineman, 1990.

Mgadla, Part Themba. *Missionaries and Western Education in the Bechuanaland Protectorate, 1859–1904: The Case of the Bangwato*. Gaborone: University of Botswana, 1989.

Moffat, Robert. *Missionary Labours in Southern Africa*. London: John Shaw, 1842.

Nkomazana, Fidelis. "Religion in Botswana." In "Culture and Heritage," *Botswana National Atlas.* Gaborone: Botswana Department of Surveys and Mapping, 2001.

Schapera, Isaac. *Tribal Innovators: Tswana Chiefs and Social Change, 1795–1940.* London: Athlone Press, 1970.

Setiloane, Gabriel M. *The Image of God among the Sotho-Tswana.* Rotterdan: Balkema, 1976.

Werbner, Richard. "Land, Movement, and Status among the Kalanga of Botswana." In *Studies in African Social Anthropology.* Edited by Meyer Fortes and Sheila Patterson. London: Academic Press, 1975.

Willoughby, William Charles. *The Soul of the Bantu.* London: SCM, 1928.

Brazil

POPULATION 176,029,560

ROMAN CATHOLIC 75.0 percent

HISTORICAL PROTESTANT 12.5 percent

PENTECOSTAL AND NEO-PENTECOSTAL 7.0 percent

SPIRIT 3.0 percent

AFRO-BRAZILIAN 1.5 percent

SHINTO, BUDDHIST, JEWISH, INDIGENOUS 1.0 percent

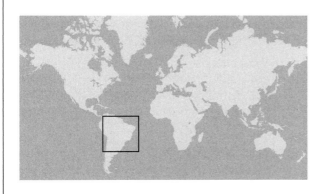

Country Overview

INTRODUCTION Brazil, known officially as the Federative Republic of Brazil, is located on the east coast of South America. It is that continent's largest country, both in area and population, and is its only Portuguese-speaking country. It has a religious landscape that reflects the successive waves of migration that brought European and Asian settlers and African slaves to inter-

act with the small (and soon to be eliminated) indigenous populations. In his first official act after claiming Brazil for Portugal in 1500, Pedro Álvares Cabral celebrated a Roman Catholic Mass. Jesuit missionaries built on this symbolic foundation to evangelize in native communities. The goal of economic development, however, has long outweighed the pursuit of doctrinal purity in Brazil. When Jesuit efforts to educate and protect indigenous peoples angered plantation owners who sought to enslave the Indians, the colonial government expelled the Jesuits in 1759. Although Brazil has grown to become the largest Roman Catholic country in the world, census figures do not capture the tendency of Brazilians to affiliate with more than one religion.

The massive importation of slaves from West Africa provided one of the most pervasive and enduring religious influences in Brazil. Slavery in Brazil surpassed slavery in the United States in both quantity and duration, and the legacy of African spirituality remains present in contemporary life. Participation in Afro-Brazilian religions, however, spans all ethnic groups and social classes and bears no stigma. Most Brazilians recognize the offerings left to African deities at crossroads or enshrined in Carnival floats. Roman Catholics may attend Afro-Brazilian ceremonies without weakening their Roman Catholic identity. In fact, the northeast, the traditional home of Afro-Brazilian religions, is also Brazil's most Roman Catholic region.

Though Roman Catholics maintain a numerical advantage in Brazil, fewer than 20 percent attend weekly Mass. Since the 1950s Protestant groups have made significant inroads among poor, urban Brazilians, eliciting such devotion that practicing Protestants may outnum-

A priestess of the Candomblé religion sits in a terreiro in Salvador, Brazil. Adherents of Candomblé, the best studied of the Afro-Brazilian religions, are also Roman Catholics and may be required to attend Mass as part of the ceremonial cycle. © BARNABAS BOSSHART/CORBIS.

ber practicing Roman Catholics. The aggressively prose-lytizing churches have taken their message to the air-waves. More recent migrants have brought Islam, Shintoism, and Judaism to Brazil. Religious syncretism in Brazil implies more than a mechanical integration of cultural traits from one faith to another. The intermingling of religions creates entirely new, coherent systems of thought that are in a constant process of renewal.

RELIGIOUS TOLERANCE After Brazil's independence from Portugal, the 1824 constitution affirmed Roman Catholicism as the state religion. With the overthrow of the emperor in 1889, the Roman Catholic Church lost its official status. Instead the new republic looked to the scientific philosophy of positivism for guidance, enshrining the motto "Order and Progress" on the national flag. Afro-Brazilian religions were seen as a source of criminality, and their meetings were subject to police raids. In the 1920s and 1930s the Roman Catholic Church sought to reinsert itself in the Brazilian national identity by erecting a statue of Christ the Redeemer on

Corcovado Mountain in Rio de Janeiro and cultivating close ties to President Getúlio Vargas. The constitution of 1934 rewarded their support with state subsidies for the Roman Catholic Church and Roman Catholic schools, though these were later nullified.

During military rule from 1964 until 1985, religious and lay leaders suffered imprisonment and torture for speaking against the dictatorship. While the 1967 constitution guaranteed the free exercise of religious expression, it was not enforced until the return to democracy in the 1980s. The government does not require religious groups to register and allows for the unrestricted establishment of places of worship. In 1977 authorities ordered the Protestant group Wycliffe Bible Translators to leave the indigenous areas where they were working. Since the early 1990s the Bureau of Indian Affairs has restricted the entry of missionaries to indigenous territories.

A national scandal followed a 1995 broadcast of the neo-Pentecostal group Universal Church of the

Kingdom of God in which a church leader kicked a statue of Brazil's patron saint, Our Lady of Aparecida. The television presenter apologized and was removed from his post. The presence of both Roman Catholic and Protestant elected officials has safeguarded government respect for religious tolerance. Efforts toward interdenominational harmony have been helped by the National Council of Christian Churches, an ecumenical group that sponsored a 2000 campaign for "human dignity and peace."

Major Religion

ROMAN CATHOLICISM

DATE OF ORIGIN 1500 C.E.
NUMBER OF FOLLOWERS 132 million

HISTORY From the beginning of Portuguese colonization in 1500, Roman Catholic evangelizers have faced significant challenges in spreading their doctrine. Unlike in Spanish America, the Portuguese crown retained complete authority over the Roman Catholic Church, including the right to appoint clergy and publish papal bulls. Since the crown collected tithes, the church never established an independent source of wealth. Spiritual life in the sixteenth and seventeenth centuries centered on the plantation, not the parish. Landowners paid priests, who celebrated Mass on the owner's property.

The Roman Catholic Church remained subject to government authorities during Brazil's first years of independence. Dom Pedro II refused to circulate a papal condemnation of Freemasonry, but several Brazilian bishops circumvented his decision by expelling Masons from their organizations. The subsequent imprisonment of two bishops and Vatican intervention contributed to the official separation of church and state in Brazil. In the veneration of a black terra-cotta Virgin Mary in São Paulo state, church leaders saw an opportunity to reassert control over popular faith. In 1929 they petitioned the pope to name Our Lady of Aparecida the patron saint of Brazil. Her shrine has become a destination for pilgrims from all over the country.

To coordinate the church's outreach efforts to poor parishioners, Brazilian bishops founded the National Bishop's Conference of Brazil (CNBB) in 1952. When the Second Vatican Council (1962–65) affirmed that the church was of this world and committed to a less rigid hierarchy, the CNBB implemented a more accessible liturgy in Brazil. Although the Roman Catholic Church had at first welcomed the military coup in 1964, it grew increasingly alarmed at the rampant human rights abuses. By 1979 four priests had been murdered and one bishop had been kidnapped, beaten, and painted red. A meeting of Latin-American Roman Catholic leaders had established a "preferential option for the poor," which energized Brazilian bishops to support the families of the "disappeared" and tortured and denounce government abuses.

Small grassroots groups called ecclesiastical base communities (CEBs) were formed to allow lay leaders to conduct religious services where priests were scarce. The shortage of priests and the vastness of the Brazilian territory has been an ongoing challenge for the Roman Catholic Church. During the 1970s and 1980s CEBs incorporated the new liberation theology into their worship, applying biblical lessons to confront contemporary conditions of inequality. At their peak 80,000 CEBs operated in Brazil. Then in the late 1980s and 1990s their popularity declined.

While many hailed base communities as the seeds for a transformative mass movement, only a small proportion of Brazilian Roman Catholics participated in them. Several other forces conspired to weaken their potential. The election of a more conservative pope distrustful of communist-inspired ideology undermined the authority of progressive bishops. Critics have also noted how the emphasis on literacy and intellectual arguments alienated many of the poor parishioners CEBs were intended to attract. Furthermore, competition increased from Protestant groups and the Movement for Catholic Charismatic Renewal, who emphasize the ecstatic gifts of the Holy Spirit. The ascendant conservatism in the Roman Catholic Church at the start of the twenty-first century has hampered its ability to connect with the large base of poor Brazilians who clamor for social change.

EARLY AND MODERN LEADERS During the years when the Roman Catholic Church fell out of official favor, some of the most charismatic Roman Catholic leaders in Brazil came from outside the church hierarchy. Antônio Maciel, known as the Counselor, attracted many followers in the northeast after a devastating drought in 1877. His reputation as a holy man derived from his austere piety and prediction that the world would end in 1900. With 20,000 followers, he refused to recognize the republic's separation of church and state and founded a utopian town (called Canudos) based on religious principles. Roman Catholic bishops regarded him as a subversive, and regional landowners feared losing workers, so the military decimated the settlement in 1897.

The northeast of Brazil, with its infusion of African religions from the slave trade and relatively rugged living conditions, spawned another Roman Catholic leader who upset the church hierarchy. Early in the twentieth century Father Cícero, a parish priest in the state of Fortaleza, earned fame for the appearance of blood on the communion wafers he distributed. When his parish in the town of Juàzeiro became a pilgrimage site, the local bishop suspended him from performing the sacraments. Even this censure did not diminish the ardor of his followers. In 1913, in response to a government attack on the town, Father Cícero led his forces to repel the soldiers and capture the state capital. His statue in Juàzeiro still draws pilgrims.

As the repressive actions of the Brazilian military increased and the Roman Catholic Church underwent reforms in the 1960s, two leaders seized on the church's potential for promoting social justice. Dom Hélder Pessoa Câmara endured the assassination of his associate as he campaigned against the imprisonment of political dissidents. Dom Paulo Evaristo Arns, cardinal of São Paulo, organized an ecumenical service to honor a tortured Jewish journalist whose death the government called a suicide. Even as soldiers circled the cathedral, Arns turned his church into a place of refuge and resistance.

The Brazilian prelates Cardinal Agnelo Rossi (1913–95) and Cardinal Lucas Moreira Neves (1925–2002) achieved high posts within the Vatican. Current voting members of the College of Cardinals who oversee dioceses in Brazil include Geraldo Majella Agnelo, Serafim Fernandes de Araújo, José Freire Falcão, Cláudio Hummes, and Aloísio Lorscheider.

At the beginning of the twenty-first century, the most visible Roman Catholic leaders were those affiliated with the Movement for Catholic Charismatic Renewal. Father Marcelo Rossi, the most successful of a cadre of singing priests, has appeared on national television and as a spokesperson for Brazil's largest Internet service provider. His compact discs have sold millions of copies. Consumers could enter a contest with the grand prize of a trip to Rome and an audience with the pope.

MAJOR THEOLOGIANS AND AUTHORS Leonardo Boff, a Franciscan theologian, sparked a debate over liberation theology that reverberated throughout the Roman Catholic Church. More than promoting a preferential option for underprivileged Brazilians, Boff published suggestions that the institution of the church itself could benefit from restructuring to favor the spiritual over the centralization of power in Rome. In 1984 Cardinal John Ratzinger summoned Boff to Rome, where he imposed a 10-month silencing on the friar, banning him from writing or lecturing during that time. Brazilian bishops including Cardinal Arns came to Boff's defense, but the sentence constituted part of a larger Vatican effort to squelch the political aspects of liberation theology. Boff has since left the priesthood, and in 1988 the Vatican divided Cardinal Arn'ss diocese, previously the world's largest, into five.

HOUSES OF WORSHIP AND HOLY PLACES The Church of Nosso Senhor de Bonfim in Salvador, Bahia, has earned a reputation for miraculous healing. Cured believers leave offerings in the ex-voto room as testament to their answered prayers. The same church is holy for followers of Candomblé, an Afro-Brazilian religion whose followers are also Roman Catholics. Every January they wash the steps of the church in Salvador in honor of the deity Oxalá. Though Roman Catholic leaders object to this reinterpretation of their shrine, they are unable to stop it.

WHAT IS SACRED? Popular Catholicism centers devotion on saints, relics, and miraculous images. During the long period of slavery in Brazil, dead slaves took on sacred associations. One figure of a female slave known as Anastacia, whose face is covered with a mask of torture, has become a national holy symbol. She became popular as an intercessory figure among Afro-Brazilians in the 1970s and then reached white middle-class followers in the 1980s. Soap opera stars declared their faith in her; samba schools incorporated her image into the Carnival floats. Her example of stoicism in the face of suffering inspired marginal peoples, from street children to gays. Although the cardinal of Rio declared that Anastacia never existed and ordered an end to her worship, sites related to her have become destinations for pilgrims. Her image appears on medallions and prayer cards and dangles from rearview mirrors throughout Brazil.

HOLIDAYS AND FESTIVALS The Roman Catholic liturgical calendar provides ample occasions for festivals. Saint's days in particular draw visitors to different regional celebrations. In July the Festival of Saint Benedict takes place in the central-western states. Traditional dances and foods such as *bolinhos* (balls of deep-fried rice or cheese) accompany this holiday. In the state of Pernambuco cattlemen gather to celebrate an outdoor Cowboy's Mass. They remain on horseback during the ceremony and receive blessings for their gear.

Every October the northeast city of Belém devotes two weeks to a celebration called Cirio de Nazare. A statue of the Virgin leaves the cathedral in a religious procession and is not returned until the end of the festival. October 12 is the festival day dedicated to the patron saint, Our Lady of Aparecida.

On New Year's Eve, Roman Catholics join followers of Afro-Brazilian religions to honor Iemanjá, goddess of the sea. Gathering on the beaches of Rio de Janeiro, millions of people dressed in white toss offerings into the water, hoping for blessings in return.

Carnival, the pre-Lenten celebration that Brazil is famous for, is only nominally a religious holiday. Roman Catholic leaders have become critical of the excesses of the five-night bacchanalia that precedes Ash Wednesday. The celebration in Rio de Janeiro culminates in a parade of elaborate floats sponsored by samba schools with nearly 100,000 spectators. Winning has become so costly that some samba schools have sought sponsors or sell spaces on their floats to affluent tourists.

Fifty days after Easter a Feast of the Holy Ghost takes place in the colonial town of Paraty, south of Rio de Janeiro. The weeklong celebration includes processions with flag bearers and folkloric dances.

MODE OF DRESS Urban Roman Catholic laity dress like the majority of Brazilians, who are known for their skin-flashing fashion, short skirts, and colorful clothes. Since much of the Brazilian population is young, denim jeans have become a de facto national uniform. Professionals dress in Western-style business suits. White clothing is associated with practitioners of the Afro-Brazilian religion Candomblé.

DIETARY PRACTICES The Roman Catholic faith does not generally restrict the dietary practices of its members. One clear distinction between Roman Catholics and Protestants is that Roman Catholic leaders place little stigma on the consumption of alcohol.

RITUALS The central ritual of Roman Catholicism is the Mass, where believers receive the host and wine as the body and blood of Christ. Many Roman Catholic rituals in Brazil bear traces of their European origin. As part of a movement to make the Roman Catholic Church more responsive to its black parishioners, Afro-Brazilian seminarians devised an Inculturated Mass, which integrates African music, clothing, and dance with the traditional dispensing of sacraments. These African Masses explicitly invoke the *orixás* of Candomblé and mimic the ecstatic experience of spirit mediums.

RITES OF PASSAGE Major life transitions have traditionally been marked by Roman Catholic ritual. Under the influence of liberation theology, some of the elaborate celebrations have been toned down. Medical anthropologists have analyzed the phenomenon of angel babies, infants who fail to thrive and are said to be called to heaven by a saintly patron. While priests once held religious funerals for the deceased children, the high rate of infant mortality in the favelas (slums) of many Brazilian cities and the de-emphasis on mystical ritual in the progressive Roman Catholic Church have meant that angel babies are buried without ceremony.

MEMBERSHIP Roman Catholic leaders and laity alike express concern at the dwindling rates of Mass attendance, a trend that has been exacerbated by migration from rural to urban areas, where the church has a less-developed infrastructure. Brazilian bishops have responded with a campaign to reenergize baptized members who no longer participate in church activities. The Movement for Catholic Charismatic Renewal does welcome former members of Afro-Brazilian religions, engaging them in exorcism-like ceremonies to induct them into a new religion.

SOCIAL JUSTICE From the time of the military dictatorship through the advent of liberation theology, the Roman Catholic Church has intervened on behalf of the underprivileged and oppressed. The Churche's Council for Missions to the Indians, founded in 1972, offers support to indigenous leaders. Bishops protested the displacement of rural workers from their land through the Pastoral Land Commission, which in turn has lent support to the Landless Workers Movement. On National Day, the commemoration of the country's independence, the Roman Catholic Church joins with civil organizations in rallies called Cry of the Excluded (begun in 1995) to remember the populations that remain outside the Brazilian mainstream.

In 2000 the Roman Catholic Church conducted a national plebiscite on conditions imposed by the International Monetary Fund to alleviate the country's external debt. More than 95 percent of those voting disapproved of the economic arrangement. The Bishop's Conference sponsors an annual brotherhood campaign during Lent, which has raised awareness of such issues as drug abuse, homeless children, and racial discrimination.

SOCIAL ASPECTS Even under liberation theology's emphasis on social justice and equality, the Roman Catholic Church has not modified its stance on female sexuality and reproduction. Despite strict doctrinal prohibitions against contraception, most Roman Catholics in Brazil do use some form of birth control, either pills or sterilization. In discussions with anthropologists, poor Brazilian Roman Catholic women make a distinction between the religious prohibition on killing life and the medical practice of preventing conception.

POLITICAL IMPACT While there is no explicit Roman Catholic caucus within the constituent assembly, the Roman Catholic Church exercises power in politics discreetly. Sympathetic legislators work to defend the teaching of religion in public schools and to prohibit the recognition of homosexual unions. The Roman Catholic Church operates a television channel, RedeVida, that broadcasts the church's message directly into households.

CONTROVERSIAL ISSUES Even as Brazil confronts a growing epidemic of HIV, Roman Catholic officials maintain strong opposition to the free distribution of condoms. The Roman Catholic Church remains staunchly opposed to contraception, and church officials argue for limiting abortions even in cases of rape. Influence from the church also made divorce illegal in Brazil until 1977.

CULTURAL IMPACT As with religious doctrine and ritual, the Iberian influence mingled with indigenous and African traditions makes it difficult to distinguish the specifically Roman Catholic contribution to contempo-

rary art. Jesuits and other early colonizers brought musical instruments from Portugal that still shape Brazilian music: flute, clarinet, *cavaquinho* (a small, four-stringed guitar), piano, violin, cello, accordion, and tambourine. Once outlawed, samba expanded from its origins in African religions to encompass members of the Brazilian upper class eager to celebrate national traditions.

Other Religions

Between 1990 and 1992, 710 new churches (about five per week) opened in Rio de Janeiro. Of those churches, 90 percent were Pentecostal denominations and only one was Roman Catholic. As the proportion of Roman Catholics in national census figures drops, the number of Protestants in Brazil has multiplied three times more quickly than the population itself. European immigrants in the first half of the 19th century established the first Protestant churches in Brazil but did not embark on a program of proselytizing. The first missionary groups arrived in the 1850s. Converts to the new churches are called *crentes* (believers) and distinguish themselves by their formal dress.

Both the variety of denominations and the number of followers proliferated in the 20th century. Growth occurred in three successive waves. The first wave, from 1910 to 1950, began with the expulsion of Swedish laborers from their Baptist congregation for speaking in tongues. Those interested in more ecstatic forms of worship joined North American–based churches such as Assemblies of God. In the second wave, from 1950 to 1970, the growth of churches corresponded with increasing urbanization and the development of mass media. The churches that succeeded were Pentecostal congregations that emphasized the gift of healing. Denominations like Brazil for Christ and God Is Love were domestic in origin. Beginning in the 1970s the final wave of churches espoused a doctrine of health and wealth that gave divine sanction to material affluence. These churches, which include the Universal Church of the Kingdom of God, are often called neo-Pentecostal.

The most visible of contemporary Protestant leaders has been Bishop Edir Macedo, founder of the Universal Church of the Kingdom of God (IURD). A former government employee, Macedo practiced both Roman Catholicism and the Afro-Brazilian religion Umbanda before becoming a Pentecostal pastor. In 1977 he bought a former funeral home in Rio de Janeiro to headquarter his own church. To gain the attention of potential converts, Macedo purchased airtime on radio stations. In the theology of IURD demons are responsible for most physical and financial problems. Church services include dramatic exorcisms and constant pleas to contribute donations. By 1990 his flock had grown sufficiently that he could afford to buy TV Record, the nation's third largest television network. During the pope's 1991 visit to Brazil, Macedo countered the massive public Mass the pope led with several prayer meetings that drew even more followers. IURD claims 6 million members worshiping in 46 countries. Migrants to Europe and the United States carry the religion with them, often turning abandoned movie theaters into spaces of worship. As IURD expands, its opponents have grown more vocal. Macedo was briefly jailed for tax evasion. The group ensures government protection by electing its own slate of candidates to public office. Twenty-six IURD-affiliated federal deputies promote religious freedom and advance a conservative social agenda.

The Pentecostal message of self-help through faith healing has been especially attractive to underprivileged urban Brazilians. In the northeastern city of Belém anthropologists have found an inverse relationship between household income and the number of Pentecostal churches in a neighborhood. To conquer pervasive alcoholism, poor Brazilians have few options—most of the poor have no access to state health care, and participation in Catholic rituals often makes alcohol consumption a virtual requirement. With the exception of the looser standards of IURD, Pentecostal churches prohibit drinking, smoking, and other harmful behaviors that exacerbate life in urban slums.

As converts become more involved in their new churches, they find succor in a mutually supportive community. Although some larger denominations have become bureaucratized, all Protestant churches offer opportunities for lay leadership and female participation that the Roman Catholic Church denies. Protestantism has also served as the springboard for political careers, not all of which are predictably conservative. General Ernesto Geisel, a Protestant, served as president during the military dictatorship. Benedita da Silva, a member of Assemblies of God and the leftist Worker's Party, became the first Afro-Brazilian woman to serve in the national congress.

Although Pentecostalism is generally hostile to the Roman Catholic Church's base communities and the practice of Afro-Brazilian religion, all seek to channel supernatural power to improve present-day conditions. They all place individual misfortune in a larger framework that gives meaning to suffering. Pentecostalism, however, has achieved the greatest following among Brazil's large class of underprivileged. Scholars have speculated that of all the religions available to the poor, Pentecostalism best prepares its followers to accept their marginal positions and to await compensation in the afterlife.

Statistically adherents of Afro-Brazilian religions represent only 1.5 percent of the Brazilian population, but the Afro-Brazilian Federation claims that followers account for 70 percent of the country's population. The magnitude and duration of the slave trade in Brazil left an indelible mark on religion. The slaves themselves represented the diverse populations of West Africa, including Sudanese peoples from Yoruba, Dahoman, and Fanti-Ashanti groups; Bantu peoples; and the Islamized peoples of Peul, Mandingo, and Hausa. Included in their numbers were animists, Muslims, polytheists, and others who practiced ancestor worship. Some historical accounts maintain that colonists prohibited slaves from observing their religious practices for fear of promoting group solidarity, while other interpretations stress that slave owners encouraged the observance of African religions as a way to promote the erotic dancing that they believed would stimulate reproduction. In either case the chaotic and disruptive nature of slavery ensured that few religious practices from Africa survived intact.

The Afro-Brazilian religions active in contemporary Brazil date from the late-eighteenth and early-nineteenth centuries. Conditions of work in the sugar-growing plantations of the northeast were more conducive to the nurturing of African traditions than mining or cattle-raising regions. In the large plantations as many as 1,000 slaves lived together under minimal supervision. In the interest of evangelizing large numbers of slaves, members of Roman Catholic religious orders allowed the practice of African customs as long as they were adapted and reinterpreted in Roman Catholic terms. *Orixás* are the intermediaries between Olorun, the supreme god of the Yoruba, and humans. This pantheon of deities came to be identified with the Roman Catholic saints and addressed as personal guardians in the same manner as saints. In different parts of Brazil an *orixá* can be paired with a different saint. Xangô, for instance, is worshiped as Saint Jerome in Bahia, Archangel Michael in Rio, and Saint John in Alagoas.

Adherents of Candomblé, the best studied of the Afro-Brazilian religions, are also Roman Catholics and may be required to attend Mass as part of the ceremonial cycle. Each *terreiro* (the home of an Afro-Brazilian religion) maintains an altar for worship of both Catholic saints and African deities and is independent of other cult houses. A hierarchy of assistants, musicians, and priests and priestesses who have undergone initiation rituals conduct the ceremonies. In private rituals initiates sacrifice animals to the *orixás*. Drumming and Yoruba chanting accompany the public rituals, which begin with an invocation of Exu, a troublesome god. As the initiates, dressed in costumes, begin to dance, some enter into a trance possessed by his or her *orixá*. Outside of Bahia, Candomblé worship goes by different names with slightly different traditions.

While Candomblé retains a strong African element, Umbanda has firm nationalist roots. In the nineteenth century the writings of Allan Kardec, a Frenchman, influenced the development of spiritism in Brazil. He posited a rational theory of reincarnation that allowed contact with souls of the dead. When spiritism arrived in Brazil at the end of the nineteenth century, its philosophical bent became less important than its role in healing. Umbanda rituals, conducted in Portuguese, combine African, indigenous, Roman Catholic, and spiritist traits to forge a resolutely Brazilian religion. It has maintained some of the ecstatic trances associated with Afro-Brazilian religion and reduced the expenses of initiation. Umbanda adds to the pantheon of saints and *orixás* locally significant spirits, like the *caboclo* and the *preto velho*, who can be manipulated through spirit possession to cure member's physical and spiritual ills. Its popularity has spread through the urban middle and popular classes since its foundation in the 1920s, and now Umbanda boasts radio programs and publications.

New Age centers have also succeeded in incorporating several strains of religious tradition into a coherent system for healing. In São Paulo holistic centers offering New Age services have attracted a predominantly educated, Roman Catholic following. Borrowing from indigenous shamanism, New Age practitioners employ visualization techniques to journey spiritually to the nonmaterial realm. Some enhance the effect with the hallucinogen ayahuasca.

More than 500 New Age centers operate in the area known as Planaltina, outside the capital city of Brasília.

One of the most successful is Valley of the Dawn, a 120-acre site founded in 1973 by a clairvoyant woman known as Tia Neiva. As many as 80,000 spirit mediums associated with Valley of the Dawn attend to the physical and mental needs of the residents of the federal district. The site itself has become a tourist attraction, well known for its powers of healing. Daily rituals seek to channel forces from an invisible spaceship that will recalibrate the internal energies of the spirit mediums. They believe that a 2,000-year cycle is coming to an end, and members must be prepared for a new planetary phase.

Peter S. Cahn

See Also Vol. 1: *Christianity, Pentecostalism, Roman Catholicism*

Bibliography

Bastide, Roger. *The African Religions of Brazil: Toward a Sociology of the Interpenetration of Civilizations.* Translated by Helen Sebba. Baltimore: Johns Hopkins University Press, 1978.

Beozzo, José Oscar, and Luiz Carlos Susin, eds. *Brazil: People and Church(es).* Translated by Paul Burns. London: SCM Press, 2002.

Burdick, John. *Blessed Anastacia: Women, Race, and Popular Christianity in Brazil.* London and New York: Routledge, 1998.

———. *Looking for God in Brazil: The Progressive Catholic Church in Urban Brazil's Religious Arena.* Berkeley: University of California Press, 1993.

Cox, Harvey. *The Silencing of Leonardo Boff: The Vatican and the Future of World Christianity.* Oak Park, Ill.: Meyer-Stone Books, 1988.

Holston, James. "Alternative Modernities: Statecraft and Religious Imagination in the Valley of the Dawn." *American Ethnologist* 26 (1999): 605–31.

Mariz, Cecília. *Coping with Poverty: Pentecostals and Christian Base Communities in Brazil.* Philadelphia: Temple University Press, 1994.

Page, Joseph A. *The Brazilians.* Reading, Mass.: Addison-Wesley Publishing Company, 1995.

Scheper-Hughes, Nancy. *Death without Weeping: The Violence of Everyday Life in Brazil.* Berkeley: University of California Press, 1992.

Wafer, James William. *The Taste of Blood: Spirit Possession in Brazilian Candomblé.* Philadelphia: University of Pennsylvania Press, 1991.

Brunei

POPULATION 350,898
MUSLIM 67 percent
BUDDHIST 13 percent
CHRISTIAN 10 percent
OTHER 10 percent

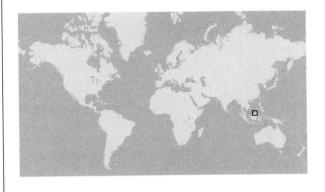

Chinese, Ibans, and Indians, principally adhere to Buddhism, Christianity, and Hinduism.

RELIGIOUS TOLERANCE Brunei is a staunchly Islamic state. The 1959 constitution stipulates that Brunei is to remain as a Malay Islamic monarchical state but guarantees freedom of worship to religious minorities. The Ministry of Religious Affairs is vigilant in enforcing Islamic practices, and special religious officers investigate any breach of Islamic law by Muslims. Thus, the sale of alcohol is banned, and consumption of meat is permissible only with the approval of state religious authorities. Conversion of Muslims to other religions is taboo.

Major Religion

SUNNI ISLAM

DATE OF ORIGIN 1344 C.E.
NUMBER OF FOLLOWERS 235,000

HISTORY Islam has been the dominant force in the state policy and social life of Brunei for more than 650 years. Yet remnants of Hindu-Brahmanic rituals of the pre-Islamic era are still evident in royal court ceremonies. The strengthening of Islamic practices took place when Shaikh Syarif Ali, an Arab immigrant, married the daughter of the local ruler and became the third sultan in the late fourteenth century. A visiting Italian sailor, Antonio Pigafetta, described Brunei in 1521 as a prosperous and thriving kingdom. Until the sixteenth century Brunei was the stronghold of Islam in Borneo, the

Country Overview

Introduction

INTRODUCTION Negara Brunei Darussalam is a tiny, oil-rich sultanate of 2,226 square miles. It is situated next to the East Malaysian state of Sarawak in the northwestern corner of Borneo. Malay Muslims form the majority of the population.

The people of Brunei enjoy a high per capita income and extensive welfare benefits. Since 1967 the head of state has been Sultan Haji Hassanal Bolkiah, the 29th in an unbroken line of sultans (Brunei's Hindu-Brahmanic and Buddhist polity was converted in mid-fourteenth century to an Islamic dynasty). Most indigenous peoples, such as the Muruts and Dusuns, have not converted to Islam. Modern immigrants, such as the

Boys celebrate at a Muslim wedding reception. Islamic reforms and modernization have simplified what were at one time elaborate rituals. Marriage ceremonies formerly lasted for more than two weeks, but have since been shortened to a few days. © DEAN CONGER/CORBIS.

Sulu Archipelago, and the southern Philippines. In 1582 the proselytizing Catholic Spanish conquerors of the Philippines clashed with the Brunei sultan. Subsequently, Islamic practices waxed and waned in an impoverished Brunei that was saved from extinction by British intervention during the nineteenth century. When a British residency system was introduced in 1906, only one dilapidated mosque was found in the Brunei capital. Except in matters of Islam, the sultan was obliged to follow the British resident's advice in administration, a policy that indirectly helped to boost the sultan's role as the defender of religion. The wealth from oil, first discovered in 1929, contributed to the revival of Islam, especially after 1950, when Sultan Omar Ali Saifuddin III (reigned 1950–67) regained authority vis-à-vis the British hegemony.

EARLY AND MODERN LEADERS In premodern times the court-appointed religious officials, especially the Pehin Menteri Agama, exercised considerable influence. After 1950 Islamic administration became thoroughly revamped and bureaucratized. The sultan, who also acts as the prime minister, functions as both the head of state and head of religion. A special Ministry of Religious Affairs looks after the day-to-day administration of religious matters, while the mufti placed under the prime minister's office issue religious edicts.

MAJOR THEOLOGIANS AND AUTHORS Foreign Islamic missionaries were active in the past. Popular works of religious scholars like Shaykh Ahmad Khatib from

the neighboring Sambas (southern Borneo) were read and interpreted in the nineteenth century by his Brunei pupils, including Dato Ahmad Banjar and Pehin Abdul Mokti bin Nassar. In the 1840s the teachings of a Brunei Sufi, Haji Mohammed, started a religious schism. Since the mid-1960s a new religious elite educated at Al-Azhar University of Egypt, Al-Juneid Madrasah of Singapore, and the newly established University of Brunei Darussalam have held important bureaucratic positions, especially in religious administration.

HOUSES OF WORSHIP AND HOLY PLACES More than 120 mosques and prayer halls, mostly built by state munificence, dot the sultanate. Especially noteworthy are the two state mosques in the capital city of Bandar Seri Begawan. Jami Asri Hassanil Bolkiah, a green-domed mosque, was built by Sultan Haji Hassanal Bolkiah in 1992, and the Sultan Omar Ali Saifuddin Mosque was built by his father, Sultan Omar Ali Saifuddin III, in 1958.

WHAT IS SACRED? As with their Southeast Asian neighbors, the acknowledged form of Islam in Brunei is Sunni Islam. Any attempt to undermine the official teachings with Wahhabism, a puritan form from Saudi Arabia, or other modernist teachings are punishable offenses. As with believers elsewhere, Malay Muslims are strict monotheists, but unlike Muslims in some countries, they do not worship saints or hold tombs or other places to be sacred.

HOLIDAYS AND FESTIVALS All major Islamic festivals are celebrated in Brunei. Of those festivals five are declared public holidays: Id al-Fitr (end of the Ramadan fast), Id al-Adzha (day of sacrifice), the Muharram (Islamic New Year, the Prophet Muhammad's birthday), Nuzul al-Koran (revelation of the Koran), and Miraj (day of the Prophet's ascension to heaven). The festival marking the end of the Ramadan fast is celebrated in grand style, when subjects and visitors personally greet the sultan and his family in his palace. The sultan also joins his followers on a long walk around the capital city on the Prophet Muhammad's birthday.

MODE OF DRESS The Islamic dress code is emphasized. Malay women wear *baju kurung*, which consists of a loose tunic, called a *baju*, over a long skirt, or they wear a sarong. The women also wear headscarves called *tudong*. Men wear a loose shirt over a sarong or a pair of trousers. To complete their ensemble, men also wear a head-dress called a *songkok*.

DIETARY PRACTICES The permissible dietary code, or *halal*, which is strictly enforced, forbids the consumption of meat not approved by state religious authorities. For example, non-Islamic establishments, such as Chinese restaurants where pork is served, must display signs stating that their foods are not suitable for consumption by Muslims. In general, *halal* certification is issued to restaurants that have Muslim owners, cooks, and managers. A special religious board oversees the import of *halal* foods, and most local meat slaughtered according to Islamic rites is permissible.

RITUALS Rituals mark many auspicious occasions and thanksgiving ceremonies, known as Doa Selamat (Conferment of Blessings). During the Ramadan fast Brunei Malays visit and clean the tombs of their ancestors. Since 1990 state officials and common people have prayed (*bertahlil*) daily near the grave of Sultan Omar Ali Saifuddin and his consort, the parents of Sultan Haji Hassanal Bolkiah, an event well covered by state television during the fasting month.

RITES OF PASSAGE In Brunei religion and local customs are sometimes combined in the celebration of major rites of passage, such as birth, death, and marriage. On the other hand, Islamic reforms and modernization have simplified what were at one time elaborate rituals. An example is the marriage ceremony, which formerly lasted for more than two weeks, from the time of the "beautification" of the bride and bridegroom (*majlis berbedak*) to the nuptial procession itself (*majlis bersanding*). In modern times this has been shortened to a few days. Burial rites in Brunei include the recitation of the Koran for seven consecutive nights in the home of the deceased, followed by ceremonies on the 40th and 100th days after death.

MEMBERSHIP State religious agencies in Brunei actively promote conversion of non-Muslims to Islam. Religious converts receive special gifts from the state and well-wishers. Conversion ceremonies are often highlighted in the state media.

SOCIAL JUSTICE Brunei is a rich welfare state, and laws favor the Malay Muslims with various benefits, including free education, medical care, and government-subsidized housing. The religious ministry collects *zakat*, tithes made by Muslim followers for distribution to the poor, which is an important religious obligation.

SOCIAL ASPECTS Although Brunei is predominantly an Islamic state, intermarriage between Muslims and non-Muslims does occur. When an interfaith couple marries, the non-Muslim converts to Islam through a process known as *masuk melayu* (to become a Malay). Children of such marriages become fully assimilated into the Malay Muslim community.

POLITICAL IMPACT Islam has been given constitutional and public recognition through the Religious Council that advises the sultan in Islamic and religious matters. The Ministry of Religious Affairs has considerable power in formulating and implementing adherence to Islamic laws. Islamic values and beliefs have increasingly been incorporated and manifested within Brunei politics and society. The sultan acts as the defender of the faith, and the constitution guarantees that "the religion of the State shall be the Muslim religion."

CONTROVERSIAL ISSUES Strict implementation of Islamic legislation creates occasional controversies. For example, unmarried Muslim couples found in *khalwat*, or close proximity to each other, can be fined and may even be imprisoned. Human rights organizations have at times expressed concern over the undue detention of individuals allegedly involved in evangelical practices forbidden by the state.

CULTURAL IMPACT Islamic Brunei has not produced noteworthy cultural achievements, although among local Malays there have been talented calligraphists and artists. The state channels artist's creativity into such religious performance arts as public recitation of the Koran. Islam also heavily influences the themes and performance of stage shows, public media, and contemporary literature. The state-built mosques display exquisite characteristics of Southeast Asian Islamic architecture.

Other Religions

The Brunei constitution guarantees freedom of practice for other religions. In 1993 the government participated in the Kuala Lumpur Declaration, which affirmed freedom of religion as well as other human rights. Because Islam is the state religion in Brunei, however, other religions are not allowed to proselytize, and occasionally foreign clergy or particular priests, bishops, or ministers are denied entry into the country. Importation of religious teaching materials or scriptures is highly controlled, as are attempts to rebuild non-Muslim places of worship.

During the period of the British residency (1906–59), Christianity did make some inroads in Brunei, although the British authorities shielded local Muslims from its impact. The pioneering Christian denominational schools, including Saint George's and Saint Andrew's in Bandar Seri Begawan and Saint Michael's and Saint Angela's in Seria, are still active. There are a number of Christian churches, many of which are Roman Catholic, including two in Bandar Seri Begawan, three in the oil town of Seria, and two in Kuala Belait.

There are three Chinese temples in Brunei; one, named Kuan Yin, or Goddess of Mercy, is in Bandar Seri Begawan, and the other two, Ching Nam in Muara and Fook Tong Temple, are in Tutong. The Chinese community has run its own denominational schools, including the well-known Chung Hwa Middle School in Bandar Seri Begawan.

Two small Hindu temples, run largely by the transient Gurkha population, are found in Bandar Seri Begawan and Seria. Minor groups like Sikhs and devotees of Sai Baba confine their religious services to their homes. A large number of the minority peoples among the Murut, Dusun, and Punan communities still adhere to their ancestral beliefs, while some choose to remain as freethinkers.

B.A. Hussainmiya

See Also Vol. 1: *Buddhism, Christianity, Islam, Sunni Islam*

Bibliography

Brunei Ministry of Finance, Statistics Division. *Brunei Darussalam Statistical Year Book.* Bandar Seri Begawan, 1992.

Hussainmiya, B.A. *Sultan Omar Ali Saifuddin III and Britain: The Making of Brunei Darussalam.* Kuala Lumpur: Oxford University Press, 1995.

Iik Arifin Mansurnor. "Historiography and Religious Reform in Brunei during the Period 1912–1950." *Studia Islamica,* 1995, 48–59.

Kershaw, Eva Maria. *A Study of Brunei Dusun Religion: Ethnic Priesthood on a Frontier of Islam.* Phillips, Maine: Borneo Research Council, 2000.

Niew Shong Tong. "Brunei." In *The Encyclopedia of the Chinese Overseas.* Edited by Lynn Pan. Singapore: Archipelago Press, 1998.

Saunders, Graham. *A History of Brunei.* New York: Oxford University Press, 1994.

Bulgaria

POPULATION 7,928,901
EASTERN ORTHODOX 82.6 percent
MUSLIM 12.2 percent
ROMAN CATHOLIC 0.6 percent
PROTESTANT 0.5 percent
OTHER 4.1 percent

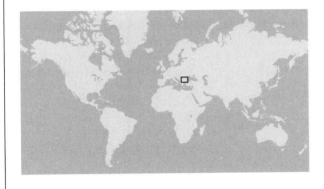

Country Overview

INTRODUCTION The Republic of Bulgaria, situated in southeastern Europe, is bordered by Romania on the north, Greece and Turkey on the south, the Black Sea on the east, and Macedonia and Serbia and Montenegro on the west. The region has always been a crossroads of different cultures and civilizations. Ancient local religions, Christianity, Islam, and Judaism have been present there. Christianity left the greatest impact on Bulgarian culture and identity, dating back to the missionary work of Saint Paul in the first century C.E.

The Bulgarian state was founded in 681 C.E., and Christianity was accepted as a state religion in the ninth century. The influence of the neighboring Byzantine Empire (fourth and fifteenth centuries) is a crucial factor for the understanding of Bulgarian medieval culture and politics, though for certain periods the Bulgarian kingdom showed its own glory.

The five centuries of Ottoman domination (1396–1878) left a significant Muslim population in the country. Jews were the third biggest religious group until 1946. The modern Bulgarian state (established in 1878) has proclaimed Orthodox Christianity as the country's dominant religion. Catholic and Protestant minorities have also had their impact on Bulgarian history. The period of Communist rule (1944–89) limited the free practice of religions. After 1989 there was a religious revival, though Bulgarian society remains highly secular. Other religions include Armeno-Gregorian Christianity, Judaism, the distinctive Bulgarian White Brotherhood, the International Society for Krishna Consciousness, and the Bahai faith.

RELIGIOUS TOLERANCE The constitution (1991) declares the division of religious institutions and the state. Freedom of conscience, thought, and religion, as well as freedom of religious and atheistic beliefs, are also proclaimed. The state is obliged to maintain tolerance and respect among all religious communities and among all believers and atheists. Eastern Orthodox Christianity is acknowledged as the country's traditional religion. This does not provide any privileged legal position, though the Law on Religions (2002), which gives preferential treatment to the Orthodox Church, has raised some controversies.

Bulgarian boys play with ritual fireballs during Sirni Zagovezni. Bulgarian families also observe the holiday by asking for forgiveness and eating the sweet dessert of white khalva. © REUTERS NEWMEDIA INC./CORBIS.

Major Religion

ORTHODOX CHRISTIANITY

DATE OF ORIGIN 870 C.E.
NUMBER OF FOLLOWERS 6.5 million

HISTORY Christianity began spreading in Bulgarian lands in the first century C.E. with the missionary work of Saint Paul. Episcopal centers date back to the second century. Christianity met with greater success after its adoption as an equal religion in the Roman Empire in the fourth century.

The first Bulgarian state was founded in 681 C.E. by Khan Asparuh. Christianity was spread in the state by Greek prisoners of war and clergy. In 864, after a period of famine and war, Prince Boris I accepted Christianity as a state religion. This act was followed by the revolts of boyars (pagan nobles) in 865–66; these were suppressed, and the insurgent boyars and their families were killed. Boris negotiated with the pope about a possible adoption of Roman Catholicism, but he committed to Constantinople (the Eastern church) in 870, and that year is considered the starting date of the Bulgarian church.

Missionary work continued until the tenth century. During this era there were major developments in Bul-garian Christianity, including the invention of the Cyrillic alphabet in the ninth century by Saints Cyril and Methodius, who also translated the major Christian books into Old Bulgarian. Their work continued with their disciples, Gorazd, Laurentius, Kliment, Naum, and Angelarius.

During Byzantine rule (1018–1185) the Bulgarian church existed as the Ohrid archbishopric. For diplomatic reasons Tsar Kaloyan in 1204 settled a union with the pope and proclaimed Bulgaria a Catholic country. The Bulgarian Orthodox patriarchate was restored in 1235.

During Ottoman rule (1396–1878) Christianity in the Bulgarian lands was under the jurisdiction of the Constantinople patriarchate. Orthodox monasteries had their own monastery schools, where Bulgarian identity was preserved. A fully independent Bulgarian exarchate (the domain of an exarch, the leader ranked above a metropolitan and below a patriarch) was created in 1870. After Bulgaria's liberation in 1878 Orthodox Christianity was proclaimed the dominant religion. It later experienced great limitations during Communist rule (1944–89). The Bulgarian patriarchate was restored in 1953.

After the collapse of Communism in 1989, the restored freedom of religion brought many Bulgarians back to the churches. A schism occurred in the Bulgarian Orthodox Church after 1990 with the appearance of two synods, each claiming to be the legitimate representative of the church (discussed below under CONTROVERSIAL ISSUES).

EARLY AND MODERN LEADERS Prince Boris I (852–889), who accepted Christianity as the state religion and converted Bulgarians to Christianity, is regarded as the Baptist of Bulgaria. Saint Kliment Ohridski (840–916), one of the prominent disciples of the brothers Saint Cyril and Saint Methodius, was the first Bulgarian bishop. Other prominent leaders included Evtimiy Tarnovski (1320–1462), a patriarch who personally participated in defending the medieval capital Tarnovo from the Ottoman conquerors. One leader who could be regarded the greatest Bulgarian revolutionary of the nineteenth century was Vasil Levski (1837–73), an Orthodox deacon.

MAJOR THEOLOGIANS AND AUTHORS Most major theologians and authors in Bulgaria have also been church and state leaders. Saint Kliment Ohridski, mentioned above under EARLY AND MODERN LEAD-

ERS, wrote the first original Bulgarian works, which described the fundamentals of the Christian faith. The Bulgarian tsar Simeon I (reigned 893–927) was the author of three collections of Christian works. Chernorizets Hrabar, a ninth-century monk, wrote *On the Letters*, which gave an alphabetic listing of the major principals of Christianity and also emphasized on the sacred character of the letters in the Cyrillic alphabet.

Teodosiy Tarnovski (1300–1362) was the ideologist of a meditative tradition called Hesychasm. The Orthodox monk Saint Paisiy Hilendarski (1722–73), author of the first Slavic-Bulgarian history, founded the Bulgarian Renaissance, the national cultural revival that took place in the eighteenth and nineteenth centuries. The Orthodox bishop Sofroniy Vrachanski (1739–1813) is regarded as the founder of the new Bulgarian literature.

HOUSES OF WORSHIP AND HOLY PLACES Among the most popular Orthodox churches in Bulgaria is the Saint Alexander Nevsky Cathedral (built 1882–1912) in Sofia, the capital city. Bulgaria has many chapels. There are also many monasteries that played a significant role in preserving Christianity during the Ottoman rule; these are usually situated in the mountains. The most significant is the Rila Monastery in southwest Bulgaria, which dates to the tenth century.

A place of worship that became popular at the end of the twentieth century is Krastova gora (Forest of the Cross) in the Rhodope Mountains, where a part of the Holy Cross is believed to have been present. Rupite in southwestern Bulgaria is a place believed to have healing power. The Church of Saint Petka, built there in memory of the fortune-teller Vanga (died in 1996), has become a popular destination.

WHAT IS SACRED? Bulgarian Orthodox Christians accept the cross as the most important sacred symbol. Icons are regarded as sacred and are often used in rituals and processions. Some churches house holy relics of saints that are kept in special places and are believed to have healing power. Distinctive relics include those of Saint Ivan Rilski, kept in the Rila Monastery, and the relics of Archbishop Seraphim, kept in the Russian Orthodox Church in the center of Sofia.

HOLIDAYS AND FESTIVALS Easter is the most celebrated Orthodox holiday in Bulgaria, as it stresses the heavenly nature of Jesus. The date is defined according to the new moon after the vernal equinox, as in other Orthodox Christian countries. Christmas is celebrated on 25 December (unlike in other Orthodox countries, where it is on 7 January).

The celebration of saints' holidays—such as those of Saint Cyril and Saint Methodius (11 May); Saint Constantine and Saint Elena (21 May); Saint Dimitriy (27 October); and Saint Ivan Rilski (19 October)—is distinctive for Bulgaria. In the Bulgarian Orthodox calendar there are 90 holidays devoted to Bulgarian saints. Certain saints' days are observed as both church and secular holidays. For example, Saint Todor's Day is celebrated by cattlemen; Saint Trifon's Day by vinegrowers; Saint George's Day by the military and shepherds; Saint Nicola's by fishermen, traders, and bankers; and Saint Cyril and Saint Methodius's Day by teachers, students, and scholars.

MODE OF DRESS Most laypersons in Bulgaria wear Western-style clothing. The Orthodox clergy wear special church clothes in most public places. The most typical are a cassock made of black cloth, a tunic worn under the cassock, a *kamelaukion* (cylindrical cap), and a skullcap. The deacons wear *sticharion*s and oversleeves, and the monks wear belts.

DIETARY PRACTICES A distinctive holiday associated with special food is Sirni Zagovezni (the Sunday before Lent), when families gather to ask for forgiveness and the sweet dessert of white khalva is eaten. Most feasts are associated with the consumption of special foods. Eggs are painted different colors, and people bake *kozunak* (Easter cakes) for Easter. A number of vegetarian dishes are put on the table on Christmas Eve, which marks the last evening of the Advent, and on Christmas Day much meat is consumed. Saint Nicola's Day is marked by the consumption of fish and Saint George's Day by eating lamb. After a funeral there is often a ritual consumption of food, especially boiled wheat.

RITUALS Liturgies and prayers are the most common forms of worship in Bulgarian Orthodox churches. The baptism of a child is one of the sacraments in the Orthodox faith. During this ceremony the child is immersed in water three times. Another ritual connected to a sacrament is the anointing; a person's forehead, chest, eyes, ears, mouth, arms, and feet are anointed with holy oil in the form of a cross in order to consecrate the mind, thoughts, heart, wishes, actions, and behavior. The sacrament of Eucharist is with bread and wine. Since 1989 participation in rituals has become popular, and politicians have used this as a part of their campaigns.

RITES OF PASSAGE There are no Orthodox rites of passage that are distinctive to Bulgaria. Church weddings have become popular since 1989. During this ceremony crowns are laid on the heads of the couple, they are blessed three times holding lit candles in their hands, and they exchange wedding rings.

MEMBERSHIP Statistics indicate that 83 percent of the population identifies as Orthodox Christian, but few people practice the faith. After 1989 many Bulgarians viewed themselves as Orthodox Christian mainly because of the deep connection between Bulgarian national identity and Orthodoxy. Because of its historical position, the Bulgarian Orthodox Church is not active in evangelization, with the exception of Father Boyan Saraev (born in 1956), who has been active in converting Bulgarian-Muslims to Orthodox Christianity.

SOCIAL JUSTICE For Orthodox Christianity in Bulgaria, national issues have always been more important than social justice. Since 1989 the church has been active in the promotion of elective religious education in schools. There are some lay Orthodox nongovernmental organizations, which run hospitals and spread Orthodox culture, but they have limited resources.

SOCIAL ASPECTS Bulgarian Orthodox Christians are expected to treat parents with respect and obedience; this is especially the case in more traditional places. Traditional family values, which are typical for most Bulgarians, have had an impact on the societal attitude toward state representatives, the military, and leaders in general.

Orthodox Christianity is one of the touchstones of Bulgarian society, which opposes modernization and preserves tradition. Modernization has challenged traditions mainly in the big cities. The church's views on marriage and the family do not differ from those of most other traditional Christian churches.

POLITICAL IMPACT Christianity has played a role in Bulgarian political life since its acceptance as a state religion in the ninth century. It gave common identity to the different ethnic groups. The Bulgarian National Revival, the struggle for independence from Ottoman rule in the nineteenth century, started with the fight for church independence in the late eighteenth century.

Today the Bulgarian government is secular, and it accepts the church as a symbol of tradition, not as a political factor. The Bulgarian Orthodox Church plays a minor role in contemporary political life. It has supported legislation limiting the function of new religious movements. Orthodox clergymen have been elected as members of parliament, but this has led to a greater political influence on the church rather than a church influence on politics.

CONTROVERSIAL ISSUES The schism in the Bulgarian Orthodox Church after 1990 is the greatest controversial issue. There appeared two synods, each claiming to be the legitimate representative of the church. The division was not for canonical reasons; rather, it occurred along political lines, with the active interference of the state and the political parties. An alternative synod questioned the legitimacy of Patriarch Maxim's election (in 1971) under the Communist regime. The government of the Union of Democratic Forces (1991–92) supported the alternative synod, while governments supported by the Bulgarian Socialist party tolerated Patriarch Maxim. The former monarch Simeon Saxecoburggotski (Tsar Simeon II, 1943–46), who returned and was elected prime minister in 2001, strongly supported Patriarch Maxim. His government took an active role in the acceptance of the new Law on Religions (2002), which granted Patriarch Maxim exclusive legitimacy. Following a dispute over church property between the two synods, police force was used in July 2004 to take the priests from the alternative synod out of their churches.

CULTURAL IMPACT The Nestinars, a spiritual community within Orthodox Christianity in Bulgaria, are widely known for dancing barefoot over burning coals while holding icons, which are believed to protect them. It has remained only as a tourist attraction. The production of Bulgarian Orthodox Christian music has a long history and is a crucial part of the work of world-renowned opera singers such as Boris Hristov (1914–93).

A number of Orthodox places of worship in Bulgaria are distinctive pieces of architecture. For instance, the Saint Alexander Nevsky Cathedral in Sofia was built in 1882–1912 in a neo-Byzantine style. It is the biggest cathedral in the Balkans. The Rila monastery is also significant; founded during the tenth century, it underwent various renovations and additions over the centuries, resulting in the large complex that exists today. The monastery's main church, built in the nineteenth century, contains a notable carved wooden iconostasis and murals signed by the renowned Zahari Zograf (but painted by many artists).

Bulgarian medieval and Renaissance literature was largely shaped by Orthodox Christian writings. The painting of icons is the most developed part of Bulgarian fine arts, and people from all over the world visit many original icons in the crypt of the Saint Alexander Nevsky Cathedral in Sofia.

Other Religions

The majority of Muslims in Bulgaria belong to the Sunni tradition, and their communities are shaped mainly along ethnic lines: Turks, Roma, and Bulgarian-Muslims. There is also a tiny Alevi-Kazalbashi minority (Muslims who profess a heterodox Islam).

The first historical data about Islam in Bulgaria date back to the eighth century C.E., when the Arabs besieged Constantinople, and Bulgarians fought against them with the Byzantines. The real spread of Islam came after the fourteenth century, when the region became part of the Ottoman Empire. Islam was the dominant religion in Bulgaria during Ottoman rule (fourteenth through nineteenth centuries).

After liberation from Ottoman rule in 1878, a large Turkish and Muslim minority remained in Bulgaria. The Bulgarian Muslim population was reduced by recurrent emigrations after the Russian-Turkish War (1877–78) and during the Balkan Wars (1912–13); there were also waves of emigration in 1930–39, 1950, 1968, and 1978. During the Communist period a campaign was launched in order to Bulgarize Muslims, first the Bulgarian-Muslims and then the Turks, whose Muslim names were changed by force. In the summer of 1989 the Communist regime initiated a forceful deportation of ethnic Turks. Many of them returned to Bulgaria after the fall of the regime in November 1989.

In 1930 the Koran was translated into Bulgarian from English. The renowned Bulgarian scholar Tsvetan Teofanov published a direct translation from the Arab original in the 1990s. After 1989 the Muslim community was able to practice its religion freely, to publish, to send students abroad to receive religious education, and to give religious instruction to Muslim children. There are three Muslim high schools and an Islamic Institute in Sofia.

In the 1990s a split occurred in the Muslim community that was similar to the schism in the Bulgarian Orthodox Church (that is, not along religious but along political lines). The authority of the old chief mufti, who was loyal to the previous Communist regime, was questioned by a new generation of leaders supported by the political party Movement for Rights and Freedoms. A third stream is represented by muftis who received Muslim education in Saudi Arabia. For a certain period of time there were three different chief muftis in Bulgaria, each questioning the other's legitimacy.

The Chief Mufti Office (the official institution of Islam) in Bulgaria is loyal to the state and to the constitutional system and is concerned about preventing the emergence of Islamic fundamentalism in Bulgaria. With the exception of Muslims in some rural areas, the majority of Muslims in Bulgaria are secular and wear Western-style clothing. The practice of Islam is mostly limited to formally participating in prayers and to avoiding consuming pork and wine; Muslim Bulgarians, however, consume other alcoholic beverages, though a strict interpretation of the Koran does not allow it. The Turkish ethnic minority has its own folklore traditions, literature, arts, and theater. Notable Muslim architecture includes the old mosques in Haskovo (from 1395) and Stara Zagora (from 1409).

Roman Catholicism has been present in Bulgaria from the very adoption of Christianity, and it was the dominant religion for short periods in the Middle Ages. Bulgarian Catholics follow the most common trends of contemporary Roman Catholicism. They received special protection from the pope during the Ottoman rule and experienced suffering during the Communist regime (1944–89). Many Catholic lay organizations have been present in Bulgaria since 1989.

Protestants are present in Bulgaria mainly through missionary activities dating back to the seventeenth century and through Bulgarians who received their education abroad. There are Methodists, Baptists, Lutherans, Seventh-day Adventists, and other churches, but the majority of Bulgarian Protestants are Pentecostals. Protestants suffered severe persecution during the Communist rule. The evangelical churches are highly active in seeking growth, especially among the country's Roma population. After 1989 the Faith Movement has become popular among the neo-Pentecostal charismatic churches, mainly through the Word of Life Church in Uppsala, Sweden. The movement, based on an idea called prosperity theology, has attracted young people with its emphasis on material well-being.

An interesting syncretism in Bulgaria is that the cross and other Christian symbols have sometimes been present in the worship practices of non-Christian adherents, such as Muslims. Krastova gora (Forest of the Cross) and Rupite, mentioned above under HOUSES OF WORSHIP AND HOLY PLACES, are also venerated by neo-Pagans and others for their healing power.

Armeno-Gregorians and Jews in Bulgaria live mostly in the big cities, and their communities are shaped along ethnic lines. They are usually professionals; many Bulgarian Jews are active in academia and politics.

The White Brotherhood was founded in the early twentieth century by Petar Dunov (1864–1944), who took the spiritual name Beinsa Duno. It is a distinctive Bulgarian spiritual community that has some common elements with theosophy and old Bulgarian Pagan traditions. Dunov was a well-known figure in the country. The Brotherhood was criticized by the Bulgarian Orthodox Church, and during the Communist regime it was prohibited. After 1989 its activities were reestablished. It has followers in most European countries and in Brazil, Australia, Canada, and the United States.

The Bahai faith has been active in Bulgaria since 1928. Jehovah's Witnesses, Mormons (Latter-day Saints), and other religions also exist in the country, as do new religious movements. The International Society for Krishna Consciousness has been officially registered since 1991, though Krishna devotees had existed in Bulgaria earlier. Other new religious movements include neo-Pagans, the Unification movement, New Age groups, Sri Chinmoy, Osho, and The Family (formerly Children of God), but their followers are small in number.

Mario Marinov

See Also Vol. 1: *Christianity, Eastern Orthodoxy, Islam*

Bibliography

"Bulgaria." In *Religions of the World: A Comprehensive Encyclopedia of Beliefs and Practices.* Edited by J. Gordon Melton and Martin Baumann. Santa Barbara, Calif.: ABC-CLIO, 2002.

Chiflianov, Blagoi. *Liturgika.* Sofia: Universitetsko izdatelstvo "Sv. Kliment Ohridski," 1996.

Höpken Wolfgang. "From Religious Identity to Ethnic Mobilisation: The Turks of Bulgaria before, under, and since Communism." In *Muslim Identity and the Balkan State.* Edited by Hugh Poulton and Suha Taji-Farouki. New York: New York University Press, 1997.

Irwin, Zachary. "The Fate of Islam in the Balkans." In *Religion and Nationalism in Soviet and East European Politics.* Edited by Pedro Ramet. Durham, N.C.: Duke University Press, 1989.

Kumanov, Milen, and Kolinka Isova. *Istoricheska entsiklopediia Bulgarii.* Sofia: Trud, 2003.

Petkov, Todor. *Putevoditel za dukhovnite obshtnosti v Bulgariia.* Sofia: zdatelska kushta Litavra, 1998.

Raikin, Spas T. "Nationalism and the Bulgarian Orthodox Church." In *Religion and Nationalism in Soviet and East European Politics.* Edited by Pedro Ramet. Durham, N.C.: Duke University Press, 1989.

Republic of Bulgaria, National Statistical Institute. *Statistical Yearbook 2001.* Sofia: Institut, 2001.

Stoyanov, Peter, ed. *Churches and Religions in the People's Republic of Bulgaria.* Sofia: Synodical Publishing House, 1975.

Tsarkovnoistoricheski i arhiven institut. *Bulgarskata patriarshia prez vekovete (sbornik).* Sofia: Sinodalno izdatelstvo, 1980.

Burkina Faso

POPULATION 12,603,185

MUSLIM 55 percent

TRADITIONAL 24 percent

ROMAN CATHOLIC 17 percent

PROTESTANT 3 percent

OTHER 1 percent

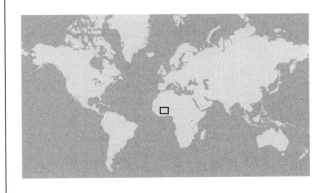

Country Overview

INTRODUCTION Burkina Faso, a country in West Africa, is surrounded by Mali on the west and north, Niger and Benin on the east, and Togo, Ghana, and Côte d'Ivoire on the south. As Upper Volta, the country gained independence from France in 1960, and it was renamed Burkina Faso in 1984. The capital and largest city is Ouagadougou. Although it has declined in importance, Bobo-Dioulasso remains the second largest city and the hub of a productive agricultural region.

About half of the population is ethnically Mose (Mossi), concentrated in the central part of the country,

but there are a number of other ethnic groups. Burkina Faso has three major indigenous national languages: Moré, the language of the Mose; Jula, the language of the western third of the country; and Fulfulde, spoken mostly in the north. The official language is French, which is the medium of the government and press and of the schools at all levels.

Although Muslims constituted only a quarter of the population in 1964, they are now a majority. Nonetheless, many observers still think of Burkina Faso as a bastion of traditional practices and as an area of success for Roman Catholic missions. The political elite and intelligentsia are mostly Catholic, and in four decades following independence only one head of state did not have a Catholic background.

RELIGIOUS TOLERANCE Burkina Faso does not have an official religion, and since independence Muslims and Christians have benefited from the benevolent impartiality of the state. Religious tolerance permeates the country, and Muslim, Christian, and traditionalist members are frequently found within the same kinship group or even family.

Major Religions

ISLAM

TRADITIONAL BELIEFS

A man stands next to an animist mascot sculpted from mud and bone and covered with fowl feathers. Traditional beliefs often involve elements of both animism and ancestor worship. © CHARLES & JOSETTE LENARS/CORBIS.

ISLAM

DATE OF ORIGIN Sixteenth century C.E.
NUMBER OF FOLLOWERS 6.9 million

HISTORY In the sixteenth century C.E., Manding-speaking traders (Yarse) from the west introduced Islam to the independent, feudal-like Mose kingdoms in the central part of what is now Burkina Faso. The traders adopted the Moré language without losing their religion and their sense of distinctiveness. By the eighteenth century there were Muslim communities in Ouagadougou, and some kings became Muslims, sent their sons to Koranic schools, and had Muslim councilors.

Islam traders of similar origin also arrived in the west. There, however, they retained their Manding speech and became organized as a type of diaspora (Jula, or Marka). Some Islamic families produced scholars who became allied as specialists to powerful traditionalist leaders. Besides educating their own, they provided services to non-Muslims, including literacy for diplomacy and correspondence and for producing charms. Muslims traveled to trade, to further their education, and for pilgrimage and thus became a conduit for news and innovations.

Some Muslims were hostile toward the French conquest of the late 1800s and in Mose country enjoined the chiefs to resist. The colonial regime treated all Muslims with suspicion, kept them under surveillance, and during the two World Wars persecuted them. Conversion to Islam accelerated in the 1950s and especially after independence.

A reform movement began in the 1950s in Ouagadougou among wealthy Muslims of Yarse and Mose origin. This was reinforced with the repatriation in the 1960s of some 200 persons from Saudi Arabia and by returning graduates of Cairo's Al-Azhar and other Arab universities. This more puritan Islam rejected the older local form and the Sufi practices that had spread in the nineteenth century. Although its critics refer to it as Wahhabism, reformers themselves do not use the term.

The reformers established national associations, and in the cities merchants and Mose chiefs turned to Islam as a counterforce to the Catholic intellectuals who had been trained in colonial schools and who were leading the country to independence. In 1973, after violent clashes with other Muslims, the reformers founded the Association Sunnite de Haute Volta. Their association received financial support from Saudi Arabia, which enabled them to build mosques, undertake development projects, and award scholarships for religious study in the Middle East.

EARLY AND MODERN LEADERS In addition to the traditional Islam of the trader communities, two Sufi orders were introduced in the nineteenth century. In the Masina region of neighboring Mali, the Qadiriyya order spread among the Fulbe through the political and military movements of Seeku Amadu (Lobbo). Another advocate of Qadiriyya was Mahamudu Karantao, of the Upper Muhun (Black Volta) Valley. In the second half of the nineteenth century, 'Umar Tall (Al-Futi), whose followers conquered the Masina, advocated Tijaniyya. During the colonial period these two orders gained many adherents, and they now constitute the majority of Muslims in Burkina Faso.

A separate branch of Tijaniyya, called Hamalliyya, or "eleven grains," was founded by Shaykh Hamahu'llah in northwestern Mali and propagated by the disciples Aboubakar Maiga, who established himself in Ouahigouya in 1920, and Abdoullaye Doukare, who settled in Djibo in 1932. In 1979 the followers of Hamalliyya established the Association Islamique de la Tijaniyya, under the leadership of Muhammed Maïga, the son of Aboubakar.

MAJOR THEOLOGIANS AND AUTHORS The traditional Sunni Islam of the trader communities seems to have originated with Al-Hajj Salim Suwari, a teacher who lived in the Masina region of Mali in the early sixteenth century. This tradition, which was adapted to living in a political environment dominated by non-Muslims, followed the Malikite school of law.

HOUSES OF WORSHIP AND HOLY PLACES Among the Mose the hallmark of Islamic identity became a personal prayer circle marked off by a line of pebbles and located outside the entrance to the family compound. The Muslim communities of the west built mosques in the Sudanic style. Since the 1960s, to fulfill the injunction to pray as a congregation on Fridays, Muslims in Burkina Faso have built hundreds of small village mosques along with a few large mosques in cities. These are structures of cement blocks with corrugated metal roofs that display little continuity with the Sudanic architectural tradition.

WHAT IS SACRED? As elsewhere, Islam in Burkina Faso does not hold animals or relics to be sacred. The epitome of the sacred is the text of the Koran.

HOLIDAYS AND FESTIVALS Muslims in Burkina Faso celebrate the standard holidays of the Islamic calendar. Traditional Jula Islam, however, adds local variation. New Year's Day, on the 10th of the Muslim month of Moharram, is locally called Jommene and is celebrated by the Zara of Bobo-Dioulasso with dances that dramatize the early eighteenth-century Kpakpale war. The anniversary of the birth of Muhammad, on the 12th of Rabi' al-Awal, is celebrated with dances, during which girls are said to choose their future husbands. The distinctive dance called the Kurubi is organized on the 27th day, Laylat al-Qadr, of the fast of Ramadan, the anniversary of the night when the first verses of the Koran were revealed to the Prophet. During the event,

which lasts from dusk until dawn, women wear their finest clothes, and unmarried women and men engage in licentious behavior in an atmosphere of carnival.

MODE OF DRESS In precolonial times, when villagers wore scant clothing, Muslims marked their identity by wearing cotton clothes. The powerful and wealthy flaunted embroidered gowns and wide turbans modeled on Middle Eastern styles, which spread as the cosmopolitan fashion. Muslim communities often included specialists in weaving, sewing, and dying cotton. Imported and locally made cloth was one of the important commodities of Muslim trade.

Since independence European-style garments have come into general use in Burkina Faso, but Muslims often still distinguish themselves by wearing better and cleaner clothing—for example, preferring flowing gowns and skullcaps to shirts and pants. Jula women are marked by fancy head coverings and dresses, but traditionally they have not worn the veil. With the growth of the puritanical reform movement, however, men can be seen wearing Saudi-style ankle-length shirts, and a few women wear the veil, occasionally even a solid black one that entirely covers the face and body.

DIETARY PRACTICES In Burkina Faso, Muslims generally abide by the interdiction against eating pork, and they avoid eating the meat of other animals, including caterpillars and arthropods, that non-Muslims in some parts of the country relish. There is even greater opposition to the consumption of alcoholic beverages, especially the traditional sorghum beer.

RITUALS Muslims in Burkina Faso are expected to perform the five daily prayers (*salats*) that are standard in Islam. In addition, the Sufi orders prescribe, as elsewhere, a ceremony (*wird*) that consists of the recitation of formulas (*dhikrs*) a specified number of times and in a specific order as a means of deepening faith and reaching salvation.

RITES OF PASSAGE In Burkina Faso, Muslims practice the circumcision of boys and sometimes of girls, although the latter is more typical of non-Muslims. The traditional Muslims of Bobo-Dioulasso perform special customs during funeral commemorations. These include dances in which grandchildren of the deceased represent them by wearing their clothes and by mimicking personal traits, as well as masquerades in which young men disguised in white cotton costumes (Do-gbe masks) perform a dance.

MEMBERSHIP The traditional Islam of Burkina Faso does not proselytize, although the Sufi brotherhoods have a more active policy of recruitment. The contemporary puritanical movement comes closer in its propaganda efforts to the missionary model. Although wealthy individuals have acted as leaders in reformist Islam, common people have also been attracted to the movement. Among converts to Islam, those belonging to disfavored, endogamous artisan castes are overrepresented.

SOCIAL JUSTICE The pronouncements of Muslim authorities in Burkina Faso include appeals to fairness and charity. Muslims have sometimes opposed traditional authorities, including Mose chiefs, but in general they do not take strong public stances on issues.

SOCIAL ASPECTS Among traditional Muslims in Burkina Faso, women are not secluded. They have freedom in matters of marriage and divorce, and some have been successful in commerce. Reformers, however, advocate the seclusion of women.

POLITICAL IMPACT As elsewhere in West Africa, winning the support of Muslims has become a significant factor in electoral success in Burkina Faso, even though most politicians have a Roman Catholic background. During the presidency of Sangoule Lamizana (1966–80), the only Muslim among the country's presidents in the four decades after independence, government contracts helped consolidate the fortunes of a group of Muslim businessmen. This resulted, however, from patronage rather than from official policy. Following the 1978 elections, with the support of the Yatenga politician Gérard Kango Ouedraogo, Muhammed Maïga received official recognition for his Association Islamique de la Tijaniyya. In 1983–87 Captain Thomas Sankara tried to promote the Communauté Musulmane de Burkina, originally founded in 1962 as a pan-Muslim association, over other organizations, both to reduce the rivalries within it and to harness it to the tasks of reconstructing and modernizing the country.

CONTROVERSIAL ISSUES One issue of national concern in Burkina Faso has been the begging in the streets of boys who attend traditional Koranic schools. They do so to supplement their living.

CULTURAL IMPACT Muslims were responsible for some of the most remarkable achievements of precolonial culture. The best known is the Sudanic style of mosque architecture, in which thick walls of unfired clay are reinforced inside with wood posts, on which rest beams supporting a flat roof. The high corner and center reinforcements produce a monumental appearance. Beautiful examples, most built in the nineteenth century, are preserved in western Burkina Faso, including the mosque of Imam Sakidi in Bobo-Dioulasso. In the 1930s this style inspired a French colonial architecture, called neo-Sudanic, like the much photographed train station in Bobo-Dioulasso. Cherished textile traditions are also associated with Muslims. They are mostly cotton weavings of narrow bands that are then sown together and dyed, but they also include silk mixed with cotton and treated with indigo to bring out a pattern resulting from the different ability of the two threads to take the dye.

In precolonial times Arabic was read and written in Muslim towns, but from colonial times onward the intelligentsia trained in French-speaking schools has been cut off from these Islamic sources. Since the 1980s graduates from Islamic institutions abroad have returned to Burkina Faso with a good command of Arabic.

TRADITIONAL BELIEFS

DATE OF ORIGIN Unknown
NUMBER OF FOLLOWERS 3 million

HISTORY Traditional beliefs in Burkina Faso involve a wide range of rituals that form a deeply anchored foundation for the population, and against them Islam and Christianity appear only as recent arrivals. Although some of the basic principles are of great antiquity, the practices have changed over time as ritual elements have been freely borrowed and adapted to local conditions.

During the colonial period regional cults, with portable shrines that involved plant roots and leaves, fashioned objects, and secret recipes, spread as they gained reputations for healing or for powers against witchcraft. People traveled to seek initiation into a cult, and, for a fee, authorities of the shrine made replicas for them. In this way they added to their existing set of ancestral and local spirit shrines. Such transfers resulted in new shrines with restricted membership, in which the key ritual offices were assumed by a few individuals.

The all-male Kono and Komo societies, which spread to western Burkina Faso from Mali, were considered serious rivals by Christian missionaries and Muslims. Some local spirit shrines and regional cults reveal an Islamic influence, indicating that they did not evolve in isolation.

EARLY AND MODERN LEADERS Because of a number of factors, including the collective nature of celebrations, the secrecy involved, the rapid diffusion of ideas, the overlap of old and new practices, and the absence of written records, it is difficult to identify individuals in the history of traditional beliefs in Burkina Faso. Colonial and missionary records provide names of locally important people, but broad movements are hard to document.

One person who influenced the western part of the country in the 1960s was the prophet Musa. From his village in northern Côte d'Ivoire, he sparked a movement against witchcraft. Thousands of people, sometimes entire villages, traveled to visit Musa and drink his special water, be purified, and prove themselves innocent of witchcraft. People burned their shrines, including some dedicated to ancestors. A vast area inhabited by the Senufo and other ethnic groups thus gave up their ritual activity and became ripe for conversion. Since then, however, some young people from these communities are reported to have sought to reconstruct the shrines.

MAJOR THEOLOGIANS AND AUTHORS The traditional practices of Burkina Faso were never systematized in what the Judeo-Christian-Islamic heritage understands as religion and thus have no theologians in the conventional sense. Decades of Christian proselytizing and conversions to Islam have inspired practitioners, however, to conceive of their activities as an alternative "religion," designated, for example, by the word *lanta* (custom).

HOUSES OF WORSHIP AND HOLY PLACES Traditional practitioners in Burkina Faso do not build specialized houses of worship. Nature spirit shrines are generally marked by a heap of stones, around which congregations gather in the open air. Ancestral shrines, where senior men perform rituals, may be kept indoors, and in the past they sometimes served as family sepulchers. The tomb of the mother of a Mose chief is often located outside the entrance to his compound, marked by a half-buried clay pot, and the chief's inherited and acquired shrines are kept in the house of his senior wife. The village shrines in western Burkina Faso characteristically are either wooden posts ending in a three-tined fork, which supports a clay pot filled with ritual plants or liquids, or columns of unfired clary in which a potent object has been buried. Shrines of the Kono and Komo, kept in miniature buildings, are carried outside for public ceremonies.

WHAT IS SACRED? Although the term "sacred" as used in the Judeo-Christian-Islamic tradition may not exactly apply, there are matters in the traditional belief systems of Burkina Faso that are held to be particularly important. Because traditional beliefs often involve elements of both animism and ancestor worship, various items associated with each are honored. Such natural features as woods and ponds, for example, may have special significance, and plants and their parts, including leaves and roots, are often considered to possess power for healing. Animals may become totems for a family. In addition, certain man-made objects, for example, amulets, are held to have the power to protect the wearer.

HOLIDAYS AND FESTIVALS Phases of the agricultural calendar are marked with rituals in Burkina Faso. For the Mose, for example, a thanksgiving ceremony, called Pelega or Basgha, begins on the night of the first moon following the harvest, with libations and sacrifices made to the ancestors of the king or chief. It continues on the following day with feasting, the drinking of beer, and the distribution of gifts. The period between the end of the harvest and the beginning of the rainy period, from December to May, is a period of major public celebrations. In western Burkina Faso these include spectacular masquerades. Great funeral commemorations, held at enormous expense, are scheduled toward the end of the period for those who have died in previous months.

MODE OF DRESS During precolonial times people in many parts of Burkina Faso covered their loins with leaves or narrow cotton bands or wore only ornaments. Hunters and warriors, however, wore cotton tunics treated in special baths and sown with amulets and charms as protection. The wearing of bracelets and necklaces for this purpose is still common. Today European-style clothing along with head scarves and cotton prints, which were originally typical of Muslim women, have spread to all groups, and so it is not as easy to distinguish traditionalists from others. On special ceremonies men don the hunter costumes of their ancestors.

DIETARY PRACTICES Followers of ancestral practices in Burkina Faso generally avoid eating the meat of an animal that provided a service to an ancestor. These bans are specifically linked to shrines with which ancestors made covenants, and they distinguish members of the various descent groups. Initiation into a shrine also carries with it such prohibitions. People follow such proscriptions to avoid retribution, however, not out of awe or devotion. A wife refrains from eating the food prohibited to her husband when she is pregnant with his child.

Local religious practices in Burkina Faso are otherwise permissive in matters of food, and there are no general constraints. The drinking of sorghum beer often accompanies various ritual shrine activities.

RITUALS Rituals among traditionalists in Burkina Faso are intended to produce beneficial effects in the present, not in a future life. It is believed that ancestors can affect the fortunes of their descendants, who invoke ancestors in specially built shrines for good harvests, health, fertility, and averting misfortune. Nature spirits are approached in sacred woods, hills, or ponds. Some cults focus on assortments of objects, often including clay pots filled with roots and water, to contact occult powers who may possess celebrants during ceremonies.

The most common shrine ritual is slitting the throat of a chicken and dripping the blood over the stones or man-made objects. At some shrines sheep, goats, and dogs are sacrificed. The Kono and Komo societies organize yearly ceremonies that involve secret costumes and headpieces and include nightlong dancing. This is followed in the morning by the sacrifice of dozens of animals, whose flesh is then eaten, and by the refreshing of the plants kept in jars and used as remedies. Some ceremonies (*salakas*) involve libations of sorghum beer and food. Before making important decisions, people consult diviners, who employ similar techniques across ethnic groups.

There is a clearly articulated idea of a single god, Wende in Moré-speaking areas and Ala in the Manding-speaking (Jula) zones of the west, with corresponding terms in other local languages. Local people take this as identical to the God of the Koran and the Bible. This god receives no ritual attention but is mentioned numerous times each day in salutations, benedictions, and

wishes. The god is conceived as the source of everything in the world, which reveals a monotheism underlying the diverse ritual practices.

RITES OF PASSAGE Young men, and sometimes women, undergo ritual initiations in Burkina Faso. These formerly took years to complete, with initiation camps serving to impart mythological and ritual knowledge and to test physical training. Where people have converted to Islam or Christianity, the ceremonies have been abandoned, but in rural areas they exist in abbreviated forms.

Traditional preparation for marriage is a lengthy process, involving at the end the ritual abduction of the woman and her presentation at the shrine of the groom's ancestors, thus beginning a period of shy cohabitation before full conjugal life. Outside the main cities these practices are still largely followed. Funerals include the burial of the body on the day of death and a major commemorative ceremony that is held later, during the dry season.

MEMBERSHIP Ancestor shrines in Burkina Faso are restricted to groups of descendants. Most other shrines are shrouded in secrets acquired by initiation. Protective or healing rituals may be available to any person in need, and custodians of shrines with great reputations receive numerous solicitations for help. Initiation into a shrine does not generally require that the person abandon previous commitments. Partly as a defense against Islam and Christianity, however, traditionalists are becoming more restrictive on this matter.

SOCIAL JUSTICE Accusations of using the power of shrines to conduct sorcery is sometimes leveled against people in Burkina Faso. In addition, the threat of mobilizing shrines for personal ends can be shrewdly used to consolidate wealth and power. Success in business or in politics is often attributed to powerful personal shrines or to the paid services of ritual doctors, who may be Muslim. Thus, much shrine ritual activity is morally ambiguous.

SOCIAL ASPECTS Ancestor veneration in Burkina Faso is closely related to social organization by descent. Relations within a family, kinship group, and village find corollaries in traditional ritual activity in a more pronounced way than in Islam or Christianity. In marriage many village traditionalists make a distinction between a first union, arranged by the senior relatives of the partners and condoned by presentation to the ancestors, and subsequent unions, which often follow divorce and which the partners enter into by mutual agreement without broader social and ritual guarantees. Outside this distinction ritual practices have little to do with regulating and legitimizing marriage, and any couple that lives together is considered to be husband and wife. Fertility is an important concern, especially in rural areas, and couples who do not have children consult diviners or try ritual medicines.

POLITICAL IMPACT Shrine activities in Burkina Faso have had greater public visibility since the 1980s. In urban areas non-Muslim, non-Christian people are increasingly becoming aware of their ability to exert political pressure. In Bobo-Dioulasso, for example, some shrine locations obliterated by urban development have been restored upon popular request, voiced mostly by Roman Catholic intellectuals who want to serve as spokespeople for traditionalists and thus gain their political support.

CONTROVERSIAL ISSUES As in other parts of West Africa, rumors of evil people conducting dark rituals periodically stir the public in Burkina Faso and are reported in the press. The most notorious of these are reports of the kidnaping of children to be used in secret rituals for the pursuit of gain. Another recurrent fear is of people believed to inflict impotence in casual interactions, including handshakes. Such fears disrupt daily life and have resulted in retaliatory mob violence. They may stem from the pressures of modernization and indicate limits to the seeming triumph of Islam and Christianity.

CULTURAL IMPACT Throughout the world carved mask headpieces and altar figurines from Burkina Faso are among the most prized African art pieces. Music that mixes drums, xylophones, and traditional wind instruments with European instruments and that combines local styles of singing and rhythms with European orchestration has developed in urban areas.

Other Religions

About 17 percent of the people of Burkina Faso are Roman Catholic. In 1900 the Society of Missionaries of Africa, known as the White Fathers, began working in Koupela and Ouagadougou. After initially stormy relations with the French colonial administration, the missionaries expanded in Mose areas and elsewhere after World War I. The priest Joanny Thévenoud, appointed a superior in 1906, became a central figure of the colonial establishment, especially after the creation of Upper Volta in 1919. Ouagadougou was elevated to a vicariate in 1921, and Thévenoud was consecrated a bishop the following year. A mission in Bobo-Dioulasso was founded in 1927. Catholics, who saw themselves in a race with Islam for the souls of the people, targeted rural areas. To create Christian communities, they recruited chief's sons among the Mose and elders and leaders elsewhere. Thévenoud influenced the appointment of colonial chiefs. The missionaries' interest in the status of young women was controversial, criticized by non-Catholics as, among other things, meddling in community affairs.

Through their schools and a seminary in Pabre, the White Fathers established a native colonial elite. In 1935 a seminary at Koumi was founded, and 48 native priests were ordained between 1942 and 1960. In 1955 the five vicariates of the colony became dioceses, and in 1956 Dieudonné Yougbaré was consecrated as bishop of Koupela. He was the first indigenous bishop in French West Africa. Paul Zoungrana was appointed archbishop of Ouagadougou in 1960 and consecrated a cardinal in 1965. Today there are ecclesiastical provinces headed by archbishops (in Ouagadougou, Koupela, and Bobo-Dioulasso), as well as nine bishoprics.

Catholic theologians in Burkina Faso have focused on reconciling indigenous culture with church doctrine. The liturgy has been thoroughly indigenized. In their churches and stations the missionaries contributed to local construction techniques, especially through the use of lateritic bricks, an inexpensive, durable material. Missionaries and nuns opened craft training centers, especially for women, and introduced innovations in agriculture and animal husbandry, including dairy production. The Catholic workers' movement was the origin of labor unions in Burkina Faso, which since 1966 have played an important role in politics. The major impact of Catholicism in the arts has been in liturgical choral music, where there has been an original blending of African with other elements.

Protestants make up 3 percent of the population of Burkina Faso, although the various denominations claim more than twice this number. The first Protestants to arrive, in Ouagadougou in 1921, were U.S. missionaries from the Assemblies of God. The Christian and Missionary Alliance, also from the United States, was established in Bobo-Dioulasso and Dedougou in 1925; the Sudan Interior Mission in Fada N'Gourma, in 1930; Wesleyan missions, in 1930; and the Yoruba First Baptist Mission, from Nigeria, in 1939. The French colonial administration viewed these English-speaking missions with suspicion, although the missionaries ignored politics and focused on converting the people and translating the Bible. Deep rivalries divided the churches. The Assemblies of God and some other churches are now controlled by Africans. In contemporary times the large numbers of converts have elevated these churches from their formerly marginal position.

Mahir Saul

See Also Vol. I: *African Indigenous Beliefs, Christianity, Islam, Roman Catholicism*

Bibliography

Audouin, Jean, and Raymond Déniel. *L'Islam en Haute Volta: À l'époque coloniale.* Paris: L'Harmattan, 1978.

Déniel, Raymond. *Croyances religieuses et vie quotidienne: Islam et Christianisme à Ouagadougou.* Paris: Collège de France, Laboratoire d'Anthropologie Sociale, 1970.

Hammond, Peter B. *Yatenga: Technology and Culture of a West African Kindgom.* New York: Free Press, 1966.

Kouanda, A. "Les Conflits au sein de la Communauté Musulmane du Burkina, 1962–1986." *Islam et Sociétés au Sud du Sahara* 3 (1989): 7–26.

Le Moal, Guy. *Les Bobo: Nature et fonction des masques.* Paris: ORSTOM, 1980.

Levtzion, Nehemia. *Muslims and Chiefs in West Africa: A Study of Islam in the Middle Volta Basin in the Precolonial Period.* Oxford: Clarendon Press, 1968.

Otayek, René. *Dieu dans la cité: Dynamiques religieuses en milieu urbain ouagalais.* Bordeaux: Centre d'Étude d'Afrique Noire, 1999.

Royer, Patrick. "Le Massa et l'eau de Moussa: Cultes régionaux, 'traditions' locale et sorcelerie en Afrique de l'Ouest." *Cahiers d'Études Africaines* 39 (1999): 337–66.

Saul, Mahir, and Patrick Royer. *West African Challenge to Empire: Culture and History in the Volta-Bani Anticolonial War.* Athens: Ohio University Press, 2001.

Skinner, Elliott P. "Christianity and Islam among the Mossi." *American Anthropologist* 60 (1958): 1102–19.

———. *The Mossi of the Upper Volta: The Political Development of a Sudanese People.* Stanford, Calif.: Stanford University Press, 1964.

Somé, Magloire. "Christian Base Communities in Burkina Faso: Between Church and Politics." *Journal of Religion in Africa* 31, no. 3: 275–303.

Burundi

POPULATION 6,373,002

ROMAN CATHOLIC 62 percent

AFRICAN INDIGENOUS BELIEFS 23 percent

PROTESTANT 13 percent

MUSLIM 2 percent

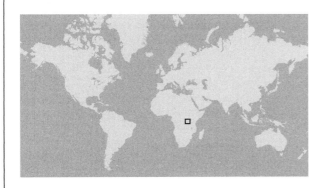

Country Overview

INTRODUCTION The Republic of Burundi is a small Central African country between Rwanda, the Democratic Republic of Congo, and Tanzania, with its southwest border along the shoreline of Lake Tanganyika. Mostly mountainous and wooded, the country has tropical rainforest in the northwest. Nineteenth-century European travelers described it as a land of almost ideal beauty, but political turmoil has rendered Burundi one of the poorest countries in Africa.

Burundi's main ethnic groups are the Hutu (the majority), Tutsi, and Twa. Though many Burundians (particularly the Twa) retain vestiges of indigenous religious practices, the country is predominantly Catholic. The White Fathers opened their first mission in Burundi 1879. The Germans colonized the region following the Berlin conference of 1885, bringing Protestant denominations. After World War I Burundi came under Belgian control. Like the Germans, the Belgians left the Tutsi king and political system in place; however, the Belgians provided the Catholic missions a more favorable climate for expansion. Burundi gained its independence in 1962. In 1966 Tutsi Captain Michel Micombero ended 400 years of Tutsi monarchy, renaming the country the Republic of Burundi.

In April 1972 the Hutu population rose against the Micombero government, killing 10,000 Tutsi. The enraged Tutsi retaliated by slaughtering more than 100,000 Hutus, including priests and nuns. Thousands, including most of the intellectuals, fled to neighboring countries. In 1976 Tutsi Colonel Jean Baptiste Bagaza took power, and in 1987 Tutsi Major Pierre Buyoya deposed him. Despite ethnic conflicts in 1988 and 1993 that killed tens of thousands, Buyoya established a committee for national unity comprising both ethnic groups and laid out plans to ensure equal opportunities in education and employment. In 1990 he replaced military rule with a democratic government.

Burundi's first democratically elected Hutu president, Melchior Ndadaye, was assassinated in 1993 after three months in office. Since then Burundi's continuing social and political turmoil has killed and sent into exile more than half a million of its population. In 1996 Buyoya staged another government takeover. In 2000 Burundi's factions agreed to work toward power sharing, and in 2003 Hutu Domitien Ndayizeye took over

Religious and military figures walk past victims of the Tutsi-Hutu ethnic conflict. Since the 1990s, Catholic Church leaders have worked with Protestant leaders on peace and reconciliation initiatives, hoping to bring about sociopolitical change in Burundi. © CORBIS SYGMA.

as transitional president and conducted talks on power-sharing. The larger of the two opposing Hutu political parties, the Forces for Defense of Democracy, negotiated with the government, and the other party, the Forces for National Liberation, promised to do so.

RELIGIOUS TOLERANCE The Burundi constitution of July 1974 states that "Burundi is a unitary, indivisible, secular and democratic Republic" and that "all Burundi have equal rights and responsibilities without distinction of sex, origin, race, religion and opinion." Although the majority of Burundi Catholics are Hutus, the ethnic intolerance in Burundi has had little to do with religious affiliation. When the Catholic Church challenged the Bagaza government over the 1977 massacre and repression of Hutus, however, 15 Catholic missionaries were expelled.

In the 1980s and 1990s tensions between church and state escalated. Bagaza felt the Roman Catholic clergy were too sympathetic to the Hutus and were trying

to tarnish his government, and he had several priests held in prison without trial. Buyoya eased up on religious repression, but civil rights were restricted and detention and torture of prisoners continued. By 1997 more than 100,000 Hutus, including priests and seminary students, had sought refuge in neighboring countries.

Major Religion

ROMAN CATHOLICISM
DATE OF ORIGIN 1879 C.E>hasis>
NUMBER OF FOLLOWERS 4 million

HISTORY Western missionaries who came with the colonial establishment in the nineteenth century introduced Christianity to Burundi. The Catholic White Fathers made their first attempt in 1879, but Arab traders (who saw the Catholic presence as a threat to their slave trade) killed two of the priests. More White Fathers came in 1884 and settled near Bujumbura. Arab traders again forced a withdrawal. The White Fathers next entered Burundi from the east, establishing a mission at Mugera in 1898. They expanded from there, opening more mission stations throughout Burundi.

When Burundi was transferred from German to Belgian rule, the Catholic Church intensified its mission activity. While the German rulers had identified with the Tutsi hierarchy, some of the Catholic missionaries regarded the Tutsi as unjust rulers who were impossible to convert, and they turned their efforts toward the Hutu. In 1922 Burundi became a vicariate apostolic, with 18 missionaries and about 15,000 Catholics. The first Burundi national was ordained into the priesthood in 1925. In the 1930s the church experienced tremendous growth with an average of 1,000 baptisms per week. The first indigenous bishop was consecrated in 1959, and Burundi became an ecclesiastical province with more than one million baptized Catholics, or 60 percent of the total population. Because of a lack of priests, the church established catechetical training centers to prepare lay leaders to instruct new converts. Such rapid growth slowed down in the succeeding years.

The life of the Catholic Church has been deeply affected by Burundi's ethnic upheavals. For many years the Catholic hierarchy failed to take a clear and vigorous position. In 1977 the missionary clergy and other Burundi low-ranking priests wrote a letter urging the archbishop of Gitega to condemn the atrocities. The archbishop and other Tutsi clergy disagreed with the missionarie's opposition to the government. The difference of opinion continued to divide the missionary religious superiors and the National Episcopal Conference of Bishops, and many missionary priests were expelled. While the church has formally taken a strong position, tensions still exist between foreign missionaries and the national clergy.

Since the 1990s Catholic Church leaders have worked with Protestant leaders on peace and reconciliation initiatives, hoping to bring about sociopolitical change in Burundi. These efforts have intensified since 2000, when Burundi's factions signed a deal that heralded a three-year transition to shared power between the Hutus and the Tutsis.

EARLY AND MODERN LEADERS Michael Ntuyahaga, the first indigenous bishop, was ordained to the newly created diocese of Bujumbura in 1959. Father Michael Kayoya, a respected clergyman and an outspoken critic of the government, was executed along with 17 other priests in 1972. The first three archbishops of Burundi were Antoine Grauls (in office 1959–1967), Andre Makarakiza (1968–82), and Joachim Ruhuna (1982–96). Archbishop Simon Ntamwana was appointed to succeed Rhuhuna in 1997; the president of the Catholic Bishop's conference in Burundi, he influences the country's sociopolitical and religious life, and politicians often seek his advice.

MAJOR THEOLOGIANS AND AUTHORS There are no Roman Catholic theologians of significance in Burundi. Michel Kayoya (1934–72), a Catholic priest, published two famous books: *Entre deux mondes: sur la route du développement* (1970) and *Sur les traces de mon père: jeunesse du Burundi à la découverte des valours* (1971; translated as *My Father's Footprints: A Search for Values*, 1973). He was executed in Burundi along with 17 other priests in 1972.

HOUSES OF WORSHIP AND HOLY PLACES The central cathedral, Regina Mundi, is situated in the capital city of Bujumbura and serves as the venue for events of national importance. The bishops in each of the seven dioceses preside over large churches. The archdiocese resides in Gitega, where the cathedral is one of the oldest and serves as the center of worship for Burundi Catholics.

WHAT IS SACRED? Devotion to Catholic Saints and ancestors is common among Burundi Catholics. Such sacred personalities and their relics are sometimes associated with miracles.

HOLIDAYS AND FESTIVALS Easter, Pentecost, and Christmas provide occasions for elaborate festivals.

MODE OF DRESS Burundi Catholic women usually wear a two- or three-piece outfit. A long piece is swathed around the lower body with a top worn loosely over it, similar to the Indian sari. The third piece is worn over one shoulder and down to the waist. The fabric is beautifully colored and the color suited to the occasion. Catholic men wear Western dress: pants, shirt, and a coat. Professional men in urban areas wear Western-style business suits. Children wear elaborate white suits or dresses during baptisms and confirmations.

DIETARY PRACTICES Like Catholics elsewhere, Burundi Catholics do not eat meat (except fish) on Fridays and fast during lent. Individuals may fast at other times in order to contemplate and pray.

RITUALS Life in Burundi is marked by traditional African and Christian rituals. The Catholic Mass often blends African and Catholic rituals. Younger Burundi priests influenced by the theology of inculturation integrate African music and dance with the traditional dispensing of sacraments. Babies are given a traditional naming ceremony as well as a church baptism. Arranged marriages are no longer common; young people select their partners. During the engagement party the parents of the bride are usually presented with a bride price (dowry) in the form of a cow or its monetary equivalent. A priest officiates at the wedding ceremony, during which the priest and an African traditionalist offer prayers. Elaborate funerary rituals may include both African traditional and Catholic rites.

RITES OF PASSAGE Burundi Catholics traditionally mark major life transitions with great ceremony. Baptism is treated as a significant rite and is followed by elaborate festivities with dancing and feasting. Adults may be baptized after a long period in catechumen classes.

MEMBERSHIP The children of Roman Catholic parents are initiated into the church through the sacraments of baptism and confirmation. Catholic schools direct this process and promote Catholic education in general. Burundi Catholics also use other institutions, such as the hospitals, as avenues for evangelism. The priests who serve in these institutions conduct Mass on the premises, introducing the faith to new people. Other avenues for evangelism are Catholic weddings and funerals. Unlike the Protestant churches, the Catholic Church does not use radio or television for evangelism.

SOCIAL JUSTICE The Tutsi-Hutu ethnic conflict has deeply affected the psyche of the people of Burundi, and the Catholic Church has been criticized for its silence throughout most of this tragic period. In the later part of the twentieth century the church finally spoke out in criticism of the government. In response to the ethnic crimes of 1986, Bishop Bernard Bududira of Bururi (the home diocese of President Bagaza) presented a public analysis of the situation. In 1990 the episcopal conference of bishops responded to Bududira's analysis by founding the Commission for Justice and Peace. They issued a call to Catholic youth, using the theme of building a new Burundi based on love and justice.

In the 1980s Burundi Catholics founded the base Christian community Inama Sabwanya in the south as a response to the call to indigenize the church. Fifty to 100 families took over the responsibilities of directing prayer, education, sacraments, charity, and finances for themselves. The church supported this ecclesial organization in its efforts toward social and economic development. Such communities have continued to provide initiatives aimed at reducing poverty throughout the country. Some of those initiatives include income-generating projects and revolving loans for women and youth.

SOCIAL ASPECTS The war in Burundi has drastically reduced the number of males and has necessarily affected Catholic values and realities concerning marriage and the family. The Catholic Church has had to deal with the increasing number of single women and single mothers. Polygamy is still practiced by a few Burundians, though both church and state discourage it.

POLITICAL IMPACT Since the 1990s the Roman Catholic Church has been vocal over the abuse of civil rights in Burundi. The bishops have repeatedly challenged President Domitien Ndayizeye's government to take responsibility for national reconciliation. The assassina-

tions of Burundi Archbishop Joachim Ruhuna (1996) and the Vatican envoy Archbishop Michael Courtney (2004) evidence the fear of the church's influence. Courtney was closely linked to the process to end the years of conflict in Burundi. President Ndayizeye recognized him as a man dedicated to peace.

CONTROVERSIAL ISSUES With the spread of HIV and AIDS, which have run rampant in Burundi, the Catholic Church's opposition to the distribution of condoms has raised controversy among Burundi Catholics. Those in high positions in the government have criticized church leaders for condemning repression and participating in negotiations for peace.

CULTURAL IMPACT The Western and Catholic influence on indigenous music is notable in the use of the accordion, piano, and guitar. Africans appropriated these musical instruments and added their own drums and rhythm, particularly with regard to church music. Church services incorporate African arts, fabrics, and drama. Burundi drawings and carvings portray Catholic themes. Initially the missionaries discouraged such art, but inculturation has made indigenous art important for the church.

Other Religions

The majority of adherents of African religions are Twa Pygmies, 90 percent of whom are traditionalists. They believe that the creator God, known in Kirundi as Imana, is normally invisible but sometimes appears to the people in the form of a white lamb. Followers address few prayers directly to Imana; rather they use an ancestral spirit intermediary, Kiranga, a former human being whose cult originated in Rwanda (where he is known as Ryangombe). Initiates known as Abana b'Imana serve as attendants or caretakers of the highly organized Kiranga cult. Kiranga periodically possesses his highest-ranked initiates, to whom special honor is accorded.

African traditional religion continues to influence all Burundi. Those who identify themselves as Christians still perform indigenous rituals and practice the veneration of ancestors. Due to the influence of traditional religion, the term Imana is used in the Catholic Church to describe God. Other similar expressions are transferred to Christianity without difficulty.

The history of the Protestant Church in Burundi dates back to the German occupation. Lutherans opened their mission in 1911. Their work ended when Belgium replaced Germany after the Second World War. In 1921 the Seventh-day Adventists arrived, followed by Danish Baptist missionaries. American Quakers and Methodists took over the old German missions and expanded to other areas. The Swedish Free Mission (Pentecostalists) began work in the Bururu region in 1935 and now has the largest Protestant community in Burundi. The World Gospel Mission and the Church Missionary Society entered Burundi in 1935. The Anglicans established churches in the south, where they gained some ground. Also in 1935 the Protestant churches formed an alliance to coordinate their respective spheres of operation, as well as to unite their voices to influence social policies. Pentecostal or charismatic renewal has spread to virtually all the Protestant churches, but civil unrest destroyed any organization the promoters had established.

Over the years the Protestant congregations in Burundi have remained small, but they are nonetheless important in their influence. Protestants are heavily involved in education and medical and social services. In 1970 the Anglicans ran 275 primary schools, 3 secondary schools, and 2 teacher-training colleges in addition to a theological college. The massacre that followed the Hutu uprising of 1972 reduced the Protestant churches by half.

Islam accounts for about 2 percent of the population. Most practitioners are Sunni Muslims, and the highest proportion of these are Africans, followed by Asians. Minority Muslims are Ismailis, Bohoras, and Kharijites. Muslims in Burundi are influential in urban centers, where they flourish economically, and maintain relations with Muslims in neighboring countries.

Samuel K. Elolia

See Also Vol. I: *African Indigenous Beliefs, Christianity, Roman Catholicism*

Bibliography

Baur, John. *2,000 Years of Christianity in Africa.* 2nd rev. ed. Nairobi: Pauline Publications Africa, 1994.

Hohensee, Donald. *Church Growth in Burundi.* South Pasadena, Calif.: William Carey Library, 1977.

Lemarchand, R. *Rwanda and Burundi.* New York: Praeger, 1970.

McDonald, Gordon, ed. *Area Handbook for Burundi.* Washington, D.C.: U.S. Government Printing Office, 1969.

Wolbers, Marian F. *Burundi.* New York: Chelsea House Publishers, 1989.

Cambodia

Country Overview

INTRODUCTION The Kingdom of Cambodia lies on the northeastern shore of the Gulf of Thailand in Southeast Asia and is bordered by Thailand to the west and northwest, Laos to the northeast, and Vietnam to the east and southeast. The greatest concentrations of population and economic activity are on the flood plains of the Mekong and Sab Rivers, which flow from Laos and the Tonle Sap lake, respectively, toward southern Vietnam and the South China Sea, merging in the vicinity of Phnom Penh. Some 75 percent of Cambodia's population is involved in agriculture, mostly in the cultivation of rice. Theravada Buddhism is the traditional religion of nearly all of the country's farmers.

As in neighboring countries, however, Buddhism is mixed with spirit practice. Hindu-Brahmanist traditions, which preceded Theravada Buddhism, still capture the popular imagination and figure in court rituals as well as in healing practices and localized cults. The cataclysmic period from 1975 to 1979, when the country (then called Democratic Kampuchea) was controlled by the radical communist Khmer Rouge movement under Pol Pot, drastically transformed all aspects of Cambodian society, including religion, and the country is still recovering from its effects.

RELIGIOUS TOLERANCE Under Pol Pot all formal religious practice was abolished, monks were defrocked, and temples were destroyed or converted to other purposes. Many Muslim Cham people were killed when they resisted state-imposed practices, such as communal meals that included pork. The socialist government of the 1980s restored religion but was strongly secular in orientation and imposed significant restrictions. Since 1989 there has been considerable religious freedom, with tolerance for a variety of practices. Buddhism became the official state religion of Cambodia in 1993.

Major Religion

THERAVADA BUDDHISM

DATE OF ORIGIN Thirteenth century C.E.
NUMBER OF FOLLOWERS 11.4 million

HISTORY Evidence of Buddhist practice in the area of present-day Cambodia dates to the third century C.E.

Buddhism arrived and developed among elites in the area at about the same time as other Indian religious practices, including the cults devoted to Vishnu and Siva. The classical Angkor Period (802–1432 C.E.), famous for its monumental religious architecture, was primarily associated with Sivaism, but Vishnuism and Mahayana Buddhism also flourished. A form of Theravada Buddhism spread to Cambodia in the thirteenth century and has been the dominant religion in the country since that time.

Until French colonial control became well established in the late nineteenth century, Cambodia was dominated at various times by the Siamese, whose presence in the country affected Buddhist practices there. In the 19th century, for example, Bangkok served as a center of monastic education for Cambodians. In the early twentieth century the French colonial government tried to reduce Siamese influence and develop a more truly Cambodian tradition. They created a Buddhist Institute and Pali schools and encouraged local religious publications. Briefly displaced by occupying Japanese forces in 1945, the French administration was subsequently challenged by a growing independence movement. The young king, Norodom Sihanouk (born in 1922), captured the momentum of the movement and negotiated independence from France in 1953.

Between 1975 and 1979 the country underwent a fundamental transformation as Pol Pot's radical Khmer Rouge government evacuated cities and reorganized all of Cambodian society around agricultural communes. Many high-ranking monks and other intellectuals were killed, and many others fled the country.

The socialist People's Republic of Kampuchea (PRK), established in 1979, restored Buddhism but placed controls on its activities. Young men were not allowed to seek ordination, for example. In 1989 constitutional changes reinstated religious freedom, resulting in dramatic increases in the numbers of people seeking ordination or a Buddhist education. The disruptions of the previous 15 years continued to be felt, however, and many believe Buddhism in Cambodia has been weakened.

EARLY AND MODERN LEADERS The Angkorean king Jayavarman VII, who reigned from 1181 to about 1215, supported Mahayana Buddhism and is still regarded as a model for Cambodian Buddhist kingship. The lesser-known ruler Ang Chan, whose reign lasted from 1516 to 1566, was also a great political and reli-

A monk prays outside of the temple of Angkor Wat. The ancient city of Angkor is famous for its monumental religious architecture. © KEREN SU/CORBIS.

gious restorer and may have laid the foundations for the Cambodian cult of Maitreya, the next Buddha, whom most members believe will be born on earth in the far distant future.

In the twentieth century Norodom Sihanouk, who abdicated the throne in 1955 to assume political leadership of Cambodia, developed a social program for the country that has often been described as Buddhist socialism. An important contemporary Buddhist leader is the monk Maha Ghosananda (born in 1929), who, after working in camps for Cambodian refugees in the 1970s and '80s, led a series of celebrated peace marches that began in 1992.

MAJOR THEOLOGIANS AND AUTHORS Several anonymous works have profoundly influenced Cambodian Theravada Buddhism. The *Reamker*, a Khmer-language version of the *Ramayana* with a Buddhist orientation, dates to the seventeenth century. By the 19th century there were important Khmer versions of the Jataka stories, which focus on the former lives of the Buddha, and *Trai Phum*, a cosmological treatise that originated in Thailand in the fourteenth century. The *Buddhamnay*, a set of prophetic texts that probably dates to the late nineteenth century, is of Cambodian origin but is similar to texts developed in neighboring countries. It exists in a variety of written and oral versions and continues to influence millennialist thinking in Cambodia.

Suttantaprija Ind (1859–1924), who was associated with the modernization of Buddhism, published an ethical treatise based on traditional fables, the *Gatilok*, in 1921. The two most prominent Cambodian Buddhist scholars of the twentieth century were Chuon Nath (1883–1969) and Huot Tat (1891–1975?), successive patriarchs of the Mahanikay order. Both wrote extensively and were associated with reform movements. Chuon Nath also organized Khmer translations of the *Tipitaka*, the canon of Theravada Buddhism.

HOUSES OF WORSHIP AND HOLY PLACES The Buddhist temple complex found in every Cambodian municipality is called a *wat* (in Khmer, *vatt*). Among the buildings in a *wat* are the *preah vihear*, a high, decorative building which houses the most important Buddha image in the *wat*; the *sala chhan*, a lower, usually open-sided building which is used for assemblies; and the *koti*, or monk's quarters.

Cambodians tend to regard elevated places as sacred. *Wats* or shrines can be found on most hills and mountains throughout the country. The most famous holy mountain is Phnom Kulen (the source of the streams that flow to Angkor), which attracts forest monks and other ascetics.

WHAT IS SACRED? Images of the Buddha, the Buddhist scriptures, and monks are all objects of reverence among Cambodian Theravada Buddhists. Many Cambodians also show great deference toward their king, which is in keeping with both Buddhist and Hindu-Brahmanist conceptions of kingship. (This level of respect for the king, however, may be declining as the country's political situation changes and as new generations emerge for whom the institution of kingship has less meaning.)

Angkorean ruins, even in small fragments, are regarded as sources of spiritual power. Cambodian villages invariably contain a shrine to the spirit of a place, or *neak ta*, which is sometimes embodied in a rough stone or crude image.

HOLIDAYS AND FESTIVALS Central to the Cambodian Buddhist calendar is the rainy season retreat, or *vassa*, (also, *vossa*) which lasts from July to September. Ritual activity intensifies during this period, and monks are forbidden to sleep outside their temples. *Vassa's* beginning and end are marked by community celebrations.

Two important holidays occur near the end of *vassa*. During the 15-day celebration of *Pchum Ben*, which is sometimes likened to the Day of the Dead celebrated in some Western countries, members of the laity take turns camping at the *wat*, where they feed the monks and make offerings to the spirits of the dead. On *Kathin*, which takes place in the month following *vassa*, robes and other necessities are presented to monks, often by a group that comes in festive procession from another community.

In February Cambodians celebrate the day of the Buddha's last sermon, and in May they observe the anniversary of the Buddha's birth and enlightenment. Another major holiday is the lunar New Year, which is celebrated in April. Although not technically a Buddhist holiday, New Year's Day is often celebrated at the *wat* in rural areas. Offerings are made to the *devata* (a deity resembling an angel) of the new year, and members of the community gather to build mounds of sand in the belief that each grain will bring greater health and happiness to their lives.

MODE OF DRESS The article of clothing most closely associated with Theravada Buddhism is the saffron robe of the monk, who also shaves his head and removes all facial hair. Laypersons abiding by the five basic precepts of Buddhism often wear white tunics and baggy black trousers. Those who have vowed to keep more precepts—usually women, who are known as *doun chi*—may dress completely in white, as is done in other Theravada countries except Myanmar. Another traditional garment is the *cong kben*, a wraparound covering that is rolled in the front, passed between the legs and tucked in at the back waist. It is often worn by classical musicians, by the bride and groom during part of the wedding ceremony, and sometimes by officiants in Brahmanic ceremonies.

DIETARY PRACTICES Cambodian Buddhism is remarkably free of dietary restrictions for the lay population, and most restrictions observed by monks have to do with the timing of meals rather than with what is eaten. The most far-reaching restriction is that monks cannot eat solid food after noon. This rule is also observed by *doun chi* and other laypersons who, either at all times or on designated holy days, keep the ten Buddhist precepts. Alcohol consumption by monks is strictly prohibited, and laypersons who follow the five basic precepts also do not drink. Alcohol is not a forbidden substance for laypersons, however, and drinking is common.

While Buddhists view the killing of animals—and orders to kill them—negatively, few Cambodians are vegetarians, and vegetarianism is not part of monastic discipline. In fact vegetarianism is thought to contradict the monastic injunction to eat indiscriminately what is given. This contradiction is partially resolved when Muslims serve as butchers and fishers in a Cambodian community; nevertheless, Buddhists do not rigidly avoid these occupations.

RITUALS Monastic communities maintain their own ritual cycle, including daily liturgies, the periodic renewal of vows, and confession. Lay participation in the ritual life of the *wat* is voluntary, and it intensifies on regular holy days (*tnghay sel*) and holidays.

Most public rituals that are considered Buddhist, whether performed at the *wat* or in a home, involve the presentation of food and other necessities to monks (in order to generate merit) and the chanting of liturgies by the monks. Ordination, one of the most important public rituals, is often an elaborate and costly ceremony. Fundraisers and ceremonies honoring parents or the dead are among the rituals commonly performed in homes. Funeral ceremonies, in which monks play a prominent role, include an elaborate procession that precedes cremation. Additional commemorative ceremonies take place on the seventh and 100th days after death.

A Cambodian wedding may include a ritual segment in which Buddhist monks receive offerings and chant blessings of the union. Weddings are not Buddhist ceremonies, however, and such a segment is likely to be overshadowed by other rituals in which spirits or Brahmanic deities are invoked.

Cambodians often seek blessings or protection from monks or lay religious specialists, either in the form of ritual anointing with water or in more elaborate ceremonies. Some argue, however, that these are not strictly Buddhist practices. Monks may also be called to ceremonies to placate or empower local spirits.

RITES OF PASSAGE In Cambodia—as in Thailand, Myanmar, and Laos—most young men join monasteries temporarily, whether they serve as novices or full-fledged *bhikkhus* (monks). Thus, a monastic education serves as a sort of rite of passage into manhood, a period in which significant markers of identity are abandoned while the young man learns discipline and the codes central to his community's ritual life. The elaborateness of the ordination ritual lends itself to this view of monastic training. The disruptions suffered by Cambodian Buddhism in the 1970s and '80s, however, have led to fewer young men entering the monasteries, and so the importance of monastic training as a rite of passage may be waning. A traditional period of seclusion once served as a parallel rite of passage for young women, but this is now rarely practiced.

MEMBERSHIP While membership in the monkhood is very strictly defined—by ordination, dress, and disciplinary practice—there is no clear definition of membership in Cambodian Buddhism, and it is often assumed that to be ethnically Khmer is to be Theravada Buddhist. As they become integrated into Khmer communities, some ethnic Chinese and hill people assimilate Theravada practices. Individuals who have taken vows to abide by five or more of the Buddhist precepts are considered especially integral to their *wat* community.

SOCIAL JUSTICE Buddhism provides the ethical basis for Cambodian concepts of social justice. In the 1950s, when Norodom Sihanouk promoted so-called Buddhist socialism, he argued that Buddhist principles could be a basis for a more equitable society. Nevertheless, it is only since the 1990s that Buddhist organizations dedicated to social activism have clearly emerged. Many of these groups had roots in the refugee camps that were set up in the 1980s on the border with Thailand. They flourished in the intense political atmosphere of the time as a result of contact with the Thai Engaged Buddhism movement and the financial support they received from international nongovernmental organizations (NGOs). The most celebrated of the organizations was the Dhammayietra movement led by Maha Ghosananda, which organized peace marches in the 1990s to promote spiritual renewal and national reintegration. Another organization with roots in the refugee camps, Buddhism for Development, has used Buddhist institutions to carry out social projects. The Association of Nuns and Laywomen in Cambodia, which is supported by international NGOs, has encouraged social activism for women's rights. In the 1990s the United Nations funded instruction for monks aimed at demonstrating that Buddhist principles are consistent with contemporary definitions of human rights and at promoting human rights in popular consciousness.

SOCIAL ASPECTS One of the five basic Buddhist precepts calls for refraining from sexual impropriety. Generally, however, Buddhism's central concern with monks rather than householders means it is custom rather than religious injunctions that gives order to Cambodian marriages and family life. Buddhism calls for devotion to parents, and shrines to "the mother" and "the father," conceived abstractly, are found in some homes and some *wats.*

Because Theravada Buddhism has traditionally not permitted the ordination of women, it is sometimes seen as having a male bias. Cambodian women are active in *wat* activities, however, and their prominent role in ritual merit making suggests that such activities can be socially empowering for them.

POLITICAL IMPACT The Cambodian monasticism is officially nonpolitical. For many young Cambodians, however, their period of service in the monastic communities is a time of intellectual exploration, and it is perhaps inevitable that young monks become interested in and involved in politics. In the early 1940s the monk Hem Chieu (1898–1943) was arrested for his nationalist activities, prompting massive demonstrations in which many other monks participated. In 1998 young monks joined protests against the outcome of national elections, in which widespread fraud was alleged. In subduing the protests government forces beat and reportedly killed some of the monks.

No prominent monks have influenced policy or political philosophy in contemporary Cambodia. Political power is perceived to be connected with spiritual power, however, and political figures may seek contact with or ritual blessing by monks or lay specialists whom they consider powerful. In addition Cambodian political figures often make public donations to *wats* or individual monks.

CONTROVERSIAL ISSUES In 1993 a transitional government administered by the United Nations broke a long-standing tradition in Cambodia by allowing monks to vote. Monks have retained this legal right, one that is supported in particular by opposition political parties; nevertheless, the monastic hierarchy opposes voting by

monks and has discouraged the practice. A controversy of longer standing concerns the lack of ordination of women, which is regularly discussed in Cambodia, as in other Theravada Buddhist countries. No concrete steps have been taken toward the ordination of women, however.

CULTURAL IMPACT Buddhist narratives—especially the Jataka stories, in oral and written form—continue to be of great popular importance in Cambodia's culture. Their significance still probably exceeds that of secular narratives, though television ownership may be changing this. Pali, the Buddhist scriptural language, has had a clear historical influence on Cambodian literary styles. Modern Cambodian literature has been little studied, and the lack of institutional frameworks since 1979 has meant that much of it has remained unpublished. At least some important writers, however, have dealt with such Buddhist themes as impermanence and the emptiness of desire.

A large proportion of plastic art produced in Cambodia since 1989 has been religious in nature. This output has been associated with the reconstruction of temples and their decoration with murals. More commercially oriented Cambodian art often draws on Angkorean iconography.

Other Religions

Religious populations other than the Theravada Buddhists have been little studied in Cambodia, and the percentages included at the beginning of this entry, which are based on published estimates and statistics describing ethnic populations, should be regarded as only rough approximations.

As in other Southeast Asian countries the ethnic Chinese in Cambodia are nominally Mahayana Buddhists, though in practice they combine Mahayana Buddhism with other religious traditions. Official figures representing Cambodia's ethnic Chinese population are quite low because of high rates of intermarriage and declines in Chinese language skills and identification with Chinese culture among young ethnic Chinese in the late twentieth century. Ethnic identity among the Chinese, who once formed a major part of Cambodia's urban population, has shown signs of rebounding more recently, however. Chinese-style Mahayana Buddhist temples are a conspicuous presence in urban centers and large market towns, and attention to Chinese temples seemed to increase in the 1990s along with the flourishing of Chinese newspapers and Chinese-language schools. At the same time some distinctions between Khmer and Chinese religious practices seemed to become blurred. Many urban homes contain Chinese household shrines, for example, whether or not the family identifies itself strongly as Chinese. Likewise, many families of Chinese extraction are active in Theravada *wats*.

Islam is practiced by the Cham and Chvea populations, groups that are often associated with river towns and urban areas. Recent research has identified a small Cham-speaking group called the Jahed that practices a heterodox Sufi-influenced form of Islam based on texts in an ancient Cham script. The Cham were treated harshly under the Pol Pot regime, and according to some estimates 70 percent of the population perished during this period. Since then, however, there has been little tension between Muslims and Buddhists. Contact with Muslims from other Southeast Asian countries has increased, perhaps facilitated by the presence of United Nations troops from Malaysia and Indonesia in Cambodia during the early 1990s.

Although there was a Christian presence in Cambodia before 1975, it was largely confined to the ethnic Vietnamese population. The Catholic cathedral in Phnom Penh, once a conspicuous landmark, was dismantled by the Khmer Rouge in the 1970s. Since 1991 Christianity has made inroads among the Khmer, largely as a result of the return of Christianized Cambodians from refugee camps and the missionary efforts of Cambodians returning home from their countries of resettlement. Estimates of the number of Cambodian Christians vary, but the actual figure is probably much less than 1 percent of the total population.

Little-studied minority peoples representing 26 different ethnic groups now exist primarily in the mountainous areas of northeastern Cambodia. The migratory disruptions of the Pol Pot period and, since then, the impact of new land policies and the intrusions of lowland populations have all led to the diminution of these groups and to their assimilation by ethnic Khmer populations. The religious beliefs of these peoples are usually classified as animist, but they vary considerably from group to group.

John Marston

See Also Vol. 1: *Buddhism, Mahayana Buddhism, Theravada Buddhism*

Bibliography

Bizot, François. *Le figuier à cinq branches: recherche sur le bouddhisme khmer.* Paris: Ecole française d'Extrême-Orient, 1976.

Chouléan, Ang. *Les êtres surnaturels dans la religion populaire khmère.* Paris: Cedoreck, 1986.

Ebihara, May. "Interrelations between Buddhism and Social Systems in Cambodian Buddhist Peasant Culture." In *Anthropological Studies in Theravada Buddhism.* Edited by Manning Nash. New Haven: Yale University Southeast Asia Studies, 1996.

Harris, Ian. "Buddhism In Extremis." In *Buddhism and Politics in Twentieth-Century Asia.* Edited by Ian Harris. New York: Pinter, 1999.

Leclère, Adhémard. *Le bouddhisme au Cambodge.* Paris: Ernest Leroux, 1899.

Marston, John, and Elizabeth Guthrie. *Cambodian Religion: Recent Studies* (forthcoming).

Ponchaud, François. *La cathédrale de la rizière: 450 ans d'histoire de l'église au Cambodge.* Paris: Le Sarment-Fayard, 1990.

Yang Sam. *Khmer Buddhism and Politics from 1954 to 1984.* Newington, Conn.: Khmer Studies Institute, 1987.

Cameroon

POPULATION 16,184,748

ROMAN CATHOLIC 34.7 percent

AFRICAN INDIGENOUS BELIEFS 26 percent

MUSLIM 21.8 percent

PROTESTANT 17.5 percent

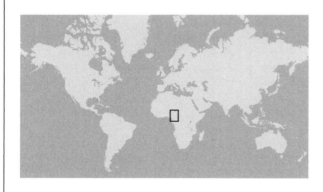

Country Overview

INTRODUCTION The Republic of Cameroon, located on the west coast of Africa on the Gulf of Guinea, is surrounded by six countries: Nigeria to the northwest, Chad and Central African Republic to the east, and Republic of the Congo, Gabon, and Equatorial Guinea to the south. Cameroon is often said to be Africa in miniature, both for its geographic diversity, which ranges from rain forests in the south to the semidesert Sahelian landscape of the north, and for its rich cultural diversity, which includes a mix of more than 150 different languages and a variety of African religious practices.

Christianity spread from the coast, and Christians predominate in the south and the west. Islam arrived from the Sahel region and from northern Nigeria, and most Muslims are found in northern Cameroon. Among African indigenous religions, the populations of the north are famous for their circumcision rites and their fertility rituals, as well as their masquerades, which are usually associated with fertility or funerary rituals in which the masks represent bush spirits or the spirits of the deceased. Societies in the western part of Cameroon also have spectacular masquerades, but these are often connected with secret societies (among, for example, the Bamiléké or the Bafut) or elaborate chiefly rituals (such as the Nguon ceremony among the Bamoun, which celebrates a dynasty claiming to be more than 600 years old). Societies in the central part of Cameroon, including the Bulu and Beti, have abandoned many of their indigenous religious traditions. Witchcraft remains a main concern for most people throughout Cameroon. The forest peoples (the so-called pygmies) of the southern and eastern parts of Cameroon continue to practice their renowned healing and hunting rituals.

RELIGIOUS TOLERANCE A secular state, Cameroon does not have a state religion, and it guarantees freedom of worship. The state, however, subsidizes a great number of Catholic and Protestant schools and hospitals that operate all over the country. Although the religious composition and history of northern Cameroon, which is predominantly Muslim, is similar to that of northern Nigeria, Cameroon has so far been spared from the religious violence that has plagued its western neighbor.

Major Religions

CHRISTIANITY

AFRICAN INDIGENOUS BELIEFS

ISLAM

CHRISTIANITY

DATE OF ORIGIN 1842 C.E.
NUMBER OF FOLLOWERS 8.4 million

HISTORY After its arrival in Cameroon, Christianity spread slowly, following the advance of colonization. Reverend Alfred Saker (1814–80), a British Baptist minister, established the first mission in the country in Victoria (now Limbe) in 1842 and then another in Douala in 1845. The Baptists were followed by American Presbyterians, who opened a missionary station in 1871. Lutheran Basel missionaries arrived in 1886, and Roman Catholic missions started in 1890. Norwegian and American Lutheran missionaries, starting in Ngaoundere in 1923, were the first to operate in northern Cameroon.

Conversion to Christianity increased after World War II, especially after Cameroon gained independence from France and Britain in the early 1960s. Along with Islam, Christianity was presented as a national and modern religion. Cameroon's first schools were controlled by Catholic and Protestant Christians, and conversion matched the spread of literacy. More recently, small missionary groups, including Jehovah's Witnesses and the Church of Jesus Christ of Latter-day Saints, have developed in some parts of the country, but their numbers remain small.

EARLY AND MODERN LEADERS Although a few theologians and priests in Cameroon have provided a political interpretation of the Bible, none has directly engaged in politics. Paul Biya, elected president of Cameroon in 1982, is Christian, but he and other political leaders have not promoted Christianity. Baba Simon (1906–75) was one of the first Cameroonian Catholic priests and was an important spiritual leader. He worked as a missionary in the Mandara mountain region and evangelized the Kirdi population. He became adored for his piety, tolerance, and compassion.

MAJOR THEOLOGIANS AND AUTHORS Jean-Marc Ela (born 1936) is one of Cameroon's most noted theolo-

A vendor sits among her wares at a fetish stall in Cameroon. These items may be used for witchcraft, divination, magic, or idol worship, all of which are practices prohibited by Christian churches. © KARL AMMANN/CORBIS.

gians. He has, together with Engelbert Mveng (1930–95) and Fabien Eboussi Boulaga, adapted the ideas of liberation theology (a school of thought, started in Latin America, arguing that the church should focus its efforts on liberating people from oppression and poverty) to the African continent. Interpreting the biblical message as having a political dimension, these theologians have aimed at freeing converts from all forms of oppression, including fears, superstitions, witchcraft, poverty, slavery, and traditions.

HOUSES OF WORSHIP AND HOLY PLACES Christians in Cameroon worship in churches. Large churches are built like those in Europe and the United States. Small village churches are long, square buildings, constructed of mud bricks and straw roofs in poor communities and of cement and tin roofs in richer communities. The biggest churches and cathedrals are found in the major cities of Yaounde and Douala.

WHAT IS SACRED? Cameroonian Christians follow the sacred beliefs of Western Christians, holding the Bible and sacraments sacred.

HOLIDAYS AND FESTIVALS Christmas, Easter, and Assumption are national holidays in Cameroon. Harvest festivals, organized by local Christian churches, are also important. Celebrated on a larger scale than are Christmas and Easter, they include big feasts that are communally organized among neighboring villages.

MODE OF DRESS There is no mode of dress distinctive to lay Christians in Cameroon. As a rule, however, Christians dress nicely to attend church services. Many churches have printed colorful cloth that church members can buy to make shirts, trousers, or robes that are worn for special church occasions. Catholic priests usually wear a chasuble during Mass. Protestant ministers often wear Western clothing, including a black jacket and tie. In northern Cameroon, where there is a large Muslim population, Protestant ministers may occasionally wear prestigious Muslim robes (*gandoura*) during worship services.

DIETARY PRACTICES As elsewhere in Africa, dietary practices follow the manner of the specific church. For example, some Protestant churches prohibit drinking alcohol and smoking, while others, such as Seventh-day Adventists, strictly adhere to Leviticus and Deuteronomy in the Old Testament, which prohibits, among other things, the consumption of pork.

RITUALS The importance given to Christian rituals varies according to the context. baptism, First Communion, confirmation, weddings, and funerals are often seen as more important in towns than in rural areas. Christian urbanites, often far from home, seldom conform to their local traditions and rely more heavily on Christian rituals. In rural areas, however, many traditional rituals are still practiced, although they are increasingly combined with Christian rituals. For example, a funeral may include traditional rituals such as a masquerade or an ancestor's cult, which involves some sacrifice to the ancestors, along with a Mass or worship service, as well as Bible readings and a Christian choir at the tomb. Many weddings in rural areas are still organized according to local customs, although they might sometimes be accompanied by a church service. The low proportion of weddings organized within churches might be explained by the fact that polygyny is still widely practiced, even in Christian communities.

RITES OF PASSAGE While some rites of passage, such as weddings, funerals, and harvest festivals, combine Christian and African indigenous rituals, baptism, First Communion, and the ordination of priests occur exclusively in church. The Christian clergy tends to disapprove of indigenous rituals. Initiations, circumcisions, and enthronement of chiefs, however, are generally performed without any reference to Christianity, although they may start or end with a collective prayer.

MEMBERSHIP In Cameroon followers are not only Christian, but they are judged either a good or bad Christian. A good Christian not only reads the Bible, attends worship services regularly, follows the example of Christ, participates in Christian rituals, and contributes to the activities of the church, but is also monogamous and refrains from participating in the traditional practices prohibited by the church, including witchcraft, divination, magic, or idol worship. Such traditional practices, however, help define ethnic identity. In short, the more western a Christian convert is in belief and behavior, the better Christian he is considered to be. This raises important questions regarding the extent to which Christian practice is compatible with the maintenance of the various ethnic identities of Cameroon.

SOCIAL JUSTICE Catholic and Protestant missionaries have often been engaged in socially progressive campaigns to free Cameroonians from traditional forms of perceived oppression, such as economic or domestic slavery, traditional forms of taxation, mandatory rites of passage, and compulsory work to be provided to traditional leaders. Christian churches have established a great number of schools and hospitals throughout the country that provide services to everybody, regardless of their religious affiliation.

SOCIAL ASPECTS Catholic and Protestant missionaries advocate to restrict sexual relationships within monogamous marriages. For example, missionaries sermonize against sex before or outside marriage, polygyny, and levirate, the marriage of a widow to her deceased husband's brother. The behavior of some missionaries, however, which has included adultery, fathering illegitimate children, and even unofficial polygyny, is a serious matter of concern discussed at the highest level of the Catholic and Protestant churches of Cameroon.

POLITICAL IMPACT Christian church leaders have been outspoken in their criticism of the government, denouncing corruption, abuse of power, and social inequalities, and the Church can be said to constitute a kind of independent democratic opposition, although it is not represented as such in the parliament. This sometimes makes the relationship between the state and the churches relatively tense. The murder of the Catholic theologian Engelbert Mveng in 1995 was still not elucidated nearly a decade later and is widely believed to have been politically motivated.

CONTROVERSIAL ISSUES Cameroon has been severely hit by acquired immunodeficiency syndrome (AIDS), and the position of various Catholic and Protestant churches in AIDS prevention has been controversial. Christian churches have not only advocated for restricting sex to monogamous relationships within marriage, but many church leaders have launched campaigns against the use of condoms, which they believe can only encourage promiscuity and sexual relationships outside marriage. As a result, some people have blamed Christian churches to bear a heavy responsibility in the death toll from AIDS, which was one of the highest in West Africa at the start of the twenty-first century.

CULTURAL IMPACT In some regions of Cameroon, especially in the southern and central parts of the country, conversion to Christianity has been accompanied by major cultural changes, such as the rejection of local religious sculptures, rituals, and rites of passages. Other regions, in particular the western part of the country, have, on the contrary, shown a great capacity to retain or adapt their cultural traditions, despite conversion to Christianity. Today, the translation of the Bible in many Cameroonian languages plays an important role in slowing down linguistic erosion. Church choirs use indigenous words and music to convey their Christian faith.

AFRICAN INDIGENOUS BELIEFS

DATE OF ORIGIN Unknown
NUMBER OF FOLLOWERS 4.2 million

HISTORY There is no written document about the history of African indigenous religions. Indigenous religious beliefs and practices generally stem from the wish to control the world, prevent misfortune, and secure good luck and abundance. Indigenous practices rest on

a belief in the efficacy of ancestors' intervention, rituals, and taboos. Rituals practiced by one group are easily adopted by a neighboring group if they are believed to have greater efficacy, even without any missionary effort. This makes the history of indigenous religions complicated. Religious practice might also become closely associated with the identity of a community. In this case, religious practices follow people wherever they go, and religious history becomes associated with the history of migrations, which is extremely complex in Cameroon. In the course of time, the religious practices of migrants can change or merge with local practices.

Although the number of followers of African indigenous religions is usually calculated by taking the total number of Cameroonians and subtracting the number of Christians and Muslims, these estimations do not account for the fact that most converts to Christianity or Islam continue to share African indigenous beliefs and to participate in some traditional rituals.

EARLY AND MODERN LEADERS Most Cameroonian traditional leaders can be said to have, in one way or another, a religious role to play. In societies that have an institutionalized chief or king, the chief fights against witchcraft and also secures abundance and fertility. Some chiefs have a "sacred power," which is often acquired through highly secret rituals in which the chief may break some of the most fundamental taboos of the society, including practicing metaphorical or real murder, incest, or cannibalism. This projects them symbolically out of the social order and allows them to control natural forces for the benefit of the society, as well as to control and prevent witchcraft. Some traditional chiefs have become modern leaders through their election as members of parliament, their nomination in a government post, or their role as high-ranking civil servants.

MAJOR THEOLOGIANS AND AUTHORS There is no major African indigenous theologian or author, although there is a renewed interest in indigenous traditions among local university students and administrative elites. There is a growing number of master theses and videos that record local traditions. Most texts on African indigenous religions, however, have been written by scholars having a Christian or Western background.

HOUSES OF WORSHIP AND HOLY PLACES Followers of African indigenous religions do not regularly worship in big communal buildings, and there is no indigenous equivalent to churches or mosques. Holy places are associated with the spiritual world. It is usually in these places, which include cemeteries, houses of skulls, sacred groves, water pools, and houses where regalia or sacred drums are kept, that rituals are performed.

WHAT IS SACRED? The sacred, defined in opposition to the profane, permeates many aspects of life. Some chiefs are considered sacred, and people have to show them respect by kneeling down in front of them, clapping hands in their presence, and avoiding touching them or looking at them directly. These chiefs have their own throne and drinking glass that no one else can use, and, depending on the ethnic group and the village, they are required to follow certain taboos.

Some animals are considered sacred. Royal animals, especially the leopard, lion, and python, must be brought to the chief, who usually retains the skin. Pregnant women and their husbands often refrain from killing aquatic animals in order not to harm the spirit of the coming child. Finally, some animals can be used in divination, as is the case with the trapdoor spider whose actions can be "read" and interpreted by a diviner in some societies of the Grassfields region near Nigeria.

Sacred objects usually include such regalia as thrones, chiefs' calabashes (drinking gourds), and leopard skins, or ritual objects, including masks, carved or clay figurines, and skulls.

HOLIDAYS AND FESTIVALS Large festivals may be organized annually around harvest or first fruits festivals, each year, every other year, or every few years when the festival requires extensive preparation and a significant amount of money to feed the numerous guests. Each ethnic group has its own festivals.

MODE OF DRESS Apart from masquerades, when participants may wear a mask with palms, feathers, or a handmade cotton cloth covering the entire body, few indigenous rituals require specific attire. People participating in rituals, such as ancestor's cults, wear everyday clothing, and they wear their best clothes at weddings, funerals, or harvest festivals. During circumcisions or some stages of rites of passages, people wear the minimum amount of clothing, appearing almost naked.

DIETARY PRACTICES There exist numerous food taboos that vary from group to group. Some lineages,

clans, or chiefs avoid eating specific animals or plants because of a mythical relationship that links the animal to an ancestor. For example, the animal may have warned or saved the ancestor of an imminent danger, or it may have taken care of a lost baby. Some categories of people avoid specific foods believed to be harmful to their condition. Leprous people might avoid hot food or animals with a red skin in order to avoid making their skin condition worse, and pregnant women might avoid some animals associated with qualities that they don't wish for their child.

RITUALS Rituals can be organized on a personal level, or at the family, lineage, clan, village, or ethnic group level. The higher the level, the bigger and more important the ritual.

Fertility rituals are performed to secure abundance. They can take the form of yearly harvest festivals, first fruits festivals, hunting rituals, or of ancestor's cults, among others. These rituals often involve prayers or offerings to bush or water spirits (*mami wata*) or ancestor's spirits that are believed to be partly responsible for the general good luck of individuals or communities. Fertility rituals sometimes replay a mythological event. They can also be accompanied by masquerades, or by the ritual washing of the skulls of dead persons.

Broadly speaking healing rituals are intended to prevent or treat misfortune, which is widely believed to have a social origin. Diseases, accidents, and bad luck may happen naturally, but can ultimately be caused by a breach of taboos, disrespect of traditional custom, or by the jealousy, greediness, and malignance of other humans. This last cause can have three different sources. First, human malignance might be caused by a curse. Second, it can come from hereditary witchcraft by which it is believed some people have an organ in their intestine that allows their spirit to leave their body at night to go harm other people. Third, human malignance can come from acquired sorcery through which some people have bought or learned how to prepare magic and poisons to harm others. A common response to these threats is to consult diviners, who can either see what is happening in the spiritual world, or communicate with spirits via spiders, drawings in the sand, magnets, or some other devices. Traditional healers prescribe protective treatments that might consist of charms that work magically to counter sorcery, and that often send the disease back to the person who first sent it. Chiefs can also provide protection against witchcraft by mystically countering sorcery through their words, rituals, or personal power. Still another type can be provided by masquerades or, as is found mainly in western Cameroon, by secret societies that can perform rituals to protect or punish people.

RITES OF PASSAGE Rites of passages mark the passage from one social status to another. They typically involve a period of seclusion that is supposed to be relatively dangerous for the individuals undergoing the passage, followed by a period of coming out and acceptance of their new status or identity.

The passage to adulthood is marked in some societies by important rituals, such as long circumcision rituals for groups of children from the same village or region who were born during the same period, which can be marked between 1 to 2 years, or between 12 to 15 years. The rituals organized during wedding ceremonies concern a contract between families or lineages, and they usually involve less emphasis on religious ritual than in the other rites of passage. Death rituals vary according to the status of the deceased. For example, in the western, central, and northern parts of Cameroon a chief may be buried in an underground chamber in a sitting position facing the east. After a period of decomposition the skull is removed from the chamber and is washed and ritually treated. The skull is then either buried again in a separate tomb or placed with the skulls of other chiefs in a house of skulls. There are usually at least two funeral ceremonies for the chief. The first, a mournful occasion, is organized during or shortly after the burial. A closing ceremony, organized between a few months and two to three years after the death, officially ends the mourning period and its mood is joyful.

MEMBERSHIP Membership in African religions is acquired through the successful completion of rites of passage, as well as by growing up in an environment wherein indigenous religion is practiced by parents, kin, neighbors, and friends. African religions are tolerant and usually not exclusive. Everybody can participate in a ritual, unless it involves some secret or requires that one has already been through a rite of passage. There is no attempt to convert other people, and nobody is prevented from participating in rituals performed in other religions. Many Muslim and Christian converts continue to practice some indigenous religious rituals because they constitute an important part of their ethnic identity.

SOCIAL JUSTICE Social values are inherent in the rituals of African indigenous religions. Initiation into adulthood, for example, usually teaches respect for elders, and equality among the people initiated at the same time. The ancestor's cult is based on a reciprocal relationship with the spirit of the dead—one remembers one's ancestors and sacrifices to them so that ancestors can remember the living and secure their success. In Cameroon witchcraft can be judged and condemned by state courts that can have recourse to local diviners to produce evidences, and convicted witches can be sent to jail.

SOCIAL ASPECTS Indigenous religions pervade all aspects of life, and it is difficult to extract indigenous religions from the general social context in which they are embedded. The practice of indigenous rituals often involves familial or lineage networks that imply local forms of solidarity. It is often believed that witchcraft is inherited from the mother. People running away from witchcraft usually find refuge among their matrikin. Success in farming or hunting is seen to depend on the good observance of taboos and rituals.

POLITICAL IMPACT Indigenous religions may play a local political role through the sacred power of chiefs, secret societies, and ritual specialists. Indigenous religions, however, play no role in national politics, although many politicians, including those at the highest spheres of the state, consult diviners and traditional healers in order to protect themselves against witchcraft or sorcery from competitors.

CONTROVERSIAL ISSUES Opinions concerning indigenous religions are often ambiguous. On the one hand, people wish to reject what they feel is bad, including the supposed practice of sorcery and witchcraft, the high cost of some major festivals, the importance of duties linked to the respect of traditions, and the abuse of power by the traditional chiefs. On the other hand, they praise such positive aspects as a high moral standard, the ritual maintenance of fertility and world order, the fight against witchcraft, and traditions that play an important part of people's ethnic identity.

CULTURAL IMPACT Wood sculpture, music, and dance, some of the most important aspects of Cameroonian art, are closely associated with the practice of indigenous religions. In this sense, the diversity of indigenous religious practices goes hand in hand with the rich artistic diversity and creativity found in the country. In many places, especially in western Cameroon, cultural traditions have successfully adapted to modern times and have shown an extraordinary vitality. Elsewhere, artists have been successful in secularizing their art, either for tourist purposes, such as in Foumban, or to create popular music genres that are based on traditional rhythms, such as Makossa or Bikoutsi.

ISLAM

DATE OF ORIGIN Sixteenth century C.E.
NUMBER OF FOLLOWERS 3.5 million

HISTORY Although Islam has been present in the northern tip of Cameroon since the sixteenth century, it was only in the beginning of the nineteenth century, when northern Cameroon was conquered by the Fulani and incorporated into the Muslim Sokoto Empire, that it began to spread to other parts of northern Cameroon. The Sokoto Empire had been created by Usman dan Fodio (1754–1817), who was successful in reforming the practice of Islam in the former Hausa Kingdoms, which he defeated and unified under his leadership. Islam spread to northern Cameroon (the greater Adamawa) by Adama of Gurim, who founded his capital in Yola in the mid-nineteenth century. Today Islam dominates the religious, political, economic, and cultural life in northern Cameroon.

EARLY AND MODERN LEADERS Usman dan Fodio and Adama are widely known historical leaders. Contemporary leaders include Fulani sultans from all the major towns of northern Cameroon. The sultan is traditionally both the religious and the political leader of his region. The sultan delegates his religious power to his imam (religious leader), who is in charge of the most important mosque in town. The sultan shares his political power with some dignitaries having a slave origin, who represent the local population's interests, and with a few dignitaries having a Fulani identity, who represent the Fulani interests. The first president of Cameroon, Ahmadou Ahidjo (served 1960–82), was a Muslim Fulani who was instrumental in encouraging the spread of Islam in northern Cameroon by subsidizing the construction of mosques and promoting new converts in the administration. In 1982 Ahidjo resigned from office and Paul Biya, a Christian from southern Cameroon, succeeded him as president. After a failed coup against

Biya in 1984, which was mainly perpetrated by Fulani northerners, the administration was purged of a great number of its Muslim civil servants.

MAJOR THEOLOGIANS AND AUTHORS Although there are a number of Muslim scholars known only in their village or town, there is no internationally recognized Muslim theologian or author from Cameroon.

HOUSES OF WORSHIP AND HOLY PLACES In villages with scattered, isolated homes, each household might have a small prayer area in the open air under the shade of a tree marked by stones and filled with sand where people make regular prayer. In villages and towns where there is a cluster of homes, the mosque is a bigger structure that is used by people living in its vicinity.

WHAT IS SACRED? As with other Islamic followers, Cameroonian Muslims consider sacred such traditional beliefs as the Five Pillars of Islam, the words of the Koran, and mosques. One difference, however, is that in Cameroon sultans are sacred kings who should be shown the highest respect and who still have, in some places, discretionary powers of life and death over their subjects.

HOLIDAYS AND FESTIVALS The Festival of the Sheep (*Tabaski*) and the end of Ramadan are public holidays in Cameroon. Both festivals have a special significance in northern Cameroon where followers begin the celebration with a communal prayer in a field situated at the outskirts of the major towns. On the way back to town, the crowd cheers when the sultan (*lamido*) passes in front of them. If the sultan is on horseback, he is preceded by a group of griots (professional musicians) who praise him and his ancestry with trumpets and songs. Everybody wears their finest attire and ceremonial weapons, and the horses are adorned with beautifully decorated saddles and harnesses. Back in town, representatives of the different groups of the sultanate walk in procession in front of the sultan to swear him allegiance. Then the young men of the sultanate compete in spectacular horse races. The festivities can last a few days and include music, dances, and rich meals.

MODE OF DRESS Muslim men usually dress in a *gandoura*, a long white robe that covers a shirt and trousers. The *gandoura* can be beautifully embroidered, expensive, and prestigious to wear, reflecting wealth and status. As such, wealthy non-Muslims may wear the *gandoura* as a sign of prestige. Muslim women usually go unveiled and there is no particular dress that is considered Muslim.

DIETARY PRACTICES Cameroonian Muslims avoid eating pork and many avoid eating bush meat under the pretense that it has not been ritually slaughtered. Some Muslims, however, eat it if the game has been killed by a Muslim hunter who recited a ritual prayer before firing his gun. The butcher trade in Cameroon is almost completely controlled by Muslims, even in those areas dominated by Christians.

RITUALS Ideally Muslims pray five times a day, and the prayer ritual does not differ from what is practiced by Muslims elsewhere, although some details can vary according to the brotherhood to which a person belongs. Most major public events in northern Cameroon are accompanied by a *doa* (or *dua*), a short Islamic prayer or blessing that includes all present whether Muslim or non-Muslim. In Cameroon the Koran is often used within the context of magic by Muslim scholars who practice divination and healing rituals. The words of the Koran are spoken in repetition; or they are written on a wooden tablet, washed, and the wash water with the sacred ink of the Koran is drunk by the scholar; or else the sacred words are written in amulets worn as protective charms.

RITES OF PASSAGE The name giving ceremony of a newborn is an important rite of passage that marks the entry of the child into the Muslim community. The child's head is shaved, and the whole community is invited to take part in a collective meal. Circumcision of boys is another important rite of passage. Muslim ulama (religious leaders or scholars) have been much more successful than Christian missionaries in eradicating traditional collective rites of passages involving the consumption of alcohol and the use of masks or charms that are associated with ancestor's cults, enthronements, and masquerades. In northern Cameroon, however, individual rites of passage, such as births, weddings, and funerals, have continued along local traditions with regard to the music, the role played by relatives, the type of gifts, and the setting.

MEMBERSHIP At the time of the conquest of northern Cameroon in the nineteenth century by the Fulani, the intent was to spread Islam. The main drive for the conquest, however, quickly became political and economic. The principal resource of the region was its slaves, and since it was forbidden to capture and sell fellow Muslims as slaves, the local populations were prevented from converting to Islam by the Muslim sultans and by the Fulani. Although the slaves working in the palaces of the sultans were superficially Islamized earlier on, it was only in the 1950s that the bulk of the rural population was allowed to convert. Conversion was seen as a social promotion that permitted people to escape their former slave status. Moreover, Islam was and continues to be closely associated with Fulani identity and conversion is often accompanied by a process of Fulanization. The Fulani have, therefore, tried to prevent the conversion of the local population to Islam, first in order to fuel the slave trade, then, when slavery was abolished, in order to maintain the social hierarchies existing between the former masters and their subjects. Some resistance to conversion of non-Fulani is still found as converts can be questioned regarding the sincerity of their faith, for the simple reason that they are not originally Fulani.

SOCIAL JUSTICE Islam defends equality and social justice among Muslims, however, it does not always do so with non-Muslims. In northern Cameroon, the spread of Islam is associated with a ruthless Fulani colonization of the area, and with the enslavement of entire communities that were sold on the slave markets of northern Nigeria. Until the 1950s, Islam was seen as an instrument of domination, as it excluded non-Muslims from any participation in the power structures and from any social recognition or prestige, relegating non-Muslims to a lower status synonymous to that of slaves. Even in modern times, societal discrimination by Muslims against Cameroonian non-Muslims is strong and widespread throughout northern Cameroon.

SOCIAL ASPECTS Conversion to Islam often leads to major social changes. For example women lose public influence and tend to avoid public spaces, patterns of Islamic law apply, and religious knowledge confers prestige and power that might counteract that of the traditional chiefs. Although Muslims are allowed no more than four wives at one time, in northern Cameroon rich Fulani can have numerous concubines.

POLITICAL IMPACT Historically Muslim identity has played a political role in northern Cameroon and the whole of northern Cameroon is often considered to be

Muslim-dominated. Ahmadou Ahidjo, the first president of Cameroon, put social policies in motion in the north that strengthened Muslim standing in Cameroon.

CONTROVERSIAL ISSUES One of the main controversial issues concerns the political and social role that Islam should play in Cameroon. The sultans have been so far relatively successful in keeping at bay the most extremist forms of Islam, although beginning in the 1990s, these ideas and movements, coming from scholars who studied in the Middle East, began to infiltrate northern Cameroon. At the beginning of the twenty-first century, the application of Shari'ah (Islamic law), however, was not on the political agenda.

CULTURAL IMPACT Koranic schools are found in all places where Muslims are numerous enough to organize them, but they are usually not subsidized by the state. Girls and boys generally attend government schools and then go to the Koranic school later that same day or on weekends. The Arabic alphabet is widely used as a means of communication in northern Cameroon, and it competes with the Latin alphabet.

Other Religions

A small number of foreign-born Hindus, Buddhists, Jews, and Orthodox Christians are found among the community of diplomats, military personnel, and businesspeople in Cameroon.

Quentin Gausset

See Also Vol. 1: *African Indigenous Beliefs, Christianity, Islam, Roman Catholicism*

Bibliography

Barley, Nigel. *Symbolic Structures: An Exploration of the Culture of the Dowayos.* Cambridge: Cambridge University Press, 1983.

Fardon, Richard. *Between God, the Dead and the Wild: Chamba Interpretation of Ritual and Religion.* Edinburgh: Edinburgh University Press, 1992.

Geschiere, Peter. *The Modernity of Witchcraft: Politics and the Occult in Postcolonial Africa.* Charlottesville: University of Virginia Press, 1997.

Laburthe-Tolra, Philippe. *Initiations et sociétés secrètes au Cameroun: Les mystères de la nuit.* Paris: Karthala, 1985.

Lode, K. *Appelés à la Liberté: L'histoire de l'Eglise Evangélique Luthérienne au Cameroun.* Amstelveen: Improcep Editions, 1990.

Mveng, Engelbert. *Album of the Centenary, 1890–1990: The Catholic Church in Cameroon—100 years of Evangelization.* Yaounde: National Episcopal Conference of Cameroon, 1990.

Ngongo, Louis. *Histoire des forces religieuses au Cameroun: de la Première Guerre mondiale à l'Indépendance (1916–1955).* Paris: Karthala, 1982.

Schilder, Kees. *Quest for Self-Esteem: State, Islam, and Mundang Ethnicity in Northern Cameroon.* Leiden: African Studies Center, 1994.

Canada

POPULATION 31,902,268

ROMAN CATHOLIC 45.7 percent

PROTESTANT 36.2 percent

OTHER 5.6 percent

NO PREFERENCE 12.5 percent

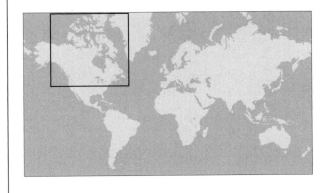

Country Overview

INTRODUCTION In area Canada is the second largest country in the world. It takes up most of the northern part of the North American continent. More than half of Canada consists of infertile permafrost and tundra. Two-thirds of the people live within 125 miles of the United States, which is a major influence upon the Canadian economy and culture.

Canada's history has produced a unique culture shaped by two successive European conquerors, first the French and then the English. French Catholicism and English forms of Protestantism have continued to act as a quiet conscience for the nation. Many of its early English-speaking settlers were opponents of and refu-

gees from the American Revolution. Further, until the twentieth century Canada remained a part of Britain and its empire, and the country has nurtured a form of government and politics distinct from the United States. Canadians have historically chosen government reform over revolution and have tended to value community over the individual and compromise over disagreement. Such attitudes are also generally reflected in its religious practices, which tend to be more accommodating and less confrontational than in many other countries.

RELIGIOUS TOLERANCE Canadians share in the worldview that distinguishes between nationhood and religion, recognizing that to belong to a nation is not the same as to belong to a particular religion. Although Christianity is the dominant religion in Canada, other religions are accepted as equal partners in the development of the country's life and culture. Canadians also share the principle that religious membership cannot be mandated by the government and that each individual must be free to join, or not to join, a religious organization as he or she wishes.

Canada does not explicitly outlaw the establishment of religion or permit its freedom. Nor does the country have a history of legal interpretation describing the relationship between the church and the state. Instead, as the Charter of Rights and Freedoms states, every person is assumed to have certain "fundamental freedoms," which include the "freedom of conscience and religion."

The ecumenical movement in Canada has, among other things, resulted in the United Church of Canada (1925), which is made up of Presbyterian, Congregationalist, and Methodist churches. (A minority of Pres-

Pilgrims line up outside of the Basilica of Sainte-Anne-de-Beaupré, located just east of Quebec City. This religious site is a healing shrine and is dedicated to the mother of the Virgin Mary. © JONATHAN BLAIR/CORBIS.

byterians remained separate, while the Evangelical United Brethren joined the United Church in 1968.) The major Christian churches, including Catholics, train their clergy in common university centers, and they also join in many social action projects. KAIROS, representing almost 70 percent of Christian adherents in Canada, is an example of such common social action. The only exceptions to both ecumenism and interfaith cooperation come from Christian evangelicals and fundamentalists, who refrain from such involvement as a matter of principle.

Major Religions

ROMAN CATHOLICISM

OTHER CHRISTIAN DENOMINATIONS

ROMAN CATHOLICISM

DATE OF ORIGIN 1534 C.E.
NUMBER OF FOLLOWERS 14.5 million

HISTORY The history of Roman Catholicism in Canada can be divided into four periods that sometimes overlap. The period of its origins ran from 1534 to 1763. The first Catholics in Canada were the French who arrived as traders and missionaries. They were eager to traverse the continent in pursuit of their goals, and as a result French Catholicism is found throughout present-day Canada. The goal of the Catholic missionaries was to create a new world free of the antagonisms and politics of the old. They failed in this, however, since the goals of the French kings were opposed to theirs. Further, in the Treaty of Paris (1763) the French lands and peoples east of the Mississippi River were ceded to Britain. With the signing of this treaty, wealthy, educated professionals tended to return to France, while the poor and their clergy remained to become citizens of a British land with its own (Anglican) church.

Thus, from 1763 French Catholics in Canada lived in a British country. Britain needed the support of Canadian Catholics to help them oppose the colonies to the south that revolted in 1776 and then, in 1812, to help fight a second war with the United States. The French bishops, who were the principal interlocutors between the colonizing British and the French Canadians, were committed to retaining the faith, language, and communal sense of the people. To do so they developed a highly centralized and disciplined Catholicism that looked to the pope in Rome as the central constituent of its identity. Catholicism was dominant in Quebec, and, by 1960, 88 percent of all Catholics in Quebec attended Mass on Sunday, and Catholic priests, brothers, and nuns ran the province's social services, which included a Catholic school system.

From 1867, when Canada became a dominion within the British Empire, Catholicism existed in a bicultural country. Catholic immigrants from countries other than France were present early in Canadian history, and there were Indians who converted to Catholicism early on. Among the numerous other Catholics who immigrated to a growing Canada were Scottish Roman Catholics, who arrived in Nova Scotia by 1780, and floods of Irish from 1820 onward. In fact, outside Quebec, Irish Catholics came to dominate the ranks of clerical and religious orders. The Catholic Church in Canada thus came to reflect the linguistic division between English-speaking and French-speaking Canadians.

There were two significant developments in Canadian Catholicism in the 1960s. First, the so-called Quiet Revolution in Quebec resulted in people taking into their own hands their ecclesial, political, and economic life. The result was that Quebecers abandoned French Catholics outside Quebec to their own fate. Second, Vatican II (1962–65) thrust the Catholic Church into an intense dialogue and involvement with the contemporary intellectual, political, and religious worlds. As a consequence, Canadian Catholics came to work more closely with one another and with other religions. At the same time the church attempted to become a servant of the people, alleviating basic human needs rather than operating as an antagonist to modern education, technology, and urban life. The result of these profound developments within the church was a breakdown of what had been a highly centralized and disciplined structure. This was reflected in various changes, including levels of attendance at Mass. In Quebec, for example, by the end of the twentieth century only 22 percent of Catholics attended Mass every Sunday, and the clergy and religious orders no longer staffed social services.

EARLY AND MODERN LEADERS A number of women have played important historical roles in the Catholic Church in Canada. They have included Marie Guyard (1599–1672), or Marie of the Incarnation, an Ursuline nun who is sometimes called the "Mother of the Church in Canada"; Marguerite Bougeoys (1620–1700), the founder of the Congregation of Notre Dame; and Marie Marguerite d'Youville (1701–71), the founder of the Grey order of nuns. François De Montemorency-Laval (1623–1708) was the first bishop of French-speaking Canada.

Twentieth-century Catholic leaders in Canada have included Paul-Emile Leger (1904–91), who left his post as a cardinal of the church in 1968 to work among the poor and needy. Jean Vanier (born in 1928) founded L'Arche, a federation of Christian communities for people with developmental disabilities that has expanded to other countries. The Canadian Conference of Catholic Bishops, which was established in 1943, has become the means through which the Catholic Church exercises its pastoral authority and responsibility for the benefit of the church and of society.

MAJOR THEOLOGIANS AND AUTHORS The Canadian Bernard J.F. Lonergan (1904–84) was an internationally known Jesuit philosopher and theologian whose writings have continued to be highly influential. The philosopher and sociologist Gregory Baum (born in 1923) has written on topics such as religion and society, social ethics, and liberation theology.

HOUSES OF WORSHIP AND HOLY PLACES In Canada church buildings are the locale of most Catholic worship. The best-known Catholic churches in Canada are the Basilica of Notre Dame (1650) in Quebec City, the Notre Dame Basilica in Montreal (1829), and the Chapel of Saint Marie Marguerite d'Youville at Notre Dame de Lourdes in Rigaud, Quebec.

There are several Catholic shrines in Canada that are popular as pilgrim destinations. Among them the best known are found in Quebec. Both Saint Anne de Beaupre, in Beaupre, east of Quebec City, and Saint Joseph's Oratory, in Montreal, are healing shrines. The Martyr's Shrine in Midland, Ontario, honors the martyrdom of Jesuits who worked among the Indians of Canada. Cap de la Madeleine, which is dedicated to Mary, the mother of Jesus, dates to 1714 and is the oldest stone church in North America.

WHAT IS SACRED? Most Catholic churches in Canada house relics in their altars. Places and waters considered especially holy are associated with the various healing shrines. In addition, the holiness of nature is emphasized in the various pronouncements of Canadian bishops dealing with the degradation of the environment. Since Vatican II there has been renewed emphasis upon the sacrality of every human being, especially the poor and needy.

HOLIDAYS AND FESTIVALS Catholics in Canada share four holidays (Good Friday, Easter, Easter Monday, and Christmas) with other Christians, and these are statutory holidays throughout the country. In addition, in the various provinces there are official holidays associated with saints. Saint Jean Baptiste Day (June 24), for example, is a celebration of Quebec identity for every Quebecer, not only Catholics, and Newfoundland observes Saint Patrick's Day (March 17). Aside from these national and provincial holidays, there are holidays celebrated by various nationalities in Canada. In Quebec, for example, March 19 is observed as Saint Joseph's Day among Italians and 16 July as Our Lady of Mount Carmel Day among both Italians and Latinos.

MODE OF DRESS There is no unique dress for the Catholic laity in Canada, either in general or during worship services. The clergy and members of both male and female religious orders do, however, sometimes wear distinctive dress. The Roman collar or the religious habit distinguishes some Catholic professionals. Nonetheless, in Canada most Catholic professionals dress as do secular professionals, even when the Vatican urges adoption of a unique Catholic dress.

DIETARY PRACTICES Catholicism in Canada participates in the common periods of abstinence and fasts as set forth in canon law. Those who are older than 14 abstain from eating meat on Ash Wednesday and on Fridays during Lent. Fasting is obligatory for those aged 18 to 69 on Ash Wednesday and Good Friday. The custom of fasting during Lent and giving the money saved to the poor has increased among Canadian Catholics.

RITUALS Catholics in Canada share in the common sacramental rituals of believers throughout the world. To some extent, however, ritual expression in Canada is shaped by ethnic heritage, by ideological perspective, and by rates of church attendance.

Ethnic heritage has continued to influence rituals for some Canadian Catholics. For example, among Sicilians the Saint Joseph altar is still found, where on Saint Joseph's Day (March 19) fresh foods are gathered to be shared with one another and with the poor. At Easter, Catholics of the Ukrainian rite and immigrants from Poland take bread to the church to be blessed before they share it with their families. Except among a small percentage of adherents, however, ethnic influences have diminished in Canada.

Compared with other Catholics, conservatives, that is, those who favor the practices of the nineteenth and early twentieth centuries, attend Mass and participate in sacramental rituals at a rate of almost two to one. Their prayers and devotions focus on saints and on life as developed in the past hundred or so years. On the other hand, liberal Catholics in Canada, as elsewhere, have joined liturgical life and social policy. Such Catholics tend to focus more on social issues like justice and peace and on the mystical life, and they favor biblical prayers such as those found in the Psalms, which have served as the basis of daily prayers for two millennia.

Weekly attendance at Mass in Canada varies widely by age. It is highest (31 percent) among those over the age of 55 and only slightly lower (30 percent) for those between the ages of 35 and 54. For younger people between the ages of 18 and 34, however, the rate is only 15 percent. These differences, of course, affect participation in church rituals.

RITES OF PASSAGE The expectation that church rituals will be a part of rites of passage varies by age among Canadian Catholics, surprisingly being much higher among teenagers (81 percent) than among adults (34 percent). The expectation is also higher among those who attend Mass weekly. The observation of rites of initiation such as baptism for infants and confirmation has grown among Catholics in Canada, thus bringing these practices in line with traditional church teachings. Baptism is a rite of passage engaged in by all Catholics since it is the means through which a person becomes a member of the church.

The Catholic Church in Canada usually requires that persons participating in rites of passage prepare for the rituals. This may involve attending classes, reading certain material, or even choosing readings and hymns to be included in the ceremony. Catholics in Canada who have stopped attending church often find the rites associated with marriage, anointing of the sick, and funerals especially disconcerting since they are not what are remembered from the past.

MEMBERSHIP There have been devastating losses of membership in the Catholic Church in Quebec, although this seems to have reached a plateau. Outside Quebec, however, Catholicism has continued to grow in Canada.

A number of Canadian bishops have urged the adoption of methods for bringing new members into the Catholic Church. Research has indicated that the best targets for evangelization are those who are no longer actively participating in the Catholic Church rather than those who have abandoned regular attendance at another church or who profess no religious affiliation. The two most reliable methods of bringing new members into the church have continued to be marriage and knowing someone who is Catholic.

SOCIAL JUSTICE The majority of early Catholic immigrants to Canada were poor, and initially the development of social services by Catholics involved creating institutions to care for their own. Toward the end of the nineteenth century there began to develop a concern for the poor, uneducated laborers who were products of the developing capitalist economy. By the time Pope Leo XIII's encyclical *Rerum Novarum* (1891; "Of New Things") brought these concerns to a worldwide audience, the clergy of Quebec had already begun to develop a social doctrine that challenged dehumanizing social conditions and supported aid to needy individuals.

The conservative nature of the Quebec hierarchy was challenged by the Jesuits' *école sociale populaire* and by political movements such as Action Libérale Nationale, Bloc Populaire Canadien, and Catholic Action, which asked followers to see, judge, and act against crushing social conditions. Caisse Populaire (Credit Union), which began with the poor sharing their pennies in church basements, has become a powerful economic force in Quebec. The Antigonish Movement, a social movement of adult education and economic reform that began in 1928, demonstrated the power of the cooperative and trained leaders throughout North America in ways of organizing the poor to improve their lives.

SOCIAL ASPECTS Until 1950 marriage and the family among Catholics in Canada reflected the traditions of ethnicity, religiosity, permanency, and fecundity. A Catholic was to marry someone of his or her own faith and ethnic heritage. People were to stay married until death and have as many children "as God provides." With Catholics in Quebec leading the way, these traditions crumbled in the last half of the twentieth century. Today there are only slight differences between Catholics and the general Canadian population in rates of divorce and remarriage and in numbers of children. Although annulment in the Catholic Church is not theologically equivalent to divorce, it has enabled many Catholics to remarry with church approval.

POLITICAL IMPACT The early conflicts between French Catholics and English Anglicans in Canada gave way, after the Treaty of Paris in 1763, to the violence inherent in the legal, economic, educational, and linguistic attempts of each side to dominate the other. These attempts gradually subsided, however, so that the dominant Christian churches in Canada have generally come to be united in their advocacy of policies promoting justice, peace, and environmental issues.

Until the Quiet Revolution of the 1960s, the clergy in Quebec, especially bishops, used their power to direct the political course of the province. They were sometimes united in their aims, but more often than not bishops vied among themselves for control of the political process. The general direction was, until the 1960s, supportive of a highly centralized and disciplined Catholicism. The thrust after the Quiet Revolution was for the clergy to listen to the people and to respect their political wishes. Bishops attempted to become more servants to, rather than generals of, the political weal.

CONTROVERSIAL ISSUES As has happened elsewhere, contemporary Catholicism in Canada is split between conservative episcopal, authoritative voices and the more liberal outlook of others. Nonetheless, contrary to the situation in some countries, Catholic bishops in Canada are more open in expressing their views on divorce, birth control, and the role of women in the church. It is not by accident, for example, that Canadian bishops voiced as much opposition as was ecclesiastically possible to Pope Paul VI's birth control encyclical *Humanae Vitae* (1968; "Of Human Life").

As with Catholicism everywhere, the official stance in Canada is that artificial birth control, abortion, divorce, and the ordination of women are forbidden. All of these official stances take on different nuances in practice, however. While women are not ordained in the Catholic Church in Canada, they do, for example, have a strong voice in, and even control of, major Catholic institutions. In addition, there are increasing numbers of parishes that have women serving as their heads, even though, because they are not ordained, the women cannot act as priests in the Mass.

CULTURAL IMPACT The construction techniques of Indians influenced the building of Catholic mission chapels in Canada in the seventeenth century. With the arrival of trained builders from France, three basic models were used to construct Catholic churches in Quebec: the Jesuit Latin cross design; the Recollet plan, consisting of a broad nave with a narrower semicircular apse; and the Maillou plan, consisting of a nave ending with a semicircular apse. These plans were abandoned in the nineteenth century as the architect Thomas Baillairge introduced ancient Greek architecture, with its columns and pillars, which dominated Quebec architecture until contemporary times. Outside Quebec, however, the Gothic Revival style gradually became identified with church buildings until, after the 1960s, modern architecture began to be used for all new buildings, especially those that replaced the longitudinal style with one focused on the central altar table. After the mid-twentieth century the difference between Catholic churches in Quebec and those in the rest of Canada faded.

The early missionaries in Canada found music to be a great tool in converting Indians to Catholicism, and the "Huron Carol," the joining of a French Christian tune with words and images of the Hurons, dates to the seventeenth century. Aside from unique situations like that of the "Huron Carol," however, the music used in Catholic churches came from Europe. In Canada as elsewhere, it was not until after Vatican II that local music in either French or English began to be used in the celebration of the sacraments.

OTHER CHRISTIAN DENOMINATIONS

DATE OF ORIGIN 1710 C.E.
NUMBER OF FOLLOWERS 11.5 million

HISTORY As with Roman Catholicism, the history of Protestantism in Canada may be divided into four periods. The first, from 1710 to 1853, was a period of Brit-

ish colonialism and Anglican domination. An Anglican thanksgiving service for capturing Port Royal (now Annapolis Royal in Nova Scotia) in 1710 inaugurated the presence of Protestantism in Canada. The Anglican Church (Church of England) became the established religion, and because of its identification with the conquerors of Quebec, it was the established church even in that Catholic area. The flood of Loyalists from the colonies to the south brought to British North America, as the area was then known, not only additional Anglicans but also Congregationalists and Baptists. These latter groups challenged not only the Anglican hierarchical mode of governance but also the Anglican claim to establishment, and they strove to share in the land, money, and political power that went to the Anglican Church. The tensions between the traditional, hierarchical Anglican Church and the newer congregation-based churches continued, but the privilege of establishment ended with the secularization of the clergy reserves in 1853. The government's withdrawal of these lands, which had been set aside for use by the Anglican Church, in effect disestablished the church.

Thus, beginning in 1853, all of the Protestant churches in Canada were forced to become self-supporting. Over time they developed democratic means of governance and the ability to listen to the voices of the people. They also came to reject the internal divisions that characterized the various Protestant churches scattered across the nation, and each of the principal denominations, including the Presbyterians, Methodists, and Lutherans, developed a national church. Conflicts within the churches were mostly between traditions that had their source in the United States and those derived from Britain. Protestants generally continued, however, to be united in their negative views of Catholics.

A new period began with Canadian confederation in 1867 and, in 1925, with the union of Presbyterian, Congregationalist, and Methodist churches as the United Church of Canada, representing just under one-third of all Protestants. Canadian Protestantism came to project a unified view best described as mainline, or consensus, Christianity. This was formalized in the establishment of the Canadian Council of Churches in 1944, to which even Catholics became associate members. The Evangelical Fellowship of Canada, however, formed in 1964 and representing 8 percent of Canadian Christians, remained a vocal opposition to the all-embracing nature of the mainline churches. Like their counterparts elsewhere, evangelicals in Canada adhered to conservative values and biblical literalism, the experience of being born again, and evangelizing.

After 1960 the divisions between mainline and evangelical churches became even stronger in Canada. Every Protestant church, except Pentecostal groups, has lost membership, although people have continued to identify with the church of their birth. In seeking renewal, the mainline churches have continued the tradition of seeing the needs of Canadian society from a Christian perspective, while the evangelical churches have emphasized the need for the individual to be reborn and to witness for Jesus as personal Savior. There is no clear evidence, however, that either approach has stopped the loss of or provided a gain in membership.

EARLY AND MODERN LEADERS Among early Protestant leaders was Charles Inglis (1734–1816), the first Anglican bishop (1787–1816) of Canada and of North America. Henry Alline (1748–84) was a charismatic evangelical who left his mark upon the Maritimes as both a preacher and an organizer.

Later Protestant leaders in Canada included Alosphus Egerton Ryerson (1803–82), a Methodist minister who, together with his brothers, was a leading figure in politics and education in Ontario. Samuel Dwight Chown (1853–1933) was an influential head of the Methodist Church who led it into an alliance with other Protestant groups in what later became the United Church of Canada.

Twentieth-century leaders in Canadian Protestantism included William Aberhart (1878–1943), an eloquent radio evangelist who became premier of Alberta in 1935 and one of the founders of the Social Credit Party. Pierre Berton (born in 1920) is a narrative historian known not only for his descriptions of key Canadian events but also for his sharp criticism of the Anglican Church in the 1960s. In 1980 Lois M. Wilson became the first woman to be chosen as moderator, or head, of the United Church of Canada.

MAJOR THEOLOGIANS AND AUTHORS There were a number of influential twentieth-century Protestant thinkers in Canada. Wilfred Cantwell Smith (1916–2000), a Presbyterian minister, Islamicist, and student of comparative religions, was one of the century's most significant thinkers on interfaith study and dialogue. George Parkin Grant (1918–88) was a Christian philosopher known for his vocal arguments against the Canadian weakness for U.S. culture and goods. The writer

John Webster Grant (born in 1919) has shaped the genre of Protestant church history in Canada.

Among Protestant writers in Canada was the novelist Lily Dougall (1858–1923). She was the author of many influential religious books.

HOUSES OF WORSHIP AND HOLY PLACES With one major exception, the tradition that each Protestant congregation builds its own house of worship has continued in Canada. The exception involves those instances where membership in the United Church of Canada has resulted in the acceptance of a common house of worship from among existing church buildings. Thus, members of the United Church have sometimes chosen as their place of worship a building from among Presbyterian, Congregationalist, Methodist, or Evangelical United Brethren churches. Because this has been a highly sensitive issue in church union, detailed means and processes for making such a choice have been developed.

WHAT IS SACRED? The sacred in Canadian Protestantism is most often expressed through its churches, Sunday worship and gatherings, and work for justice and peace. Thus, traditional embodiments of the sacred include the Bible, preaching, creeds, rituals, and declarations of moral standards.

HOLIDAYS AND FESTIVALS Protestants in Canada share with Catholics the national statutory holidays of Good Friday, Easter, Easter Monday, and Christmas. In addition, Saint George's Day (23 April), honoring the patron saint of England, is celebrated in Newfoundland. In many parts of the country Orangemen's Day (12 July) is celebrated with religious fervor by members of the Orange Order, an Irish Protestant political society.

MODE OF DRESS Members of both the mainline and the evangelical branches of Protestantism in Canada generally adhere to local styles of dress in their daily and their religious lives. In formal secular ceremonies many clergy wear a collar, and when celebrating religious rituals, they wear the traditional dress of their respective denomination. The twentieth-century liturgical movement has gradually influenced all of the mainline churches, so that the dress for leaders of religious rituals has tended to return to that of the first Christian millennium. Anglican clergy, for example, may wear a chasuble at Mass or an alb and a stole at a wedding ceremony. Clergy of the United Church of Canada also sometimes wear the alb and stole. In those traditions that emphasize preaching, many clergy wear academic robes.

There are Christian groups in Canada that are known for their distinctive dress. The simplicity of the dress of the Hutterites, a Mennonite group, and of the Doukhobors, a group of Russian origin, for example, makes these people stand out among the more modern styles of their neighbors.

DIETARY PRACTICES Canadian Protestants are not distinguished from other Canadians by the foods they eat. Among many young mainline Protestants vegetarian eating habits have increased, but this, again, does not distinguish them from others of the same age.

Early Protestants rejected the Catholic practices of fasting and of abstaining from meat during sacred periods, and these differences have continued to dominate in Canada. As part of the modern liturgical movement, however, some Protestant churches have urged a return to the practices of the first Christian millennium, and as a consequence fasting during certain periods has grown among Anglicans, among certain members of the United Church of Christ, and particularly among Lutherans.

RITUALS The ancient Christian rituals, or sacraments, are an important part of worship in mainline Protestant churches in Canada. Evangelical churches, on the other hand, although they observe many of the rituals, which they call "ordinances," emphasize the interior disposition of the person.

The two rituals that are generally observed among all Protestants in Canada are baptism and Communion, the latter sometimes called the Eucharist or the Lord's Supper. While these rituals retain the essentials of ancient Christian practices, such as water in baptism and bread and wine, or grape juice, in Communion, they have different meanings among the churches. In addition, the rituals are performed differently. Baptism, for example, is performed in some churches by sprinkling or pouring water and in others, particularly in evangelical churches, by immersing the person in water. The rituals also vary in the extent of the engagement of those participating and in their complexity and length. Communion, for example, can be as short as 20 minutes among some Lutherans or as long as three hours among Pentecostals.

RITES OF PASSAGE In a 2000 survey 80 percent of Christian teenagers in Canada expressed a desire to participate in religious rites of passage at the appropriate moments in their lives. At the same time 57 percent of adults expressed a desire for a Christian funeral. The manner of celebrating such rites is unique to each Protestant denomination while similar to the rites of coreligionists throughout the world.

Baptism is an early rite of passage for those mainline churches in Canada that baptize infants. For those churches that do not baptize children, Baptists and other evangelicals, for example, it is often an initiation ritual for teenagers. Acculturated into the born-again experience and baptism as rituals marking the entrance into adulthood, many evangelicals are baptized in their midteens.

Even Canadians who do not go to church regularly expect to be married in church and to be buried from a church. The expectation of having a church marriage is so strong that certain churches have become known as "marriage chapels." Although most funerals have come to be held in funeral homes, they include Bible readings and prayers as part of the ritual, even when they are not performed by a minister.

MEMBERSHIP Attendance at weekly services by Protestants has changed significantly in Canada since the mid-twentieth century. In 1957, 51 percent of conservative Protestants attended church weekly, whereas 58 percent did so in 2000. On the other hand, while 35 percent of mainline Protestants attended weekly services in 1957, the number had fallen to 15 percent in 2000.

While all Protestant churches in Canada actively seek new members, their methods and the intensity of their efforts vary. Evidence indicates that when a church puts its efforts into getting back those who have left it has more success than when it tries to recruit people without any religious preference.

Until the mid-twentieth century missionary activities by Protestants were intense among Indians throughout Canada and among Catholics in Quebec. Most Indians converted to Christianity while retaining and modifying their native rituals, especially those surrounding rites of passage. Early missionaries devised alphabets so that the spoken languages of Indians could be written. Indians, on the other hand, also influenced Christian practices. Among mainline Protestant churches contemporary celebrations of the sacraments include the burning of sweet grass, for example, and, in confirmation, the use of lodges associated with coming-of-age ceremonies. Few Catholics in Quebec were converted to Protestantism, since this was an affront to both their culture and their religion.

The regulations for the use of electronic media in Canada affect religious broadcasting. Canadian law requires a balanced point of view, fairness in describing views, and a demonstration that the needs of the community are being served. Especially for evangelicals, who tend to consider their view as the only correct one and who believe that those in error should be condemned, not served, it is difficult to adhere to these requirements. Consequently, the type of religious broadcasting readily found on the radio in the United States, for example, does not find a place in Canada.

SOCIAL JUSTICE In a 2000 survey, 65 percent of Canadian Protestants said that the church should be involved in social issues such as poverty, education, and human rights. With the support of the provincial governments, religious groups in Canada have traditionally taken a role in such matters, thus acting as the conscience of the nation. The mainline churches speak and act to support the rights of all people to such basic needs as food, housing, education, work, and clean air. For example, through PLURA, whose name reflects its membership (Presbyterian, Lutheran, United Church of Canada, Roman Catholic, and Anglican), the mainline churches work in regional committees to assist local antipoverty organizations.

SOCIAL ASPECTS Among Protestants in Canada views on marriage and the family are clearly split between mainline and evangelical Christians. Mainline churches have come to accept divorce under certain circumstances, whereas evangelicals are hesitant to support anything but the family styles of the eighteenth and nineteenth centuries.

POLITICAL IMPACT Although there has been a significant drop in membership and weekly church attendance among mainline Protestants in Canada, this has not been accompanied by a lessening of institutional church leadership on national issues. In addition, the anti-Catholic attitudes of Protestants in the past have given way to an ecumenical concern regarding the dominant issues of the day. Although evangelical Protestants do not participate in the ecumenical movement, they are equally involved with social issues, even though they are sometimes opposed to the views of mainline Christians.

CONTROVERSIAL ISSUES The mainline Protestant churches in Canada reflect the dominant opinion of the country in supporting the responsible and reflective use of birth control and abortion, while allowing for divorce. Evangelical Christians are generally opposed to abortion, approve of divorce only with great difficulty, and rarely adhere to a consistent position on birth control. Although all of the mainline churches ordain women, the question of who gets ordained and the consequences of ordination differ from church to church. Except in a few fundamentalist churches, women are found in leadership positions in all Protestant churches in Canada.

CULTURAL IMPACT The Palladian style of architecture is closely associated with early Anglican churches in Canada. From 1839 on, a powerful group of English theologians advocated a return to the plan of medieval Catholic churches. Their influence can be found throughout the eastern part of Canada in such churches as Saint James's Cathedral in Toronto, Christ Church Cathedral in Fredericton, New Brunswick, and the Baptist Cathedral in Saint John's, Newfoundland. The Gothic Revival can be seen in many Methodist and Baptist churches, for example, in Saint Paul's Cathedral in Regina, Saskatchewan. After World War II more modern styles struggled to gain popularity among a religious population that identified church buildings with premodern architecture. Saint James's Anglican Church (1935) in Vancouver began the modern style in church architecture in Canada.

In Canada the Anglican and Lutheran churches and the United Church of Canada favor and encourage the arts in church life. These churches see contemporary life and its cultural expressions as a road to God. Those who are part of the contemporary liturgical movement in these churches also encourage the use of dance in worship services as well as various types of contemporary music. For those Presbyterians who have remained separate from the United Church of Canada, on the other hand, the arts are incorporated into church life in only a limited fashion, with the sermon always dominating the worship service. Pentecostal Christians also fall within this tradition, for they encourage the teaching of the Bible as expressed in songs, readings, and preaching.

Other Religions

In addition to the dominant Roman Catholic and Protestant churches in Canada, there are smaller numbers of other Protestant and Christian groups. These include Baptists, Lutherans, those Presbyterians who did not join the United Church of Canada, and Pentecostals. Canada is also home to members of the Church of Jesus Christ of Latter-day Saints, or Mormons, and to Jehovah's Witnesses. Small numbers of Hutterites and of Doukhobors live in Canada. It is important to note, however, that in Canada most of these groups do not advocate the same style of confrontational advocacy and witnessing that are found among coreligionists elsewhere, including the United States. The Canadian value of compromise outweighs the belief in advocacy for a cause. It also should be pointed out that 12.5 percent of the total population of Canada, a number far greater than any of these smaller religious groups, indicate that they have no religious preference.

Orthodox Christians and Jews each make up a little more than 1 percent of the population of Canada. Over the years the Orthodox have slowly declined as a percentage of the total population, whereas Jews have remained at a consistent percentage. While most Jews live in Montreal and Toronto, their countries of origin range from Ukraine, Germany, Poland, Russia, and Romania to Israel and Morocco. Jews were among the first non-Christians to settle in Canada, and they make up the largest of the non-Christian religions. As in most of North America, Jews have struggled against the anti-Semitism of the host culture. Court cases, however, have indicated the power of contemporary Canadian law to counter anti-Semitism.

Although Canada's population is growing at the rate of about 1 percent a year, half of this growth is accounted for by immigration. For the most part immigrants come from former British and French colonies. While the first immigrants to Canada came from Europe, today many come from Asia and Africa, which has increased the diversity of the country's religious life. Just as the religious life of the first European immigrants was shaped by the geography of Canada, so the religious life of contemporary Asian and African immigrants is shaped by certain basic values that have developed in Canada. These include the emphasis on community, compromise, and good government, as well as the belief that religion involves—besides a sacred book and building, traditional rituals, and preaching—such activities as helping one's neighbor and education. It takes time, of course, for immigrants to adapt to Canadian culture, and because immigration to Canada has been continuous and intense, there is some tension between established residents and new immigrants.

Islam has grown in Canada, with Muslim immigrants coming mostly from East and Southeast Asia, Africa, and the Middle East. They bring with them variants of Islam, which sometimes results in tension. Buddhists, Hindus, and Sikhs showed a doubling in population in the late twentieth century, while those with Chinese folk religions and Bahais have tended to remain at the same levels from generation to generation.

The national numbers for each of these religions do not reflect their concentration in a particular province or city. Although Pentecostals, for example, are only 1.6 percent of the total population of Canada, 25 percent live in Ontario, and they operate their own school board in Newfoundland. Likewise, Cardston, Raymond, Magrath, and Stirling, in southern Alberta, are the homes of many of the Mormons in Canada. When the Hutterites were persecuted in the United States, they also found their way to Alberta, where they have established nearly 100 colonies. Their Anabaptist teachings, German language, and communal holdings were accepted in this nation of immigrants, and over time nearly all the world's Hutteries have come to live in Alberta. The same is the case with the Doukhobors, a Russian sect that originated in the eighteenth century and that rejects both religious and civil authority. Almost half of the Ukrainian Catholics in Canada live in Alberta and Manitoba.

Because Hinduism, Sikhism, Buddhism, and Taoism have come to Canada from Asia, practitioners of these religions make up a significant and growing minority in British Columbia. In the Vancouver metropolitan area, for example, 13 percent of the people speak Chinese in their homes, and another 12 percent speak Punjabi. Sikhs, who come from the Punjab in India, have several large temples in the Vancouver area that can each house more than a thousand congregants.

Data indicates that Canada will see a significant growth in religions outside the Catholic and Protestant mainstreams. Further, the growth rate of Christian religions overall is less than the growth rates for most non-Christian religions.

Nathan R. Kollar

See Also Vol. I: *Anglicanism/Episcopalianism, Christianity, Methodism, Reformed Christianity, Roman Catholicism*

Bibliography

Anglican Church of Canada. 22 Dec. 2003. http://www.anglican.ca.

Baum, Gregory. *The Church in Quebec.* Ottawa: Novalis, 1991.

Bibby, Reginald W. *Restless Gods: The Renaissance of Religion in Canada.* Toronto: Stoddart, 2002.

Canadian Conference of Catholic Bishops. 22 Dec. 2003. http://www.cccb.ca.

Evangelical Fellowship of Canada. 22 Dec. 2003. http://www.evangelicalfellowship.ca.

Fay, Terence J. *A History of Canadian Catholics.* Montreal: McGill-Queens, 2002.

Grant, John Webster. *Moon of Wintertime: Missionaries and the Indians of Canada in Encounter since 1534.* Toronto: University of Toronto Press, 1984.

Statistics Canada. 22 Dec. 2003. http://www.statcan.ca.

United Church of Canada. 22 Dec. 2003. http://www.united-church.ca.

Cape Verde

POPULATION 408,760

ROMAN CATHOLIC 95 percent

PROTESTANT 5 percent

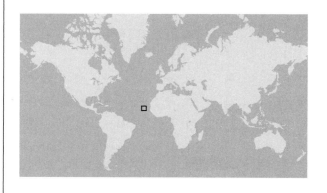

Country Overview

INTRODUCTION The Republic of Cape Verde (in Portuguese, República de Cabo Verde) comprises a group of nine inhabited islands that lie 385 miles off West Africa's coast. The Portuguese reached the islands (which were uninhabited) by 1455, and a plan of active colonization and settlement was launched in 1462. As settlers arrived in São Tiago island, they founded Ribeira Grande (now Cidade Velha), the oldest European city in sub-Saharan Africa. Cape Verde prospered as an offshore common post, particularly for the trade of slaves, ivory, and gold. The Portuguese had reluctantly abandoned the lucrative slave trade by the late 1870s.

In 1879 the colonial administration of Cape Verde was separated from that of Guinea-Bissau on the mainland. In 1956 a group of Cape Verdean and African nationalists formed an independence movement. They launched an armed struggle in Guinea in 1963 that led to the independence of Cape Verde from Portugal on 5 July 1975.

The population is mostly Crioulo, a culture and mixed language that emerged from the Atlantic slave trade during the fifteenth to nineteenth centuries. Despite the overwhelming dominance of Catholicism, the ethnic and religious diversity of this small nation is great. Most Africans arrived in Cape Verde with the beliefs and practices of African indigenous religions or Islam—both of which were widespread on the coast of Upper Guinea—and elements of these practices have been retained. In addition to a small but important presence of Judaism, there have been increasing numbers of Protestants and some Muslims.

RELIGIOUS TOLERANCE From 1462 to 1975 Roman Catholicism was the official religion of Cape Verde. Tolerance of other faiths was minimal, especially during the Inquisition. Forced expulsion of Jews from Portugal to Cape Verde and the arrival of African slaves resulted in some religious diversity. Postcolonial Cape Verde has political and constitutional provisions for religious freedom, and this has been strongly observed. There are no known cases of religious persecution in practice or in the legal arena.

Major Religion

ROMAN CATHOLICISM

DATE OF ORIGIN 1466 C.E.
NUMBER OF FOLLOWERS 390,000

HISTORY Probably the first Catholic priests in Cape Verde were those who arrived in 1466 to convert the slaves that had been taken there to work on the cotton and sugar plantations. In 1533 a bishop was appointed to Ribeira Grande, and the great Sée cathedral was initiated there; it was the first Catholic cathedral in sub-Saharan Africa.

Religious land holdings in Cape Verde were sometimes designated as *capelas,* or large church-owned slave plantations. Often these lands evolved into semiprivate *morgadio* land that was essentially feudal in ownership and social structure. The land, buildings, slaves, water rights, rents, products, and livestock were all owned by the *capelas,* giving the church and the Portuguese crown a virtual monopoly.

From 1552 to 1642 the Jesuits were prominent in Cape Verde, where they operated a mission on large land donations. By the 1620s slave smuggling and declining plantation profits had reduced their income. They finally closed their mission, and Capuchin brothers arrived in 1647. Because the Jesuits threatened the lucrative slave trade (by pressing for laws against overcrowding slave ships and laws that required slaves to be baptized), by 1759 they were resisted and suppressed by the crown. Franciscans were ready to fill this void.

In the 1940s the Catholic Church was so closely associated with colonial authorities that an anticolonial *rebelado* movement protested the abuses and rejected the authority of priests.

EARLY AND MODERN LEADERS The height of activity and construction was during the time of Bishop Vitoriano Portuense (in office 1688–1705), who was noted for his missionary work on the African coast and his strict morality in the islands. He served from 1688 to 1690 as the governor of Cape Verde, but his moral values were too strict for the islanders, and he was opposed for a second term. The Catholic Church in Cape Verde is divided into two dioceses: Mindelo, headed since 2003 by Bishop Arlindo Gomes Furtado, and Santiago de Cabo Verde, whose bishop, Paulino do Livramento Évora, was appointed in 1975.

Pope John Paul II blesses worshippers in Cape Verde in 1990. Most postcolonial governments in Cape Verde have had a polite or friendly relationship with Catholic religious authorities. © REUTERS NEWMEDIA INC./CORBIS.

MAJOR THEOLOGIANS AND AUTHORS In 1754 the cathedral at Ribeira Grande was abandoned because of French pirate attacks on the city. In later centuries religious training was based around the seminary in São Nicolau, which also trained priests for other Portuguese possessions in Africa. The writer and lawyer Baltazar Lopes da Silva (1907–89), who founded the literary journal *Claridade* (Clarity), was closely associated with the literary tradition that descended from the seminary of São Nicolau.

HOUSES OF WORSHIP AND HOLY PLACES Cape Verde's historic places of worship were at the seminary in São Nicolau (closed in 1931 and rebuilt in the 1990s) and at the cathedral in Ribeira Grande, which today stands in deteriorating ruins. Personal shrines are not uncommon in homes, and there are roadside shrines.

WHAT IS SACRED? Aspects of African syncretic religions, as well as beliefs such as sympathetic magic, divination, and notions of evil versus positive forces, survive in celebrations of saint's days. For example, Saint John is celebrated with drumming, processionals, and masks and dancing in African styles, especially on São Tiago island. Spirits are believed to live in certain areas, such as Janela on Santo Antão island.

HOLIDAYS AND FESTIVALS In Cape Verde saint's days are celebrated with festivals (*festas*), which are accompanied by drumming and processionals. The *festa* of Saint João on 24 June is especially well known for its bright banners and for a parade of model ships. The ships are worn as part of the costume of the central performers, who suspend the model on their shoulders while apparently piloting the ship. There are also *festas* for Saint António and Saint Pedro.

MODE OF DRESS There are no Catholic modes of dress that are distinctive to Cape Verde. Catholics in Cape Verde follow certain folk traditions; for instance, African and Islamic practices such as the protective eye (*mal d'ojo*) and cowries (for fertility) are supernatural supplements to dress.

DIETARY PRACTICES As in most countries, the Catholic Church in Cape Verde has suspended the practice of abstaining from meat on Friday, but some conservative believers continue the practice. Fasting and abstinence during Lent is observed.

RITUALS Cape Verdean Catholic rituals sometimes incorporate African or Moorish traditions, which may vary by island but can include smashing mustard seeds into dust and then spreading the dust on a house to protect it from evil spirits. For babies there may be special "seventh day" celebrations and prayers to drive out "witches." Some children are given belts made of fish vertebrae that are in the form of a cross; this is worn for protection under their clothes.

When a person dies, a senior member of the family may construct a simple household altar, which is sprinkled with holy water seven days after the death. Funerals may recruit or hire wailers for the *guizas*, or mourning rituals. In some Catholic cemeteries the graves can be emptied and then reused by others. The original bones and other remains are removed as early as seven years later to a common container in the cemetery.

RITES OF PASSAGE Like Catholics all over the world, Cape Verdeans often mark major stages in life by the reception (or first reception) of a sacrament. Catholic rites are performed in Cape Verde for birth, first Communion, confirmation, marriage, and the anointing of the sick. Funeral Masses are also offered for the dead, and Catholics are expected to confess their sins to a priest during the rite of Reconciliation. These practices are unique in that they rest on the use of Crioulo language and culture and celebratory informal music.

MEMBERSHIP Most Cape Verdeans are born into Catholic families and baptized as infants. Aside from formal events and rites of passage, it appears that church attendance is low, especially among youths. But the Catholic Church owns a radio station, Radio Nova, by which it can spread its message.

SOCIAL JUSTICE In Cape Verde Catholic women are especially involved in church activities, and this can empower them in some respects. Religious aspects of social service and psychological support, such as confession or counseling, are practiced.

SOCIAL ASPECTS In Cape Verde godparents (*padrinos*) are named for a child at baptism. This kinship metaphor establishes a protective relationship that results in social solidarity. The church encourages formal marriage and the strengthening of the family, but among the young in particular, informal unions and serial relationships (especially for men) are common.

POLITICAL IMPACT During the colonial period it was a serious offense to challenge either the Catholic Church or the Portuguese state. Under colonialism the church in Cape Verde expressed its opposition to musical forms that it considered subversive and "too African," such as *funana* and *batuko*. There were cases of African-style drums being smashed.

The Catholic newspaper *Terra Nova* was founded in the 1970s. Since the church had supported the colonial government, the paper created some tensions with the early postcolonial secular government and served as something of voice for the opposition in the Barlavento islands.

Most postcolonial governments in Cape Verde have had a polite-to-friendly relationship with Catholic religious authorities. Today the church is not substantially engaged in politics, except for opening prayers at some dinner meetings.

CONTROVERSIAL ISSUES Previously the Portuguese Catholic Church had been aligned with colonialism, political fascism, and slavery. Such controversial memories were noted during the secular nationalist armed struggle. The Portuguese had sought to portray the nationalists as godless communists. It was thus a great political victory when Pope Paul VI received the nationalist leader Amílcar Cabral in 1970.

After independence was achieved, the more conservative, propertied, and Catholic Cape Verdeans sometimes took issue with the government about abortion (which is not legal and avoided as an issue but which is widely practiced) and reproductive rights. Patriarchal views associated with the Catholic Church about the position of women in society or in church life are considered problematic by some.

CULTURAL IMPACT The cultural impact of the Catholic Church in Cape Verde is most evident in church architecture, religious imagery, and iconography, but it is also seen in small chapels, roadside shrines, domestic religious objects, and household shrines.

The São Nicolau Seminary proved to be a birthplace for Cape Verdean cultural and literary movements. From 1936 to 1958 the journal *Claridade* (Clarity) was the inspiration for a literary movement of the same name that has lingering influences today. It stressed a Cape Verdean, rather than Portuguese, identity.

Other Religions

As a result of proselytizing efforts from the United States, Protestant faiths in Cape Verde represent about five percent of the population, and they are growing slowly. They include the Church of the Nazarene (especially in Nova Sintra on Brava island), Jehovah's Witnesses, and Sabbatarians, as well as some of the Protestant evangelical groups. Some proselytizing efforts have been made by Mormons since the 1990s.

Many Cape Verdeans can trace Jews (known as *novos Cristãos*, or new Christians, after their forced conversions) in their ancestry from the early sixteenth century. Expelled from Portugal during the Inquisition, Jews began to settle in the region as *lançado* (outcast) traders. There are no practicing Jews in Cape Verde today, but aspects of Jewish ethnicity, family names, and folk practices can be found. The most recent Cape Verdean Jews were active in the nineteenth century; they were largely Sephardic Jews from Morocco. One hamlet in Santo Antão has retained the name Sinagoga.

Some Cape Verdean youths and about 300 African merchants in Cape Verde are followers of Islam. There are also a small number of Bahai.

Richard Lobban Jr.

See Also Vol. I: *Christianity, Roman Catholicism*

Bibliography

Carreira, António. *The People of the Cape Verde Islands.* London: C. Hurst, 1982.

Friberg, H.R. *Like a River Flowing: The Church of the Nazarene in Africa and the Republic of Cape Verde.* Kansas City, Mo.: Nazarene Publishing House, 1982.

Lobban, Richard. *Cape Verde: Crioulo Colony to Independence.* Boulder, Colo.: Westview, 1995.

Meintel, Deirdre. *Race, Culture, and Portuguese Colonialism in Cabo Verde.* Syracuse, N.Y.: Syracuse University Press, 1984.

Central African Republic

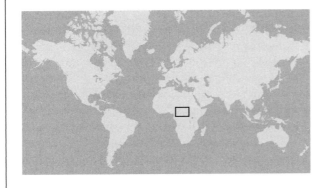

Country Overview

INTRODUCTION The Central African Republic is a landlocked country located in the middle of the continent. It is a complex nation, with at least 10 distinct ethnic groups that follow three principal religions—Christianity, traditionalism, and Islam. These various groups, living at one of the continent's most important crossroads between black Africa in the west and south and the Arab world in the north and east, were loosely united by the French beginning in 1885, culminating in the establishment of the colony of Oubangui-Shari during the 1920s. Christianity was introduced beginning in the late nineteenth century. The colonial period was relatively short, with independence coming on 13

August 1960, and it has been difficult for the government to forge a true nation capable of integrating the country's ethnic groups as well as the thousands of immigrants from Nigeria, Niger, and the Sudan, people often generally classified as Hausa or Muslim. In contrast to countries such as Chad and Nigeria, however, the postindependence leaders have never associated religion with their governance of the country.

RELIGIOUS TOLERANCE The constitution of the Central Africa Republic protects religious freedom and calls for the separation of church and state. In the history of the country, however, Christianity, especially Roman Catholicism, has been favored, with the first prominent leader, Barthélemy Boganda, having been a Catholic. Yet, except for the violent slave raids on non-Muslim communities conducted by regional sultans, the country has not had a history of religious persecution. Since independence Christians, traditionalists, and Muslims have lived together, even though ecumenism among the faiths has not been strongly promoted.

Major Religions

CHRISTIANITY

AFRICAN INDIGENOUS BELIEFS

CHRISTIANITY

DATE OF ORIGIN 1894 C.E. (Roman Catholicism) and 1924 C.E. (Protestantism)
NUMBER OF FOLLOWERS 1.8 million

HISTORY The Roman Catholic Church penetrated West Africa as early as the fifteenth century, and evidence indicates that Catholic missionaries were in Central Africa, including the Sudan and parts of Chad, during the eighteenth century. Church activity did not begin in the Oubangui-Shari region until the 1890s, however, when the first Capuchin and Saint-Esprit priests arrived and began their evangelization. Their work along the riverbanks was so promising that in 1909 the Holy See created an apostolic prefecture at Bangui, the colony's capital. The missionaries slowly penetrated farther into the interior, making major inroads into Banda and Baya country, a move that compelled the pope to create an apostolic curate in Bangui in 1937 followed by an apostolic prefecture at Berbérati. Thus, by 1940 some 45,000 people in Oubangui-Shari had embraced Catholicism.

Baptists were the first to establish Protestant missions in Oubangui-Shari, in 1932, followed by the Foreign Missionary Society of Oubangui-Shari, the Lutheran Sudan Mission at Baboua, the Central African Pioneer Mission at Carnot, and the Swedish Baptist Mission at Alindao. As an incentive to their work, both Catholics and Protestants received subsidies from the French government, although the Catholic Church enjoyed preferential treatment. In addition, both were entrusted with the primary education of the Africans and were allowed to establish hospitals in the colony.

EARLY AND MODERN LEADERS Because Christianity in the colony of Oubangui-Shari was dominated by foreign missionaries, no prominent African leaders emerged. In addition, Christianity in Oubangui-Shari did not give rise to independent, so-called Ethiopian, churches or to religious cults that might have challenged the colonial order.

There are no more than 45 Catholic priests in the Central African Republic. Since 2003 the leader of the Catholic Church has been Archbishop Paulin Pomodimo, of the archdiocese of Bangui, the capital. Catholic bishops also maintain an episcopal conference. Protestants have organized themselves into L'Église Protestante de Bangui for the discussion of ecclesiastical and social matters.

MAJOR THEOLOGIANS AND AUTHORS Given that education in the colony remained essentially at the elementary level and that the few seminarians received only the training essential for the priesthood or the ministry, Ou-

bangui-Shari did not produce distinguished church theologians or authors. The same has been true of the country since independence.

HOUSES OF WORSHIP AND HOLY PLACES Other than cathedrals and church buildings, there are no special houses of worship or holy places for Christians in the Central African Republic. In these matters Catholic churches follow the directives of the Vatican, and Protestant churches of the various foreign boards located in the United States and Europe.

WHAT IS SACRED? As in Western Christianity, there are no animals or plants sacred to Christians in the Central African Republic. Whereas relics have lost their value in many parts of the Western world, however, in the Central African Republic, as in Africa generally, Christians continue to venerate such objects. These include the relics of European saints, crosses, and necklaces and medals that have been blessed. This aspect of African Christianity is least appreciated by Protestants, who consider such practices to border on superstition and idolatry.

HOLIDAYS AND FESTIVALS The same major holidays—Christmas, Easter Sunday, Ascension, and Assumption—celebrated by the Western church are observed in the Central African Republic. The prominent role of the Catholic Church is demonstrated by the fact that it is the Catholic holidays, and not those of Protestants, that are observed. No African saints are celebrated in the Central African Republic, in spite of the fact that in some parts of the continent Charles Lwanga and the Martyrs of Uganda are honored.

MODE OF DRESS As with believers throughout the world, Christians in the Central African Republic are expected to dress modestly both inside and outside places of worship. In contrast to the West, however, where people sometimes go to church in casual clothes, Christians in the Central African Republic strive to wear their best on Sundays and religious holidays, even when they are poor.

DIETARY PRACTICES As is generally the case with Christians elsewhere, there are no taboos regarding diet for Christians in the Central African Republic. Catholics, and Protestants even less so, no longer take seriously the practice of abstaining from meat on the eve of certain sacred days. Christians are told that they should break the ethnic tradition of not hurting or eating an animal associated with their clan, but the practice has continued.

RITUALS Africans have traditionally taken rituals quite seriously, and they continue to do so. Thus, baptism, first Communion, confirmation, matrimony, and ordination to the priesthood or the ministry are great and solemn occasions for Christians in the Central African Republic, as are births and funerals. Catholic funeral services, for example, include a Mass, elaborate processions and singing, and, following the burial, a feast, from which many people come away intoxicated and with full stomachs. Death is seen simultaneously as a sad and a happy occasion, marking the time when a person has fulfilled his contribution to the survival of his lineage and stands ready to join the invisible world of his ancestors, or "heaven."

RITES OF PASSAGE Christians are forbidden to participate in the traditional initiation rites practiced by virtually every Central African ethnic group to mark the transition from childhood to adulthood. In the past any Christian participating in such "pagan" customs, as they were called, was excommunicated or disfellowshipped by the church, but such punishment is rarely carried out today. For Christians the principal rites of passage are confirmation, when a person is said to become a soldier of Christ, and matrimony, the most visible proof that a child has become an adult.

MEMBERSHIP Even though neither Catholics nor Protestants exclude any potential member, there is a major difference between the two churches in recruitment in the Central African Republic. Catholics tend to favor group membership, whereby converts are instructed together as "people of God," thus emphasizing the community of the faithful. Protestants prefer individual conversions, which may take years, in agreement with the doctrine of individual interpretation of the Scriptures.

The Catholic Church has maintained the practice of going into villages, establishing temporary conversion and teaching centers, and sending priests, often by motorcycle, to the countryside. Catechists sometimes live with potential members in rural areas until they are baptized.

SOCIAL JUSTICE Following independence, Christian churches in the Central African Republic promoted social justice and became sources of protest against government corruption and the abuse of human rights. Speaking on behalf of the poor and using their meager resources to uplift those in need have been hallmarks of the churches, even though the perpetrators of the worst crimes against Central Africans, including President Jean-Bédel Bokassa, have been Christians.

SOCIAL ASPECTS Christianity has become the principal defender of the nuclear, as opposed to the extended, family in the Central African Republic. Many Christian males, however, continue to practice polygyny, carrying on secret relationships with girlfriends and concubines. Given the low status of women, wives are powerless to stop the practice.

POLITICAL IMPACT Christianity has little political impact in the Central African Republic. The church has no political party or organization of its own, even though most political leaders are Christians, and the Catholic Church is often reminded by the Vatican to stay out of politics. At the same time relations among the various faiths have not led to civil strife or war.

CONTROVERSIAL ISSUES Christians in the Central African Republic uphold traditional teachings on matters such as divorce, abortion, birth control, and the subordinate role of women. Unlike many of their counterparts in the West, few of the country's Christians espouse one thing and live another. Catholics in the Central African Republic, for example, take the pope's messages more seriously than do many Catholics in the West.

Apart from serving as catechists, teachers, altar girls, and, in the Catholic Church, nuns, women in the Central African Republic have played an insignificant role in church affairs. There are no Christian feminists in the country.

CULTURAL IMPACT Through translations of the Bible, teaching manuals written in the vernacular, and the popularization of religious music, Christian churches have been a major force in the propagation of Sango as the lingua franca of the Central African Republic. Except for the erection of cathedrals in the Western artistic style, Christianity has had little effect on architecture. In fact, Christianity has had little impact on the arts in general, including dance, which it has tried to eliminate. On the other hand, traditional practices and artistic styles—including dancing, hand clapping, drumming and the playing of other instruments, and sculpture—have influenced the Christian churches as they strive to become Africanized.

AFRICAN INDIGENOUS BELIEFS

DATE OF ORIGIN C. 6000 B.C.E.
NUMBER OF FOLLOWERS 900,000

HISTORY The area of what is now the Central African Republic was probably inhabited as early as 6000 B.C.E. The original inhabitants are believed to have been the Aka, also known as the Babinga or the Tvide or, in the Western world, as Pygmies. Around 1000 C.E. they were overpowered by Bantu-speaking migrants who were technologically more advanced farmers and by Sudanic and Nilotic conquerors. As a result, the Babinga and others were relegated to the forests, where they have continued to live.

The events that have shaped the history of traditional religion in the region are varied. They include the arrival, in the eastern and northern parts of the country, of Islam and slavery from the Sudan and Chad, as well as the European colonial conquest and the introduction of Christianity, both of which occurred during the nineteenth century. Whereas the conditions prevailing in the area before the introduction of Islam and Christianity helped to stabilize traditional religion, the arrival of Islam, at times through violence and the enslavement of non-Muslims, and of Christianity, which was allied with the colonial state, weakened the traditional religious fabric, especially in the newly developing urban areas. This accounts for the fact that in the Central African Republic only 25 percent of the population can be considered to be truly traditional in religion.

Since the beginning the major elements of traditional religion in Africa have included the belief in a single great God, who is never referred to in the plural, along with spirit mediums and ancestors. There is, as well, belief in a "vital force," or "vital energy," that emanates from God to permeate all living and nonliving things.

EARLY AND MODERN LEADERS Because of the nonliterate nature of Central African Republic societies and the dominance of Christianity and Islam, no traditional religious leaders are remembered permanently. Generally, however, each clan and lineage recalls its most prominent priests and divine rules of the previous two generations.

MAJOR THEOLOGIANS AND AUTHORS The nonliterate nature of the societies of the Central African Republic and the absence of organized efforts at proselytizing make it impossible to cite theologians, religious authors, or renowned spiritual leaders. It should be pointed out, however, that each lineage or family has its own local priests, religious experts, diviners, healers, and magicians who control religion. At times the village chief or the clan leader enjoys the powers of a high priest, deciding, for example, when the community may plant, harvest, and fish. This is the case among the Sara in the north.

HOUSES OF WORSHIP AND HOLY PLACES In the Central African Republic, as is common in all of sub-Saharan Africa, a designated house in a family compound may serve as the place of worship for the family unit. Certain forests or parts of forest, cemeteries, specific trees and mountains, or perhaps ancestor's abodes may be held as sacred objects and places.

WHAT IS SACRED? Each ethnic group, clan, and lineage in the Central African Republic has its own sacred animal, or totem, that may not be hurt, killed, or consumed. Objects buried with the dead or those found in cemeteries or sacred forests are not to be touched, lest the person incur the ire of ancestors. Certain figurines, amulets, and special bracelets and necklaces, as well as beads worn around the waist, may also acquire a sacred character, as may objects related to fertility and maternity.

HOLIDAYS AND FESTIVALS The beginning of the harvest, the birth of a child, a successful hunting trip, the end of rites of passage, and the day of a chief's enthronement are examples of occasions that are celebrated by the village community in the Central African Republic. Unlike Islam, which holds every Friday as a day of prayer and a holiday, or Christianity, with its annual cycles of Sundays and specific days of common worship for the faithful, traditionalists observe festivals whenever there is an important social occurrence.

MODE OF DRESS There is no religiously prescribed way of dressing among traditionalists in the Central African Republic. Decency is always emphasized, and people dress in traditional attire such as a *tanga*, a cloth wrapped around the waist for women and around the body for men. Sandals may be worn to protect the feet.

DIETARY PRACTICES There are very few dietary prohibitions among the societies of the Central African Republic. Pregnant women are forbidden to eat fish or eggs or certain animal meats in the belief that the unborn may be endangered or born with physical defects. Because it is considered sacred, a totemic animal may not be consumed.

RITUALS Rituals among traditionalists in the Central African Republic follow harvests and the rhythm of life—birth, adulthood, marriage, ascent to power, elderly status, death, and migration to the world of the ancestors. Ceremonies are held to announce a child's birth, to name the child, and to present the newborn to the lineage and the community. For each of these occasions, there is usually a religious ceremony presided over by the head of the family, a priest, or the village chief, with the ancestors playing an important role.

The phenomenon of "possession"—emotionally charged dances—takes place during rituals. It is believed that spirits or ancestors speak through the person in a state of possession, although some experts say that the possessed may be in a state of self-induced ecstasy.

RITES OF PASSAGE In virtually every ethnic group in the Central African Republic, adulthood is preceded by rites of passage, which may take place over weeks or months. These initiation ceremonies, as they are generally called, usually involve seclusion from the community under the supervision of an elder—a man for boys and a woman for girls—and the learning of a new language that can be understood only by the initiated. During the time of initiation, the young people are taught to think and care about the community rather than about themselves as individuals. They are taught that society expects them to perpetuate the lineage of the clan and that death should not matter to them if they have helped the clan to survive; it is the reason they were born. In this context marriage is presented as obligatory and an abundance of children as a blessing. The young people are taught that, as adults, they will be expected to perform the tasks of fathers and mothers and perhaps, as among the Babinga, those of warriors or hunters. They learn that, as they move to the next stage, some

will be called upon to assume the responsibility of leading the community. Old age is presented as a time of experience, wisdom, and earned respect.

MEMBERSHIP Membership in a traditional African religion is automatic, and no child may question his household's teachings. This is one reason it makes no sense to speak of an atheist in traditional societies.

As is the case in all of sub-Saharan Africa, in the Central African Republic there are no traditionalist missionaries who try to convert people. Traditionalism does not prevent other religions from seeking converts in its midst, however, since traditionalists do not hold their religion to be better than that of anyone else. People convert to other religions when they become convinced that the new God is stronger than the one they have been worshiping.

SOCIAL JUSTICE A sense of justice is strong within traditionalism, and in the Central African Republic wrongs are usually addressed publicly by a presiding member of the family, the chief, or designated community leaders. Accompanying this is the principle of proportional retribution for a wrong committed, something that is well entrenched in traditional religion. Notions of justice and fairness are conveyed and reinforced through household education and consist mainly of daily observation, listening, and practice.

Traditionalists in the Central African Republic no longer shun a Western education and its social teachings. The material benefits to the family that are derived from a Western education, even if the young person rejects traditionalism and embraces Christianity in the process, are held to outweigh the negatives. Traditionalists continue, however, to find it difficult to accept the Western practice of incarceration as a proportional retribution for a horrendous crime such as murder.

SOCIAL ASPECTS Among all ethnic groups in the Central African Republic, marriage is expected of every young man and woman. Traditional society sanctions polygyny and the extended family. Having many children is considered to be a sign of a blessing from ancestors and the divine realm. The family or the community takes precedence over the individual, and a person is believed to be on earth to perpetuate the lineage. This is the order that God ordained and that he entrusted certain members of the community—priests, chiefs, diviners, ancestors, and spirit mediums—to enforce and preserve. The child also learns from the family how to acquire a sense of community responsibility and to avoid evils such as sorcery, jealousy, laziness, theft, adultery, and disrespect for human life, including murder.

POLITICAL IMPACT The political power of traditional leaders was severely curtailed and weakened by the colonial government and, later, by the nation-state. Nonetheless, chiefs and kings in the Central African Republic continue to be seen as sharing in divinity, and there have been instances in which people have cast their votes on behalf of a particular political candidate because of the advice of a chief. When this occurs, the authority of the chief is derived from his personal experience and reputation for wisdom and from the traditional belief that a chief enjoys a greater share of the vital force that is present in every living and nonliving thing.

Most of the people in power in the Central African Republic today are Christians or are mission educated.

CONTROVERSIAL ISSUES Traditional religion in the Central African Republic does everything possible to preserve the family and the clan. Modern contraceptives are proscribed, and abortion is shunned in the belief that it will bring the wrath of ancestors. Because marriage is an alliance between two families or clans, divorce is difficult, and when it does occur, the bride wealth may have to be returned. Women and men have clearly defined roles in society, with women expected to be subordinate and submissive to their husbands, a tradition that is believed to be sanctioned directly by ancestors and indirectly by God.

In spite of these prohibitions, clandestine abortions do take place, as in the case of incest, and infanticide is practiced when, for example, an abominable physical or mental handicap or disease is suspected at birth. On the advice of and with prescription by a medicine man, natural contraceptives are sometimes used.

CULTURAL IMPACT Because traditional religion permeates all aspects of daily life, its specific impact on the arts is difficult to assess. It is possible, however, to discern the religious undertones, or spirituality, of various elements of culture. This can be seen, for example, in certain songs that invoke the names of ancestors or of the great God, as well as in the reverence surrounding a house of worship or a sacred place, with its accompanying figurines and symbols, that is recognized as belonging to a specific society.

In the Central African Republic today the tendency is to move away from traditionalism to embrace Western culture. This is made more compelling by the phenomenon of globalization.

Other Religions

When Hausa traders, Arab merchants from North Africa, and migrants from West Africa, especially from the Niger and Nigerian regions, moved into Central Africa, they took Islam with them. In the Central African Republic today there are some 550,000 followers of Islam, representing about 15 percent of the population. Most of the Muslims are concentrated in the north, in the prefecture of Bamingui-Bangoran, with its capital at Ndélé, which makes up the former sultanate of Dar-al-Kuti. Even though Muslims and Christians live together in peace, the history of the Arab and Muslim slave trade has not been forgotten.

Religious instruction provided in the large Islamic households and in the few remaining *madrasahs* (Koranic schools) serve to keep Islam growing in the Central African Republic. There is little or no proselytizing. As in other parts of the world, Islam is attractive in the Central African Republic for its doctrine of equality before Allah, its theoretical aversion to racism, and its stand on human brotherhood. For the noneducated Muslim, reciting the Koran in Arabic is another factor that increases the lure and prestige of Islam, with the work of the *madrasah*s contributing to this aura. Islam allows a man to marry as many as four wives, thus complementing the sub-Saharan African tradition of polygyny. To preserve the family and promote the expansion of Islam, Muslims tend to speak out against abortion. No major leaders, theologians, or authors of the faith are celebrated in the Central African Republic.

Given their relatively small size within the population, Muslims wield little political power in the Central African Republic. There has been no Muslim presidential candidate. There is, however, a fundamentalist political party, the Union Nationale Démocratique du Peuple Centrafricain, founded in 1998 and led by Mahamat Saleh, that attracts the Muslim population in the east. Because of their low educational level, Muslims have had little influence on literature, art, and architecture in the Central African Republic, the exception being the few Middle Eastern-appearing mosques in the east and northeast. Islamic music in the country is usually a blend of Sudanese-Arabic-Nilotic rhythms, tunes, and instruments that have little resemblance to the music of the Bantu-speaking population.

There are pockets of Hindus and Bahais in the Central African Republic, but their numbers are insignificant. The Hindus mostly came from Asia during the colonial period. As in most of Africa, the Bahais are of recent arrival.

Mario J. Azevedo

See Also Vol. 1: *Baptist Tradition, Christianity, Islam, Lutheranism, Roman Catholicism*

Bibliography

Africa: South of the Sahara. London: Europa Publishers, 2003.

Hewlett, Harry S. *Intimate Fathers: The Nature and Context of Aka Pygmy Paternal Infant Care.* Ann Arbor: University of Michigan Press, 1991.

Kalck, Pierre. *Central African Republic: A Failure in De-Colonisation.* Translated by Barbara Thomson. New York: Praeger, 1971.

———. *Historical Dictionary of the Central African Republic.* 2nd ed. Translated by Thomas O'Toole. Metuchen, N.J.: Scarecrow Press, 1992.

———, comp. *Central African Republic: Bibliographical Series.* Vol. 52. Santa Barbara, Calif.: Clio Press, 1993.

Maquet, Jacques. *Africanity: The Cultural Unity of Black Africa.* London: Oxford University Press, 1972.

Mbiti, John S. *African Religions and Philosophy.* London: Heinemann, 1969.

———. *Introduction to African Religion.* London: Heinemann, 1975.

O'Toole, Thomas. *The Central African Republic: The Continent's Hidden Heart.* Boulder, Colo.: Westview Press, 1986.

Oxford Encyclopedia of Africa South of the Sahara. London: Oxford University Press, 1997.

Oxford Encyclopedia of the Modern Islamic World. London: Oxford University Press, 1995.

Parrinder, Geoffrey. *Religion in Africa.* Baltimore: Penguin, 1969.

Ray, Benjamin C. *African Religions: Symbols, Ritual, and Community.* Upper Saddle River, N.J.: Prentice Hall, 2000.

Shorter, Aylward. *African Christian Theology.* Maryknoll, N.Y.: Orbis Books, 1977.

Suret-Canale, Jean. *Afrique noire: Géographie, civilisation, histoire.* Paris: Editions Sociales, 1968.

Temples, Placide. *Bantu Philosophy.* Paris: Présence Africaine, 1959.

Thompson, Virginia, and Richard Adloff. *The Emerging States of French Equatorial Africa.* London: Oxford University Press, 1960.

Voll, John Obert. *Islam: Continuity and Change in the Modern World.* Boulder, Colo.: Westview Press, 1982.

Chad

POPULATION 8,997,237

MUSLIM 40 percent

AFRICAN INDIGENOUS BELIEFS 30 percent

CHRISTIANITY 29.9 percent

OTHER (JEHOVAH'S WITNESS, BAHAI) 0.1 percent

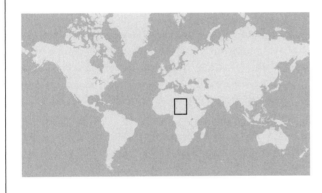

Country Overview

INTRODUCTION The Republic of Chad is a former French colony in north central Africa. Surrounded by Niger, Libya, The Sudan, Central African Republic, Cameroon, and Nigeria, Chad has mountains in the east and north; from north to south it has areas of desert, semidesert (the Sahel), savanna, and tropical rain forest. The economy is based on cotton, livestock (cattle, goats, and sheep), corn, millet, cassava, and peanuts. Water scarcity has contributed to constant movement of livestock, migration, and conflict over wells and grazing land. In 2003 Chad began pumping oil from its south-

ern lands and exporting it through Douala, Cameroon. The World Bank provided the funds for the pipeline project, and the international community hopes that revenues will change the living standards of Chadians, currently at absolute poverty level.

Prominent among Chad's more than 200 ethnicities and languages are Sara, Arab, Tubu, Moundang, Fulani, Maba, Mbum, Barma, Mubi, Hadjeray, Yedina, and Bedeyat. Chadians followed traditional African religions for centuries before the arrival of foreign faiths. Because of their proximity to Muslim communities, northern Chadians embraced Islam during the tenth century. The Muslim north took slaves from the southern traditionalist populations.

The French entered Chad in the 1890s but discouraged Christian activity until the 1920s, favoring Islam (despite its strong resistance to colonialism) as a stabilizing and civilizing religion. Only after World War I did France support missionary work, and then only in the south, with its more promising economic resources. Leaving the social and political structure of the north almost intact, France subjected the south to forced labor, military recruitment, and porterage and their assimilationist "civilizing mission," entrusting Evangelical, Baptist, and Roman Catholic missionaries with the education of the population.

Chad achieved its independence in 1960. Violent civil conflict prevailed from 1965 to 1990. Though religion was not the primary cause, it exacerbated the geoeconomic and ethnic differences between north and south, as have the policies of Christian presidents N'Garta (François) Tombalbaye (1960–75) and Félix Malloum (1975–79) and Muslim heads of state

Goukouni Oueddei (1979–82) and Hisseine Habre (1982–90). Muslim Idris Deby (born in 1952) has been Chad's president since 1990.

Since the 1970s the country has seen the emergence of Jehovah's Witnesses and the Bahai faith, but these groups have remained insignificant.

RELIGIOUS TOLERANCE According to the 1996 constitution, Chad is "a sovereign, independent, and secular republic," whose inhabitants have freedom of "opinion and expression, of conscience, and religion." The country's turbulent religious history has prevented an ecumenical movement from forming. During the 1980s southern Chadians retaliated against harsh Muslim treatment by killing hundreds of northerners living in the south. Since 1994 Christians have consistently been harassed in predominantly Muslim areas, such as Wadai. Most Chadian experts agree, however, that Islamic fundamentalism has not taken root in Chad.

Major Religions

ISLAM

AFRICAN INDIGENOUS BELIEFS

CHRISTIANITY

ISLAM

DATE OF ORIGIN Tenth century C.E.
NUMBER OF FOLLOWERS 3.6 million

HISTORY Islam entered northern Chad principally through the influence of Muslim merchants using the trans-Saharan trade routes. The conversion of the sultans of the Kanem-Bornu Empire, Bagirmi, and Wadai between the thirteenth and sixteenth centuries facilitated the spread of the religion. When the French arrived in Chad, they saw Muslims as more disciplined, cleaner, more literate, and more "civilized" than the rest of the Chadian population and accorded them the benefits of relative freedom and government employment.

The nineteenth century also saw the arrival and active work of several *turuq* (brotherhoods, or orders). The Tijaniya, a more moderate order originally from Morocco, is the most popular in the country; the Qadiriya, the oldest order, is most popular in Kanem and Chari-Bagirmi Prefectures; the Sanussiya, originally

from Libya, was the most resistant to French penetration, especially in Borkou-Ennedi-Tibesti Prefecture; the Mirghaniya is popular in Wadai; and the Tarbiya is an offshoot of the Tijaniya, which was outlawed by Christian President François Tombalbaye in 1962.

The founding of the Front de Liberation Nationale (National Liberation Front, a guerilla movement mainly in the north and east) in 1966 and its dominance over the country since the 1980s have boosted the role of Islam and sharpened the religious and political differences in the country. The three Muslim northern presidents in power from 1979 to the present have sporadically ordered recriminations against southerners. President Idris Deby (born in 1952) has been elected twice since 1996, though not everyone believes the election process was fair and just.

Still a predominantly urban phenomenon, Islam has attracted the traditionalists in Chad with its resistance to colonialism, its literacy, its use of the Arabic language, the cosmopolitan connections it had with the Middle East (especially Mecca), and its tolerance of African cultural traditions. Chadian Muslims, predominantly Sunni, are mainly drawn from the country's Arab, Fulani, Tubu, Suprême Kanembu, and eastern populations. The Conseil Suprême des Affaires Islamiques (Supreme Council of Islamic Affairs) in N'Djamena is Islam's supreme decision-making body.

EARLY AND MODERN LEADERS The Imam (Suni prayer leader) of Fort-Lamy (now N'Djamena) and the Derdei (the spiritual leader of the Muslim Tubu people) have always occupied prominent positions among Chadian Muslims. During the 1950s and 1960s Ahmed Koulamallah (1912–75), a colorful politician in the national assembly, became the de facto leader of Muslims in Chad. Imam Moussa Ibrahim in N'Djamena has been the head of the country's Islamic community since the 1980s.

MAJOR THEOLOGIANS AND AUTHORS No known Muslim theologians or authors have had a significant impact on Islamic beliefs and doctrine in Chad. A number of Chadian marabouts (holy men) and ulama (religious scholars) have attended the University of al-Azhal in Cairo, Egypt, and Islamic institutions of higher learning in Karthoum, Sudan.

HOUSES OF WORSHIP AND HOLY PLACES Chadian Muslims worship in mosques. The N'Djamena mosque is the country's most important and elaborate. Rural Muslims have no place to observe Friday worship and are often limited to using the floor of their homes for prayer. Chadian Muslims often carry a straw mat or a rug with them on which to kneel and perform daily prayers.

WHAT IS SACRED? There are no sacred books, objects, animals, plants, or relics besides the Koran and the sacred beads among Chadian Muslims. Many use and wear amulets, relics of a past when Muslims waged war against "infidels" or other Muslims.

HOLIDAYS AND FESTIVALS During a two-day celebration called Tabaski (Eid al-Adha), Chadian Muslims kill a sacrificial animal, hold a long mosque prayer, attend elaborate banquets, and visit relatives and friends to commemorate Abraham's willingness to sacrifice his son to God. Eid al-Maulud (also known as Maulud al-Nebi) celebrates the Prophet Muhammad's birthday, and Eid al-Fitri celebrates the end of Ramadan. The Deby regime has imposed all three Islamic holidays nationally on Muslims and non-Muslims. The Muslim Tubu observe the Islamized Moudou festival (the Fête de Mouton), an annual ritual consisting of the burial and the disinterment of the viscera of a lamb used to forecast one's destiny on earth.

MODE OF DRESS Most people in Chad, including Muslims, dress simply. The white or green robe and a white cap distinguish Muslim men. Women wear a long, usually dark dress and a veil that covers the head. Outside N'Djamena, where the poverty is even greater, the cap or veil (and the name) may be the only distinguishing feature of a Muslim. In the north turbans are quite common, as is the growing of a beard. François Tombalbaye's administration got into trouble in the Borkou-Ennedi-Tibesti Prefecture when he tried to force Muslims to cut their beards and remove their turbans.

DIETARY PRACTICES Muslims in Chad follow the same dietary prescriptions as Muslims elsewhere. Chadian Muslims take fasting during Ramadan so seriously that they do not even swallow saliva from sunset to sundown. As a result, they spit constantly, a practice that is repugnant to non-Muslims.

RITUALS In N'Djamena Friday service is packed, mainly with male worshipers. The morning prayers by the muezzins (Muslim criers) is a daily routine, even though nonurban Muslims never set foot in a mosque. About 10 percent of Chadian Muslims visit Mecca yearly, traveling through The Sudan. Before its civil wars Chad was on one of the most popular land routes for pilgrims going to Mecca.

Muslim funerals and marriages in Chad are short and do not require much ceremony. Against the teachings of Islam, many Muslim healers and charlatans perform the rituals common among Chadian traditionalists.

RITES OF PASSAGE Chadian Muslim rites of passage are not as elaborate as those of the traditionalist southern populations. Male circumcision is performed at birth. Among certain ethnic groups, such as the Sara and Moundang, children of the same age receive responsibilities at the same time, but no initiation ceremonies mark the transition to adulthood.

MEMBERSHIP In Chad a person who declares his belief in Allah and the Prophet, changes his name, carries the Koranic verses in his bags or pocket, and prays during the day is accepted as a Muslim. Though Islam resisted the colonial system, the French helped spread the religion in Chad by giving preference to Muslims in their bureaucracy, a policy that encouraged many to convert. The improvement of the infrastructure and the communications network also facilitated the spread of Islamic ideas through merchants, traders, and ambulant brotherhoods.

Chadian Islam continues to rely on Muslim households, which tend to have many children, for its growth. The radio and newspapers have been used with small effect, since most people cannot read and do not own a radio.

SOCIAL JUSTICE Because it considers all men to be created equal by Allah, Islam in Chad upholds a strong sense of social justice and a respect for citizen's rights, condemning racism and discrimination, especially among Muslims. Most Islamic communities in Chad, however, follow the African traditional practice in settling disputes: A group of elders or intermediaries from the litigating societies, or a Muslim court, determines the proportional and "appropriate" retribution or retaliation.

Koranic education is encouraged through the *madrasahs* (Koranic schools). Memorization is emphasized over understanding and thinking independently, so many African children recite Koranic verses in Arabic without understanding a single word. No Islamic secondary schools or institutions of higher learning exist in Chad.

SOCIAL ASPECTS The Islamic family in Chad is as extended as it is among the traditionalists. Except among the Tubu of northern Chad (who have a monogamous tradition), most Muslim households are polygynous and have many children. Female adultery is punishable by death, though the law is rarely applied. Divorce is the most common response to infidelity.

POLITICAL IMPACT Islam was always an instrument of unification and political control in the former northern kingdoms and principalities. Even before independence political parties were established in Chad on the basis of Islam. In 1981, at the insistence of Colonel Moammar Kaddafi of Libya, President Goukouni Oueddei proclaimed Chad an Islamic Republic united with its northern neighbor, but this lasted only briefly. Since the mid-1990s many eastern Chadian Muslims have demanded that Chad become an Islamic state. The government has arrested many radical Islamists and has forbidden others to preach fundamentalist doctrines. President Deby and almost all his powerful cabinet members are Muslim, and since 1979 only Muslims have been able to rise in the country's bureaucratic ranks.

CONTROVERSIAL ISSUES All Chadians believe that marriage is an obligation and that fertility and birth should not be prevented through artificial means. Muslims see family planning as a Western conspiracy to shrink the Muslim world.

Chadian Islam discourages divorce, but it is easy to obtain, especially if the husband initiates it. Despite Islam's teachings about the equality of all people before Allah, Chad's Muslim societies (with some exceptions among the Tubu, who allow women to make decisions, especially when the men are tending cattle or away looking for work) treat women as second-class citizens, and inheritance laws weigh heavily against them.

CULTURAL IMPACT Except for the rectangular, domed N'Djamena mosque, there is little Muslim architectural influence in Chad. Arabic, usually associated with North African Islam, is Chad's second official language. Except in the far north, however, newspapers of wider circulation and books are still written in French, not Arabic.

AFRICAN INDIGENOUS BELIEFS

DATE OF ORIGIN 900 C.E.
NUMBER OF FOLLOWERS 2.7 million

HISTORY People may have inhabited the region as early as 4,000 B.C.E. The Sao people established a brick-walled housing civilization around 900 C.E. The history of traditionalism in Chad, a peaceful and tolerant religion, has no landmarks. Traditional religion probably encountered its first historic challenges, slowly losing adherents, with the coming of Islam during the tenth century and Christianity during the twentieth century. It received a slight boost in the early 1970s with Christian President Tombalbaye's policy of a return to "cultural purity" or authenticity, but the effects of secular education and the relative progress of Christianity and (to a lesser degree) Islam have eroded traditionalism's grip on society, even in the south, where the religion is strongest.

Chadian traditionalists maintain the beliefs of their ancestors: in the existence of one remote Creator and Supreme Being, in the power of a hierarchy of spirits (good and bad), in the special role of ancestors (the "living dead"), in the need for physical sacrifice to placate the forces of the universe and atone for individual and community sins, and in the prevalence of special forces in the universe, ultimately emanating from the Supreme Being. Traditionalists in the south, particularly the Sara, most often call the Supreme Being Nouba, though the Moundang and others use "Allah," a proof of the cultural influence of Islam in Chad.

EARLY AND MODERN LEADERS Traditionalism in Chad has its system of priests, diviners, magicians, seers, medicine men, witches, and sorcerers, but religious leadership has resided mainly in the village and clan chief, the *mbang, ngar, nge-be,* or *ngeido-nong.* Among the Sara, the largest and most influential ethnic group in Chad, the *mbang* of Bedaya is the religious leader. The *mbang* determines when initiation ceremonies (*yondo*) and planting, harvesting, and fishing seasons will begin. Among the Moundang, another major ethnic group, the *gon lere* performs this social and political function.

MAJOR THEOLOGIANS AND AUTHORS Since traditionalism emanates from the community, where life is not compartmentalized into sacred and secular, there are no religious personalities above the chiefs, the priests, and the sacrifice officiators. Systemic changes occur mainly in response to changes in the physical environment and the intrusion of foreign philosophies, rarely through individual innovation or discovery from within.

HOUSES OF WORSHIP AND HOLY PLACES Chadian traditionalists venerate the places where ancestors and spirits are thought to congregate or live: certain mountains, cemeteries and burial places of ancestors, parts of the forest or grasslands, and certain areas of the chief's compound where sacrifices may be offered. Among the Hadjeray and Yedina the mountains and trees where the Margai (supernatural forces with power over harvests, animals, human fertility, and storms) and their priests live are sacred.

WHAT IS SACRED? Traditional Chadians hold sacred anything in a cemetery, including pots and relics; clan totems; figurines, objects, and artifacts associated with divinity and the ancestors; tools, beads, and amulets used or prescribed by a diviner; parts of the forest or mountains where sacrifices may be offered; the authority of the chief, which is thought to have been divinely bestowed on him; and the chief's official paraphernalia.

HOLIDAYS AND FESTIVALS Days of rest or celebration in traditional Chadian religion revolve around harvests, weddings, funerals, and the end of initiation for boys and girls.

MODE OF DRESS There are no dress codes that distinguish traditionalists in Chad, who emphasize decency in the midst of poverty. Western attire or a large cloth around the waist, sometimes covering the shoulder, is common and acceptable in southern Chad.

DIETARY PRACTICES As in most of Africa, carnivorous animals (especially those that eat human flesh) are not an acceptable part of a traditionalist diet, and the consumption of a totem animal is forbidden. Pregnant women may not eat eggs or caterpillars, which it is thought might abort the fetus. Some Chadian traditionalist societies do not allow woman to eat chicken. Monkey meat, popular in neighboring Central African Republic and Democratic Republic of Congo, is proscribed in Chad, as is the meat from a dog, snake, cat, vulture, fox, and a big lizard called *varan* in French.

RITUALS Chadian traditionalism requires no pilgrimages and no daily or weekly rituals. Rituals are performed for certain occasions, such as weddings, childbirth, and funerals. Sacrifices are offered at the burial of relatives or important community leaders. When someone dies far from home and the body cannot be brought back, the family performs a ritual washing of hands and makes offerings to the ancestors. During harvest and on important family occasions, part of the first produce and drinks are offered to the ancestors. The first day of the Sara new year, which occurs during the first full moon following the harvest, calls for long celebrations. Samples of the first crops and hunting and fishing catches are offered to the ancestors and consumed by the community in thanksgiving. Drinks are poured on the ground as libation.

RITES OF PASSAGE Initiation ceremonies that mark the transition from childhood to adulthood constitute the most important rites of passage among Chadian traditionalists. During *yondo* the Sara perform male circumcision and female clitoridectomy (often infibulation) and teach a new language to the initiates. *Yondo* lasts only a few weeks to avoid disrupting the student's school year.

MEMBERSHIP Traditionalism's continuation relies on the household inculturation of children, who grow up in an environment where life and religion are one and who learn from observation, listening, participation, and example. Because it does not engage in proselytizing, Chadian traditional religion has lost many of its followers to Christianity and Islam.

SOCIAL JUSTICE Traditionally southern societies in Chad were communal: people shared their agricultural produce with the poor, and the chief exacted contributions from the community to care for the underprivileged, sick, and disabled. Among the Sara successful farmers (*bra-kos,* or masters of the hoe) were expected to help the poor and the young men seeking to fulfill their bride wealth obligations before marriage. During the colonial period war veterans (*anciens combattants*) held "parties," inviting everyone and feeding the poor for a day. Because people were taught to respect others (or face the ire of the ancestors), abuses of human rights were never an issue. Education focused on how to be a useful member of the community and how to survive in an environment that one could not control. Even though these traditions continue today, the Western education system, in which individualism supersedes the needs of the community, prevails.

SOCIAL ASPECTS Among Chadian traditionalists marriage is obligatory and is an alliance between two clans or families, creating large extended families. Men may marry more than one wife, and each wife is expected to bear at least seven children. Women who cannot bear children are blamed and believed to be infertile because the ancestors are punishing them. Infertility and sterility are causes for divorce. Chiefs are expected to marry many wives. During the 1930s and 1940s, Chief Beso of Sarh had 40 wives, Chief Belangar of Koumra had 100, and Chief Tatala of Moissala had 150. These obligations are sanctioned by the ancestors. The ancestors punish women's adultery by seeing that the mixture of different types of semen in the woman's womb kills the fetus.

POLITICAL IMPACT As a religious group traditionalists have had no political impact in Chad, neither seeking office nor fighting to force their religious beliefs on others. Political leaders recruit them as party members and then pay little attention to them, because they tend to be uneducated in the Western sense and cannot articulate their views on the problems facing the country. In 1973 Christian President Tombalbaye accused General Félix Malloum of trying to overthrow the government through sorcery. Malloum reportedly used the ritual of burying a sheep alive (the incident was called he Black Sheep Plot); he was tried and jailed.

CONTROVERSIAL ISSUES Virtually all Chadian traditionalists hold the same position on what the West consider to be controversial issues: They teach against divorce (unless absolutely necessary), indiscriminate abortion (they do have natural ways of inducing one), family planning to reduce fertility, and birth control devices. Like virtually every society in Chad, traditionalism is patrilineal and has prescribed roles for women, who are expected to bear children; cook; please their husband at all costs; till, plant, and harvest; and stay out of politics. Among the Sara, for example, the chief's council of elders has never had a woman member. Westernization has not changed traditionalists dramatically.

CULTURAL IMPACT Culturally traditionalism has had a great impact in Chad, especially in the countryside, where religion and cultural manifestations are inseparable. In dancing, singing with xylophone accompaniment, worshiping, creativity in architectural design and sculpture, and the interpretation of events through unnatural causes, traditional religion has left a resilient imprint and continues to influence even generations of Christians and Muslims. African traditionalists' emphasis on the family, the community, and respect for life is, as one expert put it, "part of the religious and moral patrimony for humankind."

CHRISTIANITY

DATE OF ORIGIN 1920 C.E.

NUMBER OF FOLLOWERS 2.6 million

HISTORY The French colonial administration discouraged missionary work until the 1920s, when it allowed Christians into southern Chad, which they called *le Tchad utile* (useful Chad) because it had more promising economic resources. Baptists and Evangelicals came in 1920, and the Catholics arrived in 1925. The north remained barred to missionaries.

During the preindependence period, all southern Chadian political parties had Christian overtones, such as Baptist-educated François Tombalbaye's *Parti Progressiste Tchadien* (founded in 1947), though Muslims and traditionalists were invited to join. In 1960 Chadians elected Tombalbaye (1918–75), a Sara and a southerner, their first president. In the early 1970s Tombalbaye, increasingly anti-Western, sought to gain more acceptance within his own major constituency, who were beginning to criticize his regime. He promoted a return to some traditional African religious practices. The backlash from Christians and missionaries and the stiff measures Tombalbaye took against them (including imprisonment, expulsion of foreign missionaries, and death) is said to have contributed to his violent overthrow and assassination in 1975. The Church's opposition to polygamy also brought the wrath of the government and traditional authorities. Since the Muslim north ascended to power in the 1979, Christian influence has diminished considerably in the country and Christians have been marginalized.

Almost 2.6 million Chadians claim to be Christian (2 million Catholics), but the accuracy of this figure is debatable. Some say Chadian Catholics number no more than 750,000.

EARLY AND MODERN LEADERS Monseignor Paul Dalmais, archbishop of N'Djamena, was vocal within the Catholic Church in the 1970s, criticizing former French policies in Chad and the civil war in the country. He retired in 1981. The Most Reverend Charles Vandome (born in 1928), archbishop of N'Djamena since 1981 and head of the Episcopal Conference of Chad, has been the most influential Catholic leader since. A Jesuit, Vandome is a linguist who has authored many books on the Ngambaye language of Chad. The Entente des Églises et Missions Évangeliques au Chad (Association of Evangelical Churches and Missions of Chad), which represents some five Protestant denominations and organizations, has a more diffuse leadership.

MAJOR THEOLOGIANS AND AUTHORS The Catholic and Protestant Churches in Chad have produced no known religious thinkers or writers since their inception.

HOUSES OF WORSHIP AND HOLY PLACES Catholic and Protestant services take place in churches. Chad's best known church is the N'Djamena Catholic Cathedral, which survived the war, though it was damaged. The other denominations have smaller, lesser known churches, mostly in southern Chad. Cemeteries also command respect.

WHAT IS SACRED? Chadian Christians consider their churches and the Bible sacred. Medals of saints worn around the neck and the rosary were once common but are no longer popular. Christian behavior and practices in Chad have become increasingly secular.

HOLIDAYS AND FESTIVALS Chadian Christians celebrate Christmas, Easter, the Immaculate Conception, and All Saints' Day. Because of the predominance of Islam and the Church's diminished influence, Sundays are less sacred: Even in the conservative countryside, Christians work on Sundays when they wish.

MODE OF DRESS Chadian Christians once dressed their best on Sundays and holidays; men wore suits in the sweltering heat of the Sahel. Increased poverty and gradual secularization have resulted in decency being the only concern, though many go to church in ragged attire. Children and women dress as formally as possible for First Communions and weddings.

DIETARY PRACTICES Like traditionalists in Chad, Christians do not eat totem animals, and certain foods (such as eggs) are proscribed for pregnant women. Chadian Catholics barely observe fasting and abstinence during Lent anymore. The Protestant Churches attempted to introduce a strict code for drinking (as well as other practices, such as drum dancing), but they lost their battle during the backlash against them in the 1970s.

RITUALS Sundays and the few Christian holy days require church attendance and prayer of Chadian Christians. Weddings and funerals attract more people, because of both their social meaning and the food and beverages served. On these occasions people publicly exhibit their social status and wealth. Processions take place occasionally, as on Palm Sunday. Christians often participate in traditional animal sacrifices held to predict the future.

RITES OF PASSAGE Chadian Christians celebrate baptism, confirmation, weddings, and funerals as rites of passage. By the 1970s Christian missionaries had succeeded in abolishing the traditional initiation ceremonies that require circumcision—the *yondo*. In 1973 President Tombalbaye restored them and attempted to force them on all southern Chadians—young and old, Christian, Muslim, and traditionalist—causing a rupture within the Church, especially with the Baptists. Christians and their missionaries reacted with harsh criticism and were finally exempted from undergoing the aspects most offensive to them, such as clitoridectomy and religious activities related to ancestors.

MEMBERSHIP A three-year period of proof of conversion was once required to become a Christian in Chad, but because of the competition with Islam for converts, membership is now open. As a result of this change, many Chadian Christians do not know the most essential dogmas of their faith, and Catholics are often unable to name the pope. The most common means of recruitment is word of mouth, as in the old days.

SOCIAL JUSTICE The Church in Chad has not been particularly vocal against injustice, but its teachings continue to emphasize the basic virtues of love and care for others. Partly because they feel they are victimized by the country's Muslim-dominated government, Christians are among the few champions of human rights in Chad. Most of the leaders of Amnesty International and the League of Human Rights in Chad are Christian.

The Church continues to run schools wherever a mission exists, mostly at the elementary level (especially in remote areas), and to sponsor several health centers that provide free treatment to destitute Chadians.

SOCIAL ASPECTS Chadian Christian households maintain the traditional extended family structure. Marriage is still obligatory for young men and women as a means of preserving and perpetuating the clan and pleasing the ancestors. Family planning consists of spacing the birth of children rather than decreasing their number. Polygyny is not sanctioned, and many Christian male Chadians keep mistresses.

POLITICAL IMPACT Christian religious groups have never had a visible political impact in Chad, except when political parties were formed in the south during the 1940s and somewhat during Tombalbaye's presidency. The presence of active Islam, the French disregard for Christianity as a mobilizing force, the clashes and competition between Catholics and Protestants, and the insensitive behavior of certain Christian denominations during the clashes over *yondo* in the 1970s have rendered Christianity almost irrelevant in the country's political life today.

CONTROVERSIAL ISSUES Little family planning on the Western model exists in Chad, and Christians maintain large families. Though largely ignorant of Christian teachings against birth control, divorce, and abortion, most Christians conform to them anyway because of the unaffordability of birth control, the need for more hands in the fields, the inability to return bride wealth in divorce, and the high infant mortality rates.

CULTURAL IMPACT Christianity's cultural impact in Chad is notable in church architecture, religious rituals, songs, performances, and the use of the vernacular in the teachings of the Gospel and in Bible translations. After the Second Vatican Council (1962–65) Catholics made a major effort to adapt Christianity to African cultural traditions. Protestants have been more conservative in this respect, though they have ordained more African ministers than has the Catholic Church. Celibacy has been a major obstacle to the recruitment of Africans into the priesthood because of the African belief in family life and procreation as gifts from God.

Other Religions

During the 1970s and 1980s the Jehovah's Witnesses and some adherents of the Bahai faith, which preaches universal human brotherhood and peace in Christ, entered Chad to proselytize. Their numbers and impact have not been significant.

Mario J. Azevedo

See Also Vol. 1: *African Indigenous Beliefs, Christianity, Islam*

Bibliography

Azevedo, Mario. *Roots of Violence: A History of War in Chad.* Amsterdam, OPA: Gordon and Breach Publishers, 1998.

Azevedo, Mario, and Emmanuel Nnadozie. *Chad: A Nation in Search of its Future.* Boulder, Colo.: Westview Press, 1998.

Buijtenhuijs, Robert. *Le Frolinat et les guerres civiles au Tchad (1977–1984).* Paris: Karthala, 1987.

Collelo, Thomas, ed. *Chad: A Country Study.* Washington, D.C.: U.S. Government Printing Office, 1998.

Cordell, Dennis. *Dar al-Kuti and the Last Years of the Trans-Saharan Slave Trade.* Madison: University of Wisconsin Press, 1985.

Decalo, Samuel. *Historical Dictionary of Chad.* Lanham, Md.: Scarecrow Press, 1997.

Isichei, Elizabeth. *A History of Christianity in Africa.* Lawrenceville, N.J.: Africa World Press, 1995.

Jaulin, Robert. *La mort sara.* Paris: Plon, 1967.

Lanne, Bernard. *Histoire politique du Tchad de 1945 à 1958.* Paris: Karthala, 1998.

Mbiti, John S. *African Religions and Philosophy.* London: Heinemann, 1969.

———. *Introduction to African Religion.* London: Heinemann, 1975.

Ray, Benjamin. *African Religions.* Upper Saddle River, N.J.: Prentice-Hall, 2000.

Reyna, Steve P. *Wars without End: The Political Economy of a Precolonial African State.* Hanover: University Press of New England, 1990.

Voll, John Obert. *Islam: Continuity and Change in the Modern World.* Boulder, Colo.: Westview Press, 1982.

Chile

POPULATION 15,402,000

ROMAN CATHOLIC 77 percent

EVANGELICAL PROTESTANT 12 percent

OTHER PROTESTANT 1 percent

ATHEIST/NONRELIGIOUS 6 percent

OTHER 4 percent

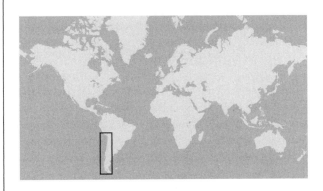

Country Overview

INTRODUCTION Chile, on the western coast of South America, is long (2,880 miles from north to south) and narrow (only 265 miles wide at its widest point). It is bordered on the west by the Pacific Ocean and on the east by the Andes Mountains. Geographically inaccessible and lacking the gold and silver reserves of colonial settlements to the north, Chile began its modern history as one of Spain's most neglected colonial outposts.

The region never possessed a large indigenous population, as did Mexico or the Northern Andean territo-

ry. Demographically, therefore, Chile is the most ethnically homogeneous country in Latin America, comprised mostly of Spanish immigrants, with some Germans and Croats, who brought their Catholic faith. While some mixing with the indigenous Mapuche population did occur, the ethnic flavor of Chile remained largely European. For these reasons, religious evangelization had not been a strong priority for the Catholic Church until the latter half of the twentieth century.

The rapid growth of evangelical Protestantism began in the 1930s and resulted in large part from the pastoral neglect of the Catholic clergy. It is estimated that there are as many practicing Evangelicals as practicing Catholics in the country, though most Chileans still declare allegiance to Catholicism. The challenge of Protestantism forced the Catholic Church to increase its efforts to re-evangelize the population and has resulted in a spiritual renaissance in the nation.

RELIGIOUS TOLERANCE In an effort to spur trade with northern Europe and the United States in the nineteenth century, Chile was one of the first Latin American countries to tolerate the religious activities of non-Catholics. Official church-state separation came in 1925, officially allowing Protestants greater religious freedom and the right to proselytize. Chile's democratic stability prior to the 1973 military coup allowed for civic tolerance between religions to develop, although the Catholic Church was given preferential legal and financial status. Catholic opposition to the military dictatorship of Augusto Pinochet (1973–90) prompted the government to crack down on progressive Catholic organizations. When democracy returned in the 1990s,

People light candles in honor of Teresa de los Andes, Chile's first saint. Local communities traditionally organize small celebrations around their patron saint. © PABLO CORRAL VEGA/CORBIS.

evangelical Protestants attained legal standing similar to that of the Catholic Church, allowing them equal access to chaplaincies in prisons, state hospitals, and the military.

Major Religion

ROMAN CATHOLICISM

DATE OF ORIGIN 1541 C.E.
NUMBER OF FOLLOWERS 11,860,000

HISTORY Catholicism arrived with the Spanish colonists in the early 1500s. Given that the indigenous population was relatively sparse and nomadic, evangelization was not a high priority for the Catholic clergy. Throughout the colonial period, financial support for the Catholic Church was granted to the Spanish crown through a legal agreement known as the *patronato.* In exchange for royal funding the crown was granted the right to appoint bishops and approve of all papal bulls that would influence the colonial church.

Following independence in 1818 the church and state wrestled over control of episcopal appointments. A simmering feud between the church and a variety of governments lasted for most of the nineteenth century. In the 1850s a dispute over the expulsion of two church canons resulted in legislation reducing some of the legal prerogatives of the Catholic Church and allowing for religious toleration of non-Catholics. Church and state were finally officially separated by the 1925 constitution. During the 1880s the church lost exclusive control over marriage and funeral services, though religious ceremonies were still performed concomitant with civil ones. Compared with other Latin American countries (e.g., Mexico), the separation of church and state was mutually amicable, and the church retained state funding and substantial control over the public education curriculum.

Given that the disestablished church retained a favorable social position among the political and economic elite, Catholic clergy generally behaved in a more conservative manner during the first half of the twentieth century. As Protestant groups began to win a substantial number of converts among the lower classes, however, the Catholic Church began paying more attention to the poor and engaging in more progressive pastoral activities, including organizing labor unions and cooperatives. Spurred on by the reforms of the Second Vatican Council of the 1960s as well as their increased activity among the poor, members of the Catholic clergy adopted a confrontational stance against the Pinochet military dictatorship (1973–90) and earned a reputation as one of the most politically progressive churches in Latin America at the time. The return of democracy in 1990 saw the Catholic Church devoting more time to pastoral activities than to political action.

EARLY AND MODERN LEADERS The relatively low-key nature of the Catholic Church throughout Chile's history has meant that it has not produced many noteworthy leaders. Rafael Valdivieso served as the first archbishop of Santiago during the mid-nineteenth century and fought for the interests of the Church during a time when various administrations expropriated the property of the church and reduced its prerogatives. Valdivieso is credited with founding *La Revista Católica* (Catholic Magazine), one of the primary publications promoting Catholicism in Chile to this day.

In the twentieth century Raúl Silva Henríquez became one of Latin America's most outspoken advocates of human rights from the 1960s through the 1980s. Appointed as archbishop of Santiago in 1960, Silva became a strong advocate for the reforms promoted by the Second Vatican Council. His leadership in the Latin American Bishop's Conference (CELAM) during the mid-1960s pushed many regional Catholic leaders to adopt a "preferential option for the poor." Shortly following the 1973 military coup, Cardinal Silva organized the ecumenical Committee of Peace, which sought to defend victims of the military coup. This organization was shut down by the military, but Silva responded by creating the Vicariate of Solidarity, which served as the principal human rights watchdog throughout the dictatorship. Cardinal Silva resigned his post in 1983, citing philosophical differences with Pope John Paul II.

MAJOR THEOLOGIANS AND AUTHORS Chile was home to one of the earliest and most influential thinkers of the progressive Catholic Church in Latin America—Padre Alberto Hurtado (1901–52). Born of a humble family, Hurtado was ordained as a Jesuit in 1933. Although serving as a university professor, Hurtado became known as an organizer of Catholic labor unions and for his pastoral work among the poor. In 1941 he penned a landmark book entitled *Is Chile a Catholic Country?* wherein he argued that the Chilean Church had taken the allegiance of the poor for granted. Hurtado's advocacy of the lower classes became the basis for progressive Catholicism and the Christian base community movement arising in the 1960s. For his tireless efforts on behalf of the poor, Hurtado was the first Chilean citizen beatified by the Vatican. His name is associated with the country's largest private charity, the Hogar de Cristo, first created by Hurtado in the 1940s as a homeless shelter.

HOUSES OF WORSHIP AND HOLY PLACES Cities and towns throughout Chile maintain a central church in the town square, as is common throughout Spanish America. Given that Spain did not invest much in this colonial region, most churches are humble structures, especially compared with the more ornate churches of Mexico and the Andes. In Santiago, the nation's capital, a statue of the Virgin Mary and a small chapel stand on top of Cerro San Cristobal, a small hill north of downtown. This site often serves as a central gathering place for religious pilgrims. The Santuario de la Tirana in northern Chile also serves as a pilgrimage site for the thousands of visitors who celebrate the Festival de la Tirana each July. The Templo Votivo de Maipu, built to honor the patron saint of Chile, the Virgen of Carmen, also draws Catholic pilgrims to its location in a southwest suburb of Santiago.

WHAT IS SACRED? Like other Latin American Catholic nations, many in the population consider the Virgin Mary to be a focus of their religious faith. It is common for individuals to set up personal shrines to the Virgin in their homes and along roadsides. This tradition likely emanated from the lack of clergy and, hence, religious services, thereby forcing individuals to create their own rituals.

HOLIDAYS AND FESTIVALS Religious festivals in Chile are largely decentralized. Local communities traditionally organize small celebrations around their patron saint. The Festival of La Tirana (mid-July) is the largest religious holiday unique to Chile and annually draws tens of thousands of pilgrims to the northern town of Iquique. Several days of feasting and dancing are followed by a trek to the site of the Virgen del Carmen. This festival is also celebrated in Santiago, though on a less grand scale. Chileans, particularly in rural areas, also celebrate the Domingo de Cuasimodo on the first Sunday following Easter with street processions. During this festival, priests are known to offer Communion to the sick and elderly who cannot regularly attend Mass.

MODE OF DRESS The Catholic Church has little influence on Chileans' mode of dress, which is similar to that in most Western Christian nations. During certain religious festivals, notably the Festival de la Tirana and Domingo de Cuasimodo, dancers and other participants will dress in traditional costumes and masks that reflect a syncretism of the indigenous Mapuche dress and colonial fashion.

DIETARY PRACTICES There are no distinctive dietary practices associated with Catholicism in Chile.

RITUALS Catholic rituals in Chile are similar to those of Catholics everywhere. While civil marriage is recognized in Chile, most marriages involve a religious ceremony similar to Catholic and Christian weddings in Europe and North America. Engaged couples will typically wear wedding bands on their right ring fingers until they are married, whereupon the ring is switched to their left ring fingers.

RITES OF PASSAGE There are no Catholic rites of passage that are distinctive to Chile.

MEMBERSHIP While more than three-fourths of the population affiliates itself with the Catholic Church, regular participation in the Mass is much lower. The 1995 World Values Survey estimated that only 21 percent of Chilean Catholics attended Mass weekly. Given that questions of religious attendance tend to elicit an upward bias, this figure should be considered a maximum. Most Chileans who affiliate themselves with the Catholic Church are baptized into the faith.

SOCIAL JUSTICE For most of its history the Chilean Catholic Church's principal connection to issues of social justice was to engage in traditional acts of charity. Under the inspiration of Padre Alberto Hurtado in the first half of the twentieth century, members of the clergy began to organize workers and students into worker's circles (labor unions) and Catholic Action groups. These groups sought to improve the lives of la-

borers and the poor. During the dictatorship of Augusto Pinochet (1973–90), the Catholic episcopacy organized the ecumenical Committee for Peace as an advocacy group for human rights. When this organization was shut down by the military, the church organized the Vicariate of Solidarity to monitor human rights abuses and lobby for the rights of the poor.

Following the end of the dictatorship, a more conservative Catholic hierarchy has stepped back from its previously strong advocacy of social justice and has focused attention on issues such as divorce and the legal status of the church. Nonetheless, the church does continue to fund charitable organizations such as the Hogar de Cristo and a variety of think tanks (e.g., Centro Bellarmino), which write extensively about social issues.

SOCIAL ASPECTS Catholicism is deeply embedded in Chilean culture. Laws making divorce and abortion difficult are heavily influenced by the Catholic culture, as well as by the lobbying efforts of the church. Crucifixes are commonplace in government offices and private homes. Priests and nuns are accorded high respect and are often included in most public ceremonies. Religious weddings are more common than civil marriages, and most parents have their children baptized shortly after birth. The strong social and political influence of the Catholic Church has made divorce legally difficult in Chile, though there has been some movement toward liberalizing these laws, in spite of opposition by church officials. The country has one of the lowest divorce rates in the Western Hemisphere. Increasing prosperity and urbanization, however, have led to one of the lowest birth rates in the region.

POLITICAL IMPACT The Catholic Church has played a low-key role in politics throughout most of its existence, becoming active only from the 1960s through the 1980s. Indirectly, however, efforts by the Catholic Church to organize students through Catholic Action groups led to the birth of the Christian Democratic Party in the late 1940s. Influenced by the social encyclicals of Pope Leo XIII and Pope Pius IX (and later the Second Vatican Council), this party became a major force of the center-left during the 1960s, when they held the presidency under Eduardo Frei (1964–70). It emerged as the dominant political party in a broad coalition of leftist and center-left organizations that held the presidency following the return to democracy in the 1990s.

The Catholic episcopacy played a direct role in criticizing the Pinochet dictatorship, and several bishops played a role in negotiating for a return to democracy between the military and civilian groups in the late 1980s. Since then the political role of the Catholic Church has become much more reserved. Chile's legal structure is still influenced, in part, by Catholic canon law.

CONTROVERSIAL ISSUES Though culturally similar to most Catholic European nations, Chile maintains a strict set of laws making divorce difficult to obtain. Couples wishing to separate legally must obtain an annulment of their marriage predicated on legal irregularities during the civil ceremony. This often requires false testimony. Several attempts over the past decade to enact a more liberal divorce statute have failed because of the powerful opposition of the Catholic prelate and the structure of the Chilean national legislature, which disproportionately favors the more conservative sectors of society.

CULTURAL IMPACT The Catholic Church has had minimal cultural impact on the arts community. While authors such as Pablo Neruda and Isabel Allende have drawn upon religious themes in their work, secular influences are more likely to predominate. Though Catholicism remains an important part of Chilean life, contemporary culture is more secular than religious.

Other Religions

Throughout its colonial existence Chile remained exclusively Catholic. Following independence in 1826, the need to establish trade with northern Europe and the United States pushed the country to accept the presence of Protestantism. Protestantism, however, remained largely a foreign phenomenon, relegated to the private practice of visiting merchants and dignitaries. Some Protestant missionizing began in the late 1800s and early 1900s but was largely unsuccessful because it targeted the upper classes, which were solidly Catholic. The lack of a large indigenous population also inhibited Protestant growth.

Protestant growth expanded rapidly after 1910. A split occurred within the Chilean Methodist Church when a group of native Chileans sought to emphasize a more emotional form of worship that would appeal to the lower classes. This group founded the National Methodist Church, which split again two decades later into competing Pentecostal camps. Once the Pentecostal split occurred in the 1930s, evangelical Protestantism spread rapidly among the ordinary people. The previous emphasis on hierarchy in the Methodist Church was replaced by a preference for autonomous, and rapidly expanding, Pentecostal ministries.

By the late 1990s roughly 12 percent of the population was Protestant, with about 90–95 percent of those representing some variety of Pentecostalism. The Church of Jesus Christ of Latter-day Saints has also made advances in recent years. The growth of evangelical Protestantism can be attributed largely to the lack of Catholic priests in poorer neighborhoods, especially during the middle of the twentieth century. An environment of religious freedom and tolerance, as well as a general separation of church and state, has also facilitated the expansion of Pentecostals. When the Catholic Church became critical of the military government of Augusto Pinochet, the dictator reached out to a small segment of Pentecostal and Evangelical ministers known as the *Consejo de Pastores* (Council of Pastors). This group provided the annual blessing (Te Deum) of the government and was rewarded with financial support, including the construction of a large church just outside downtown Santiago. Despite the connection between the military and this group of Pentecostal leaders, most Pentecostal ministers remained politically neutral, and some mainline Protestants, including the liberal World Council of Churches, even joined the Catholic Church to lobby for human rights and a return to democracy. Two ecumenical organizations, the National Committee to Aid Refugees and the Committee of Cooperation for Peace, were created in 1973 to monitor the human rights abuses of the military, but they were quickly shut down by the dictatorship.

The return of democracy to Chile in 1990 proved beneficial to the evangelical Protestant population. Their relatively large size, estimated to equal the number of practicing Catholics, has led politicians to expand religious freedom in the nation. The growing influence of Evangelicals is borne out by their ability to elect several Evangelical politicians to local and national offices and to lobby successfully for the passage of a law giving non-Catholic religious groups the same legal status as the Catholic Church. This law, passed in 1997, provides equal access for Protestants into prisons, hospitals, and the military.

Today there are approximately 250 different religious denominations in Chile, most of which are Christian. The largest include the Pentecostal Methodist Church (about 720,000 members in 1995), the Evangelical Pentecostal Church (570,000), and the Pentecostal Church of Chile (400,000). The Church of Jesus Christ of Latter-day Saints and Jehovah's Witnesses also claim significant membership—266,000 and 107,000, respectively. Membership in small, independent charismatic churches is estimated to be roughly half a million members. All these denominations can be found throughout the country, though they are mostly in the major cities of Santiago, Valparaiso, and Concepción, where the majority of the Chilean population is concentrated. While Evangelical and Pentecostal churches have succeeded most among the lower socioeconomic sectors of society in the past, they have made significant inroads among the middle classes.

Non-Christian religions make up only a fraction of Chile's population and have not had a significant cultural or political impact.

Anthony Gill

See Also Vol. I: *Christianity, Methodism, Pentecostalism, Roman Catholicism*

Bibliography

Gill, Anthony. *Rendering unto Caesar: The Catholic Church and the State in Latin America.* Chicago: University of Chicago Press, 1998.

Mecham, J. Lloyd. *Church and State in Latin America: A History of Politico-Ecclesiastical Relations.* Chapel Hill: University of North Carolina Press, 1996.

Poblete, Renato. *Crisis Sacerdotal.* Santiago: Editorial de Pacífico, 1965.

Smith, Brian. *The Church and Politics in Chile: Challenges to Modern Catholicism.* Princeton, N.J.: Princeton University Press, 1982.

Willems, Emilio. *Followers of the New Faith: Cultural Change and the Rise of Protestantism in Brazil and Chile.* Nashville: Vanderbilt University Press, 1967.

China

POPULATION 1,284,303,705

CHINESE POPULAR RELIGIONIST
29.2 percent

BUDDHIST 8 percent

ATHEIST 8.1 percent

CHRISTIAN 6.5 percent

TRIBAL RELIGIONIST 4.3 percent

MUSLIM 1.7 percent

NONRELIGIONIST 42.1 percent

OTHER less than 0.1 percent

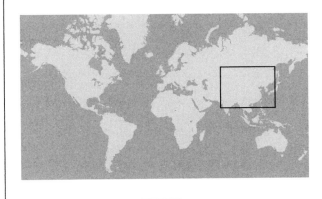

Country Overview

INTRODUCTION China is the world's most populous country and the fourth largest in area. About four-fifths of its population are peasants; one-fifth works in industry and trade in urban centers. The Han Chinese are the dominant ethnic group (92 percent), but there are more than 50 ethnic minorities (over 100 million people) in China, most of whom live in regions bordering other countries.

The country's largest faith is Chinese popular religion, a syncretic belief system that originated in the second millennium B.C.E. and that later borrowed elements of both religious (not philosophical) Taoism (Daoism) and Confucianism. Taoism, a Chinese religion founded in the second century C.E., incorporated Buddhist deities into its pantheon, and many Taoist gods and ritual practices were then amalgamated into popular religion. Today Taoism and Chinese popular religion overlap symbiotically. Taoist priests (and sometimes Buddhist monks and nuns or even Confucian ritual specialists) are hired to perform popular religious rituals.

Confucianism originated in China during the late sixth and early fifth centuries B.C.E. with the "Sage Master" philosopher Confucius. Although only a small percentage of Chinese still practice it exclusively as an ethical and ritual system, Confucianism remains a strong cultural force, and many of its beliefs and practices are widely recognized by followers of Chinese popular religion.

Buddhism was introduced into China in the first century C.E. by immigrants from Persia, Central Asia, and India; by the eighth century it was fully domesticated. In the mid-seventh century Christianity arrived from Syria. Muslim traders brought Islam from the Middle East and Central Asia to China in the late seventh century. In the mid-ninth century a Taoist Tang emperor heavily persecuted foreign religions. Buddhism went underground, and Christianity died out; indigenous Islamic converts were too few to warrant imperial attention. At the end of the thirteenth century Catholicism ap-

By dressing as angels and holding candles, these young Chinese girls participate in Christmas Midnight Mass at the Nantang Cathedral in Beijing, China. © AFP/CORBIS.

peared in China. At about the same time, a significant number of indigenous people began to be converted to Islam. Western Protestant missionaries were active in China from the beginning of the nineteenth century until the Communist People's Republic of China (PRC) expelled them in 1952.

Since the death of Mao Tse-tung, China's leader from 1949 to 1976, Christianity has been the country's fastest-growing religion. Strong revivals have occurred in the port cities along the eastern seaboard, as well as in cities and towns dotting the interior provinces. A parallel, nationwide resurgence of Pure Land Buddhism has also taken place. Meditative Chan (Zen in Japanese) Buddhism is practiced by Buddhist monks in monasteries as well as by philosophically minded lay intellectuals.

RELIGIOUS TOLERANCE The 1954 constitution of the PRC and each constitution promulgated thereafter all guarantee freedom of religion. Technically, however, the government recognizes and sanctions only five faiths—Buddhism, Taoism (Taoism stands for religious Taoism in this essay), Islam, Catholicism, and Protestantism—and religious activities are limited to state-approved fa-

cilities. Popular religion and related heterodox cults do not receive constitutional protection, but popular religionists enjoy a high degree of freedom, partly because their religious practices are based in Taoism and Buddhism and appear legal and partly because popular religionists form such a large group. Their base of more than 360 million adherents makes the government leery of losing their support.

The degree of religious tolerance since 1949 has fluctuated according to the intensity of radicalism in Chinese Communist Party (CCP) politics. During Mao's Cultural Revolution (1966–76), all religions were harshly suppressed, and religious activities went underground. Nearly all churches and temples were closed or appropriated for secular uses. In the post-Mao era religious tolerance has greatly increased, though it does not yet conform to international standards.

In 1999 the government passed an anticult (*fan xie-jiao*) law as part of a crackdown on Falungong, a popular group that promotes *qigong* (breath cultivation) combined with Buddhist-style meditation and that has a far larger membership than any other social organization or dissident movement in China. Since 2001 the government has expanded the crackdown to include certain unregistered Christian "house churches," involving millions of Protestants whose gatherings are technically illegal.

Major Religions

CHINESE POPULAR RELIGION

BUDDHISM

CHRISTIANITY

CHINESE POPULAR RELIGION

DATE OF ORIGIN c. second millennium B.C.E.
NUMBER OF FOLLOWERS 366 million

HISTORY Chinese popular, or folk, religion probably originated during the Shang period (c.1766–1122 B.C.E.). Throughout its existence it has been in flux, formed through a gradual process of incorporating newer, harmonious ideas into its ancient pristine traditions over three thousand years. During premodern times these ideas were essentially taken from Confucian ethics, Taoism, and folk Buddhism, but the religion's absorption of different forms of belief and practice is ongoing even into the contemporary period. Popular religion is followed by people of all social groups, especially in the observance of major festivals. Since the 1980s, as a legacy of the Cultural Revolution, Chairman Mao has emerged as a cult figure, his image used not only as an emblem of protection in vehicles but also as an object of worship in certain shrines established by local peasants in northern China. After their harsh repression by Mao, popular religious activities have resurfaced into public life and are booming. Devotion to local deities thrives, and the sale of objects for ritual use—incense sticks, paper money, and elaborate, miniature imitations of consumer commodities (such as furniture, for ancestors to use in the next world)—is big business. Mediums are common in rural areas and suburban centers.

At the national level Chinese popular religion is a diffused system, but it is highly organized in local communities. Because it performs the vital social function of promoting community identity and solidarity, popular religion has also been called "local communal religion." Adherents believe the universe is divided into three spheres—Heaven, Earth, and the Underworld—all governed by a supreme ruler, the Jade Emperor (Yuhuang Dadi). The counterpart of the earthly emperor, he presides in Heaven over a bureaucracy staffed by all sorts of god-officials (*shi*) and gods (*shen*). Among these are the King of the Underworld (Yanluowang) and a host of other functionaries stationed on earth, including the city god (*Chenghuang*), comparable to a human magistrate, and the local earth god (*Tudi Gong*), like a local constable. The kitchen god (Zao Jun), whose picture hangs above a peasant family's kitchen stove, is the resident agent of the Jade Emperor, watching over the daily conduct of the family members.

Under the officials are the common ghosts (*gui*)—the souls of the dead, who are confined in the Underworld. Souls of cultural heroes (for example, the mythic Yellow Emperor and Confucius) may have had their status changed from ghosts to gods (or saints) after their deification (mostly by the imperial government). Ancestors (*zu*) are those lucky ghosts whose living descendants sustain them through sacrifices. Ghosts who died without offspring are like the homeless and beggars in human society, and they are prone to make trouble for their relatives and fellow villagers; they may be propitiated, however, by community offerings at an annual festival. Notable female deities, including the Old Mother

(Laomu, counterpart of the Buddhist goddess of mercy, Guanyi), are worshiped nationally; and Mazu (Heavenly Empress), the deified spirit of a virtuous unmarried woman, is worshiped widely in the southeastern provinces.

A bewildering array of popular religious groups, commonly called "secret societies," are characterized by secret hierarchical organizational structures and are empowered by occult folk Buddhist and religious Taoist beliefs. In Chinese history these groups adopted different names, such as "society" (*hui*), "brotherhood" (*men*), "way" (*tao,* or *dao*), and "sect" (*jiao*). Major examples include the Triad (Sanhe Hui), the Universal Salvation Society (Puji Hui; named after its founder, Pu Ji), the Hong Brotherhood (Hong Men), the Unity Way (Yiguan Dao), the Nine Functions Way (Jiugong Dao), and the White Lotus Sect (Bailian Jiao).

Often linked with millenarianism (the belief in a coming messianic kingdom), secret societies may trace their origins to as far back as the third century B.C.E. Some groups became politically subversive, playing major roles in popular revolts (for example, the White Lotus Rebellion at the turn of the nineteenth century) against imperial governments. The Red Spear Society (Hongqiang Hui) sprang up in the 1930s in northern China; these were local groups formed during the Japanese occupation to defend villages against roaming bandits. In 1953 the Communist government launched a massive suppression campaign against *Hui-Dao-Men* ("Societies-Ways-Brotherhoods"), all but eradicating them from the Chinese mainland. Some of their offshoots have reappeared, reintroduced by Chinese adherents who live overseas.

EARLY AND MODERN LEADERS Only secret societies that gave birth to political movements have produced national leaders. Liu Song and Zhu Hongdeng (Zhu Fengming) were pioneers of a popular movement that led to the 1796–1804 White Lotus Rebellion. Chang Loxing led the Nien (an offshoot of the White Lotus Sect) Rebellion (c. 1853–68) against the Manchu (Qing) regime. Under a quasi-Christian ideology, Hong Xiuquan (1814–64) led the anti-Qing Taiping Rebellion (1850–64), the longest and most devastating period of civil unrest in Chinese history, nearly toppling the Qing imperial dynasty. Sun Yat-sen (Sun Zhongshan, 1866–1925), a member of the Hong Brotherhood, led the anti-Qing revolution, resulting in its final demise in 1911. Li Hongzhi (born in 1953), a former trumpet player from northeastern China, is the founder of the Falungong movement.

MAJOR THEOLOGIANS AND AUTHORS The deities in popular religion are not supported by any systematic study or documentation.

HOUSES OF WORSHIP AND HOLY PLACES For more than two thousand years the emperor (Son of Heaven) alone could officially offer sacrifices to Heaven at special altars in the imperial capital. The demise of the imperial system in 1911 ended these rituals. Thousands of household shrines and altars remain. Many of China's villages and towns have local temples, more numerous in the south and southeast. Sacred sites venerated by both popular religionists and religious Taoists outside population centers include the five (Taoist) sacred mountain peaks (*wuyue*)—Taishan (*shan* means "mountain" or "peak") in eastern Shandong, Bei Hengshan (*bei* means "north") in northern Shanxi, Nan Hengshan (*nan* means "south") in southern Hunan, Huashan in western Shanxi, and Songshan in central Henan—as well as major Buddhist sacred sites and renowned Taoist temples.

WHAT IS SACRED? Certain individual cults in popular religion are dedicated to sacred natural beings or objects, such as the god of insects, the god of horses, the tree god, the dragon king, and various astral gods (such as the Purple Emperor Star, *ziweixin*).

HOLIDAYS AND FESTIVALS The aspect of popular religion shared by all Chinese is the annual cycle of festivals, which follows the lunar calendar. The Chinese New Year (Xinnian, or Chunjie: Festival of the Spring) is the most important. Family members return home from distant workplaces, and families hold a banquet in honor of the ancestors. Held on the third day of the third lunar month, the Qingming (Pure and Clear) Festival, also known as *Hanshi jie* (Day of Eating Things Cold), is the second most important opportunity to honor ancestors; family members perform the traditional sacrificial rituals of cleaning the graves (*saomu*) and offering food. The PRC government's forcible implementation of cremation has largely eliminated private graveyards and led to a simplification of the rituals. People in southern Anhui now buy Qingming *diaozi* (threefoot-long bamboo sticks with multicolored paper strips tied to the tip) from supply stores and erect them

around family tombstones in public cemeteries. In metropolitan Shanghai families place fresh flowers around gravestones; they burn incense, offer cooked foods and wine, and light cigarettes for the deceased to enjoy.

The Ghost Festival (Guijie), which coincides with the Buddhist Ullambhana (Deliverance) Festival, is held on the fifteenth day of the seventh month. Hell is said to open its gates to release the spirits of the dead. People in suburban Shanghai entertain their ancestors with a lavish dinner and the burning of mock gold and silver ingots. They also place food offerings and burn incense outside the front door for roaming ghosts (those who died without offspring). The Hanyi jie (Sending Off the Winter Cloths), which has been revived in the north around Hebei, is celebrated on the first day of the tenth lunar month (November on the Gregorian calendar). Popular religion adherents offer mock (paper) clothing and abundant food supplies to the ancestors in preparation for winter.

On the twenty-third day of the twelfth month, it is the prescribed duty of the kitchen god to present his annual report to the Jade Emperor on the conduct of each family member. On the evening of his ascent to Heaven, family members offer him candies (*tanggua*: round, sticky candy balls shaped like miniature tomatoes) to sweeten his lips, so that he may say only good things about them.

MODE OF DRESS Lay adherents of popular religion have no dress code. When invited to preside over folk rituals, Buddhist monks wear their robes, and Taoist specialists wear standardized ritual vestments (Taoists are differentiated by the color of their headband; hence the Redhead and Blackhead Taoists). The Red Spear Society requires its practitioners to wear a red apron when they communicate with their patron deities in the sanctuary.

DIETARY PRACTICES Dietary restrictions are required mostly among members of the secret societies. The Nine Functions Way (Jiugong Dao) forbids members to eat meat, garlic, or onions; to drink wine; and to smoke tobacco. The Unity Way (Yiguan Dao) forbids the use of alcohol.

RITUALS The rituals of Chinese popular religion allow humans to interact with the spirit world. Most communal rituals are performed by Taoist priests of the Zhengyi sect (Celestial Masters Taoism). Buddhist ritual traditions are used during requiem services and Confucian rituals for rites involving animal sacrifice. Taoist priests or ritual masters are invited to perform rites in the temples on the birthdays of the local gods. They also preside over one of the most elaborate public rituals performed for a community, the *jiao* ritual of cosmic renewal. A large-scale festival involving scores of villages surrounding the central temple of the local god, the ritual may last for many days. Mass processions, sacrificial offerings, and ritual theatrical performances are staged to entertain the gods. On the third day of the festival, the Taoist priests emerge from the temple to present offerings to the superior gods in Heaven. On a different day they perform the feast for the universal deliverance of hungry ghosts (*pudu,* which means "all-ferried over"), allowing them to go to a better place in the Underworld or in Heaven.

RITES OF PASSAGE Since the Han period (206 B.C.E.–220 C.E.) birth, maturation, marriage, and burial have been regulated by sumptuary (extravagance-prevention) and ritual laws of the Confucian tradition. Today a pregnant woman no longer makes offerings to the spirit (*taishen*) believed to protect the fetus, but rites related to the recovery of the mother's health are maintained: She must rest for one month after delivery, eating special foods rich in protein and vitamins. The old rite of "capping," in which the father gave his son both a new name and a square-cornered cap, thus marking his entrance into mature manhood, was dropped long ago. Weddings are largely devoid of religious content and involve no religious functionaries. In cities businesses known as Liyigongsi (Companies of Rituals and Ceremonials) arrange for the wedding garments, transportation, and the other aspects of the event.

By contrast, the traditional funeral rite has been enhanced. Layers of white tissue paper and talismans are put over the corpse in its coffin. A Taoist priest is usually invited to perform the funeral rites at a funeral parlor. At the graveside the bereaved family ceremonially burns a paper house completely furnished with miniature lamps, stoves, refrigerators, a telephone, and reams of paper money for the bank account of the dead in hell. After the cremation, bone-ash caskets (*guhuixia*) are either stored in the village Spirits' Hall (*lingtang;* in northern China) or buried in a public cemetery (in southern China), to be visited annually during the Qingming festival.

MEMBERSHIP The participation of villagers in local religious activities is voluntary. Secret societies require an elaborate initiation procedure, including an oath of secrecy, and members' conduct is regulated by secret rules, including the ritual use of symbols and gestures as a means of communication. During times of famine or political unrest, these groups drew their members mostly from the lower stratum of the society—the poor and the unemployed.

SOCIAL JUSTICE Chinese popular religion has no systematic teachings regarding such social issues as poverty, education, and human rights. Temple networks connecting local communities in a large area function as informal local governments, collecting contributions from adherents in order to provide social services to the needy.

SOCIAL ASPECTS Chinese popular religion is centered on the family and the local community. Marriage is seen as uniting two families rather than two individuals. Sometimes two families hire a ritual specialist to conduct a spirit marriage (*minhun*)—a wedding ceremony uniting the ghost of the deceased daughter of one family with the ghost of the deceased son of the other. The PRC government's strict enforcement of its law permitting only one child per couple has undermined the value popular religion places on having more children.

POLITICAL IMPACT Throughout Chinese history perennial tensions existed between the imperial government and certain Buddhist-inspired popular secret societies, as these groups have at times inspired popular revolts. The White Lotus Sect led an eight-year mass rebellion (1796–1804) protesting political corruption and economic hardship. The Boxers, a secret religious sect whose members practiced a form of martial arts and staged occult rituals worshiping the gods, started a massive anti-foreign and anti-Christian movement in 1900. Ravaging China's northern provinces for two years, the Boxer Rebellion caused the martyrdom of hundreds of Western missionaries and thousands of Chinese Christians.

CONTROVERSIAL ISSUES In keeping with its syncretic nature, Chinese popular religion stresses compromise and harmony in its beliefs and practices; hardly any issue causes controversy among adherents. In contrast to the divisiveness the cult of Mary has brought about within

Christianity in the West, Chinese popular religion embraces and honors many prominent female deities. There are cults of Mazu and the Niangniang (a group of goddesses who grant children and protect the eyes). Women's ministry is accepted by all: Buddhist nuns may be invited to officiate at ritual events, and spirit mediums are almost exclusively female.

CULTURAL IMPACT Literature inspired by Chinese popular religion includes hagiographies (idealized biographies of saints) and ghost revenge stories. The sixteenth-century classic *Fengshen Yanyi* (The Investiture of the Gods) reflects popular religion's polytheistic ideology. Popular communal festivals and rituals have led to the creation of ritual dances, processions, and theatrical arts as corollaries to communal worship.

BUDDHISM

DATE OF ORIGIN c. 68 C.E.
NUMBER OF FOLLOWERS 107.9 million

HISTORY Immigrants brought Buddhism to China during the first century C.E. in three distinct forms: Southern Buddhism (Theravada), Tibetan Buddhism (Lamaism or Tantric Buddhism), and Han Buddhism. Theravada is practiced only among the Dai, a small ethnic group that inhabits the border region of southern Yunnan. Tibetan Buddhism, which belongs to the Mahayana school, is the religion of the Tibetans and some of China's minority nationals, such as the Mongols in the north and the Manchus in the northeast. Strictly speaking, only Han Buddhism, also of the Mahayana school, may be called "Chinese Buddhism," because it is subscribed to by the Han Chinese, who constitute over 90 percent of China's Buddhist population. Historically the two most popular forms of Chinese Buddhism were the Pure Land Sect (Jintu zong), which flourished mainly in China's rural communities, and Chan Buddhism, which found adherents among the educated in cities and towns. Pure Land Buddhism asserts that people can be saved into the "Western Paradise" through faith in the Amitabha Buddha (O Mi To Fo in Chinese; Bodhisattva of Boundless Light and Life) and repetitious invocation of his name. Chan Buddhists believe that through meditation practice, they may experience inner enlightenment, achieving Buddhahood in this life.

Buddhism became woven into the fiber of Chinese sociopolitical life by the middle of the eighth century.

Its growth and influence was abruptly arrested in the middle of the ninth century by devastating political suppression. Though "folk Buddhism" remained a vital part of rural popular culture, Buddhism as a high ideology forever lost its prestige among China's educated ruling elite. In the era of the Chinese Republic (1912–49), Buddhism experienced a small revival led by certain "monk-politicians," who helped establish the nationwide Chinese Buddhist Association (CBA; Zhongguo Fojiao Xiehui) to carry out reforms within the Buddhist sangha (Buddhist community) and to protect monastic properties from government encroachment.

When the CCP seized power on the mainland in 1949, the CBA's headquarters moved to Taiwan with the Nationalist government. The founding of the PRC fundamentally changed the socioeconomic status of Buddhism in China. The land reform law of 1950 officially deprived the large Buddhist monasteries of their land-owning rights. The state set up a new Chinese Buddhist Association (also abbreviated as CBA) in 1952 as a quasi-religious organization under the supervision of the CCP party apparatus. After 1959 the CCP's forceful application of Marxism-Leninism to all aspects of intellectual life left no room for independent thinking. During the violent years of the Cultural Revolution (1966–76), Buddhist temples were severely damaged, and monks and nuns were forced to return to laity in order to participate in productive labor. The post-Mao government considerably liberalized China's religious policies. Both Tibetan and Han Buddhism flourish in China today. Though various Han sects existed before the founding of the PRC, only the Pure Land sect remains popular, and it has experienced a strong revival throughout China, especially in rural communities. Chan Buddhism is practiced in Chan monasteries and by an undetermined number of intellectuals.

EARLY AND MODERN LEADERS Dao Cho (562–645) and Shan Dao (613–81) founded the Pure Land sect of Chinese Buddhism. Xuan Zhuang (600–64), a pioneering Chinese Buddhist pilgrim-scholar, translated the Buddhist scriptures of the School of Consciousness Only (Weishi) from Sanskrit into Chinese. Master Jian Zhen (Ganjin in Japanese; 688–763), a famous Chinese Buddhist missionary, founded the Japanese monastic Ritsu (Lü in Chinese) School in 753. The Sixth Patriarch Hui Neng (638–713) was an epic figure in Chan Buddhism. It was he who perfected the teaching of Chan.

The two leaders of the revival movement under the Chinese Republic were the progressive Abbot Taixu (Tai-hsü; 1889–1947) and the more conservative Abbot Yuanying (Yuan-ying; 1878–1953). They advocated purging Buddhism of "superstition"—getting rid of the Buddhas and bodhisattvas (Buddhas-to-be: beings who compassionately refrain from entering Nirvana in order to help others), which they considered "illusionary," and eliminating profit-making funerary rites—so that all Buddhists might find the "Western Paradise" in this world by rendering services in their local communities. They also led the founding of the CBA in 1929. During China's War of Resistance against Japan (1937–45), Monk Juzan (Chu-tsan; secular name: Pan Chutong; 1908–84), one of Taixu's prominent disciples, organized the Anti-Japan Association of Chinese Buddhists and founded the patriotic journal *Lion's Roars* (*Shizihou*). In 1950, thanks to his pro-CCP activism, Juzan was appointed editor-in-chief of *Modern Buddhism* (*Xiandai foxue*), a monthly magazine that serves as the mouthpiece of CCP's religious policy.

MAJOR THEOLOGIANS AND AUTHORS The *sida gaoseng* (four eminent monks)—Zhu Hong (1535–1615), Zhen Ke (1542–1603), De Qing (1546–1623), and Zhi Xu (1599–1655)—arose in China in the late sixteenth and early seventeenth centuries. The four advocated creating a synthesized Buddhism from Pure Land Buddhism, Chan Buddhism, and Neo-Confucianism. Under their tutelage numerous intellectuals became *jushi* (lay devotees) and helped foster the rise of the new religious phenomenon known as *jushi* Buddhism. Yang Wenhui (1837–1911) was a pivotal figure in the *jushi* tradition. Among his disciples who became renowned *jushi* scholars were four of the famous late–Qing dynasty reformers: Tan Sitong (1865–98), Liang Qichao (1873–1929), Tang Yongtong (1893–1964), and Lü Zheng (1896–1989).

The famous *jushi* Zhao Puchu (1907–2000), president of the CBA from the 1980s until his death and author of *Buddhism in China,* advanced a doctrine of "this-worldly" Buddhist thought, calling on Chinese Buddhists to pay equal attention to agricultural work (work in "this world") and Chan meditative practice (*nong Chan bingzhong*). Ren Jiyu (born in 1916), a leading philosopher and director of the Institute for Research of World Religions at the Chinese Academy of Social Sciences, directed the monumental project *Zhongguo Fojiaoshi* (*History of Chinese Buddhism*), published in 1981.

HOUSES OF WORSHIP AND HOLY PLACES Chinese Buddhist monks and nuns worship in temples or within the monastery of their residence. Lay devotees worship together at the Lay Association Hall (Jushi lin). Rank-and-file Buddhists set up family shrines or icons for worship and go to the temple only on festival days and for special purposes—for example, to ask a bodhisattva for healing. Among the most popular Buddhist worship centers in China are the various holy sites known as *zuting* (where certain patriarchs founded their sects).

Chinese Buddhists make pilgrimages to the *sida mingshan* (four famous mountains), each with devotion to a particular bodhisattva: Putuo Shan (*shan* means "mountain"), situated on an island in Eastern Zhejiang Province, is dedicated to Guanyin (Avalokiteshvara; goddess of compassion); Omei Shan in Sichuan is dedicated to Puxian (Samantabhadra, god of universal virtue); Wutai Shan in Shanxi is dedicated to Wenshu (Manjushri, god of great wit); and Jiuhua Shan in Anhwei is dedicated to Dizang (Kshitigarbha, god of specters). Song Shan—a mountain in Henan with a legendary Chan temple, Shaolin Si (*si* means "temple")—is famed for its tradition of spectacular martial arts. In southernmost China, on Hainan Island, the world's tallest statue of the goddess Guanyin was erected in 2003 (on the date Guanyin renounced her lay life) as part of the PRC's aggressive promotion of pilgrimage tourism.

WHAT IS SACRED? Some mountains are sacred to Chinese Buddhists. Certain rocks and caves may also be venerated in Tibet and other Tantric Buddhist areas. Buddhist relics, such as the tooth relic housed in the Buddha's Tooth Pagoda (a 50-meter-high structure outside Beijing, restored in 1961), are considered sacred. The tooth is revered as a *fawu* (divine object) and looked upon by the worshipers as a kind of *guanxiang*, or medium of meditation.

HOLIDAYS AND FESTIVALS Buddhist festivals in China have been largely secularized and politicized. Their dates are determined by the lunar calendar. During the lunar month of Vesakha (generally in May), Chinese Buddhists hold the Yufojie (Bathing the Buddha Festival), celebrating the day the newborn Sakyamuni ("Sage of the Sakyans"; the historical Buddha) is said to have been bathed by water sent down by gods. On the nineteenth day of the second, sixth, and ninth months of the year, Chinese Buddhists celebrate Guanyin's birth, enlightenment, and death. The Yulanpen (Ullambhana; Festival of the Hungry Ghosts) takes place on the fifteenth day of the seventh month (in August or September). At the full moon monks chant from Buddhist scripture for the hungry ghosts and put out food to feed them. Lay devotees also participate in the rites by burning large paper boats, helping "ferry across" hungry ghosts to a better world.

MODE OF DRESS Monastic dress code prohibits the use of animal products and silk. The color and pattern of garments worn by Chinese Buddhists are determined by their social status within the Buddhist community.

There are three main categories of garment. The first is called *changshan* (an informal long gown worn for most monastic work). The second is called *haiqing* or *changpao* (a gown with much fuller sleeves than the first, hanging down about 18 inches from the wrist). It might be worn alone, but for important ritual events it is always worn under the *jiasha* (*kasaya* in Sanskrit), which is the third and most formal type of garment.

Most monastic garments are grey or black, but grey is perhaps the most widely worn. Novices, nuns, and lay devotees wear the 5-strip garment (*wutiao i*), so-called because it is made from 5 strips of cloth. Fully ordained monks may wear the 7-strip garment (*qitiao i*) in any shade of yellow to light brown. The temple abbot normally wears a 25-strip red robe (*hongi*). On major ritual occasions, such as ordinations, he puts on the Ten-Thousand-Buddha garment (*qianfo i*) (a robe magnificently embroidered with numerous Buddha figures). All monks' garments have the same "Y" neck—one side crosses over the other, as with a Western bathrobe, leaving the throat bare. All ordained monks and nuns shave their heads completely.

Xiangke (literally "incense-offerers"; occasional Buddhists), particularly those in the countryside, tend to wear conservative colors: gray, black, and dark blue. Lay devotees may also wear monks' robes, but they do not shave their heads.

DIETARY PRACTICES Dietary habit in Chinese monasteries varies according to geography. In general, meat, fish, eggs, dairy products, vegetables of the onion family (including garlic and leeks), and all intoxicating beverages are forbidden or customarily avoided, as they are believed to stir up the sexual appetite. Typically the daily diet consists of rice, congee, bean curd, turnips, and mixed vegetables (*lohan zhai*, the most popular combination, consists of 18 different vegetables; 18 is the

number of *lohan*, or enlightened ones who have crossed over to "the other shore" and received eternal salvation, in the Buddhist pantheon). On the first, eighth, fifteenth, and twenty-third days of each lunar month, the diet is supplemented by somewhat better ingredients, such as mushrooms, noodles, or Chinese vermicelli. Some lay devotees observe the same dietary restrictions as the clergy; others do so only on special occasions.

RITUALS Buddhist rituals are performed both in monasteries and in the homes of the laity. When a layperson enters the *sangha* (Buddhist community), he goes through the rite of tonsure (*tidu*). Kneeling before an image of Maitreya (Milefo; the coming Buddha who will succeed the historical Buddha, or Sakyamuni), the candidate publicly renounces his lay life and his obligations in human relationships, including those to his parents, asking the master to shave his hair to symbolize this renunciation. After attaining the minimum age (usually 20), a novice becomes a monk through the rite of ordination (*shoujie*). The candidate takes a series of vows, after which "ordination scars" are burned into his scalp with moxa.

To become a lay devotee (*jushi*), a person must follow a three-step ritual: declaring faith in the Three Refuges (the Buddha, the dharma (law), and the sangha); taking the Five Vows (not to kill, steal, drink alcoholic beverages, lie, or commit sexual misconduct); and taking the Bodhisattva Vows (committing to follow the bodhisattva path in helping and saving all other creatures). Lay devotees attend worship services at the temple on special occasions and practice religious cultivation (*xiuxing*) at home, where they set up altars next to ancestral tablets for worshiping and offering incense to the Buddha image.

Increasingly popular, lay pilgrimage is a conspicuous aspect of contemporary Buddhist ritual. Tienzhu Shan in Hangzhou is one of the most visited cultic centers of the goddess Guanyin; the business that has grown up around servicing pilgrims epitomizes the secular character of contemporary lay pilgrimage in China.

RITES OF PASSAGE The life cycle of a lay Buddhist in China is marked by a set of religious rites. Buddhist mothers usually bring newborn babies to the monastery so that the abbot can touch the baby's forehead, giving a blessing for longevity. During the Cultural Revolution the Mao cult became a quasi religion, and some Buddhist adherents also performed "revolutionary wedding rites" in front of a portrait of Chairman Mao. Tibetan Buddhists still practice symbolic "kidnapping" (of the bride from her parents) as a major part of the marriage rites. Since the 1980s memorial services have replaced the traditional Buddhist funeral rite of *chaodu* (which saved the dead from being punished in hell) in most areas of China. Most Han Buddhists are now cremated rather than buried, although a simplified form of the Buddhist funeral procession remains, with Chinese and Western bands playing traditional and modern dirges.

MEMBERSHIP Proselytizing anywhere except within temples is illegal for Chinese Buddhists. Family influence has been a major factor in the growth of the Buddhist lay population. A lay devotee receives a formal certificate (*jushi zheng*, or *guiyi zheng*) after taking the Three Refuges and the Five Vows, confirming his *jushi* status and his membership in a Buddhist sangha. The overwhelming majority of lay Buddhists in China today, however, are *xiangk* (occasional Buddhists), whose affiliation with the sangha is often fluid and does not involve a membership ceremony, since they may worship other deities in popular religion as well.

Ordination is required to join a Buddhist monastery. The great shortage of Buddhist monks and nuns after the Cultural Revolution has been slowly alleviated since 1978 (two years after Mao's death, when the "reform" era began) by the restoration of Buddhist seminaries and academies, which had been in ruins.

SOCIAL JUSTICE After 1949 the Communist government decided it must rectify "feudal" abnormalities and "injustices" embedded in the Chinese Buddhist clergy's monastic life. Monks and nuns were given civil rights (to vote and hold public office), but these rights obliged them to perform the civil duties other citizens had to fulfill, such as taking part in productive work, serving in the army, and actively participating in political campaigns and movements. Today lay Buddhists are required to serve in the army, but monks and nuns are not.

Neither the CBA nor any of its leaders may engage in social reform activities. Under the doctrine of "this-worldly" Buddhism, Chinese Buddhists are now actively engaged in various voluntary social services, including medicine, education, and environmental protection.

SOCIAL ASPECTS In 1955 a group of young Shanghai monks called for a revision of the Vinaya (monastic regulations) with the hope of allowing marriage for monks and nuns. In support their request, they invoked the new marriage law of 1950, which aimed at abolishing the patriarchal and compulsory practices in the system of arranged marriages by parents. These monks compared the compulsory nature of enforced celibacy for Buddhist clerics to that of arranged marriages within the secular community. Xuyun (Hsü-yün; 1840–1959), an eminent Chan abbot and honorary president of the CBA, vetoed the request. While lay devotees can marry, he refuted, monks and nuns must remain celibate unless they give up their vocation and return to secular life (*huansu*). The new marriage law also allows lay Buddhists (like all Chinese citizens) to divorce.

POLITICAL IMPACT Individual Buddhists have had little effect on politics in China, with the exception of the Dalai Lama, who has worked peacefully for Tibetan autonomy. The CBA's main function since its founding in 1952 has been to keep the Buddhist clerical ranks free from "counterrevolutionaries" and the laity from forming "subversive" heterodox sects. The government has also used the CBA internationally to conduct "people's diplomacy," fostering closer ties with neighboring Buddhist countries in South and Southeast Asia and Japan.

CONTROVERSIAL ISSUES From the early days of the PRC, Buddhist participation in politics has caused controversy between progressive and conservative Buddhist clergy. Conservatives distrust the new constitution, which allows monks and nuns to vote and hold public office. The progressives disagree, and they have had to reinterpret the Vinaya (monastic regulations) in order to justify killing Chinese "counterrevolutionaries" or foreign enemies during war.

Compulsory abortion has been a controversial issue among lay Buddhists since the post-Mao government widely enforced the "one child only" policy after 1978. Some regard the practice as killing life.

CULTURAL IMPACT Historically Buddhism has profoundly influenced Chinese architecture, sculpture, paintings, literature, and musical traditions. Buddhist architecture introduced into China included temples, pagodas, and grottos (cave complexes hewn into cliff walls). Because dynasty emperors were often the most pious Buddhists, Buddhist temples gradually took on the design of imperial palaces, bearing little resemblance to their Indian counterparts. The most famous Buddhist temple is the Famen Si in Xi'an, Shaanxi. Notable examples of a pagoda and a grotto are the Liuhe Ta (Six Harmonies Pagoda) in Hangzhou, originally built in 971 C.E. and the Magao Grottos in Dunhuang City in the northwest, which contain Buddhist mural paintings and stucco sculptures.

Even after the founding of the PRC, Buddhist-inspired literature remained popular among Chinese readers, especially the sixteenth-century *Xiyouji* (*Journey to the West*; English translators sometimes use the title *Monkey*). This novel was Mao's favorite reading, and he promoted a revolutionary interpretation of the classic. *Fanhua* (a Buddhist painting style), *fanbei* (Buddhist music), and *chanwu* (Chan dance) are increasingly popular in China today.

CHRISTIANITY

DATE OF ORIGIN 635 C.E.
NUMBER OF FOLLOWERS 91.2 million

HISTORY Christian Nestorianism (Jingjiao, meaning "Luminous Faith") reached China from Syria in the mid-seventh century, died out after massive religious persecution in the mid-ninth century, and resurfaced in 1260. Franciscan missionaries commissioned by the pope arrived in China at the end of the thirteenth century. In both cases Christianity was accepted mostly by non-Han ethnic minorities, and it failed to survive the end of the Mongol Yuan dynasty (1271–1368 C.E.). Only at the end of the sixteenth century did the Christian faith become domesticated among the Han people, through Jesuit missionaries pioneered by Matteo Ricci (1552–1610).

Robert Morrison of the London Missionary Society was in 1807 the first Protestant missionary to reach China. Protestantism expanded steadily throughout the nineteenth century and well into the first half of the twentieth. Western missionaries established mission churches along denominational lines. In the 1920s the rising tide of anti-imperialism among China's intellectuals led to anti-Christian riots.

Meanwhile, independent Protestant churches under Chinese leadership emerged outside the mission churches; these include the Local Churches (or Local Assemblies; Difang jiaohu; a term referring to any indigenous church whose theology promotes the idea of a single, united church for each city, town, or village), the Jesus Family (Yesu jiating), and the True Jesus Church (Zhen

Yesu jiaohui). Two major ministry churches also came into being: the Christian Tabernacle (Jidutu Huitan) in Beijing and the Great Horse Station Congregation (Damazhan Jiaohu) in Gangzhou (Canton), under the ministries of Wang Mingdao (1900–1991) and Lin Xian'gao (Samuel Lamb, born in 1924), respectively.

In 1952 the Communist regime expelled all Western missionaries from China. Two quasi-religious mass organizations—the Three-Self Patriotic Movement (TSPM) for Protestants and the Chinese Catholic Patriotic Association (CCPA) for Catholics—were established under the direct supervision of the CCP, which made membership mandatory for all Protestant and Catholic churches. Some Catholics and independent Protestant groups refused to join.

During the Cultural Revolution (1966–76), public worship was forbidden, and Christians with divergent backgrounds began meeting in private homes; thus, "house churches" (jiating jiaohui) emerged all over the country. Since the death of Mao in 1976 and the "opening up" of China, the house church movement has mushroomed, and Protestant churches along the eastern seaboard and in the interior provinces (some where Western missionaries began their work in the nineteenth century and others where indigenous Christian groups flourished in the first half of the twentieth century) have experienced waves of revivals. New, unorthodox, quasi-Christian sectarian groups have also arisen.

The Chinese Catholic Church, historically under the direct control of Rome, was finally granted the status of a "national church" in 1946 and put under the formal jurisdiction of a native hierarchy. The pope ordained Thomas Tien (Tian) Gengxin (1890–1967), the bishop of Beijing, as the first Chinese cardinal. After 1949 the papacy's continuing assertion of supreme ecclesiastical authority over the Chinese Catholic Church clashed with the PRC's policy of independence in religion. The PRC government rejected Rome's authority over episcopal appointments and the ordination of priests in China. Chinese bishops who had received their appointments from the pope before 1949 were forbidden to make contact with Rome. While government-approved clergy served the "official churches" (those who had joined the CCPA) in the cities, "underground" priests (those approved by Rome) served rural Chinese Catholic congregations that had refused to join.

In the post-Mao "reform" era (since 1978), wanting to meet the severe shortage of Chinese clerics, the Vatican has waived canonical law and allowed the Chinese Catholic Church to ordain new priests on their own initiative and even consecrate new bishops. A list of Chinese episcopal nominees must first be sent to Rome for final approval through Rome's representatives in Hong Kong. Over two-thirds of the Chinese Catholic bishops currently associated with the CCPA gained Vatican approval during the early 1990s. Meanwhile, Beijing has begun to allow the consecration through the CCPA of bishops who have already openly received appointments from Rome.

EARLY AND MODERN LEADERS Of the Jesuits' early Catholic converts, the most prominent were Li Zhizao (Leo; died in 1630) and Xu Guangqi (Paul Hsü; 1562–1633), both high-ranking ministers in the Ming imperial court. Xu and the Italian mathematician Matteo Ricci translated Euclid's *Elements of Geometry* into Chinese as part of the missionary strategy of introducing Western sciences as a prelude to evangelism.

Liang Fa (Aa-fa; 1789–1855, baptized in 1816), the first ordained Chinese Protestant pastor and evangelist, was a prolific gospel tract writer. His *Quanshi Liangyan* (*Sincere Exhortations to the People of the World*) converted Hong Xiuquan (1814–1864), founder of the anti-Qing Taiping Heavenly Kingdom (Taiping Tianguo). Xi Shengmo (Shenmo means "overcoming the devil"; also known as Pastor Xi; 1830–96), the star convert of the China Inland Mission, was a legendary Christian leader and powerful evangelist.

Throughout the twentieth century Chinese Christian leaders submitted to the ruling authorities. Major conservatives (evangelicals) were Dora Yu (Yu Cidu; 1873–1931), Watchman Nee (Ni Tuosheng, 1903–72), Leland Wang (Wang Zai; 1898–1975), and John Sung (Song Shangjie; 1901–44). Major liberals were Cheng Jingyi (1881–1939), Yu Rizhang (David Yui; 1882–1936), and Wu Leichuan (1870–1944).

MAJOR THEOLOGIANS AND AUTHORS Zhao Zichen (T.C. Chao; 1888–1979), a renowned theologian and a prolific writer, was a pioneering figure in advocating for the independence of the Chinese Church under the "three-self" principle (self-governing, self-propagating, and self-financing). Wu Yaozong (Y.T. Wu; 1893–1979), a liberal theologian and a prominent leader of China's YMCA, was the main architect behind the establishment of the TSPM. Wu argued that Chinese Christians must be "politically accountable." His successor, Ding Guangxun (K.H. Ting; born in 1915),was

a consecrated Anglican bishop educated at Union Theological Seminary and Columbia University. Ding has contended that not every word in the Bible should be taken as the word of God and has advocated the remolding of Chinese Christianity as a faith that "answers to the tide of history and to the needs of the broad masses."

On the conservative side ("the spiritual group"; *shulingpai*), Reverend Jia Yuming (1880–1964) was the first Chinese theologian to introduce systematic theology (a branch of Western theology that explores Biblical doctrines analytically and thematically) into the Chinese Church. Wang Mingdao, a proponent of practical theology, emphasized moral discipline in day-to-day Christian life. Watchman Nee championed experiential theology, emphasizing a personal life of holiness, as well as the ecclesiastical theology of having only one church in each city, town, or village. Citing New Testament examples, such as the seven churches in seven localities mentioned in chapters 2 and 3 of Revelation, Nee called the idea a practical way of working out the "oneness of the Body of Christ" in a locality. This idea has contributed to the emergence of thousands of indigenous, independent Local Churches worldwide.

HOUSES OF WORSHIP AND HOLY PLACES During the darkest days of the Cultural Revolution (1966–69), faithful Christians (mainly Protestants) still managed to meet in small groups in houses, fields, or parks. They sang hymns of praise, setting the lyrics to the tunes of revolutionary songs.

In the "reform" era (since 1978) Christians in China's large cities have met in traditional chapels or cathedrals. The Mo En Church (formerly Moor Memorial Methodist Church) in downtown Shanghai accommodates thousands of Protestant worshipers on Sunday. The great majority of Christians, however, meet in homes or larger "meeting points" (*juhui dian*), particularly in rural areas.

Marian shrines at Donglu in Hebei province and Sheshan in suburban Shanghai are the most prominent sites for Catholic pilgrimages. Apparitions of the Virgin Mary are rumored to have appeared at these and other holy places.

WHAT IS SACRED? Both Chinese Protestants and Catholics treat the Communion bread and wine as sacred. Catholics also view holy pictures, as well as Marian statues and icons of saints, as sacred.

HOLIDAYS AND FESTIVALS Chinese Catholics celebrate Christmas, Easter, Pentecost, and the Assumption as the four great feast days. Those who live in the countryside also celebrate the Chinese popular festivals of the lunar calendar, from New Year's Day to the mid-Autumn festival, substituting compatible Catholic practices for the popular indigenous ones. At the Qingming Festival rural Catholics honor their ancestors with prayers in front of their graves rather than with sacrifices of food. At the Feasts of All Souls and All Saints, Catholic priests say masses for the dead.

Chinese Protestant members of official churches or of house congregations with denominational backgrounds celebrate traditional Christian holidays, such as Christmas and Easter. Indigenous independent congregations, such as the Local Churches, observe only the Lord's Day (Sunday) and reject Christmas and Easter for their "pagan" origins. They often celebrate traditional Chinese festivals by evangelizing. The Seventh-day Adventists observe the Sabbath (Saturday) instead of the Lord's Day.

MODE OF DRESS After Mao's death in 1976, Chinese Christians, like other Chinese citizens, changed their gray Sun Yat-sen uniform (made of loose pants and jacket, required clothing during the Mao era) for more Westernized dress. Especially in rural areas, Christians tend to dress conservatively, both in style and in color. Clergy in the official churches wear formal vestments during worship, according to their denominational tradition; other clergy usually dress in Western style suits.

DIETARY PRACTICES Chinese Christians follow the injunction in the New Testament (Acts 15:29) to abstain from eating the meat of strangled animals, animal blood, and foods that have been sacrificed to idols. Chinese Catholics still observe the prohibition against eating meat on Fridays. Some fast to make their prayers more effective.

RITUALS Christian worship in official Protestant churches in such urban centers as Beijing follows the practice of the pre-1949 mission churches and is patterned on a typical Western service. Baptism by sprinkling is most common, and weddings and memorial services are conducted in Western style.

Local Churches and Seventh-day Adventists in Beijing and Shanghai conduct their worship services openly and independently. The vast majority of Protestants,

however, meet at unregistered "house churches" (*jiating jiaohui*) or registered "meeting points" (*juhui dian*) in both rural communities and cities. Some Local Churches advise women to wear a head covering at meetings, often a black hairnet. The Local Church in Nanjing holds weekday evening meetings that sometimes include a sermon; sometimes the meetings are for prayers and fellowship. On Sunday mornings the church holds Holy Communion, which they call "meeting for breaking the bread" (*bobing juhui*). Baptisms are performed in a Baptismo (commonly a cement or ceramic pool). Most Local Church weddings and funerals include scriptural readings, frequently from Ephesians 5:23–27 for weddings and from I Corinthians 15:50–58 for funerals.

Since the Second Vatican Council (1962–65) Catholic priests have conducted Mass in native Chinese dialects in such major cities as Beijing and Tianjin, whereas some older priests in the countryside still hold Mass in Latin. Other aspects of the Mass have changed significantly: The altar is now set between the priest and the congregation, so that the priest faces the worshipers, and congregants may sing hymns in Chinese and participate in the reading of the Scriptures. Underground priests in rural areas conduct Mass and sacramental rituals in believers' homes.

RITES OF PASSAGE Official Protestant churches perform rites identical with their counterparts outside China, with some notable exceptions. Whether operated officially (registered) or as house churches (unregistered), Local Churches require believers who desire baptism to show evidence of having been saved and to learn the "basic truths" regarding Christ's redemptive work on the cross. Baptism is by full immersion. If a believer is called to serve the Lord full-time, a consecration meeting is conducted for his sake; in some places church elders lay hands on him and bless him so he will receive spiritual gifts to enhance his ministry. Weddings afford a couple the opportunity to consecrate their new family to the Lord. Funerals allow the living to testify to the faithful Christian service of the deceased.

Chinese Catholic children are baptized in infancy. At age seven they may begin receiving Holy Communion at Mass. Young Catholics participate in the sacrament of confirmation at the onset of puberty. Virtually all rural Catholics share some non-Catholic folk customs associated with burials: providing a funeral banquet, wearing mourning garments, and forming a procession to the grave site. Catholics, however, do not kowtow to the casket or burn incense sticks and mock paper money. Instead, Catholic peasants sprinkle holy water on the casket, say prayers for the dead, and place a simple cross on the burial mound or tombstone. When one is available, a Catholic priest attends the funeral and leads the prayers; otherwise the family of the deceased leads the service.

MEMBERSHIP Catholicism is an inherited faith in China, particularly in rural areas. Those born into Catholic families need not make any personal commitment to the church. In official Protestant churches membership is confirmed by baptism. Church membership grows through public evangelism conducted in registered meeting places and through personal contact with relatives and friends. Government regulations forbid preaching the gospel to children under 18, though the policy has been modified since the 1980s.

House church members evangelize aggressively. Young members become itinerant evangelists, boldly roaming beyond the boundaries of their native provinces in search of converts, which is against government regulations. Some young evangelists sign wills before leaving parents or spouses in anticipation of arrest and imprisonment.

SOCIAL JUSTICE The PRC's religious policy is that all religious practices must be compatible with Chinese socialism. Despite their rapid growth, contemporary Protestant and Catholic churches may not effect any social reforms and dare not publicly voice concern over rampant official corruption and social injustice. Since 1978 Chinese Protestants and Catholics have resumed some of their traditional social services, such as providing famine relief and setting up schools and orphanages.

SOCIAL ASPECTS Chinese Catholicism and Protestantism consider marriage a holy union (one of the seven sacraments for Catholics) that may be broken only in cases of adultery or death. The traditional Chinese emphasis on the family and the relationship between husband and wife (valued as one of the five cardinal bonds in Chinese society) reinforces the Christian value. Divorce—not allowed for Catholics—is infrequent among Chinese Protestants, especially among house church believers in the rural areas. Mixed marriages among urban Catholics are common, but in rural communities Catholic parents usually seek Catholic wives for their sons.

POLITICAL IMPACT Chinese government policy forbids any religious organization from interfering with the political or judicial process or from holding any activity that may have a negative impact on national unification or harmonious relationships among nationals. Even after the 1982 publication of Document 19, which embodies the government's newest and considerably liberalized guidelines governing religious affairs, little room is allowed for Christian groups to voice political concerns. The essential function of the TSPM and the CCPA is identical with that of the CBA: to implement the official guidelines contained in Document 19. At the Chinese People's Political Consultative Conference (an advisory organization whose members include high-ranking CCP officials as well as representatives from small parties and registered religious organizations), the Catholic and Protestant representatives are allowed to voice some degree of concern over political matters.

CONTROVERSIAL ISSUES Abortion is extremely controversial among conservative Chinese Christian groups, even though they have no objection to the common practice of sterilization (performed to ensure compliance with the government's "one child only" policy). Women practice ministry widely, in both official and house churches, but certain conservative groups still advise women to cover their heads and allow women to speak only to all-female audiences.

Also controversial is the legal status of "cults" (xie-jiao), which are the objects of a recent government crackdown. The government has condemned and outlawed some Christian groups as cults on the basis of their political outlook rather than their religious doctrine. It has treated some Local Church groups in Zhejiang as cults and has labeled them the "shouters sect" (Huhanpai) because they were found praying loudly en masse during their meetings. Some of these groups have been vindicated and granted legal status after registering their meeting facilities with the government. Other groups, such as the Eastern Lightning sect (Dongfang Shandian), are regarded as cults both by the government and by Chinese Christians at large. Eastern Lightning originated in Henan in 1989 and claims that Christ has already returned to earth (like the "lightning") as a woman in China (the "East"), as Jesus predicted in Matthew 24:27. The group is said to have specifically targeted house church members in the rural areas and the Catholic clergy as potential converts.

CULTURAL IMPACT Since the New Cultural Movement of the May Fourth era (1919), Christian influence on Chinese literature and music has been pronounced. The novel *Yao* (*Medicine*) by Lu Xun (1881–1936), an eminent leader of the new Chinese literary movement, portrays vividly the bold spirit of suffering of Christ. The work of Bing Xin (pen name of Xie Wanying; born in 1900), a renowned female author, was inspired by Christ's spirit of love. *Death of Jesus* by Mao Dun (1896–1981); the confessional literature of Ba Jin (born in 1905), China's St. Augustine; and the works of leading contemporary scholars, such as Zhu Weizhi and literary critic and historian Ma Jia, all attest to the profound impact of Christianity on Chinese literature.

Thousands of classic church songs and hymns by such Western composers as Charles Wesley, John Newton, Fannie Crosby, and A.B. Simpson have been translated into Chinese. In the late 1920s Chinese Christians began writing their own hymns. The 1936 hymnal *Putian Songzan* (*Hymns of Universal Praise*) and the hymnal compiled by Watchman Nee (which includes his own compositions) are widely used among Chinese Protestants. The music popular among the house churches comes from *Jianan Shixuan* (*Songs of Canaan*), composed by Lü Xiaomin, a young Chinese Muslim who converted to Christianity.

Other Religions

By the late seventh century Muslim traders had reached China by land from the west (the Silk Route) and by sea from the southeast. Foreign Muslims from the West settled in northwestern China during the Tang dynasty (618–907), and under their influence, some Chinese had converted to Islam by the eighth century. As part of the Mongol empire during the Yuan dynasty (1279–1368), China found its land and sea communications with the Muslim world greatly improved. Kublai Khan, the Mongol ruler, aggressively recruited Muslims from various parts of his empire to help his government as ministers and tax collectors, resulting in an influx of Muslims into all parts of China. Though a minority, the Muslim population increased steadily, primarily through births, intermarriages between Muslim men and Chinese women, and the adoption of Chinese male children into wealthy Muslim families as mates for their daughters.

The founder of the Chinese Ming dynasty (1368–1643) decreed that Muslims in China must adopt Chinese dress, take a Chinese name, and learn and speak Chinese. The descendants of these Chinese-speaking Muslims became known as the Hui, or Chinese Muslims. The Hui, though they complied with the decree, held tenaciously to their faith, their religious practices, and their dietary restrictions, retaining their identity as members of the Muslim world. Contemporary Hui live in nearly every urban center and town throughout China, with the largest concentrations in the Ningxia and Qinghai Autonomous Regions in the northwest. Some Mongols in Inner Mongolia on China's northern frontier are also Muslims.

Turkic-speaking Muslims, the majority of whom are Uyghurs, are concentrated in China's far northwest (Xinjiang). Both Turkic and Hui Muslims responded to repression under the Qing dynasty (1644–1911) with frequent rebellions. The legendary Hui figure, Ma Hualong (1810–71), led a major insurrection against the Qing from 1862 to 1878 that ravaged all of northwestern China. During the Republican period (1912–49) the Kazakh chieftain Osman (Usman) Bator led a full-scale rebellion in Xinjiang against the Nationalist government and formed the Eastern Turkestan Republic. Two Muslim leaders in the northwest, Burhan and Saifudin, negotiated a compact with the Communist regime, resulting in the 1955 creation of the Xinjiang Uyghur Autonomous Region. Shahidi, a Tartar general of Xinjiang and chairman of the Islamic Association of China, has supported carrying out the CCP's policies among the Turkic-Muslim population, but radical Muslims in Xinjiang have always promoted a separatist movement. The 1999 jailing of Rabiya Kadeer, a prominent Muslim businesswoman, reflects the continuing tension between non-Chinese-speaking Muslims and the PRC government.

Since the founding of the PRC, serious local disturbances have occurred frequently in the northwest between the Gedimu ("the ancient tradition"; officially recognized Islamic groups) and newer organizations, such as Sufi orders that emerged before 1949. Chinese Sufism, which originated in Central Asia, is a synthesis of Islam, Taoism, and martial arts practices; it emphasizes the inner, mystical dimension of Islam. Sufi leaders among the Uyghurs maintain influence over their adherents through tight control of sacred religious sites.

Wang Daiyu (1580–1650), acclaimed as China's most illustrious Islamic scholar, wrote the first important text in Chinese on the Islamic faith. The twentieth-century's famous four chief *ahongs* (grand imams) were

Wang Jingzhai (1879–1949), Da Busheng (1874–1965), Ha Decheng (1888–1943), and Ma Songting (1895–1992). Ma Jian (Ma Zishi, 1906–78), a prolific translator from Arabic into Chinese, was actively involved in PRC politics, and he emphasized the compatibility between the teachings of Islam and Marxism.

China's most famous mosques include Fenghuang Si in Hangzhou, Huaisheng Si in Guangzhou (Canton), Shengyou Si (Mosque of Friends of the Prophet) in Quanzhou (all three built in the eleventh century), and the thirteenth-century Xianhe Si in Yangzhou. Shrines (known as *gongbei* among the Hui and *mazar* in Xinjiang) built around the tombs of Sufi masters and other religious leaders are important sites for Muslim worshipers in the northwest. The Honglefu *daotang* (Hall of the Path or Doctrine) in Ningxia, the site of Ma Hualong's execution and tomb, regained its status as a major center of Sufi worship in the 1980s. Thousands of followers of the Zheherenye (Jahriyyah) Sufi sect from Yunnan, Xinjiang, and elsewhere gather there during major religious festivals.

Muslims in China may not consume pork or other nonhalal meat and generally eat lamb and mutton. Turkic Muslims in Xinjiang eat *polo* (pilaf, made of mutton and rice) and naan bread (baked as in northern India and Afghanistan); naan stalls are common in cities as far east as Xi'an. Major Muslim festivals observed in China are Shengjijie (Maolujie; the Prophet's birthday), Kaijaijie (the Fast-Breaking Festival at the end of Ramadan), and Guerbangjie (Corban, or Feast of Sacrifices; also called Zhongxiaojie, or Feast of Loyalty and Filiality).

Islamic worship rituals (*libai* or *baigong*) in China include the five daily prayers and the observance of Ramadan. The Hui largely ignore the traditional Muslim rites of passage, though some rural communities, such as the town of Na in Ningxia, faithfully preserve them. On the third day after the birth of each child in Na, a local *ahong* (imam) reads the scripture in the family's home and gives the child a *jingming* (Koranic name). The family also gives the child a *hanming* (Chinese name) or *xiaoming* (school name) for official purposes. All Hui boys in Qinghai undergo *gehetainai* (circumcision) when they are 12.

Hui men may be distinguished from Han Chinese by their round-topped, brimless skullcaps made of white or black cotton or wool. Beards are also an important marker, especially for older men. Turkic Muslims may be identified by their caps and ethnic dress. Men and boys favor "flower caps" (colorfully embroidered square caps) or tall fur or felt hats. Women generally wear black, white, or green kerchiefs made of silk or cotton. Sufis of the Jahriyyah orders shave the sides of their beards in memory of their founding *shaykh* (religious leader), Ma Mingxin (1719–81), whose beard was shaved off before his execution.

Taoism as a religion (Taojiao) originated in a movement during the second century called Tianshi tao (the Way of Celestial Masters). The founding of this movement is attributed to Zhang Ling (Zhang Daoling; 34–156 C.E.). Zhang claimed that the Taishang Laojun (Lord Lao the Most High: the deified title of Laozi, who lived from approximately 604 to 531 B.C.E.) bestowed the title Tianshi (Celestial Master) on him in a revelation in 142 C.E. In time the movement absorbed elements of popular religion. Wang Chongyang (1127–70), founder of the Quanzhen (Perfect Truth) sect, was the first major Taoist theologian whose ideology combined Taoist, Buddhist, and, to a lesser degree, Confucian ideas.

Taoists believe in a hierarchy of gods—including mythical figures as well as deified human beings—all under the supreme deity Yuhuang dadi (the Jade Emperor). Taoist rituals performed by individuals are generally aimed at prolongation of life or immortality. Every Taoist must perform the *zhai* (purification) rituals involving sacrifices, fasts, and mental renewal. Although Taoist beliefs and rituals, such as the *jiao* community ritual for cosmic renewal, have all been absorbed into the complex amalgam of Chinese popular religious practices, Taoism as a religion has maintained a separate institutional identity in Chinese society.

Most Taoists in China today are priests, monks, and nuns. Along with some lay devotees, they conduct their religious rituals at Taoist monasteries. The best-known Quanzhen monastery is the White Cloud Monastery (Baiyuan guan) in Beijing, which currently houses the headquarters of the Chinese Taoist Association. Other famous Taoist sacred sites (temples, pavilions, and the like) are the Yonglo gong (Chunyang gong; *gong* means "palace") in Shanxi and the Louguan tai (*tai* means terrace; also called the Ziyün lou) on the mountain Zhongnan Shan in Shaanxi. Other Taoist sacred mountains include Wudang Shan in Hubei, Mao Shan in Jiangsu, Longhu Shan in Jiangxi, Qingcheng Shan in Sichuan, and Lao Shan in Shandong.

The PRC's regulations embodied in Document 19 outlaw any public religious rituals (including Taoist) that it considers superstitious or harmful to the physical and mental health of the people. The government has also banned some traditional Taoist rituals performed for individuals, such as spirit writing (*fuluan*, a divinatory technique for communicating with gods). Local authorities may simply ignore such practices in rural communities.

Confucianism is a belief system that integrates the original teachings of Confucius (551–479 B.C.E.) and new elements advanced by later Confucian thinkers. It consists of doctrinal teachings on proper interpersonal relations within human society and ritual practices performed in relation to supernatural beings and the spirits of deceased ancestors. Many of the beliefs and practices Confucius adopted had been in existence since the Western Zhou dynasty (c. 1027–777 B.C.E.). From the eleventh century C.E. onward, because of its ideological and ritual development in response to Chan mysticism and Taoist metaphysics, the belief system became known as Neo-Confucianism. In modern times the system has taken on the name of New Confucianism.

Throughout the time of the imperial dynasties, Confucian rituals were an intrinsic part of state religion. These rituals were largely practiced among the educated elite, including officials in the imperial bureaucracy and upper-class gentry in the countryside. Until 1905 Confucianism was a basis for upward social mobility, as the civil service examination required candidates to write an essay on a phrase from a Confucian text. The Communist revolution under Mao totally reoriented Chinese social structure, and Confucian rituals were virtually abandoned. Confucius temples are still preserved (like famous Buddhist and Taoist temples) as national cultural monuments.

Confucian beliefs recognize a supreme reality (or being) in the universe known as Heaven (Tien) or Lord on High (Shangdi), as well as the existence of gods (*shen*) and spirits (*ling*). Confucians also venerate celestial and earthly deities (the sun, moon, mountains, and rivers), all of which are presumed to have the power to intervene in human affairs. Only the emperor, as the Son of Heaven (Tienzi), could conduct the grand rite of sacrificing burnt offerings in the name of the Cult of Heaven. The emperor also offered smaller sacrifices at the altars of the earth, sun, and moon located (since the time of the Ming dynasty; 1368–1644) in the imperial capital. Heaven had his own will (*tienyi*), and he issued mandates (*tienming*). As Son of Heaven, the emperor had to embody cardinal Confucian virtues, such as benevolence (*ren*) and justice (*yi*) to his people. Before withdrawing his mandate from an unworthy monarch, Heaven showed his displeasure by issuing warnings to the emperor in the form of portents, omens, and wonders (such as earthquakes, solar and lunar eclipses, and unusual and freakish occurrences in the natural world).

Confucianism also involved family rituals, the most important being ancestor worship. Various rites pertinent to the human life cycle (those surrounding adulthood, prospective marriages, funerals, and anniversaries of a death) have been absorbed into the syncretic system of popular religion. Under the PRC Kong Miao—the Confucius Temple in Qufu, Shandong (Confucius' birth place)—is a tourist site for religious pilgrimage. Some metropolitan cities, such as Beijing and Tianjin, also have Confucius temples. A small number of Confucian ritual specialists, along with Taoist and Buddhist priests, may be hired to preside over popular religious events.

Silas Wu

See Also Vol. 1: *Buddhism, Confucianism, Taoism*

Bibliography

Adler, Joseph A. *Chinese Religions*. London: Routledge, 2002.

Bays, Daniel H. "Chinese Protestant Christianity Today." In *Religion in China Today*, edited by Daniel L. Overmyer. Cambridge, England: Cambridge University Press, 2003.

———, ed. *Christianity in China: From the Eighteenth Century to the Present*. Stanford: Stanford University Press, 1996.

Ch'en, Kenneth K. S. *Buddhism: The Light of Asia*. Woodbury, N.Y.: Barron's Educational Series, Inc., 1968.

Ching, Julia. *Chinese Religion*. Maryknoll, N.Y.: Orbis Books, 1993.

Dean, Kenneth. "Local Communal Religion in Contemporary Southeast China." In *Religion in China Today*, edited by Daniel L. Overmyer. Cambridge, England: Cambridge University Press, 2003.

Dillon, Michael. *Religious Minorities and China*. Minority Rights Group International, UK, 2001.

Dunch, Ryan. "Protestant Christianity in China Today: Fragile, Fragmented, Flourishing." In *China and Christianity: Burdened Past, Hopeful Future*, edited by Stephen Uhalley Jr. and Xiaoxin Wu. Armonk, N.Y.: M. E. Sharpe, 2001.

Gladney, Dru C. 1998. *Ethnic Identity in China: The Making of a Muslim Minority Nationality*. Orlando, Fla.: Harcourt Brace College Publishers, 1998.

———. "Islam in China: Accommodation or Separatism?" In *Religion in China Today*, edited by Daniel L. Overmyer. Cambridge, England: Cambridge University Press, 2003.

Hunter, Alan, and Kim-kwong Chan. *Protestantism in Contemporary China.* Cambridge, England: Cambridge University Press, 1993.

Lai, Chi-tim. "Daoism in China Today, 1980–2002." In *Religion in China Today,* edited by Daniel L. Overmyer. Cambridge, England: Cambridge University Press, 2003.

Lambert, Tony. *The Resurrection of the Chinese Church.* London: Hodder and Stoughton, 1991.

MacInnis, Donald E. *Religion in China Today: Policy and Practice.* Maryknoll, N.Y.: Orbis Books, 1989.

Madsen, Richard P. *China's Catholics: Tragedy and Hope in an Emerging Civil Society.* Berkeley: University of California Press, 1998.

———. "Catholic Revival During the Reform Era." In *Religion in China Today,* edited by Daniel L. Overmyer. Cambridge, England: Cambridge University Press, 2003.

Naquin, Susan, and Chun-fang Yu, eds. *Pilgrims and Sacred Sites in China.* Berkeley and Los Angeles: University of California Press, 1992.

Saso, Michael. "Chinese Religions." In *A New Handbook of Living Religions,* edited by John R. Hinnells. Oxford: Blackwell Publishers, 1997.

Welch, Homes. *The Practice of Chinese Buddhism, 1900–1950.* Cambridge, Mass.: Harvard University Press, 1967.

———. *The Buddhist Revival in China.* Cambridge, Mass.: Harvard University Press, 1968.

———. *Buddhism under Mao.* Cambridge, Mass.: Harvard University Press, 1972.

Wu, Silas H. *Dora Yu and Christian Revival in Twentieth-Century China.* Boston, Mass.: Pishon River Publications, 2002.

Yang, Keli, et al., eds. *Zhongguo Isilan Baikequanshu* (Encyclopedia of Chinese Islam). Chengdu, China: Sichuan Cishu Chubanshe, 1996.

Yu, Chun-fang. "Chinese Women Pilgrims' Songs Glorifying Guanyin." In *Buddhism in Practice,* edited by Donald S. Lopez Jr. Princeton: Princeton University Press, 1995.

Colombia

POPULATION 41,008,227

ROMAN CATHOLIC 81 percent

OTHER CHRISTIAN 10 percent

EVANGELICAL 3.5 percent

OTHER 3.6 percent

NONRELIGIOUS 1.9 percent

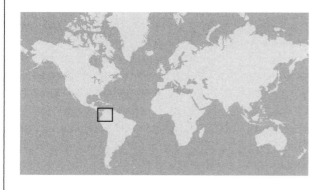

Country Overview

INTRODUCTION The Republic of Colombia, located in northern South America, is bordered by the Caribbean Sea on the north and the Pacific Ocean on the west. It also borders Panama, Venezuela, Brazil, Peru, and Ecuador. The twin chains of the northern Andes Mountains run through the country, which has thus been historically constrained by its rugged geography. Colombia also spreads over the lowland Amazon basin.

Prior to the arrival of the Spanish in the sixteenth century C.E., highland Colombia was the site of several indigenous chiefdoms. In the area around Bogotá the

Chibcha developed, while the south was a contact zone with the expanding Inca empire. The lowland area held a variety of horticultural societies centered along the rivers. Colonial economic enterprises, in which the native population was used for labor, led to a decline in the Indian population and the importation of African slaves. As a result, Colombia has a rich amalgam of populations and heritages.

The Catholic Church was one of the key institutions of colonial society in Colombia. It has maintained its strength as an important social force. In response to the interactions of local histories with metropolitan religious and historical trends, each area has developed its own variety of folk Catholicism. Other religious groups in Colombia include various Protestant churches as well as Seventh-day Adventists, Mormons, and Jehovah's Witnesses. There are also small communities of Jews, Muslims, and practitioners of indigenous and African-influenced religions.

Like other aspects of Colombian life, religion was affected in the nineteenth century by struggles between two political factions, the Conservatives and Liberals, and in the mid-twentieth century by the great social conflicts known as La Violencia (the violence). Ongoing civil wars between various guerrilla groups and the state continue to influence religion.

RELIGIOUS TOLERANCE The constitution grants the religious freedom of Colombians. The constitution of 1991 states that there is no official church, but a concordat (1973) between the Vatican and Colombia recognizes the important historical and demographic place of the Catholic Church within Colombia. The law requires religious organizations to formally register in order to have access to public institutions or to perform marriages. Despite the official freedom granted by law, religious leaders have been threatened and attacked by paramilitaries and guerrilla organizations, more often for political than for religious reasons.

Major Religion

ROMAN CATHOLICISM

DATE OF ORIGIN sixteenth century C.E.
NUMBER OF FOLLOWERS 31 million

HISTORY The Spanish conquered the region that is now Colombia in the early sixteenth century C.E. They took with them the Roman Catholic Church, whose missionaries began evangelizing to the native population. Monasteries were established for members of the various Catholic religious orders, and the first dioceses (of Santa Marta and Cartagena) were created in 1534. The Archdiocese of Bogotá was established in 1564. Throughout the colonial period the church was largely controlled by the king of Spain.

Colombia achieved independence in 1824. Throughout the nineteenth and twentieth centuries political power fluctuated between Conservatives, who supported a centralized government and a strong role for the Catholic Church in society, and Liberals, who emphasized regional governments and favored less power for the church. During the periods of Liberal rule in the nineteenth century, attempts were made to disestablish the church; the constitution of 1863 instituted a separation of church and state and guaranteed religious freedom. Two decades later the church's power was reestablished.

The single most important religious event in Colombia was the Latin American Bishop's Conference held in 1968 in the city of Medellín. The conference gathered bishops from throughout Latin America to consider urgent matters of church policy and life in the region. Social conditions in Latin America at that time were marked by increasing urbanization, revolutionary activity, and developing governmental repression of popular movements. The bishop's conference responded to these issues by claiming a "preferential option for the poor," meaning that the church stood in solidarity with the impoverished people of Latin America. The

Columbian women decorate a statue of the Virgin del Carmen with flowers for a festival in her honor. © JEREMY HORNER/CORBIS.

bishops adopted ideas from liberation theology, a previously marginal theological movement that emphasizes the church's duty to become involved in social change on behalf of the poor and oppressed.

Liberation theology became an important force within the Roman Catholic Church in Latin America, but in the 1990s the Vatican, under Pope John Paul II, increasingly attempted to shift the focus away from social and political action and back to the mysteries of the sacraments. The Vatican worked to maintain central church authority by appointing more conservative church leaders upon the retirement of those who had participated in Medellín.

Despite the adoption of progressive principles in Medellín, the Colombian Catholic Church has been known for its conservative leadership. It has, however, been affected by calls for social justice. Roman Catholicism remained the country's official religion until 1991, when a new constitution was adopted.

EARLY AND MODERN LEADERS One of the notable leaders of the Catholic Church during the colonial era was Archbishop Antonio Caballero y Góngora (1723–96), who served as viceroy of the region (which was then a part of a viceroyalty called New Granada) from 1782 to 1788. He was responsible for significant education reforms.

Isaias Duarte Cancino (1939–2002), archbishop of Cali, was known for his bold criticisms of guerillas and narcotics traffickers, despite the fact that the church has generally attempted to avoid involvement in such affairs. He was murdered by unidentified gunmen.

Colombia has 12 archdioceses and 48 dioceses. As of 2004 Colombia's cardinals (the clergy next in rank to the pope) were Darío Castrillón Hoyos (born in 1929), Alfonso López Trujillo (born in 1935), and Pedro Rubiano Sáenz (born in 1932).

MAJOR THEOLOGIANS AND AUTHORS There are academic theologians on the faculties of all of Colombia's universities. Colombia has a number of Catholic universities, the foremost of which is Javeriana University, founded by the Jesuit order in 1623. Its original campus is in Bogotá, and a second campus is in Cali.

HOUSES OF WORSHIP AND HOLY PLACES Colombia follows the traditions of international Catholicism with a hierarchy of sanctuaries and pilgrimage sites based on miraculous images of saints, the Virgin Mary, and Jesus Christ. Despite the official separation of church and state, religion saturates much of Colombian life. Thus, public spaces, both national and local, are marked by the presence of holy images, such as crucifixes or images of saints, the Virgin, or Christ. People often show their respect for such images by genuflecting and engaging in other specific rituals.

Many Catholic churches in Colombia are known for the important sacred images that they house. These include the Basilica of Nuestra Señora del Rosario (Our Lady of the Rosary) in Manizales, the Basilica of Señor de los Milagros (the Lord of Miracles) in Buga, the Cathedral of the Sagrada Familia (Holy Family) in Bucaramanga, the Sanctuary of Las Lajas in Ipiales, the Church of La Hermita (the Hermitage) in Popayán, the Church of Monserrate, and the Cathedral of Salt in Zipaquira.

WHAT IS SACRED? Colombian Catholics follow the practices designated by the international Catholic Church. In popular religiosity, indigenous and African-American practices have combined with Catholicism, influencing the concept of what is considered sacred. Thus, sacred objects, including images of saints and amulets, are deemed to have the power to bring about transformations in a person's life.

HOLIDAYS AND FESTIVALS As a result of colonial practices, each town and social organization in Colombia has a patron saint, and his or her feast day is a major social and religious event. Holy Week (the final week of Lent) has a particularly strong presence as a popular festivity in Colombia. The main site of its celebration is the city of Popayán, where large crowds gather to watch and participate in processions in which the passion (suffering and death) of Jesus is reenacted.

Colombia as a whole celebrates the following religious events as official holidays: the Feast of the Epiphany, Saint Joseph's Day, Holy Thursday, Good Friday, the Feast of the Ascension, the Feast of Corpus Christi, Saints Peter and Paul, the Feast of the Assumption, All Saints' Day, the Feast of the Immaculate Conception, and Christmas. While these increasingly are celebrated as secular holidays, with religious activities occurring in both homes and churches, traditionally they marked a relationship between the church and society. Many of these holidays involved processions and other ritual activities organized by a brotherhood, *cofradía*, which often played a secular as well as a religious role.

MODE OF DRESS Colombian Catholics generally wear secular Western clothes. Members of religious orders often wear dress appropriate for their order.

DIETARY PRACTICES Colombia follows the dietary practices of international Catholicism. This mainly entails fasting during certain periods.

RITUALS The Colombian Catholic Church follows the norms of international Catholicism in its worship services and rituals. Nevertheless, as in many Latin American countries, there is a popular Catholic religiosity that focuses on alternative spiritual forms.

There is a long tradition in Colombia of pilgrimages to shrines and sanctuaries dedicated to holy figures. For example, a church at the top of Monserrate, a hill on the outskirts of Bogotá, has been a pilgrimage destination since the colonial era. Many devout Catholics climb the hill—often on their knees, and particularly during the period between Ash Wednesday and Easter Sunday—to express devotion to a statue of El Señor

Caído (the Fallen Christ). They perform the act as penance for their sins and as part of a request for divine intervention. Other pilgrimage sites include the Church of the Divino Niño (Divine Child) in Bogotá, the Señor de los Milagros (Miraculous Christ) of Buga, the Basilica of the Virgin of Chiquinquirá in Boyaca, the Sanctuary of Las Lajas in Ipiales, and the Church of Maria Auxiliadora in Antioquia.

Popular Catholicism acknowledges popular saints who are not officially accepted by the church. Another feature of popular Catholicism is healing, which is performed by folk healers and shamans. Healers and popular saints draw the devotion of large numbers of Colombian Catholics.

RITES OF PASSAGE For most Colombians Catholic traditions mark rites of passage. These include baptism, First Communion, and marriage.

MEMBERSHIP The Colombian Catholic Church maintains an active public profile within Colombian society. To this end it has organized ministries at the archdiocesan and diocesan levels to perform outreach. At the same time it has a chain of universities and schools to train people in Catholic doctrine and to influence secular learning. The church maintains a vigorous and active presence in broadcasting and on the Internet.

Because it has maintained its strong public role, the Catholic Church in Colombia has an unusual strength in Latin America. To a greater degree than other countries in the region, it has retained its members despite the inroads of non-Catholic religions, particularly Pentecostalism.

SOCIAL JUSTICE The Colombian Catholic Church has established a strong presence in issues of social justice, poverty, migration (displaced people and refugees), human rights, and education. It has done so through operating institutions such as orphanages and hospitals and through sponsoring nongovernmental organizations that provide social benefits. This has been particularly important given the ongoing war between the state and both the guerrilla forces that control large areas of the country and the various organizations involved in narcotics trafficking.

SOCIAL ASPECTS In its views on marriage and the family the Colombian Catholic Church follows the direction of the Vatican. Many poor couples in Colombia,

both urban and rural, live together as common-law partners because they cannot afford a Catholic (nor a civil) wedding celebration. There is a gay-rights movement in Colombia that has been becoming increasingly public. The church often speaks about these, and other, social issues to the Colombian population and to the country's politicians.

An important aspect of Catholic family life in Colombia is the *compadrazgo* (copaternity) system. When a child is baptized, the parents choose his or her *compadres* (godparents), who will provide guidance and financial support for the child.

POLITICAL IMPACT From its foundation the Colombian state has had a formal relationship with the Catholic Church. The church was one of the pillars of the colonial government. After independence (1824) the country was embroiled in a long series of often violent struggles around the church's place in society and its relationship to the state. Although the country's constitution formally separates the Catholic Church from the state, the church maintains its role as a critical public voice and as a symbol of Colombian nationality and is influential in the country's political life.

CONTROVERSIAL ISSUES The Colombian Catholic Church promulgates the position of the Vatican on controversial issues such as divorce, birth control, and abortion. Colombia is a secular country with laws allowing divorce, but the church disapproves of dissolving a marriage. In practice many Catholics in Colombia use methods of contraception that are not condoned by the church. Abortion is illegal in Colombia, and efforts to legalize it have been met with protestations from the Catholic Church. In 1997 euthanasia was decriminalized in Colombia; the measure was denounced by the country's Catholic bishops.

CULTURAL IMPACT Since the colonial era the Catholic Church has been an important patron of Colombian art. The most notable architectural works of the colonial period, for instance, are church buildings. They include the elaborate Santo Domingo Church (sixteenth century) in Tunja and the baroque Palace of the Inquisition (eighteenth century) in Cartagena.

Although other institutions have risen to the fore as promoters of art in Colombia, the Catholic Church continues to occupy an important place, both as an institution and because of its prominence in Colombian

COLOMBIA

society and culture. For example, there are notable Colombian painters (such as Fernando Botero, born in
1932) who converse with the religious history of Colombian and international art even when they do not explicitly deal with religious themes.

Colombian scholarship is probably best known
through the writings of the Nobel Prize-winning novelist and journalist Gabriel García Márquez (born in
1928). One of the proponents of the school of magical
realism, a literary movement that takes seriously the
metaphysical qualities of popular Latin American religiosity, García Márquez also writes about the wars surrounding the Colombian Catholic Church in the nineteenth century.

Since the late twentieth century a number of Colombian fiction writers have addressed the important
role of popular religiosity in social and political life.
These include Laura Restrepo (born in 1950), author
of *Dulce Compañía* (1995; *The Angel of Galilea*); Fernando
Vallejo (born in 1942), who wrote *La Virgen de los Sicarios*
(1994; *Our Lady of the Assassins*); and Jorge Franco (born
in 1962), author of *Rosario Tijeras* (1999).

Other Religions

Although Colombia is strongly Catholic, it contains
much religious diversity. Part of the variety is a result
of Colombia's historical assemblage of distinct peoples,
but a significant portion also derives from the growth
of non-Catholic religions among its people since the late
twentieth century.

Colombia was the seat of important Indian chiefdoms, such as the Chibcha (also called Muisca), a people who lived in the area around modern-day Bogotá.
As a result of centuries of ethnic mixing, today almost
60 percent of the country's population is considered
mestizo, or of mixed Indian descent. Indians themselves
make up about 1 percent of the population. Colombia
received large numbers of slaves from Africa during the
colonial period. It is estimated that more than a fifth—
and perhaps as much as a third—of its population is
of African origin. Both Indians and Africans have left
their stamp on the religions of Colombia.

The influence of Indian and African culture is particularly evident in the popular Catholicism of Colombia. Indigenous and African religious practices continue
within this common, often extra-official, form of Catholicism. For instance, many Colombians of African

heritage who are officially Catholic also maintain links
to the broader culture of the African diaspora through
forms of music and dance and through a sense of religiosity related to spirits and spirit possession. Such practitioners are largely concentrated in the western department of Chocó.

Some groups in Colombia continue to practice recognizable forms of indigenous and African religiosities.
In Colombia's highlands most indigenous peoples were
assimilated into Catholicism. It took longer for lowland
peoples to be brought into the mainstream Colombian
culture, and as a result they have maintained many more
of their religious traditions, including classic Amazonian shamanism. Many peoples employ a range of hallu-
cinogenic substances as part of the shamanic journey.
Their cosmology generally builds on a stratified sequence of levels, from the world above, to this world,
to the world below. The most relevant deities are those
involved in everyday natural and social events. Indigenous mythologies are filled with tales of folk heroes.
Each group has its own history and particularity and
therefore its own distinctive form of social life and behavior.

Many indigenous groups face heavy social pressure
to become Christians from Catholic or Protestant missions situated near their villages. Interaction with the
Colombian state and the powerful missions has created
a crisis of religious identity and meaning for many peoples. This has often led to the development of amalgams
of Christianity and the indigenous norms of the converts. Sometimes the traditional religious system is
maintained on the edges of formal Christianity.

The cosmology of the central Andes—the area that
was once the Inca empire—has developed into a vital
aspect of the religious practices of the people of southern Colombia. In this region the landscape is considered
spiritually significant; mountains and other natural features are seen as sacred. Practitioners of Andean spirituality see dreams as an important means by which information about the world is communicated to humans.
They are omens that must be read upon awakening. Furthermore, the religious specialists of this region, especially those who are members of the Ingano people of
the Sibundoy valley, are known for their curative abilities and powers. People from many other areas of Colombia seek them out.

Since the late twentieth century indigenous religious practices have become increasingly popular among
urban middle- and upper-middle-class Colombians.

Such people have been particularly interested in employing the various forms of shamanism and traditional healing.

In 1822 several islands off the Caribbean coast, including San Andrés, became part of Colombia (they had previously been under English, and then Spanish, jurisdiction). These areas of largely black population are historically Protestant, an aspect that has not changed despite Catholicism's dominance in Colombia. As in other parts of Latin America, Pentecostals are largest single sector of Colombian Protestants. They are an important social force among poor city dwellers and residents of rural areas.

Colombia has a significant population of Jehovah's Witnesses. They are a thriving and important community within the country. Colombia also claims an increasing population of members of the Church of Jesus Christ of Latter-day Saints (Mormons).

Judaism was first taken to Colombia in the sixteenth century by Spanish settlers. The modern Jewish community in Colombia can be traced back to immigrants who arrived from the Caribbean islands of Jamaica and Curaçao in the eighteenth century. In the first half of the twentieth century a significant number of Jews immigrated to Colombia from the Middle East, North Africa, and Europe. Most Jewish Colombians today reside in the major cities. There has been a notable decline in the Jewish population since the 1990s, when many Jews emigrated in response to the country's violence and economic problems. In Colombia there are small communities of Muslims. Colombians, particularly middle- and upper-class urbanites, also are drawn to the range of religions found in many other cities of the Western hemisphere, such as Buddhism and New Age religions.

David Knowlton

See Also Vol. 1: *Christianity, Roman Catholicism*

Bibliography

Castillo Cárdenas, Gonzalo. *Liberation Theology from Below: The Life and Thought of Manuel Quintín Lame.* Maryknoll, N.Y.: Orbis Books, 1987.

Domínguez, Jorge I, ed. *The Roman Catholic Church in Latin America.* Garland, 1994.

Goldman, Irving. *Cubeo Hehénewa Religious Thought: Metaphysics of a Northwestern Amazonian People.* Edited by Peter J. Wilson. New York: Columbia University Press, 2004.

Levine, Daniel H. *Religion and Politics in Latin America: The Catholic Church in Venezuela and Colombia.* Princeton, N.J.: Princeton University Press, 1981.

Londoño-Vega, Patricia. *Religion, Culture, and Society in Colombia: Medellin and Antioquia, 1850–1930.* Oxford: Oxford University Press, 2002.

Reichel-Dolmatoff, Gerardo. *Amazonian Cosmos: The Sexual and Religious Symbolism of the Tukano Indians.* Chicago: University of Chicago Press, 1971.

———. *The Sacred Mountain of Colombia's Kogi Indians.* New York: E.J. Brill, 1990.

Taussig, Michael. *Shamanism, Colonialism, and the Wild Man: A Study in Terror and Healing.* Chicago: University of Chicago Press, 1987.

Comoros

POPULATION 614,382

SUNNI MUSLIM 98 percent

CHRISTIAN 2 percent

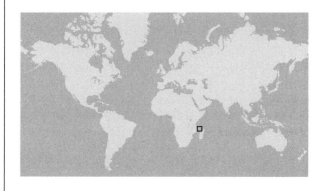

Country Overview

INTRODUCTION The Union of Comoros is a group of three islands—Njazidja (also called Grande Comore), Nzwani (Anjouan), and Mwali (Mohéli)—in the Indian Ocean between Madagascar and the East African coast. Formerly a French colony, it gained independence in 1975. A fourth island in the colony, Mahore (Mayotte), voted to remain a French territory; it is claimed by the Comoros but administered by France.

The location of the Comoros, including its relative proximity to the Arabian Peninsula, has led to a blending of Malagasy, African, and Arab cultures. Despite French colonization, Comorians are overwhelmingly Sunni Muslim. In the twentieth century Muslim brotherhoods that tolerate certain African healing and magico-religious practices have predominated. Since inde-

pendence in 1975, European trained political leaders have embraced Western secularism, while Comorians who have studied in Saudi Arabia and other Arab countries have adopted Wahhabi asceticism, contributing to tensions over political and religious leadership.

RELIGIOUS TOLERANCE Islam is the official state religion in the Comoros. The 2001 constitution provides for freedom of religion, but authorities have infringed upon this right in the past. According to the U.S. Department of State *International Religious Freedom Report* (2003), both the government and Comorian society discourage the practice of religions other than Islam. Christians are prohibited from proselytizing and face social discrimination and some police harassment. There are two Roman Catholic churches and one Protestant church in the country, but these are restricted to expatriates.

Major Religion

ISLAM

DATE OF ORIGIN 800 C.E. to 1500 C.E.
NUMBER OF FOLLOWERS 602,000

HISTORY The Comoros was settled at least a thousand years ago, first by migrants from Madagascar and later by Islamic settlers from the Persian Gulf and the East African coast. According to widely held belief, Islam was brought to the islands earlier—in the seventh century C.E., during the lifetime of the prophet Muhammad—by two Comorian nobles who traveled to Arabia. Archaeological and historical evidence suggests that Islam arrived in the Comoros between the ninth and sixteenth centuries and was introduced by Arab merchants and Shirazi princes who had been expelled from Persia.

Long before French colonization in the nineteenth century, Islam played a central role in the Comoros. Ruling families learned to speak and write Arabic, made the *hajj* (pilgrimage to Mecca), and maintained ties with other Indian Ocean Muslim communities, such as Kilwa, Zanzibar, and Oman. Several *tariqa* (Sufi brotherhoods), including the Shadiliya, the Qadiriya, and the Rifaiya, became active in the islands; these brotherhoods embraced mysticism and adopted specific rites for contact with Allah, but they also accommodated African religious and healing practices, which continued to be followed in the twenty-first century.

EARLY AND MODERN LEADERS According to legend, two seventh-century nobles, Fey Bedja Mwamba and Mtswa Mwandze, took Islam to the Comoros after their travels to Jeddah and Mecca. Hassan bin Issa, an early sixteenth-century Shirazi chief who claimed to be a descendent of the prophet Muhammad, also contributed to the Islamization of the islands by building mosques and encouraging conversion. Sheikh Abdalah Darwesh initiated the Shadiliya brotherhood in the Comoros in the late nineteenth century. Originally from Grande Comore, Sheikh Darwesh traveled throughout the Middle East and Syria, where he studied science and the Koran. He later converted Siad Muhammad Al-Maarouf (1852–1904), who became the supreme guide of the Shadiliya brotherhood, which subsequently spread from the Comoros to the East African coast.

MAJOR THEOLOGIANS AND AUTHORS Sheikh Al-Ami bin Ali al-Mazruwi (1890–1949) was the first ulama (religious scholar) of the region to use the Swahili language and to write books on Islam. Al-Habib Omar (d. 1976) was born in the Comoros and studied in Arab countries before serving as a teacher and *cadi* (Muslim magistrate) in Madagascar, Zanzibar, and, after 1964, the Comoros.

HOUSES OF WORSHIP AND HOLY PLACES There are almost 800 mosques in the Comoros, as well as numerous Koranic schools. Mosques are located in villages and towns throughout the islands and range from small, stone houses to large, elaborate palaces, such as the old

A man walks past the Old Friday Mosque in the Comoran capital, Moroni. Mosques are located in villages and towns throughout the Comoros islands and range from small, stone houses to large, elaborate palaces. © ANTONY NJUGUNA/REUTERS NEWMEDIA INC./CORBIS.

Friday Mosque on the waterfront in Moroni, the island's capital. In 1998 a new Grand Mosque, financed by the emir of Sharjah (of the United Arab Emirates), was inaugurated in Moroni.

WHAT IS SACRED? The tombs of Islamic holy men and local founders of religious brotherhoods are frequently sites of pilgrimage during holy days.

HOLIDAYS AND FESTIVALS Comorians observe the major Muslim holidays, including Id al-Adha (Feast of the Sacrifice), Muharram (Islamic New Year), Ashura, *Mawlid* (birth of the prophet Muhammad), *Leilat al-Mairaj* (Ascension of the Prophet), *Laylat al-Mi'raj* (Night of the Ascension), and Ramadan (the holy month of fasting). The entire month of the birth of the Prophet, celebrated according to the Islamic lunar calendar, is marked by a succession of celebrations at the family, quarter, and village level, culminating in a feast prepared for the ulama (community of religious men). This month is almost as sacred in the Comoros as Ramadan. Muslim brotherhoods, such as the Qadiriya, celebrate the deaths of their founder by inviting the disciples of the brotherhood in other villages to come participate.

MODE OF DRESS Traditionally men dress in trousers and light, white gowns. They also wear white jackets decorated with golden thread over the gowns, *kofias* (caps with intricate sewn designs) or fezes, and leather sandals. Today many men have adopted European dress. Women of all ages and social classes still wear the *chirumani*, a length of printed cloth wound round the body. Different colors and designs express regional and class variations.

DIETARY PRACTICES Comorians generally observe Islamic prohibitions against pork and alcohol and fast during the holy month of Ramadan. Diet reflects the history of French colonialism and, especially, the island's tropical maritime location.

RITUALS Comorians observe standard Muslim practices of prayer and devotion: prayer five times a day, Friday mosque, fasting during Ramadan, and, for wealthier Muslims, the pilgrimage to Mecca. Drawing on their African heritage, many Comorians also consult *mwalimus* or *fundi* (medicine men and astrologers learned in the use of sacred texts and knowledge) and marabouts (holy men) for divination, healing, and protection from evil spirits. *Mwalimus* perform ceremonies to activate jinni (spirit beings) to determine propitious days for holding feasts, whether a proposed marriage will succeed, or the cause of illness. *Mwalimus* also perform private and communal healing ceremonies and prepare amulets that contain Koranic texts.

RITES OF PASSAGE The major events in the life of a person—birth, marriage, and death, as well as circumcision for males—are all marked by rites of passage. After the birth of a child, the husband sends his wife's family a large quantity of bananas, sugar, rice, and a cow. Boys are circumcised before the age of 12. An illness leading to death is a private family affair, but beginning with the funerary washing of the body and continuing through the funeral prayer and burial, the entire village participates under the direction of Muslim religious men. By far the most elaborate rite of passage in the Comoros is the grand marriage that is practiced by wealthier families. Grand marriages may last up to three weeks and entail feasts, dances, parades, prayers, and gifts of jewelry, furniture, food, and other household items. Families of more modest means practice scaled-down marriage ceremonies.

MEMBERSHIP More than 98 percent of Comorians are Muslim, which attests to the overwhelming success of that religion and the inability of Christian missionaries to make significant inroads during the colonial period. Prior to French colonization, wealthy families learned Arabic, made the pilgrimage to Mecca, and maintained family and trade connections with Muslim communities throughout the Indian Ocean coastal region. Today Comorian citizens are prohibited from attending Christian church services. Wealthy urban families typically follow orthodox observances of Muslim holy days and possess a thorough knowledge of Islamic theology and law. In the countryside agricultural work schedules and poverty make for less strict observance. Nonetheless, in both rural areas and town, boys and girls begin to attend Koranic schools at about the age of seven.

SOCIAL JUSTICE Although Islam requires giving alms to the poor, the difficult economic situation and turbulent political climate since independence in 1975 have fostered neither human rights nor social justice in the Comoros. Different factions have sought to mobilize religious support both to uphold and to contest political power and social inequality. Political opponents have relied on their own interpretation of the Koran and hadith (traditions of the prophet Muhammad), advocating Shari'ah (Islamic law) in an effort to rectify government corruption, rigged elections, mismanagement, and interference by foreign mercenaries.

SOCIAL ASPECTS In accordance with Islamic law men are able to marry up to four wives, although most men in the Comoros marry only one wife at a time. Islam in the Comoros has adapted itself to the widespread practice of matrilocality, by which a married couple resides with the wife's family. When a young woman is ready to marry, her parents will build her a house or add an extension to their home. If a man marries more than one wife, his wives will live in separate households. The husband is expected to divide his time and to contribute equally among each wife's household.

Women's status is influenced by Islamic values of modesty and seclusion, although seclusion is practiced primarily in wealthy families. Wives of less affluent men circulate freely, sell at markets, and work in the fields. Although women are largely excluded from public affairs, they inherit land, houses, and jewelry and frequently finance their husband's and brother's trading and cash crop ventures. Compared with women in many Islamic societies, Comorian women have considerable influence and liberty. Family elders are highly respected and provide worldly and spiritual guidance.

POLITICAL IMPACT In precolonial times Islam served to uphold ruling nobles who claimed descent from Arab or Persian ancestors or even from the Prophet himself. Since independence competing Islamic views have entered the political scene, both to justify and to challenge government power. Government officials have adopted Western political ideologies while continuing to support the leaders of the Islamic brotherhoods.

Since independence Islamic fundamentalism and Wahhabism have grown in popularity as students have returned from Islamic studies abroad. In response to perceived corruption, injustice, hypocrisy, and chaos within the Comorian government, fundamentalists have sought to create a genuine Islamic republic with the Koran as the central guide.

CONTROVERSIAL ISSUES Because of high population density, the Comorian government has favored birth control and family planning, but Islamic reservations about contraception have made official advocacy hazardous. Abortion is authorized only for serious medical reasons and is otherwise against the law. Divorce and remarriage are accepted, but because of matrilocal residence, women retain the family home and property.

CULTURAL IMPACT While observing the Muslim prohibition against representational images, artisans produce wood carvings, jewelry, raffia weavings, and embroidery with elaborate geometric designs distinctive to the Comoros. Doors, tables, Koran and lamp holders, cabinets, and tourist art are covered with complex carved patterns. Comorian music, both popular and religious, draws on influences from the Middle East, East Africa, and Madagascar to create its own distinctive and varied styles. Many religious and theological documents, as well as poetry and literature, have been published in Swahili.

Other Religions

In the Comoros there is a small Christian presence restricted mainly to expatriates, including Europeans and residents from Madagascar and Réunion. Because of the strength of Islamic faith, Comorians resisted the influence of colonial missionaries. Comorian Muslims continue to draw on their African heritage to practice numerous agrarian and healing rituals. These include healing ceremonies and spirit possession, divination through contacting jinni, and collective end-of-year sacrificial feasts.

John Cinnamon

See Also Vol. 1: *Islam, Sunni Islam*

Bibliography

Ahmed, Abdallah Chanfi. *Islam et politique aux Comores: Évolution de l'autorité spirituelle depuis le Protectorat français (1886) jusqu'à nos jours.* Paris: Harmattan, 1999.

Newitt, Malyn. *The Comoro Islands: Struggle against Dependency in the Indian Ocean.* Boulder, Colo.: Westview Press, 1984.

Ottenheimer, Martin. *Marriage in Domoni: Husbands and Wives in an Indian Ocean Community.* Prospect Heights, Ill.: Waveland Press, 1984.

Ottenheimer, Martin, and Harriet Ottenheimer. *Historical Dictionary of the Comoro Islands.* Metuchen, N.J.: Scarecrow Press, 1994.

Costa Rica

POPULATION 3,834,934

ROMAN CATHOLIC 70.1 percent

PROTESTANT 18 percent

OTHER RELIGIONS 1.8 percent

NONRELIGIOUS 10.1 percent

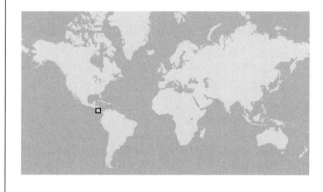

Country Overview

INTRODUCTION Costa Rica is a predominantly Spanish-speaking county located in Central America. Largely mountainous, it lies between Nicaragua to the north and Panama to the south. To the west is the Pacific Ocean, and to the east is the Caribbean Sea.

At the time of the Spanish conquest, beginning in the early sixteenth century, Costa Rica was inhabited by several ethnolinguistic groups: the Chorotegas on the north Pacific coast, the Huétares in the Central Valley and on the Caribbean coast, and the Bruncas in the southern region along the Pacific. More than half the Indians died during the 1500s because of disease or warfare with the Spaniards. By 1611 the entire Costa

Rican population was reported to be 15,000, which included Indians, Spaniards, and mixed race, called *mestizos.*

During the Spanish colonial period (1519–1821), Roman Catholicism dominated the social and religious life of Costa Rica. Beginning in the mid-1800s, however, indentured servants were imported from mainland China to provide labor for the coffee industry, and these workers took their ancient beliefs with them to the New World. During the late 1800s additional Chinese laborers arrived in Costa Rica, along with some East Indians and many Afro-American immigrants from the British West Indies, to help with railroad construction and the development of the banana industry on the Caribbean coast. Upon their arrival most of the East Indians were Hindus, and the majority of the black West Indians were Protestants. The first Protestant worship services were conducted in the nation's capital, San José, in the 1840s among English-speaking foreigners, who were mainly American, British, and German citizens.

The growth and geographical expansion of Protestant denominations, marginal Christian groups, and non-Christian religions in Costa Rica is largely a phenomenon of the post–World War II era, which also witnessed a decline in Catholic church attendance and in the observance of older Catholic traditions.

RELIGIOUS TOLERANCE The constitution of 1949 establishes Roman Catholicism as the state religion and requires that the state contribute to its financial maintenance. It also prohibits the state from impeding the free exercise of other religions that practice universal moral standards and acceptable social behavior.

Major Religion

ROMAN CATHOLICISM

DATE OF ORIGIN 1522 C.E.
NUMBER OF FOLLOWERS 2.7 million

HISTORY The Spanish conquistadors first explored the territory of Costa Rica along the Pacific coast in 1519. A participant in the González Dávila expedition of 1522 was Spanish Catholic priest Diego de Agüero, who became the first foreign religious worker to visit the territory known today as Costa Rica and Nicaragua. After exploring the northwestern part of Costa Rica, the Spaniards established a temporary settlement among the Chorotega Indians on the Nicoya Peninsula, where de Agüero claimed to have baptized nearly 6,000 individuals. The first Catholic church was built in 1544 in the village of Nicoya.

Roman Catholicism dominated the social and religious life of Costa Rica until the mid-1800s, when the population was mostly homogeneous and other religions were prohibited. The majority were poor *mestizo* farmers and laborers, while a minority were Europeans of Spanish stock who owned most of the land and controlled the country politically, economically, and socially. There were also a small number of black slaves and freedmen on the Caribbean coast and of American Indian peoples who inhabited remote parts of the country.

From the beginning of the Spanish colonial period until the mid-1800s, the Catholic Church in Costa Rica was administered as part of the episcopal province of León, Nicaragua; however, in 1850 an independent bishopric (diocese) was created by Pope Pius IX. In 1852 a concordat with the Vatican was signed in which the jurisdiction over church property and its temporal rights were transferred to Costa Rican civil authorities. In 1878 the first Catholic seminary was established for training local priests. The Archdiocese of San José was created in 1929.

Historically the Catholic Church in Costa Rica has suffered from a lack of economic resources because it depended on the tithes of a relatively small and poor population. Whereas the majority of the diocesan priests were Costa Ricans, almost all of the religious priests (members of religious orders) were foreigners from Spain, Germany, Italy, and the United States. In rural areas many Catholic priests had to serve 10 to 15 remote parishes each month.

Catholics sleep in the plaza outside of the Basilica of Our Lady of the Angels following a pilgrimage to worship "La Negrita," the patron saint of Costa Rica. AP/WIDE WORLD PHOTOS.

In 2002 the ecclesiastical province of Costa Rica consisted of 7 dioceses and 284 parishes, which were served by 561 diocesan priests and 192 religious priests.

EARLY AND MODERN LEADERS Presbyter Dr. Anselmo Llorente y Lafuente (died in 1871) was the first bishop of the diocese of Costa Rica (appointed 1851). He obtained pontifical approval for the University of Saint Thomas, founded in San José in 1843.

Msgr. Víctor Manuel Sanabria y Martínez (died in 1952) was an intellectual and author who promoted a series of social reforms during the 1930s and 1940s to counteract the growing influence of Marxist-inspired labor unions. Dr. Benjamín Núñez Vargas (1915–94) was a priest, educator, and social reformer; he helped organize the labor union Rerum Novarum Confederation of Costa Rican Workers in the mid-1940s and played an important role in the formation of the National Liberation Party.

Msgr. Hugo Barrantes Ureña (born in 1952), the sixth archbishop of San José, took office in 2002 with a promise to renew the work of the church and the conviction that priests should spend more time on the streets and with the people in order to recover lost members and attract new followers.

MAJOR THEOLOGIANS AND AUTHORS Dr. Arnoldo Mora Rodríguez (born in 1937) is a former Dominican priest, philosopher, theologian, politician, author, and art critic. Mora, who represents the progressive wing of the Catholic Church in Costa Rica, authored *Monseñor Romero* (1981), an important work about the popular reformist archbishop of El Salvador who was assassinated by right-wing elements during the civil war in 1980, and *Los orígenes del pensamiento socialista en Costa Rica* (1988; *The Origins of Socialist Thought in Costa Rica*).

Dr. Pablo Richard (born in 1939) was a diocesan priest in Chile and earned a doctorate in sociology of religion at the Sorbonne, Paris, before moving to Costa Rica in the late 1970s; he is one of the international leaders of the liberation theology movement, a socially and politically progressive Catholic movement that emerged in the 1960s in Latin America. Dr. Richard has written extensively, including such books as *La iglesia latinoamericana entre el temor y la esperanza* (*The Latin American Church between Fear and Hope*) and *Religión y Política en América Central* (*Religion and Politics in Central America*).

HOUSES OF WORSHIP AND HOLY PLACES Most of the remaining Catholic churches from the colonial era are now preserved as historical monuments, whether or not they are still in use. The Basilica of Our Lady of the Angels in Cartago, a large, ornate wooden structure built in the 1920s, is considered by Catholics to be the most sacred religious site in the country.

WHAT IS SACRED? The principal religious relic that exists in Costa Rica is a small stone statue of the Virgin Mary holding the Christ Child. Preserved in a grotto under the Basilica of Our Lady of the Angels in Cartago, the statue is located near the site where the Virgin Mary allegedly appeared in 1635.

HOLIDAYS AND FESTIVALS There are more than 2,000 towns in Costa Rica that are named after a Catholic saint, and in many of these places the most important day of the year is the celebration of their patron saint, which typically includes a parade of people carrying religious icons, as well as a carnival of other attractions. Together with the Day of the Virgin (2 August),

the most important religious holidays are Lent and Holy Week.

MODE OF DRESS Although diocesan priests in Costa Rica usually wear traditional Roman Catholic clerical garb whenever they appear in public, many priests and nuns no longer wear the traditional cassock of their respective religious orders. All active Catholics have been instructed to dress modestly, but there has never been any particular religious attire required of laypeople in Costa Rica.

DIETARY PRACTICES The only dietary restrictions among Catholics in Costa Rica today are those practiced during Lent and Holy Week, when faithful Catholics are expected to refrain from eating the meat of animals and drinking alcoholic beverages.

RITUALS Although most middle- and upper-class Catholics in Costa Rica feel obligated to observe the traditional Catholic rituals, many members of the lower socioeconomic class often do not have the resources to pay the cost of formal religious ceremonies, such as baptisms, confirmations, weddings, and funerals. Most active Catholics routinely recite formal prayers, say the Rosary, and go on pilgrimages.

RITES OF PASSAGE Like all Latin American Catholics, Costa Rican Catholics follow the basic rites of passage, including infant baptism, catechism classes, confirmation and First Communion, marriage, ordination of priests and deacons, last rites, and funerals.

MEMBERSHIP Since the 1960s the number of Catholics in Costa Rica has declined because of the growth of secularization, modernization, and new religious movements. Consequently, the Catholic Church of Costa Rica has taken a defensive stance regarding its own institutional decay and membership decline by denouncing "the invasion of the sects" and the loss of traditional moral and spiritual values. In general, the church's clerical leadership in Costa Rica has sought to deal with the problems underlying the decline by chastising the unfaithful, calling on nominal believers to take catechism classes, denouncing other religious groups, and seeking to "reevangelize those who are already baptized" as Roman Catholics.

SOCIAL JUSTICE The recommendations of the Second Vatican Council (1962–65) and the Conference of

Latin American Bishops in Medellín, Colombia, in 1968 defined a new social role for the Catholic Church in Latin America—that of the "Preferential Option for the Poor." This new option led to the development of liberation theology, which had as its goal the liberation of the poor from the socioeconomic and political structures of oppression in Latin America and the respect for human rights. The Ecumenical Department of Investigations, an independent think tank and publishing program in Costa Rica, continues the liberation theology tradition under the leadership of former priests Franz Hindelammert and Pablo Richard.

SOCIAL ASPECTS Until the 1960s the Catholic Church and popular Catholic religiosity dominated the political, social, and religious life of Costa Rica. Beginning in the 1960s a large gap emerged between the official moral and ethical teaching of the Catholic Church and the Catholic population regarding marriage and family life. A growing number of couples began choosing a civil rather than a religious marriage ceremony and started using birth control methods prohibited by the Catholic Church; divorce became more prevalent; and overall Mass attendance declined.

POLITICAL IMPACT After independence from Spain in 1821, a series of liberal parties vied with conservative ones for control of the government. Since the mid-1940s two major political ideologies have dominated Costa Rican politics: the Social Christian movement (conservatives) and the Social Democrat movement (liberals). Today the Social Christian Unity Party (known as PUSC) represents the former, and the National Liberation Party (known as PLN) represents the latter. Between 1950 and 1990, the PLN won more presidential elections than the PUSC, but during the 1990s the reverse was true.

In Costa Rica most politicians and civil servants are Roman Catholics, but priests and nuns are prohibited from serving in public office. Some church officials, however, have been accused of participating in partisan political activities and have been censured by their higher authorities.

CONTROVERSIAL ISSUES For many Costa Ricans, affiliation with the Roman Catholic Church is becoming less of a social obligation than in previous decades, with fewer than 20 percent of Catholics today regularly attending Mass. During the 1990s public opinion polls revealed that a growing number of Catholics were unhappy with the church's official policy regarding birth control, divorce, remarriage, abortion, the role of women in the church, obligatory celibacy for priests and nuns, the absolute authority of the pope and the bishops, and the lack of lay participation in decision making.

CULTURAL IMPACT Until the 1960s Catholicism had a strong influence on many aspects of Costa Rican life, but its impact on the arts was modest. Most Costa Ricans are part of a tradition of popular religiosity that views Catholicism as more of a social responsibility than a moral obligation, and this worldview is reflected in their music, art, and literature, which is more secular than religious.

Other Religions

Protestantism first arrived in Costa Rica in the nineteenth century. In response to the needs of the growing black West Indian population on the Caribbean coast, the Jamaican Baptist Missionary Society sent its first workers to Costa Rica in 1887, the British Wesleyan Methodists in 1894, the Anglicans in 1896, the Seventh-day Adventists in 1903, and the Salvation Army in 1907. By 1950 at least 15 Protestant mission agencies had begun work in Costa Rica among blacks and *mestizos*.

The first Protestant mission agency established in the Central Valley was the Central American Mission (now CAM International). CAM sent its first missionary couple, the Rev. and Mrs. William McConnell, to Costa Rica in 1891. This early missionary effort progressed slowly and with great difficulty because of the primitive conditions of the country and opposition from the Catholic clergy. In 1960 CAM organized the Association of Central American Churches (ACAM), with 27 local churches. Although nondenominational, CAM and ACAM are fundamentalist and separatist in nature and have had difficulty working with people from other denominations until the past few decades.

By contrast, the work of the interdenominational Latin America Mission (LAM), founded by Scottish Presbyterian couple Harry and Susan Strachan in 1921, has been significant in the historical development of Protestantism in Costa Rica. During the 1920s and 1930s the Strachans worked with missionaries of other Protestant denominations in San José to conduct evangelistic crusades, educate pastors and lay workers, provide medical treatment, and promote the social welfare of the general population, despite strong opposition from the Catholic clergy.

Between 1950 and 1985 a minimum of 28 other Protestant missionary societies started work in Costa Rica. Numerous church organizations came into existence as a result of the nationalization of these missionary efforts, as a reaction to missionary domination of church affairs, or as a result of independent efforts. At the beginning of the twenty-first century, there were more than 200 Protestant denominations in Costa Rica, most of which were independent of foreign support.

A small percentage of the Costa Rican population belongs to other Christian faiths, including other Catholic and Eastern Orthodox traditions, such as the Reformed Catholic Church, the Russian Orthodox Church in Exile, and the Catholic Apostolic Orthodox Church, as well as marginal Christian groups, such as Jehovah's Witnesses, the Church of Jesus Christ of Latter-day Saints, the Unity School of Christianity, Mita Congregation, Voice of the Chief Cornerstone, Light of the Word Church, Christadelphians, God is Love Church, and Universal Church of the Kingdom of God.

Costa Rica has a large number of non-Christian religions, including the Bahai faith, Buddhism, traditional Chinese religions, Hinduism, Islam, and Judaism. There are also followers of various Native American animistic religions, magic-witchcraft, ancient wisdom, and a variety of New Age Spiritualist movements. In addition, Myalism-Obeah, Rastafarianism, and Vodou are reported to exist among the black West Indian population, especially on the Caribbean coast.

At the start of the twenty-first century, approximately 10 percent of the Costa Rican population had no religious affiliation.

Clifton L. Holland

See Also Vol. 1: *Christianity, Roman Catholicism*

Bibliography

Blanco Segura, Ricardo. *Historia eclesiástica de Costa Rica: 1502–1850.* 2nd ed. San José, Costa Rica: EUNED, 1983.

Hiltunen de Biesanz, Mavis, et al. *Los Costarricenses.* San José, Costa Rica: EUNED, 1979.

Holland, Clifton L. "Religion in Costa Rica." Religion-in-the-Americas. Prolades. 10 June 2004. http://www.prolades.com.

Holland, Clifton L., ed. *World Christianity: Central America and the Caribbean.* Monrovia, Calif.: MARC-World Vision International, 1981.

Nelson, Wilton. *Historia del Protestantismo en Costa Rica.* San José, Costa Rica: Publicaciones INDEF, 1983.

Côte d'Ivoire

POPULATION 16,804,784

MUSLIM 38.5 percent

AFRICAN INDIGENOUS 31.5 percent

ROMAN CATHOLIC 19.5 percent

PROTESTANT 6.0 percent

HARRIST 1.5 percent

OTHER CHRISTIAN 3.0 percent

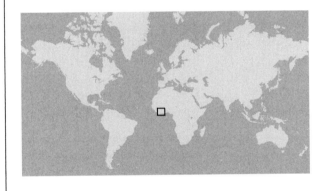

Country Overview

INTRODUCTION The Republic of Côte d'Ivoire—until 1986 also officially known by its English translation, the Ivory Coast—is a former French colony on the Atlantic coast of West Africa. Bordered by Liberia and Guinea to the west, Ghana to the east, and Burkina Faso and Mali to the north, Côte d'Ivoire is located in a low-lying region, with areas of savanna and forest. Its economy is based largely on agriculture. Ivorians include more than 60 ethnic groups, each with its own language or dialect, that fall within five large ethnic clusters: Akan,

Kru, Northern Mande, Southern Mande, and Voltaique (Gur).

Côte d'Ivoire's religious pluralism complements its cultural and linguistic diversity. Ivorians have adapted Islam and Christianity to their indigenous beliefs in a variety of ways, and many ethnic groups have incorporated selected aspects of one religion or the other. Indigenous religions and Islam have coexisted since the fourteenth century, when Islam began to penetrate the northern part of the country from the empire of Mali. Catholicism and Protestantism arrived later, between the seventeenth and nineteenth centuries. The French took over the government of the country in 1893. Since Côte d'Ivoire won its independence from France in 1960, a large number of economic immigrants, about 70 percent of them Muslim, have arrived from neighboring countries.

Geographically Muslims are concentrated in the northern half of the country, although large communities also exist in the south, especially in Abidjan, Côte d'Ivoire's commercial capital and its seat of government. Islam is the dominant religion among certain ethnic groups, such as the Juula (Dyula), Malinké, and Senoufo, that have a long-standing tradition of contact with Mali, which is predominantly Muslim. Roman Catholics and Protestants of various denominations are found mostly in the southern, central, and western regions of the country. Roman Catholicism and the Harrist Church have their largest followings among Akan- and Kru-speaking peoples, such as the Baoulé, Anyi, Guéré, and Wobé. African indigenous beliefs persist in rural areas more commonly than in urban centers.

Ivorian villagers stand in front of a mud mosque. Shrines for worship and ceremonies, usually simple mud huts with enough space for the members of an extended family, are common in rural areas. © BRIAN A. VIKANDER/CORBIS.

RELIGIOUS TOLERANCE The constitution of 2000 guarantees religious freedom. Religious groups are required to register with the authorities, but penalties are rare for those that fail to do so. Traditional religions do not officially register.

Although more than one-third of the Ivorian population practices Islam, successive pro-Christian administrations in Côte d'Ivoire since 1960 have discriminated against Muslims as well as followers of traditional indigenous religions. Some Muslims have openly accused the government of refusing to employ them and to renew their national identity cards. The government denies victimizing Muslims, but many Muslims feel that authorities use them as scapegoats for the country's political and economic problems.

Followers of traditional religions believe in egalitarianism and do not see much difference between their religion and Christianity and Islam. Biases against traditional religions exist, however. Christian and Muslim leaders have been criticized for stigmatizing those who practice traditional indigenous religions by calling them "pagans" and accusing them of involvement in black magic and human sacrifice.

Nonetheless, relations between the various religious communities remained amicable for the most part until the 2000 presidential campaign, during which the pro-Christian government disqualified the main Muslim candidate. Conflicts between Muslims and Christians have increased with Côte d'Ivoire's unstable political conditions.

Major Religions

SUNNI ISLAM

AFRICAN INDIGENOUS BELIEFS

SUNNI ISLAM

DATE OF ORIGIN 1300 C.E.
NUMBER OF FOLLOWERS 6.5 million

HISTORY Islam spread into what is today northern Côte d'Ivoire around the fourteenth century. The Malinké rulers of the empire of Mali had adopted the religion, and its influence progressively extended throughout the savanna region of West Africa. Islamized Juula traders in gold and kola nuts gradually moved southward toward the sources of gold, converting some local leaders to Islam. By the 1890s Muslim leader Samory Touré (c. 1830–1900) controlled most of the northern part of Côte d'Ivoire. The colonial administration, established in 1893, saw Islam as a threat to French rule and therefore kept Muslims under close surveillance and discouraged other Ivorians from converting to Islam.

Since the end of French rule in 1960, all the heads of state and many senior government officials of Côte d'Ivoire have been Roman Catholics. To appease the marginalized Muslims, President Félix Houphouët-Boigny (1905–93) built a grand mosque in Yamoussoukro, his birthplace, and another in Abidjan-Riviera. Nevertheless, Muslim students and other critics continued to censure Houphouët-Boigny's pro–Roman Catholic stance, underscored by the $400 million basilica he built in Yamoussoukro, a much larger structure than Saint Peter's Basilica in Rome.

The dominant strand of Ivorian Islam is Orthodox Sunni, which espouses Sufism. Sufi marabouts (holy men) organize their followers into brotherhoods, of which four exist in Côte d'Ivoire: the Qadiriya, the oldest and most influential, founded in Iraq in the eleventh century; the Tidjaniya; the Senoussiya; and the Ahmadiya, which flourished in Abidjan, especially in the 1960s and 1970s. The Ahmadiya originated in India and is the only non-Sunni brotherhood in Côte d'Ivoire and the rest of West Africa. A strain of Sunni Islam that emerged in nineteenth-century Saudi Arabia in response to maraboutism, Wahhabism arrived in Cote d'Ivoire from Mali and gained a strong foothold in Bouaké in the central part of the country.

EARLY AND MODERN LEADERS The Juula still revere Samory Touré as a brave Muslim leader who opposed French expansion into the more remote regions of the country. By the 1880s Samory had brought the numerous Juula communities under a central political authority. He used his army to implement social reforms, introduced Islamic law in the areas under his command, and built new mosques and schools to continue spreading Islam. Samory's high-handed measures, however, undermined the traditional basis of Juula communities. In 1897, for instance, he executed some 40 senior ulama (religious leaders) for showing contempt for his low level of Islamic education. Although Côte d'Ivoire became a French colony in 1893, Samory continued to resist the French until 1898, when he was finally defeated and exiled to Gabon.

The two most important leaders of present-day Côte d'Ivoire's Islamic community are Imam El Hadj Idriss Koudouss Koné, president of the Conseil National Islamique (National Islamic Council) since 1993, and El-Hadj Moustapha Koweit Diaby, chairman of the Conseil Supérieur Islamique (Islamic Superior Council) since 1990.

MAJOR THEOLOGIANS AND AUTHORS The late fifteenth-century teachings of the Soninké al-Hajj Salim Suwari guided Muslims in their interactions with non-Muslims in the gold-producing areas of the Akan. Suwari, reputed to have made the hajj (pilgrimage) to Mecca seven times, believed that unbelief stemmed from ignorance and that God willed some people to stay in ignorance longer than others. True conversion could therefore occur only at a time determined by God, and forcible conversion through a jihad (armed struggle) against unbelievers amounted to a contravention of God's will. Suwari taught Muslims that their commitment to education would ensure that they were in tune with the laws of Islam at all times.

During the eighteenth and nineteenth centuries the Juula were influenced by the teachings of the Saganogo sheikhs, including Muhammad al-Mustafa (c. 1720–76; born Abbass Saganogo). The Saganogo introduced a new phase of mosque building in Kong, Bouna, and Bondoukou and encouraged Islamic learning among the Juula.

HOUSES OF WORSHIP AND HOLY PLACES The most important center for Islamic activity in Côte d'Ivoire is the city of Bondoukou in the eastern part of the country, which has more than 30 mosques. Two of the country's most prominent mosques are in Yamoussoukro and Abidjan. In rural areas piles of neatly packed stones or inverted green bottles (half-buried in the ground to keep them in place) also constitute places of worship.

WHAT IS SACRED? Many Muslims use amulets (gris-gris) prepared by marabouts, or Muslim holy men, for a variety of purposes—to ward off misfortune, protect against diseases, and ensure happy marriages, among other things. The amulets usually contain verses of the Koran or some of the prophetic hadiths (traditions of the Prophet and his companions), making them sacred objects.

HOLIDAYS AND FESTIVALS The government did not recognize any Muslim holidays before 1974, and only since 1994 have all major Muslim holidays been observed nationally. The most important one in Côte d'Ivoire is Ramadan, when Ivorian Muslims fast from dawn to dusk for a month in accordance with the Fourth Pillar of Islam. The feast of Korité (Id al-Fitr) closes Ramadan with communal prayers, sacrifices of sheep, and visits by relatives and friends. Ivorians celebrate Tabaski (Id al-Kebir), commemorating Ibrahim's (Abraham's) obedience to God's command to sacrifice his son, by praying and sacrificing sheep.

MODE OF DRESS Traditional Muslim men favor loose-fitting, ankle-length boubous (gowns), often embroidered with elaborate Islamic designs, especially for ceremonial occasions. Younger Muslims in urban centers prefer Western-type clothing, although they may appear in boubous on Muslim holidays or at festivals. Muslim women typically avoid short dresses, although exceptions are made by urbanized young women. Women prefer long, flowing gowns and head-ties (made of strips of fabric) for ceremonial events. Veils are uncommon.

DIETARY PRACTICES Like their counterparts elsewhere in the Islamic world, Muslims in Côte d'Ivoire do not eat pork or pork derivatives and do not drink alcohol, because they believe it renders the body impure. Some

Muslims, however—especially youths and young adults in urban areas—frequent nightclubs and may drink.

RITUALS Muslims in Côte d'Ivoire observe the Five Pillars of Islam as the foundation of their rituals: submitting to the will of Allah, praying five times a day, giving alms to the poor, fasting during the month of Ramadan, and, if possible, making the pilgrimage to Mecca at least once. They pray on a prayer mat facing east toward Mecca, cleansing the body before each prayer using a specific set of procedures. During prayer they follow set rules in kneeling, bowing down, and standing up to face the sky. Despite their faith in their religion, many Muslims in Côte d'Ivoire resort to traditional religious practices when they feel it is necessary.

RITES OF PASSAGE Ivorian boys and girls as young as four years old attend Koranic schools on Saturdays and Sundays, where they learn to recite the Koran in Arabic under the supervision of a *mallam* (Islamic teacher). Some established schools in Côte d'Ivoire now offer religious instruction after normal class hours during the week.

Traditionally Muslims begin to instruct girls about womanhood as soon as they reach puberty. The parents have a strong say in the choice of a spouse for their daughter. Marriages represent the union of two families and are an occasion for an ostentatious show of wealth among affluent Muslims.

After a death, the body must be wrapped in white and buried no later than the next day without a coffin. Prayers are held in a mosque before the body is conveyed to the cemetery, and women are not allowed at the graveside.

MEMBERSHIP Since the 1980s the Muslim population has leaped from one-fourth to more than one-third of Côte d'Ivoire's total population. The number of Muslim immigrants from neighboring countries has grown since the mid-1980s, and evangelization by Muslim clerics has also been successful. As the country's political, social, and economic problems have increased, more Ivorians have been converting to Islam than to Christianity, in part because Christianity has been associated with European colonialism and the regimes of Félix Houphouët-Boigny and Henri Konan Bedié, whose pro-Catholic bias caused discontent among non-Catholics. In addition, traditionalists find Islam more compatible than Christianity with indigenous African religious values.

SOCIAL JUSTICE Many Muslims in Côte d'Ivoire give alms to the poor, in accordance with the Third Pillar of Islam. Successful Muslim businesspeople organize charitable associations to help the poor. Donations of food, money, and clothing are offered to mosques in Côte d'Ivoire to assist the needy.

SOCIAL ASPECTS Although the extended family is an integral part of the lives of most Muslims, a rapidly growing number of Muslim men in Côte d'Ivoire, hard hit by the country's economic decline since the mid-1970s, are refraining from marrying multiple wives. Arranged marriages are becoming increasingly anachronistic, especially among educated Muslims in urban areas. Divorce is generally frowned upon, but a man may ask for a divorce if his wife fails to bear children or engages in an extramarital affair. Women rarely take the initiative to seek divorce, but they may if they have strong evidence of an alcoholic or impotent husband. The use of modern contraceptive methods among Ivorian Muslim women is relatively low, though it is more likely among women in cities than those in rural areas.

POLITICAL IMPACT Ivorian Muslim communities have not shown the extremism associated with Islamic fundamentalism elsewhere, but conflicts between Muslims and Christians increased after the presidential election of 2000, when ethnoreligious fighting was not only widespread but also often fatal.

The Conseil Supérieur Islamique (Islamic Superior Council, or CSI), created by President Félix Houphouët-Boigny in 1990, mediates conflict between Muslim groups, bringing together reformists and nonreformists and helping formulate an Islamic agenda in line with government policies. Supervised by the Conseil Supérieur des Imams (Imam's Superior Council), the CSI also strives to maintain peaceful coexistence between Muslims and non-Muslims.

CONTROVERSIAL ISSUES Muslims contend that Islam has instituted equality between men and women. Muslim women, however, largely continue to play traditional roles as wives and mothers. Western-educated Muslim women in urban centers take on a variety of roles in the public sphere—as government functionaries, teachers, and nurses, for example. Others have become successful businesspeople and have performed the hajj to Mecca several times, in part to promote their businesses.

Although there is no specific reference to the practice in the Koran, some Muslims perform infibulation (female genital incision) to mark the coming-of-age for girls. A government ban in 1998 has made it less common, especially in urban centers. Believing the Koran does not endorse abortion, which is illegal but available in Côte d'Ivoire, Muslim women tend to oppose it, but most would support it if a woman's health were in danger. Traditional Muslim men generally feel that even health risks do not justify abortion.

CULTURAL IMPACT Among the better-known authors from Côte d'Ivoire, Ahmadou Kourouma stands out for his *Les Soleils des indépendences* (1968; "The Suns of Independence"), which portrays both Islamic and Malinké indigenous traditions struggling to survive in a powerful but decadent state. Muslim and traditional leaders are depicted as ineffective, but believers continue to cling to them because these authorities define the believer's essence and shape the reality of their world. Kourouma points out the cultural ambivalence of both Muslims and traditionalists.

Islamic calligraphy is part of Ivorian popular art. Artists inscribe passages from the Koran or hadiths on the walls of houses and mosques and on the sides of the minibuses that ply the routes between Abidjan and cities in the interior. A host of locally made objects, such as stools, ceramic pieces, and cushions, often display Islamic designs, with intricate patterns of squares and triangles woven together. Boubous are stylishly embroidered with Islamic motifs.

AFRICAN INDIGENOUS BELIEFS

DATE OF ORIGIN Tenth century C.E.
NUMBER OF FOLLOWERS 5.3 million

HISTORY The oral histories of various ethnic groups indicate that Côte d'Ivoire's earliest inhabitants migrated to their present settlements from the thirteenth century onward. The Senoufo, an ethnic cluster of Bambara origins, migrated into the Korhogo region of north-central Côte d'Ivoire after the decline of the empire of Mali (c. 1550s), in time choosing Islam over their traditional beliefs. Akan groups tracing their origin to the Ashanti empire in what is now central Ghana separated and dis-

persed between the mid-seventeenth and early eighteenth centuries because of conflicts with the Denkyira. The Akan took their traditional religious beliefs and practices into central Côte d'Ivoire, inhabited primarily by the Baoulé. Traditional religions are more widespread in central and western Côte d'Ivoire than in other areas.

EARLY AND MODERN LEADERS Traditional priests, lineage heads, and village chiefs carry out important roles in the indigenous religions practiced in Côte d'Ivoire, including officiating at ritual ceremonies that honor specific deities. Priests, known as Akomfo among Akan groups, undergo an extensive apprenticeship under a more established priest respected in the local community. The priest can divine the source of problems (for example, the death of a family member, a misfortune, or a disease) for his followers, often for a fee, and sometimes suggests remedies for diseases believed to have spiritual causes. Among the Lobi, in the northeastern part of the country, diviners are important religious leaders, providing spiritual guidance for the daily challenges of life rather than predicting the future.

MAJOR THEOLOGIANS AND AUTHORS Ivorian priests and elders, regarded as repositories of spiritual knowledge, pass the beliefs and practices of traditional religions from one generation to the next by word of mouth and through customs. Those given such a responsibility must make painstaking efforts to learn and carry on the oral traditions and to ensure that the right things are done to satisfy ancestral spirits and deities.

HOUSES OF WORSHIP AND HOLY PLACES Many Ivorian villages designate a sacred forest for the performance of ritual activities. Shrines for worship and ceremonies, usually simple mud huts with enough space for the members of an extended family, are common in rural areas. More affluent families may designate a room of their house as a shrine.

WHAT IS SACRED? Most Ivorian ethnic groups recognize a supreme being (Onyame in Twi, the language of the Akan), which they worship through *abosom* (intermediary ancestral spirits and lesser deities). Because ancestral spirits ensure the prosperity of the lineage and provide daily spiritual guidance, they are far more important than lesser deities. Certain trees, rocks, rivers, and lakes are associated with the spiritual life of a village or clan. Wooden masks and statues representing a deity or an ancestral spirit are sacred and may be worn only by specially trained people. When the face of a person makes contact with the inside of the mask, that person is believed to be transformed into the entity the mask represents. Traditional priests and diviners prepare amulets and necklaces of charms (gris-gris) to help ward off evil spirits or to ensure the well-being of the bearer. The people consider these sacred and keep them with great care.

HOLIDAYS AND FESTIVALS The most important communal religious gathering among the Akan peoples is the yam festival, during which they not only give thanks for a bountiful harvest but also honor the dead and solicit their protection against misfortune, disease, and evil spirits. They also express gratitude to the Akan chief who, according to tradition, first tasted the yam, at the risk of his own life, before the food was known to be edible.

The Dan and Wê celebrate a festival of masks between January and April, parading masks that represent different families and clans. In Gomon, near Abidjan, people celebrate the Fête du Dipri, during which women and children perform nocturnal rites to purge the village of evil spirits.

MODE OF DRESS Besides masks, body paintings, and costumes designed for specific rituals and ceremonies, most Ivorians who adhere to traditional religions dress like their compatriots in either Western clothing or traditional attire, which varies from one ethnic group to another. Some have adapted the Muslim boubou (gown), omitting the embroidery.

DIETARY PRACTICES Indigenous religions in Côte d'Ivoire require no dietary restrictions except during some rituals among certain ethnic groups. Among the Baoulé, for example, a widow or widower is expected to fast for six months after the death of a spouse, eating only freshly cooked food once a day at sunset.

RITUALS Traditional Ivorians perform a wide variety of divination, initiation, and funeral rituals designed to protect and strengthen the community. The Baoulé appease divinities through dance, accompanied by singing and drumming. Men perform the dance for Dyè (a deity for men), wearing a mask that embodies the deity, which women dare not look at on pain of death. Funerals generally involve mourners (usually women) and musicians, who trace the history of the deceased's family through songs. Singing, wailing, screaming, and dancing help relieve the loss of a loved one. Among the Baoulé the burial is followed by a ceremony of adoration that involves sprinkling water on the steps of the deceased's house, inviting the ancestors to receive a sacrifice (a chicken, guinea fowl, cow, sheep, or goat), and spilling the blood of the animal on a wall of the house as a permanent reminder.

RITES OF PASSAGE Among some ethnic groups in northern Côte d'Ivoire, secret societies led by community elders initiate and educate the young in the community's beliefs, practices, and history. Among the Senoufo, women's and men's secret societies—called the Sandogo and the Poro, respectively—induct the young of their gender into adulthood. Poro male initiation rituals take place in a forest, usually close to a village, where adolescent boys spend time learning adult roles and bonding with others of their age group. They finish with huge celebrations.

Marriage and death are also marked as rites of passage. When a woman gets married she leaves her father's house and moves in with her husband and in-laws. Because most ethnic groups believe in life after death, funerals mark a transition between the land of the living and the land of the dead.

MEMBERSHIP Practitioners of traditional religions in Côte d'Ivoire most often adhere to the beliefs of the ethnic group to which they belong. Evangelization is not a custom of indigenous religions.

SOCIAL JUSTICE Because communal living is an integral part of life among most Ivorian ethnic groups, especially in rural areas, indigenous religions emphasize self-reliance and selfless community service. Most groups have traditionally depended on agriculture for their livelihood, so that the spiritual well-being of the community is linked to its ability to provide for itself. Laziness is thought to lead to a life of poverty, so children are taught to be industrious from an early age. Farm work is usually shared between husband and wife, often with the bulk of it allocated to the latter. With the increasing economic hardship facing the country, school-age children often sell produce and wares in the streets of Abidjan and Yamoussoukro to help their parents meet the rising cost of living.

SOCIAL ASPECTS The religious ethos of traditional religions in Côte d'Ivoire promotes a strong sense of extended family, which includes parents, children, uncles, aunts, nephews, nieces, and grandparents. Marriage unites families and lineages as well as couples. Among the Dagaaba, though incest is taboo, cross-cousin marriages are common. Such marriages strengthen kinship ties and cement bonds between in-laws. The Senoufo exact heavy fines from those who engage in premarital sexual behavior, and even heavier fines for adultery. Because the sanctions are imposed in the name of the ancestors and the purity of the matrilineage, few commit the offenses.

The emphasis on procreation as an integral part of marriage in traditional communities means that women are treasured for their reproductive capacity; they ensure the continuation of their husband's family name. For this reason birth control and sterilization are taboo to most traditionalists. Among the Senoufo, a married woman has the right to say no to her husband's request to spend the night with her. If she has entered his bedroom, however, she cannot refuse his overtures.

POLITICAL IMPACT Indigenous religions do not have the same social status in Côte d'Ivoire as Christianity and Islam; the Ministry of the Interior does not officially register them as religions. Still, the government often invites traditional Akan chiefs, who perform religious as well as secular functions, to pour a libation to ancestral spirits at important national events.

CONTROVERSIAL ISSUES Among practitioners of indigenous religions, girls between the ages of four and fifteen go through a traditional process of circumcision arranged by their parents. Among the Dan in western Côte d'Ivoire, the event occurs at the beginning of the rice-harvesting season. Despite a government ban on infibulation, and the health risks associated with it, many Ivorians believe it will be difficult to combat the practice. Most groups that lead the campaign against infibulation operate in urban areas and do not reach the rural population. Urban parents often take their daughters to their ancestral villages for the initiation ceremonies.

CULTURAL IMPACT Traditional Ivorian music generally overlays different melodies and rhythms so that no one dominates the others. Among some traditional societies, like the Dan, music permeates every aspect of life, with births, marriages, deaths, and harvests all occasions for musical performances. The griot, or traditional bard, is omnipresent and sings to the music of locally produced instruments made of gourds and animal horns and skins. These instruments include the talking drum (tam-tam), *djembe*, and *shekere*.

The Baoulé, Dan, and Senoufo are known for their artistry, especially their wood carvings. They produce a variety of masks representing the dead or lesser deities.

Other Religions

The introduction of Christianity dates to 1637, when five French Roman Catholic missionaries arrived at Assinie, on the Atlantic coast of Côte d'Ivoire, and attempted to spread their religion—without success. Christianity began to take hold in the nineteenth century, and the first Roman Catholic mission was established in 1895. The African Mission of Lyon (France) evangelized more successfully than earlier groups and by 1911 had established a mission in the northern town of Korhogo. The first African priest was ordained in 1934. While the colonial government allowed Catholic missions to establish their own schools, it promoted a secular school system as well. After Côte d'Ivoire achieved independence from France in 1960, the Roman Catholic Church continued to run schools and seminaries throughout the country.

Protestants have not gained as much influence in Côte d'Ivoire; French colonial authorities were less supportive of them because of their English and American backgrounds. The first Protestant church was founded by British Methodists in 1924 and faced stiff competition from the Roman Catholic Church for converts. The Protestant Methodist Church of Côte d'Ivoire was born from its British predecessor and is the only member of the World Council of Churches in Côte d'Ivoire. Between the world wars the Christian and Missionary Alliance worked among the Baoulé and Toumodi. The World Evangelism Crusade, a British mission, arrived in 1934 and gave rise to the Église Protestant du Centre, which continues to operate today.

African Initiated Churches (AICs) have also had a marked impact on Ivorian religious life. The Harrist Church has commanded the largest following among the country's Protestant denominations since the 1920s. Its founder, Liberian preacher William Wadé Harris, moved to Côte d'Ivoire and began preaching just before World War I. Saying he had received a vision from God, Harris implored his followers to turn to Christianity for salvation and protection rather than using amulets, fetishes, and "witchcraft." Part of his success came from his sensitivity to indigenous religious beliefs, which he discouraged not as reprehensible but as contrary to Christian morality. He also preached at a time when traditional institutions seemed to have failed in the face of French colonialism; he offered Africans salvation from the oppressive colonial system. Harris openly approved of polygamy, but the Harrist Church does not advocate the practice.

Tamba M'bayo

See Also Vol. 1: *African Indigenous Beliefs, Christianity, Islam, Roman Catholicism, Sunni Islam*

Bibliography

Daniels, Morna. *Côte d'Ivoire*. Santa Barbara, Calif.: ABC-Clio, 1996.

Haliburton, Gordon Mackay. *The Prophet Harris: A Study of an African Prophet and His Mass Movement in the Ivory Coast and the Gold Coast, 1913–1915*. London: Longmans, 1971.

Harrison, Christopher. *France and Islam in West Africa, 1860–1960*. Cambridge: Cambridge University Press, 1988.

Kaba, Lansine. *The Wahhabiyya: Islamic Reform and Politics in French West Africa*. Evanston, Ill.: Northwestern University Press, 1974.

Launey, Robert. *Beyond the Stream: Islam and Society in a West African Town*. Berkeley and Los Angeles: University of California Press, 1992.

Levtzion, Nehemia, and Randall L. Pouwels, eds. *The History of Islam in Africa*. Athens: Ohio University Press, 2000.

Mundt, Robert J. *Historical Dictionary of the Ivory Coast (Côte d'Ivoire)*. Metuchen, N.J.: Scarecrow Press, 1987.

Walker, Sheila. *The Religious Revolution in Ivory Coast: The Prophet Harris and the Harrist Church*. Chapel Hill: University of North Carolina Press, 1983.

Croatia

POPULATION 4,390,751

ROMAN CATHOLIC 87.83 percent

EASTERN ORTHODOX 4.42 percent

OTHER CHRISTIAN 0.58 percent

OTHER 1.4 percent

AGNOSTIC, UNDECLARED, NOT RELIGIOUS, OR UNKNOWN 5.77 percent

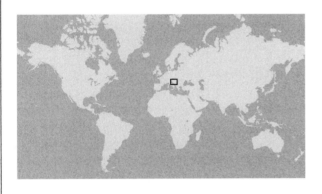

Along with language, religion has played a large part in the preservation of the national identity of Croatians. Roman Catholicism served to identify Croatians in the multinational Yugoslavia, in which Eastern Orthodoxy and Islam were also dominant religions. The fall of communism, the dissolution of Yugoslavia, and the independence of Croatia in the early 1990s strengthened the connection between national and religious identification.

RELIGIOUS TOLERANCE According to its constitution, Croatia is a secular country in which all religious communities are separate from the state, equal before the law, and free in their public action. The position and role of the Catholic Church have been regulated by four agreements that Croatia signed with the Vatican in 1996 and 1998. A 2002 law on the legal position of religious communities regulates the rights and freedoms of other religious groups.

Country Overview

INTRODUCTION The Republic of Croatia is a small country located on the Adriatic Sea in the southeast of Europe. It lost its independence as early as the twelfth century and at times has been a part of Hungary, Austria, and Yugoslavia. In addition, parts of contemporary Croatian territory were once under the control of the Republic of Venice, the Ottoman Empire, Napoleon's France, and Italy. In 1991 Croatia seceded from Yugoslavia to become an independent country.

Major Religion

ROMAN CATHOLICISM

DATE OF ORIGIN Seventh–Ninth century C.E.
NUMBER OF FOLLOWERS 3.9 million

HISTORY Croatians gradually embraced Roman Catholicism between the seventh and ninth centuries C.E. The first official church recognition of Croatia came from Pope John VIII in a letter to the Croatian ruler Branimir in 879. The term "bishop of Croats" was re-

A priest conducts Mass outside of the Chapel of Saint Jerome. The central event of religious life for Catholics in Croatia is Mass on Sunday. © JONATHAN BLAIR/CORBIS.

corded as early as the tenth century. Croatian ecclesiastical independence was furthered by the foundation of the Diocese of Zagreb in 1089–91 and by its promotion to the rank of an archdiocese in 1852. Until the twentieth century, however, it was events in neighboring countries that most influenced the history of Catholicism in Croatia, and Croatians shared the most important church events of the period with other nations. Ottoman invasions and the occupation of a large part of contemporary Croatia resulted in an emphasis on the differences between Christianity and Islam.

After the dissolution of Austria-Hungary and the formation in 1918 of what later became Yugoslavia, the Catholic Church ceased to be the dominant religion in the larger state. In 1935 Yugoslavia and the Vatican signed a concordat on the position of the Catholic Church, but because of strong resistance it was never ratified by the Yugoslav parliament. After World War

II the Communist government implemented hostile policies toward religion, and in 1952 Yugoslavia ended diplomatic relations with the Vatican. Political relations with the Vatican were reestablished in 1966, and religious life gradually became more normal. With Croatia's independence the Catholic Church once again became the dominant religious community.

EARLY AND MODERN LEADERS One of the major historical leaders of the Catholic Church in Croatia was the bishop of Djakovo, Josip Juraj Strossmayer, known for his openness to ecumenism. A participant in the First Vatican Council (1869–70), he was a prominent opponent of the dogma of the infallibility of the pope. After World War II the Communist government condemned the archbishop of Zagreb, Alojzije Stepinac, to 16 years in prison, alleging cooperation with the fascist Ustasha state during the war. In 1953 he was made a cardinal and in 1998 was beatified. His successor was Cardinal Franjo Šeper, who participated in the Second Vatican Council (1962–65) and, beginning in 1968, served as head of the Sacred Congregation for the Doctrine of the Faith. Cardinal Franjo Kuharić (1919–2002) was the archbishop of Zagreb and the president of the conference of Yugoslav bishops for many years. Josip Bozanić became the archbishop of Zagreb in 1997 and was named a cardinal in 2003.

MAJOR THEOLOGIANS AND AUTHORS During the Middle Ages and after, the reputations of such Croatian theologians as Ivan Stojković, Marko Marulić, Juraj Križanić, and Josip Juraj Bošković extended throughout Europe. The central figure in the nineteenth century was Josip Juraj Strossmayer, who was not only a bishop but also a theologian, politician, and cultural worker. In spite of the unfavorable circumstances, during the Communist period there were attempts to revise religious thought in Croatia on the basis of the Second Vatican Council, primarily through the work of such theologians as Tomislav Šagi-Bunić, Vjekoslav Bajsić, and Bonaventura Duda.

HOUSES OF WORSHIP AND HOLY PLACES Croatian Catholics gather in churches for Mass, especially on Sundays. Some churches are extremely old and have the status of protected monuments of culture. These include the basilica in Poreč, dating from the sixth century, and the Church of the Sacred Cross in Nin and Saint Donat's Church in Zadar, both from the ninth century.

During the Communist period few new churches were built, and the process of building intensified after 1990. Many churches were damaged or demolished during the war that accompanied the establishment of independence.

WHAT IS SACRED? Apart from sacred places such as churches, cemeteries, and sanctuaries, relics of the saints were popular in Croatia in the past, and they have remained so to some extent. The cult of the Virgin Mary is highly developed, with frequent prayers being made to her. In some towns processions celebrating the patron saint are still organized. Since 1990 the custom of marking the day of a profession on the feast day of its patron saint has been reintroduced. For example, policemen officially celebrate their day on the feast day of St. Michael.

HOLIDAYS AND FESTIVALS During the Communist period church holidays were not officially recognized in Croatia, although they were privately celebrated. Today they are celebrated as state holidays. The principal holidays of Christmas and Easter are celebrated by many as a part of national culture and tradition rather than for religious reasons. Other state holidays include Epiphany, Corpus Christi, Feast of the Assumption, and All Saint's Day.

MODE OF DRESS Churchgoing in Croatia is no longer marked by formal dress, and there is no religious influence on the mode of dress. Apart from the prescribed clerical dress, priests often wear civilian clothes in everyday life, although this is rare among nuns.

DIETARY PRACTICES At least to some extent, most Croatians honor the regulations on fasting, or moderation in eating, and on abstinence from meat on the holidays of Ash Wednesday and Great (Good) Friday. It is a widespread custom in Croatia to eat fish rather than meat on Christmas Eve. To a lesser extent Croatians fast on Fridays, especially during Lent, and on quaternary days (four times a year). The major church holidays, especially Christmas and Easter, are traditionally marked by formal family meals.

RITUALS The central event of religious life for Catholics in Croatia is Mass on Sunday. The number of regular participants varies, but it has been estimated that 30 percent of the population attends worship services several times a month. Approximately the same percentage prays every day outside religious ceremonies, and half the population makes a confession one or more times a year. Some people undertake pilgrimages, with one of the most popular sites in Croatia being the sanctuary of the Virgin Mary in Marija Bistrica. Since the 1980s Medjugorje, in a predominantly Croatian area of neighboring Bosnia and Herzegovina, has been a popular pilgrimage site. For many people church marriages and funerals are an important part of tradition and of national identity. Based on an agreement between Croatia and the Vatican, church marriages are recognized as if they were contracted by state officials.

RITES OF PASSAGE In Croatia the process of Catholic initiation begins with infant baptism. During the school years, which in Croatia begin at the age of 7, Communion, at about the age of 9, and confirmation, at age 14, are connected to attendance at religious education classes. During the Communist period the classes were organized exclusively by the church. Since 1991, however, religious education has been an elective subject in schools, with approximately 90 percent of all children attending classes. Attending classes in the parish is also required for receiving Communion and for confirmation.

In order to be married in the church, a man and woman must attend a course organized by the church. There also are catechism classes for adults.

MEMBERSHIP Data on church membership in Croatia, specifically on the number receiving sacraments, are recorded only at the parish level. Census data, on the other hand, show strong identification with the Catholic Church, which is often seen as a declaration of belonging to the Croatian people or as respect for tradition. Because of the overlapping of national and religious identity, newer methods of evangelization have not been developed. Nonetheless, the church has a presence in the media and owns several radio stations.

SOCIAL JUSTICE The social teachings of the Catholic Church have become more important in Croatia since independence, particularly in light of the greater inequalities that have developed. As archbishop of Zagreb, Josip Bozanić has spoken on several occasions of Croatian politics and practices that negate basic values of solidarity and public good. Nonetheless, the extent to which the church should interest itself in matters of social justice or influence social policies has itself been debated. The church in Croatia has only marginally been concerned with matters of human rights. In education the church exerts its influence mainly through religious education classes in the schools and through a small number of Catholic schools.

SOCIAL ASPECTS The negative rate of natural growth that Croatia has come to experience is among the major concerns of the Catholic Church. High rates of divorce, with marriages freely dissolved according to state regulations, and the large number of single-parent families are also of concern.

POLITICAL IMPACT Today the Catholic Church has no formal role in Croatian politics, but its political impact in the past was extraordinarily significant. Life in a multinational and multireligious Yugoslavia and under a Communist government only strengthened the political aspects of church activity. Although the war that took place in the early 1990s in the territory of Croatia and of Bosnia and Herzegovina was not strictly a religious conflict, there was a strong connection between national and religious identity. Soldiers frequently wore religious symbols in order to express their identity as a Croatian (Catholic), Serbian (Orthodox), or Bosnian (Muslim). The destruction of houses of worship and the banishment of clerics were sometimes a part of military strategy.

CONTROVERSIAL ISSUES In present-day Croatia the Catholic Church has only limited influence on its followers in such matters as birth control, abortion, and divorce. The exceptionally liberal law on abortion of 1978 remains in force, and research has shown that a majority opposes legal restrictions on abortion, even though they may share the church's moral viewpoint. The church's position on other issues, for example, post-Communist development, integration into the European Union, and the defense of national interests, are also controversial among some Croatians.

CULTURAL IMPACT The cultural impact of the Catholic Church, especially on Croatian art and architecture, has been exceptionally important historically. The remains of such pre-Romanesque buildings as Prince Višeslav's font and Archbishop Ivan's sarcophagus from the eighth and ninth centuries are witnesses to the national and religious development of the time. The first

Croatian university dates to 1495, when a Dominican institution in Zadar, then in Dalmatia, was promoted to the rank of a general European university. A special script called Glagolitic was used in Croatia until the middle of the nineteenth century, and a number of priests employed both the Glagolitic script and the Old Slavic and Latin languages in liturgy, practices that contributed to the development of a national language and literature.

In the twentieth century, however, the arts in Croatia were almost entirely separated from ecclesiastical influence and secularized. In popular culture especially, the influence of the West has become important.

Other Religions

Among other religious groups in Croatia, the most numerous are Eastern Orthodox churches, primarily the Serbian Orthodox Church. The arrival of Serbs in the territory of contemporary Croatia was linked with their flight from Ottoman rule, with the Venetian and Austrian governments often settling them in unsafe lands near the borders with the Ottomans. In the seventeenth century some of the Orthodox who settled in Croatia accepted unification with the Catholic Church, and the Greek Catholic Church (with Byzantine, or Eastern, rites but in union with Rome) still exists in Croatia today. After the war between 11 and 12 percent of all Orthodox in Yugoslavia lived in Croatia.

Throughout history the relations between Catholics and Orthodox Serbs have undergone various changes, and there was long widespread interest in Croatia for union between the two Christian groups. With the formation of Yugoslavia, however, political and national conflicts were joined to the religious differences of the Croatians and Serbs. Opposed to Croatian independence, Serbs joined in armed rebellion and occupied parts of Croatia, and after the government had retaken the lands in 1995, almost all Serbs living in the affected areas left.

The existence in Croatia of a small Islamic population, of less than 2 percent, is also linked to the Ottoman conquests and to the fact that the Bosnian people in Bosnia and Herzegovina, which borders Croatia and which was part of a common state from 1878 until 1991, are predominantly Islamic. After 1967 the designation "Muslim" was primarily used to mark the separate national and cultural identity of the Bosnian people.

A revitalization of Islamic religious life occurred in the 1980s, when a large Islamic center with a mosque was built in Zagreb, the first such building in Croatia.

As early as the first century B.C., Jews settled in what is now Croatia, and in the Middle Ages there were Jewish communities in the large cities. During World War II approximately 80 percent of the Jews in Croatia were victims of the Ustasha regime, established when the Germans defeated Yugoslavia. After the war many of the surviving Jews left. The synagogue in Zagreb, which was demolished in 1941, has not been rebuilt.

There are numerous Protestant churches in Croatia, but they are small. The introduction of Protestantism occurred in the sixteenth century on the borders of Croatia. In efforts to oppose German and Hungarian influences, the Croatian parliament long resisted Protestant activities. Only after World War I, with the formation of Yugoslavia, did Evangelic and Calvinistic churches in Croatia become independent of Austrian and Hungarian control. Today these churches have only small numbers of believers and go almost unnoticed.

The situation is similar with regard to other Christian communities, such as Baptists, Pentecostals, Mormons, and Seventh-day Adventists. Only Jehovah's Witnesses, because of their manner of evangelization, attract public attention. Jehovah's Witnesses have been officially present in Croatia since 1953, and during the Communist period some were incarcerated because they refused to serve in military forces.

Siniša Zrinščak

See Also Vol. 1: *Christianity, Eastern Orthodoxy, Islam, Roman Catholicism*

Bibliography

Malovic, Stjepan, and Gary Selnow. *The People, Press, and Politics of Croatia.* Westport, Conn.: Praeger, 2001.

Šanjek, Franjo. *Kršćanstvo na hrvatskom prostoru.* Zagreb: Kršćanska Sadašnjost, 1996.

"Vjera i moral u Hrvatskoj." *Bogoslovska Smotra* 68, no. 4 (1998): 461–700.

Zrinščak, Siniša. "Church and State in New Social Circumstances: The Croatian Story." In *Church-State Relations in Central and Eastern Europe.* Edited by Irena Borowik. Kraków: Nomos, 1999.

———. "Religion and Social Justice in Post-Communist Croatia." In *Religion and Social Change in Post-Communist Europe.* Edited by Irena Borowik and Miklós Tomka. Kraków: Nomos, 2001.

Cuba

POPULATION 11,263,000

ROMAN CATHOLIC 47 percent

PROTESTANT 4 percent

SANTERÍA (AFRO-CUBAN RELIGIONS) 2 percent

JEWISH 0.01 percent

NO STATED RELIGIOUS AFFILIATION 46.99 percent

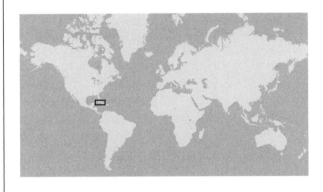

Country Overview

INTRODUCTION Cuba is the largest island in the Greater Antilles, an island range in the Caribbean Sea. It is comprised of the main island and the Isle of Youth. The capital city is Havana (La Habana).

When the European navigator Christopher Columbus encountered the island of Cuba in 1492 C.E., it was populated by the Siboney and Taino peoples, whose religious traditions have been virtually eliminated. Columbus claimed the island for Spain, and in subsequent waves of immigration Europeans, Africans, and Asians would take their religious heritages to Cuba. The British introduced Protestantism to Cuba in 1762, when they briefly occupied Havana.

While Roman Catholicism has always been statistically the majority religion of Cuba, African religious traditions—taken to the island by West African slaves—remain part of the lifeblood of the nation's religious practices. The Catholic Church banned Afro-Cuban religious practices, generically called Santería, but since the days of slavery many Cubans (primarily the poor) have disguised traditional African religious practice with an overlay of Catholic practices, notably the veneration of saints and the Virgin Mary.

RELIGIOUS TOLERANCE Religious tolerance is a rather new conception in Cuba's history. Columbus first encountered the island in 1492, but the Spanish Catholic Church did not send a bishop to oversee the island's religious life until 1516. By that time the Spanish Inquisition was investigating all "heretical" religious practices in Spain. While the full force of the Inquisition did not cross the Atlantic, freedom of religion was not extended to Cuba until 1886. Before then Catholicism was the only religion allowed to be practiced in the public sphere.

In 1991 the Cuban Communist Party lifted its 25-year ban on the admittance of religious believers to the party. The following year the Cuban constitution was amended to declare that Cuba was no longer an atheist state but rather a secular one committed to religious freedom. Article 42 was also revised to prohibit discrimination on the basis of religious beliefs. Religious adherents were promoted to full citizenship and assured equal protection under the law.

While discriminatory practices have not yet been completely eliminated, relations between religious institutions and the state continue to move forward. Christmas, after having been abolished in 1969, once again became a national holiday in 1997. In 1998, immediately before the pope's visit to Cuba, Cuban leader Fidel Castro met with Protestant leaders to elicit their ecumenical support for the visit.

Major Religion

ROMAN CATHOLICISM

DATE OF ORIGIN 1492 C.E.
NUMBER OF FOLLOWERS 5.3 million

HISTORY Cuba's religious history is dramatically different from those of most continental Latin American countries. In 1516 C.E. the Diocese of Cuba was founded; it included the Spanish colonies of Florida and Louisiana. During Cuba's occupation by Spain for the next two centuries, there was little colonization (because Cuba lacked precious metals) and less concern for developing the faith among the indigenous or slave populations. It became a port of rest for Spanish ships. The few clergy that were in Cuba were located mostly in Santiago, Havana, and other port cities. Many of the priests who served in Cuba in the sixteenth and seventeenth centuries behaved like the Spanish settlers, acquiring land, wealth, and slaves and engaging in licentious behavior. The intermittent leadership throughout this early colonial period inhibited the development of a strong church presence on the island.

In 1687 Bishop Diego Evelino de Compostela arrived to give leadership to the Catholic Church in Cuba. Compostela, who served in Cuba for 18 years, took advantage of new Spanish immigration to create 30 new parishes on the island. He developed social programs, emphasizing the church's role in education. Compostela also founded San Ambrosio seminary in 1689. Although most of these innovations affected only city dwellers, from the end of the seventeenth century until independence in 1898 the Catholic Church had absolute dominance over public religious life in Cuba.

From the seventeenth century onward West African slaves hid their religious practices from the church by

A follower of the Afro-Cuban tradition called Santería makes the pilgrimage to the icon of Saint Lazarus, which also symbolizes the deity of Babalu Ayé. © REUTERS NEWMEDIA INC./CORBIS.

overlaying the worship of their gods with devotion to Catholic saints and the Virgin Mary. These practices are discussed below under OTHER RELIGIONS.

In 1762 the British occupied Havana and took Anglican clergy there to serve the British navy. This was a blow to the Catholic Church's domination of the Cuban religious climate. Protestant colonial traders from North America flooded into the capital.

Other struggles that have plagued the Catholic Church in Cuba can be understood as a result of the church's traditionalism and conservatism. This can be seen in the major social struggles. While Cuba was under Spanish rule, the church was firmly both anti-abolitionist and anti-independence, siding with the status quo and not with the *independistas* (those who were fighting for independence from Spain). When Spain lost its colony in 1898, the Catholic Church also lost its tight grip over the Cuban population. While the church struggled to reestablish itself after Cuba's independence, it once again found its followers among the urban wealthy elite and never with the majority rural poor. Since the revolution of 1959 the church has remained disengaged from the social aims of the revolution.

While the church has strenuously advocated access to mass media and education, which the Cuban government continues to deny, Cardinal Jaime Ortega y Alamino (appointed in 1994) has also recognized that Cuba is a country that guarantees education and health care to all and has criticized the United State'ss embargo against the island. Perhaps the most historic moment for the church in Cuba was the visit by Pope John Paul II to the island in January 1998. The pope called for a renewed faith among Cubans.

EARLY AND MODERN LEADERS The Cuban Catholic Church has been known for being socially conservative, although the most notable Cuban Catholic leaders have not. Félix Varela (1788–1853), a professor of philosophy, greatly influenced his generation of Cubans. Varela believed in the abolition of slavery and in autonomy for Cuba, and he introduced bills to this effect at the Spanish parliament, to which he had been appointed in 1821. After the dissolution of the Spanish parliament in 1823, Varela was condemned to death and fled to the United States, where he edited the newspaper *El Habanero* while continuing to write on issues of justice and freedom.

By the 1950s the church had completely accommodated itself to the political elite, but Enrique Pérez Serantes (1883–1968), archbishop of Santiago de Cuba, was an exception. He rose to prominence in 1953, when he spoke out against the government's handling of prisoners from a failed coup attempt led by Fidel Castro. Most of the captured rebels were tortured and killed. Pérez Serantes helped secure a government declaration that the remaining prisoners would not be harmed. Perhaps more than any other Cuban bishop, Pérez Serantes was concerned about the plight of Cuba's poorest citizens. He urged the Cuban bishops to sign a public statement (1958) calling for the resignation of President Fulgencio Batista. In 1961 Pérez Serantes broke with Castro's government because of its increasingly radical stance.

Jaime Ortega y Alamino (born in 1936) was appointed the cardinal of Cuba in 1994.

MAJOR THEOLOGIANS AND AUTHORS The Cuban Catholic Church has not produced major theologians or authors. Probably the two most notable are Félix Varela and Archbishop Pérez Serantes, both discussed above under EARLY AND MODERN LEADERS. Pérez Serante'ss most notable writings were his pastoral letters to the Cuban churches.

HOUSES OF WORSHIP AND HOLY PLACES Most urban churches in Cuba were built between the late sixteenth and the mid-nineteenth centuries. They have a typically ornate Spanish *retablo* (altarpiece), often depicting scenes from the lives of Jesus and his mother, Mary. Rural churches are smaller and are generally simpler, except for those that were built on plantations as part of the family residence; these tend to be ornate chapels.

The first church in honor of Cuba's patron saint, La Virgen de la Caridad (the Virgin of Charity, a sacred statue discussed below under WHAT IS SACRED), was built in 1611. The statue's current sanctuary, built in 1927, is located outside of Santiago de Cuba in the small mining town of Cobre, close to where the statue was found. Pope Paul VI elevated the sanctuary to the category of basilica in 1977.

WHAT IS SACRED? In Cuba popular Catholicism centers devotion on saints and particularly on La Virgen de la Caridad (also called Nuestra Señora de la Caridad del Cobre, or Our Lady of Charity from Cobre). According to tradition, in 1606 three fishermen found a small statue of the Virgin Mary attached to a board floating in the Bay of Nipe, in southeastern Cuba, the morning after a storm. On it was written the inscription, "I am the Virgin of Charity." That the statue had survived the storm unharmed was taken to be a miracle. Because her discoverers were servants, La Cachita, as the Virgin is known, has been venerated by the downtrodden of Cuba and is considered their protector. She is said to have assisted the Cuban army during its liberation struggle against Spain. The Virgin of Charity was declared the patroness of Cuba by Pope Benedict XV in 1916 and so crowned in 1936. Pope John Paul II crowned her image the queen and patroness of the Republic of Cuba in 1998.

HOLIDAYS AND FESTIVALS Throughout the liturgical year the Catholic Church in Cuba celebrates special masses focusing on the patron saints of each bishopric. On 8 September there are celebrations throughout Cuba for La Virgen de la Caridad del Cobre. Many Cubans celebrate Christmas in their homes and put up Christmas trees; the day gifts are shared is 6 January, the holy day Epiphany, the celebration of the Three Wise Men visiting the Christ child.

MODE OF DRESS Members of the Roman Catholic laity dress like the majority of Cubans, who wear Western clothing.

DIETARY PRACTICES On Christmas day it is traditional to eat *lechon* (roasted fresh ham) with *moros y cristianos* (which literally translates as "Moors and Christians"), black beans with white rice.

RITUALS Most Cuban Catholics are baptized as infants. Now that religious practice is no longer a deterrent to occupational advancement, however, many adults also pursue a life of faith and receive the sacrament of baptism.

Because a Cuban marriage must be made official with a civil ceremony, the church service is extraneous. When a church wedding is performed, however, the bridal party usually consists of girls, rather than of women the bride's own age, so as not to detract from the uniqueness of the bride. An African influence can be seen in the use of drums and guitars in some liturgies.

RITES OF PASSAGE Among Catholics in Cuba, as in Mexico and other Latin American countries, a special mass called a *quinceañera* is usually held to bless a young woman when she comes into adulthood (at age 15). It is followed by large party for the girl and her friends. There is no equivalent celebration for boys.

MEMBERSHIP In 1961 the Cuban government banned national religious media outlets, in reaction to the increasing hostility and "counterrevolutionary" activities of many Catholics toward the government's apparent Communist leanings. Because the Catholic Church in Cuba has no public avenue to advertise its mission, there is no campaign to attract new members. For the Cuban public the major attraction to the church was the pope's visit in 1991. Signs of his visit continue to be evident in many towns and in all Catholic churches. New Catholics are also drawn to the church by friends and neighbors.

SOCIAL JUSTICE Since the mid-twentieth century the revolutionary government of Cuba has sought to repair the inequities of society. This is a marked contrast to other Latin American countries, where liberation theology had a profound impact upon Christian churches, particularly in the call for social justice on the part of the state. While the Cuban state has been culpable of some abuses and discriminatory actions, the revolutionary government's overall plan for Cuba was to create social equity; in doing so the state usurped the traditional projects of the churches, such as schools, hospitals, social service agencies, charity drives, orphanages, and homes for the aged.

SOCIAL ASPECTS Cuban family life has eroded much since the 1960s. Catholics have been affected as much as any other group by the tremendous social changes brought about by the revolution. Catholic women, who previously may have been wives and homemakers, were expected to become part of the work force.

This rapid social change did not extend to family life, where women were still expected to run the household, rear children, and perform volunteer work for the revolution. The state attempted to institute a legal solution to gender inequality, but the Catholic hierarchy in its public pronouncements did not particularly endorse the shifts in gender roles implemented by the state. Among some Cuban Catholics there is the sense that society was better off when traditional gender roles were the norm. The social liberation of women has sometimes been blamed by Catholics for contributing to the erosion of the Cuban family.

POLITICAL IMPACT Since the revolution of 1959 the Catholic Church's political influence has been mainly negative, serving to turn the revolutionary government away from active engagement with the church. Up until 1991 religious Cubans were denied the rights to run for political office or join the Communist party. From the 1960s the revolutionary government's secretary for science and culture, José Felipe Carneado, dealt with religious affairs in Cuba. In 1985 the government created an office for religious affairs, with Carneado as its head. Carneado's relationship with the church was one of the factors that led to the visit by Pope John Paul II in 1998. Since then the dialogue between the Catholic Church in Cuba and the Cuban government has been strengthened, and the church has gained renewed political rights.

CONTROVERSIAL ISSUES Although the Catholic Church rejects abortion, birth control, and divorce, all Cubans have legal rights to these activities, and in Cuban society the church has no political power to create a controversy about such issues. In Cuba women are guaranteed equal rights under the law. This, however, does not pertain to professions in the church. The Catholic priesthood in Cuba is only open to men.

CULTURAL IMPACT There is no specific impact by the Catholic Church on contemporary music, art, or literature.

Other Religions

The British occupied Havana in 1762, introducing Protestantism to Cuba. In the few months that the British were in control, Cubans experienced a wider taste of ideas and economic markets. Even after the Spanish crown regained its control over Cuba, it could not reinstitute trade restrictions, and Cuba became a country open to the enlightenment ideals of the late eighteenth century, including the ideas of laissez-faire capitalism and democracy. These ideas eventually led to an independence movement, which began in the mid-nineteenth century and lasted until 1898, when independence from Spain was won.

In 1886, shortly before Cuba's independence from Spain, the Spanish constitutional law allowing freedom of religion was extended to Cuba. In Cuba's new constitution religious freedom was guaranteed. Protestants went to the island looking for economic opportunities and were free to practice their religions.

The development of Protestantism in Cuba was greatly affected by the United State'ss proximity to Cuba. After Cuba's war for independence from Spain, the United States occupied Cuba for nearly four years (1898–1902). Hundreds of American Protestant missionaries flooded the island. They displaced the early Cuban Protestant missionaries, took over the evangelistic endeavor, and imbued it with a nineteenth-century liberal American ethnocentrism. The missionaries founded "American Schools" that attracted middle- and upper-class Cubans (as well as the families of American businessmen) until the 1930s and '40s, when leadership of these institutions was given over to Cubans. By 1959 there was a thriving Protestant community of Baptists, Presbyterians, Methodists, Episcopalians, and many smaller Christian groups.

Shortly after the revolution (1959) Cuba was established as a Marxist-Leninist (atheist) state. Nevertheless, from the 1960s to the 1980s there were religious people in Cuba who voiced their commitment both to the revolution and to their religious beliefs. The development of Latin American liberation theology, which advocated an almost Marxist economic ideology, contributed to the Cuban state's changing attitudes. These concrete examples of being simultaneously revolutionary and religious eventually led to the historic visit in 1984 of Rev. Jesse Jackson to Havana, during which Castro attended the worship service to celebrate the new Martin Luther King, Jr. Center, a Baptist-affiliated social-service center in Havana.

Religious Cubans suffered discrimination to varying degrees from 1962 to 1991. One of the religious leaders responsible for the easing of relations between the state and the faithful was the Presbyterian minister Sergio Arce Martínez. In 1965 Arce wrote a pamphlet examining the Christian mission through a sociopolitical lens, challenging the faithful to be revolutionaries and the atheists to recognize that faith and revolution were not mutually exclusive.

In 1992 the Cuban constitution was amended to provide for religious freedom, and religious adherents were given full citizenship. Shortly thereafter three Protestant religious leaders joined the Cuban Communist Party and were elected to the People's Power, Cuba's parliament: Sergio Arce Martínez, Baptist minister Raúl Suárez, and Episcopal priest Odén Marichal.

Since the 1990s Protestant membership in Cuba has been growing by the thousands each year. While support for state-run socialism has apparently been eroding among the common people, who have been living in extreme economic crisis, a new evangelistic fervor has developed. Many of the new Christians are Pentecostals who see their faith conservatively, in both social and theological arenas. On the other end of the theological spectrum, there are the faithful who adhere to the liberal leanings of Sergio Arce Martínez. These churches have also been growing but not at the rate of the Pentecostal churches. There is a belief among some religious leaders that many of the new Christians have come to the church out of expediency—for the material items made available to them through humanitarian religious circles.

Another religious movement that has grown and become more visible since 1991 is the Afro-Cuban tradition that is often called Santería. This tradition originated with the Yoruba of West Africa, who were taken to Cuba as slaves. In the eighteenth century Cuban plantation owners split up slave families in order to prevent uprisings, but the Catholic Church, in an effort to appear more compassionate, created *cabildos,* mutual aid societies for slaves. These societies were often organized by ethnic group to assist with the reconstruction of African ethnic heritage. The *cabildos* connected slaves from different parts of West Africa with each other and offered them a location to engage in rituals associated with their African religious traditions.

In the *cabildos* the slaves camouflaged their own *orisha*s (gods) as Catholic saints. For example, on the holiday for Saint Lazarus, the African slaves would appear to be venerating the Catholic saint while actually recreating a traditional African ritual for Babalu Ayé, the *orisha* of the transformative power of diseases. Today the terms *orisha* and saint are used interchangeably in Cuba. The name Santa Barbara, for instance, automatically evokes Changó, god of thunder. Oshun, goddess of the river and fresh water, is associated with La Virgen de la Caridad de Cobre, the patroness of Cuba. Lucumi, a Yoruban word meaning "friends," is another common name for this religion.

In the twentieth century Cubans continued to practice Afro-Cuban religions semi-secretively to prevent persecution by the atheist communist government. Throughout the early decades of the latter's administration (1960s to '80s) these religious traditions were heralded as national folklore, and their dances and costumes were performed by dance companies and exhibited by museums throughout the country.

Since the early 1990s, however, more middle-class Cubans have adopted Afro-Cuban practices, and practitioners have become more open about their beliefs. While the percentage of Cubans designated as practicing Santería is listed as 1 percent, in reality a significant number of Catholics also practice various Afro-Cuban religious traditions, including Regla de Ocha.

In Cuba before 1959 there were about 15,000 Jews, most of whom were from Russia and Eastern European countries. Many originally went to the island hoping their stay would lead to entrance into the United States. A number of Jews, however, found Cuba an accepting society, free from the anti-Semitism they had experienced in Europe. After the revolution of 1959 approximately 90 percent left the island, fearing persecution or preferring to live in a country with a free-market economy. Today there are only about 1,000 Jews in Cuba, mostly in Havana and Santiago de Cuba. The community has been experiencing some growth, with Jews returning to religious practice and non-Jewish spouses converting. The leadership of the Cuban Jewish community requires that persons requesting conversion must either be married to a Jew or prove their Jewishness from familial historical documents. Conversion for a heartfelt desire to become Jewish is not accepted because of the concern that the person only wants a way to leave Cuba (by emigrating to Israel).

Margarita Suárez

See Also Vol. 1: *Roman Catholicism*

Bibliography

Arce Martínez, Sergio. *The Church and Socialism: Reflections from a Cuban Context.* New York: New York CIRCUS Publications, 1985.

———. *Teología en revolución.* Matanzas, Cuba: Centro de Información y Estudio Augusto Cotto, 1975.

Arce Martínez, Sergio, and Odén Marichal. *Evangelization and Politics.* New York: New York CIRCUS Publications, 1982.

Braun, Theodore A. *Perspectives on Cuba and its People.* New York: Friendship Press, National Council of Churches, 1999.

Cepeda Clemente, Rafael, ed. *La herencia misionera en Cuba: Consulta de las iglesias protestantes realizada en Matanzas, Cuba, del 26 octubre al 3 de noviembre de 1984.* San José, Costa Rica: Departamento Ecuménico de Investigaciones, 1986.

Dewart, Leslie. *Christianity and Revolution.* New York: Herder and Herder, 1963.

Gómez Treto, Raúl. *The Church and Socialism in Cuba.* Maryknoll, N.Y.: Orbis Books, 1988.

Kirk, John M. *Between God and the Party: Religion and Politics in Revolutionary Cuba.* Tampa: University of South Florida Press, 1989.

Murphy, Joseph M. *Santería: African Spirits in America.* Boston: Beacon Press, 1993.

Pérez, Louis A. *Cuba: Between Reform and Revolution.* New York: Oxford University Press, 1995.

———, ed. *Slaves, Sugar, and Colonial Society: Travel Accounts of Cuba, 1801–1899.* Wilmington, Del.: Scholarly Resources, 1992.

Ramos, Marcos A. *Protestantism and Revolution in Cuba.* Miami: University of Miami, North-South Center for the Research Institute for Cuban Studies, 1989.

Suárez, Margarita M.W. "'Hasta la Victoria Siempre': Birthing Cuban Feminist Theology." Ph.D. diss., Northwestern University, 2002.

Yaremko, Jason M. *U.S. Protestant Missions in Cuba: From Independence to Castro.* Gainesville: University Press of Florida, 2000.

Cyprus

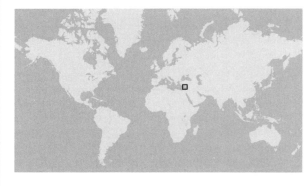

Country Overview

INTRODUCTION Cyprus is the third largest island in the Mediterranean and lies close to the southern coast of Turkey. It has had a turbulent history in which religion—particularly Eastern Orthodox Christianity—has played a pivotal role. The country is divided as a result of its invasion in 1974 by Turkish forces, which occupy 37 percent of Cypru'ss territory. In 1983 a "Turkish Republic of Northern Cyprus" was unilaterally declared; only Turkey recognizes it. The southern part of the country is called the Republic of Cyprus.

RELIGIOUS TOLERANCE Although Orthodoxy is predominant, the Cyprus constitution of 1960 guarantees

freedom of religions whose teaching and rites are not secret. Discrimination on religious grounds is prohibited. The Orthodox Church administers its affairs according to the holy canons and its charter of 1914. Because of the inseparability of Greek Cypriot and Orthodox identity, any religion other than Orthodoxy is considered a betrayal, and foreign missionaries have occasionally experienced harassment. Jehovah's Witnesses in Cyprus have been criticized for their refusal to perform the obligatory military service.

Major Religion

EASTERN ORTHODOXY

DATE OF ORIGIN 45 C.E.
NUMBER OF FOLLOWERS 600,000

HISTORY Christianity was introduced to Cyprus by the apostles Paul and Barnabas, who came to the Cypriot city of Salamis in about 45 C.E. and converted the Roman proconsul, Sergius Paulus, in Paphos. Barnabas settled in Salamis until his reported martyrdom in 57 C.E.

In the fourth century Christianity became established throughout Cyprus, whose ecclesiastical independence was ratified by the Council of Ephesus in 431 and reaffirmed by the Council of Trullo in 692. Antioch's claims to Cyprus were annulled when Barnaba'ss tomb and relics were discovered in 488, a fact indicating the Cypriot church's ancient origins and apostolicity. Emperor Zenon (reigned 474–91) subsequently finalized

Cypru'ss ecclesiastical independence. During the seventh to ninth centuries the church suffered tribulations by Arabs, leading Emperor Justinian II to evacuate Cypriots to Kyzikos (renamed New Justiniana) in 688. They returned in 698, but since then their archbishop has borne the title "Archbishop of New Justiniana and all Cyprus."

Tensions arose during the Frankish (Lusignan dynasty, 1192–1489) and Venetian (1489–1571) rules as a result of Latin efforts to convert Orthodox Cypriots to Roman Catholicism. Under the Ottomans (1571–1878) the Orthodox Church enjoyed several privileges, and the archbishop was recognized (beginning in 1660) as the ethnic spokesman. During British rule (1878–1960) the church became involved in the national cause of uniting Cyprus with Greece (the efforts were unsuccessful; Cyprus gained independence in 1960). The Turkish invasion has resulted in the smuggling of Christian art treasures abroad.

EARLY AND MODERN LEADERS Historical leaders include Spyridon, bishop of Trimythous (fourth century), and archbishops Chrysanthos (served 1768–1810) and Kyprianos (served 1810–21). The best-known leader was Archbishop Makarios III (1913–77); elected in 1950, he also served as the first president of the Republic of Cyprus from 1959 to 1977. He personified the *ethnarch*, an ecclesiastic undertaking the leadership of a nation in critical moments.

MAJOR THEOLOGIANS AND AUTHORS Important theologians who were active in Cyprus include Epiphanius of Salamis (c. 315–402) and Neophyte the Recluse (1134–c. 1220).

HOUSES OF WORSHIP AND HOLY PLACES Houses of worship in Cyprus are the churches and chapels dedicated to Christ, the Virgin Mary, or a saint. Monasteries and convents are considered holy places. The most renowned and wealthy is the monastery of Kykko, founded in the eleventh century. It houses the icon of the Mother of God, which has been traditionally attributed to Saint Luke the Evangelist. Many monasteries in the Turkish-occupied area have been deserted, pillaged, and destroyed. Some, such as the Apostle Andreas monastery in the Karpasia peninsula, have become holy even for Muslim Turks.

WHAT IS SACRED? Cypriots venerate the icons and relics of saints, but they reserve the highest reverence and

honor for the cross. The most important relics are three fragments of the holy cross that, according to legend, were transported to Cyprus by Saint Helena (c. 248–c. 330). They are kept in a church in Tochni, the monastery of Stavrovouni, and the monastery of Omodhos, where Saint Helena is said to have also left a piece of the holy hemp (the rope by which Christ was tied to the cross). A newer place of reverence is the tomb of Archbishop Makarios III at Throni, near the Kykko monastery.

HOLIDAYS AND FESTIVALS Most of the 12 public holidays in Cyprus are religious. Each Cypriot celebrates the day of the saint for which he or she was named, and on the day of the patron saint of a village there is always a religious fair. The ancient Festival of the Flood coincides with the Pentecost and is observed in seaside towns. Lasting for a few days, the celebrations include boat racing, dancing, and a singing competition of songs known as *chatista*. The most popular custom is to throw water on one another for purification. Another festival takes place in Omodhos on the Tuesday after Easter, when every family welcomes the relics of the holy cross in their house and makes generous donations to the church.

MODE OF DRESS Apart from the archbishop, who can wear imperial purple for ceremonies, Cypriot clergy of all rankings, as well as female monastics, wear the black cassock. Because of Cypru'ss position between East and West, archbishops in the eighteenth and nineteenth centuries were robed with garments representing authority in the East, such as the *kaftani*.

DIETARY PRACTICES Cypriot dietary practices follow the feasts and fasts dictated by the Orthodox calendar. In addition, various kinds of dough are baked for both religious celebrations and rites of passages. For example, at Easter *flaouna*, a pastry filled with cheese, eggs, spices, and herbs, is made; at funerals sweet pies are offered. Rites of passage are marked by the preparation and consumption of specific foods. At weddings there is a dish called *resi*, a lamb and wheat pilaf. A ritual food called *kollyva*, consisting of boiled wheat, pomegranate seeds, almonds, sesame, and raisins, is taken to church for memorial services and patron saint celebrations.

RITUALS Formal worship is a highly ritualized occasion, while popular worship consists of rituals at home, the celebration of name-days (which are considered more notable than birthdays), and the veneration of icons.

Cyprus is known as the "island of saints," and tales of miraculous events, visions, shrines, and pilgrimage sites abound. Destinations for pilgrims include the small monastery of Trooditissa (visited particularly by childless couples), the cave of Saint Neophytos (believed to cure various ailments), the monasteries of Saint Andreas and Saint Barnabas in the occupied territory, and many places known for miraculous icons of the Mother of God (such as the icon of Agia Napa).

RITES OF PASSAGE Orthodox Cypriots usually administer baptism during infancy by triple immersion in water followed by confirmation. Through baptism a child receives his or her name, which is usually related to the Virgin Mary or an Orthodox saint. Church weddings are preceded and followed by rituals ensuring material prosperity and fertility and marking changes in status. For example, the *antigamo,* observed on the Sunday after a wedding, serves to reintroduce the bride into the religious community as a wife.

Funeral services are held within 24 hours after death and are followed by immediate burial in a cemetery; cremation is discouraged. The exhumation of bones usually takes place after three years. This phase indicates the ritualistic end of mourning. Bones are afterwards washed and put in ossuaries. People hold commemoration services for the dead on the third, ninth, and fortieth day after death and thereafter once a year.

MEMBERSHIP Cypriots become members of the Orthodox Church through baptism. The church owns its radio and television station, Logos, and publishes the review *Apostolos Barnabas* as its official bulletin. Since the reign of Archbishop Makarios III, the church has supported Orthodox missions in Kenya, Uganda, and Tanzania. In 1971 an Orthodox Patriarchal Seminary was founded in Nairobi (in operation since 1981) to meet the clerical needs of East Africa.

SOCIAL JUSTICE The Orthodox Church and the monasteries, particularly that of Kykko, sponsor many social activities, from educational (Sunday schools) to charitable (orphanages). Because its higher echelons have never been the preserve of any particular social class, the church remains popular and close to the people. Through representatives laypeople are involved in the election of the archbishop. There is occasional criticism but no militant anticlericalism.

SOCIAL ASPECTS Civil marriage became valid in Cyprus in 1923. The church is concerned about beta-thalassemia, a blood disorder endemic in Cyprus. Premarital blood tests are required by the church (but not by the government), with the eugenic intent of reducing the number of affected children born.

POLITICAL IMPACT The church has provided traditional leadership for Cypriots, and in 1821 church leaders were executed during the eruption of the Greek War of Independence. Under British rule the ethnarchic tradition was transformed into nationalism, and Cypru'ss union with Greece was supported with fervor by the church even through uprisings (in 1931 by Bishop Nicodemus) and guerrilla activities (in the 1950s). Three bishops (deposed in 1973) unsuccessfully criticized Archbishop and President Makarios III for having undertaken an incompatible twofold office. After 1977 Cypru'ss leadership was assumed by politicians, but the church's opinion has continued to influence political matters.

CONTROVERSIAL ISSUES The church continues to safeguard its traditional doctrine and conservative morality. This is evident in its opposition during 1998–2000 to the decriminalization of homosexuality by the Cyprus Parliament. The ordination of women to the priesthood is also not accepted.

CULTURAL IMPACT Because of its long interplay with Cypriot history, Orthodoxy has left its imprint upon the cultural life of the island as a whole, such as in architecture (cultural sites protected by UNESCO), in painting (icons and mosaics), in Byzantine and folk music, and in religious literature.

Other Religions

The other significant religion in Cyprus is Islam, which dates back to the Ottoman period. Most Turkish Cypriots, along with settlers from Anatolia and Turkish soldiers, live in the north and follow the Hanafi school of Sunni law. Turkish Cypriots generally are not orthodox Muslims; they adhere closely to the reforms of Kemal Atatürk and are secularized in many respects. For example, they do not abstain from alcohol. Nonetheless, there exist some movements and organizations in Cyprus that foster the establishment of an Islamic society.

The highest Muslim authority in Cyprus is the mufti residing in the Turkish part of the city of Nicosia. There are important Muslim historical places of worship (the Khalat-I-Sultan Tekyé) and religious trusts (independent foundations).

The Roman Catholic community in Cyprus is concentrated in the south. Catholic Cypriots date back to the Frankish and Venetian rules and have left an imprint upon religious architecture. The community is served by Franciscans and a prior who is an accredited nuncio (papal representative).

The Maronites (Syrian Lebanese Christians who became united with Rome in 633 and who were progressively latinized) had in past centuries flourished in Cyprus despite tensions and persecutions.

The Armenian community in Cyprus dates back to the sixth century. Many Armenians fled to Cyprus to escape the genocide of 1915. Preserving a strong sense of ethno-religious identity, Armenians in Cyprus have their own churches, schools, and meeting places, and they stay in close contact with the Armenian diaspora worldwide. Although their relations to Orthodox Cypriots have been generally good, occasional tensions have occurred, and the number of mixed marriages is small.

There is also a small Anglican community remaining in Cyprus as a result of British rule.

Vasilios N. Makrides and Eleni Sotiriu

See Also Vol. 1: *Christianity, Eastern Orthodoxy, Islam, Sunni Islam*

Bibliography

Englezakis, Benedict. *Studies on the History of the Church of Cyprus, Fourth to Twentieth Centuries.* Aldershot, England: Variorum, 1995.

Hackett, John. *A History of the Orthodox Church of Cyprus from the Coming of the Apostles Paul and Barnabas to the Commencement of the British Occupation (A.D. 45–A.D. 1878).* London: Methuen and Co., 1901; New York: Burt Franklin, 1972.

Mayes, Stanley. *Makarios: A Biography.* London: Macmillan, 1981.

Meinardus, Otto. "Relics in the Churches and Monasteries of Cyprus." *Ostkirchliche Studien* 19 (1970): 19–43.

Paraskevopoulou, Maria. *Researches into the Traditions of the Popular Religious Feasts of Cyprus.* Nicosia, Cyprus: M. Paraskevopoulou, 1982.

Sant Cassia, Paul. "Religion, Politics, and Ethnicity in Cyprus during the Turkokratia." *Archives Européennes de Sociologie* 27 (1986): 3–28.

Czech Republic

POPULATION 10,256,760

ROMAN CATHOLIC 26.3 percent

CZECH EVANGELICAL CHURCH OF THE BRETHREN 1.3 percent

CZECHOSLOVAK HUSSITE CHURCH 0.9 percent

OTHER RELIGIONS (INCLUDING JEWISH, BUDDHIST, MUSLIM) 3.1 percent

UNKNOWN 10.1 percent

WITHOUT RELIGIOUS AFFILIATION 58.3 percent

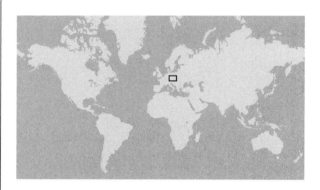

Country Overview

INTRODUCTION The Czech Republic, a mid-size country in central Europe, is bordered by Poland to the north, Germany to the west, Austria to the south, and Slovakia to the east. Formerly part of Czechoslovakia, it gained independence in 1993 as a result of the "velvet divorce," which split Czechoslovakia into two countries: Slovakia and the Czech Republic. Economically developed, the Czech Republic became a member of NATO in 1999 and the European Union in 2004.

Christianity arrived in the area in the ninth century C.E. Later, during the early fifteenth century, Jan Hus, a preacher and university master, led an effort to allow the lay public as well as the clergy to receive the Eucharist under both species, both the bread and wine, during Mass, a movement that continued through the establishment of local brethren churches. These Czech "brothers" later joined the Lutheran and Calvinist movements. With the military defeat of the Protestants in 1620, the Roman Catholic Church responded with its Counter Reformation, concluding in 1781 with the Tolerance Edict issued by Habsburg ruler Joseph II. The Roman Catholic Church supported the Habsburg monarchy, which ruled over central Europe, and was later accused of not backing a national independence movement. After an independent Czechoslovak Republic was established in 1918, part of the population left the Catholic Church and created the Czechoslovak Church, later renamed the Czechoslovak Hussite Church.

By the 1921 census 7.5 percent of the population already declared no religious affiliation. This religious decline continued, particularly during the second half of the century under the Communist government. The establishment of a democratic government in the 1990s improved the standing of the church but did nothing to halt the secularization process.

RELIGIOUS TOLERANCE Complete freedom of religion was declared in the Austro-Hungarian Empire in

1848 but truly came into effect with the Protestant Patent issued in 1861. Czechoslovakia, formed in 1918, encouraged religious freedom until 1948, when the Communist Party took power and representatives of the Roman Catholic Church began to be persecuted. Religious freedom was renewed after the collapse of the Communist government (known as the "velvet revolution") in 1989. Although the country is among the least religious in Europe, religious tolerance is an integral part of its society.

Major Religion

ROMAN CATHOLICISM

DATE OF ORIGIN 863 C.E.
NUMBER OF FOLLOWERS 2.7 million

HISTORY Christianity arrived in Bohemia and Moravia—now regions of the Czech Republic—from both the east and west in the early ninth century, spreading out after the arrival of missionaries Constantine and Methodius in 863. The power of the Roman Catholic Church peaked in the fourteenth century under Charles IV, the Czech king and Holy Roman Emperor. The Protestant Reformation, which challenged the power of the church beginning in the sixteenth century, terminated in 1624 with the Imperial Patent, which declared Catholicism the only permissible religion. Non-Catholics were to accept the Catholic faith or leave the country. Catholicism remained the official religion in the area until 1918, when an independent Czechoslovakia was established. In the first half of the twentieth century, one-quarter of the Czech population left the Roman Catholic Church.

In the 1950s conflict between the Roman Catholic Church and the Communist state led to the trials of church representatives and activists and to the abolition of the monastic orders. One group of the Catholic clergy cooperated with state power and organized an "official" Peace Movement.

Political liberalization in 1968 enabled a partial introduction of church reforms by the Vatican II council. But these efforts were short-lived, as democratic practices were gradually abolished, and in 1970 church activities were again suppressed. In the mid-1980s the Roman Catholic Church "awakened" and became a recognized human rights advocate. After the revolution in

A young girl waits to hear Pope John Paul II say mass during an official visit to then-Czechoslovakia in 1990. After the revolution in 1989, the Roman Catholic church renewed its activities in the country. © BERNARD BISSON/CORBIS SYGMA.

1989, the church renewed its activities in the country, maintaining eight dioceses, 3,100 parishes, and more than 1,800 priests.

EARLY AND MODERN LEADERS Saint Adalbert, a teacher of the faith at all levels of society, is one of the most important figures in the Czech Catholic Church. Others are the charismatic Ernest of Pardubice, first archbishop of Prague, who played a large role in founding Prague University, and F. Kordač, who in 1919 upheld the position of the church and was actively involved in social work. Cardinal J. Beran headed the church during the period of its persecution in the 1950s and was imprisoned for some time. Cardinal F. Tomášek played an important role in the battle against the Communist government during the 1980s. Cardinal M. Vlk has been the head the church since the early

1990s and, until 2001, was chair of the Council of European Bishop's Conferences.

MAJOR THEOLOGIANS AND AUTHORS Among those associated with the arrival of Christianity in Moravia are the missionaries Constantine and Methodius, brothers from Thessalonica who introduced the faith in 863. They translated the Scriptures into Slavonic and used Slavonic at Mass. Seventeenth-century Jesuit and historian B. Balbín is known for his text *Sacred Bohemia*. Notable contemporary theologians include J. Zvěřina, who has conceived his theology as "the sister of the people in search of truth," and O. Mádr, who has focused on moral theology.

HOUSES OF WORSHIP AND HOLY PLACES There are more than 6,800 churches and chapels throughout the Czech Republic, hundreds of which are of historical value and classified as state cultural monuments. Velehrad in Moravia ranks among the most significant pilgrimage sites. Founded as a Cistercian monastery in the twelfth century, it is visited by 60,000 people annually, as well as by another 100,000 during the nationwide pilgrimage. Svatá Hora at Příbram, founded in the thirteenth century, is a popular pilgrimage center in Bohemia. Historical monasteries and convents are located in 210 towns and communities. Strahov Monastery in Prague, and Teplá and Broumov in Bohemia, are particularly well known.

WHAT IS SACRED? A feature of Czech Catholic religiosity is the veneration of local historical saints. The most popular early saints are Saint Adalbert, a prince and bishop of Prague; Saint Wenceslas and his grandmother, Saint Ludmila, both murdered, though on separate occasions, for their involvement in spreading Christianity; the medieval saints Zdislava and Agnes, celebrated for their charity work; and the martyr Saint Jan Nepomuk. Roman Catholic believers venerate relics of saints in their celebrations.

HOLIDAYS AND FESTIVALS Of the Czech Republic's 13 public holidays, seven are religious and five are related to Christmas or Easter. Christmas is a family event, and Nativity scenes and mangers are traditionally built and exhibited in churches. Singing Christmas carols celebrating the birth of the baby Jesus is a widespread tradition. The *Christmas Mass* by J. Ryba, a rural eighteenth-century teacher, forms a regular part of any choral repertoire in Roman Catholic churches and concert halls during the Christmas season.

Easter is the most important holiday for Czech Catholics. On the night before Easter Sunday believers take vigil at the baptism of new church members. Easter Mass is an occasion for sanctification of meals.

The Festivity of Constantine and Methodius is a religious holiday associated with the ninth-century missionaries Constantine and Methodius. Huge annual pilgrimages are made in early July to Velehrad as homage to these patron saints of Europe.

MODE OF DRESS The Czech Republic's Roman Catholic population dresses according to personal taste rather than religious affiliation. Wearing a cross or a pendant with the figure of Mary is not necessarily an indicator of faith. It can be merely a fashion accessory or a mark of respect for family tradition. In some Moravian regions the tradition of wearing local folk costumes during important religious events and pilgrimages has survived.

In the Czech Republic, Roman Catholic priests, bishops, and other leaders wear distinctive clothing on special occasions and during different liturgical periods of the church year, such as Easter or Christmas. For divine services their clothing might differ in color (for example, white, red, or green) and they might use different insignias (such as an alb, a biretta, or a crosier).

DIETARY PRACTICES Fasting, especially during Lent, is a traditional Roman Catholic custom observed by Czech Catholics. Two one-day fasts, on Ash Wednesday and Good Friday, are more common than the original 40-day fast, which began on Ash Wednesday and involved giving up meat. Friday as a day without meat is observed by Czech Catholics throughout the year, unless it coincides with a religious holiday. Fasting as a folk custom occurs on Christmas Eve and should be held all day, typically concluding at dinner and followed by receiving Communion at midnight Mass. This fast for Czech Catholics is more than giving up meat or food—it refers to everything superfluous to life.

RITUALS A Czech Catholic's life is marked by three turning points: the birth of a child, marriage, and death. The birth of a child is an occasion for a baptism and a ceremonial Mass, commemorating the family's affiliation with the Catholic Church. Legally recognized church weddings also affirm the faith and the belief in the indissolubility of marriage. The final ritual in the life of Czech Catholics is the sacrament of anointing of the sick or elderly, providing them with strength through grace. Some apostates also seek anointing from Roman Catholic priests.

The Eucharist—receiving the body of Christ at Holy Mass—is an inherent component of Catholic life in the Czech Republic. The sacrament of reconciliation through confession is a regular ritual. Elderly Catholics, mainly women, go to confession roughly once a month; others attend generally at least once a year before Easter.

Less official rituals include sanctifications emphasizing the presence of God in daily life and the physical world. They involve blessings, consecrations, and devotions and refer to many events and locations associated with the life of the Roman Catholic Church in the Czech Republic. Consecrations, for example, may be connected with the opening of a new church or the presentation of a new bell, cross, or painting. Priests bless meals, the next crop, and the healing springs at the beginning of spa season (for example, in Karlovy Vary).

RITES OF PASSAGE People of any age in the Czech Republic may enter the Roman Catholic Church if, after serious consideration, they choose to declare their faith. Baptisms are held after individual preparation, usually at Easter.

Czech Catholic children about 8–10 years of age experience an important and festive event when they go to their first confession and, during Mass, take the first Holy Communion. Then, between the ages of 15 and 18, following a year of preparation, they attend confirmation. In this rite of passage youths confirm their baptism and church membership and their conscious decision to face life responsibly.

Marriage is an important rite of passage for Czech Catholics. The sacrament of matrimonial vows pledged by partners upon entry into marriage takes place in the presence of a priest or deacon.

MEMBERSHIP In secularized Czech society the Roman Catholic Church strives to maintain as much contact with the public and other religions as possible. A state radio station broadcasts religious programs two hours a week, and the program *Christian Magazine* airs weekly on state television. These broadcasts inform the Czech public about Catholic ideas and activities, with the goal being to increase membership. In addition, Radio Proglas (a private Christian radio station) and various Catholic magazines and websites provide information on church events and documents, life in the parishes, religious communities, and dealing with life's problems.

SOCIAL JUSTICE The Roman Catholic Church is the largest provider of non-state health and social facilities in the Czech Republic. The Czech Catholic Charity, which began work in 1918, is among the three most successful Czech charitable organizations and operates more than 200 hostels, clinics, and centers. It runs an annual fund-raiser for assisting the poor and the handicapped and provides aid to people afflicted by war (for example, in Chechnya and Afghanistan) and natural catastrophes. The organization helped many people during the 1997 and 2002 floods in the Czech Republic. Each year the well-known Epiphany Fundraiser raises about $1 million. The Prague archbishopric joined the international Distance Adoption plan and, through Czech families, pays for the education of almost 10,000 children, mainly from India, Uganda, Lithuania, or Latvia.

SOCIAL ASPECTS The family and the raising of children are important concerns of the Roman Catholic Church. In the Czech Republic different church institutions provide assistance in supporting families and children and organize a variety of related counseling services—premarital, marital, and family planning—accessible to church members and nonmembers alike. The divorce rate is similar for both Catholics and non-Catholics, with 53 marriages out of every 100 ending in divorce.

POLITICAL IMPACT Czech history is full of religious conflicts and wars. The Hussite movement arose among dissatisfied supporters of the Roman Catholic priest Jan Hus after his death in 1415. In 1420–31 the Hussite army fought five successful battles against the crusaders. The victory of the Catholic armies in 1620 at White Mountain proved a fateful event, determining the immediate future of the Czech nation. It led to the onset of the Thirty Year's War, the return of Catholicism, and the execution of 27 Czech nobles who had battled alongside the Protestants.

In the early twentieth century the Roman Catholic Church led a legal battle against T.G. Masaryk, the first president of Czechoslovakia, and lost. This, and the church's support for the Austro-Hungarian Empire, detracted from its popularity. After World War II leaders of the church, loyal to the Vatican, broke ties with the Communist regime, but since 1990 the church has worked toward a mutual understanding with the government, particularly in connection with church restitution issues.

CONTROVERSIAL ISSUES More than 60 percent of people in the Czech Republic—40 percent of Roman Catholics and 70 percent of nonbelievers—support the right of women to decide about abortion. Half the population, roughly the same among Roman Catholics and nonbelievers, expresses tolerance toward homosexuals. Parliament has several times rejected a proposed bill on registered partnerships for homosexuals. Many members of the Roman Catholic Church have declared their opposition to this through petitions.

Within the Roman Catholic Church a dispute has emerged over the second ordination of married priests who were secretly ordained under the Communist regime. The Vatican opposes this option.

CULTURAL IMPACT Art and architecture flourished in Moravia and Bohemia during the Gothic and baroque periods. The Chapel of the Holy Cross in Karlštejn Castle, with artwork by Master Theodorik, are European Gothic treasures, as is the famous painting by the Master of the Litoměřice Shrine in the Chapel of Saint Wenceslas in Saint Vitas Cathedral. Another architectural work is the Gothic and baroque star-shaped Church of Saint Jan Nepomuk in Ž'ár nad Sázavou in Moravia, built by J.B. Santíni.

Petr Brandl, a late-baroque artist, painted Saint Joachim and Saint Anna in the Prague Church of Our Lady of Victory. Sculptural masterpieces of baroque art include F.M. Brokof's early-eighteenth-century statues on the fourteenth-century Charles Bridge, as well as three reliefs carved in natural stone in eastern Bohemia by M.B. Braun. These reliefs depict the birth of Christ, the coming of the three kings, and the vision of Saint Hubert.

Other Religions

The recognition of non-Catholic churches became possible in the second half of the nineteenth century. Other faiths had long existed among the local popula-

tion, the foundations for which were laid during the attempt at reformation in the fifteenth century. Roman Catholic reformist preacher Jan Hus, inspired by John Wycliffe, proclaimed Christ as the head of the church, condemned simony as a mortal sin among priests, and called for church reform. He was condemned to death by the Church Council in Konstanz in 1415. After his death his ideas spread, and Hussite preachers demanded that the Word of God be preached freely by both the clergy and laity and that the Holy Sacrament be administered in "two kinds." In the mid-fifteenth century some of Hu'ss supporters, the Utraquists, formed a church that administered bread and wine at Communion. Another group, composed of brethren, formed the Union Fraternity, which existed for 150 years. One of the most prominent members was Petr Chelčický. He proclaimed strict evangelical humility and Christian forgiveness and perceived man as a being who, in his earthly existence, is deserving of work, respect, and protection. In the sixteenth century non-Catholic denominations expanded to include Lutherans. Religious pluralism ended with the rise of the Habsburgs, who in 1627 demanded conversion to Catholicism or exile. John Amos Comenius, a prominent teacher, a peacemaker, and the last bishop of the Union Fraternity, was among the figures forced to leave in 1628. Despite the aggressive re-Catholicization process, non-Catholic churches survived.

The Czech Evangelical Church of the Brethren was established on 17–18 December 1918 out of a merging of Calvinist and Lutheran churches. The first Mass in the reformed evangelical religion had already taken place in 1909. Now the second largest church in the Czech Republic, it has 134,000 members in 270 local chapters, which are headed by a presbytery and a priest, elected by chapter members. The church is divided into 13 seniorities, which are headed by committees made up of equal numbers of clergy and elected laypersons. The highest organ is the synod, composed of elected deputies that meet each year. The church provides its members and the general public with information through magazines and websites maintained by more than 40 local chapters. Charity work is a church tradition. The Evangelical Society for Christian Charity, founded in 1874, has 29 centers providing social services to the sick, elderly, and physically and mentally handicapped. Study in the fields of theology, philosophy, and social work is offered at the Evangelical Theological Faculty of Charles University.

The Czechoslovak Hussite Church, the country's third largest church, emerged in 1919 at the initiative of reform-minded Catholic clergy, who at Christmas held the first Roman Catholic Mass in the Czech language. The church was officially established 8 January 1920 by a group of priests, headed by Dr. K. Farský, who sought reform by demanding Mass in the national language, marriage for priests, and the democratization of church administration. At present the church has about 100,000 members in five Czech dioceses and 352 religious communities. Its position in the church spectrum is centrist: It is connected with Catholicism through its fixed liturgical order and the number of sacraments and with Protestantism through its conception of the Lord's Supper and rejection of the adoration of saints. Since 1947 women have been allowed to perform priestly duties. The church is headed by a patriarch, elected for seven years, and a central council, comprising equal numbers of bishops and elected lay members. The highest organ is the assembly, which meets irregularly. A separate Hussite Theological Faculty exists at Charles University, where students of any or no religious denomination may apply for study in Hussite theology, Judaism, religious studies, or social work. Like other churches, it runs charitable activities through the diaconate and uses modern information technology for public relations.

The Prague Jewish community is numerically small, but it boasts a rich and significant history stretching back to the tenth century. Though only a small part of the Prague Jewish ghetto (at one time the largest Jewish settlement in Europe) has been preserved, it features a number of important monuments: the thirteenth-century Old-New Synagogue, the fifteenth-century Old Prague Cemetery, and the Jewish Museum, with a collection of 40,000 exhibits and 100,000 books. Hundreds of religious figures, rabbis, thinkers, and artists are associated with the Prague Jewish community. These include the medieval rabbi Lipman Mülhausen (fifteenth century); the legendary philosopher, cabalist, and reformer Jehuda Lina Ben Becalel, otherwise known as the Rabbi Löw; or Maharal (sixteenth century); and rabbi Jechezkel Landau (eighteenth century). In the twentieth century Prague-based German-language literature, a peculiar phenomenon in world literature, gained fame. It was mostly the work of Jewish authors such as Franz Kafka, Max Brod, and Johannes Urzidil.

There are 310,000 members in the country's 19 other churches and religious societies or communities, which exist with the support of the state, their members, or foreign assistance. In the 2001 census 5.9 million people declared no religious affiliation. This very diversified group includes some 3.7 million avowed atheists. Additionally, 1.1 million people refused to declare their religion or faith.

In the early 1900s some nonreligious groups in the country founded the Free Thought movement, which later became affiliated with an international community. At the beginning of the 1950s its activities came to an end, but after 1990 the organization Free Thought of the Czech Republic, a humanist and ethical association of citizens without religious denomination, started up.

Freemasons, hermetism, and occult movements have a more than 100-year tradition in the Czech lands. Famous Freemasons include the Czech secessionist painter Alphonse Mucha. Gustav Meyrink belonged to a circle of Prague esoterics. Spiritism enjoyed popularity in the 1920s and 1930s, especially in northern and eastern Bohemia.

Many people who belong to no church become familiar with religious thought through books, courses, and even practical meditation. New trends in the area of mind and spirit, including alpha-level psychic programming, aim at the mastery of spiritual exercises and the spread of spiritual knowledge. Some healing techniques and therapies, such as Reiki, kinesiology, or holotrophic breathing, are also popular. All these methods have been referred to as secular religions.

Ján Mišovič

See Also Vol. 1: *Christianity, Judaism, Lutheranism, Reformed Christianity, Roman Catholicism*

Bibliography

Čornej, Petr, and Jiří Pokorný. *A Brief History of the Czech Lands to 2004.* Prague: Práh Publishers, 2003.

Demetz, P. *Prague in Black and Gold.* London: Penguin Books, 1997.

Filipi, P. *Křesťanstvo.* Brno: Centrum pro studium demokracie a kultury, 1998.

Halík, T. *Co je bez chvění, není pevné.* Prague: Lidové noviny, 2002.

Kadlec, J. *Přehled církevních dějin českých.* Vols. 1–2. Prague: SPN, 1977.

Kuča, K. *Atlas památek České republiky.* Vols. I–2. Prague: BASET, 2002.

Mišovič, J. *Víra v dějinách zemí Koruny české.* Prague: SLON, 2001.

Pánek, J. *Joan Amos Comenius, Teacher of Nations.* Prague: Orbis, 1991.

Polišenský, J.V. *History of Czechoslovakia in Outline.* Prague: Bohemia International, 1991.

Sayer, Derek. *The Coasts of Bohemia: A Czech History.* Princeton, N.J.: Princeton University Press, 1998.

von Kunes, Karen. *Beyond the Imaginable: 240 Ways of Looking at Czech.* Prague: Práh Publishers, 1999.

Democratic Republic of the Congo

POPULATION 55,225,478

ROMAN CATHOLIC 43 percent

PROTESTANT 22 percent

INDEPENDENT CHRISTIAN (INCLUDING KIMBANGUIST CHURCH) 30 percent

MUSLIM 1.5 percent

TRADITIONAL 3.5 percent

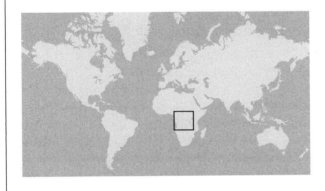

Country Overview

INTRODUCTION The Democratic Republic of the Congo (DRC) is a large, diversely populated country in central Africa. It is bordered by the Central African Republic and The Sudan to the north; Uganda, Rwanda, Burundi, and Tanzania to the east; Zambia to the southeast; Angola to the southwest; and the Republic of the Congo and the Atlantic Ocean to the west. A dense forest covers almost half of its territory. The Congo, the most powerful river in Africa, runs though the country and is endowed with an exceptional network of dams and ports.

With 359 ethnic groups and nearly 400 languages and dialects, the DRC is a complex cultural mosaic. Even so, the country has developed a distinct national identity, shaped in part by religion, education, and colonization. The current borders were established in 1884–85, when Belgium's King Leopold II formed the Congo Free State, making it his personal possession and designating himself as sovereign. Subsequent abuse of forced laborers, however, especially in the state's rubber plantations, led to outrage in Europe, and in 1908 the territory, renamed the Belgium Congo, was removed from Leopold's rule and became an official colony of Belgium. National identity was further enhanced beginning in the 1920s by Kimbanguism, an indigenous Christian movement, which preached against European culture. On 30 June 1960 the colony gained independence, initially as the Republic of the Congo. It was renamed the DRC in 1964, Zaire in 1971, and then again the DRC in 1997.

During the 1960s regional secession and rebellions caused population displacements, resulting in a considerable loss of life, deteriorating living standards, and destruction of infrastructure in more than half the country. In 1965 a military coup by General Mobutu Sese Seko embarked the country into a bleak future; poverty and misery became the daily life of the population, even though the DRC possessed substantial mineral, forest, and agricultural resources. A rebellion finally overthrew Mobutu in 1997. After a subsequent period of political unrest, revolt, military presence by neighboring coun-

Congolese Catholics take holy communion from a Priest in the Catholic Church of Nyakasanza, located in Bunia, Congo. AP/WIDE WORLD PHOTOS.

tries, and assassination, the DRC formed a government of national unity in 2002.

Today, reflecting its colonial past, the DRC is overwhelmingly Christian, with Roman Catholicism the largest of the denominations. Although only about 3 percent of the population adheres exclusively to traditional religion, the great majority still follow some aspects of traditionalism, combining both Christian and traditional practices into their daily life.

RELIGIOUS TOLERANCE The colonial state fought against all messianic movements (including the Kimbanguist and Kitawala), seeing them as a threat to peace. It also attempted to control the spread of Islam.

Since independence in 1960 the government has remained secular, and it has recognized freedom of speech and religion in its various constitutions. In 1971, however, the state passed a law regulating religious groups, which recognized only three Christian denominations: the Church of Christ in Zaire (in 1997 renamed the Church of Christ in Congo), the Roman Catholic Church, and the Kimbanguist Church. It also recognized the Muslim community. The primary concern of the law was Protestant churches, whose proliferation and internal conflicts were perceived by the government as threatening the unity of the country. The Mobutu re-

gime, moreover, organized the persecution of Jehovah's Witnesses. In 2003 the Victory Army of Fernando Coutinho Church was shut down because of its political criticism.

Today the political class is mostly composed of Christians, in particular Catholics. Even so, Christians, Muslims, and other religious groups generally live together in harmony.

Major Religions

CHRISTIANITY

AFRICAN INDIGENOUS BELIEFS

CHRISTIANITY

DATE OF ORIGIN late fifteenth century C.E.
NUMBER OF FOLLOWERS 52.4 million

HISTORY Archaeological remains, including brass crucifixes, show that Christianity had deeply influenced the people and culture of the Congo region well before the European colonization of the nineteenth century. Roman Catholic priests, including Portuguese Jesuits, were the first to evangelize the region in the late fifteenth century. Decisive events included the baptism of the Congo king Nzinga-Nkuwu and some of his court on 3 May 1491; the birth of a traditionalist party sponsored by Prince Mpanzu, who hoped to reestablish ancestral traditions ridiculed by Catholic leaders; the peak of Christianity during the rule (1506–43) of Nzinga Mbemba, baptized Alfonso I; the episcopal ordination in 1512 of Henrique (son of the king of Congo), who was appointed apostolic curate of Congo in 1521; and the unexpected decline of Christian influence beginning with the introduction of the slave trade (in which even missionaries took part). In 1596 the Catholic diocese of Congo-Angola was established. The monopoly of the Portuguese missionaries, gained from royal patronage, was lost after the arrival of the first Capuchin missionaries of Italian and Spanish origin in 1645. By that time more than 300,000 of the 2 million Congolese inhabitants had been baptized.

A second period of Catholic evangelization occurred during the latter half of the nineteenth century, when a new generation of Catholic missionaries arrived from the Congregation of the Fathers of the Holy Spirit, the Society of African Missions, the Congregation of Immaculate Heart of Mary, the Society of the Missions of Verona, and the Missionaries of Our Lady of Africa (White Fathers). Over time these settlements spread throughout all regions of the country. This second phase of evangelization coincided with the beginning of European colonization.

In the late nineteenth century Protestant missionaries also arrived in the area of the DRC: the Baptist Missionary Society in Lower Congo and Kisangani; the American Baptist Foreign Missionary Society in Lower Congo, Kinshasa, and Bandundu; the Livingstone Inland Mission in Palabala; and the Swedish Missionary Society in Kasi, Mukimbungu, and Manyanga. These missionaries adopted a critical attitude toward the colonial policy of the Congo Free State (1885–1908, led by King Leopold II of Belgium), whose atrocities against forced laborers were confirmed by an international commission in 1904. Colonial rulers thus became suspicious of Protestants and showed preference and support for the Catholics. Leopold II entrusted the evangelization of the colony to Scheutist missionaries, who were Belgian. In 1906 Leopold II granted all social work, including education and health, to churches, mainly the Catholic Church, in exchange for money. At that time missionaries were considered government and administrative agents and even held judicial power.

In the Belgium Congo the Catholic Church was organized in ecclesiastical divisions (parishes and apostolic prefectures), and by independence in 1960 the country had seven orders of brothers and approximately a hundred of sisters. Today the Catholic Church is organized into 47 dioceses.

In contrast, the Protestant Church was organized by missions, and by 1958, 45 Protestant groups were active in the area of the DRC. In 1902 various Protestant churches, under the presidency of Reverend Pastor George Grenfell of the Baptist Missionary Society, came together for the first time in Leopoldville (later Kinshasa). They decided to meet regularly in an advisory committee called the Missionary Conference of the Congo, and in 1922 the committee formed another group, the Christian Council of the Congo, renamed the Protestant Council of the Congo in 1924. In 1942 the Church of Christ in Congo was established. There were 64 Protestant communities in the DRC in 2000.

EARLY AND MODERN LEADERS Until the 1950s it was foreign missionaries, with the help of Congolese

aides, who assumed the work of Christian evangelization. The first three Congolese missionaries—Octave Kapita, Cyril Mununu, and Joseph Lutumba—made vows to the Company of Jesus in 1950. The first Dominican father, Dominique Sukula, was ordained in 1954, and the first Congolese Benedictine, Father Francois Senkoto, was ordained the same year. Father Frederic Etsou, the second Congolese Scheutist, was ordained in 1958. By 1960 the Catholic Church counted 669 mission posts served by 6,000 white missionaries, who were aided by 500 African priests.

With the ordination beginning in 1956 of Congolese bishops, including Pierre Kimbondo, Joseph Nkongolo, and Joseph Malula, a corresponding evolution occurred within the Catholic Church, culminating in the creation, by pontifical decree, of an episcopal hierarchy in the Belgian Congo and Rwanda-Urundi in 1959. Following this decree, all 32 vicariates and 7 apostolic prefectures were organized into 6 ecclesiastical provinces. In 1962 the first Catholic archdioceses and dioceses were formed. In December 1991 Laurent Monsengo Pasinya, archbishop of Kisangani, was elected president of the National Episcopal Conference of the DRC. At the start of the twenty-first century, the Catholic Church had 3,014 priests and 6,487 nuns, all coordinated by the National Episcopal Conference.

After independence a process of Africanization also took place in the Protestant Church. Pastors Pierre Shaumba Wembo, John Petelo, and Jean Bokeleale Itofo Bokambanza were the first secretaries-general and legal representatives of the Protestant Council of the Congo. In 2000 the Protestant Church had 320,101 parishes, 16,730 ordained pastors, and 1,265 missionaries. The Church of Christ of the Congo, headquartered in Kinshasa, was directed by Marini Bodho beginning in 1990s.

MAJOR THEOLOGIANS AND AUTHORS Theological education for Catholics was originally organized in small seminaries staffed by priests and later in large seminaries in such cities as Mayidi and Kabwe (the latter providing a high intellectual and spiritual education). It was in the School of Theology at the University of Lovanium in Kinshasa where the religious elite was rigorously prepared; today, however, this responsibility is assumed by a number of theology institutes. Among the most noted Congolese theologians have been Tharcisse Tshibangu Tshishiku (rector of the University of Lovanium from 1967 to 1971 and of the National University of Zaire from 1971 to 1981) and Abbé Ntedika Konde (rector of the University of Joseph Kasa-Vubu). The work of François Kabasele Lumbala and Ngindu Mushete was influential in the Africanization of religious rites in the Congolese Catholic Church.

During the period of colonial rule the Protestant Church provided only a basic education to its pastors, notably at the School of Pastors and Teachers of Kimpese. A more thorough training was provided after the Protestant Faculty of Theology was formed at the Free University of the Congo in Kisangani in 1963. This faculty exists today at the Protestant University of Congo in Kinshasa. Especially important among Protestant theologians was David Yemba Kekumba, dean of the theology department, as well as rector, at the Protestant University of the Congo.

HOUSES OF WORSHIP AND HOLY PLACES Cathedrals and churches are generally built according to requirements imposed by the Vatican or by different Protestant churches of Europe and the United States. Notable among Catholic churches are the Notre Dame Cathedral of the Congo in Kinshasa and the cathedral in Kisantu. Important among the Protestants is the Centennial Church in Kinshasa.

WHAT IS SACRED Among Catholics in the DRC, Christian relics are worshipped, and holy water and rosaries are objects of devotion. Portraits of saints, formerly depicted as white figures, have been replaced by African images. Some Congolese saints, including Bakanja and Annuarite, are now revered. Protestants in the DRC, like Protestants elsewhere, consider these practices to be idolatrous and condemned by the Bible.

HOLIDAYS/FESTIVALS In 1971 Mobutu imposed a "policy of authenticity" on the country. As a result, several religious holidays were no longer celebrated. For example, Ascension Day and All Saints' Day lost their status as legal holidays on 14 September 1972. Even Christmas was removed as a legal holiday by the Political Bureau of the Popular Movement of the Revolution on 28 June 1974, but its status was later restored. This policy also suppressed Christian first names. Today, of all the Christian holidays, only Christmas Day and Easter Monday are recognized by the DRC constitution.

MODE OF DRESS Both poor and rich Congolese Christians dress up when they go to church, particularly on Sunday. Christians wear a *pagne*—a piece of cloth wrapped around the body or fashioned into a skirt or shirt—often printed with an image of the Virgin Mary or a Congolese saint. Members of women's choirs wear *pagne*s made with patterns inspired by modern life.

DIETARY PRACTICES There are no dietary restrictions during important events of the Catholic Church; however, some conservative Catholics abstain from eating meat on Good Friday. Alcoholic beverages are traditionally prohibited for Protestants, although this requirement is not presently observed.

RITUALS The Catholic Church in the DRC, as elsewhere, generally observes seven sacraments: baptism, Eucharist, confirmation, penance, marriage, holy orders, and anointing of the sick. Only baptism, first Communion, and marriage create great occasions for family members and friends to rejoice. Once the ceremonies end, the events becomes secular, and people eat, drink, and dance. These parties take place outside of churches, in bars or at home. Protestants celebrate marriage in a similar manner as Catholics.

Traditional Congolese rites, especially for the dead, have been in conflict with Christian practices. Catholic rituals, however, have undergone profound changes since the late 1960s, when the church decided the message of Christ should be taught within the context of local cultures. In 1988 the Vatican officially accepted the Congolese Mass, the music for which includes popular African rhythms.

RITES OF PASSAGE In the DRC Christians recognize the same rites of passage as Christians elsewhere. Passage to adult Christian life is marked by confirmation for Catholics and often by baptism by Protestants. Initiations into traditional secret societies, rigorously prohibited by colonial rulers and missionaries, are no longer common, at least in cities. During colonial times Christians could be excommunicated for referring to pagan practices; this is no longer the case.

MEMBERSHIP In cities Protestants recruit new members in large public forums, at home, and even on buses. Television and radio are also used for recruitment. In villages educated catechists and evangelists enlist new members. Catholics have set up recruitment groups in most urban neighborhoods. Children are sometimes obligated to get baptized (with parental consent) before they pursue their education in Catholic or Protestant schools.

SOCIAL JUSTICE During the colonial period the Catholic Church was associated with the ruling political power and showed little concern about the exploitation of the Congolese people. By the 1950s, when decolonization was underway, the Catholic Church started to discuss problems colonized people had in working toward social and political emancipation. With the independence of the DRC in 1960, the Catholic Church began to criticize social injustice, and in 1971 Cardinal Malula, archbishop of Kinshasa, defended "distributive justice" in a speech that became the preoccupation of the National Episcopal Conference.

Although during the colonial period Protestant missionaries of the Baptist Missionary Society defended the African prophet Simon Kimbangu when he was condemned to death in 1921, most Protestant churches have avoided issues of social justice. None of them, for example, defended the Jehovah's Witnesses when they were forbidden to practice their religion, nor did they protest the banning of the Victory Army of Fernando Coutinho Church in 2003.

SOCIAL ASPECTS During the colonial period the Church promoted the development of monogamous marriages and nuclear families, and Christian villages were built for this purpose. Polygamy was discouraged through the payment of an additional tax for each wife. Today the practices of polygamy and having mistresses remain social realities against which the Church has little power, despite its homilies and sermons.

POLITICAL IMPACT Christian churches have played an important political role in the DRC. All Catholic churches denounced Mobutu's "policy of authenticity" that abolished Christian names in 1971. As a result of this criticism, Cardinal Malula was exiled to the Vatican, and some properties of the Catholic Church in Kinshasa were confiscated. On the other hand, Protestants and Kimbanguists generally supported the absolute power of Mobutu.

Regular pastoral letters and declarations by Catholic bishops have contributed to shaping the political consciousness of the DRC. The National Sovereign Conference (1991–92), attended by bishops and other church authorities, was chaired by Laurent Monsengwo Pasinya, archbishop of Kisangani. He also chaired the DRC's High Council of the Republic from 1992 to 1997. During the years 1990–97 Catholic parishes became places of political mobilization. Beginning in 2003 the Senate was presided over by Marini Bodho, national president of the Church of Christ of the Congo, while the Independent Electoral Commission responsible for preparing and organizing the elections beginning in 2005 was placed under the direction of the Catholic abbot Appolinaire Malu Malu.

CONTROVERSIAL ISSUES Catholic women's movements have fought against the exclusion of women from economic and political responsibilities. The Vatican opposition to contraception and abortion is not followed by Catholics in the DRC, and there is a conflict between traditional Christian teaching and the Congolese social practices of polygamy, cohabitation, and fetishism. In addition, cohabitation of priests has become widespread, raising the question of celibacy within the Congolese clergy.

CULTURAL IMPACT Christian churches in the DRC have been important in the dissemination of modern values and the study of local languages. In the 1960s the decision by the Catholic Church to spread the message of Christ through local cultural practices led to the introduction of Congolese music in Mass, *pagnes* as religious clothes, and processions infused with African practices.

Also in the 1960s the Catholic Education Bureau helped promote the organization of African studies throughout the country. Catholic schools now educate more than 60 percent of students in the DRC, far exceeding the number of students in Protestant and government schools. Most intellectuals in the country have been educated by the Catholic Church.

AFRICAN TRADITIONAL

DATE OF ORIGIN end of the first millennium C.E.
NUMBER OF FOLLOWERS 1.9 million

HISTORY Prior to the introduction of Christianity, traditional religion existed throughout the Congo region. It centered on the existence of a Supreme Creator—denoted by various ethnic groups as Mungu, Nzambe, Nzambi, or Imana—who was viewed as good though inaccessible to humans. Nature spirits and ancestors functioned as intermediaries between humans and the

Supreme Creator, and the ancient people of the Congo would regularly appeal to ancestors for help. They also believed that a certain evil spirit existed. All people were not considered equal; some had supernatural power that could intervene to curse or bless, to save or kill, or to influence the forces of the world beyond.

EARLY AND MODERN LEADERS All ancient Congolese societies were based on traditional religion, and their traditional chiefs—such as Nimi Lukeni of the Bakuba and Mwant Yav Tshombe of the Lunda—enjoyed both religious and sociopolitical power. Important among contemporary leaders has been Ne Muanda Nsemi, spiritual chief of the Bundu dia Kongo (Kingdom of Congo), a political-religious group that seeks the reestablishment of the ancient kingdom of the Bakongo and requires adherents to reject Christianity, Islam, and other outside religions. The teachings of Ne Muanda Nsemi rest on the traditional religious beliefs of the region.

MAJOR THEOLOGIANS AND AUTHORS Traditional religion in the Congo region is without a written heritage and thus does not have theologians in the ordinary sense. Local chiefs, however, have been important is passing down the tenets and practices of traditional religion, and they have also held many religious functions—for example, soothsayer, sorcerer, and healer—defining their intermediary role between human beings and ancestors. In the contemporary DRC many Christians, despite their faith in Jesus Christ, also look to traditional chiefs for help, especially when an illness cannot be addressed by modern medicine.

In the twentieth century many important scholars of traditional religion and life emerged. These included Gérard Bwakasa, Albert Doutreloux, Van der Kerken, the Belgian missionary J. Van Wing, K. Kia Bunseki Fu-Kiau (known for his writing on Bantu-Congo religion and philosophy), and Vincent Mulago (whose work also appears under the name Gwa Cikala Musharhamina).

HOUSES OF WORSHIP AND HOLY PLACES Sacred places inhabited by spirits and ancestors are located in forests, mountains, cemeteries, trees, water springs, and rivers, where only the initiated and their adherents can go.

WHAT IS SACRED Each ethnic group or tribe that practices traditional religion in the DRC has a sacred animal that adherents do not eat. This sacred animal, however, may be sacrificed on the occasion of great events in order to regenerate the society when it is in crisis.

HOLIDAYS/FESTIVALS Births, mourning, the end of initiation periods, and harvests are accompanied by great ceremonies, rejoicing, and the observation of a variety of rites.

MODE OF DRESS Spiritual chiefs, masters of ceremonies, and the initiated wear clothing specifically designed for religious events (such as the burial of traditional leaders and initiations into secret societies) or for their spiritual function (e.g., healing).

DIETARY PRACTICES In certain circumstances traditional religion imposes restrictions on food and sex, which are enforced by religious chiefs or designated priests. Sometimes foods useful to children or to pregnant women are forbidden to others. The consumption of dogs or cats, long ago reserved to exclusive social groups mostly in villages, now occurs in cities without much restriction, largely to meet the needs of the hungry.

RITUALS There are numerous traditional rites for birth, mourning, marriage, ancestor consultation, and other occasions. These rites are determined by the initiation societies, the circumstances, and the social practices of one's ethnic group. There are also modern adaptations; healers in the city of Kinshasa, for example, sell their services, while in the villages families tend to reward such services by giving presents. Dances are present at most rituals, and incantations not understood by the adherents give an esoteric character to these ceremonies. Special invocations or prayers are said to the Supreme Creator to request rains, fecundity, or good harvests.

RITES OF PASSAGE Initiations into adult life are found in the Kongo, Lunda, and Tshokwe societies. These rites, led by elders, provide young people with important social knowledge—such as how to avoid bad spirits—and mark the moment when they must assume responsibilities in society. They are accompanied by a traditional ceremony and music.

Circumcision for young boys was considered an important rite of passage in traditional societies. It is still practiced in villages, where traditional medicine remains an essential form of healing.

MEMBERSHIP In the DRC one is a member of traditional religion through birth and participation in family and community life, and in both cities and villages, traditional religion has governed the behavior of the whole community. Traditional religion has also served as a shared reference point among people of different ethnic backgrounds within the DRC.

SOCIAL JUSTICE In traditional societies of the DRC, social justice has been a constant concern. For example, to avoid cheating or theft, traders have threatened religious sanctions. Such practices still exist today in certain rural areas less accessible to Christian influence or in certain social groups in cities, such as the Kinshasa and Lubumbashi.

SOCIAL ASPECTS Traditional initiations have taught the young how to be responsible, how to respect life, how to control oneself, and how to avoid bad spirits, adultery, envy, and jealousy. The Supreme Creator forbids injustice and recommends love for all.

POLITICAL IMPACT In the DRC political power has been understood through the beliefs of traditional religion. Among the Bakongo, for example, the supreme creator Nzambi is the legislator; he punishes anyone who breaks his laws. In theory Nzambi's power is exercised through the chief, though this belief has diminished along with the increasing influence of Christianity. Nevertheless, current political and business leaders continue to use traditional religion as an underpinning for establishing or maintaining their power. Certain Catholic and Protestant leaders have also resorted to traditional practices. A Catholic bishop was even relieved of his duties because of these practices.

CONTROVERSIAL ISSUES Reproduction is a great concern for families and kinship networks within traditional societies, and thus obstacles to it, such as contraception and abortion, are generally not tolerated. As such, traditionalists do not take seriously the use condoms to prevent HIV/AIDS.

CULTURAL IMPACT Traditional religion has been an important influence in art, music, dance, and other cultural forms in the DRC. This is seen, for example, in the production of fetish statuettes representing human beings, animals, and spirits, especially among the Bakongo.

Other Religions

During the second half of the nineteenth century Swahili-Arabs—an ethnic group with African and Arab ancestry who spoke Swahili—began to practice Islam in the area of the DRC, principally in Kabambare, Kasongo, Kindu, Nyangwe, Kisangani, Mtoa, Kalemie, and Lokandu, the commercial centers where Swahili-Arabs traded. Swahili-Arabs were generally tolerant toward traditional religion, and some local chiefs who were interested in trading with Swahili-Arabs began adopting Islamic practices. Other chiefs, however, including Mirambo, who led a powerful kingdom in central Africa, remained hostile to Islam and put up strong resistance to Swahili-Arab merchants.

Swahili was the common language of the region, and thus Swahili-Arabs were able to communicate easily with the local population, helping Islam spread to other ethnic groups. Islam was also aided by the common practice of Swahili-Arabs marrying local women. These advantages, however, were counterbalanced by the hostility toward Islam of the Congo Free State, which viewed Islam as a threat to Christian evangelization. During the colonial period Islam was contained to two areas, Maniema and the Oriental Province, but following World War II Islamic emissaries from Zanzibar and East Africa arrived in the Congo, and after independence Islam began to flourish. In 1972 the Islamic Community of Zaire was formed. In the contemporary DRC Islam remains a notable social force—for example, in its ban on the consumption of alcohol and in its acceptance of polygamy.

The Kimbanguist Church, indigenous to the DRC, was inspired by the prophet Simon Kimbangu (1889–1951), who was born in Nkamba and later became a servant to a Baptist missionary at Ngombe Lutete. On 18 March 1921 Kimbangu received a vision and a call to perform miracles. Beginning in 1921 pilgrimages were organized to Nkamba, where Kimbangu reportedly healed the sick and even brought dead people back to life, in addition to preaching against fetishism and polygamy. The prophet declared the imminent return of Christ, who would overthrow white colonial power. Soon Catholic and Protestant conversion houses, as well as hospitals and other medical establishments, were abandoned, and people went to Nkamba for spiritual and physical healing. Followers also began to challenge colonial rule, causing concern in missionary communities. On 3 October 1921 Belgian colonial authorities charged Kimbangu with insurrection, ordering his arrest and death sentence, which was later commuted to life in prison in November 1921. Transferred first to Kisangani and then to Lubumbashi, Kimbangu died in prison on 12 October 1951.

Because it was considered a subversive movement, Kimbanguism was vigorously suppressed under Belgian rule from 1921 to 1957. Its teachings attacked the foundations of colonization; they opposed the domination and exploitation of the colonized and announced the coming reign of Africans. As a result, some 37,000 Kimbanguists were deported to regions outside of Nkamba, which unintentionally contributed to the spread of the religious movement to the rest of the DRC.

In the beginning Kimbanguism was conducted secretly, but as the country headed toward independence, the movement became more tolerated. On 25 March 1960 the body of Simon Kimbangu, which had been buried in Lubumbashi, was excavated and transferred to Nkamba, where a mausoleum was built for him. On 6 April 1960 the religious movement, renamed the Church of Christ on Earth by Prophet Simon Kimbangu, obtained legal status. Nkamba became a sacred place, the "New Jerusalem," where thousands of pilgrims from the DRC and other central African countries would go. In 1969 the Kimbanguist Church became a member of the ecumenical Council of Churches. It also spread throughout central, eastern, and southern Africa and developed a presence in western Europe and North America.

The leadership of the Kimbanguist Church has remained within the family of Kimbangu. His Eminence Diangenda Kuntima Joseph, the youngest son of Kimbangu, was the first spiritual chief. When he died in 1992, his Eminence Dialungana Salomon, the eldest son of Kimbangu, replaced him. After his death in 2001, his son Simon Kimbangu Kiangani, born the day Kimbangu died, became the spiritual chief.

The Kimbanguist Church has its own liturgy and catechism that in many ways is different from those of Catholics and Protestants, reflecting its African heritage and the political, economic, and social context in which it was founded. Among its prominent beliefs are the Trinity (God expressed as the Father, Son, and Holy Ghost) and the existence of evil spirits that can harm people. Its rejects the notion of unlimited divine love toward humanity. It does not excommunicate, nor does it adhere to the worship of saints. Sacraments in the Kimbanguist Church include baptism (by prayer and the laying on hands), marriage, ordination, and Communion, the later performed with honey and a cake made of potatoes, eggs, corn flour, and green bananas. Communion is celebrated only three times a year: 25 December (Christmas), 12 October (the anniversary of Simon Kimbangu's death), and 6 April (the anniversary of the beginning of Simon Kimbangu's ministry). Kimbanguists oppose polygamy, abortion, and contraceptives.

Like Catholics and Protestants, Kimbanguists have built an extensive educational and medical network throughout the DRC, and its schools and parishes have been subsidized by the government. In November 1970 it created a school of theology, which in 1977 became the Faculty of Kimbanguist Theology, later incorporated into the University of Simon Kimbangu. The biggest hospital, built in Kinshasa after independence, is owned and administrated by the Kimbanguist Church.

During the postcolonial period the Kimbanguist Church enjoyed substantial political support, and its secretary-general (1960–92) and legal representative, Reverend Lucien Luntadila, was appointed to high political positions. In the DRC, as well as in the neighboring countries of Angola and the Republic of the Congo, politicians have looked to members of the Kimbanguist Church for support. When, for example, the spiritual chief Diangenda died in 1992, the DRC, Angola, and the Republic of the Congo sent ministers to the funeral.

Sabakinu Kivilu

See Also Vol. 1: *Christianity, Protestantism, Roman Catholicism*

Bibliography

Adelman, Kenneth Lee. "The Church-State Conflict in Zaire: 1969-1974." *African Studies Review* 18 (1975): 102-116.

Andersson, Efraim. *Messianic Popular Movements in the Lower Congo.* Uppsala: Almqvist & Wiksells, 1958.

Asch, S. *L'Eglise du prophète Simon Kimbangu: De ses origines à son rôle actuel au Zaire.* Paris: Karthala, 1983.

Birmingam, David, and Phyllis M. Martin, eds. *History of Central Africa.* London and New York: Longman, 1983.

Braeckman, E. M. *Histoire du protestantisme au Congo.* Brussels: Librairie des Eclaireurs Unionistes, 1961.

Haddad, Adnan. *L'Arabe et le Swahili dans la République du Zaire.* Paris: Sedes, 1983.

Kabasele Lumbala, François. *Alliances avec le Christ en Afrique: Inculturation des rites Religieux au Zaire.* Paris: Karthala, 1994.

Kabongo Mbaya. *L'Eglise du Christ au Zaire: Formation et adaptation d'un Protestantisme en situation de dictature.* Paris: Karthala, 1992.

Kivilu, Sabakinu. "Kimbangu Simon." In *Encyclopaedia Africana Dictionary of African Biography.* Vol. 2. Algonac, Michigan: Reference Publications, 1979.

MacGaffey, Wyatt. *Modern Kongo Prophets: Religion in a Plural Society.* Bloomington: Indiana University Press, 1983.

———. *Religion and Society in Central Africa: The Bakongo of Lower Zaire.* Chicago: University of Chicago Press, 1986.

Wamu Oyatambwe. *Eglise Catholique et pouvoir politique au Congo Zaire: La quête Démocratique.* Paris : L'Harmattan, 1997.

Denmark

POPULATION 5,368,854

EVANGELICAL LUTHERAN 86
percent

MUSLIM 1.9 percent

OTHER 2.1 percent

NONAFFILIATED 10 percent

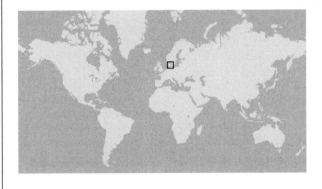

Country Overview

INTRODUCTION Forming a geographic and cultural bridge between Scandinavia and the rest of Europe, the Kingdom of Denmark lies north of Germany and south of the Scandinavian Peninsula, separated from Norway and Sweden by channels connecting the North Sea and the Baltic Sea. The country consists of the peninsula of Jutland and two large islands, Fyn and Sj'lland, as well as dozens of smaller islands. First united under Viking kings in the ninth century, Denmark was a major imperial power in northern Europe throughout the Middle Ages. It lost most of its empire between the sixteenth and nineteenth centuries, however, and has played a

minor part in the political dramas of the twentieth century.

As in most of Scandinavia, Denmark's religious world was dominated until the tenth century by Norse polytheism, which involved major gods like Odin and Thor as well as a variety of minor gods, spirits, and ancestor cults. Christianity first arrived with missionaries around 700 C.E., and it became established with the support of the crown in the tenth and eleventh centuries. In 1536 the Evangelical Lutheran Church was made the state church, which it remains today. The crown suppressed most alternative religions until the Enlightenment, though it sometimes permitted small circles of Nonconformists to practice in Copenhagen and Fredericia.

Since the late eighteenth century, Denmark has stood at the forefront of political and economic liberalization in Europe. Democracy and religious freedom were established in the constitution of 1849, and the country has been among the world's leaders in promoting gender equality and progressive social legislation since World War II. Religious groups have proliferated, though the state church still retains the vast majority of the population. While the nation is among the most prosperous in the world, economic strains in the late twentieth and early twenty-first centuries led to questions about the future of its generous welfare state. At the same time, the difficulty of absorbing immigrants into the largely homogeneous population has sparked contentious national debates about Danish culture and identity. Since most of the immigrants have been Muslims—guest workers and their families began arriving in the 1960s, and large numbers of African and Middle

Eastern refugees have since entered the country—these debates have often taken on religious overtones.

RELIGIOUS TOLERANCE The Danish constitution explicitly guarantees freedom of worship, and official discrimination against Nonconformist religions has been all but unknown. A state church does exist, and most Danes belong to it, but its leadership has no power to constrain individual religious practice or expression. Religious minorities do sometimes face discrimination by employers or private citizens, a serious problem especially for Muslim immigrants. Such discrimination is rooted primarily in cultural differences, however, with religion playing a minor role.

Major Religion

EVANGELICAL LUTHERANISM

DATE OF ORIGIN 1536 C.E.
NUMBER OF FOLLOWERS 4.6 million

HISTORY Royal support enabled Christianity to become established in Denmark in about 950 C.E. In 1536 the Evangelical Lutheran Church replaced the Roman Catholic Church as the official church in Denmark, following a two-year civil war that broke out between Catholic and Lutheran forces over the ascension of Christian III to the throne. A devout follower of Martin Luther, Christian appropriated the property of the Catholic Church, and he reorganized its structure and theology along Protestant lines. For the next three centuries the church in Denmark remained an extension of royal authority, its theological leanings following those of the monarch. During the Pietist period in the early eighteenth century, for example, the religiosity of Christian VI led to the imposition of stringent controls on church attendance and doctrine, while Frederik VI's political liberalism was associated with rationalist doctrines in the church at the turn of the nineteenth century.

Alternatives to the church's official views sometimes took the form of lay movements. In the nineteenth century, for example, two opposed lay movements known as Grundtvigianism and the Inner Mission came to dominate religious debate within the church. Denmark's 1849 constitution established religious freedom, eliminating compulsory membership in the state church.

The church, which became known as the *Folkekirke,* or People's Church, retained the allegiance of the overwhelming majority of Danes, but over the next century it gradually receded from the center of Danish life and culture. The twentieth century saw powerful trends toward secularism in Danish society, especially after World War II, and contemporary Denmark is one of the world's least actively religious nations. Despite these developments, the church remains important to Danish culture and identity, and some observers have seen signs of a return to religious observance among Danes.

EARLY AND MODERN LEADERS Some of the most important church leaders in the Danish Lutheran Church have been the kings who governed it. Christian III (1503–1559), Christian VI (1699–1746), and Frederik VI (1768–1839) all played major roles in the development of Danish religion. Influential early Lutheran clerics included the evangelist Hans Tausen (1494–1561), the bishop Peder Palladius (1503–1560), and the theologian Niels Hemmingsen (1513–1600). In the nineteenth century the priest and poet Nikolai Frederik Severin Grundtvig (1783–1872) became immensely influential in Denmark, his folk-oriented Christianity reshaping not only Danish religious thought but broader ideas about Danish identity as well. At the same time Inner Mission leader Vilhelm Beck (1829–1901) led the opposing Pietist movement. Since the establishment of the Folkekirke in 1849, some of the most influential figures in the church have been the government ministers who have overseen it, such as J.C. Christensen (1856–1930) and Bodil Koch (1903–1972).

MAJOR THEOLOGIANS AND AUTHORS In addition to those mentioned above, influential figures in Danish religious thought have included the 17th-century theologian Jesper Brochmand, the 18th-century Pietist poet Hans Adolph Brorson, and the 19th-century philosopher Søren Kierkegaard. Notable Danish theologians of the twentieth century included Vilhelm Grønbech (1873–1948), the Grundtvigian preacher Hal Koch (1904–1963), the theologian and scholar Poul Georg Lindhardt (1910–1988), and the ethical theologian Knud Ejler Løgstrup (1905–1981).

HOUSES OF WORSHIP AND HOLY PLACES Worship is conducted in the churches, one of which stands in most rural villages and in each urban parish. Country

Prince Nikolai of Denmark is christened in a Copenhagen church. Although the twentieth century saw powerful trends toward secularism in Danish society, the church remains important to Danish culture and identity. © ORBAN THIERRY/CORBIS SYGMA.

churches are usually small, and many date back to the eleventh century. Architecturally important churches include Viborg Cathedral in Jutland, Roskilde Cathedral on Fyn, and Helligåndskirken, Marmorkirken, Grundtvigkirken, Vor Frelsers Kirke, and Vor Frues Kirke in Copenhagen. Inner Mission meetings take place in spartan brick *missionshus* (mission houses) in many parishes, while Grundtvigian *forsamlingshus* (meeting houses) provide space for both religious and cultural activities.

WHAT IS SACRED? A largely secular country, Denmark has few sacred sites; while older church buildings and archaeological sites like Viking graves have sacred associations, they are not objects of pilgrimage. Historical relics, like the bloody bandages of King Christian IV in Rosenborg Castle, perhaps come closest to sacred objects.

HOLIDAYS AND FESTIVALS While Easter (*Paaske*) is the most important religious holiday in Danish Lutheranism, Christmas (*Jul*) is the most actively celebrated, with Christmas Eve constituting the high point of the season. Popular culture teems with decorations and Christmas activities, such as tree trimming and festive Christmas luncheons, from the beginning of December through Epiphany. Other important religious and cultural festivals include Shrove Tuesday (*Fastelavn*), during which costumed children go from door to door demanding treats; Midsummer's Eve (*Sankt Hans Aften*), celebrated with midnight bonfires and concerts; New Year's Eve, celebrated with fireworks and mischief by teenagers; and smaller holidays like Great Prayer Day (*Store Bededag*) and Saint Martin's Day (*Sankt Mortens Dag*).

MODE OF DRESS Lay Lutherans wear no distinctive clothing in Denmark. Lutheran priests wear black robes with pleated collars when officiating.

DIETARY PRACTICES Danish Lutheranism imposes no dietary restrictions. A number of holidays, however, involve festive meals, with large family gatherings at Christmas and Easter. Certain foods are associated with individual holidays, including special rolls (*fastelavnsboller*) on Shrove Tuesday, decorated eggs at Easter, goose dinners on Saint Martin's Day, and spherical pancakes (*æbleskiver*) during the Christmas season. Danes have not fasted at Lent since the Reformation, though some pastors have tried to revive the practice.

RITUALS Churches hold weekly services on Sunday mornings that include prayers, scripture readings, hymns, Communion, and a sermon. Attendance at most services is sparse, with fewer than 5 percent of the population attending on a given Sunday. Special holiday services, however, particularly on Christmas Eve and Easter, attract large numbers of worshipers. Weddings are often held in church, but civil ceremonies at the town or city hall are equally common. Funerals generally take place at a special church service, with interment following in the churchyard. Such rituals, which are typically brief, involve extensive family gatherings.

RITES OF PASSAGE The primary life-cycle rituals held in the Danish Lutheran church are baptisms, confirmations, weddings, and funerals. Baptism normally takes place between two and four months of age but may occur at any time. Confirmation ordinarily occurs at age

14, following religious instruction by a priest. Church weddings are usually formal affairs, with the bride dressed in white; civil marriages tend to be less elaborate, though they may be blessed at a church ceremony afterward.

MEMBERSHIP About 80 percent of Danes are baptized in the Evangelical Lutheran Church as infants. Baptism involves the sprinkling of water and requires the presence of at least three godparents. The Danish Evangelical Lutheran Church does little formal evangelization, though societies for both foreign and domestic missionary activities exist. Domestic missions, led by groups like the Church Society for the Inner Mission in Denmark, focus on reviving faith among the increasingly secularized population. In the nineteenth and through much of the twentieth century, domestic missions were powerful forces in organizing social life in many rural areas.

SOCIAL JUSTICE The Lutheran Church in Denmark has tended to follow the human rights orientation of the ecumenical organizations of the European Union. While the church has no mandate for nonreligious political activity, its clergy have often taken leading roles in the promotion of foreign relief efforts, aid for immigrants, education, tolerance, and human rights. In addition, voluntary associations led by lay persons within the church have participated extensively in human rights activities.

SOCIAL ASPECTS Danish Lutheranism has generally maintained a liberal position on marriage and the family, allowing divorce and remarriage and, in some cases, solemnizing homosexual unions. The church does not have policies opposing the use of birth control or abortion. There is debate about the church's stance on these issues, however, and some clergy, notably those affiliated with internal mission groups, have adopted a much more conservative position.

POLITICAL IMPACT The contemporary Danish church has had little political visibility beyond its general advocacy of humanitarian positions. Before the passage of the 1849 constitution, however, the church was an important arm of the state and often played a major role in political conflicts. The Protestant Reformation in Denmark, for example, was intertwined with the victory of the Protestant Christian III in the Count's War of 1534–36. While the introduction of religious freedom in 1849 diminished the direct connection between politics and the church, religious movements in Denmark continued to assume political significance at times. The theology of N.F.S. Grundtvig, for example, was the inspiration for rural reform movements in the nineteenth and early twentieth centuries, and it provided an intellectual foundation for the resistance movement during the German occupation of 1940–45.

CONTROVERSIAL ISSUES The liberal views of the Danish church on reproductive and gender issues reflect the attitudes of the Danish public. Some groups within the church, however, including some clergy, hold much more conservative views on issues like birth control, abortion, remarriage, and the ordination of women. Those associated with internal mission groups, like the Inner Mission society, tend to oppose both abortion and the ordination of women.

CULTURAL IMPACT Historically, the Lutheran church has had a profound influence on Danish literary and artistic culture. Before the twentieth century, much of the nation's great art and music had a devotional aspect; the classic hymns of composers like Thomas Kingo, Hans Adolf Brorson, and N.F.S. Grundtvig, for example, make up a major part of Denmark's musical heritage. Some of the country's great writers and thinkers, including Søren Kierkegaard, have been theologically trained. The secularizing trends of the twentieth century greatly diminished the church's influence in the arts, leaving it with relatively little visibility in contemporary cultural life.

Other Religions

While the Evangelical Lutheran Church dominates Danish religious life, the country is home to a variety of other religious groups. The largest of these are the Muslims, Roman Catholics, Baptists, Pentecostalists, Jews, Jehovah's Witnesses, and Mormons, all with populations of more than 5,000. A number of smaller groups also exist, ranging from the Salvation Army to various Eastern and alternative religions. Three of these groups have been particularly visible in Danish history and culture.

The largest minority religion in Denmark is Islam, with more than 100,000 adherents. Muslims first came to Denmark in significant numbers in the 1960s, mainly as guest workers from Turkey, Yugoslavia, and Pakistan. Such immigration was ended in 1973, but family reunification and refugee policies have enabled a continuing flow of Muslim immigrants in the decades since.

While Muslims can be found all across the country, they are most visible in several large enclaves in the Copenhagen area. Set amid an unusually homogeneous larger society, the cultural distinctiveness of Muslim immigrants has led to a variety of problems, including employment discrimination and some popular hostility toward Muslim religious practices. At the same time official discrimination has been minimal, and Islamic worship is carried out freely and publicly. Copenhagen has no major mosque; worship occurs in a variety of sites, organized in rented premises by independent local groups. Levels of observance among Muslims in Denmark range from the strongly traditional to the highly acculturated and secularized.

About 35,000 Roman Catholics live in Denmark, half of them in Copenhagen and the rest spread out over 50 parishes throughout the country. While the Reformation of 1536 effectively banned Catholicism in Denmark, the Catholic Church began rebuilding after the introduction of religious freedom in 1849. By the early 1920s the church claimed about 25,000 members, many of them immigrant agricultural laborers from Poland. The nation's Catholic population has since remained fairly stable. Today the church is administered by the bishop of Copenhagen, and it employs about 60 full-time priests. While the largest congregations are in the Copenhagen area, significant Catholic communities exist in most of the larger provincial cities.

Jews constitute the oldest and most established religious minority in Denmark. The Jewish Community of Denmark (Det Mosaiske Troessamfund) traces its origin to 1684, and Jews have enjoyed full civil rights since 1814. The nation's 7,000 or so Jews are deeply integrated into the larger Danish society, with high rates of intermarriage and low rates of religious observance. Most members of the Jewish community worship in the Great Synagogue, a large nineteenth-century building in the heart of Copenhagen; two small synagogues offer alternative services for those practicing a very strict Orthodox observance. The community also administers a number of social institutions, including a school, several day-care centers, cultural societies, and two nursing homes. All Jewish institutions follow Orthodox formats in their ritual practice.

In the twentieth century Denmark offered one of the world's most hospitable societies for Jews, with anti-Semitism all but absent. This high level of tolerance was dramatically demonstrated in October 1943, when a boatlift to Sweden organized by the Danish resistance saved almost the entire Jewish population of Denmark from extermination by the Nazis. The rescue left the Danish Jews as one of the few Jewish communities in mainland Europe to survive the Holocaust intact—and one with an extremely close tie to its Christian neighbors.

Andrew Buckser

See Also Vol. I: *Christianity, Lutheranism*

Bibliography

Balle-Petersen, Margaretha. "The Holy Danes: Some Aspects of the Study of Religious Groups." *Ethnologia Scandinavica* II (1981): 79–112.

Blum, Jacques. *Indvandrere og minoriteter: fordomme og diskrimination i det danske samfund.* Copenhagen: Gad, 1982.

Buckser, Andrew. *After the Rescue: Jewish Identity and Community in Contemporary Denmark.* New York: Palgrave, 2003.

Davidson, Hilda. *Myths and Symbols in Pagan Europe: Early Scandinavian and Celtic Religions.* Syracuse, N.Y.: Syracuse University Press, 1989.

Enoch, Yael. "The Intolerance of a Tolerant People: Ethnic Relations in Denmark." *Ethnic and Racial Studies* 17, no. 2 (1994): 282–300.

Lausten, Martin Schwarz. *A Church History of Denmark.* Translated by Frederick H. Cryer. Aldershot, England; Burlington, Vt.: Ashgate, 2002.

Lindhardt, Poul Georg. *Vækkelser og kirkelige retninger i Danmark.* Copenhagen: Hans Rietzel, 1959.

Nielsen, Ernest D. *N.F.S. Grundtvig: An American Study.* Rock Island, N.Y.: Augustana, 1955.

Oakley, Stewart P. *A Short History of Denmark.* New York: Praeger, 1972.

Salomonsen, Per. *Religion i dag: Et sociologisk metodestudium.* Copenhagen: Gad, 1975.

Djibouti

POPULATION 472,810

MUSLIM 94 percent

CHRISTIAN 6 percent

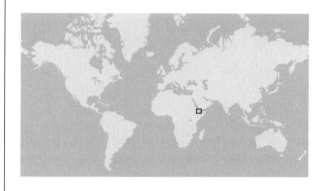

Country Overview

INTRODUCTION One of the smallest African countries, the Republic of Djibouti lies on the northeastern coast of the Horn of Africa, facing the Gulf of Aden and the Strait of Mandeb, which separates the gulf from the Red Sea. Djibouti is bordered by Eritrea to the north, Ethiopia to the west and south, and Somalia to the southeast. The land is mainly volcanic desert, and the climate is hot and arid.

Two ethnic groups form the majority of Djibouti's population: The Issa, who are of Somali origin, make up 60 percent of the population, and the Afar, who are of Ethiopian origin, make up 35 percent. The rest consists of Yemeni Arabs and Europeans, who are mostly French. While Cushitic languages are most commonly spoken, the country's official languages are Arabic and

French. Both the Issa and the Afar are Sunni Muslim, and most follow the Shafiite school of law and belong to the Qadiriyya Sufi brotherhood, which was well established in the region in the nineteenth century.

By the twelfth century Arab merchants had brought trade and the Islamic faith into the interior. Later, the coastal cities became important destinations for camel caravans emerging from the desert. The ancient trade patterns shifted when, in the late nineteenth century, the French colonial government created the port of Djibouti as the terminal for a new railroad connecting Djibouti with Ethiopia. French rule was accompanied by the arrival of Catholic missionaries, who first established Christianity in Djibouti in 1885.

RELIGIOUS TOLERANCE While Djibouti's constitution declares Islam to be the state religion, it also provides a restricted freedom of religion for others. The government generally claims to respect this right, but, in practice, proselytizing by non-Islamic religious groups is discouraged. In essence, Islam has not served to unite the Afar and the Issa peoples, but neither has it inspired any fanaticism for ethnic cleansing.

Major Religion

ISLAM

DATE OF ORIGIN Twelfth century C.E.

NUMBER OF FOLLOWERS 444,440

HISTORY Due to the proximity of the Horn of Africa to the Arabian Peninsula, its peoples were among the

Every town and village in Djibouti has a mosque. Due to the proximity of the Horn of Africa to the Arabian Peninsula, its peoples were among the first on the African continent to adopt Islam. © WOLFGANG KAEHLER/CORBIS.

first on the African continent to adopt Islam. The region's first contact with Islam can be traced back to the seventh century C.E., during the lifetime of the prophet Muhammad, when persecuted Muslims fled Arabia and took refuge in the Horn, then known as Al-Habashi. By the twelfth century merchants and clerics from the Arabian Peninsula were proselytizing extensively along the coast, where local clans established small Muslim emirates. The greatest Islamic impact, however, is attributed to the Muslim merchants who traveled into the interior. Gradually Islam expanded, and the local Muslims established Islamic states separate from the Christian state of Abyssinia, which had previously controlled the whole region. These small Muslim states eventually coalesced into the three sultanates—Tadjoura, Rahayto, and Bobaad—that make up what is now Djibouti.

Arabs controlled trade in what is now Djibouti until the sixteenth century, when the Portuguese made a brief appearance there. As the Portuguese began making conquests farther east, however, the Arabs resumed their domination of the Red Sea and the Gulf of Aden. Caravans into the hinterland carried mainly imported cloth, firearms, and slabs of salt from Lake Assal. On their return to the coastal markets, they carried coffee, wax, hides, perfumes, and, above all, slaves.

Following the arrival of French imperial authorities in the region, the Catholic Church established its mission in 1885 through Capuchin missionaries from the province of Strasbourg. By the late 1880s France had expanded its protectorate to include the shores of the Gulf of Tadjoura and the hinterland, designating the area French Somaliland. Following World War II the Afar and the Issa pressed the French government for independence, which was finally granted in 1977. Hassan Gouled Aptidon, a senior Issa politician, became the first president of the Republic of Djibouti. Aptidon was elected to three consecutive six-year terms before stepping down in 1999, when Ismail Omar Gelleh was elected to the presidency.

EARLY AND MODERN LEADERS Ali Mirah, Ahmad Ibrahim al-Ghazi, and Ahmad Gran are noted heroes of the sixteenth-century strife between Muslims and Christians. Ali Aref and his contemporary Hassan Gouled Aptidon are highly respected for their roles in the negotiations that led to independence from France in 1977. All of the current sheikhs are also highly respected for their knowledge of Islam.

MAJOR THEOLOGIANS AND AUTHORS The highest Muslim authority is the *qadi* of Djibouti. The main duty of this high-ranking religious leader is to preside over the Shari'ah (Islamic law) court, though he also celebrates marriages and registers divorces and wills. Mogue Hassan Dirir is the current *qadi* of Djibouti. Ongoure Hassan Ibrahim is an Islamic judge and politician of great influence.

HOUSES OF WORSHIP AND HOLY PLACES Every town and village in Djibouti has a mosque. The most famous are the Haaji Diide and the Masjid of Balbala.

WHAT IS SACRED? The tombs of those considered holy are treated as sacred spaces. An example is the tomb of Sheikh Abu Yazid in the Goda Mountains. Residents and visitors stream to this location every year to honor the fifteenth-century religious leader.

HOLIDAYS AND FESTIVALS The general Islamic holy days, including every Friday and the month of Ramadan, are strictly observed by Muslims in Djibouti's urban centers. In addition to the Islamic calendar, Djiboutian Muslims also observe New Year's Day (1 January), Labor Day (1 May), Independence Day (27 June), and Christmas Day (25 December). In some cases rural people, who are mostly nomadic, alter the timing of Islamic festivals to suit their traditional ritual calendar, which is dictated by natural cycles as well as ancient traditions that honor their ancestors.

MODE OF DRESS The distinctive dress of the Afar and the Issa reflects the hot climate. The men wear a piece of checkered cloth wrapped loosely about the loins that hangs below the knees. In addition, a cotton robe is thrown over one shoulder like a Roman toga. In most cases a traditional knife is added as an accessory. The women wear long skirts that are often dyed brown using mimosa bark. In addition, married women wear a piece of transparent cloth on their heads and sometimes over their shoulders and upper body. Young and unmarried women do not usually cover their heads, particularly in the interior. Traditional Arab dress (*ihran*) is worn at certain religious festivals and especially in preparation for the hajj.

DIETARY PRACTICES There are no Islamic dietary practices that are distinctive to Djibouti.

RITUALS The high Islamic festivals, such as the Id al-Fitr and the Id al-Adha (Feast of the Sacrifice), are an important aspect of Muslim self-awareness and solidarity in Djibouti. Some aspects of religious life have been altered by urbanization, however. In contrast to their urban compatriots, for example, people in rural areas have continued to regulate their religious lives according to the ritual calendar. The veneration of saints, which is linked to the traditional cult of the ancestors, is also observed.

RITES OF PASSAGE There are no rites of passage that are distinctive to Djibouti.

MEMBERSHIP In a general sense every native Djiboutian is considered a Muslim. A Muslim resurgence in the country has been evident in the proliferation of mosques and Koranic schools funded by Saudi Arabia and Kuwait.

SOCIAL JUSTICE More than any other region of the continent, the Horn of Africa has endured the debilitating effects of conflict, which have led to complex humanitarian emergencies during the last three decades. With Muslim political and local leaders acting as fa-

cilitators, joint relief partnerships have negotiated with warring parties to facilitate the movement of humanitarian supplies across the lines of battle.

SOCIAL ASPECTS Islam has made the greatest strides in family, inheritance, and ritual law. Although the Issa and the Afar consider themselves to be deeply Muslim, the harsh conditions of their nomadic existence leave them little time to adhere to the details of Islamic practice, such as the observation of Ramadhan or frequent prayers. Furthermore, in most cases of conflict between Koranic law and tribal law, custom usually prevails. In cases of adultery, for example, Afar law applies the harsher punishment to the guilty man, in contrast to the general Islamic law. On the other hand, women who are guilty of adultery are either reprimanded by their husbands or, at most, divorced. In another example, instead of recognizing three categories of homicide—namely, premeditated, involuntary, and voluntary—Afar and Issa Muslims seek to avenge all murders.

POLITICAL IMPACT Despite the political borders separating Djibouti's ethnic groups from their counterparts in other parts of the Horn, Djiboutians maintain close cultural and religious contacts through their clan networks. Furthermore, since the 1990s contacts with the Middle East and North Africa have helped to energize movements for Islamic renewal and political reform, particularly among unemployed youth. Djibouti's youth also study abroad at centers of Islamic learning. Several Arab countries, including Saudi Arabia and Kuwait, have provided financial incentives to support such ventures. In 1992 Imam Muhammad University in Riyadh established an Arab Islamic institute in Djibouti to promote Islamic and Arabic-language education. In May 1999 the president, Ismail Omar Guelleh, declared Islam to be a central tenet of his government and named the *qadi* as the country's senior judge of Islamic law and minister-delegate for Islamic affairs under the Ministry of Justice.

CONTROVERSIAL ISSUES Some clergy have advocated the state's adoption and application of Islamic law in Djibouti. The government has resisted such moves, however. Interpretations of jihad, or holy war, have generated debate since the bombing of the World Trade Center in New York City in September 2001. The treatment of refugees fleeing conflicts and drought in other parts of the Horn continues to be a major social problem.

CULTURAL IMPACT Much of Djibouti's art is still preserved in oral form, particularly song. The native languages in which Djiboutian's songs and poems are expressed contain numerous Arabic loan words. The country's significant literary artists include Raage Ugaas, an Issa poet whose works often focused on family life. In the 1940s the art of "miniature" poetry was introduced by Abdi Deeqsi, a young truck driver of great insight. His popular *balwo*, short poems not more than two lines in length, express deep feelings of love, affection, and the agonies of passion. Abdourahman A. Waberi has produced works of literature on such themes as exile, nomadism, and cultural conflict, including *Le Pays sans ombre* (1994), *Cahier nomade* (1996), *Balbala* (1997), and *Moisson de crânes: textes pour le Rwanda* (2000).

Examples of the influence of French and Islamic cultures on architecture in Djibouti are visible in buildings featuring Art Deco plasterwork around doors and windows or the delicate motifs and calligraphic elements of Islamic design.

Other Religions

Christians make up about 6 percent of Djibouti's population. The Roman Catholic Church, introduced during the period of French rule, claims the majority of the country's Christians and is the most active of the churches. It is the only church that has found converts among the local population. The country's Orthodox Christian community is composed of the Greek Orthodox and Ethiopian Orthodox churches. The sole Protestant body in the country, the Protestant Church of Djibouti, dates from World War II. It is related to the Reformed Church of France, and its small membership consists entirely of Europeans. Most of the Christian churches in Djibouti serve the spiritual needs of foreigners, while the participation of others is largely restricted to the churche's humanitarian services.

Samuel K. Elolia

See Also Vol. 1: *Islam*

Bibliography

Coates, Peter D. "Factors of Intermediacy in Nineteenth-Century Africa: The Case of the Issa of the Horn." In *Proceedings of the Second International Congress of Somali Studies.* Edited by Thomas Labahn. Vol. 2. Hamburg: H. Buske, 1984.

Englebert, Victor. "The Danakil: Nomads of Ethiopia's Wasteland." *National Geographic Magazine* 147, no. 2 (1970): 186–212.

Lewis, I.M. *Islam in Tropical Africa.* London: Oxford University Press, 1966.

———. *Peoples of the Horn of Africa: Somali, Afar, and Saho.* London: International African Institute, 1955.

Shehim, Kassim. "The Influence of Islam on the Afar." Ph.D. diss., University of Washington, 1982.

Thompson, Virginia, and Richard Adloff. *Djibouti and the Horn of Africa.* Stanford, Calif.: Stanford University Press, 1968.

Trimingham, J. Spencer. *The Christian Church and Missions in Ethiopia (Including Eritrea and the Somaliland).* London; New York: World Dominion Press, 1950.

———. *The Influence of Islam upon Africa.* New York: Praeger, 1968.

———. *Islam in East Africa.* New York: Books for Libraries, 1980.

Dominica

POPULATION 70,158

ROMAN CATHOLIC 70.0 percent

SEVENTH-DAY ADVENTIST 4.7 percent

PENTECOSTAL 4.3 percent

METHODIST 4.2 percent

BAPTIST 2.8 percent

ANGLICAN 0.7 percent

OTHER (INCLUDING BAHAI, MUSLIM, RASTAFARIAN) 13.3 percent

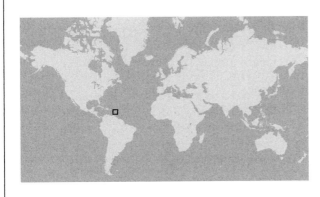

Country Overview

INTRODUCTION The Commonwealth of Dominica, an island in the Caribbean, was known as Waitikubuli when first sighted by Christopher Columbus in 1493. It was renamed Dominica, or Dies Dominica (Day of the Lord), in thanksgiving to God.

Part of the Lesser Antilles, the island lies between Guadeloupe to the north and Martinique to the south. It is mostly volcanic, mountainous, and densely covered with lush virgin rainforests. The topography of the island made colonization difficult for both the French and the British, who laid claim to the island and fought at various times for possession of it during the seventeenth and eighteenth centuries. Finally, in 1783, after five years of French occupation, the British took permanent possession of Dominica as stipulated by the Treaty of Versailles. By then French influence already had a tremendous impact on Dominica's cultural development. From as early as the seventeenth century, the Caribs, the indigenous inhabitants, were exposed to French Catholic missionaries, who had come with the purpose of converting them. The French priests were also instrumental in converting the slaves to Catholicism.

In the eighteenth century Protestantism was introduced to Dominica, but it never took a firm hold there, as is evident by the small number of practitioners. Since the 1980s both Catholicism and mainstream Protestantism have lost ground to the Pentecostals, Baptists, and Seventh-day Adventists. Other groups include Muslims, Hindus, Bahais, Buddhists, Rastafarians, and folk religionists.

RELIGIOUS TOLERANCE Despite the heavily Roman Catholic influence, Dominica does not have an official state religion. Religious freedom is guaranteed by the constitution. Prior to 1829 the British forbade Catholics to hold government jobs or have political representation, privileges reserved specifically for members of the Church of England and other Protestant sects. In

This Catholic church bears a mural of Christopher Columbu'ss landing on the island in 1493. Since his arrival, the Roman Catholic Church has played an important role in the development of Dominica. © DELLA ZUANA PASCAL/CORBIS SYGMA.

1829 the Roman Catholic Relief Act gave Roman Catholics the right to hold office and to obtain government jobs.

More recently the Rastafarian movement encountered fierce opposition from both the political and social establishments. The Prohibited and Unlawful Societies Act of 1974 was passed to contain the social and political activism of the Rastafarians and the offshoot Dreads. (Unlike the Rastafarians, who had Afrocentric beliefs, the Dreads had strong Christian beliefs and were considered to be dangerous.) By 1975 the government had declared a truce, appointed a committee that met with the Dreads, and made recommendations to ameliorate the social and economic conditions on the island.

Major Religion

ROMAN CATHOLICISM

DATE OF ORIGIN 1646 C.E.
NUMBER OF FOLLOWERS 49,100

HISTORY From the arrival of Christopher Columbus in 1493, the Roman Catholic Church has played an important role in the development of Dominica. During the French colonization the Catholic Church became firmly entrenched as the dominant denomination. Beginning with Father Raymond Breton in 1646, French priests proselytized the indigenous inhabitants. Unlike the British, the French priests, under the Code Noir of 1688, baptized slaves, allowed participation in the Mass, and gave religious instruction. The Catholic Church was officially established in Dominica in 1730. In 1783, when the British captured Dominica from the French, the church and the French priests were discriminated against and refused political representation because of their relationship to France and the pope.

During the late nineteenth and early twentieth centuries, Catholic priests were the organizing forces in village life, developing schools and organizing social services throughout the island. By the mid-twentieth century, especially since the 1980s, church membership declined as more young people became attracted to other religious denominations.

EARLY AND MODERN LEADERS Father Raymond Breton of the Dominican Order and Brother Charles were the first missionaries to instruct the Caribs in Roman Catholic religious rites, and in 1646 they celebrated the first Mass among them. During the 1800s the church's expansion was driven mainly by the work of Bishop Charles Marie Poirier, who divided Dominica into 12 parishes, each with a parish priest, a church, and an elementary school.

Philip Schelfhaut, the fifth bishop of Roseau (from 1902 until his death in 1921), constructed many churches, including the Cathedral, and was responsible for establishing Saint Anthony's Society, an insurance organization that provided medical attention and paid burial expenses.

By the mid-twentieth century the Roman Catholic Church encouraged the ordination of local priests, leading eventually to the ascendancy of Bishop Bowers Lane and Archbishop Kelvin Edward Felix. Since 2001 Archbishop Emil Paul Tscherrig and, since 2002, Bishop Gabriel Malzaire head the church.

MAJOR THEOLOGIANS AND AUTHORS In 1909 Bishop Philip Schelfhaut began the *Dominican Chronicle,* a newspaper still published today, although under different ownership. The bishop also published the *Ecclesiastical Bulletin,* a monthly journal that provided instruction for Catholics.

Father Raymond Proesmans, an archivist, is credited with contributing to the preservation of Dominican history. Father Clement Jolly wrote weekly articles on religious topics and two books relating to Christian life in Dominica.

HOUSES OF WORSHIP AND HOLY PLACES The main church, the Cathedral, is located in Roseau, but each parish or region has its own church.

WHAT IS SACRED? Dominicans follow the established practices of the Roman Catholic Church and have no sacred relics peculiar to the island. Anthropologist Anthony Layng, who studies the Caribs, states that the sacraments are magical. In his study of Carib magic, Layng points out that some Carib tales or legends include the appearance of a white man who possesses magical power.

HOLIDAYS AND FESTIVALS The Roman Catholic Church in Dominica celebrates Fête de la Saint Pierre (Feast of Saint Peter) in all the fishing villages. The festival begins with a Mass, continues with a procession to the handsomely decorated boats, and ends with a lively village party. Dominicans also travel the length of the island to the shrine of Our Lady of Lourdes and La Salette to commemorate the Virgin's appearance at Lourdes and La Salette in France.

MODE OF DRESS The older Roman Catholic parishioners in Dominica attend church formally dressed. The older men often wear suits and ties, and the older women wear hats. Young people attend church in less formal attire.

DIETARY PRACTICES Roman Catholics in Dominica do not have any strict dietary restrictions. During Lent, however, many of the older generation and the more devout abstain from eating meat.

RITUALS The rituals of the Roman Catholic Church include prayers of novenas to the saints and Jesus. The church encourages its members to observe the Stations of the Cross during Lent, and confession of sins is heard daily. Death is celebrated for nine nights by offering prayers, singing hymns, drinking, dancing, and telling stories.

RITES OF PASSAGE Roman Catholics in Dominica baptize their children during infancy, and first Communion is given around age seven, when children are be-

lieved to have reached the age of reason. The clergy confirms young adults into the faith between the ages of 12 and 14, signaling the transition from childhood to adolescence.

MEMBERSHIP Despite losing some young members to other sects, the Roman Catholic Church in Dominica works hard to retain members and attract new ones. It reaches out to the community through *The Voice of the Island,* a radio program that provides information and religious instruction to Catholics. Each weekend the church sponsors other radio programs that deal with issues important to the religious community.

SOCIAL JUSTICE The Roman Catholic Church has always been instrumental in the educational and social welfare of the island. It has established many charities and organizations to meet the needs of its congregation. The church also encourages its followers, especially the more affluent, to contribute time, money, and clothing to the less fortunate, including the indigenous Caribs. The church promotes human rights by encouraging its members to respect and protect the rights of others.

SOCIAL ASPECTS Although the church actively encourages marriage, there remain a large number of single-headed households. The church is also concerned with the preservation of the family and, working in conjunction with other Caribbean territories, issues guidelines regarding the duties and responsibilities of Catholics in maintaining the family structure.

POLITICAL IMPACT The Roman Catholic Church has always played a role in the development of Dominica but does not encourage the clergy to get involved in island politics. During the 2000 election campaign the bishop issued orders to priests and lay associates to desist from participating in partisan politics. Nevertheless, Bishop Gabriel Malzaire, along with other bishops of the eastern Caribbean, issued a statement of support and reaffirmed their commitment to the agenda of the Organisation of Eastern Caribbean States, which was established to promote and enhance the overall development of the smaller Caribbean islands.

CONTROVERSIAL ISSUES The Roman Catholic Church in Dominica does not support abortion or the ordination of women to the priesthood. Dominicans have been receptive to the church's position on child abuse and violence against women. The church offers special retreats for fathers and sons to help them deal with their anger toward women and children. The church has been less successful in its efforts to get Dominicans to marry, even though priests preach about this issue during Sunday Mass.

CULTURAL IMPACT Dominicans did not have much exposure to the arts and literature until recently. French priests and nuns introduced the traditional Christmas carols during the times of slavery (c. 1780–1834). The best-known Christmas carol, the "Cantique de Noel," sung after Midnight Mass at most homes, is no longer part of the tradition in Dominica. Religious songs and hymns are sung at wakes and during the parish fetes.

Other Religions

Anglicanism remains the religion of the small landowning British elite. Anglicans are presently part of the Church in the Province of the West Indies. Methodism first appeared on the island in the early nineteenth century and flourished in the northeastern Dominican villages of Wesley and Marigot. It is generally associated with the mixed-race, or mulatto, class, thereby separating this class from the poorer black and Carib classes.

The Pentecostals, Baptists, and Seventh-day Adventists arrived in Dominica early in the twentieth century but were initially unsuccessful because of opposition by the Catholic Church and, in the case of Pentecostals and Seventh-day Adventists, because of their religious practices. The latter two groups require practitioners to abstain from drinking alcohol, smoking, and having extramarital sex. Because they are not as strict or concerned with such behaviors, Baptists have been somewhat more successful, especially among the Caribs. Nonetheless, since the 1980s these religious sects have grown throughout the island, with many villages having at least one charismatic church built within their communities.

During the 1970s many young Dominicans were dissatisfied with the Catholic Church and, for inspira-tion and guidance, turned to Rastafarianism, a religious movement originally from Jamaica. Rastafarianism emphasizes Afrocentric beliefs and local traditions and encourages a return to the land.

Obeah, a form of sorcery introduced to Dominica by the slaves, is still practiced, even though it is illegal. It is difficult to determine how much influence obeah has had on Dominican worldview. Though obeah is reported to be on the decline, plant remedies, teas (tisanes), and baths are still used for protection against evil spells or for good luck by Dominicans. These are usually given during specific times of the year and are associated with certain phases of the moon.

Maritza Straughn-Williams

See Also Vol. 1: *Christianity, Roman Catholicism, Seventh-day Adventist Church*

Bibliography

Atwood, Thomas. *The History of the Island of Dominica.* London: Frank Cass and Co., 1971.

Barrett, David B., George T. Kurian, and Todd M. Johnson, eds. *World Christian Encyclopedia.* 2nd ed. New York: Oxford University Press, 2001.

Cracknell, Basil E. *Dominica.* Harrisburg, Pa.: Stackpole Books, 1973.

Honychurch, Lennox. "A to Z of Dominica Heritage." A Virtual Dominica. 20 Feb. 2004. http://www.avirtualdominica.com/heritage.htm.

————. *The Dominica Story: A History of the Island.* Roseau: Dominica Institute, 1984.

————. *Our Island Culture.* Roseau: Dominica Cultural Council, 1982?

Layng, Anthony. "Religion in the Carib Reserve." Paper presented at the 77th annual meeting of the American Anthropological Association, Los Angeles, November 1978.

Salter, Richard. "Dominica." In *Religions of the World.* Edited by Gordon J. Melton and Martin Baumann, 403–5. Santa Barbara, Calif.: ABC-CLIO, 2002.

Dominican Republic

POPULATION 8,721,594
ROMAN CATHOLIC 89.3 percent
PROTESTANT 8.1 percent
OTHER 2.6 percent

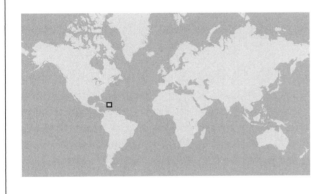

Country Overview

INTRODUCTION The Dominican Republic, located in the West Indies, consists of the eastern two-thirds of the island of Hispaniola and several small islands. Haiti occupies the western third of Hispaniola, with the Atlantic Ocean lying to the north and the Caribbean Sea to the south. The capital is Santo Domingo.

Christopher Columbus first reached Hispaniola in 1492, and Santo Domingo became the first European colony in the New World. From the beginning efforts were undertaken to convert the native Taino to Roman Catholicism, but they were decimated by warfare and disease. Aspects of the Taino heritage have been retained, particularly in the southwest, which was their political and ceremonial center. As early as 1502 Christian slaves of African origin arrived from Spain, and shortly thereafter slaves were introduced directly from Africa. The Spanish blacks established religious brotherhoods (*cofradías*) that served as mutual aid and burial societies. Africans also introduced healing and divination societies characterized by spirit possession (called *vodú*, or voodoo).

In 1697 France gained control of the western third of the island, organized the colony of Saint-Domingue, and imported more than a million African slaves. The slaves eventually revolted, establishing the Republic of Haiti in 1804. From 1822 to 1844 Haiti occupied the whole island, and during this period Haitians were encouraged to settle in the Spanish region. In 1844 Santo Domingo gained independence from Haiti as the Dominican Republic, but control returned to Spain from 1861 to 1865.

The late nineteenth and early twentieth centuries were a period of political and economic instability. The United States occupied the country from 1916 to 1922, and U.S. influence contributed to the rise of Rafael Trujillo, dictator from 1930 to 1961. The following period was dominated by Trujillo's right-hand man, Joaquín Balaguer, until his death in 2002. From the mid-twentieth century Haitian seasonal workers (*bracerosa*) were brought for sugarcane harvests, and others came illegally. The Haitian system of voodoo influenced its Dominican counterpart, and the related *rará* (Dominicanized as *gagá*) religious societies, with carnival-like celebrations during Lent, developed in worker's settlements.

A follower of folk Catholicism chants during a Christmas service. Folk Catholicism incorporates elements of vodú *and has flourished in contemporary times.* © TONY ARRUZA/CORBIS.

RELIGIOUS TOLERANCE By a concordant with the Vatican, Roman Catholicism is the state religion of the Dominican Republic, although it is not so designated by the constitution. Protestants and others are free to practice their religion and to proselytize. They do not, however, enjoy the same degree of state support, for example, of churches and schools, and Protestants do not figure as highly in the political, economic, or social hierarchies. Edicts during both the colonial and republican periods have banned *vodú* and the performance of its music using long-drums. This reflects the policy of *hispanidad*, which promotes the Spanish racial and cultural heritage in opposition to the African heritage of Haiti. In contemporary times, however, proscriptions against *vodú* have been overlooked, and the practice has flourished.

Major Religion

ROMAN CATHOLICISM

DATE OF ORIGIN 1492 C.E.
NUMBER OF FOLLOWERS 7.8 million

HISTORY The Roman Catholic Church was officially established in the West Indies by a 1504 bull of Pope Julius II that founded two dioceses in Santo Domingo, one in the city itself and the other in Concepción de La

Vega, and another diocese in San Juan, Puerto Rico. The Diocese of Santo Domingo was elevated to an archdiocese in 1546. The emphasis initially was on the expansion of parishes, and during this period Franciscans, Dominicans, and Jesuits arrived on the island. A provincial council, which included Santo Domingo and other colonies, was held to address the "two slaveries," of the native Indians and of African blacks, in the Caribbean.

The political instability of the nineteenth century sometimes hindered the church in its pastoral work, and the shortage of priests and inadequate training contributed to the rise of folk Catholicism, which incorporated elements of *vodú*. Since the late nineteenth century, however, the church has been strengthened, particularly with the expansion of the clergy and the founding of Catholic schools. The church looked the other way with respect to the human rights abuses of Rafael Trujillo, while the dictator managed the church astutely, signing an agreement with the Holy See in 1954. Relations soured in 1960, however, when the episcopate took a stance against Trujillo, which led to deportations.

Since the assassination of Trujillo in 1961, church and state have had a close relationship, with the church hierarchy playing a significant role in Dominican politics. Beginning in the 1970s, some clergy adopted liberation theology, and bishops issued statements calling for a better standard of living for peasants and supporting labor organizations for sugarcane workers. Pope John Paul II visited three times, in 1979, 1984, and 1992. The 1992 visit was in celebration of the quincentenary of Columbu's voyage and included the Fourth General Latin American Episcopal Conference.

EARLY AND MODERN LEADERS In 1548 Francisco de Liendo became the first native-born Dominican to be ordained. During the early eighteenth century the archbishop of Santo Domingo, Francisco Rincón, dominated intellectual life. Pedro Valera y Jiménez was appointed archbishop in 1811, and he held the post until forced into exile in 1830 under the Haitian occupation. During the republican era Tomás Portes e Infante celebrated the first diocesan synod of the nineteenth century (1851). In 1880 Fernando Arturo de Meriño began serving simultaneously as archbishop and president, a dual role also occupied by Adolfo Alejandro Nouel beginning in 1913.

During the Trujillo dictatorship, the church was apolitical, particularly under Archbishop Ricardo Pittini (1953–61), when concessions and privileges were granted to the church to reinforce its neutrality. Octavio Antonio Veras was the first cardinal (1961–81) in the Dominican church. Nicolás de Jesús López Rodríguez, archbishop since 1981, is also a cardinal.

MAJOR THEOLOGIANS AND AUTHORS During the first years of the colony, Antón de Montesinos (died in 1540) set forth in his sermons a defense of the Taino. He was supported by Bartolomé de las Casas (1474–1566) in *Brevísima relación de la destruición de las Indias* (1552).

HOUSES OF WORSHIP AND HOLY PLACES The First Cathedral of the Americas (1541) is located in Santo Domingo. National pilgrimage sites include the church of the patron saint, Nuestra Señora de las Mercedes (Our Lady of Mercy; 1616), on Santo Cerro (Holy Hill), near La Vega. The old church (1572) and new basilica (1971) of the unofficial patron saint, Nuestra Señora de la Altagracia (Our Lady of High Grace), is in Higüey.

WHAT IS SACRED? In formal Roman Catholicism in the Dominican Republic, the host and images of the saints in churches, particularly at pilgrimage sites, are held to be sacred. Touching the images is thought to bless a person through "contagious magic."

There are a number of sacred elements in folk Catholicism. They include lithographs of the Virgen de la Altagracia and of other saints. The most popular of these is San Miguel Arcángel (Saint Michael the Archangel), who represents the Yoruba deity Ogún. Stones, particularly neolithic axes called "thunderstones," are thought to thwart the evil eye when used by healing practitioners. To some extent the long-drums used by the Afro-Dominican brotherhoods are held to be sacred.

HOLIDAYS AND FESTIVALS The national pilgrimage to the Dominican patron saint, Virgen de las Mercedes, takes place on 24 September on Santo Cerro. The pilgrimage to the unofficial patron saint, Virgen de la Altagracia, who receives even wider devotion, takes place on 21 January in Higüey. Other pilgrimages include those to Santo Cristo de los Milagros (Holy Christ of the Miracles), in Bayaguana, on 28 December and to Cueva de Bánica (Cave of Bánica), in Elías Piña province, on 4 October for San Francisco (Saint Francis).

Christmas Eve (Nochebuena) is celebrated with a midnight Mass, although it is largely a secular family gathering. Holy Week has become a beach season for the urban bourgeoisie. In sugarcane communities Haitian and Haitian-Dominican *gagá* societies end the Lenten season with a carnival, the height of their ritual season, and in Cabral there is a three-day post-Lent carnival.

Among practitioners of *vodú*, major celebrations include the saint's day of San Miguel Arcángel, on 29 September. Among secondary celebrations are those on 25 July for Santiago (Saint James), fused with Ogún Balenyo and called by his nickname Papá Ogún, and those on 26 July for Santa Ana, called Anaísa Pié. There are also celebrations for several other prominent deities of the *vodú* pantheon.

MODE OF DRESS In the Dominican Republic the dress for Roman Catholics on religious occasions is formal and includes shoes. Black is the color of mourning in urban areas and white in Afro-Dominican rural areas; men wear black trousers and a white shirt with a small black cross of cloth affixed. White is the general color for vows and pilgrimages. In many cases, however, specific colors, combining both African and European associations, are worn for pilgrimages, vows, or *vodú* celebrations. For example, dark blue, the color of Ogún, is worn for Santiago. Mediums wear color-encoded head scarves during ritual events.

DIETARY PRACTICES On Good Friday salted cod or herring may be cooked in a *locrio* (rice and meat or fish dish). A dish of sweetened red beans with spices, sweet potatoes, and crackers (*dulce de habichuelas*) is also prepared on Good Friday. A late-night family meal is customary on Christmas Eve, featuring roast pork.

RITUALS Parishes in the Dominican Republic have annual processions on their patron saint's day. Processions are also held for the patrons of the Afro-Dominican brotherhoods. Those who incur vows with a saint for healing may pay by sponsoring a festival, which then becomes an annual event. *Vodú* societies celebrate initiations, healings, and their saint's days.

Catholic children are generally baptized and thus acquire godparents and ritual kin. Long-drums may also be baptized. The other Catholic sacraments are practiced more by the urban elite than by rural dwellers and the urban lower classes, who are often of rural origin.

RITES OF PASSAGE The elite and upper middle class in the Dominican Republic have church weddings. People in rural areas do not marry in church but rather enter into common-law marriages, which may later be legitimized as civil unions.

For the elite and middle class, death rites include nine novenas. For rural and lower-class urban Dominicans this is done at home by a male folk priest, the *rezador*. When a person is a member of a brotherhood or so requests, long-drums are played during the death ritual. If a child dies before the first Communion, at about the age of seven, rural communities traditionally hold a wake for the *angelito* (little angel), sponsored by the godparents and accompanied by children with colored banners.

MEMBERSHIP As elsewhere, children become Roman Catholics in the Dominican Republic through baptism. The Afro-Dominican brotherhoods are based on the extended family, and so people are born into them, but many keep track of membership and charge an annual fee, with the money supporting death expenses. *Vodú* mediums receive a "calling," revealed, for example, through an illness, and then are trained before they are initiated at the spiritual center where they were healed.

The Dominican Catholic Church does not engage in evangelization but rather, through catechism, emphasizes the training and education of children. The church has six radio stations that provide religious as well as social services, such as teaching literacy. The publications of the church can be found in the remotest corners of the country and are sometimes the only printed material in a rural home.

SOCIAL JUSTICE The Roman Catholic Church and members of the clergy have often defended the people against governmental and individual abuse. The church provides social services, mainly through hospitals and schools, but also through such agencies as Cáritas and Servicio Jesuita a Refugiados (Jesuit Refugee Service).

SOCIAL ASPECTS As elsewhere, the Roman Catholic Church in the Dominican Republic holds the stable, nuclear family as the model and encourages marriage. In cities there are courses to help couples strengthen their unions.

POLITICAL IMPACT At times during Dominican colonial and republican history, church and state have virtu-

ally been one and the same. Sometimes, however, there has been discord, as when church officials were harassed by the government in the 1840s and 1850s or when Catholic radio stations were censored in the late twentieth century. At other times the church has tacitly supported unjust governments, as during the dictatorship of Rafael Trujillo. In contemporary times Archbishop Nicolás de Jesús López Rodríguez has taken public stands on political and economic matters, and Agripino Núñez Collado, president of the Pontifical Catholic University Madre y Maestra, has been involved in settling political disputes.

CONTROVERSIAL ISSUES Although it is not recognized by the Roman Catholic Church, divorce is legal in the Dominican Republic. The church opposes birth control and abortion, but both are practiced extensively. In the church women have only assistant and auxiliary roles. They sometimes form organizations such as the Comunidad Cristiana, in Tamayo, which has demonstrated to demand social services from civil authorities. Women are the leaders in folk religion. They are the traditional hereditary heads of the Afro-Dominican brotherhoods and of perhaps 80 percent of all *vodú* societies.

CULTURAL IMPACT The colony of Santo Domingo was the site of the first cathedral and many of the first churches built in the New World, and since the earliest years Roman Catholic churches have supported musicians. Among twentieth-century composers, José de Jesús Ravelo (1876–1951) wrote masses, a requiem, and other religious works. Literature and the visual arts, specifically painting, have been Dominican strengths in modern times, yet the themes are rarely religious. An exception is the contemporary interest in illustrating folk religious practices, such as the prizewinning paintings of Ricardo Toribio that depict *gagá* and the paintings and installations of Charo Oquet that depict *vodú. In addition, there are paintings and music inspired by the early twentieth-century healer and messianic leader Olivorio Mateo (Papá Liborio).*

Other Religions

Protestantism entered Hispaniola in 1824 with the arrival of 6,000 U.S. freedmen, and beginning in the late nineteenth century, Protestants from the English-speaking Lesser Antilles arrived to work in the sugarcane industry. In 1919 a consortium of churches was formed in New York to establish the Iglesia Evangélica Dominicana (Dominican Protestant Church; 1922). In the 1960s the Iglesia Evangélica Dominicana, together with the English-speaking Episcopal Church, formed Servicio Social de Iglesias Dominicanas to provide well-baby clinics and other medical and social services. Other services include family planning and a publisher and bookstore. Protestantism has grown especially among young women and the urban lower classes.

Pentecostalism in the Dominican Republic was the product of foreign missionaries. The movement was first introduced by Salomón Feliciano, from Puerto Rico, in 1918. It was Francisco Hernández, however, who reintroduced Pentecostalism in 1930 and who became known as the father of the movement in the Dominican Republic. The four main denominations, established between 1930 and 1956, are the Asambleas de Dios (Assemblies of God), Iglesia de Dios (Church of God), Iglesia de Dios de la Profecía (Church of God of Prophesy), and Iglesia de Dios Pentecostal (Pentecostal Church of God). Since the death of Rafael Trujillo in 1961, others have been established. Missionary efforts during the twentieth century have established a proliferation of other Christian denominations and religions. These include Baptists, the Church of Jesus Christ of Latter-day Saints (Mormons), Seventh-day Adventists, and Jehovah's Witnesses. There are also Bahais, Hindus (Hare Krishna), and Buddhists.

Jewish converts were among the first colonizers of the island. In 1939 a small colony of German Jewish refugees settled in Sosúa, but the number of Jews today is small. Islam was introduced in 1979 by foreign medical students.

There also are followers of Rosacrucianism in the Dominican Republic, as well as Freemasonry, which was introduced in 1803. All nineteenth- and early twentieth-century presidents except Fernando Arturo de Meriño were said to have been Masons. The practice of Kardec spiritism is a phenomenon of the urban elite and the middle class, whose practitioners for the most part identify themselves as Catholics. A counterpart of Brazilian *umbanda*, it is commonly mixed with Dominican *vodú*, although its practitioners reject the use of the term.

Martha Ellen Davis

See Also Vol. 1: *Christianity, Roman Catholicism*

Bibliography

Davis, Martha Ellen. *Afro-Dominican Religious Brotherhoods: Structure, Ritual, and Music.* Ann Arbor: University Microfilms, 1976.

———. *The Dominican Southwest: Crossroads of Quisqueya and Center of the World.* Gainesville, Fla.: Ethnica Publications, 2004. Video.

———. *La otra ciencia: El vodú dominicano como religión y medicina populares.* Santo Domingo: Universidad Autónoma de Santo Domingo, 1987.

———. *Vodú of the Dominican Republic.* Gainesville, Fla.: Ethnica Publications, 1996.

Deive, Carlos Esteban. *Vodú y magia en Santo Domingo.* Santo Domingo: Museo del Hombre Dominicano, 1975.

Lockward, George. *El Protestantismo en Dominicana.* Santo Domingo: Editora Educativa Dominicana, 1982.

Lundius, Jan. *The Great Power of God in the San Juan Valley: Syncretism and Messianism in the Dominican Republic.* Lund, Sweden: University of Lund, 1995.

Lundius, Jan, and Mats Lundahl. *Peasants and Religion: A Socioeconomic Study of Dios—Olivorio and the Palma Sola Movement in the Dominican Republic.* London: Routledge, 1999.

Martínez, Lusitania. *Palma Sola, opresión y esperanza: Su geografía mítica y social.* Santo Domingo: Academia de Ciencias, 2003.

Pérez Memén, Fernando. *La iglesia y el estado en Santo Domingo, 1700–1853.* Santo Domingo: Universidad Autónoma de Santo Domingo, 1984.

East Timor

POPULATION 792,000
ROMAN CATHOLIC 94.6 percent
OTHER 5.4 percent

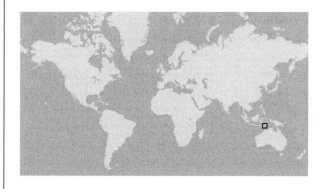

Country Overview

INTRODUCTION The Democratic Republic of Timor-Leste (the Portuguese term for "East Timor"), located in Southeast Asia, is bounded by Indonesia on the west, the Timor Sea on the south, and the Banda Sea on the north. Its territory (5,736 square miles) includes the eastern half of Timor Island, the islands of Jaco and Atauro, and Oecussi, an enclave within Indonesian Timor. Most of the country is ruggedly mountainous. The climate is tropical with a dry and a wet season. East Timor is underdeveloped, and potential economic resources include oil and gas reserves, coffee, sandalwood, marble, and tourism. On 20 May 2002, after more than 350 years of Portuguese colonialism, 24 years of Indonesian occupation, and two years of administration by the United Nations, East Timor became an independent nation.

The majority of the population is Roman Catholic. Other religions represented in East Timor include Protestantism, Islam, and Hinduism and Buddhism (the latter two typically discussed as one group in East Timor). Catholicism, introduced by the Portuguese during the sixteenth century, initially spread to the coastal regions because the mountainous interior provided a geographical barrier. At the time of the 1975 Indonesian invasion nearly three quarters of the East Timorese population were animists. During the Indonesian occupation the Catholic Church protected the East Timorese people from Indonesian abuses; this support precipitated the large conversion to Catholicism.

RELIGIOUS TOLERANCE The East Timorese constitution (ratified in 2002) provides for the separation of church and state and recognizes religious freedom and tolerance. Since independence was declared, majority and minority religions have coexisted peacefully, although cases of property destruction at mosques have been reported.

Major Religion

ROMAN CATHOLICISM

DATE OF ORIGIN 1515 C.E.
NUMBER OF FOLLOWERS 749,000

HISTORY Portuguese colonists took Roman Catholicism to East Timor in 1515, and the arrival in 1556 of a Dominican friar, António Taveira, started a more widespread missionizing effort. Because the conversion of local chiefs often inspired many conversions among the general population, the church's earliest efforts were focused on the coastal kingdoms. By 1640 there were 10 missions and 22 churches.

The next wave of Catholic expansion began in 1697 with the arrival of the Portuguese friar Manuel de Santo António, and by 1702 Carmelite missions had followed. Seminaries had been established in Oecussi and Manatuto by 1747. Tense relations with the colonial government, however, hampered Dominican missionary activity. In 1834 the government expelled the Dominicans and replaced them with Jesuits. Missionizing was also curtailed by continual local rebellions and by the rugged mountain ranges.

Substantial conversion did not occur until after the Indonesian invasion in 1975. The East Timorese became subject to the state law requiring all Indonesian citizens to be members of a world religion. The Catholic Church served during this time as the primary protector of the East Timorese from the brutalities of the Indonesian army. These factors propelled a substantial conversion to Catholicism. By 1981 the Tetun language (the lingua franca of East Timor) had replaced Portuguese as the vernacular of Catholic rites. East Timor separated from Indonesia in 1999 and officially became independent in 2002.

EARLY AND MODERN LEADERS The initial efforts to spread Catholicism in East Timor can be attributed to Friar António Taveira, Bishop Manuel de Santo António (who served there from 1697 to 1722), Bishop António de Castro (who served in the 1740s), and Father José António Medeiros (who arrived in 1875).

Martinho da Costa Lopes (the native apostolic administrator for East Timor) and his successor, Bishop Carlos Ximenes Belo (the 1996 Nobel Peace Prize Laureate), have had tremendous impact in the years following World War II. As a consequence of their efforts to defend the East Timorese during the Indonesian occupation, Catholicism became established as the majority religion. Bishop Basílio do Nascimento was appointed apostolic administrator in 2002.

MAJOR THEOLOGIANS AND AUTHORS There have not been any theologians of particular significance in East Timor.

A mother and child light candles at an East Timor grave site. East Timorese Catholics view church buildings, cemeteries, and the personages and objects associated with these places as sacred. AP/WIDE WORLD PHOTOS.

HOUSES OF WORSHIP AND HOLY PLACES European-style cathedrals are found in the larger cities of East Timor. The churches in district administrative centers vary in size and elaborateness, and villages have small chapels. Churches display the mark of local craftsmanship; significant cultural symbols are incorporated into decorative carvings and paintings.

WHAT IS SACRED? East Timorese Catholics view church buildings, cemeteries, and the personages and objects associated with these places as sacred. Their conception of "sacred" is influenced by the indigenous notion of *lulik*, potent spiritual power associated with certain places, objects, or persons.

HOLIDAYS AND FESTIVALS Catholic holidays in East Timor include Christmas, Good Friday, Easter, Assumption Day, All Saint's Day, and the Day of the Immaculate Conception. The Virgin Mary is a special focus of local Catholic veneration, and during May both the Marian Festival and the Feast of the Rosary venerate Mary. A family grouping (such as a village hamlet or a clan) sponsors rosary prayer sessions that center on a statue of Mary and that move from house to house. This culminates in a ritual procession that ends at the local church or at a mountainside grotto outside the village, where the statue is deposited and a Mass is held.

MODE OF DRESS For church services East Timorese Catholics wear Western-style clothing in the city and *tais* (a traditional handwoven and dyed textile) in rural areas. The mode of dress for village women consists of a Timorese *tais* or Indonesian batik skirt, an Indonesian-style top (*kebaya*), and a lace shawl head covering (usually black) of the old Portuguese style. Priestly vestments have also incorporated *tais* textiles.

DIETARY PRACTICES East Timorese Catholics tend to abstain from eating meat on Fridays (especially on Good Friday) and on Ash Wednesday. Some elders also keep meat abstinence during Lent. The strictness about avoiding meat, however, varies greatly and indeed is often superseded by the traditional feasts that accompany marriages and death rituals.

RITUALS Most people in East Timor attend Sunday Mass, which is also the main social venue in rural areas. Baptism, first Communion, confirmation, marriage, and funeral are the main Catholic rites in East Timor. Offerings made during Mass include currency and local produce such as rice, eggs, and bananas. During Mass the priest also blesses bowls of flower petals, which are then taken to the grave of a loved one.

RITES OF PASSAGE Catholic baptism in East Timor takes place when a child is between three months and seven years old. It usually follows various traditional East Timorese life-cycle rituals that secure the child's soul and introduce him or her to the community and the ancestors. When children are about 7 to 12 years old, they receive catechism training, after which the first Communion is administered with much pageantry. Confirmation ceremonies take place during an East Timorese Catholic's teenage years.

Marriage for the East Timorese is an alliance between social groups (houses and clans). Thus, traditional marriage processes (which vary widely among cultures within East Timor) precede Catholic rites. After Catho-

lic funeral services the deceased are buried in Christian graves. These rites, however, are just the first phase of protracted traditional funerary ritual processes.

MEMBERSHIP Catholics in East Timor do not proselytize.

SOCIAL JUSTICE Throughout the Indonesian occupation the church defied the state through nonviolent resistance and was the main critic of Indonesian military brutality. The church has been vocal in its human rights advocacy.

SOCIAL ASPECTS East Timorese Catholic marriage requires both partners to be of the same faith, to lead a Christian life, and to raise the resulting children as Catholics. Many of the local customary life-cycle rites have been syncretized with Catholic rites of passage. Thus, the traditional social obligations of specific categories of kin (for example, a mother's brother) to sponsor life-cycle rituals continue through Catholic rites.

POLITICAL IMPACT Throughout Portuguese colonialism and the Indonesian occupation, the Catholic Church in East Timor was a staunch supporter of the people, providing the vehicle for resistance to oppression. In 1999, during the UN-administered "popular consultation" process that led to East Timor's independence from Indonesia, the church participated in voter education. Militia and Indonesian military rampages after the election drove many East Timorese to the sanctuary of churches, where priests and nuns risked their own lives to protect them.

CONTROVERSIAL ISSUES The East Timorese Catholic Church's stances on birth control, divorce, and abortion follow those of the Vatican and are not considered controversial. Local church leaders do not openly confront these issues. Many East Timorese Catholics have remarried after divorce. While these marriages are not recognized by the church, they are legitimized through a civil court or through customary law.

CULTURAL IMPACT Catholicism is an important aspect of East Timorese national and cultural identity, which was forged historically vis-à-vis relations of political power and resistance to oppression. Catholic practice has had no clearly evident effect on East Timor's music, art, or literature, all of which are heavily influenced by various traditional belief systems.

Other Religions

Information is lacking about the uniquely East Timorese features of Protestant, Muslim, Hindu, and Buddhist practices. Hinduism and Buddhism, often discussed in a combined manner, are practiced in East Timor by people of Balinese origin. Protestants mainly come from West Timor, because during colonial times the Dutch converted the West Timorese to Protestantism. A small number of Protestant missionaries operate in East Timor. It has been estimated, however, that after independence the size of the congregation was halved. With the exception of minor tensions between Protestant missionaries and Catholics in the Baucau region, the two Christian branches appear to coexist peacefully. Isolated incidents of vandalism to Muslim mosques in Dili and in Baucau have been reported. There have also been tensions between Muslims of Arabic descent and Muslims of Malay migrant descent.

Animistic beliefs focusing on ancestors have a strong presence in East Timor. Catholicism is highly syncretized with local traditional beliefs. The concept of *lulik* (the sacred power of places, objects, and persons) is important. Sacred places are mountains, forests, and rivers associated with the founding ancestors and the Creator God. Ancestral heirlooms are also considered sacred. The most significant ancestor-focused rituals are the funerals that include large-scale animal sacrifice. Other notable rituals center on the sacred founding houses (*uma lulik*), which play an important role in maintaining traditional social structures and kinship relations.

Andrea Molnar

See Also Vol. I: *Christianity, Roman Catholicism*

Bibliography

Cardoso, Luis. *The Crossing: A Story of East Timor.* Translated by Margaret Jull Costa. New York and London: Granta Books, 2002.

Carrey, Peter. "The Catholic Church, Religious Revival, and the Nationalist Movement in East Timor, 1975–98." *Indonesia and the Malay World* 27, no. 78 (1999): 77–95.

Kohen, Arnold S. *From the Place of the Dead: The Epic Struggles of Bishop Belo of East Timor.* New York: St. Martin's Press, 1998.

Lennox, Rowena. *Fighting Spirit of East Timor: The Life of Martinho da Costa Lopes.* New York: Zen Books, 2000.

Marker, Jamsheed. *East Timor: A Memoir of the Negotiations for Independence.* Jefferson, N.C.: McFarland and Company, 2003.

Ecuador

POPULATION 13,447,494

ROMAN CATHOLIC 87 percent

PROTESTANT 10 percent

NONRELIGIOUS 2 percent

OTHER 1 percent

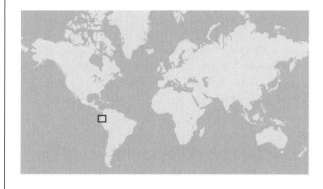

Country Overview

INTRODUCTION Nestled on the equator (from which the country takes its name) in South America, the Republic of Ecuador is bounded by the Pacific Ocean on the west, Colombia on the north, and Peru on the east and south. It contains some of the highest mountains on Earth. The Sierra, one of the country's three regions, is composed of the high plateaus and valleys between the massive twin mountain ranges of the Andes. This area was the core of ancient civilization in South America and was one of the centers of the Inca empire (fifteenth–sixteenth centuries C.E.). The other two regions are the coastal lowlands (known for plantation agriculture, especially bananas) and the Amazon lowlands (known for oil production and various forms of subsistence horticulture).

Ecuador claims one of the largest percentages of Indians of countries in the Americas. A strong Indian movement has been influential in Ecuadorian politics, social policy, and culture. The great majority of Ecuadorians are Roman Catholic; Catholic beliefs and practices are sometimes combined with those of indigenous religions. A growing number of people in Ecuador have been converting to Protestant faiths, and the Mormons have established a presence in the country. There are also small numbers of Jews, Baha'is, Muslims, Buddhists, and Hindus.

RELIGIOUS TOLERANCE Despite the state's long relationship with the Catholic Church, which was a pillar of colonial and republican society, Ecuador enshrines freedom of religion in its constitution. The state works to ensure religious tolerance in policy and in practice.

Major Religion

ROMAN CATHOLICISM

DATE OF ORIGIN sixteenth century C.E.
NUMBER OF FOLLOWERS 11.7 million

HISTORY Once a center of an indigenous state, part of the area that is now Ecuador was conquered in the fifteenth century C.E. by the Incas, who established their state religion of the Sun God. In the early sixteenth century the Spanish conquered the Incas and the indigenous people and took Catholicism to Ecuador. By 1546 the bishopric of Quito had been founded. During colonial times the Catholic Church was an important mainstay of the state and of society, and religious orders such as the Jesuits and the Dominicans expanded Christianity among Ecuador's indigenous population. The church was responsible for education and for much of the social welfare. By the end of the colonial period it had acquired enormous wealth—much if not most of it gained through coerced labor performed by indigenous people and Africans imported as slaves.

The region, as part of Gran Colombia, won independence from Spain in 1822; it split from Colombia to became the Republic of Ecuador in 1830. Ecuador's early republican period was marked by struggles between liberals and conservatives over the place of the church in civic life. By the end of the nineteenth century the liberals had obtained the upper hand. Religious pluralism was guaranteed in Ecuador, and the relationship of the church to the state was severely limited. The state abolished tithing (taxing to support the church) and established a system of secular public schools.

Nonetheless, the Catholic Church as an institution maintained considerable influence in Ecuador. In the mid-twentieth century the church became interested in issues of social welfare and in the problems faced by the numerous poor Ecuadorians and began organizing social assistance. It also became concerned about the place of Indians in Ecuadorian society. This coincided with the rise of a powerful Indian movement in the country and the rapid growth of Protestantism among indigenous peoples. A high point of Ecuadorian church life was the 1985 visit of Pope John Paul II. He toured the country, bringing a substantial public visibility to Ecuadorian Catholicism.

EARLY AND MODERN LEADERS The first bishop of Quito, García Díaz Arias (died 1562), was appointed in 1546. Initially the cathedral in Quito was made of adobe walls and a thatched roof. It was Díaz Arias who began construction of the present cathedral in the city.

At the turn of the twenty-first century the leaders of the Catholic Church in Ecuador included four archbishops—Raúl Vela Chiriboga (born in 1934; appointed an archbishop in 2003), Antonio Arregui Yarza (born in 1939; made archbishop in 2003), Vicente Cisneros Durán (born in 1934; appointed archbishop in 2000), and José Mario Ruiz Navas (born in 1930; became an archbishop in 1994)—and one emeritus arch-

The Virgin Mary is carried from home to home in a religious procession in Ecuador. © PABLO CORRAL VEGA/CORBIS.

bishop, Luis Alberto Luna Tobar (born in 1923; archbishop 1981–2000.

MAJOR THEOLOGIANS AND AUTHORS Leónidas Proaño (1910–88), bishop of the Ecuadorian diocese of Riobamba, influenced the development of liberation theology in Latin America. He is commonly known as the "Bishop of the Poor" and the "Bishop of the Indians." He believed the church had an obligation to encourage the development and organization of disadvantaged people. Bishop Proaño's work included strong support for indigenous Ecuadorians.

The Instituto de Pastoral Latinoamericano (Latin American Pastoral Institute), established in the early 1960s, played an important role in the formation of liberation practice by providing information and training for priests and nuns and by encouraging pastoral innovation.

HOUSES OF WORSHIP AND HOLY PLACES Catholicism in Ecuador maintains a hierarchy of places of worship, from cathedrals to local chapels. There are also shrines that house figures of particular importance to the country; significant examples include the Sanctuary of the Virgin of Quinche (which contains the image of the patroness of Ecuador) and the seventeenth-century Sanctuary of Guapulo in Quito (which contains an important image of Our Lady of Guadalupe).

WHAT IS SACRED? Ecuadorian Catholics maintain devotional practices similar to those of Catholics around the world. To this end, they have a network of holy patrons. The country as a whole, as well as each region and each town, has its patron; this is either a saint, a particular apparition of the Virgin Mary, or a figure of Jesus. The national patroness is Nuestra Señora de la Presentación del Quinche (the Virgin of Quinche). This image of the Virgin Mary was carved in the sixteenth century and is associated with legends of the Virgin's miraculous appearance to a group of Indians. As the patron saint, she connects a history of her image with the national history in ways that are highly significant for many of the country's Catholics. In the month of November the Virgin of Quinche draws pilgrims from the major ethnic groups of Ecuador; she thus serves as an image of an ethnically united nation.

HOLIDAYS AND FESTIVALS Ecuadorian Catholics recognize the standard holidays of international Catholicism. Given the historical connection between Ecuador and the Catholic Church, some festivals (such as All Souls' Day and Christmas) are also official holidays. Standard festivals from the Catholic calendar, including the Feast of the Epiphany and Holy Week, are celebrated in Ecuador. Also important are feasts for local patrons, such as the Virgin of Quinche (in November) and Saint John in Imbabura (in June).

In addition, these festivals overlap with folkloric events that draw on Catholic tradition. A well-known example is the Mama Negra (black mother) Festival in Latacunga, which combines a celebration of the Earth's fertility with honoring the Virgin of Mercedes, the town's patron saint.

MODE OF DRESS Ecuadorian Catholics do not wear any clothing distinctive to their religion. Particular groups of highland Indians, such as the Saraguros and the Otavalos, have distinctive forms of dress, and these are worn by Catholics from these communities.

DIETARY PRACTICES Ecuadorian Catholics do not have particular food restrictions. Certain traditional dishes are served for particular feasts. For example, during Holy Week (Easter) Ecuadorians serve *fanesca* (a stew made of fish and a number of grains), and in the area around the city of Cuenca it is customary to eat *mote pata* (a dish made with hominy and pork) during Carnaval, the festival preceding Lent.

RITUALS Catholicism in Ecuador follows the standard rituals of international Catholicism. In addition, there is a history of popular devotion and ritual that stems from two sources: historical Iberian Catholic practice and syncretism with indigenous traditions. Popular religiosity stresses many public acts of devotion, such as pilgrimages and participation in patron saint festivals, as well as domestic rituals of devotion to religious figures (including popular saints).

RITES OF PASSAGE For Catholics in Ecuador, the standard rites of the Catholic Church (including baptism, first Communion, and marriage) mark the major rites of passage. In rural popular Catholicism and portions of urban Catholicism, it has long been an important rite of passage to sponsor feasts tied to patron saints. This system connects secular and political prestige with religion. The growth of secularity and non-Catholic religion has somewhat weakened this system.

MEMBERSHIP After the Latin American Bishops' Conferences in Medellín, Colombia (1968), and Puebla, Mexico (1979), the Ecuadorian church concerned itself with issues of social injustice. As a result, it developed particular pastoral approaches directed at strengthening membership among Ecuador's Indian and black populations as well as at social issues affecting these groups, such as poverty and migration. Among other things, the church embraced the notion of inculturation, the idea that, rather than being bound to a single vision of Catholic life and practice, the gospel may be understood within the cultural norms and practices of the different groups that compose a country. Thus, the Euadorian church has developed a theology and practice for Ecuador's Indians and another for its black population.

The Catholic Church uses media such as radio to communicate with the Ecuadorian people. Catholic universities, including the Salesian Polytechnic University and the Catholic University of Ecuador (both in Quito), are also influential in maintaining the church's membership.

SOCIAL JUSTICE The Catholic Church has been a critical voice of social justice in Ecuador, supporting the organization and political action of the indigenous population as well as being deeply concerned about the welfare of the country's poor. It has organized nongovernmental organizations to participate in social development. It also maintains a network of schools as well as one of radio stations and other media to educate the Ecuadorian people.

The order of Salesians in particular were notable for their indigenous advocacy efforts. These included forming the Shuar Federation in 1964, primarily to preserve the native Shuar people's land rights, and creating an indigenous-based publication series called Mundo Shuar.

SOCIAL ASPECTS The Ecuadorian Catholic Church follows the social teachings of the Vatican. The majority of Catholic families in Ecuador are nuclear families, but a common practice is to augment the family support system by naming *compadres* (godparents) for a child at his or her baptism.

POLITICAL IMPACT Given the historical relationship between the Catholic Church and the nation, as well as the fact that the vast majority of Ecuadorians are Catholic, Catholicism is prominent in political life. The constitution separates church and state, but, nonetheless, the Ecuadorian Bishops' Council gives pastoral comments on social and political affairs in the country. As mentioned above under SOCIAL JUSTICE, the church provided a foundation for the Indian movement, which became a powerful political force in the 1990s.

CONTROVERSIAL ISSUES It has been estimated that at least half of Ecuadorians use some form of contraceptives, even though the Catholic Church forbids it. Abortion remains illegal under Ecuadorian law. While the Catholic Church in Ecuador takes a conservative stance on a range of social issues, such as sexuality, marriage, and the family, it also opposes the dominant social and economic order, and many Ecuadorians see this as controversial.

CULTURAL IMPACT Many aspects of Ecuadorian national culture developed in the embrace of Catholicism. Quito, the capital of Ecuador, was an important colonial city. It became a center for a style of colonial religious art called the Quiteño school, which combined European baroque with indigenous elements and is known for its brilliant colors. The religious buildings of the colonial era were often elaborately decorated in this style, as seen in the rich interiors of many of the churches in Quito's historical center. The colonial period left gems of religious architecture that today serve as symbols of Ecuadorian national culture. One example is the Metropolitan Cathedral, in the center of Quito, which dates back to the sixteenth century. In the religious feasts held during popular festivals, a style of music and dance developed that now forms one of the main elements of the national folklore.

Other Religions

Indigenous religiosity is an important part of Ecuador's religious life. While much of it—particularly in the case of highland Indians—has been embedded within Catholicism as a form of what is called popular Christianity, it also maintains a recognizable indigenous form. With the development of a strong Indian movement (beginning in 1964 with the establishment of the Shuar Federation), there has been pressure to organize an Indian religion separate from Christianity.

A resurgence of indigenous-based forms of religiosity has converged with the Ecuadorian indigenous political movement, with the international indigenous movement (particularly around 1992, with the observation in the western hemisphere of the Columbian Quincentenary), and with a global New Age movement tied to environmentalism and tourism. Indians and their religious expression are idealized perhaps as never before, which serves to simultaneously distort and protect them.

Indigenous religiosity of the highlands emphasizes a notion that people are related to the landscape and the elements of nature, such as the earth, sky, sun, moon, and stars. The mountains, for example, are thought to contain the principles of life and to be greater than human beings. As a result, offerings are often made to each mountain to bring it into a social relationship and to guarantee its goodwill toward people. The best known of these mountains is perhaps Mount Imbabura in northern Ecuador, which is believed to have the power to impregnate women who travel alone and unprotected in its flanks.

Dreaming is important as a means of divining the immediate future and the conjunction of forces in the world around an individual. The world is seen as filled with omens, some portentous and some beneficent. Religious specialists and healers are contracted to divine and transform the balance of forces in the world for the benefit of individuals, families, and communities.

While the majority of Ecuador's Indians reside in the highlands and speak one form or another of Quichua (a type of Quechua, of which there are many versions throughout the Andes), there is also a significant and different population of Indians in the eastern lowlands (such as the Shuar, the Achuar, and the Huaorani) and smaller groups of indigenous peoples (such as the Tsáchila and Chachi) in the western Andean foothills and Pacific coastal area. These groups maintain a distinctive cosmology related to that of other Amazonian peoples. An important part of their religious life involves shamans who often ingest hallucinogens, such as *ayahuasca* (a drink produced from the vine *Banisteriopsis caapi*), as part of their shamanic journey to confront the universe and to bring order to human lives.

While indigenous religions continue to maintain their power, large numbers of Indians in Ecuador have converted to various forms of evangelical Christianity. Different regions have been heavily influenced by one missionary organization or another (such as the Gospel Missionary Union, World Vision, and the Summer Institute of Linguistics). There also has been a growth of indigenous Ecuadorian Protestantism. As in other Latin American countries, Pentecostalism has become increasingly important among Ecuadorians. The Church of Jesus Christ of Latter-day Saints has also substantially grown in Ecuador, developing a notable presence among the Otavalo Indians of Imbabura province. Ecuador's Jewish community is mainly concentrated in Quito. Small numbers of people in Ecuador are Baha'i, Muslim, Buddhist, and Hindu.

David Knowlton

See Also Vol. I: *Christianity, Roman Catholicism*

Bibliography

Bottasso, Juan. *Los shuar y las misiones: Entre la hostilidad y el diálogo.* Quito: Mundo Shuar, 1982.

Crespi, Muriel. "St. John the Baptist: The Ritual Looking Glass of Hacienda Indian Ethnic and Power Relations." In *Cultural Transformations and Ethnicity in Modern Ecuador.* Edited by Norman E. Whitten, Jr. Urbana: University of Illinois Press, 1981.

Goffin, Alvin M. *The Rise of Protestant Evangelism in Ecuador, 1895–1990.* Gainesville: University Press of Florida, 1994.

Harner, Michael. *The Way of the Shaman: A Guide to Power and Healing.* New York: Harper & Row, 1980.

Jouanen, José. *Los Jesuitas y el oriente ecuatoriano: Monografía Histórica 1868–1898.* Guayaquil, Ecuador: Editorial Arquidiocesana, 1977.

Moya, Luz del Alba, ed. *La fiesta religiosa indígena en el Ecuador.* Cayambe, Ecuador: Abya Yala Press, 1995.

Muratorio, Blanca. *The Life and Times of Grandfather Alonso: Culture and History in the Upper Amazon.* New Brunswick, N.J.: Rutgers University Press, 1991.

Salomon, Frank. "Killing the Yumbo: A Ritual Drama of Northern Quito." In *Cultural Transformations and Ethnicity in Modern Ecuador.* Edited by Norman E. Whitten, Jr. Urbana: University of Illinois Press, 1981.

———. "Shamanism and Politics in Late-Colonial Ecuador." *American Ethnologist* 10, no. 3 (1983): 413–28.

Egypt

POPULATION 70,712,345

MUSLIM 90.0 percent

COPT 9.0 percent

OTHER (ANGLICAN, ARMENIAN CATHOLIC, ARMENIAN ORTHODOX, GREEK CATHOLIC, GREEK ORTHODOX, JEWISH, MARONITE, PROTESTANT, ROMAN CATHOLIC, AND SYRIAN CATHOLIC) 1.0 percent

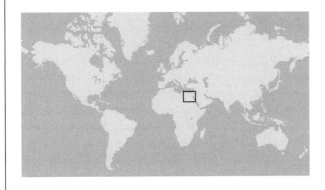

Country Overview

INTRODUCTION The Arab Republic of Egypt is the most populous Arab-Muslim country in the world. Located in the heart of the Middle East, on the crossroads between Africa and Asia, it is bordered to the north by the Mediterranean Sea, to the northeast by Israel, to the east by the Red Sea, to the south by The Sudan, and to the west by Libya.

Egypt's unique strategic location has made it of great economic, political, and cultural importance. Fertile land around the Nile River allowed the development of one of the world's great civilizations (from 3000 B.C.E.). Saint Mark is believed to have brought Christianity to Egypt in the first century. By the time the Muslims arrived in 639 C.E., most of Egypt's population was Christian. Harshly persecuted under Roman and Byzantine rule, the Copts (Egyptian Christians) found little reason to resist the Muslims, who gained control of the country by 642. They established a new center near the old part of Cairo and turned Egypt into a major economic and military resource for the Muslim Caliphate. Slowly the population converted to Islam, and by the thirteenth century Muslims outnumbered Christians.

Most of contemporary Egypt's population is Sunni Muslim. The Orthodox Copts are the largest Christian group. Both Islam and Christianity have witnessed revivals in Egypt since the 1960s. This is reflected in the increasing significance of the mosque and the church in people's daily lives; the growing interest in performing religious duties; the widespread display of religious symbols in private and public spaces; the proliferation of religious organizations that offer educational, health, and social services; and the increasing number of television and radio programs and audiotapes that communicate religious information to Muslims and Christians.

RELIGIOUS TOLERANCE Historically relations between Egyptian Muslims and Copts have been characterized by peaceful coexistence, despite occasional tension and conflict. Muslims and Copts share a common

Egyptian Muslim women perform prayers for Eid el-Adha, or the Feast of Sacrifice, outside a mosque in Cairo, Egypt. Muslims celebrate the feast to mark the end of the hajj (pilgrimage to Mecca). AP/WIDE WORLD PHOTOS.

language, culture, heritage, and national identity. One incident that demonstrated some of these shared traits was the 1968 appearance of the Virgin Mary in a church named the Holy Virgin in Cairo. Both Muslims and Christians flooded the church to observe the apparition. This incident, which took place 10 months after the devastating 1967 war with Israel and while the nation was in a state of great despair, was interpreted by both Muslims and Copts as a sign that God had abandoned the nation and that the Virgin Mary was there to comfort and reassure them.

Despite the fact that the constitution grants religious freedom to all Egyptian citizens, the Copts suffer from direct and indirect discrimination. A main source of frustration for many Christians is the restrictions placed on the construction of churches. Permission from the president of the country is needed for such construction. Various writers and religious figures have been critical of these restrictions, which are based on

Ottoman laws that date back to 1856. They believe that such restrictions have contributed to the growing militancy of the church and the escalation of conflict between Muslims and Copts since the early 1970s. In the 1980s and '90s the Copts suffered several deadly attacks, especially in Upper Egypt, by extreme Muslim groups.

There are various groups in Egypt, including the government, who draw on religion to support their projects and claims. While most Muslim activists use peaceful means to achieve what they see as "the true Islamic society," there are some radical groups who believe that violence is a legitimate way to change the political system and establish social justice. In recent years radical groups have been weakened by the tough measures taken by the government, the lack of popular support, and the expanding influence of moderate Islamic groups.

Major Religion

ISLAM

DATE OF ORIGIN Seventh century C.E.
NUMBER OF FOLLOWERS 63.6 million

HISTORY When the Muslims arrived in 639 under the leadership of Amr ibn al-As, Egypt was controlled by the Byzantine Empire. There are indications that many among its Coptic population welcomed the arrival of the Muslims. Unlike the Byzantines, the Muslims were more tolerant of religious differences and did not impose heavy taxation on the indigenous inhabitants. Several Coptic rebellions during the eighth century, however, indicate that there was resentment of the discriminatory regulations of some Muslim rulers. Islam slowly spread in Egypt, and by the twelfth century the Coptic language (a form of ancient Egyptian written in Greek letters) lost prominence to Arabic, which became the language spoken by all Egyptians. The use of Coptic is now limited to liturgy.

From 969 to 1171 Egypt was ruled by the Fatimid Dynasty, which followed the doctrine of Ismaili Shiism. Despite the fact that Sunnism was officially outlawed, most Egyptians continued its practices, and Egypt officially reverted to Sunni Islam by the end of the Fatimid's rule. In addition to the building of Cairo and several important monuments, the Fatimids created an enduring legacy when they founded al-Azhar mosque and university in 972. It is considered the oldest university in the world, and over the years it has trained and employed some of the most prominent Muslim scholars and leaders.

Throughout the years Islam has been used by Muslim rulers, foreign invaders, and opposition leaders to legitimize their actions and to subordinate or empower Egyptians. For example, to establish and reinforce their rule, successive rulers, who were usually of foreign origin, drew on the support of the ulama (religious scholars). The Europeans also drew on Islam to justify their colonial projects. Napoléon Bonaparte tried to present himself as a true Muslim who came in 1798 to liberate Egyptian Muslims from the tyranny of the Mamluks. The British also used religious tradition to justify their colonization of Egypt. For instance, veiling was seen as backward and a sign of the subordination of women. British leaders like Lord Cromer used such arguments to legitimize the British presence in Egypt. Religion also played an important role in the resistance against European colonization. It was the ulama of al-Azhar who led the resistance against the French and the British. Such Muslim leaders and scholars as Jamal al-Din al-Afghani, Muhammad Abduh, and Hasan al-Banna drew on Islam in their attempts to empower Egyptians in the face of European domination.

In the 1950s the ulama supported Gamel Abdel Nasser in his attempt to build an independent nation, but soon conflict erupted between Nasser, who chose a socialist and secular ideology, and Muslim activists, especially those who belonged to the Muslim Brotherhood, an organization that draws on Islamic principles to transform social and political life. Some of the members of this group, such as Sayyid Qutb, became radical in their views and directed their rage primarily at the Egyptian leadership. After an attempt by members of the Muslim Brotherhood to assassinate him, Nasser banned the group, had most of its leaders arrested, and ordered the executions of some of them.

In the early 1970s President Anwar el-Sadat used religion to contain the power of the left and to weaken the supporters of the late president Nasser. He built his legitimacy in part through public religious performances, such as praying in mosques and observing religious holidays. Religious activism flourished during this period, and soon religious groups, both moderate and radical, started competing with the government over who held the legitimate right to rule Egypt. Various religious and secular groups attacked Sadat for his open-door policy (encouraging foreign investment), which increased economic, social, and political inequalities, and for the 1979 peace agreement with Israel, which alienated Egypt from other Arab countries. Outraged by such criticisms and believing that Muslim and Christian groups were conspiring against him, Sadat ordered the arrest of thousands of intellectuals and religious figures, both Muslim and Christian. This created an uproar in the country, and in 1981 Sadat was assassinated by Muslim religious extremists.

Radical groups posed a serious threat to the leadership of Hosni Mubarak, who became president following Sadat's assassination. They started a wave of armed attacks that targeted government officials, liberal writers, Christian citizens, and Western tourists. Their goal was to use economic and military pressure to destabilize the government and initiate their own Islamic rule. The government, through its repression of the radicals and support for more moderate religious groups, managed to weaken the extremist groups. In 1998 al-Gamaat al-Islamiyya (Muslim Groups) announced an end to the use of violence by its members. Various groups have continued to draw on religion to peacefully assert their opposition to the government and what they view as un-Islamic aspects of society.

EARLY AND MODERN LEADERS The official religious leadership in Egypt is crystallized in two important positions. The first is the grand mufti of Egypt, the main religious adviser to the Egyptian judiciary. The mufti issues opinions about controversial issues, often in favor of the government's position. Sheikh Ali Goma became grand mufti in September 2003. Sheikh Al-Azhar, who is appointed by the Egyptian president, is another highly important position. This sheikh enjoys tremendous religious authority that extends beyond Egypt to shape religious debates and views in various Muslim countries. Muhammad Sayed Tantawi became Sheikh Al-Azhar in 1996.

Another prominent position that is not linked to the government is that of the head of the Muslim Brotherhood. Its founder, Hasan al-Banna, who was assassinated (most likely by secret agents) in 1949, continues to be seen as the Supreme Guide (political and spiritual leader) of this group. Al-Banna was born in 1906 in a small village in northern Egypt. He was trained as a teacher in a college in Cairo, and then he studied at al-Azhar University. Al-Banna started the Muslim Brotherhood as a youth organization in 1928. Its main objectives were the encouragement of social and moral reforms according to Islamic values and thought. Inspired by the work of Muhammad Rashid Rida (1865–1935), al-Banna advocated the value of learning from the acts and sayings of al-Salaf al-Salah (the pious predecessors) in enabling Muslims to resist Western hegemony and to lead a true Muslim life. The group turned into a political organization in 1939. Its ideology extends beyond Egypt to include struggles in various Muslim countries. The group became an ally of the national movement and supported the 1952 revolution, but members were disappointed when the new government under Gamal Abdel Nasser adopted a socialist and secular ideology. Banned by Nasser in 1954, the organization was revived when Anwar el-Sadat became president. He released all of the group's members who were in prison and promised to implement the Shariah (Islamic law). The movement went underground until it was legalized as a religious group in 1984. Despite many restrictions by the security apparatus, the Muslim Brotherhood is still active in Egypt and enjoys strong popular support.

Born in 1906 and executed in 1966, Sayyid Qutb, another famous member of the Muslim Brotherhood, continues to be highly influential in Egyptian religious movements. While a government employee in the Ministry of Education, Qutb visited the United States for two years and was deeply offended by the racism, materialism, and open relationships between the sexes there. He cut his visit short and joined the Muslim Brotherhood upon his return to Egypt. He shifted from moral writing into a more revolutionary discourse inspired by the ideas of Ibn Taymiya (1268–1328) and Sayyid Maududi (1903–79). Sayyid Qutb spent 11 years in prison and then was executed under Nasser for his radical views, which encouraged people to use force to change the government. Qutb wrote several important books in Arabic, including *Social Justice in Islam* (1970), *In the Shade of the Qur'an* (1997), and *Milestones* (1981).

MAJOR THEOLOGIANS AND AUTHORS Sheikh Muhammad Abduh (1849–1905) is the best known modern religious reformer in Egypt. He was influenced by the teachings of Jamal al-Din al-Afghani (1837–97), who believed that Muslims should first reform themselves in order to be able to resist Western colonization. Abduh argued that Islam was compatible with science, reason, and modern forms of government. He was exiled by the British in 1882 for his political activism. During his exile Abduh directed his attention to educational and theological concerns and worked to reform religious thought to meet the challenges of modernity. He returned to Egypt in 1892 and became its grand mufti. He wrote several important books, including *Risalat al-Tawhid* (Theology of Unity). He trained several influential scholars, among them Muhammad Rashid Rida, who in turn inspired the activism of Hasan al-Banna. Abduh's views continue to inform various debates on the role of religion in contemporary Muslim societies.

Mahmud Shaltut (died in 1963) was influential in reforming al-Azhar and in arguing against extreme elements. Muhammad al-Ghazali (died in 1996) was another activist from the Muslim Brotherhood who also served in high government positions. He wrote some 40 books on the role of Islam in public life.

In contemporary Egypt there are many individuals—both religious scholars and laypersons—who circulate interpretations of the sacred texts. They communicate their views through various channels, such as pamphlets, weekly lessons in mosques, audiotapes (which are effective in communicating with a wide illiterate audience), and television programs. One sheikh, Muhammad al-Sharawi (died in 1998), was loved by many people for his ability to use television to communicate accessible religious explications to the general public. Sheikh Yusuf al-Qaradawi (born in 1926) has appeared on various satellite channels to discuss contemporary challenges and how Muslims can deal with them. Zaynab al-Ghazali (born in 1917), a female activist influential in the Muslim Brotherhood, founded the Muslim Women's Association. She preaches in a local mosque to a large number of women and strongly advocates women's participation in public life in ways that do not contradict Muslim laws.

HOUSES OF WORSHIP AND HOLY PLACES Cairo is home to thousands of spectacular old mosques, such as Ibn Tulun and Sultan Hassan. Some of these mosques became shrines because people believed they contain the remains of members of the Prophet's family, such as the Prophet's grandchildren, al-Hussain and Sayyida Zaynab. Such mosques and many "saint" tombs, which are found throughout Egypt, have a special place in the religious imagination. People visit them to ask the "saints" buried there to help heal a sick child, cure an infertile daughter, or bring back a missing son. Some of these shrines are the sites of annual festivals called *maw-*

alid (singular *moulid*), which attract thousands who seek spiritual and physical healing and/or entertainment.

WHAT IS SACRED? Muslims in Egypt follow two of the four Sunni legal schools: the Hanafite or the Shafiite. They share with other Muslims an emphasis on the unity of God. While often dismissed by official Muslim leaders, there is also a strong popular Islam that pays close attention to holy men, miracle works, mystical visions, and visits to the tombs of famous Sufis and other religious figures.

A *wali* (friend of God; plural *awliya*) is any man, woman, or child who is granted special powers by God. A *wali* acquires his or her status because of genealogical relationship to the Prophet Muhammad and/or extreme devotion and spiritual discipline. A *wali* is capable of receiving mystical illumination, working miracles, and mediating on behalf of those in need. *Awliya* continue to be powerful after death. Their tombs are often turned into shrines that are visited by many to show devotion and to ask for help in troubling matters. Two of the most famous shrines are the tombs of Ahmad al-Badawi (died in 1276) in Tanta and Ibrahim al-Dasuqi (died in 1296) in Dasuq.

There are also several Sufi orders (*tariqas*) in Egypt. The largest of these are the Rifaia, the Ahmediya, and the Shadhiliyya. Their rituals, especially *dhikr* (also *zikhr*; the remembrance of God), are occasions for the healing of the sick, the pacification of the troubled, and the dispersion of *baraka* (blessing).

HOLIDAYS AND FESTIVALS The most colorful holiday in Egypt is *Mawlid al-Nabi* (also *Moulid al-Nabi*), the annual celebration of the birth of the Prophet Muhammad. Multicolored decorations appear in the streets and buildings, and special sweets are offered as gifts to relatives. Id al-Fitr (also Eid al-Fitr; celebrating the end of Ramadan) and Id al-Adha (also Eid el-Adha; the Feast of Sacrifice, which follows the pilgrimage to Mecca) are joyful occasions. Special cookies are served during the former while meat dishes are served during the latter. During al-Adha families who can afford it slaughter a sheep, a goat, or even a cow as a sacrifice to God. Special dishes made of meat and thin bread, which are called *ruqaq*, are traditionally consumed as part of the feast.

The *mawlid* is an important part of religious life in Egypt. It is an annual celebration of the birth of a religious figure or holy person. The big *mawalid* can last for weeks and attract people from different parts of the country. They may combine Sufi *dhikr* (remembrance of God); entertainments, such as music and singing; and the initiation of young boys through circumcision and introduction to the holy person for blessing. Vendors sell different types of foods, sweets, drinks, and toys. The biggest *mawalid* are those of Sayyida Zaynab, al-Hussain, and al-Shafai (in Cairo) and of al-Badawi (in the city of Tanta).

MODE OF DRESS Class, more than religion, shapes the dress code in Egypt. Upper-class Muslims usually dress in Western-style clothes. The working-class and rural populations tend to wear more "traditional" Egyptian clothes that are not religiously marked. Since the early 1970s the head cover (known in the West as the veil and in Arabic as *hijab*) has been worn by many women in Egypt. In urban areas different types of veiling may signify modesty, piety, religiosity, a political viewpoint, or regional origin (especially rural versus urban). Most women wear a simple cover while more devout women wear the *khimar*, a garment wound tightly around the face to cover the hair that then flows down to cover most of the upper part of the body. Few wear the *niqab*, a veil that covers the hair and face. Some men wear a long white robe and grow a beard to signify their devotion to the Prophet and his traditions.

DIETARY PRACTICES Most Muslims in Egypt follow the restrictions Islam imposes on the consumption of pork and alcohol. While some Muslims, especially among the upper class, may drink and serve alcohol, the restriction on the consumption of pork is more closely observed. Animals are slaughtered according to the Islamic way, which includes a special prayer before the throat of the animal is slit. People mention the name of God at the beginning of a meal and thank him after finishing it.

RITUALS Many Egyptian Muslims observe the five daily prayers, especially the communal prayer on Friday. Ramadan is a special month in Egypt. Fasting during the day, most Egyptians visit and socialize during the night. Plenty of foods and sweets are prepared, and relatives and friends invite one another for fancy meals to celebrate the break of the fast. Performing the hajj (pilgrimage to Mecca) is highly regarded, and those who perform it acquire extra prestige and honor. The *zakat* (alms) is either given to the poor directly or is dispersed through a charitable organization or a local mosque.

RITES OF PASSAGE Marriage and death are the two most important life transitions that are marked by religious rituals. Most marriages have a religious and a secular component. The marriage itself is contracted by a religious figure, while the wedding celebration is often a public social event that includes music and dancing. Some religious families have shifted to religious music and singing and insist on separating men and women during the celebration. Death is another important rite of passage. Egyptians believe that the corpse should be buried as soon as possible. After the body of the deceased is washed and dressed in a special white shroud, special prayers are performed in the mosque. Some prayers are also whispered in the ear of the deceased before burial.

MEMBERSHIP When a child is born, the father—or another male relative—whispers the prayer call in the ear of the newborn, who is considered a Muslim from birth. After one week, most families have a secular celebration called *subu,* but some families have moved to a more religious celebration called *aqiqa.* Whereas *subu* involves singing, dancing, and distributing sweets and popcorn to neighbors, relatives, and friends, *aqiqa* consists mainly of cooked foods—usually rice, meat, and some kind of sweet—that are taken to a local mosque to be consumed by attendees.

All male babies are circumcised. Most are circumcised during the first week of their life, while many girls are circumcised between the ages of 8 and 10. While both practices have religious meanings, female circumcision is controversial, and many religious figures do not see it as part of Islam. Conversions to Islam among Egyptian adults are few.

SOCIAL JUSTICE Various religious groups and charities are trying to improve the conditions of the poor in Egypt. They use various spaces and methods to provide affordable educational and health services. Some big mosques have integrated such services within their domains. During Ramadan families who can afford it provide free food to the needy. Some groups, such as the Muslim Brotherhood, have been so successful in providing needed services, especially after the 1992 earthquake that struck Cairo, that the government has issued laws to restrict such activities.

SOCIAL ASPECTS Divorce and marriage in Egypt are largely regulated by Muslim laws. Marriages are often planned and arranged by the families involved. The couple and their families usually share the expenses and work together to secure the establishment of a new home for the newly married. While divorce is allowed and easy to get, mainly for men, it is not common. *Kul* is a recent law that allows women to go to court to get a divorce. Such attempts to give women more power in divorce and custody cases are faced by strong resistance from conservative religious and secular elements. One problem is the growing number of children born to Egyptian mothers and non-Egyptian fathers. Such children do not have Egyptian citizenship and are often treated like foreigners, which restricts their access to various services and resources. Attempts to grant them citizenship rights have been unsuccessful.

POLITICAL IMPACT Religious figures and groups are directly and indirectly active in Egyptian political life. Many groups are trying to push the government toward implementing more of the Shariah in public life. Members of the Muslim Brotherhood and independent Muslim activists have sought public office in national and local elections. They also control several professional syndicates and associations.

CONTROVERSIAL ISSUES There are intense debates over the nature of the political system in Egypt and its relationship to Islam. Various authors have written about the relationship between modernity and Islam and between Egypt and the West. Many attempts to change the legal status of women have been met with strong resistance by individuals and groups, who provide specific interpretations of the Koran and *sunnah* (the Prophet's sayings and deeds) to support the status quo. Feminists have increasingly tried to present alternative interpretations of the religious texts to support women's rights. The role of the religious authorities in monitoring and censoring books, novels, and films has been another controversial matter.

CULTURAL IMPACT From the beginning Islam made a lasting impact on Egyptian music, art, literature, and architecture. Islamic forms and motifs were integrated in metal works; the decorations of mosques, houses, and palaces; calligraphy; and arabesques, a style of decoration based on intricately interwoven plant motifs and geometrical shapes. Egypt is the leading Arab country in music production. Its music incorporates folk, classical Arabic, and Western music. Um Kulthum (died in

1975), the Diva of the East, began as a Koran chanter and went on to become the most famous Egyptian singer, enjoying massive popularity in the Arab world. Some extreme groups have discouraged people from listening to music because it distracts them from worshiping. Still, religious music has continued to grow in importance. Religious songs, accompanied by such instruments as the tambourine, are increasingly heard at weddings and various gatherings and even on buses. Some Sufi groups use music in their gatherings and sessions dedicated to the remembrance of God.

Other Religions

The Copts are the second largest religious group in Egypt. Most Copts belong to the Coptic Orthodox Church. There are also communities of Coptic Catholics, Roman Catholics, Anglicans, Greek Orthodox, Armenian Orthodox, Maronites, Syrian Catholics, and Protestants. The number of Jews decreased sharply after the creation of Israel, and only a small number of them still reside in Egypt.

The Copts consider themselves "the true Egyptians," who have preserved the heritage of the pharaohs by not intermarrying with Arabs. They live throughout Egypt but are best represented in Cairo and Upper Egypt, especially in Asyut and Minya. They have been traditionally associated with commerce, banking, and the civil service.

The year 284 marks the beginning of the Coptic calendar, for it was in that year that Diocletian, who brutalized the Copts, became emperor of Rome and that many men, women, and children lost their lives for their faith. Such tremendous sacrifice made martyrdom central to the history and religious imagination of the Copts.

Despite harsh persecution under the Romans and Byzantines, Christianity flourished in Egypt, and by the third century ascetic Christians had developed the monastery system, a major contribution of the Copts to Christianity. There are at least 12 monasteries in Egypt, the largest and most famous being at Wadi al-Natroun.

Most Egyptians converted to Christianity in the fourth century. Disagreements over the nature of Jesus at the Council of Chalcedon in 451 led to the creation of the independent Coptic church. It was considered a Monophysite church because of its belief that Christ had only one (divine) nature. The Copts themselves argue that they were misunderstood by others, that they have always maintained that Christ was perfect in his humanity and divinity, and that the human and the divine were united in the mystery of Incarnation. The Byzantines considered the Copts heretics and treated them accordingly.

Under Muslim rule the Copts were granted protection and freedom to worship in exchange for paying a poll tax (*jizya*). Many rulers treated them fairly, granted them freedom to worship, and employed them as civil servants. Others treated them extremely harshly. The deranged Fatimid ruler Al-Hakim (reigned 1012–15), for example, persecuted and heavily taxed them, destroyed their churches, and confiscated their property.

The Coptic Orthodox Church has its own pope, who is seated in Alexandria. The church has witnessed a spiritual and political revival manifested in the growing number of young men and women who have joined monasteries and in the church's increasing role in public life. The roots of this revival can be traced back to the end of the nineteenth century, when the church, under the leadership of Pope Kyrillos IV, started a reform movement. A major factor in this revival was the Sunday School Movement. These schools, which spread throughout the country, emphasized Christian education and promoted the study of the Bible. They became central to the education of young Copts, teaching them about their church and community's past and religious heritage.

Since 1971 Shenouda III (born 1923) has been the leader of the Coptic Church. He believes in a strong role for the church in defending the rights of Copts in Egypt. Since his selection he has been working to restructure the church and to increase its role in the Coptic community and public life. This led to a strong confrontation with President Anwar el-Sadat, who in 1981 exiled the pope to the monastery of Saint Bishoi outside Cairo. He stayed in exile until 1985, when President Hosni Mubarak reinstated him. Since then he has been active in strengthening relations with Muslims and other Christian communities and in expanding the church inside and outside Egypt.

Copts have a strong identity that draws closely on religious symbols. Icons of saints are clearly visible in Christian homes, vehicles, and shops. Many Copts wear a cross around the neck or tattoo it on their wrists. This serves to display their religious identity and to protect them from evil spirits. Copts spend more than half of the year fasting. This includes abstaining from food for several hours each day and from eating any animal products and such other products as wine and coffee. Marriage is limited to the community; other Christians who marry Copts are required to convert and be rebaptized in the Coptic Church.

The Copts celebrate Christmas on 7 January, Epiphany on 19 January, and the Annunciation on 21 March. Their festivals include *mawalid*, which are similar in many ways to the Muslim *mawalid*. The *mawalid* of Saint George and the Holy Virgin are especially popular and are attended by both Muslims and Christians.

Farha Ghannam

See Also Vol. I: *Coptic Christianity, Islam*

Bibliography

Abdel Fattah, Nabil, ed. *Al-Halah al-Dinyah fi Misr.* Cairo: Al-Ahram Center for Strategic and Political Studies, 1995.

Daly, M.W., ed. *Modern Egypt from 1517 to the End of the Twentieth Century.* Vol. 2 of *The Cambridge History of Egypt.* Cambridge: Cambridge University Press, 1998.

Doorn-Harder, Pieternella van. *Contemporary Coptic Nuns.* Columbia: University of South Carolina Press, 1995.

Esposito, John L., ed. *The Oxford Dictionary of Islam.* Oxford: Oxford University Press, 2003.

Hoffman, Valerie J. *Sufism, Mystics, and Saints in Modern Egypt.* Columbia: University of South Carolina Press, 1995.

Ghannam, Farha. *Remaking the Modern: Space, Relocation, and the Politics of Identity in a Global Cairo.* Berkeley: University of California Press, 2002.

Kamil, Jill. *Christianity in the Land of the Pharaohs: The Coptic Orthodox Church.* London: Routledge, 2002.

Meinardus, Otto F.A. *Two Thousand Years of Coptic Christianity.* Cairo: The American University Press in Cairo, 1999.

Petry, Carl F., ed. *Islamic Egypt, 640–1517.* Vol. I of *The Cambridge History of Egypt.* Cambridge: Cambridge University Press, 1998.

Rodenbeck, Max. *Cairo: The City Victorious.* Cairo: The American University in Cairo Press, 1998.

Sayyid-Marsot, Afaf Lutfi. *A Short History of Modern Egypt.* Cambridge: Cambridge University Press, 1985.

El Salvador

POPULATION 6,353,681

ROMAN CATHOLIC 56.7 percent

PROTESTANT 17.8 percent

NONDECLARED 23.2 percent

OTHER 2.3 percent

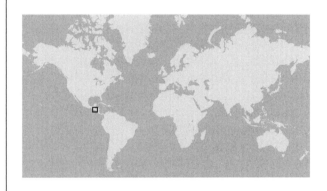

Country Overview

INTRODUCTION The Republic of El Salvador, is Central America's smallest country, but it has its greatest population density. It was Christianized in the sixteenth century as a result of Spanish conquest and colonization. In pre-Columbian times groups belonging to three different aboriginal civilizations lived in the current territory of the republic. The Maya inhabited the northwestern part of the country near Lake Guija. The Pipil, a group belonging to the Nahuatl ethnolinguistic family that also included the Toltec and the Aztec, migrated from central Mexico in successive waves that lasted from the ninth to the thirteenth century C.E. They founded the chiefdom of Cuzcatlán in the center of the

country and gradually displaced other groups from most of the territory. The Lenca, a group of South American origin that was strongly influenced by Mayan culture, settled in the eastern part of the country across the Lempa River. These group's religious practices were documented beginning in colonial times.

Many archaeological sites now attest the importance of religion among the aboriginal cultures. The Pipil worshiped a supreme deity (Teotl), the earth (Tal), the sun (Tonal), and the moon (Meztli) and shared the cult of the mythical cultural hero Quetzalcoatl with other groups in the region. Totemic affiliations linked families and individuals to spiritual entities often incarnated in animals. The current heritage of aboriginal religion is limited to a few legends (Sipitío, Cadejo, Ciguanaba), which are still widespread as children's lore. The imposition of the Roman Catholic faith and extensive intermarriage led to the gradual extinction of aboriginal religious practices throughout the colonial period.

Presently the majority of the country's population is Roman Catholic. Protestantism was introduced in El Salvador in the late nineteenth century; in recent decades evangelical groups have experienced considerable growth. The remnants of aboriginal religion that had survived the colonial period were obliterated as a consequence of swift land expropriation carried out by the government of Gerardo Barrios (president from 1860 to 1863). A group of powerful families, including relatives of Barrios, obtained the country's most fertile lands in order to implement the cultivation of coffee. This consolidated the hold of a powerful elite on the country's economy and its dependence on coffee as the main

A woman holds a photo of Monsignor Oscar Arnulfo Romero during a Mass held on the anniversary of his assassination. Romero was the most influential figure of the Salvadoran church in the twentieth century. © AFP/CORBIS.

export product. These events, and the harsh military repression of the 1932 communist-led insurrection, extinguished the last forms of communal land property inherited from pre-Columbian times, turning most of El Salvador's rural population into a landless peasantry.

RELIGIOUS TOLERANCE El Salvador's constitution established the lay character of the state before other Latin-American countries; nevertheless, the Roman Catholic Church has continued to enjoy especial status in the country. Other denominations are tolerated and guaranteed freedom of cult (religion is not enforced by the state). The Ministry of the Interior, by virtue of a 1996 law, authorizes and regulates the operation of religions other than Catholicism. No instances of sectarian religious persecution have been recorded in recent years. It should be noted, though, that the social and political

involvement of some sectors of the Roman Catholic Church before and during the civil war of 1980–91 clashed with the views of conservative landowners, entrepreneurs, and the army. This led to persecution and notorious acts of violence against priests, nuns, and lay church workers.

Major Religion

ROMAN CATHOLICISM

DATE OF ORIGIN 1525 C.E.
NUMBER OF FOLLOWERS 3.6 million

HISTORY As in other Latin-American countries, the origin of Roman Catholicism in El Salvador was a direct consequence of the Spanish conquest. Pedro de Alvarado, a lieutenant of Mexico's conquistador Hernán Cortés, landed on the coast of Cuzcatlán in the early fifteenth century intending to extend the Spanish crown's domination over the territory. The Pipil forces, under the leadership of Atlacatl, defeated the Spaniards at Acaxual (currently the port of Acajutla) on 8 June 1524. Alvarado's return in force in 1525 marked the onset of the colonial regime. Soon afterward Spanish priests set to the task of implanting Roman Catholicism in the context of colonial institutions such as the *encomienda*, which dislocated aboriginal society and subjected the population to exploitation. El Salvador was a province under the administration of colonial authorities based in Guatemala. The province's main economic activities were the production of indigo colorant, balsam, and subsistence crops. In religious matters El Salvador was also subordinated to Guatemala's authority, and the latter, in turn, to Spain's. As in the rest of Spanish America, the king of Spain chose all bishops throughout the colonial period. The Council of Indies directed the church's activities and administered matters such as the founding of dioceses, missionary activity, and discipline among the clergy.

After independence the church continued to support the established social system. Pastoral activity promoted an interpretation of the faith that stressed piety and mystical detachment from the world and that also stressed fatalistic compliance with the prevailing social order. The church hierarchy blessed each new government in a Te Deum ceremony, which consolidated the church's links to the state and the rigid socioeconomic order.

EARLY AND MODERN LEADERS José Matías Delgado (1767–1832) was a leading figure of the independence movement. He and other Salvadoran *próceres* (founding fathers) were key actors in Central America's emancipation from Spanish colonial rule in 1821 and became founders of the short-lived Federation of Central American States. Father Delgado addressed San Salvador's population in the famous call of 5 November 1811 and became a member of the federation's legislative assembly in 1823. He struggled to obtain the status of diocese for San Salvador. The ecclesiastical authorities in Guatemala were adamantly opposed to this, and finally Pope Pius VIII intervened by excommunicating Father Delgado for contumacy.

Monsignor Luis Chávez y González was archbishop of San Salvador from 1939 until 1977. During his tenure the Salvadoran church underwent significant changes. The marginal condition of the peasantry, which had been taken for granted by the church's hierarchy, became a source of concern. The traditional approach of charity was seen as ineffective; the growth of Protestantism loomed as a threat to the Roman Catholic faith in the country. The monsignor addressed this situation by promoting the organization of cooperatives in the countryside. Vatican II in 1965 and the 1968 conference of Latin-American bishops in Medellín, Colombia, provided further impetus to the church's social awareness.

Monsignor Oscar Arnulfo Romero (1917–80) was the most influential figure of the Salvadoran church in the twentieth century. He served 35 years as a relatively conservative priest and seven years as a bishop. His three-year tenure as archbishop, mostly held during the chaotic pre–civil war period, left a lasting spiritual and social legacy. He became increasingly concerned with the country's social conditions amidst the explosive political situation and the first major engagements between the army and the leftist guerrillas. Romero preached at San Salvador's Metropolitan Cathedral. His sermons, broadcast on a Roman Catholic radio station, became an eloquent medium of protest against the country's severe inequality, poverty, and human rights violations. El Salvador's conservative sectors interpreted his exhortations to the army, police, and right-wing death squads to stop violence and repression as yet another form of Marxist propaganda. Romero was seen as inciting the populace to armed insurrection, which turned him into a target of the death squads. He was assassinated while saying Mass in 1980. His successor, Monsignor Arturo Rivera y Damas, was a key figure in the negotiations of the peace accords that brought about the end of the civil war in 1991. Archbishop Monsignor Fernando Sáenz Lacalle (born in 1932) started his tenure in 1995.

MAJOR THEOLOGIANS AND AUTHORS Father Ignacio Ellacuría (1930–89), born in Spain, was sent to El Salvador at age 17. He studied philosophy in Ecuador and held a doctorate from the Universidad Complutense in Madrid, Spain. A Jesuit priest, he left an important philosophical and theological legacy and is considered one of the most important figures of recent Salvadoran history. Ellacuría's role as an educator and political actor was also outstanding. Under his direction, amidst the turbulence and violence of the 1970s and 1980s, the Universidad Centroamericana José Simeón Cañas became one of the most prestigious institutions of higher education in Latin America. His theological and philosophical approach, centered on dialogue and understanding as preconditions for social change, earned him criticism from the radical left and fatal enmity from the right. He was assassinated in 1989 during anti-insurgency operations at the Central American University.

HOUSES OF WORSHIP AND HOLY PLACES The most important churches in the country are the cathedrals of San Salvador, Santa Ana, and San Miguel. Also notable are the Sagrado Corazón, Vírgen de Guadalupe, El Calvario, and Don Rúa churches in San Salvador and churches in the provincial capitals, such as in Zacatecoluca. Some of these churches are fine examples of colonial architecture; most of the churches built during that period were destroyed in earthquakes. The statue of the World's Savior in San Salvador honors Jesus as the capital's and the country's patron saint.

WHAT IS SACRED? The effigy of the Divine Savior of the World, kept at the Metropolitan Cathedral in San Salvador, is an object of great fervor among the faithful as explained below under HOLIDAYS AND FESTIVALS. Also notable among Salvadoran Catholics is the pilgrimage to the town of Esquipulas in western Guatemala, site of a black effigy of Jesus Christ (Cristo Negro) since 1595.

HOLIDAYS AND FESTIVALS The Feast of the Transfiguration of the Savior of the World, celebrated 1–6 August, is, along with Easter, one of the most salient religious events in the country. During this period celebrations in honor of Jesus, who is the patron of the nation (El Salvador means "The Redeemer" in Spanish), are held in San Salvador (Holy Redeemer). Most of these celebrations are of a secular nature (fairs, civic parades, and so on), but religious fervor is heightened during the ceremony of the *bajada* (descent) of the effigy of the Divine Savior of the World. The effigy, covered in a special tunic, is brought down from its pedestal at San Salvador's Metropolitan Cathedral and carried in a procession. This festivity has its origin in the foundation of the city of San Salvador by the Spanish on 6 August 1525.

As in the rest of Central America, Easter is celebrated by Salvadoran Catholics through reenactments of Jesus Christ's *via crucis* (Way of the Cross) and processions in all major cities and towns. Nochebuena (Christmas Eve) is celebrated on 24 December. People sing traditional Christmas carols, create *Nacimientos* (miniature scenes of Jesu's birthplace and surroundings), and attend midnight Mass.

The feast of Our Lady of Guadalupe, is celebrated on 12 December. It commemorates the appearance of the Virgin Mary to an aboriginal named Juan Diego near Mexico City in 1531, and it is one of the most popular Marian feasts in Latin America. Children wear modified versions of aboriginal attire and participate in festivities worshiping the Virgin. The historical reference to the conversion of aboriginals is evident. Parents and their children visit the Basilica of the Virgin of Guadalupe.

The feast of the Finding of the Holy Cross, which in El Salvador also celebrates the conversion of the aboriginals, is observed on 3 May. All Soul's Day, also popular in Mexico as the "Day of the Dead," is celebrated on 2 November with visits and flower offerings to the tombs of relatives.

MODE OF DRESS No particular way of dressing distinguishes Salvadoran Catholics from other denominations.

DIETARY PRACTICES Roman Catholic injunctions to abstain from eating meat on Friday and during Lent are largely ignored in El Salvador. There is no religious significance attached to particular dishes.

RITUALS The current practice of Roman Catholicism in El Salvador does not involve rituals other than the

standard liturgy. In contrast to Guatemala, Mexico, and Andean countries, no instances of religious syncretism combining pre-Columbian and Catholic rituals subsist.

RITES OF PASSAGE The same rites of passage that characterize the initiation of Roman Catholics throughout the world—baptism, first communion, and confirmation—are practiced in El Salvador. In El Salvador confirmation is a Catholic rite of passage practiced by youths between ages 12 and 15 after the celebration of first communion. Young people prepare for this sacrament over a period of two years under a catechist's direction. Confirmation, which is administered only among a fervent minority of Salvadoran Catholics, is considered an important event in a person's life. Only high-ranking priests are authorized to furnish the sacrament.

MEMBERSHIP The Salvadoran Catholic Church practices extensive missionary work, community organizing, seminars, and other forms of proselytizing. Radio, television, and the Internet are used to extend the church's reach. The church's participation in education is paramount. Several Catholic elementary and high school institutions have traditionally been viewed as the country's best educational options. The most prestigious schools include Liceo Salvadoreño, Externado de San José, and Colegio Santa Cecilia, for boys; and Colegio La Asunción, Colegio Sagrado Corazón, and Colegio Sagrada Familia, for girls.

SOCIAL JUSTICE The creation of rural communities in the countryside, promoted by Monsignor Chávez y González in the 1960s, was followed by the formation of Catholic base communities. These forms of organizations were influenced by the renovated social thinking of the Latin-American Roman Catholic Church after the 1968 Medellín Conference, which included approaches such as the theology of liberation advocated by Gustavo Gutiérrez in Peru and the work of Brazilian Bishop Helder Camara. A large sector of the Salvadoran church opposed these tendencies, but the archdiocese of San Salvador committed itself to change, in the context of the increased polarization of political events throughout Latin America. Numerous peasants were thus encouraged to find transcendence in the message of a socially engaged Jesus and to seek liberation from economic and political oppression. This had significant repercussions. The practice of Catholicism in the base communities became a political act. As the armed skirmishes between the army and the Marxist-inspired guerrillas turned into civil war in the 1970s, the Catholic base communities radicalized their activities. Associations of peasant groups became powerful leagues that provided support for the leftist coalition Frente Farabundo Martí para la Liberación Nacional (FMLN).

SOCIAL ASPECTS Common-law couples, fathering children outside marriage, and abandonment of children—especially by their fathers—are entrenched practices among the urban and rural poor. Illiteracy, poverty, inadequate housing, and machismo are factors that hinder the campaigns undertaken by the church and government to address these problems.

POLITICAL IMPACT Since the civil war (which ended in 1991) the Catholic Church has continued to influence the country's politics, but not to the extent of the 1970s and 1980s. Possible explanations are a shift toward more conservative positions among the church's hierarchy and erosion of popular support for the Christian Democratic Party (CDP). Christian Democrats, inspired by a nonradical reading of the Catholic Church's social ideas, have participated in the country's politics since 1960 and won the 1972 elections without actually reaching office. The CDP's leader, Napoleón Duarte, was named president of the governing junta in the turbulent year of 1980. He won the 1984 presidential election, enjoying the support of the United States, which viewed the CDP as a moderate political option that could bring about a solution to the civil war. The CDP's agenda of social and economic reforms, however, was fiercely opposed by both the Marxist insurgency and the ultraconservative elite.

CONTROVERSIAL ISSUES The position of the Salvadoran church on issues of abortion and contraception echoes the views of the Vatican.

In 1989 six Jesuit priests affiliated with the Central American University, including the university's rector, Ignacio Ellacuría, along with a female employee and her daughter, were assassinated during anti-insurgency operations in San Salvador. The conservative media and the military establishment accused the priests of subversion, hence making these crimes appear to be "normal" war events. The low-ranking military accused and convicted in this case were subsequently freed under the amnesty law negotiated in the 1991 peace accords. The universi-

ty, which had formally accused the armed forces high command of planning and coordinating the murders, has asked for a review of this case.

Another case of violence against the Roman Catholic Church during the civil war involved the assassination of four American Maryknoll nuns in 1980. National Guardsmen were convicted of these murders in 1984. The minister of defense and the head of the National Guard were sued by the nun's families in a Florida court in 2000 for their responsibility as commanding officers during the crimes.

CULTURAL IMPACT Architecture and liturgical art, especially from the colonial period, have been the most noticeable cultural manifestations of Roman Catholicism in El Salvador. The cathedrals of Santa Ana, Metapán, and San Vicente are fine examples of colonial architecture. Also notable are more recent constructions, such as the tower and dome of the Don Rúa Church in San Salvador. Previous versions of San Salvador's Cathedral (now Metropolitan Cathedral) in downtown San Salvador were destroyed by an earthquake (1873) and fire (1951). In the 1990s it was completely repaired from the damages of a 1986 earthquake.

Other Religions

A 1995 survey conducted by the Central American University reported 17.8 percent of El Salvador's population to be Protestant. This figure includes Baptists, Presbyterians, Lutherans, and several Evangelical groups, such as the Church of Jesus Christ of Latter-day Saints (Mormons) and Seventh-day Adventists. Small numbers practice Judaism and Islam, though most of the Middle Eastern immigrants who settled in the country belonged to or converted to Roman Catholicism.

The first Protestants in El Salvador were German and British immigrants who arrived at the end of the nineteenth century. Some accumulated considerable wealth and became part of the coffee-growing elite. The first Protestant mission in the country, the Central American Mission, was established in 1896. The Seventh-day Adventists, the Baptist Church, and the Assemblies of God subsequently arrived. All of these groups enjoyed substantial financial support from North America and managed to attract a large constituency during the twentieth century. In the 1970s and 1980s Protestantism, particularly the evangelical churches, achieved unprecedented rates of conversion. The practice of stricter moral codes involving abstinence from alcohol and reduction of family violence may also have contributed to the rise of Protestantism.

Initially Protestant churches in El Salvador distinguished themselves from Roman Catholicism because of their neutral political stance and emphasis on personal salvation. In recent years they have focused more on social action and participated in ecumenical networks aimed at improving the country's endemic poverty and dismal environmental conditions. Protestant participation in education has grown at the elementary, high school, and university levels.

Benjamín Amaya

See Also Vol. 1: *Baptist Tradition, Christianity, Lutheranism, Reformed Christianity, Roman Catholicism*

Bibliography

Brierly, Peter, ed. *World Churches Handbook.* London: Christian Research, 1977.

Dussell, Enrique. *History and the Theology of Liberation.* New York: Orbis Books, 1976.

Holland, Clifton L., ed. *World Christianity: Central America and the Caribbean.* Monrovia, Calif.: MARC-World Vision, 1981.

IUDOP (Instituto Universitario de Opinión Pública). "La religión de los salvadoreños en 1995." *Estudios Centroamericanos* 563 (1995): 849–62.

"La Iglesia Salvadoreña en el siglo 20." *Proceso* 696 (February 1996).

Mecham, J. Lloyd. *Church and State in Latin America.* Chapel Hill: University of North Carolina Press, 1966.

Patterson, Anna L. *Martyrdom and the Politics of Religion.* Albany: State University of New York Press, 1997.

Sobrino, J., et al. *Companions of Jesus: The Jesuit Martyrs of El Salvador.* Maryknoll, N.Y.: Orbis, 1990.

Equatorial Guinea

POPULATION 498,144

ROMAN CATHOLIC 80 percent

PROTESTANT 5 percent

MUSLIM 4.1 percent

AFRICAN TRADITIONAL 3.4 percent

ANIMIST 2.1 percent

BAHAI 0.5 percent

NONRELIGIOUS 4.9 percent

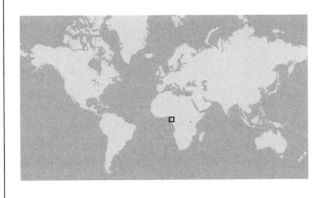

Country Overview

INTRODUCTION The Republic of Equatorial Guinea consists of a number of islands and islets—including Bioko (previously known as Fernando Po), Annobón, Corisco, and the two Elobeys—off the west coast of Africa in the Gulf of Guinea. In addition, the country includes the mainland enclave of Río Muni (also known as Mbini), which is bordered by Cameroon to the north and Gabon to the east and south.

At the time of its discovery by Portuguese mariners in the 1470s, Fernando Po was inhabited by Bubi speakers who sought to avoid Europeans during the Atlantic slave trade period. Inhabitants in heavily forested Río Muni—including Ndowe and other coastal groups, Bayele, and the majority Fang ethnic group—entered into sustained contact with Europeans in the nineteenth century. Missionary efforts by Protestants began on Fernando Po in the 1820s and on the mainland in 1875. Lasting Catholic presence dates from the 1850s on Fernando Po, which became known as Bioke in 1979.

In 2004 there were three Roman Catholic dioceses in Equatorial Guinea: Bata and Ebebiyin in Río Muni, as well as the archdiocese of Malabo on Bioko. The Spanish colonial government hampered Protestant missionary efforts, but today there are a growing number of Christian groups, including Seventh-day Adventists, Assemblies of God, Jehovah's Witnesses, and nondenominational evangelical groups. Fang speakers, many of whom also belong to Christian churches, practice the Bwiti religion, which combines elements of ancestor veneration and Christian beliefs and rituals.

RELIGIOUS TOLERANCE Although a 1992 law states official preferences for the Catholic Church and the Reform Church of Equatorial Guinea, other Christian groups operate without government interference. Freedom of worship is protected by law, but the government imposes restrictions on clergy critical of the regime. Religious organizations must register with the Ministry of Justice and Religion, a process that may take several years.

Pope John Paul II visits Equatorial Guinea in 1982. Although Catholics faced severe persecution under President Macías Nguema, the Catholic Church was able to pursue its activities in the 1980s and 1990s without major governmental interference. © VITTORIANO RASTELLI/CORBIS.

Major Religion

CHRISTIANITY

DATE OF ORIGIN Fifteenth century C.E.

NUMBER OF FOLLOWERS 399,000

HISTORY Although Portuguese Catholic missionaries visited Fernando Po as early as the late fifteenth century, no lasting Christian influence took place until the nineteenth century, in part because of the violence of the slave trade and the reticence of the Bubi peoples on the island. British and, later, Jamaican Baptist missionaries worked on Fernando Po from 1827 until expelled by the Spanish in 1858. American Presbyterians served on Corisco Island from 1850 to 1875 and then in Río Benito on the mainland until 1924. Sustained Roman Catholic presence on Fernando Po dates from the beginnings of Spanish colonial activity in the 1850s. During the colonial period from the 1850s to 1968, the Catholic Church, along with the colonial administration and commercial interests, played a crucial role in strengthening Spanish influence. At the time of independence in

1968, the Catholic Church played a strong and vital social role in the country.

During the turbulent dictatorship of Equatorial Guinea's first president, Francisco Macías Nguema (ruled 1968–79), all sectors of society, including Christian churches, were severely oppressed. Foreign priests were expelled; Guinean clerics were imprisoned, tortured, forced into exile, and sometimes killed. In 1978 all Church activities were banned. With the 1979 overthrow of Macías by his nephew, Lt. Col. Teodoro Obiang Nguema, the most severe religious restrictions were lifted. Missionaries returned, and religious activities resumed. Nonetheless, the Obiang government, which held power at the start of the twenty-first century, remained extremely sensitive to political criticism, including that coming from the Catholic clergy.

EARLY AND MODERN LEADERS Rev. John Clarke directed Jamaican Baptist missionary efforts in Fernando Po and the adjacent mainland from 1841 until 1858, when Protestant missionaries were expelled by the Spanish. Clarke and his associates opened a number of mission stations on the island. He gained a sympathetic linguistic and cultural understanding of the Bubis and the Fernandinos (descendants of freed slaves and laborers from the West African mainland).

Ildefonso Obama Obono (born in 1938) became Catholic archbishop of Malabo in 1991. Prior to that he served as bishop of Ebebiyin from 1982 to 1991. He has advocated human rights and democratic reforms.

MAJOR THEOLOGIANS AND AUTHORS Ikengue Ibiya (or Ibia J'Ikengue, 1834–1901), a Benga from Corisco Island, was trained by the American Presbyterians; in 1875 he became the first Protestant pastor from the future Equatorial Guinea. His Benga-language *Customs of the Benga* excoriates Benga religious and cultural practices as superstition and idolatry while making a strong case for Christian evangelization.

Spanish Claretian missionary Pedro Armengol Coll (1859–1918) served from 1904 to 1918 as the first bishop of the Apostolic Vicariate of Fernando Po. His 1911 memoirs recount Catholic missionary work on the island.

HOUSES OF WORSHIP AND HOLY PLACES There are cathedrals in Malabo, Bata, and Ebebiyin, as well as numerous Catholic and other Christian churches and chapels throughout the country. Malabo Cathedral, completed in 1916, is in the Spanish gothic style. During the Macías era Malabo Cathedral was desacralyzed and turned into an arsenal. Other churches were turned into cocoa sheds. Since Macía'ss overthrow in 1979, such churches have returned to their original religious function.

WHAT IS SACRED? Christian churches in Equatorial Guinea contain standard sacred objects, such as Communion bread and wine, as well as crosses and religious medallions. During the Macías era the president sought to impose his own personality cult and proclaimed himself the "unique miracle of Equatorial Guinea"; his portrait had to be hung in all Christian churches.

HOLIDAYS AND FESTIVALS Equatorial Guineans celebrate standard Christian holidays, including Christmas, Easter, Good Friday, Easter Monday, and, among Catholics, Immaculate Conception. Holidays, including secular holidays such as Independence Day (12 October), Human Rights Day (10 December), and President Obiang's birthday (5 June), are marked by religious services and traditional dances.

MODE OF DRESS Today Guinean Christians have largely adopted Western-style dress, as well as West African styles made from brightly colored imported cloth.

DIETARY PRACTICES Under the Spanish colonial system, educated Catholic Africans could become emancipated, making them honorary Spaniards who could consume the bread and wine of the Mass. Aside from Catholic dietary restrictions during Lent, which include fasting on Ash Wednesday and Good Friday, most Christians do not eat a special diet.

RITUALS Catholics in Equatorial Guinea practice standard weekly and daily Mass and prayer services. High Mass is performed at the cathedrals of Malabo, Bata, and Ebebiyin. Adherents of the syncretic Bwiti religion incorporate Christian prayers, biblical readings, and hymns into all-night rituals that include ingestion of the hallucinogen *iboga*.

RITES OF PASSAGE Aside from standard Catholic sacraments such as baptism, first Communion, confirmation, reconciliation, marriage, Holy Orders, and anointing of the sick, there appear to be no distinct Christian rites of passage in Equatorial Guinea. Male children are circumcised. Marriage may entail transfer of bride wealth (goods and money) from the groom's family to the bride's family. Like other central Africans, Equatorial Guineans practice end of mourning ceremonies up to a year or more after the death of important adults. These ceremonies involve dances, feasting, performances (of the Mvett epic), and Christian observances.

MEMBERSHIP Equatorial Guinea has the highest proportion of baptized Catholics on the African continent, which indicates the success of evangelization efforts during the colonial period. Although Catholics faced severe persecution under Macías Nguema, the Catholic Church was able to pursue its activities in the 1980s and 1990s without major government interference. Because of the high percentage of Catholics in the country, church membership is transferred within families rather than through active proselytizing.

Methodists are the principal Protestant group on Bioko. The Evangelical Church, supported by the Presbyterian Church of the United States and the Worldwide Evangelization Crusade of the United Kingdom, are the largest Protestant denominations in Río Muni. Protestant evangelization efforts were impeded by the Spanish colonial government and under Macías Nguema. Protestant groups have been able to operate more freely since 1979, when Obiang Nguema assumed office. The Spanish-language version of Christian Broadcasting Network's 700 Club is broadcast daily via satellite television.

SOCIAL JUSTICE During the colonial period the Catholic Church ran almost all of the schools, hospitals, and orphanages in Equatorial Guinea. After independence in 1968 social and educational efforts were severely disrupted under Macías. Clerics were silenced, often through arrest, expulsion, and violence. The Vatican misunderstood the gravity of the situation, advising priests and seminarians who had fled to return to Equatorial Guinea, where they were often arrested. In the 1970s the papal nuncio in Yaoundé, Cameroon, advised the Catholic Church to remain quiet in order not to endanger religious personnel who had remained in the country. With the arrival of Obiang Nguema in 1979, overseas missionaries and exiled priests returned. In the 1990s priests and even Archbishop Ildefonso Obama Obono denounced government persecutions and human rights abuses and continued to face government intimidation, arrest, and torture.

SOCIAL ASPECTS Most Christian denominations in Equatorial Guinea oppose polygamy, which nevertheless remains widespread. In the nineteenth century women unhappy in polygamous unions sometimes sought refuge in neighboring mission stations. Today among most ethnic groups except the Bubi, women, in the case of marital dissolution, are required to return bride wealth given to their family at the time of marriage. In most cases the husband maintains custody of children born during the marriage, while the wife's family retains custody of children born prior to the marriage. Women have the legal right to own and inherit property but in practice have few opportunities to accumulate wealth.

POLITICAL IMPACT As early as the 1850s the Catholic Church enjoyed privileged relations with the Spanish colonial government, which, in an effort to weaken British presence in Fernando Po, expelled Protestant missionaries. During the colonial period the Catholic Church remained a pillar of the Spanish colonial system, and at the time of independence the church was perhaps the strongest and most unifying institution in the country. Macías Nguema, who saw the church as a threat, unleashed successive waves of restrictions, persecution, and violence against clerics. In 1976 Bishop A.M. Ndongo of the Bata Diocese was killed while in a Bata prison. Bishop Nzé Abuy and numerous other religious personnel, including Protestants, were forced into exile.

In 1991 President Obiang agreed to a multiparty political system but has continued to use the state security apparatus and electoral fraud to maintain a firm grip on power. Throughout the 1990s, while many priests practiced self-censorship, those who did speak out against the political situation frequently faced harassment and arrest. In 1998 Archbishop Obama denounced persecution and ill treatment of Catholic priests and nuns. He also called for free and fair presidential elections.

CONTROVERSIAL ISSUES The Catholic Church opposes divorce, abortion, and most forms of birth control. As a testament to long-term Catholic influence in Equatorial Guinea, Spanish laws that prohibited abortion remained in effect until 1991. Since then new laws have continued to prohibit abortion and impose harsh penalties upon both those who perform abortions and women who consent to them. Abortions, however, may be carried out to save the life of a woman or to preserve her mental or physical health.

CULTURAL IMPACT Christian artists in Equatorial Guinea have painted biblical scenes with African participants and settings. Catholic and Protestant hymns have been translated into Bubi, Fang, Benga, and other African languages. Hymns are also performed using African tones and rhythms, while contemporary Guinean music draws on African as well as Catholic and Protestant choral traditions.

Other Religions

Prior to Christian evangelization ethnic groups in Equatorial Guinea practiced African traditional religions. The Bubi of Fernando Po revered the Supreme Creator, *Dupe*, and worshiped the elements. The high priest conserved the sacred fire and blessed the yam plantations. Fang peoples on the mainland conserved ancestor relics (*byeri* in Fang), particularly crania of prominent forebears and accompanying statues, that were placated, fed, and consulted before important undertakings, such as hunting expeditions, marriage, and war. Fang also believed in the supernatural efficacy of many medicines or charms (*byang*) composed from a wide variety of ingredients: plants, animals, humans, and manufactured objects. Many precolonial Fang religious practices required elaborate rites of purification and sacrifice to the ancestors. Antiwitchcraft ceremonies also entailed rituals to identify and combat suspected evildoers.

Well into the twentieth century Fang speakers still practiced a number of initiation rites, which continue to inform beliefs about wealth, power, and social success. Young men underwent initiation in *melan* ceremonies in which they consumed a plant with hallucinatory properties. *Ngil*, or *Ngyi*, was a men's initiation society devoted to settling judicial affairs and combating witchcraft. Women were initiated into *Mevungu*, a society devoted to fertility and protection.

The Bwiti religion is also practiced by Fang speakers. Originally an ancestor religion among peoples in southern Gabon, Bwiti spread to Fang migrant laborers in the early twentieth century and eventually to Río Muni. Bwiti, which draws on ancestor religions and Christianity, requires substantial initiation rites, including ingestion of the hallucinogen *iboga*, which enables initiates to contact the spirits.

In the slightly more open political climate since the 1990s, political opponents have denounced ritual murders, which in some cases involved the removal of the victim's organs to make "medicines." Some ritual crimes are thought to have political significance.

Since 1970 the number of Muslims has grown, mainly due to the influx of West African merchants. Their practices are similar to Muslims in neighboring countries in the region.

John Cinnamon

See Also Vol. 1: *Christianity, Roman Catholicism*

Bibliography

Ensema, Nzang M. *Cien años de evangelización en Guinea Ecuatorial.* Barcelona: Editions Claret, 1983.

Fegley, Randall, comp. *Equatorial Guinea.* World Bibliographic Series, vol. 136. Oxford: Clio Press, 1991.

Fernández, C. *Misiones y Misioneros en la Guinea Española.* Madrid: Editorial COCULSA, 1962.

Liniger-Goumax, Max. *Historical Dictionary of Equatorial Guinea.* 3rd ed. Lanham, Md.: Scarecrow Press. 2000.

Martín de Molono, A. *La ciudad de Clarence: Primeros años de la actual ciudad de Malabo, capital de Guinea Ecuatorial, 1827–1859.* Madrid-Malabo: Centro Cultural Hispano-Guineano, 1993.

Perrois, Louis, and Marta Sierra Delage. *The Art of Equatorial Guinea: The Fang Tribes.* New York: Rizzoli, 1990.

Eritrea

POPULATION 4,465,651

SUNNI MUSLIM 50 percent

ORTHODOX CHRISTIAN (TEWAHDO) 40 percent

EASTERN CATHOLIC (EASTERN RITE) AND ROMAN CATHOLIC 5.5 percent

PROTESTANT 2.4 percent

AFRICAN INDIGENOUS BELIEFS 1 percent

SEVENTH-DAY ADVENTIST 0.5 percent

JEHOVAH'S WITNESS 0.5 percent

OTHER (BUDDHIST, HINDU, BAHAI) 0.1 percent

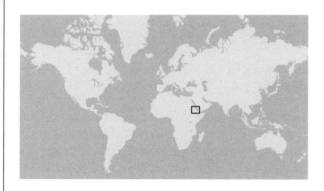

Country Overview

INTRODUCTION Eritrea is a small country in the region of northeast Africa known as the Horn of Africa. Its eastern border stretches 600 miles along the coastline of the Red Sea, and its neighboring countries are Ethiopia, The Sudan, and Djibouti. Eritrea's predominantly rural population lives by agriculture and animal husbandry. Its terrain is roughly divided into highlands occupied by farmers and lowland plains inhabited by people who practice mixed farming and herding.

Italy originally established Eritrea's borders and ruled the country as an Italian colony from 1889 to 1941. During World War II the British army defeated the Italians in Eritrea, governing the area as a protectorate until 1952. The United Nations then established Eritrea as an autonomous unit in federation with Ethiopia, but in 1962 Ethiopia annexed Eritrea as a province. From 1961 to 1991 Eritreans fought a war of independence from Ethiopia. Finally, in May 1993 Eritrea declared its official separation from Ethiopia and was admitted to the United Nations. One of the least developed countries in the world, Eritrea was left with its infrastructure largely destroyed and its economy crippled by war. A Christian-dominated government ruled Eritrea as a one-party state.

Historically a crossroads between Africa and the Middle East, Eritrea has long been home to both Christianity and Islam. Eritrean Muslims are Sunnis, and many are members of Sufi orders or brotherhoods. Religion predominates over other forms of group identification, including kinship, ethnic, and national.

RELIGIOUS TOLERANCE The Eritrean government officially recognizes four religions: Orthodox Christianity, Islam, Catholicism, and Evangelical Christianity. The religious holidays of these four groups are celebrated nationally, and their adherents are free to practice their respective religions, but they may not proselytize by radio, newspaper, or Internet. The government does not allow religious schools for either Christians or Muslims.

In general, the Eritrean government has been tolerant of Christian and Muslim groups, but it has restricted the freedom of religion and movement of groups it perceives as opposing the government. In 2002 the government closed twelve Pentecostal and charismatic churches and arrested men, women, and children who practiced what the government labels "new religions." The government has arrested without trial members of the Jehovah's Witnesses, some Muslims, and in 2003 hundreds of members of new Protestant churches, including the Full Gospel (Mulu Wengel), Kale Hiwot, and Rema churches. It has banned some religious organizations, shut down health clinics run by foreign religious organizations, and refused visas to foreign churches and mission workers. Religion-based political parties are banned by the Eritrean constitution, but the government has postponed implementing the constitution indefinitely, citing the 1998–2001 border war with Ethiopia and the continuing tensions as reasons for its decision.

Major Religions

SUNNI ISLAM

ORTHODOX CHRISTIANITY

SUNNI ISLAM

DATE OF ORIGIN Ninth century C.E.
NUMBER OF FOLLOWERS 2.2 million

HISTORY Eritrean Islam dates nearly to the inception of Islam in nearby Mecca in the Arabian peninsula. In the early seventh century Muhammad's companions (sahaba) crossed the Red Sea to the Eritrean coast, seeking refuge in what was then Abyssinia. In the eighth century Arab Muslims settled off the Eritrean coast on the Dahlak Islands, which became a center of trade between Abyssinia, Yemen, Egypt, and India and a gateway for Islamic holy men to enter coastal Eritrea.

By the thirteenth century coastal peoples including the Afar, the Saho, and some Beja converted to Islam. A Muslim ruler, Ahmed b. Ibrahim al-Ghaza, came to power in Ethiopia in the sixteenth century, and some

The minaret of a mosque stands before the steeple of an Orthodox church in Keren, Eritrea. Historically a crossroads between Africa and the Middle East, Eritrea has long been home to both Christianity and Islam. AP/WIDE WORLD PHOTOS.

Christian highland populations converted. Both the Turkish Ottoman Empire (which controlled the Eritrean coast from the mid-fifteenth to the mid-nineteenth century) and Egypt (which ruled coastal and western Eritrea from 1840 to 1885) helped spread Islam in Eritrea.

After World War II a majority of Eritrea's Muslims wanted independence for their country, while the Christian population favored unity with Christian-dominated Ethiopia. When Ethopia annexed Eritrea, many Eritrean Christians gained educational and economic opportunities, and Muslims were marginalized.

In the 1960s Ethiopian rule was contested by armed Eritrean nationalist movements, which originated in predominantly Muslim regions. Though they were both ostensibly secular movements with diverse bases of support, the Eritrean Liberation Front was often associated with Muslims, and the Eritrean People's Liberation Front (EPLF) was more closely identified with Christians. In time both movements became national and claimed Christian and Muslim members in almost equal numbers. The EPLF, however, emerged dominant, went on to defeat the Ethiopian army, and formed the national leadership. The leadership of the EPLF has tended to come from a Christian background and has treated the majority Muslims as a minority group. After their decline under Ethiopian rule, however, Eritrean Muslim institutions, including Shari'ah courts, regional Islamic councils, and the office of mufti, have been revived since independence.

EARLY AND MODERN LEADERS Jamal al-Din Ibrahim, born in Ethiopia 1865, was appointed in 1897 as the *qadi* (Islamic judge) for the Afars in Eritrea. Jamal al-Din introduced religious reforms to this nomadic population, discouraging non-Koranic beliefs and practices.

Sheikh Ibrahim al-Mukhtar (1909–69) became the country's first grand mufti in 1940. Sheikh Ibrahim reformed Eritrea's Shari'ah (Islamic) courts and centralized local *waqf* (financial endowment) committees in the 1940s. In the 1950s he regularized the training of *qadis* and court procedures and emerged as an outspoken nationalist, working for Eritrean independence, despite persecution, for the rest of his life.

Sheikh Alamin Osman Alamin was appointed by President Isaias Afworki in 1992 as the first grand mufti of independent Eritrea, becoming the final authority on important religious questions and rules for Eritrean Muslims. Although Islam does not recognize the distinction between church and state, Sheikh Alamin holds that the Eritrean government must remain secular in order to represent both major religious communities fairly.

MAJOR THEOLOGIANS AND AUTHORS Jamal al-Din Ibrahim (b. 1865) studied in Ethiopia and Mecca and settled in Eritrea on the coast of the Red Sea. He wrote religious poetry and a book of prayers for travelers to Mecca. Among other important Eritrean Muslim writers, Jibril Hajji Abubaker, a twentieth-century author, published five books on Islam in the Tigrinya language.

Sheikh Ibrahim al-Mukhtar, Eritrea's most distinguished Muslim scholar as well as its first grand mufti, published numerous articles and books in Arabic on Islam. After studying the Koran in Eritrea, Sheikh Ibrahim studied Islamic teachings in The Sudan and gradu-

ated from al-Azhar University in Cairo. He helped found more than a dozen Islamic religious institutes (*mahad*) and schools throughout Eritrea and nurtured a relationship between al-Azhar University and the *mahad* King Farouk in Asmara, whose graduates were admitted to al-Azhar.

HOUSES OF WORSHIP AND HOLY PLACES The Masjid al-Khulafa al-Rashideen, the grand mosque in Asmara, is the most prominent mosque in Eritrea. Several important Muslim shrines attract pilgrims, who visit to worship and to seek cures from sickness. These holy places include the shrines of Sheikh Alamin in Embereme, Sheikh Muzamil in Adi Itay, Sheikh Said Becri in Keren, Sheikh Abdelkadir in Asmara, Sheikh Yakub in Tifreria, Sheikh Abd Allah Salem near Addi Kerez, and Sheikh Mussa in Mareb.

WHAT IS SACRED? Like Muslims worldwide, Eritrean Muslims consider the Koran sacred. The space within the mosque may also be considered sacred; men must remove their shoes before entering, and women are generally prohibited from entering. The shrines of certain holy men are sacred to some Eritrean Muslims.

HOLIDAYS AND FESTIVALS The most important holidays for Eritrean Muslims are Ramadan, Id al-Adha (commemorating Ibrahim's willingness to sacrifice a son), and Id al-Mawlid (the Prophet's birthday). Muslims celebrate these days with special sermons at mosques and feasting at homes throughout Eritrea. Eritrean Muslims make *ziyaras,* special visits to the tombs of holy men, on specific days of the year. The most important *ziyaras* are associated with holy men of the Khatmiyya *tariqa* (Sufi brotherhood) and the Ad Shayke family. These pilgrimages attract people from all over the Eritrean lowlands, as well as some from the highlands.

MODE OF DRESS Eritrean Muslims are ethnically diverse and dress in a variety of ways. Jeberti men and women wear clothes similar to the Orthodox Christian *kedan Habesha* (Abyssinian dress). Jeberti men add a *kufyet* (Islamic skullcap) and an *imama* (a long piece of cloth wrapped around the head like a turban). Beneath their shawls, Jeberti women wear colorful veils known as *meqna'at* or *reshewan* that cover their faces. Rashaida men wear white cotton robes called *jubba* and a head cover called a *kufya,* while Raishaida women wear long black robes and hoodlike headdresses that cover their faces completely. Muslim Bilen women do not cover their heads at all and wear bright, colorful shawls and dresses. Bilen men wear the white tailored cotton trousers typical of Eritrean Orthodox Chistians. Some Eritrean Muslims have adapted new styles from the Gulf States and The Sudan.

DIETARY PRACTICES Eritrean Muslims are forbidden to drink alcohol and to eat pork and any other meat not slaughtered according to Islamic halal practices. Historically Eritrean Muslims and Christians did not share meals. Within the liberation fronts Muslims and Christians were expected to eat the same food, and the same expectation exists in such national institutions as Asmara University, a sign that food taboos dividing Muslims and Christians are breaking down.

RITUALS Like Muslims worldwide, devoted Eritrean Muslims are expected to recite the *shahadah* (a profession of faith: "There is no god but God [Allah], and Muhammad is the messenger of God"), give alms to the poor, fast during daylight hours in the month of Ramadan, and make a pilgrimage to Mecca at least once in their lifetime, if possible. They are expected to engage in ritual prayer five times a day. On Fridays Muslim men gather to say midday prayers communally in the mosque. Muslim women are directed to follow the same ritual observances as men, but they generally do not enter mosques. Eritrean Muslims also make *ziyaras,* specific visitations or pilgrimages to tombs of holy men.

RITES OF PASSAGE Eritrean Muslims span diverse cultural groups, and religion and cultural practices have become intertwined. Thus, within Eritrea what it means to be a Muslim varies considerably. A child's *semaya,* or naming day, is celebrated on the sixth or seventh day after birth with feasting and the sacrifice of an animal. The child's name is often taken from the Koran and may combine a prefix such as *abd* (servant) and one of the names of God. Both boys and girls are circumcised when they are still young, though the age varies. Female genital cutting among Muslims ranges from clitoridectomy to infibulation. Boy's circumcisions are attended by larger celebrations than girl's.

Marriage contracts are formalized in the mosque, where the bride is represented by a male relative. Marriage celebrations vary by ethnicity and wealth as well as between urban and rural areas. A death is marked by collective mourning at the family home followed by a funeral procession to a burial ground, where graves are unmarked. Women do not take part in the procession.

MEMBERSHIP Because Christians rarely convert to Islam in Eritrea, the main concern of Eritrean Muslims is not to recruit new members but to keep those who espouse the faith unified and practicing in accordance with orthodox beliefs.

SOCIAL JUSTICE Muslim Eritreans are enjoined by their religion to give alms (*zakat*) to the poor and to regard all Muslims as their spiritual equals. The rich often invite the poor to their homes to celebrate during holidays and give them money and gifts to celebrate in their own homes.

The Eritrean government has always offered Arabic schools to accommodate the wishes of Muslims, even during the war for independence, but the schools did not receive much support. Since 2000 the government has implemented a policy of primary education in the mother tongue (local indigenous languages) for all elementary school children. Many Muslims have resisted this policy. Muslim Eritreans are divided across many ethnic groups that do not share a common language. They want their children to be educated in Arabic, a language that came to Eritrea with Islam over a thousand years ago and that evokes strong feelings among Eritrean Muslims. They pray in Arabic, their religious leaders use Arabic in mosques, and their judges use it in administering Shari'ah law in Islamic courts. Many Muslim children study Arabic in *khalwa* (Islamic preschools). At the elementary school level, religious schools are not permitted, so some parents send their children to Arabic private schools.

Like most Orthodox Christians, Eritrean Muslims tends to be conservative, upholding tradition rather than advocating for social change or human rights.

SOCIAL ASPECTS While Islam permits men up to four wives at a time, most men do not exercise this right because of lack of resources. Polygyny was illegal under the Eritrean People's Liberation Front's (EPLF's) marriage law and was prohibited in the EPLF's 1977 constitution. The ban continued until Eritrean independence. Since then the government has said little about it, and there are no constitutional or civil codes banning it. It is becoming rare nonetheless.

Muslim principles dictate a traditional division of labor in the family, and Eritrean Muslim women have historically been less involved in work outside the home and in public affairs than Eritrean Christian women, but Muslim women have begun to participate in all arenas of life. Moreover, during the war for independence, Muslim women fought side by side with men in the Eritrean People's Liberation Front. Also since the 1960s, however, many Eritrean Muslims have been influenced by labor migration, exile, and refugee experiences in The Sudan and the Gulf States, where gender segregation is practiced more strictly.

POLITICAL IMPACT Islam has played an important role in Eritrean politics. Muslims were the first to agitate for independence from Christian-dominated Ethiopia, and many Eritrean Muslims feel alienated from the Christian-leaning government. In 1988 the Eritrean Islamic Jihad Movement broke off from the Eritrean Liberation Front because of its secularity and later splintered into competing political movements for Muslim rights, Harakat Alkas al-Islami al-Eritree (the Eritrean Islamic Salvation Movement, or EISM) and Harakat al-Islah al-Islami al-Eritree (the Eritrean Islamic Reform Movement, or EIRM). Both the EISM and the EIRM aim to unite Eritrean Muslims and establish an Islamic state, promising to safeguard the right of Christians to practice their religion within that state. Although many Muslims would not publicly reject either movement, neither has widespread popular support. Many find their programs too extreme and fear they create new divisions among Eritreans and further fragment the Muslim community. The movements serve to articulate some of the grievances of Eritrean Muslims clearly.

Muslims in Eritrea have also agitated for recognition of Arabic as a national language. Unlike the Tigrinya-speaking Christians, Eritrean Muslims are linguistically diverse and have difficulty making their voices heard at the national level. Arabic is not widely spoken in Eritrea, and few Eritreans are native speakers, but because it is the holy language of Islam, Arabic symbolizes the Muslim voice.

CONTROVERSIAL ISSUES Because Eritrean Muslims are a political minority, the main controversies that arise concern how to deal with the secular state. In its everyday practices the government encourages desegregation of men and women, and Muslims have reacted in different ways. Practices of secluding women and restricting their access to public spaces vary among Muslim communities in Eritrea. Bilen Muslims allow men and women to mix freely, while the rest of Eritrean Muslims practice segregation of men and women.

The state initiated National Youth Service in 1994, requiring all women and men eighteen years and older to undertake six months of military training and a year of work on national reconstruction. Many Muslim families have refused to send their daughters to participate in the National Youth Service on religious grounds. The government has not enforced its policies in places it has encountered resistance.

Although in many parts of the country the government has gradually introduced basic reforms—including banning forced marriages, discouraging female circumcision, instituting equal rights for men and women to initiate divorce, permitting abortion in cases of rape and incest, and allowing women the right to vote and participate in village councils and national assemblies—these reforms have not been imposed on regions where Muslims predominate. In some Muslim areas there has been resistance to teaching boys and girls together in government schools. The government has been flexible in implementing its reforms in order to avoid confrontation with Muslim communities.

CULTURAL IMPACT Arabian control of the now Eritrean Dahlak Islands, the port city of Massawa, and parts of the Eritrean coastline from the eighth and ninth centuries to the sixteenth century left many Islamic cultural imprints. Elaborate Arabic inscriptions adorn the Dahlak burial grounds. Islamic influence is most visible along the coast of the Red Sea, particularly in Massawa, where Islamic architecture dominates the old town. Massawa has three mosques: Masjid Abu Hanif, built in 1203; Masjid Sheikh Mudui ,built in 1503; and Masjid Hamal, built in 1543. The influence of later Turkish (1557–1846) and Egyptian (1846–1965) Islamic rule is also visible in Eritrean architecture.

Cultural contact between Eritrean Muslims and Muslims in neighboring regions is reflected in Eritrean music, which draws particularly on the rich heritage of Islamic musical traditions from the Sudan region and Egypt. Not all culture comes from outside; Muslims who speak Afar, Saho, and Tigre have their own traditions that may be defined as Eritrean Muslim culture.

ORTHODOX CHRISTIANITY

DATE OF ORIGIN Fourth century C.E.
NUMBER OF FOLLOWERS 1.8 million

HISTORY Orthodox Christianity came to Eritrea in the fourth century, when parts of present-day Eritrea and Tigray (a neighboring region of Ethiopia) formed the center of the powerful Christian kingdom of the Aksum. Eritrean Orthodox Christians were isolated from Orthodox Christians in the Middle East, North Africa, and the Greco-Byzantine empire, however, by the rise and spread of Islam throughout the region in the seventh century. The Christian Eritrean highlands were on the periphery of the Ethiopian empire, and inhabitants belonged to the Ethiopian Orthodox Church. In 1889 Italy took political authority over the Christian regions of Eritrea from Ethiopia, but the Eritrean Orthodox Church did not officially separate from the Ethiopian Orthodox Church until Eritrean independence in 1993.

The Eritrean Orthodox church is one of the six Oriental (lesser Eastern or pre- or ante-Chalcedonian) Orthodox churches, including the Coptic, Syrian, Armenian, Ethiopian, and (Indian) Malankara, that are in communion with each other.

EARLY AND MODERN LEADERS Abune (Bishop) Filipos (c.1323–1406) founded the most prestigious monastery in Eritrea, Debre Bizen (Place of Vision). The monastery prospered under his leadership, claiming nearly 900 monks around 1400 C.E.

Keshi (Reverend) Dimetrios Gebremariam, a twentieth-century Christian reformer, founded Mahaber Hawariat, a religious order that reformed church services and administration, introduced a new architectural style for churches in many parts of Eritrea, and sponsored a new translation of the Bible into Tigrinya that has gained wide acceptance. Gebremariam is also credited with converting many Kunamas (a small ethnic group in Eritrea who have continued to practice their own indigenous African religion) to the Orthodox faith.

Abune Filipos (born Aba Tewelde Berhan; 1905–2002) became the first patriarch of the Eritrean Orthodox Church in 1998. Filipos was ordained deacon in 1919 and joined the Debre Bizen monastery in 1929, serving as abbot of the monastery until 1990. In 1990 (when Eritrea was still part of Ethiopia) he was ordained to the episcopate as the bishop responsible for Ethiopian monasteries, and in 1991 he became the archbishop of Eritrea.

MAJOR THEOLOGIANS AND AUTHORS Abune Ewostatewos (Eustathius; 1273–1352), born in Tigray, Ethiopia, helped found monastic communities in Eritrea, preaching that spiritual autonomy required isolation from the state and society and asking his disciples not to rely on charity from their congregations or take donations from nobles. He advocated strict adherence to the teachings of Christ and, in his efforts to abolish non-Christian practices and beliefs, is believed to have uprooted 12 sanctified groves of trees dedicated to African gods. Ewostatewos also opposed the slave trade and condemned the rulers who were involved in it.

HOUSES OF WORSHIP AND HOLY PLACES Orthodox Christian churches are ubiquitous in Eritrea. The important monasteries in Eritrea include Debre Bizen, Debre Libanos, Debre Maryam, Debre Menkarios, and Debre Sina. The monasteries serve as centers of worship, prayer, and religious culture; they are famous for producing writings and paintings and as repositories of knowledge regarding law, history, and the grammar of the ancient religious language, Geez. The monasteries also train the priests who serve the various parishes throughout Eritrea.

WHAT IS SACRED? Eritrean Orthodox Christians regard the church as a sacred place and treat it with great solemnity. It is not uncommon to see men and women kissing the walls of the church and praying while touching the church walls. The *tabot*, which the followers believe to be a copy of the Holy Ark of the Covenant, is the most consecrated object in the religious ritual of the Mass.

HOLIDAYS AND FESTIVALS Saturday and Sunday are both sabbath days for Eritrean Orthodox Christians. The most important holidays are Leddet (Orthodox Christmas) on 7 January, Timket (Orthodox Epiphany) on 19 January, Fessika (Orthodox Easter) in the spring, Kedus Yohannes (Orthodox New Year) on 11 September, and Meskel (the Finding of the True Cross) on 27 September. Easter is venerated more than Christmas. The night before Christmas and Easter, priests conduct masses from late evening until midnight, when the congregation is blessed and allowed to break a month-long fast. The strictly religious break their fast by eating porridge with butter, spices, and yogurt. Early in the morning believers sacrifice a goat, sheep, or chicken, sometimes inviting the poor to a meal or giving them some meat from the sacrifice. Some families build a small hut of leaves and branches for receiving guests, covering the floors and the seats with leaves and bulrushes. The feast ends by sunset.

Each Eritrean Orthodox Christian village and urban neighborhood has its own patron saint. The saint's day is celebrated with a feast called *negdet* (pilgrimage), when people living away from their community customarily return.

MODE OF DRESS Many Eritrean Orthodox Christians wear Western-style clothing and reserve their traditional dress, called *kedan Habesha* (Abyssinian dress), for special occasions. Christian women's *kedan Habesha* is a long white dress of fine, hand-woven cotton with a fitted bodice and a full skirt, often with colorful embroidery at the hemline or down the center of the dress. A *netsela* (shawl) made from the same material is worn over the head and shoulders. Women sometimes wear *netsela* with Western clothing. During holidays women wear more elaborately embroidered shawls and dresses called *zuria*. Historically many Orthodox Christian women had an elaborate Orthodox cross tattooed on their forehead.

Traditional dress for Christian men consists of white cotton trousers that fit tightly from knee to ankle (resembling jodhpurs) and a tunic-like, long-sleeved, fitted white shirt. The men drape a white *netsela* around their shoulders and torso. Orthodox priests wear a version of this outfit with a headdress similar to a turban.

DIETARY PRACTICES Eritrean Orthodox Christians do not eat pork and regard hoofed animals, such as horses and donkeys, and birds other than chicken as similarly unclean and unsuitable for eating. These food taboos date from pre-Christian-era rulings in the Old Testament.

Orthodox Christians do not eat or drink from dawn to sunset during Lent, the fast of the Apostles, the fast of the Assumption, Advent, Epiphany, and the fast of Nivereh (which commemorates the preaching of Jonas). After dark they may eat vegetarian meals, including lentils, ground split peas, and vegetable stew. During nonfasting periods they abstain from eating meat and dairy products on Wednesdays and Fridays. Orthodox Christians will not eat meat slaughtered by a Muslim.

RITUALS Eritrean Orthodox Christians worship every day, removing their shoes before entering the church and sitting according to gender. A head priest, an assistant, and three deacons must be present to conduct a service. Pilgrimages to distant shrines, to monasteries (which prohibit all females, human and animal, from en-

tering), and to Jerusalem (where there is an ancient monastery) are highly valued.

During pregnancy Orthodox Christian women wear amulets in the shape of a cross to ward off spirits that might harm their unborn children. Christians pray constantly to Saint Mary (Mariam) to protect their children, who are seen as particularly vulnerable to spirit possession and other dangers that could cause sickness or death.

RITES OF PASSAGE The major rites of passage for Eritrean Orthodox Christians occur at birth, baptism, circumcision, confirmation, holy communion, marriage, and death. Visitors after a birth eat *gaat* (a thick wheat porridge), thank Saint Mary for the safety of mother and child, and often sing and dance around the two in celebration. The parents name the baby immediately, usually either taking a name directly from the Bible or combining a biblical names with a prefix, such as Gebre (servant; Gebremariam means "male servant of Saint Mary"), Wolete (servant; Woletemariam means "female servant of Saint Mary"), Tekle (plant), and Tesfa (hope).

Five to seven days after birth children of both genders are circumcised. Herbs and garlic are mixed and buried along with the excised flesh. Circumcision is regarded as a necessary procedure to make a child a proper male or female and is not marked by any special celebration. Female circumcision is slowly disappearing.

Orthodox Christian boys are baptized 40 days and girls 80 days after birth, and confirmation takes place right after baptism. The service ends with the priest tying a string of silk called a *mateb* around the child's neck, symbolizing membership in the church.

Marriages and deaths are consecrated with a mass before the wedding or burial.

MEMBERSHIP Children born to Eritrean Orthodox Christian families become members of the church through baptism, and others may convert through baptism at any time. The Eritrean Orthodox Church does not proselytize.

SOCIAL JUSTICE Most Eritrean Orthodox Christians are poor and find solace for their suffering in active membership in their religious communities. Churches provide shelter for destitute and homeless people, but Orthodox Christianity in Eritrea encourages acceptance of social hierarchies as ordained by divine authority. Inequality between men and women is institutionalized.

SOCIAL ASPECTS The Eritrean Orthodox Church recognizes only marriages conducted in the church and forbids polygamy as well as marriage between minors and between relatives within seven generations. It recognizes few grounds for divorce, but widows and widowers may remarry. Orthodox Christianity supports a traditional division of labor in the family, but in rural areas women work side by side with men in farming.

POLITICAL IMPACT While neither Orthodox Christianity nor its religious leaders hold great sway in Eritrean politics, Orthodox Christians have historically dominated Eritrea's political life. The ranks of the secular People's Front for Democracy and Justice (the rulers of Eritrea's one-party state) are drawn disproportionately from the highland Orthodox Christian population, presenting a serious challenge to Eritrea's national unity and political stability.

CONTROVERSIAL ISSUES Many young Orthodox Eritreans have found the teachings in traditional Geez and Geez-rite liturgies too arcane and have introduced masses in Tigrinya accompanied by more contemporary music played on electronic keyboards. Many have started debating a reform of the church, calling their movement *tehadso* (renewal movement), and have begun practicing charismatic forms of worship. The leadership of the Orthodox church has rebuffed and excommunicated these reformers, labeling them "Pente," meaning that they belong to the persecuted Pentecostal Church. As a result, many have joined existing Pentecostal churches. This process has opened up discussion of how to reform the Orthodox church and its centuries-old practices.

Other controversial issues have involved cultural practices involving weddings, funerals, and *tezkar* (remembrance of the dead). With the full cooperation of the priests of the Orthodox church, these public events have become increasingly expensive and extended (sometimes over several days), with little religious content or merit. For example, in addition to the immediate burial and mourning of the dead, depending on their age and social status, religious tradition calls for ceremonies to remember them after two weeks (*asur*), after 40 days, after six months, after a year (*tezkar*), and every year thereafter. Reform-minded religious leaders have attempted to streamline these traditions, with minor success.

CULTURAL IMPACT Contemporary artwork, music, and literature in Tigrinya reflect the legacy of Orthodox Christianity. Eritrean jewelry, textiles, and decorations of various kinds, including traditional tatoos, use the Orthodox cross as a motif. The Orthodox cross has many variations, but all are complex and ornate.

Religious chants called *zema* are an integral part of Eritrean Orthodox Christian rituals. *Zema* are chanted in Geez by a group of people and are often accompanied by various instruments, such as the *tsenatsel* (sistrum), *kebero* (a large drum), and hand bell.

Over the centuries Eritrean Orthodox Christian priests and monks have produced elaborate handwritten prayer books, scrolls, and other religious texts in Geez. The most famous manuscripts are the *Gadla Samaetat* (Acts of Martyrs) recorded between the fifth and the fifteenth centuries, some of which are believed to have been translated from Greek and Arabic. Many illuminated manuscripts are decorated with miniature paintings in what is known as the "Eustathian" style, named for Abuna Ewostatewos, and are believed to be the first paintings that show portraits of lay people, not just saints. The walls of churches and monasteries are also decorated with religious paintings, often depicting scenes from the lives of saints.

Other Religions

Adherents of all other religions combined make up only 10 percent of Eritrea's population, and some religions, like animism, are declining. Even though only a small sector of the Kunama ethnic group is still overtly practicing African animist religions, animism is indigenous to Eritrea, and most Christians and Muslims have integrated some animist practices into their beliefs.

Besides Islam and Orthodox Christianity, the Eritrean government recognizes Evangelical Christianity and Catholicism and allows adherents to practice freely and celebrate their holidays. The Evangelical Lutheran Church (Makene Yesus) was brought to Eritrea by Swedish Lutheran missionaries in 1886. Roman Catholicism was first introduced into Eritrea in the sixteenth century by Portuguese priests, but most of the conversions among the local population took place when the Italians reintroduced Catholicism into Eritrea in the nineteenth century during the colonial period. Because most of the its members were originally Orthodox Christians who accepted the pope of Rome as their spiritual leader, the Eritrean Catholic church is an Eastern Catholic, or Eastern Rite, church.

The ranks of Protestant churches are growing as some Orthodox Christians are attracted to what they perceive as a less conservative church. Protestantism was born in Eritrea when Haileab Tesfai (1846–76) founded a religious reform movement in the 1860s after studying a Bible translated into Amharic. Orthodox Christian priest's familiarity with the Bible had been limited by the rarity and expense of the handwritten Geez texts and by the fact that Geez was no longer spoken in the region; priests also used other sacred texts such as Haimanot Abew (the Book of the Faith of the Fathers) and the Apocrypha. Haileab argued that the Bible was the sole authority, that according to the Bible Christ was the only mediator with God, and that the Bible did not sanction certain Orthodox practices, such as the excessive veneration of the *tabot* (ark), the Virgin Mary, and the saints. Haileab and his followers were excommunicated from the Orthodox Church and founded the Evangelical Church of Eritrea.

Among Protestant Eritreans, a progressive reform movement called Mulu Wengel (Full Gospel) developed in the 1990s seeking to reduce hierarchy within the church and make Christianity more accessible and responsive to the masses. A very small number of Eritre-

ans are members of Seventh-day Adventist, Jehovah's Witness, Bahai, Hindu, and Buddhist churches.

Victoria Bernal and Tekle Woldemikael

See Also Vol. I: *Christianity, Islam, Sunnism*

Bibliography

Aren, Gustav. *Evangelical Pioneers in Ethiopia: Origins of the Evangelical Church Makene Yesus, 1898–1936.* Stockholm: EFS Forlaget; Addis Ababa: The Evangelical Church Makene Yesus, 1978.

Miran, Jonathan. "Islam in Eritrea: An Historical Overview." In *L'Erythree Contemporaine.* Edited by Marc Lavergne and Marie-Claude Simeone-Senelle. Paris: Karthala, 2003.

Miran, Jonathan, and R.S. O'Fahey. "The Islamic and Related Writings of Eritrea." In *Arabic Literature of Africa: The Writings of the Muslim Peoples of Northeastern Africa.* Compiled by R.S. O'Fahey. Leiden and Boston: Brill Academic Publisher, 2003.

Osthathios, Geevarghese Mar. "Oriental Orthodox Churches." In *Dictionary of the Ecumenical Movement.* Edited by Nicholas Lossky et al. Geneva: WCC Publications; Grand Rapids, Mich.: Eerdmans Publishing, 1991.

Trimingham, J.S. *Islam in Ethiopia.* London: Oxford University Press, 1952.

Wondmaegnehu, Aymro, and Joachim Motovu. *The Ethiopian Orthodox Church.* Addis Ababa: The Ethiopian Orthodox Mission, 1970.

Estonia

POPULATION 1,415,681

LUTHERAN 14.0 percent

ORTHODOX CHURCH 13.0 percent

OTHER CHRISTIAN 1.4 percent

JEHOVAH'S WITNESSES 0.3
  percent

MUSLIM 0.1 percent

ANIMIST 0.1 percent

ATHEIST 6.1 percent

OTHER RELIGIONS 0.2 percent

**RELIGIOUSLY INDIFFERENT OR
  UNDETERMINED** 64.8 percent

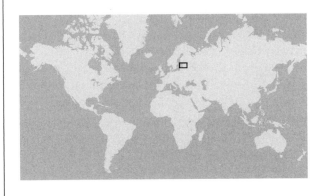

Country Overview

INTRODUCTION The Republic of Estonia is a small country in northern Europe on the coast of the Baltic Sea. To the north is the Gulf of Finland, to the east are Lake Peipus and Russia, and to the south is Latvia.

About 65 percent of the total population are ethnic Estonians. The second largest ethnic group is Russians (28 percent). Estonians belong to the Finno-Ugric linguistic family and have a language and ethnic identity different from their neighbors. Estonia was Christianized in the thirteenth century and became a part of Roman Catholic Europe until the Reformation when it converted to Lutheranism.

On 24 February 1918 Estonia declared itself independent from Russia. In 1940 Estonia was occupied by the Soviet Union. The Soviet state decimated the Estonian population through deportation and emigration, among other factors, leading to a loss of about a quarter of the total population. As a result of the several decades of Soviet occupation, with its atheist propaganda and hostility toward Christianity, most of the people became alienated from the church.

Over the years, as the Soviet Union gradually declined, Estonia's independence from Moscow increased. On 20 August 1991, after the collapse of the Soviet Union, the Estonian parliament passed a resolution reestablishing national independence. Church attendance and other religious activities increased explosively in the early 1990s, only to decline beginning in the mid-1990s.

RELIGIOUS TOLERANCE Estonia's constitution prohibits religious discrimination, as well as incitement to religious hatred, violence, and discrimination, and establishes every individual's freedom of conscience, religion, and thought. Estonia has no state church. Affiliation with churches and congregations is voluntary. Everyone has the right to observe religious rituals, either alone or

The Alexander Nevsky Cathedral in Estonia was built in the nineteenth century. The Orthodox Church in Estonia made considerable gains after Estonia's annexation to the Russian Empire. © JOHN D. NORMAN/CORBIS.

with others, provided they do not interfere with law and order, health, or morals.

Major Religion

CHRISTIANITY

DATE OF ORIGIN Early Thirteenth century C.E.
NUMBER OF FOLLOWERS 402,000

HISTORY Estonians first had contact with Christianity, from the West as well as East, more than a thousand years ago. It was not, however, until the thirteenth century, after the German and Danish crusaders conquered the country, that organized activity was begun, with the Roman Catholic Church founding three episcopates (in Tallinn, Tartu, and Saare-Lääne). Since the thirteenth century Estonia has sometimes been called Saint Mary's Land.

The Lutheran Reformation took hold of Estonia in 1524–25. The Lutheran movement, reinforced with

the ministry of the Moravian Brethren, consolidated the position of the formal church establishment to such an extent that it was regarded as a considerable power in society and its standards seen as the basis of Christian life until the nineteenth century. After the First Church Congress in 1917, the Lutheran Church became the Free People's Church, uniting 127 congregations with a membership totaling about 920,000.

The Orthodox Church in Estonia made considerable gains after Estonia's annexation to the Russian Empire in the Northern War (1700–21). The organization of Orthodoxy in Estonia started in 1850 when the Riga Diocese was established, accompanied by a wave of conversion from other denominations to the Orthodox Church. A second Orthodox church, the Estonian Apostolic Orthodox Church, recognized as an autonomous church under the Constantinople patriarchate, was created in the early 1920s. By the year 2000 the religious tradition enjoying the largest following in Estonia was Lutheranism, followed by Orthodoxy, the free church movement, and Roman Catholicism.

EARLY AND MODERN LEADERS Among the leaders of the Estonian "national awakening" movement of the mid-nineteenth century were several Lutheran pastors of Estonian ancestry, the most important being Jakob Hurt and Villem Reimann. Leaders of the twentieth century include Professor Johan Kõpp, founder of the Faculty of Theology at the University of Tartu and later the archbishop of the Estonian Evangelical Lutheran Church (EELC).

Prominent contemporary church leaders include Jaan Kiivit, Jr., archbishop of the EELC, and Einar Soone, bishop of the EELC and president of the Estonian Council of Churches. As of 2003 the Estonian Orthodox Church under the Moscow patriarchate was headed by Metropolitan Cornelius, and the Estonian Apostolic Orthodox Church under the Constantinople patriarchate was headed by Metropolitan Stephanus.

MAJOR THEOLOGIANS AND AUTHORS The heyday of Christian theology in Estonia was the nineteenth century, when the leading lights were Theodosius Harnack (practical theology), Maritz Engelhardt (church history), Alexander von Oettingen (systematic theology), and Karl Gustav Girgensohn (psychology of religion). The top names of twentieth-century Estonian theology were Uku Masing (the Old Testament, Semitic languages, and comparative theology), Artur Võõbus (the history of the Syrian Church), Elmar Salumaa (systematic theology), and Toomas Paul (the history of Estonian Bible translation).

HOUSES OF WORSHIP AND HOLY PLACES Christians hold their divine services in church buildings, prayer houses, or rented rooms. There are two nunneries in Estonia: the (Orthodox) Pühtitsa Mother of God's Dormition Convent at Kuremäe and the (Roman Catholic) Most Holy Savior of Saint Bridget's Convent at Pirita. The medieval sacred buildings are protected by the governmental Preservation of Antiquities Act. Pilistvere is home to an interesting sacred place for Estonians: a large pile of granite topped by a cross, established in 1988 in memory of the victims of Soviet repressions.

WHAT IS SACRED? For Christians the triune God is holy. Sociological surveys show that the image of God among Estonian high school students is relatively vague and rather anthropomorphic. It is common among the Estonians, a highly individualistic people, to have personal holidays and sacred places. Among sacred personal holidays are anniversaries of a loved one's death and of political (Communist) repressions. Personal sacred places include one's birthplace or graves of one's parents.

HOLIDAYS AND FESTIVALS The greatest holidays for Christians in Estonia are Christmas and Easter. Lighting a candle on the graves of loved ones has become a widespread tradition on Christmas Eve. Also important is Midsummer Day (24 June), or Saint John the Baptist's Day, which is celebrated as a family holiday and traditionally includes the lighting of the Midsummer Eve bonfire. Both the Christmas Eve and Midsummer Eve traditions appear to bear some relationship to the ancient pre-Christian celebrations of the winter and summer solstices.

The pre-Christian and Christian traditions are intertwined in the celebration of All Soul's Day (2 November), a day reserved for the remembrance of the dead. People traditionally light a candle in a window of their home.

In the Orthodox Setu County in southeastern Estonia, deceased loved ones are commemorated in the graveyard during religious holidays. On these occasions a table is laid on the grave; the feast is attended by relatives living both nearby and far away.

Somewhat unusual holidays of the popular calendar are Saint Martin's Day (10 November) and Saint Catherine's Day (25 November), when it is customary for children to wear costumes as they go from door to door wishing well to the families. The children sing songs, dance, and perform dramatic pieces in return for small gifts.

MODE OF DRESS The clergy of Estonian churches wear clerical garb in keeping with their ecclesiastical tradition. In the Lutheran Church the black gown has been supplanted by the white alb with several accessories (the stole, the *casula*, and so on). The churches that have traditionally avoided special attire, such as Baptists and Pentecostals, have increasingly adopted some elements of ecclesiastical garb (for example, the clerical collar and the alb). The centuries-old tradition of wearing special festive church clothes went into recession in recent times and is barely noticed today.

DIETARY PRACTICES Dietary practices are a form of Christian piety and, in Estonia, are important especially in the Orthodox and Roman Catholic churches, which observe fasting rules. Advent church members abstain from eating pork and drinking coffee.

The greatest church holidays are associated with traditional foods; for example, a traditional Christmas meal consists of blood sausage with sauerkraut and potatoes. So strong was the association of blood sausage with Christmas that the Soviet occupants prohibited its sale before and during the season. Another food prepared for Christmas is gingerbread. The traditional Easter meal is the sweet *pasha* made from curds. An integral ingredient of the Easter table is colored eggs (traditionally dyed using onion skins).

RITUALS As a rule religious services are held on Sunday mornings. Services start with the ringing of church bells. Since the late 1990s some 40 percent of the funerals and 10 percent of the weddings in Estonia have been ecclesiastical. The second period of independence, begun in 1991, has seen the emergence of the custom of consecrating memorials and new buildings, including private homes. Republic of Estonia anniversary celebrations traditionally involve divine services and military parades that include a short prayer. Going to the sauna is an old Estonian tradition. The sauna was a place for healing procedures, to give birth to children, and to die.

RITES OF PASSAGE The traditional rites of passage are baptisms, confirmation classes, weddings, and funerals. During the Soviet era participation in church ceremonies could result in repressions. Secular ceremonies were promoted as a counterbalance. Baptisms were replaced with secular name-giving ceremonies, confirmation camps with youth summer days, and church weddings with secular marriage registration procedures; furthermore, secular funeral services were introduced. All categories of church ceremonies experienced an exponential growth in the first years following the regaining of independence in 1991. Since 1995, however, a downward trend has been observed, although the number of child baptisms has continued to rise.

MEMBERSHIP Prior to the Soviet occupation the membership of the largest church, the Estonian Evangelical Lutheran Church, amounted to more than 80 percent of the total population. The subsequent discrimination against the church, and the massive Soviet atheistic propaganda, led to a drastic decline in membership.

In contemporary Estonia, where only about 28 percent of the population are church members, various missionary activities are undertaken. The Estonian Evangelical Alliance, founded in 1991, is striving to coordinate and facilitate ecumenical evangelization efforts. All the churches organize evangelization weekends and outreach programs for special target groups, such as youths or families. Various media are used in attracting new members. Two Christian radio stations, Family Radio and Radio 7, are engaged in reaching a larger audience. About 40 Christian publishers issue theological literature.

SOCIAL JUSTICE Christian churches play a weighty role in social welfare programs. Soup kitchens and shelters run by churches provide support to poor and needy people. Chaplains extend their services to prisons. Churches have been actively involved in the development of religious education in the schools. School religious education is nonconfessional and essentially ecumenical. This is seen as a guarantee of the protection of the basic principle of religious freedom.

SOCIAL ASPECTS In Estonia 56 percent of marriages end in divorce. An important message of the church is emphasizing the value of marriage and family. Many churches run children's Sunday school and youth groups, which advocate the virtues of a stable family.

POLITICAL IMPACT The government and the parliament are secular in Estonia, yet there are Christians among the members of both. Christian values have been explicitly advocated by Isamaaliit (Pro Patria Union) and Eesti Kristlik Rahvapartei (Estonian Christian People's Party). The latter unites Christians from different churches; however, being a small party, it has no representation in the parliament. Although there is no state church in Estonia, the government signed cooperation protocols with the Estonian Evangelical Lutheran Church in 1995 and the Estonian Council of Churches in 2002. The Lutheran Church has set up a committee for promoting cooperation with the state.

CONTROVERSIAL ISSUES The Roman Catholic Church has explicitly opposed euthanasia and abortion. The ordination of women has been introduced in practice only in the Lutheran Church (since 1967), which, as of 2003, had 18 women ministers.

A much-debated issue in Estonia since the 1990s has been religious education, currently taught as an optional subject in about 70 (of some 700) schools. Religious education has been defined as a nonconfessional and essentially ecumenical discipline, the purpose of which is imparting knowledge about different religions and contributing to the moral development of the student. The tradition of nonconfessional religious education in Estonian schools dates back to the early 1920s. During the Soviet period religious education was banned from schools.

CULTURAL IMPACT The earliest Estonian-language book preserved to date is a translation of Martin Luther's *Small Catechism* printed in 1535. The translation of the Bible has had a major impact on the Estonian literary language. The first translation of the entire Bible into Estonian was published in 1739. The Lutheran principle that every Christian should be able to read the Scriptures gave rise to a network of peasant schools in the late seventeenth century. The history of high school education in Estonia goes back to 1583 (at a Jesuit seminary in Tartu). Higher education in theology has been provided in Estonia since 1632, when a university (Academia Gustaviana) was established in Tartu.

Lutheran pastors played a prominent role in the Estonian "national awakening" of the mid-nineteenth century. Pastor Jakob Hurt initiated the Estonian folklore collection campaign in the 1880s, resulting in one of the most voluminous folklore archives on the globe.

The church music practice gave birth in 1869 to the magnificent song festival tradition, which continues to this day and can boast of choirs featuring as many as 30,000 singers at nationwide song festivals. The Christian message wrapped in the medium of music has played a remarkable role in Estonian culture through the work of such celebrated composers as Rudolf Tobias (1873–1918), Arvo Pärt (born in 1935), and Urmas Sisask (born in 1960).

Other Religions

There has been a rise in non-Christian religions and religious movements since the 1990s. Estonia today has about 50 religious groups. Most of these, representing social movements, do not have their own organizations. Apart from Christians there are Muslims, Jews, Bahais, Buddhists, and Hindus. The Estonian Islamic Congregation has slightly more than 1,400 members and unites both Sunnites and Shiites. Jews in Estonia have founded three congregations. Orthodox Judaism is represented by the Estonian Jewish Congregation, which dates its establishment back to 1856. The Progressive Jewish Congregation in Tallinn and the Jewish Progressive Congregation Gineni in Narva have been active since 1992.

One Bahai, one Hindu, and three Buddhist congregations operate in Estonia. Their memberships range from a few dozen to a few hundred. The congregations are run by ethnic Estonian leaders.

The earth-worship movement, which pursues the restoration of ancient pagan religion, is experiencing a renaissance. Currently the movement has a couple hundred adherents. It is formally represented by the House of the Earthen Realm of Taara Worshipers and Earth Worshipers, founded in 1995. Taara worshipers emphasize the value of the ancient Estonian worldview and the secret knowledge handed down from generation to generation. Earth worshipers consider it important for humans to be bonded to the earth they live on. Humans can accumulate the energy necessary for their development from the surrounding natural environment.

Tõnu Lehtsaar and Pille Valk

See Also Vol. 1: *Christianity, Lutheranism, Eastern Orthodoxy*

Bibliography

Au, Ilmo, and Ringo Ringvee. *Kirikud ja kogudused Eestis.* Tallinn: Ilo, 2000.

Kulmar, Tartmo, Urmas Petti, and Alar Laats. "Eesti teoloogia ajalugu." In *Encyclopedia Estonica.* Vol. 11. Tallinn: Eesti Entsüklopeediakirjastus, 2002.

Lehtsaar, Tõnu. "Why Do People Join Churches in Estonia?" *Religion in Eastern Europe* 4 (1997): 1–9.

Liiman, Raigo. *Usklikkus muutuvas Eesti ühiskonnas.* Tartu: Tartu University Press, 2002.

Salo, Vello. "The Struggle between the State and the Church: A Case Study of a Soviet Republic." In *The Estonian SSR.* Boulder, Colo.: Westview, 1978.

Valk, Pille. "From Soviet Atheism to National Identity: A Specific Background for the Religious Education in Estonia." *Panorama: International Journal of Comparative Religious Education and Values* 12, no. 1 (2000): 78–93.

Valk, Pille, and Tõnu Lehtsaar. "Developments of Practical Theology in Today's Estonia." *International Journal of Practical Theology* 7, no. 1 (2003): 101–30.

Ethiopia

POPULATION 65,892,000

ETHIOPIAN ORTHODOX CHURCH
48 percent

ISLAM 34 percent

EVANGELICAL/CHARISMATIC 12
percent

NEO-CHARISMATIC 0.5 percent

ROMAN CATHOLIC 1.5 percent

INDIGENOUS RELIGIONS 4 percent

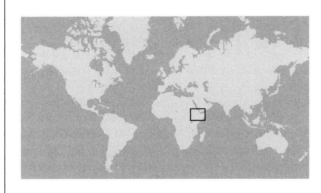

Country Overview

INTRODUCTION The Federal Democratic Republic of Ethiopia, located in eastern Africa, is home to some 81 distinct ethnic groups. It is bordered by Eritrea to the north, The Sudan to the west, Kenya to the south, and Somalia and Djibouti to the east. To the north, beyond Eritrea, is the Red Sea. Most of Ethiopia's culturally diverse population resides on a great mountain massif, usually well watered by rain that provides ample water for irrigation projects in the western and eastern lowlands.

Ethiopia has been a religious battleground for centuries. Christianity penetrated the Axumite Kingdom in northern Ethiopia in the fourth century. When Islam was first launched in Arabia in the seventh century, persecuted followers of Muhammad fled to Axum for refuge. The peaceful coexistence between Christians and Muslims was short lived, as the Muslims soon cut both the east and west Axumite trade routes by controlling the Red Sea. The armed Axumite response initiated a retaliatory jihad by the Muslims. Eventually Christian Axum was encircled and weakened by Islamic sultanates. In the ninth century Queen Guedit, a pagan from the south, invaded Axum, further weakening Christianity there. Reportedly churches were burned, Christians were enslaved, and Christian practice was nearly obliterated. It was during this dark age that historian Gibbon wrote, "Encompassed on all sides by the enemies of their religion, the Aethiopians slept near a thousand years, forgetful of the world by whom they were forgotten." The Axumite's only relations with other Christians during this time was with the Coptic Church of Egypt, from whom they received their bishop.

These dark ages revealed the resilience of Christianity. The Christian movement shifted further south, and a new heartland was established in Lasta, where it lasted for over a century. In the thirteenth century an indigenous Abyssinian Christianity emerged, as did the Abyssinian nation. The thirteenth-century document *Kibre Nagast* (The Glory of the Kings), which unites Ethiopian royalty to the Old Testament Solomonic dynasty, became an Ethiopian mythology that bound Ethiopia to ancient Israel. Orthodox Christianity dominated the religious terrain of Ethiopia until the fall of Haile Selassie I in 1974.

RELIGIOUS TOLERANCE Until 1977 the Ethiopian Orthodox Church (EOC), the largest of the five Oriental Orthodox branches, was the state church of Ethiopia. The constitution now guarantees freedom of religion, which has helped bring about a genuine respect for those with different religious practices and traditions. Even so, the EOC remains a strong public presence in the country. The Orthodox church liturgy can be heard over loudspeakers several mornings a week, and Muslims are called daily to 5:00 A.M. prayers. Charismatic churches have also installed high-powered speaker systems that herald their joyful songs into the surrounding neighborhoods every Sunday morning.

Major Religions

ETHIOPIAN ORTHODOX CHURCH

ISLAM

ETHIOPIAN ORTHODOX CHURCH

DATE OF ORIGIN 327 C.E.
NUMBER OF FOLLOWERS 31,628,000

HISTORY Around 320 C.E. Christianity was brought to the Axumite court by two Syrian lads, Frumentius and Aedisius, whose ship was plundered off the Red Sea coast. The king of Axum, Ezana, eventually forsook the cult worship of the *arwe,* depicted in ancient Ethiopian art as a dragon with four legs. The mythology of the Orthodox Church shows Saint George mounted on his white horse spearing the dragon. King Ezana proclaimed Christianity as the court religion. Written documents verify that Frumentius was appointed bishop (*Abun*) of Axum by St. Athanasius of Alexandria. This initiated the EOC's 1,600-year ecclesiastical dependency on the Egyptian Coptic Church for their bishop. In 1959 the last Egyptian bishop withdrew from Ethiopia.

This ancient African church displayed tenacious endurance. A sixteenth century jihad, launched from eastern Ethiopia with the assistance of Ottoman soldiers and firearms, practically devastated Ethiopia's rich cultural and spiritual heritage. The intervention of 400 Portuguese armed soldiers in 1541 eventually pushed

Men line up during a religious service outside of Saint Mary's, the oldest and most revered of all churches in Ethiopia. It dates back to the sixth century and is believed to be the repository of the Old Testament Ark of the Covenant. © CORBIS SYGMA.

back the Islamic threat, but not before a significant number of Christian communities in the north converted to Islam.

The isolation of the EOC within its mountain strongholds, surrounded on three sides by Muslim sultanates, has been a significant factor in the indigenization of the EOC. Through the centuries, as the church and state moved south, it was inevitable that traditional religious belief systems found their way into church practice.

Prior to 1974 being a true Ethiopian meant one was a member of the Ethiopian Orthodox Christian church. As the church expanded into the south, where traditional religion and Islam were predominant, many converts to the EOC were given a Christian name. Emperor Haile Selassie I was the last king of this ancient dynasty; he was overthrown in 1974 by the Dergue, a military group with Marxist-Leninist leanings. Supported by the Soviet Union, this dictatorship remained in power until 1991, when the Soviet Union collapsed. In 1994 the Ethiopian government hammered out a constitution that ensured a republican form of government, guaranteed sovereignty for each of the nine Ethiopian nation-states, and assured every Ethiopian citizen religious freedom.

Significant ecclesiastical reforms were instituted during the reigns of Yekuno Amlak (1270–85), Zara Yaeqob (1434–68), Tewodros II (1855–68), Yohannes IV (1871–89), and Haile Selassie I (1930–74).

EARLY AND MODERN LEADERS After the initial evangelization of the Axumite Kingdom in the fourth century, the "Nine Saints" arrived from Syria in the late fifth century. Their distinct contributions were the founding of monasteries, the translation of the Bible from the Syriac into Geez (the Semitic language of the Axumites), and the development of the Geez liturgy, which was subsequently refined by their student, Yared. His creative church liturgy and hymns have been handed down through the centuries and, to this day, lift the spirits of the faithful.

The reading of Psalms and the Lives of the Saints has promoted religious piety within the EOC. The most significant of these dozens of extant biographies are those of Anthony (d. 356; written by St. Athanasius of Alexandria), Tekle Haymanote (d. 1313), and Ewostatewos (d. 1352). A devotional book handed down from the fourteenth century, the *synkessar*, has an appropriate reading for each day of the Ethiopian calendar.

A significant EOC leader, Abba Walde Tensae (d. 1998), conducted a healing ministry in Woliso, 110 kilometers (68 miles) west of Addis Ababa, for some 40 years. With the blessing of the EOC hierarchy, this ministry brought faith and healing to thousands.

MAJOR THEOLOGIANS AND AUTHORS The majority of contemporary EOC scholars write from a perspective of defending the faith against the inroads historically made by Catholics and presently being made by the growing "New Church Movement" of Charismatic Evangelicals. Because church communication is in Amharic, a language unknown outside Ethiopia, there is minimal written theological debate with international Christian communities. A respected and renowned British-educated theologian, writer, and teacher within the EOC is Seifu Sellassie Yohannes. Another renowned teacher is Abba Gebre Sellassie of Saint Paul's Theological Seminary. The holy lives and teachings of EOC theologians at the Holy Trinity Theological College in Addis Ababa are making a strong impact on the next generation of EOC leadership.

Influential EOC religious magazines that are read by urbanites include *Smeha Tsiiq* (Witness of Righteous Truth) and *Hamer* (The Ark), published by Maheber Qedusan. Readers tend to be zealous, educated young people intent on retaining the traditions and teaching of the EOC while modernizing the church's management. Several religious books by Archbishop Shenouda III, of the Coptic Church of Alexandria, have been translated into Amharic.

HOUSES OF WORSHIP AND HOLY PLACES The Ethiopian Orthodox Church has more than 32,000 places of worship, usually constructed on promontories, which also serve as burial sites for the faithful. The walls of many churches contain biblical frescoes, which have been a source of religious enrichment for a basically nonliterate society. The majority of churches are located in the northern regions of Tegrai, Wollo, and Amhara.

Since 1991 fifteen new EOC structures have been erected in Addis Ababa—several of enormous size. The eleven rock-hewn churches at Lalibela, constructed in the twelfth century, are a proud heritage of the EOC and a growing tourist attraction. The oldest and most revered of all churches is that of Saint Mary's in Axum. It dates back to the sixth century and is believed to be the repository of the Old Testament Ark of the Covenant, which holds the two tablets of the law given to Moses. It is estimated that there are more than 800 EOC monasteries, the most ancient and famous of these being Debre Damo in Tegrai (sixth century), Debre Libanos in Amhara (thirteenth century), and Debre Bizan in Tegrai (fourteenth century). These monasteries continue to play a significant role in the ecclesiastical life and spirituality of the EOC.

Annual pilgrimages are made to the following shrines named after angels, holy saints, and Mary: Lalibela (in Lasta), Geshen Maryam (in Wollo), Qulube (near Harrar), Axum (in Tegrai), Debre Libanos (north of Addis Ababa), and the Zuqwala monastery (located on a volcanic promontory south of Addis Ababa).

WHAT IS SACRED? Every Orthodox church is sacred, as it contains a replica of the authentic Ark of the Covenant, which the faithful believe is presently housed in Saint Mary's Church at Axum. Every devout EOC follower gives obeisance to the ark when passing by an Orthodox church because therein dwells the presence of God. Priests carry a small silver cross with which they bless the faithful. In respect to that which is holy, members will kiss the cross. As Patriarch Paulos said, "Everything is religious in Ethiopian tradition. The songs, the salutations of the people—everything is so deeply biblical."

HOLIDAYS AND FESTIVALS The Ethiopian liturgical calendar is replete with church holidays. Of the 30 days in each month in the Ethiopian calendar, 12 are set aside as holy days on which certain saints or divinities are honored. Each month no work is performed and the faithful fast on the following days: the birth of Mariam, day one; the Nine Saints, day five; the Trinity, day seven; Michael, day twelve; Grace or Righteousness, day sixteen; Gabriel, day nineteen; Mariam, day twenty-one; St. Giorgis, day twenty-three; Holy Savior of the World, day twenty-seven; Emmanuel, day twenty-eight; and the Day of God, day twenty-nine. During a fast no meat or dairy products are to be eaten until 3:00 P.M.

In addition to the above, nationally honored church holidays include Lideta (Christmas), Timqet (the baptism of Jesus), Fasika (Good Friday and Easter), and Meskel (the finding of the true cross). Fifty-five days prior to Fasika, all EOC members are to fast. No weddings are performed during this Lenten period. The most joyous festival is Meskel, celebrated soon after the beginning of the Ethiopian calendar year (mid-September), when all members of every household light a bundle of sticks and dance around it.

MODE OF DRESS The Ethiopian Orthodox Church does not prescribe a particular mode of dress for men and women. Women worshipers wear a head covering and white shawl to church. Ordinarily Ethiopian men and women dress in Western clothing. On special EOC holidays the men wear a white tunic and jodhpurs with a white shawl draped over their shoulders. Women dress in white dresses and shawls with ornately embroidered borders. Educated EOC young people are adopting modern dress that often shocks their elders.

DIETARY PRACTICES Because the EOC has an uncritical reverence toward the Old Testament, members of the EOC strictly follow the dietary regulations specified in Leviticus. Thus, pork is forbidden. Approved animals must be properly slaughtered and bled. EOC members look upon the lax eating habits of non-Christians with disgust. For example, the pastoralist cattle herders along the Omo River drink the mixed blood and milk of their cattle, and the Nilotic Gumuz residing along the Blue

Nile River eat rats and snakes. Rigid fasting from all animal products during EOC holy days is observed by all EOC members except pregnant women and small children.

RITUALS The church and monastery are the centers of Orthodox spirituality. The faithful are called to worship at the church on Sunday and on the special holy days designated for each of the saints. Like that of the Egyptian Coptic Church, the EOC Eucharist Liturgy is conducted reverently, with colorful pageantry, music and bells, smoking incense, and the choreography of robed priests circling the altar. Many of the faithful spend the entire night in the precincts of the church offering prayers of thanksgiving to saints. Menstruating women are forbidden to enter into the church compound. Shoes must be removed before entering the church. Ritual fasting is demanded of all the faithful; every Wednesday and Friday are prescribed fast days. There are more than a hundred other holy days, including the Easter Lenten period.

RITES OF PASSAGE EOC families initiate the membership of their infants into the church through the rite of baptism. Infant males are inducted by baptism 40 days after birth, and infant girls are baptized 80 days after birth. Adult converts are baptized after receiving catechetic instruction from a priest.

A church wedding, which includes the liturgy, demands that a couple remain together until death. At death the church assumes the responsibility of assuring the soul safe passage to heaven. The deceased must be buried in a churchyard or within the confines of a well-known monastery. *Teskar* is celebrated 80 days after death, when the priests usher the soul into heaven by special prayers. Seven years after death there is another religious celebration of remembrance.

MEMBERSHIP Children baptized into the EOC are assigned a local church priest as a spiritual father (*nefs abat*). Adult converts from indigenous religions or Islam are first taught the five Pillars of the Faith (the Trinity, the incarnation of Jesus, baptism, the Eucharist, and the life hereafter), after which they may be baptized and appointed a priest who is "the father of their soul." The growth of the EOC is mainly biological and not through overt evangelism, as it was in previous decades among those of traditional religions or Islam. The media are not used in outreach to the non-EOC population. Dignified burial within the confines of an EOC church is a means of retaining membership of the elderly. EOC membership among Ethiopian young people is declining, as a growing number are converting to Islam in order to find lucrative jobs in Arab countries.

SOCIAL JUSTICE In centuries past Ethiopian monarchs headed both church and state and so were the final court of appeal in judicial matters. The *Fetha Nagast*, a traditional legal code based on canon and civil laws compiled in medieval Egypt, has served as a legal source in court decisions. Though there is now separation of church and state, the EOC continues to have an impact on judicial matters in Ethiopia.

SOCIAL ASPECTS Prior to 1950 nearly all primary education was provided by EOC priests in church schools. With modernization the Ethiopian government and EOC missions have established hundreds of schools. In efforts to curb the widespread incidence of HIV and AIDS, the EOC is attempting to bring about behavioral change through moral teaching.

The social structure of Ethiopian society is imbued with the Orthodox teaching of the sanctity of monogamous marriage and wholesome family life. Priests in local EOC parishes continue to teach respect for the elders, care of the dying, and the close supervision of young people until they are married.

POLITICAL IMPACT From the fourth century to 1974 the Ethiopian church and state were melded together. During these centuries the EOC had a profound political impact upon Ethiopian society. In more recent years religion has had an impact on politics indirectly through EOC members who hold significant government portfolios.

CONTROVERSIAL ISSUES In centuries past the nature of Christ and the keeping of the Sabbath were disputed within the EOC. At the end of the nineteenth century Emperors Yohannes IV and Menelik II settled these issues by adopting the *Tewahido* doctrine of Christ's united divine and human natures. Sunday, not Saturday, was proclaimed the day of worship.

Since the fourteenth century the religious community known as Beita Esrael has been a constant nuisance to the EOC because of its quasi–Old Testament practices. This community, known as Falasha to outsiders, pursues a Judaistic faith modeled after the institutions of the Hebrew Scriptures. Since the 1990s thousands of the Beit Esrael have been airlifted to Israel to become full-fledged Jews, an action questioned by Ethiopian authorities.

In modern times the issue of abortion has been debated in the Ethiopian parliament. Religious leaders continue to argue against abortion, upholding the sanctity of the lives of the unborn. Other aspects of modern life have intruded into Ethiopia, posing a challenge to EOC clerics, most of whom attempt to retain the ancient traditions of the church. Educated EOC youth have struggled with church leaders to make their Orthodox faith relevant in a rapidly changing society.

CULTURAL IMPACT Because the church has had a deep and pervasive impact on Ethiopia for more than sixteen centuries, all Ethiopians living in the highlands have been influenced by EOC culture. Only the Muslim Affar, the Somalis in the eastern lowlands, and the indigenous religionist ethnic groups residing along the Omo River have not been influenced by Orthodox culture in a significant manner.

The Orthodox Church has had a significant influence on the arts in Ethiopia. The interior walls of most local Orthodox churches are painted with beautiful murals having biblical motifs. Church music continues to influence contemporary popular music in Ethiopia.

ISLAM

DATE OF ORIGIN Seventh century C.E.
NUMBER OF FOLLOWERS 22,403,000

HISTORY Muslims first arrived in Ethiopia in the seventh century, during the lifetime of Muhammad, when about a hundred Muslim refugees fled from Arabia and were given refuge by the Christian King of Axum. From the seventh century Muslims were traders along the Red Sea. During the sixteenth century, a time of Islamic military expansion in Ethiopia, Ahmed bin Ibrahim, from the Muslim sultanate of Adal, rallied around him Affar and Somali clans. Ibrahim used Turkish firearms to make a jihad into the Orthodox highlands, where hundreds of churches were plundered; under threat of death many Orthodox Christians converted to Islam. It took the recruitment of 400 Portuguese musketeers to overcome the Muslims in Christian Abyssinia. There remained, however, significant pockets of loyal Muslims in Wollo and Tegrai.

Islam in Ethiopia has not been a single coherent system. Sufi teachers spread Islam, and over the centuries Sufism developed into several distinct, regional orders, each with its own sheikhs. Over time, as Sufism gained popularity, important sheikhs came to be regarded as saints endowed with the power of healing; they were deified after death, and their tombs became centers of worship.

Abyssinian rulers continued to be wary of Muslims. In 1668 King Yohannes I restricted Muslim residence within cities and forbade them to own land. By 1855 Emperor Tewodoros threatened expulsion and attempted to convert the Muslims to the Orthodox faith. In 1878 Emperor Yohannes IV went further, issuing an edict to force all Muslims to embrace Christianity. In 1886 some 20,000 Muslims who refused to become Christians were put to death.

EARLY AND MODERN LEADERS Christian emperors Menelik II (reigned 1889–1913) and Haile Selassie I (reigned 1930–74) were more tolerant toward their Muslim subjects. Muslims were granted freedom of worship but were still denied rights given to Christians. Under the Dergue regime (1974–91) Muslims achieved true equality. Muslim holy days were recognized as national holidays. Since 1994 the Ethiopian constitution has made no religious distinction among citizens. Restrictions on travel to Mecca have been lifted, and censorship of imported religious literature has been repealed. The Ethiopian Muslim Youth Association has been given official permission to organize. Modern influential Islamic teachers in Ethiopia include Emom Noweye, Hadj Abdul Nassir, and Afif Abdulfetah Tebari.

MAJOR THEOLOGIANS AND AUTHORS At Islamic educational centers in Addis Ababa, Harar, and Wollo, an orthodox form of Sunni Islam has been preserved, and cultural and religious links with the outside Islamic world have been retained. Ethiopian scholars working at these centers have produced an indigenous and popular Islamic literature. These scholars include Emom Noweye, Negussu Nejash, Dr. Amdurah Rephed, Afif Abdulfetan Tebari, and Hadj Abdul Nassir, whose work has been widely distributed.

HOUSES OF WORSHIP AND HOLY PLACES Mosques are located in all urban centers and in Muslim-populated areas in the countryside; the faithful attend worship every Friday. The most significant Muslim shrine is the Sheikh Hussein tomb in Bale region, visited by thousands of pilgrims each year. Other important shrines are the Faraqasa pilgrimage centre in Arsi region, as well as the sanctuary of Gata and the shrine of Jama Negus, both located in Wollo region.

WHAT IS SACRED? The Koran is the most sacred object for Ethiopian Muslims. Selected texts of the Koran are tied as amulets onto the arms of the faithful. Each mosque, with its fenced compound, is also sacred territory from which women are barred.

Pre-Islamic and indigenous religious elements have been incorporated into Ethiopian Islam and made holy. Natural springs whose water is believed to have healing powers are now venerated and given Arabic names. Oxen are sacrificed by the graves of ancestors, and songs in praise of Sheikh Hussein are sung in eastern Ethiopia. Islamic burial sites are revered as holy places.

HOLIDAYS AND FESTIVALS In 1991 the Ethiopian government declared three Islamic holy days as national holidays. The first, Id al-Fitr, is a three-day celebration, with feasting, the giving of alms to poor relatives, and gifts of cakes, dates, wheat, and money. It marks the end of Ramadan, the Muslim month of fasting. Keeping the fast is one of the Five Pillars of Islam. During the month-long fast Muslims abstain from all food, drink, tobacco, sexual relations, and other indulgences during the daylight hours. Children under eight and pregnant or nursing women are exempt from fasting. In Ethiopia Id al-Fitr is sometimes mistakenly called Ramadan.

The second, Id al-Adha (called Arafa in Ethiopia), marks the end of the hajj, the annual pilgrimage to Mecca. Communal prayers are made, and at the mosque the imam sacrifices a sheep on behalf of the community. Later in the day each family will kill a sheep, a camel, or an ox as a sacrifice on behalf of the family. The meat is shared with neighbors or the poor. Muslims then visit nearby shrines, where they offer prayers.

The third national Islamic holiday is Mawlid, the birthday of Muhammad. On this day Ethiopian Muslims join street processions that include the singing of epic poems recounting the life of Muhammad. Modern Wahhabi teachers have attempted to suppress this unorthodox levity.

MODE OF DRESS Since 1991 the government policy of freedom of religion has allowed Ethiopian Muslims to wear flowing white robes and the white *kofia* on their heads. It is customary for Muslim women to cover their heads with a white shawl. In recent years the fanatical Wahhabi sect prescribed a strict dress code among Muslims, stressing that women must wear long, black *burka*s (dresses) with headgear that covers all but their eyes. There is a growing sentiment among Ethiopian Somalis against this imposed mode of dress.

DIETARY PRACTICES Only meat slaughtered by a Muslim religious leader may be eaten by Muslims. Pork is forbidden, though camel meat is a delicacy for highland Muslims.

RITUALS Before a Muslim male enters the precincts of the mosque to pray, he must wash his hands, feet, ears, and nose. Ethiopian Muslims also practice the Five Pillars of the Faith, which include prayer five times a day, giving of alms to the poor, fasting on holy days, pilgrimages, and the jihad. These are community rituals and are not meant to impose on the inner spiritual life of the individual, which is a private matter.

RITES OF PASSAGE Soon after the birth of a child, parents take the infant to the mosque and, with several other families, prepare a sumptuous feast that is eaten by the clergy and parents. The child is given a name at this feast. At puberty, children of both sexes are circumcised. Muslim weddings are another rite of passage. Two or three days after the wedding feast, a sheikh performs the *lika* (covenant) between the bride and groom. The final rite is observed at death, when the clergy perform an elaborate religious ceremony, lasting several days, to usher the soul into paradise, after which a gravestone is erected.

MEMBERSHIP Ethiopian Muslims do not actively seek members. In modern Ethiopia a person gains membership in the Muslim community when born into a Muslim family. Young people are gradually assimilated into the faith by initially observing the *tsalat* (prayers) five times a day. Some young people from the EOC are converting to Islam in order to work in Saudi Arabia. These converts change their name and swear allegiance to Allah.

SOCIAL JUSTICE Shariah (Islamic law), especially as it concerns the family, is practiced in some Ethiopian Islamic communities with the consent of the Ethiopian government. Shariah is thought to bring stability to Muslim society, but in Ethiopia Christians strongly oppose any form of its national imposition.

SOCIAL ASPECTS Among developments affecting Muslim families has been the opening of Muslim kindergartens and elementary schools in urban areas. Ethiopian Muslims have also been offered scholarships to Saudi Arabia's Islamic universities. Young scholars returning from these universities have become the new clergy at Ethiopian mosques, replacing the older, uneducated sheikhs.

Muslims have also organized nongovernmental social services, such as food aid and medical care, providing help to families in depressed areas of Ethiopia. In general, the status of women is lowest in the most orthodox Muslim communities.

POLITICAL IMPACT The Supreme Council of Islamic Affairs, given legal status by the government in 1992, provides guidance on religious matters. Internal struggles emerged in 1995, climaxing in a clash between Muslims and the Addis Ababa police at the al-Anwar mosque. Under the supervision of the Ethiopian government, new elections were held to replace members of the Supreme Council, leading some Muslims to complain of government interference in the internal affairs of the council.

CONTROVERSIAL ISSUES Throughout much of its history Islam in Ethiopia did not undermine the traditional worldview of the Oromo and other peoples in the country. There was, in fact, a symbiosis between the traditional indigenous religion and Islamic Sufi teaching. Ethiopia's young, elite Wahhabi teachers, however, are promulgating a strict orthodoxy, which is being resisted by the older generation of Ethiopian Muslims, who are reluctant to let go of their belief in indigenous gods and to accept only Allah. Young sheikhs are also putting pressure on traditionalists to forsake their worship at shrines and at tombs of the ancestors. Zealous Muslims have molested pilgrims worshiping at the Sheikh Hussein shrine in Bale.

CULTURAL IMPACT In recent times the Ethiopian government has granted new freedoms to the Muslim community. Restrictions on importing of religious literature have been repealed. The Ethiopian Muslim Youth Association now produces the magazine *Dawa*, and additional Islamic publishing houses have been established in Addis Ababa. The overwhelming majority of Islamic publications are Amharic translations of religious Islamic material from Arabic and English. The writings of the popular South African Islamic activist and debater Ahmed Deedad are also being translated into Amharic. The great influx of Islamic magazines and books in Amharic, Oromifa, and other Ethiopian languages is informing educated Ethiopian Muslims about Islamic dogmas and practice.

Other Religions

The first Jesuit missionaries arrived in Ethiopia in the sixteenth century with the goal of bringing Ethiopian Christianity into the Roman Catholic fold. After a popular uprising in 1632, the Jesuits were evicted from the country. They were followed in the mid-eighteenth century by Catholic missionaries, who established several ministries.

When Haile Selassie I became emperor in 1930, the Catholics were invited to expand their educational and medical services. But despite the significant Catholic resources invested in Ethiopia, the Catholic Church has not gained a large or vibrant indigenous following. Catholics have erected large churches in urban centers of the Southern Nations region, and the clerics of these parish churches are without doubt the most highly trained in Ethiopia, particularly compared with EOC or Evangelical clerics.

Protestant English and German missionaries entered Ethiopia in the nineteenth century. Their goal was to build a relationship with the EOC and assist in its spiritual development by introducing the Amharic Scriptures. Ethiopian clerics, however, were mistrustful of the Protestants.

In 1991 the Evangelical Churches Fellowship of Ethiopia was formalized. There are now seventeen denominations cooperating in this organization. The two largest denominations are the Ethiopian Kale Heywet Church (KHC) and the Ethiopian Evangelical Church, or Mekane Yesus (EECMY). The KHC has its roots in an interdenominational mission agency called SIM International, which began operations in Ethiopia in 1927. SIM's goal was to launch new churches among the indigenous religionists of southern Ethiopia. The EECMY evolved in 1959 from Lutheran missionaries, who came to Ethiopia from Norway, Denmark, Germa-

ny, and the United States after the Italian occupation of the country (1935–41).

Smaller church groups arose from Baptist, Mennonite, Pentecostal, Brethren, and other mission agencies. Under the Marxist/Leninist Dergue government (1974–91), the new churches came under attack. Though they were ordered to be closed, Evangelicals began meeting in houses.

An indigenous charismatic movement, calling itself Mulu Wengeil (Full Gospel), evolved among Ethiopian university students in the mid-1960s. One of their lasting contributions to the Evangelical movement was the emergence of a new, creative, and indigenous church hymnody, which helped maintain spiritual passion during Communist rule. Following the downfall of the Dergue in 1991 and the granting of freedom of worship, a sense of true ecumenism grew among the Evangelicals. An enthusiastic, charismatic style of worship became common to all these churches, with special evenings set aside for healing and the casting out of evil spirits. The Evangelicals have even launched the Ethiopian Graduate School of Theology in Addis Ababa.

A growing religious group in Ethiopia since 1970 has been the Hawariat Beit Kristian (Jesus Only Church). The creed of this neo-charismatic group is non-Trinitarian. They owe their unusual popularity among Ethiopians to their synthesis of charismatic Christianity and indigenous religious belief and practice.

Each year there is a worldwide gathering of Rastafarians in Shashemane, south of Addis Ababa. The original, small Jamaican community arrived in Ethiopia around 1960 to honor Emperor Haile Selassie I (before his 1930 coronation he was known as Ras Teferi), whom they considered a Messiah. Saturday worship is conducted at the group's large, New Jerusalem temple in Shashemane.

The indigenous Ethiopian religion teaches a four-tier cosmology. The "high god" (having different names in different ethnic groups) dwells at the highest level. The second tier is home to benevolent spirits to whom invocations are made for wealth, peace, or offspring. The third tier is that of the ancestor spirits who are appeased by annual offerings of butter and grain. In the fourth tier resides the malevolent spirit, *shaytan*, who must be appeased, often with blood sacrifice, to avoid harm. With modernization and the spread of Evangelical Christianity, many indigenous religionists have converted to Christianity and, to a lesser extent, Islam.

E. Paul Balisky

See Also Vol. I: *Christianity, Coptic Christianity, Eastern Orthodoxy, Islam*

Bibliography

Aren, Gustav. *Envoys of the Gospel in Ethiopia.* Stockholm: EFS Forlag, 1999.

Balisky, Lila W. "Theology in Song: Ethiopia's Tesfaye Gabbiso." *Missiology* 25, no. 4 (1997).

Crummey, Donald. *Priests and Politicians: Protestant and Catholic Missions in Orthodox Ethiopia, 1830–1868.* Oxford: Clarendon Press, 1972.

Eide, Oyvind. *Revolution and Religion in Ethiopia.* Addis Ababa: James Currey, 2000.

Fargher, Brian L. *The Origins of the New Churches Movement in Southern Ethiopia, 1927–1944.* Leiden: E.J. Brill, 1996.

Ibrahim Idis. "Freedom of Religion and Secularization of State: The Legal Status of the Islamic Law and Shariat Courts in Ethiopia." In *Proceedings of the 12th International Conference of Ethiopian Studies.* East Lansing, Mich., 1994.

Kaplan, Steven. *The Monastic Holy Man and the Christianization of Early Solomonic Ethiopia.* Wiesbaden: Franz Steiner Verlag, 1984.

Pankhurst, Richard. *The Social History of Ethiopia.* Addis Ababa: Institute of Ethiopian Studies, 1990.

Sergew Hable Sellassie. *The Church of Ethiopia.* Addis Ababa: United Printers, 1970.

Taddesse Tamrat. *Church and State in Ethiopia.* Oxford: Oxford University Press, 1972.

———. "Ethiopia, the Red Sea, and the Horn." In *Cambridge History of Africa.* Vol. 3. Edited by Roland Oliver. Cambridge: Cambridge University Press, 1977.

Trimingham, J. Spencer. *Islam in Ethiopia.* London: Oxford University Press, 1952.

Ullendorff, Edward. *The Ethiopians: An Introduction to Country and People.* London: Oxford University Press, 1960.

Fiji

POPULATION 856,346

CHRISTIAN 54.9 percent

HINDU 36.6 percent

MUSLIM 7.7 percent

OTHER 0.8 percent

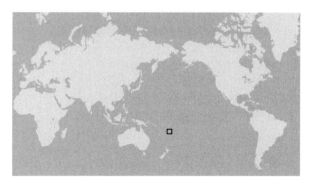

Country Overview

INTRODUCTION The more than 300 islands that make up the Republic of the Fiji Islands (known as the "crossroads of the Pacific") lie some 1,300 miles north of Auckland, New Zealand, and include include a mixture of Polynesian, Melanesian, and Indian cultures. Fiji's multiracial population is divided between Fijians, who are indigenous Pacific Islanders (51 percent); Indo-Fijians, largely descendants of indentured workers from India (46 percent); and small percentages of Europeans, Chinese, and Rotumans and other Pacific Islanders. The bulk of Fiji's citizens reside on the three largest islands—Viti Levu, Vanua Levu, and Taveuni—and a majority live on Viti Levu, where the capital city, Suva,

is located. English is the official language, but Fijian and Hindi are spoken in 94 percent of the households. There are several dialects of Fijian, the dominant being Bauan. The economy is large agricultural.

Contacts with Western explorers began as early as the seventeenth century, and in 1874 Fiji became a crown colony of Britain. Fiji became independent in 1970, adopting a bicameral parliament modeled on the Westminster system. Democratic rule was disrupted by Fijian-led coups in 1987 and again in 2000. After a period of turmoil following the 2000 coup, in which Fiji's first Indo-Fijian prime minister was ousted, Fijian politicians emerged victorious in the 2001 elections.

An overwhelming majority of the country's Christians are Fijians, and more than two-thirds of Fijians are Methodists. By contrast, virtually all Hindus, Muslims, and Sikhs are Indo-Fijians, with heavy concentrations on western Viti Levu and on Vanua Levu. The country's military is almost completely Fijian (99 percent), and a majority of soldiers are Methodists.

RELIGIOUS TOLERANCE The 1997 Fijian constitution provides for freedom of religion, and civil authorities have generally respected this right in practice. Although there is a general climate of religious tolerance, shortly after the 1987 coups, which were led by a Methodist lay preacher, a ban was introduced on all unofficial travel, business, and recreational activity on Sunday, including public celebrations by Hindus. Ecumenical and interfaith groups perform joint services for Independence Day celebrations. They also have denounced incidents of vandalism and desecration of Hindu, Muslim, and Roman Catholic worship sites.

The chief of a Fijian village holds the tabua *(whale's tooth). Perhaps the most sacred symbol in Fijian culture, exchange of the* tabua *symbolizes respect, acceptance, forgiveness, and an ironclad social bond between parties.*
© ANDERS RYMAN/CORBIS.

Major Religions

CHRISTIANITY

HINDUISM

CHRISTIANITY

DATE OF ORIGIN 1830 C.E.
NUMBER OF FOLLOWERS 470,100

HISTORY The first Christian missionaries, three Tahitians, arrived in Fiji in 1830. Sent by the London Missionary Society, they laid the foundation for the first Wesleyan missionaries—the Englishmen William Cross and David Cargill—who arrived in 1835. Assisted by Tongan missionaries, Cross and Cargill soon established a printing press, and the Scriptures were translated into the Bauan dialect. Following the conversion of the most powerful chief in 1854, Christianity spread rapidly throughout Fiji, and by 1875 there were more than 900 churches and 1,400 village schools. In 1977

the Methodist Church became wholly autonomous, and its leadership is completely local. Fijian Methodist missionaries are sent to other islands in the Pacific and the Caribbean.

The first Catholic missionaries—Marists from France—arrived in Fiji in 1844, but the first permanent sanctuary was not built until 1878. Nuns from the Missionary Sisters of Mary opened schools in 1885. During the twentieth century Irish priests began to succeed French missionaries, and the first Fijian priest was ordained in 1939. By 1966 the Catholic Church had grown to 40,000 members, the Archdiocese of Suva was established, and there was a proliferation of religious orders, lay movements, and schools, including the Pacific Regional Seminary.

Since the 1960s the Assemblies of God has been the fastest growing religious group, increasing membership 10-fold. The Seventh-day Adventists, who began work in Fiji in 1891, quadrupled their number of churches in the last four decades of the twentieth century. The growth of the Methodist and Anglican churches, however, has fallen below the rates of population increase.

EARLY AND MODERN LEADERS Although William Cross and David Cargill are legendary Wesleyan figures in Fiji, other missionaries were prominent later in the nineteenth century. The most notorious may have been Thomas Baker, the only missionary to be killed in Fiji, when, according to legend, he insulted a chief by touching his head. Another Wesleyan, Hannah Dudley, the first Australian missionary of any denomination in Fiji, established circuits of churches among Indo-Fijians. Josateki Koroi and Manasa Lasaro, successive presidents of the Methodist Church, were embroiled in highly publicized divisions in the 1980s, with the latter's Christian nationalist agenda gaining ascendancy.

Archbishop Petero Mataca was appointed in the late twentieth century to oversee the Archdiocese of Suva. At the time of the 1987 military coups, the Fijian nationalists Inoke Kubuabola, a Baptist lay preacher, and Tomasi Raikivi, a Methodist minister, headed the Fiji Council of Churches, which consisted of seven churches, including Roman Catholics.

MAJOR THEOLOGIANS AND AUTHORS Paula Niukula, a former president of the Methodist Church, Sevati Tuwere, a former president of the church and the principal of the Pacific Theological College (PTC), and

Jovili Meo, also a former principal of the PTC, are among a growing number of emerging Fijian theologians. Niukula, who died in the mid-1990s, is best known for his critical reflections on the role of the church in the 1987 coups. Tuwere has written on the theology of the *vanua* (the land), relating indigenous concepts of church and culture to Western theologies. Meo has written a number of articles on theology and Christian education. Kevin Barr, a Catholic priest, has published research on urban poverty and on the social and political impact of right-wing fundamentalism on religious life in Fiji.

HOUSES OF WORSHIP AND HOLY PLACES Christians in Fiji gather in various types of churches, from a huge, ornate cathedral in Suva to small, modest parish buildings in rural areas. Several sanctuaries, such as the quaint Saint Andrew's Presbyterian Church in Suva, are modeled on nineteenth-century European architectural designs. Village churches are adorned with elements of Pacific culture, including decorative mats, carved wooden crucifixes, and leis constructed of native flora. The Samoan Congregational Church in Suva is built in the shape of a turtle, an important indigenous religious symbol. The Levuka Church of the Holy Redeemer, built in 1904 to commemorate Queen Victoria's Diamond Jubilee, was the first Anglican church of stone in the western Pacific. The open-air Catholic chapel at the Pacific Regional Seminary contains numerous carvings of indigenous symbols.

WHAT IS SACRED? Fijians have integrated Christian sacred symbols, such as the Bible and eucharistic elements, with indigenous cultural and religious symbols. Important church meetings entail gathering around a *tanoa* bowl, a receptacle used for drinking *yaqona*, which is prepared from the root of the kava plant. According to legend, *yaqona* was given to Fijians by the ancient god Degei. In lengthy speeches associated with formal *yaqona* ceremonies, there are references to the sacredness of ancient ancestral spirits and of the *vanua* (the land and everything associated with it). The *tabua* (whale's tooth) is perhaps the most sacred symbol in Fijian culture. Its exchange symbolizes respect, acceptance, forgiveness, and an ironclad social bond between parties. In some cases the *tabua* has been Christianized by using it in the context of a church ritual. Similarly, on rare occasions coconuts are substituted for the wine and bread in Communion services.

HOLIDAYS AND FESTIVALS In addition to Christmas, Good Friday, and Easter, Christians in Fiji celebrate local secular holidays, such as the Bula (Hello, or Good Day), sugar, and hibiscus festivals, as well as the birthdays of Queen Elizabeth II and Prince Charles. Since *kerekere* (the giving and receiving of gifts) is so much a regular part of Fijian life, Christmas focuses primarily on a quiet meal among friends. Vestiges of the ancient Fijian festival of the first fruits continue in harvest services, in which Christians lay the best of their new crops at the altar. Although many Christians deny belief in the traditional *vu* (ancestors), important community leaders continue to be venerated in memorials spoken on festival occasions. Christians sometimes join interfaith celebrations associated with Hindu and Muslim holidays, which are official public holidays.

MODE OF DRESS Christian men in Fiji generally wear the *sulu*, a rectangular piece of cloth about two yards long. For church services men combine Western and indigenous styles by wearing a *sulu* wrapped around the waist in combination with a white shirt, tie, and suit coat. Women, who are expected to dress modestly, wear full-length white dresses and hats and cover their shoulders and legs. For formal occasions men wear a gray or black kiltlike garment, called a *sulu vakataga,* and women wear a two-piece ankle-length dress called a *sulu-i-va.* Both men and women wear black for 100 days following a death in the family. A bride occasionally wears a traditional Fijian skirt of dried leaves, but such indigenous costumes are increasingly associated with the tourist industry. Western-style clothing is popular with the young.

DIETARY PRACTICES The diet of most Christians in Fiji is determined by regional availability, not religious prescription, and is heavily based on starches. Some Christians are vegetarians. A few groups, such as Seventh-day Adventists, reject pork and stimulants and do not drink *yaqona,* although it is widely consumed by Christians.

RITUALS Mainline Christian worship services in Fiji are generally solemn affairs, patterned after missionary styles and emphasizing prayers, liturgical readings and responses, sermons, announcements, and singing. In the Methodist Church it is not infrequent for the Sunday morning service to last two or more hours and for members to remain or return for additional, often livelier, services in the evening. Catholic Masses are less lengthy and are performed at various times during the week. Many Christians continue to conduct weekday family prayers at dusk, at which a senior male leads devotions in the home. Christians participate in an annual ecumenical prayer festival.

Girls in Fiji traditionally underwent the *veiqia*, a prolonged and painful initiation into adulthood that entailed elaborate tattooing of the pubic area. Boys endured the initiation of circumcision and proved their manhood by killing an enemy. Killings are now outlawed, but remnants of tattooing and circumcision continue. The practices have steadily diminished, however, although some tattooing has been revived.

RITES OF PASSAGE If a family has the means, a person's 21st birthday is marked with an elaborate ceremony that includes speeches, feasting, and dancing. Births are similarly celebrated. Fijian weddings are large communal affairs, at which the groom's relatives present numerous gifts (especially fine mats and foodstuffs), there is feasting and drinking of *yaqona*, and the bride and groom consummate the marriage. In some rural areas the sheet on which the couple have intercourse is examined to verify the virginity of the bride.

Funerals involve two or three days of visits to the family of the deceased by various constituencies, all of whom bring mats and foodstuffs prior to the actual service. The church service itself varies in length and content, depending on the status of the deceased, and many dignitaries, in addition to family members, may give lengthy eulogies. At the graveside service hymns are sung while the casket is covered with dirt, and a feast follows.

MEMBERSHIP Because the vast majority of Christians are Fijians and most services are conducted in the Fijian language, there are strong links between church membership and ethnic identity. Nevertheless, some church broadcasts are in English, and there are missionary activities directed toward Indian converts.

SOCIAL JUSTICE Following the 1987 coups, a small group of Christians, along with Hindus and Muslims, established Interfaith Dialogue of Fiji as a way of seeking ethnic and racial unity. During the 1990s the Fiji Council of Churches, through its Research Institute, sought to promote social justice by collecting and disseminating data on the positions of Fiji's major political parties on such issues as land tenure, racism, and

women's rights. Nevertheless, since the Fiji constitution provides for an ethnically based electoral system that mandates special protections for indigenous Fijians, most of whom are Christian, the constitution is partial to Christians.

SOCIAL ASPECTS Fijian Christians identify with *vanua* (understood in terms of particular land areas), the Fijian people as a whole, and a complex traditional social structure that is made up of various levels of kin-based units and other groups in which persons trace their lineages to common ancestors. Obligations link Fijians to chiefs associated with the land and the district. Thus, Fijian Christians are expected to behave according to *vakaturaga* (chiefly norms and values), which include respect, deference, humility, loyalty, honesty, togetherness, love, and kindness. Fijians are free to choose their spouses, and although the vows are exchanged in churches, weddings also include elaborate cultural celebrations.

Christianity has generally been more affected by Fijian culture than vice versa, although the early missionaries obliterated certain practices, such as cannibalism and mutilation rituals, while introducing such Western values as radical individualism and capitalism. Chiefs and teachers, as well as pastors, are recognized as leaders of rural communities. Christian teachings regarding human rights in general and the value of women in particular have been reflected in the establishment of ecumenical social action groups sponsored by the Fiji Council of Churches and the Pacific Conference of Churches.

POLITICAL IMPACT The Methodist Church is supported by a majority of the country's chiefs and thus remains influential in the Fijian community, especially in rural areas. In addition, in collusion with allied political parties, the Methodist Church has continued to work to establish a Christian state. The Methodist Church, however, experienced deep divisions in 1988–89 when dissidents set up roadblocks to protest a relaxation of the Sunday decree (which forbid certain activities on Sunday), were temporarily jailed, and later seized control of the church. In 2000 Tomasi Kanilagi, head of the Methodist Church, publicly declared his intention to use the church as a forum under which to unite all ethnic Fijian political parties for the 2001 elections.

CONTROVERSIAL ISSUES Although a few women have been ordained in the Methodist Church, they have not been assigned to the more prestigious congregations. The church's control of large landholdings remains a highly sensitive issue, since Fijians communally hold more than 80 percent of the land. Among questions debated by Christians are whether or not pastors and priests should consume *yaqona* on a regular basis, the legitimacy of homosexuality as an alternative sexual orientation, the impact of modern Western values on traditional culture, and relations with Indo-Fijians.

CULTURAL IMPACT Christianity has had an impact on several aspects of Fijian culture, especially by instituting the strict observance of Sunday as a day of rest, free from virtually all commercial and organized sporting activities. While some of the early missionaries sought to eliminate indigenous dancing, and some features were effectively stopped, dancing has continued to be a key element in Fijian artistic expression. Many Methodists condemned the use of tobacco and the chewing of betel nuts, although *yaqona* has kept a respected place among island Methodists. The Methodists also established annual choir competitions that blend Western Christian hymns with traditional Fijian musical forms.

HINDUISM

DATE OF ORIGIN 1879 C.E.
NUMBER OF FOLLOWERS 313,422

HISTORY Hinduism was the main religion of the indentured laborers (*girmits*) taken to Fiji to work sugarcane plantations beginning in 1879. There was also some free migration from India that included Hindus and small numbers of Muslims and Sikhs. Hindu beliefs and practices in Fiji vary according to the parts of India from which the migrants came. At the end of the indenture system in 1920, many *girmits* became small farmers on leased land, although those from Gujarat and Punjab tended to go into business. A strike by sugarcane workers in 1921 divided the Indian community, with the Sanatani, who were orthodox Hindus and who worshiped several deities, becoming distinct from the Arya Samaj, a monotheistic reformist sect. Political division between the two has continued to the present, although without rancor. Indo-Fijians today adhere to one of the many sects of Hinduism that developed during the twentieth century.

By the time of Fijian independence in 1970, Hindu migrants and their descendants formed close to 50 percent of the population. After the 1987 coups, however, a significant number of Indo-Fijians left to establish communities in Australia, New Zealand, Canada, and elsewhere.

EARLY AND MODERN LEADERS In the 1920s Sadhu Bashishth Muni led the Sanatanis in Fiji, while later Vishna Deo became prominent as a supporter of the Arya Samaj sect. Today Harish Sharma and Kanilesh Arya, respectively, are leaders of the two groups.

MAJOR THEOLOGIANS AND AUTHORS There are no major Indo-Fijian theologians. Sadhus and holy men and women from India have visited periodically, and their influences have resulted in the establishment of several sects, such as Hare Krishna, Divine Life Society, and Sai Baba. Among both immigrants and those born in Fiji, Mahatma Gandhi's influence has remained strong, particularly for his ideas on nonviolence and self-sufficiency and his anti-British stance. The Ramayana is a major holy text for Sanatanis.

HOUSES OF WORSHIP AND HOLY PLACES Every Hindu home in Fiji has its shrine where prayers (*puja*) are said each day. Each Indian settlement has two or three centrally located *mandap*s, places where the community worships with a learned man called a pandit. There are temples in major settlement areas. In some sects the home of a community leader becomes the place of worship.

WHAT IS SACRED? Orthodox Sanatanis in Fiji practice a Brahmanical form of Hinduism, with emphasis on vegetarianism, cleanliness, and ritual worship. Bhakti (devotion to a deity) supported by *shloka*s (sacred words) is central to the faith. The cow is revered by Hindus in Fiji, and cow dung is considered clean. The coconut tree is a symbol of the continuity of the family, and the coconut is considered the purest offering, while rice symbolizes fertility.

HOLIDAYS AND FESTIVALS Diwali (Festival of Lights) is celebrated widely among Hindus in Fiji. This festival celebrates the Indian New Year, in which Lakshmi, the goddess of fortune, is invoked to watch over everyone for the coming year. Holi (Festival of Colors) is a spring festival in which an effigy of a witch is burned and special songs are sung, while participants go from house to house spraying one another with colored water. The birthdays of Rama and Krishna also are celebrated. The festival of Tazia, in remembrance of forebears who arrived in Fiji during indenture, is no longer observed.

MODE OF DRESS The traditional dress for Indo-Fiji men included the *kurta* (a cap), lioncloth (dhoti), and *pagri* (long shirt). Women wore a *lahanga*, a long dress with pantaloons, together with an *orhni*, or shawl. Today men wear the dhoti and some women the sari mainly on religious and high public occasions.

DIETARY PRACTICES Indo-Fijians have continued the practice of vegetarianism, setting aside special days when no meat is eaten. Because the cow is regarded as holy, beef is avoided by strict Sanatanis. Special sweets and vegetables are distributed during the major festivals.

RITUALS Indo-Fijian rituals vary among the different sects. Prayers for the gods Sayanarayan and Hanuman are led by a family priest or a pandit under a mango tree. In villages and urban communities Hindus come together to recite the Ramayana. These recitals reinforce ancestral beliefs, with Rama as the model man. Readings of other holy texts are important community rituals. Firecrackers are used to mark special occasions.

Fire walking, said to have arrived with migrants from South India, is an annual purification rite that acknowledges Maya Devi (Great Mother). Preparation includes body piercing as well as sexual abstinence and dietary restrictions. Today fire walking is performed by Fijians for tourists, but this should not be confused with the Indo-Fijian ritual.

RITES OF PASSAGE For Indo-Fijians special rites mark pregnancy and births, weddings, and funerals. On the sixth day after birth a ceremony is performed by a priest, and gifts are given and the child introduced to the world. The child receives the appropriate astrological sign, and a grandparent suggests a name. During indenture children began to be named for gods, following a practice in parts of India.

The marriage ceremony in Fiji lasts three days, with the man being washed ritually by his family and rubbed with turmeric and oil. The throwing of unhusked rice (*lawa bhijni*) into the fire marks the beginning of the ceremony, which takes place on the village *mandap*.

Cremation takes place over a funeral pyre soaked in ghee and lit by the oldest son. Camphor and incense are used to ignite, maintain, and cleanse the fire. The bones and ashes of the deceased are collected by the family to be scattered with flowers on a river. For the following 13 days the family and adherents perform rituals.

MEMBERSHIP Any increase in the numbers of Indo-Fijians comes from births or from migration from India. Hindus do not actively seek to increase membership by mission, although recruitment practices vary among the several sects.

SOCIAL JUSTICE Although some Indo-Fijians are now fifth-generation residents, marginalization remains a problem. In the debate over a new constitution, beginning in the 1990s, Indo-Fijians have expressed their desire for the power to exercise basic human rights and for a share in decision making.

Since the end of indenture, growing sugarcane and vegetables has been the main source of livelihood for many Indo-Fijians. Land leases restricted to 30 years, however, have thwarted attempts at agricultural development. Although access to government schools was initially restricted, education has improved through the establishment of Indo-Fijian schools in which both the language and religious practices are part of the curriculum. At the same time, more than 50 percent of Indo-Fijian households in both urban and rural areas fall in the lowest income category. This is caused by low prices for sugarcane and by difficulties in gaining employment in urban areas.

SOCIAL ASPECTS The caste system has been displaced in Fiji, but the family, supported by religious practices, has remained a strong feature of Indo-Fijian life. Families in rural areas live in settlements, with the households established amid their lands and at some distance from neighbors. Families are tightly bonded to one another, as well as to the region in which they have become established. Each settlement has its own pandit and *mandap*.

Because migrants came from different geographical areas of India, the Hindu caste system broke down in Fiji. There emerged a taboo on marriage between those who had come on the same ship, however, as they were considered to belong to the same family. Intercultural marriages are still rare, and Sanatanis tend not to marry Arya Samajis. Likewise, Hindus tend not to marry Muslims, and *girmits* generally do not marry those who came as free migrants.

POLITICAL IMPACT Although Indo-Fijians are seen as an ethnic bloc in opposition to other Fijians, they share key political goals, including concern for Fiji as a nation and the desire for a harmonious life. Nonetheless, the division between Sanatanis and Arya Samajis has prevented the emergence of strong Indo-Fijian leadership and been a deterrent to political development.

CONTROVERSIAL ISSUES In the discussion over a new constitution, political representation for Indo-Fijians remains a difficult issue. The various Hindu sects in Fiji have their own positions on political representation, however, and their leaders are not united. Indo-Fijians also see access to resources, especially land, as key to their long-term future.

Abuse of women among Indo-Fijians was particularly marked in the early days, and even today cultural practices continue to restrict women from wider community participation. Very few Indo-Fijian women are able to have a career, and beginning in the 1980s, prostitution became a problem in urban areas. Although Indo-Fijian women at the University of the South Pacific, in Suva, share levels of success with male students, they find it harder to succeed after graduation. Access to government scholarships for education overseas is difficult for all Indo-Fijians.

There is debate among Indo-Fijians over the option of leaving Fiji and their heritage. Some businessmen have decided to leave and start again elsewhere. Others have chosen to stay, despite concern for the security of their children and themselves.

CULTURAL IMPACT Many Hindu practices have been incorporated into everyday life in Fiji. Major events, such as Constitution Day, include Indo-Fijian ceremonies, dancing, dress, and food. Thus, the impact of the various Hindu groups that have developed in Fiji has been widespread. Despite the divisiveness of the coups of 1987 and 2000, the ideology and rituals of Hindus are by and large respected.

Other Religions

The Muslims of Fiji form the largest single Islamic community among Pacific Island countries. They worship in numerous green and white mosques found primarily in cane-growing areas. There also are small number of Sikhs who have migrated from India.

Nancy J. Pollock

See Also Vol. I: *Christianity, Hinduism*

Bibliography

Derrick, Ronald A. *A History of Fiji.* Suva: Government Press, 1946.

Ernst, Manfred. *Winds of Change.* Suva: Pacific Council of Churches, 1994.

Gillion, K.L. *Fiji Indians: Challenge to European Dominance, 1920–1946.* Canberra: Australian National University Press, 1977.

———. *Fiji's Indian Migrants: A History to the End of Indenture in 1920.* Melbourne: Oxford University Press, 1962.

Katz, Richard. *The Straight Path: A Story of Healing and Transformation in Fiji.* Cambridge, Mass.: Addison-Wesley, 1993.

Lal, Brij V. *Girmityas: The Origins of the Fiji Indians.* Canberra: Journal of Pacific History, 1983.

Mavor, J.E., ed. *Traditional Belief and the Christian Faith.* Suva: Lotu Pasifika Productions, 1977.

Ravuvu, Asesela D. *The Fijian Way of Life.* Suva: University of the South Pacific, Institute of Pacific Studies, 1983.

Reed, A.W., and I. Hames. *Myths and Legends of Fiji and Rotuma.* Auckland: Reed Books, 1967.

Sanadhya, Totaram. *My Twenty-one Years in the Fiji Islands.* Suva: Fiji Museum, 1991.

Subramani, ed. *The Indo-Fijian Experience.* Saint Lucia, Australia: University of Queensland Press, 1979.

Thornley, Andrew, and Tauga Vulaono, eds. *Mai Kea Ki Vei?—Stories of Methodism in Fiji and Rotuma.* Suva: Fiji Methodist Church, 1996.

Tuwere, Ilaitia Sevati. *Vanua: Towards a Fijian Theology of Peace.* Suva: University of the South Pacific, Institute of Pacific Studies; Auckland: College of Saint John the Evangelist, 2002.

Wood, A.H. *Overseas Missions of the Australian Methodist Church, Fiji.* Vol 2. Melbourne: Aldersgate Press, 1978.

Finland

POPULATION 5,183,545

EVANGELICAL LUTHERAN 84.9
   percent

ORTHODOX CHRISTIAN 1.1 percent

PENTECOSTAL 1 percent

OTHER 1.1 percent

NONAFFILIATED 11.9 percent

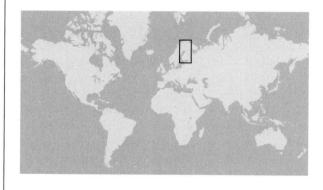

Country Overview

INTRODUCTION Situated in northern Europe between Sweden and Russia, Finland has been strongly influenced by both of these countries throughout its history. It was ruled by Sweden from the 1320s until 1809, when it became an autonomous grand duchy of the Russian Empire. Independence from Russia in 1917 was followed by a brief but devastating civil war in 1918 and, finally, confirmation of the constitution of the Republic of Finland in 1919.

In 1157 the Swedes launched the first of three crusades into Finland in an attempt to gain control of the country and to spread the word of Christianity there. Ultimately the Swede's Roman Catholicism replaced the indigenous religions of the Finns. Even before the arrival of the Swedes, Orthodox missionaries from Russia had worked in eastern Finland, notably the area around Lake Ladoga in Karelia. These developments laid the foundations for Finnish religious culture.

After the Reformation, the Lutheran Church became dominant in Finland, replacing Catholicism entirely by the mid-sixteenth century. The Lutheran Church has also played a central role in the larger Finnish culture, serving as the major provider of social services and education before these functions were taken up by the state. Recent decades have seen a slow but steady decline in the number of Lutheran adherents, a slowly emerging religious pluralism, and the growth of the nonaffiliated population.

RELIGIOUS TOLERANCE Until passage of the Dissenters Act of 1889, the two national churches in Finland—the Lutheran and the Orthodox—were the only approved religious institutions in the country. The 1889 law allowed Protestant dissenters—most significantly, the Baptists and Methodists—to organize into religious communities. Complete religious freedom was introduced with the Freedom of Religion Act of 1922, which took effect in 1923. This law secured the rights to form religious communities, to practice any religion publicly as long as no laws or public standards of decency were violated, and to have no religion at all. Although Finland became religiously neutral with this amendment to its constitution, the Lutheran Church and the Orthodox Church remained in their positions as the two na-

A clergyman prays at the Valamo monastery—the only monastery of the Finnish Orthodox Church. Although it has only about 60,000 members, the Orthodox Church in Finland is significant because of its long history and the special legal standing it retains alongside the Evangelical Lutheran Church.
© CHRIS LISLE/CORBIS.

tional churches, retaining their special relationship with the Finnish state, with their legal status defined in separate laws.

Although other of the world's major religious traditions and many new religious movements are currently represented on the Finnish religious scene, their numbers of adherents remain small. The Lutheran Church's reaction to the emergence of religious pluralism in Finland has been mostly neutral. A member of the World Council of Churches and the Lutheran World Federation, the church is active in the ecumenical community.

Major Religion

LUTHERANISM

DATE OF ORIGIN 1527 C.E.
NUMBER OF FOLLOWERS 4.4 million

HISTORY The Reformation officially reached Finland in 1527 when Gustavus Vasa, the king of Sweden, declared that Christianity should be preached in the form of the Protestant churches that followed the teachings of Martin Luther. This top-down reformation was partially motivated by the prospect of confiscating the great wealth of the Roman Catholic church, but the ideas of the Reformation also came to Finland with students and churchmen who had studied in the Protestant universities of Germany.

The Reformation in Finland could be described as moderate, the change being gradual and nonviolent. The church retained some aspects of Catholicism, such as the ministry of bishops. The major changes were that the Mass was now said in the native language, which at the time was often Swedish, and the New Testament was translated into Finnish. With the crown's confiscation of the Catholic Church's property, the decorative trappings of Catholicism disappeared and the church buildings became plain, which is how they have remained to this day.

The Lutheran Church retained its dominant position under Russian rule. Although the Russian Empire was overwhelmingly Orthodox, its rulers and the Russian Orthodox church did little to change the religion of the Finns. Since the early twentieth century—especially since the Freedom of Religion Act of 1922—the major challenge to the hegemony of the Evangelical Lutheran Church in Finland has been the steady growth of the percentage of people with no religious affiliation.

EARLY AND MODERN LEADERS Mikael Agricola (died in 1557) has been called the "father of the Finnish Reformation." Agricola studied under Martin Luther in Wittenberg and later became the first bishop of Turku. The founders of the various revivalist movements—including Paavo Ruotsalainen (1777–1852), who founded the movement simply called Pietism (Revivalism), and Lars Levi Laestadius (1800–61), who founded Laestadianism—also exercised a strong influence on Finnish Christianity.

Mikko Juva (born in 1918) and John Vikström (born in 1931), both emeritus archbishops of the Evangelical Lutheran Church, have played an important role in public discussion. They have also established themselves among leading Finnish intellectuals.

MAJOR THEOLOGIANS AND AUTHORS Reformer Mikael Agricola published a Finnish translation of the New Testament, his most important work, in 1548.

Because universities in Finland are state institutions, many contemporary Finnish theologians who are affiliated with them have not taken offices in the church, though most have been ordained. Among the most notable are Heikki Räisänen (born in 1941), an internationally known Bible scholar; the late Seppo A. Teinonen (1924–95), whose Finnish introduction to Christian dogmatics is a classic; and Simo Knuuttila (born in 1946), an expert on Aristotle as well as the history and the philosophy of mind. Raija Sollamo (born in 1942), a former vice-rector of the University of Helsinki, is one of the most influential women among Finnish theologians.

HOUSES OF WORSHIP AND HOLY PLACES The most notable Lutheran churches in Finland are the ancient Cathedral of Turku, the seat of the archbishop of the

Evangelical Lutheran Church of Finland, and the Cathedral of Helsinki. Also worth mentioning is the Kerimäki Church, the world's largest wooden church. There is no specific tradition of holy places in Finnish Lutheranism.

WHAT IS SACRED? In addition to religious holidays, the ceremonies of the Lutheran Church are considered sacred. There are no holy pilgrimage sites, and reverence of Bibles or relics is absent from mainstream Lutheranism. Individual congregations, particularly among revivalist groups, may consider a local place sacred, but as a rule sacredness lies in the functions of the church, especially the sacraments.

HOLIDAYS AND FESTIVALS The majority of public holidays in Finland are related to the Christian annual cycle, the central events being Christmas and Easter. Saint John's Day on the eve of the summer solstice is also widely celebrated as Juhannus, the Midsummer festival, but almost always without reference to any religious meaning.

MODE OF DRESS There is no dress code associated with the Lutheran faith. Finns of all faiths usually dress in casual Western or European clothing. The only visible sign of Christianity or Lutheranism might be a cross worn around the neck, a common confirmation gift for Finnish Lutherans. The members of Pietism, one of the revivalist movements in Finland, wore distinctive—usually plain black—garments until casual clothing replaced traditional dress in the mid-twentieth century.

Lutheran priest's clothing is quite plain, usually consisting of a white alb, or robe, and a stole, a long band worn around the neck. The garments that bishops wear during special holiday ceremonies are more elaborate. During the week priests usually wear black attire and a distinctive white collar. Different offices in the church are distinguished by different shirt colors; for example, ordinary priests wear black shirts, while bishops wear violet shirts.

DIETARY PRACTICES There are no dietary restrictions or practices associated with the Evangelical Lutheran Church of Finland. Prayer before lunch was once common in public schools, but now individual teachers may decide whether to say a prayer. Recent years have witnessed a slight resurgence of the Easter fasting tradition.

RITUALS Baptism, Holy Communion, confirmation, marriage, confession, ordination, and the last rites are central ceremonies in the Evangelical Lutheran Church of Finland. As in other Lutheran churches, only baptism and Holy Communion are sacraments. Public prayer is rare outside the Mass, but according to surveys, many Finns pray when alone. Attendance at regular Mass on Sundays is particularly low, but some new, innovative forms of worship have become popular, especially with the younger generation. These include popular music with Christian themes, dancing, and often active participation in these activities by members of the congregation.

RITES OF PASSAGE Certain rites of passage form the core functions of the Evangelical Lutheran Church of Finland. Whereas only 1 to 2 percent of members attend Mass on Sunday, approximately 90 percent of Finns have been baptized or confirmed (usually at the age of 15), and 70 percent have had a Lutheran marriage ceremony. In 2001 approximately 98 percent of the dead were buried in Lutheran cemeteries.

MEMBERSHIP Although the percentage of Finns belonging to the church has waned in recent decades, its members still make up 85 percent of the population. The minuscule attendance at Mass implies that, for many people, membership is more a social custom than a measure of devotion. In the context of certain rites of passage, however, the church is still seen as important.

The Evangelical Lutheran church actively supports missionary activity, both abroad and at home. Especially in the traditional revivalist areas, large gatherings of the faithful are common in the summertime. Some parishes publish weekly or monthly papers, and most have their own Internet sites.

SOCIAL JUSTICE The Evangelical Lutheran Church has taken a very active role in charitable activities. Although social security is a responsibility of the state, the church's social services complement those of the government. Examples include food rations for the homeless, assistance for the elderly with their day-to-day activities, play groups for children, and afternoon clubs for youth. The current bishops have been outspoken in the media on issues of social justice and the welfare state. The Lutheran Church also works with other churches and religions to promote awareness of human rights issues in Finland and abroad.

SOCIAL ASPECTS Marriage and the family are featured strongly in the message of the Evangelical Lutheran Church. In an era of increasing divorce rates, the church offers marriage counseling and support for divorced persons. Although secular marriage has been possible since the Freedom of Religion Act of 1922, most Finns choose church weddings.

The Lutheran Church offers activities for children and adolescents, the most visible of these being the traditional confirmation school. The school most often takes the form of a summer camp and has been, and continues to be, very popular among adolescents.

POLITICAL IMPACT Through much of Finland's history, religion and politics have shared strong ties. In contemporary Finnish politics, the historical impact of religion is identifiable in the rhetoric of politicians who, especially before elections, try to prove that their views represent "Lutheran values," which are often equated with "Finnish values."

CONTROVERSIAL ISSUES In 2001 homosexual couples in Finland were given the legal right to register their relationships. They were not given the right to use the term marriage to describe their relationships, however, and the Lutheran Church will not bless same-sex relationships. This has become one of the central controversial issues in the church. The rights of homosexual employees of the church have also become an issue of public debate. Concerning issues like abortion, birth control, and divorce, the mainstream church's attitude could be described as moderate. But individual leaders, especially in areas where the revivalist movements are strong, have often condemned such practices.

Although women have been ordained since 1986 in the Evangelical Lutheran Church, some conservative vicars have refused to say Mass together with a female priest. There is also a faction in the church's politics that actively opposes women's ordination.

CULTURAL IMPACT The traditional slogan "Home, Religion, and Fatherland," used to denote the nationalistic ethos of independent Finland, acknowledges the Lutheran Church as one of the foundations on which the nation has built its identity. Nowadays contested by religious pluralism and multiculturalism, the sentiment embodied in the expression has nevertheless been a great source of inspiration for the arts as well as Finnish culture in the wider sense. Väinö Linna's *Tuntematon sotilas* (1955; *The Unknown Soldier*, 1968), a historical novel of World War II, is an example of a work that combines these themes in a classic interpretation of the spirit of Finnishness.

Other Religions

One peculiar characteristic of Finnish Lutheranism is the revivalist phenomenon that was sparked by late-17th-century Pietism, a reaction against the increasing secularization of the Lutheran church. The peculiarity arises from the fact that, unlike revivalist movements in many other countries, the Finnish movements have not formed their own religious communities but instead have stayed within the fold of the Evangelical Lutheran Church. This has given rise to interesting tensions between the often more conservative revivalist movements and the mainstream church.

Four of the traditional revivalist movements—Pietism, Laestadianism, Evangelicism, and Supplicationism (Knee-Praying)—were born in the nineteenth century. The later, so-called fifth revivalist movement, organized after World War II, was influenced by the international neo-Pietistic movement, which stressed the importance of repentance and of faith as a personal decision. All of the revivalist movements emphasize personal commitment to one's faith and the authority of the Bible. Support for the revivalist movements is nowadays found in all parts of the country, but it remains focused primarily in rural Finland. An exception to this rule is Laestadianism, which has a strong, politically influential base in the capital.

Although it has only about 60,000 members, the Orthodox Church in Finland is significant because of its long history and the special legal standing it retains alongside the Evangelical Lutheran Church. The two are the only religious institutions in Finland, for example, for which the state collects taxes. The rituals and tradition of pilgrimage for which the Orthodox Church in Finland is known have lately attracted the interest of large numbers of nonmembers.

The historical influence of the Orthodox Church is strongest in North Karelia and South Karelia, which lie along Finland's eastern and southeastern border. Orthodox monks established a steady mission in historic Karelia in the twelfth and thirteenth centuries, though the first signs of Orthodox influence there can be traced to the tenth century. Having maintained the right to practice their religion under Catholic and, later, Lutheran Sweden, Orthodox believers in the area became orga-

nized as a church only in 1896, when the diocese of Karelia was established. Finland lost most of Karelia to the Soviet Union during World War II, and it has been estimated that during the war years, approximately 70 percent of the Orthodox population there immigrated to other parts of Finland. Organizationally the Finnish Orthodox church is an autonomous church under the patriarch of Constantinople, the head of the Eastern Orthodox churches. Bithynia Johannes (born 1923), the archbishop of Finland from 1987 to 2001 and the metropolitan of Nicaea since 2001, has strengthened the role of the canonical tradition in the Finnish Orthodox church and developed the church's inter-Orthodox and ecumenical relations.

Jews first came to the eastern parts of the Kingdom of Sweden at the end of the eighteenth century. These people were mostly skilled craftsmen from mainland Sweden. Later, under Russian rule, the Jewish population grew as soldiers from the tsar's armies settled in Finland. Although Jews were judicially prohibited from practicing their religion until passage of the Freedom of Religion Act of 1922, members of the small community lived peacefully alongside Lutheran and Orthodox Christians.

The center of Finnish Judaism is Helsinki, the national capital. In addition to the Orthodox synagogue, a Jewish school, hospital, and nursery are also located there. In recent years the number of Jews in Finland has dwindled because of intermarriage, a declining birth rate, and emigration.

Following their modest beginnings in 1910, Finland's Jehovah's Witnesses officially registered as a religious community in 1946 after being banned by the government from 1942 to 1945. They have since become one of the fastest growing religious groups in the country.

The organization of the Jehovah's Witnesses in Finland is hierarchical, with the country being divided into chapters. Local chapters are kept small in order to preserve a "family connectedness" among members. As in the international movement, the message of the Jehovah's Witnesses in Finland emphasizes millennial themes and the coming of the Last Judgment.

Pentecostalists make up the third largest religious population in Finland, and many members of the country's Christian Democratic Party come from Pentecostalist groups. The Pentecostalist movement was established in the early 1900s when some groups began celebrating their own Communion and adopted the practice of baptizing the faithful. A central figure in the movement was T.B. Barratt (1862–1940), a former Methodist preacher from Britain who, after his Pentecostal baptism in the United States in 1906, established charismatic groups in all of the Nordic countries.

What separates Pentecostalism from mainstream Finnish Lutheranism is the baptism of the faithful and the emphasis on charismatic gifts, such as speaking in tongues. The importance of charismatic gifts has waned since the formation of the movement, but occasional revivals bring them to the fore.

The first Islamic community in Finland was officially established in 1925, though a small number of Muslim Tatars from Russia had been living in the country since the latter half of the nineteenth century. Ethnic background has subsequently been a major factor in the formation of Islamic communities in Finland, since the Tatars have accepted only Muslims who share their ethnicity. Later Muslim immigrants, especially the Arabic-speaking groups and the large numbers of immigrants from Somalia, have formed new, often mixed communities. The majority of Finnish Muslims are Sunni Muslims, though there are also small communities of Shias and Sufis.

Muslims in Finland are concentrated in major urban areas, and most are immigrants. Their places of worship are usually on premises converted for the purpose, since no separate mosques have been built. Muslim children attend state schools, but their communities also offer instruction in the Koran and in Arabic. Most Somali women dress in the traditional costume of their country of origin and wear the veil. Women of other ethnic groups and many Somali teenage girls often adopt Western styles of dress. The growing Muslim presence has aroused occasional public debate concerning the ritual slaughter of animals, the wearing of the veil, female circumcision, and the link between terrorism and some fundamentalist Muslim groups.

Titus Hjelm

See Also Vol. 1: *Christianity, Lutheranism, Russian Orthodoxy*

Bibliography

Heininen, Simo, and Markku Heikkilä. *Suomen kirkkohistoria.* Helsinki: Edita, 1996.

Heino, Harri. *Mihin Suomi tänään uskoo?* Porvoo: WSOY, 1997.

Klinge, Matti. *A Brief History of Finland.* 10th ed. Translated by David Mitchell. Helsinki: Otava, 1994.

Lampinen, Tapio. "Civil Religion Proclamation of Church and State in Finland." In *The Church and Civil Religion in the Nordic Countries of Europe.* Edited by Béla Harmati. Geneva: Lutheran World Federation, 1984.

———. "Finland: The Land of the Church and of Church Sociology." *Sociological Analysis* 51, no. 1 (1990): 53–62.

Ramet, Pedro, ed. *Eastern Christianity and Politics in the Twentieth Century.* Durham, N.C.: Duke University Press, 1988.

Seppo, Juha. "The Freedom of Religion and Conscience in Finland." *Journal of Church and State* 40, no. 4 (1998): 847–872.

Singleton, Fred. *A Short History of Finland.* Cambridge: Cambridge University Press, 1998.

France

POPULATION 59,765,983

ROMAN CATHOLIC 85 percent

MUSLIM 5 percent

PROTESTANT 2 percent

JEWISH 1 percent

OTHER (HINDUISM, BUDDHISM, TAOISM, AND CONFUCIANISM) 2 percent

UNAFFILIATED 5 percent

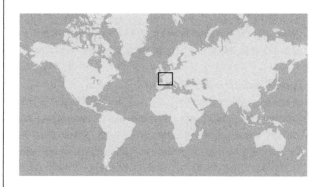

Country Overview

INTRODUCTION Roman Catholicism is by far the largest religion in the French Republic. Because of its geographic location as a passageway between northern and southern Europe, the country has lent itself to strong external influences. Shaped like a hexagon, it has a coastline on both the Atlantic Ocean (the Bay of Biscay and the English Channel) and the Mediterranean Sea and shares land frontiers with eight modern states: Andorra,

Belgium, Germany, Italy, Luxembourg, Monaco, Spain, and Switzerland.

Christianity entered the region from the east near Lyon and the south along the Mediterranean shores. Judaism made its way into Antique Gaul from Germany when Hebrew merchants established their colonies near Strasbourg and Metz. Islam arrived from the south in the eighth century when Muslims crossed the Pyrenees in an attempt to conquer France but failed at Poitiers. Protestantism came close to dominating the country in the sixteenth century when Anglo-Saxon reformers tried to support the French Huguenots (Protestants) by sending, unsuccessfully, the English fleet to La Rochelle on the Atlantic coast.

While Roman Catholicism has had a determining impact on French culture and identity, its faith has spread unevenly throughout the entire territory. According to the *Carte Boulard,* France's best-known map of religious geography, the most fervent regions have traditionally been Brittany, the Massif Central, the Western Pyrenees, the Midi, Alsace-Lorraine, and parts of the Alps. The least fervent ones included, until the 1970s, the Limousin and the Parisian Basin. Nowadays the overall tendency is toward indifference in religious behavior among the former Catholic population.

RELIGIOUS TOLERANCE Tolerance was first instituted in 1598 under the Edict of Nantes, which allowed Protestants to practice their faith. Afterward, however, the state and the Roman Catholic Church remained so intertwined that France had to go further than other countries in separating matters of state and matters of reli-

Notre-Dame-en-Vaux is one example of the Gothic cathedrals found in France. The Gothic style came about in the twelfth century in the region around Paris. © ELIO CIOL/CORBIS

gion. This separation started with the Revolution of 1789 and was made final by law in 1905.

Modern France is constitutionally a secular state with individual religious freedom enshrined in article I [changed from article 2] of the constitution. Secularism (*laïcisme*) as defined by the French state means neutrality of the public authority toward beliefs and juridical guarantee of free expression and exercise of religion. The banning of visible religious symbols, such as the wearing of headscarves in public spaces, is a way to reaffirm the neutrality of lay institutions. In 2001 the French government passed an anticult bill to "reinforce the prevention and repression of groups of a sect-like character." As of early 2004 some 150 cult groups have been investigated for use of cruelty, harassment, and other unfair pressure to secure conversion.

Major Religion

ROMAN CATHOLICISM

DATE OF ORIGIN c. late second or early third century C.E.

NUMBER OF FOLLOWERS 50.8 million

HISTORY The starting point for Christianity in Gaul (as France was called then) has been dated to the late second or early third century C.E., when the Roman army arrived and converts, such as Martin of Tours and Ambrose of Milan, started to preach the new faith in the region. At the end of the fifth century, Clovis, the leader of the ethnic Franks, was baptized along with more than 3,000 soldiers. Shortly afterward, at the beginning of the sixth century, the Burgundian princes, who occupied the Rhône River valley, swore in their first Catholic king. Charlemagne's reign (768–814) marks a turning point, as he was fully supported by the Roman Catholic Church. His coronation as emperor by the pope made him the uncontested political leader of Western Christendom.

Starting in the eleventh century French sovereigns preached the Crusades against the Eastern infidels by providing funds, encouraging prayers, and giving administrative support. With their peoples and armies they embarked on long and costly expeditions to Palestine to rescue the Holy Sepulchre (the tomb in which the body of Christ was laid) from the Muslim tribes. The Crusades lasted well into the thirteenth century and ended with the death of the "holy king" Louis IX (1226–70). Within France the Crusades became divisive when Pope Innocent III used them against the Cathari of southern France. The French followers of Catharism—also known as Albigenses, from the southern French town of Albi—were a powerful Christian sect that emerged as a resistant movement against the clergy. The Cathari were especially numerous in the southern provinces of Languedoc and Provence. They were tolerated until Innocent III came to the papacy in 1198 and summoned the Albigensian Crusade against them. The human cost was extremely high. Some 20,000 people were massacred in Bezier. It was also the Catharist movement that occasioned the establishment of the Inquisition, an ecclesiastical tribunal using torture and death to purge the population of its "heretics" (mainly Jews and Huguenots) and "witches" (mainly women). For years the Inquisition tyrannized western Europe and sent millions of people to be tortured or to the stake. One of its victims was Joan of Arc. She was a blend of religious faith and nascent nationalism. Considered a heretic by the Inquisition, Joan was burned at the stake in 1431.

The 1500s were the century of religious wars (seven of them from 1562 to 1598) pitting Protestants against Catholics. It was in response to growing Protestantism that the ecumenical Council of Trent (1545–63) redefined the doctrines of Catholicism and executed a thorough reform of the inner life of the church by removing the numerous abuses that had developed in it. The darkest period of the sixteenth century was marked by the Massacre of Saint Bartholomew's Day in 1572, leading to the murders of approximately 50,000 Huguenots.

For many centuries the French kings were among the strongest allies of the Roman Catholic Church.

Starting as early as the fourteenth century, however, loyalty to Rome started to erode in the kingdom. French monarchs were becoming more interested in consolidating their own power than in supporting Christendom. As a result, they began to contest the supreme power of the pope and to resent the exercise of authority by ecclesiastics in civil spheres. The monarchy's aspirations for independence over religious and territorial matters eventually led in 1682 to the Declaration of the Clergy of France, whereby the Church of France, known as the Gallican Church, clearly expressed its position regarding the restrained authority of the pope in the French Church in favor of that of France's bishops and temporal leaders. It should be noted, however, that while French sovereigns grew increasingly hostile to papal authority and sought to restrict the intervention of Rome within their frontiers, they never demanded separation from Rome, as was the case in England.

In 1789, when the French Revolution overthrew the monarchy, the National Assembly (French government) considerably weakened the power of the Roman Catholic Church. The church regained some of its influence under Napoleon Bonaparte with the 1801 Concordat with the Vatican, which restored Catholic worship in France in order to bring some peace to the country. In the course of the nineteenth century, once a republican constitution was adopted (1875), the traditional power of the church diminished gradually, leading to the official separation of church and state in 1905. Yet the greatest challenges in the French Roman Catholic Church occurred after Vatican II (1962–65). In the 1970s and '80s French Catholicism posed a potential threat to the Roman church because of the emergence of a fundamentalist schism under the leadership of Archbishop Marcel Lefebvre (1905–91), who openly rejected Rome for its liberalism. While this traditionalist movement has received some popular support among French Catholics, a new movement has since emerged. This movement is made up of younger clerics seeking to develop a more evangelistic Roman Catholic Church whose mission is to serve the larger community. Since 2003 this shift toward pastoral commitment seems to have had a profound impact on all levels of the church, from the bishops to the laity.

EARLY AND MODERN LEADERS Saint Martin lived in the fourth century. In France he is considered to be the first Christian who evangelized the countryside. A basilica was constructed in 1014 in Tours where he rested, and the sanctuary became a pilgrimage center until its destruction in 1562, during the Wars of Religion.

Saint Bernard was born in 1093 of a noble Burgundy family. At the age of 21 he founded the monastery of Cîteaux, and he served as abbot of Clairvaux from age 25 until his death in 1153. He was an effective orator and a powerful writer. So inspiring was his mysticism that hundreds of Cistercian monasteries were founded after him throughout Europe.

Saint Louis (or Louis IX) was the son of Blanche of Castile and Louis VIII. He devoted himself to government, charity, and piety. During his reign (1226–70) France waged no war against other Christian neighbors. He died in a Crusade, and after his death the Crusades ended. A fervent supporter of the arts, he was the king who commissioned the building of the Sainte Chapelle in Paris as a shrine to house the relics of Christ's crucifixion, including the Crown of Thorns.

Saint Joan of Arc, known in France as la Pucelle (the Maid), was a visionary shepherdess who believed that God had sent her on a mission to save France from the English invaders. Born in 1412 in a peasant family from the village of Domrémy, Joan was only 13 when she became aware of God's prophecies. She herself went to battle, was arrested, and was finally condemned to death in Rouen. She was only 19 years old. In 1909 she received beatification by the Roman Catholic Church.

Saint Vincent de Paul was born in 1580, was ordained in 1600, and died in 1660. He devoted his life to the poor. He worked with convicts who were kept in abject conditions in the galleys; built hospitals for them in Paris and Marseille; established the Congregation of Priests of the Mission; and, with Louise de Marillac Legras, founded the community of the Sisters of Charity, which she directed until her death (in 1660). He started soup kitchens for the poor, gave shelter to young, homeless women, and sent missionaries abroad to help some 30,000 slaves on the Barbary Coast (in Tunis, Algiers, and Bizerte), who had been kept captives by the Turks.

Saint Bernadette (Bernadette Soubirous) was 14 in 1858 when, in Lourdes, her first apparition (of about 18) of the Blessed Virgin Mary occurred. A church was built on the spot where the visions took place, and in 1873 the most important French pilgrimage was inaugurated. More than a million pilgrims travel annually to Lourdes, and more than 4,000 cures have been witnessed at the shrine.

Saint Thérèse of Lisieux (Thérèse Martin) was born in 1873 and died in 1897 at Lisieux, where she had spent 11 years as a Carmelite nun. At the convent she took the name Sister Thérèse of the Child Jesus and the Holy Face. Remembered as "the little flower," she was canonized in 1914 and was considered by Pope Pius X to be "the greatest saint of modern times."

MAJOR THEOLOGIANS AND AUTHORS At the height of France's power during the Middle Ages (twelfth and thirteenth centuries), its scholastic Roman Catholic philosophers contributed greatly to the development of Western thought. Among these scholars were Anselm, Roscelin, and Peter Abelard.

In the sixteenth century Agrippa d'Aubigné expressed in poetry the terrible horrors and tragedies generated by the Wars of Religion. The following century gave birth to Jacques-Bénigne Bossuet (1627–1704), one of France's most celebrated orators. Then during the eighteenth century Honoré Tournely distinguished himself by the brilliance of his treatises and lectures delivered at the Sorbonne, where he worked for 24 years. In 1802 François-René de Chateaubriand showed (in *Genie du Christianisme*) that Christianity could be a source of artistic inspiration. At the end of the nineteenth century Louis Baunard, rector of the Catholic University of Lille, wrote extensively on the religious history of modern France.

After World War II an important voice on the Catholic left was Emmanuel Mounier. In the review *Esprit*, Mounier became a strong proponent of social Catholicism, which now identifies itself with France's political left.

HOUSES OF WORSHIP AND HOLY PLACES For French Roman Catholics the church is the place of worship. Pilgrimages as a form of devotion to saints and the Blessed Virgin Mary are still popular. In France, Lourdes in the Hautes-Pyrénées is the most famous and best-attended pilgrimage, held for the apparition of the Blessed Virgin to 14-year-old Bernadette Soubirous in 1858. Paray-le-Monial in the department of Saône-et-Loire, where apparitions to Saint Margaret Mary Alacoque occurred, has been a much-frequented place of pilgrimage since 1873. Another well-known pilgrimage center is Lisieux in Normandy, where the shrine to Saint Thérèse is located.

WHAT IS SACRED? The French Roman Catholics have a long-standing tradition of believing in miracles and the intercession of the saints. From the early days of Catholicism, French churches and cathedrals have contained sacred relics from the saints. Such relics are found frequently in rural parishes, where the cult of the saints was strong and usually approved by the church. For centuries devotional objects were more important than the official liturgy to ordinary Catholics. Among others these devotional objects included the rosary, the cross, religious medals, representations of saints, the Immaculate Heart of Mary, and the Sacred Heart of Jesus. This interest in devotional objects started to diminish in France after the Second Vatican Council (1962–65).

HOLIDAYS AND FESTIVALS On the Sunday closest to Epiphany (6 January), Roman Catholics in France celebrate the Feast of the Kings (Fête des Rois) by serving a sweet pie (*galette des rois*). This dessert is baked with a bean (*fève*) inside it. Whoever finds the bean is the king for the day.

Ash Wednesday, the first day of Lent after Mardi Gras, is not a national holiday, but devout Catholics go to church and get their foreheads marked with an ashen cross. Palm Sunday, the last Sunday of Lent and the beginning of the Holy Week, is celebrated by taking a twig of boxwood to church to be blessed. Good Friday is a holiday, and many Catholics still participate in the Stations of the Cross. On Easter Sunday fervent Catholics attend Mass to take Easter Communion. Easter Monday and the Ascension are holidays.

Traditionally Whit Sunday (Pentecost) and Whit Monday are celebrated in France. In 2003 a serious political crisis was created when more than 13,000 elderly died during a summer heat wave. This disaster led the French government to look for ways to pay for an assistance program for the elderly. As a consequence, Whit Monday was designated a bank holiday on which employees would work to fund this initiative in the name of national public solidarity. Corpus Christi (also known as Fête-Dieu) is a holiday that takes place on the Thursday following Pentecost. In some parts of France (such as Aix, in Provence) festivals are held for the occasion.

The Assumption of the Blessed Virgin Mary (15 August) is a national holiday, as is All Saint's Day (1 November). On All Saint's Day older people usually visit cemeteries to put flowers on their family graves. Christmas is an important family day. Some people go to church late at night on 24 December or in the morning the next day. The family eats a large meal (called *réveillon*) late on Christmas Eve. Gifts are presented on either Christmas Eve or the morning after.

Since 1806 in France, Christmas, Fête-Dieu, the Ascension, the Assumption, and All Saint's Day still follow the ecclesiastical calendar. The other feasts have been transferred to Sunday.

MODE OF DRESS Traditionally, French Roman Catholic clerics wore vestments suited to their position and as prescribed in the canons. In public priests used to wear the soutane, or cassock, which has been replaced by the Roman collar. Members of French Roman Catholic orders wore distinct habits, such as a loose frock over which was thrown a hood with a cape.

In modern times the dress code is much less rigorous than in the past, and many members of the clergy are now dressed in lay clothes of a sober or black color. At Mass, however, the officiating priest still uses the traditional vestments, including a toga covered by alb, chasuble, maniple, cincture, and stole. Some orders continue to wear their specific garbs.

DIETARY PRACTICES In the past for Roman Catholics in France, all Fridays were supposed to be meatless, and throughout the 40 days of Lent no meat, eggs, or cheese were to be eaten. Nowadays meat prohibition on Friday is occasionally observed in traditional Roman Catholic families.

RITUALS In France only about 20 percent of Roman Catholics regularly attend Mass on Sunday. Attendance increases on holidays and for family celebrations. Since the Second Vatican Council (1962–65) France has witnessed a de-Christianization of society, and the tendency within the Roman Catholic Church has been to deritualize religious practice. For instance, praying, popular devotions, and the blessing of houses and religious medals are less practiced, and street processions have disappeared.

Over the centuries pilgrimages have been important expressions of worship and ways to fulfill a penance or a vow. People would go on a pilgrimage seeking a miraculous cure or hoping to earn an indulgence. The earliest recorded pilgrimages in France date back to pre-Christian days. These journeys remain popular and usually draw pilgrims from many parts of France.

RITES OF PASSAGE The majority of French Catholics are only "seasonal Catholics" (*conformistes saisonniers*) in that they see their contact with the church as being confined to baptism (which gives full membership in the Roman Catholic Church), confirmation (traditionally considered a rite of passage into adulthood), marriage, and religious funerals. This decline in the practice of the Catholic faith seems to suggest that the church has little relevance in the personal life of its membership.

MEMBERSHIP The French Roman Catholic Church is actively involved in a revival of Catholic faith at home and still campaigns actively for conversion in the developing world. Catholic missionaries abroad consider evangelization as one of their chief activities.

SOCIAL JUSTICE It was in medieval times that women started to bind themselves by vows to corporal and spiritual service of mercy. For instance, the Sisters (also called Daughters) of Charity of Saint Vincent de Paul (founded in 1633 by Saint Vincent de Paul and Louise de Marillac Legras) worked with orphans, the poor, and the sick. Other such organizations included the Sisters of Saint Thomas, the Sisters of Saint Charles, and the Vatelotte Sisters, all devoted to teaching and hospital work. Madeleine-Sophie Barat founded the Society of the Sacred Heart in 1800, and Jeanne Jugan founded the Little Sisters of the Poor in 1839.

Today regarded as the national defender of the poor, Abbé Pierre (born Henri Groues in 1912) tackled the problem of poverty in France after World War II. By having companions live and work with the destitute, he was able to help these people find work and a place to live as well as regain dignity and self-esteem. In 1949 he founded Emmaus, which became an international movement for self-support communities for the homeless. As of the early twenty-first century, the movement (which celebrated its 50th anniversary in 1999) was secular rather than religious and had 400 communities in 44 countries.

SOCIAL ASPECTS In France during the Middle Ages the Roman Catholic Church controlled family relationships: marriages, annulments of marriages, questions of legitimacy, and inheritance of personal property. Starting in the 1970s the church's power has been limited mainly to baptism, confirmation, marriage, and funerals. Practicing Catholics are frequently uncomfortable with positions taken by the church. This is illustrated by the controversy reported in the press in 2003 over a French bishop who defended a parish priest in northern France for having refused to officiate at a marriage because the couple planned not to have any children. The French Catholic Church's vision of marriage still requires the procreation of children.

POLITICAL IMPACT The French government is secular, and the Roman Catholic Church is not directly involved in French political life. While the church establishment is still conservative, it is not automatically on the side of the French government. Ever since the close of the Second Vatican Council in 1965, the church has made public declarations against human rights violations of immigrant workers and refugees. The church has also even taken a stance on certain political issues, as seen in its denunciation in the 1970s of the use of nuclear weapons by the French government of the time. Some protests, however, were not always welcomed by the Vatican. For instance, Jacques Gaillot, the Roman Catholic bishop of Evreux, in Normandy, who frequently campaigned in favor of immigrants, the homeless, and homosexuals, was dismissed from the French Roman Catholic Church in 1995. His dismissal came shortly after Charles Pasqua, the French minister of the interior, had met with the pope and complained about the bishop. Although the Roman Catholic Church is no longer the conservative force it used to be, public polls tend to indicate that the majority of the French population feel that Roman Catholicism has little influence on their political allegiance.

CONTROVERSIAL ISSUES A serious internal problem agitating the church has been reports of sex scandals. The news agency Zenit reported in *CathNews* (August 2002) that 118 priests were under investigation for pedophilia, 30 had been convicted, and 11 were jailed. The French bishops, under the leadership of Bishop Jacques David of Évreux, responded with a dossier titled *Combating Paedophilia: Points of Reference for Educators*. Such sex scandals have severely eroded the former prestige of the clergy. There is growing public agreement that today's practice of celibacy is difficult to observe for many priests. Other challenging issues for the Catholic Church include the clerical role of women, family planning, contraception, abortion, divorce, and same-sex marriage.

CULTURAL IMPACT The Roman Catholic Church has played a crucial role in the development of French art.

Merovingian times (from the fifth to the eighth century) gave birth to Latin hymnody (liturgical poetry), when devoted ecclesiastics started using songs and hymns to praise God in their worship. During the Carolingian era (from the eighth to the tenth century) classical learning was encouraged, leading to the emergence of religious scholasticism. By the eleventh century cathedral schools had achieved international renown, especially the cathedral schools in Chartres and Paris. Troubadour poets dominated the French literary movement from the eleventh to the thirteenth century. They introduced the chanson de geste, an early epic literary form emerging at the time of pilgrim shrines and the Crusades.

Traditionally the Catholic press has been represented by a number of newspapers and periodicals, among which two leading Parisian journals stand out: *Liberation* (formerly the *Univers*, published since 1833) and *La Croix* (published since 1900). Since about 1970 educated Catholics have tended to choose their periodicals according to their occupational backgrounds. For instance, French Roman Catholics in managerial positions tend to read *La Vie* and *Le Pélerin*, professors and teachers tend to read *Le Témoignage Chrétien*, and lawyers and those in the medical professions tend to read *La France Catholique.*

Religious architecture in France is best represented by the art of the Gothic cathedrals as found in Chartres, Reims, Paris (Saint Denis and Notre-Dame de Paris), Amiens, and Lyon. The Gothic style came about in the twelfth century in the region around Paris. Verticality, light, and color were the artistic qualities best reflecting the divine spirit of the time. The builders were highly skilled artisans—freestone masons who had been emancipated from the control of local guilds in order to travel freely. They formed a trade society of their own with their secret knowledge. After the decline of Gothic architecture, they became part of the Freemasonry movement.

Other Religions

Islam is occasionally regarded as France's second religion. Most of its adherents are French citizens from immigrant backgrounds who originally arrived in the 1960s and '70s as low-paid and unskilled laborers from Algeria, Morocco, and Tunisia (former French colonies in North Africa). There is no central mosque in France. In 2003 three municipalities—Strasbourg, Paris, and Marseille—agreed to build local mosques. Because of their disparate origins and recent arrival in France, Muslims are still in the process of forming a national integrated Islamic community. Furthermore, secular France is reluctant to accept their increasingly visible role in national society. This was evidenced in the mid-1990s when Muslim female students who wore the *hijab* (Islamic headscarf) in class were expelled from public schools.

Beginning during Francis I's reign (1515–47), the Protestant Reformation gained strong support, and its adherents became known as the Huguenots. Their first leader was Lefèvre d'Étaples, a scholar and the editor of French translations of the Bible. The history of the French Reformation movement may be divided into four major periods: (1) the militant period from 1559 to 1598, which led to the Massacre of Saint Bartholomew's Day (in 1572) and its aftermath; (2) the Edict of Nantes period from 1598 to 1685, a period of tolerance when the Huguenots gained political security and the right to freely exercise their religious worship; (3) the period between 1685 and 1789, from the revocation of the Edict of Nantes (by Louis XIV) to the Revolution, which destroyed the political power of the Huguenots and forced thousands to emigrate (primarily to England and also to the Americas) or else to go underground; and (4) the period from the 1789 Revolution to the secularization of the state in 1905, during which, in order to pacify the nation, Napoleon Bonaparte imposed upon the Protestants a new organizational structure leading to the creation (in 1849) of the Union of the Free Evangelical Churches of France. At present Protestantism counts about 1 million adherents.

Jewish communities appeared early in western Europe. In Gaul, Jewish merchants arrived in the second century C.E. By 600 C.E. there were Jewish communities in all the major Gallic cities. Early harassments were reported under the Merovingian kings but seemed to have disappeared with Charlemagne, who gave them limited protection. The ninth and tenth centuries were peaceful times for the French Jewry, who enjoyed some degree of autonomy in worship and education and worked actively in commerce, industry, and trade. During that time many turned to finance and became moneylenders to the kings. Bloody outbreaks of anti-Semitism became common during the mythic exaltation of the Crusades, which led to repeated invasions of Jewish settlements in Anjou and Poitou and to the eventual slaughter in 1236 of some 3,000 people at Bordeaux and Angoulême. Although the king of France expelled them in 1306, some

Jewish communities protected by the pope were able to survive in Avignon, Cavaillon, and L'Isle-sur-la-Sorgue. Starting in the sixteenth century until the end of the eighteenth century, Portuguese and Spanish Jews, forced to convert to Catholicism but still practicing their religion, came to establish themselves in the southwestern cities of Bordeaux and Bayonne. Anti-Semitism was reignited during the Dreyfus Affair, which began in the late 1880s when the French army wrongly accused a Jewish officer, Captain Alfred Dreyfus, of treason. After spending years in jail, Dreyfus was exonerated in 1906 and decorated with the Legion of Honor. World War II was a dark period for French Jews because many of them fell victim to the pro-Nazi Vichy government and were deported to die in concentration camps. The survivors were stripped of their property and had to leave the country. Today France has the largest Jewish population in the European Union. Emigration of French Jews to Israel increased drastically in 2001 in the wake of a string of anti-Semitic attacks on several members of their community.

Since the 1970s modern France has experienced a great deal of ethnic diversity, with immigrants still claiming religious affiliations with their former cultures. For instance, in Paris and many other major urban centers, a large segment of the Asian population continues to practice Hinduism, Buddhism, Taoism, or Confucianism. Additionally, and despite increased secularization, New Age movements (usually from North America) have attracted large groups of followers. Unlike mainstream religions, New Age movements have encouraged individuals not to blindly adhere to a faith but instead to engage in renewed inquiry and search for nondogmatic expressions of the divine through a plurality of forms and paths that seem to respond well to the needs of the times.

Christiane Paponnet-Cantat

See Also Vol. 1: *Roman Catholicism*

Bibliography

The Catholic Encyclopedia. 20 June 2004. http://www.newadvent.org/cathen.

Durant, Will. *The Age of Faith: A History of Medieval Civilization—Christian, Islamic, and Judaic—from Constantine to Dante: A.D. 325–1300.* New York: Simon and Schuster, 1950.

Hen, Yitzhak. *Culture and Religion in Merovingian Gaul, A.D. 481–751.* Leiden and New York: E.J. Brill, 1995.

Kingdon, Robert M. *Myths about the St. Bartholomew's Day Massacres, 1572–1576.* Cambridge, Mass.: Harvard University Press, 1988.

Ravitch, Norman. *The Catholic Church and the French Nation, 1589–1989.* London and New York: Routledge, 1990.

Strayer, Joseph R. *Western Europe in the Middle Ages.* 2nd ed. Englewood Cliffs, N.J.: Prentice Hall, 1974.

Gabon

POPULATION 1,355,246

CHRISTIAN 90.6 percent

MUSLIM 4.6 percent

AFRICAN INDIGENOUS BELIEFS
3.1 percent

NONRELIGIOUS 1.1 percent

OTHER 0.6 percent

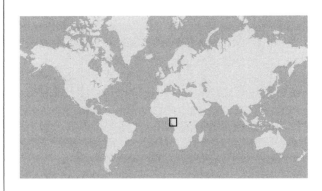

Country Overview

INTRODUCTION The Gabonese Republic straddles the equator on the West African coast and is surrounded by Equatorial Guinea, Cameroon, the Republic of Congo, and the Atlantic Ocean. The land is heavily forested. Prior to French colonization, which began in the 1840s on the coast and expanded inland until the eve of World War I, Gabonese peoples (including Fang, Mbede, Punu, Eshira, Nzabi, Myene, Kota, Obamba, and Teke) hunted; fished; practiced shifting cultivation, iron metallurgy, and trade; and collected forest products. Rural populations continue to hunt, fish, and culti-

vate, as well as planting some cash crops (cocoa, coffee, hevea, market foodstuffs). Half of Gabon's population lives in two coastal cities, Libreville (the capital) and Port Gentil.

Before Christian missionaries arrived in the 1840s, inhabitants practiced a range of African religions, including ancestor religions and initiation societies. In the early twentieth century intense colonial exploitation, impoverishment, famine, and disease led to depopulation and social crisis, as well as widespread conversion to Christianity. During this time Catholic and Protestant mission churches and schools were established in most major towns. By evangelizing and educating several generations of Gabonese intellectuals and colonial and postcolonial administrators, the mission stations have played an important role in reshaping Gabonese society.

France granted Gabon independence in 1960 but has continued to exercise important political, economic, and cultural influence. Following independence Gabon developed a strong presidential regime. The Parti Démocratique Gabonais ruled from 1968 to 1990 under a one-party system. El Hadj Omar Bongo (born Albert-Bertrand Bongo) has been in power since Gabon's first president, Léon M'Ba, died in 1967. Gabon's National Conference in 1990 instituted a multiparty system. Because of its low population and abundant natural resources, including timber, manganese, and especially oil, Gabon has enjoyed one of the highest per capita incomes in sub-Saharan Africa. Since the mid-1980s, however, economic mismanagement, foreign debt, price fluctuations, and gradually depleting oil reserves have contributed to increasing economic hardship.

Most contemporary Gabonese are at least nominally Christian, while up to 40 percent continue to draw on African religious practices, divination, and healing, which have in turn incorporated elements of Christianity. West African and Lebanese merchants living in coastal cities and provincial towns practice Islam. A small number of Gabonese, including President Bongo, have converted to Islam. Since the 1980s there has been an increase in evangelical revival movements and Pentecostalism, especially in Libreville.

RELIGIOUS TOLERANCE The Gabonese constitution protects freedom of worship, a right generally respected by the government. The Ministry of the Interior keeps a registry of religious groups but does not register "traditional" religious groups. Since 1983 the government has banned Jehovah's Witnesses (ostensibly because the church did not protect nonmembers who disagreed with the group's views) and the Salvation Army. In the 1980s three small local churches (Christianisme Celeste, Church of the Cherubim and Seraphim, and Order of the Temple of Jerusalem) were also banned along with two international evangelical movements (Bethany Church and Full Gospel). The government saw these movements as a threat because they attracted Gabonese dissatisfied with the entrenched ruling class. With the arrival of a multiparty system in 1990, restrictions were lifted.

Major Religion

CHRISTIANITY

DATE OF ORIGIN Seventeenth century C.E.
NUMBER OF FOLLOWERS 1.2 million

HISTORY Portuguese, Italian Capuchin, and French Catholic missionaries visited the coast of Gabon in the seventeenth and eighteenth centuries, with no lasting results. More permanent missionary work began with the establishment of American Protestant missionaries in 1842 and French Catholic missionaries in 1844. American Congregational and Presbyterian missionaries established a mission station in present-day Libreville and sought to evangelize Mpongwe, Kele, and Fang peoples on the coast and in the Gabon River estuary. In 1874 Presbyterian Pastor Robert Nassau founded the first mission station on the Ogooué River. In 1844 Father

Gabonese villagers watch a dancer perform in the early twentieth century. The combined impact of Christianity and Western modernity have substantially weakened masked dance and sculptural traditions that addressed ancestors, the spirit world, and initiation societies. © SCHEUFLER COLLECTION/CORBIS.

Jean-Rémy Bessieux of the Congregation of the Sacred Heart of Mary founded a mission post in Libreville not far from the French naval fort. He opened a boy's school and Saint Mary's church and arranged for the arrival of the Immaculate Conception Sisters in 1849.

Nineteenth-century conversion rates were slow, in part because of the resiliency of traditional practices and in part because of Protestant opposition to polygamy and the consumption of alcohol. As the colonial era and mission education took root, conversions increased. The first Gabonese Catholic priest, André Raponda-Walker, was ordained in 1899. Today the bishops of Oyem, Mouila, and Franceville and the archbishop of Libreville are Gabonese, but three-quarters of the Catholic clergy are foreign. The first African Protestant pastors were Ibia J'Ikengue from Corsico Island, ordained in 1870, and Ntâkâ Truman, a Mpongwe from Libreville, ordained in 1880.

By 1913 the American Presbyterian missionaries, facing increasing restrictions from the French colonial administration, relinquished their Gabon operations to the Paris-based Société des Missions Évangéliques (SME), which had taken over the Presbyterian Ogooué Mission stations in 1893. The SME subsequently expanded mission operations into the northern Woleu-Ntem region and south to Port Gentil. After Gabonese independence the SME turned over its operations to the Evangelical Church of Gabon.

Two other major Protestant churches have operated in Gabon since the colonial period. The Christian Missionary Alliance (later renamed the Christian Alliance Church) has operated in southern Gabon since the 1930s. Since the 1970s this conservative, biblically literalist church has expanded to Libreville to serve growing urban populations from the south. In the mid-1930s Swiss SME missionary Reverend Gaston Vernaud broke away to found the Pentecostal Evangelical Church (later affiliated with the Assemblies of God Churches) after leading a "Great Revival" centered on possession by the Holy Spirit. In the climate of increasing economic hardship since the 1980s, Libreville residents have turned to evangelical and Pentecostal churches, which have a less hierarchical structure than the Catholic Church and the Église Évangélique. Without formally renouncing their Christian faith, some Gabonese have turned to neotraditional or syncretic healing and initiation religions, which draw on both Christianity and spirit veneration.

EARLY AND MODERN LEADERS Jean-Rémy Bessieux (1803–76), a crucial influence in Roman Catholic efforts during the formative early missionary work, was named the first bishop of Gabon in 1848. American John Leighton Wilson (1809–86) founded the American Protestant mission in Gabon in 1842.

Albert Schweitzer (1875–1965) first came to Gabon in 1912 as a medical missionary under the auspices of the SME. In 1924 he founded his own hospital on the Ogooué River at Lambaréné, financing it through lectures and organ concerts in Europe and the United States.

In 1899 André Raponda-Walker (1871–1968) became the first Gabonese ordained as a Catholic priest. During his long career he studied the history, cultures, languages, and flora of Gabon and published numerous works, many reissued since the 1990s by the André Raponda-Walker Foundation in Libreville.

Monsignor Basile Mvé Engone (born in 1941 near Oyem) succeeded André Fernand Anguilé (from Libreville, in office 1969–98) as archbishop of Libreville in 1998. Monsignor Mvé is well known and respected for having presided over Gabon's National Conference in

1990, which instituted a multiparty political system after 22 years of single-party rule.

MAJOR THEOLOGIANS AND AUTHORS As soon as they arrived in Gabon in the 1840s, Protestant and Catholic missionaries began to translate portions of the Bible and liturgy into Mpongwe and other Gabonese languages. Nineteenth- and twentieth-century missionaries—including American Protestants John Leighton Wilson and Robert Nassau, French priests Henri Trilles and Maurice Briault, and French and Swiss Protestant missionaries Samuel Galley and Fernand Grébert—published abundantly on theology, evangelization, and Gabonese culture. Albert Schweitzer wrote both theological studies and paternalistic accounts of his dealings with Africans.

HOUSES OF WORSHIP AND HOLY PLACES Christian houses of worship in Gabon range from the ornately carved open-air Église Saint Michel in Libreville to rustic wattle-and-daub chapels where village catechists or evangelists lead morning and Sunday prayers. Priests and missionaries used African labor to build a number of churches and mission schools in the interior towns. With the spread of independent evangelical and Pentecostal groups, especially since the 1980s, new Christians hold services and prayer meetings wherever possible, including in private homes.

WHAT IS SACRED? Gabonese Christians recognize as sacred those things that are holy to Christians elsewhere, including the seven sacraments among Roman Catholics. Many Christians continue to revere their ancestors by constructing expensive cemented tombs and holding lengthy, elaborate mourning ceremonies that combine traditional and Christian rites.

HOLIDAYS AND FESTIVALS Christian holidays, including Assumption, All Saint's Day, Christmas, Easter, Ascension, and Pentecost, are marked by church services and family feasts. Holidays and even ordinary Sundays are important in both villages and cities for visiting, drinking, and sharing meals.

MODE OF DRESS Christian dress has become substantially Westernized in Gabon since the nineteenth century. Many Protestants wear brightly colored cotton choir gowns to service. Both Catholic and Protestant clergy follow European conventions.

DIETARY PRACTICES Evangelical churches discourage alcohol consumption. Aside from voluntary abstinence during Lent, most Christians face no special dietary restrictions.

RITUALS Christian rituals in Gabon include morning and evening prayer and Sunday service or Mass. Periodic revival meetings occur throughout the country. Clergy and lay members of the Église Évangélique, for example, meet to review policy, iron out differences, and renew their faith.

Gabonese Christians have traditionally performed elaborate rituals associated with weddings and funerals. Families went through intricate bride-wealth negotiations and ceremonies, the groom's kin transferring goods and money to the bride's kin to cement the union. Although officially illegal, bride-wealth transfers are still important in certain parts of the country. Church weddings occur, but separate civil ceremonies are necessary to legalize marriages. Funeral and mourning rites involve wakes, expensive transport of remains to villages of origin, and ritual purification of close kin. Elaborate and expensive end-of-mourning ceremonies take place a year or more after the death.

RITES OF PASSAGE Gabonese Christian rites of passage include baptism, first Communion, confirmation, marriage, and extreme unction. Initiation into revitalization movements, such as Bwiti and Mimbiri, include Christian prayers and hymns. Certain Gabonese groups—Christian Kota, Kele, and Kwele—practice elaborate male circumcision ceremonies outside Christian institutions.

MEMBERSHIP Since the 1980s membership in evangelical and Pentecostal groups has increased. The Catholic Church in Libreville maintains an active printing press for both religious and cultural materials. Christian television and radio stations transmit mainstream Catholic and Protestant religious broadcasts daily. Catholic and Protestant churches do not actively compete for converts; relatively few unevangelized people remain in Gabon.

SOCIAL JUSTICE Protestant and Catholic churches have played a leading role in education since the mid-nineteenth century and continue to run primary and secondary schools throughout the country alongside the public school system. Certain dissident Gabonese priests have denounced inequitable income distribution, poverty, and human rights abuses, but the Catholic Church has generally supported the status quo.

SOCIAL ASPECTS Both Catholic and Protestant Churches promote faithful, monogamous marriage, education for women, personal spiritual growth, and economic prosperity while opposing polygamy (which is legal in Gabon) and the physical abuse of women, both of which are common, even among practicing Christians. The Catholic Church has officially opposed abortion, birth control, and divorce, while Protestant missions accept divorce in cases of polygamy, physical abuse, and infidelity. Divorce and childbirth outside marriage remain frequent. Since the nineteenth century the majority of Catholic and Protestant church members have been women, who see the church as a space of relative freedom and benefit from missionary instruction, fellowship, and spiritual growth outside the daily constraints of marriage.

POLITICAL IMPACT In spite of tensions between missionaries and colonial administrators over morality and colonial policy, neither Catholics nor Protestants actively challenged French colonial interests. In the 1970s a handful of Gabonese priests began using the church to challenge the one-party Gabonese state. Father Paul Mba-Abessole had to flee the country after disputing President Bongo's right to run unopposed for the presidency in 1973. Mba returned from exile in 1989 to help establish the multiparty system. He was the leading opposition candidate in the disputed 1993 presidential elections, officially garnering 26.5 percent of the vote. After serving as mayor of Libreville from 1997 to 2002, he rallied to the Bongo "presidential majority," becoming a government minister and vice prime minister. Catholic bishop Monseigneur Basile Mve, President of the Bishop's Conference, mediated negotiations for the multiparty system and chaired the Democratic Transition Conference in 1990.

Since taking office in 1967 President Bongo has worked to maintain cordial ties with Catholic and Protestant leaders, intervening to contain leadership and factional struggles within the Église Évangélique, for example.

CONTROVERSIAL ISSUES Though both the Roman Catholic Church and conservative Protestant denominations oppose polygamy, churches allow men with more than one wife to attend services. Because of concern over high levels of infertility, the Gabonese government has outlawed abortion except in cases where a woman's life is in danger. Most Gabonese Christians value children and oppose birth control and abortion, but in recent years the high cost of living and increasing economic hardship have driven Gabonese to try to limit childbirths.

CULTURAL IMPACT The efforts of missions and, later, public schools in Gabon have resulted in high literacy rates. Early Gabonese intellectuals learned to read the Bible and drew on it to reinterpret their own history and culture. Today biblical traditions inspire Gabonese oral traditions, which frequently claim historical connections to ancient Egypt and Israel. Christian music draws on both European hymns, often translated into Gabonese languages, and African rhythms. The combined impact of Christianity and Western modernity, however, has substantially weakened masked dance and sculptural traditions that addressed ancestors, the spirit world, and initiation societies.

Other Religions

Prior to Christian evangelization Gabonese peoples belonged to both men's and women's initiation societies. These kin-based societies believed that ancestors participated actively in the world of the living. Initiates appealed to ancestors and spirits (who were subordinate to one Supreme Being, creator of man and the universe) for protection and prosperity and to strengthen social solidarity. People conserved relics of illustrious ancestors as sources of morality, protection, and power and as concrete representations of the ancestors. Healers (*nganga* in various Bantu languages) used divination, trancing, ritual, and forest plants to treat illnesses and to counteract sorcery. A wide variety of protective and harmful medicines and charms were composed of plant, animal, natural, manufactured, and human materials. Traditional Gabonese religions recognized many sacred objects and dietary interdictions, especially with regard to certain species of game. The flesh of certain animals was forbidden, for example, to men and women of child-bearing age. Traditional art, famous in Gabon, had an impact on European circles after a spiritual mask stolen from Gabon around 1904 was brought to the attention of Pablo Picasso, Matisse, and others.

Christian missionaries perceived the traditional religious reliance on relics as fetishism or demon worship and combated these practices with increasing success through the colonial period. Healers, however, continue to play an active role in both urban and rural Gabon. As a response to unprecedented wealth accumulation, social inequality, and the unrealized promises of modernity, fears of sorcery and ritual murders have increased since independence. Those who consult African healers (as well as members of initiation religions) follow food interdictions identified by their initiating priest or priestess. In both villages and towns food interdictions, traditional medicine, and charms are used alongside Christianity. Certain Gabonese groups (including Kota, Kele, and Kwele) continue to practice elaborate male circumcision ceremonies, considered crucial for successful accession to social adulthood. Urban dwellers return home to take part and to have their sons circumcised. Celebrations include feasting, drinking, dancing, and teaching of the candidates, both prior to the operation (performed by a specialist) and during the healing period. In the past women also celebrated first menses, which led to initiation into women's initiation societies. Female circumcision was not practiced.

The most spectacular and well-documented religious practice in present-day Gabon is Fang Bwiti. Originally a men's initiation society practiced in southern Gabon by Tsogho and Apinji peoples (who continue the practices), Bwiti was adopted by Fang men who worked in early twentieth-century Ogooué River and coastal-region logging camps. Initiates participated in all-night ceremonies that involved elaborate rituals and ingestion of *tabernanthe iboga*, a hallucinogen deemed sacred in Bwiti because it is thought to enable contact with the spirits. Initiates drew on elements of Bwiti to reconcile traditional Fang practices and the altered circumstances of the colonial situation. Bwiti continues to flourish alongside mainstream Christian churches. A syncretic movement, it has also drawn substantially on Christianity by incorporating prayers, hymns, and a strong faith in God.

Muslims have been present in Gabon since the early colonial period when West African soldiers accompanied French explorers into the area. During the 1970s and 1980s thousands of West African Muslims, including Senegalese, Malians, and Hausa merchants, came to Gabon attracted by the country's oil wealth. Muslim holidays include Id al-Fitr and Id al-Adha.

John Cinnamon

See Also Vol. I: *Christianity*

Bibliography

Fernandez, James. *Bwiti: Ethnography of the Religious Imagination in Africa*. Princeton, N.J.: Princeton University Press, 1982.

Gardinier, David. *Historical Dictionary of Gabon*. 2nd ed. Metuchen, N.J.: Scarecrow Press, 1994.

Perrier, André. *Gabon, un réveil religieux, 1935–1937*. Paris: Harmattan, 1988.

Raponda-Walker, André, and Roger Sillans. *Rites et croyances des peuples du Gabon: Essai sûr les pratiques religieuses d'autrefois et d'aujourd'hui*. Paris: Présence Africaine, 1962.

Tonda, Joseph. *La guérison divine en Afrique centrale (Congo, Gabon)*. Paris: Karthala, 2002.

Gambia

POPULATION 1,455,842

ISLAM 90 percent

CHRISTIAN 9 percent

AFRICAN INDIGENOUS BELIEFS 1
percent

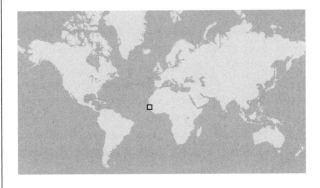

Country Overview

INTRODUCTION The Republic of the Gambia, located in western Africa, is shaped like a finger and is surrounded by Senegal on the north, east, and south and by the Atlantic Ocean on the west. A tropical country, it took its name from the Gambia River, which flows through it westward into the Atlantic.

The Gambia was a British colony until it gained independence in February 1965. Colonial rule had a significant impact on religious life, helping both Islam and Christianity develop throughout the region. Religion continues to be an important element in Gambian society and politics.

In the Gambia are several important ethnic groups, including the Mandingo (42 percent of the population), Fulani (18 percent), Wolof (16 percent), Jola (10 percent), Serahuli (9 percent), and non-Africans (1 percent). Although English is the official language, 16 indigenous languages are also spoken in the country.

RELIGIOUS TOLERANCE The Gambia has a remarkable legacy of religious tolerance. Religious freedom is guaranteed by the constitution. Christians and Muslims live peacefully together, interacting freely in daily life, be it in the market square, schools, political parties, or business ventures. This hospitable environment has created conditions in which Islam and Christianity have been able to thrive. Christians and Muslims have maintained their religious particularities while engaging in an ongoing dialogue about life and faith. Religious tolerance is also extended to adherents of African traditional religion.

Major Religion

ISLAM

DATE OF ORIGIN c. 1600 C.E.
NUMBER OF FOLLOWERS 1.3 million

HISTORY Islam in the Gambia dates back to the medieval empires of Ghana and Mali. It arrived in the Senegambian region (Senegal and the Gambia) in the ninth century, presumably (according to a general consensus among scholars) by virtue of itinerant traders, marabouts (Islamic scholars), and Islamic jihad (struggle, or holy war). The earliest accounts of Islam in the Gambia are from the travel journals of the fifteenth-century Portuguese explorer Alvise Cadamosto.

In the nineteenth century, as holy wars continued, Islam became fully established in the Senegambian region, and Islamic states were founded. By the mid-nineteenth century these powerful Islamic forces had to wrestle with non-Islamic groups in the region, as well as with the rising tide of European traders along the African coast. By the close of the nineteenth century, Gambian Muslims were, for all intents and purposes, under the hegemony of the British Empire, and Muslim leaders had to live side by side with this imperial power.

Islam at the beginning of the twentieth century was not a state religion but rather a religion of faithful believers who associated with different Sufi orders, such as the Tijaniyah, Qadiriyah, or Muridiyah. British colonial policies, however, created the perfect ambience for Islam to flourish. For example, by providing road networks and creating an access to the Gambia River, the British allowed Muslim leaders and merchants to connect with one another and to become part of the broader *ummah* (Islamic community). This gave Gambian Muslims the confidence to practice their religion without fear of reprisals or antagonism. Islam eventually became the religion of the elite as well as the common people, and Koranic schools provided the basic instruction of the faith. When the Gambia gained independence in 1965, Muslims constituted about 80 percent of the total population.

EARLY AND MODERN LEADERS In the Gambia a prominent spokesperson for Islam has been President Yahya Jammeh, who came to power in July 1994. He has been a strong supporter of religious tolerance.

MAJOR THEOLOGIANS AND AUTHORS Two noted contemporary scholars of religion from the Gambia are Lamin Sanneh (Yale University, New Haven, Connecticut) and Sulayman Nyang (Howard University, Washington, D.C.). Both Sanneh and Nyang have been prolific writers in the study of Islam, politics, and culture in the Gambia.

HOUSES OF WORSHIP AND HOLY PLACES In the Gambia the most important place of worship for Muslims is the mosque. The voice of the muezzin summons people to prayer at specific times during the day. Con-

Buckets are used to form a line for people waiting to get water from a mosque in the Gambia. In the Gambia, the most important place of worship for Muslims is the mosque. © NIK WHEELER/CORBIS.

temporary architectural designs for mosques generally follow patterns from the Middle East. Within some of the big mosques are Koranic schools where young people are given religious instruction and memorize verses from the Koran. The mosque provides a place for people to socialize, meditate, and perform the obligatory daily prayers.

WHAT IS SACRED? There is no element of the sacred distinctive to Islam in the Gambia. The mosque is the house of prayer and thus a sacred place.

HOLIDAYS AND FESTIVALS In the Gambia, Muslims celebrate the Id al-Adha (Feast of Sacrifice) and the Id al-Fitr (the end of the fasting month of Ramadan). For the Id al-Fitr businesses and government offices are closed, and invitations are extended to friends, neighbors, and family to join in celebrations. The Gambia is probably the only Muslim nation in the world that observes as public holidays Christian feasts, such as Good Friday and the Feast of the Assumption of the Blessed Mary. Christians and Muslims celebrate these festivals with pomp and pageantry. It is customary for Christians and Muslims to visit one another during these religious celebrations.

MODE OF DRESS In the Gambia many Muslims still dress in a traditional Islamic fashion. For instance, women often wear a scarf or another form of Islamic head covering as a visible way of affirming their identity. With the influence of modernity and globalization, however, it is now common for some Gambian Muslims to wear Western clothing.

DIETARY PRACTICES There are no dietary laws specific only to Gambian Muslims. Islamic dietary restrictions, however, are strictly observed in the Gambia. Animals must be properly slaughtered, and Muslims are forbidden from eating pork or drinking alcohol.

RITUALS In the Gambia, as in other countries, Muslims come together for the Jumat (the Friday noon prayer). The mosque is the center for worship and fellowship for Gambian Muslims, and prayer is central and paramount to their lives. The basic rituals before and after the *salat* (prayer) are strictly observed.

Gambian Muslims see the marriage ceremony—a celebration involving music, dance, and food—as the best way to bring families together. Islam in the Gambia has been influenced by the African ethos of communal commitment and connections. Muslim marriages reflect this aspect of African culture.

RITES OF PASSAGE The traditional stages in life (birth, marriage, death) in Islam are still observed by Muslims in the Gambia, though Gambian Muslims view these stages within the particular traditional teachings of their ethnic group. Muslims place tremendous emphasis on marriage. A dowry is required for a marriage to be legitimate. When a person is about to die, it is customary for a family member to turn the dying person's face toward Mecca and recite the first *shahadah* (Islamic declaration of faith), "There is no god but Allah."

MEMBERSHIP The Gambia Muslim Congress, a group concerned with Islamic *dawah* (missionary work), propagates Islamic values and teachings in the Gambia. Their primary goal is to bring new members to Islam. Other

organizations engaged in *dawah* include the Gambia Muslim Association, the Gambia Islamic Union, and the Supreme Islamic Council. In order to compete with Christian missionaries from the West, many international (including Middle Eastern) Muslim organizations have boosted their activities in The Gambia.

SOCIAL JUSTICE By the 1920s young Muslims obtained a basic education in Islamic schools. This educated class of Muslims established the Young Muslim Society in 1929. In the 1950s this organization was renamed the Gambia Muslim Congress. The organization's objectives were to promote and safeguard the interests of Muslims and ensure that Muslims occupied key positions in the government and civil service.

Nowadays such Muslim organizations as the Gambia Muslim Association, the Gambia Islamic Union, and the Supreme Islamic Council are involved in issues concerning social justice, human rights, equality, and total well-being for Muslims.

SOCIAL ASPECTS Gambian Muslims are encouraged to marry and have children. Celibacy and renunciation of sexuality are forbidden. Marriage is a solemn union sanctioned and blessed by God. As in traditional African culture, Muslim men in The Gambia can have more than one wife. Children are enrolled in Koranic schools at an early age.

POLITICAL IMPACT The availability of Islamic literature and increased globalization have helped raise political awareness within Gambian Muslim communities. Young people within national Muslim groups, such as the Gambia Muslim Association, the Gambia Islamic Union, and the Supreme Islamic Council, are politically conscious and raise questions about the political and economic policies of the nation's government.

CONTROVERSIAL ISSUES Controversial among Gambian Muslims is the status of women in religion and society. Although traditional social views have led to discrimination against women in education and employment (for example, just one-third of high school students are girls), the atmosphere of tolerance in The Gambia has encouraged open dialogue on the issue.

CULTURAL IMPACT In the Gambia a wide range of Islamic literature, in both English and Arabic, has become available, which has led to a growing intellectual depth in how people understand the religion. This literature has especially influenced young people in the Gambia.

Other Religions

In 1458 Diogo Gomez, a Portuguese explorer, arrived in the Gambia. According to written accounts, Gomez was the first Christian in the country. He met and discussed religious issues with a Mandingo chief, Nomimansa, who eventually converted to Christianity and begged Gomez to baptize him. Because he was not a priest, Gomez could not fulfill this request, so he sent the Abbot of Soto de Cassa to instruct Nomimansa on the basic tenets of the Christian faith.

Portuguese communities emerged in the Gambia shortly after Gomez's arrival. Settlers married into local families and established their own communities. They built houses and churches in the Portuguese architectural style. Priests from the island of Cape Verde, who maintained a regular staff of 12 friars, periodically served the new churches.

Although Christianity was received positively by the indigenous people, it did not enjoy major success until the early nineteenth century, when Protestant missionary activity started in the Gambia. Catholic and Protestant missionaries subsequently established schools in the area.

In contemporary Gambia the Christian community is largely Catholic. Other significant Christian denominations include Methodists and Anglicans. Catholic schools are prominent in the country. The government does not put restrictions on religious instruction, which is made available in both public and private schools.

African traditional religion is the faith of a tiny percentage of the population. Many Muslims and Christians, however, follow traditional rituals and practices during important events in their lives, especially birth, marriage, and death.

Akintunde E. Akinade

See Also Vol. I: *Christianity, Islam*

Bibliography

Anderson, J.N.D. *Islamic Law in Africa.* London: Colonial Research Publications, 1954.

Gailey, Harry. *A History of the Gambia.* London: Praeger, 1964.

Nyang, Sulayman S. "A Contribution to the Study of Islam in the Gambia." *Pakistan Historical Journal* (April 1977): 125–38.

———. "Gambia." In *The Oxford Encyclopedia of the Modern Islam World.* Edited by John L. Esposito. New York and Oxford: Oxford University Press, 1995.

———. "Gambia: A State in Search of Viability." *Africana Marburgensia* 8, no. 1 (1975): 3–25.

Sanneh, Lamin. *Piety and Power: Muslims and Christians in West Africa.* Maryknoll, N.Y.: Orbis Books, 1996.

Ungar, Sanford J. *Africa: The People and Politics of an Emerging Continent.* 3rd rev. ed. New York: Simon and Schuster, 1989.

Georgia

POPULATION 4,960,951

GEORGIAN ORTHODOX 70 percent

MUSLIM 10 percent

ARMENIAN APOSTOLIC 8 percent

RUSSIAN ORTHODOX 5 percent

OTHER 7 percent

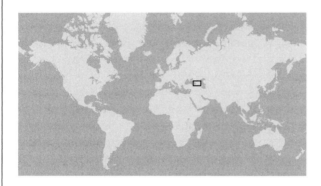

Country Overview

INTRODUCTION The Republic of Georgia is situated to the south of the Caucasus Mountains. It is bordered by Russia to the north, Armenia and Turkey to the south, Azerbaijan to the east, and the Black Sea to the west.

The Georgians represent one of the indigenous peoples of the Caucasus region, and the Kartvelian languages that they speak have not been conclusively linked to any other language family. Eastern Georgia (referred to as "Iberia" in older documents) was in the Persian sphere of influence, whereas western Georgia, including

the ancient kingdoms of Colchis and Lazica, had been in contact with the Greeks since Homeric times. After centuries of Arab and Turkish occupation, King David the Rebuilder (reigned 1089–1125) recaptured the capital, Tbilisi (Tiflis), ushering in a vibrant, but short-lived, period of territorial expansion and flourishing artistic and intellectual life.

The Georgian golden age reached its apogee under Queen Tamar (reigned 1184–1212) but soon thereafter succumbed to Mongol invaders from the east. Georgian lands saw little respite from warfare, devastation, and conquest in the following centuries, as Tamerlane's hordes and then the Safavid Persians swept through the east and the Ottoman Turks extended their hegemony through the west. In hopes that the protection of a more powerful Christian nation would bring peace, the east Georgian king placed his realm under Russian suzerainty in 1783; by the mid-nineteenth century all of Georgia had been incorporated into the Russian Empire. In the wake of the collapse of the czarist regime in 1917, Georgia declared its independence. In 1921 the Red Army invaded Georgia, and it, along with Armenia and Azerbaijan, was annexed to the Soviet Union. In 1991 Georgia seceded from the U.S.S.R.

RELIGIOUS TOLERANCE Georgia's constitution guarantees freedom of speech, thought, conscience, religion, and belief and prohibits discrimination on those grounds. The constitution asserts the separation of church and state, but it also recognizes the "special importance of the Georgian Orthodox Church in Georgian history." Traditionally—and as a whole, even now—Georgians are not given to religious fanaticism and are generally tolerant of the confessional diversity that has been part of their history for centuries.

Major Religion

GEORGIAN ORTHODOX CHURCH

DATE OF ORIGIN C. 326 C.E.
NUMBER OF FOLLOWERS 3.5 million

HISTORY According to tradition the apostle Saint Andrew the First-Called brought the gospel to Georgia. Other accounts mention the apostle Saint Simon, who is said to have been buried in Abkhazia, and the saints Bartholomew and Thaddeus, who are also credited with the introduction of Christianity to the Armenians. Certainly Christianity was present in Georgia by the end of the fourth century, as evidenced by the earliest known churches.

The adoption of Christianity as the state religion in Iberia (eastern Georgia) occurred perhaps as early as 326, a quarter century or so later than in Armenia. It was from Armenia that Saint Nino the Enlightener entered Georgia and, after performing several miracles, succeeded in converting the king and queen of Iberia to the new faith. The archbishops of Iberia, whose see was in Mtsxeta, were subordinate to the Patriarchate of Antioch until 468, when the Georgian church acceded to autocephalous (independent) status within the Orthodox communion. There is some evidence that Monophysitism was introduced into Georgia during the sixth century, probably from Syria, but by the end of that century the Georgian hierarchy had clearly sided with the Chalcedonian doctrine that Jesus Christ had two natures, divine and human.

The earliest Georgian-language texts date from the fifth century, but it was after the Arab conquest of Tbilisi in 645, when the centers of intellectual and monastic activity shifted to the southwestern provinces (in what is now Turkey) or to Georgian monastic communities in Syria and Palestine, that the greatest monuments of Georgian ecclesiastical writing were produced. This was also a time of active church building and icon making, which continued through the Georgian golden era.

In 1811, several years after the annexation of Georgia to the Russian Empire, the autocephaly, or independence, of the Georgian Church was abrogated by orders

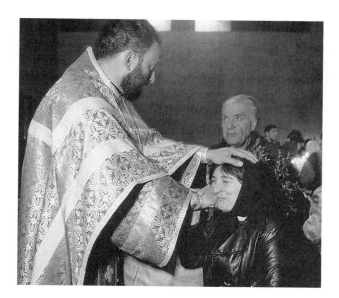

A Russian Orthodox priest blesses a woman during a religious service in Georgia. Russian Orthodoxy was introduced upon the annexation of Georgia by the Russian Empire in 1917. © PETER TURNLEY/CORBIS.

of the czar. For more than a century the church was governed by exarchs (bishops) appointed by the Moscow Patriarchate, of which all but the first were ethnic Russians. During this period the ancient frescoes in many Georgian churches were whitewashed, and old stone iconostases (icon screens) with the wooden ones preferred by the Russian authorities. Immediately after the declaration of Georgian independence from Russia in 1917, autocephaly was restored.

EARLY AND MODERN LEADERS P'et're I (467–74) was the first catholicos (primate) of the autocephalous Georgian Orthodox Church. After Bagrat III succeeded in uniting the kingdoms of eastern and western Georgia, Melkisadek' I (1010–33) became the first prelate to hold the dual title catholicos-patriarch of all Georgia. Since 1977 the catholicos-patriarch and archbishop of Mtsxeta-Tbilisi has been Ilia II (born Irakli Gudushauri-Shiolashvili in 1933).

Many Georgian monarchs took an active interest in ecclesiastic affairs. In the early fifth century King Archil is said to have convened the Georgian clergy in order to reject the Arian heresy, and King David the Rebuilder announced his reforms of the civil (and church) administration at the Council of Ruisi-Urbnisi in 1103. Also worthy of mention are the religious and civil leaders who founded monasteries in Georgia and abroad: Grigol Xandzteli, who established monastic communities in

T'ao-K'larjeti (southwest Georgia) during the ninth century; the scholar Ioane and the military leader Tornike, who undertook the construction of the famous Iveron ("Iberian") Monastery on Mount Athos (built 980–983); and the Byzantine general Grigol Bakurianisdze, founder of the Petritsoni Monastery in Bulgaria (1083). Over the centuries a number of Georgians have been recognized as saints, including the author and social activist Ilia Ch'avch'avadze (Saint Ilia the Righteous), who was assassinated in 1907, and Patriarch Ambrose Xelaia (served 1921–27).

MAJOR THEOLOGIANS AND AUTHORS The leading intellectual figure of the early Georgian church was P'et're the Iberian (411–91), the founder of several monasteries in Jerusalem and elsewhere in Palestine. Numerous monastic writers contributed to the rich corpus of classical Georgian literature, including the poet and hymnographer Ioane-Zosime (tenth century), the translators Euthymius the Athonite (955–1028) and Giorgi Mtat'smindeli (tenth century), and the philosophers Ephrem Mtsire (eleventh century) and Ioane P'et'rit'si (early twelfth century).

HOUSES OF WORSHIP AND HOLY PLACES It has been asserted that more than 10,000 churches and monasteries have been constructed in Georgia, many of them now in ruins. Some of the earliest appear to have been made of wood, such as the fourth-century construction uncovered on the site of the Svet'itsxoveli cathedral in Mtsxeta. Many fifth- and sixth-century stone churches, such as Sioni (Bolnisi) and Anchisxat'i (Tbilisi), were three-aisled basilicas, a style which subsequently evolved into the larger-scale three-naved design represented by the seventh-century church at Nek'risi. Also in the early seventh century a number of churches were laid out in a circular or octagonal ground plan, including the celebrated Jvari church overlooking Mtsxeta, the three tiny conjoined chapels at Old Shuamta, and the ruins of the cathedral at Bana in eastern Turkey. Beginning in the tenth century and throughout the golden age, great cruciform cathedrals with high domes were constructed throughout Georgia, notably Alaverdi, Svet'itsxoveli, the Bagrat cathedral at Kutaisi, and the uncommon brick church at Q'int'svisi, renowned for its frescoes. Among the numerous Georgian monasteries, mention should be made of those built next to—or even into—cliffs, with caves used as cells: Davit-Garedji and Shio-Mghvime (both begun in the sixth century) and the extraordinary complex at Vardzia near the Turkish border (twelfth–thirteenth centuries).

WHAT IS SACRED? As elsewhere in the Orthodox world, icons are displayed in great numbers inside all functioning churches, and most believers also have icons at home. Relics are not as prominent as in Latin Christianity, but several are displayed in Georgian churches or referred to in chronicles.

HOLIDAYS AND FESTIVALS The Georgian Church observes, by and large, the same holy days, fasts, and commemorations of the dead as do other Orthodox communities and establishes their dates according to the Julian calendar, which is thirteen days behind the modern (Gregorian) calendar. Easter is the greatest of the holy days, celebrated in a liturgy that begins at midnight with the solemn procession of icons around the church and lasts almost until daybreak. Some of these observances have distinctly local features, such as the strewing of box tree branches on the church floor on Palm Sunday (in Georgian, Bzoba [the Box Feast]). The principal Orthodox fasts are during Lent (Didi marxva), Advent, the two weeks preceding the Dormition of Mary (Mariamoba, 28 August [15 August îO. S.ï]), and from the Monday eight days after Pentecost until the feast of Saints Peter and Paul (P'et're-p'avloba, 12 July [29 June îO. S.ï]). Departed souls are commemorated on Meatfare Saturday (Xortsielis shabati), nine days before Lent; Soul Saturday (Sulis shabati), the day before Pentecost; and on the second, third, and fourth Saturdays of Lent. Of special significance to Georgians are Saint Nino and Saint George, each of whom has two feast days each year. Major cathedrals also have annual celebrations.

MODE OF DRESS Georgian liturgical vestments are comparable to those in other Orthodox churches. As ordinary garments, clerics of all ranks wear black robes with head coverings. All bishops wear cylindrical hats of roughly similar shape; that of the catholicos-patriarch is adorned with a large cross, whereas those of archbishops have smaller crosses, and those of bishops are unmarked. Georgian prelates also wear elaborate pendants and crosses—those of highest rank may wear as many as three—and carry a staff.

DIETARY PRACTICES Except for fasts, which are regulated by Orthodox conventions, Georgians are not subject to any special dietary restrictions.

RITUALS The Georgian Orthodox liturgy continues to be celebrated in the classical Georgian language of the ninth through the twelfth centuries, written in the old ecclesiastical script (*nusxuri*) rather than the secular *mxedruli* script that has been used to write Georgian since the Middle Ages. The modes and polyphony of Georgian liturgical chant are distinctive and share some features with Georgian folk song.

On feast days, especially in rural areas, numerous popular observances not sanctioned by the Orthodox hierarchy still occur at or near churches. Worshipers commonly circumambulate the church three times counterclockwise, sometimes leading animals to be slaughtered, whose meat will be served at a banquet (*supra*) within or near the church precincts. Even in Tbilisi, on the feast of the Dormition of Mary, worshipers leading sheep or bearing chickens crowd into churchyards, where they light candles and present written prayer requests to the priest. Some churches are pilgrimage sites, especially for people seeking healing or the birth of children. One widespread practice, even when little remains of the church save a pile of stones, is the lighting of beeswax candles, which are then affixed to the wall and left to burn out. As in some neighboring regions, Georgians visiting a shrine or other sacred site may tear off a strip of fabric from their clothing and tie it around a branch of a nearby tree known as a "wish tree" (*nat'vris xe*).

RITES OF PASSAGE The sacrament of baptism is administered according to Orthodox norms and is followed by chrismation (the equivalent of Catholic confirmation). Although it is normally a ritual for infants, because of Soviet-era restrictions on the practice of religion, many adolescent or even adult Georgians have only recently been baptized, including former members of the Communist Party. During the Orthodox wedding ceremony, the couple wear crowns and are referred to as "king and queen" (*mepe-dedopali*) for a short while afterward.

After death the body is exposed in the home for a day or two so that family members, friends, and neighbors can pay their respects. A funeral service may be held in the church, but this is not obligatory. Before taking the coffin out of the house, the pallbearers carry it around the room three times counterclockwise. Funeral banquets take place after burial, on the 40th day after death and, finally, on the first anniversary, to mark the end of mourning. On subsequent anniversaries of a person's death, family members will visit the grave site, light candles, and eat a small commemorative meal there.

MEMBERSHIP In principle anyone can become a member of the Georgian Orthodox Church through conversion and baptism, but the contemporary church has been strongly linked to Georgian ethnic consciousness and has few non-Georgian members. In earlier times this relation was conceived in quite different terms. The tenth-century writer Giorgi Merchule defined Georgia as the land "where the liturgy is celebrated in the Georgian language." At the time those lines were written, and especially in the following centuries, a wide variety of home languages were spoken by those who heard the divine liturgy in Georgian. Even as recently as the seventeenth century Georgian villagers were said to refer to all Orthodox Christians as *Kartvelebi* (that is, Georgians) regardless of their language or nationality.

SOCIAL JUSTICE Since the end of Soviet rule, the Georgian Orthodox Church has undertaken a number of humanitarian activities, such as operating soup kitchens, homes for the elderly, and a shelter for homeless children.

SOCIAL ASPECTS Under the Georgian constitution the church has no role in regulating marriage, divorce, and related matters. There is some opposition to abortion among believers, but it remains legal in Georgia.

POLITICAL IMPACT The Orthodox Church was integrated into the feudal politico-economic order of medieval Georgia. Many monasteries and bishoprics held fiefs, along with the serfs living on the land, and some accumulated sizable holdings through gifts and bequests from the nobility. In 1103 King David the Rebuilder granted the powerful office of *mt'signobart-uxutsesi* (grand chancellor, first in rank among the royal ministers) to his close advisor Giorgi, bishop of Ch'q'ondidi. For centuries afterward the chancellorship was combined with the west Georgian episcopal see in question. Under the Soviet and post-Soviet administrations the church leadership has had no official political role, but the catholicos-patriarch Ilia II has been a highly visible public figure for many years, and his opinions have considerable influence.

CONTROVERSIAL ISSUES In contemporary Georgia the Orthodox Church has been caught in the crossfire between traditionalists, who oppose ecumenism, and representatives of the minority religious communities, especially the newly arrived Protestant churches, who object to what they see as the favored status of the Orthodox Church. In 1997, under pressure from the traditionalists, the Holy Synod of the Georgian Orthodox Church withdrew its membership in the World Council of Churches. In September 2003 thousands of Georgians took to the streets to protest a proposed agreement on religious matters between the Georgian state and the Vatican, which was canceled soon afterward by representatives of the Georgian president. On the other hand, the church leadership has condemned the activities of the most extreme self-proclaimed defenders of Orthodoxy, such as the Basilists (violent splinter groups inspired by the excommunicated priest Basili Mkalavishvili).

CULTURAL IMPACT As in Armenia and the Slavic lands, the introduction of Christianity to Georgia was accompanied by the creation of an alphabet for the purposes of translating the Scriptures and other religious texts into the vernacular. Surprisingly the oldest known inscriptions in Georgian, which date to about 430–40, are located in what is now Israel. Within a couple of generations after the adoption of Christianity, communities of Georgian monks were active in Palestine and Syria, where, over the centuries, they translated numerous works from Greek, Syriac, and other languages and also wrote original hagiographies of Georgian saints. In the tenth and eleventh centuries major monasteries were established on Mount Athos and in Bulgaria, and these attracted some of the most gifted translators and philosophers of the period. At the same time, centers of learning were founded within Georgia, of which the most celebrated were the academies at Gelati and Iq'alto.

The first Georgian printing press was installed during the reign of King Vakht'ang VI (reigned 1711–24). Many of the books produced by this press were intended for use in the monastery schools and seminaries then being opened at the initiative of Patriarch Doment'i III (served 1704–25). This educational work was continued by the distinguished patriarch Ant'on I (served 1744–88), who was himself the author of many books, including a highly influential grammar of the Georgian written language.

Other Religions

The medieval Georgian chronicles mention military campaigns to subdue unruly "pagans" dwelling in the remote highland valleys of northern Georgia. Some mountain tribes accepted the state religion; others, however, resisted or fled further upland. A handful of Georgians living in the northeastern mountain provinces of Pshavi and Xevsureti have continued to practice a syncretic religion centered on the veneration of divine beings known as "children of God" (*xvtishvili*) or "icons" (*xat'i*). The Pshav-Xevsur religious system appears to have resulted from the restructuring of inherited pre-Christian beliefs in light of concepts appropriated from Orthodox Christianity and medieval Georgian feudalism. The highland communities imagine themselves to be the "vassals" (*q'ma*) of their tribal *xat'i*, which in turn is subordinate to God, the invisible sovereign of this cosmological hierarchy.

The first of the world religions to establish itself in Georgia was Judaism. A Jewish community has been present since ancient times in the old capital of Mtsxeta; synagogues are also found in major cities, such as Tbilisi and Kutaisi, and even in the town of Oni in the highlands of northwestern Georgia. It has been estimated that as many as 100,000 Jews once lived in Georgia. After Soviet authorities relaxed emigration restrictions in the 1970s, most Jews left the country, and fewer than 10,000 remain. In September 1998 the Georgian government officially celebrated 2,600 years of Judaism in Georgia.

Islam has been present on Georgian territory since shortly after the time of Muhammad, brought by the Arab armies who conquered much of the eastern half of the country. A significant portion of the Georgian populace later converted in those ancient southwestern provinces that were incorporated into the Ottoman Empire. Some of these lands were returned to Georgia in the nineteenth century, and they now constitute the autonomous region of Adjaria (Ach'ara). Most Georgian Muslims, however, remain within the borders of Turkey. The majority of Muslims residing in the Georgian republic are Azeris or members of other traditionally Muslim ethnic groups.

Other religions that have long-standing roots in Georgia include the Armenian Apostolic Church (the majority faith of Georgia's Armenian community, which is centered in Tbilisi and the districts adjacent to the Armenian border) and Yezidism (the syncretic religion practiced by most of Georgia's Kurdish population). European missionaries first introduced Roman Catholicism in the thirteenth century. The present-day Catholic community has been estimated to number about 50,000.

Russian Orthodoxy was introduced upon the annexation of Georgia by the Russian Empire, and it assumed a hegemonic status when the autocephaly of the Georgian church was abolished from 1811 to 1917. Since the restoration of autocephaly, the practice of Russian Orthodoxy in Georgia has continued, mostly among ethnic Russians. Also introduced during the czarist period were small numbers of Old Believers and the pacifist Dukhobors, who settled in the Ninot'sminda district of southwest Georgia about 150 years ago to escape persecution. In the late Soviet period as many as 6,000 Dukhobors lived in the village of Gorelovka and several adjacent hamlets. Since the breakup of the Soviet Union, about two-thirds of the Dukhobors have left Georgia.

Since independence a number of new religious communities have appeared in Georgia. Some of these were introduced by foreign missionaries, while others seem to have arisen through local initiative. The Jehovah's Witnesses, who have an estimated membership of between 15,000 to 36,000, have drawn the most attention. This religion has had a measure of success among marginalized segments of the population but has provoked the opposition—on occasion expressed through physical violence—of ultra-Orthodox zealots. Attempts have also been made by traditionalist politicians to ban the Jehovah's Witnesses. Other recently introduced Protestant denominations include Baptists, Seventh-day Adventists, the Salvation Army, and various Pentecostal churches. Their combined membership probably numbers a few tens of thousands. Since the last years of Soviet rule, a small number of young urban Georgians have become interested in Buddhism and other Eastern religions. A Hare Krishna temple has opened in Tbilisi, and this group has also been involved in charitable work.

Kevin Tuite

See Also Vol. 1: *Christianity, Eastern Orthodoxy, Islam*

Bibliography

Allen, W.E.D. *A History of the Georgian People from the Beginning down to the Russian Conquest in the Nineteenth Century.* London: Kegan Paul, 1932.

Charachidzé, Georges. *Le système religieux de la Géorgie païenne: Analyse structurale d'une civilisation.* Paris: F. Maspero, 1968.

Janasvili, Mose. *Sakartvelos saek'lesio ist'oria.* 1886. Reprint, Tbilisi: Ekvtime Xeladzis st'amba, 1990.

Lang, David Marshall, trans. *Lives and Legends of the Georgian Saints.* 2nd ed. London: Mowbrays, 1976.

Lomouri, Nodar. "Sakartvelos krist'ianobis saxelmt'sipobriv religiad gamotsxadeba" and "Sakartvelos ek'lesia da misi avt'ok'epalia." In *Sakartvelos ek'lesiis k'alendari, 2001* 111–46. Tbilisi: Sakartvelos sap'at'riarkos gamomtsemloba, 2001.

Menabde, Levan. *Dzveli kartuli mt'serlobis k'erebi sazghvargaret.* Vol. 2 of *Dzveli kartuli mt'serlobis k'erebi.* Tbilisi: Tbilisi State University Press, 1980.

Mepisashvili, Rusudan, and Vakhtang Tsintsadze. *The Arts of Ancient Georgia.* Leipzig: Edition Leipzig, 1979.

Nutsubidze, Shalva. *Kartuli pilosopiis ist'oria.* Tbilisi: Metsniereba, 1985.

Tuite, Kevin. 2004. "Lightning, Sacrifice, and Possession in the Traditional Religions of the Caucasus." Parts 1 and 2. *Anthropos* 99 (2004), no. 1: 143–59; no. 2: 481–98.

Germany

POPULATION 83,251,851

ROMAN CATHOLIC 34.8 percent

EVANGELICAL CHURCH IN GERMANY (EKD) 34.4 percent

EVANGELICAL FREE CHURCHES 1.8 percent

OTHER CHRISTIAN 1.8 percent

OTHER RELIGIONS 3.2 percent

NO RELIGIOUS AFFILIATION 24.0 percent

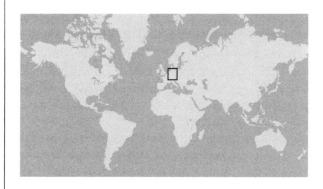

Country Overview

INTRODUCTION The Federal Republic of Germany is located in Central Europe between the Rhine River in the southwest, the Oder and Neisse Rivers in the east, the North and Baltic Seas in the north, and the Alpine foothills in the south. Lowland is predominant in the north, and in the middle and south are wood-covered low mountain ranges, such as the Harz and Black Forest.

Germany borders on France and the Benelux countries (Belgium, the Netherlands, and Luxembourg) in the west, on Denmark in the north, on Poland, the Czech Republic, and Austria in the east, and again on Austria and also Switzerland in the south. The German-speaking area transcends the German borders. Most parts of the country are economically highly developed.

Historically Germany has been influenced by a variety of regional traditions, which built the ground for principalities formed in the Middle Ages. These principalities became subdivisional territories of the Holy Roman Empire of the German Nation and were reorganized in the early 1800s. Since 1871 the princely territories have been federal states of the German Empire. In the organization of the federal states after 1945, the older traditions can still be recognized.

Since the Reformation of the sixteenth century, Germany has been bidenominational (*bikonfessionell*). A territory's affiliation with either Roman Catholicism or a Protestant denomination (Lutheran or Reformed) was determined by the Peace of Augsburg (1555) in the political principle *cuius regio eius religio* (the population's religious affiliation has to adjust to that of the prince). Only the hostility of National Socialism (the Nazi party) and, in East Germany, the Communist regime toward religion had a comparably great impact.

In Germany about 76 percent of the population is affiliated with an institutional religion, mainly represented by Roman Catholic or Protestant Christianity. Some 29 million people are affiliated with the Roman Catholic Church, and some 28.6 million belong to one of the member churches of the Evangelical Church in Germany (EKD). The EKD comprises Lutheran and

People participate in a procession for Leonhardi, the patron saint of horses, cattle, and prisoners. Places of pilgrimage are especially significant in the Roman Catholic church. © FRANZ-MARC FREI/CORBIS.

Reformed churches, as well as churches resulting from nineteenth-century unions between Lutheran and Reformed churches. There are striking differences, though, between the areas constituting the Federal Republic until 1990 and the former German Democratic Republic (under the Communist government). For example, in what was formerly West Germany, some 42.3 percent of the population is Roman Catholic, 36.8 percent is affiliated with churches belonging to the EKD, and 13.1 percent declares no religious affiliation; the figures for the former East Germany are 2.8 percent, 24.2 percent, and 70.7 percent, respectively.

Other Christian churches and communities exist in Germany, though their membership, compared with that of the Roman Catholic Church or the EKD, is small. The Old Catholics numbered about 25,000 members in 1999–2001. The small Protestant communities include the free churches of Anglo-Saxon origin and new Pietistic, fundamentalist, or charismatic communities, as well as such specific communities as the New Apostolic Church or Jehovah's Witnesses. In total, membership in these groups adds up to about 1.1 million. The free evangelical communities have been growing, while all other groupings have stagnated or lost members. The Baptists have about 87,000 members,

and the Methodists about 64,000. Among the specific Christian communities, the New Apostolic Church is the largest (with 388,000 members), followed by Jehovah's Witnesses (with 164,000). The different churches of Orthodox Christianity are also represented in Germany with about 920,000 members; the strongest are the Ecumenical Patriarchy of Constantinople, the Serbian Orthodox Church, the Romanian Orthodox Church, and the Russian Orthodox Church. Their membership mirrors the migration movements of the second half of the twentieth century.

Since the early 1960s the religious landscape in Germany has undergone remarkable changes, including an increase in the variety of religious lifestyles. This variety is mainly determined by a growing presence of world religions, Islam in particular. Nevertheless, Germany is not an especially multireligious country. It is still culturally Christian.

RELIGIOUS TOLERANCE Prior to 2002 religious groups that were organized according to Germany's association law—which provided legal recognition of different associations, including sports clubs or charity associations—were highly protected. Then in 2002 the following regulation was introduced: Even if associations declare themselves to be religious, they may be prohibited if they are suspected of opposing the constitution. Thus, religious communities that accept the German state constitution have religious freedom. The state monitors cases of suspected terrorist support and of suspected psychological manipulation, especially of young people.

The relationship between the Roman Catholic Church and the various Protestant denominations is marked by a climate of intense ecumenism. The rapprochement between Catholics and Protestants is practiced even more on the congregational level than on the level of bishops and other church leaders.

Constitutionally there is no state church. Legally the Roman Catholic dioceses and the Evangelical Church in Germany, as well as their subdivisions and unions, have a public status (they are corporations under public law). This is true also for some of the other Christian communities, above all the Christian free churches. Non-Christians, including Muslims, are mostly organized according to association law. Judaism and humanist communities, having a public status, are the exceptions.

With the growing number of Muslim immigrants since the 1960s, Islamophobia (bias against Muslims) has spread among the population. In the public sphere anti-Semitism is taboo but sometimes may be found in private discussions in combination with nationalist sentiments.

Major Religion

CHRISTIANITY

DATE OF ORIGIN Third century C.E.
NUMBER OF FOLLOWERS 57.6 million

HISTORY Only few regions of present-day Germany belonged to the Roman Empire and, thus, to an area of early Christian expansion. The actual Christianization started from the south and the west and reached northern Germany during the eighth century. The western parts of Germany that belonged to Charlemagne's empire were Christianized at the beginning of the ninth century and were mainly organized into parish churches (*parochias*). The Christianization of eastern Germany was linked with its colonization by Germanic tribes, which began in the seventh century and got to a certain closure in the twelfth century (Cistercian monasteries in northern and eastern Germany). Christianization in Germany did not focus on individual conversion but on the prince's conversion and, thus, subsequently, on the conversion of their subjects.

Historically Germany's Christianity is mainly characterized by the sixteenth-century Reformation. Influenced by their princes, some of the German territories converted to Protestantism, while fewer remained Catholic, together with the emperor. In the sixteenth century already, and especially in the seventeenth century, heavy military actions between Protestant and Catholic territories arose—for example, the Thirty Year's War (1618–48). In the eighteenth century the Catholic faith was revitalized, as the splendor of baroque church architecture convincingly shows. Protestantism also gained new inspiration, above all by the religious movement of Pietism.

Much ideological, political, and social upheaval was seen at the end of the eighteenth and nineteenth centuries as a result of the Enlightenment movement, the French Revolution, Napoleon, the German Revolution of 1848, urbanization, and industrialization. Religion and Christianity lost significance, and Protestantism identified itself with nationalist movements. In what was called Kulturkampf (culture battle), the state sought to limit the public importance of Catholicism. Various Christian groups and individuals tried to deal with the negative consequences of this social change. When Germany was politically restructured after World War I (1914–18), the Catholic and Protestant churches lost their status as state churches yet stayed corporations under public law; that is, they were still autonomous legal communities with public functions (education and welfare).

The age of National Socialism (Nazism) had a great impact on religious life. Only a minority of church leaders, pastors, and laypeople were critical from the beginning, although the fundamental opposition of National Socialism toward religion became increasingly more explicit. Members of this minority founded an emergency league. Later the Confessing Church arose. In 1934 the Barmen Theological Declaration was formulated in an attempt to minimize the influence of National Socialism and the state on the Evangelical Church and theology. The Christian churches in general put up with the government's actions against Jewish residents, or at least did not firmly fight against them.

As a result of general restorative tendencies, church life experienced an upswing after World War II. From the late 1950s on, the Christian influence subsided again, and fewer people participated in the Christian community life. The situation in the Communist part of Germany developed separately, and the number of church members decreased drastically. Even after the country reunited, this development continued.

EARLY AND MODERN LEADERS The history of Christianity in Germany is intrinsically linked with the lives of its religious figures. From the Middle Ages two saints of the Catholic Church deserve mention: the Benedictine nun Hildegard of Bingen (1098–1179) and Elisabeth of Thuringia (1207–31), born a Hungarian princess. Hildegard was a prophet and a mystic whose spirituality integrated different spheres of life. Elisabeth stood out because of her charitable actions.

From the sixteenth century on, Germany was dominated by the great Protestant leaders, above all Martin Luther (1483–1546). His Bible translation had an enormous impact on the development of a German standard language. His companion was the humanist Philipp Melanchthon (1497–1560), who worked toward the creation of Protestant educational institutions. The German Pietist movement is characterized by three personages: Philipp Jakob Spener (1635–1705), who formed Bible study groups; August Hermann Francke (1663–1727), known for his charitable and educational work in Halle; and Nikolaus Ludwig von Zinzendorf (1700–60), who founded the community Unitas Fratrum in Herrnhut.

In the nineteenth century some Christians challenged and promoted the charitable and philanthropic activities of the churches: On the Protestant side was Johann Hinrich Wichern (1808–81), and on the Catholic side, Adolf Kolping (1813–65) and Wilhelm Emmanuel von Ketteler (1811–77), bishop of Mainz. Some twentieth-century Christians became known because they embodied the resistance against National Socialism and paid for it with their lives. Among these were Dietrich Bonhoeffer (1906–45), the Protestant pastor Paul Schneider (1897–1939), the Catholic priest Alfred Delp (1907–45), and Jewish philosopher and later Carmelite nun Edith Stein (1891–1942), who was murdered in the concentration camp Oswiecim. Standing out among church leaders were the Protestant bishops

Theophil Wurm (1868–1953) and Hans Meiser (1881–1956) and the Catholic cardinals Konrad Earl of Preysing (1880–1950) and Clemens August Earl of Galen (1878–1946). In postwar Germany the Protestant bishops Otto Dibelius (1880–1967), Hanns Lilje (1899–1977), and Kurt Scharf (1902–90), in addition to the president of the Evangelical Church in Hesse and Nassau, Martin Niemöller (1892–1984), can be regarded as the most important Protestant church leaders. Important Roman Catholic leaders were the cardinals Josef Frings (1887–1978) and Julius Döpfner (1913–76).

MAJOR THEOLOGIANS AND AUTHORS In its several historical periods German Christianity has produced a great variety of theologians. In the Middle Ages German mysticism proved important. It was represented by the Dominicans Meister Eckhart (c. 1260–1327) and Johann Tauler (c. 1300–61), among others. Since the sixteenth century Martin Luther and Philipp Melanchthon, as well as numerous other Protestant scholars, can be considered significant. In the nineteenth century the Protestant theologian Friedrich Schleiermacher (1768–1834) paved the way for a theology reflecting the Christian faith against the background of modernity. In about 1900 scholars such as Adolf von Harnack (1851–1930) and Ernst Troeltsch (1865–1923) inherited this theological tradition. The 1920s saw a period of theological revision in different perspectives. Up to the second half of the twentieth century, the Swiss scholar Karl Barth, professor of theology in Göttingen, Münster, and Bonn (until 1935), was quite influential in Germany. U.S. emigrant Paul Tillich (1886–1965) was rediscovered in Germany in the late 1950s. Both formatively influential and controversial was the New Testament scholar Rudolf Bultmann (1884–1976), whose intention was to present the historical insights of the Bible in an existentialist way with regard to mastering the problems of life—for example, finding identity, overcoming illness, and approaching death.

On the Catholic side some scholars in the second half of the twentieth century stand out: the religious philosopher Romano Guardini (1885–1968), the dogmatist Karl Rahner (1904–84), and the social ethics scholar Oswald von Nell-Breuning (1890–1991). Cardinal Joseph Ratzinger (born in 1927), the prefect of the papal Faith Congregation, was a German professor of theology and an archbishop in Munich before the Vatican appointed him. The Swiss theologian Hans

Küng (born in 1928), who lives in Germany, represents an open dialogic Catholicism.

HOUSES OF WORSHIP AND HOLY PLACES Sacred architecture in Germany conforms with Old European traditions. Usually the churches consist of the nave for the lay assembly and the choir, with an altar. Besides the altar, the font and the pulpit are important basic elements. In the age of the Reformation, Protestants took over the Catholic churches.

During each period of Western architectural history since the early Middle Ages, churches were built in villages, country towns, and cities. Therefore, many churches of Romanesque, Gothic, and Renaissance style may be found. Only a few churches were erected during the period of classicism. In the last decades of the nineteenth century, the neo-Romanesque, neo-Gothic, and neo-Renaissance styles were predominant. In the beginning of the twentieth century, Jugendstil churches were constructed. A last heyday for church architecture was the postwar period after 1950, when new "modern" churches were built. Since the end of the nineteenth century, parish halls used for the different parish activities (and partly for worship services) were built.

WHAT IS SACRED? In the Roman Catholic tradition, the elements that are consecrated in the Eucharist liturgy are considered sacred. Sacred places are consecrated ones—thus, above all, churches and cemeteries. Places of pilgrimage are especially significant—for example, Altötting in Bavaria. In Protestantism there is no consecration of places, although the Protestant churches as places of worship and preaching, and the cemeteries as burial grounds for the dead, are highly regarded.

HOLIDAYS AND FESTIVALS The temporal structures of week and year in German Christianity are completely rooted in Christian traditions. Among the churches, Sunday is considered to be the first day of the week and is a reminder of the resurrection of Christ. The year recapitulates salvation history as the four Gospels tell it: Advent and Christmas remind of the coming of Christ, Lent and Easter remind of the salvational death and the resurrection, and Ascension Day and Pentecost remind of the elevation of Christ and the coming of the Holy Spirit. In the remaining time of the ecclesiastical year, there are only a few feasts.

Not least because of a strong Protestant influence, Sunday has continued to be a collective day off for busi-

nesses. Shops, offices, schools, and industrial plants are closed. The big church holidays are public holidays. Christmas, Easter, and Pentecost are each celebrated with two days off. Good Friday and Ascension Day are further public holidays. In German federal states with a Catholic majority, such Catholic holidays as Corpus Christi and All Saint's Day are also public holidays. In the more Protestant federal states, such Protestant holidays as Reformation Day and Repentance Day are public holidays. Some of the Catholic holidays, especially those of Saint Mary, are celebrated only by the church—there are no days off.

MODE OF DRESS Today sacred robes are used only in liturgical performance—for example, the Mass robes of the Catholic priests and the usually black robes of the Protestant pastors. German Protestantism has no specific episcopal robes and no robes for the lay actors in the worship services. In general, priests and bishops only occasionally wear professional robes in nonceremonial situations. In everyday life priests and pastors, as well as members of religious orders, cannot be recognized by their clothing, although there are nuns who wear a uniform. Like Catholic nuns, Protestant sisters sometimes wear a special uniform if they have committed themselves to lifelong ministry.

DIETARY PRACTICES Dietary and fasting practices are of minor significance in German Christianity. In the first half of the twentieth century, Roman Catholics still abstained from meat on Fridays. Protestants did the same only on Good Friday. Fasting during Lent is rarely practiced; only the Catholic clergy may do it. There are some efforts in both Roman Catholic and Protestant churches to revive fasting practices.

RITUALS The most eminent ritual in both Catholicism and Protestantism is the Sunday morning worship service, which Catholics normally celebrate as a Mass and Protestants as either a worship service with the Lord's Supper or a preaching service. Protestant weekday services are rare; Catholics celebrate them as Masses. In both churches special prayer services are mostly linked with specific occasions—for example, a prayer for peace.

In general, Catholic and Protestant worship life is highly influenced by local and regional traditions. This is also true for Roman Catholic pilgrimages. Places of pilgrimages are mostly located in southern and western

Germany. Every so often there are also pilgrimage tours to other European places (such as Lourdes, France). The Protestant *Kirchentage* and the Catholic *Katholikentage* represent a modern form of pilgrimage. They are places of political and social discussions and of spiritual reassurance and take place every other year. In the last decades of the twentieth century up to 100,000 people participated in the Protestant *Kirchentage*.

RITES OF PASSAGE Rites of passage still enjoy great significance in Christian Germany. Roman Catholicism calls baptism, confirmation, marriage, and anointing of the sick (also understood as accompanying dying people) sacraments. In Protestantism baptism is the only rite of passage considered to be a sacrament. In both churches baptism is mostly practiced as infant baptism, although it currently tends not to occur close to the day of birth but, rather, during the first year of life and sometimes even later. Catholic confirmation takes place around the age of 10, while Protestants celebrate it during adolescence. Protestant and Catholic church members strongly approve the confirmation rite. In the former German Democratic Republic the Socialist-Communist ritual *Jugendweihe* was a substitute for Protestant confirmation. Even today many young people in East Germany participate in this humanist ritual, but not in confirmation.

Christian marriage ceremonies are common, although the participation rate is lower than with baptisms and Catholic and Protestant confirmations. One reason for this is that an increasing number of couples (heterosexual and homosexual) prefer a committed relationship to a legal marriage. Homosexual partnerships have recently been given greater value by the German government, and homosexual partners may have a legal relationship comparable with marriage.

Finally, burial ceremonies are predominantly performed by Protestant or Catholic clerics. There are differences, though. In rural areas the percentage of Christian burial ceremonies is higher than in urban centers. For instance, in Hamburg and Berlin a growing number of church members prefer to have a secular leader perform the burial ceremony rather than a pastor. The secular ceremonies, however, exhibit a variety of elements derived from Christian tradition—for example, the Lord's Prayer.

In general, religious Christian celebrations are embedded into a wide range of activities, including such civil elements as eating together or exchanging gifts.

MEMBERSHIP Participation in church activities is low in Germany. Only 16.5 percent of all Catholics and 4.2 percent of Protestants attend an average Sunday worship service. Increasing the number of church members is an aim more of the free churches and not so much of the established churches, although even there regular evangelization events take place.

According to theological convictions, membership in a Christian church (which is acquired by baptism) is valid for a person's entire lifetime. People can legally end their membership by making a formal declaration at a state office. In 2000 more than 129,000 Catholics (almost 0.5 percent of the members) left the Catholic Church, and 188,000 members (0.7 percent) left one of the churches of the Evangelical Church in Germany (EKD). In contrast, few new people joined the Catholic Church or one of the EKD churches.

SOCIAL JUSTICE Among the German Christian organizations that are actively involved in humanitarian and sociopolitical work are Caritas Germany (on the Catholic side) and the Protestant Diakonisches Werk (Christian Social Services of the Evangelical Church in Germany). Their work, along with that of smaller Christian churches and organizations, represents a significant contribution to the German welfare state. Both Caritas Germany and Diakonisches Werk are umbrella organizations for numerous Catholic and Protestant associations or groups on the local, regional, and national level working in the field of social services. The larger of these run hospitals, schools and training centers for social work professionals, and homes for the handicapped, senior citizens, children, or the homeless.

The Catholic and the Protestant churches have bodies responsible for running international development aid programs, including Bread for the World and Church Development Service for the Protestants and Caritas Internationalis and Misereor for the Catholics. Both churches are engaged in assistance programs for eastern Europe. Furthermore, they contribute actively to forming public opinions on social and human rights topics. In addition to the church organizations, numerous smaller, nongovernmental organizations inspired by Christian ideals participate in national and international aid programs, doing grassroots work in poor countries, providing help for children, women, and the jobless.

In the field of education, many Christian congregations run kindergartens. Both churches and free Christian groups maintain Christian schools. Church colleges are mostly set up to train social workers. Besides that, a small number of church-run theological seminaries exist. Normally priests and pastors are educated in theological departments of state universities.

SOCIAL ASPECTS In the legislation of the old Federal Republic of Germany (West Germany), Catholic social teaching—above all, the principle of subsidiary—was influential. According to this principle smaller social units, such as families, should preeminently get supported by the state or the municipalities.

In general, marriage and family-building are highly valued by the Christian churches. Therefore, the indissolubility of marriage is emphasized. In practice, however, there is a high number of divorces, and church teaching holds little influence over the actual behavior of church members.

POLITICAL IMPACT Beginning in the fourth century Christianity was the exclusive state religion in Europe, initially in the Roman Empire. This cooperation, or sometimes antagonism, of secular and sacred power also existed during the Middle Ages and was mostly adopted in the Protestant territories. During the Thirty Year's War (1618–48), which took place in central Europe, principally in Germany, armed conflicts erupted between Catholic and Protestant territories.

The religious uniformity of the German territories was dissolved by the territorial reforms of the early nineteenth century. States that were biconfessionally oriented (having Catholic and Protestant church bodies) and that usually also had Jewish communities came into being. In former purely Protestant territories the prince continued to be head of the Protestant state church. The year 1918 marked the end of the German state churches; nevertheless, the big Christian churches remained privileged corporations under public law. Only in the course of the following decades did other religious communities, above all the Christian free churches, attain the same legal status.

Today Germany represents a corporatist model: The Christian churches are considered to be partners of the state, especially concerning social and educational work. Christian (that is, Catholic or Protestant) instruction is part of the ordinary curriculum in public schools. The Catholic Church and the Evangelical Church of Germany are also officially included in the process of social legislation. In special cases (for instance, bioethical problems) church leaders are members of advisory boards of the government. Both large churches have their offices for church-state relations in Berlin. They try to influence the public sphere in all political decisions of ethical importance.

CONTROVERSIAL ISSUES In Germany theological and ethical controversies exist both between the Christian denominations and within them, especially between those holding more conservative positions and those oriented toward modernization. When, in the 1990s, the Lutheran World Federation sought a consensus with the Catholic Church concerning the doctrine of justification (the central point of Martin Luther's theology, that justification means salvation by faith, not by moral life or religious activities), an intense discussion arose among German Protestant theologians. Another controversial topic between Catholics and Protestants has been the issue of a common Eucharist, which the Catholic Church has rejected, despite an ecumenical *Kirchentag* (church congress) that took place in 2003. Furthermore, the question of women's role in the ministry is controversial between the two Christian churches. While the Roman Catholic Church refuses it, many female pastors work in the Protestant federal churches, and quite a few women hold other positions of leadership.

Ethically German Catholics and Protestants share many of the same convictions—for example, in the field of bioethics. Many German Protestants agree with the Catholic Church in rejecting homosexuality, and whether homosexual couples should be blessed in a special church service similar to a marriage ceremony is also controversial among Protestants. The Protestant free churches, especially those of a Pietist or fundamentalist orientation, are strongly in favor of conservative norms (justified by their way of interpreting the Bible) regarding, for example, sexual behavior, homosexuality, and abortion. Concerning the problem of abortion, conservative Protestants make the same critical arguments as the Catholics.

Pregnancy counseling (*Schwangerschaftskonfliktsberatung*) is the most difficult controversy among Catholics. Since 1993 abortion has not been subject to prosecution within the first 12 weeks of pregnancy (though only if a counseling session takes place beforehand and the procedure is carried out by a physician). This kind of session was offered by Catholic and Protestant counseling centers. Among the German [Catholic] Bishop's Conference, pregnancy counseling by Catholic centers was controversial, and in 1999 the pope demanded that the Catholic Church stop participating in abortion counseling. Subsequently a Catholic lay initiative arose and founded the association Donum Vitae to continue with Catholic counseling work, though under their responsibility, not that of the bishops. Canon law of the Catholic Church does not accept this association, and it is also contested among the German Catholics. Pregnancy counseling within the state-regulated procedure by Protestant centers has not been affected by the Catholic decisions.

CULTURAL IMPACT The Christian influence on cultural development, philosophy, and the arts in Germany has been significant—not in the same way in all historical periods, but continuously up to modern days. Church architecture of the Romanesque, Gothic, and baroque periods and in the styles of classicism and historicism demonstrate this, as do the new church buildings erected after 1945. Critical references to Christianity are typical of the philosophy of German Enlightenment, German Idealism (Immanuel Kant, Georg Wilhelm Friedrich Hegel, Johann Gottlieb Fichte, and Friedrich Wilhelm Josef Schelling), and subsequent streams during the nineteenth century (Ludwig Feuerbach, Karl Marx, Friedrich Nietzsche, and others). The fine arts up to modernity refer to biblical motifs (as in the work of Emil Nolde). The Nazarenes of the nineteenth century painted biblical stories: Julius Schnorr of Carolsfeld (1794–1872), for example, became the most important Bible illustrator of German Protestantism. Another significant cultural contribution of German Protestantism was its church music, including that of Johann Sebastian Bach (1685–1750) and his predecessors and direct successors. The Mass remained a popular form into the eighteenth and nineteenth centuries (notably in the music of Wolfgang Amadeus Mozart, Ludwig van Beethoven, and Franz Schubert). Throughout its history German literature has expressed familiarity with, and mirrored, the critical arguments over Christianity.

Other Religions

Judaism, looking back on a history of a thousand years, is the oldest of the country's non-Christian religions. Its first communities were established along trade routes and rivers. The cities of Mainz, Speyer, and Worms were centers of Jewish life. In the eleventh cen-

tury participants in the Crusades caused pogroms against Jews, and in the mid-fourteenth century further riots took place. Even if the presence of Jews was tolerated, they had to pay extremely high taxes. The Reformation did not bring about any fundamental change. Because they were driven out of the cities (fifteenth and sixteenth centuries), the Jewish residents had to settle in the countryside. In addition, there was a small group of "court Jews" who lived at the courts of princes. State regulations for Jewish life existed from the end of the Thirty Year's War (1618–48).

The Enlightenment in Germany finally resulted in a growing tolerance and in the political emancipation of the Jews, which continued over the course of the nineteenth century. Although anti-Semitism never completely ceased, German Jews gradually identified themselves with German culture, even with the German state, to a remarkably high degree during the nineteenth and early twentieth centuries. At the same time, the search for a Jewish identity went on. Within and between the Jewish communities, some tensions between conservative and orthodox members existed.

The policy of the National Socialists was at first aimed at driving the Jews away from the country's social and political life and was subsequently intended to make them emigrate. Then on 9 November 1938 the persecution of Jews worsened: Synagogues were burned down, Jewish shops and apartments were rifled, and thousands of Jews were arrested, later to be sent to concentration camps. From 1941 until 1945 the National Socialist policy was to exterminate German and European Jews. Of the German Jewish population (more than 500,000 in 1926), only 5,000 to 7,000 survived the Holocaust, according to reliable estimates. The conscious decision of Jews after 1945 to stay in Germany or to return there led to the development of new Jewish communities. Since the early 1990s there has been a notable growth in the Jewish population because of immigrating Jews from eastern Europe. In 2000 there were about 180,000 Jews in Germany. Of these 100,000 were affiliated with Jewish communities.

Most of the Jewish communities in Germany are united communities; that is, they consist of Jews of divergent religious orientations. During the 1990s single, autonomous, liberal communities were founded. Regional associations, corresponding to the areas of the federal states (along with the individual large, Jewish communities in big cities, such as the one in Frankfurt am Main), are member organizations of the Central

Committee of the Jews in Germany, which publicly functions as an umbrella organization. Legally the Central Committee, the regional associations, and, usually, also the communities themselves are corporations under public law. Thus, their legal status corresponds with that of the Christian churches and communities. Other Jewish institutions include the Central Welfare Office of the Jews in Germany, a philanthropic organization; the Central Archive for the Research into the Jew's History in Germany; and the College for Jewish Studies in Heidelberg. There is also a Jewish newspaper. Early in 2003 the Federal Republic of Germany signed a state contract with the Central Committee of the Jews, in which the government committed itself to supporting the establishment of Jewish communities.

Jews in Germany have significantly contributed to cultural development. Notable are Moses Mendelssohn (1729–86), philosopher of the Enlightenment; Karl Marx (1818–83), who came from the Hegelian left-wing tradition; Georg Simmel (1858–1918), the co-founder of German sociology; the neo-Kantian scholar Hermann Cohen (1842–1918); Franz Rosenzweig (1886–1929), who, together with Martin Buber, translated the Hebrew Bible anew into German; and the most important representatives of critical theory, namely Theodor W. Adorno (1903–69) and Max Horkheimer (1895–1973). Also important are the writer Heinrich Heine (1797–1856), the composer Felix Mendelssohn (1809–47), the painter Max Liebermann (1847–1935), and the scientist Albert Einstein (1879–1955). With the rise of Zionism in the late nineteenth century and the experiences of World War I, a new reflection on the Jewish tradition began, as seen in the work of Cohen and Rosenzweig, the latter mainly in connection with Buber. Two outstanding scholars of the 1930s and the post–World War II period who are rooted in the traditions of German Judaism are the rabbi Leo Baeck (1873–1956) and Gershom Scholem (1897–1982).

Islam in Germany is relatively new. Since the end of the eighteenth and beginning of the nineteenth century, there have been a small number of Muslims in the country—such as embassy members, emigrants from Islamic countries, and German converts—but these numbers increased significantly after the State Agreement of 1961 between Germany and Turkey, which permitted and promoted the migration of workers from Turkey to West Germany. By 2001 the Muslim population in Germany had reached about 3.2 million; of these some 2.2 million were Sunnite Muslims, mainly Turks. About

310,000 Muslims held German nationality, with only 11,000 coming from ethnic German families.

In Germany the largest Islamic organizations are the Turkish-Islamic Union of the Institution for Religion (DITIB), Islamic Community Milli Görüs (IGMG), and the Association of Islamic Cultural Centres (VIKZ). Since the 1970s Muslims in Germany have also formed umbrella organizations on the national level. The most important organizations are the Central Committee of Muslims in Germany and the Islam Council for the Federal Republic of Germany. The policies of these organizations are different, and there is no agreement even on issues such as being recognized as a corporation under public law and establishing Islamic instruction in public schools. (Although in some federal states Islamic instruction is conducted in public schools, it more commonly takes place in Koran schools. The family is the main body responsible for Islamic socialization.) Only 10–30 percent of German Muslims are affiliated with the above organizations. The participation rate in Friday prayers is higher.

During the early 1960s, when the first Turkish migrants settled in Germany, Islamic places for prayer were inconspicuous, some being located in deserted factory buildings. This remains true, though in cities mosques have increasingly been built in the Muslim architectural tradition. In everyday life a Muslim woman's headscarf attracts attention. Young women wear a headscarf often to express an autonomous religious-cultural identity. It is controversial for Islamic public school teachers to wear headscarves, and the federal states have different regulations concerning them. In German public life the Islamic calendar of feasts is hardly noticed.

More than 90,000 German residents are Hindu; most are originally from Sri Lanka or India. In addition, about 160,000 people in Germany are affiliated with the different branches of Buddhism; of these 40,000 to 50,000 are of German origin. Another 30 organizations and groups belong to new religious movements, free religious movements, or different kinds of syncretism—for example, the Christengemeinschaft, a religious community that combines Christianity with Rudolf Steiner's anthroposophy.

Besides these religious communities, there are groups that do not consider themselves religious, yet provide spiritual support around the issues of healing, wellness, meditation, and self-realization. A conscious atheism is less common today than during the era of National Socialism and Communism. Some 18 percent of the population (almost 10 percent of West Germans but more than 53 percent of East Germans) state that they do not believe in God.

Karl-Fritz Daiber

See Also Vol. 1: *Christianity, Islam, Judaism, Lutheranism, Roman Catholicism*

Bibliography

Conway, John S. "Germany." In *Encyclopedia of Christianity*, Vol. 2, 398–408. Grand Rapids, Mich., Leiden, and Boston: Eerdmans and E.J. Brill, 2001.

Daiber, Karl-Fritz. "Evangelical Churches and Catholic Church in Germany." *Journal of Empirical Theology* 7, no. 2 (1994): 5–20.

———. "Religion and Modernity in Germany." *Social Compass* 43, no. 3 (1996): 411–23.

Evangelical Church in Germany. *Statistik über Äusserungen des kirchlichen Lebens in den Gliedkirchen der EKD.* Corr. ed. Hannover: Office of the Evangelical Church in Germany, 2002.

Oakes, Edward T., ed. *German Essays on Religion.* New York: Continuum, 1994.

Reynaud, Michel, and Sylvie Graffard. *The Jehovah's Witnesses and the Nazis: Persecution, Deportation, and Murder, 1933–1945.* Translated by James A. Moorehouse. New York: Cooper Square Press, 2001.

Scribner, Robert W. *Religion and Culture in Germany (1400–1800).* Leiden: E.J. Brill, 2001.

Sen, Faruk, and Hayrettin Aydin. *Islam in Deutschland.* Munich: C.H. Beck, 2002.

Smith, Helmut Walser, ed. *Protestants, Catholics, and Jews in Germany, 1800–1914.* Oxford, N.Y.: Berg, 2001.

Steigmann-Gall, Richard. *The Holy Reich: Nazi Conceptions of Christianity, 1919–1945.* New York: Cambridge University Press, 2003.

Williamson, George S. *The Longing for Myth in Germany: Culture, Religion, and Politics from Romanticism to Nietzsche.* Chicago: University of Chicago Press, 2004.

Wolfart, Johannes C. *Religion, Government, and Political Culture in Early Modern Germany: Lindau, 1520–1628.* New York : Palgrave, 2001.

Ghana

POPULATION 20,244,154

MUSLIM 16 percent

ROMAN CATHOLIC 15 percent

AFRICAN INDEPENDENT CHURCHES 14 percent

PRESBYTERIAN 12 percent

AFRICAN INDIGENOUS BELIEFS 21 percent

PENTECOSTAL 8 percent

METHODIST 7 percent

OTHER 7 percent

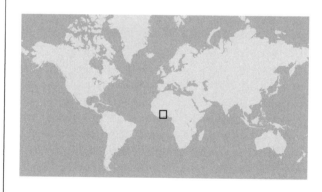

Country Overview

INTRODUCTION The Republic of Ghana, located in West Africa, is bordered by Côte d'Ivoire (Ivory Coast), Burkina Faso, Togo, and the Atlantic Ocean. Its capital, Accra, is on the coast. The land is characterized by tropical rain forest in the south and wooded savanna in the north, and the inhabitants live mainly by subsistence agriculture, cocoa cultivation, fishing, petty retail trade, and food processing. Gold, timber, and cocoa constitute the bulk of exports. The major ethnic groups include the Akan (49 percent), Moshi-Dagomba (16.5 percent), Ewe (13 percent), Ga-Dangbe (8 percent), Guan (4.4 percent), and Gurma (4 percent).

Owing to outsider patterns of conquest and evangelization, Christianity is found mostly in the south and center of Ghana and Islam in the north, while practitioners of indigenous beliefs live mostly in rural areas. One group of traditionalists, the Afrikan Renaissance Mission (ARM, or Afrikania), claims four million followers, but this claim has not been independently verified.

Traders and accompanying clerics brought Islam to northern Ghana in the fifteenth century. In 1482 Portuguese explorers established the first European foothold on the southern coast at El Mina, where the first Catholic mass was conducted. With the rise of the slave trade in the 1500s, the Dutch, English, Danes, and Swedes vied for control of the Gold Coast (the name given to the West African coastline from Côte d'Ivoire to Togo because of the vast quantities of gold being extracted inland). The Dutch eventually wrested control of the coast from the Portuguese and continued extracting gold and other wealth, doing little proselytizing. By 1875 the British had taken over the coastal fortresses, from which they exerted military, economic, and social dominance over the Gold Coast. The sixteenth through the nineteenth centuries saw the arrival of many Protestant denominations, but only after the arrival of the Basel Presbyterians in 1828 and the Wesleyan Methodists in 1835 did Christian churches take root. Mission schools effectively proselytized and furthered colonialism.

Ghanaians earned their independence peacefully in 1957. After the newly elected legislature passed a resolution calling for independence, the Gold Coast attained full independent membership in the Commonwealth of Nations under the name of Ghana—the first colony in sub-Saharan Africa to gain its independence. Ghana's first president, Kwame Nkrumah, was overthrown after attempting to marginalize Christian churches, which he believed had not played an active role against colonial domination. None of the several military and civilian governments since 1966 have been oriented toward any religion.

RELIGIOUS TOLERANCE Constitutional guarantees of the right to practice religion freely are generally respected. Religious institutions wanting formal government recognition must register. Few traditional religions were registered. Several missionary groups operate throughout the country with few restrictions.

Inter- and intrafaith tensions exist, although governmental and nongovernmental organizations advocate ecumenical harmony and religious tolerance. A ban on drumming and noise making before the yearly Homowo (harvest) festival in Greater Accra has raised objections from Christian charismatic churches, who argue that the ban is unconstitutional and prevents them from holding full worship services. Public and traditional authorities have intervened, and local committees have conducted public awareness campaigns and enforced the rules.

Muslims have objected to the widespread practice of prayer in public meetings and the requirement that all students attend devotional services that include the Lord's Prayer, Bible readings, and a blessing. A petition by the Muslim Students Association in 2000 and public advocacy by the African Renaissance Mission (a traditionalist group) resulted in government permission for Muslim students to practice daily prayers and to be exempt from nondenominational services in government boarding schools.

Major Religion

CHRISTIANITY

DATE OF ORIGIN c. 1482 C.E.
NUMBER OF FOLLOWERS 14 million

A Ghanian chief presides over his village. The leaders of African traditional religions are priests, chiefs, elders, and lineage heads. © PENNY TWEEDIE/CORBIS.

HISTORY Portuguese explorers brought Christianity to the Gold Coast in 1471. In 1482 a Portuguese fleet established the A Mina (El Mina) settlement, and sailors attended the first Catholic mass on Ghanaian soil. They reportedly prayed for the souls of the natives and for their conversion from idolatry. In 1503 the Portuguese clergy conducted a mass baptism for the first 300 Catholic converts—the King of Efutu, his palace officials, and their families. Historical evidence indicates that the Portuguese baptized and catechized slaves before shipping them to the New World.

Missionary efforts by the Catholic Augustinians and Capuchins in the sixteenth and seventeenth centuries produced little fruit. In 1752 the Anglican Society for the Propagation of the Gospel in Foreign Parts conducted missionary work in the interior of the country, but the effort ended in 1816 with the death of its leader. The Protestant Moravians also established missions in the eighteenth century. Of nine Basel missionaries sent to Christiansborg (a Danish fort overlooking the Atlantic Ocean at Osu, present-day Accra) between 1828 and 1840, not one made a convert, and several died of malaria and other tropical diseases.

The nondenominational, ecumenical Basel Mission Society, founded in 1815 in Switzerland, began working in the Gold Coast in 1827. After 1835 the Akwapim (an Akan people dwelling north of Accra) became the target of their efforts. They founded a boy's school in 1843 and a girl's school in 1847. They had by 1881 almost 50 schools and by 1900 two teacher colleges, from which many Ghanaian leaders have graduated. The Wesleyan Methodists arrived in 1835, followed by the Bremen missionaries in 1847, the Lyons Fathers in 1880, and the African Methodist Episcopal Zion in 1898. The Anglican Society returned in 1904.

Along the coast and among the Akwapim, Presbyterian and Methodist schools replaced indigenous beliefs with Christian worldviews, taught Western curricula, and began to train future clerks and other professionals, some of whom would become government officials and form a class of elites. In 1920 the Colonial Report counted 198 mission schools and only 19 government schools. Under the Education Act of 1960, the state assumed financial and curricular control for all formal instruction, but nearly all secondary schools today, particularly the non-coed schools, are mission and church-related.

In 1929 Christian churches founded the Christian Council of Ghana, an advisory body that presently represents 14 member churches and links them to the World Council of Churches and other ecumenical bodies. The National Catholic Secretariat, established in 1960, coordinates the 4 archdioceses and 14 dioceses. The Anglican Communion belongs to the Church of the Province of West Africa, which includes a missionary region and 13 dioceses, of which 9 are in Ghana.

Protestant Pentecostals and Independent African Churches are the fastest growing Christian churches. Between 1960 and 1985 the number of Pentecostals increased from 2 to 8 percent of the general population, and the numbers of African Independent Church members increased from 1 to 14 percent. The growth of these churches may stem from a view of Western church denominations as symbols of a colonial past and therefore alien to Ghanaians cultural and spiritual needs. The independent churches have shown an ability to harmonize Biblical teachings with traditional beliefs about divination, ancestor worship, and evil. Traditional remedies, libation rituals, chants and spells, communion with ancestors, and cultural displays are embraced to varying degrees in these churches. For example, rival drum societies and singing groups in the African Independent and Pentecostal churches are extremely popular among youth, who get from these activities a new sense of embracing Christianity without abandoning the indigenous faith of their ancestors. Mainstream churches have a tendency to see independent churches as apostate (defectors).

EARLY AND MODERN LEADERS Philip Quaque (1741–1816), the first African ordained as an Anglican priest, was a pioneer in education and missions. Thomas Birch Freeman (1809–90), born in England of an African father and an English mother, was instrumental in expanding the Methodist missions on the Gold Coast. Theophilus Opoku (1824–1913), a native of Akuropon, was the first African ordained as a minister in the Gold Coast by the Basel Mission. He was followed by David Asante (1834–92), educated in the Basel school in Akuropon and in Switzerland, who wrote on African religion.

William Wadé Harris (1865–1929), a Liberian by birth, began preaching along the Gold Coast in 1912 and became the first major African leader-prophet. He is recognized by the separatist churches in Ghana and Côte d'Ivoire as their founder.

The Reverend Robert Aboagye-Mensah, general secretary for the Christian Council of Ghana and president of the Methodist Church in Ghana since 2002, is the founder and executive director of the Ghana Institute for Biblical Exposition and Teaching. Bishop Kobina Quashie, consecrated in 1992 as the second Anglican bishop of the diocese of Cape Coast, became the archbishop of the Province of West Africa and bishop of Koforidua for the Anglican Church in 2003. The Most Reverend Peter K. Appiah (Cardinal) Turkson (born 1948), who was appointed archbishop of Cape Coast for the Catholic Church in 1992 and elevated to cardinal in 1993, presides at the National Catholic Secretariat. Dr. Mensa Otabil, founder of the International Central Gospel Churches, has since 1997 been chancellor of Central University College in Accra.

MAJOR THEOLOGIANS AND AUTHORS Mercy Amba Oduyoye, a highly respected theologian, has enriched Western Christianity with African thought and has authored several books on women and theology in Africa. She also directs a World Council of Churches task force to encourage women to take up theology as a discipline. Among Oduyoye's books is *Hearing and Knowing: Theological Reflections on Christianity in Africa* (1986).

HOUSES OF WORSHIP AND HOLY PLACES For Ghanaian Protestants and Catholics churches are sanctuaries and holy places. Many Independent African churches begin by meeting outdoors under trees; as membership grows and the church becomes more financially solvent, the congregation constructs a building for its sanctuary. In 2004 the Church of Jesus Christ of Latter-day Saints (Mormons) dedicated a temple in Accra, one of 120 such temples in the world and only the second in Africa.

WHAT IS SACRED? Ghanaian Christians consider the Bible to contain the divinely inspired, infallible word of God. Catholics and Protestants consider the sacraments sacred, and Catholics venerate saints. Such independent churches as the Twelve Apostles Church, Divine Faith Healing Church, Musama Disco Christo Church, and the Church of the Messiah emphasize spiritual gifts, including divine healing, prophecy, visions, dreams, and speaking in tongues.

HOLIDAYS AND FESTIVALS Ghanaian national holidays include Christmas and Easter, when Christians and non-Christians visit family and relatives. The annual Catholic festival of Corpus Christi, celebrated in Kumasi on the last Sunday of the church calendar, combines the feasts of Corpus Christi and Christ the King. Christians also celebrate traditional feasts, such as the Homowo harvest (a festival of the Ga people) and the Akan festival of Odwira, a traditional harvest feast.

MODE OF DRESS Ghanaians adopted Western-style suits and dresses from the missionaries, though on any given day, Christians might also choose to dress in Ghanaian style. Christianity has reinforced Ghanaian traditional modesty in dressing styles; for example, it is considered indecent for women to wear shorts in public, and men do so rarely.

During Catholic Mass in Asante, priests wear colors that reinforce the indigenization of the Mass. Cassocks of woven kente cloth are yellow for royalty and green for newness, vitality, and fertility—symbols of great importance to the Akan.

DIETARY PRACTICES Ghanaian Catholics do not eat meat on Fridays, especially during Lent, to remind themselves of Christ's suffering and death on the cross. In the south, where fish is an important part of the diet, this interdiction causes little disruption in the routine. Pentecostals may not use alcohol or tobacco. Some Christians who draw on traditional beliefs and practices to deepen their spiritual life observe other food taboos.

RITUALS Ghanaian Pentecostal and African Independent Churches have exuberant worship services with drumming, clapping, speeches, and offerings. Time is set aside for testimonials, prayer, and speaking in tongues. Mainstream Christian church services are typically three or more hours long. Protestants and Catholics file to the front of the church to present offerings.

Many Ghanaian Catholic churches have "authenticated" the Mass. In some churches in the Kumasi diocese, the priest and congregation recommit their vows using the language that devotees to a shrine would use to renew their oath of allegiance to a king or chief. They incorporate drums and song and dance that resembles the dance of a traditional priest; offerings of fruit, plantains, cassava, rice, eggs, and chicken are literally the fruits of parishioner's labor. Healing may include the sprinkling of holy water believed to protect one from evil spirits. Invoking the saints is seen as a way to stay in touch with ancestors.

Christians in the Asante region celebrate ritualized weddings, healings, funerals, and the Corpus Christi festival in ways that reflect traditional beliefs about witchcraft and the spirit world. A church wedding is typically preceded by a ceremony in which the family of the groom offers a bride price to the family of the bride. A Catholic lay church member offers a libation and says a prayer as in traditional practice but without the usual curse on the celebrant's enemies at the end of the prayer.

RITES OF PASSAGE Concerted missionary efforts to ban traditional cultural practices weakened without eradicating the influence of Ghanaian naming ceremonies, puberty and nobility rites, sacrifices, libation rituals, and funeral rites. Many Ghanaian Christians have fused the two sets of beliefs in their observance of baptism, marriage, and funerals. Catholics accord the sanctity of a sacrament to each of these rites of passage; Protestants do so only for baptism. During infant baptism the sprinkling of water symbolizes the parent's commitment to the Christian upbringing of the child, and although not expressly acknowledged, it is believed to protect newborns from evil spirits, sorcery, and other harm. Pentecostals and certain other Christian faiths practice adult baptism.

Passage from life to death is accorded great significance, especially among the Akan, as reflected in their elaborate funerals. At Christian funerals someone may speak to the corpse, wishing the departed rest and asking the cause of death. If sorcery or malevolence was involved, the deceased is implored to reveal those responsible before taking leave. The body is buried with the feet facing the bush, so that when the person wakes, he will head for the wilds. Some funerals affirm life and joy: modern bands, drumming, dancing, and refreshments are meant to appease the dead while assuring them of their continuity with the living. Funerals are both religious and social events where Ghanaians want to be seen and young people may meet members of the opposite sex. Saturdays and Sundays are funeral days, and many Ghanaians spend their weekends in some way participating in funerals. Those attending funerals are recognizable by their uniform dress, which may be black and red or black and white, depending on the region.

MEMBERSHIP Christian churches maintain and expand membership in a number of ways, infant baptism foremost among them. Protestants tend to pursue the biblical injunction to evangelize with greater vigor than Catholics. The Catholic diocese of Kumasi conducts outreach through the feast of Corpus Christi (the body of Christ), with its procession that moves through the streets with regalia fit for the Asantehene (king). Some churches, such as the Church of Jesus Christ of Latter-day Saints, require missionary work. Faith-based television and radio programming and crusades featuring world-class evangelists have become commonplace. Ghanaian missionaries live in New York and other eastern seaboard cities, where they minister primarily to immigrant communities.

SOCIAL JUSTICE Ghanaian Christians are exhorted to treat others as they would be treated, to be meek in spirit, to help the sick and downtrodden, to seek justice, and to minimize wealth and worldly pursuits for spiritual gain. In practice this belief system fits with traditional African attitudes requiring obligation to one's family, clan, community, and ethnic group.

Historically medical missionaries practiced social justice, introducing Western medicine into the Gold Coast in the nineteenth century. Until World War I missionaries were among the few providers of health care. Christian groups now provide modern medical facilities, including Catholic-affiliated hospitals in Sunyani and Tamale and the Presbyterian hospital at Agogo.

The Catholic Church promotes social justice through its Justice and Peace Commissions, found throughout individual dioceses with varying levels of activism. The Catholic labor union federation, an umbrella organization linked to European labor unions, protects the rights of individual workers.

SOCIAL ASPECTS Christianity introduced new sets of values about the family. When graduates of mission schools took jobs, they became less dependent on and less obliged to conform to tradition. Increasingly few Christian marriages follow traditional prescription, and some no longer involve payment of a bride price by the groom's family to the bride's family. Many Christian churches refuse to offer the sacraments to those in polygamous marriages, including the first wife, even though she is not responsible for her husband's taking of a second wife. Divorce and artificial birth control are proscribed by the Catholic Church and strongly discouraged by some Protestants.

POLITICAL IMPACT During the colonial period Ghanaians educated in Christian secondary schools often became the intermediaries between the rulers and the indigenous peoples. No longer dependent on lineage patterns for wealth and status, these new elites were able to become urbanized and enter into the market economy and later into modern politics. Kwame Nkrumah, Ghana's first president, was a product of missionary schools.

The Catholic Bishops Conference and the Christian Council of Ghana have occasionally used their influence to advocate for political reforms. In 1991 these organizations pressured the military government of the Provisional National Defense Council (PNDC) to return the country to civilian rule and forced Flight Lieutenant Jerry Rawlings (leader of the PNDC) to make several concessions. Among these was a new constitution, signed in 1992, which safeguarded civil rights, paved the way for multiparty elections, and opened the arena for new decentralization laws. A Catholic newspaper, *The Standard*, has often criticized the government.

CONTROVERSIAL ISSUES Some hard-line Christians and their churches have adopted intolerant attitudes toward traditional practices, branding them pagan, heathen, and antithetical to Christianity. This view is in part the legacy of foreign missionaries and teachers, who punished children for watching puberty rites and fetish dancing, as well as for eating food used in traditional rites and sacrifices, which the missionaries felt was subject to the influence of evil spirits. In 2001 the Local Council of Churches in Sunyani called for an end to the pouring of public libations in state ceremonies, claiming the practice was primitive, backward, misleading to illiterates, and a hindrance to national development.

CULTURAL IMPACT Christian missionaries equated Ghanaian traditional art with fetishes, sacrifices to pagan gods, and heathen depravity. Christian teachings and values suppressed "living" art forms such as masks, brass gold weights with carved figurines, stools, and bracelets decorated with animals, all inspired by traditional religious beliefs. As a result, contemporary blacksmiths, sculptors, carvers, weavers, and painters produce objects to satisfy the demands of Western tourists. Crucifixes, medallions with the likeness of the Virgin Mary, and other religious objects are also available. Artists have woven wall hangings for churches depicting Christ and the saints.

Christianity has also left its imprint on music. In many churches Ghanaians perform Western-style music, from gospel to Christian pop, besides the popular hymns. Funerals are as likely to have gospel music as hymns. Christianity has also assimilated Ghanaian culture: At the Corpus Christi festival, Asante musical instruments (*kete*), such as flutes, pipes, and drums, are played much as they were for the Asantehene's (king's) court, only now they proclaim Jesus Christ as king.

Other Religions

African traditional religion (ATR) and Islam have fewer members than Christianity but are extremely influential in Ghanaian life—ATR for its deeply rooted belief system (which concerns all aspects of life) and Islam for the unifying role it plays in the social, economic, and political spheres in the predominately Muslim north.

The practice of ATR in Ghana is ancient. It is anchored in the belief in a Supreme Being (Nyame in Akan; Mawu in Ewe) far removed from human existence yet linked to human beings by lesser deities in their natural surroundings and accessible most directly to people through their ancestors. The living carefully avoid actions that may adversely affect the spirits of the departed. Ancestors can support the prosperity and good health of the lineage and offer protection from evil; they may be reincarnated through the birth of one's children.

The leaders of ATR are priests, chiefs, elders, and lineage heads. Priests, who learn to be diviners and healers, are associated with simple shrines that may be no more than mud huts in reed-fenced enclosures. Here Ghanaians come for healing, advice, and assistance in controlling their fortunes and destiny. The spirits of the lesser deities are believed to communicate through the priests. Many places are sacred; Bosumtwi Lake, for example, is sacred to the Asante. The general population participates in ATR through such annual festivities as the Odwira of the Akan, the Homowo of the Ga-Adangbe, and the Aboakyir of the Efutu people of the coast (Guan). Priests and lineage heads make sacrifices and pour libations during these celebrations to strengthen people's relationship with their ancestors.

One controversial element of ATR in Ghana has been the practice of Trokosi (or Fiashidi), a form of religious servitude, which some have labeled slavery. Practitioner families, mainly among the Ewe in the Volta region, send a virgin girl, sometimes under the age of 10, to a shrine for several weeks or as much as three years or more to atone for an allegedly heinous crime committed by a family member. The girls, who often stay with a family in the village who are members of the shrine, are charges of the priests and under their religious instruction. They help with the maintenance of the shrine, drawing water, working on the shrine's garden, and doing agricultural or household labor. If the girl's family is unable to provide the gifts required for her final release, she may remain at the shrine indefinitely—hence the charge of slavery. Some priests have reportedly taken sexual advantage of their charges, but there is little evidence of this as a widespread practice. A U.S. State Department investigation revealed that around 100 girls were serving at two dozen active Trokosi shrines in the Volta Region in 2001 and 2002.

Another controversy has evolved over the treatment of elderly rural traditionalist women, often widows, who are accused of witchcraft and sometimes beaten or lynched. In 2003 as many as 850 women may have been banished from their villages to live in "witch camps" in the north of the country.

Islam spread into the ancient Ghana Empire of West Africa in the ninth century, mainly as a result of trade with North African Muslims. It arrived in the northern territories of present-day Ghana around the fifteenth century through Mande and Wangara traders and clerics. In the northeast, Islam gained acceptance from people who had escaped the Hausa jihads of northern Nigeria in the early nineteenth century.

Aside from the north, Muslims are concentrated in urban centers such as Accra, Kumasi, Sekondi-Takoradi, Tamale, and Wa. Most Ghanaian Muslims are Sunni of the Maliki legal tradition; a minority of Muslims subscribe to the Shafi'i school of thought. While the mystical brotherhoods (*tariq*) are scarce among Ghanaians, the Tijaniyah and the Qadiriyah brotherhoods are more popular. A Shiite sect called the Ahmadiyah, which originated in India in the nineteenth century and was brought to Ghana by Pakistani missionaries in 1921, is the only non-Sunni order in the country. Officially Muslims account for 16 percent of the population, but the Coalition of Muslim Organizations considers the 2000 national census flawed and estimates the number to be approximately 30 percent.

Muslims are united under the Muslim Representative Council in Accra, which guides them in religious, social, and economic matters, mediates conflicts between Muslims of different strands of Islam, and arranges pilgrimages to Mecca. The council also provides for basic Koranic instruction in Islamic schools. One of the challenges facing the council and Muslims generally is the relative scarcity of natural resources and the low level of economic development in the northern regions of the country. The Ahmadiyah movement has built vocational training centers, hospitals, and some secondary schools and teaches the Western curriculum in an effort to narrow the gap between the Muslim north and the more economically developed and prosperous predominately Christian south. One of the nationally recognized festivals in Ghana is the Damba festival in Wa, which commemorates the birth of the prophet Muhammad.

Other non-Christian religions with small followings in Ghana include the Bahai faith, Buddhism, Judaism, Hinduism, Shintoism, Nichiren Shoshu Soka Gakkai, Sri Sathya Sai Baba Sera, Sat Sang, Eckanker, the Divine Light Mission, the Hare Krishnas, and Rastafarianism.

Robert Groelsema

See Also Vol. I: *African Traditional Beliefs, Christianity, Islam, Roman Catholicism*

Bibliography

Africa South of the Sahara 2004: The Republic of Ghana. 33rd ed. London: Europa Publications, 2003.

Berry, La Verle, ed. *Ghana: A Country Study.* Area Handbook Series. Washington, D.C.: U.S. Government Printing Office, 1995.

Dictionary of African Christian Bibliography. 10 Sept. 2004. http://www.gospelcom.net/dacb/index.html.

Obeng, Pashington. *Asante Catholicism: Religious and Cultural Reproduction among the Akan of Ghana.* Leiden: E.J. Brill, 1996.

Owoahene-Acheampong. *Inculturation and African Religion: Indigenous and Western Approaches to Medical Practice.* American University Studies, Series XXI: Regional Studies, vol. 16. New York: Peter Lang, 1998.

Owusu-Ansah, David, and Daniel Miles McFarland. *Historical Dictionary of Ghana.* No. 39 of *African Historical Dictionaries.* Lanham, Md., and London: Scarecrow Press, 1995.

Greece

POPULATION 10,645,343

EASTERN ORTHODOX 97 percent

MUSLIM 1.3 percent

ROMAN CATHOLIC 0.6 percent

PROTESTANT 0.2 percent

JEWISH 0.05 percent

OTHER 0.85 percent

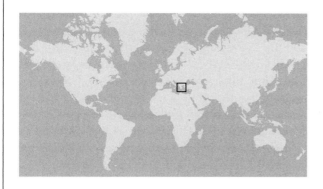

Country Overview

INTRODUCTION Greece (formally known in English as the Hellenic Republic) is located in the southern Balkan Peninsula. A mountainous country, it is bordered to the east by the Aegean Sea, to the south by the Mediterranean Sea, and to the west by the Ionian Sea. To the north it shares land borders with Albania, Macedonia (FYROM), Bulgaria, and Turkey. Its territories include more than 2,000 islands.

Greece is known as the cradle of ancient Hellenic civilization, and yet, since the Byzantine period, Ortho-

dox Christianity has been the dominant religion. Following the emergence of Greece from centuries of Ottoman control and the foundation (1828), international recognition (London Protocol of 1830), and territorial expansion of the Greek state, the Orthodox Church became closely associated with the state, and it has often fallen victim to Greece's turbulent politics. In the early twentieth century the clash between Prime Minister Eleutherios Venizelos and King Constantine, who was supported by the Church hierarchy, and the internal partitioning of Greece from 1915 to 1917, are examples of this, as is the period from 1967 to 1974, when a military dictatorship controlled the country. While these events affected the public image of the Church as an institution to some extent, they had no visible negative impact upon the overall significance of Orthodoxy for the Greek people.

RELIGIOUS TOLERANCE The Greek constitution of 1975 recognizes Orthodoxy as the prevailing, established religion and the Orthodox Church as a public entity with legal privileges. Orthodoxy is not the official state religion, yet many politicians and believers—and the Church itself—act as if it were so because of its overwhelming presence in Greek history. Consequently, although the constitution guarantees freedom of conscience and of all recognized religions and prohibits proselytism and discrimination on religious grounds, Orthodoxy enjoys many special privileges. Religious minorities—the Jehovah's Witnesses, for example—have protested this, and Greece was condemned in the 1990s by the European Court of Human Rights for religious discrimination. Despite these problems, the Church has frequently shown a tolerant and supporting face toward

Greek Orthodox priests bless the sea on the Holy Day of Epiphany by throwing a cross into the water. Swimmers compete to retrieve the cross that, according to legend, brings health and happiness to whomever finds it. © AFP/CORBIS.

non-Orthodox Greek citizens—toward the Jewish population, for example, during World War II. The Greek Church is a founding member of the World Council of Churches and seeks ecumenical dialogue, though some hard-liners, including monks and nuns, are critical of this ecumenical spirit.

The calendar reform of 1924 caused an internal schism in the Greek Church, since it meant adopting the Gregorian calendar, which had been in use in the west since the sixteenth century, but which had been developed under the aegis of the papacy. The Old Calendarists, the self-named True Orthodox Christians of Greece, consist of several independent groupings that control many monasteries and convents, and they claim about one million adherents, though their number is actually much smaller—between 300,000 and 500,000. They still use the old Julian calendar.

Major Religion

GREEK ORTHODOX CHURCH

DATE OF ORIGIN 49 or 50 C.E.
NUMBER OF FOLLOWERS 10.3 million

HISTORY The Greek Church considers itself to be in direct continuity with the early Christian communities of Philippi, Beroea, Thessaloniki, Corinth, and Athens,

which were founded by the apostle Paul. Two known Christian apologists of the second century, Athenagoras and Aristeides, were from Athens. At the time the Greek language was an important medium of communication and marked the fruitful encounter of Christianity with Hellenism, which was, however, far from peaceful. Tension between the two prevailed throughout late antiquity and beyond, despite the wider Christianization of the Greek area that began in the fourth century and the official prohibition of paganism by the Byzantine emperor Theodosius I, who ruled the eastern Roman Empire from 379 to 392 and both the eastern and western empire from 392 to 395. The part of Greece that belonged to the Exarchate of Eastern Illyricum was jurisdictionally subject to the bishop of Rome, but it became dependent on the Patriarchate of Constantinople in 732. During the Byzantine period (330–1453), which was occasionally interrupted by Slav and Frankish occupations, Greece did not play a major role in Church politics, with the exception of the bishopric of Thessaloniki, the despotate of Epirus, and the monasteries that began to develop in the tenth century, which included Hosios Loukas, Athos, Daphni, Kaisariani, Patmos, Mystra, Meteora, Nea Moni on the island of Chios, and Vlatadon in Thessaloniki. Under Ottoman rule (1453–1821) Greece remained ecclestiastically dependent upon Constantinople, while the Church undertook many nonreligious functions with respect to the subjugated Orthodox population. Following the birth of Greek nationalism and the achievement of independence, the Church was unilaterally declared autocephalous (self-governed) in 1833, after the arrival of Greece's first king, Otto Wittelsbach of Bavaria. This separation was formally approved by Constantinople in 1850. During the nineteenth century the Greek Church was weakened through its subjection to, and control by, the state, but it still managed to remain influential because of its strong involvement in Greek irredentism. Despite Greece's territorial expansion in the nineteenth and twentieth centuries, some of the acquired lands—mainly in Epirus, Macedonia, and Western Thrace—remained under the spiritual, but not administrative, jurisdiction of Constantinople. Crete retains a semiautonomous status under Constantinople, while the remaining areas, which include Mount Athos and the Church of the Dodecanese, are directly subjected to it. Despite problems in its relations with the Greek state and other tribulations, the Church's social and legal position gradually ameliorated during the twentieth century. According to its holy canons and its charter of 1977, the Church is governed by a 12-member permanent Holy Synod of metropolitans, who serve in one-year rotations under the presidency of the archbishop of Athens and all Greece.

EARLY AND MODERN LEADERS Many Greeks have held important ecclesiastical posts and have played leading roles in their country's history. For example, Gregory V, patriarch of Constantinople, was hanged by the Turks in 1821 after the eruption of the Greek War of Independence and is now honored as an ethnomartyr. Archbishop Damaskinos (1891–1949) served as viceroy for a short period after World War II. Athenagoras, patriarch of Constantinople from 1948 to 1972, was known for his ecumenical endeavours, including the rapprochement achieved between Orthodox Christians and Roman Catholics after many centuries of schism. Many contemporary Greek prelates—including Anastasios Yannoulatos (born in 1929), archbishop of Tirana and all Albania, and Demetrios Trakatellis (born in 1928), archbishop of the Greek Orthodox Archdiocese of America—have established international reputations.

MAJOR THEOLOGIANS AND AUTHORS Leaving aside the numerous known Greek theologians of the past—from Andrew of Crete (died in 740) and Gregory Palamas (1296–1359) to Eugenios Voulgaris (1716–1806) and Nikiphoros Theotokis (1736—1800)—and concentrating on the contemporary period, there are several theologians who have become known beyond Greece's borders. These include Hamilcar Alivizatos (1887–1969), Nikos Nissiotis (1925–1986), Savas Agourides (born in 1921), John Zizioulas (born in 1931), and Christos Yannaras (born in 1935). There are two theological schools in Greece at the university level, in Athens (since 1837) and in Thessaloniki (since 1942), instructing both clergy and laypeople. Many Greek theologians have completed postgraduate studies in western Europe and the United States. The Church itself supports several seminaries for the training of parish priests, though the priests often lack good education, while the best-trained theologians are laymen.

HOUSES OF WORSHIP AND HOLY PLACES Greek Orthodox houses of worship are the churches and chapels dedicated to Christ, the Mother of God, or a male or female saint. Monasteries and convents are also considered holy places. Most churches are dedicated to the Mother of God, who is depicted in numerous icons, is characterized by numerous specific attributes, and represents the most popular figure within Greek Orthodoxy. Her most popular pilgrimage site, on the Aegean island of Tinos, is associated in many ways with Greece's recent political history. There, in 1823, her miraculous icon, allegedly painted by the evangelist Saint Luke, was unearthed.

Pilgrimage sites in Greece are usually associated with miraculous healings and votive offerings. Many famous monasteries, including those of Mount Athos and Meteora, as well as the monastery of Saint John the Theologian on the island of Patmos, are important places of pilgrimage. According to Byzantine tradition women are not allowed access to the monastic complex on Mount Athos. Popular pilgrimage sites on the islands of Aigina and Mytilini are dedicated, respectively, to Saint Nectarios and to Saints Raphael, Nicolaos, and Irene.

WHAT IS SACRED? The Greek landscape as a whole can be considered sacred since it is filled with churches, chapels, monasteries, convents, and shrines. This phenomenon has its antecedent in ancient Greece, though sacredness, including that of nature, was understood differently then. More specifically, Greek Orthodox venerate the icons and the relics of saints as well as such sacred objects as fragments of the Holy Cross. Most of these are preserved in the monasteries, though they are occasionally brought to the greater urban areas to be revered by the masses. Stories, legends, and traditions surrounding extraordinary deeds and miracles associated with such sacred objects abound in Greece.

HOLIDAYS AND FESTIVALS Most public holidays in Greece are religious in nature, including Easter Sunday and Monday, Christmas Day and Second Christmas Day, Epiphany, Whitsunday and Whitmonday, and the Dormition of the Mother of God. State holidays and their official ceremonies often coincide with Orthodox feast days. The Annunciation feast (25 March) is celebrated alongside the anniversary of the beginning of the Greek War of Independence. The anniversary of the entrance of Greece into World War II (28 October) coincides with the feast of the Protecting Veil of the Mother of God, while the Dormition of the Mother of God (15 August) is celebrated simultaneously with the day of the armed forces. There are also many popular local festivals and rituals associated with patron saints, which often exhibit pre-Christian elements. The coexistence of popular and official religion has not been problematic in most cases, though tensions may sometimes arise. For example, the popular northern Greece fire-walking practices called Anastenaria, which take place on the feast day of Saints Constantine and Helena (21 May), have been denounced by the Church.

MODE OF DRESS Clergymen of all rankings, as well as female monastics, wear the black cassock, a long-sleeved, full-length garment, while the head, in the case of unmarried clergymen and the nuns, is covered by a garment resembling a black hood that hangs low over the head and flares onto the back. Married priests wear a tall black, pipelike hat. Liturgical vestments are much more elaborate and colorful. All religious vestments are imbued with great symbolic meaning, for they transform the wearers into representatives of the Kingdom of God and reflect otherworldliness.

DIETARY PRACTICES Dietary practices are determined to a great extent by the feasts and fasts dictated by the Orthodox calendar. In a year there are 110–160 days of fasting, and observances may vary from light to strict. Light fasting observances require abstinence from eating meat and other animal products, such as eggs and dairy products. More strict observances forbid the consumption of fish and even olive oil. Strict fasting is required on the day before Holy Communion, while light fasting is practiced on Wednesdays and Fridays. The three main times for fasting are the Great Lent, which lasts through the six weeks between Green Monday and Easter; the 40-day period before Christmas; and the period between 1 and 15 August for the Dormition of the Mother of God.

RITUALS Greeks retain a fairly passive attachment to Orthodoxy, attending church mainly on Sundays. The rate of religious practice in Greece is higher than in other European countries, and church attendance between 1985 and 2000 showed signs of growth. Church attendance is particularly high on religious holidays, as religious allegiance is manifested above all on special occasions. Thus, the rites of passage are almost universal, particularly baptisms, marriages, and religious burials, as are popular religious and national festivals and major feasts of the Christian year that highlight the importance of popular religion in Greece. This moderate religiosity among the majority of Greeks shows that they find in Orthodoxy a spiritual and ethical context and a link to tradition and the Greek cultural heritage.

RITES OF PASSAGE The main rites of passage in the Greek Church are those of baptism, marriage, and death. Baptism is one of the seven essential sacraments of the Greek Orthodox Church and is usually performed when the child is a few months old. It is done by immersion and involves the sacramental acts of anointment with oil and pronouncement of the name. In the case of a first-born child, the name given is usually that of the grandfather or grandmother on the father's side.

Marriage symbolizes the passage to adulthood. Up to that point most people live in the parental home. The majority of the people prefer a religious wedding over a civil one. The wedding service includes the following basic steps: the betrothal, the lighting of the candles, the joining of hands, the crowning, scriptural readings, drinking from the common cup, the dance of Isaiah, and the proclamation of marriage. Important to both baptism and marriage is the institution of god-parenthood, a created kinship that is considered higher than relationships in the social world.

Death for the Orthodox marks the separation of the soul from the body, which is usually buried within 24 hours after death. Funeral events include a vigil, a funeral service at the church, burial, a meal, prayers at the graveside on the third and ninth days after death, and memorial services on the fortieth day after death and on the first anniversary. The bones are usually exhumed after three years. The Church may deny an Orthodox burial to unbaptized infants and those who have committed blasphemy or suicide, denied their faith, or accepted cremation.

MEMBERSHIP Greeks become members of the Orthodox Church through baptism. During the twentieth century a number of influential lay semimonastic movements of private initiative—Zoe (founded in 1907), for example—carried out, with their affiliated organizations, extensive internal missions (through Bible study groups and Sunday schools) as well as philanthropic activities throughout the country. To some extent these movements resulted from the ineffectiveness of the Church. The official organization, Apostoliki Diakonia, did not become active until after 1950. The Church, in cooperation with the Patriarchates of Constantinople and Alexandria, has engaged in extensive missionary and charitable activities since the twentieth century, particularly in Africa (Congo [Kinshasa], Ethiopia, Madagascar, Kenya, Uganda, and Tanzania) and in Asia (India, Indonesia, the Philippines, Hong Kong, Japan, and

South Korea). It also uses all modern communication technology, including the Internet, for its purposes.

SOCIAL JUSTICE Although the Church did not play a crucial role in earlier public debates on social policy and welfare, it did develop a social consciousness of its own. Dioceses and monasteries are centers of philanthropic activity, both on a regular basis as well as during emergencies. Since the 1980s there have been attempts to formulate a more concrete social doctrine from an Orthodox point of view. This effort has been influenced by earlier analogous attempts among private Orthodox movements and by the socialist's coming to power for the first time in 1981. Some Orthodox bodies engaged in social activities avoid any type of public visibility, retaining an inward focus and cooperating minimally with nonreligious organizations involved in similar activities. The Church has created its own committees to address various contemporary social issues, such as bioethics.

SOCIAL ASPECTS In 1982 an optional civil marriage ceremony was introduced by the socialistic government, yet the numbers of Greeks choosing civil marriages has remained limited, a fact indicative of the bond between Orthodoxy and the Greek population. This is because Orthodox marriage is not a religious ritual alone but includes many other cultural elements, so that it is transformed into a major cultural event for the community. Generally Orthodoxy remains popular, and there is no organized and militant anticlericalism, though some diffuse anticlerical sentiments are found among the population. Historically the clergy has not formed a separate, privileged social class, and for parish clergy the possibility of marriage remains open, a fact that reflects their closeness to the laypeople.

POLITICAL IMPACT Steeped in the long tradition of the harmonious collaboration between the emperor and the patriarch, Greece, like most predominantly Orthodox countries of eastern and southeastern Europe, does not separate church and state. Intellectuals, jurists, and theologians who favor an administrative or even a thorough formal separation of church and state represent a minority. Church and state in Greece are inextricably intertwined in numerous ways, and both profit from this situation, despite the occasional and, at times, serious conflicts between them. The state often proclaims that it guards the traditions of Orthodoxy and Hellenism. Despite the fact that Christianity was generally a nonna-

tional religion in the past, the Greek Church has been transformed since the nineteenth century into a strong nationalistic church and has identified itself with the relevant aspirations of the state, such as territorial expansion and union with Cyprus. The Church's strong involvement in the crisis over the recognition of Macedonia (FYROM) and the "Macedonian question" of 1992–93 was a case in point. The Church has also often suffered for national causes and can identify many victims among its ranks—from World War II and the subsequent Greek Civil War (1946–1949), for example.

CONTROVERSIAL ISSUES The Greek Church has not allowed the ordination of women as priests and, despite occasional political and social pressure, does not intend to liberalize its doctrine and ethics relating to sexual matters. Many issues, like the omission of religious affiliation from identity cards in 2000, have resulted in tensions between the Church and the state. The intention of the archbishop Christodoulos (elected in 1998) to demarginalize the Church and play a more central role in the public sphere has met with resistance from many politicians and intellectuals, who want to restrict the Church's influence to the religious domain alone.

CULTURAL IMPACT Orthodoxy has left its imprint on all major aspects of Greek cultural life—in the architecture of churches and monastery complexes, Byzantine and folk music, iconography, religious literature, and numerous aspects of popular custom and religiosity. For this reason many Greeks—even atheists—consider Orthodoxy not so much a specific religious tradition but an integral part of their cultural repertoire.

Other Religions

Muslims in Greece, who number about 140,000 and constitute the country's largest religious minority, are Sunnis of the Hanafite rite, who live primarily in Western Thrace and are mostly Turks, Pomaks, and Rom (gypsies). The Great Mufti of Greece is the recognized leader of Greek Muslims. Jews flourished earlier in Greece, particularly in Thessaloniki, but since World War II the 75,000-member community has been reduced to about 5,500. The historical community of Roman Catholics (primarily of the Latin rite but also of the Byzantine and Armenian rites) has existed since the times of the Crusades in the Ionian islands and central Aegean islands, as well as in Crete. There are about 65,000 Catholics in Greece, and the Holy See retains diplomatic relations with the country. There are two main Protestant denominations, the Greek Evangelical Church (founded in 1858) and the Free Evangelical Churches of Greece (founded in 1908), as well as some minor groups. Altogether there are between 16,000 and 18,000 Protestants in Greece. The Jehovah's Witnesses, with about 30,000 members, have grown to more than 300 congregations.

Vasilios N. Makrides and Eleni Sotiriu

See Also Vol. 1: *Christianity, Eastern Orthodoxy*

Bibliography

Alivizatos, Nicos. "A New Role for the Greek Church?" *Journal of Modern Greek Studies* 17 (1999): 23–40.

Basdekis, Athanasios. "Between Partnership and Separation: Relations between Church and State in Greece under the Constitution of 9 June 1975." *The Ecumenical Review* 29 (1977): 52–61.

Carabott, Philip. "Politics, Orthodoxy and the Language Question in Greece: The Gospel Riots of November 1901." *Journal of Mediterranean Studies* 3 (1993): 117–38.

Clogg, Richard, ed. *Minorities in Greece: Aspects of a Plural Society.* London: C. Hurst and Co., 2002.

Danforth, Loring M. *Firewalking and Religious Healing: The Anastenaria of Greece and the American Firewalking Movement.* Princeton, N.J.: Princeton University Press, 1989.

Dubisch, Jill. *In a Different Place: Pilgrimage, Gender, and Politics at a Greek Island Shrine.* Princeton, N.J.: Princeton University Press, 1995.

Frazee, Charles A. *The Orthodox Church and Independent Greece, 1821–1852.* London: Cambridge University Press, 1969.

Georgiadou, Vasiliki. "Greek Orthodoxy and the Politics of Nationalism." *International Journal of Politics, Culture, and Society* 9 (1995): 295–315.

Kitromilides, Paschalis M. *Enlightenment, Nationalism, Orthodoxy: Studies in the Culture and Political Thought of South-eastern Europe.* Aldershot, England: Variorum, 1994.

Kokosalakis, Nikos. "Church and State in the Orthodox Context with Special Reference to Greece." In *Identità europea e diversità religiosa nel mutamento contemporaneo.* Edited by Peter Antes, Pietro de Marco, and Arnaldo Nesti, 233–57. Florence: A. Pontecorboli, 1995.

———. "The Political Significance of Popular Religion in Greece." *Archives de Sciences Sociales des Réligions* 64 (1987): 37–52.

———. "Religion and Modernization in Nineteenth-Century Greece." *Social Compass* 34 (1987): 223–41.

Makrides, Vasilios N. "The Orthodox Church and the Post-War Religious Situation in Greece." In *The Post-War Generation and Establishment Religion: Cross-Cultural Perspectives.* Edited by Wade Clark Roof, Jackson W. Carroll, and David A. Roozen, 225–42. Boulder, Colo.: Westview Press, 1995.

———. "Orthodoxy as a Conditio Sine Qua Non: Church and State/Politics in Modern Greece from a Socio-Historical Perspective." *Ostkirchliche Studien* 40 (1991): 281–305.

Molokotos-Liederman, Lina. "Identity Crisis: Greece, Orthodoxy, and the European Union." *Journal of Contemporary Religion* 18 (2003): 291–305.

Pollis, Adamantia. "Greek National Identity: Religious Minorities, Rights and European Norms." *Journal of Modern Greek Studies* 10 (1992): 171–95.

Stavros, Stephanos. "Human Rights in Greece: Twelve Years of Supervision from Strasbourg." *Journal of Modern Greek Studies* 17 (1999): 3–21.

Stewart, Charles. *Demons and the Devil: Moral Imagination in Modern Greek Culture.* Princeton, N.J.: Princeton University Press, 1991.

Winterer-Papatassos, Mary. *Experiencing the Feast Days of the Festal Menaion in Greece.* Minneapolis: Light and Life, 1987.

Grenada

POPULATION 101,400
ROMAN CATHOLIC 54.3 percent
ANGLICAN 20 percent
OTHER 25.7 percent

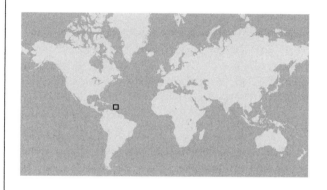

Country Overview

INTRODUCTION A densely forested, mountainous island in the Caribbean Sea, Grenada is the most southerly of the group known as the Windward Islands. Some
islands of the Grenadines group, including Carriacou
and Petit Martinique, are within its jurisdiction. About
80 percent of the people are of African origin (descendants of slaves); the rest are either mixed or of some less
prominent grouping, such as East Indians (descendants
of indentured laborers) or Europeans.

In the mid-1650s C.E. Grenada was colonized by
the French, who established Roman Catholicism as the
island's religion. The island was captured by the British
in 1762, opening the door to non-Catholic Christians,
and the island rapidly became pluralist in its religious

manifestations. These include Anglicans, Methodists,
Presbyterians, and various other evangelical and Pentecostal groups.

The British also imported many slaves from Africa.
In 1795–96 there was an uprising against the British,
part of a wave of unrest that was related to the French
Revolution and French antislavery sentiments. Slavery
was abolished in Grenada in 1834.

Grenada became self-governing in 1967 and gained
independence in 1974. For more than a decade the political life of the island was controlled by Prime Minister
Eric Gairy, who in 1979 was ousted by the radical leader
Maurice Bishop. In turn the Bishop regime was undone
by the more radical element of his People's Revolutionary Government. The assassination of Bishop and some
other ministers in 1983 was followed by the American
invasion, which removed the radicals and their Cuban
supporters. Disapproval of the Gairy and Bishop regimes united Christians of all persuasions in a way that
their common faith never had. Other religions in Grenada include non-Christian groups such as Shango, Hindus, Muslims, and Rastafarians. All of these give the island a character of great diversity.

RELIGIOUS TOLERANCE During the late eighteenth
and early nineteenth centuries religious tolerance was
not characteristic of church life in Grenada. When the
island passed from French to British hands, religious life
was affected by the concept of establishment, in which
the Anglican Church came to be regarded as preeminent
and was funded by the state, despite having a small following. Roman Catholicism, with more members and
a long history on the island, was marginalized by the

A view of Saint Patrick's Catholic Church in Grenada. Altogether there are thirty-six Catholic places of worship in Grenada. © JAN BUTCHOFSKY-HOUSER/CORBIS.

government. Religious groups—both Christian and non-Christian—function today in an atmosphere of tolerance, which has been enshrined in the constitution of the country (1974).

Major Religion

CHRISTIANITY

DATE OF ORIGIN Seventeenth century C.E.
NUMBER OF FOLLOWERS 75,340

HISTORY Christianity was introduced to Grenada during the late seventeenth century C.E. by French Catholics who emigrated from the nearby island of Martinique in order to minister to the needs of their compatriots. Catholicism became and remained the sole expression of Christianity in the colony until after 1763, when the British assumed control of the island. The church buildings were immediately taken over and used for the Church of England, or Anglican Church, which then became the official church establishment of the island.

During this period the Roman Catholic Church was harassed by civil officers, who were probably more interested in pushing them out than in supporting the

Church of England. The Catholics never gave up, and by the early nineteenth century they had begun to reestablish themselves. By that time there were not only Anglicans in Grenada but Methodists and Presbyterians as well. In less than a hundred years the island had changed from being Catholic to being multi-denominational.

The growth of the Roman Catholic Church in Grenada continued into the twentieth century, during which time it was administered as part of the Archdiocese of Port of Spain (the capital of Trinidad and Tobago). In 1956 a diocese was instituted in Grenada's capital, Saint George's; it consists of the islands of Grenada, Carriacou, and Petit Martinique.

The Anglican Church in Grenada forms part of the Diocese of the Windward Islands, which also includes the islands of Saint Vincent and Saint Lucia.

The Methodist Church arrived in the late eighteenth century, when Methodist missionary Thomas Coke (1747–1814) paid his first visit to the island. In 1833 the Presbyterians opened a church, Saint Andrew's, to cater to Scotsmen who lived on the island. After operating for several years under the Scottish Presbytery, it became attached to the Canadian Presbytery in Trinidad. By the 1980s a desire for autonomy had become evident, and in 1986 the church in Grenada became an independent presbytery.

A wide variety of other Christian groups formed in Grenada, including Spiritual Baptists (an Afro-Christian body); Seventh-day Adventists, Pentecostals, the Plymouth Brethren, the Salvation Army, Jehovah's Witnesses, and the Church of God.

EARLY AND MODERN LEADERS The first bishop of the Catholic diocese of Saint George's was Justin Field, whose tenure lasted from 1957 to 1969. Others holding that office were Patrick Webster (1970–75) and Sydney Charles (appointed in 1975). Bishop Charles held office during the trying years of the Maurice Bishop regime, and it was during his tenure that the Catholic Church became one of the founding members of the Grenada Council of Churches. A Grenadian, Vincent Matthew Darius, was appointed bishop in 2002. Besides being a prior of his order, Bishop Darius also served as spiritual director of his alma mater, the Regional Seminary of Saint John Vianney in Trinidad.

In all churches local leadership is being fostered, though not exclusively so. Several of the clergy are from Europe or other areas.

MAJOR THEOLOGIANS AND AUTHORS There have been no major theologians or authors in Grenada.

HOUSES OF WORSHIP AND HOLY PLACES The main Catholic church is the Cathedral of the Immaculate Conception, located in the capital, Saint George's. Altogether there are 36 Catholic places of worship in Grenada. Included among these is the National Shrine of our Lady of Fatima at Battle Hill. There are a variety of other places of worship in the capital, such as Saint George's Anglican Church (built in 1825) and Saint Andrew's Presbyterian Church (built in 1831), known as Scots' Kirk.

WHAT IS SACRED? There are no distinctive sacred elements in the practice of Christianity in Grenada.

HOLIDAYS AND FESTIVALS The major holy days for Christians in Grenada are Christmas; Saint Patrick's Day, observed in honor of the Irish (of whom the priesthood and the religious orders of the Catholic Church boast a few); Good Friday; Easter; Pentecost (Whitsunday and Whitmonday), commemorating the coming of the Holy Spirit in its fullness; and Corpus Christi, commemorating the Body of Christ. Christmas and Easter are occasions of great festivity for all Grenadian Christians and are observed with additional services. Roman Catholics observe Corpus Christi with great ceremony, which includes a Mass, benediction, and procession through the streets, and it typically attracts a greater attendance by the faithful than is customary during the year. They are usually regarded as public holidays.

MODE OF DRESS In Grenada there is no special dress for Christians. Ministers wear a variety of dress for their formal functions in worship. These vary from the black gown worn by Methodists and Presbyterians to the Eucharistic vestments worn by Anglicans and Roman Catholics. These vestments are usually worn over a robe called an alb, which is typically white in color and symbolic of purity.

DIETARY PRACTICES There are no special dietary practices in the churches in Grenada. Members are encouraged to use their discretion and to avoid excess, which is regarded as sinful. Christians continue to follow the custom of observing Wednesdays and Fridays as days of comparative fasting, when staunch members eat fish instead of red meat. During Lent Christians practice fasts of varying intensity.

RITUALS Since the 1960s services of a nonliturgical nature have become frequent in Christian churches in Grenada. These services do not have a fixed structure or ceremonials, and they emphasize teaching and prayer. Among the groups that meet for such services are those with a charismatic leaning. In the Roman Catholic Church charismatic groups form part of the renewal movement that started in the 1970s, in which efforts were made to revitalize the faith and practice of members.

Matrimony is usually administered to Catholics within the Mass. To those who, as nonmembers, marry Catholic partners, certain prescriptions may apply.

RITES OF PASSAGE There are no Christian rites of passage that are distinctive to Grenada. Incorporation into a Christian church is by baptism, and all major churches in Grenada practice infant baptism. In some this is followed by confirmation, which in the Roman Catholic Church is preceded by first Communion.

MEMBERSHIP The Roman Catholic Church is not obviously aggressive in its attempts to gain converts, but its methods of evangelization are wide-ranging. In commending its faith, the diocese operates a radio station, Good News Grenada Radio; a television station called Catholic Television; and a newspaper, *Catholic Focus*. It maintains a Web site with a program called "Know Your Faith," in which members are asked to submit questions of concern to be answered by one of the staff. The church also administers a bookshop in Saint George's. The Catholic Church in Grenada makes a strenuous effort to nurture of the children of their members, encouraging them to remain faithful to the Catholic Church.

Since the 1980s the Anglican, Methodist, and Roman Catholic churches in Grenada have all experienced a decline in numbers as a result of the growth and activity of the Pentecostals, Seventh-day Adventists, and Spiritual Baptists. These groups are aggressive in their proselytizing in a way that the older churches are not. Characteristic of their approach is the tendency to make derogatory remarks about those churches that do not hold the faith as they interpret it. Thus, the Anglicans and Roman Catholics are the objects of great hostility and propaganda. The newer churches' methods also include regular crusades in tents, especially where they see a vacancy occurring in the pastorate of another church.

SOCIAL JUSTICE A major part of the Catholic Church's work in Grenada is in education, because it has habitually built schools to cater to the youth in the communities where it ministers. Today the church administers several primary and secondary schools. It also encourages a vibrant Catholic Teachers' Association, which facilitates discussion and communication among its teachers and fosters commitment to the church.

The Grenadian Catholic Church is also engaged in social work. Since the early years it has operated organizations such as the Saint Vincent de Paul Society and the Madonna House Apostolate. There is a Cheshire Home for disabled persons, two homes for the aged, and two retreat centers. These efforts serve the wider community as well as church members.

Adventists in Grenada are engaged in education, administering schools in the capital. They also operate a dental clinic there.

SOCIAL ASPECTS The Catholic Church in Grenada remains firm in its views on marriage, which it regards as an inviolable sacrament. It considers marriage as vital to the well-being of both the individual and the society, and it encourages support for conjugal and family life. The church does not support divorce. There is a belief among non-Catholics in Grenada that the Catholic Church's stance on mixed marriage is harsh, in that it expects the children of such marriages to be brought up in the Catholic tradition. The church is prohibitive toward abortion, which it regards as a plague and an abominable crime.

POLITICAL IMPACT During the closing decades of plantation slavery (1808–33), relations between the churches in Grenada were not cordial; a general atmosphere of intolerance pervaded the region. When slavery finally ended, there persisted a spirit of rivalry, which became intense in the late nineteenth and early twentieth centuries. Other groups nevertheless established themselves in the island. The late twentieth century witnessed a new spirit, in which churches made efforts to work together despite denominational differences. The Grenada Council of Churches was formed to facilitate dialogue and cooperation among the churches.

The years of the Gairy and Bishop governments caused considerable political division among churches in Grenada. Some, such as the Anglicans and Roman Catholics, were critical of the Bishop regime and of the support being given to it by the Caribbean Conference of Churches. In turn, the People's Revolutionary Government became suspicious of the Council of Churches in Grenada. Other churches, such as the evangelicals, regarded support for those in authority as a scriptural demand based on Romans 13:1–7. The overthrow of Eric Gairy in 1979 changed the political atmosphere in the island. Church leaders were staunchly opposed to the apparent Communism of the new regime, and the regime decried the churches' refusal to support the revolution. The Council of Churches resisted the government and ultimately gave their support to the American invasion of Grenada in 1983.

CONTROVERSIAL ISSUES The churches in Grenada continue to compete with each other and do so more fiercely than before. Even though the rate of population growth has declined and public schools are amply available, churches maintain religiously affiliated schools. Newer churches perceive the older churches as being too liberal and believe that there is a need for a revival of a Christianity that would not compromise with the world. This exacerbates the tension between churches.

The ordination of women is another controversial issue, one that has been intensified by the 1995 decision of the Anglicans in the West Indies to admit women to the priesthood. Mixed marriages also pose a serious problem, because the Roman Catholic Church expects the children of such unions to be brought up in the faith of the Catholic partner; the non-Catholic partner is expected to comply. It is an issue for all the Caribbean islands, but it is not often publicly debated.

CULTURAL IMPACT The architecture for Christian places of worship in Grenada is predominantly European, though that has been changing as new places of worship are built. As elsewhere in the region, an attempt is being made to use music of a Caribbean flavor in church services. At present this involves the hymns and some other parts of the liturgy that are sung. The process of incorporating local musical styles continues to be somewhat limited, however.

Other Religions

There are a number of other religious groups operating in Grenada. The most prominent is the Afro-Christian group called the Spiritual Baptists. The belief system of this group is a mixture of Christianity and traditional African religions. Entry is through baptism by immersion; it also has a practice called mourning, a kind of discipline in which the individual is completely dependent on other members of the church. As part of this mourning the devotee has visions and receives a "gift," which indicates that individual's future role in the church. The interpretation of the vision is the responsibility of the person who is guiding the devotee in mourning.

In addition to this group, there are small numbers of Hindus, Muslims, Rastafarians, and devotees of the African god Shango (Sango). The Hindus and Muslims are descendants of people who had been taken to the region as indentured laborers in the nineteenth century or of others who have since migrated to the island. Their impact on Grenadian culture is negligible. Devotees of the African god Shango, the god of thunder, follow beliefs and practices that largely reflect traditional African ancestral worship. Their major rituals are providing offerings of food to spirits and pouring libations. The religion reflects close affinities with groups such as the Spiritual Baptists, whose activities they sometimes patronized to obtain certain "gifts."

The Rastafarian movement originated in Jamaica in the 1950s. The prophecies of Marcus Garvey (1887–1940) led them to believe that an African king was to be their savior. They considered this messiah to be Prince (Ras) Tafari Makonnen (Ethiopian emperor Haile Selassie I, 1892–1975). Rastafarians are, for the most part, vegetarian and live off the produce of the land. One of their most prominent practices is smoking marijuana, which they regard as having medicinal characteristics.

Noel Titus

See Also Vol. 1: *Anglicanism/Episcopalianism, Christianity, Roman Catholicism*

Bibliography

[Ali, Arif]. *Grenada, Carriacou, Petit Martinique.* London: Hansib Publishing, 1994.

Searle, Chris. *Grenada: The Struggle against Destabilization.* London: Writers and Readers Pub. Cooperative Society, 1983.

Simpson, George Eaton. *Black Religions in the New World.* New York: Columbia University Press, 1978.

———. *Religious Cults of the Caribbean.* Rio Piedras: Institute of Caribbean Studies, University of Puerto Rico, 1980.

Sinclair, Norma. *Grenada: Isle of Spice.* London: Macmillan Caribbean, 1987.

Sunshine, Catherine. *The Caribbean: Survival, Struggle, and Sovereignty.* Washington, D.C.: EPICA, 1988.

Guatemala

POPULATION 13,314,079

ROMAN CATHOLIC 51 percent

MAYA SPIRITUALITY 24 percent

EVANGELICAL 24 percent

OTHER 1 percent

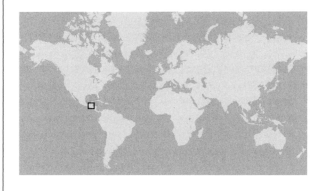

Country Overview

INTRODUCTION The Republic of Guatemala, bordered to the west by the Pacific Ocean (between Mexico and El Salvador) and to the east by the Caribbean Sea (between Belize and Honduras), is the most populous and religiously diverse country in Central America. Guatemala's several mountain ranges have historically made transportation and communications somewhat difficult. Mestizos (usually called Ladinos), people of mixed Spanish and native origin, have dominated the country politically since the Spanish invasion in 1524 C.E. The Spanish imposed Catholicism on the majority Maya population, who now speak 21 distinct languages and comprise 55 to 60 percent of the population. Other

groups include the Garifuna on the Caribbean coast, the small Xinca population in the eastern lowlands, and several immigrant populations, of whom the Germans (who began arriving in the 1830s) are the most notable.

A 36-year civil war ended in 1996, when the Guatemalan government and the Guatemalan National Revolutionary Unity (URNG) signed a peace accord. The Maya were historically discriminated against and excluded from power, and ethnic tensions continue to shape social relations. During the 1980s and 1990s Maya groups began to assert the right to practice their religious traditions openly; the Maya Movement seeks to make connections between the various Maya groups in the country. This has somewhat paralleled the growth of many forms of Protestantism, which has received attention from outside the region and has made Guatemala one of the two Latin American countries with the largest percentage of evangelicals. There are also small communities of Jews, Muslims, Mormons, and Spiritists in Guatemala.

RELIGIOUS TOLERANCE Religious tolerance was formally established by the liberal government of President Mariano Gálvez in 1832. A more cited decree establishing freedom of worship was issued in 1873. These decrees essentially deestablished the Catholic Church as the official religion of Guatemala and opened the door for a significant influx of Protestant missionaries at the end of the nineteenth century.

The 1985 constitution (amended in 1993) guarantees freedom of religion. It also acknowledges the legality (*personalidad jurídica*) of the Catholic Church. Other churches and religious associations have the right to be

Kites are flown in the Santiago Sacatepequez Cemetery during the Day of the Dead celebrations. The kite is said to be a mode of communication with departed relatives. AP/WIDE WORLD PHOTOS.

recognized. In 1995, as part of the peace process, the government and the URNG signed the Accord on the Identity and Rights of Indigenous Peoples, which affirms the native population's right to practice their own traditions without interference or prejudice and guarantees the protection of Maya sacred sites. Few aspects of the accord have been legally codified.

Major Religions

ROMAN CATHOLICISM

MAYA SPIRITUALITY

EVANGELICALISM

ROMAN CATHOLICISM

DATE OF ORIGIN 1524 C.E.

NUMBER OF FOLLOWERS 7 million

HISTORY In 1524 C.E. Spain, led by the conquistador Pedro de Alvarado, invaded the territory that would be-

come Guatemala. During the subsequent colonial period the Catholic Church was an agency of the crown, although the friar's evangelization methods sometimes occasioned conflict. Catholicism in Guatemala developed around veneration of saints; local sodalities (lay religious associations) called *cofradías* were charged with caring for saint's images in local communities. *Cofradías* in Guatemala are a mix of Spanish and indigenous practices.

In the post-independence era (beginning in 1821) the Catholic Church was pressured by Guatemalan liberal governments determined to "modernize" the country and break the power of the church. The church experienced a resurgence during the tenure (1838–65) of conservative *caudillo* (strongman) Rafael Carrera. The liberals took power again in 1871, and Justo Rufino Barrios (1873–85) set the stage for modern church-state relations by again attacking the Catholics and inviting the first Protestant missionary to Guatemala. The church generally supported succeeding governments until dictator Jorge Ubico was overthrown in 1944.

When this revolution ended in a 1954 coup, the church lent its support to those who had ousted the elected but left-leaning government of Jacobo Arbenz.

The *aggiornamento* (updating) of the church that came with the Second Vatican Council (1962–65) dovetailed with aspects of the older Catholic Action movement's agenda; there was a push for more direct pastoral involvement with social concerns. In Guatemala this resulted in a spate of cooperative and social organizing. This movement was attacked in the late 1960s and again in the late 1970s and early 1980s, when many priests and religious were killed or threatened. All religious workers were pulled from the Diocese of El Quiché in 1980. Some formed the Guatemalan Church in Exile and continued to try to draw international attention to the conflict.

During the peace negotiations (1987–96) the Catholic Church assumed a high profile. It issued statements designed to focus attention on inequities in Guatemalan society, and it brought civil society together to make its demands heard.

EARLY AND MODERN LEADERS Father Francisco Marroquin was the first bishop of Guatemala (1535–63). Beginning in 1537 Dominican friar Bartolome de las Casas, known as the "Defender of the Indians," applied methods of peaceful evangelization in the area known as Verapaz (literally, "true peace").

Pedro de San José Betancur (died in 1667) was respected for his concern for the poor and infirm; he founded a hospital and is sometimes called the "Saint Francis of the Americas." He was canonized by Pope John Paul II in 2002, becoming Guatemala's first saint. In the early eighteenth century the Catholic priest Francisco Ximénez (1666–1729) discovered the *Popol Vuh*, the sacred book of the K'iche' Maya—sometimes referred to as the Mayan Bible—in the town of Chichicastenango. He copied it in the K'iche' language and translated it into Spanish.

Bishop Alvaro Leonel Ramazzini (born in 1947) and Bishop Julio Edgar Cabrera (born in 1939) have been strong voices for social justice in the Guatemalan Episcopal Conference, as has Archbishop Victor Hugo Martínez Contreras (born in 1930). During the peace negotiations of the 1980s and '90s Rodolfo Quezada Toruño, a Catholic bishop (appointed a cardinal in 2003), was the chief negotiator for several years. Bishop Juan Condera Gerardí (1922–98) directed the Recovery

of Historical Memory project (REMHI, its Spanish acronym), which documented human rights abuses that had taken place during the civil war. Gerardí was murdered two days after presenting the REMHI report.

MAJOR THEOLOGIANS AND AUTHORS Ricardo Falla (born in 1932), a priest and anthropologist, has written about religious change and Catholic Action in a K'iche' village as well as on experiences with the Popular Communities in Resistance movement during the 1980s and 1990s. Carlos Rafael Cabarrús Pellecer (born in 1946), a priest, has written on Maya spirituality among the Q'eqchi'; he founded the Central American Institute of Spirituality in 1993. José Parra Novo (born in 1950) has addressed the topic of inculturation (the presentation of Catholicism in terms of indigenous norms).

HOUSES OF WORSHIP AND HOLY PLACES A characteristic of most towns and villages in Guatemala is that a Catholic church is situated on the central square or plaza. The Metropolitan Cathedral (original construction 1782–1815) in Guatemala City is a sign of the historical presence of the Catholic Church in the life of the nation.

WHAT IS SACRED? Sacredness for Guatemalan Catholics revolves around the sacraments and images of the saints and the Virgin Mary. People often maintain personal connections to particular saints in their home community or elsewhere, and some saints are considered to have healing powers or the ability to intervene in human affairs. Throughout the year many Guatemalan Catholics make pilgrimages to certain sacred images, where they burn candles (the colors of which signify special needs), say prayers, and make *promesas* (promises).

HOLIDAYS AND FESTIVALS Major townships throughout Guatemala have patron saints. Each year festivals are held for a week or so on each side of the saint's day. Celebrations of Holy Week (*Semana Santa*, the week before Easter) are particularly important in Catholic liturgical life. The best-known Holy Week events are the processions in the colonial city of Antigua, in which people arrange *alfombras* (sawdust and flower-petal carpets depicting religious symbols) along the parade routes.

Celebrations of the Day of the Dead (*Día de los muertos*), which is a combination of Catholic and Mesoamerican traditions, are held in conjunction with All

Saint's Day and All Soul's Day (1 and 2 November). People decorate graves and share meals with dead relatives. The town of Sumpango is known for kite flying during this time; the kite is said to be a mode of communication with departed relatives. During the Christmas season churches and homes in Guatemala frequently display *nacamientos* or *Belenes* (Bethlehems), elaborate scenes of the birth of Christ.

MODE OF DRESS Guatemalan Catholics dress in the style of the ethnic group to which they belong. Among Ladinos this is a Westernized style, including some business attire in cities. Some older women continue the practice of covering their heads in church.

DIETARY PRACTICES There are no dietary practices specific to Catholicism in Guatemala. A common food served in homes during Day of the Dead celebrations in urban areas is *fiambre*, a cold meat and salad dish.

RITUALS Besides the Mass and other rituals related to the liturgical calendar, the most important Catholic rituals in Guatemala are those related to the celebration of Holy Week and to the annual pilgrimage to the image of El Señor de (the Lord of) Esquipulas in the city of Esquipulas near the Honduran border (15 January, but the season extends through Holy Week). Images of the Lord of Esquipulas are found in many local sanctuaries.

RITES OF PASSAGE Rites of passage in Catholicism center on the sacraments, particularly baptism, first Communion, marriage, and death. In Guatemala the social traditions surrounding these events can change depending upon ethnic context or the place where they are observed (rural or urban).

MEMBERSHIP In many Guatemalan communities leadership created through the Catholic Action movement has confounded the authority of *cofradías* (local religious associations), as has the presence of evangelicalism. The Catholic Church sometimes responds to evangelicals with missives and more attention to pastoral work, but a perpetual shortage of priests hinders these efforts.

The nature of evangelization in a pluricultural society has become a central issue for the Catholic Church. This can be seen in its emphasis on inculturation (presenting the faith in terms more acceptable to the country's indigenous population). There has also been a growing Catholic charismatic presence that shares simi-larities with evangelical practices yet allows Catholics to remain in their own tradition.

SOCIAL JUSTICE In Guatemala groups associated with the Catholic Church work on issues such as land rights and education. During the late 1970s many people throughout Latin America began to participate in forms of Catholicism associated with liberation theology. In Guatemala the military and the government repressed social organizing, largely preventing the use of liberationist terminology. The Guatemalan Episcopal Conference wrote a series of pastoral letters designed to give the population hope during the years of repression. In 1990 the Archbishop's Office for Human Rights was established as an instrument for documenting human rights violations. In the post-conflict period it has continued to speak out on human rights issues and provided the auspices for the Project on the Recovery of Historical Memory, a truth commission formed following the peace agreement.

SOCIAL ASPECTS In general, Guatemalan Catholics emphasize the sacramental nature of marriage and see the family as a central institution for raising children. The extended family is important for reinforcing social structure in the country as a whole.

POLITICAL IMPACT The Christian Democracy Party of Guatemala (DCG), which is based on Catholic ideology, was founded in 1955. The first president in Guatemala's transition to democracy was Christian Democrat Vinicio Cerezo (1986–91). Support for the party in national elections has been minimal, however. In contemporary Guatemala the primary political involvement of the Catholic Church has been watching over the peace process and facilitating the documentation of human rights violations.

CONTROVERSIAL ISSUES The Catholic voice in Guatemala is often fragmented as Catholics respond to social concerns. Individual Catholics frequently hold opinions that diverge from the hierarchy, and the hierarchy itself is not always unified. Within the Catholic Church in Guatemala social stances on issues such as abortion, ordination of women, and divorce tend to mirror those of the Vatican. Abortion is illegal in the Guatemalan Penal Code, but family planning is available in much of the country. In 2001 the Catholic hierarchy in Guatemala opposed a congressional law designed to make contraceptives more accessible to women.

CULTURAL IMPACT The city of Antigua, the former capital, was largely destroyed by an earthquake in 1773. It is now notable for its colonial architecture (some in ruins and some well preserved), which contains a significant Catholic aspect. Since the colonial period Catholic themes—at times mixed with elements of indigenous culture—have been a predominant feature of Guatemalan art, especially in the paintings and altarpieces in churches. Catholicism has provided background and source material for many Guatemalan writers, including poet and novelist Miguel Ángel Asturias (1899–1974), who won the Nobel Prize for Literature in 1967. Local arts and crafts, such as wood carvings and paintings, often have Christian themes.

MAYA SPIRITUALITY

DATE OF ORIGIN 900 C.E.
NUMBER OF FOLLOWERS 3.2 million

HISTORY By the middle of the Formative period (2000 B.C.E.–250 C.E.) private and local shamanic practices had begun to be overlaid with a common spiritual tradition that linked political power and ancestor veneration in elite ceremonial centers. The majority of the population continued to live outside these centers and to practice a religion somewhat removed from that of the aristocracy. These traditions were maintained until the time of the Spanish invasion (sixteenth century C.E.). After 1541 the Catholic Church began organizing dispersed Maya villages into *reducciones*, village centers established in the Spanish grid pattern. Maya religious practices, condemned as pagan and idolatrous, were forced underground, where they survived for more than five centuries, in some cases modified by contact with Catholicism. The condemnation of Maya spirituality continued with the arrival of the evangelicals in the nineteenth century.

In about 1990 Maya spirituality started being openly practiced in the context of the Maya Movement. This has resulted in a resurgence of interest in the practice of the Maya spiritual guides as well as a *reivindicación* (rediscovery and reaffirmation) of Maya culture and religion more generally. Many Catholics and evangelicals in Guatemala also affirm aspects of Maya spirituality, although they may not always openly acknowledge it.

EARLY AND MODERN LEADERS The most numerous leaders of Maya spirituality on the local level are sha-

mans (also known as daykeepers [*aj q'ijab*], spiritual guides, or even Maya priests), who conduct ceremonies and serve as focal points for Maya practices. They are primarily diviners who deal with a range of personal and community issues and have been the guardians of Maya religious traditions for generations.

Prominent names associated with Maya spirituality include Tecum (usually referred to as Tecún Umán), a K'iche' warrior and prince who in 1524 was killed in the initial encounter with the Spanish. Tecum represents the historical and mythological importance of Maya traditions in conflict with outside forces. Legend has it that the national bird, the Quetzal, obtained its brilliant red breast when it alighted on the dying Tecum. Rigoberta Menchú (born in 1959), a Maya K'iche' woman, has been a prominent spokesperson for indigenous issues; she won the Nobel Peace Prize in 1992.

MAJOR THEOLOGIANS AND AUTHORS Adrián Inés Chávez, the leading Maya intellectual during the first half of the twentieth century, was an educator and Maya shaman. Chávez translated the *Popol Vuh*, the sacred Mayan text, into Spanish (1979). Antonio Pop Caal (1941–2002), a lawyer and Maya spiritual guide, was influential in the public resurgence of Maya spirituality for decades before his kidnaping and murder. Victor Montejo (born in 1951), a Popti' Maya who was forced into exile during the 1980s, has written several books, including an eyewitness account of the Guatemalan army's razing of a Maya village during the civil war and collections of legends from the Maya tradition.

HOUSES OF WORSHIP AND HOLY PLACES For those who practice Maya spirituality, holy places tend to be altars or sacrificial places in the mountains or near other natural areas, such as lakes, streams, caves, or trees. Some of these places are located in archaeological zones (for instance, the ancient Kaqchikel capital of Iximche'). Those concerned with Maya rights demand access to such sites. Among the Maya sites that are particularly well known are the shrine to Pascal Abaj in Chichicastenango and the hill called Paklom in Momostenango. In some communities a representation of San Simón (commonly known as Maximon) unites Maya spiritual traditions with the veneration of a Catholic saint. Sometimes portrayed as a Judas figure (betrayer of Christ), Maximon receives attention from both Maya and Ladinos.

WHAT IS SACRED? In the sacred Mayan text, the *Popol Vuh*, humans are made from maize (corn). This link emphasizes human's connection with nature and the need to respect the environment. The *mundo* (earth) is considered sacred, and there is much reflection on the "heart of Heaven" and the "heart of the Sky" in Maya cosmology. Crosses are important symbols in Maya tradition; they are associated with the four cardinal directions and with the "world tree" that links the sky, the earth, and the underworld. Also important are the sun and the moon, which are sometimes associated with Jesus and the Virgin Mary but are often seen as complementary aspects of the divine.

Time and the marking of time are highly important for practitioners of Maya spirituality. The movement of the cosmos and an individual's destiny are both linked to the *cholq'ij*, a ritual calendar of 260 days. Ancestors are respected as bearers of knowledge and tradition.

HOLIDAYS AND FESTIVALS The Maya's 260-day ritual calendar coordinates with its 360-day solar or agricultural calendar in 52-year cycles that are significant in the Maya understanding of history. Each renewal of the 260-day calendar falls on the day known as 8 Batz, or Waq'xaqib B'atz'. This is an important day for celebration, as is Wayeb', the 5-day period that follows the end of the 360-day year. This period was formerly considered to be unlucky and even dangerous, but now it is celebrated as a time of preparation for the coming year. Planting ceremonies have been noted in much of the literature surrounding Maya spiritual practices. These involve giving thanks to mountain spirits and to the earth itself for permission to plant or harvest.

MODE OF DRESS Maya men typically use Western dress, but traditional attire is common in some areas. Even male spiritual guides often wear Western clothing, although they wear a head covering and a sash around the waist during ceremonies. Women often continue to wear their *traje* (customary dress), which includes a blouse (*huipil*) and a skirt (*corte*) that is often handwoven.

DIETARY PRACTICES In Maya spirituality corn is sacred and is equated with the very essence of life. This parallels its importance as a dietary staple. Alcohol is consumed in rituals, although much modern observance tends to downplay its use.

RITUALS Ceremonies at sacred sites involve offerings of *copal* (pine resin) incense, candles, flowers, and other items. These are sacrificed in a fire erected on a base representing the four cardinal directions. The center of the fire-base is associated with the "navel of the world." The fire is "fed" *copal* and candles representing the need being addressed, and the daykeeper who performs the ceremony makes a reading of the fire as it consumes the offerings. The ceremony may simply be an offering or sacrifice that a person wishes to make in response to some benefit received in life.

RITES OF PASSAGE Birth is particularly significant, because when a person is born, his or her destiny is tied to the particular day and number in the ritual calendar. This is related to the "Day Lord" and the spirit (*nawal*) given to the newborn. The date of birth can also reveal whether a person is suitable for the office of daykeeper. Following a period of apprenticeship, the daykeeper receives a *vara* (technically a "staff" but in reality a divining kit consisting of beans and other paraphernalia) as a sign of office.

In Maya cosmology departed ancestors remain present in the ongoing life of the community. As guardians of esoteric knowledge and progenitors of the community, the "grandparents" (*abuelos*) assume a significant role in establishing values and the way of life of the people.

MEMBERSHIP Maya spirituality is the practice of an ethnic group. A person learns how to perform or take part in the rituals through *costumbre*, custom handed down from prior generations. The religion is sometimes ecumenical in that, with permission and proper respect, it will allow non-Maya participants in ceremonies.

SOCIAL JUSTICE A primary concern among the Maya population in Guatemala is the right to use customary Maya law (*ley consuetudinario*) in the adjudication of crimes committed within community boundaries. The idea is to maintain ties between a person who has committed a crime and his or her community.

SOCIAL ASPECTS Arranged marriages remain common among the Maya. Married couples tend to live with the husband's parents immediately after marriage, later establishing independence with their own home. Marriage is traditionally facilitated through an intermediary contracted by the potential husband's family. Divination plays a role in assessing if the proposed couple is a good match. Although different roles are assumed by women and men in the family, when forums are held to discuss Maya culture and religion, gender inequality and patriarchy are increasingly discussed.

POLITICAL IMPACT In Guatemala the political impact of the Maya and of Maya cultural practices has been growing. Since the final peace accord (1995) more Maya candidates have been running for local public office, and in a number of areas in the highlands civic committees engage in political action in ways that challenge party-based politics. The Academy of Maya Languages, established in 1990, promotes legislative recognition of the place of Maya languages in Guatemalan society.

CONTROVERSIAL ISSUES Among the controversial issues facing the Maya in Guatemala is the struggle for the legal codification of their right to practice their religion and cultural traditions. A second issue with religious overtones is the role of women in Maya society. Guatemala's discouraging social indicators (literacy, health care, per capita income, and access to economic opportunity) highlight the problems of Maya women, who are considered doubly oppressed because they are both female and indigenous.

CULTURAL IMPACT One long-term impact of Maya spirituality has been in the realm of performing arts, where Maya and Catholic traditions have come together in traditional dances associated with both Maya culture and the Spanish influence on it. Some dances, such as the Dance of the Conquest, are related to history, while others relate more directly to saint's images and Maya culture. Performances are often accompanied by instruments such as the marimba and the oboe-like *chirimia*.

EVANGELICALISM

DATE OF ORIGIN 1882 C.E.
NUMBER OF FOLLOWERS 3 million

HISTORY Although several Bible salesmen (*colporteurs*) spent time in Guatemala during the first half of the nineteenth century, the formal date of the Protestant arrival in Guatemala is 1882 C.E., when Presbyterian missionary John Clark Hill arrived in an entourage of then-president Justo Rufino Barrios. The five "historical" denominations in Guatemala were the Presbyterian Church in the United States of America, the Central

American Mission, the California Friends, the Church of the Nazarene, and the Primitive Methodists. All had a presence in the country by 1914. Pentecostals first arrived in Guatemala in 1916.

Evangelical growth was slow until the late 1960s, when the pace quickened, especially after a massive earthquake in 1976 opened Guatemala to all kinds of relief work. Evangelicalism also grew as a result of the instability created by the war, when Catholics were persecuted. Its growth reached a peak in the late 1980s and had begun to taper by about 1993.

Today Pentecostals comprise more than 70 percent of the country's evangelicals. Guatemalan evangelicals also include many independent congregations and neo-Pentecostal churches. The latter has been characterized by large churches in elite neighborhoods, mostly in the capital, but this has been changing as neo-Pentecostal churches expand throughout the country and involve themselves in educational and foreign missionary activities. A number of evangelical denominations now present in Guatemala are indigenous to Central America. Throughout the Mesoamerican region evangelical growth has been most prominent among the indigenous population and the urban poor.

EARLY AND MODERN LEADERS Evangelicalism in Guatemala is characterized by the fact that there is no single voice that can claim to speak for the community as a whole. Important historical figures include the early Presbyterian missionaries Edward Haymaker (1859–1948) and Paul Burgess (1886–1958); both supported work among the indigenous population. Albert Bishop arrived in Guatemala in 1899 and, along with Cameron Townsend (1896–1982), was an early representative of the Central America Mission. Townsend arrived in Guatemala in 1917, promoted the use of native languages in evangelization, and founded the Wycliffe Bible Translators, now known as the Summer Institute of Linguistics. Ruth Esther Smith of the California Society of Friends arrived in Guatemala in 1906 and was an important figure in the eastern town of Chiquimula until her death in 1947.

Contemporary leaders include General Efraín Ríos Montt, an elder in El Verbo (The Word), a neo-Pentecostal church; he became president of Guatemala following a coup in 1982 and occupied that office during some of the worst violence of the civil war (until 1983). He has been accused of genocide. From 2000 to 2004 he served as president of Guatemala's unicameral congress. Franciso Bianchi, a neo-Pentecostal businessman, led largely unsuccessful efforts to form a political party based on biblical principles during the 1999 and 2003 national elections. Kaqchikel Presbyterian minister Vitalino Similox became the executive secretary of the Guatemalan Conference of Churches in the late 1980s.

MAJOR THEOLOGIANS AND AUTHORS Lay theologian and poet Julia Esquivel (born in 1930) is known internationally for her reflections about war and violence in Guatemala. Emilio Nuñez of the Central American Theological Seminary in Guatemala City is an evangelical theologian (active since the 1970s) recognized throughout Latin America. Virgilio Zapata produced an important history of the evangelical movement (1982). Harold Caballeros, the minister of the neo-Pentecostal El Shaddai Church in Guatemala City since the 1980s, propounds a doctrine of spiritual warfare, in which true Christians are seen as engaged in a fight with spiritual forces of evil. Kaqchikel Presbyterian minister Antonio Otzoy was trained as a Maya spiritual guide, and since the 1990s he has been working to link evangelical theological beliefs with elements of Maya spirituality.

HOUSES OF WORSHIP AND HOLY PLACES In Guatemala *templos* (local churches)—typically small, brightly colored buildings—are places where evangelicals gather to worship, study, and make personal contact. Baptisms are often held at resorts with swimming pools, near springs and rivers, and at the seashore. While these places are not considered sacred as such, they assume a sacred character while the community is gathered there.

WHAT IS SACRED? To be an evangelical is to link one's destiny to the Gospel revealed in the Bible. Hence, evangelical churches in Guatemala often have open Bibles painted on the building's exterior and scripture verses painted on the interior walls.

HOLIDAYS AND FESTIVALS Religious holidays and festivals are not highly important in the Guatemalan Evangelical community. Day of the Dead services and Holy Week observances are seen at best as giving entirely too little attention to the Resurrection and to God's presence in the here and now. Christmas and Easter are acknowledged, but even these are not much celebrated in local congregations.

MODE OF DRESS Everyday dress is common among evangelicals in Guatemala. This includes Maya dress in Maya communities (although it is sometimes restricted in schools with evangelical connections) and Western dress in non-Maya settings. Some Pentecostal churches discourage women from using makeup and wearing pants.

DIETARY PRACTICES There are no strict dietary practices or restrictions across the wvangelical spectrum. Use of alcohol and tobacco is discouraged. Periods of fasting (*ayuno*) and prayer are common during vigils in local congregations.

RITUALS A believer's baptism is the most common ritual in evangelical congregations in Guatemala, including historical denominations. Healing, speaking in tongues, and congregational prayer (wherein congregants pray at the same time in their own words) are common in Pentecostal worship services. Sabbath observance is strongly encouraged.

RITES OF PASSAGE Among evangelicals the most common rites of passage are birth, entrance into the church through baptism, and marriage. Newborns are not baptized but are prayed for and presented publicly to congregations.

MEMBERSHIP The rate of evangelical growth in Guatemala slowed in the 1990s. Because of the evangelical belief that individuals have access to the truth through personal biblical interpretation, avenues for personal faith sharing and proselytizing are common, and evangelical communities have a tendency to fragment. Guatemalan evangelicals are heavily involved in educational endeavors, usually with a religious component. Because such education is associated with national or Western culture, the churches have sometimes been viewed as facilitating assimilation. Conversely, some evangelical communities are committed to using Bibles that have been translated into Maya languages; this strengthens cultural identity. The evangelical presence in television, publishing, and especially radio make evangelicalism a prominent and unavoidable presence in the life of the nation.

SOCIAL JUSTICE Evangelical groups are often said to be focused more on morality than on structural issues affecting society. While the neo-Pentecostal churches in the capital of Guatemala tend to represent upper-class values of "health, wealth, and success," some evangelicals address issues such as social well-being, the clarification of events that took place during the war, and indigenous rights. Other congregations, including Pentecostal groups in poor neighborhoods, provide community support and a religious presence for members as they try to survive in difficult circumstances.

SOCIAL ASPECTS Family networks often form the backbone of congregations in smaller communities in Guatemala. Women play a particular role in holding congregations together, but they are frequently prevented from holding ministerial positions. The service role of the deacon is common for women.

POLITICAL IMPACT Evangelicals tend to have a reputation for being either conservative or apolitical. In a repressive environment such as Guatemala before the end of the war, this reputation implies support for the status quo. There is no evangelical political party, and studies have shown that there is no evangelical voting bloc in Guatemala.

CONTROVERSIAL ISSUES One divisive issue is the United Nations-sponsored Code of Children and Youth, which was passed by the Guatemalan congress in 1996 and was supposed to have taken effect in 1997. Many evangelicals were concerned that the code was too focused on the rights of children and compromised parental authority. In late 1999, in an unusual display of ecumenical agreement, a group of evangelicals and Catholics produced a document intended to serve as an alternative to the proposed law. In 2000 the congress indefinitely postponed the law's implementation.

CULTURAL IMPACT In Guatemala evangelical culture has reshaped both the physical and the spiritual landscape. The Protestant emphasis on literacy and education—there are now two universities with roots in the evangelical community—has been continuous. Traditional Guatemalan musical forms, such as music played on the marimba, were initially shunned by some missionaries because of the connection with native culture. Such music is now laden with evangelical themes of salvation and life in Christ. As in many parts of the world, evangelicals in Guatemala have also adapted contemporary music styles for their own purposes.

Other Religions

A number of other religions and religious groups are present in Guatemala. These include small Jewish and Muslim communities, neither of which has more than 1,500 members. Judaism was first brought to Guatemala by German emigrants in the nineteenth century. The majority of Guatemalan Jews today are descendants of Middle Eastern, German, and eastern Europeans who arrived in the early twentieth century. The majority live in Guatemala City. Although the Jewish community is theologically traditional, some of its members participated in ecumenical discussions before the peace accords. The Guatemalan Muslim community proselytizes, but there is some emphasis on peace and dialogue with other traditions. Other groups associated with Christian beliefs—Seventh-day Adventists, Jehovah's Witnesses, and Mormons—have been growing and sometimes cause tensions because of their persistent proselytization.

Spiritism, associated with Allan Kardec (1804–69) and claiming to present universal truths from the spirit world, is a diffuse presence influencing personal spirituality throughout the country. A mural (inaugurated in 1992) by Roberto González Goyri (born in 1924) in the National Museum of Archaeology and Ethnology in Guatemala City is a unique public affirmation of religious pluralism in Latin America. Although the sequence of panels begins and ends with aspects of ancient and contemporary Maya belief and practice, the mural also depicts Muslims, Jews, evangelicals, and Mormons.

C. Matthew Samson

See Also Vol. 1: *Christianity, Evangelical Movement, Roman Catholicism*

Bibliography

Adams, Abigail. "Making One Our Word: Protestant Q'eqchi' Mayas in Highland Guatemala." In *Holy Saints and Fiery Preachers: The Anthropology of Protestantism in Mexico and Central America*. Edited by James W. Dow and Alan R. Sandstrom. Westport, Conn.: Praeger, 2001.

Annis, Sheldon. *God and Production in a Guatemalan Town*. Austin: University of Texas Press, 1987.

Berryman, Philip. *Stubborn Hope: Religion, Politics, and Revolution in Central America*. Maryknoll, N.Y.: Orbis Books, 1994.

Chiappari, Christopher. "Toward a Maya Theology of Liberation: The Reformulation of a 'Traditional' Religion in the Global Context." *Journal for the Scientific Study of Religion* 41, no. I (2002): 47–67.

Cook, Guillermo, ed. *Crosscurrents in Indigenous Spirituality: Interface of Maya, Catholic, and Protestant Worldviews.* New York: Leiden, 1997.

Falla, Ricardo. *Quiché Rebelde: Religious Conversion, Politics, and Ethnic Identity in Guatemala.* Translated by Philip Berryman. Austin: University of Texas Press, 2001.

Garrard-Burnett, Virginia. *Protestantism in Guatemala: Living in the New Jerusalem.* Austin: University of Texas Press, 1998.

Scotchmer, David G. "Life of the Heart: A Maya Protestant Spirituality." In *South and Meso-American Native Spirituality.* Edited by Gary H. Gossen with Miguel León Portillo. New York: The Crossroad Publishing Company, 1993.

Steigenga, Timothy J. *The Politics of the Spirit: The Political Implications of Pentecostalized Religion in Costa Rica and Guatemala.* Lanham, Md.: Lexington Books, 2001.

Tedlock, Dennis, trans. *Popol Vuh.* Rev. ed. New York: Touchstone, 1996.

Watanabe, John. *Maya Saints and Souls in a Changing World.* Austin: University of Texas Press, 1992.

Wilson, Richard. *Maya Resurgence in Guatemala: Q'eqchi' Experiences.* Norman and London: University of Oklahoma Press, 1995.

Guinea

POPULATION 7,775,065
MUSLIM 85 percent
CHRISTIAN 10 percent
OTHER 5 percent

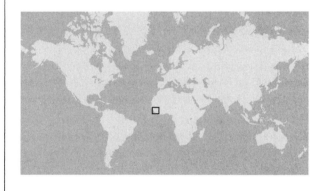

Country Overview

INTRODUCTION The Republic of Guinea, located in western Africa along the Atlantic Ocean, is bordered by six countries: Guinea-Bissau, Senegal, and Mali to the north; Côte d'Ivoire to the east; and Liberia and Sierra Leone to the south. The country is divided into four natural geographic regions: Lower Guinea (Maritime Guinea, or the Coastal Region), Middle Guinea (the Fouta Djallon), Upper Guinea, and the Forest Region. Each of the regions is home to a major ethnic group or cluster of closely related groups.

Guinea is one of the most Islamic countries in West Africa; the majority of citizens are Sunni Muslims. The Shia branch has been increasing in number but is still small. Christianity in Guinea is most prevalent where European influence was strongest—in the Coastal Region and Forest Region. Muslims and Christians in Guinea remain partly animist. As a result of civil wars and conflicts, some 500,000 people from Sierra Leone, Liberia, and Côte d'Ivoire have sought refuge in the south of Guinea. They are predominantly Christians and practitioners of traditional beliefs.

RELIGIOUS TOLERANCE Guinea is a secular state and does not have an official religion. The constitution provides for freedom of worship, permits faith communities to govern themselves without government interference, and prohibits discrimination on the grounds of religion. These rights are generally respected.

In order to benefit from certain government privileges, including tax benefits and energy subsidies, all recognized Christian churches in Guinea are required to belong to the Association of Churches and Missions. The state requires missionaries to declare their aims and activities to the Ministry of the Interior or to the National Islamic League (La Ligue Islamique), a cabinet-level government office. The government has at times restricted the activities of Jehovah's Witnesses, but Roman Catholic, Pentecostal Assemblies of Canada, Philafricaine (for the treatment of leprosy and other diseases), and various American missionary societies operate freely in the country.

Major Religion

SUNNI ISLAM

DATE OF ORIGIN 1100 C.E.
NUMBER OF FOLLOWERS 6.6 million

HISTORY Islam was introduced to Guinea and other parts of West Africa during the Almorayide (militant Muslim) invasions of the Ghana Empire in 1076. The efforts of Almorayide missionaries were extended by traders, courtiers, and rulers, who spread Islam along trade routes and to far-flung seats of government.

Islam continued to spread throughout the savannah region of Guinea, which was part of the Mali and Songhai empires from the thirteenth to the seventeenth centuries. In the sixteenth and seventeenth centuries migrating Fulani (also called Peul, or Fulbé) pastoralists and militant proselytizers conquered the indigenous population and confiscated their land. Religious leaders (*karamokos*) founded a theocratic kingdom (1725–1896) in the Fouta Djallon region and selected Karamoko Alfa (Ibrahima Musa, or Alpha Ibrahima) as their *almamy* (military and spiritual king) and leader of the jihad.

In 1751 Karamoko Alfa's successor, Ibrahima Sori, revitalized the jihad, which led to a great religious revival throughout West Africa. The Fouta Djallon was all but converted to Islam when, in about 1850, Al Haj Oumar Tall launched a holy war against the French, the traditional nobility of the Senegal-Niger region, and the dominant Qadiriya theocracies. Islam was further consolidated in Upper Guinea and the Forest Region during wars of conquest led by Samory Touré in the 1870s. In the twentieth century the French colonial administration's anti-Catholic policies inadvertently accelerated the acceptance of Islam. Guinea gained independence from France in 1958.

EARLY AND MODERN LEADERS In the propitious environment of the Theocratic Kingdom of the Fouta Djallon, Karamoko Alfa conducted jihads, bringing Islam to Fulani peoples in Senegal and the Gambia and throughout coastal West Africa. The Toucouleur Muslim scholar and military chief Al-Hajj Oumar Tall established the Tijaniya Sufi order in the western Sudan (now Mali, Senegal, and Guinea) in the mid-nineteenth century.

The Mandingo warrior Almamy Samory Touré, known for resisting French and British imperialism in

Islamic holy men place a body in a grave during a Guinean funeral. Guinean Muslims observe at least six rites of passage, one of them death. AP/WIDE WORLD PHOTOS.

the 1880s and 1890s, founded an independent state in 1875. Stretching from present-day Bamako (in Mali) to northern Liberia, the empire lasted only four years, but it contained a brief interlude of theocratic rule during which Touré imposed Islam, outlawed pagan customs, destroyed symbols of animism, and built mosques.

Religious leadership is shared by the secretary-general of the Islamic League; the leaders of Guinea's regional cultural associations; the grand imams of Conakry, Labé, and Kankan; and a diverse group of scholars and teachers.

MAJOR THEOLOGIANS AND AUTHORS Karamoko Alfa, educated in the great Islamic learning center of Bhourya, is credited with translating the Koran into Pulaar, the Fulani language. Al-Hajj Oumar Tall came under the influence of the Tijaniyya brotherhood in the Fouta Djallon. He taught and preached before he began his jihad against the pagan Bambara kings of Ségou and Kaarta in 1852. Some 20 works have been attributed to this mystic-pilgrim and influential sheik, who, more than any other Guinean author, shaped Islam in Guinea.

HOUSES OF WORSHIP AND HOLY PLACES The Great Mosque is located in the capital city, Conakry, and the oldest mosque is outside of Pita in the Fouta Djallon.

Muslims regard the village of Touba in the northwest Fouta Djallon as holy. Touba was founded in 1823–24 by Al-Hajj Salimou, a Muslim teacher. It is home to Diakhanké Muslim scholars and teachers of the Qadiriya brotherhood, a group that dates to the late fifteenth century. Touba has become a destination for pilgrimages, and many of the faithful send their children there for religious instruction.

The village of Fougoumba holds special significance because of the role it played during the Theocratic Kingdom. *Almamys* were installed in Fougoumba, which served as neutral ground where free men assembled and provincial armies gathered prior to jihads.

WHAT IS SACRED? The words and texts from the Koran written upon prayer recitation boards are thought to have a supernatural power, and the water used to wash them from the board may be captured in a bowl and consumed, conveying power to the person who drinks it. Some Guinean Muslims believe that the pig, which once befriended the Prophet Muhammad, is sacred.

HOLIDAYS AND FESTIVALS The government recognizes Muslim and Christian holidays, which are celebrated widely by people of both faiths. One popular Muslim holiday is the *Fête de Tabaski* (known elsewhere as Id al-Adha), commemorating Abraham's willingness to sacrifice his son, believed by Muslims to be Ismael. On Tabaski it is customary to kill a ram or sheep and eat mutton, and it is charitable for those of means to offer a sheep or goat to the less fortunate. Tabaski is also a day to give and receive gifts and to wear new clothes.

Another feast occurs at the end of Ramadan, a month of fasting from sunrise to sunset. Work assumes a slower pace during Ramadan, and nightlife quiets as people typically eat and drink at home to recover their strength. In spite of the physical deprivation, many Guineans look forward to spiritual renewal and approach Ramadan with great anticipation. A third important holiday is Mawloud, the Prophet Muhammad's birthday. People celebrate by attending mosque, visiting friends and family, and feasting. The dates are determined by the lunar calendar.

MODE OF DRESS Muslim Guineans wear *boubous*, garments that are slipped over the head and worn over matching pants. They vary from simple cuts of cloth with little or no decoration to beautifully embroidered cotton robes. The full-length cut of the *boubou* reflects an Islamic injunction recommending long garments to protect the body. Leather, open-heeled, pointed slippers may be worn with the *boubou*. Women may wear matching scarves or turbans, while men wear Muslim skullcaps, which are either of a simple round design and usually white or tailored to match their tunics. They may also wear felt caps. In the Fouta Djallon *boubous* are tailored with distinctive Fulani patterns and styles and are particularly associated with Islamic practice.

DIETARY PRACTICES Some Guinean Muslims publicly follow Islam's dietary restrictions on alcohol and pork, while at home they may not strictly observe them. Generally Muslims from the Forest Region and some modern urbanites are less rigid about their dietary practices. Before and after meals, which are eaten with the right hand only, a bowl of water is made available for washing hands. This is a Muslim practice that in Guinea has become a cultural norm. Gratitude to Allah for the meal is expressed using the Arabic term *albarka*.

RITUALS The National Islamic League estimates that 70 percent of Guinean Muslims practice their faith regularly through observance of Islamic rituals. These include the Five Pillars of Islam. In Guinea prayer time is observed quite strictly, and it is not unusual to interrupt work or other activities to say prayers.

In times of illness or uncertainty Muslims seek the advice of *marabouts*—religious teachers, medicine men, and soothsayers who are considered intermediaries between Allah and his people. The rituals that *marabouts* prescribe often combine traditional religious practices with aspects of Islam. For instance, depending on the need, they may ask their followers to wear an amulet with a verse from the Koran inside or to drink the words of a text washed from a prayer board and collected into a bowl.

RITES OF PASSAGE Guinean Muslims observe at least six rites of passage: birth, circumcision, a complete reading of the Koran, marriage, being an elder, and death. Birth is validated by baptism and the naming ceremony. The Malinke conduct a naming ceremony seven days after the birth of a child; the father whispers the name into the baby's ear so that the child is the first to hear his or her name.

Both male and female children are circumcised, but the dates for performing the rite vary by ethnic group and community and, increasingly, according to the wishes of the parents. Although observed less than in the past, circumcision traditionally confirms knowledge of the faith and marks the passage to adulthood (hence, it must be performed before an individual can marry). The complete reading of the Koran by age 15 marks the passage to young adulthood, when preparations begin for marrying and establishing a household.

Guinean Muslims between 35 and 40 years of age are expected to bridge younger and older generations. Men typically begin to attend prayers regularly, and as they age they may be welcomed into elder's associations. Many elders are able to recite lengthy passages from the Koran.

MEMBERSHIP Converts from other beliefs are welcomed into the faith, but Guinean Muslims seldom proselytize. Making a pilgrimage to Mecca enhances a Muslim's membership status. Additional recognition may be bestowed upon theologians, imams, and scholars who are able to recite the entire Koran.

SOCIAL JUSTICE Guineans have traditionally had an accepting attitude toward poverty. Acts of charity are required by the Koran and by traditional social norms. It is commonplace to give alms to street beggars and to those gathered at the doors of the mosque. On feast days the wealthy are expected to give alms commensurate to their ability.

SOCIAL ASPECTS All Guineans are born into relationships through clan and kinship and are bound by their age set or peer group (karé, or sérè). Children circumcised in the same group may form mutual help associations and cooperative work parties. Guineans see these traditional institutions as consistent with teachings in the Koran.

Malinke and Fulani societies continue to reflect their once highly stratified class structure. During the jihads of the eighteenth and nineteenth centuries, various communities were assimilated or enslaved. In the Fouta Djallon a feudal society evolved that was composed of Fulani overlords, freeborn Fulani, Fulani of the bush, and non-Fulani serfs. As a result of this stratification, many serf villages do not have mosques.

POLITICAL IMPACT Given the Sunni influence, no Islamic party or significant fundamentalist movement exists in Guinea. Islam does influence politics, however, and to some extent the former ruling party (Parti Démocratique de Guinée) has competed with Islamic leaders for leadership.

Since the advent of multiparty politics in 1992, parties have aligned themselves with regional cultural associations, whose leaders include clerics and theologians. Following the December 1993 elections (during which some street violence occurred), Fulani leaders appealed for peace, admonishing that outcomes were Allah's will. Some analysts regarded this fatalist view as the equivalent of giving the incumbent carte blanche to manipulate the elections.

The National Islamic League, whose mandate is to reach out to Muslims and to coordinate with other faith communities, has cabinet-level status in the government. The league distributes rice to Islamic groups, supports mosque construction, arranges annual charter flights to Mecca, and contributes to strengthening the political base of the regime.

CONTROVERSIAL ISSUES Although Islam has generated little controversy in state and social relations, government support for the National Islamic League has led to complaints that the state favors Muslims over non-Muslims. Furthermore, in deference to the Islamic communities of the Fouta Djallon and parts of Upper Guinea, the government refrains from making appointments of non-Muslim leaders in these areas. In April 1999 government ministers were required to take an oath on either the Koran or the Bible, a gesture that provoked some criticism from those insisting that such practices violated the secular nature of the state.

Both Islamic and Christian leaders condemned the fighting between Muslims and Christians in the Forest Region in January 2000. National Muslim leaders attributed the violence to long-unsettled land disputes and not to religion.

CULTURAL IMPACT Islam has had a great effect on the language, alphabet, and intellectual thought of the Fulani people. Arabic was used to transcribe Pulaar (the Fulani language) into written form, into which the Koran was translated word for word. Arabic was the language of the Koran; hence, the close relationship of Arabic script to that of Pulaar encouraged the spread of Islam through increased facility in reading the Koran. Because the Fulani are so Islamicized, many of them master the Arabic alphabet as well as their own language. In Koranic schools children are taught to read and write Arabic from an early age so that later they can read and interpret the Koran and religious works written in Arabic.

Fulani poetry is highly lyrical and expresses religious, philosophical, and social themes. Arabesque designs embellish many mosques throughout the Fouta and other parts of the country. Leather craftsmen design cases for the Koran, and musicians compose religious music, which is played on locally made violins, lyres, flutes, maracas, and calabashes (which are used as drums).

Other Religions

Christian groups in Guinea include Roman Catholics, Anglicans, Baptists, Jehovah's Witnesses, Seventh-day Adventists, and evangelicals. Portuguese explorers landed on the coast of West Africa in the late 1400s, but it was not until 1877 that the Holy Ghost Fathers established the first Catholic mission at Boffa. Because of resistance in the Fouta Djallon and parts of the Forest Region, evangelization was restricted to coastal areas. After World War II the rate of conversions slowed as a result of the continuing spread of Islam and competition between Catholic and Protestant missionaries from Sierra Leone. Despite these hindrances the impact of Christianity has been intensified by the influence of missionary schools, where many political leaders have received their training.

Some 10 percent of Guineans describe themselves as Christians, and the vast majority of these are Roman Catholics. The Guinean Catholic Church is presided over by an archbishop in Conakry and two bishops in Kankan and N'zérékoré. Protestants, numbering perhaps a few thousand, are mostly Anglicans. Relations between Christians and Muslims have been generally amicable. Like Muslims, Christians in Guinea blend elements of traditional African religion into their faiths.

About five percent of the Guinean population adheres to traditional indigenous beliefs. The exact origins of traditional religion in Guinea are unknown, but it likely dates to the Stone Age. The Malinke, the Fulani, and other African groups shaped religious systems from the tenth century onward.

Guinean indigenous religions share common characteristics with the traditional beliefs of sub-Saharan Af-

rica. At the apex is a God or Supreme Being, who, like the God of Islam and Christianity, is omnipotent and timeless. Similarities diverge at this point. The African God is remote and seldom worshiped. People pray and sacrifice to intermediate divinities that take the form of animate or inanimate objects, which, living or dead, each have a force called *nyama* (spirit, will, personality, and distinctiveness). Pre-Islamic Fulani revered the bull and used sour milk in life-cycle ceremonies. Coastal peoples believe in a water genie, Sata-Bo. Malinke rites, which are connected with the earth, sometimes involve worship of the crocodile. *Marabouts*—clerics, fortune tellers, healers, and teachers—perform rituals, decipher signs, unravel mysteries, assign blame, prescribe medicines, cast spells, and advise on important decisions.

The belief in ancestral homelands is a determining factor for the location and movement of people. The shrine of the ancestors unites a clan or kin group with the head of the family lineage, its chief priest. Rituals in the Forester Toma group are practiced in forest clearings known as the "Sacred Forest." These groves are off-limits to women and strangers. The Forester Toma bury family members around the foundation of the home, because their spirits are believed to be present in the village.

In the Forest Region and the Coastal Region are found mystery cults, or "secret societies," such as the Poro society for men and the Sande society for women. Membership is by initiation and takes place at puberty. Beliefs and practices are not shared with members of the opposite sex or with uninitiated children. When performing official functions, cult leaders wear masks representing the cult object. These masks are considered sacred. The cult leaders, usually the society's elders, exercise a controlling influence over cult members, dictating their stances in elections and political affairs.

In the 1960s President Sékou Touré, a member of the Malinke group, conducted a debunking campaign to strip away the powers of the cults. Sacred forests were burned and planted over with banana and coffee plantations, and sacred objects were destroyed. Foresters blamed the Fulani for tacit approval of the desecration. The campaign was only partly successful. After Touré's death in 1984, cult leaders who had fled to neighboring countries returned to Guinea, and traditional practices reemerged. Many Foresters continue to harbor deep distrust of the Malinke and Fulani and have refused to support their political candidates.

In Guinea traditional initiation and caste associations have exerted more influence on music, the visual arts, and oral literature than Islam and Christianity have. Traditional sculpture, masks, jewelry, and musical instruments are attributed special powers when they are worn or displayed during initiation ceremonies and the like. As such, they exercise political, social, religious, and cultural power via rituals. Malinke musicians draw on the glory of the Mali Empire (c. 1230–c. 1450). Malinke literature—epitomized by Camara Laye's *L'Enfant noir* (1953; *The African Child*)—reflects the staying power of taboos and the spirit world.

A small number of Bahai exist in Guinea but are not officially recognized. Among the expatriate community (mainly composed of traders from Asia) are Hindus, Buddhists, and practitioners of traditional Chinese religions. There are few atheists.

Robert Groelsema

See Also Vol. I: *African Indigenous Beliefs, Christianity, Islam, Roman Catholicism, Sunni Islam*

Bibliography

Binns, Margaret. *Guinea.* World Bibliographical Series, vol. 191. Oxford: Clio Press, 1996.

CultureGrams 2002. Vol. 2, *Africa, Asia, and Oceania.* Orem, Utah: CultureGrams, 2002.

Nelson, Harold D., et al. *Area Handbook for Guinea.* 2nd ed. Washington, D.C.: U.S. Government Printing Office, 1975.

O'Toole, Thomas, and Ibrahima Bah-Lalya. *Historical Dictionary of Guinea.* 3rd ed. African Historical Dictionaries, no. 16. Lanham, Md.: Scarecrow Press, 1995.

Suret-Canale, Jean. "Touba in Guinea: Holy Place of Islam." In *African Perspectives.* Edited by Christopher Allen and R.W. Johnson. Cambridge: Cambridge University Press, 1970.

Trimingham, J. Spencer. *A History of Islam in West Africa.* London: Oxford University Press, 1962.

Guinea-Bissau

POPULATION 1,345,479

AFRICAN INDIGENOUS BELIEFS 65
percent

ISLAM 30 percent

**CHRISTIANITY (ROMAN CATHOLIC
AND PROTESTANT)** 5 percent

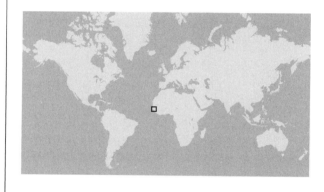

Country Overview

INTRODUCTION The Republic of Guinea-Bissau (formerly Portuguese Guinea) is a small West African nation on the Atlantic Coast south of Senegal and west of Guinea. The coastal regions of the country comprise rivers and swampland, while forest and savanna cover the interior. The people make their living primarily by subsistence farming and herding. The country is home to more than 30 different ethnic groups, the principal ones being the Balanta (27 percent), Fula (23 percent), Mandinga (12 percent), Manjak (11 percent), and Pepel (10 percent). Brames, Beafada, Bijagos, Felupes (Mankanya), and migrants from neighboring countries

make up the rest of the population. Although Portuguese is the official language, less than 10 percent of Gunieans speaks it. Kriolu—a blend of Portuguese and indigenous languages—is widely spoken, and each ethnic group also has its own language.

The first inhabitants of the area practiced indigenous African religions. Traders brought Islam to the area in the tenth century. In 1250 Mande warriors founded the Gabu kingdom, characterized by an indigenous animism. Political divisions and trade disputes weakened the kingdom in the late 1700s, and in 1867 it failed in the face of Islamic jihads throughout West Africa. The Portuguese arrived in the area in 1446. Throughout the colonial period they attempted to form an elite group of "assimilated" Guineans with Portuguese ancestry who spoke Portuguese and converted to Christianity. Portuguese influence did not extend beyond this small group. Guinea-Bissau gained independence from Portugal in 1974 after an eleven-year war of liberation.

The majority of Guineans practice indigenous African religions; these traditionalists are scattered throughout the country. The Muslim one-third of the population (the Mandinga, Fula, and Beafada peoples) lives mainly in the north and northeast. Despite Portugal's 500-year presence, Christianity is not widespread, and most Christians reside in the capital city of Bissau. Muslims and Christians in Guinea-Bissau continue to practice their indigenous religions, emphasizing "old" traditions in some contexts and "new" traditions in others.

RELIGIOUS TOLERANCE Guineans strive to uphold the ideal of unity through diversity. The constitution of

1984, amended in 1996, guarantees religious freedom, and the government's attitude toward religious expression is officially one of tolerance and neutrality. It has criticized some traditional practices, such as delayed burial and female circumcision. Not much effort has been made to bring the country's religions together, and the cultural divide between them is readily observable in daily life. The capital city of Bissau is divided into Muslim, Christian, and traditionalist neighborhoods, and intermarriage between groups is often discouraged. In 1999 President Kumba Yala (a Christian Balanta) angered some Muslims by expelling the Ahmadiyya (a Muslim reform sect from Pakistan) from the country, a decision that was overturned by the Supreme Court. Despite divisions, overlap in religious practice is common. Muslims and Christians consult traditional African healers, and traditionalists and Christians commonly send their sons to Muslim initiation rituals. This translates into an ethos of religious harmony.

Major Religions

AFRICAN INDIGENOUS BELIEFS

ISLAM

AFRICAN INDIGENOUS BELIEFS

DATE OF ORIGIN 900 C.E.
NUMBER OF FOLLOWERS 875,000

HISTORY From 900 to 1400, the inhabitants of the area, adherents of traditional African religions, maintained peaceful contact with Muslim Berber and Djula traders who traveled through the area. Although between 1250 and 1867 the Mandinga conquered and converted many peoples in and around present-day Guinea-Bissau to their indigenous religion, other groups escaped their influence by fleeing to coastal areas, where they continued to practice their own traditional religions.

Indigenous beliefs and practices played a prominent role in the eleven-year war of liberation. Guineans fought against Portugal beginning in 1963. Both African and Portuguese soldiers consulted local healer-diviners to aid them in planning war strategies or to acquire amulets thought to offer protection against knives and bullets. In 1998, when a military junta attempted to oust the country's president, several diviners were said

An initiate of a religion indigenous to Guinea-Bissau. Male initiation rituals are practiced throughout Guinea-Bissau, and most involve circumcision. © DAVE G. HOUSER/CORBIS.

to have predicted the length and outcome of the conflict.

EARLY AND MODERN LEADERS Because they are egalitarian and noncentralized, African indigenous religions lack individually recognized leaders. Ancestors, elders, and diviners play important local roles. Many people carve wooden posts representing ancestors, to which they make sacrifices to ensure health and success. Elders and diviners act as mediators between the human and spirit worlds, determining when and how such sacrifices should be made.

MAJOR THEOLOGIANS AND AUTHORS Religious knowledge among traditionalists in Guinea-Bissau is spread and passed on orally rather than in writing. Healer-diviners (*djambakus* in Kriolu) study their craft intensively over a number of years through apprenticeship and train the next generation of specialists.

HOUSES OF WORSHIP AND HOLY PLACES Sacrifices to ancestral or other spirits to prevent or address misfortune are performed at local shrines, which are sometimes natural (trees and water sources) and sometimes man-made (carved ancestor posts, wells, and containers). Elders of some ethnic groups gather to make sacrifices or discuss religious matters in small thatched huts built around a central shrine or assemblage of shrines. The actions performed at shrines are thought to connect human and spirit worlds and to ensure harmony to the living.

WHAT IS SACRED? Indigenous religions in Guinea-Bissau assert an interconnectedness of the human and spirit worlds. People, places, and things are sacred when they evoke this relationship. Specific trees and water sources are sacred in that spirits are believed to reside there. Members of some ethnic groups hold certain animals sacred and prohibit the consumption of their meat. Such man-made items as amulets, wells, and containers are sacred when they are used to place humans in contact with spirits. More generally, all natural things—the earth, the sky, animals, and plants—are thought to be sacred, and specific rules govern people's contact with them.

HOLIDAYS AND FESTIVALS Practitioners of indigenous religions in Guinea-Bissau follow a calendar relating to the agricultural cycle. Members of most ethnic groups perform ceremonies before beginning such agricultural work as clearing fields, ploughing, or harvesting. Ceremonies may also be held when the first rains arrive, in times of drought, and after a successful harvest.

MODE OF DRESS Traditional dress for ritual or ceremonial occasions varies by ethnic group in Guinea-Bissau and may include grass skirts, cowry shells, headdresses, and white clay (used as body paint). Women often wear dyed or patterned wraparound skirts (*panu* in Kriolu) and matching shirts or one-piece dresses (*spera* in Kriolu), accented with colorful head ties and bead jewelry. Men wear patterned cotton pants and shirt outfits or European-style clothing and hats, depending on ethnic group affiliation and the occasion.

DIETARY PRACTICES Among many ethnic groups in Guinea-Bissau, pregnant women commonly observe food taboos, avoiding eggs, fruit that has fallen on the ground, and the meat of animals with claws, fangs, or slippery skin, since these are thought to produce fetal abnormalities. Adherents of traditional religions drink alcohol (usually palm wine, sugarcane alcohol, and cashew fruit wine) on ritual occasions, often in vast quantities.

RITUALS Many indigenous rituals are linked to the agricultural cycle. Before ploughing rice fields, the Balanta hold *baloba* ceremonies to combat evil spirits. Sacrifices may be performed to control the rains or to ensure a successful harvest. Rituals are also performed in times of crisis. When faced with misfortunes, such as illness, death, theft, infertility, or social conflict, people consult healer-diviners, who communicate with *iran* (ancestral or other spirits) to uncover the cause and prescribe appropriate remedial action.

Many rituals center on such life events as birth and death. Funerary rituals are often elaborate, and many involve delayed burial. Members of several ethnic groups perform the *djongajo* ritual, in which men hold the corpse on a bier and ask it the reasons behind the death and whether sorcery was involved. The forward or backward movement of the bier indicates positive or negative responses.

RITES OF PASSAGE Male initiation rituals are practiced throughout Guinea-Bissau, and most involve circumcision. The age varies with the ethnic group. The Bijagos people hold especially elaborate initiation rituals for both genders, teaching traditional skills and values in various stages over several months. Every twenty to twenty-five years Manjak hold an initiation ceremony for young males in a sacred forest in each Manjak "land." Emigrant Manjak from Senegal and Europe return to their home villages to participate in this all-important rite of passage, which lasts up to a couple of months.

Marriage is often arranged and includes ritual exchanges between the groom's and bride's families, as well as dancing and feasting. Funerary rituals (*toka tchur* in Kriolu) are thought to facilitate the entrance of the soul of the deceased into the next world. Relatives and friends gather to dance, feast, and drum throughout the night. Animal sacrifices are especially important, and the number of cows killed often reflects the social status of the deceased. Many indigenous religions of Guinea-

Bissau hold that the deceased are reembodied in new-born infants.

MEMBERSHIP Practitioners of indigenous African religions do not see themselves as members of a religion, and Guineans do not convert to such beliefs. Religious identity is acquired by birth into a particular ethnic group (some who believe in reincarnation believe it is acquired before birth). Although adherents of traditional religions commonly see converts to Islam and Christianity as turning their backs on tradition, the converts rarely abandon their old beliefs, and conversion rarely precludes participation in indigenous rituals.

SOCIAL JUSTICE Indigenous religions in Guinea-Bissau place a strong moral obligation on helping others. Those who share are respected and can count on the future help of others. The attainment of material wealth and power is often associated with witchcraft, especially when it is acquired quickly, effortlessly, or at other's expense.

SOCIAL ASPECTS Practitioners of indigenous religions in Guinea-Bissau see marriage as the ideal state and expect it of everyone. Among many ethnic groups, individuals are not considered full adults until they are married and have children, and traditional initiation rituals often prepare people for these roles. Marriages are arranged among many groups, although "love" marriages have become common in urban areas. Polygyny is common among members of some ethnic groups. The primary purpose of marriage is to produce children, and both men and women value children highly, especially given that infant mortality rates are high. Children bring joy and happiness, contribute to agricultural labor, increase one's social status, and ensure that one will be cared for in old age and remembered after death. "May you have many children" is a common blessing throughout the country.

POLITICAL IMPACT Since independence, political power has remained in the hands of adherents of traditional religions, who openly profess their reluctance to relinquish it to the Muslims, "those who wear the hats." JoÂo Bernardo "Nino" Vieira, Guinea-Bissau's president from 1980 to 1999, was said to have consulted numerous healer-diviners (ironically some of them Muslims) to maintain power in the face of growing local discontent.

CONTROVERSIAL ISSUES In precolonial times Guinean practitioners of traditional religions often killed breach babies (born feet first) and twins, associating these with the animal world. Although some claim that infanticide still occurs today, such infants are more commonly washed with an herbal mixture thought to neutralize their ambiguity and danger. Babies born with physical deformities or other anomalies may be suspected of being *iran,* or spirit children, said to be created when a spirit enters a pregnant woman's body and changes places with the human fetus.

Development workers and government officials in Guinea-Bissau are critical of such practices as polygyny and delayed burial, associating the latter with disease. The Balanta people are criticized for ritualized cattle stealing, a practice associated with boy's initiation rites.

CULTURAL IMPACT The influence of indigenous African religions is evident in nearly every aspect of culture in Guinea-Bissau. The Pepel weave cloth with intricate designs for use during funerary ceremonies. The Bijagos and Nalu peoples are famous for their wooden carvings of animals representing spirits, which are used in rituals. Several contemporary music groups have preserved indigenous musical styles, including *ngumbe,* fast-paced music using drums and other percussion instruments. They often sing in Kriolu. Wooden carved ancestor posts, spirit houses, and medicine bundles are common features of traditional Guinean architecture and have both practical purpose and aesthetic appeal.

ISLAM

DATE OF ORIGIN Tenth century C.E.
NUMBER OF FOLLOWERS 404,000

HISTORY Berber and Mande traders brought Islam to the area beginning in the tenth century. Although Guineans gradually began adopting aspects of the religion as early as the twelfth century, most did not define themselves as Muslims until the nineteenth century, when Islamicized Fula from the Futa Jallon (present-day Guinea) began waging jihads. In 1867 the Fula put an end to the 600-year-old traditionalist Gabu kingdom, a tributary of the Mali empire, and they converted many local people (mainly Mandinga and Beafada) to Islam.

The Ahmadiyya, a Muslim reform sect from Pakistan, first arrived in Guinea-Bissau in the mid-1980s. Although this reform movement has since been slowly gaining popularity, traditional Muslims vehemently oppose it.

EARLY AND MODERN LEADERS Leadership in Guinea-Bissau is tied to kinship and age rather than to personal achievements. Muslim men who are Koranic scholars or healer-diviners or who have made the pilgrimage to Mecca hold considerable power and influence. Leaders of local mosques are influential and provide balance to political leadership by asserting their spiritual influence.

Members of the Mandinga Sane and Mane clans, who ruled the various provinces of the Gabu kingdom during the fifteenth and sixteenth centuries, are respected for their historical leadership. The founder of the Muridiyya brotherhood of Senegal, Ahmadu Bamba Mbacke (1853–1927), is remembered for his piety and anticolonial teachings, and Muslims in Guinea-Bissau sing praises to him on Islamic holidays.

MAJOR THEOLOGIANS AND AUTHORS Some local holy men (*muru* in Kriolu) have earned national or international reputations. Before Konchupa Faati's death in the late 1990s, pilgrims traveled to his village near Bafata to receive blessings, delivered through his breath and spittle. Some holy men study in North Africa and the Middle East, returning to Guinea-Bissau to establish their own Koranic schools. The Koranic school of Al-hadj Fodimaye Ture (born sometime between 1919 and 1939) in the Oio region draws thousands of pilgrims annually to receive blessings and celebrate Gammo, the Prophet's birthday. Holy men double as Muslim healers, treating clients for a host of afflictions, and divine the future using sand, cowry shells, and dreams.

HOUSES OF WORSHIP AND HOLY PLACES Guinean cities, towns, and villages in Muslim areas or with significant Muslim populations have at least one central mosque and may have smaller ones that serve specific neighborhoods. As mosques are generally reserved for Friday worship, people pray in their homes or central compounds on other days. Guinean Muslims travel to villages with famous Muslim healers to receive blessings or make requests. Alhadj Fodimaye Ture's village (near Farim) is the most popular Muslim pilgrimage site.

WHAT IS SACRED? Sacred objects include the Koran, prayer beads, and protective amulets that encase Koranic verses. White things, such as rice, milk, sugar, salt, kola nuts, and cloth, are also deemed sacred and are commonly offered as sacrifices or charity.

HOLIDAYS AND FESTIVALS Ramadan (Jun-Jun) is the most important holiday for Muslims in Guinea-Bissau. People break their daily fast with *moni* (millet porridge), drunk from a common calabash using small ladles. On Laila, which coincides with Ramadan, Muslims gather at sunset and chant until dawn, believing that the suffering endured on this single night is worth more than a thousand days of fasting in the eyes of God. On Gammo (the Prophet's birthday) Muslims travel to local pilgrimage sites where they stay awake for three nights, recounting the life of the Prophet and singing praises to local or regional saints. At a *bunya*, which celebrates the yearly return of the Mecca pilgrims, people sing praises to the returnees, receive blessings, and share a feast.

MODE OF DRESS *Ropa garandi* ("big clothes") is the Kriolu term for modest attire, a distinguishing feature of Muslim identity in Guinea-Bissau. For women this consists of colorful African dresses and matching head ties. Older women may drape Arab-style scarves over their head ties, especially for prayer and ritual occasions. Women accentuate their dress with gold or bead jewelry and protective amulets that hold Koranic verses. Muslim men wear African or Arab-style long robes, often with pants underneath. Footwear consists of locally made leather sandals or colorful shoes from Saudi Arabia. Men accentuate their dress with embroidered hats, fezzes, or Saudi-style head coverings, silver bracelets (gold is reserved for women), protective amulets, and sunglasses.

DIETARY PRACTICES Muslims in Guinea-Bissau have a unique local explanation for the Muslim prohibition on pork. The Mandinga people believe that, long ago, their journeying ancestors, near death from dehydration, encountered many animals that knew of a nearby water source but were too selfish to disclose its location. Finally a pig selflessly led them to water. Out of respect for the pig, rather than because of its uncleanness, Mandinga refrain from eating pork.

Animals with claws or fangs and carrion are also taboo. Chinese green tea, flavored with sugar and mint leaves and brewed ceremonially in three rounds, is drunk widely, especially by men. Tea, kola nuts, and local tobacco are essential features of rituals and other celebrations. Guinean Muslims say they follow the Muslim prohibition on alcohol, though some are said to drink in secret.

RITUALS In preparation for Koranic school in Guinea-Bissau, a holy man writes Koranic verses on a child's palm with ink, sprinkles salt over the ink, and instructs the child to lick his hand. Circumcision for both girls and boys is linked to religious purity and is followed by a coming-out ceremony, involving dancing and feasting. Although circumcision used to be performed at puberty, it takes place more commonly now between the ages of 6 and 10.

Marriage occurs in two stages. The parents of the bride and groom exchange kola nuts to "tie" the marriage, allowing the couple to procreate. The "bringing of the bride," when relatives and guests accompany the bride from her father's to her husband's house, may occur between one and seven years later.

At death the corpse is washed, dressed, and buried according to Islamic doctrine. Graves are unmarked and virtually unrecognizable. Funerary ceremonies are held one week, one month, three months, and one year after the burial. People gather in memory of the deceased to read the Koran, receive blessings, and hold a feast.

RITES OF PASSAGE Muslims in Guinea-Bissau consider infants pure until they cut their first tooth, an event associated symbolically with the ability to lie and the loss of innocence. Children of both sexes enjoy a relatively carefree existence until age 7, when they develop social sense and their behavior is more restricted: Girls help their mothers with domestic chores, and boys study the Koran. Adulthood for both genders is marked by the birth of the first child. During their childbearing years, women focus more on their roles as wives and mothers than on their spiritual lives, while their husbands become increasingly devout. Men and women become elders when their children have children. Elders of both genders enjoy reduced workloads and elevated social status. Elderhood for women is marked especially by an intensification of religious practice.

MEMBERSHIP What makes one a Muslim is the subject of lively debate in Guinea-Bissau. Many believe that religious identity begins at conception, when the sexual fluids of a Muslim man "mix" with the blood of a Muslim woman and Allah breathes life into the fetus. A baby born headfirst is said to accept Islam, while a breach baby (born feet first) is said to refuse Islam. Muslim

mother's breast milk is believed to transmit Muslim identity even to non-Muslim infants.

A more practice-based understanding of Muslim identity asserts that life course rituals inscribe it on the body, and daily prayer, fasting, and the observation of food taboos are signs of piety. Although they occur on occasion, mixed marriages are considered problematic since, in the eyes of many, conversion alone does not render one a true Muslim. For this reason Guinean Muslims do not actively proselytize.

SOCIAL JUSTICE Muslims in Guinea-Bissau are often members of socially stratified societies, consisting of groups of nobles, artisans, and descendants of slaves. Although membership is conferred at birth and marriage outside one's group is discouraged, social relations between groups reflect an ethos of respect and interdependence.

Material wealth, power, and fame are thought to be blessings from God. Guinean Muslims believe good fortune should be shared with others and discourage violence of all kinds, since the taking of human life is reserved for Allah. Despite these ideals, sorcery and spirit contracts (in which individuals make deals with spirits for wealth and power) are common among Muslims in Guinea-Bissau, even among those who deem such activities "un-Islamic." Those who accumulate money, power, and fame quickly and effortlessly or at other's expense are suspected of such nefarious activities.

SOCIAL ASPECTS Muslims in Guinea-Bissau place great importance on family and expect everyone to marry and have children. As gifts from God, children are highly desired and contribute to one's social status and economic situation. From initiation onward men and women maintain relatively separate lives and roles. Men are responsible for providing financially for the family, and motherhood is a woman's most important role. Women are free to engage in economic activities outside the home and may keep their earnings. Marriages are commonly arranged, and men may marry up to four wives. Co-wife relations are often harmonious. Children belong to their father's lineage, a law that discourages women from instigating divorce. A widow is encouraged but not obligated to marry a brother of her deceased husband. Foreign development organizations have waged campaigns to change local attitudes toward arranged marriage, polygyny, family planning, and female circumcision, but Muslims have been especially resistant to these efforts.

POLITICAL IMPACT Islam has had little influence in national politics in the post-colonial era. In 1998 Ansumana Mané, a Muslim Mandinga from neighboring Gambia, led a popular rebellion against President "Nino" Vieira. Although Mané sought regime change rather than political power, practitioners of indigenous religions feared the possibility of a Muslim takeover, while Muslims (though skeptical) delighted in this possibility. Support for the rebellion did not follow religious lines, however, and was estimated at 98 percent of Guinea-Bissau's population. Nino was ousted in 1999, and his successors have been non-Muslims.

CONTROVERSIAL ISSUES Increased migration in Guinea-Bissau has raised awareness of how Islam is practiced elsewhere, and Guinean Muslims have become more concerned with their place in the *ummah*, the global community of Muslims. Some contend that traditional African practices, such as initiation rituals, are "un-Islamic" and should be ended, while others argue that such rites confer Muslim identity. Adherents of the Ahmadiyya reform movement pray with their arms folded and oppose many local "African" practices, such as female circumcision and the use of amulets. Some men are now aware that female circumcision is not an official Muslim practice and are open to change, but women explicitly link the practice to Muslim identity and are reluctant to end it.

Although the Ahmadiyya reform movement is gaining support by building schools and mosques throughout the country, they face significant opposition by local elders, who fear their power and influence.

CULTURAL IMPACT Islam brought a profound appreciation for writing to Guinea-Bissau. Koranic students and holy men dedicate much of their lives to learning to write Koranic verses from memory in classical Arabic. Written with ink onto wooden tablets, these texts are thought to be both beautiful and powerful.

Masquerades associated with initiation rituals are still prevalent despite the fact that many deem them "un-Islamic." Drumming still occurs in some Muslim ritual contexts, but this traditional African holdover is often debated and may be accompanied or replaced altogether by Muslim chants.

Guinean Muslims sometimes paint the mud-brick walls of their traditional African-style houses white with a blue stripe as is common in parts of the Middle East, and they decorate the interiors of their houses with wall hangings from Mecca, prayer beads, and protective amulets encasing Koranic verses.

Other Religions

Christianity came to Guinea-Bissau in the 1500s with Portuguese traders and explorers, but the religion did not have a significant impact until the 1900s, when the Franciscans started the first schools. Christianity is most common among the Kriolu population—the urban elite, who maintained close ties with the Portuguese during the colonial period. Protestant churches are steadily gaining in popularity, but most Guinean Christians are Roman Catholics. Pope John Paul II visited Bissau in January 1990, saying Mass for thousands of Catholics and speaking on social justice. While Catholics in Guinea-Bissau persist in many indigenous beliefs and practices, Protestants are more inclined to view indigenous religions as conflicting with Christianity.

Carnival, which developed out of pre-Lenten parades in the 1950s, is Guinea-Bissau's most distinctive "Christian" celebration. Despite its Catholic roots, Carnival has an African flavor, and Guinean traditionalists celebrate it as enthusiastically as Christians. Children create giant masks out of paper, clay, a paste made from the baobab fruit, and paint. Common mask themes are cow heads (resembling the Pepel initiation masquerade figure) and "devils" (representing *iran* spirits). Masks may also be political in nature, representing colonial or contemporary political leaders. Carnival in Bissau is a hybrid blend of indigenous, Portuguese, and even Brazilian elements, with some people parading the streets in traditional ethnic clothing and others dressed as popular cult figures, such as Michael Jackson. The three-to five-day celebration culminates in an official carnival procession; all neighborhoods participate, and prizes are awarded to the best masks.

Michelle C. Johnson

See Also Vol. 1: *African Indigenous Beliefs, Islam*

Bibliography

Brooks, George. "Historical Perspectives on the Guinea-Bissau Region, Fifteenth to Nineteenth Centuries." In *Mansas, Escravos, Grumetes e Gentio: Cacheu na Encruzilhada de Civilizações.* Edited by Carlos Lopes. Bissau: Instituto Nacional de Estudos e Pesquisa, 1993.

Crowley, Eve Lakshmi. "Contracts with the Spirits: Religion, Asylum, and Ethnic Identity in the Cacheu Region of Guinea-Bissau." Ph.D. diss., Department of Anthropology, Yale University, 1990.

Forrest, Joshua. *Guinea-Bissau: Power, Conflict, and Renewal in a West African Nation.* Boulder, Colo.: Westview Press, 1992.

Gable, Eric. "Women, Ancestors, and Alterity among the Manjaco of Guinea-Bissau." *Journal of Religion in Africa* 26, no. 2 (1996): 104–21.

Johnson, Michelle C. "Being Mandinga, Being Muslim: Transnational Debates on Personhood and Religious Identity in Guinea-Bissau and Portugal." Ph.D. diss., Department of Anthropology, University of Illinois at Urbana-Champaign, 2002.

Scantamburlo, Luigi. *Etnologia dos Bijagos da Ilha de Bubaque.* Bissau: Instituto Nacional de Estudos e Pesquisa, 1991.

Guyana

POPULATION 698,209

HINDU 35.0 percent

ANGLICAN 13.8 percent

ROMAN CATHOLIC 10.0 percent

ISLAM 8.0 percent

PENTECOSTAL 7.5 percent

SEVENTH-DAY ADVENTIST 4.5 percent

METHODIST 2.6 percent

OTHER CHRISTIAN 4.5 percent

NOT STATED/OTHER 11.0 percent

NONE 3.1 percent

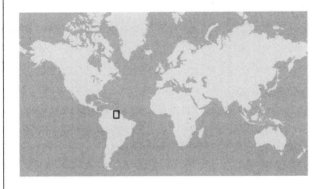

Country Overview

INTRODUCTION The Co-operative Republic of Guyana, located in northern South America, is bordered by Venezuela to the west, Brazil to the west and south, and Surinam to the east. Most residents live in the coastal region facing the Atlantic Ocean.

Guyana was occupied by Amerindians before the Dutch established the first durable settlements in about 1580. The Dutch and then the British imported Africans to work on the sugar estates from 1603 until slavery was abolished 1838. The freed Africans were reluctant to work on the sugar estates. Thus, the planters imported indentured laborers from Africa, China, India, and the Portuguese island of Madeira.

This importation of laborers transformed Guyana into a racially and culturally diverse society, resulting in a variety of religious practices. The arrival of the Portuguese (from Madeira) led to the establishment of Roman Catholicism in Guyana. Some of the Chinese were Christians upon arriving in Guyana, and others became Christians, primarily Protestants, once there. Africans and Indians (South Asians) brought Comfa, Hinduism, and Islam to Guyana; many of their descendants have continued these religious practices, though others have converted to Christianity. Anglicanism was the religion of the British, who oversaw a colony in Guyana from 1831 to 1966.

The People's Temple, an American church headed by the Reverend Jim Jones, established an agricultural community (Jonestown) in Guyana's jungles in the 1970s. In November 1978 an American congressman visited the community to investigate claims it was operating like a concentration camp. Jones, after ordering the congressman killed, led to a mass suicide of the community; 914 people, including 276 children, died.

RELIGIOUS TOLERANCE Until Guyana gained independence from Britain in 1966, African religions and culture were maligned and suppressed. Hinduism and Islam, arriving from India, were also seen as inferior and idolatrous, but evangelism by Christian missionaries gained little success among the Indian population. Guyana's 1966 constitution guarenteed freedom of worship to all religions.

Major Religions

HINDUISM

PROTESTANTISM

HINDUISM

DATE OF ORIGIN 1838 C.E.
NUMBER OF FOLLOWERS 244,400

HISTORY Of the various subgroups of Hinduism, it was the Sieunaraini panth, a Vaishnavite sect, that took root in Guyana and the Caribbean. This panth was widely held by the majority Chamars and other lower-caste groups in the area. It did not require the leadership of high-caste men or professional priests to function.

Not all Indian Hindus who went to Guyana were Sieunarainis. Toward the end of the nineteenth century, temples dedicated to the worship of Rama and Krishna began to appear, and Arya Samajist missionaries visited. The Arya Samaj, a reform movement within Hinduism (founded in India in 1875), was anti-Christian in bias and strongly opposed to Western culture. The Tamils from Madras introduced into Guyana the unorthodox Tantric branch of Hinduism known as Kali Mai.

The Guyana Sanatan Dharma Sabha (Eternal Religion Society), formed in Guyana in 1927, was influential in moving Guyana back toward a more orthodox Hinduism. As a result, the caste system, which had broken down in Guyana, began to be reconstituted. Orthodox Hindus in Guyana saw themselves as belonging to the two highest castes, the Brahmans and the Kshatriyas. With respect to the rest of society, Indians became the "white" race (Brahmans), and the others, predominantly those of African descent, became the "black" race (the outcastes).

LEADERS In the 1940s a Kali pandit (priest), Kistima Rajgopal, struggled to eliminate all forms of discrimina-

A Catholic nun supervises the education of her Guyanese students. Ten percent of Guyana's population adhere to the Roman Catholic faith. © GIRAUD PHILIPPE/CORBIS SYGMA.

tion in Hindu practice. As a result, Kali pandits of different races, castes, and genders emerged.

Pandit Reepu Daman Persaud has been an influential member of the Guyana Sanatan Dharma Sabha. He was appointed the minister of agriculture in 1992 and became the minister of parliamentary affairs in 2001.

MAJOR THEOLOGIANS AND AUTHORS There are no major Hindu theologians or authors in Guyana.

HOUSES OF WORSHIP AND HOLY PLACES Places of worship can be in the home, where altars are set up; in temples; or at any waterside, such as the sea, a river, or a canal. The god worshiped in the home relates to the planet under which a person was born. Found in Guyanese temples are symbols of the gods Hanuman, Durga, Shiva, Ganesh, Lakshmi, and Surujnaraine.

WHAT IS SACRED Although cows are sacred in Hinduism, they are slaughtered and eaten by Hindus in Guyana. Cow manure is lit in rituals, and adherents of the Kali Mai sect bathe in milk. Water, representative of the Hindu goddess Ganga Mai, is also sacred, and practitioners go to the sea for a spiritual bath to wash away their sins.

HOLIDAYS/FESTIVALS Two Hindu festivals, Phagwah and Diwali, became public holidays in 1964. Phagwah, lasting for seven days, celebrates the burning of the demon Holika, symbolizing the triumph of good over evil. The first day, the public holiday, is the most visible; devotees gather to throw colored powder or colored water on each other. The festival of Diwali, lasting five days, also celebrates the triumph of good over evil. In Diwali darkness represents evil, and light is used to welcome the goddess Lakshmi. Homes and businesses are lit with electric lights and oil lamps known as *diyas.*

MODE OF DRESS Hindus in Guyana normally wear Western-style clothing. Some Hindu men and women wear traditional Indian clothing (saris and dhotis, respectively) to *mandir*s (temples) and to Hindu events, such as weddings, funerals, and social gatherings.

DIETARY PRACTICES The diet of Guyanese Hindus is not based on religious prescription. Although some Hindus are vegetarians, most in Guyana eat various types of meat. Others adopt a vegetarian diet for nine days prior to a *puja* (a religious offering to a god).

RITUALS A religious offering to a god, or *puja*, may be held at conception. On the birth of the child, the parents go to a pandit, who selects a name. Sometimes the baby's head is shaved at the ninth month. The hair is placed in a dough made of flour and water and taken to the sea.

Hindu marriages take place on Sundays, though the ritual process begins on Friday with the planting of the bamboo (the center pole of the wedding tent). During the ceremony the couple walks around the bamboo and repeats the seven vows for living well with each other and their in-laws. After the Hindu ceremony the couple changes from Hindu to Western bridal wear, which they wear while cutting the wedding cake.

At death some Hindus are buried in a cemetery. Others are cremated, and the ashes are scattered in the sea.

RITES OF PASSAGE There are no distinctive Hindu rites of passage in Guyana. The family, however, may hold a yearly *puja* (a religious offering to a god) to Rama or Krishna to thank them for blessings for the past year.

MEMBERSHIP Hindus in Guyana do not proselytize. Hindus are usually born into the religion, though people who want to become Hindu may do so. In the Kali Mai sect, Guyanese of African descent can participate and become priests.

SOCIAL JUSTICE Because in Hinduism a person's position is determined by actions in a previous life, there are few teachings or activities concerning poverty and human rights. In 2002 a private school was opened with the purpose of creating an East Indian collective political identity built around the notion of East Indian–Hindu racial, cultural, and religious superiority. The school was intended to play a role in reinvigorating the East Indian Hindu mind-set by reinstilling a pride and appreciation in the people.

SOCIAL ASPECTS Among Hindus marriage is seen as a sacred duty, and it is embarrassing to a family if a child does not marry. Because arranged marriages have become less common and because of increased access to education, some Hindus are not getting married as young as in times past. Some Hindu children have been disinherited for marrying a member of another caste or ethnic group, especially if the person is African.

POLITICAL IMPACT In Guyana the reorganization of the Hindu caste system into two groups—Indians (the "white" race) and others, especially Africans (the "black" race)—has since the 1960s led to racial conflict and riots between Africans and Indians. The country thus tends to divide itself politically along ethnic lines, with Africans voting for the African-dominated People's National Congress and Indians voting for the Indian-dominated People's Progressive Party. Religion has been the basis in attempts to create a racial rather than a class-based society.

CONTROVERSIAL ISSUES In Guyana, Hinduism takes no stance on issues such as birth control, divorce, and abortion. A role of women is to clean and prepare the temple, or *mandir,* and to cook for special occasions. They can also give lectures if they have the knowledge.

CULTURAL IMPACT Hinduism is represented in Guyana in the architecture of the *mandirs,* in sculptures and paintings in the *mandirs,* and in music and dance. Hindus can learn the language, music, religious songs, and dances of India and learn to play Indian musical instruments at Georgetown's Indian Cultural Center. The culture is continued in the popular songs from India, which are heard on the radio, and in films, which can be seen at cinemas or on Guyanese television.

PROTESTANTISM

DATE OF ORIGIN 1616 C.E.

NUMBER OF FOLLOWERS 229,710

HISTORY Protestantism of the Calvinistic tradition began in Guyana with the Dutch in 1616. The Dutch Reformed Church's demise began when the colonies were passed to the British in 1803; the church went out of existence in 1860. The Moravians sent missionaries to the county of Berbice in 1738. They were the first to teach the Christian precepts to African slaves and Amerindians. Intending to convert and educate the slaves, the Congregationalists, sponsored by the London Missionary Society, established missionaries not far from Georgetown in 1808–09. The Scots went to Guyana following the British conquest of the colonies, leading to the formation of the Scots Presbyterian Church in 1816. A visit to Guyana in 1880 by John Morton of the Canadian Presbyterian Church convinced him that missionary work should be done among the East Indians. The Methodists first arrived in 1805 but were not allowed to minister to the people until 1821. Anglicanism was taken to Guyana by the early English settlers who went in 1843 in response to a call from the Dutch governor. The foundations of the Anglican Church in Guyana were laid from 1781 to 1814, with the diocese established in 1842. The Pentecostal churches became noticeable in the late 1950s. At first regarded with derision, church leaders came to be respected in their communities for their opinions and decision-making skills. The largest Pentecostal churches in Guyana are the Assemblies of God and the Full Gospel Assembly.

LEADERS Reverend John Smith, a missionary who served in the Congregational Church, was jailed for not divulging information relating to the 1823 slave revolt. He died in jail of tuberculosis before a reprieve arrived. Bishop Alan John Knight was the Anglican bishop of

Guyana from 1937 to 1979 and archbishop for the West Indies from 1950 to 1979. During his tenure the Anglican Church is said to have moved from being an English church to a West Indian one in that he created a West Indian bench of bishops (the organization of bishops for legal purposes) and the number of West Indian priests increased throughout the region. In 1980 the Right Reverend Randolph George became the first Guyanese and locally elected bishop.

MAJOR THEOLOGIANS AND AUTHORS There are no major Protestant theologians or authors in Guyana.

HOUSES OF WORSHIP AND HOLY PLACES There are no holy places in Guyana. Churches are the houses of worship. Pentecostal services were initially conducted in bottom houses. (Many homes in Guyana are built on stilts; the bottom house is the open area between the stilts.) This progressed to where individuals rented small houses in which they held weekly services. A Pentecostal church is now a distinct concrete building, with the main churches being air-conditioned with built-in baptism pools.

WHAT IS SACRED The Bible is the sacred book for Protestants in Guyana.

HOLIDAYS/FESTIVALS The major Christian holidays are Christmas and Easter. Christmas is now mainly a commercial enterprise, but it has always been an occasion for Guyanese family members and friends to get together and for cleaning and refurnishing the home. Easter Monday is a public holiday in Guyana and is an occasion for kite flying.

MODE OF DRESS The vestments worn by priests in the mainstream Protestant churches are in keeping with those in Western societies. Pentecostal priests wear suits. Formal Western-style attire is normally worn by those attending church services.

DIETARY PRACTICES The diet is based on Guyanese cultural practices and not on religious prescription. Until recently it was imperative that Christians only eat fish on Good Friday.

RITUALS Weddings are conducted according to standard Protestant precepts. At the home of the bride in families of African descent, there may be an African-derived ritual known as Kwe-Kwe the night before the wedding. In addition to its entertainment value, the ritual serves to emphasize new relationships created by the union, provide instructional and psychological preparation to the couple for married life, and resolve social conflicts in the community.

Protestants in Guyana are buried at death. Cremation is rare. The night before burial family and friends gather for a wake at the deceased's home.

RITES OF PASSAGE In the mainstream churches children about three months old are baptized. Confirmation takes place at about age 12. In the Pentecostal churches children are "offered up" (the pastor prays over the child) when they are about one to two months old. There is no confirmation, but from the age of seven children may decide if they want to be baptized in the church.

MEMBERSHIP Membership in Protestant churches is open to all ethnic groups in Guyana. The mainstream churches do not actively seek growth, but the Pentecostals do by visiting homes in their neighborhoods on Saturdays. Their membership has been steadily increasing over the years, drawing from the mainstream churches.

SOCIAL JUSTICE In the mainstream churches, beginning with the Anglicans in the 1820s, wherever a mission began, a school was started. A 1976 education act issued by the government ended the dual control of schools, and the government assumed mandatory management and control of buildings and their sites. Since 1992 private schools began again but mostly by individuals rather than the churches. Anglican and Catholic bishops were vocal and militant during the authoritarian rule of the African-dominated People's National Congress from 1968 to 1992 and were central in the formation of the Guyana Human Rights Association to fight for the return of free and fair elections in Guyana.

SOCIAL ASPECTS Although churches place a value on commitment, there is no emphasis as such on marriage and family. An exception to this is found within the Anglican Church. The Mother's Union, an international Anglican organization of mothers, focuses on upholding marriage and living according to Christian principles.

POLITICAL IMPACT The mainstream churches in Guyana were silent on the issue of freedom of slaves, perhaps because the churches were subsidized by state funds and membership was made up primarily by the planter class. Through religious instruction and education, the mainstream churches played an important role in producing ideological acceptance of the status quo among the nonwhite population during the colonial era. The church establishment has been conspicuously silent regarding the oppression currently taking place, perhaps because some members of the establishment are employed by the government.

CONTROVERSIAL ISSUES There is no apparent official stance on birth control, divorce, or abortion. Unlike some other Caribbean countries, the Anglican Church still refuses to allow women to become priests.

CULTURAL IMPACT The cultural impact of the churches is essentially in architecture. Older mainstream churches are wooden and in keeping with the colonial architecture of Guyana. Some of the newer Pentecostal churches tend to be made of concrete, which reduces the cost of maintenance. The Anglican Saint George's Cathedral was, until recently, the tallest wooden building in the world.

Other Religions

Roman Catholicism had its origins in the fifteenth century with the arrival and settlement of Europeans, but it was the arrival of Portuguese (from Madeira) as indentured laborers between 1834 and 1885 that led to the establishment of the church. A vicariate was set up in 1837 and a diocese in 1956. Benedict Singh, the first Guyanese bishop, was ordained in 1972. He retired in 2003 and was replaced by Francis Dean Alleyne from Trinidad.

The arrival of East Indians as indentured servants from 1838 led to the establishment of Islam in Guyana. Several Islamic organizations were founded for the purpose of promoting Islamic education and economic empowerment, providing recreational and sporting activities, and encouraging the development of youths in positive and productive ways. Membership in the religion is open to all ethnic groups.

A distinctive religion practiced in Guyana is Comfa, which has about 10,000 practitioners. It is an African-derived religion incorporating aspects of Christianity, Hinduism, and Islam and features of the cultures of the various ethnic groups associated with Guyana. The word *comfa* is derived from the Twi (a West African language) *o'komfo* (meaning priest, diviner, or soothsayer). Similar to African religions, Comfa is oral and eclectic, making it open to change and constantly being adapted to meet participant's needs.

The philosophical framework of Comfa is Bantu and is associated with the Central Africans who went to Guyana as indentured laborers between 1838 and 1865. The hierarchy of forces in Bantu ontology has been transformed in Guyana. At the top of the celestial realm is God. At the bottom of the scale, in the terrestrial realm, are the Amerindians, who in Guyanese society do not have political or economic power to influence other's lives. Like the Bantu religion, the complexity of Comfa, falling under the label of "obeah," derives from the manipulation of the universe in the making of various charms for embodying and directing spirits. The obeah rituals form the core of the Comfa religion.

Comfa has also borrowed from Hinduism, especially the Tantric branch of Kali Mai, which is based on the belief that there is constant interaction between the physical or material world and the spiritual world. The actions and general life patterns of peoples are believed to be governed by spirits and demons.

The Jordanite religion, unique to Guyana, began about 1882 with conversations between a Grenadian (Joseph MacLaren) and an East Indian laborer (Bhagwas Das). MacLaren went to Guyana in 1895 and proceeded to win converts to his new religion, the Church of the West Evangelical Millennium Pilgrims. Nathaniel Jordan joined the faith in 1917 and made such an impact that by the time he died (1928), people had begun to identify the movement by his name.

Some Jordanite religious beliefs relate to the Guyanese sociocultural context. Many practices resemble East Indian ones. Baptism by immersion is found in African religions as well as in the New Testament and in fundamentalist Christianity among whites.

Being religions of the economically powerless, Comfa, Jordanite, and Kali Mai lack prestige and have had no political impact on the society. They all show cultural synthesis and the undeniable support each culture gives to the other rather than viewing another as intrinsically inferior. This view counters the divisive ideology of orthodox Hinduism currently operating in Guyana.

Until the work of missionaries the Amerindians worshiped a god, but they believed—and continue to believe—in the Peaiman, a priest or magician who cures by ritual, and the Kanaima, the evil spirit. All evil is blamed on Kanaima, and the only cure is found through the Peaiman.

Kean Gibson

See Also Vol. I: *Christianity, Hinduism*

Bibliography

Arthur, Kerry. "Islam's Good Society." *Guyana Review* (November 2001): pp. 28–36.

Bisnauth, Dale. *A History of Religions in the Caribbean*. Kingston, Jamaica: Kingston Publishers Ltd., 1989.

———. *A Short History of the Guyana Presbyterian Church*. Georgetown, Guyana: Labour Advocate, 1970.

"Blessed Assurances: Dynamic New Churches Play Proactive Social Roles." *Guyana Review* (November 2002): pp. 24–29.

Duke, Blanche Emmeline. *A History of the Anglican Church in Guyana*. Georgetown, Guyana: Red Thread Women's Press, 2000.

Gibson, Kean. *Comfa Religion and Creole Language in a Caribbean Community*. Albany: State University of New York Press, 2001.

———. *The Cycle of Racial Oppression in Guyana*. Lanham, Md.: University Press of America, 2003.

Haiti

POPULATION 7,063,722

VODOUIST 80 percent

CHRISTIAN (ROMAN CATHOLIC, PROTESTANT) 93 percent

OTHER (JEWISH, SANTERIAN, RASTAFARIAN, MORMON) 7 percent

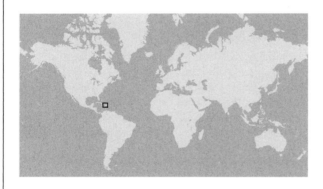

Country Overview

INTRODUCTION Haiti occupies the western third of Hispaniola, the second largest island in the Caribbean. Its original inhabitants were Taino Indians, whom the Spanish first encountered during Columbu'ss initial voyage in 1492, then enslaved, and, finally, decimated—all within a generation. After the Taino genocide the island became a Spanish colony with plantations worked by African slaves, who were first imported in about 1512. Haiti became a French colony in 1697, and a century later it became the second independent republic in the New World and the only nation in history to be

born out of a successful slave revolt (1791–1804). Although French slave law (Code Noir) required that slaves be baptized into the Roman Catholic Church, most had continued to practice some form of African ancestral religions, which by the end of the eighteenth century had coalesced into a religion called "voodoo" by terrified white colonists. By the end of the Haitian Revolution, most Catholic priests, along with most white settlers, had disappeared from the island. The Catholic Church was reinstated as the official state religion via a Vatican concordat in 1860, and soon afterwards Episcopal and then Baptist missionaries arrived from the United States. By the mid-twentieth century American Pentecostals had launched a major missionary effort that drew many Haitian converts. Despite the reestablishment of Catholicism and the introduction of other Christian missions, the overwhelming majority of Haitians retained links to Vodou while simultaneously practicing some form of Christianity. Such bi-religiosity is normative in many Black Atlantic cultures.

RELIGIOUS TOLERANCE For most of Haiti's history Vodou has been denied or persecuted by the government. From the 1920s through the 1940s, in collaboration with the Catholic Church and occupying United States armies, successive governments undertook several "anti-superstition campaigns," which sought to eradicate Vodou temples and to force practitioners to renounce the Vodou spirits. It was only with the adoption of the 1987 constitution that Vodou was recognized as a "national patrimony." In 2003 the government of President Jean-Bertrand Aristide, a former Catholic priest, recognized Vodou as a religion on par with Catholicism and that of the various Protestant sects. While

Episcopal and many Catholic bishops, priests, and churches have found ways to accommodate Vodou practices, Pentecostals and Baptists have continued to condemn these practices as Satanic.

Major Religions

VODOU

CHRISTIANITY

VODOU

DATE OF ORIGIN Sixteenth century C.E.
NUMBER OF FOLLOWERS 5.7 million

HISTORY Vodou entered history in August 1791 by means of a ceremony for the "hot" *Petwo lwa* (also *Petro loa;* divine spirits) held in Bwa Caiman (Crocodile Forest) by a *manbo* (also *mambo;* priestess) named Cecile Fatiman and an *oungan* (also *hungan;* priest) named Boukman Dutty. Inspired by this ceremony, slaves in Haiti began a revolt that became a revolution under the brilliant leadership of Toussaint L'Ouverture, a fervent Catholic who secretly served the *lwa,* as many Haitians still do. Vodouists have credited victory over Napolean's forces to Ogou, the *lwa* of war, and his consort, Ezili Danto, the spirit of hardworking peasant women. During and after the war many Haitians fled to New Orleans, where Vodou was reestablished and championed by the *manbo* Marie Laveau in the mid-nineteenth century.

Although many of Haiti's rulers practiced Vodou in secret, Catholicism was reinstated as the state religion in 1860. Thereafter Vodou was alternately ignored or suppressed, especially during the "anti-superstition" campaigns of the 1920s and 1940s. During the presidencies of François (Papa Doc; 1907–71) and Jean-Claude (Baby Doc; born in 1951) Duvalier, which together lasted from 1957 to 1986, many Vodou practitioners were co-opted by the government, though neither president formally acknowledged his links to the religion. Vodou priests who were associated with the Duvaliers suffered accordingly after Jean-Claude Duvalier was deposed in the *dechoukaj* (uprooting) of 1986. Vodou has flourished both culturally and politically under President Jean-Bertrand Aristide (1991–96; reelected 2001).

EARLY AND MODERN LEADERS Vodou is a religion of oral tradition; thus, its history has most often been

Haiti is dotted with pilgrimage sites considered sacred to the most important lwa. The waterfall in Sodo is where Ezili Danto, the spirit of hardworking peasant women, is honored every July 17. AP/WIDE WORLD PHOTOS.

transmitted through legend. The names of its greatest prophets—who reestablished their African religious practices in Haiti and melded them with parallel Taino beliefs and rituals and the rites and practices of Roman Catholicism, Freemasonry, and other systems—may never be known. A few names, however, are still remembered: Dom Petro (or Dom Pedro), possibly an African ritual specialist from the Dominican Republic, is said to have devised the "hot" Petwo rites of the religion in the eighteenth century. The passion of those rites was personified in Makandal, the leader of a band of maroons (runaway slaves), who is credited with a plot to liberate Haiti by employing Petwo medicines against slave owners in the mid-eighteenth century. Similarly motivated were the priests at Bwa Caiman, including the legendary Cecile Fatiman.

Contemporary leaders of Vodou include the *oungan* Max Beauvoir, who has drawn media attention in his efforts to revitalize the religion; Aboudja (Ronald Derenencourt), emperor of the temple at Soukri, who has expressed the religion through music; and the *manbo* Alourdes Champagne, who is celebrated in a biography by Karen McCarthy Brown titled *Mama Lola: A Vodou Priestess in Brooklyn* (1991).

MAJOR THEOLOGIANS AND AUTHORS Most theologies of Vodou have been written by nonpractitioners. Jean Price-Mars began a modern effort to reevaluate the religion as part of an African continuum in *Ainsi parla l'oncle . . .* (1928; *So Spoke the Uncle*, 1983). Milo Rigaud merged Vodou esoteric tradition with New Age jargon in *La Tradition Voudoo et le Voudoo haïtien* (1953; *Secrets of Voodoo*, 1969). Foreign observers have also been important interpreters of Vodou, especially the anthropologist Alfred Métraux (*Vaudou haïtien*, 1958; *Voodoo in Haiti*, 1959) and the dance ethnographer and filmmaker Maya Deren, whose personal and passionate *Divine Horsemen* (1953) is probably the most influential book on Vodou written in English. The most incisive contemporary interpreter of the religion may be Laënnec Hurbon, the author of many works that focus on the nexus of Vodou, culture, and politics in modern Haiti.

HOUSES OF WORSHIP AND HOLY PLACES Ceremonies for the *lwa* are carried out in temples called *ounfo*, which are found in every corner of the island and throughout the Haitian diaspora. A *ounfo* is divided into a public area (*peristil*) for dancing, singing, and sacrificing to the *lwa*, and private altar areas (*djevo*) dedicated to the various pantheons of the religion. Haiti is also dotted with pilgrimage sites considered sacred to the most important *lwa*. The most popular of these sites are Sodo, a waterfall north of Port-au-Prince where Ezili Danto is honored every 17 July, and a village called Plaine du Nord, where pilgrims gather each 25 July to immerse themselves in mud holes marking the terrestrial emergence points for Ogou, the *lwa* of war.

WHAT IS SACRED? Dividing lines between the sacred and the profane are extremely permeable in Haiti. Whatever pleases the *lwa* may be sacred. This may include liquors, cigarettes, perfume, costumes, or jewelry. Dolls may sometimes be used to embody the *lwa*, but the so-called voodoo doll stuck with pins is largely a fantasy concocted by Hollywood and promoted by tourist shops in New Orleans. Diverse propitiatory objects are gathered on altars arranged for the *lwa* in the *ounfo* or in the privacy of bedroom shrines. Other sacred meeting spaces in Haiti include cemeteries, large trees, watersides, or crossroads, where spirits of the dead and the *lwa* may be encountered. Sacrifices to these spirits may include fruit or animals—usually chickens but sometimes goats or bulls, which are ritually slaughtered and then shared between spirits and humans.

HOLIDAYS AND FESTIVALS The Vodou festival calendar is synchronized with the great feasts of the Roman Catholic Church, just as each of the major *lwa* has a counterpart among the Roman Catholic saints. For instance, ceremonies for Ogou, the general of the Vodou pantheon, are celebrated on 25 July, the feast of St. James Major, Ogou's Catholic counterpart. Sometimes this synchronization is imperfect. During Lent Vodou altars are covered with cloth, and no ceremonies are conducted in the *ounfo*, but this is also the time for Rara, when raucous bands of revelers march through the streets during the 40 days preceding Easter Sunday. All Saint's Day and All Soul's Day (1 and 2 November) are dedicated to Gede, the trickster divinity of death and sexuality. These celebrations are national holidays and involve parading and much public tomfoolery. Christmas is associated with Saint Nicholas, who is revered as the father of the *marasa*, the sacred twins who, together with the *lwa* and the dead, constitute the sacred trinity of Vodou.

MODE OF DRESS *Ounsi* (also *hunsi; members of the* Vodou temple society) generally dress in white for ceremonies and dance around a center pole (*poto mitan*) in the *peristil* as they await the arrival of the *lwa*. Each *lwa* has his or her own ritual costume, which is kept in the private altar rooms of the temple. When the *lwa* "mount" the bodies of their worshipers in trance possession, the "horse," or possessed person, is dressed in appropriate sacred attire—a sword and military insignia for Ogou, a red dress and head tie for Ezili Danto, or a black top hat and sunglasses for Gede. During Rara, marching societies are often attired in elaborate quasimartial, sequined outfits. On pilgrimage penitents sometimes wear multicolored strips of cloth called *rad penitens* (cloth of penance).

DIETARY PRACTICES In a hungry nation like Haiti, food preferences are a luxury reserved for the gods—who do have strong tastes. Ezili Danto, for instance, likes pork and raw rum, while her pleasure-loving sister Freda prefers orangeade and white hen. Danbala, the snake deity, eats raw egg, and the trickster, Gede, likes hot red peppers and cassava cakes. These foods are offered to the *lwa* and then shared by the *ounsi*. Similarly, certain animals are ordained for sacrifice to certain divinities: Ogou likes the bull; Gede, the black goat; and Ezili Danto, the black pig. Food for the gods does not come cheap.

RITUALS The most important Vodou ceremony is the *manje lwa*, the feeding of the gods. The ceremony is a kind of divine dinner party to which a particular *lwa* is invited by singing his or her favorite songs, drumming his or her beats, dancing his or her steps, or drawing his or her *veve*, a mystical design traced on the floor of the temple with cornmeal, charcoal, or coffee grounds. At these ceremonies the favored *lwa*, along with other divinities, may arrive via spirit possession. Sacrifices are made, and the meat of the sacrifice is then enjoyed by the *ounsi* in a communal feast. To participate in the *manje lwa*, one must be initiated, and ascendance to participation in higher rituals requires further initiations—all the way to the taking of the *ason*, the beaded calabash rattle, which is the most sacred implement of the *oungan* and *manbo*. *Ounsi* may marry their patron *lwa* in a special ceremony that parallels a secular wedding. When someone is dying, a priest may be called in to withdraw the soul from the body and to conduct it to its underwater home, where it will remain for a year and a day before being called back in a special ceremony (*retirer d'en bas de l'eau*) and ensconced in a *govi*, or sacred jar. The *govi* is then placed on the Vodou altar, and its contents are revered as a recovered ancestral essence.

RITES OF PASSAGE The most important Vodou rites of passage are contained in the ascending degrees of initiation into the mysteries of the priesthood, from *ounsi* to *oungan* or *manbo*. During these initiations songs and dance steps are learned, *veve* are transcribed into notebooks, the initiate's head is dressed to bear the burden of spirit possession, and one endures various tests, such as the *bruler zin*, in which the initiate shows newly acquired strengths by thrusting a hand into a metal pot full of boiling porridge.

From baptism to marriage to funeral, every Vodou rite of passage may be reinforced by performing parallel rites in the Catholic Church. At the end of life burial in a Catholic cemetery may be attended by a Vodou priest, who safeguards the transition of the deceased's soul from those *malfacteurs* (evildoers) who might wish to transform it into a *zonbi* (zombie). *Zonbi* are captured souls who are forced to work for their *malfacteurs* until freed by their deaths or some other intervention.

MEMBERSHIP Like most other religions of the African diaspora, Vodou does not proselytize. Membership is a familial privilege: A person's *lwa* is inherited from his or her parent. Initiation is often preceded by some physical or mental affliction that is interpreted as a call from the *lwa* for formal participation in the rites of the religion. There are a few initiates who are not Haitian and who have apprenticed themselves to some charismatic *oungan* or *manbo*. It is understood that initiates have already been baptized into the Catholic Church. An affiliation with Protestantism is considered antithetical to serving the *lwa*.

SOCIAL JUSTICE The morality of Vodou is expressed through a practitioner's fulfilling obligations to his or her Mèt Tèt (master of the head), or guardian *lwa*. The moral pillar of a temple is its priest: The *oungan* or *manbo* is expected to ensure justice among society members and to do what is necessary to ensure that the society is run for the mutual benefit of its members.

SOCIAL ASPECTS Vodou has no decalogue. It does not prescribe marital arrangements. Few Vodouists can afford church weddings, and common-law arrangements are normative. Perhaps because of Haiti's extreme poverty, children's lives are considered especially sacred, and feeding their spiritual guardians (*manje marasa*) is considered a profound act of piety.

POLITICAL IMPACT Although it has been often denied or suppressed, Vodou always has been the critical factor in Haitian politics. From the revolution to the presidency of Jean-Bertrand Aristide, political leaders have used this popular religion but have given little back to it in return.

CONTROVERSIAL ISSUES Because each Vodou temple is independent of any central authority, there is no forum for organized debate on issues affecting the development of the religion. Within the last generation, however, such Haitian intellectuals as Max Beauvoir and

Ronald Derenencourt (also known as Aboudja), who are also Vodou priests, have sought to "Africanize" the religion by stripping it of such syncretic elements as lithographs of Catholic saints, but these continue to be popular in most Vodou altars and temples.

CULTURAL IMPACT It has always been impossible to imagine Haiti without Vodou, but the field of Vodou's cultural impact is in fact much wider. In musical forms, such as jazz, blues, and rock and roll; popular sequined arts and "naive" painting; dances like the Charleston, swing, jitterbug, and meringue; and spiritual philosophies, Vodou has made incomparable contributions to world culture. Much of the brilliance of this religious-cultural tradition was captured in the exhibition *Sacred Arts of Haitian Vodou*, which toured the United States from 1995 to 1999, and in the accompanying catalog of the same title.

CHRISTIANITY

DATE OF ORIGIN Early sixteenth century C.E.
NUMBER OF FOLLOWERS 6.6 million

HISTORY Christianity has gone through three epochs in Haiti. From 1697 to 1804 it was represented by a French clergy who mostly served the white settler population. Jesuit missionaries, who made an effort to catechize African slaves, were expelled for their efforts in 1763. All foreign clergy were driven out from newly independent Haiti by 1804, and they did not come back until a concordat was signed with the Vatican in 1860, ending what Haitians term the "great schism" from Rome. During this second epoch, American Protestant missionaries also entered Haiti and made ready converts, despite the official status of Catholicism. The present epoch began during the rule of François Duvalier, who Haitianized the Catholic hierarchy. The most important contemporary trends include the rapid spread of Pentecostalism among the urban poor and the growth of the Liberationist "Little Church" (Ti Legliz) movement among socially active Catholic priests.

EARLY AND MODERN LEADERS Christianity as practiced in Haiti has its roots and draws its leadership from elsewhere. For Catholics that leadership is in Rome, and indeed the words of certain popes, including John Paul II, have carried great religious and political weight in Haiti. Following the *dechoukaj* (uprooting) of 1986,

Archbishop François Gayot of Cap-Haïtien (consecrated 1974; retired 2003) was widely considered to be "the pope's man" in Haiti. The Liberationists in Haiti have been inspired by similar movements in other Latin American countries. Their contemporary champion has been Bishop Willy Romélus (consecrated 1979) of Jeremie. The Protestant and Pentecostalist churches in Haiti represent, for the most part, branches of American missionary movements.

MAJOR THEOLOGIANS AND AUTHORS As with church leadership so too is Christian theology a foreign import, aside from such grotesque aberrations as François Duvalier's editing the Paternoster to read "Our Papa Doc Who Art in Port-au-Prince . . . ." The Haitianization of Christian liturgy to include Kreyol (Haitian Creole) song, music, and dance was undertaken seriously only within the last generation, mostly under the influence of Liberationist priests. Jean-Bertrand Aristide, the most famous of these priests, published a book of his sermons and opinions, *In the Parish of the Poor* (1990). Episodes in Aristide's religious and political life have already entered into popular hagiography.

HOUSES OF WORSHIP AND HOLY PLACES Interesting Catholic churches remain from the colonial period, including a Gothic imitation of Mont-Saint-Michel at Miragoane. The most important survivor of the colonial period had been the old wooden cathedral in Port-au-Prince, which was being restored by UNESCO when it burned down during a 1991 political riot. The most artistically important church in Haiti is the Episcopal Cathedral of Sainte Trinité in Port-au-Prince, whose vault is covered with biblical paintings in a Vodou style that were commissioned from the leading painters of the Haitian Renaissance (1945–60). Pentecostal churches often operate in storefronts or revival tents.

WHAT IS SACRED? Reflecting their French origins, and perhaps the desires of Catholicism's Vodouist constituency, Catholic expressions of the sacred are deeply material, with statues and other representations of the saints and Jesus, rosaries, crucifixes, and related sacramental objects employed in most public and private rituals. Episcopalians share in this sort of material Christianity, while Baptists and, especially, Pentecostals are fervently iconoclastic. "Down with statues of the Saints" is a favorite graffito that is often spray-painted in Kreyol on Catholic church walls.

HOLIDAYS AND FESTIVALS Christmas, Easter, All Saint's Day, All Soul's Day, Carnival, and Ash Wednesday are public holidays in Haiti, as is the feast for Our Lady of Perpetual Help (27 June), the patroness of Haiti. The great saint's days are also occasions for important Vodou ceremonies, especially the feasts for Saint Joseph the Worker (1 May), Saint John the Baptist (24 June), Our Lady of Mount Carmel (17 July), and Saint James Major (25 July). Perhaps no Christian holiday is as raucously celebrated as All Soul's Day (2 November), which is also the feast for Gede, the Vodou divinity of sex, death, and laughter.

MODE OF DRESS Pentecostals and other Protestants in Haiti favor the formality of American-style church wear, while clothing worn at Catholic Masses mirrors the bourgeois class rankings of the congregation. Catholic priests favor the white soutanes of the French clergy or the jeans and sandals of the hip Liberationists.

DIETARY PRACTICES There are no prescribed dietary restrictions for Haitian Christians, though Pentecostals abjure alcohol.

RITUALS Most Catholic rituals in Haiti—including the processions for important saint's days and the Way of the Cross pageants that take place on Good Friday—have been borrowed from French Catholicism. In most areas of Catholic observance, these rituals have been syncretized with Vodou ceremonies. Perhaps the most important ritual among Pentecostals is "getting the Holy Ghost," which is analogous to spirit possession among Vodouists.

RITES OF PASSAGE For the majority of Haitian Catholics, birth is marked by baptism and death by a requiem Mass in a church. The observance of first communion and confirmation is rarer, though if a family can afford to celebrate these sacraments, they do so with feasting, and they have the events videotaped. Because of the expenses involved, church weddings are usually reserved for members of the middle classes. Sacraments such as baptism and the Eucharist are also incorporated into Vodou initiation rites.

MEMBERSHIP While participation in various Catholic services and feasts is commonplace at all levels of society, church membership is more often a class entitlement. Catholic rites serve to sanctify secular social and national transactions while providing a major sacramental resource for Vodou. Affiliation with Protestantism is associated with individualism, literacy, a lifestyle of white shirts and ties, and, most important, abjuration of the *lwa*. While one must be a Catholic to practice Vodou, Protestants may never serve the *lwa*.

SOCIAL JUSTICE Christianity has been little concerned with social justice in Haiti. During colonial times the Jesuits championed slave's participation in the church, which led to their being thrown out of the country. Since the reinstallation of the Catholic Church, the Catholic hierarchy has been socially conservative and politically aligned with the various oligarchies. Protestants and Pentecostals preach individual salvation but have not been associated with political movements for social change. In the wake of the Haitianization of the Catholic clergy under Duvalier, an increasing number of young priests became engaged in the Liberationist movement, most prominently Jean-Bertrand Aristide, whose fiery sermons on social justice led to his election as president of Haiti in 1990. Under intense pressure from the Vatican, Aristide resigned his priesthood shortly thereafter.

SOCIAL ASPECTS Christianity has had little impact on social arrangements in Haiti. Weddings are more a matter of financial, rather than religious, concern. Few outside the small elite class can afford church weddings, and common-law marriages are the most common. While men may support several common-law wives, households are not polygamous. Each wife maintains her own home, and the husband provides what he can toward the maintenance of the ménage.

POLITICAL IMPACT Until the regime of François Duvalier, the Catholic Church exercised considerable influence in Haitian politics. Duvalier outmaneuvered Rome, gained the right to name bishops, and curbed the number of foreign clergy. Jean-Claude Duvalier carried on his father's policies but was badly shaken by the 1983 visit of Pope John Paul II, who criticized the regime in both French ("Il faut que quelque chose change ici" ["Something must change around here"]) and Kreyol ("Min mouen, kote nou?" ["Here I am; now where are we?"]). Through their popular radio stations, Soleil (Catholic) and Lumière (Protestant), the churches were actively engaged in the overthrow of the Duvalier regime in 1986. Both were also active in the anti-Vodou pogroms that followed, especially via the incitements of Radio Lumière.

CONTROVERSIAL ISSUES For Christians the most controversial issues involve ways of addressing the fact that Haiti is the poorest country in the hemisphere. Should the various churches engage in social justice issues, even at the cost of jeopardizing existing social and political structures? The question is more divisive for Catholics than for Protestants, who have traditionally been quiescent in the political arena. Questions concerning the Christian-Vodou relationship also persist, with some opening toward Vodou on the part of younger Catholic priests. Finally, there is the Catholic-Protestant rivalry, with the situation in Haiti forming one aspect of a regional phenomenon that is neatly expressed in the question, Is Latin America going Protestant?

CULTURAL IMPACT Whatever impact Christianity has had on Haitian culture has been filtered through Vodou. The effects are expressed visually—in the appropriation of Catholic imagery to represent the Vodou *lwa,* for example, or in sculptural works like those of Georges Liautaud (1899–1992), who incorporated myriad elaborations of the Christian cross in Vodou icons. As Archbishop Gayot of Cap Haitien has noted, "We let [the Vodouists] into the church, and they stole the furniture."

Other Religions

There are small numbers of other religions present in Haiti, reflecting the cosmopolitan nature of its history and its geographic position at the center of the Caribbean. Practitioners of other black diaspora religions, such as Santeria, have opened up botanicas in Port-au-Prince. Jewish and Syrian Maronite Catholic merchants dominate the large urban retail markets. American Mormon missionaries in their standard black pants and white shirts are a common sight both in the cities and in rural areas. The long-standing middle-class tropism for New Age theologies and transcendentalism is reflected in the large Rosicrucian temple in the Delmas district of Port-au-Prince, as well as in the speculations of such Haitian religious writers as Milo Rigaud. There has also been a growing fascination with Rastafarianism, as evidenced by the popularity of reggae music, Rasta T-shirts, and the dreadlocks sported by increasing numbers of the urban young.

Donald Cosentino

See Also Vol. 1: *African Indigenous Beliefs, Christianity, Pentecostalism, Roman Catholicism*

Bibliography

Aristide, Jean-Bertrand. *In the Parish of the Poor: Writings from Haiti.* Translated and edited by Amy Wilentz. Maryknoll, N.Y.: Orbis Books, 1990.

Beauvoir-Dominique, Rachel. *L'Ancienne Cathédrale de Port-au-Prince: Perspectives d'un vestige de carrefours.* Port-au-Prince: Henri Deschamps, 1991.

Brown, Karen McCarthy. *Mama Lola: A Vodou Priestess in Brooklyn.* Berkeley and Los Angeles: University of California Press, 1991.

Cosentino, Donald, ed. *Sacred Arts of Haitian Vodou.* Los Angeles: UCLA Fowler Museum of Cultural History, 1995.

Desmangles, Leslie G. *The Faces of the Gods: Vodou and Roman Catholicism in Haiti.* Chapel Hill: University of North Carolina Press, 1992.

Ferguson, James. *Papa Doc, Baby Doc: Haiti and the Duvaliers.* Oxford and New York: B. Blackwell, 1988.

Hurbon, Laënnec. *Les Mystères du Vaudou.* Paris: Gallimard, 1993.

Rigaud, Milo. *La Tradition Voudoo et le Voudoo Haïtien: Son temple, ses mystères, sa magie.* Paris: Niclaus, 1953.

Honduras

POPULATION 6,560,608

ROMAN CATHOLIC 86 percent

PROTESTANT 11 percent

SPIRITIST 1 percent

BAHAI 0.5 percent

NONRELIGIOUS AND OTHER 1.5 percent

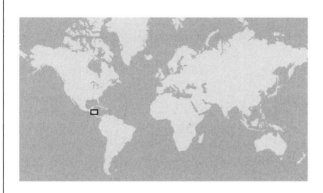

Country Overview

INTRODUCTION The Republic of Honduras is the second largest country in Central America, behind its neighbor to the southeast, Nicaragua. With access to both the Pacific Ocean to the southwest and the Atlantic Ocean through the Caribbean Sea to the north and east, it might be thought that Honduras would have emerged as a regional economic power. The rugged mountainous terrain that covers more than three quarters of the country, however, has hampered access to water and trade routes. The difficult terrain also has accentuated regional pretensions to superiority between

the capital, Tegucigalpa, in the south and the northern industrial and economic center of San Pedro Sula.

While their history has not been interrupted by war or violent revolution as often as for many of their Central American neighbors, political instability has been an ever present reality for Hondurans. Since the country gained independence from Spain in the early nineteenth century, there have been hundreds of internal coups and rebellions and more than 100 different political administrations. In addition, poverty remains high in spite of international efforts to spur the economy. Bananas, the most important crop in Hondura'ss modern economy, have not produced much local progress either. The mostly U.S.-based companies that run the banana plantations have been a boon for landowners and public officials, but the vast majority of the Honduran workforce has not benefited from this so-called green gold.

Thus, political, social, and economic hardship has been a way of life for most Hondurans, which has presented religious leaders with both opportunities and obstacles. The calls for social justice that are so indicative of much of Latin-American Christianity have not been as prevalent in Honduras, even though political instability and the lack of development have created conditions ripe for social discontent. Honduran churches have been more focused on belief and spiritual development than on religiously inspired social reform.

RELIGIOUS TOLERANCE Honduras was established in the 1820s as part of the short-lived United Provinces of Central America, and within that coalition Roman Catholicism was established as the state religion. Church and state were not legally separated until 1880. Later

A young girl readies to participate in the celebration of San Miguel Archangel—the patron saint of Tegucigalpa. Roman Catholics in numerous Honduran towns and villages hold feasts and festivals for their patron saints. © REUTERS NEWMEDIA INC./CORBIS.

constitutions guaranteed freedom of religion, and for the most part the government has respected this right. At the institutional level, however, there are many connections between church and state. Church schools receive government aid, and even public school classes begin with readings from the Bible. By law practitioners of any sort of witchcraft can be deported. Relations among religious groups are generally positive, and there is some cooperation on matters of mutual interest, such as regional development and disaster relief.

Major Religion

ROMAN CATHOLICISM

DATE OF ORIGIN 1520 C.E.
NUMBER OF FOLLOWERS 5.6 million

HISTORY Roman Catholicism arrived in what is now Honduras in the sixteenth century alongside the Spanish conquerors. Within a century it had become the dominant religion in the land, replacing the polytheistic and decentralized religions practiced by the native pre-Columbian peoples. Although Catholicism was established as the state religion in the early years of the repub-

lic, a series of conflicts later in the nineteenth century led to the stripping away of much of the church's power in the 1880s.

Two things stand out in the modern history of Catholicism in Honduras. First, the church has always been chronically understaffed. In the 1970s, for example, it was estimated that there was only one priest for every 10,000 Catholics. This long-standing problem led to the founding of the Delegates of the Word, a lay group charged with carrying out the work of the church in areas where clergy were unavailable. Although started in Honduras, the Delegates of the Word has spread throughout Central America. Second, as some members of the clergy began speaking out against social injustice, wealthy landowners reacted violently out of fear of losing their position. Most famously, in the 1975 massacre in Olancho department, local elites brutally murdered a number of peasants, priests, and students. This effectively curtailed, at least for a time, the efforts of the church in Honduras to promote social justice.

EARLY AND MODERN LEADERS One of the most notable features of Catholicism in Honduras is the absence of a key personality. This is not to say, however, that the church has been without leadership. Father José Trinidad Reyes, for instance, founded the National Autonomous University in the middle of the nineteenth century and was noted for his leadership in the arts. Bishops are under the leadership of Oscar Andrés Cardinal Rodríguez Maradiaga in the Archdiocese of Tegucigalpa. Appointed archbishop in 1993, he became the first Honduran cardinal, in 2001. A number of priests have become well known for social criticism, leading, in the case of some, to their martyrdom. These have included Father Ivan Betancur, who was murdered in the Olancho massacre of 1975, and Father James "Guadalupe" Carney, who disappeared in the early 1980s.

MAJOR THEOLOGIANS AND AUTHORS There are no theologians of international importance in Honduras. The most influential school of thought to have come out of Latin America has been the theology of liberation, identified with Gustavo Gutiérrez of Peru among others. Although much of Catholicism in Central America has been influenced by this school's emphasis on social and economic justice, the major statements of liberation theology have come from outside Honduras. Even among the population, liberation theology has not taken root in Honduras as it has in other developing countries.

HOUSES OF WORSHIP AND HOLY PLACES All dioceses in Honduras are under the Archdiocese of Tegucigalpa. Well-known churches include San Francisco, the oldest church in Tegucigalpa, which dates from about 1592. The San Miguel Cathedral, built in 1782, is also located in Tegucigalpa, as is the impressive basilica of the Virgin of Suyapa, which is Hondura'ss most important Catholic landmark.

WHAT IS SACRED? Honduran Catholicism is similar to the Catholicism of the rest of Central America. It operates on the basis of the Christian year, and apart from shrines of particular local importance, such as the basilica of the Virgin of Suyapa, there is little innovation in Honduras. There is some blending of Catholicism and native religion, much of which finds its origin in the great Mayan civilization that flourished from the third through the ninth centuries. Mayan religion was polytheistic and stressed the roles of various gods in the patterns of nature. Elaborate rituals guaranteed the favor of the gods, and through them the sun and rain that agrarian civilization depended on, and elements of these practices have been preserved in Honduran festivals.

HOLIDAYS AND FESTIVALS As with Christians elsewhere, Christmas and Easter are the major religious holidays in Honduras, with Good Friday, the day on which Christ was crucified, often receiving special commemoration. On the local level numerous towns and villages hold feasts for their patron saints, but the largest of these is the anniversary of the Virgin of Suyapa, which begins in the first week of February. Thousands of people travel to Tegucigalpa during the festival, which celebrates the finding of a small cedar statue of the virgin by a peasant farmer in the mid-eighteenth century. After a pilgrimage from El Piliguin, where the statue was reportedly found, the discovery of the virgin is reenacted and miracles attributed to her recounted. The tradition has been celebrated annually in Honduras for more than 250 years.

MODE OF DRESS Clothing in Honduras is influenced more by availability and practicality than by religion, with Western fashions predominating, especially among the upper classes. Particularly for girls, however, the clothing surrounding festivals, which often reflect Mayan or other native influences, is colorful and celebratory. Contests are occasionally held in connection with these festivals, with young girls dressing as representatives of different agricultural products or areas.

DIETARY PRACTICES The diet of Hondurans is determined primarily by economic factors and not by religious beliefs. Although agriculture is the backbone of the economy, farming conditions are not good, and most Hondurans work small plots of land they seldom own. Malnutrition is rampant, and access to potable water is limited, particularly in rural areas. Corn, beans, and rice are the staples of the Honduran diet, with meat and fish being infrequent supplements.

RITUALS Given the chronic shortage of priests in Honduras, regular religious services are not available to the entire Catholic population. In rural areas especially, formal Masses may be celebrated only infrequently. Lay leaders such as representatives of the Delegates of the Word help carry out the work of the church on a more regular schedule.

Many of the rituals familiar to Hondurans are connected to major events in the life cycle or to religious and secular holidays. As with Catholics everywhere, the baptism of infants is common and is often followed by family celebrations. Pilgrimages are common on major holidays. Each village has its own patron saint, and people often travel to nearby towns for local celebrations.

RITES OF PASSAGE For girls in their early teens the transition to womanhood is marked by a coming-out party called La Fiesta Rosa. Despite church teachings, in rural areas common-law marriages are widespread and are generally viewed as being legitimate.

MEMBERSHIP All children born to Catholic parents and baptized into the church are considered to be Catholic, which in part explains the dominance of the Catholic faith and the lack of strict adherence by much of the population. The Catholic Church made a major evangelistic push in the middle of the twentieth century as a way of shoring up support in the face of growing Protestant churches. The Delegates of the Word have contributed to this effort by serving as a bulwark against Catholic losses in those areas where the shortage of priests is most chronic. In 1998 the government approved the Solidarity Catholic Channel, a broadcast service to compete with a Protestant channel and with various cable stations.

SOCIAL JUSTICE Aggressive resistance on the part of local landowners has hampered Catholic efforts at social justice in Honduras. Events like the Olancho massacre and other persecutions have suppressed much of the vocal criticism coming from the church. Human rights violations are common in Honduras, and legal redress is largely unavailable because of inequality and official corruption. Fear of persecution has not hampered all Catholic activities for social justice, however. The church has been active in education through parochial schooling. Efforts at disaster relief, as, for instance, in the response to Hurricane Mitch in 1998, have also been noteworthy. Catholic Relief Services has programs in place to promote nutritional education, debt relief, and sustainable agriculture as a means of fighting environmental degradation. As a highly indebted poor country, Honduras was often cited in Jubilee Year 2000 pronouncements on debt relief and sustainable development.

SOCIAL ASPECTS Family ties are strong in most Central American cultures, and Honduras is no exception. Multigenerational households are common, as are other forms of extended family living. The Catholic Church has reinforced this strong sense of family life with its teachings on parental authority and on responsibility for passing on the faith. Family life in Honduras does not always live up to the ideal, however. Common-law marriages are frequent, and single motherhood is also widespread, as is domestic abuse against women. Women comprise only about one-third of the formal labor force, and in rural areas the numbers are even lower.

POLITICAL IMPACT The Catholic Church has always been a powerful social institution in Honduras, dating to its establishment as the state religion in the nineteenth century. It also has wielded great political influence. The church's role in political affairs was more powerful, however, before the social reorganization of the late nineteenth century, when it was stripped of some of its land and influence. Even though diplomatic relations between Honduras and the Vatican have been maintained and the presence of the church continues to be a force in politics, it no longer has direct influence over legislative and other government affairs.

CONTROVERSIAL ISSUES The opposition of the Catholic Church to birth control has been controversial in Honduras, as it has been in many poor countries because of the links between poverty, single motherhood, and a high birthrate. In 1994 Pope John Paul II praised the Honduran priesthood for affirming the importance

of family stability and responsible Christian parenthood as the building blocks for Honduran society, and he specifically praised their opposition to artificial means of birth control. Abortion is illegal in Honduras unless the health of the mother is threatened, and family planning groups are often critical of the church's opposition.

CULTURAL IMPACT Honduran culture is a blend of Catholicism and native religious experiences. Folk music and the dances that accompany them, for instance, betray both Spanish and Indian influences. This is not surprising since more than 90 percent of the population is mestizo, a blend of European and native Indian ancestry. Dances are a part of most celebrations, religious and secular, and are sometimes accompanied by brightly colored masks and fireworks. Many of the cultural artifacts that come from Honduras are related to the Indian civilizations that thrived in pre-Columbian times. Catholic churches in Honduras are noted for their elaborate wood carvings, though some gold and silver artifacts can also be found, mostly in the cities. Christian art in Honduras began more than 500 years ago and is exemplified through the work of artists like José Miguel Gómez.

Other Religions

Although Catholicism dominates the religious landscape of Honduras, Protestants have made impressive numerical and institutional strides. The earliest Protestant activity in Honduras dates to missionary activity in the middle of the nineteenth century, but sustained work by Protestant groups is barely a century old. In 1896 Cyrus Scofield founded the Central American Mission, inaugurating a slow but steady stream of Protestant activity in Honduras. The comparatively little international attention given to Honduras in contemporary times has perhaps led to less missionary activity than in neighboring states like Guatemala or El Salvador. Hurricane Mitch, however, along with the relief work in Honduras that followed the devastation, brought renewed efforts by numerous Protestant groups from North America.

Estimates of the number of Protestants in Honduras vary, but there are perhaps a half million or so belonging to various denominations, sects, and independent churches. There are dozens of Protestant groups working in Honduras, some with close ties to North American churches, others entirely independent. These include groups such as the Church of God, Southern Baptists, Mennonites, and Assemblies of God. There are also numerous splinter groups from the more established denominations, and no one Protestant body can claim a privileged position. Besides developing their own congregations, Protestant groups work together on various issues, including theological education. In 1998 the first ecumenical seminary in Honduras, called the Honduran Theological Community, began operation on the outskirts of Tegucigalpa. Protestants also have a strong presence on radio and television, and they have prepared for continued growth.

In much of Central America during the late twentieth century, Pentecostalism, and charismatic Christianity more generally, emerged as the dominant religious development, but this seems not to have drawn the attention of religious observers in Honduras. Many contemporary discussions of the explosion of Pentecostalism in Latin America barely mention Honduras or even omit it entirely. Nevertheless, as a renewal movement Pentecostalism has reached every corner of Honduran Christianity, influencing perhaps 1 million believers across several denominations.

Outside Christianity there has been something of a revival among Hondurans of native religions as a means of reconnecting to the culture. The influence of these traditional religions extends beyond their practitioners, who make up less than 1 percent of the population. Only small minorities, most of them Indian tribes, practice traditional religions, but some of these people

are counted among the Catholic population as well. The confusion is more than just numerical, for, as noted above, religious life in Honduras is often a blend of Catholicism and native religions, with the influence going both ways. The Garifuna, for instance, observe Catholic holidays but practice native rituals and celebrations as well, and other such native groups include the Miskito and the Lenca. Spiritists are mostly non-Christian adherents of African and Caribbean cults, although these attract some nominal Catholics. Since the 1960s the number of Bahais has grown dramatically.

Steven Jones

See Also Vol. 1: *Christianity, Pentecostalism, Roman Catholicism*

Bibliography

Acker, Alison. *Honduras: The Making of a Banana Republic.* Boston: South End Press, 1988.

Charles, Cecil. *Honduras: The Land of Great Depths.* Chicago: Rand McNally, 1890.

Martin, David. *Tongues of Fire.* Oxford: Blackwell, 1990.

Meyer, Harvey K. *Historical Dictionary of Honduras.* Metuchen, N.J.: Scarecrow Press, 1976.

Norsworthy, Kent, and Tom Barry. *Inside Honduras.* Albuquerque: Research Center Press, 1994.

Peckenham, Nancy, and Annie Street, eds. *Honduras: Portrait of a Captive Nation.* New York: Praeger, 1985.

Hungary

POPULATION 10,075,034

ROMAN CATHOLIC 51.9 percent

REFORMED 15.9 percent

LUTHERAN 3.0 percent

GREEK CATHOLIC 2.6 percent

NONRELIGIOUS 25.4 percent

OTHER 1.2 percent

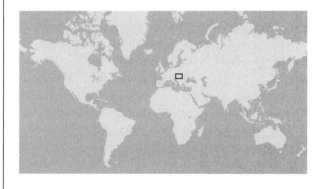

Country Overview

INTRODUCTION The Republic of Hungary is located in central Europe. It is bordered by Austria and Slovenia to the west, Slovakia to the north, Ukraine and Romania to the east, and Croatia and Serbia and Montenegro to the south.

The area was occupied by the Roman Empire at the end of the first century B.C.E. Roman soldiers imported the ancient Roman religion and the other main religions of the empire, including Christianity, the Mithras cult, and the Isis-Osiris cult. After the collapse of Roman power in the region, it was invaded by German tribes, who were expelled by the Avars in the sixth century. Christianity had disappeared almost totally by the time the Hungarian pagan tribes arrived (sometime before the tenth century). The Kingdom of Hungary was founded in 1000 when the first Hungarian Christian king, Saint Stephen, was crowned.

The independent Kingdom of Hungary collapsed during the sixteenth century in the wake of the Turkish invasion. Hungary was divided into three parts until the end of the seventeenth century. The lack of central power facilitated the spread of the Protestant Reformation. Although the western areas close to Vienna remained loyal to Catholicism, the eastern regions (Transylvania) and the southern and central part (occupied by the Turkish Empire) became Reformed. By the end of the sixteenth century the country was mostly Protestant. At the end of the seventeenth century the country became a part of the Habsburg Empire, and the country has been predominantly Catholic ever since. Catholicism in Hungary includes both Roman and Greek Catholics.

The Communist Party took power in 1948. The party-state fought against religiosity and tried to control churches. Since the mid-1980s there has been a religious revival in Hungary. The elimination of the State Church Office resulted in religious freedom, which made local parishes one of the strongest parts of civil society. Since 1989, when the Communists relinquished their monopoly on power, new religious communities have emerged, mainly in large cities. Some of them have come from the large churches, while many (such as Mormons) have arrived from the West.

RELIGIOUS TOLERANCE The movement for religious tolerance in Hungary began with the Reformation. Gradually Lutheranism, and later Calvinism and Unitarianism, joined Catholicism as official denominations. In 1568 the parliament in Torda formed a resolution on religious freedom that granted disparate communities the right to choose their own preachers.

The constitution of Hungary guarantees the right to freedom of thought, conscience, and religion as well as the separation of church and state. The law concerning religious tolerance is Act IV/1990, which not only declares the right of Hungarians to the free and undisturbed exercise of religion but also oversees the registration of churches. The latter has become a serious issue in the discussion of religious tolerance, because churches in Hungary must be registered in order to obtain tax-exempt status and access to state subsidies.

Major Religion

ROMAN CATHOLICISM

DATE OF ORIGIN Tenth century C.E.
NUMBER OF FOLLOWERS 5.5 million

HISTORY Christianity was taken by Roman soldiers into the Roman province of Pannonia (western Hungary) during the second century. When Saint Stephen founded the Hungarian kingdom in 1000, the Catholic Church's center was established in Esztergom. According to tradition Saint Stephen offered Hungary to the Blessed Virgin, and therefore Hungary used to be called *Regnum Marianum* (Mary's Kingdom). Since the reign of Saint Stephen, the king of Hungary has been called apostolic because of his particular rights in the Catholic Church, including the right to call national synods and to sit in judgment on Catholic clergy.

Catholic bishops and clergy were loyal to the Habsburgs during the several rebellions of the sixteenth through eighteenth centuries. In the nineteenth century, however, the clergy opposed the political, social, and economic reforms suggested by the aristocracy. This opposition led to the Kulturkampf, when the Protestant political elite separated the Catholic Church from the state. Until World War II, however, the Catholic Church maintained its important political and social role as well as its economic and cultural influence.

As the largest land owner and political rival, the church was attacked by the Communist Party after

The Holy Crown of Saint Stephen. Because of its political significance, the cult of the Holy Crown is widespread among both Catholics and non-Catholics in Hungary. © REUTERS NEWMEDIA INC./CORBIS.

World War II. Most church land, schools, and hospitals were confiscated between 1945 and 1949. After the Communist coup in 1948 churches were repressively controlled by the State Church Office, with close cooperation from the secret police. Communist authorities closed cloisters and monasteries, forced monks and nuns to leave the country, and imprisoned hundreds of priests, even the cardinal-primate József Mindszenty and József Grósz, the archbishop of Kalocsa. During the 1960s and 1970s Hungarians became increasingly secularized. The earlier importance of religious practices and symbols in everyday life declined because they were cleansed from the public sphere.

EARLY AND MODERN LEADERS As the foremost leader of the Counter-Reformation in Hungary, the cardinal-primate Péter Pázmány (1570–1637) persuaded the majority of the aristocracy to adopt Roman Catholicism. He was also renowned for his brilliant essays.

The most influential Catholic priest of the twentieth century was József Mindszenty, also a cardinal-primate. He was an outspoken opponent of Communism and Nazism, and in 1949 the Communist government convicted him of treason. He was imprisoned until 1956 when he was freed for a short period of time by the forces of the anticommunist revolution. As Soviet troops reasserted their authority, he fled to the U.S. legation, where he remained for 15 years as a symbol of Soviet oppression. In 1971, at the urging of the Vatican, he left Hungary for Vienna, where he died in 1975.

Another leader was Áron Márton (1896–1980), the Hungarian Catholic bishop of Alba Iulia (in Romania). By refusing to sign the concordat between the Romanian party-state and the Catholic Church (to give up fundamental rights of Catholics to the Communist state), he fought for the rights of the Hungarian minority and for freedom of consciousness and religion. Márton protested against the nationalization of denominational schools and institutions. In 1948 he published his pastoral letter opposing the union of the Greek Catholic Church with the Orthodox Church. Márton was imprisoned between 1949 and 1955, and until 1967 he was not allowed to leave his residence.

MAJOR THEOLOGIANS AND AUTHORS Although some universities were founded in Hungary before the seventeenth century, none of them survived. Thus, many Hungarian theologians, including Salamon de Hungaria (thirteenth century), Paulus de Hungaria (fifteenth century), Andreas Pannonius (fifteenth century), and Michael Pannonius (also known as Ascenius; eighteenth century), studied and lived outside the country. Nevertheless, some lived in Hungary, such as Osvát Laskai (sixteenth century); Pelbárt Temesvári (died in 1504), author of *Sermones* ("Sermons"); Karthauzi Névtelen (sixteenth century), who wrote *Erdy Codex*; Péter Pázmány (1570–1637), author of *Igazságra vezérlö kalauz* ("Guide to the Truth"); and Ferenc Faludy (1704–79), author of *Szent ember, Téli éjszakák* ("Winter Nights").

During World War II Hungarian Catholic theologians and philosophers were forced abroad by the political situation in Hungary rather than by the lack of universities. Among these intellectuals were Antal Schütz, Sándor Horváth, László (Ladislaus) Boros, Szaniszló (Stanley) Jáki, Tamás Molnár, and Balázs Mezei.

HOUSES OF WORSHIP AND HOLY PLACES Few Roman or Gothic churches in Hungary survived the Turkish invasion of the sixteenth and seventeenth centuries. The most formidable are Saint Stephen's Cathedral in Budapest and Saint Peter's Cathedral in Esztergom, modeled after Saint Peter's cathedral in Rome. Hungarian Catholic churches more commonly reflect the baroque style of architecture.

Hungarian Catholics often install crosses along main roads and build Calvaries, representing the crucifixion of Christ, on rural hillsides. The latter sites are visited by pilgrims, usually on Easter Saturday.

WHAT IS SACRED? In addition to the typical sacred relics of Catholicism, Hungarian Catholics venerate a number of Hungarian saints (including Saint Stephen, Saint Ladislaus, Saint Imre, Saint Elisabeth, and Saint Margaret). Hungarian Catholics also honor the right hand of Saint Stephen, a relic that leads the procession on Saint Stephen's Day.

The Holy Crown of Saint Stephen was probably manufactured later in the eleventh century. Its symbolic meaning (as the Hungarian state, its laws, and its traditions) emerged after the thirteenth century. Because of its political significance, the cult of the Holy Crown is widespread among both Catholics and non-Catholics in Hungary.

HOLIDAYS AND FESTIVALS Beyond the universally celebrated Catholic holidays, such as Christmas and Easter, Hungarians honor Saint Stephen, the first king of Hungary, on 20 August with an open-air Mass at Saint Stephen's Cathedral in Budapest, after which is a procession and fireworks. Because of Saint Stephen's political significance, national leaders are expected to observe this holiday regardless of their religious affiliations.

Hungarians also celebrate All Saint's Day on 1 November by visiting cemeteries and adorning graves with flowers and candles. Originally a Catholic custom, the holiday is widely celebrated today among Protestants and nonbelievers as well.

MODE OF DRESS Hungarian Catholics dress on the conservative side of European fashion. Catholic schools prescribe decent hair style, minimal makeup, and long skirts for girls, and they discourage students from wearing jewelry.

DIETARY PRACTICES Fasting is rare among Hungarian Catholics today, but some dietary customs are upheld. Catholics do not eat meat on Christmas Eve, on Good Friday, or on Easter Saturday. The Christmas Eve menu is fish and sweets (mainly sweet bread with mashed poppy seeds or nuts). While the Christmas menu is typically a Catholic custom in Hungary, the traditional menu on Easter Sunday, which includes smoked ham, boiled eggs, and sweet bread, is common among most Christians.

RITUALS The Roman Catholic Mass was reformed according to the "Constitution on the Sacred Liturgy" of the Second Vatican Council (1962–65). In some churches in Hungary there is traditional organ liturgical music; gospel music and Taizé (an international ecumenical movement) songs have been gaining popularity.

Since the 1980s basis communities, or prayer groups that meet weekly, have spread among young—mainly urban and educated—Catholics seeking more intensive prayer activity, community life, and social responsibility. Some basis communities, mainly the Bokor network, have clashed with the church leadership, criticizing its pre-1990 cooperation with the socialist party-state, its wealth, and its hierarchical structure. The Bokor network of communities nearly broke with the church, but after the political changes of the 1990s it did not become a separate sect. Instead, it stayed in the church.

Hungary has numerous well-known pilgrimage sites, all of them connected to the cult of the Blessed Virgin; they include Kisczell, Máriaradna, Máriapócs, Besnyö, and Máriaremete. Hungarians also make pilgrimages to two sites outside of the country's borders: Mariazell (in Austria) and Csíksomlyó (in Transylvania, Romania).

RITES OF PASSAGE Although fewer than half of Hungarian Catholics attend church regularly, most favor religious funerals and weddings. The columbariums—chambers for cinerary urns—built in the basement of new Catholic churches are also popular among nonreligious Hungarians because these places are meant to be permanent depositories for the remains. In public graveyards, plots are sold only for 25 years.

MEMBERSHIP The Catholic Church in Hungary proselytizes mainly through its extensive network of schools, which offer open enrollment and welcome nonreligious pupils. Catholic outreach is also conducted through short programs on public television and through a number of publications, including the weekly newspaper *Új Ember* ("New Man"). In 2000 the church founded Radio Pax. The church engages in some missionary activities with gypsies, but since the political changes of 1990 it has been focused on reconstructing its own institutional network.

SOCIAL JUSTICE In 1990 the Hungarian Catholic Church launched a concerted effort to reclaim its

schools and hospitals, which had been confiscated under Communist rule. By 2002 the church owned 50 kindergartens, 96 primary schools, 55 secondary schools, 43 other types of schools, 1 university, and 1 college. That year 368,856 pupils received Catholic religious education in Hungary.

Church organizations, such as the Maltese Association, as well as individual parishioners, offer a wide range of social services in Hungary. Local parishes are especially involved in the care of elderly people. While donations collected in parishes help the needy in Hungary, these funds are also designated to support social and educational institutions in Ukraine and Romania.

SOCIAL ASPECTS Catholics in Hungary are traditional with respect to marriage and family life. Big families (at least four or five children) are popular among young Catholics. Committed Catholics reject consumer society, and the emphasis on children and faithful family life forms the basis of Catholic identity. Gender roles are also traditional among Catholics, with more Catholic women staying at home than is true of Hungarian women in general.

POLITICAL IMPACT Following the fierce religious wars of the sixteenth and seventeenth centuries, Catholics and Protestants forged a peaceful coexistence. During the Kulturkampf, at the end of the nineteenth century, the Catholic Church was separated from the state.

After the 1920 Trianon Treaty, "Christian-national" thinking became the dominant ideology in Hungary. Between the two world wars, political influence was cooperatively shared by the Protestant political elite, the mainly Jewish business elite, and the Catholic clergy. Between 1945 and 1949 political Catholicism was represented by the Democratic People's Party. Rightist parties and voters are still influenced by the (basically Catholic) Christian Democratic ideology. Since 1990 religiosity has been one of the main divisions between leftist and rightist voters in Hungary. A Catholic left is practically nonexistent in Hungary.

CONTROVERSIAL ISSUES Present-day church controversies are rooted in the country's Communist past. One unpleasant issue is the lustration of the Catholic clergy—that is, the publication of documents revealing priests who cooperated with the Communist secret police and the State Church Office. In this controversy the moral authority of priests is at stake. Since 1990, when the Catholic Church began reclaiming its confiscated property, there has been debate about the sum of state subsidy to be allotted for repair of church buildings and for the so-called social functions performed by church institutions, such as education, health care, and social care.

Because the country was separated from the West, and because religious life was strictly checked under Communism, the aggiornamento (revisions of church doctrine laid out in Vatican II) has had little impact on Catholic thinking in Hungary. The segment of the Catholic community that defends traditional Catholicism is larger than the segment that accepts the resolutions of the Vatican II, although issues of private life are rarely discussed. Hungarian Catholics condemn divorce, homosexuality, and abortion—issues that create continuous fights between Catholics and the laicized part of society.

CULTURAL IMPACT Present in Hungary for a thousand years, Catholicism has permeated the culture of the country at all levels. The most renowned Catholic poets are Miklós Zrínyi (1620–64), Mihály Babits (1883–1941), and János Pilinszky (twentieth century), but because the relative obscurity of the Hungarian language, they are not well known outside of Hungary.

Hungarian Catholic composers such as Ferenc Liszt (1811–86), who became a deacon in the Cchurch, and Zoltán Kodály (1882–1967) have had a significant impact on Western culture as a whole. Liszt was not only the greatest piano virtuoso of his time but also an original composer and a principal figure in the Romantic movement. Kodály was a prominent composer and an authority on Hungarian folk music.

Other Religions

Only 2.6 percent of Hungarians are Greek Catholics. While they recognize the pope as head of the Catholic Church, they follow the Orthodox liturgy. The only differences between Roman and Greek Catholics in Hungary are the liturgy and matters of church hierarchy; for instance, Greek Catholic priests may marry, but Roman Catholic priests must be celibate. The Greek Catholic community in Hungary is generally less wealthy and more traditional than the Roman Catholic community.

The Reformed Church in Hungary has about 1.5 million members. It was founded in about 1552, with its strongest roots in eastern Hungary and Transylvania. Indeed, Debrecen was often called the "Calvinist Rome." This area was favorable for religious inventions and freedom; Transylvania had two Unitarian princes, and the founder of Unitarian Church, Ferenc Dávid, lived there. The Reformed Church in Hungary has maintained the bishopric system.

The Catholic Counter-Reformation narrowed the religious freedom of Protestants until 1781, when they were emancipated. The Reformed Church maintained good relations with the elite in the nineteenth and twentieth centuries. Secularization had stronger effects among Reformed Christians than among Catholics. The lifestyle and customs of the Reformed are so assimilated to those of Catholics that today the members of these two communities hardly can be differentiated from each other.

The history of Reformed Christians was so deeply interwoven with the formation of Hungarian national identity that this denomination is often called "Hungarian religion." The first Hungarian version of the Bible was translated in 1590 by Gáspár Károli, and Refomed thought defined the emergence of Hungarian identity; for example, the national anthem of Hungary was written in 1823 by Ferenc Kölcsey, a Reformed poet. Reformed Christians have had decisive roles in the literature and politics of the country. The most respected Reformed clergyman of the post-Communist period was László Tökés, who unleashed the Romanian Revolution of 1989 from a Hungarian parish in Timisoara, Romania.

Jews had settled in Hungary as early as the third century B.C.E., when the area belonged to the Roman Empire's province of Pannonia. The Jews of Hungary lived under considerably safer conditions than their brethren elsewhere in Europe. Hungarian Jews were mostly engaged in the commerce of agricultural produce. The Toleration Decree (1781) allowed their settlement in the free royal towns as well as the establishment of their own schools, and it also enabled Jews to engage in trade and commerce and to possess landed property. The half century preceding World War I was a period of prosperity and achievement for Hungarian Jewry, most of whom belonged to the Reform wing. The founder of Zionism (the movement to establish a Jewish homeland), Tivadar (Theodor) Herzl (1860–1905), was born in Budapest. During World War II Hungarian Jews suffered under German Nazism and the reign of terror inflicted by the Hungarian Nazis. Ultimately, several hundred thousand Hungarian Jews perished in the Holocaust. Judaism has about 13,000 members in present-day Hungary.

The land of Hungary was under Byzantine influence even before the Hungarian tribes arrived there. Although Saint Stephen joined the Catholic Church, the Byzantine political and religious influence was strong until the end of the twelfth century. Thereafter, Orthodoxy existed only among the Romanian minority in Transylvania until the eighteenth and nineteenth centuries, when Serbs, Greeks, and Bulgarians moved into Hungary, keeping their own denominational affiliations. There are several different kinds of Orthodoxy in Hungary, including Russian, Serbian, Bulgarian, Romanian, and Greek Orthodoxy. These communities today are divided in terms of authority. Hungarian Orthodox Christianity has about 15,000 members.

About 14,000 people are members of other religions in Hungary. Since the mid-1980s—when the party-state began liberalizing its cultural and religious policy—some Eastern religious movements have arrived in Hungary. Several New Age practices (such as transcendental meditation and yoga) as well as indigenous shamanism and witchcraft have emerged. Muslim and Buddhist communities also exist in Hungary. The largest and most-discussed groups are the Church of Krishna Consciousness and the Church of Scientology, each of which has a few thousand members in Hungary. The proselytizing activity of these two churches has provoked keen reactions in public life. Civil organizations, journalists, and politicians have attacked these groups

and called for their administrative restriction or prohibition.

Attila Karoly Molnár

See Also Vol. 1: *Christianity, Eastern Rite Churches, Judaism, Reform Judaism, Reformed Christianity, Roman Catholicism*

Bibliography

Déri, Erzsébet, ed. *Calvinist Churches in Hungary*. Budapest: Hegyi, 1992.

———, ed. *Catholic Churches in Hungary*. Budapest: Hegyi, 1991.

Gereben, Ferenc, ed. *Hungarian Minorities and Central Europe: Regionalism, National and Ethnic Identity*. Piliscsaba, Hungary: Pázmány Péter Catholic University, 2001.

Ecumenical Council of Churches in Hungary. *Religious Freedom in Central and Eastern Europe after the Collapse of Communism*. Budapest: The Council, 1998.

Kool, Anne-Marie. *God Moves in a Mysterious Way: The Hungarian Protestant Foreign Mission Movement, 1756–1951*. Zoetermeer, Netherlands: Boekcentrum, 1998.

Schanda, Balázs. *Legislation on Church-State Relations in Hungary*. Budapest: Ministry of Cultural Heritage, 2002.

Tomka, Miklós. *Religion und Kirche in Ungarn*. Vienna: Ungarische Kirchensoziologischen Institut, 1990.

Zombori, István, Pál Cserépfalvy, and Maria Antoinette De Angelis, eds. *A Thousand Years of Christianity in Hungary*. Budapest: Hungarian Catholic Episcopal Conference, 2001.

Iceland

POPULATION 290,570

EVANGELICAL LUTHERAN CHURCH OF ICELAND 86.6 percent

OTHER EVANGELICAL LUTHERAN 4.3 percent

ROMAN CATHOLIC 1.8 percent

OTHER PROTESTANT (PENTECOSTAL, SEVENTH-DAY ADVENTIST, OTHER) 1.3 percent

MORMON 0.2 percent

JEHOVAH'S WITNESS 0.2 percent

ORTHODOX (RUSSIAN AND SERBIAN) 0.1 percent

OTHER (BUDDHIST, MUSLIM, BAHAI, ASA) 0.6 percent

NOT REGISTERED 4.9 percent

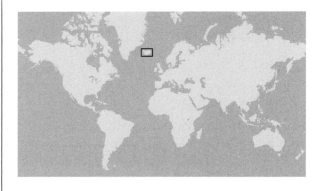

Country Overview

INTRODUCTION The Republic of Iceland is a highly developed Scandinavian country in the Atlantic Ocean on the northern outskirts of Europe. Fjords, mountains, glaciers, volcanoes, and deserts characterize the island, leaving most of the inhabitable areas near the coast. Although the economy depends largely on the fishing industry, most Icelanders are employed in business, education, technology, and other professional occupations. Only 6 percent live in rural areas, while 62.3 percent live in the region surrounding the capital, Reykjavík.

The first settlers arrived in Iceland in the ninth century C.E.. The majority were from Scandinavia (primarily Norway), while others came from Britain and Ireland. The Vikings brought most of the latter as slaves. Some settlers and most slaves were Christian; the rest followed the Viking's Asa beliefs. Under pressure from the King of Norway, Iceland's Althing, a political assembly of independent chieftains, adopted Christianity as the country's official religion in 999 or 1000. The first Roman Catholic bishopric was established in 1056.

Iceland's "golden age" of settlement (the free state period) lasted until the country joined the Norwegian kingdom in 1262 after a long civil war. The Danish kingdom absorbed Iceland in 1380, cut Iceland's ties to the Catholic Church during the Reformation, and enforced Lutheranism as the state religion in 1551. The royal administration dismantled other traditional national institutions, such as the Althing at Thingvellir and the old bishoprics at Hólar and Skálholt.

In the 1830s Icelanders living in Copenhagen, inspired by democratic and nationalist ideals, began agitating for Iceland's political independence. Iceland adopted a constitution in 1874, becoming an independent state in royal union with Denmark in 1918. In 1944 the restored Althing declared Iceland a republic and elected the first president.

The few representatives of other churches to arrive in Iceland before the mid-twentieth century (Pentecostals, Seventh-day Adventists, Plymouth Brethren, Mormons, Jehovah's Witnesses, and Bahais) met with suspicion and opposition, though Icelanders accepted the social work of the Salvation Army, which arrived from Denmark in 1895 and operated under the auspices of the national church. The 1970s saw an attempt to renew the old Norse Asa beliefs. Because of its geographical isolation, Iceland has retained the old Norse language and cultural identity, and this movement aroused some interest. Buddhism came to Iceland in the 1980s, Islam in the 1990s, and Orthodox Christianity since then.

RELIGIOUS TOLERANCE While guaranteeing religious freedom, the Icelandic constitution of 1874 defines the Evangelical Lutheran Church of Iceland as the national church, legitimized by its historical role as the guardian of culture and its maintenance of religious services throughout the country. The constitution aimed at providing greater separation of church and state, which some Icelanders are still struggling to bring into being. Although only 25 religious organizations are now registered by the statistical bureau, the country has up to 200 religious movements and groups, most of them small.

Major Religion

EVANGELICAL LUTHERAN CHURCH OF ICELAND

DATE OF ORIGIN 1551 C.E.
NUMBER OF FOLLOWERS 252,000

HISTORY In 1551 King Christian III of Denmark forcibly replaced the Roman Catholic Church in Iceland with Lutheranism, abolishing the monasteries and appropriating a considerable portion of church land. The publication in Icelandic of the New Testament (1541) and the Bible (1584) are milestones in Iceland's Lutheran history. The Icelandic parish clergy were in the forefront of the national independence and social movement starting in the 1830s, consolidating it and giving it its

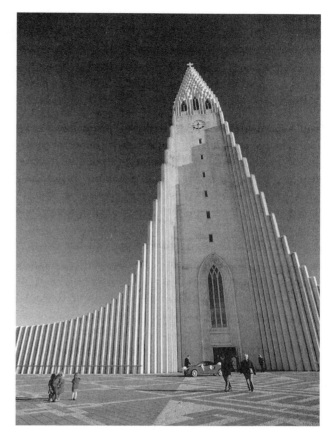

Worshippers walk outside of the church named after Reverend Hallgrímur Pétursson. © CATHERINE KARNOW/CORBIS.

relatively nonrevolutionary character. The Icelandic constitution in 1874 restored the Althing as a legislative body in internal affairs, including church matters.

At the beginning of the twentieth century, leading Icelandic theologians introduced German and English liberal theology within the national church, hoping to prevent the secularization of the society and secure Christian influence on modern culture. Almost simultaneously an influential group of politicians, intellectuals, and respected theologians began advocating spiritualism and psychic research, hoping to get empirical proof of the miracles in the Bible. Although both liberal theology and spiritualism met with strong opposition from Lutheran orthodoxy, they remained influential among the clergy well into the second half of the century.

After World War II more Icelanders felt that material well-being and modern thought went hand in hand with secularization, and church policy gradually set aside liberal theology and emphasized the church as an autonomous and more institutionalized part of society.

EARLY AND MODERN LEADERS Reverend Haraldur Níelsson (1868–1928) translated the Old Testament of the latest Icelandic Bible edition and was later a professor of theology at the University of Iceland. Though controversial for advocating spiritualism and psychic research, he was a highly regarded teacher and preacher. Translations of his books are still published all over the world.

Reverend Fridrik Fridriksson (1868–1961) founded the Icelandic YMCA and YWCA in 1899. An important public figure and religious leader, he opposed liberal theology and spiritualism and emphasized evangelical revival Christianity.

Bishop Sigurbjörn Einarsson (born in 1911), a former professor of theology, became an influential church leader in the late 1950s. He stressed the classical values of the orthodox Lutheran faith, including confession and the liturgy, while relating it to modern cultural and social issues.

MAJOR THEOLOGIANS AND AUTHORS Until the late nineteenth century, orthodox Lutheran literature, such as the passion hymns of Reverend Hallgrímur Pétursson (1614–74) and the sermons of Bishop Jón Vídalín (1666–1720), were read in almost every home in the sparsely populated rural areas. Hallgrímur Pétursson's hymns have been reprinted many times and translated into several languages and are still read on national radio during Lent.

HOUSES OF WORSHIP AND HOLY PLACES Thingvellir, the residence of the Althing (the old parliament, founded in 930), is the nation's most sacred place, related through history to the introduction of Christianity around 1000 C.E.. In 1987 Iceland's largest church was consecrated on a hill in the center of Reykjavík and named after Reverend Hallgrímur Pétursson.

Iceland's oldest churches are generally small turf-and-timber buildings. The urban churches built during the latter half of the twentieth century are usually large, concrete structures with a congregational hall for social activities. Many Icelanders visit churchyards to remember and pray for deceased friends and family members.

WHAT IS SACRED? The most sacred values of the Icelandic people reside in the remembrance of ancestors and national legends and heroes. The old manuscripts of the Eddic poems and Icelandic Sagas and other medieval literature, generally kept in the Árni Magnússon Institute, are considered sacred. During the Reformation Skálholt and Hólar became Lutheran bishoprics, and these spots are holy to all Lutherans.

HOLIDAYS AND FESTIVALS National holidays are usually celebrated in church, and attendance reaches its peak during Christmas. The birthday of Jón Sigurdsson (1811–79), the leader of the national liberation movement, is celebrated on 17 June. The first Sunday of June (Seaman's day) is dedicated to those working on fishing boats and transportation vessels. The opening session of the parliament starts each year with a religious service in the cathedral in Reykjavík.

MODE OF DRESS Icelanders dress like other people in northern and western Europe. Liturgical dress in Iceland was inherited from (and is identical to that worn in) the Danish Evangelical Church tradition.

DIETARY PRACTICES Many Icelanders celebrate Saint Thorlákur's Day (23 December) by eating specially prepared kæst skata (fish). Thorlákur was a twelfth-century Icelandic saint. Manure-smoked lamb is common at Christmas dinner.

RITUALS Only 10 percent of Icelanders attend Sunday services regularly, though many go on Christmas, New Year's Eve, and Easter. The first Sunday in December is another popular service, with special musical programs.

Surveys show that about 80 percent of Icelanders believe in God as a creator and benevolent spirit they can relate to in their prayers. Many say that in times of hardship and sorrow they pray and God hears their prayers. Seventy-five percent say they get comfort and strength from their religion, as compared to 26 percent of Swedes. Icelanders surveyed relate their religion more to a happy life than to judgment and death: 60 percent believe in the existence of heaven and only 15 percent in the existence of hell.

The early-twentieth-century interest in spiritualism no longer has admirers among the ministers of the church, but one-third of Icelanders report that they have attended séances, and the majority of people believe it is possible to contact the dead.

RITES OF PASSAGE More than 90 percent of newborn children in Iceland are baptized and as many young people are confirmed in the national church. Both occasions involve large family celebrations. Until 1926 the national church's confirmation program was included in the primary school curriculum.

Up to 90 percent of marriages involve a church ceremony. Funeral services are important social gatherings, and most include a Christian service with one of Hallgrímur Pétursson's seventeenth-century hymns, a reception in a congregational hall, and an obituary in the *Morgunbladid*, the largest newspaper.

MEMBERSHIP The national church has become aware of the need to reach the younger generation and has begun to offer courses and social events.

SOCIAL JUSTICE Since the inception of the Evangelical Lutheran Church, its administrative network and social work have formed the backbone of Icelandic society. Historically local ministers of the national church visited every household once a year and reported cases of abuse and immorality to the civil authorities; in the most sparsely populated areas, ministers still do this. Civil authorities responsible for caring for the poor are advised by local clergy. Although the church formally separated itself from the educational system in the 1920s, local Evangelical Lutheran Church ministers supervised public education until the middle of the twentieth century.

SOCIAL ASPECTS Iceland's national church emphasizes the importance of marriage and family life but generally tolerates cohabitation before marriage, increasingly common and accepted since the later nineteenth century. In Iceland, however, one-third of marriages end in divorce. The church offers family counseling and administers a church aid program for families with social problems.

POLITICAL IMPACT Evangelical Lutheran ministers played leading roles in the nationalist movement that began in 1830. Clergymen and theologians constituted a considerable proportion of the elected members of Iceland's parliament. The church has avoided major conflict with society. Clergymen have been close allies of politicians who needed ties with the public. Even the labor unions have seldom spoken against the church.

CONTROVERSIAL ISSUES Since the beginning of the twentieth century, Icelandic Lutherans have debated the validity of Christian doctrines by setting them against scientific and humanistic approaches to life. Their questioning lead many into spiritualism. In the 1940s and 1950s Lutherans questioned the expense of building the big church in Reykjavík in light of Christian ethics on caring for the poor. In the 1980s the Icelandic Christian peace movement met with severe criticism from conservative politicians. In the 1970s and 1980s Lutherans debated abortion rights, and the debate on homosexual marriages continues.

Politicians and others have become increasingly concerned that the privileged position of Iceland's national church violates religious freedom and the equality of religious communities. Pressure groups formed in the 1990s to promote the total separation of church and state. The Society for Humanistic Ethics provides secular rites of passage for those who want an alternative to the Lutheran confirmation ritual.

CULTURAL IMPACT Christian institutions brought the written word to Iceland, a crucial step in the cultivation of national culture and literature, notably in the conservation of the Icelandic language. Churchmen and monks commonly recorded the old Icelandic poetry and sagas.

To legitimize its political claims against Denmark during the struggle for independence, the Icelandic nationalist movement reembraced the ideal of the heroic and independent settlers, creating a cultural foundation for their political program.

Other Religions

Roman Catholicism was absent from Iceland from 1551 until 1857, when two Catholic priests arrived to assist French fishermen. Icelandic officials and clergy, not accepting the religious freedom declared by the Danish constitution of 1849, fiercely opposed their missionary efforts. Catholic missionaries left in 1875 and only returned to the country in 1897, gradually gaining success at that time. Approximately half the members of Iceland's Catholic Church are immigrants from Poland and the Philippines, most of whom work in the fishing industry in various villages and towns.

The Seventh-day Adventists and Plymouth Brethren came to Iceland around 1900 and established themselves in Reykjavík. In the early 1920s Pentecostals had some success among women in expanding fishing communities, notably Vestmannæyjar. Until World War II these groups led isolated lives under the leadership of foreign missionaries. The 1960s saw a Pentecostal revival centered in Reykjavík. The charismatic movement reached Iceland in the 1970s, inspiring members of the Evangelical Lutheran YMCA and YWCA to split off and found Youth with a Mission, which itself split into various independent Pentecostal churches.

In 1851 two Icelandic apprentices returned home from Copenhagen after having converted to the Church of Jesus Christ of Latter-day Saints (Mormons). Their missionary efforts also met with strong opposition. Most of the Mormon converts soon left the country for the promised paradise in Utah. With the outbreak of World War I in 1914, the Mormons abandoned Iceland. In the 1970s Mormon missionaries arrived from the United States and had greater success.

During the 1930s Bahais and Jehovah's Witnesses worked in Iceland but only had success much later. The first Icelanders were baptized as Jehovah's Witnesses in the 1950s. The Bahais found converts in the 1970s.

In 1972 a group founded to revive the old Asa beliefs of the Vikings aroused considerable attention. Little, however, is known about Asa, and most sources on the faith are heavily influenced by Christianity.

During the 1980s immigrants began establishing various Buddhist groups. More than 600 people—the vast majority of them (460) in the Theravada Buddhist Association of Iceland—belong to registered and unregistered groups. The Muslim Association was established in the 1990s. Russian and Serbian immigrants have established two ethnic Orthodox churches in Iceland.

Pétur Pétursson

See Also Vol. 1: *Lutheranism*

Bibliography

Björnsson, Björn, and Pétur Pétursson. Trúarlíf Íslendinga. *Ritröd Gudfrædistofnunar 3.* Reykjavík: Háskóli Íslands, 1990.

Fell, Michael. *And Some Fell Into Good Soil: A History of Christianity in Iceland.* New York: Peter Lang, 1999.

Jónsson, Fridrik H., and Stefán Ólafsson. *Úr lífsgildakönnun 1990: Lífsskodun í nútímalegum thjódfélögum.* Reykjavík: Félagsvísindastofnun, 1991.

Nordal, Jóhannes, and Valdimar Kristinsson, eds. *Iceland: The Republic.* Reykjavík: The Central Bank of Iceland, 1996.

Pétursson, Pétur. *Church and Social Change: A Study of the Secularization Process in Iceland, 1830–1930.* Reykjavík: Háskólaútgáfan, 1990.

Valdimarsdóttir, Thórunn, and Pétur Pétursson. *Kristni á Íslandi IV: Til móts vid nútímann.* Reykjavík: Althing, 2000.

India

POPULATION 1,045,845,226

HINDU 80 percent

MUSLIM 14 percent

CHRISTIAN 2.4 percent

SIKH 2 percent

BUDDHIST 0.7 percent

JAIN 0.5 percent

OTHER 0.4 percent

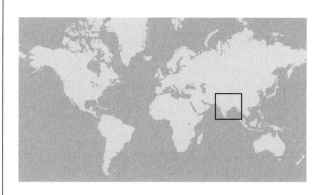

Country Overview

INTRODUCTION The Republic of India is situated in the Indian subcontinent in South Asia. It is bordered to the north and northeast by China, Nepal, and Bhutan; to the west by Pakistan and the Arabian Sea; to the east by Bangladesh, Myanmar, and the Bay of Bengal; and to the south by the Indian Ocean. The Indo-Gangetic plain and the Himalayas are the birthplace of Hinduism, Buddhism, and Jainism. With well over 800 million adherents Hinduism is by far the most widely

practiced religion in India. Buddhism and Jainism arose in the sixth century B.C.E. in North India. Buddhism spread first to Sri Lanka and then by various routes to Southeast Asia, China, and Japan, and today the majority of Buddhists live outside of India. Sikhism originated in northwestern India in the late fifteenth century.

Islam, with more than 100 million followers in contemporary India, arrived in waves from the Arabian Peninsula, Central Asia, and Afghanistan, beginning in the eighth century. The earliest Muslims to arrive in India came via the Arabian Sea. From the tenth to the eighteenth centuries Islamic peoples crossed the Himalayas from the northwest (primarily through the Khyber Pass) into North India. From the thirteenth to the eighteenth centuries Muslims established empires that dominated North India, and Hindu kingdoms were overthrown with varying degrees of intensity by their Muslim conquerors. Many Muslims who found their way into the Indian subcontinent throughout this period settled there, and Islamic traditions and tastes became mixed with those of the Hindu population. Although Islam has always been a minority religion in India, its impact on Indian history and culture has been immense. Today India has the second-largest population of Muslims of any country in the world. Other religions transported to India include Judaism, whose origins there date to the first century C.E.; Zoroastrianism, which arrived in the eighth century; and Christianity.

The Portuguese, French, and British arrived in India by sea, beginning in the seventeenth century. Eventually, the British East India Company, a trading company, came to dominate the subcontinent. Tensions between British interests and the indigenous population erupted

The Vishvanath temple, dedicated to Shiva, is one of several important temples in the sacred city of Varanasi (Kashi), Uttar Pradesh, India.
© DAVID CUMMING; EYE UBIQUITOUS/CORBIS.

in 1857 in what is known as the Sepoy Mutiny or the First Indian War of Independence. Many lives on both sides were lost. From 1858 to 1947, when it gained its independence, India was ruled by the British crown. In 1947 the subcontinent was partitioned, and the two nations of India and Pakistan were born.

RELIGIOUS TOLERANCE Although Hinduism is the dominant religion, there is no official religion in India, a secular state where freedom of worship is guaranteed and discrimination on the basis of religion is prohibited. India has endured long-standing and sometimes violent religious tensions, however. In 1947 the subcontinent was partitioned along religious lines, and Muslims in Kashmir and Sikhs in the Punjab have fought for decades to secede from India. Overall, there has been an increase in violent clashes between Hindu, Muslim, and Sikh communities in recent decades, and this reflects a decrease in the levels of religious tolerance. The incidence of anti-Christian violence has also increased.

Major Religions

HINDUISM

ISLAM

HINDUISM

DATE OF ORIGIN 1500 B.C.E.
NUMBER OF FOLLOWERS More than 835 million

HISTORY Hinduism in India is not an organized religion, and its history and practices vary from region to region. Its beginnings can be traced from the Indus Valley civilization (3200–1600 B.C.E.) through to the composition of the Vedas, which began in about 1500 B.C.E. The culture of the Indus Valley, known to the modern world through its archeological remains (including impressive urban structures, pottery, inscriptions, and other artifacts), represents one of the most advanced civilizations in the world from these early times. Research on sites in the Indus Valley is ongoing, but reflections of this important culture are discernible throughout the history of the religious and literary development of India. The Indo-Aryan authors of the Vedic texts developed the Brahmanic, or Vedic, religion, an early form of Hinduism. During these early phases a number of philosophical schools of thought and practices—including yoga, meditation, and asceticism—also developed. The two major Hindu epics, the *Mahabharata* and the *Ramayana*, which draw on early periods in the development of Hinduism, evidence the importance of narrative in transmitting traditional and religious knowledge. The *Bhagavad Gita* gave Hinduism a distinctive flavor in its articulation of the three paths of religiosity—action, knowledge, and devotion.

In the fourth and fifth centuries C.E. the Gupta Dynasty dominated the north; Pallava kings, the south; and the Chalukyas, the Deccan (India's southern peninsula). During this period classical Hinduism flourished. The following centuries gave rise to disparate kingdoms that patronized different sects of Hinduism. From early times the relationship between the political and the religious had been an intimate one, and systems of divine kingship (*devaraja*) were instituted in some locations. This period was also dominated by traditions of bhakti (devotion) in Hinduism. Islam grew to have a defining influence on Hinduism, particularly from the twelfth through the sixteenth centuries, when Muslim empires came to dominate northern India. The majority of Hin-

The Kumbha Mela, a bathing festival celebrated every 12 years in Allahabad, attracts to the Ganges River large numbers of renouncers and pilgrims from throughout India and abroad. AP/WIDE WORLD PHOTOS.

dus did not convert to Islam, but many Islamic traditions—Sufism, for example—blended with Hindu traditions, most notably those of devotional Hinduism. The European domination of India led to a series of reforms of Hinduism that included the abolition of suttee (a widow's sacrificing herself on her husband's funeral pyre) and the lifting of the prohibition against widow's remarrying. At the same time Hinduism continued to be redefined under the leadership of several important reformers, nationalists, and freedom fighters.

Perhaps the most significant event in the history of Hinduism in the modern era was the partition of the subcontinent in 1947. The change gave impetus to Hindu and Muslim political parties in India, though Jawaharlal Nehru (1889–1964), an advocate of secular socialism, became the country's first prime minister. Atal Bihari Vajpayee (born in 1924), a founder of the Hindu nationalist Bharatiya Janata Party (BJP), became prime minister in 1998. The BJP's ideology is known as Hindutva, and its agenda is to transform India into a Hindu state.

EARLY AND MODERN LEADERS Candragupta II, who reigned from about 380 to about 415, and other kings of the Gupta Dynasty patronized the arts and established several centers of learning during what is known as the golden age of Hinduism. King Harsha, who ruled in the seventh century, is also noted for his patronage of Hinduism. Seeking to revitalize Hinduism in India, Ram Mohun Roy (1772–1833), rejecting image worship and caste divisions and accepting monotheism, founded the Brahmo Samaj, and Dayananda Sarasvati (1824–83), advocating a strict adherence to the Vedas and a purification of Hindu practice, founded the Arya Samaj. In the struggle for independence Lokmanya Tilak (1856–1920), along with many others, called for *swaraj* (self-rule) and *svadeshi* (self-reliance). Mahatma Gandhi (1869–1948) is considered the father of India. Among Gandhi's many contributions is his well-known philosophy of satyagraha, or "holding firmly to the truth" through the practice of nonviolence (ahimsa) and self-sacrifice, which became a powerful course of action in the independence movement. Jawaharlal Nehru, as

India's first prime minister (1947–1964), advocated secular socialism and sought to modernize his country. He is known as the chief architect of India's domestic and foreign policy. Immediately after independence B.R. Ambedkar (1891–1956), India's first minister of law, spoke out for the rights of the *dalits* (untouchables), and in 1956 he converted to Buddhism, inspired by the Buddha's protest against inequality. Sarvepalli Radhakrishnan (1888–1975), India's president from 1962 to 1967, emphasized the role of social institutions and ethical action in religious practice. Atal Bihari Vajpayee (born in 1924), prime minister since 1998, adheres to a Hindu nationalist agenda.

MAJOR THEOLOGIANS AND AUTHORS Major figures that continue to have an impact upon Hindu thought in India are too numerous to mention, but they include the sages Valmiki, who composed the *Ramayana*, and Vyasa, who composed or compiled the *Mahabharata*, as well as Panini, the Sanskrit grammarian; Patanjali, who wrote the *Yogasutras*; Manu, to whom is attributed the *Laws of Manu*; and the prolific and prominent fifth-century poet and dramatist Kalidasa. Important also are Shankara (788–820), the founder of the influential school of Advaita (nondual) Vedanta; Ramanuja (1017–1137), the founder of the Visishtadvaita (qualified nondual) Vedanta; Madhva, the thirteenth-century founder of Dvaita (dual) Vedanta; Abhinavagupta, who is known for his works on aesthetic theory; and Tulsidas (died in 1623), the author of the *Ramacaritmanas*. The Nayanars (Tamil Shaiva poet-saints) and the Alvars (Vaishnava poet-saints) appealed to popular audiences and sparked a religious renewal from the fifth through the tenth centuries. In the devotional tradition Caitanya (1486–1533), Basavanna (1105–1167), Mira Bai (1516–1546), Tukaram (died in 1649), and Jnaneshvar (thirteenth century) are also well known.

In the nineteenth and twentieth centuries the message of Ramakrishna (1836–86) that all religions lead to the same goal resulted in the establishment of the Ramakrishna Mission. One of Ramakrishna's disciples and founder of the mission, Swami Vivekananda (1863–1902), is well known for his interpretation of Hinduism for Western audiences. Other teachers famous in India and the West include A.C. Bhaktivedanta Swami Prabhupada (1896–1977), who founded the International Society for Krishna Consciousness (ISKCON), commonly known as the Hare Krishna movement; Maharishi Mahesh Yogi (born in 1911?), who introduced

Transcendental Meditation (TM) to the West; Swami Sivananda (1887–1963), who founded the Divine Life Society; Swami Chinmayananda (1916–93), who founded the Chinmaya Mission; Sathya Sai Baba (born in 1926); and Ramana Maharshi (1879–1950).

HOUSES OF WORSHIP AND HOLY PLACES Many Hindu homes in India have a shrine or sacred space set aside to honor deities who are believed to protect the family and engender good fortune. Household shrines incorporate images relevant to all the members of the household and are tended to daily. Hindus also worship in temples, which are found throughout the country. Important temples and temple complexes include the Minakshi temple, dedicated to the goddess Minakshi, in Madurai, Tamil Nadu; the Chamundeswari, dedicated to the goddess Chamundi, in Mysore, Karnataka; the Jagannath temple, dedicated to the god Jagannath, in Puri; and the multitude of temples in Bhubanesvar, Orissa, which include the Lingaraj temple. The Vishvanath temple, dedicated to Shiva, is one of several important temples in the sacred city of Varanasi (Kashi), Uttar Pradesh.

Also well known are the many temples at Vrindavan and Mathura dedicated to Krishna in Uttar Pradesh and at Dwarka in Gujarat; the Shiva temple in Somnath, Gujarat; the Nataraja temple, dedicated to Shiva, the cosmic dancer, at Chidambaram, Tamil Nadu; the Ranganatha temple, sacred to followers of Vishnu, in Srirangam, Tamil Nadu; the Kalighat temple, dedicated to the goddess Kali, in Calcutta (Kolkata), Bengal; and the Kamakhya Devi temple, dedicated to the goddess Shakti, in Guwahati, Assam. The Venkatesvara temple, dedicated to Lord Venkatesvara and said to be the wealthiest temple in India, is in Tirupati, Andhra Pradesh. Temples and temple complexes throughout the subcontinent are important sites of pilgrimage, though pilgrims also converge at other holy sites, including those along the Ganges river, especially the holy cities of Varanasi and Allahabad and the shrines at Badrinath and Kedarnath.

WHAT IS SACRED? India is sacred to Hindus, and its mountains, rivers, and other physical features are revered. The mere sight of the Ganges, which flows from the Himalayas across the northern plains and into the Bay of Bengal, is considered beneficial. It is believed to be particularly auspicious to be cremated along the river's banks or to have one's ashes immersed in its waters. Mountains, particularly the Himalayas, are venerated as abodes of the gods.

All life is sanctified in Hinduism, but cows are regarded as especially holy. Scriptures—particularly the Vedas but also the *Bhagavad Gita*—are considered sacred. The syllable "om" is believed to be the root syllable of the universe, and its repetition is auspicious. The swastika is an ancient symbol in Hinduism that represents power, strength, and goodness. Holy ash, *rudraksha* beads, the trident, and the lingam (a phallic symbol) are sacred to followers of Shiva, and the conch and the wheel (*chakra*) are held sacred by followers of Vishnu. In almost all cases ritual is the means through which the sacred is encountered in Hinduism.

HOLIDAYS AND FESTIVALS Hindu holidays are celebrated according to the lunar calendar. Holi is the festival of color marking the advent of spring. Celebrants sing, dance, and throw colored powder or water on one another, and sometimes social roles are reversed. Pongal in South India, Onam in Kerala, and Baisakh in the Punjab are harvest festivals. Many Hindus celebrate the birthdays of important deities, including Rama, Krishna, and the elephant-headed Ganesha. People light oil lamps, electric lights, and candles and set off fireworks during Diwali, the Festival of Lights. Dussehra is a ten-day festival marking the victory of Rama over the ten-headed demon, Ravana. In Bengal Dussehra is celebrated as Durga Puja in honor of the goddess Durga and her victory over the buffalo demon, Mahisha. Shivatratri is dedicated to Shiva and commemorates his marriage to the goddess Parvati. The celebration of the Rathayatra, a chariot festival dedicated to Lord Jagannath, takes place in Orissa in June and July. The Kumbha Mela, a bathing festival celebrated every 12 years in Allahabad, attracts large numbers of renouncers and pilgrims from throughout India and abroad.

MODE OF DRESS Hindu women in India wear saris in many different colors, fabrics, and designs. Hindu widows wear white saris. In some regions married women wear the *mangala sutra,* a necklace of gold and black beads, as the equivalent of a wedding ring, and they apply vermilion to the parting of the hair. Hindu women also decorate their hands and feet with henna designs on auspicious occasions and wear *bindis,* which are colored dots, on their foreheads. The traditional *bindi* symbolizes marriage, but contemporary Hindu women, both married and unmarried, wear *bindis* of different colors and shapes.

Hindu men wear Western clothing or the traditional dhoti. In South India many men wear a *lungi,* a wide strip of cloth wrapped around the lower body. Hindu men wear a variety of headgear, including turbans. Mahatma Gandhi sported a distinctive cap (*topee*) that became a symbol of the freedom struggle. Temple priests mark devotees with a small spot, a *tilakam,* symbolizing the mystic third eye of wisdom, between their eyebrows. The *tilakam* may take various shapes. Sometimes Vaishnavites mark their foreheads with vertical lines, and Shaivites may mark theirs with horizontal lines. Vaishnavites wear beads made of *tulsi* (basil), while Shaivites wear *rudraksha* beads, which function as aids to meditation. Some monks shave their heads and wear saffron-colored robes.

DIETARY PRACTICES Food in Hindu India tends to be spicy and sometimes very hot, particularly in South India, where meals are often served on banana leaves and eaten with the hands. Indians are particularly fond of rich sweets made from milk, ghee (clarified butter), and nuts, and these delicacies are often included in offerings. Food that has been first offered to a deity is known as *prasad.* Offering and eating sweets on festival days is an important practice.

Perhaps because of traditional rules regarding caste, Hindus often eat alone rather than in groups. All guests are treated as if they are gods, however, and Hindus offer food to their guests as a religious obligation. Fasting is common on certain days as a matter of religious observance. Because the cow is sacred in India, Hindus do not consume beef. The Hindu doctrine of ahimsa (nonviolence) is sometimes interpreted as prohibiting the slaughter and consumption of any animal, and because of this many Hindus are vegetarians.

Hinduism categorizes foods as *sattvic* (pure, healthy), *rajasic* (active, spicy), and *tamasic* (heavy, unhealthy). Traditional Indian medicine (*ayurveda*) identifies many foods, such as turmeric and ginger, as having medicinal value. *Ayurveda* also defines foods as hot and cold, depending upon their effects on the mind and body.

RITUALS Hindus in India perform a wide variety of rituals for purification, to fulfill vows, as acts of devotion, and to accumulate merit. Placing offerings of grains, ghee, and other sacred substances in a fire is a practice that dates to ancient times. The Hindu ceremony of *puja,* in which a deity is honored with a consecrated image, is one of the most fundamental of Hindu rites, though its practice varies considerably throughout the country. Hindus choose their deities individually, and domestic shrines incorporate images reflecting the choices of household members. Many Hindus perform *puja* in their homes. A god may be attended with such daily rites as bathing, dressing, decoration with flowers and vermilion, and offerings of flowers and food. Key to this ritual is taking *darshana* (literally, "seeing"), in which the devotee sees the deity and is in turn seen by the deity, and *prasada*, the devotee's receiving of food symbolic of the deity's grace. Hindus also perform *puja* in temples, where priests officiate. Pilgrimages are undertaken to holy sites throughout the country. Spiritual discipline (*sadhana*), including the practice of yoga and meditation, characterizes Hindu ritual practice. Austerities known as *vrats* (vows) structure the religious practice of many Hindus, especially women, and often consist of fasting, the recitation of mantras, and meditation. *Shraddhas* are important rituals performed to assist the dead in making rebirth transitions.

Dawn is an auspicious time for Hindus. At this time women draw geometric designs in chalk or rice flour on the floor or the doorstep. Some Hindus recite the sacred Gayatri mantra at dawn and dusk. In the evenings devotees may gather at the temple or in one another's homes to sing praises to the gods.

RITES OF PASSAGE Hindus in India identify four *ashramas*, or stages of life: student, householder, forest-dweller, and renouncer. This system is followed by males belonging to the first three castes, though others also pass through these stages. Initiation into the first stage is called *upanayana*, during which young boys receive a sacred thread, worn over the left shoulder, marking them as "twice-born." This ritual signifies their entrance into the religious community. Between 12 and 14 additional rituals known as *samskaras* mark major life transitions from conception to death. For a Hindu woman the most important rite of passage is marriage, which is generally arranged by her parents. Each phase of the ceremony, which may last for several days, has religious meaning.

Most Hindus cremate their dead, and the eldest son traditionally lights the funeral pyre. Afterwards the ashes are collected and immersed in a holy river, preferably the Ganges. After-death rituals (*shraddhas*) are performed for several days thereafter and on the first anniversary of the death.

MEMBERSHIP There are many different ways of being a Hindu in India, and a variety of different religious practices are prescribed in different sects of Hinduism. Hindus generally do not proselytize. Notable exceptions to this rule include the Ramakrishna Mission and the Hare Krishna movement. Some, but not all, Hindu sects accept converts. Because many Hindus believe in the existence of a Supreme Being and the ability of this being to manifest itself in this world in different forms and at different times, they accept other religious paths as true and valid. According to this mindset other religions are essentially Hindu; thus, there is no need for conversion. Some Hindus accept Jesus, for example, as an avatar, or incarnation, of God. Furthermore, many Hindus believe that Sikhism, Buddhism, and Jainism are different forms of Hinduism, though Sikhs, Buddhists, and Jains do not necessarily agree.

SOCIAL JUSTICE Poverty, access to education, and discrimination based on caste, gender, religion, and economic status are major problems in India. Indian reformers of the nineteenth and twentieth centuries laid the groundwork for social reforms that have led to numerous constitutional and legal protections for the disadvantaged. Social justice is high on the agenda of many Hindu groups that mount programs of charity and volunteer activity and work for the betterment of society. These organizations include the Satya Sai Baba Organization, the Divine Life Society, and the Ramakrishna Mission. There are numerous organizations that focus on women's issues, including the Centre for Women's Development Studies in Delhi, and efforts on this front are ongoing.

SOCIAL ASPECTS Marriage in Hindu India is considered a sacred duty, and Hindu women are often understood as fulfilling their spiritual destiny through marriage. Women are often assigned the role of guardian of tradition, and their domestic and ritual activities are believed to facilitate their husband's salvation. Marriages are often arranged, and it is uncommon for Hindu women to remain unmarried. As mothers, women are culturally esteemed, and mother figures in politics, religion, and the Hindu pantheon command reverence. The agenda of the modern Hindutva movement calls for the return of women to traditional Hindu roles within the family. Many women in India are active in the promotion of this agenda, affirming their roles as mothers, wives, and daughters, while others continue to agitate for reform.

POLITICAL IMPACT The Indian constitution describes India as a socialist secular democratic republic. The Congress Party, which dominated Indian politics from independence to the early 1990s, focused on the principles of secular socialism. In the late 1980s the growing strength of the Hindu nationalist Bharatiya Janata Party (BJP) brought Hinduism to the fore of national politics. The BJP and its affiliates, the Rashtriya Swayamsevak Sangh (RSS) and the Vishva Hindu Parisad (VHP), make up the *sangh parivar,* a dynamic political force in India that seeks to restore what it sees as essential to the grandeur of the Hindu tradition. The fusion since the late 1990s of Indian politics and Hinduism has caused friction between Indian Muslims and the national government and has encouraged some Sikhs to fight for an independent Sikh state.

CONTROVERSIAL ISSUES Discrimination on the basis of caste (casteism) and community (communalism) and the treatment of women are controversial issues in Hindu India. The caste system is a strong organizing force, and those outside the system and at its lowest levels are particularly disadvantaged. These groups include the Scheduled Castes (SC; formerly known as untouchables and also referred to as Dalits), Scheduled Tribes (ST), and Other Backward Classes (OBC). Caste discrimination is illegal in India, but it persists. Since the late nineteenth century a series of measures aimed at improving the condition of underprivileged groups has been put in place. Central to these measures is a system of "reservations" (a form of affirmative action) that provides for special representation of certain underprivileged groups in the domains of employment, governance, and education. The Indian constitution includes a reservation policy that has been refined and expanded by both the central and state governments. Responses to these reforms have often been controversial. For example, Prime Minister V.P. Singh's attempt in 1990 to implement the 1981 recommendations of the Mandal Commission by increasing the number and scope of reservations was met with resistance, some of which was extremely violent.

Communal tensions, especially between Muslim and Hindu communities, that erupt in violence seem to be on the increase. Social practices that result in poor treatment of women—child marriage, for example, or dowry—are also controversial. There are numerous cases of disputes over dowry, and thousands of widows relocate to pilgrimage centers every year for relief from abuse at home. The term suttee means "good woman," but it also refers to the practice of women immolating themselves on the funeral pyres of their husbands. Although suttee is illegal, the death of Kuttu Bai on her husband's pyre in 2002 indicates that the practice has not been eradicated.

CULTURAL IMPACT Indian crafts include pottery, sculpture, painting, jewelry, and weaving. Sculptures depicting gods, goddesses, and other figures from Hindu mythology ornament Hindu temples in India. The movements and gestures of classical dance accompany traditional Hindu stories. Ravi Shankar, one of India's most esteemed sitar players and composers, has introduced millions around the world to Indian music. Vocal music is also an important art form in Hinduism. The Indian film industry, which dates to the beginning of the twentieth century, is one of the world's most prolific. Satyajit Ray (1921–1992) is recognized as one of the world's great filmmakers. Many Indian films tell stories from Hindu mythology and feature songs with Hindu-based lyrics. Television productions of the *Mahabharata* and the *Ramayana* are also extremely popular. The paintings of Raja Ravi Verma (1848–1906) are well known for their European-style depictions of scenes from the Hindu epics. Prominent literary figures include Rabindranath Tagore (1861–1941), winner of the Nobel Prize for Literature in 1913, R.K. Narayan (1906–2001), and Arundhati Roy (born in 1946), winner of the Booker Prize in 1997.

ISLAM

DATE OF ORIGIN Eighth century C.E.
NUMBER OF FOLLOWERS 140 million

HISTORY Many Muslims in India trace their origins to the Arabian Peninsula and Central Asia; others are converts from the indigenous population. Islam arrived in Sindh in the eighth century, and at about the same time, Arab traders brought their religion to the southern coast of Kerala. Since then Turkish, Afghani, and Mongolian Muslims have entered India. Politically and culturally, Islam has had its greatest impact in North India. By the eleventh century Muslim rulers had established their capital at Delhi, and various Islamic dynasties retained Delhi as their capital. The Moguls controlled India from the sixteenth to the mid-eighteenth century, and it was during this period that many Islamic monuments, including the Taj Mahal, were constructed. The eighteenth century saw the rise of the Muslim-dominated states of Hyderabad in the Deccan under Nizam-ul-Mulk (1671–1748) and Mysore in South India under the rule of Hyder Ali (1722–82). Islamic political control of India officially ended in 1857, when the British deposed Bahadur Shah Zafar (1775–1862), the last Mogul ruler.

Muslims played an active role in India's struggle for independence. The All-India Muslim League, later known simply as the Muslim League, was founded by Aga Khan III (1877–1957) in 1906 in order to safeguard the political rights of Muslims in India. After partition the Muslim League became the major political party of the newly formed Pakistan. The Khilafat movement of 1919–24 upheld the solidarity of Muslim and Hindu nationalists in its support of the Turkish sultan—who, as caliph, was the head of the worldwide Muslim community—against the British. The Khilafat movement brought the Muslim clergy into the political arena, where their presence continues to be felt. Partition split the Muslim community, with most of British India's Muslims ending up in Pakistan. Although Muslims in India are a minority, they are a diverse population with a distinctive cultural identity.

EARLY AND MODERN LEADERS The sixteenth-century ruler Akbar (1542–1605) is remembered for consolidating the Mogul empire and for his tolerance toward other religions. Akbar founded a new religion, Din-i-Ilahi, that drew heavily on the teachings of Islam, Hinduism, Zoroastrianism, and Christianity, but it did not survive beyond his death. Included among the Muslim rulers of South India are Tipu Sultan (1753–99) in Mysore and, in the Deccan, the Nizams of Hyderabad. Muslims who played key roles in the struggle for independence include Hasrat Mohani (1878–1951); the Ali brothers, Muhammad Ali (1878–1931) and Shaukat Ali (1873–1938); and Maulana Muhammad Ali (1874–1951). Maulana Abul Kalam Azad (1888–1958) espoused the cause of secular nationalism and served as India's first education minister. Muhammad Ali Jinnah (1876–1948) played a determining role in the establishment of Pakistan; Liaquat Ali Khan (1895–1951) served as the first prime minister of Pakistan; and Zakir Husain (1897–1969), a staunch advocate of Muslim education and a former vice-chancellor of Jamia Millia Islamia, served as president of India from 1967 to 1969. Avul Pakir Jainulabdeen Abdul Kalam (born in 1931) was inaugurated as president of India in 2003.

MAJOR THEOLOGIANS AND AUTHORS Sufism flourished in India, drawing heavily on the devotional tradition of Hinduism. Among the hundreds of popular and influential Sufi *pirs* (living saints) are Khwaja Moinuddin Chishti (1115–1229) of Rajasthan, Shaikh Ahmad (died in 1624) of Sirhind, the fifteenth-century saint Khawaja Habib-ullah Attar of Kashmir, and Sultan Bahu (1628–91) of the Punjab. The great poet Amir Khusrau (1253–1325) was associated with the royal courts of the Delhi sultanate and is recognized as the father of the Urdu language. In the nineteenth and twentieth centuries Syed Ahmed Brelavi (1789–1831) and Maulana Muhammad Ilyas (1885–1946) founded, respectively, the Indian Wahhabi movement and the Tablighi movement, both with the objective of purifying Islamic practice. The poetry of Muhammad Iqbal (1877–1938) centers on themes of love and freedom, and he is recognized as the spiritual founder of Pakistan. Syed Ahmad Khan (1817–1898) sought to revitalize the study of Islam in India through secular education, establishing Aligarh Muslim University, which became the center for Islamic politics in India in the first half of the twentieth century. Abdullah Yusuf Ali (1872–1952) is known for his 1934 English translation of, and commentary on, the Koran.

HOUSES OF WORSHIP AND HOLY PLACES The Jama Masjid in Delhi, India's largest mosque, was built by the Mogul emperor Shah Jahan (1592–1666) and accommodates up to 25,000 people. Other popular mosques include the Hazratbal Mosque in Srinagar, which houses the sacred hair of Muhammad; the Mecca Masjid in Hyderabad; the Moti Masjid (Pearl Mosque) in Agra; the Haji Ali mosque in Bombay; and the Thousand Light Mosque in Madras (Chennai). Numerous tombs that function as tributes to the Islamic presence in India include the Taj Mahal in Agra and Humayun's (1508–56) Tomb in Delhi. The dome of the tomb of Mohammed Adil Shah (died in 1656) in Bijapur is second in size only to the dome of Saint Peter's Basilica in Rome. Perhaps the most important Sufi shrine is the tomb of Khwaja Moinuddin Chishti in Ajmer, which rests on a silver platform and is covered with a marble dome.

WHAT IS SACRED? Muslims in India, like Muslims all over the world, hold the name of God, the prophet Muhammad, and the Koran as sacred. They maintain the sanctity of their mosques, mausoleums, and Sufi *dargah*s (shrines). The Qutb Minar, an impressive red sandstone tower built in Delhi in the thirteenth century, symbolizes the power and majesty of Islam in India. The Taj Mahal, the mausoleum built by Shah Jahan for his wife Mumtaz Mahal in the seventeenth century, evidences the Islamic sensibility of beauty, proportion, and austerity. Haji Ali's mosque and tomb in Bombay, which can only be reached at low tide, is an example of the richness of the popular tradition that reveres the Indian saints of Islam. The Hazratbal shrine in Srinagar is an important pilgrimage site for Muslims.

HOLIDAYS AND FESTIVALS Id al-Fitr celebrates the end of the fast of Ramadan and is a national holiday in India. Id al-Adha marks the ritual sacrifice of Abraham and is commonly called Bakr-Id in India because of the tradition of sacrificing a goat (in Urdu *bakr*). On the tenth day of Muharram Shiite Muslims all over India dress in black to mourn the death of Husayn (born in 626), the son of 'Ali and the grandson of Muhammad. Bamboo and paper replicas of the martyr's tombs (*taziya*s) and green standards like those of Husayn's army are carried in procession through the streets, and participants enact battle scenes. People of all denominations fill the streets in Lucknow, Srinagar, Hyderabad, Bombay, and Delhi to witness the processions and demonstrations of grief, which include self-flagellation, body piercing, and fire walking. On the occasion of Mawlid al-Nabi Muslims celebrate the birth of Muhammad; and in the Hazratbal Mosque in Srinagar, a holy hair from his beard is displayed. On this day in some parts of India a replica of the horse on which Muhammad is believed to have ascended to heaven is placed next to a stone tablet engraved with the symbolic footprints of the Prophet and is anointed with sandalwood paste. This ritual is called the sandal rite. Annual festivals marking the death anniversaries of Sufi saints are called *urs*. The best known of these are held at the *dargah* of Hazrat Nizamuddin Auliya (1236–1325) in Delhi and at the Chishtiyya shrine in Ajmer, Rajasthan.

MODE OF DRESS Muslim men and women in India wear clothing similar to their Hindu counterparts. Muslims brought stitched garments to India and adapted them to local styles and materials. The *salwar kameez,* an outfit consisting of a long tunic and loose pants that taper to the ankle, originated in the Muslim courts and is now popular throughout India. Islamic dress for both men and women is based on principles of modesty. Many Muslim women in India cover their heads with a *hijab*, or headscarf. In families that observe purdah,

women wear a formless garment called a *burqa* when they go out. Some Muslim men wear skullcaps with intricate embroidery and raised patterns. Many styles of coats, cloaks, vests, shawls, handbags, and hand pouches have also been heavily influenced by Islamic designs. Tablighi Muslims in India follow dress codes consistent with Islamic law: men sport beards, wear simple robes, and avoid jewelry, and women cover their bodies completely.

DIETARY PRACTICES Muslims in India generally follow Islamic food laws. The consumption of pork and alcohol is forbidden. Unlike their Hindu counterparts Muslims usually eat in groups, a practice that reflects the Islamic emphasis on equality. Once in India the Moguls adapted the cooking styles they brought from Afghanistan and Persia. The resultant cuisine is called Mughlai, and it is one of the richest in India. In contrast to the Hindu preference for vegetarian foods, meat is a staple in Mughlai food.

RITUALS Muslims pray communally at mosques, but it is only recently that women in India have been allowed to do so. Women pray regularly at the Jama Masjid in Delhi and at some other mosques throughout India. The hajj, or pilgrimage to Mecca, is the quintessential Muslim ritual, and every Indian Muslim aspires to make this pilgrimage at least once. The Indian government provides subsidies for approximately 120,000 hajj pilgrims every year, and planes and ships are specially scheduled for the pilgrimage.

Sufi centers of pilgrimage attract large numbers of devotees. There is at least one major *dargah* housing the tomb of an important Sufi saint (*pir*) in every region of India. These sites tend to be centers of religious practice for Muslim women and are well known as sources of favors and healing. Pilgrims and devotees hang *kalawas,* or petitions for favors, on the walls or pillars of the shrine. They also commonly touch or kiss the tomb. Amulets that have been touched by the hand of a descendant of the saint or that have been placed on the tomb are sometimes distributed. The annual celebration of the *pir*'s death is a major event, sometimes lasting for several days. Fakirs, or Sufi mystics, often attend these rituals, and there are public demonstrations of self-mortification and spirit possession. Music and dance encourage a state of ecstasy in participating Sufi holy men (dervishes), who may become so entranced that they whirl in frenzy.

RITES OF PASSAGE Circumcision of male children between the ages of seven and twelve is the norm for Muslims in India, though the procedure varies from region to region. In most Muslim communities a doctor or surgeon performs the circumcision, and women are not permitted to observe. Indian Muslim marriages are generally arranged and consist of civil contracts signed by both sides. The marriage ceremony is simple, but it is preceded and followed by celebrations that can last several days. Divorce is allowed in Islam, but in India it is frowned upon.

Perhaps because sons are considered assets, the birth of a daughter is sometimes greeted with sadness. In many families a girl who has reached puberty is subject to certain restrictions and is gradually confined to the female section of the house, rarely leaving home unescorted. At marriage she moves to her husband's home, returning to her parent's home for the birth of her first child. Once she has produced a child, her status increases, especially if she gives birth to a son.

MEMBERSHIP Islamic communities in India are extremely diverse. The Muslim Mapillai communities of Kerala are the descendents of Arab traders who arrived in the eighth century; the Pathans trace their origins to Afghanistan; the Khojas belong to the community of Shiite Isma'ilis; and the Memons belong to the Sunni Hanafi tradition. Ahmadi Muslims accept the works of the Punjabi prophet Mirza Ghulam Qadiani (died in 1908). Islam is a proselytizing religion, and many Indians converted to Islam between the thirteenth and eighteenth centuries, when Islam was politically dominant. The number of converts—and the extent to which the conversions were forced—has recently been the subject of much debate in India. Many reform movements—including the Wahhabi movement, which came to India in the nineteenth century, and one of its variations, the Deoband school—have focused on establishing religious schools (*madrasas*) for Muslims in India. At about the same time leaders of the Tablighi movement began to teach mass gatherings (*jama'at*) of Muslims the details of orthodox religious practice.

SOCIAL JUSTICE Poverty, lack of education, and discrimination are major problems faced by Indian Muslims. India has job quotas for many groups, and the absence of such quotas for economically backward Muslims has been a point of contention. Education is a primary concern of the Muslim community in contemporary India. The literacy rate among Muslims is lower than the already low national average. Lack of education is especially acute among girls.

There are hundreds of Islamic religious training institutes (*madrasas*) in India. Aligarh Muslim University and Jamia Millia Islamia are the main Muslim institutions of higher education.

Although the Islamic faith stresses the equality of all believers, some Muslim communities have adopted a caste system. The two major castes are the elite Ashraf, who are considered to be descendants of either the Prophet's family or of immigrants from the Middle East, and the Ajlaf, who are descendants of local converts. Generally, these two groups do not intermarry or mix socially.

SOCIAL ASPECTS In many Muslim families early marriage for females is relatively common. From infancy through adolescence girls remain in their parental homes, but after marriage they move to their husband's homes. Women's status increases as they pass through the stages of daughter-in-law, mother, mother-in-law, and grandmother.

POLITICAL IMPACT Despite the fact that Muslims and Hindus in India have lived together for centuries, relations between them in modern India continue to be volatile at times, and communal violence has been on the rise. The polarization of India's relations with Pakistan since the 1990s has further fueled tensions between the two groups, and the strengthening of links between religion and politics in India since the late twentieth century has increased Muslim's sense of unease. Yet, despite the rise in communal tension—and even though their representation in parliament, the state legislatures, the civil service, and educational institutions does not reflect their numbers—many Muslims have confidence in the democratic tradition of the Indian state.

CONTROVERSIAL ISSUES Issues relating to Muslim Personal Law, which is based on the Islamic Shari'ah and protected by the Indian legal system, have been much disputed. The 1985 Shah Bano controversy illustrates this point. Shah Bano, an elderly Muslim woman, went to court when her husband divorced her but refused to pay alimony. The court ruled that even though separate civil law structures applied to Hindus and Muslims, all citizens should be treated equally. The following year, however, legislation was enacted removing

Muslim divorce cases from the review of Indian civil courts.

The practice of purdah is also controversial. Muslim purdah begins at puberty, and its purpose is to protect women from men outside the family. It separates women from the rest of society by means of veiling and the construction of separate living quarters for women, or zenana. Purdah is considered a sign of economic status, but it also entails restrictions upon women's education, health care, and economic status, and has made it difficult for Muslim women to engage in public political or economic activities.

CULTURAL IMPACT The Islamic influence on Indian music, art, architecture, and crafts is reflected in the blending of Persian and Afghani techniques and designs with indigenous ones. Muslims introduced abstract decorative ornamentation, geometric designs, calligraphy, new inlay techniques, glass engraving, enameling, carpet weaving, embroidery, damascening, miniature painting, and papiermâché. The Peacock Throne of the Moguls is one of the finest examples of gem inlay work and metal crafts. *Qawwali* (devotional songs) and *ghazals* (love songs) are two popular Muslim vocal forms that were brought to India from Persia. The classical Persian poetry of the Mogul court provided a foundation for Urdu literature.

Salman Rushdie (born in 1947) is famous both for his Booker Prize–winning novel, *Midnight's Children* (1981), and for the fatwa issued against him in 1989 by Ayatollah Ruhollah Khomeini of Iran following the publication of the novel *The Satanic Verses* (1989). Maqbool Fida Husain (born in 1915) is renowned for his sometimes controversial paintings. Among the most respected Muslim classical musicians in India are instrumentalists Zakir Hussain (born in 1951), Ali Akbar Khan (born in 1922), and Bismillah Khan (born in 1916).

Other Religions

Buddhists, Jains, Christians, and Sikhs—as well as small communities of Zoroastrians, Jews, and Bahais—lend a distinctive flavor to the religious composition of India. Although Buddhism is no longer a major religion in India, the country still contains pilgrimage sites that are important to Buddhists all over the world. These include Bodh Gaya, where Siddhartha Gautama attained enlightenment; Nalanda, the site of the famous Buddhist university that flourished from the fifth to the eleventh century C.E.; and Sanchi, with its monumental Buddhist stupas (dome-shaped shrines). The Mauryan emperor Asoka, who ruled almost all of India in the third century B.C.E., was a great patron of Buddhism. His rock and stone pillar inscriptions, proclaiming Buddhist teachings, are found throughout India.

Jainism, like Buddhism, arose in India in the sixth century B.C.E. In keeping with their dedication to nonviolence, Jains are strict vegetarians. Wheat, rice, lentils or pulses, beans, and oil-seeds are considered noninjurious foods, as are fruits and vegetables that ripen on plants or fall from the branches of trees. Respecting all life is a major principle of Jainism, and enterprises that improve the quality of life—like hospitals, schools, and animal care facilities—are funded by the Jain community throughout India.

Jains built temples and monoliths, and cut structures out of rock. Caves like the ones in Orissa were constructed to house Jain monks. Jain temples and temple complexes are characterized by lavish carvings in marble and granite. Among the most impressive of these are the massive Svetambara temple complex in the Satrunjaya hills near Palitana, Gujarat; the Ranakpur temple complex in Rajasthan; and Mount Abu in Rajasthan. The most famous Jain monolith is the Digambara shrine in Sravanabelgola, Karnataka. This massive nude sculpture of the Jain saint Gomateswara was built in the tenth century. Every 12 years, during the Mahamastakabhisheka ceremony, the statue is purified with tons of coconut milk, curd, bananas, milk, and saffron. Jain pilgrims from all over the world gather to witness the celebration.

Jews began arriving in India in the first century C.E., others fled the Arabian Peninsula in the seventh century, and still others arrived from other Middle Eastern countries in the eighteenth century. The three main Jewish groups in India are the Cochini, Bene Israel, and Baghdadi.

Zoroastrians, known as Parsis in India, arrived from Persia in the eighth century C.E. Fire is sacred to the Parsis, and it is classified according to grades. There are eight fires of the highest grade (Atash Behrams) in India, all in the states of Maharashtra and Gujarat. The most ancient of these, which according to tradition was transported from Persia, is located in the village of Udwada, a center of pilgrimage for Parsis. While a Fire Temple is a place for religious worship, a Tower of Silence (*dakh-*

ma) is a place where the dead are left to be devoured by vultures. In 1673 the British ceded land in the Malabar Hills of Bombay to the Parsi community for the establishment of their first Tower of Silence.

The first Christians in India, at least according to legend, were converted by the apostle Thomas on the Malabar coast in the first century C.E. The Nestorian Church, an ancient Christian church also known as the Persian, Assyrian, or East Syrian Church, has roots in India dating to the sixth or seventh century C.E. Beginning in the sixteenth century Christian missionaries from Europe converted Indians to Roman Catholicism and various denominations of Protestantism. Perhaps the most unique festival celebrated by Christians in India is the Goa Carnival. The rowdy celebrations that begin three days before Lent feature street plays, songs, dances, feasts, and processions. Each year someone is elected to lead the main parade as Momo, the king of the underworld.

Because Christianity is a proselytizing religion, and because Christian missions in India have had some appeal, particularly among the lower classes, it is sometimes viewed with suspicion. Although Christians account for only a small percentage of the population, anti-Christian violence has been on the rise in India. Some state governments have passed legislation banning conversions to non-Hindu religions. For example, in 2003 Tamil Nadu passed a bill banning conversions that are based on force, fraud, or allurement. Other states have passed similar legislation designed to prevent conversions to Buddhism, Islam, Christianity, and Sikhism, particularly mass conversions of disadvantaged groups, which are often political in nature.

Sikhism has had a significant impact on the history and public life of India. Most Sikhs live in the Punjab, and many of them have aspired to establish an independent homeland, Khalistan, there. In the early 1980s Sikh militants mounted a campaign for autonomy, and in 1984 Jarnail Singh Bhindranwale (1947–84) and his followers occupied the Golden Temple at Amritsar. Prime Minster Indira Gandhi ordered the Indian army into the temple. Gandhi's assassination by two of her Sikh security staff on 31 October 1984 brought in its wake heavy reprisals for the Sikhs. The rioting was especially acute in Delhi, where numerous Sikhs lost their lives.

Many Indian sites sacred to the Sikhs are associated with the lives of the founders and saints of Sikhism. Examples include Guru Gobind Singh's (1666–1708) birthplace in Patna; Keshgarh, Punjab, where Gobind Singh founded the Khalsa, an order of Sikkhism; and Hazur Sahib in Maharashtra, where he died. By far the most important Sikh holy site is the Golden Temple in Amritsar. The temple is built on the banks of a lake where Guru Nanak (1469–1539), the founder of Sikhism, lived for some time. The dominant features of the temple are its massive golden dome and the square of marble on which it stands. The Sikh sacred scripture, the Guru Granth Sahib, is set on a jewel-studded platform inside the temple.

Sikh celebrations at Amritsar are elaborate, involving large numbers of pilgrims and devotees. On Guru Nanak's birthday the Guru Granth Sahib is carried through the streets of Amritsar. Sikhs all over the Punjab erect roadside stalls offering sweetened milk to passersby in remembrance of the martyrdom of Guru Arjun, the fifth Sikh guru. Sikhs in India also celebrate the Hindu festival Diwali, illuminating their houses with candles and electric lights.

With slightly more than 1.5 million members, India's Bahai community is the largest in the world. The Lotus Temple in Delhi is a popular pilgrimage site for Bahais throughout the country. The Bahais are strong believers in education and have established many educational institutions in India.

Leona Anderson

See Also Vol. 1: *Buddhism, Hinduism, Islam, Jainism, Saivism, Sikhism, Vaishnavism, Zoroasterianism*

Bibliography

Ahmed, Akbar S. *Religion and Politics in Muslim Society: Order and Conflict in Pakistan.* Cambridge: Cambridge University Press, 1983.

Basham, A.L., ed. *A Cultural History of India.* 1975. Reprint. London: Oxford University Press, 1984.

Brown, Judith M. *Modern India: The Origins of an Asian Democracy.* 2nd ed. New York: Oxford University Press, 1994.

Hardy, Peter. *The Muslims of British India.* London: Cambridge University Press, 1972.

Hasan, Mushirul. *Legacy of a Divided Nation: India's Muslims since Independence.* Boulder, Colo.: Westview Press, 1997.

Hollister, John Norman. *The Shi'a of India.* 2nd ed. New Delhi: Oriental Books Reprint, 1979.

Khilnani, Sunil. *The Idea of India.* 1997. Reprint. London: Penguin Books, 2003.

Kinsley, David R. *Hinduism: A Cultural Perspective.* 2nd ed. Englewood Cliffs, N.J.: Prentice Hall, 1993.

Madan, T.N., ed. *Muslim Communities of South Asia: Culture, Society, and Power.* Rev. ed. New Delhi: Manohar, 1995.

Majumdar, Dhirendra Nath. *Races and Cultures of India.* 4th ed., rev. and enl. New York: Asia Publications, 1961 (reprinted 1973).

Rahman, Fazlur. *Islam.* London: Weidenfeld & Nicolson, 1967.

Richards, John F. *The Mughal Empire.* Cambridge: Cambridge University Press, 1993.

Schimmel, Annemarie. *Islam in the Indian Subcontinent.* Leiden: E.J. Brill, 1980.

————. *Mystical Dimensions of Islam.* Chapel Hill: University of North Carolina Press, 1975.

Indonesia

POPULATION 231,328,092

MUSLIM 88.8 percent

PROTESTANT 5 percent

CATHOLIC 2.9 percent

HINDU 2.4 percent

BUDDHIST 0.7 percent

OTHER 0.2 percent

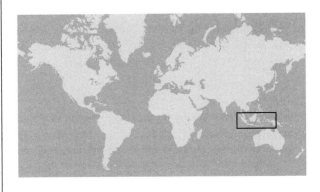

Country Overview

INTRODUCTION The Republic of Indonesia, located in Southeast Asia between the Pacific and Indian Oceans, is an archipelago of more than 13,000 islands, about 6,000 of which are inhabited. To the north is the Philippines, and to the south is Australia. Its people speak more than 200 languages, with Indonesian being the official national language. Java, the most populous island in the archipelago, is the principal locus of economic and political power. Formerly known as the Dutch East Indies, the islands were named Indonesia in 1884 C.E.

The country became independent from the Netherlands in 1945.

In Indonesia there are traces of ancestral cults and spirit worship dating back to the prehistoric Stone Age and Bronze Age. Such indigenous religions have shaped almost all later introduced religious beliefs and practices. Hinduism and Buddhism were taken to the islands beginning in the first or second century C.E. and were the dominant religions until the sixteenth century.

As early as the seventh century several Indonesian islands, especially Sumatra, were visited by Persian and Arabian traders, among them Zoroastrians, Nestorians, Christians, and Muslims. As Muslim traders settled in Indonesia, Islamic communities were established in the coastal areas. Sufi Muslim missionaries spread the religion to the rest of the region in the late fifteenth century, and it soon replaced Hinduism and Buddhism. Despite the presence of Christian traders—the Catholic Portuguese (in the fifteenth through sixteenth centuries) and the Protestant Dutch (in the seventeenth through twentieth centuries)—Islam has overwhelmed any competing religions up to the present day. The majority of Indonesia's population is Muslim.

Islamic practice in Indonesia is largely popular and nonlegalistic in nature, a characteristic often explained by the fact that the first Islamic religious teachers came from the Sufi, or mystical, tradition in Islam. Sufism has been notably compatible with the previous religious traditions of the indigenous Indonesians, including ancestor worship, Hinduism, and Buddhism.

RELIGIOUS TOLERANCE Officially the foundation of the Indonesian state and nation is based on a national ideology of *Pancha Sila,* the Five Principles. They are belief in one God; humanitarianism; national unity; democracy based on the people's sovereignty; and social justice. The 1945 constitution guarantees freedom of religion to every resident. The Indonesian government officially recognizes Islam, Protestantism, Catholicism, Hinduism, and Buddhism, observing most of the major holy days of these religions as national holidays.

Major Religion

ISLAM

DATE OF ORIGIN Eighth century C.E.
NUMBER OF FOLLOWERS 205.4 million

HISTORY Early in the eighth century C.E. Islam was taken to Indonesia by Persian and Arabian traders who landed on Indonesia's islands en route to India, Pakistan, and China. They established Muslim communities along the coasts, but the religion was not spread widely in the islands until the thirteenth century, when local rulers began to convert to facilitate trading.

In the late fifteenth century the Muslim settlers, in cooperation with the rulers, penetrated the hinterlands to promote Islam. Subsequently Islam was established and popularized mainly through the missionary work of the Wali Allah (friends of God), most of whom belonged to the Sufi tradition. The Nine Walis (Wali Sanga) in late-fifteenth-century Java, for example, were the first Muslim preachers who astutely adopted indigenous cultures, religious practices, and beliefs to draw people to Islam. By the early sixteenth century Islam—and its interrelated social, economic, and political life—had gained a wide influence among the Indonesian ruling classes. This facilitated the spread of Islam, because in Indonesia the ruler's religion was traditionally also the official religion for the ruled people.

Hinduism and Buddhism were superseded, although elements of these religions were incorporated into Islamic practices. Many regions have developed their own hybridized versions of Islam (a syncretism of indigenous, Hindu, and Islamic beliefs and practices), and this has contributed to the pluralism that exists in Indonesian Muslim society today. The popular Islam practiced by the Javanese people has been shaped by indigenous folklore, miracle stories, and myths that are not in accord with orthodox Islamic teachings.

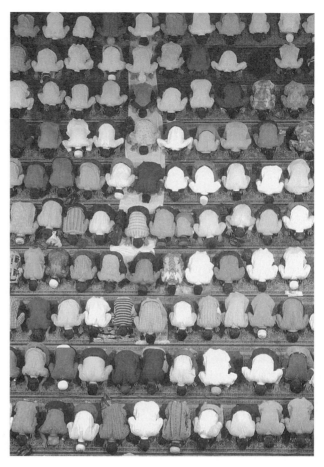

Muslim men bow toward Mecca during prayers at the Istiqlal Mosque in Indonesia. The Istiqlal Mosque is sacred to Muslims and is also one of the largest in Southeast Asia. AP/WIDE WORLD PHOTOS.

The Indonesian Muslim reform movement Muhammadiyah (Followers of Muhammad) was founded in 1912. It advocates reforming Islam by aligning it with the original Arabic religious sources and by attacking Islamic syncretism. In its first years it strongly opposed traditional Indonesian Islamic education as well as Dutch secular and Christian education. Early Muhammadiyah followers were mostly traders and urban people who promoted modern education, health services, and the adoption of Islamic religious law by Muslim communities. Today Muhammadiyah followers and supporters are usually urban, educated, and entrepreneurial.

The movement drew a strong reaction from the leaders of traditional Indonesian Islam, who in 1926 established Nahdatul Ulama (NU; literally "awakening of the religious teachers"), a conservative, rural-based organization. NU reformed its own traditional institutions, such as the *pesantren*s, Islamic boarding schools usually located in rural areas. The NU was usually tolerant of popular syncretistic Islamic practices, and its ulamas (*kyai*, or religious teachers) and *ummah* (the religious congregation) felt satisfied with its limited influence on political, economic, and social life. NU Muslims played a major role in the struggle for Indonesian independence. Nevertheless, when independence was proclaimed in 1945, the national leaders, led by Sukarno and Mohammad Hatta, formed the Republic of Indonesia based on a nationalist ideology rather than establishing an Islamic country (to avoid alienating Christians and practitioners of indigenous religions who were dominant in several areas outside Java). Retired army general Suharto became president in 1967, and for the next 30 years his New Order military regime attempted to maintain a delicate balance, acknowledging and in certain respects encouraging Islam's religious and cultural influence among the population while at the same time limiting its political influence.

Since independence certain radical Islamic parties in the parliament have often promoted the observance of Shari'ah (Islamic law) for all Indonesian Muslims, but such efforts have not been successful. Outside the NU and Muhammadiyah membership, a larger population of secular and "nominal" Indonesian Muslims has made it difficult for the Islamic political parties to win the support of the majority of Indonesians.

The JIL (Jaringan Islam Liberal, or Liberal Islamic Network) was founded in 2001. It has promoted alternative interpretations of Islamic teachings, directing them especially toward younger Indonesians. Its presence is part of the Indonesian Muslim intelligentsia's reaction to contemporary radical and fundamentalist Islamic movements.

EARLY AND MODERN LEADERS Ahmad Dahlan (1868–1923), who regarded the established Islamic community in Indonesia as syncretic and degenerate, founded the reform movement Muhammadiyah in 1912. He called for a return to the pristine teachings of the Koran and sunnah (the customs of Muhammad) and for modern *ijtihad* (independent interpretation through reasoning).

In 1984 Abdurrahman Wahid (also known as Gus Dur; born in 1940) became the head of the Muslim organization Nahdatul Ulama. He served as the fourth Indonesian president in 2000–01. A liberal, intellectual Islamic leader, Gus Dur firmly opposed Islamic radicals

or militants, espousing instead the idea that Islam must absorb modern methods, techniques, and knowledge.

MAJOR THEOLOGIANS AND AUTHORS Religious education, conducted through a system of *pesantren*s (Islamic boarding schools), has shaped the development of Islam in Indonesia. There are three distinctive components of a *pesantren*: students (*santri*), boarding facilities (*pondok*), and *kyai* (teachers). A *kyai* is the center not only of the *pesantren* but also of the community—religiously, intellectually, socioeconomically, and sometimes politically.

Certain *pesantren* graduates have gained public attention, especially among educated Muslims, for their promotion of Islamic reform. One such reformer, a voice of the new Islamic middle class in Indonesia, is the scholar and writer Nurcholish Madjid (born in 1939). Since the 1980s he has worked to develop a pluralistic interpretation of Islam, seeking to learn from the views of different sorts of Muslims as well as from adherents of other religions and secularists. His books include *Pembaharuan Pemikiran Islam* (1970; "Renewal of Islamic Thinking") and *Islam: Doktrin dan Peradaban* (1992; "Islam: Doctrines and Civilization").

HOUSES OF WORSHIP AND HOLY PLACES The tombs of regional Islamic saints—the beloved Sufi religious teachers who lived in and served local communities—are holy places, or shrines, for Sufi worship. In Java, for example, there are the graves of the Nine Walis (fifteenth and sixteenth centuries): Maulana Malik Ibrahim, Gunung Jati, Muria, Ampel, Drajad, Kudus, Kalijaga, Bonang, and Giri. Usually placed next to the local mosques, the tombs serve not only as places for official daily prayer but also as local gathering places and pilgrimage destinations. Because the shrines of Muslim saints also reflect political concerns and are related to notions of local power and hierarchy, many non-Muslims celebrate the birth or death anniversaries of various saints.

According to popular Islam in Indonesia, the completion of seven pilgrimages to the Demak mosque in Central Java, which is believed to have been built by one of the Nine Walis, is equal to making the hajj (pilgrimage to Mecca, one of the Five Pillars of Islam). The monumental marble Istiqlal Mosque (built in 1978) in Jakarta is also sacred to Muslims; it is one of the largest mosques in Southeast Asia.

WHAT IS SACRED? The Koran is the original and most sacred religious article for all Muslims. A calligraphic painting of the revealed Words is held to be visible sacred. Although such Islamic art is less common in Indonesia because of the people's unfamiliarity with Arabic literature, certain Sufis and other believers keep such articles to express that the calligraphic words themselves have been the manifestation of a spiritual feeling rather than just the vehicles of the literal meaning of the text.

HOLIDAYS AND FESTIVALS Indonesian Muslims observe annual celebrations based on the prophet Muhammad's life. The most important annual ritual celebrated by Indonesian Muslims, however, is Id al-Fitr (called Lebaran in Indonesian), the first day after the fasting month (Ramadan). During a weeklong Lebaran celebration, Muslims put on new clothes, visit relatives, neighbors, and friends, promote forgiveness, and exchange gifts—usually festive foods such as cookies and wrapped steamed rice. The week is also celebrated with fireworks and outdoor *dangdut* (Malay-Indian pop music) shows. Visiting relatives' tombs during Lebaran is an act of piety believed to earn God's reward in this world as well as on the Day of Judgment. Celebrating the *mawlid* (birthday of the prophet Muhammad) is also considered to merit a spiritual reward. Indonesian Muslims, mostly the peasantry, have developed their own idiosyncratic form of religious celebration as a way of maintaining their cultural identity.

MODE OF DRESS Since the 1990s significantly more young female Indonesian Muslims have begun wearing the *jilbab*, a scarf that covers the hair, neck, and chest. A modified veil, the *jilbab* is a highly visible symbol of Muslim identity in Indonesia and throughout the world. In Indonesia, however, women's "conversion" to proper Islamic clothing is understood as an act by which modern Muslim women signify personal identity and spiritual self-mastery—not as a sign of subjugation. It is believed that women will be able to apply this experience of spiritual autonomy in making other modern social, political, and cultural choices. In this context, donning the *jilbab* is imagined as a step toward the transformation of the society at large.

DIETARY PRACTICES Indonesian Muslims follow the general Muslim practices of fasting and observing prohibitions such as pork and alcohol. Moreover, in Indonesia (as in other Southeast Asian countries, India, and China), abstinence and asceticism are also ways to attain divine blessings, graces, or other spiritual favors. Consuming only water and plain rice on Monday and Thursday of certain weeks is practiced to receive spiritual favors and wishes.

RITUALS Because few Indonesian Muslims can afford to perform the hajj (pilgrimage to Mecca in Saudi Arabia), they regularly visit instead the tombs of regional Islamic saints. Many pilgrims bring offerings, such as incense, rice, flowers, and fruits, to the shrines. These offerings, which were common in the pre-Islamic traditions of Indonesia, are typical of popular religion, even while they contradict the conventions of orthodox Islamic ritual practice.

The syncretic nature of Islam in Indonesia is also reflected in the *slametan* (as it is called in Javanese) or *kenduri* (in Indonesian), a communal feast that incorporates the recitation of Islamic chants. The guests include community members and spirits, who come together in order to support the host. *Slametan,* which means asking for *selamat* (peace, safety), symbolizes the mystical and social unity of those participating in the ritual.

A person hosts a *slametan* with the hope that potential uncertainty, tension, and conflicts—which may result from events such as birth, house moving, or bad dreams—may be minimized. A *slametan* requires special food (coned steamed rice and its garnishes), incense, Islamic chants, and a formal speech by the host. The participants serve as witnesses that all kinds of invisible beings arrive and sit with the congregation. The spirits supposedly eat the offered food, its aroma in particular. What is left is distributed to the participants. That is why the food, and not the prayer, is the heart of the *slametan.*

RITES OF PASSAGE There are four main stages of the Indonesian life cycle: childhood, youth, maturity, and old age. Before and during childhood there are two popular Muslim rites. In the first seventh months of pregnancy, a rite is conducted to ask God's blessing for a safe birth. When a family's first child is seven months old, there is a ritual in which his or her feet are placed on the earth for the first time. This was originally an indigenous ritual, but the traditional understanding (introducing the baby to the Mother Earth) has been replaced by an Islamic interpretation (that the vulnerable child needs God's blessing and protection).

The rite of circumcision is performed when a boy—by his primary school graduation—leaves childhood and is acknowledged as both a young man and a Muslim. The boy thus enters the liminal period of youth, with a status of being "no longer a child and not the father of children yet." A *pesantren* (Islamic boarding school) has been considered the most suitable place for a young man or woman while he or she prepares for the maturity stage. By the end of their *pesantren* years the students are expected to be familiar with a mystical experience of tolerance (acknowledging the radical interdependence of all that exists). Thus, a graduate hopefully can transcend the potential contradictions and conflicts in daily life—in the plurality of religious traditions in particular.

MEMBERSHIP In general, organized proselytizing is rare among any of the religious communities in Indonesia. After quelling the 1965 Communist coup, the New Order military regime banned Communism and required every Indonesian citizen to subscribe to a religion. As a result, in the 1970s new converts to Islam were mostly former "atheists" (usually Communists) as well as indigenous tribal people.

Islamic missionary work focuses primarily on encouraging nominal or syncretic Indonesian Muslims to become faithful and devout believers who eat *halal* (pure) food and drink, wear proper Islamic dress, read Islamic books and magazines, and engage in regular public prayer. These practices are also encouraged by various vested-interest industries (local food and beverages companies that target their products specifically at Muslims living in urban areas).

SOCIAL JUSTICE In an effort to better serve the vast number of Indonesians, especially Muslims, who belong to the rural underclass, beginning in early 1980s many *pesantrens* were modified as multipurpose schools where *santri* (students) would be trained to become agents of social and economic development. The *kyai* (religious teachers) and other Muslim leaders wanted to assuage the common misperception—among *santri* as well as villagers—that modernization was merely an abandonment of traditional life in favor of a Western way of life and thinking. Thus, in an effort to promote self-reliance and sustainability in rural areas, the "modern" *pesantrens* began to teach the fundamentals of agro-economy and business (in addition to the high-school education and religious training they usually provided).

SOCIAL ASPECTS In Indonesia family networks may rely on a wide range of relationships—including extended family, relatives, neighbors, *kyai* (teachers at *pesantrens*), colleagues, and friends—as resources for handling the affairs of daily life. The husband-wife relationship in Indonesia is based on the traditional notion of *abang* (older brother) and *adik* (younger sister). This approach to the relationship, though hierarchical, implies tolerance and intimacy; it is thus seen as a means of preventing family estrangements such as polygamy and divorce, which are legally acknowledged in Islam.

POLITICAL IMPACT In general, Muslim leaders (such as *kyai* and Islamic political party chairpersons) in Indonesia recognize and avoid criticizing the established government, but they hope that policies will be favorable to the interests of the Muslim majority. Young, educated Muslims, concerned about the welfare of the lower strata of society, tend to advocate instead a bottom-up approach based on the promotion of sustainable growth. To this end, a nongovernmental organization called P3M (Perhimpunan Perkembangan Pesantren dan Masyarakat, or Association for the Development of Pesantren and Society) was established in 1983 as an adjunct to the official Nahdatul Ulama (NU) organization. P3M's main task is to coordinate and facilitate projects—including liberation education, small cooperative enterprises, small-scale rural industry, and legal aid—to support *pesantren*-based community development.

As Muslim nongovernmental organizations have multiplied, each has developed a specialized interest, such as public health, gender issues, and education about liberation and empowerment. Further, several groups have cooperated with and accepted aid from "other social and racial classes," including expatriate scholars and Chinese businesspeople. Some Indonesians interpret this cooperation as a public declaration that Islam is based on egalitarianism.

CONTROVERSIAL ISSUES In Indonesia issues regarding women have become a locus of important conflicts between Muslims and the state. Since the 1990s controversies over birth control, abortion, and divorce have threatened to disrupt the uneasy mutual accommodation between the state and the Islamic movement. Various Muslim women's nongovernmental organizations—such as Fattayat and Aisyah (the sister organizations of NU and Muhammadiyah, respectively)—have challenged government policies on these issues by promoting notions of responsible womanhood and empowering communities to solve their own problems. To increase awareness about these issues, Muslim women's groups have focused not only on disseminating knowledge but also on fostering a new feminine subjectivity—one in which individual women take responsibility for their own actions. Further, such organizations have participated in interfaith networks and forums with women of various religious backgrounds.

CULTURAL IMPACT Within the Indonesian (Javanese in particular) traditional performing arts the artistic medium of *wayang*, the leather puppet show, is most popular. The puppets are played in front of a lamp so that their shadows fall onto a screen, which is viewed from the other side. It is popularly believed that the first Muslim preachers in Java, the Wali Sanga, invented *wayang* theater and used it to propagate their faith. *Wayang* actually came from a long historical tradition of Malayo-Polynesian ancestral worship and was then adapted by Hindus. Most *wayang* stories are based upon the Indian epics (the Ramayana and Mahabharata) as well as on indigenous Indonesian myths. The Islamic versions tell stories about Amir Hamzah (or Menak), uncle of the prophet Muhammad.

Sufism in Islam influenced one of *wayang*'s meanings—namely, the mystical relationship between human beings and their creator, God. The Muslim use of *wayang* as a vehicle for religious propaganda and a source of morality and philosophy has led other religious groups, including Catholics and Protestants, to develop their own particular forms of *wayang*.

An important contemporary Indonesian voice is that of Ahmad Tohari (born in 1948), a fiction writer whose novels portray religious and political issues that resulted from the New Order military regime's exploitation of Islamic teachings and rituals from the late 1960s until 1998. His novels include *Ronggeng Dukuh Paruk* (1982; "Paruk Village Dancer") and *Bekisar Merah* (1993; "Red Wild Rooster").

Other Religions

Although Indonesia's government is officially secular and sympathetic to pluralism, non-Muslim Indonesians are well aware of their minority status. Christians, both Catholics and Protestants, live mostly on the islands of Flores, Timor, New Guinea (the Indonesian part is Papua), Celebes, Sumatra, Moluccas, and Borneo. On Java, the most developed and populous island in Indonesia, Christians account for only about 1 percent of the population.

Christianity was first taken to Indonesia in the sixteenth century by Portuguese Catholic missionaries. They were known for imbuing their pastoral work with an appreciation for local religious traditions. In the early seventeenth century the Netherlands established control over the islands' trade, and the Catholic missionaries were forced to leave. Protestantism was subsequently taken to Indonesia by a colonial coalition of Dutch merchants, missionaries, scientists, soldiers, and government officials. The Dutch Reformed Church was the main form of Christianity in Indonesia for the following three centuries. When they began their work, Christian missionaries usually provided schools, hospitals, and other social economic activities as a means of proselytizing to the natives.

Since 1945, when Indonesia gained independence, Indonesian Christians—both Catholics and Protestants—have participated wholeheartedly in various national modern development programs. There has been a growing number of indigenous religious ministers and native Catholic bishops.

During the celebration of Holy Week and Easter, Indonesian Christians participate in various rituals that often combine modern, traditional, imported, and indigenous forms. These may vary from church to church. In Toba Batakland, North Sumatra, the traditional practice of performing sacred dances and chanting lamentation poems is added to the Good Friday celebration. Christmas is celebrated with festive talent shows and by exchanges of forgiveness, even between Christians and their non-Christian relatives, neighbors, and friends. Indonesian Catholics and Protestants have adapted *wayang* (puppet theater) to their religion, making the stories about biblical heroes.

For Catholics in Indonesia, May and October (the beginning and the end, respectively, of the dry season in most areas) are dedicated to the Virgin Mary. Although her apparition has never been sighted in Indonesia, pilgrims travel to several shrines of the Virgin throughout the archipelago, seeking comfort and assistance for typical family problems. The pilgrimage and procession ritual are also attended by non-Christians. The shrine of Sendang Sono, in Central Java, is considered the oldest and highest-ranked Marian shrine (shrine dedicated to Mary) in Indonesia.

In 1995 the Conference of Indonesian Catholic Bishops established a crisis center in Jakarta and a network of offices in cities throughout the archipelago. Other religions have participated in the center's activities. The center also deals with urgent events caused by natural disasters or ethnic and religious conflicts.

Through trade contacts with India, Hinduism and Buddhism were adapted beginning in the first century C.E. by several coastal as well as inland kingdoms. Adaptation occurred because the worship of various Hindu or Buddhist deities was considered similar to practices of indigenous ancestral cults, which included the veneration of deceased kings. There was a constant movement of priests, monks, and pilgrims between Indonesia and other centers of Hinduism and Buddhism in India, Southeast Asia, and China. By the sixth century they had become the dominant religions in the islands, and they remained so until the sixteenth century, when Islam largely supplanted them.

The influence of Hinduism and Buddhism are seen in their great sanctuaries, such as Prambanan Temple (a Hindu temple to Siva built in the tenth century) and Borobudur (a Buddhist monument built in the eighth or ninth century) in Central Java. Because of the Islamization of important Javanese kingdoms in the sixteenth century, most Hindus moved to Bali.

Hinduism in Indonesia is shaped by notions of hierarchical status of Indian origin, but its polarity of divine and demonic matter is typically indigenous. Indonesian Hindus believe that beauty is the attribute of gods, princes, and higher human beings; ordinary human beings and other lower creatures have cruder features and behaviors. The Indonesian Hindus, most of whom are Balinese, have seen the world as being populated by this variety of creatures, each with their allotted place in the universe. In general, Balinese Hindu practice is devoted to keeping those forces and beings in their place through personal and communal ritual acts of offerings. In a certain sense, ritual, performance, and art are more central than theology in Balinese Hinduism.

The indigenous religion—as it is defined, for example, in the context of shamanism—has continued to be practiced in various ways in Indonesia. A central belief is that, through his or her original ancestor, a shaman (curer) has access to a supernatural power and its related matters in human daily life. The indigenous religious practices are based on a belief that a spirit outside the shaman takes possession of him or her and that he or she thereafter operates only when motivated by the spirit. Contemporary ministers or other religious leaders in Indonesia (including Buddhist, Hindu, Catholic, Protestant, and Muslim) are also appreciated by their congregation as "shamanistic" persons.

Budi Susanto

See Also Vol. 1: *Islam*

Bibliography

Anderson, Benedict. *Language and Power: Exploring Political Cultures in Indonesia.* Ithaca, N.Y.: Cornell University Press, 1990.

Atkinson, Jane Monnig. *The Art and Politics of Wana Shamanship.* Berkeley: University of California Press, 1989.

Brenner, Suzanne. "Reconstructing Self and Society: Javanese Muslim Women and 'the Veil.'" *American Ethnologist* 23, no. 4 (1996): 673–97.

Fox, James J., ed. *Religion and Ritual.* Vol. 9 of *Indonesian Heritage.* Singapore: Archipelago Press, 1998.

Geertz, Clifford. *The Religion of Java.* Chicago: University of Chicago Press, 1960.

Hefner, Robert. *Hindu Javanese: Tengger Tradition and Islam.* Princeton, N.J.: Princeton University Press, 1985.

Holt, Claire. *Art In Indonesia: Continuities And Change.* Ithaca, N.Y.: Cornell University Press, 1976.

Keeler, Ward. *Javanese Shadow Plays, Javanese Selves.* Princeton, N.J.: Princeton University Press, 1987.

Lombard, Denys. *Nusa Jawa: Silang Budaya.* Jakarta: Gramedia, 1996.

Metcalf, Peter. *A Borneo Journey into Death: Berawan Eschatology from Its Rituals.* Philadelphia: University of Pennsylvania Press, 1982.

Rodgers, Susan, and Rita Kipp, eds. *Indonesian Religions in Transition.* Tucson: University of Arizona Press, 1987.

Siegel, James T. *The Rope of God.* Ann Arbor: University of Michigan Press, 2000.

Volkman, Toby Alice. *Feasts of Honor: Ritual and Change in the Toraja Highlands.* Urbana: University of Illinois Press, 1985.

Iran

POPULATION 66,622,704
SHIITE MUSLIM 91 percent
SUNNI MUSLIM 7.8 percent
OTHER 1.2 percent

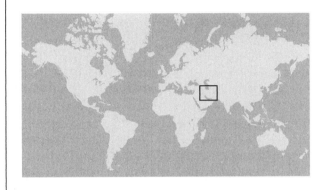

Country Overview

INTRODUCTION The Islamic Republic of Iran is a country in southwestern Asia. It is bordered on the east by Afghanistan and Pakistan, on the south by the Persian Gulf and the Gulf of Oman, on the west by Iraq and Turkey, and on the north by Armenia, Azerbaijan, the Caspian Sea, and Turkmenistan. Iran is located on a plateau that is ringed by mountains. Much of the country is dry, and more than half is wasteland. There are important oil deposits, especially in the southwest. The capital is Tehran. The official language is Persian (Farsi).

Iran (Persia) is an ancient land, with a rich historical and religious background. It was the birthplace of Zoroastrianism, and throughout history it has been a host to several religions. Iran's religious mosaic is reflected in the diversity of its religious monuments. These include the remains of prehistoric temples of Anahita, a goddess of fertility, in the provinces of Kerman, Fars, and Kermanshah; the remnants of Zoroastrian pilgrimage sites and fire temples, as well as those still active in Yazd and Kerman; a shrine in the city of Shush dedicated to the biblical prophet Daniel; the many historic Christian churches in the provinces of Azerbaijan and Esfahan; and several Islamic monuments.

Islam was introduced to the region in the seventh century C.E., during the first wave of the Arabic Islamic conquests. It took more than a century, however, for the majority of the population to embrace Islam. Throughout the formative years of Islamic civilization, Iranian culture played a significant role in its development, first by sharing its rich experience in administration and institution building and later by producing a number of outstanding Muslim scholars, philosophers, scientists, mystics, and poets, among them such figures as al-Farabi, Ibn Sina (Avicenna), al-Ghazali, al-Razi (Rhazes), and Rumi. Shiism, the branch of Islam holding to hereditary succession from Ali (the cousin and son-in-law of Muhammad and the fourth caliph), became the official religion of Iran in the sixteenth century, during the reign of the Safavid dynasty. The particular sect practiced in Iran is known as Twelver Shiism, based on belief in the succession of 12 imams (leaders) beginning with Ali. Today Iran is the only country in the world with Shiah Islam as its official religion. Other religions practiced in Iran include Christianity (mostly Armenian), Judaism, and Zoroastrianism, as well as the Bahai faith, which originated in Iran.

Iranian men prepare vegetable soup on the first day of the holy month of Ramadan. As with Muslims elsewhere, Shiites in Iran observe the Five Pillars of Islam, and they fast during the month of Ramadan. AP/WIDE WORLD PHOTOS.

RELIGIOUS TOLERANCE According to Islamic law, People of the Book—Jews, Christians, and Zoroastrians—are held to be protected minorities, with a degree of religious and legal autonomy. On the other hand, the Bahai movement, from its birth as an offshoot of Shiism to its later phase, when it declared itself an independent religion, has been outlawed in Iran, and except for a short period in the 1970s its followers have often been persecuted.

Both the 1911 and 1979 constitutions of Iran recognized religious and cultural autonomy for religious minorities, but these rights have not always been free of restraint. The restrictions, however, have varied from period to period, locality to locality, and issue to issue. Although freedom of religion is granted, for example, proselytizing is forbidden, and Christian churches are not allowed to accept Muslims in their congregations.

When appearing in public, women of religious minorities are required to observe the same dress code as Muslim women. Under the Islamic republic, Jews have faced difficult times, largely because of the anti-Zionist and anti-Israeli policies of the government.

Major Religion

SHIA ISLAM

DATE OF ORIGIN Seventh century C.E.
NUMBER OF FOLLOWERS 61 million

HISTORY From the first century of the Islamic calendar (the seventh century C.E.), adherents of Shiism lived as a minority in parts of Islamic Persia. Shiism may still have been in a minority when the earliest Shiite dynasties ruled areas of Persia. The strongest of these was the Buyid dynasty (945–1055), which governed the northern provinces along the coast of the Caspian Sea. Although the Buyids dominated the Sunni Abbasid caliphate in Baghdad, they did not officially overthrow the Abbasids but preferred to rule by manipulating the caliph. It was not until the sixteenth century that Shiism was adopted and promoted by the Safavid dynasty as the official religion.

Under Safavid patronage there began a systematic effort to develop the Shiite tradition. The Safavid monarchs invited leading Shiite scholars from Lebanon and Iraq and established major religious educational centers in Esfahan, their capital city. There, under the auspices of the Safavid court, a major school of philosophy flourished. This school was significant in maintaining the continuity of Islamic philosophy after it had gone into abeyance in other parts of the Muslim world. Also in Esfahan, major works of Shiite theology, as well as collections of the imam's sayings (*ahadith*), were produced. At the same time extensive building programs were carried out at the shrines of the Shiite imams both in Iran and Iraq, while influential *madrasahs* (theological schools) were constructed, among the best known being the Madrasah Chahar Bagh in Esfahan.

The nineteenth century saw two important events. One was the emergence of the Babi movement, an offshoot of Shiism that gradually distanced itself from Islam and developed into a new religion, the Bahai faith. The second was a confrontation between two schools of thought in jurisprudence, which ultimately gave rise to the institution of the *marja al-taqlid* (source of emulation) and to the ayatollah as the highest rank in the Shiite clergy and the highest religious authority. Throughout the eighteenth and nineteenth centuries the Shiite authorities lived mostly in Iraq, but early in the twentieth century the city of Qom in Iran became prominent as a center for their work. Ayatollah Hairi Yazdi, who resided there, reorganized its seminary, and since then Qom has functioned as one of the most important centers of Shiite education.

The significance of Qom's religious circle increased after the 1979 revolution, when the Shiite clergy assumed an extraordinarily important role in the Iranian government. This unprecedented involvement of Shiite authorities in politics occurred after Ayatollah Ruholla Khomeini had developed his theory of *vilayat-e faqih* (guardianship of jurists) in the early 1970s. According to this theory, which became the cornerstone of the constitution of the Islamic republic, political authority in the absence of the Twelfth Imam (who has been in concealment since 878 and will not return until the end of time) is the prerogative of Shiite jurists.

EARLY AND MODERN LEADERS There were a number of twentieth-century ayatollahs prominent in Iranian Shiiism. They included Akhund Khorasani and Naini, who played leading roles in the revolution of 1906–11 that established a constitutional government; Hairi Yazdi and Boroujerdi, the most important *marja*s of the century, whose educational contributions consolidated the position of the religious seminaries of Qom; and Ruholla Khomeini, who led the 1979 revolution and established the Islamic republic. Although in the West his name is most often associated with politics, Khomeini was among the most prominent Shiite scholars and *marja*s of the century. A jurist and mystic, he taught in the Shiite seminaries of Iraq during his exile in the 1960s and 1970s.

Among nonclerical figures who have made important contributions to modern developments in Shiite Islam, two prominent Iranian intellectuals may be singled out. The first of these is Ali Shariati, a sociologist whose innovative political interpretation of Shiite Islam became the religious ideology of the 1979 revolution. Translations of his work continue to inspire young Muslims outside Iran. The second is Abdolkarim Soroush, a postrevolutionary philosopher whose theories have challenged traditional interpretations of Islam and the rule of the clergy. His ideas have provided the intellectual basis for a reform movement in Iran directed at making religion less ideological and political.

MAJOR THEOLOGIANS AND AUTHORS The majority of the theologians and scholars of classical Shiism were of Iranian origin. Some, like Ibn Babuyah and Allameh Majlesi, lived and are buried in Iran, and their tombs are visited by many. The most celebrated Shiite scholar of modern times was Ayatollah Muhammad Hussein Tabatabai (died in 1980), an Iranian jurist, philosopher, and mystic who devoted his life to learning and teaching. His best-known work, *Tafsir al-Mizan,* is a voluminous exegesis that remains one of the most authoritative Shiite interpretations of the Koran in modern times. Ayatollah Murtada Mutahhari (died in 1979), Tabatabai's disciple, was another prolific and well-known scholar. During the 1970s, when the Iranian intellectual milieu was filled with Western liberal and Marxist ideologies, Mutahhari's works, written in simple and nontechnical Persian, served to defend and popularize basic principles and issues of Islamic theology and philosophy.

HOUSES OF WORSHIP AND HOLY PLACES There are a number of historic mosques in Iran. The Jame (Grand) mosques in Kerman, Yazd, and Tabriz and the Goharshad Mosque in Mashhad are among the best known. Esfahan, one of 10 cities designated by the United Nations Educational, Scientific and Cultural Organization (UNESCO) as a World Heritage Site, contains some of the oldest Islamic monuments. They include the Jame Mosque, built during the tenth and eleventh centuries, and the Royal Square, built by the Safavids. The two great mosques known as the Shah and Shaykh Lotfollah, built in the late sixteenth and early seventeenth centuries, face the square.

There are a number of Shiite holy sites in Iran. Among them are two shrines that attract millions of pilgrims from Iran and other countries throughout the world. These are the shrine of the eighth imam, Hazrat-e Reza, located in Mashhad, and the shrine of Imam Reza's sister, Hazrat-e Masumeh, in Qom. Throughout Iran there are also a number of minor shrines, known as Imamzadeh, attributed to one or another of the descendants of Shiite imams. Imamzadehs are usually popular pilgrimage destinations for local populations. Three of these shrines, however, are particularly well known: Shahzadeh Abdulazim in Ray, south of Tehran; Shah-e Cheraq, in Shiraz; and Shah Reza, near Esfahan. In the desert outside Qom is the region known as Jamkaran. The Twelfth Imam, who is believed to be in occultation (concealment), has reportedly been seen in the region. Thus, some devotees of the Twelfth Imam consider Jamkaran a holy area, and every week large crowds visit the region. They hold prayer ceremonies and night vigils, hoping that they may see him again or at least receive blessings from his spiritual presence.

WHAT IS SACRED? Iranian Shiites, like those elsewhere, venerate relics of the imams and their descendants. One of the most common holy items for a devout Iranian Shiite is a small piece of cloth, usually green in color, taken from the cover that drapes Imam Reza's tomb. This is a symbolic object that carries with it the blessings of the imam.

HOLIDAYS AND FESTIVALS Many of the major religious holidays and festivals in Iran are the same as those of other Muslim countries. Some, however, are unique to Shiite communities. The latter include commemoration of the martyrdom in 680 of Hussein, Ali's son and the grandson of Muhammad, by Sunni forces in the Battle of Karbala in Iraq. The event is remembered in Iran with a 10-day period of mourning in the month of Muharram that includes passion plays and public self-flagellation. In addition, Shiites hold a feast called Id al-Ghadir that commemorates the Prophet's designation of Ali as his legatee and successor at Ghadir-e Khomm. The birthday of the Twelfth Imam is celebrated as a joyous occasion in the month of Shaban.

There are also Iranian national festivals, including Jashn-e Mehregan, a feast of thanksgiving at the autumn equinox, and Naw Rouz, a New Year celebration. Both have religious elements, and although the holidays are of Zoroastrian origin, they were continued after the arrival of Islam. Naw Rouz, which falls on the first day of spring, includes Zoroastrian customs such as setting up a special table called Haft Sin (Seven Sins). The Haft Sin has seven flowers, fruits, and herbs whose names begin with the letter *s* (*sin*). In Muslim families the Haft Sin includes a copy of the Koran, and Islamic prayers are said at the table. Prior to Naw Rouz, on the last Wednesday of the year, there is a public celebration of Zoroastrian origin called Chahar Shanbeh Suri. On this occasion people jump over bonfires while repeating a mantra that is believed to empty them of all distress as they gain energy and life from the fires. Such practices, although they are considered heretical by some Mus-

lims, particularly outside Iran, are commonly accepted parts of the national culture and are not seen as violating Islamic doctrines or law.

MODE OF DRESS The traditional form of *hijab* (veil) among urban Shiite women in Iran has been the black chador, a loose covering from head to toe that is held by one hand under the chin and wrapped tightly around, but not covering, the face. Among some provincial and rural women the chador has taken on a variety of colors and forms. Following the 1979 revolution, the government enforced a dress code that requires all women wear the *hijab* in public. Men are expected to dress modestly in public.

The clergy are distinguished from laypersons by their dress, which includes a long gown (*aba*) and either a black or a white turban (*ammamah*). A black turban indicates that the person is a sayyid—that is, one who claims genealogical ties to a descendant of the Prophet Muhammad.

DIETARY PRACTICES Shiite Muslims in Iran follow Islamic dietary regulations, such as abstaining from pork and alcohol. Otherwise, there are no particular dietary restrictions related to Shiism.

RITUALS As with Muslims elsewhere, Shiites in Iran observe the Five Pillars of Islam, and they fast during the month of Ramadan. If possible, during his or her lifetime each Shiite makes the *hajj*, the pilgrimage to Mecca. Shiites also make pilgrimages to the shrines of imams, particularly to that of Hazrat-e Reza in Mashhad. The *sufreh* (table), a thanksgiving ritual at which female clergy recite special prayers, is popular among women.

RITES OF PASSAGE Among Shiites in Iran it is the custom for the family to hold a party to celebrate a newborn. This usually occurs around 10 days after birth, when the baby is given a name. Family and friends bring gifts.

In the twentieth century it became popular to hold a special celebration, Jashn-e Ibadat (Celebration of Worship), for girls entering the age of puberty, who from that point on are expected to observe religious commandments. At the ceremony, usually an all-female gathering, the girl says her prayers in public and recites passages from the Koran. This is followed by a gift shower, at which the girl receives an embroidered head covering and a prayer mat. There is a parallel ceremony for boys, although celebrations for boys are traditionally held on the occasion of circumcision.

The traditional marriage ceremony lasted from three to seven days, with large gatherings and parties at the houses of both the bride and the groom. In modern times, however, this has been shortened. It begins with a small gathering at the home of the bride, where the wedding is officiated by a clergy. A reception is held in a hotel or a public hall or private house.

There are at least three gatherings of mourning with the family of a deceased person. They are held on the third, seventh, and fortieth days after death, and another gathering is held on the first anniversary of the death. The mourning family wears black for at least a few months.

MEMBERSHIP The majority of Iranians are Shiites by birth, but conversion of people from other religions has always been welcome. In the 1950s and 1960s some Shiite clergy and religious centers established organizations for promoting the religion. Rather than aiming to proselytize non-Muslims, however, they concentrated their efforts toward strengthening the faith of the young against Bahai teachings and against the spread of secular ideologies. After the 1979 revolution the Sazman-e Tablighat-e Islami (Organization for Islamic Propaganda) was established as an official institution for promoting Islamic ideology both inside and outside Iran.

SOCIAL JUSTICE Shiite ideals of a just society and a just ruler were among the strongest sources of inspiration for the two revolutions of modern Iran, those of 1906–11 and of 1979. Social welfare has long been the province of the Shiite ulamas (religious scholars), who, as the recipients of religious taxes, have been responsible for distributing funds to the needy. Since the 1979 revolution the Kumiteh-e Imdad-e Imam Khomeini (Imam Khomeini's Aid and Relief Committee), a nongovernmental organization, has collected charity donations nationwide for relief projects, health care, and housing for the underprivileged. Iran's holy shrines, particularly that of Imam Reza, have enormous endowments that operate charitable foundations specifically designated to help the poor. Throughout the country a large number of popular societies and orphanages are run in the names of various imams. The societies constitute a wide network of nongovernmental charitable organizations that provide, among other assistance, no-interest loans for such purposes as marriage, buying a house, and education.

SOCIAL ASPECTS The requirements and constraints of modern life have dictated a different ethic of social relations than those of traditional life. Nevertheless, in Iran the family continues to constitute the most important social unit of society. Marriage, a tradition encouraged by the Prophet Muhammad, is considered to be a holy bond. Children are treasured, and the elderly are generally taken care of within the extended family.

Although families seek compatible marriage partners for their children, and while their views may affect the final choice, there are no arranged marriages as such in contemporary Iran. Polygamy, once outlawed, was reintroduced with minor restrictions after the 1979 revolution. The practice of *mutah,* temporary marriage for a period agreed to by the couple, is allowed in Shiite law and practiced by some. Polygamy and *mutah* carry social stigmas, however, and are not widespread. Divorce continues to be based on Islamic law, although efforts by women's rights organizations have resulted in changes. Among these are custody rights for mothers in special cases and greater financial support for wives after divorce.

POLITICAL IMPACT Iran is a distinctly Muslim country, with Shiism constituting one of the central components of national identity and culture. Iran's distinction as a Shiite nation, however, has sometimes produced isolation, if not hostility, from its Sunni Muslim neighbors. Nonetheless, its large Muslim population, rich oil resources, and strategic location in the Middle East make Iran an undeniable force in regional and global politics.

Since the establishment of the Islamic republic in 1979, Shiite clerics have exercised an unprecedented role in Iranian politics under the system of government known as *vilayat-e faqih* (guardianship of jurists), a form of theocracy. Beginning in the mid-1990s there developed a reform movement aimed at reducing the power of the conservative ruling clergy and at implementing a more moderate version of Islam in politics and society.

CONTROVERSIAL ISSUES Especially since the beginning of the twentieth century, Iranian women have been socially and politically active. During certain periods in Iranian history, religion has not only not restricted women but also has inspired them to take an active role in events, as in the revolutions of 1906–11 and 1979. Nevertheless, progress in the development of women's rights has been neither swift nor fundamental. There are various reasons for this, some cultural, some political, some religious, and some involving the regional situation of women in general.

Under the secular modernization of the Pahlavi regime (1926–79), the status of women in Iran improved to an unprecedented degree. With the advent of the Islamic republic, however, there came a backlash, and a number of social and legal restraints were reimposed. Yet Iranian women have continued the attempt to attain greater social recognition and legal rights. There are a number of women in parliament and among senior government bureaucrats. There are also a number of women's organizations and women's rights groups. Indeed, activists for women's rights, so-called Islamic feminists, represent one of the strongest religio-political forces in the country pushing for democratic reforms.

The lawyer Shirin Ebadi won the Noble Peace Prize in 2003. She was cited particularly for her efforts to improve the rights of women and children and for representing dissidents against the government.

While abortion is considered a sin by Shiites and is legally banned in Iran, it is permitted in the event that the mother's life is endangered. Several methods of birth control are legally available to Iranian couples.

CULTURAL IMPACT Before the advent of film and television, and long before the adoption of Western-style theaters, *taziyah*s (religious passion plays) were the only popular form of performance art in Iran. The *taziyah*s reenacted the events of the Battle of Karbala, in which the Imam Hussein and his family were martyred. Traditional music and literature in Iran are highly influenced by religious and mystical themes and by the rhetoric of love, ecstasy, and sacrifice for the sake of the beloved.

Work on holy shrines and mosques has attracted the best Iranian artisans, who have made these sites masterpieces of architecture. Mosques are distinguished by their large round domes and by two high minarets that are decorated with Persian designs made of blue tiles. Iranian artists excel in the painting of miniatures, in calligraphy, and in work in gold, silver, and glass.

Other Religions

Sunni Muslims, Christians, Jews, and Zoroastrians are officially recognized minorities in Iran. The Bahais living in Iran do not have legal status.

Sunni Muslims in Iran are mainly associated with ethnic groups concentrated in the provinces of Kurdistan (northwest), Sistan and Baluchistan (southeast), and Khuzistan (southwest). The constitution of Iran recognizes the main four Sunni schools of law, and Sunni Muslims have the right to perform their religious rites and practice their own canons.

As People of the Book, Christians, Jews, and Zoroastrians are recognized as protected religious minorities. Since the seventh century, when Islam became the official religion of Persia, these religious groups have lived in Iran according to the regulations set by Islamic law. The Iranian constitutions of 1911 and 1979 recognized the religious and cultural autonomy of these minorities and granted them the right to be represented in the national parliament by a proportional number of elected deputies.

The Christian community, which is the largest of these minorities but which makes up less than 1 percent of the population, is spread throughout the country, but its members are mostly concentrated in the cities of Esfahan, Tehran, Urmia, Tabriz, and Ahvaz. Iranian Christians are divided along several ethnic and confessional groups, such as Armenian, Assyrian, and Chaldean, each with various denominations that include Apostolic, Roman Catholic, Protestant, and Russian Orthodox.

Armenians constitute the largest Christian population, and probably the largest non-Muslim community, in Iran. The presence of the Armenian population dates to the early seventeenth century, when Shah Abbas, the Safavid monarch, transferred large groups of people from Armenia to Iran for political and economic reasons. They were settled in Julfa, on the outskirts of Esfahan, where they rebuilt their community and contributed enormously to Iranian culture and industry. Some of their oldest churches in Julfa, such as Vank and Bethlehem, are among the most frequently visited historical monuments.

The presence of Jews in Persian territory dates at least as early as the fourth century B.C.E., when Cyrus the Great conquered the Babylonian empire. While maintaining a distinctive identity throughout the centuries, Jews have participated in various aspects of Iranian life, particularly in business and trade. The Jewish population is concentrated mainly in Tehran and in the cities of Shiraz, Hamadan, and Esfahan.

Persia was the birthplace of Zoroastrianism, an ancient religion named for the prophet Zoroaster (Zarathushtra), who is believed to have lived between 1800 and 1000 B.C.E. in what is today northeastern Iran. From 559 B.C.E. to 642 C.E., Zoroastrianism was the official religion of three Persian empires: the Achaemenian, Parthian, and Sasanian. After the Muslim Arab conquest of Persia in the middle of the seventh century, Zoroastrianism gradually lost its dominance. Today Zoroastrians in Iran are concentrated in the cities of Tehran, Yazd, Kerman, Esfahan, Shiraz, Zahedan, and Ahvaz, where centers of worship are located. In Yazd there is an Atesh-e Behram, a fire temple of the highest level of sanctity, and there are a number of fire temples with varying degrees of sanctity in other cities.

All of the legally recognized religious minorities in Iran have associations that take care of the general affairs of their communities. These include such bodies as social and sporting clubs, publishing enterprises, and private schools, all of which provide venues for protecting and promoting cultural distinctiveness and communal life. Personal and family matters, such as marriage, divorce, the custody of children, and inheritance, are dealt with by committees under the supervision of the religious authorities of each community. The rulings of these committees then go to a civil court for official approval.

Because these religions have long existed in Iran, they have had a considerable impact on Iranian life and culture. The most significant impact, however, has come from Zoroastrianism, evident particularly in the country's national holidays. Through ancient myths and epics, Zoroastrian ideas and characters have found their way into Iranian literature and art, and some Zoroastrian concepts appear in Muslim ethical, philosophical, and mystical discourse. It is a well-accepted tradition for Iranian Muslims to name their children after figures in Zoroastrian mythology.

Bahais are the only nonrecognized religious minority in Iran. As such, adherents of the Bahai faith do not enjoy constitutional rights. There are both political and religious reasons for this situation. Since the religion's origin in the nineteenth century, there have been political allegations made against Bahais, including association with foreign powers. In the nineteenth century, for example, Bahais were charged with being agents of British imperialism. Since the mid-twentieth century they have been linked with the United States and with Zionism, charges that resulted from the support and protection Bahais received during the 1970s under Mohammad Reza Shah, the last Pahlavi monarch. A more important motivation for outlawing the Bahai tradition in Iran, however, has been religious. The Bahai belief in continuing revelations, in an open-ended succession of manifestations of God through prophets (including Bahaullah, the founder of the tradition), contradicts one of the fundamental beliefs of Islam: that Muhammad was the final prophet. Thus, the public persecution and even executions of Bahais have always been justified by charges of heresy and apostasy. Nonetheless, the Bahai faith has found both rural and urban followers inside Iran.

Forough Jahanbakhsh

See Also Vol. 1: *Islam, Shia Islam*

Bibliography

Akhavi, Shahrough. *Religion and Politics in Contemporary Iran.* Albany: State University of New York Press, 1980.

Arjomand, Said Amir. *The Turban for the Crown.* New York: Oxford University Press, 1988.

Cole, Juan. *Modernity and the Millennium: The Genesis of the Baha'i Faith in the Nineteenth-Century Middle East.* New York: Columbia University Press, 1998.

Iran Yearbook. Bonn: MB, Medien and Bücher, 1981.

Kamalkhani, Zahra. *Women's Islam: Religious Practice among Women in Today's Iran.* New York: Kegan Paul, 1998.

Malandra, William W., ed. *An Introduction to Ancient Iranian Religion: Readings from the Avesta and Achaemenid Inscriptions.* Minneapolis: University of Minneapolis Press, 1983.

Momen, Mohan. *An Introduction to Shi'i Islam.* New Haven: Yale University Press, 1987.

Netzer, Amnon. "Anjoman-e Kalimian." In *Encyclopaedia Iranica.* Edited by Ehsan Yarshater. Vol. 2. London: Routledge and Kegan Paul, 1983–90.

Sanasarian, Eliz. *Religious Minorities in Iran.* Cambridge: Cambridge University Press, 2000.

Schwartz, Richard Merrill. *The Structure of Christian-Muslim Relations in Contemporary Iran.* Halifax: Saint Mary's University, 1985.

Shahrokh, Shahrokh, and Rashna Writer, eds. and trans. *The Memoirs of Keikhosrow Shahrokh.* Lewiston, N.Y.: Edwin Mellen Press, 1994.

Shaked, Shaul, ed. *Irano-Judaica: Studies Relating to Jewish Contacts with Persian Culture.* Jerusalem: Ben-Zvi Institute, 1982.

Smith, Peter. *The Babi and Baha'i Religions: From Messianic Shi'ism to a World Religion.* New York: Cambridge University Press, 1987.

Yacoub, Joseph. *The Assyrian Question.* Chicago: Alpha Graphics, 1986.

Iraq

POPULATION 24,001,816

SHIITE MUSLIM 55 percent

SUNNI MUSLIM 40 percent

CHRISTIAN AND OTHER 5 percent

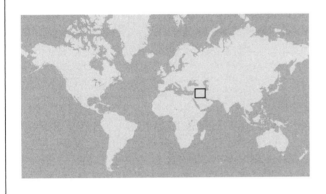

Country Overview

INTRODUCTION Lying in southwestern Asia, Iraq is bordered to the east by Iran, to the north by Turkey, to the west by Syria and Jordan, and to the south by Saudi Arabia and Kuwait. The country consists of desert west of the Euphrates River, a broad central valley between the Euphrates and the Tigris River, and mountains in the northeast. Because it embraces a large part of the alluvial plains of the Tigris and Euphrates, Iraq has been known from ancient times as Mesopotamia, "the land between the rivers."

As long ago as 5000 B.C.E. cult centers such as Eridu served as important sites of pilgrimage and devotion in Iraq. By 4000 B.C.E. an advanced civilization existed at Sumer. The Sumerians were pantheistic, and their reli-

gious beliefs also had important political aspects. The priests ruled from their temples, called ziggurats. The Code of Hammurabi (1792–1750 B.C.E.), however, evidences a more pronounced separation between secular and religious authority in Babylonia (southeastern Mesopotamia) than had existed in Sumer.

Sometime after 2000 B.C.E. Mesopotamia became the center of the ancient empires of Babylonia and Assyria. It was conquered by Cyrus the Great of Persia in 538 B.C.E., and by Alexander the Great in 331 B.C.E. In 637 C.E. the land came under the rule of Arab Muslims. The Abbasids overthrew the ruling family, the Umayyads, in 750, and in 762 they founded Baghdad as the new capital of the Muslim caliphate. The city fell to the invading Mongols in 1258. From 1533 until 1918 Iraq was part of the Ottoman Empire.

Following British occupation during World War I, Iraq elected a king, Faisal I, in 1921 and became independent in 1932. In 1958 the Republic of Iraq was declared after a successful military coup against the monarchy. Subsequent coups in 1963 and 1968 brought the Baath Party to power. Ahmad Hassan al-Bakr headed the Baathist government from 1968 to 1979, when he was ousted and replaced by Saddam Hussein. Marked by severe repression and the invasions of neighboring Iran and Kuwait, Hussein's regime was toppled in 2003 when a U.S.-led coalition force invaded and occupied Iraq.

Besides Sunni and Shiite Muslims, other religious groups in Iraq include Christians, who make up about 3 percent of the population; about 100,000 Yazidis, who, though small in number, are important in understanding the history of religions; and about 20,000

An Iraqi child worships at the Shrine of Imam Hussein, grandson of the Prophet Muhammed. Iraqi Shiites hold sacred the shrines and tombs of the imams and saints in Najaf, Karbala, Kazimayn, and Samarra. AP/WIDE WORLD PHOTOS.

Mandaeans. There are also about 2,500 Jews in Baghdad.

RELIGIOUS TOLERANCE The exclusion of Iraqi Shiite Muslims from positions of power began under the rule of the Sunni Turks. The level of intolerance increased after the 1958 revolution and especially after the Baathist coup in 1968. Successive governments confiscated Shiite religious institutions and increased the restrictions on visiting holy places. In 1969 the Iraqi Shiites rebelled under the leadership of Grand Ayatollah Sayyid Muhsin al-Hakim, whom the authorities later detained in his home. Hakim's son, Mahdi, was declared an American spy and was to be executed. Mahdi escaped to London but was assassinated in The Sudan in 1988 by Hussein's agents. Tensions increased from 1970 through 1974, when riots erupted again. The government crushed the riots, executed Sheikh Aref Al Basri

(a leader of the uprising), and clamped down on Shiite institutions.

In 1977, as in many other years, the authorities prohibited Shiites from observing a festival in Karbala'. The Shiites defied the order, the army crushed their protests, and the government arrested, sentenced, and executed many of them. Sayyid Mohamed Baqir al-Sadr, a prominent opponent of the Baathists, was given a life sentence. Five months after the Iranian Revolution, Saddam Hussein came to power. In April 1980 he ordered the execution of Sadr and his sister. The oppression of Shiites increased throughout the Iran-Iraq War (1980–88). As a punishment to Sadr's close associate, Ayatollah Sayyid Mohamed Baqir al-Hakim, who opposed the Iraqi dictator from his exile in Iran, Hussein in 1983 had 90 members of Hakim's family arrested and six of them executed.

Following the crushing defeat of invading Iraqi forces in Kuwait in early 1991, Iraqi Shiites rebelled against Hussein's regime in March. Hussein's troops massacred the rebels, bombarding Shiite cities with Scud missiles and napalm, murdering the medical staffs of hospitals, and raping and torturing people. Both Dar El Hikma, which contained 60,000 books (20,000 of them handwritten), and Dar El Ilm, which held 38,000 books (7,500 handwritten), were burned to the ground. Homes, schools, libraries, mosques, and shrines were also razed. The 92-year-old Grand Ayatollah Sayyid Abu al-Qasim al-Kho'i was arrested with his family and followers and held in a special prison in Baghdad, where he remained until his death in 1992.

In 2004 the Iraq Interim Governing Council, appointed by U.S. authorities in occupied Iraq and representing the country's different ethnic and religious groups, drafted a new constitution. The document makes Islam the state religion, but it guarantees freedom of belief and practice to all religions and denominations.

Major Religion

ISLAM

DATE OF ORIGIN 637 C.E.
NUMBER OF FOLLOWERS 22.8 million

HISTORY By 637 C.E. Mesopotamia had come under Arab Muslim rule. After the assassination of the third caliph, Othman Ibn Affan, Ali Ibn Abi Talib, the prophet Muhammad's cousin, became the fourth caliph. He soon faced political opposition led by Muawiya Ibn Abi Sufyan, which resulted in the assassination of Ali in Kufa in 661 and the rise of Muawiya as the next caliph and the founder of the Umayyad Caliphate (661–750).

In 680 Muawiya died after naming his son, Yazid, as his successor, thereby transforming the Islamic caliphate into a monarchy. Hussein, the son of Ali and the grandson of the Prophet, disputed Yazid's claim to power and confronted him militarily in Karbala'. There Hussein, a number of his family, and all of his supporters were ruthlessly murdered. In 750, however, Abu El Abbas, a descendant of the Hashemites, the clan of the Prophet, succeeded in destroying the Umayyad Caliphate and establishing the Abbasid Caliphate in Iraq.

In 762 Baghdad was founded as the capital of the Abbasid Caliphate. It became a prominent commercial, cultural, and educational center, as well as the intellectual center of the world, where great civilizations met and interacted during the Middle Ages. Baghdad is still remembered as the pinnacle of glory in Islam's history. Scholars, philosophers, scientists, poets, and spiritual leaders found their refuge in the city. Scholars of all races and religions were invited to work in the Beit Al Hikma (Academy of Wisdom). They were concerned with preserving the intellectual heritage of the known world by translating classic texts into Arabic.

Nomadic Mongol tribes swept through the Islamic world from the Far East, reaching Baghdad in 1258. They killed the caliph, filled Baghdad streets with the corpses of hundreds of thousands of its inhabitants, set fire to its libraries and cultural centers, and ultimately brought down its glorious civilization.

From the sixteenth through the early twentieth centuries, the Shiite Safavid Empire in Iran and the Sunni Ottoman Turks disputed control of Iraq. The 1722 capture of Isfahan, Iran, by Sunni Afghans, along with attempts by Nadir Shah to promote Sunni-Shiite rapprochement and to expropriate most of the Shiite endowments in Iran, led the Iranian Shiite clergy to flee to Iraq between 1722 and 1763, thus shifting the center of Shiite scholarship first to Karbala' and then to Najaf. The Persian ulama (religious leader) took advantage of the instability in Iraq, pushing the Arab ulama aside and dominating the country's religious circles. Iraqis were predominantly Sunni until the late nineteenth and early twentieth centuries, when the bulk of Sunni tribes in central and southern Iraq converted to Shia Islam.

During World War I British forces invaded southern Iraq in 1914 and occupied Baghdad in 1917. In 1920 the Arabs of southern Iraq began military actions against the British, who had not fulfilled their promises to leave control of the area to the locals after the Turks were defeated. The British military responded but soon realized that it would be impossible to maintain control. After a popular election in 1921, Prince Faisal of Hijaz, who won 96 percent of the ballots, came to power as the king of Iraq. On 3 October 1932 Iraq, under Faisal's regime, was declared an independent kingdom.

In 1941, during World War II, Iraq again fell into the grasp of British forces. In 1958 General Abdul Karim Kassim led a successful military coup against the monarchy and declared Iraq a republic. A group of officers led by Abdul Salam Arif overthrew Kassim in 1963. In 1968 a third military coup by Baath Party members brought Ahmad Hassan Al-Bakr to power. In 1979 Bakr was stripped of all powers and placed under house arrest, and Saddam Hussein became the new president.

Hussein led his country into a fierce war with Iran that lasted from 1980 to 1988 and claimed the lives of 1.5 million soldiers. In 1990 the regime—known for its repression, human rights abuses, and terrorism—invaded Kuwait. In 1991 a U.S.-led military coalition liberated Kuwait and drove the Iraqi troops out of the country. In the same year, both Shiites in the south and Kurds in the north rebelled against Hussein, but he relentlessly crushed them. Hussein's regime finally fell when a military coalition led by the United States and Britain invaded and occupied Iraq in March 2003. Sovereignty was restored in June 2004.

EARLY AND MODERN LEADERS Two Abbasid caliphs profoundly shaped the history of Iraq. Abu Jafar Al-Mansour (754–75), who was known as an excellent orator and administrator, was the founder of Baghdad. Al-Mamoun (813–33) was largely responsible for cultural expansion, including the translation of Greek works into Arabic. He founded the Beit al-Hikma (Academy of Wisdom) in Baghdad, which soon became an active scientific center.

From 1955 to 1970 Grand Ayatollah Muhsin al-Hakim was the preeminent leader of the Shiite world. In the late 1950s his son, Ayatollah Sayyid Mohamed Baqir al-Hakim (born in 1939), cofounded the Islamic political movement in Iraq with Ayatollah Sayyid Mohamed Baqir al-Sadr (1936–80) and other scholars.

The Grand Ayatollah Ali Al-Sistani (born in 1930) has become increasingly influential in Iraq's politics since the demise of Saddam Hussein. A native of Iran, Sistani studied in Najaf under Grand Ayatollah Sayyid Abu al-Qasim al-Kho'i (1899–1992). Although he adopted Kho'i's belief that clerics should distance themselves from politics, he was nevertheless harassed by the Baath Party, imprisoned briefly after the First Gulf War, and targeted by several would-be assassins in the 1990s. He succeeded Kho'i as grand ayatollah and has exerted great control over the majority of Iraq's Shiite population. Despite his seclusion and inaccessibility, he has become an important political figure in contemporary Iraq.

MAJOR THEOLOGIANS AND AUTHORS Sheikh Ahmed al-Qubaisi (born in 1934) is the most famous Iraqi Sunni scholar in contemporary Iraq. He has written more than 30 works about such subjects as women and politics in the beginning of Islam, the philosophy of the family system in Islam, family laws in *fiqh* (Muslim jurisprudence), and Islamic criminal law. Qubaisi is known for his courageous and unorthodox ideas, which are well grounded in Islamic scholarship. In his writings he emphasizes the plurality of Islamic views and tends toward moderate fatwas that reconcile modern life with the Shari'ah (Islamic law).

As Iraq has two important Shiite theological centers in Najaf and Karbala', it is not strange that it is home to many important Shiite scholars. Grand Ayatollah Sayyid Abu al-Qasim al-Kho'i was one of the most prominent Shiite scholars of the twentieth century. Kho'i was recognized as a marja' (a religious authority) after the death of Grand Marja' Isfahani in 1945. In his life Kho'i tried, as much as possible, to avoid involvement in the political turmoil of Iraq. He focused mainly on developing his scholarship, teaching his many students, and founding well-financed charitable institutions. Unlike Ayatollah Ruhollah Khomeini and Ayatollah Sayyid Mohammad Baqir al-Sadr, Kho'i maintained that the authority of a marja' is less political and more spiritual and religious, granting political authority to the *ummah* (Islamic community) itself.

A second prominent Shiite scholar is Ayatollah Sayyid Muhsin al-Hakim (died in 1970). Hakim became the absolute religious authority, *marja' mutlaq,* after the death of Ayatollah Brujerdi in 1961. Hakim opposed

the Arab union and the Iranian recognition of Israel and expressed his hostility toward the Iraqi president, Abdul Karim Kassim. Nonetheless, Hakim maintained good relations with many Arab leaders in Egypt, Jordan, Lebanon, Saudi Arabia, Morocco, and Algeria. He succeeded in building up and extending a network of agents (*wukala*), who promoted his school among a new generation of young scholars. He also founded the Group of Scholars to fight Communism. He did not subscribe to militant Islam and even did his best to nip the Daawa Party, a militant Islamic political party, in the bud.

The Shiite marja' Ayatollah Mohamed Baqir al-Sadr was a student of Hakim. Sadr was a forerunner in advocating an active role for the people in the political sphere both before and after the establishment of an Islamic state. In his outline of the struggle for an Islamic political system, jurists cooperate with intellectuals in guiding and leading the Islamic movement. Once the Islamic state has been established, the grand jurist shares power with the people. Sadr advocated the organization of an ideological political party to mobilize the masses in their struggle. He cofounded the Daawa Party in Iraq and later became the head jurist and sole ideologue of that organization, setting its political agenda and supervising its activities. Many scholars recognize his influence on Khomeini's thought.

HOUSES OF WORSHIP AND HOLY PLACES Iraq's holy cities are Najaf, Karbala', Kazimayn, and Samarra. The most prominent is Najaf, where many Shiite pilgrims come to the holy shrine of Ali ibn Abi Talib. The city's large cemetery, Wadi al-Salam, is considered the holiest and most highly sought-after burial place among Shiites. Located 120 miles south of Baghdad, Najaf escaped effective control under the Ottomans, and by the early twentieth century the city exercised an enormous religious and political influence that extended far beyond Iraq.

Fifty miles south of Baghdad is the city of Karbala', whose prestige derives from the shrine of Hussein, the son of Ali and the grandson of the Prophet, and the shrine of Abbas, Hussein's half brother. The city is famous for its Persian character. In fact, at the turn of the twentieth century, three-quarters of its population of 50,000 were Persians. Traditions attach blessing to the city's water and soil. Wadi al-Iman, its cemetery, stands second in sanctity only to Wadi al-Salam.

Kazimayn's importance stems from its shrine, which contains the tombs of Musa al-Kazim, the seventh of the twelve Shiite imams, and Mohamed al-Jawwad, the ninth imam. Samarra contains the tombs of the tenth and eleventh imams, Ali al-Hadi and his son, Hassan al-Askari. It is also believed to be the birthplace of Mohamed al-Mahdi, the twelfth imam, who allegedly disappeared and is expected to return at the end of days as the Mahdi, or messiah.

Although orthodox Sunni Islam does not tolerate tomb building or reverencing places where scholars, imams, or the Prophet's companions are buried, Abu Hanifa Mosque in Baghdad is considered an important mosque for Iraq Sunni Muslims. The mosque contains the relics of Imam Abu Hanifa (699–767), a prominent Muslim jurist who founded the Hanafite system of Islamic jurisprudence, one of the four main systems in Sunni Islam. The mosque was damaged during the U.S.-led invasion of Baghdad in 2003.

WHAT IS SACRED? Iraqi Shiites hold sacred the shrines and tombs of the imams and saints in Najaf, Karbala', Kazimayn, and Samarra. They also believe in the blessing of the soil of these holy cities.

HOLIDAYS AND FESTIVALS Both Sunni and Shiite Muslims celebrate the festivals of the Id al-Fitr, which follows the fasting month of Ramadan, and the Id al-Adha, which commemorates the anniversary of the prophet Ibrahim's offering of his son, Isma'il, as a sacrifice. The most important Shiite festival is that of Ashura, which commemorates the anniversary of the martyrdom of Hussein, the prince of martyrs, in Karbala'.

MODE OF DRESS Both male and female Muslims, whether Shiite or Sunni, are instructed to be modest in their dress. Females have to cover the entire body except the face and hands. Nevertheless, traditional Iraqi women also cover their faces. Western styles are commonly worn by men and women in contemporary Iraq.

DIETARY PRACTICES Islam proscribes the consumption of alcohol, blood, carrion, and pork.

RITUALS Besides the five daily prayers, fasting during Ramadan, *zakat* (almsgiving), and pilgrimage to Mecca, which are observed by both Sunni and Shiite Muslims, Iraqi Shiites observe the ritual of Ashura. Ashura commemorates the Tragedy of Karbala', the murder of Hussein, his supporters, and a number of his family members, including children. It is observed somewhat differently in Iran and Iraq.

In Iraq the ritual is divided into two parts. First, there is the visitation, or pilgrimage, to the shrines of the imams and saints. The second major part is Aza, an assembly for mourning the martyrdom of Hussein. The latter custom began late in seventh century when the first "wailing assembly" was organized together with the recital of the story of "The Death of Hussein." The first official ceremony, however, was in 963, when Baghdad's *suq* (marketplace) was closed down and contingents of wailing women marched the streets, beating their cheeks and reciting death poetry. Over time the ritual evolved into popular, folkloric ceremonies and assumed various forms: assemblies of condolence, processions of condolence, and passion plays, particularly in central and southern Iraq. Various contemporary ulama, however, have opposed the head cutting and self-flagellation that are included in the ceremony.

Besides the visitation during Ashura, Shiites visit the tombs of imams and saints at all times of the year. The visitation is intended to acknowledge the authority of the imams following the death of the Prophet; to maintain the contact between the Shiite believer and his or her imam, who is capable of interceding with God on the day of resurrection; and to preserve the collective Shiite memory and group identity.

Iraqi Sunnis have no specific rituals distinguishing them from other Sunni Muslims.

RITES OF PASSAGE The rites of passage in Iraq are not much different from those of any other Islamic country. There is, however, one interesting and unique rite that Iraqi Shiites observe: the corpse traffic. In Shia Islam the shrine cities emerged as the preferred burial grounds, for they allowed Shiites to pass the interval between death and resurrection in the vicinity of their imams. The corpse traffic gained momentum in the nineteenth century as the bulk of Iraq's tribes converted to Shiism. The four major consecrated cemeteries in the shrine cities, in the order of their importance, were Wadi al-Salam at Najaf, Wadi al-Iman at Karbalaa, Maqabir Quraysh at Kazimayn, and al-Tarima at Samaraa.

One Shiite tradition holds that burial in the vicinity of Ali will eliminate the ordeal of the dead in the grave and reduce the interval (*barzakh*) between death and resurrection. According to another tradition, attributed to the sixth imam, Jaafar al-Sadiq, being next to Ali for one day is more favorable than 700 years of worship.

MEMBERSHIP It was only in the nineteenth century that Iraqis began to convert from the Sunni to the Shiite denomination. Motivated by a number of factors, the massive conversion of central and southern Iraqi tribes took place in a short period of time. At the core of this process were the Wahhabi reform movement's attacks on Najaf and Karbala'. The attacks reinforced the sectarian identity of the Shiite ulama and increased their motivation to convert the tribes in order to gain their protection. Other factors included the emergence of Najaf and Karbala' as Iraq's major desert market towns; a change in the flow of the Euphrates, which encouraged a transition from a pastoral to an agricultural way of life in which Shiism ultimately became more attractive to the common tribespeople; and, most important, the Ottoman policy of tribal settlement dating from 1831. The transition of the tribes from a nomadic life to agricultural activity disrupted tribal order and created a major crisis among the tribespeople, forcing them to reconstruct their identity and to adjust to major social changes brought about by their new economic situation. The conversion was facilitated by the proliferation of *sayyid*s (descendants of the Prophet), whose authority, recognized by all of the settled tribespeople, enabled them to soothe the fragmentation of the tribal system.

In contemporary Iraq interdenominational conversion and missionary work are insignificant.

SOCIAL JUSTICE Islam instructs its followers to pay attention to the poor and give them what the Koran calls "their rights." Almsgiving (*zakat*) is one way this is done. Since the beginning of Islam Muslims have maintained the institution of *waqf* (endowment), through which money and properties are allocated to specific noble ends that help preserve social justice in the community. Secular regimes in Iraq, however, gave up collecting *zakat* and confiscated both Sunni and Shiite endowments.

In Iraq and Iran Shia Islam has developed financial institutions that do not exist in Sunni Islam. There are seven types of religious payments, which fall into three categories. The first category is the obligatory payment of one-fifth of a believer's net income. One-half of this payment, *sahm al-Imam*, is paid directly to the *mujtahid*, the great scholar whom the believer follows. The rest, *rad al-mazalim*, is paid to the *mujtahid* as a compensation for oppressive wrongs. In some cases Iranian or Lebanese Shiites may make their payments to Iraqi *mujtahid*s.

The second category includes three types of payment. First, there is *haqq al-wasiyya*, in which one-third of a deceased person's heritable properties is paid to the *mujtahid* and usually dedicated to a specific purpose. *Sawm wa salat* is a payment made to the *mujtahid* to hire a third party to observe fasting and prayer on behalf of the deceased, who missed some of these observances. With the third type of payment, leading *mujtahid*s receive money in return for aiding a believer's recovery from sickness or escape from danger.

Like the payments in the second category, the two payments in the third category are voluntarily paid, but they are paid to the custodians of the shrines, not the *mujtahid*s. First, there is the payment for the distribution of water to the poor of Najaf. This is especially important because it reminds Shiites of Imam al-Hussein, who was thirsty for one day before he was murdered. The second type of payment covers the cost of lighting the shrines and maintaining the tombs.

SOCIAL ASPECTS The extended family is central to the social organization of Iraqis. They maintain loyalty to their clans and count on kinship relations in finding appropriate spouses as well as business partners. Increasing urbanization, however, has allowed people to diversify their relations and loyalties.

Although in cities marriage depends on the free choice of the two partners, they still need the approval of their parents. As in other Muslim countries, marriage is regarded as a civil contract in Iraq. After the 1958 revolution, women's status in Iraq improved dramatically. The 1959 family law granted women many rights in such areas as inheritance, child custody, and divorce. The wars waged by President Saddam Hussein in the 1980s brought women to the socioeconomic foreground to replace the absent men.

POLITICAL IMPACT Despite being secular, the Baath Party under Saddam Hussein's regime adopted a national discourse full of Islamic rhetoric. It used this discourse to justify its wars against both Kurdish and Shiite Iraqis and against Iran and Kuwait.

On the other hand, Iraq witnessed the emergence of many sociopolitical movements that also relied on Islam to further their views and ground their discourses. The Islamic Daawa Party (basically a Shiite party), the Muslim Brotherhood (a Sunni group), and some fundamentalist Kurdish movements are prominent examples.

Unlike Sunni Islam, Shia Islam has developed a hierarchical clergy and provided their imams with both religious and political authority through the system of marja'ism. This system attributes to the imam the functions of leading wars, dividing war booty, leading the Friday prayer, putting judicial decisions into effect, imposing legal penalties, and receiving the religious taxes of *zakat* and *khums.*

The Shiite tradition of *taqlid* (emulation) instructs every Shiite to choose a highly prominent imam to follow in his theological and mundane political opinions. Although this tradition grants imams a supreme power and would seem to lend the Shiite community strong solidarity, in practice it has not been so fruitful. On the one hand, all Shiites could not come to the same *mujtahid* as their imam, something that has always resulted in the fragmentation of their views. On the other hand, the system has provoked opposition from governments that saw in the tradition a challenge to their own power.

CONTROVERSIAL ISSUES Two distinctive and frequently misunderstood Shiite practices are *muta'ah* (temporary marriage) and *taqiyah* (religious dissimulation). *Muta'ah* is a fixed-term contract that is subject to renewal. It differs from permanent marriage in that its duration can be as short as one evening or as long as a lifetime. The offspring of such arrangements are the legitimate heirs of the man.

Taqiyah, condemned by the Sunnis as cowardly and irreligious, is the hiding or disavowal of one's religion or its practices to escape the threat of death from those opposed to the faith. The persecution of Shiite imams during the Umayyad and Abbasid caliphates reinforced the need for *taqiyah.*

Shiite practice differs from that of the Sunnis concerning both divorce and inheritance in that it is more favorable to women. The reputed reason for this is the high esteem in which Fatima, the wife of Ali and the daughter of the Prophet, was held. The self-flagellation and head cutting practiced during Ashura is condemned by many Shiite scholars.

In Iraq the relation between Islam and the state has been a highly controversial issue. The positions of both Iraqi Sunnis and Shiites on this issue represent a continuum ranging from a strongly secular position stressing the complete separation between the two to that which calls for an Islamic state.

CULTURAL IMPACT Having witnessed a variety of civilizations and having a mosaic society in terms of religion and ethnicity, Iraq's culture has reflected a rainbow of customs, cuisines, dress styles, and domestic architectural styles. Iraq has always been considered a center of literary creativity, particularly in poetry and, in recent years, children's literature. In the second half of the twentieth century, its educators played a crucial role in the educational development of most of the Persian Gulf states.

During the Abbasid caliphate (750–1258 C.E.), Iraq became the birthplace of what is now known as classical Arabic music. *Maqamat, monologat,* and *pestat* are three kinds of Iraqi music that developed during this time and were disseminated through the Arab world by Iraqi musicians and their disciples.

Other Religions

The Iraqi state officially recognizes 14 local Christian communities. The largest by far is the Chaldean Catholic Church. Other denominations include the Assyrian (Nestorian), Syrian Orthodox, Syrian Catholic, Armenian Orthodox, Armenian Catholic, Greek Orthodox, Greek Catholic, Coptic, Roman Catholic, Seventh-day Adventist, and National Evangelical Protestant. The Iraqi church has apostolic roots that are 2,000 years old, with Assyrian liturgies spoken in the same ancient Aramaic dialect used by Jesus and his disciples.

Iraq's Assyro-Chaldean community embraced Christianity 2,000 years ago and broke with the Western Christian church in the fifth century. Although historically the Chaldeans, as opposed to the Assyrians per se, are former heretics who later reunited with the Roman Catholic Church, both terms—Chaldean and Assyrian—are now used interchangeably to designate the Aramaic-speaking people who live in Mesopotamia.

The Assyro-Chaldeans have had uneasy relations with their neighbors in recent history. In the troubled years that preceded the demise of the Ottoman Empire, Assyrians and Armenians alike fell victim to the genocidal policy decreed by the Young Turk government and implemented by Turkish troops and the Kurdish tribes of eastern Anatolia. The Assyrians endured additional persecutions under the modern Turkish republic. In addition, mass emigrations of Assyro-Chaldeans took place during the 1961 Kurdish uprising and during the war between Iraq and Iran in the 1980s.

The Jewish community of Iraq long maintained a compact, assiduous, self-sufficient status, with members serving in the government, dominating many of the markets, and owning property. Shops and hotels, many of them owned and operated by Jews and Christians, multiplied in Baghdad. In 1947 Iraqi Jews numbered 117,000, or 2.6 percent of the population. Anti-Jewish feeling was growing, however, because of Zionist activities in Palestine, particularly during the 1936–39 Arab uprising there. There were incidents of hooliganism against the Jews—attacks on persons and property that the government did little to prevent. After the foundation of the state of Israel, the hostile pressure increased, and for most Jews the only tolerable solution was to emigrate. Eventually, more than 85 percent of the community left.

Estimates of the number of practitioners of the Yezidi religion worldwide range from 100,000 to 800,000. The largest group lives in Iraq, near Mosul. There are also small communities in Syria, Turkey, Georgia, and Armenia. The Yezidi creed features elements of Zoroastrianism, Manichaeism, Judaism, Christianity, and Islam. The two religious books of the Yezidis, the Book of Revelation and the Black Book, are written in Arabic, though the Yezidis themselves are Kurdish speakers.

The Yezidi pantheon places God at the top, but he is believed to have been only the creator and is no longer an acting force. The active forces are represented by Malak Ta'us and Sheikh Adii. Sheikh Adii may have been the caliph Yazid, a man believed to have risen to divinity through the transmigration of his soul and to now be an active and good deity. Sheikh Adii acts in cooperation with Malak Ta'us, the peacock angel, who fell into disgrace but then repented. Over 7,000 years Malak Ta'us filled seven jars with tears. His tears were used to extinguish the fire in hell; thus, there is no hell in Yezidism. Yezidis also honor six other minor deities.

The prayer in Yezidism must be performed twice a day in the direction of the sun and at a distance from non-Yezidis. The prayer is dedicated to Malak Ta'us. Saturday is the day of rest, but Wednesday is the holy day. In December a three-day fast is observed.

There is an annual pilgrimage to the tomb of Sheikh Adii, north of Mosul, which lasts for six days in August. This pilgrimage is Yezidism's most important ritual. Central to the celebration are bathing in a river, the washing of figures of Malak Ta'us, processions, music, hymns, ecstatic songs, and dances performed by priests. Other elements include the lighting of hundreds of oil lamps at the tombs of Sheikh Adii

and other saints, offerings of special foods, and the cooking of a sacrificed ox. Important parts of these rituals have never been seen by outsiders and are therefore unknown to the wider world.

Childhood baptism is important in Yezidism and is performed by a sheikh (a religious leader). Boys are usually circumcised soon after baptism, but this is not compulsory. Immediately after death, the deceased person is buried, with his or her hands crossed, in a conical tomb.

The Yezidis believe that they are the descendants of Adam only, while the rest of the world are descendants of Eve and, hence, inferior. It is impossible to convert to Yezidism. The strongest punishment among Yezidis is expulsion, which means that the soul of the expelled person is lost forever. Monogamy is practiced, but chiefs have the right to take several wives. Divorce is difficult to obtain, as it is allowed only in cases of adultery and requires three witnesses. But if a husband stays abroad for more than a year, he is automatically divorced from his wife, and he also loses the right to remarry inside the Yezidi community.

The Mandaeans, practitioners of the only surviving gnostic religion, live in southern Iraq and southwestern Iran. They number about 20,000, and their main city is Nasiriyya. Mandaeans are often called the Christians of Saint John, as he is held to be a highly sacred person, though not indispensable, in their theology. Jesus is also a central figure, but he plays a totally different role than in religions like Christianity and Islam, being considered a false prophet who is almost depicted as evil.

The Mandaean's central religious book is the *Ginza* (Treasure), which contains mythological and theological moral and narrative tracts, as well as hymns to be used in the mass for the dead. There are many other, less central books, mainly written in East Aramaic (or Mandaean, as the language is also called). The content of these books varies, with many containing magical texts and exorcisms.

According to the Mandaeans, the cosmos is made up of two forces: the world of light, located to the north, and the world of darkness, located to the south. Each world has a ruler, and around the rulers are smaller gods, called kings. The two forces are mutually hostile, and it was through their fighting that the world was created, though without the consent of the ruler of light. Man was thus created by the forces of darkness, but in every person is a "hidden Adam," the soul, which has its origin in the world of light.

Mohamed Mosaad

See Also Vol. I: *Islam, Shia Islam, Sunni Islam*

Bibliography

Abdul-Jabar, Faleh, ed. *Ayatollahs, Sufis, and Ideologues: State, Religion, and Social Movements in Iraq.* London: Saqi, 2002.

Encyclopaedia of the Orient. 13 Sept. 2004. http://www.i-cias.com/e.o/index.htm.

Farouk-Sluglett, Marion, and Peter Sluglett. *Iraq since 1958: From Revolution to Dictatorship.* London and New York: I.B. Tauris, 1990.

Hopwood, Derek, Habib Ishow, and Thomas Koszinowski, eds. *Iraq: Power and Society.* Reading: Published for St. Antony's College, Oxford, by Ithaca Press, 1993.

Ibrahim, Ferhad. *Sectarianism and Politics in the Arab World: A Case Study—Shiites in Iraq.* Cairo: Madbouli, 1996.

Longrigg, Stephen Hemsley. *Iraq, 1900 to 1950: A Political, Social, and Economic History.* London and New York: Oxford University Press, 1953.

Mackey, Sandra. *The Reckoning: Iraq and the Legacy of Saddam Hussein.* New York: Norton, 2002.

Nakash, Yitzhak. *The Shi'is of Iraq.* Princeton, N.J.: Princeton University Press, 1994.

Roux, George. *Ancient Iraq.* Cleveland: World Pub. Co., 1965.

Tripp, Charles. *A History of Iraq.* 2nd ed. Cambridge and New York: Cambridge University Press, 2002.

Yasin, Baqir. *History of Bloody Violence in Iraq.* Beirut: Dar al-Kunooz al-Adabiyya, 1999.

Ireland

POPULATION 3,883,159

ROMAN CATHOLIC 90 percent

ANGLICAN (CHURCH OF IRELAND)
2.7 percent

PRESBYTERIAN 0.75 percent

METHODIST 0.13 percent

JEWISH, MUSLIM, AND OTHER
6.42 percent

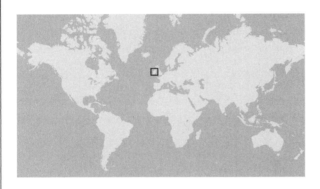

Country Overview

INTRODUCTION The Republic of Ireland, located off the northwestern coast of Europe, occupies the second largest and westernmost island of the British Isles. Shaped like a bowl, it has a low central plain ringed by limestone mountains. The republic controls all but the northeastern corner of the island, which is occupied by Northern Ireland, a part of the United Kingdom. The Irish Sea separates the island from the United Kingdom to the east.

Officially known as Eire, the Republic of Ireland attained complete independence from the United Kingdom in 1949. The majority of the population is Roman Catholic. Most Protestants on the island, who are predominantly Presbyterian or Church of Ireland Anglicans, live in Northern Ireland. Religion is a powerful force in Ireland, and the split between Catholicism and Protestantism has formed the major social and economic divisions of the country.

RELIGIOUS TOLERANCE For centuries the Roman Catholic peasantry suffered religious prosecution by the British. A new constitution in 1937, however, ended the power of the British crown and made Roman Catholicism the established religion. This caused some southern Protestants to flee to the six northern counties (Northern Ireland), where they would not be a minority, and some northern Catholics migrated south. Friction still exists in Northern Ireland between Roman Catholics who want to join the republic and Protestants who wish to remain part of the United Kingdom.

Major Religion

ROMAN CATHOLICISM

DATE OF ORIGIN 432 C.E.
NUMBER OF FOLLOWERS 3.5 million

HISTORY Catholicism reputedly arrived in Ireland with its first bishop, Saint Patrick, in 432 C.E. In fact, Patrick was the successor to Palladius, an emissary from the

Gaulish church, who died shortly after his arrival in Ireland. Pre-Christian practices and shrines were adapted to the new religion. At the Synod of Whitby in 664, Irish clerics rejected the decision by the church of Northumbria to follow Roman church customs, and by 750 the *Collectio canonum hibernensis,* the compilation of Irish canon law, was completed, establishing a Celtic Church that did not submit to Roman jurisdiction until the twelfth century.

Henry II of England established the lordship of Ireland in the twelfth century under the authority of the only English pope in history. Roman control of the Celtic Church was accepted at the Synod of Cashel in 1172, and the English government began appointing Englishmen to Irish dioceses. A series of apartheid-like laws followed, establishing a caste system that separated Britons and Gaels. The Tudor monarchs, who ruled from 1485 to 1603, established the kingship of Ireland and destroyed many of the monasteries. Under Oliver Cromwell (1599–1658), the crushing of Catholicism in Ireland was considered a "holy war." Following the final conquest of Ireland under William of Orange at the end of the seventeenth century, the anti-Catholic Penal Laws were enacted. According to the laws, should a member of a landowning Catholic family become Protestant, rights of ownership and disposal passed to the convert. Bishops and higher Catholic clergy were banished upon threat of death, and only a limited number of registered priests were permitted. The Penal Laws began to ease by the 1801 Act of Union and were abolished by the mid-1840s. Although leaders of the nineteenth-century Gaelic Revival, a movement to revive Irish culture, were predominantly Protestant, the resulting political revolution ended with Roman Catholicism being written into the 1937 constitution of independent Ireland. The church's power began to wane only in the late twentieth century.

EARLY AND MODERN LEADERS During the Dark Ages Irish scholar-monks known as *peregrini* helped keep learning alive throughout Europe, founding some of the greatest seats of European scholarship. The more famous peregrini include the ninth-century theologian John Scotus Erigena; Columba (also Columcille; died in 597), who founded the monastic center at Iona, the base from which Scotland and northern England were converted to Christianity; and Columbanus (died in 615), who founded monasteries in France and Switzerland. Early on, women held high positions in the Celtic

A devotee of Saint Patrick kneels during his pilgrimage on Croagh Patrick. Pilgrims ascend the 2,510 feet to the mountain's summit on their knees, praying the rosary. © GIANSANTI GIANNI/CORBIS SYGMA.

Church. For example, in the fifth century Saint Brigid held bishoplike authority at a mixed-sex monastery at Kildare.

After Catholicism was outlawed in Ireland during the sixteenth-century English Reformation, few Catholic Church leaders remained. Many Irish political leaders and revolutionaries were now Protestant. Finally, in 1828 the Catholic lawyer Daniel O'Connell won election to Parliament. O'Connell rallied the oppressed majority to campaign for Catholic emancipation. Following the establishment of Protestant universities in Ireland, a Catholic university was established in Dublin in 1850 by John Henry Newman (later Cardinal Newman; 1801–90). In 1866 Paul Cullen (1803–78) of Dublin became the first Irish cardinal and set about strengthening Roman authority in Ireland.

Contemporary Catholic leaders in Ireland include Cardinal Cahal B. Daly (born in 1917), the retired archbishop of Armagh and primate of all Ireland; Sean Brady (born in 1939), archbishop of Armagh and primate of all Ireland since 1996 and chairperson of the Irish Episcopal Conference; Diarmuid Martin (born in 1945), archbishop of Dublin since 2004; and Michael Neary, archbishop of Tuam since 1995.

MAJOR THEOLOGIANS AND AUTHORS Many of Ireland's greatest theologians lived prior to the Norse incursions in the ninth century and are discussed above in EARLY AND MODERN LEADERS. Contemporary Irish theologians include Eugene Duffy and Attracta Shields of the Western Theological Institute in Galway and David Blake, Eamonn Conway, and Michael Culhane of the University of Limerick. In 2001 a theological university was established in County Mayo.

HOUSES OF WORSHIP AND HOLY PLACES In the early days of Irish Catholicism the center of worship was the monastery. The backbone of Roman Catholicism today is the parish church, which is led by a pastor (canon) and one or more assistant priests (curates). Ireland's parishes form 26 dioceses, which are organized into four provinces under archbishops. The primacy is reserved for the archbishop of Armagh, though the most populous and influential archbishopric is that of Dublin.

People make pilgrimages to holy wells and shrines, which range from small roadside shelters dedicated to individual saints to Knock Cathedral, the site of an appearance of the Virgin Mary. There also are holy mountains, such as Croagh Patrick in Mayo, where pilgrims ascend the 2,510 feet to the summit on their knees, praying the rosary.

WHAT IS SACRED? Human life is considered sacred; thus, abortion is illegal in Ireland. The sacraments are also believed to be sacred, especially the Mass. The sacredness of marriage has been questioned since the legalization of divorce in the 1990s.

HOLIDAYS AND FESTIVALS The most important holiday in Ireland is Easter. Christmas (Nollaig; 25 December) is also a major holiday. On Christmas Eve families set a tall candle in a window to light the path for Mary and Joseph. On Saint Stephen's Day (26 December) boys traditionally have gone from door to door carrying a dead wren on a pole or holly bush and asking for treats and coins. Saint Bridget's Day (1 February)—the pagan holiday Imbolc on the pre-Christian calendar—marks the beginning of the agricultural season. Traditionally people braid small straw crosses to hang in their houses. Saint Patrick's Day (17 March) is not celebrated in Ireland as it is in the United States. People attend Mass on the holy day of the country's patron saint, and anyone avoiding alcohol during Lent may drink. The Feast of Saint John (24 June) probably originated in the Celtic midsummer celebration. The Feast of the Assumption (8 December) is a popular holiday in rural districts. Farm families do their Christmas shopping then because they must come to town to attend Mass.

MODE OF DRESS There are no clothing regulations for the Irish Catholic laity. Priests still wear black suits and shirts. Many nuns, however, no longer wear habits.

DIETARY PRACTICES Fasting is required only during Lent and on certain holy days. On Shrove Tuesday people eat pancakes in symbolic preparation for the Lenten fast.

RITUALS The seven sacraments of Roman Catholicism are practiced in Ireland, with attendance at Sunday Mass being the most widely practiced. In recent decades the number of people choosing a religious vocation has dropped. Compared to the United States, however, Ireland has an unusually high percentage of people who have entered holy orders.

RITES OF PASSAGE Irish Catholics have the same rites of passage, such as First Communion and confirmation, as Catholics elsewhere.

MEMBERSHIP Children of Irish Roman Catholics are expected to be raised as Catholics. As most people in the republic already are Catholic, little evangelization is necessary. Most Irish evangelization has been in the form of foreign missions to former British colonies.

SOCIAL JUSTICE Since the days of the Penal Laws, the Catholic Church has been active in social programs, supporting orphan schools, hospitals, organizations that care for the poor, and old-age homes. Although the Irish can be accepting of those of lower economic status, such acceptance has not been extended to the Traveling People, also known as Itinerants or Tinkers. Travelers are seminomadic people who travel the country in barrel-topped wagons doing odd jobs and begging. Although legislation has been changing in their favor since the 1960s, historically they have been subjected to discrimination, refusal of service, accusations of thievery, and physical assault.

SOCIAL ASPECTS Arranged marriages have nearly disappeared in Ireland, although exceptions do occur. A priest at Knock Cathedral is known for arranging marriages, and an international matchmaking event occurs each year in County Clare. Traditionally married women were expected to cook, clean house, and care for children. In the early twentieth century many working women had to leave their jobs if they married. Men were expected to provide for their families. An unexpected side effect of legalized divorce has been the court-ordered sale of family farms—many held for generations—as terms of property settlements. As a consequence, older farm owners have rewritten their wills, excluding married heirs from the patrimony in order to preserve it.

POLITICAL IMPACT The Catholic Church was written into Ireland's 1937 constitution, and its political impact has remained pervasive. The 1929 Censorship of Publication Act, which banned all sexually related written materials, stood unaltered until 1967. Reports from the mid-twentieth century held that individuals might be committed to mental institutions if they openly defied parish priests. The decline in the church's power in the late twentieth century can be seen in the 1996 legislation allowing divorce, as well as in the decline in the clergy's reputation following reports in the 1990s of child abuse in church-run orphanages and schools.

CONTROVERSIAL ISSUES A large part of the Irish population today is at odds with the church's ban on birth control. Birth control is now legal in the republic, and although abortion is illegal, women are no longer prosecuted for going abroad to seek one.

CULTURAL IMPACT Ireland's greatest treasures are works of Christian art, from high crosses to the Chalice of Ardagh and the Book of Kells. Much of the surviving medieval art in Ireland consists of carved stonework from ancient monasteries. Catholicism's impact on art has extended to modern broadcast media: The Angelus, a daily devotion commemorating the Incarnation, is broadcast on RTE, the national radio and television network.

Other Religions

The Church of Ireland, an independent member of the Anglican Church, came to Ireland during the Reformation in 1537, when the Irish Supremacy Act made

the English monarch the head of the church. The reconquest of Ireland by William of Orange in 1690 asserted Anglican control through the Penal Laws. Most of the laws were abolished by the 1801 Act of Union, which established the United Church of England and Ireland as the official church, a status it retained until disestablishment in 1870. The Church of Ireland has been independent since 1871. The presiding archbishop of Armagh, the Most Reverend Robert Eames, is the leader of a synod composed of 2 archbishops, 10 bishops, and clergy and lay members from 33 dioceses. Dioceses are composed of individual parishes, each led by a priest and a vestry.

The 1607 "Flight of the Earls," the escape to the continent of about a hundred leaders of an Irish rebellion against English rule, led to the forfeiture of more than 2 million acres of land, which was settled by 40,000 Presbyterian Scots by 1618. In 1642 they formed the Presbyterian Church in Ireland. The Presbyterian "new lights" joined the Roman Catholic majority in the 1798 Irish Rebellion, leading the rebel forces in Ulster. Following the defeat of the rebels, the Reverend Henry Cooke sought an alliance between Presbyterians and Anglicans against the Catholics, an alliance that has continued. Presbyterians form the largest Protestant denomination in Northern Ireland.

The structure of the Presbyterian Church in Ireland consists of more than 560 local congregations led by "kirk sessions" composed of presbyters (elders) and a minister. Local congregations elect the members of the 21 presbyteries and 5 regional synods. The General Assembly, the supreme governing council, is led by an elected moderator. The ministry was opened to women in1972. The Reverend Donald Watts became the church's general secretary in 2003.

The Methodist Church in Ireland was created in 1738 following a series of speaking tours by John Wesley. Methodists in Ireland separated from the established church in 1878. The church consists of local congregations formed into 76 preaching circuits, which in turn form 8 districts. Legislative matters are treated at an annual conference of district synods. At this conference the church president is elected. The Reverend W. James Rea was elected president in 2003.

The earliest recorded Jewish presence in Ireland dates to 1079. Although the Jewish population in Ireland is very small (only 0.1 percent of the population), it maintains six synagogues in three cities: four in Dublin and one each in Cork and Belfast. The only Jewish school in Ireland is Stratford School. Prominent Irish Jews include the former lords mayor of Dublin Robert Briscoe (1894–1969) and his son, Ben Briscoe (born in 1924). Chaim Herzog (1918–97), former president of Israel, was born in Belfast and educated in Dublin.

Islam has also maintained a small presence in Ireland. The Belfast Islamic Centre is a charitable institution led by the imam Sheikh Hasrizal Abdul Jamil. It provides worship services and activities for Irish Muslims and a part-time Islamic school for children aged 5 to 16.

Michael J. Simonton

See Also Vol. 1: *Roman Catholicism*

Bibliography

Archdiocese of Armagh official Web site. 20 August 2004. http://www.armagharchdiocese.org.

Arensberg, Conrad M. *The Irish Countryman: An Anthropological Study.* Garden City, N.Y.: Natural History Press, 1968.

Brady, Ciaran. *The Encyclopedia of Ireland: An A–Z Guide to Its People, Places, History, and Culture.* New York: Oxford University Press, 2000.

CatholicIreland.net. 20 August 2004. http://www.catholicireland.net.

Delaney, Mary Murray. *Of Irish Ways.* Minneapolis: Dillon Press, 1973.

Gmelch, George. *The Irish Tinkers: The Urbanization of an Itinerant People.* Prospect Heights, Ill.: Waveland Press, 1985.

Gmelch, Sharon. *Nan: The Life of an Irish Travelling Woman.* Prospect Heights, Ill.: Waveland Press, 1986.

Mac Gréil, Mícheál. *Prejudice and Tolerance in Ireland: Based on a Survey of Intergroup Attitudes of Dublin Adults and Other Sources.* Dublin: Research Section, College of Industrial Relations, 1977.

Messenger, John C. *Inis Beag: Isle of Ireland.* Prospect Heights, Ill.: Waveland Press, 1983.

Nolan, A.M. *A History of Ireland.* Chicago: J.S. Hyland, 1913.

O'Brien, Máire, and Conor Cruise O'Brien. *A Concise History of Ireland.* New York: Beekman House, 1972.

O'Rourke, Fergus. *The Fauna of Ireland: An Introduction to the Land Vertebrates.* Cork: Mercier Press, 1970.

Power, Patrick. *Timetables of Irish History: An Illustrated Chronological Chart of the History of Ireland from 6000 B.C. to Present Times.* London: Worth Press, 2001.

Israel

POPULATION 6,116,533

JEWISH 80.1 percent

MUSLIM 14.6 percent

CHRISTIAN 2.1 percent

OTHER 3.2 percent

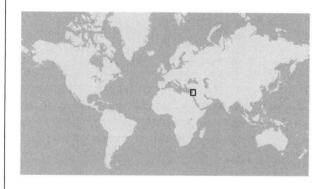

Country Overview

INTRODUCTION In the 1880s the founders of the State of Israel began to settle in Palestine—a small strip of territory located on the east coast of the Mediterranean Sea—joining a small Jewish population already living there. Jewish immigrants (mainly from Eastern Europe), inspired by Zionism (a movement to create a Jewish nation in Palestine) and escaping from anti-Semitism, went there in increasing numbers. They formed a community called Yishuv, creating many social and political institutions and developing a new national language (modern Hebrew), culture, and nationalism. Their goals and interests, however, clashed with those of the local Arab population.

The Holocaust in Europe during World War II greatly increased Jewish migration to Palestine and strengthened Western support for the state-building project. In 1947 the United Nations General Assembly voted to partition Palestine into two states (one Jewish, one Arab) and to make Jerusalem an international city. The Jews accepted the motion, and the Arabs, a two-thirds majority of the country, rejected it. The rejection was followed by intercommunal and interstate wars, leading to the uprooting of 700,000 Palestinian Arabs and the creation of a Jewish state within enlarged borders. The new state, founded in 1948, won diplomatic recognition from both the United States and the Soviet Union. Arab residents of Palestine and many surrounding Arab states remained opposed, however, and war ensued. Following the Six-Day War (1967) Israel captured the whole territory of historic Palestine.

Today about 80 percent of Israel's population is Jewish. The rest are mostly Palestinian Arabs, the majority of whom are Muslim. A minority of the Palestinian Arabs are Christian (including Greek Catholics, Greek Orthodox, and Roman Catholics) and Druze. There are also non-Arab Christians, Circassians (non-Arab Muslims), and members of the Baha'i faith living in Israel.

Since 1993 some efforts have been made to reach a political agreement between Israel and the Palestinian population. Proposed solutions have included granting self-determination to the Palestinians or creating spatial separation between them and Israel.

RELIGIOUS TOLERANCE The State of Israel officially guarantees freedom of worship for all its citizens, a commitment generally respected. In practice, however,

A man touches his prayer shawl to the Torah while men and women look on at the Western Wall, also called the Wailing Wall, in Jerusalem, Israel.
© PAUL A. SOUDERS/CORBIS.

many Muslim religious endowments have been confiscated or restricted, and Christian missionary activities are not tolerated. The non-Orthodox streams of Judaism (traditionalist, Reformist, and Reconstructionist) are prevented from performing legal marriages, divorces, and conversions in Israel.

Major Religion

JUDAISM

DATE OF ORIGIN first century C.E.
NUMBER OF FOLLOWERS 4.9 million

HISTORY Although the Jewish State of Israel was not established until 1948, small Jewish groups have existed in the area (called the Holy Land or Palestine) almost uninterruptedly for nearly 4,000 years.

Present-day Jewish religion in Israel is the rabbinical Judaism that was formed incrementally between 70

C.E. and c. 700 C.E. It was founded theologically on a codification of the religion based on the oral Torah (the Mishnah), the Babylonian (and Jerusalemite) Talmud, and responsa of great religious authorities. Rabbinical Jewish religion (sometimes equated with Judaism, a Hellenistic [ancient Greek] term for a civilization that included many secular cultures) had a social structure that centered around a synagogue (or number of synagogues), a *mikveh* (ritual purification bath), and one or several rabbis. This structure continues to be maintained today. The rabbis function as spiritual leaders of the community, exercise social control over its members, maintain the community's social boundaries, and sometimes represent the community to the outside world.

All of the Jewish communities were destroyed during the Crusades (1099–1110). Following the relative religious tolerance of the Latin Kingdom of Jerusalem, they were gradually rebuilt. With the Muslim reconquest of the country (1187) the Jewish presence expanded considerably.

In 1517 the territory became a part of the Muslim Ottoman Empire, which had seized it from the Mamlukes (the rulers of Egypt). Jews were recognized as a protected but subordinate religious minority (*dhimmi*) in exchange for paying a special tax and wearing distinctive clothing. After the Ottoman conquest Jews began settling in Hebron, Safed, and Tiberias in large numbers.

Beginning in the mid-1860s the Ottomans introduced reforms to grant Jews religious autonomy, empowering the community to register marriages and burials; to maintain autonomous (rabbinical) courts for the administration of internal issues and matters of personal status (such as divorce and adoption); to operate its own educational system; and to impose internal taxes. This legal status was also maintained while the territory was governed by the British (1919–48), and it was partially incorporated into the modern Israeli state's legal system.

In the Jewish religion there is no supreme religious authority. In the 1920s, however, efforts were made in Israel to construct a countrywide religious authority (the Chief Rabbinate) as part of the state bureaucracy. Israeli Jewish religion is officially subdivided into two rites, and accordingly the Chief Rabbinate has two chief rabbis: one Sephardic (later known as Mizrahi), the other Ashkenazi. The former represents the Jews of the Mediterranean and North African tradition, and the latter represents the Jews who follow the central and eastern European tradition. Both chief rabbis are considered civil servants, though they usually also possess considerable stature as religious authorities.

The Jewish religious tradition that came out of Muslim countries was considered less strict than the European version of Orthodoxy, which had endured the stress of the Enlightenment and other movements that encouraged assimilation and secularization. These differences led to the separation between Ashkenazi and Mizrahi Orthodoxy that exists in contemporary Israel. The Orthodox Jews who immigrated to Israel—mainly those from Lithuania—established their traditional "learning society" in which the majority of men are involved in scholastic study at yeshivas (or, in the case of married men, *kollelim*), while the women are responsible for child-raising and for the family's livelihood, working in part- or full-time "women's occupations" outside the home. Much of Lithuanian Orthodoxy in Israel continues to be organized around this lifelong learning process for men only.

In the 1980s Ovadia Yosef (born in 1920), the former chief rabbi of Egypt (and later Sephardic chief rabbi

of Israel), founded a social and political movement called Shas, the main purpose of which was to defend the interests of Sephardic Jews, a largely peripheral and underprivileged ethnic class. Throughout the 1980s and 1990s Shas expanded its political power, becoming the third-largest party in Israel.

EARLY AND MODERN LEADERS Lithuanian Rabbi Eliezer Menachem Shach (Shbtai Hacohen; 1898–2001) was a fervent opponent of Jewish secularism. Shach was an unchallenged authority on Holy Scriptures, but being highly conservative, he never composed responsa or interpretations that could be regarded as innovations. Rabbi Yosef Shalom Elyashiv (born in 1910) is considered his successor. In addition to the Lithuanian Orthodox community, Orthodoxy in Israel also includes historically rival Hasidic communities, which are led by dynasties of charismatic leaders called *rebbes* (*admors*).

Following a battle over the "Jewish character" of the would-be Jewish state during the fifth Zionist Congress (1901), the Zionist religious movement (first called the Mizrahi, later the National Religious Party) was founded. It was led primarily by Rabbi Isaac Jacob Reines (1839–1915). The National Religious community never established a paramount institution like a council of rabbis, but it did receive counsel from spiritual rabbinical authorities. In addition to Reines and Rabbi Abraham Isaac Kook, discussed below under MAJOR THEOLOGIANS AND AUTHORS, the National Religious community greatly esteemed Rabbi Abraham Yeshayahu Karelitz (1878–1953), known as the Hazon Ish, and Rabbi Shlomo Goren (1917–94), the first chief rabbi of the Israeli military and later the Ashkenazi chief rabbi of Israel. Goren led a stream of modern and religiously more moderate Orthodoxy.

MAJOR THEOLOGIANS AND AUTHORS A theological revolution occurred in Palestine in the late 1920s, led by Rabbi Abraham Isaac Kook (1865–1935), the first Ashkenazi chief rabbi of Palestine. Traditionally the fulfillment by all Jews of the 613 commandments listed in the Holy Scriptures was the condition for the coming of the Messiah, the return of all Jews to Zion (the Jewish homeland), and full redemption. Rabbi Kook reversed the causality, declaring that when as many Jews as possible fulfill the one commandment to "settle the Holy Land," the Messiah will appear to redeem "his people" and will make them adhere to all of his commandments and precepts. A cosmic redemption of the whole world will then follow. This new perception granted religious meaning and legitimacy to secular nationalism by making it part of a divine project of redemption. The Kookian theological revolution laid the foundation for its followers' participation in the secular Israeli state and society. Kook's basic theological tract is *Orot* (1961; "Lights").

The most original religious thinker of Israel was Yeshayahu Leibovich (1903–94), who perceived the Jewish religion as the rigorous fulfillment of the 613 commandments. For this reason he opposed the sanctification of the Jewish state and of the land, the colonization of the occupied territories, and even praying at the Western Wall, considering these to be pagan cults and major deviations from the Jewish religion.

HOUSES OF WORSHIP AND HOLY PLACES The entire land of Israel is considered by Jews to be holy, but its boundaries are not clearly defined, and it is uncertain what this holiness necessitates. Jerusalem, at the center of the land, is holiest. The most sacred shrine of the Jewish people as a whole is the Temple Mount (in Jerusalem), which is the presumed location of King Solomon's Temple and of the Second Temple. The part of the Temple Mount known as the Western (Wailing) Wall has become the central location for Jewish prayer. The wall is considered by Jews to be the last remnant of the Second Temple, which was the most sanctified space of ancient Israel. The Second Temple is also considered a symbol of the link between the land and the modern Jewish nation. Rabbinical authorities have prohibited access to the Temple Mount for observant Jews until the place can be "purified" according to the Halakhic laws.

The second-holiest place for individual prayer, after the Western Wall, is the Patriarchs' (Machpela) Cave (known to Muslims as Ibrahimiya, or the Prophet Abraham's tomb), located in the Hebron (West Bank) area. In Judaism it is considered to be the tomb of most of the patriarchs and matriarchs (Abraham, Isaac, Jacob, Leah, and Rebecca). The Matriarch Rachel's Tomb, located in the Jerusalem area, is considered the third-holiest shrine in Jewish religious tradition.

WHAT IS SACRED? Israeli religious Jews consider sacred the land of Israel, the Torah and other scrolls of Holy Scripture, and Jewish human remains. If Holy Scriptures are damaged, they must be buried as if they are human corpses.

HOLIDAYS AND FESTIVALS The State of Israel has adopted the Jewish religious (lunar) calendar and the major holidays. There are also secular holidays rooted in religion (such as Independence Day and commemoration days for fallen soldiers and victims of the Holocaust); these include some religious ingredients, such as recitations of the Kaddish (a Jewish prayer associated with mourning).

The Shabbat is the weekly complete day of rest (when all work is prohibited) and is considered a holiday in Israel. The High Holy Days are Rosh Hashanah (the first day of the Jewish New Year), followed ten days later by the Day of Atonement (Yom Kippur). In Israel the holidays of Pesach (Passover), Sukkoth, Shabuoth, Hanukkah, and Purim are considered less critical.

The fifteenth (*Tu*) of Av (a month of the Jewish calendar) has secondary importance within the contemporary Jewish state in general but not among strict observers of the religion. The intermediate days (*chol ha'moed*)—the second through seventh days of Sukkoth and of Passover—are partial holidays. Israeli Jews do not observe the second day of celebration of certain holidays, as Jews in the Diaspora do.

Lag b'Omer (the thirty-third day of Omer, the period of semimourning that follows Passover) was never a major holiday in Judaism, but in Israel it has taken on importance in popular religious practices that involve saint veneration as the ultimate *hillula* (popular festival). The festivities usually center on a pilgrimage to a holy person's presumed burial site and often involve building bonfires.

MODE OF DRESS In Israel there are diverse traditional Jewish religious modes of dress. In addition, modern clothing accompanied by a knitted skullcap has become the "uniform" of National Religious men in Israel as well as their social and political symbol. Modern Orthodox men who do not identify themselves politically or theologically with the "knitted skullcap wearers" wear black silk skullcaps or other variations. Members of the Mizrahi population do not necessarily wear any visibly distinctive garment, and their observance of various laws is selective and a matter of convenience or familial tradition. This selectivity does not exclude them from the

Mizrahi believers' community, as is the case in Ashkenazi Orthodoxy.

DIETARY PRACTICES All public kitchens in Israel are obliged to serve only kosher foods and to employ a *kashruth* (dietary laws) supervisor. Factories and suppliers of food in Israel—as well as suppliers abroad who send food to Israel—are obliged to employ, at their own expense, such supervisors. It is the municipalities' and the local authorities' privilege to allow or forbid the sale of nonkosher meat. The sale of such meat sometimes provokes harsh conflicts between secular and religious Jews because half of the Jewish population of Israel observes *kashruth*, while the other half does not. There is a range of adherence to *kashruth*, and various ultra-Orthodox groups dispense stricter *kashruth* (*glatt kosher*) certificates. The matter of kashruth is an example of the social boundaries in Israel that are based on degrees of perceived religious strictness.

RITUALS The most significant rituals for Jewish Israelis are affixing a mezuzah (a small case containing a scroll with handwritten holy text) to the front doorposts of their homes; participating in a Passover meal and abstaining from leavened bread during Passover; fasting on Yom Kippur; refraining from eating nonkosher food; lighting Shabbat candles; and having separate sets of dishes for meat and dairy foods (not strictly obligatory for Sephardic Jews).

RITES OF PASSAGE Most Israeli Jews observe the traditional rites of passage celebrated by all Jews (circumcision, bar mitzvah, burial, and mourning). The conscription into military service (at age 18) for Jewish males and females is sometimes perceived as a rite of passage in the Israeli militaristic culture.

MEMBERSHIP In Israel a person is considered a Jew if born to a Jewish mother or if he or she has converted (usually according to the Orthodox version of Halakhah, the body of religious law). Rabbinical Judaism does not encourage conversion (*giyyur*), and converts (*gerim*) are informally considered second-class Jews. Persons or communities suspected of not being truly Jewish (such as Ethiopian Jews or Judaized sects from India) are symbolically or practically converted.

Since the 1990s—in reaction to the so-called "demographic problem" caused by the inclusion of Muslim and Christian Palestinian Arabs in the Israeli control

system (which includes the West Bank and Gaza Strip, called also "Greater Israel") and the relative abatement of Jewish immigration—some national religious leaders in Israel have sought the conversion of non-Arab gentiles. Another phenomenon is the aggressive internal missionary activities of many religious organizations devoted to persuading secular Jews to "return" (or become "reborn") to the religion. This includes various methods of evangelization, including traditional missionary activities and using modern broadcast media, satellite television, and the Internet.

SOCIAL JUSTICE There is an ethnocentric element to Jewish religion, and in general there is not a deep concern about universal human rights and democracy (which are not considered "Jewish values"), but some Israeli Jewish religious leaders and their followers do manifest such concerns. Education is considered fundamental for the continuity of Jewish groups and movements. Most religious streams possess their own school systems. Some provide daylong scholastic activities and lunch for their students, thus mainly attracting students from lower-income families. Because both the ultra-Orthodox and the traditionalist Mizrahi Jews belong to the neediest sectors of Israeli society, most religious communities and groups run charity foundations.

SOCIAL ASPECTS The family remains a central institution in Israeli society. Because marriage and divorce are limited to the jurisdiction of the rabbinical courts, there is a class of people prohibited from marrying (*pesuley chitun*), such as couples composed of a cohen (a person whose ancestry is traced back to Aaron, who was Moses's brother and the first Jewish priest) and a divorced woman. This has resulted in a fast-growing phenomenon of cohabiting couples and single-parent families. Israel does, however, recognize non-Orthodox marriages and civil weddings conducted outside Israel.

POLITICAL IMPACT One of the major consequences of the self-definition of Israel as a Jewish state is the fact that there is no separation of religion and state. This political position is mainly manifested within the sphere of personal status (registration of marriages, divorces, and burials), which is subject to the ancient Jewish body of laws in its strict Orthodox interpretation. These issues are under the jurisdiction of religious courts and judges (*dayanim*), whose verdicts are enforced by state agencies. This system is controlled by the Chief Rabbinate, which is a part of the state bureaucracy but has full autonomy.

CONTROVERSIAL ISSUES The major controversies that arose among the religious communities at the beginning of the modern Jewish colonization of the Holy Land were practically but not theologically solved. The first issue was the cultivation of the land and the use of its fruits during fallow or sabbatical years (*shnat shmita*), a Biblical command designed to protect the land from depletion through overuse. Implementation of this law, however, endangered the profitability of Jewish agriculture in Israel. To date, every seventh year the strictly observant do not exploit the country's agricultural yield and instead consume only imported or hydroponic produce.

There is a highly emotional theological controversy about the cause and responsibility for the Holocaust. Some Orthodox rabbis (including Satmar leader Joel Moshe Teitelbaum [1897–1978] and Shas leader Ovadia Yosef) blamed the Holocaust on Zionist Jews or on secular, Reform, and Conservative Jews. In this ultra-Orthodox theodicy (argument defending God's goodness), the Jews of Europe were sinners who deserved to die. Opposed to this view were redemptionist Zionists (such as Rabbi Mordecai Atiyah [1897–1979]), who saw the Holocaust as a punishment for the Jewish unfaithfulness to the land of Israel.

Another ongoing controversy surrounds the Western (Wailing) Wall, which is sacred for Jews because it is the only remnant of the ancient Second Temple. For Muslims the wall is the outer rim of Haram al-Sharif, the third-holiest site in the Islamic world, where, according to Islamic legend, the prophet Muhammad tethered his horse during his Night Journey. Muslims built the Al-Aqsa Mosque and the Dome of the Rock on Haram al-Sharif. Religious Jews as well as several nationalist groups believe that Jewish redemption will be accompanied by the rebuilding of the Temple on the site of the mosque. Fear of destruction of the mosque remains a major concern for local Muslim Arabs and the entire Muslim world. This anxiety adds an additional religious dimension to the Jewish-Arab conflict.

Another controversial issue for some Israelis is the role of women. They are excluded from participating in the administration of state-funded religious services as well as from filling salaried public religious roles as rabbis or *dayanim* (judges), but they are accepted into local religious councils.

CULTURAL IMPACT In order to avoid pagan worship and idolatry, the Jewish religion prohibits sculptures and paintings of human figures or icons. This has imposed heavy restrictions on religious Jewish artists. Israeli contemporary culture, however, is secular and scarcely influenced by Judaism. The Jewish liturgy, for example, remains mainly within the walls of the synagogue and is used for prayer. Some of the liturgical themes have, however, found their way into pop culture.

Many Israeli artists, writers (including Nobel Prize laureate S.Y. Agnon [1888–1970]), sculptors (such as Yaacov Agam [born in 1928]), and painters (such as Reuben Rubin [1893–1974] and Marcel Janco [1895–1984]) have used Jewish religious symbols and metaphors in their works. The synagogue at Hadassah—Hebrew University's hospital—incorporates stained-glass windows (1962) by the renowned French painter Marc Chagall (1887–1985) that represent ancient Israel's Twelve Tribes (the offspring of the Patriarch Jacob's twelve sons). Another salient architectural achievement is the campus of Hebrew Union College (which includes a synagogue), a branch of the Jewish Reform Movement's rabbinical seminary. Opened in 1963, it is the major presence of this unrecognized Jewish religious congregation in Israel.

Other Religions

Before the war of 1948 the territory of Palestine that would become Israel was populated mostly by Sunni Muslim Arabs. Following the war their vast majority was uprooted, and their relative proportion was drastically reduced by massive waves of Jewish immigration. Today Muslims constitute some 15 percent of Israel's citizens.

Upon the establishment of the British administration in the early 1920s, Islam in Palestine lost its primacy within the *millet* system that had been implemented by the Ottomans; it was instead included on an equal basis with the other ethnoreligious communities. In 1922 the Supreme Muslim Council was created as an autonomous body to manage the needs of the country's Muslims according to the Shari'ah (Islamic law). The council was presided over by the grand mufti of Jerusalem, who was entitled to nominate all of the Muslim religious clerks—including muftis, *qadis* (judges), and teachers at traditional schools—in the country and to manage and control the *waqfs* (religious endowments).

With these resources, the Supreme Council gained extensive political power and was at the forefront of the nascent Palestinian national movement. Upon the establishment of Israel, the *millet* structure remained an organizational principle for the Muslim religious community as well, but it was completely depoliticized.

Between 1948 and 1967 Muslims in Israel were prevented from performing the hajj, the pilgrimage to Mecca that all Muslims must make at least once. It was made impossible mainly by the refusal of the Arab states to grant them passage and Israel's anxiety about allowing its citizens to travel to enemy countries. During this period the Muslims in Israel also lacked access to Islam's third-holiest shrine, the Haram al-Sharif, located in the Jordanian region of al-Quds (Jerusalem). After the war of 1967 partial access was permitted to Mecca (via Jordan) and to the Haram al-Sharif.

The Israeli Islamic Movement that exists today is divided between a moderate branch and a more militant one in the south. The movement provides charitable, educational, and other communal services (including a soccer league separate from the Israeli one) and controls many municipal councils. Because it does not recognize the legitimate existence of a Jewish state on what is defined as an all-Arab land, the movement does not run for the Israeli parliament.

The Druze, some 80,000 Arabic speakers living in 22 villages in northern Israel, are a religious community similar to Islam but separate from it. While the Druze religion is not accessible to outsiders, one known aspect of its theology is the concept of *taqiyya*, which calls for the complete loyalty of its adherents to the rule of the country in which they reside. For this reason, the Druze are conscripted by the Israeli military.

The Circassians, some 3,000 people concentrated in two northern villages, are Sunni Muslims, although they share neither Arab origin nor the cultural background of the larger Islamic community. Their place of origin is the Caucasus (the region between the Black and Caspian seas). Circassians participate in Israel's economic and national affairs while maintaining a distinct ethnic identity; they do not assimilate into Jewish society or into the general Muslim community.

Christian Arabs, with a population of some 150,000, constitute Israel's second-largest minority. They live mainly in urban areas, including Nazareth, Shfar'am, and Haifa. The majority of Israeli Christians are affiliated with the Greek Catholic (42 percent), Greek Orthodox (32 percent), and Roman Catholic (16 percent) churches. The Armenian Patriarchate (in East Jerusalem) is considered the second most important Armenian community in the world.

Because all Christian churches consider the land of Israel and Palestine the Holy Land, most denominations and derivatives of Christianity maintain at least one representative structure in the country. For instance, the Mormons built a university in Jerusalem in the 1980s. The Roman Catholic Church has traditionally provided schooling and various educational services to the Arab Christian (and non-Christian) population and has regarded itself as the guardian of Christian holy shrines.

On the eve of World War I the Christian population stood at some 70,000 (10 percent of the population). During the course of the twentieth century, while the general population of the Holy Land grew, the relative number of Christians there declined. The continuous deterioration of the Christian presence in the Holy Land has caused deep concern throughout the Christian world. By 1947, on the eve of Israeli independence, the Christian population in colonial Palestine numbered 143,000 (7 percent of the total population). Within the borders of the State of Israel 34,000 Christians remained (less than 3 percent of the population). Today, within the borders of what was historical Palestine (Israel, the West Bank, and the Gaza Strip), there is a total of 180,000 Christians, just over 2 percent of the total population.

The majority of the Christians in Israel are officially Arab; a smaller number declare themselves non-Arab. Many of the latter went to Israel with their Jewish spouses during the waves of immigration in the 1980s and '90s, mainly from the former Soviet Union and Ethiopia. Ethiopian immigrants were mainly the Falashmura (Ethiopian Jews who had converted to Christianity). Although most Christians in Israel are Arab, their demographic profile (their education, income, and modernity) differs from that of the Muslim population and more closely resembles that of the Jewish population.

In Israel the main Christian holy sites, which are popular pilgrimage destinations, are the Church of the Nativity (Jesus' birthplace, in Bethlehem in the West Bank); the Basilica of the Annunciation; the Grotto of the Virgin in Nazareth (where, according to tradition, the Virgin Mary met the angel who announced to her that she would be a mother); the Church of Saint Joseph, the supposed location of Jesus' carpentry shop (in Nazareth); the Church of the Holy Sepulcher in Jerusalem, where Jesus was crucified by the Romans; and the Via Dolorosa (way of sorrows), the path Jesus walked from Pontius Pilate's judgment hall to Calvary carrying his cross (in Jerusalem). These latter events are commemorated by the Fourteen Stations of the Cross, nine of which are related in the Gospels and five by tradition. The first two are located in the vicinity of Ecce Homo Convent, the next seven along the street, and the last five within the Holy Sepulcher. The most prominent leaders of local Christianity at the beginning of the twenty-first century were the Latin patriarch of Jerusalem, Michel Sabbah (born in 1933); the Greek Orthodox patriarch, Irineos I (born in 1939); and the Armenian patriarch, Torkom II Manoogian (born in 1919).

The Baha'i faith's Universal House of Justice is located on Mount Carmel in Haifa and administrates the world affairs of some five million believers. The Baha'i faith maintains that there is one universal God and embraces the principles, holy fathers, and prophets of the world's monotheistic religions as well as of Buddhism and other Eastern religions. It also accepts the Holy Land as such.

Baruch Kimmerling

See Also Vol. I: *Judaism*

Bibliography

El-Or, Tamar. *Next Year I Will Know More: Literacy and Identity among Young Orthodox Women in Israel.* Detroit: Wayne State University Press, 2002.

Friedman, Menachem. "The State of Israel as a Theological Dilemma." In *The Israeli State and Society: Boundaries and Frontiers,* edited by Baruch Kimmerling, 165–215. Albany: State University of New York Press, 1989.

———. *Ha-Hevrah ha-haredit: Mekorot, megamot ve-tahalikhim.* Jerusalem: Jerusalem Institute of Study of Israel, 1991.

Kimmerling, Baruch. "Religion, Nationalism and Democracy in Israel." *Constellations* 6, no. 3 (1999): 339–63.

Levy, Shlomit, Hanna Levinson, and Elihu Katz. *A Portrait of Israeli Jewry: Beliefs, Observance and Values among Israeli Jews, 2000.* Jerusalem: Guttman Center of the Israeli Democracy Institute and Avi-Chai Foundation, 2002.

Liebman, Charles S., and Eihu Katz, eds. *The Jewishness of Israelis: Responses to the Guttman Report.* Albany: State University of New York Press, 1997.

Ravitzky, Aviezer. *Messianism, Zionism, and Jewish Religious Radicalism.* Chicago: University of Chicago Press, 1996.

Italy

POPULATION 57,715,625

ROMAN CATHOLIC 98 percent

OTHER 2 percent

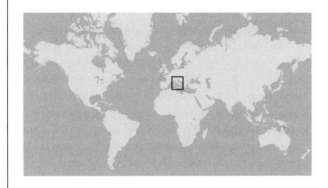

Country Overview

INTRODUCTION Occupying a peninsula that extends into the Mediterranean Sea, the Italian Republic is the third most populous country of continental Europe after Germany and France. Its religious tradition is strongly rooted in the Roman Catholic Church. Catholicism imparts a strong sense of collective identity, which has been reinforced by the growing presence of other religions, particularly Islam.

Italy was not unified as a nation until 1870, and compared with other European countries, the process of industrialization, and therefore of entry into modern

times, manifested itself late. Between 1955 and 1985 the country's industrial system, particularly in the north, underwent intense development, which produced great internal migration from the south. This was accompanied by a new phenomenon for Italy, secularization and a resulting crisis in traditional religious practice. The introduction in the 1970s of laws permitting abortion and divorce represented the most obvious signs of these changes. Although 98 percent of Italians continue to be baptized in the Catholic Church, upwards of 10 percent consider themselves without religious affiliation. Attendance at religious services is at around 30–35 percent. By the end of the twentieth century, Italy appeared to be aligned with the advanced industrialized nations of the West.

RELIGIOUS TOLERANCE Because of its cohesive Catholic tradition, Italy generally has not experienced internal religious controversies. The Protestant Reformation did not enter Italy, although the Waldenses, a Protestant sect living in the valleys of the Piedmont, suffered persecution until 1848, when Charles Albert, king of Sardinia-Piedmont, permitted them to practice their religion freely. Beginning in the late twentieth century, however, immigration from Islamic countries has raised the issue of religious tolerance. The Italian constitution (1948) declares that "all citizens have equal social dignity and are equal before the law without consideration of sex, race, language, religion, political opinions, personal and social conditions." Religious minorities have freedom of worship in Italy, and they are generally accepted with tolerance.

The rituals of Holy Week are particularly treasured in some regions of Italy. Here a group of celebrants carry the statue of the Christ and Our Lady during a procession in the village of Nocera Terinese in Italy. © REUTERS NEWMEDIA INC./CORBIS.

Major Religion

ROMAN CATHOLICISM

DATE OF ORIGIN 42–67 C.E.

NUMBER OF FOLLOWERS 56.6 million

HISTORY The origins of the Catholic Church in Italy coincide with the origins of Christianity in Rome, where it arrived with Saint Peter and Saint Paul. According to a tradition dating to the fourth century, Peter lived in Rome from 42 to 67 C.E., and the origins of Christianity in Italy can be traced to this period. Notwithstanding the recurrent presence of heresies, for a full millennium—until the separation of the churches of the East in the Schism of 1054—the history of the Church of Rome was identified with the history of Christianity.

The break with the East and, five centuries later, the break with the Protestant churches of northern Europe account for the fact that the history of Christianity in Italy was, until the twentieth century, the history of the Catholic Church itself.

After three centuries of persecution, the spread of Christianity in Rome led to the conversion of the Roman Empire, backed by the Edict of Milan issued in 313 by the emperor Constantine. In 380 the emperor Theodosius elevated Christianity as the religion of the state. A decisive moment in the Christianization of the barbarian populations was the encounter between the Church of Rome and the Franks, a Germanic tribe, which achieved its symbolic conclusion in 800 with the coronation of Charlemagne as emperor by Pope Leo III in Saint Peter's in Rome. In the following centuries the Roman papacy was engaged in stemming the hegemonic claims of the emperor and in vindicating the preeminence of the spiritual over the temporal sphere. The Investiture Controversy involved two popes, Gregory VII (1073–85) and Innocent III (1198–1216), who were the defenders of the idea of the *plenitudo potestatis* (complete power) of the Roman papacy. The reign of Innocent III saw the birth of the Franciscan movement, which, by exalting a return to evangelical poverty, represented a response to the centrifugal and heretical forces present in the medieval church. In addition, the mendicant Dominican and Carmelite orders were born during this period.

In the thirteenth century universities were established in which the Catholic Church, through the diffusion of Scholastic philosophy, presented a unitary vision of the world, of which Saint Thomas Aquina'ss *Summa Theologiae* and Dante's *Divine Comedy* represent the highest expressions. In the same century a serious crisis began in medieval Christianity, leading to the transfer of the papal court to Avignon in 1309 under the control of the king of France. The work of Saint Catherine of Siena contributed to the return of the papal seat to Rome by Pope Gregory XI in 1377. The difficulties of the Church of Rome were not resolved, however, as the need for reform swelled, leading a century and a half later to the rift with the German world and to the birth of the Protestant Reformation in 1517 through the work of Martin Luther. The Catholic Church responded with an effort at internal reform, the Counter-Reformation, which was based on the results of the Council of Trent (1545–63) and which was the starting point of modern Catholicism.

In the following centuries nationalist movements in other countries sought to maintain political power with the support of ecclesiastical doctrines. The movements took the name of Gallicanism in France and of Josephinism in Austria. In Italy, however, such trends did not meet with good fortune, for the presence of the Papal States obstructed national unification. The Italian Risorgimento concluded with the occupation of Rome in 1870 by the troops of the young Kingdom of Italy, and the Catholic Church, after approximately a thousand years, lost temporal power. From that date the pope did not leave the Vatican until a concordat was signed in 1929 that regulated relations between the state and church. In 1984 a new concordat declared the state and the church, each in its own framework, to be independent and sovereign, while abolishing the clause stating that Catholicism was the sole religion of Italy.

EARLY AND MODERN LEADERS Catholicism is a religion whose hierarchy follows a pyramidal model. At the top is the pope, who is elected by the Sacred College of Cardinals and who, in Catholic doctrine, descends directly from the apostle Peter, to whom Jesus Christ entrusted the nascent church. The pope is considered to possess dogmatic infallibility in the enunciation of the most important principles of faith. The founders of the monastic orders have also responded to pastoral needs and have proposed models of behavior for the Catholic Church. In addition, the saints represent heroic religious testimonials, tied closely to their times but with a universal message. Among these are the martyrs of the early centuries, first of all Saint Peter and Saint Paul, the founders of the Church of Rome; Saint Polycarp; Saints Perpetua and Felicity; and Saint Cipriano. All testified to the truth of their faith by sacrificing their lives.

Among the Italian founders of religious orders, Saint Benedict (fifth–sixth centuries) was a charismatic leader who founded Benedictine monasticism, which spread throughout Europe, and who established a rule for his order that joined prayer with work (*ora et labora,*) and that was renowned for its moderation. Among the founders of religious orders in the Middle Ages, Saint Francis of Assisi (1181–1216) is universally renowned for simplicity and purity, the intensity of his union with Christ, his absolute dedication to the ideals of poverty and love for others, and his profound affinity with nature.

In the modern era renewal in the church has brought about the birth of many religious orders in Italy, the founders of which were all declared saints. Among them were Saint Gaetano from Tiene (died in 1547), founder of the Oratorio of Divine Love; Saint John of God (died in 1550), founder of the Fatebenefratelli, a hospital order; and Saint Angela Merici, founder in 1535 of the Ursuline order. Beginning in the nineteenth century, the new religious orders had, above all else, educational goals for a society in which industrialization was creating marginalization and widespread religious crisis. Of note was Saint Giovanni Bosco (1815–88), founder of the Salesian Congregation, whose purpose was the religious and professional training of youth. Among later leaders was Padre Pio of Pietralcina (died in 1968), a Capuchin monk who lived in Saint Giovanni Rotondo (Puglia) and who has remained the object of veneration by an immense number of devotees. Another extraordinary figure was Angelo Giuseppe Roncalli (1881–1963), who as Pope John XXIII not only changed the style of the Roman Curia but also summoned the Second Vatican Council, the most important and revolutionary event of the Catholic Church in the twentieth century.

MAJOR THEOLOGIANS AND AUTHORS Italian theology had its most influential exponents during the period of its origins up to the time of the Counter-Reformation, after which it fell into a dark period that lasted several centuries. In the late twentieth century, however, a new generation of theologians emerged who brought to fruition the lessons of the Second Vatican Council and who attained international renown.

The greatest Italian Catholic theologian and philosopher of all time was Thomas Aquinas (1225–74). He was an extraordinary mediator between Aristotle and Saint Augustine, giving to medieval theology its most perfect development and creating a vast and profound foundation for the Catholic concept of the world of his time. Further, his life was consecrated to an intimate and profound religiosity. For these merits and for his universally known didactic authority he was called Doctor Angelicus, and Italian theology remained faithful to the canons of Thomism until contemporary times.

In 1869 Pope Pius IX convoked the First Vatican Council, whose proclamations included the doctrine on papal infallability. Later in the nineteenth century Pope Leo XIII became the promoter of a rebirth of Thomist theology in opposition to the atheistic philosophies that had emerged after the Enlightenment. It was in this climate that the Catholic University of the Sacred Heart was founded in Milan in 1921 with the purpose of revitalizing Catholic thought, mostly on the philosophical front. Contemporary Italian theologians of international importance include Bruno Forte (born in 1952), author of multiple volumes on the nature of revelation and of the church, and Piero Coda (born in 1955), a distinguished scholar of Catholic doctrine who has also engaged in dialogues with other religions.

HOUSES OF WORSHIP AND HOLY PLACES Rome is home to Saint Peter's Basilica, built in the sixteenth century and Christianity's greatest temple. Among Italy's other grand churches are the Gothic Duomo in Milan, Saint Maria Novella and Saint Maria del Fiore in Florence, Saint Mark's Basilica in Venice, and Saint Anthony's in Padova. Churches where great artists worked are interspersed throughout the country.

The cult of the Virgin Mary and the veneration of saints, which date to the origins of Christianity, are widespread and deeply rooted in Italian religious life. Of the more than 200 shrines in Italy, the vast majority are dedicated to the Madonna, often under various names and commemorating an apparition by her or miracles that occurred on the site. The landscape is also strewn with shrines dedicated to the Virgin and saints, whose memory is thus kept alive and who are held to be intercessors on behalf of supplicants. Among the most important shrines in Italy are those of the Madonna of Loreto (Marche), where a small rustic house is maintained that, according to tradition, was the abode of Mary, transported by angels from Palestine. The shrine of Saint Anthony of Padua is visited by some 4 million people a year.

WHAT IS SACRED? The practice of Catholicism in Italy, as in many other countries, has moved toward a clearer separation of the private sacred and the public secular realms. Places of worship and shrines continue to be held sacred, as are dates established by the liturgical calendar, such as Christmas and Easter. During the twentieth century secularization accelerated the relegation of the sacred to the private sphere, even though local public celebrations of the Virgin Mary and of patron saints have remained vital, especially in the south of Italy.

HOLIDAYS AND FESTIVALS The structure of the ecclesiastical year in Italy does not differ from that of other predominantly Catholic countries. The principal holidays are Christmas, preceded by the four Sundays of Advent, and Easter, preceded by the four Sundays of Lent. In Italy, in addition to the fixed holidays recognized throughout the Catholic world, there are so-called holy days of obligation, on which the faithful have the duty to participate in the Mass. For example, the Madonna is venerated on the feasts of the Immaculate Conception (December 8) and the Assumption (August 15), both considered holy day of obligation. There are also many other holy days, on which local (particularly patron) saints are remembered. Saint Francis of Assisi, the patron saint of Italy, is honored on October 4, and each city and town has its own patron saint, whose day is generally celebrated by suspending work and closing schools. This is the case, for example, with Saint Ambrose in Milan (December 7), Saint Petronius in Bologna (October 4), Saint Anthony in Padua (June 13), Saint Gennaro in Naples (September 19), and Saint Agatha in Catania (February 5). There are local holidays for shrines dedicated to the Virgin.

MODE OF DRESS Catholics in Italy do not wear special types of clothing unless it is done in homage to local traditions. During religious ceremonies, however, dress distinguishes the celebrant priest from the worshipers. The essential element of the celebrant's clothing is the chasuble, a sleeveless outer vestment, the color of which changes according to the liturgical period. In solemn ceremonies the chasuble is replaced by the cope, a mantle made in the form of a semicircle. The cope is rich in embroidery and decoration, and its colors change throughout the year to match those of the chasuble.

DIETARY PRACTICES Catholicism in Italy does not prohibit and does not impose any type of food. No food is considered impure. Rather, forms of fasting that replicate Jewish practices have been observed, with various adaptations, since antiquity. The original Christian days of fasting were Wednesday and Friday. Later, however, the obligation to abstain from meat was consolidated on Fridays and on Ash Wednesday, which follows the end of Carnival. These obligations have an essentially symbolic nature. At the popular level local eating habits in various regions are observed in conjunction with canonical and patron feasts, as well as with the cycles of the ecclesiastical year. For example, *abbacchio* (roasted lamb) is traditional on Easter for people in Rome and the south of Italy, and in many parts of the north the meal on Christmas Eve consists of pickled fish and dried fruit.

RITUALS The most important Catholic rite for Italians, as for Catholics generally, is the Mass, in which, according to church doctrine, the sacrifice of Christ is re-created in a bloodless manner with the transformation of unleavened bread and wine into his body and blood. There also are rites connected to the seven sacraments that accompany each adherent from birth (baptism) to death (anointing of the sick). Other rites have changed in time and according to cultural traditions. They can also become obsolete, as is the case with the *beneditio mulieris post partum* (blessing of the mother after giving birth), which has not been practiced in Italy since the 1970s. Particularly treasured in some regions of Italy are the rituals of Holy Week, in which there is widespread popular participation. Certain rituals, such as those tied to the New Year, Carnival, harvests, and patron saints, have to some degree fallen out of use or, particularly in the south of Italy, been reintroduced as tourist attractions.

RITES OF PASSAGE Approximately 98 percent of all Italians are baptized, although it is often merely from a sense of tradition. Fewer participate in confirmation, penance, and the Eucharist, but between 70 and 80 percent of marriages continue to be celebrated with a religious ceremony. The religious crisis in Italy has significantly reduced the number of priests being ordained, and the anointing of the sick (extreme unction) is administered to fewer than 50 percent of Italians.

MEMBERSHIP Evangelizing in Italy depends upon the situations in which priests find themselves. The trend is away from direct conversion and toward sharing people's problems without consideration of their religious or political ideology. The contemporary Catholic style in Italy is based more on friendship, dialogue, and reciprocal trust than on coercive attempts to impose the Catholic view on others.

SOCIAL JUSTICE The social teachings of the Roman Catholic Church are, above all, aimed at reducing the gaps between economic classes and between rich and poor countries. A number of enterprises of the church are oriented toward these goals. The organization Caritas and church missions, for example, are engaged in countries of the Third World. The church also works to reduce conflicts between Islam and countries of the West.

SOCIAL ASPECTS Italian Catholic doctrine follows the directives of the church on moral issues. The church fought the referendums that allowed the legalization of divorce (1974) and abortion (1981), although these proposals passed since many Catholics voted in favor of them. Moreover, according to the directives of Pope Paul VI's encyclical *Humanae Vitae* (1968; "Of Human Life"), Italian Catholicism is officially opposed to all forms of birth control except the rhythm method. Nonetheless, there have been significant changes in sexual and marital practices in Italy, with so-called de facto marriages becoming more frequent, and some of the more progressive sectors of the hierarchy and Catholic clergy issue pastoral policies addressing divorced people and nontraditional unions.

POLITICAL IMPACT On the one hand, the conquest of Rome by Italian troops in 1870 allowed the political unification of Italy, but, on the other, it opened up a long conflict between the church and state. This would eventually be settled by the concordat of 1929 (Lateran Pact), which was revised in 1984. The concordat recognized the civil validity of religious marriage ceremonies, gave legal recognition to Catholic schools, exempted priests from military service, and regulated the teaching of religion in state schools.

The long conflict that preceded the Lateran Pact pushed Italian Catholics to form cooperative associations that gained social and political representation. In 1919 Luigi Sturzo, a priest from Caltagirone (Sicily), founded the Popular Party, which had as a guiding principle the social doctrine expounded by Pope Leo XIII in the 1891 encyclical *Rerum Novarum* ("Of New Things"). In 1924 the party was suppressed by the Fascist government, but it was reborn after World War II as the Christian Democratic Party under the leadership of Alcide De Gasperi. The Christian Democrats were the majority party until the early 1990s.

The period between 1945 and 1990 was marked by confrontations between Christian Democrats and communists. In their opposition to the Italian Communist Party, which had the largest membership in Western Europe, Christian Democrats had the support of the Catholic Church. The party's political vision was reformist and supportive of all social classes. As a result of the collapse of communism in Eastern Europe, the Christian Democrats became fragmented, and the communists themselves adopted a reformist platform. As a result, the Italian political and religious framework underwent a radical transformation. Religious life became more of a personal expression; traditional morality changed markedly, with an increase in civil marriages, common-law unions, divorce, and legal abortion; and new religious movements began to spread more aggressively.

CONTROVERSIAL ISSUES While the doctrines of the Catholic hierarchy in Italy regarding birth control, divorce, and abortion have remained unchanged over time, with the church maintaining staunch opposition, social changes have occurred rapidly, even among believers. Thus, there is an ever-widening divide between the practices of observant Catholics and ecclesiastical directives. Further, women remain confined to secondary roles in the church. Although Catholic women in Italy are more and more involved in all sectors of politics, industry, education, and service occupations, they have not been offered opportunities to increase their role in the church.

CULTURAL IMPACT The impact of Catholicism on art in Italy began in early Christian times in the catacombs and the Roman basilicas and with the great Byzantine architecture of the northeast, culminating in the diffusion of Romanesque and Gothic structures throughout the peninsula. A parallel phenomenon in music was the emergence of Gregorian chant, practiced in particular in monasteries. A subsequent phase was represented by the great baroque and late baroque architecture of the sixteenth and seventeenth centuries that was widespread in the south of Italy and in Sicily, where important examples remain in Lecce, Catania, and Noto. The Italian period of great religious painting and sculpture spans the Middle Ages and the Renaissance, with Giotto (1266?–1337), Giovanni Cimabue (c. 1251–1302), Michelangelo (1475–1564), Leonardo da Vinci (1452–1519), Titian (c. 1488–1576), and Giovanni Battista Tiepolo (1696–1770) among the best-known representatives.

With the Counter-Reformation the Catholic Church strove to attain consensus. Threatened by internal disputes, the Protestant Reformation, and new scientific discoveries, the church at first imposed the ethical and doctrinal discipline promulgated by the Council of Trent. Later there developed the great decorative manner of the baroque, which was aimed at involving spectators and moving them at the most intimate levels of emotion. In music polyphonic compositions known as madrigals and new forms of sacred music triumphed, among which the greatest composers were Ludovico Grossi da Viadana (1564–1645), Gesualdo da Venosa (1560–1613), Giovanni Pierluigi da Palestrina (1524–94), and Claudio Monteverdi (1567–1643).

From the second half of the eighteenth century, religious art declined in Italy. It lost the energy it had once had and came to be devoid of authentic inspiration. In the nineteenth century some great Italian musicians, among them Giuseppe Verdi (1813–1901), composed music with religious content, mostly as requiem Masses. Beginning in the 1970s, there were attempts to promote modern religious architecture and figurative arts, but these experiments have generally not been considered successful.

Other Religions

Roman Jews arrived in Italy long before the birth of Christianity, and today there are some 35,000 Jews living in the country. Roughly 70 percent of all Jews live in Rome and Milan. Rome is the seat of a rabbinical college, and the Jewish community distributes several publications, including the *Monthly Review of Israel,* the *Milan Jewish Community Bulletin,* the *Ha Keillah* from Turin, and *Jewish Florence.*

The Waldensian Church represents the exceptional case of a Protestant community that spread throughout the Italian peninsula more than three centuries before the reforms of Martin Luther. The original settlement took place in various Piedmont valleys. The community, which together with Methodists has approximately 25,000 members, has its historical seat in Torre Pellice, where the Waldensian Table meets. Rome is the seat of the Waldensian Faculty of Theology, which publishes the magazine *Protestantism.*

Other Christian groups in Italy include Pentecostals and Seventh-day Adventists. Jehovah's Witnesses have been particularly successful in recruiting members from the lower classes.

There are more than 60 Orthodox communities in Italy, including Greek, Romanian, Russian, and Serbian groups. Some of the communities belong to the Orthodox Patriarchate, founded in Venice in 1991.

The presence of Islam in Italy is a new phenomenon, brought about by immigration particularly from North and Central Africa and from Pakistan, Bangladesh, and Indonesia. The Islamic Cultural Center of Italy, located in Rome, is associated with the Grand

Mosque of Monte Antenne, which was constructed under the auspices of Arab embassies in Italy. The Islamic Center of Milan publishes *The Messenger of Islam*.

New religious movements, which are found mostly in cities in Italy, include Scientology and Transcendental Meditation. There also are small numbers of Buddhists.

Carlo Prandi

See Also Vol. I: *Christianity, Roman Catholicism*

Bibliography

Allievi, Stefano, Gustavo Guizzardi, and Carlo Prandi. *Un Dio al plurale*. Bologna: EDB, 2002.

De Franciscis, Maria Elisabetta. *Italy and the Vatican: The 1984 Concordat Between Church and State*. New York: Peter Lang, 1989.

De Rosa, Gabriele, Tullio Gregory, and André Vauchez, eds. *Storia dell'Italia religiosa*. 3 vols. Bari: Laterza, 1994.

Marthaler, Berard et al., *New Catholic Encyclopedia*. 2d ed. 15 vols. Detroit: Gale, 2002.

Hebblethwaite, P. *Paul VI: The First Modern Pope*. New York: Paulist Press, 1993.

Introvigne, Massimo, Pierluigi Zoccatelli, and Nelly Ippolito Macrina. *Enciclopedia delle religioni in Italia*. Torino: Elledici, 2001.

Scaraffia, Lucetta, and Gabriella Zarri, eds. *Women and Faith: Catholic Religious Life in Italy from Late Antiquity to the Present*. Cambridge, Mass.: Harvard University Press, 1999.

Smith, Denis Mack. *Modern Italy: A Political History*. Ann Arbor: University of Michigan Press, 1997.

Jamaica

POPULATION 2,680,029

PENTECOSTAL 33.29 percent

SEVENTH-DAY ADVENTIST 10.84 percent

BAPTIST 7.27 percent

ANGLICAN 3.6 percent

RASTAFARIAN 0.93 percent

OTHER 23.12 percent

NONRELIGIOUS 20.95 percent

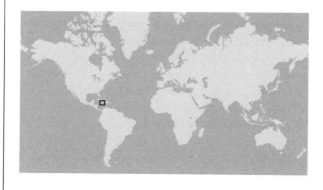

Country Overview

INTRODUCTION Jamaica, an island in the western Caribbean approximately 90 miles south of Cuba, features a rich and diverse religious legacy. Roman Catholicism was taken to Jamaica in 1494 by Christopher Columbus on his first expedition to the island. When Great Britain conquered the island in 1655, Anglicanism became the sole religion until the coming of Moravian missionaries in the 1750s. In the last two decades of the eighteenth century, other groups such as Methodists, Presbyterians, and Baptists began missionary activities among the slaves. The Baptists became numerically the most successful.

Myal, a new religion based on an African cosmology, took root in Jamaica from the mid-seventeenth century. Open to outside influences, it absorbed Christian elements, in the process becoming known as the New Baptist movement and then Revivalism. Although European Christian denominations, which were more socially acceptable, accounted for the nominal membership of the overwhelming majority of Jamaicans, it was the less esteemed Revivalism that answered to their spiritual needs. By the mid-twentieth century adherents of Revivalism discovered Pentecostalism, a group that shared the practice of spirit possession while at the same time had the respectability of origin in the wealthy, white United States. Pentecostalism grew rapidly at the expense of the European Christian denominations.

In the 1930s a new religion, Rastafarianism, was founded in Jamaica. Proclaiming the emperor of Ethiopia as God, it ushered in a period of heightened racial consciousness and desire for decolonization, growing from a small cult to a social movement by the 1960s. Today it accounts for adherents in many parts of the world.

Numerous other religious groups, mainly North American in origin, such as Seventh-day Adventists and the Church of Jesus Christ of Latter-day Saints (Mormons), are also represented in Jamaica.

RELIGIOUS TOLERANCE Freedom of religion is enshrined in the constitution, which took effect 6 August

1962, the day Jamaica became independent from Great Britain. A clause in the constitution, however, allows for all laws in force on that date to take precedence in the event of a conflict. For example, under the Night Noises Act, the police may curtail religious worship if in their opinion the law is being violated. Most affected have been Revival and some Pentecostal groups, which use vigorous drumming and amplified shouting, singing, and preaching in their services.

Generally speaking there is not only great tolerance of but also respect for all religions. In order to receive privileges such as tax exemption, a religion must be incorporated by an act of Parliament.

Major Religion

PENTECOSTALISM

DATE OF ORIGIN c. 1900 C.E.
NUMBER OF FOLLOWERS 892,000

HISTORY Africans who were taken to Jamaica as slaves during the seventeenth and eighteenth centuries came from coastal and hinterland areas of Africa. Out of the underlying worldview they shared, there emerged by the middle of the seventeenth century a new religion called Myal, which unified them into a moral community and empowered them to challenge the political order. Myal transformed itself into what became known as the Native Baptist movement by absorbing elements from Christianity, such as conversion by immersion, sacralizing of the Bible, and recognition of such figures as Jesus, John the Baptist, the Holy Spirit, Isaiah, and Jeremiah. These elements were integrated into a West African cosmology, spirituality, and aesthetics, resulting in an outlook that denied an opposition between otherworldly salvation and this-worldly well-being, as preached by the European missionaries. It instead saw religious life as a quest for spiritual empowerment through spirit possession and sacrifice. Stimulated by slaves from Central Africa who had been liberated at sea, Myal joined the Christian revival movement that swept Jamaica in 1860 (called the "Great Revival"), which involved emotionally charged services and the use of Jamaican instruments and music. Myal thus transformed itself into what is now known as Revivalism.

Pentecostalism, a religious movement originating in the United States, became the framework through which

A baptism is held at a church in Kingston, Jamaica. Baptism is one of the main rituals common to Pentecostal adherents. © DANIEL LAINÉ/CORBIS.

tenets and practices of Revivalism were institutionalized and given social respectability. From the Church of God in Cleveland, Tennessee, founded in 1904 by A.J. Tomlinson, came two streams of the Pentecostal faith, the New Testament Church of God, incorporated in Jamaica in 1949, and the Church of God of Prophecy, incorporated in 1964.

It is through Revivalism that Pentecostalism became indigenized and attracted the largest following of adherents in Jamaica. Given the high social status of the European churches and the low status of Revivalism, most people used to claim nominal membership in the former while retaining active membership in the latter. Pentecostalism, with its American origin and access to substantial material resources, was able to gain higher social standing, without any loss of emphasis on spiritual empowerment, its most central distinguishing feature.

According to scholars, Pentecostalism's phenomenal growth from a mere 4 percent of the population in 1943 to more than 20 percent in 1970 and 33 percent in 2001 has been a result of the indigenization of the movement. Under Jamaican leadership, adherence to a Puritan ethic of moral discipline as the guarantee of salvation in the next world has been supplanted by a joy and perfection in this life, and emphasis is placed on the ritual and spiritual healing of body and spirit.

EARLY AND MODERN LEADERS Among the early Pentecostal preachers were Raglan Phillips, the founder of City Mission in Kingston in 1924; George Olson, who was sent by Holiness Church of God in Indiana in response to an appeal for help in the wake of the 1907 earthquake; and George White, a Jamaican, who, with his wife, evangelized large sections of the country under the Pentecostal Assemblies of the World.

The best-known contemporary leader of the Pentecostal movement in Jamaica is Bishop Herro Blair (born in 1946), whose Deliverance Temple in Kingston is the largest church in the country. A highly rated televangelist, Blair has had a history of activism in the wider political arena.

MAJOR THEOLOGIANS AND AUTHORS Pentecostal sects do not produce theologians in the traditional sense; their approach is opposed to intellectualizing and in favor of experience. Jamaican Pentecostals maintain these same attitudes.

HOUSES OF WORSHIP AND HOLY PLACES Pentecostal churches, including those in Jamaica, tend to be large, simple structures. Religious art is confined to murals of the Last Supper or the Apocalypse adorning the altar. A simple platform on which the preacher, elders, and deacons sit, the altar is a sacred space where God and humankind meet in prayer, healing, and confession.

WHAT IS SACRED? Jamaican Pentecostals follow Pentecostal doctrine, which holds the Holy Bible as the sacred word of God. They also generally do not observe any form of taboo toward material objects, whether living or inanimate; however, in some Jamaican churches, uncovered female head hair is taboo.

HOLIDAYS AND FESTIVALS In keeping with Pentecostals internationally, Jamaican Pentecostals do not observe any holidays or festivals outside of Christmas and Easter.

MODE OF DRESS In general, women dress conservatively in Jamaican Pentecostal churches, avoiding suggestive styles, cosmetics, or jewelry. Only since the 1980s have some accommodated straightened or short hair. White is the preferred color of dress for the Eucharist. A distinct feature of women's attire in Jamaican churches and those founded by Jamaicans in Great Britain is the wearing of hats or other hair covering. It is a tenet that

women cannot minister or be members of the church without covering their hair, and this practice may be derived from Pentecostalism's roots in Revivalism, whose cosmology attributes power to female head hair. Pentecostal men do not dress distinctively.

DIETARY PRACTICES Consuming alcoholic beverages is the only dietary practice proscribed in Pentecostalism, which emphasizes the need for spiritual power acquired through prayer and fasting.

RITUALS Baptism, Communion with Jesus through the enactment of the Last Supper and the washing of the feet, and Sunday morning worship are the main rituals common to Pentecostal adherents. Baptism is by complete immersion, for which a special pool is built inside the church. Dressed in white, the converts descend into the pool, where they are received by the pastor who, with one hand holding their clasped hands and the other their back, dips them below the surface, while reciting "I baptize you in the name of the Father and of the Son and of the Holy Ghost."

What is distinctly Jamaican in the Pentecostal Sunday morning worship, or Divine Service, is the aesthetic of music, song, and dance that accompanies the Bible lessons, testimonies, and sermon. In a country where sexual relations, cohabitation, and childbearing are separated from legal marriage and where popular dance hall culture exalts sexuality, the successful Pentecostal preacher must place emphasis on the sin of fornication and the call to righteousness. The success of a sermon is often measured by the response to his altar call—that is, his invitation to those in need of salvation, sanctification, or healing to rise and stand before the altar. There he prays for them, lays his hands on the head of each one, and, in cases where he has a reputation for healing, anoints them with consecrated oil.

RITES OF PASSAGE In a simple ritual of blessing conducted before the altar, Jamaican Pentecostals dedicate rather than baptize babies. It is the emphasis on marriage, however, that distinguishes the Pentecostal movement in Jamaica, a country where marriage is the last in a series of arrangements between couples (beginning with a visiting relationship and moving into cohabitation) and where there is no taboo against pregnancy outside wedlock. By "preaching fornication"—that is, preaching against premarital sexual relations—a watchful pastor exerts pressure on his followers to maintain their status as brides of Christ (the divine bridegroom) or to elevate their social status by marrying before the church.

In Jamaica there are three phases of observing a death: the wake, in which the community expresses its solidarity with the deceased; the ninth-night ceremony to enact the final separation of the deceased spirit; and the interment. Both the wake and the ninth-night ceremony involve singing, playing games, and feasting. Pentecostals in Jamaica observe this three-phased rite of passage but substitute religious hymns for the traditional folk songs.

MEMBERSHIP Only adults and adolescents can become members of the Pentecostal faith in Jamaica; prepubescent children are simply "dedicated." With a history in Jamaica of canvassing highways and byways, preaching on buses, and conducting wayside preaching, Pentecostal male and female evangelists target the communities of the urban and rural poor, spreading the word of God through "crusades," intense recruitment campaigns lasting a week or two.

SOCIAL JUSTICE Pentecostalism in Jamaica is not generally known for any developed teaching or activism concerning poverty, social justice, education, or human rights. In 1926, however, the Church of God in Jamaica founded the Ardenne High School, which continues its mission in the twenty-first century.

SOCIAL ASPECTS Because sexual intercourse outside marriage is deemed sinful in the Pentecostal church, an unwed pregnant woman is routinely suspended from church until the baby is born, she can confess her sin, and she can be born again with the "infilling" of the Holy Spirit. Infilling is the experience of an internal spiritual movement by the Holy Spirit, which usually comes during rituals, and is signaled by trance-like states, the gift of tongues, or other manifestations of spirit possession. The church also prohibits its members from gambling, smoking, going to dance halls, and drinking.

Male leadership with a large female following is a social characteristic of Jamaican Pentecostalism. The larger more organized churches actually promote a male pastorate. Bishops, pastors, and deacons are predominantly male, while all those with spiritual gifts such as healing and prophesying are women. Although there is no doctrine against female leadership, the female founder of a Pentecostal church will appoint a male as pastor, while she settles for the honorific but still powerful status of "Mother." Women serve in secondary and minor roles, but as the collective mainstay of the church, they wield considerable power over the male leadership, including defrocking a pastor.

POLITICAL IMPACT Pentecostalism in Jamaica has generally eschewed comments and positions on political issues. One diverging instance was when Bishop Herro Blair took a public stand against the democratic socialist government of Michael Manley in the late 1970s. The Pentecostal churches across the island supported Bishop Blair and viewed his position as a struggle against godless Communism.

CONTROVERSIAL ISSUES Jamaican Pentecostalism allows married members to use contraceptives and will even tolerate divorce, but it is uncompromisingly hostile to abortion.

CULTURAL IMPACT Pioneering musical groups like the Insight Gospel Group and the Grace Thrillers, both from the 1970s, and since the 1990s born-again artists like Papa San, Lieutenant Stitchie, Chevelle Franklin, and Judy Mowatt have brought the influence of gospel, popular reggae, and dance hall rhythms into Jamaica Pentecostalism.

Other Religions

From emancipation from slavery in 1834 to independence from Britain in 1962, European missionary churches were in the vanguard of educational development in Jamaica. Most primary schools were attached to and run by a church, and many of the leading high schools were staffed and run by Christian denominations. Independence merely added more schools without diminishing church control over those they had founded.

The role of European Christian churches in social development has been equally impressive. After emancipation Baptist and other missionaries purchased large properties and organized the settlement of free villages, which became the backbone of a free peasantry. European denominations generally remained missionary up to the decades following World War II, when a native clergy began to emerge. Roman Catholicism, however, which was reintroduced in 1850 by Jesuits, nearly two hundred years after the British seized the island from Spain in 1655, is still unable to exist without a foreign clergy. Activities of the European-derived religions have been influenced by liberation theology, which in the context of a post-slavery and post-colonial society, has sought to come to grips with a predominantly black society riddled by color and class prejudices. Faced with declining membership, they have searched for meaning in a fresh outlook that emphasizes the ministry to the body and not just the soul and that has sought to renew itself through liturgical innovations as well.

Another religious movement born out of Revivalism and Christianity is Rastafarianism, whose membership remains very small but whose national and international influence is great, primarily because of its impact on culture and identity. Begun in the 1930s in Jamaica, the movement grew out of the work of Marcus Garvey, whose Pan-African activities sought to reverse the racist colonial legacy of denigration of the black persona, to uphold the essential unity of the African race, and to project Africa as a spiritual home to be proud of and return to. The coronation on 2 November 1930 of Ras Tafari Makonnen as Emperor Haile Selassie I of Ethiopia was interpreted as an event of deep religious significance. The emperor's titles, "King of Kings, Lord of Lords, Conquering Lion of the Tribe of Judah," and his claim to be a direct descendant of the Judaic King Solomon and the Queen of Sheba, were seen as proof that the Messiah had returned to redeem those Africans exiled into slavery in the West.

Based on its critique of the system of race and color prejudice and its trenchant anticolonial rhetoric, the movement spread among the Jamaican urban underclass. In the early 1950s the Rastafarians made two innovations. First, with black African hair universally regarded as "bad," they adopted the uncombed, matted hairstyle that became known as dreadlocks. Second, in their sacralization of cannabis, a banned but culturally approved substance, they pitted themselves against the authority of the state. By the 1960s this positioning by the Rastafarian made them attractive to the alienated youth, who now found a critique of "Babylon," the society that holds the "children of Israel" captive, and a vision of a new life in "the promised land," Africa. With this critique and this vision such artists as Bob Marley, Peter Tosh, Burning Spear, and Dennis Brown took the emerging popular reggae beat to new heights, becoming in effect the new missionaries, spreading the word all over the black world and beyond. By the 1980s groups proclaiming themselves Rastafarian appeared in Brazil and other countries of Latin America, as well as in Africa, Europe, North America, and Asia.

Seventh-day Adventism is the largest single denomination in Jamaica. Originating in the United States, it first spread to Jamaica in 1894. Adventists are identified by their Sabbath (Saturday) observance and a lifestyle that prohibits alcohol, coffee, pork, tobacco, cosmetics, jewelry, gambling, cinemas, and other secular forms of entertainment.

Non-Christian religions in Jamaica include Judaism, Islam, the Bahai faith, and Hinduism. Judaism, with a five-hundred-year old history in Jamaica, numbers no more than three hundred members today. Although some of the enslaved Africans, and after slavery some of the indentured Indians, were Islamic, only in the late twentieth century did Islam become a practicing community. The overwhelming majority of Indian indentured workers who came in the nineteenth century were Hindu. Most of them converted to Christianity, but there exists a small practicing community belonging to the Sanatam Dharma. Bahai adherents also are few.

Barry Chevannes

See Also Vol. 1: *Adventists, Christianity, Pentecostalism*

Bibliography

Austin-Broos, Diane. *Jamaica Genesis: Religion and the Politics of Moral Order.* Kingston: Ian Randle Publishers, 1997.

Hollenweger, Walter. *Pentecost between Black and White.* Belfast: Christian Journals Limited, 1974.

La Ruffa, Anthony. "Culture, Change, and Pentecostalism in Puerto Rico." *Social and Economic Studies* 18, no. 3 (1969): 273–81.

Stewart, Robert. *Religion and Society in Post-Emancipation Jamaica.* Knoxville: University of Tennessee Press, 1992.

Japan

POPULATION 126,974,628

SHINTOIST AND/OR BUDDHIST 90
percent

"NEW RELIGIONS" c. 10 percent

CHRISTIANITY c. 1 percent

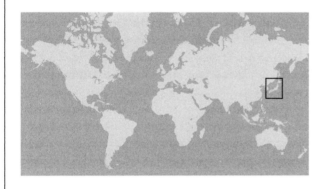

Country Overview

INTRODUCTION The nation of Japan is an archipelago off the east coast of Asia, bounded by the Pacific Ocean to the east and the Sea of Japan to the west. Approximately the size of California, Japan consists of four main islands (from north to south: Hokkaidō, Honshū, Shikoku, Kyūshū), the Ryukyu Islands (Okinawa), and thousands of small islands. Hundreds of sacred mountains and natural hot springs dot the landscape. The center of the ancient *kami* (native deities) cults and early Japanese Buddhism stretches from Mount Hiei (headquarters of Tendai Buddhism) in the Nara-Kyoto area to Ise (site of the Great Imperial Shrines) and Kōya-san (Mount Koya; headquarters of Shingon Buddhism).

Japan's population is concentrated in major urban areas, including Tokyo, Yokohama, Osaka, Nagoya, Kobe, Kyoto, and Fukuoka.

It is impossible to break down Japanese religious affiliation into a neat percentile ranking. Unlike adherents of the monotheistic faiths of the West, most Japanese do not identify with, or participate in, only one religion. Rather, most participate in aspects of both Shinto and Buddhism. Alternatively they may belong to one of the "new religions," largely lay-based movements blending elements of Shinto, Buddhism, and Neo-Confucianism with popular or folk religion. The percentages cited at the start of this essay represent only rough estimates of the number of nominal or "loose" adherents. Such persons may participate occasionally in religious celebrations, rituals, or rites of passage but do not think of themselves as "religious" or as members of a religion. Most Japanese get married in a Shinto service (coupled, perhaps, with a Western-style wedding ceremony), but they will have a Buddhist funeral. In a 1994 survey conducted by NHK, the Japanese national broadcast system, only 31 percent of the respondents indicated they had visited a shrine or temple in the past year to pray for safety, prosperity, or success in educational entrance exams.

Most Japanese participate in cultic activities associated with Shinto. Many homes include a *kami-dana* (domestic Shinto shrine for ancestral rites) or a *butsudan* (alcove housing ancestral tablets used in Buddhist rites). Various forms of Buddhism are also prominent in Japan and played a major role in shaping Japanese culture. From the seventeenth century on, Neo-Confucianism has played a central role in forming the modern Japanese

Followers of Shinto perform the purification ritual during New Year's celebrations at the Teppozu Shrine in Tokyo, Japan. This ritual is intended to remove defilement, illness, and misfortune. AP/WIDE WORLD PHOTOS.

value system and social structure. Popular nonsectarian forms of religious beliefs and practices, including divine possession, mediumship, and faith healing, have survived and blended with imported religious traditions.

RELIGIOUS TOLERANCE The postwar Japanese constitution guarantees freedom of religion to all citizens and requires the separation of religion and the state. Nevertheless, aspects of State Shinto, the national cult established by the Meiji government in the 1860s, survive in Japan and remain a source of political controversy. Most notably, visits by postwar prime ministers and other government officials to Tokyo's Yasukuni Shrine (dedicated to honoring the spirits of the deceased in Japan's wars, including spirits of convicted war criminals) have provoked angry responses domestically and internationally. Some Buddhist "new religions" have also been active politically. In the late twentieth century Soka Gakkai had its own political party for years before controversy caused the leadership to sever formal relations with the party.

Major Religions

SHINTO

BUDDHISM

SHINTO

DATE OF ORIGIN c. 400 C.E.
NUMBER OF FOLLOWERS 112 million

HISTORY The term "Shinto" (which can also be read as *kami no michi*) was coined in ancient Japan either to distinguish the cults of native deities (*kami*) from those of Buddhism or, according to the scholar Kuroda Toshio, to refer to Chinese Taoism. Nationalist Shinto apologists have long argued that Shinto represents a timeless pure Japanese spirituality, but this clearly is not defensible in historical terms. For the purposes of this entry, "Shinto" is used as shorthand for the *kami* cults. For most of Japanese history, Shinto did not exist as an independent religion as such. Rather, in the lives of the people, Buddhism, Taoism, and Neo-Confucianism have all blended with the *kami* cults.

In prehistorical Japan, people organized themselves into extended clans (*uji*) based on shared communal worship of local deities. The political leader of each clan also served as the chief ritualist. Women served as mediums, calling down the gods, who then possessed them and revealed knowledge to the people. When one clan (later to be styled "the imperial family") gradually gained hegemony over others, an imperial cult was created, elevating its local clan *kami* to universal and cosmological status. The date of c. 400 C.E. as the origin of Shinto indicates this historical process. The myths preserved in the *Kojiki* (712) and the *Nihon shoki* (720) were designed to provide a national religio-political framework for ordering society and governing the state. Thus, from the seventh century the imperial cult sought to associate worship of Amaterasu (the sun goddess at the head of the pantheon) with reverence for the emperor (the head of state).

In the Heian (794–1185) and medieval periods, Tendai Buddhist scholars promulgated the theory of *honji suijaku*, which argued that Japanese *kami* were "trace manifestations" of buddhas and bodhisattvas. That is, Japanese deities were spatially and temporally local forms of universal Buddhist divinities. For their part many Shinto shrine priests began to incorporate Chinese geomancy, yin-yang practices, and Taoist concepts into their own religious practices. Some adopted and adapted Confucian ideals and concepts to explain their belief system. Most importantly the priests of the *kami* cults made accommodation with Tendai and Shingon forms of Buddhism. Some offered their own version of the identity of the *kami* and buddhas in a theology known as Ryōbu Shinto, which argued the *kami* were the primary form and the Buddhist deities were secondary manifestations. The most important such identification in political terms equated Amaterasu Ōmikami (the sun goddess) with the Great Sun Buddha. This allowed the emperor to represent himself as not only a living *kami* but also an incarnate buddha.

In 1868, as a part of the Meiji Restoration of imperial rule, the national government forcibly separated Shinto from Buddhism. Cultic sites for the worship of *kami* were to be free of Buddhist elements. At this time the government created State Shinto, a national religious and ideological cult that was legally dissolved after Japan's defeat in World War II, although certain aspects survive today. Shrine Shinto as it exists in Japan is in large part a nineteenth-century creation rather than a timeless religious tradition.

EARLY AND MODERN LEADERS Shinto has traditionally been a locally based religion. Nevertheless, a few figures have played significant roles in Shinto history. Nakatomi Kamatari (614–669) was the primary author of the Taika Reforms, which sought to establish a polity of dual bureaus: the *Jingi-kan* (Bureau of Rites Dedicated to the Kami of Heaven and Earth) and the *Dajō-kan* (Bureau of State Affairs). In the 1860s Meiji government officials attempted to reinstate this system but without long-term success. Yoshida Kanetomo (1435–1511) was the founder of Yoshida, or Urabe, Shinto, a form of esoteric religion that presented itself as Yuitsu (the One-and-Only) Shinto. It mixed esoteric Buddhist, Taoist, and Confucian elements with the *kami* cults and was influential in the late medieval period. There is no single figure one can point to as the leader of Shinto in the modern period.

MAJOR THEOLOGIANS AND AUTHORS There are few Shinto theologians per se in Japan today. This is because, in Shinto, orthodoxy (authorized or correct doctrinal belief) is less important than is orthopraxis (correct ritual practices). A number of modern scholars have been influential interpreters of Shinto to the West, however. These include Kato Genichi, Ono Sokyo, and Muraoka Tsunetsugu on the history and essence of Shinto; Murakami Shigeyoshi on State Shinto and Shinto in the modern world; Kuroda Toshio on the conjoining of Shinto and Buddhist institutions; Joseph Mitsuo Kitagawa and Sonoda Minoru on Shinto history and Shinto in history; Umehara Takeshi on Shinto as timeless spiritual essence of the Japanese people; and Shimazono Susumu on Japanese "new religions" and postmodern religion.

HOUSES OF WORSHIP AND HOLY PLACES There are approximately 100,000 Shinto shrines (*jinja*) in Japan, ranging in size from massive shrine complexes to small, even miniature, sites of worship. The former are represented by, among others, the Grand Imperial Shrines of Ise, the Izumo Shrine, the Meiji Shrine, and the Yasukuni Shrine. Shrines today are usually marked by the presence of *torii* (distinctive gates or arches at the entrances of shrine grounds or over walkways), *shimenawa* (sacred ropes tied around trees and used to mark off sacred areas), prayer strips, and running water for worshipers to purify themselves. Many shrines are located at the foot of a mountain, on a mountain summit, or in other sites in nature. Still others are found tucked into urban neighborhoods.

WHAT IS SACRED? Various things are considered sacred in Shinto, including such natural phenomena as mountains, waterfalls, trees, caves, the sun, the moon, rock formations, and so on. Certain individuals can also be sacred, ranging from the persons of the Ise Virgin and the emperor to priests and shrine maidens. These persons are permitted into sacred areas that ordinary persons cannot enter. Also considered sacred may be specific manufactured objects, such as *magatama* (small crescent-shaped stones), brass mirrors, bows and arrows, and statues. Finally, at some shrines specific animals, including deer, foxes, dogs, and snakes, are sacred, as are mythical creatures, such as dragons, giant catfish (*namazu*), and *kappa* (water creatures).

HOLIDAYS AND FESTIVALS Every shrine in Japan has its own annual festival (*matsuri*), as well as a local calendar of monthly ritual events, specific to the different *kami* (native deities) enshrined there. Imperial and national shrines follow the ritual calendar of the Grand Imperial Shrines of Ise. There are, however, some festivals and ritual events of national scope, although they may not be celebrated at every shrine, and the date may vary by region. Some of the most popular festivals include New Year's; *setsubun* (3 February), the "change of seasons" exorcism in which dried beans are thrown in houses to chase away evil spirits; *hina matsuri* (3 March), the Doll Festival for girls; *otaue-sai*, the rice-planting ritual; *oharae* (30 June and 31 December), the Great Purification Ritual; and *shichi-go-san no matsuri* (15 November), the coming-of-age ritual for girls age seven and three and boys age five. Other major festivals and rituals, such as the Gion Festival in Kyoto, draw national crowds.

MODE OF DRESS Worshipers at Shinto shrines are not required to wear any special clothing. In Shinto weddings, however, the bride will wear an elaborate silk wedding kimono, with all the trimmings, as well as a wig and hair combs in the fashion of Heian aristocrats. The groom will wear either a kimono or a tuxedo. During festivals many participants wear *happi* coats (bright colored loose tops tied with a sash) and cloth headbands with writing on them. Pilgrims often wear white clothing and headbands; those attending a funeral wear white.

The distinctive dress of a Shinto priest includes his white silk robe, *hakama* (silk pantaloons worn over the robes, with the color marking the priest's rank), black *eboshi* hat (or, on special occasions, a *kanmuri* hat), and the ritual wooden paddle (*shaku*) he carries in his right hand. Shrine priestesses also wear white robes and a flowered headdress, recalling their traditional ritual role in calling down the *kami* (native deities).

DIETARY PRACTICES There are no standard dietary practices for worshipers in Shinto. Local shrines, however, may have specific restrictions (for example, a shrine may prohibit a specific foodstuff because of a myth or legend associated with the site). Alcoholic beverages are not prohibited; indeed, large bottles or barrels of sake (rice wine) are often offered to shrines by worshipers. Shinto priests may abstain from specific foods in preparation for performing a major ritual.

RITUALS The ritual calendar of each shrine is different, and consequently so are the specific rituals performed. There are, however, some fundamental ritual acts that all lay worshipers perform that deserve mention. Visiting a shrine to worship there is known as *omairi*. Many Japanese will visit a shrine during the New Year's celebrations, which last for five days, to pray for health and prosperity. The most commonly performed ritual is purification (*harae* or *harai*), which is intended to remove defilement, illness, misfortune, and so on. This includes the obligatory act of washing one's hands and mouth at the basin or spring at the entrance to every shrine. People who wish to petition the *kami* (native deities) will face the sacred center of the shrine, clap their hands, bow their heads, and pray to the deity.

Individuals sometimes make vows and undertake austerities (for example, making a pilgrimage to sacred sites or crawling on one's knees in prayer and penance) in order to move the *kami* to help them. Shrines also sponsor sacred dance performances (*kagura*) by community members, recalling the mythic episode when another *kami* performed the first such dance before the cave in which the sun goddess had secluded herself. During shrine festivals, young men often carry a portable shrine (*mikoshi*), containing the *shintai* (literally the body of the deity, or the object in which the *kami* resides) in raucous processions through the streets.

RITES OF PASSAGE The first rite of passage is *hatsumiyamairi*, an infant's first visit to a shrine. This is generally performed on the 33rd day after birth for boys and the 32nd day for girls. This is followed by *shichi-go-san no matsuri* in November for girls age seven and three and boys age five. Today a national civic Coming-of-Age Day is celebrated for all those persons who have attained adulthood. Marriage is perhaps the most important Shinto rite of passage. Because of the associated pollution, few shrines perform funerals.

MEMBERSHIP During the Tokugawa period (1600–1868), the government required all citizens to be registered as members of a Buddhist parish. In the Meiji period (1868–1912), however, this was reversed and all persons were required to participate in Shinto shrine activities. Today there is no legal requirement that individuals or families belong to any religious group. Shinto is not evangelistic. Just as one is a Jew by birth rather than by having to profess specific religious beliefs or by observing specific ritual obligations, in Japan Shinto is thought of less as a religion per se than as just a part of being Japanese. The few Shinto-based "new religions" that have tried to missionize overseas have had limited success in attracting members.

SOCIAL JUSTICE Historically the ethnocentric nature of Shinto has not led to a theology of social justice for all persons. Few Shinto religious leaders in the twentieth century, for instance, spoke in opposition to the systematic discrimination practiced against the Ainu (an ethnically distinct native people), the *burakumin* (a class of outcastes that has existed for centuries), or Koreans originally brought to Japan as forced laborers and their descendants. Only recently have the Japanese people and the government begun to address the rights of the physically and mentally impaired and the other groups traditionally discriminated against. The primary impetus for this did not come from religious groups but from citizen activists. When the need arose in the late twentieth century to appoint a new saishu, or supreme priestess, of the Grand Shrines of Ise (*saishu*), a position held by a female member of the imperial family, the only available candidate was handicapped. Although eventually it was decided that a physical disability did not necessarily disqualify an individual, some priests vigorously disagreed with this stance.

SOCIAL ASPECTS Shinto today remains a largely patriarchal system, not unlike Japanese society in general. In the mythology of the *Kojiki* and *Nihon shoki,* patriarchal

values color the creation myth. There a male and a female *kami* (native deity)—Izanagi and Izanami, respectively—descend from the high heavens to create this world. When the woman speaks first in the creation ritual, a monstrous child is created. Only when the ritual is performed anew with the male speaking first does creation go well. The sacred texts, thus, make it clear that male precedence is the proper order of things. Shinto also stresses traditional hierarchical Confucian values. These include reciprocal duties and obligations between superiors and subordinates or inferiors. The most important relations include those between ruler and subjects, husband and wife, parent and child, and elder and younger persons.

POLITICAL IMPACT Shinto has tended to be a conservative political force in Japanese history. Already in prehistorical and early historical Japan, the extended clan system united *kami* (native deity) worship with sociopolitical organization. Later in the emperor system religious rituals (*matsuri*) and political administration (*matsuri-goto*) were theoretically both under the authority of the emperor, who expressed the divine will. The union of Shinto and the state (*saisei-itchi*) was attempted again in the Meiji era. In the guise of State Shinto, the government controlled shrine rites and had the imperial myths from the *Kojiki* and *Nihon shoki* taught as history in all Japanese schools. In the modern age of Japanese imperialism, many members of Shinto organizations were jingoistic nationalists. Recently some Shinto priests have become active in the ecological movement in Japan and, increasingly, in international forums, where Shinto is portrayed as a "green" religion.

CONTROVERSIAL ISSUES One of the most important legal controversies in the late nineteenth and twentieth centuries in Japan centered on the legal definition and status of *shukyō* (religion). This is a neologism created in response to nineteenth-century Western concepts of "religion" and of the proper relationship of religion and the state in the modern world. The question of whether Shinto is a religion or not—and consequently whether the separation of religion and the state is at issue in cases such as government support for the Yasukuni Shrine—has been argued all the way to the Supreme Court. Similarly, at times the status of the Grand Imperial Shrines has been controversial. Some have argued that these are the private family shrines of the imperial family; others counter that if the courts accept this position, then no government funds should be used to support the shrines or to rebuild them every 20 years.

The religious and legal status of some archaeological sites in Japan has also become embroiled in controversy surrounding the imperial cult. The Imperial Household Agency has successfully blocked the excavation of certain sites by academic archaeologists by arguing that they are private tombs belonging to the imperial family. Critics counter that the real reason for blocking the excavation of burial tumuli and other sites is because scientific study would disclose embarrassing facts (for example, the purported tomb of an early emperor might be shown not to be an imperial tomb at all, or clear evidence of Korean influence or presence might be demonstrated, putting the lie to the myth of Japanese racial purity).

CULTURAL IMPACT Shinto has influenced Japanese art, architecture, music, dance, and sports. Shinto has also fostered a sense of appreciation of the natural world and the seasonal cycle. Shinto architectural style has influenced a preference for simple designs that blend into the natural setting and open, airy spaces. Shinto concepts of purity and pollution have informed domestic architecture in Japan, the utilization of space, and the concept of cleanliness.

Heian court music, known as gagaku, is performed in many Shinto rituals and is a distinctive part of Japanese traditional music. At a more popular level, *taue uta* (rice-planting songs) accompanied this agricultural labor, although they are performed today in only a few rural areas. *Kagura*, or sacred dances, are the most common form of traditional Japanese dance performed today. *Kagura* may be performed by shrine priestesses and maidens or by laypersons on special dance platforms connected to shrines. *Kagura* are also performed in neighborhoods around the country in communal dances during the festival of *obon,* when the spirits of the deceased return and are entertained. Shinto has also played a role in the history of Japanese wrestling, or sumo. Matches were traditionally held on shrine grounds during festivals as part of the entertainment for the *kami* (native deities) as well as for the gathered crowds. The salt the wrestlers scatter over the wrestling ring is a Shinto act of purification. Today a shrine roof hangs over the indoor rings of the professional tour.

BUDDHISM

DATE OF ORIGIN 538 C.E.
NUMBER OF FOLLOWERS 112 million

HISTORY Buddhism was officially introduced to Japan in 538 C.E. when the king of Paekche in Korea presented Buddhist sutras and images to the Japanese court. The influential Soga clan adopted a buddha as its clan deity in the sixth century. Prince Shōtoku (573–621) was a serious Buddhist practitioner who sought to create a centralized political system based on the Chinese model. For him Buddhism represented the epitome of a great civilization. The early Japanese turned to Buddhism for this-worldly benefits, including good health, longevity, prosperity, and protection from lightning, fire, and pestilence.

Buddhism flourished under government sponsorship and the patronage of the powerful Soga family in Nara, the first permanent capital, established in 710. Over time major temples established far-flung networks of associated temples and shrines and came to control vast estates.

The capital was moved to Heian-kyō, present-day Kyoto, in 794, inaugurating the golden age of Japanese cultural history. The esoteric Tendai and Shingon schools of Buddhism were the most influential in this period. They emphasized meditative practices utilizing mandalas (elaborate pictorial representations of the Buddhist cosmos, multiple heavens, and their inhabitants) and mantras (magically powerful words or phrases). The recitation of the *nembutsu,* a simple expression of faith in the saving power of the bodhisattva Amida, grew in popularity, as did the Heart Sutra and the Lotus Sutra. Buddhist teachings, practices, and miraculous tales were disseminated by not only ordained monks and nuns but also a variety of associated lay figures.

Medieval Japanese Buddhism affirmed this world and life as good while stressing the ephemerality, evanescence, and ultimate emptiness of all material things (*mujō*). Cultured persons cultivated the religio-aesthetic sense of *mono no aware,* or the pathos of the impermanent world. This was not merely an aesthetic response but a religious sense that plumbed deep Buddhist truths. Unlike the South Asian Buddhist ideal of achieving complete equanimity or balance in the face of the fluctuating conditions of life, medieval Japanese Buddhists actively sought to evoke specific emotional experiences that were religiously valued.

The Kamakura (1192–1333) through the Muromachi (1392–1568) period saw the rise of numerous new Buddhist movements, including the Pure Land, True Pure Land, Ji-shū, and Zen. The older schools of Buddhism did not disappear but shared the "religious marketplace" with these newer groups. With the decline of the imperial court and the concomitant rise of samurai warriors to power, the vast Buddhist estates and armed monks came to be viewed as threats to the military leaders. The military dictator Ōda Nobunaga (1534–82) sacked and burned the Tendai headquarters; he also destroyed the power bases of other Buddhist schools. Buddhism experienced another dramatic decline in its power during the Meiji period (1868–1912) and underwent significant change after the government established State Shinto and removed its support of Buddhism. In 1872 state enforcement of the Buddhist precepts for monks and nuns, including the ban on eating meat and on marriage, was ended. As a result, 90 percent of the Buddhist clergy today are married, and vegetarianism is not required of all priests. The government also turned a blind eye to the destruction of many Buddhist temples and artifacts by nationalist zealots in parts of Japan.

While the traditional schools of Buddhism have not recovered their former preeminence, Buddhism remains an important cultural force in Japan. Several Buddhist lay movements, based on the Lotus Sutra, gained prominence in the twentieth century, including Soka Gakkai, Reiyū-kai, and Risshō-Kōsei-kai.

EARLY AND MODERN LEADERS Saichō (Dengyō-daishi; 766–822) founded the Tendai school of Buddhism and introduced formal ordination practices to Japan. The Tendai headquarters on Mount Hiei outside the capital grew into a massive complex with hundreds of buildings. Saichō also worshiped the *kami* (native deities), including Sannō, the king of Mount Hiei. He prepared the way for the Tendai teachings of Sannō Ichijitsu Shinto, which identified the *kami* with Buddhist deities. Tendai clerics also promulgated the broader concept of *honji-suijaku*, which claimed that Japanese *kami* were the spatially and temporally local manifestations of universal and eternal Buddhist deities.

Kūkai (Kōbō-daishi; 773–835), the founder of Shingon Buddhism, was a brilliant thinker who produced many important works on esoteric Buddhism and philosophical issues, including *Jūjūshinron* ("Treatise on the Ten Stages of Consciousness") and *Sokushin-jōbutsugi* ("The Doctrine of Becoming a Buddha in This Body in Time"). The latter doctrine is unique to Japanese Buddhism. Kūkai's mausoleum on Mount Kōya remains a major pilgrimage site today.

Hōnen (1133–1212), the founder of Pure Land Buddhism, was originally a Tendai monk. After reading *Ōjō-yōshū* ("The Essentials of Salvation") by the monk Genshin (942–1017), he became convinced that one should seek rebirth in the bodhisattva Amida's Pure Land rather than seek enlightenment through traditional practices.

Shinran (1173–1262), Hōnen's disciple, stressed that absolute faith in the saving power of Amida's bodhisattva vow was the only path to salvation. Like Martin Luther in the West, he rejected the exclusive claims made for the role of priests and their rituals in gaining salvation. He also rejected clerical celibacy. His movement was known as True Pure Land, or Shinshū.

Nichiren (1222–82) believed that only the Lotus Sutra contained the truth, while all other religions were either false or marred by errors. He read Japanese history as a part of soteriological history in which he was destined to play a central role. Nichiren Buddhism was and is a militant evangelistic religion. The faithful repeatedly recite a *nembutsu*-like prayer, substituting the Lotus Sutra for Amida as the locus of salvation.

Zen schools of meditation played a profound role in late medieval and early modern Japan. Eisai (1141–1215) founded Rinzai Zen, while Dōgen (1200–53) founded the Sōtō school. Dōgen taught that only seated meditation (*zazen*) was efficacious and could lead to gradual enlightenment. Eisai used koan, or logical conundrums (for example, "What is the sound of one hand clapping?"), to help break Zen practitioners out of ordinary consciousness and forms of thought. Rinzai teaches that enlightenment happens instantly. Eisai also introduced the tea ceremony and Neo-Confucian thought to Japan.

MAJOR THEOLOGIANS AND AUTHORS In addition to the major Buddhist theologians already mentioned above under EARLY AND MODERN LEADERS, numerous other figures bear mention. Ippen (1239–89), the founder of the itinerant Ji sect, was a proponent of the salvific power of the *nembutsu*. Kamo no Chōmei (1153–1216) authored *Hōjōki* ("An Account of My Hut"), a famous essay on the Buddhist concepts of ephermerality and the transience of life. Rennyō (1414–

99) systematized the doctrines and practices of Jōdo Shinshū Buddhism following the death of Shinran (1173–1262). Hakuin (1685–1768) did much to popularize the practice of Rinzai Zen. Nanjō Bunyū (1849–1927) introduced Western forms of scholarship into the study of Buddhism. In the contemporary period, Ikeda Daisaku (born in 1928), the head of the Soka Gakkai lay Buddhist movement, has written many works on Buddhism for lay readers. Masao Abe (born in 1915) has been a major practitioner of interfaith dialogue, especially with Western scholars and Christian theologians.

HOUSES OF WORSHIP AND HOLY PLACES Thousands of Buddhist temples dot the Japanese landscape. These range from massive structures and complexes, such as Tōdaiji, Honganji, and Kōya-san, to small single structures. Many temples are located in the mountains, although many others are in villages, towns, and cities. Holy places include natural sites (for example, waterfalls, mountains, caves), as well as pilgrimage sites and gardens. The most famous pilgrimage is the Shikoku pilgrimage, associated with Kūkai or Kōbō-daishi, with 88 major holy sites. The burial sites or mausoleums of famous figures, including those of Kōbō-daishi and Shinran, attract many pilgrims even today.

WHAT IS SACRED? Japanese Buddhists worship before statues (wood, bronze, and stone) of buddhas and bodisattvas, which are believed to embody these deities. From the Kamakura period on, statues of Buddhist prelates also were fashioned and became objects of worship. In Tendai and Shingon Buddhism, mandalas are also sacred objects. Mountains and the surrounding valleys may be sacred, as are the tombs or grave sites of famous religious figures. In an important sense in Japan, the Mahayana Buddhist stress on nonduality led to the dissolution of all distinctions, including those between the sacred and the profane and form and emptiness.

HOLIDAYS AND FESTIVALS Japanese Buddhists celebrate the birthday as well as the enlightenment of Siddhartha Gautama, the Buddha. The followers of specific schools will celebrate the anniversary of the death of the founder of the school (for example, Shingon Buddhists observe special rites for Kōbō-daishi). The most important Buddhist festival is *ōbon*, the festival of the dead, when the spirits of the deceased are invited back and entertained with song and dance, before being sent off

again. Each Buddhist temple will also have its own liturgical calendar. Some festivals, like the Gion Festival in Kyoto, focus on syncretic Shinto-Buddhist deities.

MODE OF DRESS Buddhist monks and nuns have shaven heads and wear distinctive robes, beads, and wooden sandals (*geta*). Itinerants or pilgrims may carry a special staff or a wooden backpack for sutras, small statues, and other ritual paraphernalia. Laypersons, however, do not usually wear any special clothing unless they are on a religious pilgrimage or attending a funeral.

DIETARY PRACTICES Buddhists are traditionally vegetarians, but not all modern Buddhists are observant. Priests in sacred sites such as Kōya-san maintain vegetarian diets.

RITUALS Buddhism today is identified in the minds of most Japanese with mortuary rites. After a death the family displays a picture of the deceased with black bunting in the home. Incense is burned and food offerings are made at this temporary shrine. After the Buddhist funeral and cremation of the corpse, the priest gives the deceased a posthumous name, which is written on a small flat stick that is deposited in the family Buddhist altar. Prayers are offered daily before this altar. Special memorial services are held on the first, third, and fifth anniversary of the death. After approximately 33 years the stick with the deceased's posthumous name is burned. Thereafter the deceased receives worship only together with other ancestors. The spirits of the dead are believed to return to this world during the festival of *ōbon*, usually celebrated in late summer.

Japanese Buddhists practice diverse forms of meditation, ranging from Zen meditation to esoteric forms in Tendai and Shingon temples. Some faithful—especially the followers of Shugendō, or mountain, Buddhism—also undertake regimens of asceticism in the mountains, including taking repeated ice water baths in the winter and fasting.

RITES OF PASSAGE Taking the tonsure is the most important rite of passage for those entering the priesthood or becoming a Buddhist nun. For most Japanese, however, the extended funerary and memorial rituals, described briefly above under RITUALS, constitute the most important rite of passage. In essence these rites move the deceased from the world of the living into the spiritual world and the status of an ancestor.

MEMBERSHIP For many centuries all Japanese were required by the government to be registered with a local Buddhist temple. Through this system Buddhist institutions were used by the government to maintain a census and the tax role. In exchange Buddhist temples had received government recognition and legal protection, as well as funding in some instances. This system was ended in the late nineteenth century. Today membership is voluntary, although many families retain a traditional affiliation with a local temple. Buddhist temples generally do not actively recruit new members. There are exceptions, however, especially among the "new religions" (mainly lay-based movements), such as Soka Gakkai.

SOCIAL JUSTICE Over the centuries many Buddhists have taken the ideal of compassion for all living beings as a mandate to engage actively in social causes. Others, however, have opted to separate themselves from the world (*shukke*) in order to pursue enlightenment (*satori*), which would then allow them to aid others to escape the world of karma. Recently Buddhists have helped to lead the pacificist movement in Japan in opposing the nation's rearmament. Younger Buddhists clerics have also begun to challenge their leadership openly and argue for the need to create an "engaged Buddhism."

SOCIAL ASPECTS Prior to the nineteenth century, priests only of the Jōdo Shinshū sect married. Today most priests are married. As a result, the management of many local temples is handed down from father to son. Japanese Buddhists generally embrace marriage and the extended family as a social unit, which is especially important in performing rites for ancestors.

POLITICAL IMPACT Throughout most of Japanese history Buddhist institutions played important political roles. In some cases Buddhism provided a universal and cosmological support for the sacral emperor system. In other cases, as in the Heian and Askiga periods, major Buddhist sects (Tendai, Shingon, Pure Land) represented significant loci of political, military, and economic power that challenged central authority and, later, the samurai lords. In modern Japan, Buddhist institutions have played a less conspicuous political role, although the lay Buddhist group Soka Gakkai created its own political party, Komeito, in the second half of the twentieth century.

CONTROVERSIAL ISSUES In the modern period the extent to which Buddhist institutions should support governmental and nationalistic policies has been a major point of contention. Overt opposition has been relatively rare. In the latter part of the twentieth century, some temples began offering new rites of pacification for the spirits of aborted fetuses (*mizuko kuyō*). Abortion itself is not controversial in Japan, but the "business" of *mizuko kuyō* created media controversy over whether priests were exploiting vulnerable individuals for monetary purposes. Another ongoing source of controversy is the role of the military in Japan. Many Buddhists have promoted pacifist policies, while others have supported nationalist policies of rearmament.

CULTURAL IMPACT The cultural impact of Buddhism on Japanese culture cannot be overstated. After the capital's move to Heian-kyō (present-day Kyoto) in 794, Japanese painting, calligraphy, and sculpture reached new heights, while Japanese *waka* (31-syllable verses), *kanshi* (Chinese poems), prose, and prose-and-poetry tales, such as the *Ise monogatari* and *Genji monogatari,* were developed into exquisite art forms. Many Buddhist priests and nuns were active as poets.

Buddhists introduced anthropomorphism (the representation of divinity in human form) to Japan. In medieval Japan the practice of many different art forms was undertaken as a form of religious discipline (*michi* or *dō*). The way of tea, the way of poetry (*kadō*), and the way of archery are only a few examples of this. In general, these forms of religio-aesthetic practice sought to focus the mind and to achieve a psychosomatic state in which action was egoless. Buddhism influenced the forms of Japanese stage, including *nō*, Kabuki, and the puppet theater, as well as the art of garden and landscape design, ranging from the earliest temple-shrine complexes, such as that in eighth-century Nara, to Zen gardens in the late medieval and early modern periods. Today Buddhist influence continues to be found in film, the theater, literature, painting, comics and anime, and other arts.

Other Religions

Besides Shinto and Buddhism, Taoism, Neo-Confucianism, and Christianity have also contributed significantly to Japanese cultural history. One will find no Taoist and few Confucian temples in Japan, however. The influence of these Chinese traditions has been much more in terms of influencing Japanese social, political, and moral values and the shape of the social structure. Confucian social values have been especially important, particularly from the seventeenth century. For instance, Confucian thinkers assumed that a social and political hierarchical system was necessary for harmonious social relations from the national level down to the family. Subordinates owed loyalty and obedience to superiors in return for the care, protection, and benevolence shown them, whether those involved be daimyo (provincial military leaders) and their foot soldiers or husband and wife. This is a patriarchal system, which privileges the male over the female. In addition, elder individuals (for example, siblings) are hierarchically superior to younger ones. Younger siblings are to show deference to elder siblings, just as younger students are to show deference to their senior students as well as teachers. The pervasive influence of this structuring system may be seen in Japanese business organizational principles. The relationship between a major company and its subsidiaries is spoken of, and acted on, as that between the parent company (*oyagaisha*) and children companies (*kogaisha*).

Christianity entered Japan in the sixteenth century and was a vehicle for the transmission of Western thought, values, science, and technologies. Japanese rulers have not always been comfortable with Christianity, and there was severe religious persecution in the seventeenth century. Christian churches found in Japan date from the nineteenth and twentieth centuries. Perhaps the most influential Christian institutions in Japan have been private church-related universities, including Doshisha University in Kyoto, Nanzan University in Nagoya, and Rikkyū University and Sophia University in Tokyo. Although Japanese Christians constitute about 1 percent of the population, they have been leaders in higher education, in protecting the pacifist clauses in the postwar constitution, and in legal issues related to separation of church and state. Furthermore, numerous well-known novelists in the nineteenth and twentieth centuries were Christian.

Gary Ebersole

See Also Vol. 1: *Buddhism, Mahayana Buddhism, Shinto, Theravada Buddhism, Tibetan Buddhism*

Bibliography

Abe, Ryūichi. *The Weaving of Mantra: Kūkai and the Construction of Esoteric Buddhist Discourse.* New York: Columbia University Press, 1999.

Bock, Felicia G. *Classical Learning and Taoist Practices in Early Japan.* Tempe: Arizona State University, 1985.

Davis, Winston B. *Japanese Religion and Society: Paradigms of Structure and Change.* Albany: State University of New York Press, 1992.

Ebersole, Gary L. *Ritual Poetry and the Politics of Death in Early Japan.* Princeton, N.J.: Princeton University Press, 1989.

Hardacre, Helen. *Kurozumikyō and the New Religions of Japan.* Princeton, N.J.: Princeton University Press, 1986.

———. *Marketing the Menacing Fetus in Japan.* Berkeley: University of California Press, 1997.

Heisig, James W., and John C. Maraldo, eds. *Rude Awakenings: Zen, the Kyoto School, and the Question of Nationalism.* Honolulu: University of Hawai'i Press, 1995.

Kitagawa, Joseph M. *Religion in Japanese History.* New York: Columbia University Press, 1966.

LaFleur, William R. *The Karma of Words: Buddhism and the Literary Arts in Medieval Japan.* Berkeley: University of California Press, 1983.

Nelson, John K. *A Year in the Life of a Shinto Shrine.* Seattle: University of Washington Press, 1996.

Philippi, Donald L., trans. *Kojiki.* Tokyo: University of Tokyo Press, 1968.

———, trans. *Norito: A New Translation of the Ancient Japanese Ritual Prayers.* Tokyo: Institute for Japanese Culture and Classics, 1959.

Reader, Ian. *Religion in Contemporary Japan.* Honolulu: University of Hawai'i Press, 1991.

Reader, Ian, and George J. Tanabe, Jr., eds. *Practically Religious: Worldly Benefits and the Common Religion of Japan.* Honolulu: University of Hawai'i Press, 1998.

Ruppert, Brian. *Jewel in the Ashes: Buddha Relics and Power in Early Medieval Japan.* Cambridge, Mass.: Harvard University Press, 2000.

Smith, Robert J. *Ancestor Worship in Contemporary Japan.* Stanford, Calif.: Stanford University Press, 1974.

Tamaru, Noriyoshi, and Daivd Reid, eds. *Religion in Japanese Culture: Where Living Traditions Meet a Changing World.* Tokyo: Kodansha International, 1996.

Jordan

POPULATION 5,611,202
SUNNI MUSLIM 93 percent
CHRISTIAN 5.5 percent
SHIITE MUSLIM 1 percent
DRUZE 0.3 percent
BAHAI 0.2 percent

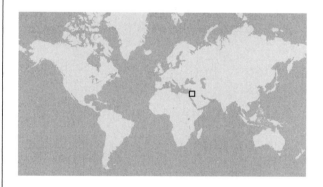

Country Overview

INTRODUCTION Jordan, situated in southwestern Asia, is one of the countries that make up the Middle East. It is bordered to the north by Syria, to the east by Iraq, to the southeast and south by Saudi Arabia, and to the west by Israel and the area known as the West Bank, control of which was officially relinquished by Jordan in 1988.

Jordan is rich in religious history. Considered part of the Holy Land, it is sacred to Jews and Christians for its connection to the Jewish prophets Abraham and Moses as well as such Christian biblical figures as John the Baptist. Many biblical events took place in the region. Jordan is important to Muslims because some of Muhammad's companions are buried there. In antiquity the area of present-day Jordan was ruled at various times by the Nabataeans, Greeks, Romans, and Byzantines.

It was in Jordan that the non-Arab world first came into contact with Islam more than 1,500 years ago. Arab armies carried Islam north and east from Arabia, entering the region of Jordan in 633 C.E. In the contemporary Hashemite Kingdom of Jordan, Islam is the state religion. The majority of Jordanians profess the Sunni branch of Islam, though there are a few thousand Shiite Muslims in the country as well. Also extant in Jordan are two religious groups historically associated with Islam: the Bahais and the Druze. The main Christian denominations represented in Jordan are Eastern Orthodoxy and Roman Catholicism, along with a lesser number of adherents to the Anglican and various Protestant churches. Religion is a strong element in the identity of most Jordanians and dictates much of the activity in their daily lives.

RELIGIOUS TOLERANCE Although Islam is the state religion, Jordan's 1952 constitution guarantees adherents of other religions the freedom to build their own houses of worship, to meet freely, and to practice their religious beliefs. Each religion has the right to regulate such personal matters as marriage, divorce, and inheritance according to its laws. Christians are affected by some practices of Islam. For example, the strict observance of Ramadan prohibits restaurants from serving alcohol to Christians during the fast. In general, there has been little conflict among religious groups or among the

A Jordanian man stands next to a monument that sits at the burial site of Abraham. Jordan is also sacred to Jews and Christians for its connection to the Jewish prophets Abraham and Moses. © DEAN CONGER/CORBIS.

various factions of Muslims. To be recognized by the state and to receive state protection, minority religious groups must be registered with the Jordanian Ministry of the Interior.

Major Religion

ISLAM

DATE OF ORIGIN 633 C.E.
NUMBER OF FOLLOWERS 4.9 million

HISTORY Since Islamic armies conquered the area in 633, Islam has been a social, religious, and economic force in what is now Jordan. Before the twentieth century, the country was mostly an appendage of more powerful kingdoms and empires. At the beginning of the six-

teenth century, it was incorporated into the Ottoman Empire. After World War I and the disintegration of the Ottoman Empire, the region including Jordan was divided between France and Britain. Transjordan, as the country was known from 1921 to 1949, was under British mandate. The country's borders, arbitrarily created by the British, became those of independent Jordan in 1946.

In 1952 the country became a constitutional monarchy. The constitution stipulated that the king must be Muslim and a son of Muslim parents. The Shari'ah (Islamic law) influences both religious and civil courts in cases concerning individual conduct.

EARLY AND MODERN LEADERS As an independent country, Jordan is quite young, and famous leaders are few. King Hussein (1935–99; reigned 1953–99), though a secular leader, was an observant Muslim, as is his son, King Abdullah II (born in 1962). The mufti of the kingdom is Sheikh Muhammad Abdo Hashem, and the director of the Shari'ah courts is Sheikh Subhi al-Muwqqat. Sheikh Izzedin Al-Khatib At-Tamimi is the chief justice and president of the Supreme Muslim Secular Council.

MAJOR THEOLOGIANS AND AUTHORS There are few Jordanian theologians or religious authors, and none who are widely known outside their own country. Jordanians have continued the long-standing Arab tradition of poetry, though their poems are not necessarily religious. The best-known Jordanian poet is Mustafa Wahbi Al-Tal. Yousef Al-Admah is a major religious essayist.

HOUSES OF WORSHIP AND HOLY PLACES Jordanian mosques may have flat or domed architecture, with a minaret for the call to prayer. Many mosques have educational centers attached for teaching the Koran and Muslim beliefs and practices. Two of Jordan's largest and most frequented mosques are in Amman: the Jam'a Al Hussani, a traditional mosque, and the Jam'a Al-Malak Abdullah Alawal, a modern mosque built in the mid-1990s. Jordan has several shrines and tombs of saints, which devotees consider holy and which they visit to invoke special blessings.

WHAT IS SACRED? In addition to mosques and the Koran, Jordanian Muslims consider sacred the tombs of such prophets as Aaron, Jethro, and Joshua and those of martyred companions of the prophet Muhammad, including his adopted son Zaid ibn Harithah, his cousins Ja'far ibn Ali Talib and Amir bin Abi Waqqa, and Abdullah ibn Ruwahah. Many Jordanians and Muslims from other countries make pilgrimages to these sites to pray and show reverence to the dead.

HOLIDAYS AND FESTIVALS Holidays include a strong social component for Jordanian Muslims, who visit relatives and friends on the major holidays—the Id al-Fitr, Id al-Adha, Islamic New Year, birthday of Muhammad, and Leilet al Meiraj (Ascension of the Prophet). Coffee, fruit juice, and candy and other sweets are served at these gatherings. Telephone calls and E-mail are used to connect with family members who live too far away to visit.

MODE OF DRESS Dress in Jordan varies according to religiosity, location, class, and other factors. Many Jordanians, especially urbanites, have adopted Western dress styles. Men often wear the traditional white or red-checkered kaffiyeh (headdress) with Western-style clothes. In rural areas women wear traditional Islamic floor-length dresses and head scarves, while styles of dress and headgear for boys and men vary widely. The youth enjoy European fashions, though shorts are worn only during sports activities. Most Bedouins still dress in flowing robes and head coverings.

Since the 1980s an Islamic revival has occurred in Jordan, as in many other Arab countries, and many women have begun wearing the veil or head scarf again. Controversy surrounds the use of the veil, especially as a covering for all or most of the face, whether it is worn for religious or cultural reasons. Many women now work in the public sphere, where they feel more comfortable wearing long-sleeved, full-length dresses with a scarf covering their hair.

DIETARY PRACTICES Religious Jordanians follow the Islamic prescription that food should be halal—that is, acceptable and properly prepared. They see a healthy lifestyle and the consumption of wholesome food as religious obligations. Lamb and chicken, the most common meats, are served with rice, vegetables, and seasonal fruits. Al-Mansaf, the national dish of Jordan, consisting of lamb cooked in dried yogurt and served with seasoned rice on flat bread, is served on religious holidays and special family occasions.

RITUALS Observant Muslims in Jordan practice the five pillars of Islam: faith, prayer, concern for the needy, self-purification, and the pilgrimage to Mecca. Other ritual acts include the sacrifice of the Id al-Adha, prayers about personal problems, and the recitation of the Koran.

RITES OF PASSAGE At birth it is customary in Jordan to whisper the shahadah ("There is no god but God [Allah] and Muhammad is the messenger of God") in the ears of newborns. On the birth of the first male child, a large celebration takes place. For the first female child, family members give gifts of gold or other precious metals, usually in the form of rings, earrings, or necklaces with verses of the Koran attached. Boys are circumcised as babies and may receive gifts on the occasion. There is no rite of passage marking puberty, but marriage, which gives adult status to both female and male, is a time of joy and great celebration. The custom of arranged marriage still exists in towns and rural areas. Death is the first stage of the journey to eternity, and as a "last rite," the dying person recites the shahadah, if possible.

MEMBERSHIP Considered Muslim from birth, a Jordanian Muslim commits a sin if he or she converts to another religion. Jordanian Muslims vary in their degree of religious observance; nevertheless, no matter how observant a person is, he or she will identify himself or herself as a Muslim.

SOCIAL JUSTICE The giving of alms (zakat) is one of the pillars of Islam, and Jordanian Muslims can pay alms directly to the poor, to travelers, or to the state of Jordan. Alms may take various forms, including money, animals (especially cattle), agricultural products, and gold and silver. The amount paid varies, with each individual calculating his or her own zakat. The payment of alms is not practiced fully by all Muslims in Jordan or elsewhere.

According to the Jordanian constitution, discrimination on account of race, religion, or language is forbidden. As far as possible, equal opportunities in work and education are afforded to all. Although Palestinian refugees can become citizens, there has been some discrimination against them. For the most part, however, human rights have been respected, especially in recent years.

SOCIAL ASPECTS The family is the foundation of Islamic society, and the extended family is unquestionably the most important social unit in Jordanian society. Children are treasured, and adults lavish time and attention on them, though women are the primary caregivers. Likewise, the elderly are greatly respected by everyone and are cared for by their children.

Marriage is a social and religious duty. The prospective groom takes a large group with him to seek permission for the marriage from the girl's eldest male relative. When a settlement is reached, coffee is served amid much socializing and celebration. Wedding celebrations typically last three days. In rural areas marriages usually take place on a Thursday evening, and a big meal is served on Friday, while in cities the marriage may take place on any day, though there is always a large crowd present and plenty of food, coffee, and sweets. A married woman's life is mostly dictated by her husband, though this is slowly changing, with the change more apparent in Jordan than in some other Muslim countries. Children also enhance a married woman's status.

POLITICAL IMPACT Because Islam is the state religion and the monarch must be Muslim, religion plays a significant role in Jordanian politics. Members of Jordan's legislature represent a spectrum of Muslims. Political parties were banned until 1992, but since then numerous parties have been established. They include nonreligious groups, such as Marxists, Pan-Arabists, socialists, Arab and social democratic parties, and the Jordanian National Alliance. A few fundamentalist or Islamist parties have also come into existence. The Muslim Brotherhood, which has used violence in other Arab countries, has worked within the system in Jordan to accomplish its work. By allowing the group to form a party and have a say in the government, King Hussein largely avoided rebellions and other physical violence. The Islamists have some legislative representation, but violent revolutionary forces are dealt with severely. In recent years Muslim extremists from Jordan have been active in other countries and more so in Jordan, which may present a challenge to the government.

The Jordanian civil legal system represents a combination of the French legal code and Islamic law. Many of the country's laws are based on the Koran and hadith, the traditional account of the words and deeds of the prophet Muhammad. These laws are enforced in the Shari'ah courts, which have jurisdiction over the conduct of individuals in both secular and religious matters.

The standards and activities of the government and the civil courts are greatly influenced by Islam.

CONTROVERSIAL ISSUES Most controversies revolve around gender. The patriarchal nature of Islam and of Arab culture puts limitations on women. Husbands have power over their wives, and gender-related violence is quite common. It is easier for a husband to obtain a divorce than for a wife to do so, and divorced fathers are often given custody of children. Divorced women are viewed as outcasts. Nevertheless, Jordanian women have opportunities to become educated and can work in most types of jobs, except night jobs and jobs that are dangerous—mining, for example.

A highly controversial issue in Islamic countries, including Jordan, is that of honor killing. The honor of a family is believed to rest upon its women, and if a single woman's chastity is compromised, a male relative may feel obligated to murder her to save the family's honor. Although nothing in Islamic law gives permission for such killings, honor killing has often been associated with Islam, and Jordanian courts are usually lenient with the murderers.

CULTURAL IMPACT Architecture is the predominant visual art associated with Islam, partly because Islam forbids the depiction of living things. Complex calligraphy and geometric designs commonly adorn buildings, especially mosques and shrines. A rich blend of Arab and Islamic imagery is reflected in such Jordanian crafts as handblown glass, earthenware, basketry, carpet weaving, and embroidery. Villagers have special songs for birth, circumcision, weddings, funerals, and harvesting. Several types of dances, accompanied by the rhythmic stomping of feet, are performed on festive occasions.

Other Religions

Christians form the largest non-Muslim religious group in Jordan. The East Bank's indigenous Christians are mainly concentrated in such small towns as Al Karak, Madaba, As Salt, and Ajlun, and there are several communities in Amman and other major cities. Jordanian Christians are descended from the ancient Palestinian and Transjordanian inhabitants of the apostolic era. The survival of Christianity in this increasingly Muslim area is explained by the extraordinary zeal of the Orthodox clergy and by the existing tribal structures, which stabilized the various religious allegiances. It was among the farmers (fellahin) in the villages that Christianity was best preserved in the past. Now Christians are found in all levels and classes of society. A number of Christians have emigrated from Jordan because of the Palestinian conflict and economic concerns.

The largest Christian denomination in Jordan is the Greek Orthodox Church, which is headed by the patriarch of Jerusalem. The parish priests and the laity are, for the most part, Palestinian Arabs, whereas the patriarch, bishops, and monks are Greeks. The patriarchate sponsors numerous schools, an orphanage, and a home for the aged. Other Christian denominations represented in Jordan include the Armenian Catholics, Roman Catholics, Greek (Melchite) Catholics, and various Protestant groups. The Protestants are mostly converts from the Catholic churches. Armenian Catholics are found on both sides of the Jordan, while Maronites and Syrian Catholics are confined to the West Bank. The Armenian patriarch resides in Jerusalem. The Armenian Church has suffered more from emigration than any other church. It operates one parish school and a charitable relief service. The Roman Catholic Church is well established and has many members. Its success in Jordan can be attributed to the extraordinary missionary efforts of the Franciscans following the medieval Crusades and the restoration of Jerusalem's Latin patriarchate in 1947. Greek Catholics are led by the patriarch of Antioch, Jerusalem, and Alexandria. The Catholic Melchite hierarchy has a more indigenous membership and is more open to change than its Greek Orthodox counterpart. The Catholic churches are subordinate to Rome, and the Holy See has diplomatic relations with Jordan.

Protestant groups in Jordan include the Anglicans, Episcopalians, Evangelicals, Assemblies of God, Lutherans, Southern Baptist Convention, Conservative Baptists, and Seventh-day Adventists. These were generally established through North American and European missionary activity. Most have founded schools, hospitals, and charitable programs and have constructed church buildings. In the 1990s the Pentecostal/charismatic renewal movement spread rapidly through most of the older churches, gaining thousands of adherents.

Among the non-Christian religious minorities in Jordan is a small community of Druze, who live in an area near the Syrian border. They are members of a sect that originally derived from the Isma'ili branch of Shia Islam; however, their current beliefs and practices, many of them secret, differ widely from those of modern Islam. The number of practitioners of the Bahai faith in Jordan has steadily increased since the 1970s, when they first settled in the northern Jordan Valley.

Connie Lamb

See Also Vol. 1: *Islam, Sunnism*

Bibliography

Dallas, Roland. *King Hussein: A Life on the Edge.* New York: Fromm International, 1999.

Glassé, Cyril. *The New Encyclopedia of Islam: A Revised Edition of the Concise Encyclopedia of Islam.* Walnut Creek, Calif.: AltaMira Press, 2001.

Handal, Nathalie, ed. *The Poetry of Arab Women: A Contemporary Anthology.* New York: Interlink Books, 2001.

"Jordan." In *CultureGrams: The Nations around Us.* Vol. 2. Provo, Utah: D.M. Kennedy Center for International Studies, Brigham Young University, 2002.

"Jordan." In *The Middle East and North Africa.* 49th ed. London: Europa Publications, 2003.

Metz, Helen Chapin, ed. *Jordan: A Country Study.* Washington, D.C.: Federal Research Division, Library of Congress, 1991.

Moaddel, Mansoor. *Jordanian Exceptionalism: A Comparative Analysis of State-Religion Relationships in Egypt, Iran, Jordan, and Syria.* Houndmills, Basingstoke, Hampshire; New York: Palgrave, 2002.

Sahliyeh, Emile. "Jordan and the Palestinians." In *The Middle East: Ten Years after Camp David.* Edited by William B. Quandt, 279–318. Washington, D.C.: Brookings Institution, 1988.

Schmidt, Darlene. "Jordan." In *Countries and Their Cultures.* Edited by Melvin Ember and Carol R. Ember, Vol. 2, 1159–65. New York: Macmillan Reference USA, 2001.

Sonbol, Amira El Azhary. *Women of Jordan: Islam, Labor, and the Law.* Syracuse, N.Y.: Syracuse University Press, 2003.

Kazakhstan

POPULATION 16,741,519

MUSLIM 63 percent

ORTHODOX CHRISTIAN 32 percent

CATHOLIC 3 percent

PROTESTANT 1 percent

OTHER 1 percent

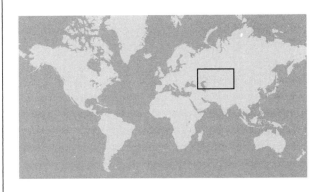

Country Overview

INTRODUCTION The Republic of Kazakhstan is the largest country in Central Asia. It is bordered to the northwest and north by Russia; to the east by China; to the south by Kyrgyzstan, Uzbekistan, Turkmenistan, and the Aral Sea; and to the southwest by the Caspian Sea.

With the second largest population among Central Asian countries, Kazakhstan is also the most ethnically and religiously diverse country in the region. Its religious divisions closely coincide with ethnicity. While

Kazakhs, who make up about 53 percent of the population, and members of 23 other ethnic groups are considered Sunni Muslims of the Hanafi tradition, East Slavs (mainly Russians) in the country profess Orthodox Christianity, and Germans and Poles profess Catholicism or Protestantism. In practical terms, however, 10 to 15 percent of Kazakhs—and a larger percentage of Russians—characterize themselves as nonbelievers. Many more are Muslims or Christians only in the nominal sense. No more than 20 to 30 percent of Kazakhs strictly observe the prescriptions of Islam in their everyday lives.

RELIGIOUS TOLERANCE Kazakhstan is a constitutionally secular state. Its constitution guarantees freedom of worship and forbids discrimination on religious grounds. Proselytism has been insignificant, and the level of mutual religious tolerance has remained rather high. Both the Muslim and the Russian Orthodox religious establishments, however, have strongly opposed the missionary activities of the so-called nontraditional religions—such as the Bahai faith, Krishnaism, and the New Age religions—and have appealed to the state to curb their activities.

Major Religions

ISLAM

EASTERN ORTHODOXY

A Muslim cemetery in Kazakhstan. Religious Kazakhs bury their deceased relatives in Muslim cemeteries, which are not uncommonly located near the graves of holy men. © DAVID SAMUEL ROBBINS/CORBIS.

ISLAM

DATE OF ORIGIN Late eighth century C.E.

NUMBER OF FOLLOWERS 10.5 million

HISTORY Islam was brought to Central Asia—the northern part of which, in historical and cultural respects, comprises the Kazakh territory—by Arab conquerors in the seventh century C.E. From the late eighth century to the fifteenth century, Islam spread throughout the territory of Kazakhstan. Islamization of the Kazakh nomads took place only in the fifteenth and sixteenth centuries, however, mostly as a result of the missionary activities of the Yasawiya and Naqshbandiya Sufi orders. In the eighteenth century and the first half of the nineteenth century, learned Tatar Muslims contributed to the further dissemination of Islam among the Kazakhs. By the beginning of the twentieth century, the general level of religiosity had increased, though it still remained much lower than in the settled parts of Central Asia.

There was a great difference between the scripturalist Islam of the religiously educated minority and the folk Islam of the majority, which retained many pre-Islamic notions, traditions, and rites. During the Soviet period (1920–91), Muslims were severely persecuted, which resulted in the drastic diminishment of its role in public life. The Soviet's atheist ideology failed to penetrate deeply into the private sphere, however. Since declaring its independence in 1991, Kazakhstan has witnessed an Islamic revival, especially of Islamic institutional forms. The Central Mosque, which can accommodate 3,000 people, was opened in Almaty in 1999, along with institutions of higher religious education. The number of Muslim periodicals has also grown. Since 1997 the religious administration of Kazakhstan has issued the magazine *Islam Alemi* (The World of Islam), among other publications.

EARLY AND MODERN LEADERS Traditionally most of the ulama (Islamic scholars) in Kazakhstan were members of non-Kazakh ethnic groups. In 1943 the Muslims of Kazakhstan were placed under the jurisdiction of the Spiritual Board of the Muslims of Central Asia and Kazakhstan, headquartered in Tashkent, Uzbekistan. Most of the mullahs in the country were Uzbeks. Following independence, most of the Uzbek mullahs were replaced by Kazakhs. In 1990 the religious hierarchy of Kazakhstan became independent, and the new Spiritual Board of the Muslims of Kazakhstan was established. Its first supreme mufti, Ratbek Nysanbai Uli, was not held in high esteem by most believers. In 2000 he was replaced by Absattar-kazhi Derbisaliev, a former employee of the diplomatic service who lacked religious education.

The level of knowledge among the Islamic religious establishment is rather low. Since independence a number of Kazakhs have graduated from religious schools in the Arab countries, Pakistan, and Turkey. Their efforts to persuade believers to adhere more strictly to Muslim precepts have been viewed with suspicion by the country's leadership. In any case, they do not occupy important positions within the religious establishment. On the local level, the mullahs play a more significant role. Although they are not always recognized by the official ulama, they are respected by ordinary Kazakhs. Many of them have preserved the Sufi tradition and have associated their activities with specific holy places.

MAJOR THEOLOGIANS AND AUTHORS Kazakh Islam has lacked major theologians and authors with a high reputation in the Muslim world. The Kazakhs revere as their own, however, the twelfth-century Turkish Sufi poet and mystic Akhmat Yasawi, who contributed to the dissemination of Islam amongst the Turkic nomads, including the ancestors of the Kazakhs.

HOUSES OF WORSHIP AND HOLY PLACES As elsewhere in the Muslim world, the house of worship is the mosque. In 1985 there were only 65 officially registered mosques in Kazakhstan; by 1999 there were 1,000, with an additional 4,000 unregistered.

Mazars (tombs) of saints and holy men are venerated and attract a large number of pilgrims. Especially revered is the mausoleum of Akhmat Yasawi in the city of Turkestan (formerly Yassy). Built in the fourteenth century, it was recently restored with assistance from Turkey. Many people visit the mausoleum in the belief that their pilgrimage there might substitute for the hajj to Mecca. The necropolises Beket-ata, Shopan-ata, Aisha-Bibi, and others are also considered holy places.

WHAT IS SACRED? The embodiment of sacredness in Islam is the Koran, which is regarded as the ultimate essence of divine revelation. To Muslims religion is inseparable from any context of human life and must conform to the larger whole—the Islamic faith. This is a far cry from current realities in Kazakhstan. Most Kazakhs have extremely vague ideas of the main dogmas of Islam and its notions of sacredness. Observance of the major tenets of Islam is low, especially in the larger cities. Only a few hundred people a year make the hajj. Twenty-five made the journey in 1991, while about 500 did so in 2001. Although every faithful Muslim is expected to memorize and recite the Koran in Arabic, the vast majority of observant Kazakhs just learn the Koran's formulas and prayers for performing *namaz* (daily worship) by heart and consider this sufficient. Although Kazakh Muslims recite in Arabic, they pronounce the words in accordance with the phonetics of the Kazakh language.

HOLIDAYS AND FESTIVALS Nonworking days in Kazakhstan are Saturday and Sunday, not Friday, as in most Muslim communities. All state holidays are secular, with the exception of Nawruz, which is commemorated on 22 March. Nawruz signifies the coming of the New Year and dates back to pre-Islamic times, but it underwent a certain transformation when it was embraced by Islam. Its celebration is accompanied by the singing of special songs (*zharapazan*) and the exchange of gifts. Even among observant Muslims, fewer than 10 percent strictly observe fasting during the month of Ramadan. More are observant of Uraza Bairam, or the Id al-Fitr, the feasting that takes place at the end of Ramadan, and Kurban Bairam (the Id al-Kabir or Id al-Adha), the festival of sacrifice, during which Muslims visit the tombs of relatives.

MODE OF DRESS Most Kazakhs, especially those in the cities, wear Western-style clothing. Traditional Kazakh hats and robes are worn mainly by the elders in rural areas, but these lack religious symbolism. Kazakh women never veil their faces or wear ritual coverings; however, religious women frequently cover their hair.

DIETARY PRACTICES With but a few exceptions, even secular Kazakhs do not eat pork. Very few, however, follow the Muslim prescriptions for the slaughter of animals. Although some schools of Islam disapprove of the consumption of horse flesh, it is the most favored kind of meat in Kazakh cuisine. The consumption of alcohol is also widespread.

RITUALS Rituals are mainly confined to the family sphere and are connected with the most important events in the life cycle. Sometimes Islamic traditions are combined with civic ones, as in the case of marriage. Recently participation in such rituals as the Muslim name-giving rite and Muslim marriage ceremonies has become more frequent. Many ordinary Kazakhs perceive such customs as circumcision and religious funerals as national rather than Muslim rituals, explaining "such is the custom" or "such is the behest of our forefathers."

RITES OF PASSAGE The most important rites of passage for Muslims are connected with birth, marriage, and death. Of these, only circumcision (*sundet*) is universally observed. Islamic tradition is also quite conspicuous in burial rites. As a rule, religious Kazakhs bury their deceased relatives in Muslim cemeteries, which are not uncommonly located near the graves of holy men. Grave monuments are often expensive and are frowned upon by adherents of normative Islam.

MEMBERSHIP Islam is an important marker of ethnic boundaries within Kazakhstan. All Kazakhs, even secular ones, are considered Muslim by birth in the ethnic community and regard Islam as their national religion. In their everyday speech, many Kazakhs like to use Muslim verbal formulas, such as "Allah Akbar" (God is great) and "Bismillah" (in the name of Allah).

SOCIAL JUSTICE The Islamic ideas of the *ummah* (community of believers) and social justice have had little impact on the everyday lives and attitudes of Kazakhs. For example, only a few follow the rule of *zakat* (donations for the benefit of the poor). The egalitarian appeal of Islam has gained some popularity, however, mainly among dispossessed and deprived peoples who are dissatisfied with the growing economic and social differentiation in society and with the country's authoritarian government.

SOCIAL ASPECTS In the eighteenth and nineteenth centuries Kazakh legal culture was based on *adat* (customary law). *Adat* was somewhat influenced by Shari'ah (Islamic law) but was never replaced by it. Many Kazakh traditions and customs—for example, the seven-generation exogamy rule, which forbade even distant rel-

atives to marry—were in contradiction with normative Islamic law. The role of the Shari'ah in contemporary Kazakhstan has been insignificant. The status of women in Kazakhstan is higher than in other Central Asian countries. Polygamy is not practiced. Children usually decide themselves whom to marry or at least are involved in the choice.

POLITICAL IMPACT The role of politicized Islam in Kazakhstan has remained negligible. The law forbids religious associations to participate in political activities. The official ulama prefer to rely upon the secular leadership of the country. In its turn, the latter has demonstrated a benevolent and paternalistic attitude toward Islam. Since 1995 Kazakhstan has been a member of the Islamic Conference Organization and of the Islamic Bank of Development. Within the country, however, the state wants to keep Islam under control. All religious associations have to register with the government.

CONTROVERSIAL ISSUES The post-Soviet religious revival in Kazakhstan contains the potential danger of extremist and fundamentalist Islam penetrating into the country. Many foreign missionaries have come into the country, and several Muslim countries have established religious schools and centers there, some of which propagate Sunni Islam of the Hanafi tradition. A number of these institutions were recently closed by the government "for promulgating ideas of religious radicalism and constituting a threat to the country's sociopolitical stability." So far, radical Islamic groups and movements have gained a certain degree of influence only in southern Kazakhstan, mainly among the Uzbek minority. The most noticeable of these groups are the Wahhabis, who preach a return to "pure Islam," and Hizb ut-Tahir, an underground organization whose goal is the establishment of an Islamic state based on the Shari'ah over all of Central Asia.

CULTURAL IMPACT Traditional Kazakh culture was oral. It was represented by *aqyns* (poets) and *zhyraus* (storytellers), who were influenced to some extent by Muslim literary culture. As a result, Islamic topics were integrated into Kazakh myths, legends, and lyrics. From its emergence in the nineteenth century, Kazakh professional culture was under the strong influence of Russian culture, and in the Soviet period it acquired predominantly secular forms. This situation has held since independence. Attempts to introduce Islamic elements in the literature, architecture, and performing arts of modern Kazakhstan have had only limited success.

EASTERN ORTHODOXY

DATE OF ORIGIN Eleventh century C.E.
NUMBER OF FOLLOWERS 5.4 million

HISTORY Orthodox Christianity was brought to Kazakhstan in the nineteenth century by Russian colonizers and settlers and, in the Soviet period, by the mass migration of Slavs into the country. During the Soviet period most Orthodox churches were closed (or even destroyed), parishes were abolished, and many clergy were imprisoned. In the post-Soviet period Orthodoxy has experienced a revival, though the actual number of its followers has been decreasing because of Slavic emigration. The revival of Orthodoxy among Russians and other East Slavs in the country has been partly connected with its perception as an ethnic religion and marker.

The Russian Orthodox Church issues periodicals and maintains a number of parochial schools. It trains the priests at the Almaty Theological School and sends some of its students to pursue further education at the Moscow Theological Seminary.

EARLY AND MODERN LEADERS No Orthodox leaders of note have emerged in Kazakhstan. In administrative and ecclesiastical matters, Orthodox Christians in Kazakhstan are directly subordinated to the Moscow patriarchate. In 1991 the latter rejected the idea of creating a semi-independent ecclesiastical body in the country.

MAJOR THEOLOGIANS AND AUTHORS Kazakhstan has always lacked theologians of high reputation in the Orthodox world.

HOUSES OF WORSHIP AND HOLY PLACES The house of worship is the church. Some Orthodox church buildings, including the main cathedral of Ascension in Almaty, which were confiscated in the Soviet period, have been returned to the church. Construction of new churches has been insignificant, mainly due to the lack of funds. There are also three Orthodox monasteries and three nunneries in Kazakhstan.

WHAT IS SACRED? In this regard there are no differences between the Orthodox Christians of Kazakhstan and their coreligionists in Russia.

HOLIDAYS AND FESTIVALS There are no Orthodox Christian holidays that are distinctive to Kazakhstan.

MODE OF DRESS Practically all Orthodox Christians in Kazakhstan, with the exception of the Cossacks, wear Western-style dress. The Cossacks, who formed a privileged military and social stratum in the Russian Empire, the descendants of which still strive to maintain their cultural and other separateness, have retained some peculiarities in their dress, including the Circassian coat, a long-waisted outer garment, and characteristic headgear.

DIETARY PRACTICES There are no foods that Orthodox Christians are forbidden to eat.

RITUALS The level of everyday observance has remained rather low among the Orthodox in Kazakhstan, though nowadays a significant number of Russians observe the major religious holidays, especially Christmas and Easter. There are no Orthodox rituals specific to Kazakhstan, however.

RITES OF PASSAGE Such Orthodox rites of passage as baptism, religious marriage, and funerals have become somewhat more conspicuous in post-Soviet Kazakhstan.

MEMBERSHIP Besides the Russians, the majority of Ukrainians and Belorussians in Kazakhstan profess Orthodox Christianity, as do the Turkic-speaking Chuvash, whose traditional homeland is in the Middle Volga region of Russia. In 1996, however, only about 60 percent of Russians in Kazakhstan described themselves as Orthodox Christians. Since then the percentage has increased somewhat, but no reliable statistics are available.

SOCIAL JUSTICE Specifically Orthodox Christian ideas of social justice have had little impact on the everyday lives and behavior of the Orthodox community in Kazakhstan. Although the charitable activities of the church have increased in the post-Soviet period, they have continued to be limited by financial constraints.

SOCIAL ASPECTS No specific characteristics of the Orthodox Church in Kazakshtan are worthy of mention in this regard.

POLITICAL IMPACT In administrative and ecclesiastical matters, Orthodox Christians in Kazakhstan are directly subordinated to the Moscow patriarchate. In 1991 the patriarchate rejected the establishment of a semi-independent ecclesiastical body in Kazakhstan and, instead, subdivided the single Orthodox diocese in Kazakhstan into three new ones—Almaty and Semipalatinsk, Shimkent, and the Urals—with the obvious intention of keeping the Orthodox Church in Kazakhstan under its control. This decision was received with a certain dissatisfaction by Kazakhstan's government. Since the Orthodox Church does not intervene in the country's political process, however, its hierarchy—especially its local leader, Archbishop Alexei—has remained on good terms with the country's leadership.

CONTROVERSIAL ISSUES Although the decision to keep the Orthodox Church in Kazakhstan under the control of the Moscow patriarchate was not well received by Kazakhstan's government, this has remained a minor issue. To demonstrate its loyalty to the country and its leadership, the Orthodox hierarchy has maintained a certain distance from the Cossacks and has condemned their appeal for territorial separatism.

CULTURAL IMPACT Although the impact of Russian and other European cultures was—and has remained—great, it has always been largely secular in nature and has never contained specifically Orthodox traits.

Other Religions

The first Catholics in Kazakhstan settled in the region before the revolution, though most Catholics in contemporary Kazakhstan are people who were deported to the country during the Soviet period or their descendants. Official sources have estimated the number of Catholics in the country at more than 300,000. The vast majority are of Polish, German, and West Ukrainian origin. Among the Ukrainians is a small group of Eastern-rite (Uniate) Catholics. The number of Catholics in Kazakhstan has been decreasing due to the emigration of people of German descent to Germany. Proselytizing by Catholics is virtually nonexistent.

Currently there are about 40 Catholic churches and 200 chapels and meeting houses in the country. There are also about 250 parishes, 90 Catholic communities, and 160 visiting groups, which are served by three bishops, more than 60 padres, and 70 sisters of charity. The first Catholic theological seminary in Kazakhstan was founded in 1998. The Roman Catholic administration publishes the monthly newspaper *Credo* in Karaganda.

Catholics prefer not to intermarry with other Christian denominations, though there are many exceptions to this rule. Marriages with Muslims are extremely rare. Relations between Catholics and the government are amicable because the Catholic community does not intervene in the political process. Their influence is more important with regard to foreign relations. Diplomatic relations between Kazakhstan and the Vatican were established in October 1992, and Pope John Paul II visited the country in 2001. In 1999 the apostolic nunciature, the papal ambassador's office, was established in Almaty; it later moved to the new capital, Astana.

The most populous Protestant group in the country is the Baptists. In addition to Germans, this group includes some Russians and Ukrainians. In the past there was a certain tension between the authorities—especially on the local level—and Protestant associations like the International Council of Churches of Evangelical Christians/Baptists and the Jehovah's Witnesses, which refused to register with the government for ideological reasons. Their congregations were routinely pressured or fined. In April 2002, however, Kazakhstan's Constitutional Council threw out the law requiring the registration of religious communities. Since then there have been no recorded cases of bans or legal cases against Protestant associations.

Anatoly M. Khazanov

See Also Vol. 1: *Christianity, Eastern Orthodoxy, Islam*

Bibliography

Anurova, A.A. *Dialog of Religions.* Almaty: Center for Foreign Policy and Analysis, 2001.

Deweese, Devin A. *History of Islam in Central Asia.* Leiden and New York: E.J. Brill, 2000.

Lewis, David C. *After Atheism: Religion and Ethnicity in Russia and Central Asia.* St. Martin's Press, 2000.

Kenya

POPULATION 30,766,000

CHRISTIAN 66 percent

AFRICAN TRADITIONAL BELIEFS
  28.7 percent

MUSLIM 5 percent

OTHER 0.3 percent

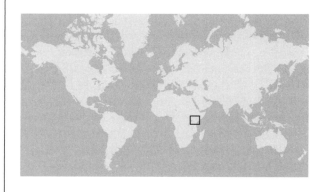

Country Overview

INTRODUCTION The Republic of Kenya, located along the East African coast, is a microcosm of cultural diversity. It is bordered by the Indian Ocean and Somalia to the east, Ethiopia and The Sudan to the north, Uganda and Lake Victoria to the west, and Tanzania to the south.

Kenya has some 44 ethnic groups. The largest are the Kikuyu, forming 20 percent of the population, the Luya, 14 percent; the Luo, 12 percent; the Kalenjin, 11 percent; and the Kisii, 6 percent. Depending on their language and the origin of their migratory pattern about a thousand years ago, ethnic groups in Kenya are classi-

fied as Bantu-speakers (69 percent), Nilotic (27 percent), or Cushitic (3 percent).

Islam was introduced to Kenya by Middle Eastern merchants and Islamic brotherhoods beginning in the seventh century, as well as by Somali Muslims who consistently migrated into northern Kenya. Prior to Islam most Kenyans held traditional, indigenous religions. By the time the Portuguese arrived, following Vasco da Gama's successful maritime voyage to India in 1498, most of the Kenyan coast had already converted to Islam, though the religion had little impact in the interior.

The attempt of the Portuguese crown to Christianize coastal Kenya was short lived, mainly because of the hostility of coastal Arabs and the lukewarm activity of Roman Catholicism in the area. European exploration of Africa increased during the mid-1880s and after the subsequent Berlin Conference (1884–88), which recognized the Kenyan coast (leased from the Sultan of Zanzibar in 1888) as a British sphere of influence. The opening of the coast to British settlers—who expropriated the best land from the Africans, especially the Kikuyu, and forced many Kenyans to farm tobacco, coffee, and tea—paved the way for the reintroduction of Christianity in the form of Anglicanism and Roman Catholicism. Later confrontation between Christians, especially the Anglican Church, and the local population, the Kikuyu in particular, combined with dissatisfaction over the British colonial system, culminated with the so-called Mau Mau Rebellion in 1952–56, leading to Kenya's independence on 12 December 1963.

Although most Kenyans today claim to be Christian, Muslims are a vocal minority on the coast, and there are pockets of Hindus, Buddhists, Taoists, and Jews in parts of Kenya, most notably in Nairobi. Although traditionalists have been losing ground to Christianity and Islam, Kenya is one of the few countries in Africa where there is a growing movement to preserve and strengthen indigenous religion.

RELIGIOUS TOLERANCE Kenya's constitution is clear in its separation of church and state. Government leaders, however, speak so often in Christian terms that Muslims and traditionalists complain that the legal separation is meaningless in practice. Moreover, the "Christian Church," a group of Christians who enjoy the support of the Methodist and several Pentecostal churches, has demanded that Kenya be declared a Christian state. The influential Catholic and Anglican churches, as well as the Muslim minority, oppose this change.

Since 1943 there has been an active National Council of Churches in Kenya, now led by Rev. Joseph Waithonga, which comprises 38 full and 8 associate members. Although there is an ecumenical movement in the country, several factors have hampered the effort to bring religious leaders together. These include the 1994 bombing of the American Embassy in Nairobi, killing 254 people and injuring 5,000, which was attributed to Muslim fanatics; the establishment of a strictly Muslim party in the country; a series of incendiary statements made by Roman Catholic bishops, who have been accused of disrespecting the prophet Muhammad; and the increasing impact of the charismatic movement, which has sharpened rather than toned down doctrinal differences among the churches in Kenya. Indeed, Muslims and Christians have burned each other's places of worship, and Muslims have physically assaulted Christians, as, for example, on Good Friday in 2003, when 500 Christians, including Bishop Nicodemus Kirima and a nun, were stoned and injured in Nyeri. Muslims claim that Christians have been attacking their mosques and disrupting their Friday prayers with loud speakers and other noises. The Catholic Church has apologized to the Supreme Council of Kenya Muslims (SUPKEM) for some of the incidents.

Relations among Christians and between Christians, Muslims, and traditionalists in Kenya have deteriorated since the 1990s. Traditionalists, too, have been looked down upon as ignorant and superstitious, good only for conversion to Christianity or Islam. Among Christians and Muslims, traditionalism is not considered a legitimate religion to be accepted and understood.

Kenyans leave a Catholic church after mass. Christian missions have a long history in Kenya, dating back to the fifteenth century. © JEFFREY L. ROTMAN/CORBIS.

Major Religions

CHRISTIANITY

AFRICAN TRADITIONAL BELIEFS

CHRISTIANITY

DATE OF ORIGIN 1880 C.E.
NUMBER OF FOLLOWERS 20,306,000

HISTORY During the fifteenth century Portuguese missionary activity along the Kenyan coast resulted in failure, especially after Yusuf bin Hassan massacred Christians in 1631. The German missionaries Ludwig Kraft and Johan Rebmann of the Church Missionary Society (CMS) started their work on the coast and in Ukamba in 1844. The United Methodist Church entered the area as early as 1862, working among the Misikenda in eastern Kenya. Catholic missionaries, including the

Holy Ghost Fathers, came from Zanzibar and Tanzania in 1892, established their Saint Austin's Mission in Kiambu, and expanding their work in the region. Then came the Hill Mill Fathers from Uganda, joined by the Consolata Missionaries from Turin, Italy, to central Kenya. Thus, between 1884 and 1914 Catholics, Presbyterians, and other Protestant denominations fiercely vied for converts, who were particularly attracted by the missionarie's philanthropic work, such as the establishment of schools and hospitals. At the turn of the twentieth century the CMS, the Church of God, the Gospel Missionary Society, the Seventh-day Adventists, the Friends Mission (evangelical Quakers), and the African Island Church were active over most of Kenya.

During the late 1920s and 1930s Christians and traditionalists clashed over the traditional practices of circumcision and clitoridectomy. This conflict led to the establishment of independent churches on Kikuyu land in the Central Province. In the process 90 percent of the Kikuyu left the CMS in 1929. Rather than sign a pledge not to participate in these rites of passage, 80 percent of the schoolchildren were also removed from the church. Thereafter, more independent churches and schools (*Karinga* schools, as they came to be known) spread to other parts of Kenya. The conflict was eventually resolved to the satisfaction of the churches, and by the 1950s most Kenyans had become Christian, at least in name.

EARLY AND MODERN LEADERS Very little is known about historical Christian leaders in Kenya. Significant in the twentieth century have been Anglican Archbishop David Mukuba Gitary; Johnson Mbillah, director, Project for Christian-Muslim Relations in Africa; Catholic Archbishop Ndingi Mwana a Nzeki; and Cardinal Maurice Michael Otunga.

MAJOR THEOLOGIAN AND AUTHORS The term "theologian" is used loosely in East Africa, often meaning someone who teaches church doctrine, writes popular works on religion, preaches outside the church, or studied some type of theology somewhere, usually abroad. Among the most important Kenyan theologians and authors are Musimbi Kanyoro, Karim Kinoti, and Rev. Ngoy David Mulunda-Nyanga.

HOUSES OF WORSHIP AND HOLY PLACES For both Protestants and Catholics worship is held in churches and chapels that have been consecrated by the church hierarchy. While some places of worship are elaborate—such as the All Saint's Cathedral of the Anglican Church and the Holy Family Basilica of the Catholic Church, both in Nairobi—others, especially in the countryside, may be made of mud and straw.

WHAT IS SACRED? Churches and chapels are sacred to Kenyan Christians. Although cemeteries, relics of saints (which do not exist yet in Kenya), the rosary, the crucifix, a saint's medal, and the Bible are also venerated and respected by Christians, reverence for them has been diminished by secular culture.

HOLIDAYS AND FESTIVALS Apart from Sundays, Kenyans do not celebrate many Christian holidays. Only Good Friday and Easter Monday are truly national Christian holidays, even though Catholics are asked to observe, to the extent possible, Assumption, Immaculate Conception, and Ascension, among others. On these days Christians attend church service and are not to engage in manual labor. Both Catholics and Anglicans wish each other "good tidings" during Christmas, which is considered to be primarily a family celebration, during which families drink abundantly, visit each other, and exchange gifts, as in the West.

MODE OF DRESS Christianity has little influence on dress in Kenya. Kenyans tend to be Westernized and formal on holy days. Most men wear a suit on Sundays, and women wear dresses and hats. The less wealthy wear shorts and a shirt or a colorful cloth wrapped around the body. Attire is always clean and ironed, even among those in the countryside.

DIETARY PRACTICES Both Christians and traditionalist Kenyans do not eat animals that consume human flesh. Monkeys, zebras, dogs, cats, and snakes are forbidden in the diet. Only truly devout Christians observe days of fasting and abstinence. Christians are among the heaviest drinkers in Kenya.

RITUALS In addition to going to church (a recent survey reported that only 9 to 12 percent of Christians attend Sunday service), Kenyan Christians pray before meals (if they are with their family) and may also go to great lengths to have a wedding that everyone invited will remember—one that offers plenty of food and beverages and is interspersed with speeches and prayers. Both in the Anglican and Catholic churches a Christian wedding, which usually lasts a whole day and evening, starts with a mass or a church service, with most guests dressed formally, and ends with a reception that resembles a Western wedding.

Kenyans do not undertake pilgrimages, and less than 5 percent visit the Holy Land or the Vatican in any given year. Funerals are elaborate, beginning with a church service and ending at the cemetery; they are usually accompanied by songs and a reception.

RITES OF PASSAGE Among Kenyan Christians baptism, confirmation, weddings, church funeral services, and ordination to the ministry mark the transition from one physical and spiritual stage to another. Christians are not allowed to participate in such traditional practices as clitoridectomy and infibulation, circumcision (when unhealthy and dangerous), initiation ceremonies that require acknowledging the power of the ancestors, and the offering of sacrifices to the spirits or the African god.

MEMBERSHIP In Kenya there is stiff competition for membership between Protestants and Roman Catholics and between Christians and Muslims. Often the number of followers is more important than their Christian fervor; this is reflected among the faithful in their lack of knowledge of essential Christian teachings and in their tendency, after conversion, to continue practicing traditional rituals—for example, sacrifice to ancestors, belief in unnatural causes for death and illness, polygamy, and dances that are seen as immoral by the church. Membership recruitment is done mostly by word of mouth, though Christian radio and television programs exist. In 2003 the Catholic Church, after years of waiting, acquired its own radio station in Nairobi.

Notable in Kenya is the emergence of the charismatic movement. Though supported by some in the Christian hierarchy as a way of reviving Christianity and the liturgy, it is mistrusted by many Catholics, who believe that it misrepresents the nature and role of the Holy Spirit. Under the acronym FIRE (Faith-Intercession-Repentance-Evangelization), the movement has been backed by American evangelicals and has promoted the assimilation of local culture into Christian practices. It also encourages the free expression of emotions during church service through dancing, hand clapping, loud and prolonged singing, and speaking in tongues. FIRE has reportedly been spreading rapidly in the country, forcing many Catholics and Protestants ei-

ther to join charismatic churches or to remain unenthusiastic members of their longstanding parishes.

SOCIAL JUSTICE There is a strong sense of social responsibility among Kenyan Christians. The clergy, for example, has been highly critical of human rights abuses by the government. The tradition of *Harambe* (self-help) and *Umoja* (togetherness) have also been embraced by Kenyan churches, and charity and generosity are not uncommon in the country.

In Kenya health services and education are the most important social contributions by the Christian ministry, and the denomination or congregation that offers the most social services tends to attract the most converts. A recent service by the Anglican Church is the Urban Development Program, which was intended to relocate slum-dwelling families (regardless of religious denomination) who lost their homes in government demolition projects in central Nairobi. The new settlement plans included input from the families on various issues, such as water supplies, education, and income-generating initiatives.

SOCIAL ASPECTS Christian churches in Kenya promote large, strong, monogamous families, although members often deviate considerably from the norm. The Catholic Church upholds priestly celibacy and condemns all polygamy. The Anglican Church allows ordination of monogamously married bishops, priests, and deacons, though they are in danger of being defrocked if they do not maintain monogamy. Anglicans also permit converted polygamous husbands to keep all their wives as long as they and their children are baptized and the man promises not to marry more women. Any Anglican woman marrying a polygamist is subject to excommunication.

All Christians in Kenya are taught not to engage in premarital sex, not to marry during their teen years, and to maintain marital fidelity and loyalty. Such teaching, however, is usually ignored among the Maasai warriors and the Samburu who have converted to Christianity.

POLITICAL IMPACT Christians have had tremendous political impact in Kenya. The first nationalist associations were organized by Christians. Virtually all political leaders (except for a few Muslims and Indian Hindus) have been Christian, and politicians have not been shy in boasting about their faith. Christian organizations have brought much pressure to bear on government abuses and injustices, and they have been instrumental in the movement toward true democracy in Kenya. This has often placed the Church at odds with the government.

CONTROVERSIAL ISSUES Some Kenyans, led by a group called Catholics for a Free Choice (CFFC), have taken to the streets to demonstrate against the church's condemnation of contraceptives, such as condoms. Following the public burning of condoms by Archbishop Ndingi Mwana a Nzeki and his followers, intended to dramatize the Catholic Church's opposition to contraceptives, the CFFC led a march under the slogan "Banning Condoms Kills." To frustrate the church, Sobbie Mulindi, director of the National AIDS Committee, announced in 1998 that, of the 800,000 Kenyans infected with HIV/AIDS, the majority were Catholic. The archbishop fired back, noting that the Catholic Church launched a campaign against AIDS long before the government was willing to admit its prevalence in the country. In Kenya many Christians have accepted family planning in order to limit the number of children.

Both the Anglican and the Catholic churches have rejected in vitro fertilization, newly introduced in Kenya, as an attempt by the West to replace God. Rev. Alfred Chipman of the Anglican Church argued that in vitro fertilization posed a "great danger ethically, morally, and socially to Kenyan society."

The Catholic, Anglican, and Methodist churches have all condemned homosexuality. The Kenyan Anglican Church rejected the ordination of Gene Robinson, a gay U.S. bishop, in 2003 and cut ties with his Diocese of New Hampshire. Kenyan Christians have been conservative on other sexual issues as well. The Catholic Church, for example, has condemned the writings of Chinua Achebe, an internationally renowned novelist, which it views as pornographic. The church has asked that his books be banned from public school libraries in Kenya.

CULTURAL IMPACT Christianity, along with Westernization, has had significant cultural impact in Kenya, more so than in most neighboring African nations. Church services are very colorful and replete with traditional European Christian songs and lyrics. Christian authors, such as Ngugi Wa 'Thiongo, have been important in Kenyan literature, often defending or attacking the Christian perspective. Christianity has had less influ-

ence in the visual arts, where traditional African styles and themes, particularly in sculpture, have dominated.

AFRICAN TRADITIONAL BELIEFS

DATE OF ORIGIN 800–1000 C.E.
NUMBER OF FOLLOWERS 8,830,000

HISTORY Indigenous religious beliefs in Kenya appeared with the first humans in East Africa, most likely about 200,000 years ago. The present structure of Kenya's traditional religion, however, can be traced back to the arrival of the country's predominant Bantu speakers, who settled as agriculturalists in the area around 800–1000 C.E. and assimilated with the indigenous inhabitants. Around the same time, the southerly migrations of the Cushitic and pastoralist Nilotic populations from the Sudan and the Horn of Africa, which continued for centuries, contributed to the complexity of the region's religious system.

The intrusion of Islam during the seventh century and of Christianity, the religion of European colonialism, during the nineteenth century resulted in the conversion of many traditionalists to the new faiths. Moreover, colonial rule—involving forced labor, taxation, Western education, the introduction of cash crops, political oppression, economic exploitation, and cultural subjugation—was intended to eradicate certain cultural elements in Kenya, including polygamy, drum dancing, "pagan" activities, local languages (which at best were to be relegated to an inferior position), indigenous rites of passage, and African religions as a whole, which Westerners called pure superstition or ancestor worship.

Despite the subsequent weakening of traditionalism, nearly 9 million people in contemporary Kenya still worship in the ways of their ancestors, and even the great majority of Kenyan Christians have not completely abandoned the religious ideas and practices of their communities and ethnic groups. These include the existence of one supreme being, creator of the universe; the power of spirits (good and evil); a divinely infused vital force that permeates every existing thing; and the critical role ancestors play in guaranteeing social tranquility and the survival of the community and its mores.

EARLY AND MODERN LEADERS Traditionalism in Kenya has been marginalized by the government and the Western-educated elite, who are mostly Christian. It has therefore remained a less organized religion than Christianity and Islam, and those who practice it and ensure that it is maintained as a viable and relevant religion are not celebrated publicly. Yet the major diviners, the powerful medicine men, the elders, and the heads of family who officiate over prayer and sacrifice remain vital leaders of Kenya's indigenous religion.

MAJOR THEOLOGIANS AND AUTHORS As with other traditional African religions, one learns about religion in day-to-day life, not from priests and missionaries. In this context the "theologians" are parents, elders, officiators over prayer and sacrifice, ancestors, and traditional political authorities who are considered to be divine, as they share the highest level of the universal vital force that comes from the highest supernatural being, God, known as *Ngai* or *Murungu* among several Kenyan peoples.

HOUSES OF WORSHIP AND HOLY PLACES Traditionalist Kenyans have many places they consider to be sacred or holy and where they perform rituals. These include cemeteries, burials inside houses (as is the case among the Akamba), parts of certain forests, mountains (such as Mount Kenya, God's dwelling place among the Kikuyu), and trees under or on which sacrifices to the ancestors are offered. Maasai people, for example, place the deceased's body under a shade tree, which is symbolically "cool," and leave it there for hyenas or other predators to devour. Kenyan traditionalists do not have formal or "handmade temples," as do some West African societies.

WHAT IS SACRED? In traditional Kenyan religion all animals associated with an ethnic group or clan are sacred. Certain amulets prescribed by a medicine man or diviner are sacred, and so are all objects left in a cemetery or associated with a shrine (mountains, trees, and ancestral sites). Apart from these, there are virtually no sacred animals, plants, or relics in Kenyan traditionalism.

HOLIDAYS AND FESTIVALS Traditionalist days of rest in Kenya do not fall on a specific day of the week or month. Days of community atonement, the first days of the planting season and harvest, the day of the chasing of the illnesses (an activity in which the whole community participates), and the end of the initiation ceremonies may be considered traditionalist holidays or festivals.

MODE OF DRESS There are no distinctive dress codes that distinguish a traditionalist from a Christian. Yet because most traditionalists tend to be illiterate, poor, and live in nature, they are more prone to be raggedly dressed, even though they are conscious of the need to be clean. Men wear shorts and shirts. Women commonly wrap one cloth around the body and another rolled around the head. During religious rituals the officiating elder, chief, or head of family may wear special attire, such as an animal skin and a cap, or carry, as a symbol of his authority, the dried tail of an animal.

DIETARY PRACTICES Traditional religion imposes few dietary taboos. Carnivorous animals, especially those that eat human flesh, are avoided. Monkeys, snakes, lions, leopards, hyenas, dogs, cats, zebras (despite their abundance in the land), bats, crows, and owls are also not for human consumption. The most common diet of a traditionalist Kenyan consists of a type of heavy porridge made from flour and served with cooked greens and, on important occasions, with local beer. Invoking the ancestors as the initiators of the practice, adults maintain that the intestines and other animal organs (e.g., liver, kidney, brain, and sex organs) can be eaten only by males or adult females. This is in keeping with the tradition common among the Kikuyu and the Luo, which states that only officiating elders or the elect are allowed to partake of certain parts of an animal being sacrificed to a spirit, an ancestor, or God.

RITUALS Traditionalists do not have specific dates or times of worship and prayer. Prayer to the High God is rare and occurs only when the community as a whole is threatened. Sacrifices, purification ceremonies, harvest thanksgiving activities, libations, and the expulsion of evil spirits symbolized by sticks, clubs, knives, and spears are usually accompanied by the killing of a lamb, whose intestines are tied around a tree and whose flesh is consumed by the elders, the chief, and a select few. Among the Kikuyu the elders are not to engage in sex during the six nights preceding a ritual and during the two subsequent nights.

Weddings and funerals are quite elaborate, but the ceremonies are generally brief, except when they are for chiefs or people of authority. Weddings are often accompanied by music and dancing that may involve the whole village. Drumming is common after the wedding. Dances and other activities are typical at funerals, and loud mourning and crying are allowed. The dead are usually buried with some of their most important belongings, such as pots and body accessories (e.g., necklaces, beads, and amulets), so they can use them in the spirit world they will inhabit.

RITES OF PASSAGE All Kenyan societies have initiation ceremonies, most of which include circumcision for boys and clitoridectomy for girls. The most elaborate rites of passage are those marking the transition from childhood to adulthood. Among the Maasai, for example, a boy goes through six major rites in his lifetime, from child to *moran* (warrior), adult, leader, elder, and eventually ancestor.

MEMBERSHIP Followers of traditional religion in Kenya do not seek converts, either by themselves or through priests or missionaries (neither of which exist). Children grow up in an implicitly religious atmosphere where little distinction is made between the secular and the spiritual and where they learn from listening daily to elders and parents and from their own experience.

SOCIAL JUSTICE As they grow older and participate in rites of passage, children in traditionalist Kenya are taught to respect human life and the rights of others, to maintain the primacy of the community over the individual, to help the needy and the old, to listen to the elders, and to tell the truth. If an individual hurts another, he or she makes his family or community responsible for the act, which often elicits a proportionate response, retribution, and compensation. All this is sanctioned by the will of the ancestors.

SOCIAL ASPECTS In traditionalist Kenya marriage is obligatory and forges an alliance between families. An unmarried person is seen as sexually impotent or infertile. A woman is expected to have as many children as possible, and a man may marry more than one wife, although fewer than one-third of traditionalist Kenyan men do. Parents are to be obeyed unconditionally, and families care for old people and the disabled.

POLITICAL IMPACT Traditionalists have had little political impact in Kenya because they have not been organized as a religious group. Yet recently some traditionalists have come together to formulate a philosophy to preserve and make their religion relevant. This group cherishes traditional African songs and dances and other practices, such as "snuffs" tobacco; abhors organized churches and Western-style government; and rejects foreign ideology. It also supports female circumcision, as well as the ethnic oath used by participants in the Mau Mau Rebellion (1952–56). Members would like to see socialism and meaningful political and socioeconomic changes enacted in Kenya.

CONTROVERSIAL ISSUES Core traditionalists speak out against abortion (except if it is known or suspected that the child will be born with severe defects), contraceptives, and Western-style family planning. Divorce is discouraged and difficult because it affects the whole family or clan, and once the marriage is dissolved, bridewealth may have to be returned to the groom's parents. Women play a subordinate role in decision making and are expected to look after the children and day-to-day household chores.

CULTURAL IMPACT Indigenous religion permeates cultural life in the Kenyan countryside. There music, art, architecture, and other traditions are still determined by a traditionalist frame of mind. Music is monophonic, rhythmic, and instrumental; sculpture is stylistic rather than realistic; houses are rectangular or circular and constructed from traditional materials; knowledge, poetry, proverbs, and riddles are transmitted orally from one generation to the next; and dance forms are participatory. All these cultural forms reflect traditionalist points of view and practices, in which the secular and the spiritual often overlap. Indeed, as it is commonly said, in religiously traditional Africa, religion is life and life is religion.

Other Religions

Islam constitutes only 5 percent of the population, yet Muslims have been vocal in Kenya, and some have embraced and preached a fundamentalist brand of Islam, at times defending the activities and philosophy of the al-Qaeda leader Osama bin Laden. Thus, many have not condemned the 1994 bombings of the American embassies in Nairobi and Dar-es-Salaam, and some shouted down President Daniel arap Moi when he urged Kenyans to demonstrate against the 11 September 2001 attacks in New York and Washington, D.C. Muslims are highly critical of the government, and they have formed their own Islamic political party—the Islamic Party of Kenya (IPK). This opposition to the government, along with the implementation by Muslims of important social programs, has made Islam popular along the coast, especially in Mombasa and Malindi, and in certain sectors of Nairobi.

The militancy of Kenya's Muslims, however, has put Islam on a collision course with Christianity, especially the Catholic Church, and this conflict has alienated a majority of Kenyans. Muslim militancy has weakened the ecumenical movement, even though Muslim clerics, such as Shaikh al-Amin bin Ali Mazrui and Sheikh Abdullah Saleh Farsy, have tried to modernize Islam and its teachings in Kenya. There is a vocal Supreme Council of Kenyan Muslims (SUPKEM), which is chaired by Abd Al-Ghafur al-Busaidi.

Less than 1 percent of the Kenyan population is Buddhist, Taoist, or Jewish, and these are mostly foreigners and temporary expatriates working on international projects. Hindus, an influential group of Indian descent, have been in Kenya since the early 1900s, when Indians immigrated to Kenya (then a British protectorate) primarily to improve their economic status by working on the Mombasa–Nairobi Railway Project. Because these faiths generally do not proselytize, no noted Kenyans have held membership in them.

Mario J. Azevedo

See Also Vol. 1: *African Traditional Beliefs, Christianity*

Bibliography

Azvedo, Mario J. *Kenya: The Land, the People, and the Nation.* Durham, N.C.: Carolina Academic Press, 1991.

Bravman, Bill. *Making Ethnic Wars: Communities and Their Transformations in Taita, Kenya, 1800–1950.* Oxford: Heinemann, 1998.

Burgman, H. *The Way the Catholic Church Started in Western Kenya.* London: Mission Book Service, 1990.

Isichei, Elizabeth. *A History of Christianity in Africa.* Lawrenceville, N.Y.: Africa World Press, 1995.

Kenyatta, Jomo. *Facing Mt. Kenya.* New York: Vintage Books, 1932.

Maxon, Robert M., and Thomas P. Ofcansky. *Historical Dictionary of Kenya.* 2nd ed. Lanham, Md.: Scarecrow Press, 2000.

Mbiti, John S. *African Religions and Philosophy.* London: Heinemann, 1969.

———. *Introduction to African Religion.* London: Heinemann, 1975.

Ocheng, William R. *Times in Kenyan History.* Nairobi: Heinemann, 1990.

Oded, Arye. *Islam and Politics in Kenya.* Cambridge: Cambridge University Press, 2000.

Parrinder, John. *African Religion.* Baltimore: Penguin, 1969.

Presley, Cora Ann. *Kikuyu Women, the Mau Mau Rebellion, and Social Change in Kenya.* Boulder, Colo.: Westview Press, 1992.

Ray, Benjamin. *African Religions.* Upper Saddle River, N.J.: Prentice-Hall, 2000.

Sabar, G. *Church and Society in Kenya.* London: Frank Cass, 2001.

Shorter, Aylard. *African Christian Theology.* New York: Orbis Books, 1977.

Kiribati

POPULATION 100,000

ROMAN CATHOLIC 53.5 percent

KIRIBATI PROTESTANT 39.2
percent

BAHA'I 2.4 percent

SEVENTH-DAY ADVENTIST 1.9
percent

MORMON 1.7 percent

CHURCH OF GOD, ASSEMBLY OF
GOD 1.3 percent

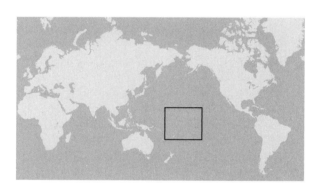

Country Overview

INTRODUCTION The Republic of Kiribati is an independent nation in the central Pacific Ocean (between Hawaii and Australia) consisting of the Gilbert Islands, Phoenix Islands, Line Islands, and Banaba. For the I-Kiribati, or people of Kiribati, the environment produced a spiritual landscape shaped by the sea and a dynamic culture that survived centuries of scarcity and drought. Officially colonized by Britain in 1892, the Gilbert Islands achieved independence in 1979 and became the Republic of Kiribati.

In the late nineteenth century Protestant missionaries from the American Board of Christian Foreign Missions and the London Missionary Society arrived to convert the Gilbertese. Catholicism was introduced about a decade later to counter Protestantism's growing power. By 1945, 95 percent of the island group was Christian. Other Christians on Kiribati include Seventh-day Adventists, Mormons, and members of the Church of God and the Assembly of God. There are also I-Kiribati who adhere to the Baha'i faith.

Most I-Kiribati continue to acknowledge the existence of the indigenous gods and spirits; Christianity and modernity are usually held in tandem with indigenous culture and spirituality. While the population of Kiribati includes Tuvaluan, Chinese, and Europeans, ethnically it is relatively homogenous, and genealogical lines connect people on most islands. Religious values and practices pervade every aspect of life. For example, all formal gatherings, including government and family events, begin with a prayer.

RELIGIOUS TOLERANCE The constitution of Kiribati provides for freedom of religion, but historically there has been tension and competition between Roman Catholics and Protestants. A step toward tolerance was taken in 1975, when the first combined church service was held in the Catholic Cathedral at Teoraereke on Tarawa. In 1989 the Roman Catholic Church and the Kiribati Protestant Church founded the Kiribati National Council of Churches to promote unity among the

Christian denominations. The council is open to all churches that accept the Trinity and Jesus Christ as the Son of God.

Major Religions

ROMAN CATHOLICISM

KIRIBATI PROTESTANT CHURCH

ROMAN CATHOLICISM

DATE OF ORIGIN 1881 C.E.

NUMBER OF FOLLOWERS 53,500

HISTORY In 1881 two catechists, Betero and Tiroi, took Catholicism from Tahiti, where they had worked on European plantations, to Nonouti in the Gilbert Islands. They baptized more than 500 people and then wrote to the Apostolic Vicar for Central Oceania asking for a priest. The first priests in the Gilberts began their work on Nonouti in 1888. The first mass was held on a ship in the middle of the lagoon at Nonouti, and the first Catholic station was established at Tebuange village. It was later transferred to Umantewenei village, where the priests built a church. The faith soon spread to the islands of Nikunau and Butaritari. Joseph Leray, one of the priests who had arrived in 1888, eventually became the first bishop in the Gilbert Islands.

The Catholic priests were more tolerant of Gilbertese cultural practices than the Protestants. They also distributed gifts to people and therefore became more popular. Today the Catholic Church membership includes more than half the population of Kiribati.

EARLY AND MODERN LEADERS Father Edward Bontemps was an important figure in the spread of Catholicism throughout the Gilbert Islands. He arrived on Tabiteuea in 1892 and eventually converted 3,600 people and baptized 600. Bishop Paul Mea (born in 1939), an I-Kiribati, was appointed head of the Catholic Church in Kiribati in 1979.

MAJOR THEOLOGIANS AND WRITERS Father Ernest Sabatier (1886–1965) created the first concise Kiribati-French dictionary. He also wrote a history of the Gilbert Islands in French, *Sous L'equateur du Pacifique* (1938) (published in English as *Astride the Equator* in 1977). Sister Alaima Talu is a well-known Kiribati historian of Tuvaluan heritage.

In Kiribati, the Catholic Church has been accommodating of indigenous cultural practices, such as dance. This tolerance has been important in maintaining its solid membership. © CHARLES & JOSETTE LENARS/CORBIS.

HOUSES OF WORSHIP AND HOLY PLACES The headquarters of the Kiribati Catholic Church are located in Teaoraereke on South Tarawa and include the Sacred Heart Cathedral. Church services in most parishes are slightly different from those in other countries but similar to many parts of the Pacific; the church often does not have seats, and the congregation sits or kneels on the floor.

WHAT IS SACRED? Most Catholics in Kiribati have in their houses a homemade shrine to Jesus, Mary, or the Holy Spirit. Sometimes these consist of a statue surrounded by plastic flowers and other decorations.

HOLIDAYS AND FESTIVALS There are no Catholic holidays that are distinctive to Kiribati. The most significant holidays are Good Friday, Easter, and Christmas.

MODE OF DRESS There is no special mode of dress for Catholic I-Kiribati; they dress in Western-style clothing, as is common in most Pacific Island countries.

DIETARY PRACTICES The Catholic Church does not restrict the diet of its members, but fasting is practiced during Lent or as a way to strengthen prayer. Fasting is especially significant in a country where food is considered central to hospitality and to the maintenance and demonstration of kin relationships. Catholics are discouraged from holding major social functions, such as weddings and birthdays, during Lent, because they require consumption of huge quantities of food.

RITUALS The various elements of the Catholic Mass have been indigenized in some places in Kiribati, and Kiribati cultural elements are involved in the service or in daily home rituals. Traditional elements include liturgical dancing in traditional costume, particularly during the offertory procession. Most Catholic communities include a charismatic song and dance group that leads meetings and other feasts. During Communion, as in most Pacific churches, Catholics usually just receive bread (the body of Christ) but not wine (the blood of Christ). The absence of the wine is mainly for economic reasons. Catholic weddings are often a syncretic blend of Kiribati and Catholic practices; they typically involve traditional feasting, singing, and dancing.

RITES OF PASSAGE Catholic rites of passage include the sacraments of baptism, first Communion, confirmation, and marriage. There is nothing distinctive about their practice in Kiribati.

MEMBERSHIP Unlike the Kiribati Protestant Church, the Catholic Church has been accommodating of indigenous cultural practices, such as dance. This tolerance has been important in maintaining its solid membership.

SOCIAL JUSTICE The Catholic Church in Kiribati runs four secondary schools, which take in almost one-third of the secondary school population. The nuns of Our Lady of the Sacred Heart support Te Itoi ni Ngaina, a women's collective at Teoraereke, Tarawa, that promotes local women's art, craft, and cooking.

SOCIAL ASPECTS For Catholic I-Kiribati families, which are characteristically large, it is an honor to have a family member who devotes his or her life to the church. In a devout Catholic family at least one son or daughter becomes a priest or nun. This is seen as adding to the spiritual wealth of the family.

POLITICAL IMPACT The Catholic Church has played a major role in politics in Kiribati since the early days of conversion. In most communities church leadership maintains the foremost position of power, ahead of both the national government and the island councils. If a constituency is primarily Catholic, it will likely support a Catholic candidate for office.

The church became directly involved in political controversy in the mid-1980s when the bishop of Tarawa created a manifesto condemning the government's negotiation of a fishing agreement with the Soviet Union. Catholics throughout the nation protested the negotiations, claiming an association with the communist Soviet Union would jeopardize the spiritual well-being of the Kiribati people.

CONTROVERSIAL ISSUES In Kiribati a major controversy surrounds the issue of family planning. The Catholic Church in Kiribati (like the church in rest of the world) frowns upon preventative methods such as the pill or condoms. It actively promotes the Billings Method and the rhythm method; Catholic medical and paramedical staff in Kiribati are instructed to promote the Billings Method to Catholics. The church in Kiribati has fought attempts to introduce sexuality education in schools. In a country with a small land area and a rapidly increasing population, the issue of birth control assumes great significance.

CULTURAL IMPACT Over the course of the twentieth century the Catholic communities have developed contemporary Kiribati music using string bands and singing groups, both in Kiribati and on Rabi in Fiji, where many I-Kiribati live. This kind of music became popular particularly because it is livelier than traditional music or Protestant music. Alphonsis Kanimea (1916–97) was an I-Kiribati catechist who composed a significant number of hymns in the Kiribati language. His compositions are widely sung in Catholic communities in Fiji and Kiribati.

KIRIBATI PROTESTANT CHURCH

DATE OF ORIGIN 1852 C.E.
NUMBER OF FOLLOWERS 39,200

HISTORY Protestantism arrived in the Gilbert Islands in 1852. The first missionaries, from the American Board of Christian Foreign Missions (ABCFM), were not successful at converting the Gilbertese. The American missionary Rev. Hiram Bingham arrived on Abaiang in 1857 and made converts through a rigorous educational program that included translating the Bible into the local language. One of the ABCFM's primary goals was to encourage literacy in order to train potential Gilbertese pastors. The ABCFM also used Pacific Islander missionaries, particularly Hawaiians, who were left in charge of ministries in the southern Gilberts. The missionaries made some conversions, but their strict requirements for Sunday observance and their opposition to dancing and smoking were not attractive to most Gilbertese.

The London Missionary Society (LMS) arrived in the Southern Gilberts in 1870. The first contingent included a number of Samoan pastors; it has been noted that the Samoans' success was helped by the existence within Gilbertese mythology of a land called "Tamoa."

The ABCFM transferred ministerial duties to the LMS in 1917. By then the Gilbert Islands were governed by the British. In the 1960s newly trained Gilbertese pastors replaced the Samoan ministers. The Gilbert Islands Protestant Church was formed in 1968. At that time approximately half of the population was Protestant. At independence in 1979 it became the Kiribati Protestant Church.

I-Kiribati pastors are trained at Tangintebu Theological College on Tarawa and the Pacific Theological College in Fiji. In the 1980s the Kiribati Protestant Church (KPC) embarked on a series of ambitious building projects, which put great financial pressure on its members, leading, among other things, to a membership decline. It is in the membership of the KPC that new religious movements find potential converts. Nevertheless, the KPC continues to maintain great support and to wield significant cultural and political clout throughout Kiribati.

EARLY AND MODERN LEADERS In 1857 a mission was established at Koinawa, Abaiang, by ABCFM minister Hiram Bingham, Jr. (1831–1908), with the help of a Hawaiian missionary named Kanoa. Bingham built a church there and also began to create a Gilbertese orthography. The first LMS missionaries to the Gilberts (in the 1870s) included Rev. S.J. Whitmee and a Gilbertese man named Tanre.

Prominent Kiribati Protestant Church ministers in the late twentieth and early twenty-first centuries have included Rev. Bureieta Karaiti, the church's general secretary, and Rev. Baiteke Nabetari, moderator of the KPC.

MAJOR THEOLOGIANS AND AUTHORS Kambati Uriam, a KPC minister (active beginning in the late twentieth century), is a historian of Gilbertese oral traditions. Many I-Kiribati theologians have emerged in the late twentieth and early twenty-first centuries after graduating from the Pacific Theological College.

HOUSES OF WORSHIP AND HOLY PLACES The main KPC church building is located in Antebuka, Tarawa. Its architecture is in a conventional Western style. The church's name—Bangotan Kristo— initially provoked controversy. The Kiribatese word *bangota,* meaning "shrine," was usually associated with ancestral worship. Many objected to giving a Christian church a "pagan" name. People later began to accept a Christian interpretation of the word.

WHAT IS SACRED? The Bible is seen as the absolute authority for the KPC. Sundays are honored with church attendance and abstinence from work.

HOLIDAYS AND FESTIVALS KPC members celebrate the same holidays and festivals as Protestant Christians in other countries.

MODE OF DRESS Protestants in Kiribati typically wear white to church, distinguishing them from Catholics. Church attire for Protestant men is usually a *lavalava* (cloth sarong) and a collared shirt, and women wear either a formal dress or a blouse with a skirt or *lavalava.* Protestant pastors wear a *sulu* (a type of skirt), suit jacket, and tie; now, however, several of them (including the head of the KPC) wear garments that resemble those of Catholic priests.

DIETARY PRACTICES Protestants are expected to refrain from consuming alcohol. The church in Kiribati has criticized the increasing consumption of kava, or *yaqona,* a traditional drink (made from the *Piper methysticum* plant) with sedative properties; it is imported from Fiji.

RITUALS KPC rituals, including Sunday service, are the same as those of other Protestant churches. Kiribati engagements and weddings, however, exhibit practices that combine Christian and indigenous cultural elements. For example, engagement celebrations usually occur over the course of a week and include dancing and feasting in which the bride's family lavishes gifts on the groom-to-be. The Christian elements lie mainly in the marriage ceremony.

RITES OF PASSAGE Potential members are interviewed by the minister, and then his or her name is brought before the church meeting. After some training the person must make a public confession before being admitted as a member.

MEMBERSHIP The KPC has been faced with losing members to groups such as the Mormons and the Baha'is. Efforts to gain and retain members include religious instruction in public schools, outreach programs in hospitals and prisons, and radio broadcasts of Christian programs. In an effort to draw youth to the church, the KPC has encouraged the use of new music forms, such as rap music, in worship services.

SOCIAL JUSTICE The KPC takes an active role in youth education and sports and organizes large annual dance competitions. The KPC also runs three high schools.

SOCIAL ASPECTS In general, the KPC promotes nuclear and extended family values along with patriarchal ideas of authority. Adultery, divorce, and having children out of wedlock are frowned upon.

POLITICAL IMPACT The KPC plays a major role in politics, often supporting certain political candidates. Kiribati Protestants tend to be more conservative politically than Catholics.

In the early days of ABCFM missionary activity, two Hawaiian missionaries, Kapu and Nalimu, facilitated the conversion of most of the islands of the Tabiteuea group and in 1881 led a religious war that successfully converted the so-called "pagan," or Tioba, adherents in the southern islands. Over the course of the war thousands of southern Tabiteueans were killed, and their land was claimed by the northerners and their Hawaiian leaders. The religious war forever changed land ownership across Tabiteuea Meang (North) and Tabiteuea Maiaki (South).

CONTROVERSIAL ISSUES The early Samoan pastors who won converts were treated with great respect, but they insisted on a life of leisure outside their pastoral duties; this became increasingly problematic, even while it served as a model for Gilbertese pastors. The Samoans also heavily taxed people's resources; the people had to provide the church with money, food, and labor. The many demands of the Protestant Church have generally contributed to its declining membership.

Given the patriarchal structure of the church, women's efforts within the KPC have been significant. The Protestant Women's Fellowship, or Reitan Aine ki Kamatu (RAK), was founded by pioneer missionary wives. Today the RAK plays a major role in financially supporting the church, and on most islands it is directly charged with the welfare of the pastor. After years of women struggling for equality in the church, Tenikotabare Bokai of Tabiteuea and Nei Ota Tioti of Onotoa were ordained in 1984, becoming the first women pastors in the KPC.

CULTURAL IMPACT Members of the KPC are often exposed to new cultural ideas through interactions with different churches and members of the KPC living overseas. These exchanges are particularly manifested in new forms of dance and music, which are shared at social gatherings or dance competitions.

Other Religions

The short-lived Tioba religion was taken to Tabiteuea in the nineteenth century by two Gilbertese who had learned of the religion in Tahiti and Fiji. The religion was then also known as Te Buraeniman and was a syncretic blend of European ideas, Catholicism, and indigenous religious practices. Through the religious wars in the 1880s, all members of the Tioba religion were killed or forcefully converted to Protestantism.

Traditional authority, especially in the southern islands, was vested in the *mwaneaba*, or meetinghouse, headed by a group of male village elders (*unimwane*) and sanctioned by both ancestral spirits and indigenous gods. The *mwaneaba* system has changed considerably since British colonialism and Christian conversion in the late nineteenth century. While meetinghouses continue to exist, the use of the *boti* (traditional sitting places) and the different roles of village clans have changed. Generational differences have been growing as I-Kiribati youth question the authority of their elders. Women's decision-making roles, previously marginalized under both *mwaneaba* authority and Christianity, have also been transforming as more women become educated in institutions shaped by Western values.

In 1947 Pastor John Howse took the Seventh-day Adventist (SDA) Church to Abemama in the Gilbert Islands. Howse converted a small number of Catholics and founded a Sabbath school in 1948. In 1954 the Kiribati Mission was formally organized under the jurisdiction of the Central Pacific Union (headquartered in Fiji). In 1972 the Kiribati Mission transferred to the Western Pacific Union (headquartered in the Solomon Islands). The SDA Church moved to Tarawa in 1966, and churches were established at Tarawa, Kauma on Abemama, and Kuria Island between 1978 and 1982. The church runs Kauma High School on Abemama.

In 1954 Roy and Elena Fernie of the National Spiritual Assembly in Panama took the Baha'i faith to Abaiang in the Gilbert Islands. The Baha'i faith became a legal religion in 1955. In 1957 a wealthy nurse, Mabel Sneider, moved the Baha'i headquarters from Abaiang to Bikenibeu in Tarawa. In 1967 the first Pacific National Spiritual Assembly was formed in the Gilberts; it became the National Spiritual Assembly of Kiribati when the country achieved independence in 1979. It continues to attract a small but committed number of I-Kiribati.

In 1976 indigenous students returning from Liahona College, the Mormon school in Tonga, took the Church of Jesus Christ of Latter-day Saints to the Gilbert Islands. The Mormon Mission in Tonga sent an American couple, Elder Hallet and his wife, to assist the students. They took over a private school at Eita, Tarawa, erecting new classrooms, dormitories, and staff quarters. The Mormons provided opportunities for I-Kiribati students to study overseas, which contributed to a growing membership. The Mormon school on Tarawa, Moroni High School, stands out because its facilities are above the standards of other Kiribati schools. In the 1980s there was much tension between the growing Mormon presence and the Kiribati Protestant Church. The latter even distributed anti-Mormon propaganda. Many Mormon students study at universities in Hawaii and Utah and are encouraged to return to Kiribati for missionary work.

Despite the introduction—and now the dominance—of Christianity in these islands, indigenous beliefs have never been relinquished. People's daily lives continue to be shaped or directed by ancestors or pre-Christian deities. Dreams in particular are taken seriously. Many I-Kiribati (particularly those on the outer islands) engage in divining, magic associated with dance and sports competitions, and rites of passage beyond those of the churches. *Bangota*, sacred places devoted to indigenous gods, exist on most islands, and in some villages the bones or skulls of the ancestors are kept and cared for in the village meetinghouse, or *mwaneaba*. All these practices exist alongside Christianity, and few I-Kiribati see such multiple loyalties or practices as problematic. Indeed, a few Christian ministers have been known to practice magic.

Katerina Teaiwa

See Also Vol. 1: *Christianity, Roman Catholicism, Protestantism*

Bibliography

Finau, Makisi, Teeruro Ieuti, and Jione Langi. *Island Churches: Challenge and Change.* Edited by Charles W. Forman. Suva, Fiji: Institute of Pacific Studies, 1992.

Macdonald, Barrie. *Cinderellas of the Empire: Towards a History of Kiribati and Tuvalu.* Canberra: ANU Press, 1982.

Sabatier, Ernest. *Astride the Equator: An Account of the Gilbert Islands.* New York: Oxford University Press, 1977.

Talu, Alaima, et al. *Kiribati: Aspects of History.* Tarawa: Institute of Pacific Studies, USP and the Ministry of Education, Kiribati Government, 1979.

Teaero, T. "Poetry of Drifting Islanders on Oceania." *Pacific Journal of Theology,* ser. 2, no. 18 (1997): 103–12.

Uriam, Kambati. *In Their Own Words: History and Society in Gilbertese Oral Tradition.* Canberra: Journal of Pacific History/Asian South Pacific Cultures Fund, 1995.

Kuwait

POPULATION 2,111,561

SUNNI MUSLIM 59.5 percent

SHIITE MUSLIM 25.5 percent

BUDDHIST, CATHOLIC, HINDU, PROTESTANT, SIKH, AND OTHER
15 percent

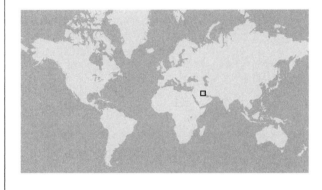

Country Overview

INTRODUCTION Kuwait is a small country situated on the eastern coast of the Arabian Peninsula at the head of the Persian Gulf. It is bounded by Iraq to the north and west and by Saudi Arabia to the south. Its territories include the islands of Bubiyan, Warba, and Faylaka, as well as other islands and islets. Its land is mainly flat and arid with little ground water.

Although it never played a major role in the strategic Persian Gulf region until the twentieth century, Kuwait was important in the religious development of the area's nomadic Arab tribes. When Islam spread to Iraq and Persia, Kuwait functioned as a passage for Muslim

missions, armies, and trade. During the medieval Islamic period, Kuwait remained an indistinguishable tribal land. The development of Kuwait proper, especially its religious character, did not occur until the economic and political prospects of the gulf region as a whole changed in the eighteenth century, by which time migrating 'Utub tribesmen from eastern Arabia were increasing their control over Kuwait. More specifically, the 'Utub were determined to defend Kuwait against attacks by Wahhabi reformists.

Despite the increasing proportion of expatriates in Kuwait's population (more than 60 percent in late 2003), Muslims continue to make up the great majority of its inhabitants. Indeed, all but a few Kuwaiti citizens and most non-Kuwaiti Arabs in the country are Muslims. The vast majority of non-Muslims in contemporary Kuwait consists of expatriates from South and Southeast Asia, Lebanon, and the West.

RELIGIOUS TOLERANCE The Kuwaiti spirit of tolerance inherited from the pristine teaching of Islam, as elaborated in the teachings of the imam Malik ibn Anas (died in 797), is captured in Kuwait's 1962 constitution. Article 29 states, "All people are equal in human dignity, and in public rights and duties before the law, without distinction as to race, origin, language, or religion." Article 35 is more specific: "Freedom of belief is absolute. The state protects the freedom of religious practice in accordance with established customs, provided that it does not conflict with public policy or morals."

Kuwait's constitution, however, specifies that Islam is the state religion. Islamic law, the Shari'ah, is "a main source of legislation." The ruling Sabah family and many other prominent Kuwaiti families belong to the Sunni tradition of Islam. Some 25 to 30 percent of the population belong to the Shiite tradition.

From 1911 Shaykh Mubarak Al-Sabah (died in 1915) welcomed the Dutch Reformed Church of the United States, which opened hospitals in the capital, Kuwait. The presence of more Christians resulted in the erection of a church adjacent to the hospitals in 1931. Since that time the church has been known as the National Evangelical Church, and it offers services in both Arabic and English.

There are several legally recognized expatriate congregations and churches in contemporary Kuwait, including a Catholic diocese and several Protestant churches. Expatriates who are members of such other religions as Hinduism, Sikhism, and Buddhism may not build places of worship but may worship privately in their homes. The government prohibits missionaries from proselytizing among Muslims; however, missionaries may serve expatriate congregations. The government also prohibits Muslims from converting to other religions.

The law does not allow religious education for religions other than Islam, though this statute does not appear to be rigidly enforced. In addition, non-Muslims may not become citizens.

Kuwait has enjoyed amicable relations among its various religionists. Indeed, Kuwaiti citizens generally are open and tolerant of other religions, though there is a small minority of ultraconservatives opposed to the presence of non-Muslim groups.

Major Religion

ISLAM

DATE OF ORIGIN mid-seventh century C.E.
NUMBER OF FOLLOWERS 1.8 million

HISTORY Islam spread to the Persian Gulf region as early as the 630s, during the reigns of the caliphs Abu Bakr (died in 634) and 'Umar ibn al-Khattab (died in 643). But the formation of Kuwait as a political entity began only with the migration of the loose tribal confederation known as the 'Utub from eastern Arabia toward the end of the seventeenth century. The tribesmen

Muslims at Kuwait City's Grande Mosque pray on the last Friday of Ramadan. AP/WIDE WORLD PHOTOS.

succeeded in maintaining a dual orientation toward nomadism and a seafaring way of life. With the growth of regional trade and increasing stability in the region—particularly after the arrival of the Portuguese, Dutch, and British—some 'Utub settled in what eventually became known as Kuwait around the beginning of the eighteenth century. From that time Islam, buttressed by Arab tribalism, was endorsed as the basis of the new state.

Responding to the existing pearling industry and trade, the settled 'Utub tribesmen developed Kuwait as a port in the eighteenth century. In 1756 the Sabah dynasty of the 'Utub was established. Toward the end of the century, the 'Utub succeeded in defending the port against the onslaught of the Wahhabis; however, it did not entirely escape their radical Islamic reformism. Nevertheless, Kuwait's rulers insisted on maintaining the country's association with the Malikite legal school, which gave it a distinctive Sunni-Malikite identity. Benefiting from the thriving regional trade in the nineteenth century, Kuwait skillfully maintained close diplomatic ties with the Ottoman authorities in Basra and Baghdad as well as British interests in the Persian Gulf. The port attracted diverse trading communities and job seekers, including Shiites from other gulf countries.

In response to pressure from Islamist groups like the Islamic Reform Society, the Islamic Heritage Revival Society, and the Shiites in the late 1970s, Kuwait's government made positive symbolic gestures toward Islamization. For example, the government tightened the ban on alcohol, increased religious broadcasting, and supported the Islamic Finance House (Bayt al-Mal), which derives most of its funds from the religious taxes paid by Muslims in the country. In the 1980s the Iran-Iraq War forced the government to take harsher measures against the Shiites, who were suspected of launching violent attacks on important facilities in the capital, particularly after the closure of the Assembly in July 1986. More and more Kuwaiti Shiites were suspected of supporting the regime of Ayatollah Ruhollah Khomeini in Iran and thus suffered discrimination or deportation. Indeed, indirect Iranian attacks on Kuwait's institutions and missions worsened conditions for Shiites in Kuwait, forcing them to become more adaptive toward—or even loyal to—the Kuwaiti government.

In contemporary Kuwait the Shiite community has faced a similar predicament. For instance, until recently Shiite leaders have claimed that Shiites who aspire to serve as imams have been forced to seek appropriate training and education abroad because of the lack of Shiite jurisprudence courses at Kuwait University. A plan thus is underway to establish a private college for the training of Shiite clerics within the country. If approved, the new college could reduce Kuwaiti Shiites' dependence on foreign educational institutions, particularly in Iraq and Iran, for the training of their clerics.

EARLY AND MODERN LEADERS The dominance of the ruling class in a relatively small country like Kuwait undermined the growth of an autonomous religious establishment. Religious leaders in Kuwait emerged among functionaries appointed by the ruler. Indeed, before 1969 the state mufti was appointed by the ruler. For instance, Sheikh 'Abd Allah ibn Khalid al-'Adsani (died in 1917), the first state mufti, was appointed by Sheikh Salim al-Mubarak al-Sabah (reigned 1916–20). Interestingly, the ruling class generally has avoided any direct exercise of authority in purely religious matters.

Muslim leaders in Kuwait have come from the ranks of Malikite scholars. Yet the customary reliance on the existing Malikite texts concerning various religious matters and issues has limited the emergence of well-known independent scholars.

A watershed in the field of religious ruling in Kuwait came in 1969, when the government formed a committee on the subject under the Ministry of Awqaf and Islamic Affairs. Sheikh 'Abd Allah al-Nuri (died in 1981) was among the most influential members of this committee.

After independence in 1961, Kuwait experienced intensive religious ties with other Muslim countries, which led to the expansion of various modern Islamic organizations in the country, including the Egypt-based Muslim Brothers and the self-proclaimed scripturalists, the Salafis. The Muslim Brothers formed the Social Reform Society, which was led by Yusif Jasim al-Hajj, who later led the Ministry of Awqaf and Islamic affairs.

Prior to the Iranian Revolution in February 1979, Shiites in Kuwait formed a political group under the leadership of such religious and merchant families as the al-Kazimi, Ma'rifi, Bahbahani, Qabazard, and Dashti. Indeed, with government support, in 1975 the Shiites won ten seats in the 50-seat Assembly. When the younger generations, responding to the revolution in Iran, wanted to alter this leadership, the government adopted stern countermeasures, including the deportation of the exiled Iranian 'Abbas al-Mahr in September 1979.

In recent years Kuwait has seen the emergence of Islamist leaders with interests in both regional and international affairs. Contemporary Shiite leaders like Muhammad Baqir al-Mahri and Abu al-Qasim Dibaji, for example, were critical of the harsh policies of the Baathist regime toward the Shiites in southern Iraq. Al-Mahri has gained prominence as a spokesman for Grand Ayatollah Ali al-Sistani of Najaf.

MAJOR THEOLOGIANS AND AUTHORS Under the conservative political regime, the Sunni majority in Kuwait has had little reason to oppose the ruling class, especially after a conservative religious bureaucracy was established, first under the mufti and, later, under the powerful Ministry of Awqaf and Islamic Affairs. One of the leading muftis, Sheikh al-Nuri, published his religious rulings in a book titled Sa'aluni (1971; They Asked Me).

More recently Kuwait has seen the emergence of promising Islamic writers. In 1999 Yusuf bin Eisa al-Qana'i (died in 1973) was awarded a national medal

(Wisam al-Takrim) for his contribution to the advancement of the study of modern Islamic thought. Sheikh Khalid Rashid writes a regular Islamic column in the well-known journal *al-Wa'y al-Islami* (Islamic Awakening).

Proponents of the orthodox school and the more reformist or literalist advocates, which include the Muslim Brothers and Salafis of different shades, have engaged in debate concerning faith and creed. For example, 'Abd al-Razzaq ibn Khalifah Shayiji defended the status quo against the radical Salafi movement in two works published in 1994 and 1996.

HOUSES OF WORSHIP AND HOLY PLACES Built near the the emir's palace in Kuwait City in 1986, the grand mosque of Kuwait has become the main venue for worship and religious celebrations. In addition, more than 1,350 local mosques, including 39 specifically for Shiites, have been built.

WHAT IS SACRED? Under the increasing influence of Salafism (fundamentalism), Kuwaitis have abandoned most un-Islamic signs of sacredness as well as the religious veneration of certain objects and, especially, those practices that are considered to be the results of superstition or accretion (corruption of the pure faith through extraneous additions). Nevertheless, the Shiites continue to venerate such objects as papers or stones taken from the holy centers of Najaf and Karbala' in Iraq. Moreover, the expression of reverence for the Koran can be found in its daily recitation, the artistic presentation of its verses in important places, and the presence of copies of the Holy Scripture in living rooms, cars, and shops.

HOLIDAYS AND FESTIVALS The Muslim festivals celebrated annually in Kuwait are common to all Islam. At the popular level, celebrations associated with the births and deaths of local religious figures are commonly organized, though major public celebrations have almost disappeared. Shiites in Kuwait enthusiastically commemorate famous moments in the lives of their imams, particularly the martyrdom of Imam Husayn near Karbala', the focus of the Ashura celebration, and the Prophet's declaration of Imam Ali's leadership, marked in the Ghadir Khum festival on 18 Dhu-l-Hijja (the month of pilgrimage). Nevertheless, the greatest festivals for all Muslims in Kuwait, as for those in other Middle Eastern countries, remain the celebration of the

Days of Sacrifice (Id al-Adha), which begins on 10 Dhu-l-Hijja and lasts for four days, and the end of the fasting month of Ramadan (Id al-Fitr).

MODE OF DRESS Proud of their Bedouin Arab culture, Kuwaiti men and women commonly dress in traditional garb. More and more Kuwaitis, however, particularly youths and students, have become accustomed to wearing clothes of Western design. Working women often prefer to wear Western-style clothing in their offices and then change into the long dress and *abaya* (a silky black cloak) for shopping and other activities.

Most Kuwaiti men wear a distinctive, floor-length white robe (*dishdasha*) and pristine headdress, a symbol of national unity. During summer a white cotton blend fabric is preferred. When the temperature drops, a wide variety of colors appear, especially dark blues, grays, tans, and browns in soft wool blends.

DIETARY PRACTICES As Muslims the Kuwaitis are expected not to drink alcohol or consume pork. The consumption of pork is, practically speaking, impossible; however, abstinence from alcohol has become a challenge for some Kuwaitis, as it is available at major establishments that cater to Westerners.

RITUALS Kuwaitis undertake five daily prayers. The majority perform them privately, while others pray in congregation at mosques. The Friday prayer, which is preceded by a sermon, must be offered in a special congregation at the mosque. Sunnis have had their Friday prayer since Islam's beginning, but the Shiites have had a formally organized Friday prayer only since September 1979, when Ayatollah Ruhollah Khomeini authorized a Kuwaiti Shiite leader named 'Abbas al-Mahr to publicly lead the prayer in congregation. Kuwaitis also perform pilgrimages to Mecca and Medina. In addition, Kuwaiti Shiites travel to Iraq and Iran to visit the tombs of Shiite imams, especially those of Imam Husayn at Karbala', Imam Ali at Najaf, and Imam Musa at Kazimayn near Baghdad.

The social institution known as the *diwaniya*, a place for informal get-togethers, has a long tradition in Kuwait. For men the *diwaniya* has been a common custom throughout the country's history. Women also have their own gatherings for socializing.

Large weddings are also a tradition in Kuwait. Men and women gather separately for the occasion, and the women's reception usually lasts through breakfast the next morning. Such all-night celebrations, in which both families as well as the bride and groom participate, show the continuing strength of the family in Kuwaiti society.

RITES OF PASSAGE Kuwaitis, like other Arabs, have introduced Islamic elements into major life transitions, including birth, adolescence, and death. Customary rites related to birth and adolescence have disappeared or are performed only among core family members at home, as most Kuwaiti children are now born in hospitals, and boys are circumcised in clinics at a young age. When a person dies, the funeral occurs soon after, for burial normally takes place within a few hours of death. Given the increasing importance of the family home as a setting for the performance of certain rites of passage and the effects of modernization and Islamic reformism, many facets of public rites have been reduced or even abandoned.

MEMBERSHIP Kuwaitis, like Muslims elsewhere, have no special occasion to mark the admission of new members, except in the case of adult conversion, which is customarily accompanied by a ceremony and the recitation of the two confessions (*shahadatan*). Children of Muslim parents—or at least Muslim fathers—are Muslim by default and, as babies, are given Islamic names, which are recited with the call to prayer (*adhan*) and the two confessions.

Since January 1982 private organizations, in cooperation with the Ministry of Awqaf and Islamic Affairs, have launched alms centers to help the needy, especially orphans, and to support missionary activities among expatriate workers abroad in Africa and other parts of Asia. With the strong financial support generated by the centers, Muslim groups have established organized missionary activities via the distribution of aid, publications, and the Internet.

SOCIAL JUSTICE Islamic social justice has been implemented in Kuwait by the ruling family through the state welfare system. The Islamic religious tax (*zakat*) obliges Muslims to put aside a portion of their income for the needy. Since January 1982 alms centers have been set up to mobilize and distribute religious tax revenues and alms more effectively in Kuwait and abroad. For example, during the month of fasting in 2003 a religious ruling (*fatwa*) was issued by the Fatwa Unit requiring delivery of *zakat* to the Palestinians.

Contemporary affluence and the continuing need for an expatriate work force have created social ambivalence among Kuwaitis. On the one hand, they offer lucrative incomes to expatriate workers; on the other hand, they are uneasy with the dominance of expatriates in key professions and in production. Several mechanisms, indeed, work negatively for the work conditions and rights of these expatriates. For example, in order to secure a supply of jobs for Kuwaiti nationals, expatriate workers are subject to vague labor laws that allow their exploitation—even deportation. In response to the problems faced by expatriates and their children, Islamic organizations, such as the various Salafi movements and the Ministry of Awqaf and Islamic Affairs, have collected special funds to assist with their education, training, and socioreligious activities.

SOCIAL ASPECTS Social arrangements involving family and marriage have grown out of traditional intergroup relations in Kuwaiti society. Indeed, the tribal worldview and traditions, more than anything else, continue to inspire Kuwaiti social organization, especially at the level of family and kinship relations. Families remain influential in the choice of spouses, reflecting the traditional emphasis on maintaining and strengthening kinship ties.

POLITICAL IMPACT The obvious and deep impact of Islam on political life in Kuwait can be seen in the emergence of the al-Sabah dynasty. The emirate, or *dawla,* inherited the political principles endorsed for centuries by diverse Islamic polities in the region. Maintaining tribal loyalty and promoting Islamic solidarity, al-Sabah won the sheikhdom and loyal subjects. In other aspects of government and state, Islam inspired the Kuwaitis after World War I to demand political representation in the form of an assembly and to organize their community life based on Arab tribalism and Islamic teachings.

The causes of Shiite social and political activism in Kuwait are complex and partly homegrown. Their struggle for political recognition embodied the Shiites' collective frustration with their exclusion and second-class status and provided an alternative to the dominant state ideology. Shiite leaders in the country have, however, prudently avoided openly criticizing the prevailing socioreligious arrangements supported by the Sabah regime.

In the Kuwait-Iraq war of 1991, Kuwaiti Shiites found themselves in conflict with the mostly Shiite Iraqi army. Iraq may have hoped to neutralize, at least, the

Kuwaiti Shiite population. Overall, however, Kuwaiti Shiites demonstrated loyalty to the state.

In addition to Islamist and secularist approaches to statehood, a third platform has emerged on the Shiite political scene in Kuwait. It advances a secularist—or, at least, non-Islamist—agenda but is nevertheless committed to promoting Shiite interests and redressing grievances. This pioneering platform faced uncertainty following elections in July 2003, when Islamist candidates—Sunni and Shiite—won 17 of 50 seats in the National Assembly. Moreover, the religio-political environment in the gulf region following the downfall of Saddam Hussein's regime in Iraq has paved the way for increased political solidarity among Shiites.

CONTROVERSIAL ISSUES The first carriers of HIV/ AIDS in Kuwait were discovered in 1984. By the mid-1990s most noncitizen carriers of the disease had been deported. By late 1998 some 40 Kuwaiti citizens had died as a result of the AIDS infection. The overwhelming majority of Kuwaitis consider the religious community and Islamic values important in AIDS prevention.

Cases of drug addiction in Kuwait have increased since Operation Desert Storm in 1991, when a U.S.-led military force drove the invading Iraqi army from Kuwait. The government, through the Ministry of Awqaf and Islamic Affairs, and the Salafi movements have called for the eradication of drug abuse and the moral and religious reeducation of addicts and have urged the public, especially families, to take an active role in preventing such abuse among loved ones.

Women in Kuwait have continued to experience legal and social discrimination. For example, in the family courts, which operate primarily according to Islamic law, one man's testimony is sometimes given the same weight as the testimony of two women. In the civil, criminal, and administrative courts, however, the testimony of women and men is considered equally. Unmarried women 21 years of age and older are free to obtain passports and travel abroad at any time. In accordance with Islamic law, however, a married woman who applies for a passport must obtain her husband's signature on the application.

CULTURAL IMPACT Closely connected geographically and culturally to the Arab world, itself almost synonymous with Islam, Kuwait is fully immersed in Arabo-Islamic culture. Its literature, architecture, painting, dance, and music grow in breadth along with Arab cul-

ture in general. Yet, Kuwait has developed certain traits and characteristics, especially in architecture, related to its own environment and interaction with the wider world. Arabo-Islamic expression in architecture can still be observed in mosques and houses, however, despite the onslaught of modern architecture.

Islam's impact on Kuwaiti music and dance can be seen in the strength of the traditional form in these fields. For example, despite the influence of Indian and East African music, the dominance of the oud (a lutelike instrument) in Kuwaiti music shows the strong presence of Arabo-Islamic elements. In dance Kuwaitis closely follow and elaborate such tribal and war dances as 'Arda (a war dance accompanied by poetry reading) and Samri, Khamari, and Tanburi, which predominate at weddings and other family and social gatherings.

Although calligraphy has been traditionally favored among Arabo-Islamic formative arts, in recent years, especially since the oil boom, Kuwait has produced internationally recognized painters and paintings.

Muslim prayer beads (*misbah*) have occupied a special place in Kuwaiti culture. Traditionally, the beads are strung in sets of 33, 66, or 99 to correspond with the names of God. The 33-beaded *misbah* is the most popular among Kuwaitis. A devout Muslim customarily touches each bead in sequence, reciting "Glory to Allah" (*subhana Akbar*) 33 times, and then repeats the process with the phrases "Praise to God" (*al-hamd lillah*) and "God is the Greatest" (*Allah Akbar*). Twirling the beads has become a popular pastime, though many still use them for religious purposes.

Other Religions

The immigration of workers to Kuwait has had a major impact on the fluctuating percentages of Muslims and non-Muslims in the country. The total number of non-Muslims in Kuwait changes rapidly and frequently.

Estimates of the nominal Christian population range from 250,000 to 400,000 and include approximately 200 citizens, most of whom belong to 12 large families. Kuwait's Christian community includes the Anglican (Episcopalian) Church; the National Evangelical Church; the Roman Catholic Church, with two churches and an estimated 100,000 members; and various Orthodox churches.

There are many other unrecognized, and thus unregistered, Christian denominations in the country, with tens of thousands of members. These denominations include Seventh-day Adventists, the Church of Jesus Christ of Latter-day Saints (Mormons), the Mar Thoma Church, and the Indian Malankara Orthodox Syrian Church.

Also in Kuwait are members of religions predominant in other pasts of Asia, such as Hindus, Sikhs, Bahá'ís, and Buddhists. They may not build places of worship but are allowed to worship privately in their homes. In January 2002, in the face of mounting pressure from Kuwaiti residents in the district of Salwa, the government ordered the closure of the Sikh temple Gurudwara.

Several ministries and other government agencies handle non-Muslim affairs in Kuwait. Officially recognized churches must deal with a variety of government entities for permits. In contemporary Kuwait seven Christian churches have some form of official recognition and thus are able to operate openly. Interestingly, the three oldest churches in the country have traditionally enjoyed some recognition by the government and are allowed to operate compounds officially designated as churches: the Roman Catholic Church (including the Maronite Church), the Anglican Church, and the National Evangelical Church of Kuwait. Although the Greek Orthodox and Catholic churches are allowed to operate openly, hire employees, and invite religious speakers, their compounds are, according to government records, registered only as private homes. No other churches have legal status in Kuwait, but they are allowed to operate in private homes. Their adherents are able to worship without government interference, provided that they do not disturb their neighbors and do not violate laws regarding assembly and proselytizing.

Informal instruction in non-Muslim religions is permitted in private homes and church compounds without government interference. From time to time government inspectors make on-the-spot checks in public and private schools outside church compounds to ensure that non-Islamic religions are not being taught.

Although there is a small community of Christian citizens, a law passed in 1980 prohibits the naturalization of non-Muslims. Citizens who were Christians before 1980 (and children born to such citizens since that date) are allowed to transmit their citizenship to their children. According to the law, a non-Muslim male must convert to Islam when he marries a Muslim woman if the wedding is to be legal in the country. A non-Muslim female is not required to convert to Islam to marry a Muslim male, but it is to her advantage to do so. Failure to convert may mean that, should the couple later divorce, the Muslim father would be granted custody of any children.

The Roman Catholic embassy accredited to Kuwait, Bahrain, and Yemen was upgraded from chargé d'affaires to full ambassadorial status in September 2001. The Vatican ambassador to all these countries resides in Kuwait City.

Iik A. Mansurnoor

See Also Vol. 1: *Islam, Shiism, Sunnism*

Bibliography

Burrell, R.M. "al-Kuwayt." *Encyclopaedia of Islam.* Vol. 5. Leiden; London: Brill, 1986.

Crystal, Jill. *Oil and Politics in the Gulf: Rulers and Merchants in Kuwait and Qatar.* Cambridge and New York: Cambridge University Press, 1990.

Fuller, Graham E., and Rend Rahim Francke. *The Arab Shi'a: The Forgotten Muslims.* New York: St. Martin's Press, 1999.

Lawson, Fred H. "Gulf States." In *The Oxford Encyclopedia of the Modern Islamic World.* Edited by John L. Esposito, Shahrough Akhavi, et al. Vol. 2. Oxford: Oxford University Press, 1994.

Russell, Sharon S., and Muhammad A. al-Ramadhan. "Kuwait's Migration Policy since the Gulf Crisis." *International Journal of Middle East Studies* 26 (1994): 569–87.

State Department, Bureau of Democracy, Human Rights, and Labor. "Kuwait." *International Religious Freedom Report.* Washington, D.C.: U.S. Government Printing Office, 2002.

Tétreault, Mary Ann. "A State of Two Minds: State Cultures, Women, and Politics in Kuwait." *International Journal of Middle East Studies* 33 (2001): 203–22.

Vine, Peter, and Paula Casey. *Kuwait: A Nation's Story.* London: Immel Publishing, 1992.

Ziadeh, Farhat J. "Law: Sunni Schools of Law." In *The Oxford Encyclopedia of Modern Islamic World.* Edited by John L. Esposito, Shahrough Akhavi, et al. Vol. 2. Oxford: Oxford University Press, 1994.

Kyrgyzstan

POPULATION 5,059,000

MUSLIM 85 percent

CHRISTIAN 13 percent

OTHER 2 percent

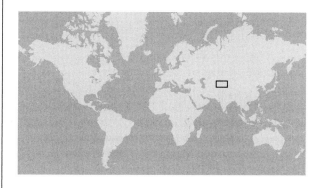

Country Overview

INTRODUCTION Kyrgyzstan is a small, mountainous country in southeastern Central Asia. It is bordered to the northwest and north by Kazakhstan, to the southeast and south by China, and to the south and west by Tajikistan and Uzbekistan. The country has served as a crossroads for several religions: Zoroastrianism, Buddhism, Manichaeism, Christianity, and Islam. In ancient and medieval times adherents of these religions and other groups built their cities and settlements along the ancient trade route of the Silk Road.

Muslims are by far the largest religious group in the Kyrgyz Republic. The Sunni Hanafi school of Islam is a major feature in the identity of the Kyrgyz people. Islam has been the religion of peoples living in Kyrgyz territories since the eighth century. The northern portion of the country adopted Islam as an official religion in the tenth century. It was not until the sixteenth century, however, that people in remote parts of the country were Islamized. Among some groups in the mountains, traditional Islam still bears traces of pre-Islamic beliefs, including faith in Tengry and Umay and other supernatural beings of the ancient Turkic pantheon. Before the atheism campaign conducted by the Soviet-controlled government in the 1920s, the Sufi brotherhoods were popular in Kyrgyzstan.

RELIGIOUS TOLERANCE The Kyrgyz Republic is constitutionally a secular state. The constitution guarantees freedom of worship and prohibits discrimination on the grounds of religion. Religious prayer is outlawed in public schools. The State Commission on Religious Affairs was established in 1996 to support freedom of conscience and religious tolerance; later it moved from the capital to the south of the country, where Muslims are traditionally more zealous and the numbers of mosques and *madrasah*s are greater.

On the whole, relations between different religious groups, mainly Muslim and Christian, are good in Kyrgyzstan. The country's two traditional religious groups, Muslims and Russian Orthodox Christians, have expressed their respect for each other and confirmed their complete avoidance of proselytism. Both groups do not welcome conversions to Protestantism; Protestant missionaries have worked among Muslims and Orthodox Christians since the country gained its independence in 1991. Besides Islamic institutions, 43 Orthodox Christian churches and 215 Protestant and other Christian

A grave at a Muslim cemetery in Kyrgyzstan. It is believed that the numerous cemeteries containing arbaks, *the souls of dead ancestors, are holy places.* © DAVID SAMUEL ROBBINS/CORBIS.

organizations also enjoy freedom of conscience in Kyrgyzstan. The country is a multiethnic state, including, besides Kyrgyz and Russians, such Muslim peoples as Uzbeks, Uighurs, Tatars, Turks, and Dungan (in Pinyin, Tonggan), the latter from China in the nineteenth century. To promote ethnic and religious tolerance, the political leadership of Kyrgyzstan created the Kyrgyzstan People's Assembly in 1992.

Major Religion

ISLAM

DATE OF ORIGIN Eighth century C.E.
NUMBER OF FOLLOWERS 4.3 million

HISTORY The Kyrgyz include many tribes and ancient peoples who lived in the vast territory that stretched from Lake Baikal in Siberia to the valleys and mountains of modern Central Asia. In the mid-nineteenth century Kyrgyzstan became a part of the Russian Empire and, later, the Soviet Union. Under the Soviet regime all religions were severely repressed. Many mosques, mausoleums, *madrasah*s, and churches in Kyrgyzstan were destroyed or converted to warehouses and secular museums. Many religious leaders were killed or exiled.

Seventy years of the Soviet policy of mass atheism severely weakened the country's religious institutions and led to a lack of knowledge about the basic principles of the traditional religions and to ritualism in the practice of Islam.

In 1991 the Kyrgyz Republic gained its independence. The newly independent state recognized freedom of conscience, and its leaders emphasized their Muslim identity. For the first time a Muslim leader, the mufti of Kyrgyzstan, was elected. Since independence, when there were 37 mosques in Kyrgyzstan, more than 1,500 mosques have been established. Because of the emigration of Christians, including Russians and others, and the arrival of Muslims from neighboring Tajikistan, the population share of Muslims has steadily increased in Kyrgyzstan. Whereas the majority of non-Muslims live in urban areas, the rural population is overwhelmingly Muslim and preserves traditions related to both Islam and ethnic culture.

EARLY AND MODERN LEADERS Among Kyryzstan's well-known leaders of the nineteenth and early twentieth centuries are Ormon Khan (1791–1854), Shabdan (1839–1912), Baitik, and Kurmanjan Datka (1811–1907). Kurmanjan Datka (1811–1907), a woman, was an eminent ruler of the southern provinces of the country. Madali Dukchi Ishan, a Muslim spiritual leader, declared *gazavat* (a holy war against non-Muslims) and headed a revolt against Russian colonial policy in 1898 in the Ferghana Valley. Askar Akayev (born in 1944), president of the Kyrgyz Republic since independence in 1991, has promised to launch democratic reforms. The internationally known writer Chyngyz Aitmatov (born in 1928) is deeply respected in his native Kyrgyzstan.

MAJOR THEOLOGIANS AND AUTHORS Called the Kyrgyz encyclopedia, the venerated epic trilogy *Manas* has a 2,000-year history. One of the world's longest epics, it includes a half million verses. The *Manas* depicts the history, culture, and religious beliefs of the Kyrgyz, and it illustrates their liberation from external enemies and the processes of Islamization among them. A *manaschi*, or *Manas* storyteller, has always been the most respected man in the local community. Famous *manaschi*s of the past include Nooruz, Jaisan-yrchy, Sagymbay Orozbak uuly, Togolok Moldo, and Saiakbay Karalaev.

Jusup Balasagun wrote "Kutadgu Bilig" ("Knowledge bringing happiness"), the first poem written in a Turkic language, which describes the philosophical, ethical, and political beliefs of the Kyrgyz in the eleventh century.

HOUSES OF WORSHIP AND HOLY PLACES Mosques are numerous in the Kyrgyz Republic, especially in the south. In 2002 official sources estimated that there were 1,388 mosques, 22 *madrasahs*, and 8 Islamic institutions of higher education registered in southern Kyrgyzstan. Every locality has its own *mazar* (holy place), or a set of *mazar*s. *Mazars* have a number of important functions in the spiritual life of the Kyrgyz and of Uzbeks living in Kyrgyzstan. For example, they may serve as places for prayer and healing and as repositories for local historical records. Among the most venerated holy places are the mausoleum of Manas in Talas province in western Kyrgyzstan, as well as Suleiman Mountain and the village of Safid Bulend in the south.

WHAT IS SACRED? *Mazar*s are sacred in the traditional Islam of the Kyrgyz. It is believed that the numerous cemeteries containing *arbak*s, the souls of dead ancestors, are holy places. The water of Lake Yssyk Kul, in northeastern Kyrgyzstan, is held sacred by the Kyrgyz, who believe the lake should not be polluted.

HOLIDAYS AND FESTIVALS There are no Islamic holidays that are distinctive to Kyrgyzstan.

MODE OF DRESS Muslim women in traditional Kyrgyz families usually wear modest European or traditional dress, but Kyrgyz youth—especially in the cities—follow Western European fashions. Muslim Kyrgyz women have never covered their faces. In traditional communities, mainly in the south and in rural areas, married Muslim women cover their heads with scarfs. Kyrgyz men cover their heads with the traditional ethnic *ak kalpak,* a white felt hat with black decoration, in all weather. All Muslim men and women cover their heads when praying.

DIETARY PRACTICES Animals that are to be eaten are slaughtered according to Muslim law. Muslims accept only the meat of lambs, horses, cows, and, in some cases, turkeys and chickens. Reflecting the country's pastoral past, the traditional cuisine includes plenty of lamb, horse, and beef combined with noodles. Horse meat is the favorite delicacy and is often offered in rituals during festivals and collective mourning dinners.

RITUALS Ash and Toy are the most important ritual gatherings among the Kyrgyz. Ash, devoted to the commemoration of the death of a man or a woman, is a key obligation for Muslim relatives of the deceased, who invite a mullah and many guests and offer a generous amount of food, including a ritual meal. Ash starts with a collective prayer. According to custom a horse and sheep are slaughtered for the meal. Given the widespread poverty that has accompanied the country's transition to a market economy, however, many people have been forced to abandon this tradition. In 2002 the Muftiyat (Islamic directorate) of Kyrgyzstan revised the rules concerning burial and funeral rites for Muslims. According to the revised rules the deceased should be buried on the same day on which death occurs, or at the latest on the next day, and there must not be any lengthy funeral rites at his or her home. Prior to this change, according to long-standing nomadic custom, the Kyrgyz had waited three days after death to bury the deceased so that relatives who had to travel long distances could attend the burial.

Toy is associated with such happy events as weddings and the births of sons. A Muslim wedding in Kyrgyzstan includes many expensive ceremonies involving mutual gift giving between relatives of the bride and groom. For many poor families this ancient custom is also a costly burden.

RITES OF PASSAGE Several moments in a child's life are celebrated as important events among traditional Kyrgyz, including Muslims. These include the birth of a son, a child's first steps, the naming of a child, a child's first haircut, and the circumcision of a son. All male children are usually circumcised before they reach school age.

MEMBERSHIP All newborns in Muslim Kyrgyz families are automatically accepted as Muslims. According to oral law (Adat), Muslim women in Kyrgyzstan, especially in rural areas, are encouraged not to marry non-Muslims.

SOCIAL JUSTICE Wealthy members of extended Muslim families are expected to help their poor relatives and neighbors. This practice has been slowly changing due to the introduction of a market economy, which has been destructive to the traditional system of mutual help and redistribution of wealth among Muslim families. Since the re-Islamization of the country after the demise of the Soviet regime, well-off Muslims donate to mosques and give alms to poor Muslims.

The exchange of gifts at many social gatherings is still common among the Kyrgyz. *Ashar,* a system of mutual help that is sometimes used in activities requiring collective efforts, is widely practiced at the community level and among close neighbors within the Muslim community.

SOCIAL ASPECTS Marriage among Muslims in Kyrgyzstan is an important step for the whole community of relatives. Often civil and religious registrations (*nikah*) are combined. The groom's family may kidnap the bride before the wedding, according to custom. The kidnaping may be mutually accepted by a couple who wish to avoid lengthy ceremonies and the intervention of their parents in marriage-related decisions, or it may be a violent action that occurs without the bride's consent. The deep-rooted tradition of *qalyn* (compensation for a bride given to her parents by the family of the groom) is common among Muslims in Kyrgyzstan. Depending on the wealth of the groom, *qalyn* may be offered in the form of currency, livestock, or other goods.

Elderly people in Kyrgyzstan are generally much respected by families and communities. To prevent juvenile delinquency and petty crime, the Court of Elders, a traditional village institution, has been restored. The members of this court can oblige a culprit to obey their decisions, rendering justice through the levying of fines, for example.

POLITICAL IMPACT No political party based on religious principle is allowed to function in Kyrgyzstan. Since the end of the 1990s Islam has been politicized by some small groups in the south. As members of the imported Hizb ut Tahrir (Party of Liberation), an illegal Islamic party, they propose the creation of a World Islamic Caliphate by nonviolent methods, though they do not participate in elections or in political life. On the whole, Islamic leaders have almost no impact on political life in the country.

CONTROVERSIAL ISSUES The weakening of the position of the official Muslim clergy under Soviet rule has contributed to the low resistance of younger generations in Kyrgyzstan to imported religious extremism. The activity of such underground groups as Hizb ut Tahrir is seen as a political tool and an outlet for the expression of social and political dissatisfaction among young, unemployed people.

Although laws in Kyrgyzstan treat men and women as equals, a majority of traditional Muslim families follow customary laws restricting the rights of women, girls, and young people. Despite such democratic reforms as the privatization of land ownership, customary limitations on women's access to land have complicated economic liberalization in the country.

CULTURAL IMPACT The influence of Islam in the Kyrgyz Republic is exhibited in the country's architectural monuments, several of which are among the greatest architectural masterpieces in Central Asia. These include the Minaret Burana near Tokmok and the Shakh-Fazil Mausoleum in Safid Bulend, both dating from the eleventh century; three mausoleums and a minaret from the eleventh and twelfth centuries in Uzgen; and the fourteenth-century Kymböz (Mausoleum) of Manas in Talas province.

A rich cycle of oral epics and tales still popular among the Kyrgyz is preserved by *akyns* (minstrels). For example, *Janyl Myrza,* an oral epic about a woman who became a military leader and liberated her people, illustrates the status of women in Muslim nomadic society. The works of well-known poets—including Kalygul (1785–1855), Togolok Moldo (1860–1942), and Moldo Kylych (1866–1917)—reflect the Muslim and ethnic identity of the Kyrgyz and their concern to preserve their faith and national character.

Other Religions

Before the Russian colonization of Kyrgyzstan in the mid-nineteenth century, its entire population was Muslim. Following Russia's annexation of Kyrgyz territories, many Russians migrated to Kyrgyzstan, and Orthodox Christian churches were built in the country. There are numerous missions from the West and from South Korea in contemporary Kyrgyzstan, and they have converted thousands of Kyrgyz and Russians to Protestant Christianity. Besides Muslims, Christians, and nonbelievers, there are tiny groups of other believers, such as Bahais and Buddhists, in Kyrgyzstan.

Anara Tabyshalieva

See Also Vol. I: *Christianity, Islam*

Bibliography

Central Asia: Islam and the State. Brussels: International Crisis Group, 2003.

Ro'i, Yaacov, ed. *Muslim Eurasia: Conflicting Legacies.* London: Frank Cass, 1995.

Strasser, Andrea, Siegfried Haas, Gerhard Mangott, and Valeria Heuberger, eds. *Central Asia and Islam.* Hamburg: Deutsches Orient-Institut, 2002.

Tabyshalieva, Anara. "The Kyrgyz and Spiritual Dimensions of Daily Life." In *Islam and Central Asia: An Enduring Legacy or an Evolving Threat?* Edited by Roald Sagdeev and Susan Eisenhower, 27–38. Washington, D.C.: Center for Political and Strategic Studies, 2000.

———. "Political Islam in Kyrgyzstan." In *OSCE Yearbook: Yearbook on the Organization for Security and Co-operation in Europe,* 89–99. Hamburg: Institute for Peace Research and Security Policy, 2002.

Laos

POPULATION 5,777,180

THERAVADA BUDDHIST 60 percent

CHRISTIAN (ROMAN CATHOLIC, LAO EVANGELICAL CHURCH, SEVENTH-DAY ADVENTIST) 2 to 3 percent

OTHER (HINDU, BAHAI, CHINESE RELIGIONS, MUSLIM, MAHAYANA BUDDHIST, AS WELL AS INDIGENOUS RELIGIONS INVOLVING SPIRIT BELIEFS AND/OR ANCESTOR WORSHIP AMONG THE TAI DAM, KHMU, HMONG, MIEN, LAO HUAY, ETC.) 37 to 38 percent

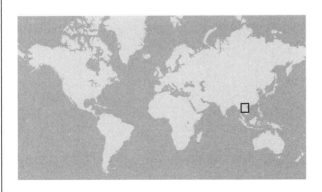

Country Overview

INTRODUCTION Laos (formally the Lao People's Democratic Republic, LPDR), an inland nation in mainland Southeast Asia, is bordered by China, Vietnam, Cambo-dia, Myanmar (Burma), and Thailand. It is a mountainous, tropical country, formerly covered with forest but now extensively harvested. The major cultivable areas lie along the Mekong River bordering Thailand and along smaller rivers and streams.

The Lao constellation of Theravada Buddhist, spirit, and ancestral beliefs and practices has emerged in the context of migration, imperial expansions, wartime displacement, cultural encounters, and the policies of a Communist regime since 1975. As elsewhere in Southeast Asia, Laos inherited an ethnic diversity that has challenged national programs of cultural and political integration. Today ethnic tensions continue amid attempts to define a national identity unified in part through Theravada Buddhism while acknowledging the many non-Buddhist minority groups.

The LPDR comprises at least 47 ethnic groups from four major linguistic families. Tai speakers represent more than 60 percent of the country's population; the largest Tai group is ethnic Lao and primarily Buddhist. The migration of Tai peoples from China and northern Vietnam peaked between the eleventh and thirteenth centuries. During this period ethnic Lao, with irrigated wet rice cultivation, moved into the lowland river valleys and established dominion over Mon-Khmer shifting cultivators, who practiced various types of ceremonies to propitiate spirits connected to the land, the village, and forces of nature. Diverse Mon-Khmer groups, such as the Khmu, constitute 24 percent of the population. Beginning in the early 1800s the Lao Huay, Hmong (also known as Miao), and Mien (also known as Yao) peoples, together accounting for 6 to 10 percent of the population, and the Tibeto-Burman (Akha and

Kho) peoples, 3 to 4 percent, migrated into the mountainous regions. A number of these groups, which have developed distinctive forms of spirit worship, include ancestors in their religious observances.

Western colonization and colonial-era national boundaries divided otherwise homogenous populations sharing closely related traits. Ethnic Lao share cultural as well as Theravada Buddhist roots with the Central Thai of Thailand, the Tai groups of northern Vietnam, the Shan of Burma, and the Dai people of southwestern China. Thailand contains more than five times as many ethnic Lao as the LPDR. Lowland Lao groups, Hmong, and Mien have migrated as well to the United States, France, and Australia.

RELIGIOUS TOLERANCE Historically religion has not represented a source of conflict between the ethnic groups of Laos, where Theravada Buddhism coexists with the worship of *phii* (spirits and ancestors). The LPDR constitution of 1991 protects religious freedom and prohibits religious discrimination. Islamic mosques, Mahayana Buddhist temples, Bahai assemblies, and Roman Catholic, Lao Evangelical, and Seventh-day Adventist churches operate openly in Vieng Chan (Vientiane) and other urban areas. The government, however, has moved against unregistered Christian evangelical groups purporting to be humanitarian organizations, accusing them of secrecy and fomenting "political dissent and internal disorder" among ethnic minorities. In the 1990s incidents of arrest, detention, and deportation of pastors associated with foreign-based diasporic communities earned Laos a reputation for religious persecution by Amnesty International and the U.S. State Department.

Major Religion

THERAVADA BUDDHISM

DATE OF ORIGIN 1340–50 C.E.
NUMBER OF FOLLOWERS c. 3.5 million

HISTORY Although Mahayana Buddhism had been present in Laos from at least the twelfth century, Fa Ngum's expeditions along the Mekong River (1340–50) established the kingdom of Lan Xang (Land of a Million Elephants) and Theravada Buddhist preeminence. He founded his capital at Luang Prabang in

Thousands of people from the countryside stream into Vieng Chan (Vientiane) during the That Luang Festival. At the Stupa, participants make donations, gamble and socialize, and view exhibits of national development programs. © NEVADA WIER/CORBIS.

1353 and instituted annual rituals reenacting the donation by the hill peoples of low-lying lands to the Lao, certifying continuing exchanges between high- and lowlanders of resources, goods, services, and respect for each other's religions. These ceremonies continued until the Pathet Lao victory in 1975.

Fa Ngum's son Xetthathirat moved the kingdom's capital to Vieng Chan (Vientiane) and built Vat Phra Keo to house the Emerald Buddha, now in Thailand. He also built the Pha That Luang stupa, which remains today the architectural and unifying symbol of the Lao nation. The Vieng Chan kings built stupas along the Mekong River, including Pha That Phanom, the grand stupa in northeast Thailand, to signify the extent of the Buddha's and their own reigns.

Intermittent attacks from Siam and Vietnam weakened Lan Xang, which in 1690 split into three principalities, centered at Luang Prabang, Vieng Chan, and Champassak. After wars in the late eighteenth to the early nineteenth century, the Siamese dethroned the Lao ruler, Chao Anou, and nearly destroyed Vieng Chan. The Siamese ruled over Lao principalities until the 1900s, when the French assumed control over Vietnam, Cambodia, and the Lao lands east and north of the Mekong, leaving the Khorat Plateau (where, even today, most ethnic Lao live) part of Siam (now Thailand). The French encouraged the rituals of the Lao kings of Luang Prabang and Champassak and rebuilt Vat Phra Keo and Pha That Luang, serving to bind religion and polity together.

The tight interpenetration of state and Theravada Buddhism loosened when the Lao Communist regime came to power in 1975, partly because of non-Buddhist minority support for the Pathet Lao. To conserve national and village resources, the Pathet Lao regime restricted major festivals and even daily merit-making rituals. Since 1985 the government has relaxed its disapproval of Theravada Buddhism; government officials now openly worship as Buddhists. The Lao people remain oriented toward merit making, seeking better lives in traditional Buddhist terms.

EARLY AND MODERN LEADERS Fa Ngum imported Theravada Buddhism into the territory of Laos from the Khmer Empire in the fourteenth century. His expeditions along the Mekong River established the kingdom of Lan Xang.

MAJOR THEOLOGIANS AND AUTHORS No major theologians of Theravada Buddhism have emerged in Laos.

HOUSES OF WORSHIP AND HOLY PLACES Many Lao Buddhist households maintain a household altar, *hing phra*. This shelf holds a small Buddha statue, pictures of deceased relatives, and other images that are worshiped each *wan phra* (Buddha day).

The *vat* (temple complex) forms the center of Theravada Buddhist religious observances and village social life. *Vat* residents include ordained monks, novices, and laymen who keep *vat* grounds and assist the monks. The most sacred ceremonies, including ordinations, are held in the *sim* (ordination hall).

Pha That Luang, a large lotus bud–shaped stupa located outside of Vieng Chan (Vientiane), stands as the symbolic center of state power and the national symbol of Buddhism. Vat Srisaket, the only structure not destroyed by the Siamese in 1828, remains a major artistic monument and center of religious observance. In Luang Prabang, Vat Xieng Thong (first constructed in 1560) exemplifies the ornate, low, swept-roof temple style in the former royal capital. Stupas and caves containing Buddha images along the Mekong denote the expansion of Lan Xang. Wat Phu, near Champassak in the south, represents the premier Angkorean ruin in Laos.

WHAT IS SACRED? In general relics (for example, slivers of bone or a hair) of the Buddha or of important monks are considered sacred. The Pha That Luang stupa is believed to contain a Buddha relic. Since 1991 this stupa, symbolizing the nation, has appeared on currency and official documents.

All images of the Buddha command respect and receive offerings, usually of candles, flowers, and incense. According to Lao legend the Phra Bang Buddha image, in Khmer style but reputedly cast in Sri Lanka, possesses heightened powers and remains the protective symbol of the nation. Now at the Luang Prabang Royal Palace Museum, the image plays a major role in Lao New Year's lustration rituals. Its washing symbolizes the coming of the rains and continuing success in agriculture.

HOLIDAYS AND FESTIVALS *Hiit sip song, kong sip sii* (12 rituals, 14 things), the traditional Lao annual cycle of rituals, is keyed to the agricultural calendar and dictates of the Buddha. Because a monsoon climate, similar to where Buddha founded his religion, regulates Lao agriculture, important ceremonies (*boun*) occur around the time of the Rains Retreat (July to October). Dry season rituals tend to be localized, sponsored by villages that, in rotation, invite members of neighboring villages. Boun Phavet (February to March) focuses on the retelling of the Vessantara Jataka by Buddhist monks, with donors sponsoring the recitation of specific passages. New Year's (mid-April) connects the advent of rains with the renewing, cleansing, and magical powers of water. The Pha That Luang festival, held in the twelfth lunar month (around October to November), has become the premier national festival, when thousands of people stream into Vieng Chan (Vientiane) from the countryside to make donations at the stupa, gamble and socialize, and view exhibits of national development programs.

MODE OF DRESS Lao monks wear attire based on South Asian dress prescribed by the Buddha—cut, sewn, and saffron-yellow–dyed robes reinforcing their separation from lay life. Contemporary industrial production has replaced most handwoven textiles with factory-produced robes, ready for purchase and donation.

When attending temple ceremonies, laity dress modestly, wearing their best clothes. White clothing is preferred when observing the precepts and when spending considerable time in the temple. The *phaa biang* (diagonally draped shoulder cloth), also worn by Buddha images installed in Lao temples, is essential for women on visits to the *vat* (temple complex) and other religious occasions.

During the liminal period of ordination rituals, ordinands, called *naak* (serpents), usually wear men's clothing of densely patterned silk woven by their mothers or other female relatives. These clothes gain spiritual power through association with this change in status and are frequently saved. During a Lao funeral this clothing, worn by the deceased, is cleansed of its defilement by being tossed over the cremation pyre, after which it can be reused in other important ceremonies.

DIETARY PRACTICES Because monks are forbidden from cooking, the food they eat must be presented as gifts. This creates a field of merit, providing daily opportunities for laypeople, especially women, to obtain merit through gifts of food. As in other Theravada Buddhist societies, monks may eat one or two meals before noon. While monks generally adhere to the doctrine of Mang Yang Sip Yang, listing 10 kinds of animals considered sacred and thus inedible, vegetarianism is not a significant aspect of everyday Lao Buddhist practice.

RITUALS As in neighboring Theravada Buddhist societies, Lao Buddhist rituals, whether of household, village, or nation, have profound social as well as spiritual meanings concerned with the accumulation of religious merit. Merit making (*haet boun*), acts of generosity that improve one's karma, increases one's chances for a better position in a future life and provides a sense of individual well-being. Doing good works for the *vat* (temple complex) or ordaining as a monk often enhances a man's *piap* (social prestige). Ritualized daily gifts of food to monks support the sangha (community of monks) at the community level. Local festivals at village *vat* provide occasions for wealth redistribution. Major Buddhist festivals have legitimated the rule of kings and the social hierarchy of different ethnic groups and enhanced the solidarity of the nation.

Household Buddhist rituals include preparing rice and other dishes to give to monks on their morning alms rounds, maintaining the house shrine, observing the *sin haa* (Lao; *pancha sila*, Sanskrit; five ethical precepts, or the basic ethical guidelines for the layperson) once a week on *wan phra* (Buddha day), and giving a son to the sangha as a monk. The most important household-based ritual occurs at the time of the death of one of the household members. Family members mobilize support to attend to the deceased, erect the cremation pyre, and provide food, money, and an audience to recognize the deceased's importance, assure the deceased's spirit that it can depart this world and search for its next life, and listen to the monk's chanting. The procession to the cremation grounds, the communal ignition of the pyre, and watchful waiting while the cremation begins and the monks chant show communal support as well as celebrate the household of which the deceased was a part.

The Lao often practice the *sukhuan* or *bacii* (soul-tying) ceremony, when white cotton strings are tied around a person's wrists (or other joints) with the intended effect of binding the soul to that person. While not strictly Buddhist, this ritual partly defines Lao culture. It often includes chanting by Buddhist monks and also the presentation of an elaborate offering constructed of banana leaves and flowers. Such ephemeral offerings often grace the shrine areas in Buddhist *vat*, where the images are installed.

RITES OF PASSAGE As in other Southeast Asian Theravada Buddhist societies, the passage of young men through the monkhood has traditionally been the major ritual by which they reach maturity, moving from the status of *dip* (raw, untested, immature) to *suk* (cooked, tempered, sufficiently mature) to become married householders. No similar explicitly religious transition to connote adulthood is available for women.

As in other Theravada Buddhist contexts, Lao funerals and ceremonies commemorating ancestors are important means of ensuring the articulation of this world with the next and the cycle of rebirths.

MEMBERSHIP Lowland Lao and almost all Tai speakers have been and continue to be, by virtue of birth and upbringing, Theravada Buddhists. Lao Buddhism, however, does not preclude other kinds of worship, including *phii* (spirit and ancestor) worship.

Prior to Western contact *satsana*, the Lao word for religion separate from life itself, did not exist. With the arrival of the French, Lao recognized that religion could be a matter of belief, faith, and choice. Conversion to another religion became possible, although prior to independence the vast majority of those exemplifying Christianity were foreigners, either French or Vietnamese.

Lao Buddhists do not proselytize. Overseas Lao establish Buddhist temples to unify their communities. Such temples generally welcome non-Buddhist visitors, offer meditation classes, sponsor religious and cultural festivals, and maintain websites as a means of attracting adherents to "The Way." In Laos, Buddhist temples have become major tourist sites, introducing foreign visitors to Buddhist sacred sites, art, and practice.

SOCIAL JUSTICE *Dana* (giving), the laity's dominant mode of Buddhist practice, provides a channel for people to redistribute wealth. Monks, who have goods and money donated to them daily, monthly, and at special festivals, redistribute these to the needy. Additionally, poor people, especially men, can go and live in temples as *dek vat* (temple "children"), cleaning and repairing temples, attending temple schools, or going from the temple to local schools.

The abbot of a *vat* (temple complex), the *chao ao vat*, tends to be a respected figure and is often an *ex officio* member of a community group. *Vat* provide venues for Lao to organize themselves for projects, such as festivals, development schemes, and building activities. Such works add to the store of merit of each participant and household and to the progress of the nation. In this manner Buddhist concepts of a moral community (accumulating merit through acts of material generosity and selflessness) meshed with aspects of the "new socialist man" proposed by the Pathet Lao regime, especially abolishing private property and inculcating devotion to a common good.

SOCIAL ASPECTS Even though Buddhist precepts are couched in individualistic terms leading to one's eventual separation from this world, the maintenance of Lao Theravada Buddhism depends on marriage, family, and household continuity. Thus, the third of the *sin haa* (five precepts) forbids sensual excesses, which monks often interpret to lay worshipers to mean marital fidelity.

While monks may bless couples prior to and after marriage, these ceremonies are not part of religious ritual; monks do not officiate in marriages. Monks do participate in household blessings. The ability of a household to sponsor an event to which monks are invited shows other members of the community the progression of family members toward their religious goals. This same dynamic of upholding communal religious values applies when married children of a household provide elderly parents with time and gifts so they can live comfortable lives and participate in temple ceremonies.

POLITICAL IMPACT Buddhist merit-making activities, especially involving sponsorship of *vat* (temple complex) construction and renovation and giving legitimacy to powerful persons and institutions, have flourished under conditions of economic growth in Laos since 1986. The Lao Communist Party acknowledges that Theravada Buddhism provides a fundamental mechanism for ethnic Lao to demonstrate allegiance to the state. Even though Laos reinstituted Theravada Buddhism as the major religion of ethnic Lao and Tai, the government still feels competition from Theravada Buddhism, as witnessed by its attempt to establish centers for the celebration of the "cult" of Phomvihane, a founder of the LPDR.

CONTROVERSIAL ISSUES Lao Theravada Buddhists experience no significant public controversies. Sangha (community of monks) reforms undertaken in the 1990s indicate a concern with the erosion of its authority within Lao society. Some measures address the education of monks. These include increasing the number of religious educational institutions, opening a theological academy and a teacher-training institute in Vieng Chan (Vientiane), and refocusing monastic study on Buddhist doctrine and teachings, instruction in the performance of key Buddhist rituals, and attention to techniques of preaching and meditation. The sangha has also instituted new disciplinary statutes and restrictions on entry into the monkhood to prevent those evading the law or involved in substance abuse from undermining monastic standards.

CULTURAL IMPACT Through the ages the Lao have made aesthetic enhancements and embellishments to Buddhist *vat* (temple complexes). These include carvings and castings of Buddha images, carved wooden and stucco ornamentation, carved *naga* (serpent) balustrades, mural paintings and mosaics, window and door carvings, hand-copied sacred manuscripts, cloth paintings or scrolls of Buddhist narratives (especially the Prince Vessantara tale), temple furniture, and the design of *vat* buildings. Many Lao Buddha images appear in the Maravixay (Defeat of Mara) posture, emphasizing the ethic of making merit. The Lao also commonly depict Buddha making the Calling for Rain gesture, holding his arms straight down and slightly away from his sides.

The skills required of Lao women to produce yarn and weave cloth have traditionally served merit-making purposes. Donated cloth plays major roles in Buddhist ordinations, in ongoing support of monks (who do not weave cloth), and in decorating the *vat.* Additionally, this weaving has served as a way for young women to indicate that they are ready for marriage. Ordination for men and weaving for women signify the skills and discipline required to manage a household and raise and provide for children. Complex silk and cotton weaving and elaborate needlework play a central role in Buddhist rituals as gifts and as the clothing sons wear as *naak* (serpents) during their ordinations as monks. These rites of passage, as a result of economic, political, social, and cultural forces, have been undergoing changes in Laos.

Other Religions

Buddhism and the belief in *phii* (ancestors and spirits) coexist throughout Laos, although in varying balance and expressive forms among its many different ethnic groups. As Buddhism spread throughout Laos, it combined with local indigenous religious traditions. The adoption of Buddhism has provided a means of establishing state authority over various ethnic groups. Buddhism connects local communities with the larger polity and the outside world, while spirit beliefs and practices concern the internal forces affecting the local community. Also, while Buddhism provides an ethos or orientation for the moral actions that individuals can control, beliefs in *phii* enable individuals to encounter and manage the impersonal forces beyond their control.

All Lao cultures—the majority Buddhist ethnic Lao as well as ethnic minorities, such as non-Buddhist Tai (the Tai Dam), Mon-Khmer (Khmu), Hmong, and Mien—give prominence to the potential protection or possible malfeasance of *phii* affecting everyday life. Different groups emphasize different spirits, but collectively they include spirits of place, spirits of natural forces, and spirits of the deceased. The original founders of a village become, upon their death, guardian spirits of the village (*phii baan*); other spirits include the spirit of the

house (*phii huan*), the spirit of the rice fields (*phii ta hek*), and so on. Spirits are sometimes seen as inherent in various natural forces: lightning, thunder, rivers and streams, fields, and earthquakes. Spirits are also specific to crops, especially rice, which provides the major sustenance for all Lao. Upon death the spirits of individuals remain active in family affairs. The spirits of powerful individuals—noblemen or kings—may remain present in human affairs as *phii.*

Contented spirits ensure continuing health, abundant harvests, prosperity, and the success of specific endeavors—from journeys to building projects and beyond. Hungry or otherwise displeased spirits cause illness, failed crops, accidents, natural disasters, and other misfortunes. Divination rituals, including reading the bones of a sacrificial chicken, may identify the particular aggrieved spirit. Healing rituals performed by specialists, such as *mo cham* (shamans), involve trances that represent travel to the spirit world.

To keep spirits happy, households of many ethnic groups maintain altars, supplied with regular offerings of food, flowers, and candles. Such altars may also contain Buddha images. Farmers of all ethnic groups perform spirit propitiation ceremonies during the agricultural cycle—for example, before clearing forest, sowing paddy, or transplanting or harvesting rice. Some groups require animal sacrifice (perhaps chickens, pigs, or water buffalo) to honor and feed important territorial spirits. The raucous Lao Boun Bang Fai (Rocket Festival), from mid-May to early June, promotes fertility of the land, as it ushers in the rice-nourishing rains.

Villagers of many ethnic groups also erect and maintain *ho phii baan,* simple wood and bamboo huts located in the forest to honor the village's protective spirits, representing an equivalent to the communal *vat.* The Lak Muang, a pillar on the grounds of Vieng Chan's (Vientiane's) Vat Si Muang, receives offerings from pilgrims honoring the spirit of the capital city.

Male shamans (*mo cham,* or *chao cham*) perform rituals feeding village spirits. Female spirit mediums (*nang thiam*) contact the spirit world directly, becoming possessed by spirits of *naga* (serpents) or channeling powerful political individuals. As *nang thiam,* women perform essential roles in supernatural belief systems denied them in the formal institutions of Lao Buddhism.

The Hmong, Mien, and Lao Huay (6 to 10 percent of the total population) concern themselves with spirit realms involving souls, death, and an afterlife—with spirits less accessible than territorial or nature spirits, thus requiring contact through shaman intermediaries. Ancestral spirits actively participate in the daily affairs of humans; they must be fed, celebrated, and consulted on important changes, such as relocating a village. In addition, the Mien and Lao Huay incorporate Chinese-based neo-Taoist elements into their rituals, including the use of books written in archaic Chinese script and scroll paintings depicting figures central to the "spirit government."

Members of many ethnic groups also believe people have a soul (*khuan*) or souls—the number varies—that can be enticed by malevolent spirits to leave the physical person, thus causing illness or misfortune. The *sukhuan* or *bacii* (soul-tying) ritual is prominent among all Lao peoples. Lao perform the *bacii* during life transitions (for example, when embarking on travel or beginning new projects). Chanting by Buddhist monks often accompanies this ritual.

Illness results from wandering souls, requiring the intervention of "spirit doctors," or shamans. Healing ceremonies, sometimes called soul-calling, involve travel to the spirit world. Hmong shamans sometimes construct wooden bench horses for their travel; Mien rituals often involve the construction of wooden bridges linking this world to the spirit world. During these ceremonies Hmong and Mien shamans enter trance states as they travel to the spirit world, attempt to locate the patient's errant souls, and strive to entice them to return to restore health.

As for other religions with some presence in Laos, eight Mahayana Buddhist temples in Vieng Chan serve the Lao-Vietnamese and Lao-Chinese communities. Three Christian denominations—Roman Catholics, Lao Evangelicals, and Seventh-day Adventists—constitute approximately 2 to 3 percent of the total population. Roman Catholics have established four dioceses. Many Roman Catholics are ethnic Vietnamese, concentrated along the Mekong River. Others are Hmong and Khmu. Between 250 and 400 Protestant congregations with well over 40,000 members belong to the Lao Evangelical Church (LEC) and operate in central and southern Laos but are concentrated in Vieng Chan province. The LEC serves members of Mon-Khmer ethnic groups, some lowland Lao, and Hmong. Seventh-day Adventists claim about 1,000 members in two congregations in Vieng Chan. As many as 10,000 adherents of the Bahai faith worship in four assemblies, in Vieng Chan, Vieng Chan province, and Pakse. The few thousand Muslims in Laos, largely of South Asian or Cambodian (ethnic Cham) origin, worship at two mosques, both in Vieng Chan.

Sandra Cate and Leedom Lefferts

See Also Vol. 1: *Buddhism, Theravada Buddhism*

Bibliography

Archaimbault, Charles. *Structures religieuses lao (rites et mythes).* Vientiane: Vithagna, 1973.

Condominas, Georges. "Phiban Cults in Rural Laos." In *Change and Persistence in Thai Society: Essays in Honor of Lauriston Sharp.* Edited by G. William Skinner and A. Thomas Kirsch. Ithaca, N.Y.: Cornell University Press, 1975.

Evans, Grant. *Lao Peasants under Socialism.* New Haven, Conn.: Yale University Press, 1990.

———. *The Politics of Ritual and Remembrance: Laos since 1975.* Honolulu: University of Hawai'i Press, 1998.

Fadiman, Anne. *The Spirit Catches You and You Fall Down: A Hmong Child, Her American Doctors, and the Collision of Two Cultures.* New York: Farrar, Straus, and Giroux, 1997.

Gittinger, Mattiebelle, and H. Leedom Lefferts, Jr. *Textiles and the Tai Experience in Southeast Asia.* Washington, D.C.: Textile Museum, 1992.

Mayoury Ngaosyvathn. *On the Edge of the Pagoda: Lao Women in Buddhism.* Working Paper Series/Thai Studies Project, Women in Development Consortium in Thailand, paper no. 5. Toronto: York University Press, 1990.

Stuart-Fox, Martin. *Buddhist Kingdom, Marxist State: The Making of Modern Laos.* Bangkok: White Lotus Press, 1996.

Tambiah, Stanley J. *Buddhism and the Spirit Cults in North-east Thailand: A Study in Charisma, Hagiography, Sectarianism, and Millennial Buddhism.* Cambridge: Cambridge University Press, 1970.

Thao Nhouy Abhay. *Buddhism in Laos.* Saigon: Ministry of Education, Literary Committee, 1958.

Latvia

POPULATION 2,366,515

EVANGELICAL LUTHERAN 26.4 percent

ROMAN CATHOLIC 17.3 percent

ORTHODOX 8.7 percent

JEWISH 0.02 percent

OTHER, INCLUDING UNAFFILIATED, 47.58 percent

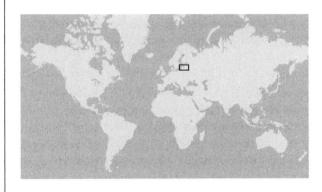

Country Overview

INTRODUCTION The Republic of Latvia, one of the smallest countries of the world, is located in northeastern Europe on the Baltic Sea. At various times throughout its history, the country has been subject to the control of its neighbors, particularly Germany, Sweden, and Poland to the west and Russia to the east, all of which have influenced its religious history. In 1918, at the end of World War I, Latvia became independent. In 1940 it was occupied by the Soviet Union under the Molo-

tov-Ribbentrop Pact of 1939. Independence was restored in 1991.

Latvia has several Christian faiths, including Evangelical Lutheran, Roman Catholic, Russian Orthodox, Baptist, and various free churches. There also are several legally registered nontraditional religions, including Islam, Vaisnava (Hare Krishna), Buddhism, Latvian paganism, Jehovah's Witnesses, and Mormonism. According to Latvian legislation, members of the Unification Church (Moonies), Scientologists, satanists, and followers of certain other sects are considered destructive and are therefore illegal. Most of these latter groups operate as secular social or "scientific" societies. The majority of the nonbelievers in Latvia, which make up 43.7 percent of the population, prefer to identify themselves not as atheists but as "agnostics," "freethinkers," "believers in their own way," or the like.

RELIGIOUS TOLERANCE Latvia is a secular state, with the constitution guaranteeing freedom of worship and prohibiting discrimination on the grounds of religion. On the request of parents, religious instruction is allowed in public schools. Latvian society is highly tolerant, and the spirit of ecumenism is widespread. There have not been religious wars in the country's history.

Major Religion

EVANGELICAL LUTHERANISM

DATE OF ORIGIN 1521 C.E.
NUMBER OF FOLLOWERS 625,000

The steeple of St. Jacob's Church rises above the city of Riga, on the Daugava River in Latvia. At one time a Lutheran church, it now serves as a Catholic cathedral. © STEVE RAYMER/CORBIS.

HISTORY Although for most Latvians religion no longer forms a strong element in their identity, its historical role has been great. When Roman Catholicism was introduced by the German Knights of the Teutonic Order in the thirteenth century, it became the official religion of Latvia (then Livonia). The Reformation had reached Riga, the capital, by the early 1520s, but the countryside was not evangelized until the seventeenth century. During the European wars of the seventeenth and eighteenth centuries, Latvia was divided between Poland and Sweden, with the respective parts of the country converted to Catholicism or Evangelical Lutheranism. Latgallia (modern Latgale), southeast of Latvia, became a province of Poland, and during the Counter-Reformation Catholicism was reestablished there. In the northwest Livland, or Vidzeme, was controlled by Sweden, and there the Lutheran faith was established. After 1721, when the Russian Empire began to annex territories

held by the Latvian people, Russian immigrants introduced Orthodoxy into the area. Judaism had an ancient presence in Latvia, dating perhaps to the fourteenth century.

From 1520 to the late nineteenth century, Lutheranism became the dominant religious affiliation in Latvia, and it provided a philosophical and ethical base for the country's political development and social organization. Through the Peace of Nystad in 1721, the Baltic was declared a Russian province. The Russian tsar, however, granted special rights and privileges to the Lutherans, which allowed the church to continue to develop. In 1918, when the independence of Latvia was proclaimed, it had a population that was 56 percent Lutheran. During the two decades of independence, from 1918 to 1940, the Lutheran Church was slowly Latvianized. Clergy educated in Latvian schools replaced many German pastors, and the 1689 translation of the New Testament was reissued in a modern version, reflecting the Latvian literary language.

After occupation by the Soviet Union in 1940, the property of the Lutheran Church was confiscated. The church was compelled to pay rent for the use of it former premises, religious instruction in the schools was forbidden, and pastors were dismissed. Religious meetings other then regular church services were prohibited. A great number of church buildings were turned into storehouses or were destroyed. Children and young people were systematically estranged from the church and rigorously indoctrinated in atheistic materialism.

In 1991 Latvia regained its independence, and the end of the communist regime allowed a new affirmation of faith by all religions. Nevertheless, religion in Latvia has not recovered to become a major influence, and the overwhelming majority of the population is not involved in religious activities.

EARLY AND MODERN LEADERS The first leaders of the Reformation in Riga and of the Evangelical Lutheran Church in Latvia were Andreas Knopke and Silvester Tegetmeyer. Knopke arrived in Riga in the early 1520s from Wittenberg, with credentials received from Philipp Melanchthon, the German reformer. The first Latvian bishop, Karlis Irbe, was elected in 1932. During the Soviet occupation, the most prominent leader of the church was Archbishop Gustavs Tūrs (1948–70). Nominated by the Soviet authorities, he nonetheless turned out to be the most independent of the Lutheran leaders under the communist regime. After independence, in 1993, Jānis Vanags, a popular young spiritual leader of the national independence movement, was chosen archbishop. Archbishop Vanags is the informal leader of the major Christian confessions of Latvia.

MAJOR THEOLOGIANS AND AUTHORS The long period of the Lutheran Church's lethargy under the communist regime did not stimulate theological thought in Latvia. Only those Latvian theologians in exile, working in Western universities, could develop their thinking. During this time Haralds Biezais (1909–93) was a prominent author who wrote extensively about the religion of the Baltic peoples. Karlis Kundziņš (1883–1967) was a coauthor with the German theologian Rudolf Bultmann. The most popular of contemporary Lutheran theologians and authors in Latvia is Juris Rubenis (born in 1961). The church historian Egils Grislis (born in 1928), who lives in Canada, has achieved worldwide recognition.

HOUSES OF WORSHIP AND HOLY PLACES In Latvia as elsewhere, the Lutheran house of worship is the church building. Some churches have inherited their names from the pre-Reformation age, while new congregations sometimes choose the name of a particular apostle or a popular saint. Although Lutheran church buildings are not normally considered sacred, some pastors have cultivated the attitude of Catholics and the Orthodox that such a building be considered a sacred space.

WHAT IS SACRED? In mainstream Lutheranism only the Bible is considered sacred. The conservative and mixed confessional background of Latvia, influenced by Catholic and Orthodox traditions, however, tends to make the elements of the Eucharist sacred as well. The altar of the church is often considered a holy place, with laypersons not allowed to touch it without a serious purpose.

HOLIDAYS AND FESTIVALS Of the 10 public holidays in Latvia, five are religious holidays. Good Friday, Easter, and Christmas are the most popular holidays, and on these days Lutherans attend church services. Saint John the Baptist Day, however, is celebrated mostly as a summer solstice and pagan festival. Special celebrations take place on 14 August in Ikšķile, where the Latvian apostle Saint Meinhard preached.

MODE OF DRESS Latvians wear conventional European dress, not influenced by religion. Elderly women in the countryside, however, wear the babushka, a triangularly folded kerchief, or another type of covering for the head, to church.

DIETARY PRACTICES The diet of most Lutherans in Latvia is based on local tradition, not religious prescription. Nevertheless, during Lent a minority of Lutherans, following the traditions of Catholics and Orthodox, fast by abstaining from meat and sometimes from milk products, as well as from alcohol and social gatherings.

RITUALS There are no peculiarly Latvian elements in Lutheran services, which normally do not differ from those of Lutheran churches elsewhere. Nevertheless, during the 1990s elements of Catholic and Orthodox practices were introduced for special periods of the church year. One example is an all-night service at Easter and the progression to the stations of the cross, which are erected outside church buildings.

RITES OF PASSAGE Rites of passage for Lutherans in Latvia do not differ from the mainline practice. Church authorities insist, however, that a person undergo religious instruction and join a congregation before the rites of passage are performed. Although baptism is observed even by nominal Lutherans, weddings are much less often celebrated, with many couples not even legalizing their marital relations. Funerals depend greatly on the person's religious beliefs during life. Secular funerals, which were introduced by the Soviets, remain popular even among some nominal Christians. At the following dinner an empty plate with a lit candle, and sometimes a glass of liquor (often vodka), is placed at the head of the table.

MEMBERSHIP In Latvia a person normally becomes a member of a Lutheran church by baptism. To become a regular member of a particular congregation, however, it is necessary to register and pay an annual fee. The church seeks only slow growth, and the number of adherents generally remains constant. Lutherans in Latvia publish two weekly newspapers and are active in radio, television, and Internet missionary work.

SOCIAL JUSTICE Lutherans in Latvia work to help the less advantaged members of their congregations. Issues of human rights, however, are not considered the business of the church. Members of Lutheran churches are active in religious education and in programs giving aid to the unemployed, prisoners, and other groups at risk.

SOCIAL ASPECTS In the local Lutheran tradition marriage is not considered a sacrament, as it is in the Catholic Church. Lutheran clergy, however, try to prevent married couples from divorcing. This is a serious problem in Latvian society, where the divorce rate is just over 60 percent.

POLITICAL IMPACT Although Latvia is a secular state, the president pays respect to the Lutheran Church on special occasions, for example, on Independence Day (18 November), when the chief of state takes part in a solemn service at Assumption Cathedral in Riga. The church does not permit acting ministers to take part in politics. If a pastor is elected to political office, he is asked to interrupt his pastoral duties for the term.

During certain periods in history the political role of the church has been critical. In the late 1980s, for example, Lutheran pastors were among the leaders of the movement for independence. Church leaders initiated a national campaign against corruption that greatly influenced local and national elections in 2001–02, and a political party created by Protestant ministers was successful enough to enter the ruling coalition in 2003.

CONTROVERSIAL ISSUES Conservative religious traditions, common to many postcommunist societies, are a considerable influence on the stand of the Lutheran Church in Latvia. Since 1993, for example, women have not been ordained. On this particular issue there is strain in the relations of the Lutheran Church in Latvia with a number of more liberal Lutheran churches elsewhere in the world.

CULTURAL IMPACT The impact of the Christian West on architecture, the arts, and everyday life in Latvia has created a typical western European society, greatly different from the Eastern Orthodox society of neighboring Russia. The beginnings of the Latvian literary language, for example, were formed by the translation of the Bible into Latvian and by the first religious writers, who were German pastors. A number of Latvian writers have created fiction influenced by Christian ideas and history, with Apsimacr;šu Jēkabs (1858–1929), Rūdolfs Blaumanis (1863–1908), and Jānis Rainis (1865–1929) among the best known. The same is true of classical Latvian visual artists, who include Kārlis Hūns (1830–77) and Kārlis Miesnieks (1887–1977).

Other Religions

Latvia became Roman Catholic in the thirteenth century but was forced to become Protestant in the sixteenth century. Then during the Counter-Reformation, under King Stephan Bathory (1533–86) of Poland, Latgallia in the southeast returned to Roman Catholicism. In the period from 1940 to 1990, the year in which religious restrictions were lifted, Catholics offered a more vital resistance to the Soviets than did Protestants, with guidance from Rome giving the clergy a measure of protection against direct manipulation by communist functionaries. Since Latvia has regained its independence, the Catholic Church has become the most consolidated and dynamic religious group in the country.

The most prominent leader of Latvian Catholics has been Cardinal Julians Vaivods (1895–1990), who managed to make the Diocese of Riga the center of the church in the Soviet Union (except for Lithuania, which had its own hierarchy). Cardinal Jānis Pujāts (born in 1930) succeeded him. The most prominent Latvian Catholic theologian is Stanislavs Ladusāns (1912–93), who worked from 1983 in Rio de Janeiro.

Compared with Europeans or Americans, Latvian Catholics are conservative. Most women cover their heads in church, and during solemn processions women wear the national costume or a white dress similar to the garb of medieval monks. Dietary restrictions are still popular, despite the fact that church authorities do not insist on them, and Latvians tend to follow pre-Vatican II practices. There are two fasting seasons, one 40 days before Easter and the other four weeks during Advent. Fasting takes the form of abstinence from meat three days a week (Wednesday, Friday, and Saturday during Lent), and believers also abstain from social gatherings. The rituals of Roman Catholics in Latvia tend to maintain Tridentine and Vatican I devotions, litanies, and novenas. Local religious festivals at minor places of pilgrimage, such as at Kraslava and Skaistkalne (Schoenberg), with services that are 40 hours long, have remained popular. The holiest place for Latvian Catholics is the Our Lady of Aglona sanctuary in the southeast, with its miraculous Byzantine icon. Every year on 15 August, when the Assumption of Our Lady is celebrated, thousands of faithful gather for a three-day festival.

Because Roman Catholics in Latvia have high rates of church attendance and trust in their spiritual leaders, they have achieved significant political influence. Catholic authorities do not act publicly, however, and unlike

Protestants do not have a political party. Instead, Catholics lobby for such interests as abortion laws and religious instruction in schools through sympathetic governmental officials.

The Roman Catholic faith in Latgale is deeply interwoven with the local culture and way of life. In the course of history Catholic rituals became mixed with local pre-Christian beliefs and traditions to create a syncretic religion there. During the five decades of Soviet rule, this region was affected the least. The local people's resistance to communist authorities protected church buildings from destruction, and the tradition of performing such rites of passage as baptisms, marriages, and funerals in church was never interrupted.

The Orthodox Church in Latvia is mainly the religion of Russian immigrants. Although Orthodoxy first appeared in Latvia through the work of missionaries in the eleventh century, it was the support the Orthodox Church received from the Russian government beginning in 1832, when by law it became the national church, that established it as an important force. The Lutheran population of Latvia was urged to convert to Orthodoxy, and tens of thousands followed the appeal. Orthodoxy reached its greatest influence at the end of the nineteenth century, when churches were built in every town of any size. The huge immigration of Russians, most of whom were atheists, after 1940 did not seriously alter the Protestant-Catholic identity of Latvia, however.

The mystical theology of Orthodoxy has appealed to those Lutherans and Catholics in Latvia who dislike the liberal tendencies in their own faiths. It is for this reason that conversions to Orthodoxy are not unusual. There are no significant differences between Orthodoxy in Latvia and Russia. The only peculiarity in Latvia are the couple of congregations in which the Holy Liturgy is conducted not in Old Slavonic but in the Latvian language. Jānis Pommers (1876–1934), archbishop of the Latvian Orthodox Church, was murdered by Soviet agents and canonized by the local church in 2001.

After Latvia regained its independence from the Soviet Union, nontraditional religions appeared. Immigrants from the former Soviet republics of Central Asia established Islamic communities. Buddhists, Hindus, Mormons, Methodists, Jehovah's Witnesses, New Age movements, and other groups emerged from western Europe, the United States, and Canada. The largest of the nontraditional religious communities in Latvia consists of members of the Church of Jesus Christ of Latter-day Saints (Mormons) and Methodists. The most rapidly expanding Pentecostal group is called New Generation and attracts mostly ethnic Russians. New Age ideas picked up from various sources commonly are joined with conventional Christian teachings to create a mixture of religious ideas. Some of these ideas may be accepted by established churches, but they generally do not take the shape of independent religious movements.

Leons Taivans

See Also Vol. I: *Christianity, Lutheranism, Roman Catholicism*

Bibliography

Babris, Peter J. *Silent Churches: Persecutions of Religions in the Soviet-Dominated Areas.* Arlington Heights, Ill.: Research Publishers, 1978.

Dreifelds, Juris. "Religion in Latvia: From Atrophy to Rebirth." *Lutheran Theological Review* 8, nos. 1–2 (fall/winter 1995–spring/summer 1996): 52–82.

Mezezers, Valdis. *The Herrnhuterian Pietism in the Baltic.* North Quincy, Mass.: Christopher Publishing House, 1975.

Pavuls, Laimons. "Lutheran Church of Latvia." In *The Encyclopedia of the Lutheran Church.* Edited by Julius Bodensieck. Vol. 2. Minneapolis: Augsburg Publishing House, 1965.

Talonen, Jouko. *Church under the Pressure of Stalinism: The Development of the Status and Activities of Soviet Latvian Evangelical Lutheran Church during 1944–1950.* Rovaniemi: Historical Society of Northern Finland, 1997.

Lebanon

POPULATION 3,677,780

SHIITE MUSLIM 41 percent

SUNNI MUSLIM 27 percent

MARONITE 16 percent

DRUZE 7 percent

GREEK ORTHODOX 5 percent

GREEK CATHOLIC 3 percent

OTHER 1 percent

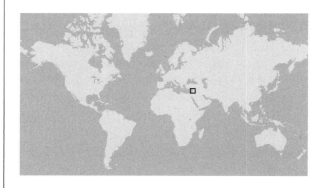

Country Overview

INTRODUCTION The Lebanese Republic, located on the eastern shore of the Mediterranean Sea, is bordered by Israel on the south and Syria on the north and east. Modern Lebanon is characterized by its diversity of ethnic and religious groups, most of which have inhabited the country since the seventh century C.E. Muslim Shiites and Sunnis moved to Lebanon in the seventh century. In the second half of the seventh century Maronite Christians fled to Mount Lebanon from Syria. Other groups include Greek Orthodox, Christian Melchites (later known as Greek Catholics), and the Druze, a splinter Muslim group that fled to Lebanon in the eleventh century.

In modern Lebanon religion is a mark of a person's identity and a major reference point in social interaction. Sectarian communities have historically evolved into semiautonomous communities with distinct political and administrative functions. In 1918 Lebanon was mandated to the French, who created Greater Lebanon (now called the Lebanese Republic) in 1920 by including Mount Lebanon, Beirut, Sidon, Tyre, southern Lebanon, the Bekaa valley, and the Akkar plain in the north. They granted each community the right to establish its own religious courts and to codify and regulate its own laws concerning marriage, divorce, and other personal matters.

The informal National Pact of 1943 made political representation proportional with community numbers. The pact failed at bridging divisive issues among the sectarian communities, however. Communal loyalties and identities hardened and precluded any hope for national integration—a fact attested to in the long civil war (1975–90). The Taif Accord (1989) ended the war and reconciled the warring factions into accepting an agreement in which Muslims were given greater representation in the government.

RELIGIOUS TOLERANCE Lebanon is a secular state but formally recognizes 18 religious groups. All Lebanese citizens are considered equal before the constitution. Public law applies to all Lebanese citizens. Inequity surfaces, however, when dealing with personal status laws, such as marriage, divorce, inheritance, child custody, and death, where citizens must refer to religious courts. Otherwise, Lebanon is a safe haven for many religious groups and prides itself on a long history of religious tolerance.

Major Religion

ISLAM

DATE OF ORIGIN Seventh century C.E.
NUMBER OF FOLLOWERS 2.5 million

HISTORY Islam spread to Lebanon during the Arab-Islamic conquests of the region in 632–34 C.E. Shiites arrived in Lebanon from Iraq in the middle of the seventh century. They congregated in eastern and southern Lebanon as well as in few places in the north. The Shiites occupied the lowest rung of the socioeconomic and political ladder.

During the Umayyad reign in Syria (661–750) and the Abbasid reign in Iraq (750–1258), the Sunni population grew in Lebanon and settled in eastern, central, and southern Lebanon. They were mainly prosperous merchants. Their identification with the Sunni population of the Arab world and with the Ottoman Empire (1516–1918)—Sunnis belonged to the official state religion—helped them to become the dominant political class.

The demise of the Ottomans at the end of War World I (1918), French colonialism, and the creation of Greater Lebanon (in 1920) curbed Sunni political domination in Lebanon. The Shiite community began mobilizing in the 1960s, when the area of southern Lebanon called Jabal Amil became the battleground between the Israeli army and Palestinian guerillas. The Shiite cleric Musa al-Sadr galvanized the Shiite community in Lebanon, transforming it socially, economically, and politically. In the wake of an Israeli invasion of southern Lebanon in the 1980s, another Shiite militant group, Hizb Allah (Party of God), vied for Shiite following. The renaissance the Shiite community underwent from the 1960s to the 1990s helped it to become one of the most potent communities in Lebanon. The Shiites in Lebanon are predominately Twelvers (who believe there were 12 divinely ordained successors of the Prophet).

The grand mufti, or religious head, leads the Supreme Islamic Council. This body oversees Sunni inter-

A Lebanese man beats a drum to wake up Muslims to have a meal before sunrise during the holy month of Ramadan. AP/WIDE WORLD PHOTOS.

ests and directs a number of *waqf* (endowments) that have established and maintained hospitals, schools, cemeteries, and mosques. Since the 1980s there have been a number of Sunni fundamentalist groups in Lebanon with a variety of religious inclinations and tendencies.

EARLY AND MODERN LEADERS The cleric Musa al-Sadr became the head of the Shiite community in 1957, after which he began a project of political and socioeconomic reform. In 1968 he established the Higher Shiite Council, an autonomous administrative group. He also reformed and mobilized the Shiite community through education. In 1975 he established the Lebanese Resistance Detachment (Afwaj al-Muqawamah al-Lubnaniyyah), also called Amal (Hope). Al-Sadr disappeared in 1979 while on a trip to Libya.

Although he is not a religious leader, Nabih Berri (born in 1938) has been influential in the Lebanese Shiite community. In 1980 he became the leader of its political movement, Amal. Berri was elected speaker of the Lebanese parliament in 1992.

Mufti Hasan Khaled (died in 1989) was the most powerful leader of the Sunni community in Lebanon. He played an important political role during the 1975 civil war and also led the Islamic Grouping, which consisted of Sunni traditional leaders.

Another important contemporary leader was Lebanese prime minister Rafiq al-Hariri (served 1992–98; reappointed in 2000; assassinated 2005). Although he was from outside the religious circles, he had played a significant role in the Sunni community. Known for his wealth and political influence, he supported a number of charitable and educational organizations.

MAJOR THEOLOGIANS AND AUTHORS The Lebanese Shiite cleric Muhammad Husayn Fadl-Allah (born in 1935) called for the rethinking of major Islamic issues and for reclaiming Islam as a religion compatible with changing circumstances and capable of serving humanity. He published books dealing with sociopolitical and religious issues, including the role of women in Islam.

Subhi al-Saleh was a well-known and prolific Sunni theologian and author who advocated peace and women's rights. In the 1980s he was vice president of the Supreme Islamic Council. Al-Saleh was assassinated in 1986.

HOUSES OF WORSHIP AND HOLY PLACES The Safa Mosque, in Beirut, is one of the prominent Shiite mosques in Lebanon. Shiites frequent Husayniyyas (halls named after their third imam, Husayn), where certain social functions, such as memorials and commemorations, are held. Jamal Abd al-Nasir Mosque and Aisha Bakkar Mosque (both in Beirut) are two important Sunni mosques in Lebanon.

WHAT IS SACRED? Lebanese Shiites, like Shiites everywhere, visit the tombs and shrines of their saints and imams. Sunnis in Lebanon do not put much emphasis on saints or visits to the tombs or shrines of saints.

HOLIDAYS AND FESTIVALS *Ashura* is the commemoration by the Shiite community of the massacre of the Prophet's grandson Husayn and members of his family in 680 C.E. For 10 days Shiites wear black and hold passion plays reciting the events in which Husayn and his family members died. The commemoration culminates in a parade of chest beating and crying. A small number of Lebanese Shiites participate in a special procession of self-mutilation and flagellation that is usually held in the southern town of Nabatiyyeh. Such practices are abhorred by the majority of Lebanese Shiites and are prohibited by Shiite religious leaders.

Sunnis share with the Shiites major Islamic holidays, such as Id al-Fitr (Feast of Breaking the Fast). Sunni celebration of the birth of the Prophet includes *salat al tarawih* (a special form of prayer performed only during Ramadan) and singing upbeat *mawlid* (songs recounting Muhammad's birth). Sunnis may also use certain musical instruments in their celebrations. Shiites read excerpts from the Prophet's life and sing *tawashih diniyyah* (special chants that are sometimes accompanied by music).

MODE OF DRESS Lebanese Muslim Shiite and Sunni women dress in a variety of wardrobes; some are Western, and some are specific to a person's religious traditions. Most Lebanese Muslim Shiite and Sunni women wear any kind of Western dress, and others simply cover their heads with scarves and wear Western clothes while adhering to the prescribed dress codes of modesty.

A minority of Shiite observant women wear the *abayah* (a black robe that covers the head and overflows to cover the whole body) or the *hijab shar'i* (a headscarf and a long robe over pants). Some Sunni observant women wear the headscarf and a long robe. Wearing the *abayah* is not a common custom among Sunni women in Lebanon. Some Sunni Kurdish women wear colorful long and baggy dresses with a colorful *mindil* (rectangular scarf).

DIETARY PRACTICES There are no dietary practices specific to Lebanese Muslims.

RITUALS Shiite and Sunni prayer rituals are the same in Lebanon as elsewhere.

RITES OF PASSAGE In Lebanon both Shiite and Sunni parents may celebrate the birth of a child by cooking a special sweet dish called *mughli* (hot rice cereal). Some Sunni families go as far as celebrating with a *mawlid*, in which people gather in the house of the newborn to recount the life of the prophet Muhammad and sing songs in praise of him.

MEMBERSHIP Muslims in Lebanon use various means to seek converts. Shiites use the Internet, the radio station al-Nur, and television stations such as al-Manar and NBN to disseminate Shiite ideas. These stations, however, represent the political views of their owners and not those of the Shiite community at large. Sunnis sometimes air their religious teachings on the secular Sunni Television al-Mustaqbal (Future TV) and on the radio station Sawt al-Iman (Voice of Faith). Koran studies are usually offered in the mosque. Although these classes are not restricted, the majority attending them are Sunni.

SOCIAL JUSTICE For Shiites the Lebanese Resistance Detachment (Afwaj al-Muqawamah al-Lubnaniyyah), also called Amal (Hope), is connected with social justice. Its founder, Musa al-Sadr, called for the defense of any oppressed person regardless of nationality, ethnicity, religion, or gender.

Among the Lebanese Sunni community there is great emphasis on public order; political dissidence against an oppressive Muslim ruler is not acceptable if it leads to public disorder and community discord. Since the 1980s, however, many Sunni fundamentalist movements, such as Harakat al-Tawhid al-Islami (the Islamic Unity Movement), have taken a different stance on accepting a corrupt leader for the sake of order. Among Sunnis there is also great emphasis on charitable works and on care for the poor and the needy—a fact attested to by the many social and charitable institutions in the Sunni community, such as the Hariri Foundation (which supports education) and Jam'iyyat al-Maqasid al-Khayriyyah (Islamic Society of Benevolent Intentions).

SOCIAL ASPECTS In the 1990s debates emerged in Lebanon about gender roles and their implications for women. A number of Shiite women have successfully integrated modernity into their spiritual lives and have demanded equal rights and full participation in their communities. Some change has taken place on the theoretical level—such as a wife's right to stipulate favorable conditions within the marriage contract—but such change has been slow on the practical level. Polygamy, although not widely practiced in Lebanon, remains a contentious issue for Lebanese Sunni women.

POLITICAL IMPACT Although Lebanon has no official state religion, its government is based on a "confessional" system, which allocates political power according to religious affiliation. This system was established by the National Pact of 1943, which stated that the president must be a Maronite, the prime minister a Sunni Muslim, and the speaker of parliament a Shiite Muslim. Thus, religion can influence Lebanese politics, especially when political and religious interests coincide. The religious impact on politics is illustrated by President Elias Hrawi's proposal in 1998 to enact a common law for personal status matters. Various religious groups, fearing loss of control of their respective communities, lobbied together to prevent such a bill.

CONTROVERSIAL ISSUES Within the Shiite community of Lebanon there is disagreement about various cultural issues, including women's rights. Also controversial is the Shiite practice of *mut'ah,* or temporary marriage (a marriage contracted for a specified period of time).

Issues commonly debated within the Sunni community are the Arab identity of Lebanon, the role of women in society, and the influence of modernity and secularism. One of the most controversial issues among Sunnis in Lebanon is a woman's right to assume political leadership. In the past religious prescriptions prohibited women from leadership positions, but this ruling has been reversed, and Lebanese Sunni women fully participate in politics. For example, Prime Minister Rafiq al-Hariri's sister, Bahiyya Al-Hariri, became a member of the parliament in 1998.

CULTURAL IMPACT Since the 1980s a number of religious songs and chants have been recorded in Lebanon that celebrate prophets, saints, and certain religious events. There are also poems dealing with spirituality and faith. In the 1980s popular songs were often adapted to better fit Islam. For instance, a folkloric song celebrating life was revised to celebrate pilgrimage to Mecca. Other religious songs that are popular among Muslims in Lebanon date back to early Islam. An example is "tala'a al-badru alayna" ("The Moon has Come upon Us"); the moon here refers to the prophet Muhammad returning to Mecca from his émigré city (Medina). Paintings of mosques and of the Dome of the Rock (where Muhammad ascended to heaven, according to Muslim tradition), as well as calligraphy (painting of Arabic script or Koranic verses), have also become more common.

Other Religions

Among the other religious groups in Lebanon, the Maronites are the most visible on the national scene. Lebanon is the center of the Maronite Church, an Eastern-rite Christian community that is believed to have originated in the fourth century C.E. with the Syrian hermit Saint Maron. The Maronites moved from the Syrian interior into Lebanon in the second half of the seventh century because of their differences with the Jacobite Church and to escape persecution by the Byzantine government. Led by the patriarch Yuhanna Marun (died in 707), they sought safety in the rugged terrain of Mount Lebanon.

In the twelfth century the Maronites backed the Crusaders against Arab Muslim attacks. Such support helped them forge strong ties with Rome, leading to a partial union with the Vatican in 1439 (full union was achieved in 1736). Their independence and attachment to their land developed into a strong sense of territorial and ethnic nationalism. Even today the idea of an independent Maronite State in Mount Lebanon continues to have an impact on Lebanon.

The seat of the Maronite Church is in Bkerke, near Beirut. There are a number of important Maronite churches in Lebanon, such as Saint Mary (Saydeh) Maronite Church and the Church of Saint Maron. Maronites emphasize community cooperation and help for the poor and the needy. Today the president of Lebanon must, according to the National Pact of 1943, be a Maronite. The patriarch (Mar Nasrallah Butrus Sufayr, appointed in 1987) is another important figure; he has led the Maronites in a campaign to request Syria's withdrawal from Lebanon. Maronites have influenced music and art in Lebanon, notably with liturgical songs and paintings of saints.

Greek Orthodox Christians are the second-largest Christian group in Lebanon. Urban and educated, Greek Orthodox Christians in Lebanon emphasize their Arabic heritage; because of their identification as Arabs, they often serve as a bridge between the Christian community and the Arab world. Other Christian groups include Greek Catholics, Assyrians, Protestants, and Copts; there are a very small number of Armenian Catholics in Lebanon.

The Druze are an offshoot of the Shiite Isma'ili sect. They are concentrated in Lebanon, with smaller populations in Syria and Israel. The Druze fled from Egypt to Lebanon in the eleventh century C.E. with their leader, Muhammad al-Darazi (hence the name Druze). Central to their belief is that al-Hakim, the sixth caliph (996–1021) of the Fatimid dynasty, did not die and will return to establish justice and order in this life.

In addition to celebrating the Muslim holidays Id al-Fitr and Id al-Adha, the Druze honor other prophets, such as Shuayb (Jethro). Observant women wear a white *mindil* (a rectangular scarf that covers the hair and the face) and a long black dress. Observant men wear a small white hat and traditional loose black pants. Laypeople often opt for Western clothes. Druze are secretive about their religion and do not accept conversion; membership is through birth only. Sheikh Behjat Ghayth has been the highest Druze authority since 1992. The Druze community in Lebanon is represented politically by Walid Junblatt, a Druze government official.

Moulouk Berry

See Also Vol. 1: *Islam, Shia Islam, Sunni Islam*

Bibliography

Abul-Husn, Latif. *Lebanese Conflict: Looking Inward.* Boulder, Colo.: Lynne Rienner Publishers, 1998.

Esposito, John L. *Islam: The Straight Path.* Oxford: Oxford University Press, 1988.

Norton, Augustus Richard. *Amal and the Shia: Struggle for the Soul of Lebanon.* Austin: University of Texas Press, 1987.

Shehadeh, Lamia Rustum, ed. *Women and War in Lebanon.* Gainesville: University Press of Florida, 1999.

Lesotho

POPULATION 2,207,954

CATHOLIC 50 percent

EVANGELICAL 25 percent

ANGLICAN 10 percent

AFRICAN INDIGENOUS BELIEFS 9
percent

OTHER PROTESTANT 5 percent

MUSLIM, BAHAI, AND OTHER 1
percent

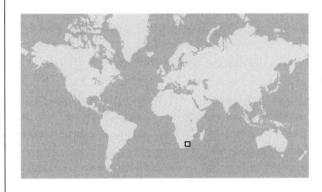

Country Overview

INTRODUCTION The Kingdom of Lesotho (known before independence as Basutoland) is completely surrounded by the Republic of South Africa. Its small size, position on a high plateau on the Drakensberg Mountain's eastern escarpment, and alpine climate give it the names "little Switzerland of Africa," "roof of Africa," and "kingdom in the sky." The people of Lesotho constitute a single ethnic group, the Sotho ("Mosotho" is

used to refer to a single member of that group; "Basotho" refers to two or more Sotho persons or to items and practices particular to the Sotho), 90 percent of whom identify themselves as Christian. Though only 11 percent of the land is arable, 85 percent of the population practices subsistence agriculture, growing corn, sorghum, wheat, peanuts, beans, potatoes, vegetables, and fruits. Livestock raising supports less than 10 percent of the population. About 17 percent of the work force works in South African mines. Water, the good climate, and newly discovered diamonds are the country's major resources. Lesotho has a literacy rate of 71 percent, one of the highest in Africa.

The Khoi and the San who first inhabited the region lived as fruit gatherers, hunters, and cattle herders and followed traditional African religions. In the tenth century the Basotho, immigrant farmers with more advanced tools and weapons, moved into the area from the Southern African high plateau south of the Limpopo River. By the sixteenth century they had settled there permanently, and during the nineteenth century they became the dominant ethnic group on the high veld (grassland) of present South Africa.

King Moshoeshoe (1786–1870) founded the Basotho kingdom during the 1820s. To protect it against constant raids by the Nguni, the Ndebele, and the Boers of South Africa, Moshoeshoe requested that it become a British protectorate, which it did in 1868. The British prohibited the expropriation of land by white settlers. In 1952 political parties began to emerge, but the monarchy survived even after independence in 1966. A five-year-period of forced military rule lasted from 1988 to 1993, when Letsie III (born in 1963) was crowned

Children play in front of a church. First Communion and Confirmation are important rites of passage for Christian children in Lesotho. © DAVID TURNLEY/CORBIS.

king, ruling Lesotho as a constitutional monarchy. Bethuel Pakalitha Mosisili (born in 1945), leader of the Lesotho Congress for Democracy, became prime minister in 1998.

Christianity arrived in Lesotho in 1833. Until 1900 most Basotho remained traditionalists, but the competitive efforts of Protestant and Catholic missionaries eventually succeeded overwhelmingly. A few hundred Muslim Asians live mainly in northeastern Lesotho, and the Bahai faith has recruited a small number of people.

RELIGIOUS TOLERANCE The Lesotho constitution, adopted in 1933, does not explicitly separate church and state, but it upholds freedom of religion and freedom of conscience. Virtually every member of the government is a Christian, however, and looks at social mores through the prism of Christianity; the Christian elite has consistently marginalized adherents of traditional African religions. Yet in spite of more than a century and a half of Christian tradition in Lesotho, a vast

majority of Christians persist in indigenous beliefs and practices that orthodox Christianity proscribes.

The ecumenical movement among the major Christian denominations is strong. The Christian Council of Lesotho has six full- and four associate-member churches. The tension prevalent between Christians and Muslims during the 1990s, when Christians accused Muslims of embassy bombings in East Africa, has subsided as a result of efforts designed to establish a meaningful dialogue among the various faiths.

Major Religion

CHRISTIANITY

DATE OF ORIGIN 1833 C.E.
NUMBER OF FOLLOWERS 2 million

HISTORY Intrigued by the work of missionaries in the Cape Colony and Natal (two British territories on the west and southeast African coasts) and for security reasons, King Moshoeshoe invited the Paris Evangelical Missionary Society (PEMS) to establish a mission near his palace on Mount Thaba-Bosiu in 1833. The PEMS sent three pioneering missionaries. One, Jean Eugène Casalis, so impressed the king that he was made royal advisor and secretary. The missionaries built a church and an elementary school. The king sent a large number of young Basotho to the school, along with two of his sons, Letsie and Molapo.

A shrewd politician, Moshoeshoe decided to limit the power and influence of the PEMS (known in the Sesotho language simply as the Church of Lesotho), especially Casalis, who at times treated him disrespectfully; he invited Roman Catholic missionaries to open a mission at Tloutle, later called Roma, seven miles southeast of his residence. In 1862 the Roman Catholic Church sent two Canadian members of the Congregation of the Oblates of Mary Immaculate, who had been working in Natal for many years. They were followed by members of other Catholic orders.

The competition between the two churches for Basotho converts and influence over the royal authorities became so divisive that Lesotho Christians were classified either as BaRoma (the Romans) or BaFora (the French). The PEMS retained the upper hand for several decades, but Moshoeshoe's death in 1870 deprived them of their influence at court. The Catholic Church, which appeared to be more tolerant of African customs and traditions and which mustered more financial resources, eventually predominated. Catholics argued that their church hierarchy resembled Sotho society and that it had roots as far back as the leadership of Peter the Apostle, a story that pleased the new monarch and his entourage.

Other denominations—Anglicanism, Methodism, and Dutch Reformism—arrived later and have remained smaller. In 1850 Moshoeshoe asked Bishop Robert Gray of the Church of England in Southern Africa to open a mission in Lesotho. The first Anglican missionaries were not posted to Lesotho until 1875, however, after the king's death. Reverend E.W. Stenson and the priests of the Brotherhood of Saint Augustine first worked as itinerant missionaries in Maseru, founding two permanent missions in 1876. The Boers, who were at war with Lesotho, expelled the Anglican missionaries and destroyed their establishments during the Gun War of 1879–80, only allowing them to return in 1883. The Anglican Church was later incorporated into the Church of the Province of South Africa.

The Methodists, affiliated with the American African Methodist Episcopal (AME) Church, entered Lesotho at Matelite in 1908 through the initiative of Reverend Dr. Cramer Sebeta. They later spread their work to Maseru and other parts of the kingdom but have remained a tiny minority. Until 1975 every AME bishop was an American. Methodism in Lesotho also includes the African Methodist Church and the Methodist Church of Southern Africa at Maseru. The Dutch Reformed Church was barred from working in Lesotho for a long time because of its support of apartheid. In 1957 it was allowed to minister to the Basotho living along the border with South Africa. The work of the Seventh-day Adventist Church began in Kolo, Mafeteng District, in 1896, but it had little success until 1920.

Also present in Lesotho are the Apostolic Church, the Assemblies of God, the Full Gospel Church of God, and several African Independent Churches, represented by the African Federal Church Council in Peka, Lesotho, north of Maseru, the capital city.

The work and impact of Christian churches on Lesotho's culture and practices cannot be overestimated. Besides converting the majority of the Basotho people to Christianity, the churches established schools and hospitals; taught the people how to use the oxen plow for agriculture; introduced such new crops and fruit plants as wheat, seed potatoes, apples, and peaches; helped improve the domestication and breeding of dogs, cats, ducks, geese, horses, and pigs; introduced the first flour mill into the country; and trained Basotho as tailors, masons, and carpenters.

EARLY AND MODERN LEADERS Christianity in Lesotho has retained the memory of its founding fathers. The two non-Basotho pioneers of the Catholic Church who arrived in Lesotho in 1862 were Bishop Francois Allard (1806–89) and Father Joseph Gérard (1831–1914). The first Mosotho priest, Father Raphael Mohasi (1896-1954), was ordained in 1931, and the first Sotho bishop, Reverend Emmanuel Mabathoana (1904–66), was consecrated in 1953. The PEMS Church pays special homage to non-Basotho pioneers Reverends Jean Eugène Casalis (1812–91) and Thomas Arbousset (1810–77), along with their first Mosotho minister, Edward Motsamai, ordained in 1900. The Anglican Church recognizes its pioneer, non-Basotho Reverend E.W. Stenson (1830-1900), and its first Mosotho priest, John Velaphe, ordained in 1913.

The current leader of the Catholic Church is Mosotho Reverend Bernard Mohlalisi (born in 1933), archbishop of Maseru. Reverend G.L. Sibolla, a Mosotho, is president of the Lesotho Evangelical Church (which became autonomous from the PEMS in 1964); Bishop Mahapu Tsubella, also an African, leads the Anglican Church of Lesotho; and Reverend D. Senhane is the highest authority of the Methodist Church of Southern Africa.

MAJOR THEOLOGIANS AND AUTHORS Christianity in Lesotho produced no celebrated theologians but several known religious writers. The Evangelical leader Eugène Casalis published a pioneering ethnography, *Les bassoutos* (1859), and his memoirs, *Mes souvenirs* (1882; translated as *My Life in Basuto Land,* 1889). The Evangelical Reverend Edward Motsamai published devotional manuals, short stories, and a biography of Morena Moshoeshoe (1942).

The Catholic Church takes pride in Father Joseph Gérard (1831–1914), long considered a saint by many Lesotho Catholics, who published several hymns, prayer books, and the first Roman Catholic book in Sesotho (the Sotho language) in 1865. In 1988 Pope John Paul II beatified Father Gérard in Rome after a reported miraculous eyesight recovery by a Mosotho girl, blind since age six, who had prayed to the beatified priest.

During his lifetime Father Gérard was called *Ramehlolo* (Father of Miracles) by Basotho Catholics.

HOUSES OF WORSHIP AND HOLY PLACES Cemeteries and churches, including the famous nineteenth-century brick Our Lady of Victory Roman Catholic Cathedral in Roma, the Saint James Anglican Cathedral in Maseru, and the Evangelical Church's establishment at its Morija headquarters, are holy to Basotho Christians. For Catholics the tomb of Father Gérard is uniquely sacred; they consider the deceased priest to be a saint even though Rome has not yet canonized him. Many Catholics are said to have taken soil from his tomb after his burial in 1914, believing the it had supernatural powers.

WHAT IS SACRED? Lesotho Christians consider churches, chapels, the Bible, and objects associated with the Mass (Catholic and Anglican) and religious observances (incense and priestly vestments) sacred. Catholics also revere saint medals, images of saints in sculpture or on cards, and the crucifix. Some Catholics wear a medal or a crucifix around their neck, though the practice is waning. Other Christians avoid anything resembling idolatry. Very rarely does one see a Presbyterian with saint cards in his or her prayer book. To a few Protestant denominations, notably the Evangelical Church of Lesotho, the dove is a sacred bird.

HOLIDAYS AND FESTIVALS Three of seven national holidays in Lesotho—Good Friday, Easter Monday, and Christmas—are derived from the Christian tradition. Christians are instructed not to work on those days, but many do. Ash Wednesday, Palm Sunday, and Christmas (the latter two celebrated with processions, lit candles, and palm tree leaves) are the most colorful annual Christian festivals. Some Protestants celebrate the Ascension.

MODE OF DRESS Christians from different denominations and the rest of the population, including traditionalists and atheists, dress similarly, although many Christians still wear the distinctive Basotho conical straw hat—the *mokorotlo*, or *molianyeoe*—and may wrap a light blanket around their bodies, especially during winter. Basotho Christian men are expected to wear Western attire, usually a suit or shorts and a shirt, to church services, while women wear dresses and cover the head with a thin veil or a Western hat. Women may not wear pants during services. The Bomabana (Children's Moth-

ers; women with or without children who maintain good standing in the Christian community) of the Methodist Church, also known as the Elder Women, wear white uniforms on Sundays.

DIETARY PRACTICES Among some Lesotho Protestants, including Presbyterians, the dove (also the pin symbol of the Bomabana) may not be killed or consumed. While Catholics are told they may drink moderately, Protestants preach total abstinence from drinking and smoking, though few observe the rule.

Christians are not expected to respect indigenous dietary traditions, but many still do. As in most of sub-Saharan Africa, animals associated with the history of a clan and totem animals (*seboko*) may not be killed or consumed. Lesotho has several traditional totems: the crocodile (the royal symbol, despite the fact that there are no crocodiles in the kingdom), elephant, baboon, monkey, lion, and hippopotamus. In addition, many Christians, like traditionalists, won't eat animals that consume human flesh or blood (lions, crocodiles, and vultures) or are man's special friends (dogs, cats, eagles, owls, and crows).

RITUALS Christians in Lesotho perform special rituals at birth, adulthood, marriage, and death, all of which require elaborate church services and blessings from church officials. Ordination into the priesthood (in the Catholic Church) or the ministry (among the Protestant denominations) and consecration to the bishopric are great occasions that require solemn rituals (singing, praying, kneeling, lying on the floor, a series of sermons, Bible reading, and a procession). Despite the long-standing Christian legacy in the country, young men who wish to marry must still pay bride-wealth to the bride's family. Since some of these rituals are among the oldest Christian practices, and some have long been abandoned in Western churches, Lesotho Christians often say that Africans are the true bearers of Christianity and should therefore evangelize the West.

RITES OF PASSAGE Infant baptism in Lesotho still requires godparents, unlike in some Western countries. First Communion and Confirmation for children age seven and older is marked by a long church service, with the participants usually dressed in white. Puberty does not call for a special ceremony in Lesotho Christian circles. Marriages, now rarely prearranged by parents, are solemn celebrations that include a long church service, eating, and dancing. Funerals are also usually long, and both men and women participate in the burial of their loved ones. Assuming a new lay position, even in the church, does not require the pomp and ceremony common in Lesotho traditional society.

MEMBERSHIP Though the large size of Christian families in Lesotho guarantees a numerical increase in practitioners, Christianity remains a strongly proselytizing religion in Lesotho. The competition among denominations has caused the churches to shorten the catechumenate period, contributing to ignorance of essential church teachings among newly converted or newly baptized Basotho.

The social benefits provided by organized churches (education, health, recreation, prestige, social status, and financial resources) have often determined the popularity of a given denomination, which explains the phenomenal growth of the Catholic Church, as well as the strong influence of the Church of England and the Evangelical Church of Lesotho. Because of their reputation of rigorous academic programs, discipline, and effective outcomes, church-run schools, hospitals, and social services have drawn those who can afford them away from government-run institutions.

Christian schools, hospitals, and the like, the main means of propagating the faith in Lesotho are word of mouth, newspapers, and the radio (in 1996 there were 100,000 radios in the country and only 50,000 television sets). The PEMS newspaper, *Leselinyana* (The Little Light of Lesotho), founded by Reverend Adolphe Mabile (1836–94) in 1863, is still published today; it and the still-circulating nineteenth-century Catholic paper *Moeletsi oa Basotho* (Counselor of the Basotho) strengthen the churche's influence in Lesotho.

SOCIAL JUSTICE The work of the Church in education and health and its advocacy on behalf of the poor have had perhaps more impact in Lesotho than anywhere else in southern Africa. During the 1970s the Catholic Church had 4 teacher training schools, 26 secondary schools, 3 vocational schools, 4 hospitals, and several convents, seminaries, book shops, and printing offices and ran the Pius XII University College, founded by Bishop Bonhomme in 1945 (after independence it became the University of Botswana, Lesotho, and Swaziland). The role of the Catholic Church has not decreased over the years. Although with less success, the other Christian churches (especially the Anglican and the Evangelical Churches) have not been less involved in similar social activities, such as education and health, and have contributed to intellectual advancement, democratic reform, and sound agricultural practices even among noneducated Basotho.

SOCIAL ASPECTS The Christian churches in Lesotho uphold monogamy and the large family. A Basotho Christian is expected to marry into a Christian family, and a wife must obey her husband, who is the sole head of the family. Unlike other Christians in the country, Lesotho Catholics are still taught that it is a sin to divorce. Theoretically every Christian denomination in Lesotho preaches against abortion, homosexuality, and polygamy. Monogamy is more common in Lesotho than in most of Southern Africa. Following the advice of the PEMS missionaries, King Moshoeshoe weakened the practice of polygamy by allowing both Catholic and Protestant converted women to seek divorce, while still maintaining the bride-wealth and land they owned or were given by the family they married into. Bride-wealth and the teachings of the Church often caused women to feel obligated to their husbands, so they rarely initiated divorce proceedings. As an example to his people, King Mosoeshoe released some of his wives. Yet he maintained that a chief or a king should only be monogamous by choice. This was the main reason he never converted to Christianity, despite his great admiration for it.

The use of contraceptives for family planning and prevention of infection and disease (such as condoms against HIV/AIDS) has created confusion among all Christian denominations. Said to be one of the four most HIV/AIDS-affected countries in the world, Lesotho has an estimated infection rate of 31 to 37 percent among 15- to 49-year-olds. While most of the Catholic leadership, through its Southern African Bishop's Conference, condemns the use of condoms, some Catholic bishops (including the Most Reverend Kevin Dowling of Rustenberg, South Africa, a prominent member of the Conference) see them as preventing "the transmission of potential death." Within the Anglican and Evangelical Churches, the clergy is more divided. Some religious leaders, including the head of the Anglican Church in Southern Africa, Bishop Ndungane, favor the use of condoms even though they preach that the ideal prophylactic is still abstinence. In the context of these divisions, Catholics are accused of contributing to the spread of sexually transmitted diseases and death through their intransigence on the issue of condoms.

The Catholic Church in Lesotho still lags behind civil society in promoting women's participation in church affairs. In most Protestant churches women may serve as assistant pastors, preach, lead Sunday services, and preside over weekly social and religious activities.

POLITICAL IMPACT Over the past century and a half, the Christian churches have had a profound impact on politics in Lesotho. Many of the royal decisions, as well as the negotiations with the British that led to Lesotho becoming a protectorate, were sanctioned by the Church and drafted with input from powerful missionaries. Moshoeshoe cherished the clergy's advice, not only because most Basotho could not read or write at the time but also because the missionaries understood their white brethren better and, in the eyes of the monarch, were using their social and political clout to benefit the Basotho kingdom.

Before and after independence the two major parties, the Basutoland Congress Party (BCP) and the Basutoland National Party (BNP), were propelled, maintained, strengthened, or vociferously opposed by the churches, especially the Catholic Church, whose priests openly campaigned for the BNP and its leader, Leabuoa Jonathan, because of his strong anti-Communist stance. The official stance of the Catholic Church, expressed in many papal encyclicals and bishop's pastoral letters since the nineteenth century, has always been uncompromisingly anti-Communist, to the extent that any Catholic who espoused Communism would be excommunicated. The Catholic Church's open involvement in politics during the 1960s and 1970s further divided the Christian community, however, compelling the Anglican Church to support the BCP, whose most prominent leaders were Protestant. King Letsie III is a Catholic, and his prime minister is a member of the Evangelical Church of Lesotho. Some tension still exists because of the Church's interference in political matters.

The continuing role of the Catholic Church in Lesotho politics is evident in the official selection—by politicians, the military, and the king—of the Catholic Most Reverend Sebastian Koto Khoarai (born in 1929, ordained bishop in 1978) as a mediator to bring about understanding among the three, who continue to resolve the traumatic results of the period of forced military rule (1988–93).

The Methodists, Seventh-day Adventists, Presbyterians, and others have not been as involved in Lesotho politics as the three major Christian denominations.

CONTROVERSIAL ISSUES Besides the devastating HIV/AIDS pandemic, which takes up much of the attention of the country's politicians and religious leaders, a major controversy among Lesotho churchgoers is the position of women, who for centuries have been treated as second-class citizens. Basotho women do not hold significant positions in society, including in the church. Though wife beating is a criminal offense in Lesotho, spouse abuse is common even in Christian households. Rape, sexual harassment, and prostitution are illegal, but women remain insecure in their homes and in the streets. A 1998 study found that of the 100 cases of human rights abuses identified in the country, 90 were related to domestic violence against women in the form of beatings, rape, and sexual harassment. Many Basotho believe that bride-wealth is at fault—that the obligation to their husbands it confers on women contributes to women's silence about abuse, a silence that allows husbands to go unpunished. Many educated Basotho would like to see bride-wealth eliminated. Many Christian males, however, still believe that wife beating is an acceptable cultural and intellectually justifiable practice.

Basotho Catholics and Anglicans criticize the Evangelical Church of Lesotho for permitting emotional (non-Christian) outbursts in liturgy and for promoting the Holy Ghost as the overriding force of the church. Critics say these lapses can lead to heretical behavior, such as the spirit possessions that occur during some community church services. Others argue, however, that what occurs among Evangelicals today conforms to African cultural traditions, which should be encouraged rather than suppressed.

CULTURAL IMPACT Since the 1830s hymns, prayers, the Bible (the New Testament was translated into Sesotho as early as 1845), and devotional and secular books have been either translated into or written in Sesotho. The books of Sotho novelist and politico-historian Thomas Mofolo (1875–1948)—especially *Pitseng* (1910), a Sesotho version of *The Pilgrim's Progress,* and *Chaka* (1931), a historical romance—have been hailed by both Christians and non-Christians. *Chaka* is considered a masterpiece of nineteenth-century southern African traditions and values.

European-looking churches, some built in Gothic style and some in modern styles, are scattered all over the country. The organ, the piano (competing with the traditional *mbila*), and Christian choirs abound, and traditional dance, considered in the past to be inspired by the devil, has slowly been adapted to Christian worship, especially in the Catholic Church.

Other Religions

Traditional African religions in Lesotho combine the religious beliefs and practices of the earliest inhabitants of the area, the Khoi and the San. Basotho traditionalists believe in one (male) Supreme Being (*Molimo* in Bantu) in a world of good and evil spirits; in ancestors (*balimo,*) who are the intermediaries between the forces of nature and the spirit world; in the power of sorcerers, witches (*boloi*), and others responsible for evil occurrences in the world (*thkolosi*); and in healers, medicinemen, herbalists, diviners, and rain-makers (*lingaka* or *sangoma*), who are able to overcome evil forces. King Moshoeshoe outlawed the killing of sorcerers and witches, whom he considered charlatans.

Traditionalists still practice rituals associated with rites of passage and agriculture. Traditional Basotho boy's initiation rites (*lebollo*) include circumcision. King Moshoeshoe worked to weaken the practice, outlawing it during the 1840s at the insistence of the Evangelical Church, especially Reverend Casalis. The king refused to send his sons to *lebollo* or to call a national initiation ceremony for the kingdom; lesser chiefs might decide to hold their own, but these were not as majestic as one proclaimed by the monarch. Weddings (which still require intricate negotiations regarding bride-wealth from the groom) and funerals involve elaborate religious rituals. Adherents of the Basotho religion traditionally buried their dead in a fetal sitting position, facing the rising sun, so that they would be ready to "to leap up when called" by the spirit world; few traditionalists now follow the practice. A sacrifice, usually involving cattle, may be offered at burials to allow the dead to join the ancestors. Rain-making ceremonies are important occasions in Sotho villages, involving prayers to God and the ancestors; sometimes men take the first turn, and if they fail, young village women take over the ritual.

Traditionalists consider cemeteries, certain parts of the forest, shrines, and designated mountains (where God or the ancestors are thought to reside) as sacred. They uphold polygyny, proscribe the use of artificial means for family planning, and make divorce difficult, given that marriage is an alliance between two families and that divorce may involve the return of the bride-wealth (*bohali*). In the past the bride-wealth was paid to the groom's family in the form of a number of head of cattle. Today, money exchange is the most common means of satisfying this obligation.

Because the traditional Basotho religion is not a proselytizing religion, its future in Lesotho is bleak. The Christian churches and the government have continued Moshoeshoe's policy of marginalizing it, and many would like to see it disappear altogether. Given that most of its members are poor and illiterate, traditionalism in Lesotho will remain an "invisible institution." Yet many of its elements remain in the religious repertoire of even the most devout Basotho Christians.

The few thousand Muslims in Lesotho entered the country from South Africa and are mostly Asians and other foreigners, with the result that few Basotho consider Islam suitable for them. This is true even among the urban poor, who have provided the most fertile ground for Islamic recruitment in other countries. The Bahai faith has made some inroads among pacifists, humanitarians, and idealists who are looking to promote human solidarity, brotherhood, and love. The majority of the Basotho people consider the Bahai faith a brotherhood movement that uses religion as a springboard for the advancement of its secular goals.

Mario J. Azevedo

See Also Vol. I: *African Indigenous Beliefs, Anglicanism/ Episcopalianism, Evangelical Movement, Roman Catholicism*

Bibliography

Ebewo, Patrick, and Chris Dunton, eds. *Na le Vena: Anthology of Creative Writing in Lesotho.* Roma: National University of Lesotho, 1995.

Eldridge, Elizabeth. *A South African Kingdom: The Pursuit of Security in Nineteenth-Century Lesotho.* Cambridge: Cambridge University Press, 1933.

Haliburton, Gordon. *Historical Dictionary of Lesotho.* Metuchen, N.J.: Scarecrow Press, 1977.

Knappert, Jan. *Myths and Legends of Botswana, Lesotho, and Swaziland.* Leiden: E.J. Brill, 1985.

Machobane, L.B.B.J. *Basotho Religion and Western Thought.* Edinburgh: Centre of African Studies, 1995.

Mbiti, John S. *Introduction to African Religion.* London: Heinemann, 1975.

Sanders, Peter, and Basil Thompson. *Moshoeshoe: Chief of the Sotho.* New York: Holmes and Meier Publishing, 1975.

Shorter, Aylward. *African Christian Theology.* Maryknoll, N.Y.: Orbis Books, 1977.

Thompson, Leonard. *Survival in Two Worlds: Moshoeshoe of Lesotho (1789–1870).* Oxford: Oxford University Press, 1975.

Turner, Barry, ed. *Southern Africa: Essential Facts on Society, Business, and Politics in Southern Africa.* New York: St. Martin's Press, 2000.

Liberia

POPULATION 3,288,198

CHRISTIAN (LUTHERAN, BAPTIST,
   EPISCOPALIAN,
   PRESBYTERIAN, ROMAN
   CATHOLIC, UNITED METHODIST,
   AFRICAN METHODIST
   EPISCOPAL [AME], AME ZION)
   40 percent

AFRICAN TRADITIONAL BELIEFS
   40 percent

MUSLIM 20 percent

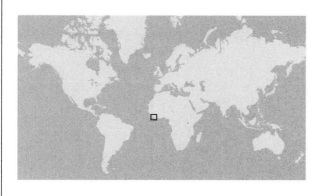

Country Overview

INTRODUCTION The Republic of Liberia in West Africa borders the North Atlantic Ocean, Côte d'Ivoire (Ivory Coast), Equatorial Guinea, and Sierra Leone. Originally called the Grain Coast and subsequently the Slave Coast, the country has a population that is ninety-five percent from indigenous groups, including Kpelle, Bassa, Gio, Kru, Grebo, Mano, Krahn, Gola, Gbandi,

Loma, Kissi, Vai, De, Mande, Mandingo, and Bella. The remaining 5 percent is almost evenly split between Americo-Liberians (descendants of former American slaves) and Congo people (descendants of former Caribbean slaves).

Liberia has the closest historical ties to the United States of all the African nation states. In the first decades of the nineteenth century, American freed slaves wanted to return to West Africa, their presumed homeland, and white Americans wanted to secure that return. In 1822 the American Colonization Society (established in 1816 by Robert Finley) sent the ship *Elizabeth* with three white agents and 88 black emigrants to West Africa. After a number of setbacks, including the death of all three whites and 22 emigrants from Yellow Fever, the party established a settlement at Mesurado Bay, naming it Perseverance. The settlers brought Christianity with them and treated the indigenous population and their traditional religion with contempt. Islam, which arrived four centuries earlier, was already well established among the Mandingo and Vai peoples in northern Liberia and was not challenged by the settlers.

Although less than 5 percent of the total population, the Americo-Liberians secured Liberian independence from the United States in 1847 and granted the first black governorship to Joseph Jenkins Roberts (an illegitimate son of Thomas Jefferson; Jefferson is said to have sent him to Liberia to keep him out of the public eye). The capital city, Monrovia, was named after President Monroe of the United States.

Liberian politics have been tumultuous since the later twentieth century. In the 1970s Master Sergeant Samuel Kanyon Doe (from the Krahn tribe) came to

The oldest church in Liberia, the Old Baptist Church, dates back to the mid-nineteenth century. GETTY IMAGES.

power in a coup. In 1989 Charles Taylor led a rebellion against Doe. Taylor's national patriotic front executed Doe and overran the countryside before the rebels split into factions. Taylor, a Christian, became president in 1997, but international pressure forced him to leave office in 2003. The United Nations has given the new government, headed by Chairman Gyude Bryant, two years to rebuild Liberia.

RELIGIOUS TOLERANCE The Liberian constitution, drafted in 1944, recognizes religious freedom as a fundamental right and prohibits the establishment of a state religion. Moreover, no leader of a religious organization may hold political office. The constitution reserves the right, however, to deny any religious practice that may threaten public safety, health, morals, or the freedoms of others. Religious groups, except indigenous religions, must register with the government and provide a statement of purpose. No complaints have been issued about the process, which all agree is quick and fair.

Historically relations between Americo-Liberian Christians, Muslims, and indigenous peoples have been uneasy. Laws have benefited the ruling elite, who have looked down on even converted indigenous people. Despite the ban on state religion, public ceremonies always open with prayers and hymns, most often Christian, but sometimes Muslim. Muslims complain that the Sunday closing law is discriminatory and that the government does not allot jobs fairly to them. Some Christians criticized the Taylor government for sponsoring over 100 pilgrims to Mecca. Muslim-Christian tensions are highest in the northern areas where most Muslims live. Taylor's government waged war against insurgents there, most of whom are Mandingo Muslims. The Mandingos accused Taylor of human rights abuses in his campaign.

Problems in southeastern Liberia center on frequent reports of ritual murders and cannibalism by members of some indigenous religious groups. The Catholic Church has opposed government policies, and the government tried to shut down the Catholic radio station on charges of illegal operation. Christian and Muslim leaders have sought to improve relations by organizing an interfaith council to bring together leaders from every religion in Liberia.

Major Religions

CHRISTIANITY
AFRICAN TRADITIONAL BELIEFS

CHRISTIANITY

DATE OF ORIGIN 1822 C.E.
NUMBER OF FOLLOWERS 1.3 million

HISTORY Christianity arrived in Liberia in 1822 with the freed slaves from America and the Caribbean. The original Americo-Liberian emigrants considered Christianity a mark of civilization and saw African indigenous religions ("paganism") as shameful; more importantly, they believed that the perseverance of traditional religion prevented European countries and the United States from respecting Liberia. The conversion to Christianity and Western values of the people in the hinterland was a prime goal of the elite rulers in Monrovia and other cities, who began their work by establishing a network of schools. The government encouraged both local and foreign missionaries, who spread various versions of the religion.

The superior attitude of the Americo-Liberians, who mocked indigenous culture and regarded it as worthless, often retarded the mission. The Americo-Liberians wanted the privileges associated with white Americans, and they practiced the racism they had suffered in the United States against the indigenous population in Liberia. To protect their distinctive identity, the settlers erected social and economic barriers, institutionalizing segregation. Indigenous people could not sit next to them at church, and Christian Africans had to enter Americo-Liberian homes through the back door. Liberia's first three constitutions restricted the rights of Africans, who had to prove they were civilized and owned property to become full citizens.

In the early twentieth century Liberian William Wadé Harris began spreading an African version of Christianity throughout West Africa. Harri'ss great success in Liberia was in large part a reaction against the segregationist policies of Americo-Liberians.

Over the years African-American missionaries and white missionaries from Europe and the United States have established Roman Catholic, Methodist, Baptist, Presbyterian, Lutheran, and Episcopalian missions. In the 1950s Mormons from America entered the mission field. The Church of the Lord (the Aladura movement) also has a number of churches of various sizes that promote large, ecstatic gatherings for communal worship.

EARLY AND MODERN LEADERS Born in the Liberian hinterlands, William Wadé Harris (c. 1860–1929) founded the Harrist movement and was unquestionably the most successful Christian missionary in Africa. His goal was to make Christianity African. At the onset of his work, most Catholic and Protestant missionaries dismissed Harris. In 1913–14 he went into areas of Liberia where no missionary had gone before, baptizing over 100,000 Africans within an eighteen-month period. Influenced by Edward Blyden, who came to Liberia from the Virgin Islands and decried Western imperialism, including the missions, Harris believed that only a British Protectorate in Liberia could save the country. He used violence, threats, and magic to attempt to bring Glebo chiefs into a plot to bring Blyden to power. After the coup failed, Harris left Liberia and traveled throughout West Africa, using any means he could to bring about conversions, with great success.

Current Christian leaders in Liberia include Michael Kpakala Francis, who became archbishop of Monrovia in 1977, and Bishop Sumowood Harris of the Methodist Episcopal Church, who took on the presidency of the Liberian Council of Churches in 2003.

MAJOR THEOLOGIANS AND AUTHORS The Harrist Church of William Wadé Harris was a unique local religious movement that unified a number of ethnic groups in their religious practices. The Ten Commandments were their religious law, Sunday was their day of worship, and the institution of the church was their place of worship. The Bible was the only sacred book and the cross the basic symbol. Baptism signified a break with fetishes and other objects and practices Harris felt were based on superstition. He continued to allow animal sacrifice and traditional song and dance for prayer.

HOUSES OF WORSHIP AND HOLY PLACES Churches, chapels, and other Christian houses of prayer exist throughout Liberia. Many of William Wade Harris's churches still dot the landscape. Many newer churches are built along his church's simple lines to fit into the African landscape.

WHAT IS SACRED? The usual Christian symbols are found in Liberia's Christian churches: crucifixes, crosses, statues of Jesus and saints, and other symbols according to denomination. The Bible is sacred, and Sunday is generally the day of worship.

HOLIDAYS AND FESTIVALS Liberian Christians celebrate the various Christian holidays—including Christmas, New Year's, various saint's days, and other Christian feasts—according to Christian denomination. The Catholic Church celebrates All Saint's Day, the Assumption, the Immaculate Conception, and other holy days.

MODE OF DRESS Christians tend to dress in Western-style clothing or an adapted African style: long shirts and loose fitting trousers.

DIETARY PRACTICES Liberian Christians have no special dietary practices except to abstain from eating meat during Lent.

RITUALS Liberian Christians use the same seven sacraments as other Christians, often adding traditional African elements to the sacramental rituals, including singing and dancing. The Harrists routinely use African forms of worship, including aspects of Sande and Poro rituals. For them traditional singing and dancing take the place of Protestant services. Roman Catholics and High Church Episcopalians offer the Sacrifice of the Liturgy (the Mass). Others follow various Protestant services that feature Bible reading and sermons.

RITES OF PASSAGE Christians in Liberia celebrate the usual Christian rites of passage. Baptism, confirmation, marriage, funerals, and other sacramental rituals mark life-stage changes.

MEMBERSHIP In Liberia Christianity actively seeks new members. Indigenous, African-American, and European Christian missionaries often travel to remote places, translate the Bible into indigenous languages, and seek to understand the daily lives of the people. Missionaries produce radio programs or run radio stations, build schools and hospitals, and conduct other welfare activities, often in remote rural areas. Christian schools have long been an integral part of increasing the denomination's numbers and influence.

SOCIAL JUSTICE Sharing is part of African traditional morality, and Liberian Christianity has built on this foundation. Christians preach the need to help the poor and other members of their communities. Christian schools have long traditions in the country that are integral parts of spreading their churche's faiths. A number of religions and missionary groups have radio stations that promote social justice. ELWA (Eternal Love Winning Africa), a Sudan Interior Mission International (now Society of International Ministries) station, once broadcast from Liberia to all of West Africa. Their studios were destroyed in 1990 during the civil war. The station has resumed broadcasts but only within Liberia.

SOCIAL ASPECTS Most Liberian Christians oppose both abortion and birth control, and many oppose divorce, believing in the permanence of marriage. In theory Liberian men head their families and expect obedience from their wives and children, although in practice, especially among farmers, married couples tend to form partnerships that strengthen family ties, dividing labor between them. Children are taught by their families to respect elders and to follow their proverbs.

POLITICAL IMPACT Because Christians are in power in Liberia, much of the economy is slanted toward Christian development, and Christians can obtain better jobs than non-Christians. Much of the opposition to the government, including armed opposition, has come from Muslim centers and draws on Muslim resentment of the Christian-controlled government.

CONTROVERSIAL ISSUES In Liberia a person who has any "white blood" at all is regarded as white, and anyone who eats, dresses, and talks like someone from Europe is called a European. A person who is black in the United States may be white in Liberia and may attain privileges no African Liberian is granted. This cultural racism has caused much pain within the Christian community.

Christianity has been somewhat more open in Liberia to women's participation in a variety of arenas than in many other African countries. Christian women are more likely to hold political office and to advance in the modern economy than are Muslim or traditional women.

CULTURAL IMPACT The original Liberian Christians sought to imitate American and, later, European models of behavior and aesthetics. Liberian churches were built to look like those in the United States. Music and manners were European in style. Education followed American models: There were American-style colleges, newspapers, and cotillions. Constant contact with American missionaries and educators, many of them African-American, encouraged this attitude. American currency is still the official currency of Liberia.

AFRICAN TRADITIONAL BELIEFS

DATE OF ORIGIN 1500 B.C.E.
NUMBER OF FOLLOWERS 1.3 million

HISTORY The basic outlines of Liberian traditional religion were present in West Africa from about 1500 B.C.E. The Sky God religion seems to have originated in eastern Africa and spread rapidly to the West. The indigenous religion that developed in Liberia centers on a god who is somewhat removed from his creation and aided in his work by subordinate spirits in charge of various aspects of the creation. The religion is taught through proverbs and other verbal devices. Followers recognize little, if any, separation between religion and other aspects of life. Estimates of the number of adherents vary greatly (from 20 percent to 70 percent of the population), because many Christians and Muslims still practice some forms of traditional rituals.

Many Liberian traditional groups have secret societies with religious as well as social, political, legal, and educational functions. These societies deal with particular aspects of religion, such as medicine and controlling snakes, lightning, and witches. Those who wish to be members must undergo a particular initiation ritual and must keep secret the way in which the society works. The men's Poro and women's Sande secret societies are the most widespread. The Poro and the Sande combine religious and political power, settling local disputes and regulating markets and other aspects of daily life.

EARLY AND MODERN LEADERS Liberian traditional religion has no prominent historical figures. Clan members fill positions of authority within traditional communities.

MAJOR THEOLOGIANS AND AUTHORS Because it is an oral tradition, Liberian indigenous religion has no written documents, and the myths that provide a religious basis for traditional social life have no authors. As religious practitioners the Kpelle have shamans of both sexes, some associated with the Poro and Sande secret societies, some connected with specific medicine societies, and some who are independent. The first two mainly conduct rituals, while members of the third category (as well as some from the second) are healers. There are also diviners who analyze and solve problems.

HOUSES OF WORSHIP AND HOLY PLACES Almost every village has its own traditional shrines, which combine African traditional elements with Christian or Islamic elements.

WHAT IS SACRED? Liberian traditional religion reveres ancestral spirits, cows, chickens, rivers, trees, and other aspects of the natural world. Twins are sacred throughout Liberia. The Mande believe in *nyama*, a sacred power that animates the world and is present in all natural objects. *Nyama* is a kind of super soul that controls the forces of nature.

HOLIDAYS AND FESTIVALS In addition to the national Islamic and Christian holidays, different ethnic groups celebrate their own farming occasions, market days, naming festivities for newborns, initiation periods for young men and women, and family holidays.

MODE OF DRESS Traditional Liberians dress in either African or Western-style dress. During rituals certain religious practitioners dress according to the needs of their duties. Members of the Poro and Sande secret societies, for example, wear traditional dress and masks.

DIETARY PRACTICES Liberian food taboos that have religious underpinnings help preserve species and maintain ecological relationships. The religion of certain ethnic groups forbids them to eat panthers. Some may not eat certain plants because of the group's relationship to the spirit or god associated with the plant. Respect for these taboos contributes to the health of the overall community.

Traditionalists usually eat beef only ceremonially. These cows are not milked and are used mainly for bride prices and sacrifices.

RITUALS Kpelle rituals focus on God, the ancestors, and forest spirits. Members of the Poro and Sande secret societies are prominent in these rituals, wearing masks to represent the spirits. Diviners sometimes prescribe ritual sacrifices, to occur at such places as crossroads.

During initiation into the Poro or Sande secret societies, after initiates have been separated from the community for some time, a major coming-out ritual is performed. Members reenter society and are introduced in their new guises.

RITES OF PASSAGE Liberian traditional secret societies initiate young people between the ages of seven and twenty into full ritual membership. The Poro and Sande educate these adolescents as proper adults and society members. Masked figures carry out both male and female initiation. The initiation takes about three years. Clitoridectomy and labiadectomy are integral parts of female initiation.

MEMBERSHIP Liberian traditional religion takes its members from local villages, where people are born into the religion and pass through various steps into full membership. Traditionalists often combine their practice with aspects of Islam or Christianity, sometimes both. Adherents of traditional religion in Liberia do not proselytize.

SOCIAL JUSTICE Traditional Liberian views of justice promote reconciliation, healing breaches, and bringing people together. Someone caught in the act of stealing or adultery might be punished immediately, but the general practice is to find ways to forget old breaches of the law and bring people together.

Religion in traditional communities seeks to give each person his or her due while stabilizing the ethnic group and its component kinship groups. Private individuals and their kin groups might bring legal actions; authorities seek to restore social relationships. Diviners help restore justice by discovering the witch or other antisocial agent who wittingly or otherwise spoiled a relationship. Compensation and ritual feasting, supported by religion, play a prominent role in the healing process.

SOCIAL ASPECTS Liberian traditional society is based on polygynous marriage and the patrilineal-patrilocal family: Descent groups are traced through the father's line and residence is based on those descent principles. Most traditional Liberian groups prefer marriage through bride price, in which the groom's family compensates the bride's family for the loss of the woman's work and children. The Poro and Sande societies work to keep marriages together and maintain social stability in families. Liberians in general have a taboo prohibiting sexual intercourse during the entire time a woman is breast-feeding. This institutionalized abstinence helps create space between children.

POLITICAL IMPACT The Poro and Sande religious societies found throughout Liberia exert both traditional and modern political power. Besides regulating activities and solving disputes within local groups, they support or oppose national policies from these local bases.

CONTROVERSIAL ISSUES Like other non-Christians in Liberia, traditional peoples feel that the Christians who have controlled the government since Liberia's founding discriminate against them. They also believe that government-supported efforts to convert them to Christianity violate their religious freedom. Many have supported rebels against the current government. The Liberian government looks on the traditionalist secret societies as sources for spreading discontent and rebellion.

CULTURAL IMPACT African traditional religion in Liberia influences many Christians and Muslims. The old beliefs appeal to many Africans, as do their moral teachings. New religious movements in Liberia have incorporated traditional belief in their doctrines. Liberian universities are teaching traditional religion as a respected course of study. Traditional teachings have influenced people not only in Liberia but also in Europe and America as people rethink Christianity.

Other Religions

Liberia is home to about 658,000 Muslims. Islam came to the Mandingo area of northern Liberia in the fourteenth and fifteenth centuries and has remained strong in that area. Mosques, Islamic crescents, turrets, and other Muslim symbols (such as pieces of the Koran worn on the forehead to ward off evil spirits) are common in the region.

Liberian Muslims celebrate Ramadan, the Prophet Muhammad's birthday, and other Islamic holidays common throughout the world. Many Liberian Muslim men wear long, flowing robes and turbans or other head coverings; women wear modest dress and are kept relatively sheltered (when wealth permits) and subordinate to men. As elsewhere, Liberian Muslims fast during Ramadan, refrain from eating pork, and only eat meat from ritually slaughtered animals. They are enjoined to make the pilgrimage to Mecca; to keep the Islamic rites of passage, including the naming rituals and the purification of women after childbirth; and to give 10 percent of their wealth to the poor. Muslim men may marry up to five wives; divorce is common.

The Vai ethnic group has become Islamic but retains its ties with traditional peoples and rites. A group that has suffered from strong competition between country and clan chiefs, the Vai have not gained in political unity through adopting Islam.

Throughout the history of the Liberian state, Muslims have been subjected to discrimination and contempt. Opposition to the Christian president Charles Taylor, strong in Muslim areas, coalesced in a group called Liberians United for Reconciliation and Development.

Frank A. Salamone

See Also Vol. 1: *African Traditional Beliefs, Christianity, Islam*

Bibliography

Creevey, Lucy, and Barbara Callaway. *The Heritage of Islam: Women, Religion, and Politics in West Africa.* Boulder, Colo.: Lynne Rienner, 1994.

Gershoni, Yekutiel. *Black Colonialism: The Americo-Liberian Scramble for the Hinterland.* Boulder, Colo.: Westview Press, 1985.

Glazier, Stephen D., ed. *Anthropology of Religion: A Handbook.* Westport, Conn.: Praeger, 1999.

Gorman, G.E., and Roger Homan, eds. *The Sociology of Religion: A Bibliographical Survey.* New York: Greenwood Press, 1986.

Johnson, Robert. *Why Blacks Left America for Africa: Interviews with Black Repatriates, 1971–1999.* Westport, Conn.: Praeger Publishers, 1999.

Karp, Ivan, and Charles S. Bird, eds. *Explorations in African Systems of Thought.* Bloomington, Ind.: Indiana University Press, 1980.

Matthews, Donald H. *Honoring the Ancestors: An African Cultural Interpretation of Black Religion and Literature.* New York: Oxford University Press U.S., 1998.

Olson, James S. *The Peoples of Africa: An Ethnohistorical Dictionary.* Westport, Conn.: Greenwood, 1996.

Parrinder, Geoffrey. *African Traditional Religion.* London: Hutchinson's University Library, 1954.

Staudenraus, P.J. *The American Colonization Society: The African Colonization Movement, 1816–1865.* New York: Columbia University Press, 1961.

Libya

POPULATION 5,368,585

MUSLIM 98 percent

CHRISTIAN 1 percent

OTHER 1 percent

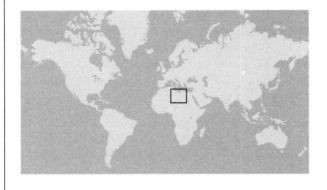

Country Overview

INTRODUCTION Known officially as the Great Socialist People's Libyan Arab Jamahiriya, Libya extends from the Mediterranean Sea well into the Sahara. The country, which is located at a strategic crossroads of Europe, Africa, and the Middle East, has experienced many invaders, with Arabs eventually having the greatest impact on the indigenous Berber people. Beginning in 642 C.E., Arab Muslims swept across North Africa and eventually occupied the area. The Fatimid dynasty, established in North Africa by 910 C.E., then extended its control eastward across Libya. A century later the Fatimids responded to growing Berber opposition by bringing in members of two bedouin tribes, the Beni Hilal and the Beni Sulaim, from Arabia to quell the revolt. Successive

waves of Arab invaders stamped their character on the Libyan people, but it was the Beni Hilal and the Beni Sulaim that ensured the Arab and Muslim character of the country.

The Italian occupation, which began in 1911, took some 35,000 immigrants to Libya over the next three decades. Mostly Christian, the Italian population shrank to a few hundred after the revolutionary government seized power in 1969. Similarly, a Jewish population numbering about 35,000 in 1948 shrank to no more than 100 residents by 1973. The non-Muslim population today consists largely of expatriates drawn from countries in Africa, Europe, and East Asia.

RELIGIOUS TOLERANCE The 1951 constitution of Libya, adopted at independence, declared Islam to be the religion of the state. When the monarchy was ousted by the Great September Revolution of 1969, the revolutionary government issued a constitutional proclamation that made Islam the religion of the state and Arabic, the language of the Koran, the country's official language. The 1977 Declaration of the Establishment of the People's Authority, which amended the constitutional proclamation, made the Koran the law of society in Libya.

Beginning in the 1940s, the Jewish population of Libya suffered increasingly harsh treatment. After centuries of relative tolerance, anti-Jewish riots broke out in late 1945 when the Muslim majority, in the wake of almost three decades of Italian colonial rule, moved to restore what it viewed as the proper order of sovereignty. In consequence, Jews began to emigrate in increasing numbers, with many finding a new home in Israel. Anti-

Jewish violence erupted again in 1967, and in 1970 the government confiscated most Jewish property, driving out the remaining Jewish population.

Major Religion

SUNNI ISLAM

DATE OF ORIGIN 642 C.E.
NUMBER OF FOLLOWERS 5.3 million

HISTORY With the Arab conquest of North Africa in the seventh century, Islam penetrated Libya, and in the course of the next 1,200 years Libya assumed a distinct Arab and Muslim character. In 1842 Sayyid Muhammad bin Ali al-Sanusi founded the Sanusi order. Sanusism was an Islamic revival movement, and for many decades religion in Libya felt its influence. Centered in Cyrenaica, in what is now eastern Libya, the order later spread to the Fezzan in the south. More a religious than a political movement, Sanusism sought to purify Islam and to educate the Libyan people in Islamic principles. Most Libyans today belong to the Sunni branch of Islam and adhere to the Malikite school of Islamic law. One of four orthodox Sunni schools, the Malikite rite holds the Koran, the sacred book of Muslims containing the word of God as revealed to and recited by the Prophet Muhammad, and especially the hadith, the traditions of the Prophet, to be the principal sources of truth.

In response to the Italian invasion of Libya in 1911, the Libyan people declared jihad (struggle), viewing the harsh colonial policies of the occupiers as an attack on Islam. In this context it was more religious zeal than nationalism that motivated the resistance to occupation. Islam as epitomized in the Sanusi movement later provided the monarchy, established at the time of independence in 1951, with legitimacy. After independence the role of religion as a legitimizing force declined for a number of reasons, including increased education and urbanization. Nevertheless, Islam has continued to exert a major influence on the history and society of Libya. Conservative attitudes dominate, and people's values and behavior remain very much a function of their religious background and attachment.

EARLY AND MODERN LEADERS Sayyid Muhammad bin Ali al-Sanusi advocated a combination of Sufism,

A young man stands in front of a poster of Libyan leader Mu'ammar al-Qaddafi. His government's unorthodox interpretation of Islam often put the government in conflict with the traditional religious leadership in Libya. © PETER TURNLEY/CORBIS.

or mysticism, and orthodoxy attractive to the bedouins of eastern Libya. After his death in 1859, the brothers of the order, known as *ikhwan,* carried his message to large parts of Africa, eventually establishing 146 *zawaya,* or lodges.

With the outbreak of World War I, Sayyid Muhammad Idris al-Mahdi al-Sanusi, grandson of al-Sanusi, assumed the leadership of the Sanusi order and concluded peace agreements with Britain and Italy. These arrangements brought diplomatic and political status to the order, but they did not bring peace to Libya. When Italy resumed its conquest of Libya, Idris fled to Egypt, leaving more martial members of the order to wage a fruitless war against Italy. During World War II, Idris pressed for an independent Libya, and in so doing he was increasingly accepted as the one

Libyan able to unite the country. Libya achieved independence in 1951, with Idris as head of state.

With the overthrow of the monarchy in 1969, the leader of the revolution, Muammar al-Qaddafi, moved to reinstate Shariah, Islamic law based on the revelations of the Prophet Muhammad, and to abrogate the European laws imported by the Idris regime. In the process he created the impression that his regime had imposed Islamic law in Libya, when in fact its real accomplishments were more modest. In the subsequent decades opposition to Qaddafi based on Islamic precepts increased steadily but never posed a cohesive, serious threat to the regime. Qaddafi successfully steered a middle course between hardline religious opponents and the Libyan population as a whole, which was largely opposed to militant Islam.

MAJOR THEOLOGIANS AND AUTHORS Rebuffed by the clerics, the revolutionary government of Muammar al-Qaddafi undertook a determined assault on the religious establishment of Libya. He was largely successful in neutralizing the ulama (religious scholars), and Islamic opposition to the Qaddafi regime became fragmented under constant pressure from government security forces. Although there have been influential ulama, such as Shaykh al-Bishti, the former imam (religious leader) of Tripoli, there are no contemporary theologians or authors in Libya with influence remotely similar to that of Sayyid Muhammad Idris al-Mahdi al-Sanusi.

HOUSES OF WORSHIP AND HOLY PLACES As in other Muslim countries, the mosque is the house of worship in Libya. Mosques are found throughout the country. Those of notable architectural or historical interest include Al-Jami al-Atiq in Awjilah; Ahmed Pasha Karamanli, Al-Naqah, Draghut, and Gurgi in Tripoli; and Sidi Abdulsalam in Zliten.

WHAT IS SACRED? Islam traditionally recognizes no distinction between church and state. Religious and secular life merge, as do religious and secular law. A Muslim stands in a personal relationship to God, and there is neither an intermediary nor a clergy in orthodox Islam. In line with their orthodox beliefs, Libyan Muslims practice the Five Pillars of Islam. Otherwise, Islam imposes a code of ethical conduct that encourages generosity, fairness, honesty, and respect.

HOLIDAYS AND FESTIVALS Like most Muslim countries, Libya observes the main Islamic festivals as holi-

days. Ramadan, the ninth month of the Muslim, or Hegiran, calendar, is a month of fasting. Some Libyan males, even though they may consider themselves unique and lead a debauched life during the rest of the year, conduct themselves with piety during Ramadan. The festival of Id al-Fitr marks the official end to the fast and is celebrated with a feast. Other religious holidays include the Feast, or Festival, of the Sacrifice (Id al-Adha), also called the Major Festival, which is celebrated on the 10th of Dhu al-Hijja, the last month of the Islamic year. Marking the end of the annual pilgrimage, the principal observance is in a village near Mecca, in Saudi Arabia, but Muslims around the word, including those in Libya, celebrate with a feast. Libyans also celebrate the Islamic New Year, although the birthday of the Prophet Muhammad is not a religious holiday in Libya. Friday is a day of rest, on which public offices are closed.

MODE OF DRESS The traditional Libyan dress for men is the *barakan*, a length of woven material that is wrapped around the head and body. When men visit mosques or other religious shrines, the emphasis is on clothing that is clean, neat, and respectful. Western-style attire, including business suits, is common in offices. The Islamic dress code for women emphasizes modesty. The use of the veil is not common in Libya, but traditional women often cover the head in public. There is no prescribed dress for religious leaders, and they tend to wear the national dress, with a cap covering the head.

DIETARY PRACTICES Islam proscribes the consumption of alcohol, blood, carrion, and pork. While the proscription of alcohol is irregularly enforced in many Muslim countries, the government in Libya is strict in ensuring that the prohibition is effective.

RITUALS Muslims throughout the world follow the same basic set of rituals, with variations in detail generally the result of the various schools of practice. In Libya, where the Malikite school is dominant, these rituals include male circumcision, weddings, religious festivals, funerals, and mourning. At such times it is common in Libya to offer hospitality and food, including sweets and delicacies. Like most Arabs, Libyans value generosity, and an ample table is a mark of good breeding. As elsewhere in the Islamic world, Muslims in Libya observe the Five Pillars of Islam, which include professing their faith, giving alms, praying five times daily, fasting during the month of Ramadan, and making a pilgrimage to Mecca.

RITES OF PASSAGE Special occasions in the lives of Muslims in Libya have both religious and secular significance. These include birth, circumcision for males, marriage, and death. In addition to their obvious religious overtones, these events are also important social rites for Libyan families, the larger clan of relatives, and often the entire neighborhood or village. In Libya, as in most Muslim countries, an event in which a family takes special pride is a child's memorization of the entire Koran.

MEMBERSHIP Islam has no ordained priesthood or other sacerdotal institution, and God is equally accessible to all. There are no consecrated centers of worship, the mosque being simply a public hall in which prayers are conducted. The local community normally cares for the mosque, but it does not form a particular community or parish. Consequently, religious life in Libya, as in other Islamic countries, is not strongly congregational.

The Sanusi movement actively proselytized in eastern and southern Libya for much of the nineteenth century, but its efforts largely ended with the Italian occupation. After 1969 the revolutionary government established the Islamic Mission Society to repair and construct mosques and educational institutions around the world. In addition, it organized the Islamic Call Society, ostensibly to serve as a missionary body, although it also engaged in political activities in host countries.

SOCIAL JUSTICE In its early statements the revolutionary government emphasized the indigenous nature of Libyan socialism, arguing that it stemmed from the heritage of the Libyan people and the heart of the nation. At the same time it gave socialism a strong Islamic basis, depicting Libyan socialism as derived from Islam. Thus, over the next two decades wealth was redistributed and private enterprise virtually eliminated in Libya. The revolutionary government also advanced education, providing free schools at all levels and largely merging religious and secular education. The government developed a poor human rights record, however. Under financial pressure in the 1990s, the Libyan government began to reverse many of the socialist policies it had earlier advocated.

SOCIAL ASPECTS Some of the practices instituted in Libya by the regime of Muammar al-Qaddafi contradict both the letter and the spirit of Islam and thus, from an Islamic point of view, are seen as violations of human rights. The revolutionary government enacted several laws to improve the legal status of women with respect to marriage and divorce. Restrictions were imposed on Libyan men marrying non-Libyan women, and men employed by the state could not marry non-Arab women. Women in Libya today enjoy divorce rights nearly equal to those of men. On the other hand, while children born of Libyan men are eligible for Libyan citizenship, this is not true of those born of non-Libyan men and Libyan women. Although the overall legal status of women has improved, in traditional sectors of Libyan society there is a reluctance to acknowledge the changes, and many Libyan women are hesitant to claim their privileges.

Marriage in Libya is more a family than a personal affair and more a social contract than a sacrament. With limited contact permitted among the sexes, young men and women enjoy few acquaintances with members of the opposite sex. Consequently, marriages are often arranged by the parents through either friends or a professional matchmaker. The law provides that a couple must consent to a union, but in practice they often play little part in the arrangements.

POLITICAL IMPACT Religion played a central role in the politics of Libya after independence in 1951, and its role increased after the revolutionary government came to power in 1969. In the Third Universal Theory, set forth in the early 1970s as an attempt to provide a theoretical underpinning for the revolution, Muammar al-Qaddafi argued that nationalism and religion were the paramount drivers of history and mankind. His thoughts on religion focused on the centrality of Islam to religion and of the Koran to Islam. Rejecting formal interpretation of the Koran as blasphemy, he also criticized the hadith on the grounds that the Koran was the only true source of God's word. The revolutionary government's unorthodox interpretation of Islam, coupled with its efforts to use Islam to support the revolution, often put the government in conflict with the traditional religious leadership in Libya.

CONTROVERSIAL ISSUES One controversial issue in Libya has been the attempt by Muammar al-Qaddafi to manipulate Islam in support of the revolution and for his own ends. Although this has generated considerable internal opposition to the regime, dissent has been neither cohesive nor a part of larger movements outside

Libya. Important opposition groups include Apostasy and Migration, Fighting Islamic Group, Islamic Liberation Party, Islamic Martyr's Movement, Libyan Islamic Group, and Muslim Brotherhood.

CULTURAL IMPACT Because Muslims have traditionally looked askance at the representation of human and animal figures, orthodox Islamic art, including that of Libya, seldom pictures living beings. Since independence Libya has witnessed a modest revival in the pictorial arts, especially calligraphy and painting, but there has been little activity in the fields of theater or film for many years. Traditional Islamic architecture, manifesting itself in places of worship as well as in secular buildings and urban planning, has enjoyed a long, fruitful history in Libya. Traditional folk culture, with Islamic overtones, has remained alive and well, with music and dance troupes often performing at festivals.

Other Religions

No more than a handful of Jews remain in Libya. The resident Christian community, numbering some 50,000, are mainly expatriates working in the petroleum industry. A variety of Christian denominations are found in Libya, with Roman Catholicism, reflecting the relatively large expatriate Italian community, being the most common.

Once dominant throughout Libya, Berbers today largely inhabit desert localities or remote mountainous areas. Unlike the Arabs of Libya, who tend to view themselves as members of the Arab nation, Berbers find identity in a particular group, typically a clan or a tribal section of a small village. Most Berbers belong to the Kharijite sect of Islam, which emphasizes the equality of believers to a greater extent than does the Malikite rite.

A small community of Tuareg nomads, claiming kinship to the larger Tuareg population in Algeria and elsewhere in the Sahara, are scattered in the southwestern desert of Libya. They adhere to a form of Islam that incorporates nonorthodox magical elements. In Tuareg society women enjoy a high status compared with those in other North African societies. Marriage is monogynous, and inheritance is through the female line. A few hundred Tebu also live in small isolated groups in southern Libya. Converted to Islam by the Sanusi movement, they retain some of their earlier beliefs and practices.

Ronald Bruce St. John

See Also Vol. I: *Islam, Sunnism*

Bibliography

Ayoub, Mahmoud Mustafa. *Islam and the Third Universal Theory: The Religious Thought of Muammar al-Qadhdhafi.* London: KPI Limited, 1987.

Deeb, Marius K. "Militant Islam and Its Critics: The Case of Libya." In *Islamism and Secularism in North Africa.* Edited by John Ruedy, 187–97. New York: St. Martin's Press, 1986.

Felice, Renzo de. *Jews in an Arab Land: Libya, 1835–1970.* Austin: University of Texas Press, 1985.

Goldberg, Harvey E. *Jewish Life in Muslim Libya: Rivals and Relatives.* Chicago: University of Chicago Press, 1990.

Joffé, George. "Qadhafi's Islam in Historical Perspective." In *Qadhafi's Libya, 1969–1994.* Edited by Dirk Vandewalle, 139–54. New York: St. Martin's Press, 1995.

Mason, John Paul. *Island of the Blest: Islam in a Libyan Oasis Community.* Papers in International Studies, African Series, no. 31. Athens: Ohio University Center for International Studies, 1977.

Peters, Emrys L. *The Bedouin of Cyrenaica: Studies in Personal and Corporate Power.* Cambridge: Cambridge University Press, 1990.

St. John, Ronald Bruce. *Historical Dictionary of Libya.* 3rd ed. Lanham, Md.: Scarecrow Press, 1998.

———. *Qaddafi's World Design: Libyan Foreign Policy, 1969–1987.* London: Saqi Books, 1987.

Vikor, Knut S. *Sufi and Scholar on the Desert Edge: Muhammad b. Ali al-Sanusi and His Brotherhood.* Evanston, Ill.: Northwestern University Press, 1995.

Ziadeh, Nicola A. *Sanusiyah: A Study of a Revivalist Movement in Islam.* Leiden: E.J. Brill, 1983.

Liechtenstein

POPULATION 32,842

ROMAN CATHOLIC 78 percent

PROTESTANT 8 percent

MUSLIM 5 percent

EASTERN ORTHODOX 1 percent

NOT RELIGIOUS 3 percent

OTHER OR NO ANSWER 5 percent

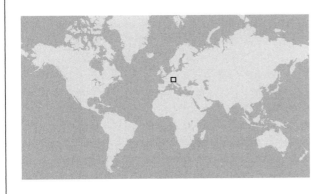

Country Overview

INTRODUCTION The Principality of Liechtenstein, a small European country located in the Rhine Valley of the Alps, is bordered by Switzerland to the west and south and Austria to the east. It has an area of just over 61 square miles, two-thirds of which is mountainous. Only one-third of the land is suitable for settlement. Foreigners, mainly Swiss, Austrians, and Germans, make up a third of the population.

The principality was founded in 1719. In 1806 Liechtenstein became a sovereign state, and in 1921 it became a constitutional monarchy governed as a parliamentary democracy. The country consists of 11 communes, which enjoy a high degree of independence. Vaduz is the capital.

Liechtenstein is overwhelmingly Roman Catholic. Church parishes form part of the political order, and officeholders of the Catholic Church are employees of the municipalities. The principal, or ruling, family is traditionally Catholic. For more than 1,500 years Liechtenstein formed part of the neighboring Diocese of Chur, now in Switzerland. The Archdiocese of Vaduz, which includes all of Liechtenstein and which is directly responsible to the Holy See in Rome, was established in 1997.

RELIGIOUS TOLERANCE The constitution of Liechtenstein establishes the Roman Catholic Church as the official state church (*Landeskirche*). It also provides for freedom of religion and conscience, and all levels of government strive to protect these rights. Catholics, Protestants, and members of other religions cooperate amicably on an ecumenical basis. All religious groups enjoy a tax-exempt status.

Major Religion

ROMAN CATHOLICISM
DATE OF ORIGIN Fifth century C.E.
NUMBER OF FOLLOWERS 25,600

HISTORY The territory of present-day Liechtenstein was Christianized during the early Middle Ages by peo-

The traditional rites of passage, including baptism, continue to be widely observed by the Roman Catholic population of Liechtenstein. © CORBIS SYGMA.

ple who came from the Roman province of Chur. Since the fifth century the Church of Saint Peter at Schaan has been a regional center of Christianity and a baptistery. Liechtenstein, not initially an autonomous church district, was instead divided into several deaneries. In the nineteenth century, when Liechtenstein became independent, it became a regional vicariate of the Diocese of Chur. Through this administrative measure the Diocese of Chur, then entirely Swiss, maintained its links to the country of Liechtenstein. During this time state and society were significantly shaped by the Catholic Church, particularly through its influence on the educational sector.

In 1971 Liechtenstein became a deanery of the Diocese of Chur. Because this administrative unit had exactly the same boundaries as the principality, it exercised a broader than usual range of tasks. Every dean, for example, maintained pastoral relations with the members of the ruling family. Further, delegates of the deanery often cooperated with political committees of Liechtenstein, especially in the areas of education and social policies. First financed by parish contributions and later also by payments from the state, the deanery was officially in charge of educational programs for adults, religious education, youth work, such relief organizations as Car-

itas and Justitia et Pax, and pastoral assistance to foreigners.

On 2 December 1997 Pope John Paul II officially established the Archdiocese of Vaduz and appointed the bishop of Chur, Wolfgang Haas, a citizen of Liechtenstein, as the archbishop. The action was taken after diplomatic efforts had failed to ease tensions in the Diocese of Chur, where Haas, a traditionalist in church matters, had encountered open opposition. The action was presented to the ecclesiastical and political institutions of Liechtenstein as a fait accompli, prompting many people to ask if international law had been violated. With the foundation of the Archdiocese of Vaduz, opponents of the appointment of Haas formed the Verein für eine Offene Kirche (Association for an Open Church), which counts approximately 1,000 people among its members.

EARLY AND MODERN LEADERS During the Middle Ages the bishops of Chur sometimes came from Liechtenstein. Among them was Lord Ortlieb von Brandis, bishop from 1458 to 1491 and a humanist and lover of art. The first regional vicar from Chur was Canon Joseph Anton Mayer (1811–26), and the last was Johannes Tschuor (1952–71). The first dean was Engelbert Bucher (1970–78), a diocesan priest from Chur. Franz Näscher, born in Liechtenstein, was dean twice, first from 1978 to 1986, but during his second term, from 1994 to 1997, the deanery was dissolved. Wolfgang Haas has headed the Archdiocese of Liechtenstein since 1997. A traditionalist, he has close ties to the conservative Catholic organization known as Opus Dei and manages religious affairs in Liechtenstein according to his own convictions. Haas has become a figure of attraction for conservative Catholics at home and abroad, particularly from the area around Lake Constance.

MAJOR THEOLOGIANS AND AUTHORS Liechtenstein has not produced any major theologians or authors.

HOUSES OF WORSHIP AND HOLY PLACES Each Roman Catholic parish in Liechtenstein has its own church, in addition to the small chapels, usually consecrated to the Virgin Mary, that stand along the roads and paths connecting the various parts of the parish. After the establishment of the archdiocese, Saint Florinus, the parish church at Vaduz, was raised to the status of a cathedral. Both the castle in Vaduz, seat of the ruling family, and the secondary school there have their own chapels. Monasteries and convents also play important roles as holy places in Liechtenstein.

WHAT IS SACRED? Roman Catholics in Liechtenstein honor a number of saints. Luzius, a missionary and martyr who spread the faith during the early period of Christianization, has been the patron saint of Liechtenstein since the late eighteenth century. Florinus, who worked as a priest during the seventh century, is the patron saint of the Cathedral of Vaduz. On 25 March 1940 Duke Franz Joseph II solemnly assigned the land and the people of Liechtenstein to the protection of Mary, the Mother of God. The Holy Virgin is the patron of the archdiocese, her day celebrated on 8 September. Nicolas von der Flüe (1417–87), the charismatic national saint of Switzerland, also is honored in Liechtenstein.

HOLIDAYS AND FESTIVALS Roman Catholics in Liechtenstein observe the common feasts of the ecclesiastical year, including Christmas, Easter, and Pentecost. In addition, the day of the Assumption of Mary (15 August), which also is observed as the birthday of the duke of Liechtenstein, is a popular festival that is deeply rooted in the cultural life of the nation. On this day the archbishop celebrates Mass in the castle at Vaduz, to which everyone in Liechtenstein is invited, and this is followed by a festival in the town.

MODE OF DRESS Official Roman Catholic ecclesiastical dress is observed by only some of Liechtenstein's clergy. Archbishop Wolfgang Haas, however, takes the dress code of the church seriously and, particularly on liturgical occasions, insists that all prescribed vestments be worn.

DIETARY PRACTICES As elsewhere, the Roman Catholic practice of abstaining from meat on Fridays and during periods such as Lent is seldom observed in Liechtenstein. The tradition is now sometimes practiced in a way that combines religion with alternative health regimes.

RITUALS Roman Catholic parishes in Liechtenstein offer a number of services on Sundays. Attendance, however, depends to a great extent on the religious orientation of the particular parish priest. Many parishioners who dislike traditionalist clergy attend services in neighboring Austria or Switzerland.

During the twentieth century a number of pilgrimages were undertaken by Roman Catholics in Liechten-

stein. These included a pilgrimage to the gravesite of Nicolas von der Flüe, Switzerland's patron saint, in 1947; a pilgrimage to Rome in 1983; and a pilgrimage of the deanery to La Sallette, a Marian sanctuary in France, in 1996. Pope John Paul II visited Liechtenstein in 1985.

RITES OF PASSAGE The traditional rites of passage, including baptism, first Communion, weddings, and funerals, continue to be widely observed by the Roman Catholic population of Liechtenstein. There are no specific local customs that influence the rituals associated with these rites. Feasts are celebrated in much the same way as in other countries of the Alps, particularly Switzerland and Austria.

MEMBERSHIP Wolfgang Haas, archbishop of Vaduz, has understood missionary work in terms of Pope John Paul II's "New Evangelization," which encouraged newer and more effective ways of reaching secular culture. Because of its close connection with the Vatican, the archdiocese became known beyond the boundaries of Liechtenstein as a center of conservative Roman Catholicism. More traditional missionary work, by both men and women from Liechtenstein, is carried out particularly in Africa and Latin America.

SOCIAL JUSTICE The Roman Catholic Church in Liechtenstein has traditionally promoted social justice, mainly from an international perspective. In 2000 Archbishop Wolfgang Haas established a local relief organization, the Kirchliche Stiftung Katholisches Fastenopfer Erzbistum Vaduz (Archdiocese of Vaduz Church Foundation for Lenten Offerings). In response, other Catholics in Liechtenstein have maintained an alternative relief organization, Das andere Fastenopfer (Other Sacrifice of Lent), which cooperates with its Swiss counterpart, Fastenopfer.

SOCIAL ASPECTS As in many European countries, there is a clear split among Roman Catholics in Liechtenstein between church teachings on the one hand and everyday practices on the other. This is particularly the case in marriage and family life, including divorce, birth control, and the raising of children.

POLITICAL IMPACT As the official state church, Roman Catholicism has always held considerable political influence in Liechtenstein. This was particularly apparent during the nineteenth century, when the church put its stamp on the Liechtenstein educational system, partly through the establishment of Catholic schools. Today, however, both the political and religious leadership of Liechtenstein favor the separation of church and state.

CONTROVERSIAL ISSUES In ethical questions, including controversial issues such as birth control, abortion, divorce, and the role of women in the Roman Catholic Church, Archbishop Wolfgang Haas strictly represents the official viewpoint of the Vatican. This has produced serious tensions between church officials and more progressive church members, who clearly form a majority among Catholics in Liechtenstein.

CULTURAL IMPACT In Liechtenstein the cultural influence of the Roman Catholic Church is seen most clearly in its religious influence over the Catholic part of the population. In the area of architecture, historical and modern church buildings dominate the appearance of all municipalities.

The establishment of the Archdiocese of Vaduz deepened the cultural and religious split within the population of Liechtenstein. About one-fifth of Catholics support Archbishop Wolfgang Haas, while a large majority favors a more liberal church. This has become particularly clear in the area of education, where older students, from the 10th grade and up, and their parents have largely rejected the official religious educational programs offered by the church, preferring instead the course "Ethics and Religious Studies" offered by the state.

Other Religions

The Reformation never took hold in Liechtenstein, and Protestants have been a part of the population only since the late nineteenth century, when they arrived as immigrant laborers. The Protestant Church, which has legal standing as an organized religion, is financed through voluntary contributions from members. For Protestants the worship service is at the center of parish life. The church attends to ecclesiastical matters through such rites of passage as baptisms, weddings, and funerals, which continue to be important in member's lives. The small Orthodox Church receives pastoral assistance from Switzerland, with services offered several times during the year.

The Islamic community in Liechtenstein regularly offers religious services. Followers of the Bahai faith meet regularly for public prayers and educational seminars, and Bahais celebrate feast days in private homes and at public places. Zen meditation has a following in Liechtenstein.

Michael Krüggeler

See Also Vol. 1: *Roman Catholicism*

Bibliography

Biedermann, Klaus. *Das Dekanat Liechtenstein 1970 bis 1997: Chronik des kirchlichen Lebens.* Vaduz: Schalun Verlag, 2000.

Kranz, Walter, ed. *The Principality of Liechtenstein: A Documentary Handbook.* 5th rev. and enl. ed. Translated by J.A. Nicholls. Vaduz: Press and Information Office of the Government of the Principality of Liechtenstein, 1981.

Wille, Herbert, and Georges Baur, eds. *Staat und Kirche: Grundsätzliche und aktuelle Probleme.* Vaduz: Verlag der Liechtensteinischen Akademischen Gesellschaft, 1999.

Lithuania

POPULATION 3,601,138

ROMAN CATHOLIC 72.6 percent

ORTHODOX CHRISTIAN 6.5 percent

PROTESTANT 1.6 percent

MUSLIM 0.1 percent

JEWISH 0.1 percent

ETHNORELIGIOUS 0.1 percent

UNAFFILIATED 19 percent

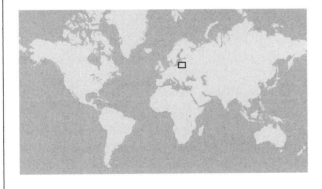

Country Overview

INTRODUCTION The Republic of Lithuania, a small country with an area of 25,000 square miles, is located on the Baltic Sea. From 1940 to 1990 it was one of 15 republics of the Soviet Union. Lithuanians and Poles make up 83 and 7 percent, respectively, of the country's population, and both profess Roman Catholicism. For several centuries Lithuania and Poland were united as one kingdom, and it was Jogaila, grand duke of Lithuania, who agreed in 1385 to submit his nation to Catho-

lic baptism when he accepted the crown of Poland. The Catholic Church subsequently became by far the largest and most influential religious organization in Lithuania.

RELIGIOUS TOLERANCE Lithuania does not have a state religion. The constitution guarantees freedom of conscience, and there are amicable relations between the various faiths. The constitution and the Law on Religious Communities give special status, however, to nine religious groups: Roman Catholic, Greek Catholic, Russian Orthodox, Orthodox Old Believers, Evangelical Lutheran, Evangelical Reformed, Jewish, Sunni Islam, and Karaite. These so-called traditional religions are eligible for governmental financial assistance and enjoy privileges such as tax exemptions, permission to teach religion in public schools, and time on national television.

Major Religion

ROMAN CATHOLICISM

DATE OF ORIGIN 1387 C.E.
NUMBER OF FOLLOWERS 2.6 million

HISTORY Roman Catholicism in Lithuania began with the baptism in 1251 of Mindagas, the first ruler of a united Lithuania, and the legal acts of Grand Duke Jogaila that made Christianity the established church in 1387. During the Reformation, Protestantism was initially successful, especially among the nobility, but because of the missionary and academic activities of Jesu-

Pope John Paul II leads a procession through the so-called Hill of Crosses. The site, near the town of Šiauliai, is covered with approximately 60,000 crosses that have been stuck into the ground by pilgrims as expressions of faith, love, and sacrifice. © REUTERS NEWMEDIA INC./CORBIS.

its, it failed to put down lasting roots, and the Catholic Church had secured its prevailing position by the end of the sixteenth century. The constitution of 1791 declared Catholicism to be the dominant religion, and Catholics were prohibited from converting to another faith.

After the partition of the Polish-Lithuanian state in 1795, the Russian Empire annexed most of Lithuania. Until World War I the Catholic Church played a significant role in the Lithuanian independence movement, including unsuccessful uprisings in 1831 and 1863, and in preserving national identity.

Lithuania was an independent state from 1918 to 1940, and a concordat was signed with the Vatican in 1927. This was canceled, however, following Soviet occupation in 1940. The rights of churches as legal entities were rescinded, religious education was banned in schools, and pastoral care in hospitals and prisons was abolished. During the Soviet era the Catholic Church again became a symbol of underground resistance. In 1987 the 600th anniversary of Lithuania's baptism was observed in Rome simultaneously with celebrations in Vilnius, although the latter were strictly censored by Soviet authorities. In 2002 three agreements were signed between the Vatican and the Lithuanian state, symbolizing the importance of the Catholic Church in independent Lithuania.

EARLY AND MODERN LEADERS Saint Casimir (Kazimierz; 1458–84) is the only Lithuanian to have been canonized. He was the son of Casimir IV (1427–92), the Grand Duke of Lithuania and King of Poland, in whose reign the Church flourished. Saint Casimir is considered the patron saint of Lithuania and is respected for his exemplary chastity and piety.

The outstanding twentieth-century Catholic leader was Archbishop Jurgis Matulaitis (1871–1927). He is honored for his efforts in charity and social justice, for the reviving of the monastic Marian order in Marijampolė, for the administration of the Vilnius diocese during the tumultuous period from 1918 to 1925, and for the preparation of the first Lithuanian concordat. Matulaitis was beatified by Pope John Paul II in 1987.

MAJOR THEOLOGIANS AND AUTHORS The Jesuit order played a distinctive role in the development of academic and theological studies in Lithuania. In 1570 the Jesuits established a college in Vilnius that later became a university. It was influential throughout the Baltic region and beyond, as far east as Moscow.

The writings of Archbishop Jurgis Matulaitis are widely known. His book *Uzrasai* consists of reflections and inspirations, reports on visits to Rome, and recollections of major events from his years as bishop of Vilnius. While not strictly theological in its content, *Uzrasai* is honored as a source of spiritual education.

HOUSES OF WORSHIP AND HOLY PLACES In Lithuania, as in other Catholic countries, the primary place of worship is the local parish church, which is dedicated to a specific saint. The cult of the Virgin Mary is especially widespread among Lithuanians. One of the oldest shrines to Mary is the image of Our Lady of Trakai, which is venerated as a protector of Lithuania. The tomb in Marijampolė containing the relics of Jurgis Matulaitis is also venerated.

The 19 small chapels located on the hills surrounding the town of Žemaiciu Kalvarija (Samogitian Calvary) are called the Stations of the Crosses. Believers go to Žemaiciu Kalvarija to retrace Jesu's path to Calavary, climbing from one hill to another and singing songs called "The Hills of Žemaiciu Kalvarija." The places for the chapels are chosen and the steps are counted so that there is correspondence with the original path of Christ's sufferings in Jerusalem.

WHAT IS SACRED? In addition to those objects venerated by Christians generally, there are sacred items particularly identified with Lithuania. These include wayside crosses, chapels, and religious statues, which are prevalent throughout the landscape. Lithuania has become known as the "Country of Crosses." The so-called Hill of Crosses, a unique site near the town of Šiauliai, is covered with approximately 60,000 crosses that have been stuck into the ground by pilgrims as expressions of faith, love, and sacrifice.

HOLIDAYS AND FESTIVALS Of 12 national holidays in Lithuania, 5 are religious festivals. These are Saint Mary's Day (January 1), Easter Monday, Assumption Day (August 15), All Saint's Day (November 1), and Christmas (December 24–25).

Christmas Eve is the most popular festival in Lithuania and is considered even more important than Christmas Day itself. The Catholic Church has abolished the requirement of fasting, but Lithuanians still follow the custom, abstaining from meat on Christmas Eve. The house is cleaned, bed linens changed, and a handful of hay spread on the table as a reminder that Jesus was born in a stable. On this day all family members must be home for a special meatless supper called *kûeias*. Afterward, the adults attend a midnight Mass, which is called *berneli mioios* (shepherd's Mass).

Catholic traditions are still frequently fused with pre-Christian customs in Lithuania. The feast of Saint John in late June, for example, is celebrated with bonfires, play on swings and seesaws, and dances, manifestations of an ancient midsummer festival. Assumption Day is also known as the celebration of meadow grass. Even Easter, the most important annual church event, includes many elements of folk tradition that symbolize the rebirth of nature after winter.

MODE OF DRESS In contemporary Lithuania people wear mainly Western-style clothing. There is no special dress associated with church attendance or church festivals, and there are no differences between the clothing of the Catholic clergy in Lithuania and those in other countries.

DIETARY PRACTICES *Kûeias*, the traditional meatless supper on Christmas Eve, is still observed in Lithuania. It begins with the passing of wafers and with wishes for each family member. To represent the 12 apostles, 12 different dishes are normally served. The principal dish traditionally was *kucia*, a porridge made of wheat, barley, and oats and eaten with poppy seed milk. Other choices may include fish (pike or herring), a compote of dried fruits, a salad of pickled vegetables, beet soup with dried mushrooms, oatmeal pudding with sweetened water, potato pancakes, *sližikai* (biscuits served with poppy seed milk), and thick, sour *kisielius* (cranberry jelly). It is essential for a person to taste everything since it is believed that whoever skips any dish will not survive until the next Christmas Eve.

RITUALS The tradition of pilgrimages to sacred places remains very much alive in Lithuania. In addition, many churches have special wall panels covered with silver or gold hearts on which names have been inscribed. People bring the hearts as an expression of thanks to Jesus or the Virgin Mary for healing, rescuing, and other blessings.

Death and burial are important in Lithuanian religious culture. Cemeteries are peaceful places situated on hills and covered with trees. In Lithuanian folklore the term *high hill* is synonymous with the word *cemetery*. The dead are dressed in their best clothes, and religious articles such as rosaries and pictures of saints are placed inside the coffin. Three handfuls of earth are poured over the coffin as a reminder that people come from dust and return to dust. Inviting everyone from the cemetery to a funeral dinner is seen as a way of carrying out the last wishes of the dead person.

All Soul's Day (November 2) is celebrated throughout Lithuania. Both believers and nonbelievers visit family grave sites to decorate them with flowers and candles, and requiem Masses are held in churches.

RITES OF PASSAGE The first Holy Communion is an obligatory Catholic sacrament that is usually observed in Lithuania shortly after the seventh birthday. The sacrament of Confirmation represents the conveying of the Holy Spirit to those who have already undergone baptism and hence symbolizes the entering of a new stage of life.

MEMBERSHIP In general, the traditional notion of membership in the Catholic Church includes an affiliation with a particular parish, regular attendance at Mass, and certain financial contributions to the church. In Lithuania, however, 50 years of atheistic policy under the Soviet regime challenged this sense of belonging. Although most Lithuanians are Catholics by birth and by cultural identification, only 10 percent attend services weekly.

The Catholic Church generally does not proselytize in Lithuania. The most important Catholic mass media are the monthly publication *Sandora* (Covenant) and the daily radio program *Mazoji Studija* (Small Studio).

SOCIAL JUSTICE Generosity to people in need is a general teaching of the Catholic Church, a doctrine of social justice that has been a tradition for the past century. Under the Soviet regime, however, the church in Lithuania was forced to refrain from charitable and other social activities. Today the major Catholic charity organi-

zation is Caritas, which is subordinated to the Lithuanian Catholic Bishop's Conference. Its programs focus on such matters as the reduction of poverty, the strengthening of the family and community, and education. The Malta order and the Lithuanian Community of Samaritans, known for ecumenical cooperation in charity activities, offer relief services, and monastic orders such as the Salesians, Congregation of Saint John, and Sisters of Mother Theresa work in various social areas.

SOCIAL ASPECTS Before World War II various Catholic lay organizations had about a million members, a third of Lithuania's population. From 1940 to 1990, however, the Communist authorities implemented policies that isolated the Catholic clergy from believers, and a result was the loss of a sense of social community within the church. The formation of lay movements, as well as the fostering of the Catholic Church's role within society, has been among the highest priorities in independent Lithuania. Youth and family centers have been established in all Catholic dioceses, and the organization Actio Catholica Patria aims to involve those young people without an interest in religion itself in various church-sponsored educational and charity projects.

The implementation of decisions of Vatican II, which dealt with the modern policies of the Catholic Church on various social issues, was belated in Lithuania because of the Soviet occupation. Hence, Lithuanian Catholics demonstrate more conservative attitudes on questions such as marriage, family, and the role of women than do their counterparts in western Europe or in North America.

POLITICAL IMPACT Under Communism active participation in lay Catholic activities was seen as an expression of political rebellion in Lithuania, and the movement Eucharistijos Bièiuliai (Friends of Eucharist) became a unique underground Catholic association. In contemporary Lithuania, despite the constitutional separation of church and state, Roman Catholicism is a de facto part of politics and society. The Catholic Church is the only religious organization whose relations with the state are regulated by official agreements. The subjects of the concordats signed in 2002 are the juridical aspects of the relation between the church and the state, cooperation in education and culture, and the pastoral care of Catholics serving in the army. Only the Catholic Church has ordinaries in the Lithuanian army. Further, a person designated by the Catholic Church occupies the position of government adviser for religious affairs.

CONTROVERSIAL ISSUES A controversial issue in Lithuania is the relationship between church and civil marriages. According to the constitution, both are valid, but there is no legal provision for divorce in the case of those church marriages that have not been registered by the state, and from the viewpoint of Catholic canon law the state cannot terminate church marriages.

CULTURAL IMPACT Catholicism has had a significant impact on Lithuanian sculpture and painting, which are closely connected with church architecture. The Petrus and Paulus Cathedral in Vilnius is recognized as an outstanding example of the harmony of architecture with the arts of sculpture and painting. Of the country's various folk arts, wooden sculpture, which often depicts biblical personalities and themes, has been particularly influenced by Catholicism.

Other Religions

Some Lithuanian religious groups are mainly ethnically based. Orthodox Christianity is represented by the Russian Orthodox Church and the Old Believers. Members of the Old Believers, a dissident branch of Russian Orthodoxy that did not accept the church reforms introduced by Patriarch Nikon in 1666, fled Russia and thus are concentrated in the east, particularly along the border with Belarus. Although most Orthodox Christians in Lithuania are Russians and Belarusans, there also are some Orthodox Ukrainians.

Lithuanian nobles, returning from study in Germany, brought Protestantism to Lithuania in the 1520s. In 1564, Sigismund II Augustus, the king of Poland and Lithuania, began implementing the decisions of the Council of Trent (1545–63), which aimed to reform the Catholic Church and thereby stop the spread of Protestantism. In contemporary Lithuania, Protestantism is represented by various denominations. The largest are the Lutheran Church, with some 30,000 members, and the smaller Evangelical Reformed Church.

The Jewish community was nearly destroyed by the Holocaust in the 1940s, when some 200,000 Lithuanian Jews were killed. Whereas 10 percent of the population was Jewish before World War II, only about 5,000 Jews live in Lithuania today. The small Islamic community members consists of Tatars, who have had a presence in Lithuania since the fifteenth century, and Uzbeks and Azerbaijanis, who immigrated in the twentieth century. The Karaites, a unique ethnoreligious group of only a few hundred members, have been in the country since 1397. They speak a Turkic-based language but use the Hebrew alphabet, and their religion, which is based on the Old Testament, is considered by some to be a branch of Judaism. A religious group unique to Lithuania are the neopagans known as Romuva.

Alexei Krindatch

See Also Vol. 1: *Christianity, Roman Catholicism, Russian Orthodoxy*

Bibliography

Balodis, Ringolds. *State and Church in the Baltic States.* Riga: Latvian Association for Freedom of Religion, 2001.

Glodenis, Donatas, and Lahayne Holger, eds. *Religijos Lietuvoje.* Šiauliai: Nova Vita, 1999.

Rimaitis, J. *Religion in Lithuania.* Vilnius: Gintaras, 1971.

Suziedelis, S. *The Sword and the Cross: A History of the Church in Lithuania.* Huntington, Ind.: Our Sunday Visitor, 1988.

Tishkov, V. *Narody i Religii Mira: Enzyclopedia.* Moscow: Bolshaja Rossijskaja Encyclopedia, 1998.

Luxembourg

POPULATION 448,569

ROMAN CATHOLIC 65.9 percent

PROTESTANT 1.2 percent

JEHOVAH'S WITNESS 0.8 percent

MUSLIM 0.7 percent

JEWISH 0.5 percent

ORTHODOX CHRISTIAN 0.5 percent

OTHER 0.9 percent

NONRELIGIOUS 29.5 percent

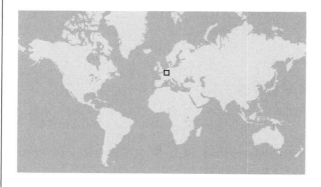

Country Overview

INTRODUCTION The Grand Duchy of Luxembourg, covering just 998 square miles (2,586 square kilometers), is situated between France, Belgium, and Germany. Before the Roman conquest (58–50 B.C.E.) under Julius Caesar, the area was inhabited by a Celtic tribe, the Treveri, who practiced a polytheist Celtic faith. After the conquest this faith evolved into a Gallo-Roman religion. The Titelberg Mountain near Rodange was the main *oppidum* (political, religious, and industrial center) of the Treveri. Beginning in the third century C.E. Christianity progressively supplanted the Gallo-Roman religion. An invasion of German tribes two centuries later brought extensive political and cultural changes.

The Spanish Habsburgs ruled Luxembourg from 1506 to 1684, and the Austrian Habsburgs ruled from 1698 to 1795. During this time Roman Catholicism became a state religion. With the French occupation beginning in 1795, a slow process of secularization began. In 1815, after the defeat of Napoleon, Luxembourg became a grand duchy, initially in union with the kingdom of The Netherlands. As part of a greater rebellion against The Netherlands, Luxembourg lost its western portion to Belgium in 1830. European powers granted Luxembourg independence in 1867. The current ruling family was established in 1890, when William III of The Netherlands died and the duchy was passed to Adolf, duke of Nassau.

By the 1970s the pace of secularization had increased, but Catholicism remained deeply rooted in the culture of Luxembourg. Even today, though religious practices have lessened among the youth, Catholicism continues to be the dominant religion, principally among older generations and the Portuguese community.

RELIGIOUS TOLERANCE Freedom of religion is enshrined in the constitution of Luxembourg. Although Catholicism is not a state religion, it permeates much of the national culture. The various other faith communities in the country, including Protestant, Jewish, Orthodox Christian, and Muslim, coexist amid a secular climate of tolerance and respect.

Major Religion

ROMAN CATHOLICISM

DATE OF ORIGIN Second century C.E.
NUMBER OF FOLLOWERS 296,000

HISTORY Christianity first arrived in Luxembourg in the second and third centuries from the episcopal cities of Metz (France) and Trier (Germany); however, its real expansion began with the conversion of Clovis, a Frank king (reigned 481–511), to Christianity. The abbeys of Echternach and Saint Maximinus in Trier, built in 698 and 633, respectively, became major spiritual centers of the area. Under the successors of Charlemagne (emperor of the Holy Roman Empire, 800–814), Luxembourg became a part of the kingdom of Lorraine in the ninth century in what is now northeastern France.

Beginning in the early sixteenth century the duchy of Luxembourg was ruled first by the Spanish Habsburgs (1506–1684) and then by the Austrian Habsburgs (1698–1795). Both the Spanish and Austrian Habsburgs introduced a number of measures opposing the Protestant Reformation, including the establishment of popular Jesuit missionaries. The duchy of Luxembourg was occupied by France from 1684 to 1698 during the reign of Louis XIV. Beginning in 1795, France's revolutionary troops occupied the country and led the first phase of secularization in Luxembourg, mainly by selling off the goods of monasteries.

In 1815, after the defeat of Napoleon, Luxembourg became a grand duchy and was given as a possession to William I, king of the Netherlands. In 1870 Luxembourg became an autonomous diocese of the Catholic Church, whose boundaries matched those of the state. During World War II Nazi Germany annexed Luxembourg. This period of suffering contributed to Luxembourgers regaining a strong sense of Catholicism, particularly devotion to the Virgin Mary. Luxembourg became an archdiocese of the Catholic Church in 1988.

EARLY AND MODERN LEADERS Saint Willibrord (658?–739) founded the Echternach Abbey in 698 and led the first important mission in the territory of the present Grand Duchy of Luxembourg. Several leaders

Members of the Luxembourger royalty are greeted by a Catholic priest. Although Catholicism is not a state religion, it permeates much of the national culture. © REUTER RAYMOND/CORBIS SYGMA.

of that abbey distinguished themselves as historians and opponents of the witch hunts.

MAJOR THEOLOGIANS AND AUTHORS Significant Luxembourgish authors include Johannes Bertels (1595–1607), an abbot of the Echeternach Abbey, who wrote the first history of Luxembourg, *Historia Luxemburgensis.* Antonius Hovaeus (died in 1568), also an abbott at Echeternach, opposed witch trials; his works include *De arte amandi deum* and *De temporis nostri statu ac conditione.* Abbott André Heiderscheid wrote *Aspects de Sociologie Religieuse du Diocèse de Luxembourg,* a study published in two volumes in 1961 and 1962.

HOUSES OF WORSHIP AND HOLY PLACES Veneration of the Virgin Mary appeared in Luxembourg in the Middle Ages. The altar in the crypt of what is now Saint Michael's Church (in the city of Luxembourg) was dedicated to Mary the Mother of God in 987. The Gothic cathedral Our Lady of Luxembourg in Luxembourg city was completed in 1621. The cathedral, which houses the statue of Mary as Comforter of the Afflicted, has been a pilgrimage site since the early seventeenth century. Veneration of Mary is linked to Marian shrines and statues throughout Luxembourg.

WHAT IS SACRED? The worship of saints has been and continues to be important in Luxembourg. Many saints undoubtedly replaced pre-Christian gods, as is the case with Saint Donat, the patron saint of thunderstorms, and Saint Martin, the patron saint of winter. Sacred trees and Celtic springs, such as Saint Mary's trees or Saint Willibrord's and Saint Martin's springs, continue to be venerated. Luxembourg's most sacred statue—of Mary as Comforter of the Afflicted—is found in the cathedral Our Lady of Luxembourg. Under the Nazi regime, when hymns to the Virgin Mary were banned, the veneration of Mary became an important aspect of Luxembourg's identity.

HOLIDAYS AND FESTIVALS The calendar in Luxembourg is punctuated with Christian feasts, and public and school holidays are largely based on the liturgical year. Traditionally each village celebrates the feast of the local church's patron saint (*kermesse*). A number of feast days have retained their importance in Luxembourg, despite having lost their strictly religious significance. For example, on the Feast of the Three Kings (6 January), the day of the Epiphany, people eat a Three King's cake that contains a bean, and the one who finds the bean is king for a day.

MODE OF DRESS Luxembourgers dress in typical European style. Civilian dress, possibly with a small cross, has generally replaced the cassock and even the clerical collar among Catholic diocesan priests.

DIETARY PRACTICES Religious dietary practices have become rare. Among a rapidly diminishing minority, adherents fast and abstain from eating meat during Lent (*Carême*) and on Good Friday.

RITUALS The annual bonfire Buergbrennen, which is based on pre-Christian rituals, is held on the first Lenten Sunday after Ash Wednesday. On Ash Wednesday itself adherents receive an ashen cross on their foreheads as a sign of human mortality. On Palm Sunday the priest dedicates palm fronds made of boxwood, which are hung up in people's homes for protection.

The Octave, a pilgrimage to Our Lady of Luxembourg in Luxembourg city, has been practiced since the early seventeenth century, when the people of Luxembourg gave Mary the title of Comforter of the Afflicted. Luxembourgers from villages all around the country have regularly gone on a pilgrimage to the statue of the Virgin Mary. The Octave, which lasts two weeks from the third to the fifth Sunday of Easter, ends with a major closing procession through the city center.

The Sprangprocessioun, an ancient pilgrimage in honor of Saint Willibrord that dates back to 1497, is held on Pentecost Tuesday in Echternach. Pilgrims process through the town toward the basilica where Saint Willibrord's tomb is located.

RITES OF PASSAGE Catholic rites of passage, including baptism, first Communion, marriage, and funeral services, are still important in Luxembourg despite a significant drop in weekly church attendance.

MEMBERSHIP In Luxembourg people are socialized as Catholics through transmission of the faith within families and through catechism organized by the church and incorporated in the public school curriculum. The Catholic Church seeks to remain as present as possible in civil society and in the country's culture. To this end it makes use of modern media, including the press, Internet, television, and radio.

SOCIAL JUSTICE The Catholic Church in Luxembourg plays a significant role in the field of justice and social works, both through its public statements and through the social services it offers to the public.

SOCIAL ASPECTS The teachings of the Catholic Church on family life and marriage, though still in force in Luxembourg, are increasingly disregarded by the country's Catholic population. Individualism and modern and secular views on family and sexual morals have gradually supplanted the church's official and traditional doctrines.

POLITICAL IMPACT The history of Luxembourg has from its origins been marked by close relations between the Catholic Church and the state. The clergy has been influential among political leaders, although this influence began to diminish after World War II. There are still strong political links between the church and state, especially through the Christian trade union and the Christian Social Party, which has taken part in all but one of the governments since World War II.

CONTROVERSIAL ISSUES Controversial issues within the Catholic Church in Luxembourg include the status of women in the church, divorce, marriage of priests, and democratization of church organizational structures. In addition, the funding of churches by the state is increasingly being called into question by a majority of the population.

CULTURAL IMPACT Christian art in Luxembourg dates back to the writing school of the imperial abbey at Echternach. It was here in the scriptorium that the country's most famous artifact, the Luxembourg Gospels, or Codex Aureus, was created in 1030. The Luxembourg Gospels are now located in the Germanic National Museum in Nuremberg, Germany.

Other Religions

In Luxembourg religious groups other than the Catholic community are very small, each having scarcely more than 1,000 members.

The Protestant community was established following the Congress of Vienna (1815), which gave Luxembourg to the king of the Netherlands but also placed it within the German Confederation, leading to a Prussian (and thus Protestant) garrison in the city of Luxembourg. The first sovereigns of the Grand Duchy of Luxembourg (1815–1908) were Protestants. The number of Protestants increased somewhat with the arrival of immigrant workers and technicians in the steel industry at the end of the nineteenth century. Protestantism was officially recognized by the state in 1894. Lutherans and Calvinists are the largest Protestant groups in Luxembourg.

Jews have lived in Luxembourg at least as far back as the thirteenth century. Until the area came under French rule in 1795, the Jewish presence remained marginal and limited to a few families. In the Napoleonic period (1799–1815) Jews acquired civic rights, and their community expanded. The period between the First and Second World Wars saw a large influx of Jews who had fled eastern Europe and neighboring regions incorporated by Germany. The annexation of the Grand Duchy of Luxembourg by Nazi Germany marked the beginning of a dark period for Luxembourg's Jewish community. From 1940 to 1945 one-third of Luxembourg's Jewish population fled or was killed.

A few small Islamic groups were established in Luxembourg in the 1960s and 1970s. Luxembourg's Islamic community first began to organize itself in the early 1980s. By the early 1990s the Islamic community was predominantly made up of Bosnian and Montenegrin refugees from the former Federal Republic of Yugoslavia. At the start of the twenty-first century, Islam had not been granted recognition as an official religion by the Luxembourg state.

Jehovah's Witnesses have been present in the country since the 1930s. Their 32 assemblies have Kingdom Halls in all regions of Luxembourg.

Aloyse Estgen, Paul Estgen, Michel Legrand

See Also Vol. 1: *Roman Catholicism*

Bibliography

Barteau, Harry C. *Historical Dictionary of Luxembourg.* Lanham, Md.: Scarecrow Press, 1996.

Legrand, M., ed. *Les valeurs au Luxembourg: Portrait d'une société au tournant du 3e millénaire.* Luxembourg: Editions St-Paul, 2002.

Newcomer, James. *The Grand Duchy of Luxembourg: The Evolution of Nationhood, 963 A.D. to 1983.* Lanham, Md.: University Press of America, 1984.

———. *The Nationhood of Luxembourg: Eight Essays on the Grand Duchy.* Echternach, Luxembourg: Editions Phi, Centre National de Littérature, 1998.

Polfer, Michel, ed. *L'Evangélisation des régions entre Meuse et Moselle et la fondation de l'abbaye d'Echternach (Ve–IXe siècle).* Luxembourg: Imprimerie Linden, 2000.

Trausch, Gilbert. "L'Eglise et la nation au Luxembourg de 1839 à 1989: Relations complexes en pays catholique." *Nos Cahiers Luxembourg* (December 1991): 61–75.

———, ed. *Histoire du Luxembourg: Le destin européen d'un petit pays.* Toulouse: Edition Privat, 2002.

Index

3HO. *See* Sikh Dharma movement
The 180 Precepts of Lord Lao, **1**:531, 543

A

à Kempis, Thomas, **1**:114, **3**:129
Aaronistas. *See* Light of the World
 Church
Abbas. *See* Abdul-Baha
Abbas, Ferhat, **2**:14, 16
Abbasid dynasty, **1**:357, **2**:505, 507,
 511
Abbeys, Taoist, **1**:539–540
ABCFM (American Board of Christian
 Foreign Missions), **2**:571, 572, **3**:115
Abdel Qadir, **2**:14
Abdirrahman Abdullah, **3**:347
Abduh, Muhammad, **1**:364–365, 394,
 2:320
Abdul Aziz ibn Saud, King, **3**:295, 297
Abdul-Baha, **1**:23, 26–27, 28
 Bahai doctrine and, **1**:31, 32
 on Bahai prayers, **1**:40
 on controversial issues, **1**:43–44
 on dietary practices, **1**:40
 Guardians and, **1**:29
 holidays and festivals, **1**:39
 holy places and, **1**:38, 45
 literature and, **1**:36
 pictures of, **1**:35
 sacred books and symbols, **1**:30, 35,
  39
 on social justice, **1**:42
 on Universal House of Justice, **1**:38
Abdullah, Muhammad ibn. *See*
 Muhammad, Prophet
Abhidhamma Day, **1**:66
Abhidhamma Pitaka, **1**:61
Abhidharma, **1**:53, 66
Abhinavagupta, **1**:334, 337, 338
Abhyagiriya order, **3**:375
Abimbola, Wande, **1**:13
Abiodun, Joseph, **3**:154
Ablutions (Islam), **1**:*354*, 361, 372

Aboriginal cultures
 Australia, **2**:*46*, 47, 52
 El Salvador, **2**:325, 326
Abortion
 Angola, **2**:25
 Argentina, **2**:38
 Bahai faith, **1**:43
 Baptist tradition, **1**:152
 Buddhism, **1**:71, 91, 98
 Central African Republic, **2**:203
 China, **2**:227
 Church of Jesus Christ of Latter-day
  Saints, **1**:159
 Côte d'Ivoire, **2**:255
 Croatia, **2**:262
 Equatorial Guinea, **2**:334
 Ethiopia, **2**:254
 Evangelicalism, **1**:188
 Germany, **2**:402–403
 Hinduism, **1**:328
 Islam, **1**:377, 388, 396
 Jainism, **1**:418
 Judaism, **1**:451
 Lutheranism, **1**:202
 Palau, **3**:190
 Pentecostalism, **1**:218
 Reform Judaism, **1**:474
 Roman Catholicism, **1**:249
 Saint Lucia, **3**:277
 Shiism, **1**:388
 Sikhism, **1**:517
 Slovakia, **3**:334
 South Korea, **3**:362, 365
 Sunnism, **1**:396
 Taiwan, **3**:428
 Uruguay, **3**:539
 Zimbabwe, **3**:588
Aboudja, **2**:456, 458
Abraham ben David of Posquieres,
 1:442
Abraham (Biblical figure), **2**:549, *550*,
 3:543
 Judaism and, **1**:423–424, 434
 Muslims and, **1**:350, 352, 372
Abravanel, Isaac, **1**:431

Abstinence and fasting
 Afghanistan, **2**:4
 Albania, **2**:9
 Andorra, **2**:20
 Angola, **2**:24
 Bahai faith, **1**:39–40
 Bahamas, **2**:66
 Barbados, **2**:82
 Belarus, **2**:87
 Bhutan, **2**:111
 Bosnia and Herzegovina, **2**:123–124,
  126
 Botswana, **2**:131, 134
 Brazil, **2**:143
 Brunei, **2**:145, 147
 Burkina Faso, **2**:157, 160
 Burundi, **2**:165
 Cambodia, **2**:170–171
 Cameroon, **2**:176, 178, 181
 Canada, **2**:186, 190
 Cape Verde, **2**:196
 Chad, **2**:207, 209, 211
 China, **2**:222, 226, 230, 233
 Christianity, **1**:122, 123–124
 Comoros, **2**:244
 Coptic Christianity, **1**:164
 Costa Rica, **2**:248
 Côte d'Ivoire, **2**:253, 256
 Croatia, **2**:261
 Czech Republic, **2**:276
 Democratic Republic of the Congo,
  2:284, 286
 Dominica, **2**:301
 East Timor, **2**:310
 Eastern Catholicism, **1**:170
 Eastern Orthodoxy, **1**:179–180
 Egypt, **2**:321, 323–324
 Equatorial Guinea, **2**:333
 Eritrea, **2**:339, 341, 342
 Ethiopia, **2**:353, 355
 fasting to death ritual, **1**:415–416,
  419
 Fiji, **2**:364
 France, **2**:376
 Gabon, **2**:383, 384

Germany, **2:**398–399, 403
Iraq, **2:**512
Libya, **2:**618–619
Luxembourg, **2:**635
Morocco, **3:**87
Switzerland, **3:**411, 416
United States, **3:**519, 534
Uzbekistan, **3:**541
Antigua and Barbuda, **2:***30,* **30–33**
Antinomianism, doctrine of, **I:**254
Antioch, John of. *See* Chrysostom, John, Saint
Antioch IV, Ignatius of, **I:**178
Antiochian Orthodox Christian Archdiocese, **I:**176
Antiochus IV Epiphanes, **I:**436
Antony of Egypt, **I:**177
Anuvrat movement, **I:**411
Anuyogas, **I:**410
Anzimba, **3:**240, 247
Apartheid, South Africa, **3:**350, 351, 352, 354, 355, 356
Apocrypha, **I:**116, 177, 439
    Protestantism and, **I:**222
    Roman Catholicism and, **I:**246
Apologetics
    Confucian, **I:**280
    Evangelicalism and, **I:**186
Apostasy, Jehovah's Witnesses and, **I:**193
Apostle to the Gentiles. *See* Paul
Apostle's Creed, **I:**111, 141, 244
Apostolic Church
    Lesotho, **2:**605
    New Zealand, **3:**135
    Nigeria, **3:**153, 155
    Slovakia, **3:**335
    Zimbabwe, **3:**586, 587, 588
Apostolic lineage
    Buddhism and, **I:**537–538
    Taoism and, **I:**537
Apostolic Pentecostals. *See* Oneness Pentecostals
Apostolic sees (Christianity), **I:**105
Aptidon, Hassan Gouled, **2:**296
Aquinas, Thomas, Saint, **I:**114, 119, 121, 246, **2:**528, 529
    moral code of conduct and, **I:**245
    on sacraments, **I:**124
Aquino, Benigno S. Jr., **3:**218
Arabesque, **I:**378
Arabia
    Islam in, **I:**353–357
    pre-Islamic, **I:**352–353
Arabic language
    Eritrea and, **2:**339, 340
    Guinea and, **2:**437–438
Arabs
    Algeria and, **2:**13

Djibouti and, **2:**295, 296
Israel and, **2:**519, 523, 524, 525
Aranyakas, **I:**302
Aräpasu, Teoctist, **3:***250,* 251
Arce Martínez, Sergio, **2:**268
Arceo, Sergio Méndez, **3:**62
Archbishop of Canterbury, **I:**139, 142–143
Archepiscopacies, major, **I:**169
Architecture
    Algeria, **2:**16
    Andorra, **2:**20
    Argentina, **2:**38
    Armenia, **2:**42
    Bangladesh, **2:**78
    Baptist churches, **I:***148,* 151
    Belarus, **2:**88
    Bosnia and Herzegovina, **2:**125, 127
    Buddhist, **I:**72
    Bulgaria, **2:**152–153
    Burkina Faso, **2:**158
    Cambodia, **2:**169, *169*
    Canada, **2:**188, 191
    China, **2:**227
    Christianity and, **I:**134–135
    Confucianism and, **I:**296
    Croatia, **2:**262
    Czech Republic, **2:**278
    Djibouti, **2:**298
    Eastern Orthodoxy and, **I:**181–182
    Ecuador, **2:**315
    Egypt, **2:**322
    El Salvador, **2:**329
    Eritrea, **2:**340
    France, **2:**378
    Georgia, **2:**392
    Germany, **2:**400, 403
    Gothic, **I:**121, 135, 136
    Guyana, **2:**452
    Hinduism and, **I:**321
    Iran, **2:**502
    Israel, **2:**524
    Italy, **2:**532
    Kuwait, **2:**579
    Kyrgyzstan, **2:**584
    Madagascar, **3:**12
    Malawi, **3:**21
    Mali, **3:**39
    Morocco, **3:**89
    Myanmar, **3:**107
    New Zealand, **3:**136
    Oman, **3:**175, 177
    Poland, **3:**227
    Portugal, **3:**234
    Reformed Christianity, **I:**232
    Romania, **3:**251
    Saudi Arabia, **3:**300
    Serbia and Montenegro, **3:**309, 311
    Seychelles, **3:**316

Shinto, **I:**488, 494
Sudan, **3:**387
Sunnism, **I:**396–397
Swaziland, **3:**400
Sweden, **3:**407
Taiwan, **3:**428
Thailand, **3:**448
Tunisia, **3:**472
United Arab Emirates, **3:**506
United Kingdom, **3:**512
United States, **3:**522–523, 526–527
Uzbekistan, **3:**543
Vietnam, **3:**564
Yemen, **3:**574–575
Zoroastrianism and, **I:**563
Aref, Ali, **2:**296
Argentina, **2:***34,* **34–39**
ArhatsI (worthy ones), **I:**53, 58, 74, 79
Arinze, Francis, **3:**154
Aristide, Jean-Bertrand, **2:**454, 455, 457, 458, 459
Aristocracy, *vs.* meritocracy, **I:**294
Aristotle, Islamic philosophy and, **I:**367–368
Arius, **I:**160
Arjan, Guru, **I:**501, 502
Arjuna, **I:**314–315
Ark of the Covenant, **2:**352
Armenia, **I:**551, **2:***40,* **40–44**
Armenian Apostolic Church
    Armenia, **2:**40, 41–43
    Georgia, **2:**394
    Israel, **2:**525
Armenian Catholic Church
    Armenia, **2:**43–44
    Jordan, **2:**553
    Lebanon, **2:**602
    Poland, **3:**223, 224
Armenian Church, **I:**166, 169–172
Armenians
    in Cyprus, **2:**273
    Iran and, **2:**502
    in Turkey, **3:**474
Armeno-Gregorian Church, Bulgaria, **2:**154
Arminianism, **I:**111, 204, 269, 271, **3:**127, 129
Arminius, Jacobus, **3:**127, 129
Army of Shiva. *See* Shiva Sena movement
Army of the Followers of the Timeless One, **I:**509, 517
Arnot, Frederick Stanley, **3:**578
Arns, Paulo Evaristo, **2:**140
Art
    African, **I:**12, 20
    Angola, **2:**25
    Argentina, **2:**38
    Australia, **2:**50

Bahubali, statue of, I:*403*, 413
Baisakhi Day, I:511
Baitul Mukarram (Bangladesh), 2:77
Balaguer, Josemaría Escrivá de, 3:371
Baldwin, Elizabeth, 3:68
Baldwin, Jane, 3:68
Balmes, Jaime Luciano, 3:371
Balubaale, I:8
Bamba Mbacke, Ahmadu, 3:303
Bambara, I:9
Ban Zhao, I:276
Banana, Canaan Sodindo, 3:586, 588
Bangladesh, 2:*74*, 74–79
Bangladesh National Party (BNP), 2:78
Baniyan, 3:575
Bantu, 2:453
    Mozambique, 3:95
    Tanzania, 3:439, 440, 441
    Zambia, 3:582
Baoulé, Côte d'Ivoire, 2:251, 255, 256, 257
Baptism
    Anglicanism, I:143
    Angola, 2:29
    Bahamas, 2:66
    Baptist tradition, I:151
    Belarus, 2:87
    Bulgaria, 2:151
    Burundi, 2:165
    Canada, 2:186, 190
    China, 2:230
    Christianity and, I:113, 124, 125–126
    Church of Jesus Christ of Latter-day Saints, I:158
    Cuba, 2:267
    Cyprus, 2:272
    Czech Republic, 2:276, 277
    Democratic Republic of the Congo, 2:284–285
    Denmark, 2:292, 292, 293
    Eastern Catholicism, I:171
    Eastern Orthodoxy, I:180
    Eritrea, 2:342
    Ethiopia, 2:353
    Evangelicalism, I:187
    Georgia, 2:393
    Germany, 2:401
    Ghana, 2:409–410
    Jamaica, 2:*535*, 536
    Jehovah's Witnesses, I:192, 194
    Liechtenstein, 2:*624*
    Lutheranism, I:199, 201, 225
    Methodism, I:209
    Moldova, 3:75
    Namibia, 3:112
    Netherlands, 3:130
    Norway, 3:169
    Panama, 3:194

Papua New Guinea, 3:201
Pentecostalism, I:212, 214, 215, *215*, 217
Peru, 3:213
Philippines, 3:219
Protestantism, I:225
Reformed Christianity, I:233
Religious Society of Friends, I:237
Republic of the Congo, 3:243
Roman Catholicism, I:248
Russia, 3:*256*, 258–259
Rwanda, 3:265
Saint Vincent and the Grenadines, 3:280, 281
Serbia and Montenegro, 3:*308*
Seventh-day Adventists, I:256
South Africa, 3:353
Swaziland, 3:399
Sweden, 3:408
Switzerland, 3:413–414
Uganda, 3:495
United Kingdom, 3:513
Uruguay, 3:538
Venezuela, 3:558
Zambia, 3:580–581
Baptist Faith and Message, I:152
Baptist Missionary Society, I:150
Baptist Peace Fellowship (United States), I:152
Baptist Tradition. *See* Baptists
Baptist World Alliance, I:150
Baptists, I:113, 125, **146–152**, *147*, *148, 149*, 224
    Bahamas, 2:65–67
    Belize, 2:98, 100
    Bolivia, 2:119
    Central African Republic, 2:199
    Dominica, 2:299, 302
    El Salvador, 2:329
    Equatorial Guinea, 2:332
    Finland, 2:366
    Georgia, 2:395
    Germany, 2:397
    Grenada, 2:420, 421, 422–423
    Guinea, 2:438
    Haiti, 2:454, 455, 458
    Honduras, 2:465
    Jamaica, 2:534
    Jordan, 2:553
    Kazakhstan, 2:559
    Latvia, 2:593
    Liberia, 2:613
    Mexico, 3:65
    Micronesia, 3:66
    Moldova, 3:72, 76
    Mongolia, 3:86
    New Zealand, 3:136
    Nigeria, 3:153
    Norway, 3:170

Palau, 3:191
Panama, 3:195
Rwanda, 3:263
Saint Kitts and Nevis, 3:269, 273
Saint Lucia, 3:277
Saint Vincent and the Grenadines, 3:279
Slovakia, 3:335
South Africa, 3:351
Suriname, 3:393, 395
Sweden, 3:409
Taiwan, 3:429
Tajikistan, 3:433
Turkmenistan, 3:485
Ukraine, 3:503
United Kingdom, 3:510
United States, 3:*519*, 521, 522, 523
Uzbekistan, 3:545
Bar Kokhba, Simeon, I:426, 437
Bar mitzvah, I:449, 473
Baraawi, Awes Muhammad, 3:347
Baraka (blessing), I:395
Barashnum, I:561
Barbados, 2:*80*, 80–83
Barbour, Nelson, I:190
Barbuda. *See* Antigua and Barbuda
Barclay, Robert, I:237, 238
Bardo Thosgrol, I:98
Barelvi order, 3:183
Barff, Charles, 3:284
Bari, 3:388
Barnabas, Saint, 2:270
Baroque period, Roman Catholicism and, I:244
Barr, Kevin, 2:361
Barratt, T. B., 2:371
Barrett, David B., I:212, 217
Barrios, Geraldo, 2:325
Barth, Karl, I:108, 119–120, 232, 233, 3:412–413
Bartholomew I, Patriarch, 3:*250*
Bartholomew of Braga, 3:232
Bartolome de las Casas, 2:426
Basant, 3:183
Basava, I:335, 337
Base communities
    Belgium, 2:92
    Brazil, 2:139
    Burundi, 2:166
    El Salvador, 2:328–329
    Hungary, 2:469
    Mexico, 3:64
    Nicaragua, 3:142
    Peru, 3:214
    Uruguay, 3:538
Basel Mission Society, Ghana, 2:406, 408
Basil, Saint, I:160, 162, 178
Basilian monastic order, I:170

Worldmark Encyclopedia of Religious Practices

Hagiographa. *See* Writings (Ketuvim or Hagiographa)

Haidara, Kontorfilli, **3**:319

Haile Selassie I, **2**:257, 351, 352, 357, 538, **3**:468

Haileab Tesfai, **2**:344

Hair, Sikhism and, **1**:504, 511

Haiti, **2**:303, *454*, **454–460**

Hajj, **1**:362, 372–373
    See also Pilgrimages

Hakim, Mohamed Baqir al-, **2**:506, 507–508

Hakim, Muhsin al-, **2**:506, 507, 508

Halakhah, **1**:423, 432, 433, 450

Halal, **1**:392–393

Halal food. *See* Dietary practices

Halevi, Judah, **1**:441

Half-Way Covenant, **1**:271

Hall of Perfection and Equalization (Seoul), **1**:297

Hallelujah, I Love Her So (song), **1**:133

Halveti order, Macedonia, **3**:5, 6

Hamalliyya order, **2**:157

Haman, **1**:447–448

Hamas, **1**:361

Hammer of Witches. See Malleus Maleficarum

Han Buddhism, China, **2**:224, 227

Han dynasty
    Confucianism and, **1**:274, 276, 284, 285, 290, 291
    Taoism and, **1**:522

Han Xiaoling, Emperor, **1**:274

Hanafi Sunnism. *See* Sunnism

Handel, George Frideric, **1**:226

Hands of the Cause of God, **1**:26, 28, 29, 30–31, 36, 37

Handsome Lake (Seneca chief), **3**:529, 530, 531

Hanh, Thich Nhat, **1**:70

Hannington, James, **3**:492, 493

Hanukkah, **1**:436, 447

Hanyi jie Festival (China), **2**:222

Happiness ages, Jainism and, **1**:406

Har Krishan, Guru, **1**:502

Har Rai, Gurug, **1**:502

Harae. *See* Purification, Shinto

Harakat al-Islah al-Islami al-Eritree, **2**:340

Harakat Alkas al-Islami al-Eritree, **2**:340

Haram (forbidden), **1**:392, 393

Harappa (India), **1**:302

Hare Krishnas. *See* International Society for Krishna Consciousness

Haredi community (Judaism), **1**:462, 466, 468

Hargobind, Guru, **1**:502, 511

Hari Raya Aidilfitri, **3**:25

Haribhadra, **1**:411, 417

Harimandir. *See* Golden Temple

Hariri, Rafia al-, **2**:600

Harmony
    Confucianism, **1**:276, 281, 282, 291, 293
    Taoism, **1**:522

Harms, Claus, **1**:198

Harris, Barbara C., **1**:142

Harris, William Wadé, **1**:134
    Côte d'Ivoire and, **2**:257–258
    Ghana and, **2**:408
    Liberia and, **2**:613

Harrist Church
    Côte d'Ivoire, **2**:251, 257–258
    Liberia, **2**:613–614

Harsha, King, **2**:479

Harsha-vardhana, **1**:63

Harvest festivals. *See* Holidays and festivals

Hasan, Muhammad ibn 'Abd Allah, **3**:347

Hasidei Ashkenaz, **1**:428, 442

Hasidism, **1**:433, 443, 462
    dress mode, **1**:448
    early and modern leaders, **1**:465
    Holocaust and, **1**:444–445
    holy places, **1**:466
    Israel, **2**:521
    music and, **1**:452
    Ukraine, **3**:503

Hasmoneans, **1**:436

Hataria, Manekji Limji, **1**:557

Hatha Yoga, **1**:311

Hats, Shinto, **1**:491

Hausa, Nigeria, **3**:149, 150, 151, 153

Havea, Amanaki, **3**:460

Hayford, Jack, **1**:216

Haymaker, Edward, **2**:430

Head coverings
    Coptic Christianity, **1**:164
    Judaism, **1**:434, 448, 459, 466
    Shinto, **1**:491

Healing and healers
    African traditional religions, **1**:13
    Angola, **2**:*23*, 23–24, 25
    Benin, **2**:104
    Bolivia, **2**:119
    Botswana, **2**:130
    Cameroon, **2**:178
    Colombia, **2**:239, 241
    Comoros, **2**:244, 245
    Gabon, **2**:384
    Guinea-Bissau, **2**:441–442
    Hinduism, **1**:304
    Laos, **2**:591, 592
    Liberia, **2**:615
    Malaysia, **3**:25
    Pentecostals, **1**:215
    Rwanda, **3**:266

Vanuatu, **3**:547
Zimbabwe, **3**:588

Healthy Happy Holy Organization. *See* Sikh Dharma movement

Heart-mind
    Confucianism, **1**:281, 287, 289
    Taoism, **1**:522, 534, 536

Heart of Jesus Christ and the Virgin Mary, **1**:168

Heaven
    Confucianism, **1**:276, 280, 289, 290, 293
    Hinduism, **1**:310
    Mandate of, **1**:276, 282
    See also specific religions

Heavenly principle *(tianli)*, in Confucianism, **1**:287

Hebrew Bible, **1**:116, 432, 438–439
    Muslims and, **1**:350, 358–359
    in Reform Judaism, **1**:471

Hebrew prayer book, **1**:440

Hebrew tradition, Christianity and, **1**:127–128

Hegel, G. W. F., **1**:119

Heian period, **1**:480–482, 487, 489

Heiderscheid, André, **2**:633

Das Heilige (The Idea of the Holy), **1**:489

Hekhalot ("Supernal Palaces") literature, **1**:442

Helena, Flavia Iulia, **1**:118, 121

Hell
    Hinduism, **1**:310
    Jehovah's Witnesses, **1**:190
    See also specific religions

Hellenism, **2**:414, 417, **3**:430

Hellenization, of Jews, **1**:436

Helwys, Thomas, **1**:146

Hemachandra, **1**:411

Henríquez, Raúl Silva, **2**:215

Henry VIII, **3**:511

Henry VIII, King, **1**:107, 120, 139

Herald of Gospel Liberty (newspaper), **1**:269

Herbalism, South Africa, **3**:355

Herbalists, **1**:15

Herbert, George, **1**:133

Herbs, in African traditional religions, **1**:15

Hereodox movements, Zoroastrianism, **1**:551–552

Heresy
    Christianity, **1**:126–127
    Judaism, **1**:431
    Zoroastrianism, **1**:551–552
    See also specific religions

Hernández, Francisco, **2**:307

Hernández, José Gregório, **3**:558

Herod, King, **1**:436–437

Herodotus, **1**:550

Heschel, Abraham Joshua, **I**:446, 457

Hesychasts, **I**:115, 119

Hezbollah, **I**:361

Hicks, Edward, **I**:241

Hicks, Elias, **I**:235

Hicksite Friends. *See* Friends General Conference

Hidden imam, **I**:24

High-church Anglicanism, **I**:142

Hijab (veil), **I**:395

Hijra (migration), **I**:356

Hildegard of Bingen, Saint, **2**:399

Hillel the Elder, **I**:439

Hills, Hindu houses of worship and, **I**:321

Hinayana Buddhism. *See* Theravada Buddhism

Hinckley, Gordon B., **I**:156

Hindu Marriage Act of 1955-1956, **I**:328

Hinduism, **I**:**301–330**, *303*, *304*, 331–339, 340–348

  Afghanistan, **2**:6

  Bangladesh, **2**:79

  Bhutan, **2**:113

  Botswana, **2**:135

  Brunei, **2**:148

  Buddhism and, **I**:47–48, 55, 56, 60, 69

  Canada, **2**:192

  central doctrines, **I**:306–312, 333, 342–343

  vs. Christianity, **I**:111

  Confucianism and, **I**:286

  controversial issues, **I**:328–329, 338, 348

  cultural impact, **I**:329, 338–339, 348

  dietary practices, **I**:323–325, 336, 346–347

  dress mode, **I**:322–323, 336, 346

  early and modern leaders, **I**:316–317, 335, 344

  East Timor, **2**:311

  Estonia, **2**:349

  Fiji, **2**:359, 363–365

  France, **2**:379

  Germany, **2**:404

  Grenada, **2**:419, 423

  Guinea, **2**:439

  Guyana, **2**:448, 449–451, 453, 454

  history, **I**:301–302, 304–306, 331, 333, 340, 342

  holidays and festivals, **I**:322, 336, 346, 511

  houses of worship and holy places, **I**:320–321, 335–336, 345–346

  India, **2**:477, 478–483

  Indonesia, **2**:490, 491, 496

  Jainism and, **I**:327, 399, 405, 407, 412, 415, 418

  Jamaica, **2**:538

  Kenya, **2**:561, 567

  Kuwait, **2**:575, 580

  Latvia, **2**:597

  Madagascar, **3**:14

  major theologians and authors, **I**:317–318, 335, 344–345

  Malaysia, **3**:23, 27

  Maldives, **3**:33

  Mauritius, **3**:52, 53–54

  membership, **I**:326–327, 337, 347

  Mexico, **3**:59, 65

  moral code of conduct, **I**:312–313, 334, 343–344

  Mozambique, **3**:100

  Myanmar, **3**:102, 103, 107

  Namibia, **3**:110, 113

  Nauru, **3**:114

  Nepal, **3**:119, 120–122, 124

  Netherlands, **3**:126, 131

  New Zealand, **3**:133, 137

  Niger, **3**:148

  Oman, **3**:172, 173, 178

  organizational structure, **I**:318–320, 335, 345

  Pakistan, **3**:179, 185, 186

  Palau, **3**:191

  Panama, **3**:192, 196

  Papua New Guinea, **3**:203

  Paraguay, **3**:209

  Philippines, **3**:216, 221

  Poland, **3**:223

  Portugal, **3**:235

  Qatar, **3**:236, 239

  religious tolerance, **I**:327, 337, 347, 417

  rites of passage, **I**:326, 337, 347

  rituals, **I**:*305*, 325–326, 336–337, 347

  sacred books and symbols, **I**:313–316, 321–322, 334–336, 344, 346

  Saint Kitts and Nevis, **3**:273

  Saint Lucia, **3**:277

  Saint Vincent and the Grenadines, **3**:282

  Samoa, **3**:286

  Seychelles, **3**:313, 315, 316

  Sikhism and, **I**:327, 515, 517

  Singapore, **3**:327, 330

  Slovenia, **3**:340

  social aspects, **I**:327–328, 337, 347–348

  South Africa, **3**:350, 351, 354, 356–357

  Spain, **3**:373

  Sri Lanka, **3**:375, 376, 380, 381

  Suriname, **3**:390–394

  Sweden, **3**:409

  Switzerland, **3**:411, 516–416

  Tanzania, **3**:441

  Thailand, **3**:442, 448

  Trinidad and Tobago, **3**:463, *464*, 465, 466–467

  United Arab Emirates, **3**:505, 508, 509

  United Kingdom, **3**:516

  United States, **3**:533, 534

  Yemen, **3**:575

  Zambia, **3**:583

  Zimbabwe, **3**:585, 591

Hindustanis, **3**:390, 391, 392, 394

Hinfelaar, Hugo, **3**:579

Hinn, Benny, **I**:214

Hirata Atsutane, **I**:485–486

Hires, Charles, **I**:239

Hirsch, Samson Raphael, **I**:444

Hirth, Jean-Joseph, **3**:264

Hitogami (*kami* in human form), **I**:475, 478, 489

Hizb-u-Tahrir, **3**:541

Hlond, August, **3**:225

Ho Chih-chang, **I**:544

Hoa Hao, **3**:567

Hodge, Charles, **I**:186, 232

Hogar de Cristo (Chile), **2**:215, 216

Hola Mahalla (holiday), **I**:511–512

Holi, **I**:322

Holidays and festivals

  Afghanistan, **2**:4

  African traditional religions, **I**:15–16

  Albania, **2**:9

  Algeria, **2**:15

  Andorra, **2**:19, 20

  Anglicanism, **I**:143

  Angola, **2**:24, 26–27

  Antigua and Barbuda, **2**:31–32

  Argentina, **2**:37

  Armenia, **2**:42, 43

  Australia, **2**:48, 51

  Austria, **2**:*54*, 56

  Bahai faith, **I**:39–40

  Bahrain, **2**:71

  Bangladesh, **2**:77

  Baptist tradition, **I**:151

  Barbados, **2**:82

  Belarus, **2**:86

  Belgium, **2**:*90*, 91

  Belize, **2**:96

  Benin, **2**:103

  Bhutan, **2**:111, 113

  Bolivia, **2**:117, 119

  Bosnia and Herzegovina, **2**:123, 126

  Botswana, **2**:131, 133

  Brazil, **2**:141

Kharatara Gaccha, **I**:399, 402, 403

Kharijites, **2**:13, 622
    Oman, **3**:173
    Tunisia, **3**:470, 473
    Yemen, **3**:570

Khatris (warriors), **I**:515, 516

Khema, Ayya, **I**:64, 71

Khilafat movement, **I**:366, **2**:484

Khisrav, Nasser, **3**:432

Khmer Rouge, **2**:168, 169, 173

Kho'i, Abu al-Qasim al-, **2**:506, 508

Khojas, **I**:387

Khomeini, Ayatollah Ruhollah, **I**:366,
    383, **2**:499, **3**:181, 184

Khomiakov, Alexis, **I**:178

Khublai Khan. *See* Qubilai

Khums, **I**:362, 386, 387

Kidgo, Angélique, **2**:105

Kidowon. *See* Prayer

Kievan Orthodoxy, **I**:176

Killing
    Buddhism, **I**:61, 67, 71, 80, 88
    Jehovah's Witnesses, **I**:193–194
    Roman Catholicism, **I**:249

Kim Il Sung, **3**:159, 161–164

Kim Jong Il, **3**:161, 162, 164

Kimbangu, Simon, **I**:134, **2**:285, 287–
    288, **3**:247

Kimbanguism
    Democratic Republic of the Congo,
      2:281, 282, 285, 287–288
    Republic of the Congo, **3**:240, 242,
      247

Kimbanguist Church (Africa), **I**:134

Kimilsungism. *See* Juche

Kindi, Yaqub ibn Ishaq as-Sabah al-,
    I:366–367

King, Boston, **3**:324–325

King, Martin Luther, Jr., **I**:118, 223

King of dharma. *See* Dharmaraja

Kingdom Halls, **I**:193

Kingdom of God, **I**:113
    See also specific religions

Kingdom of Israel, **I**:435

Kingdom of Judah, **I**:435

Kings
    African traditional religions, **I**:13
    Buddhism, **I**:55, 63
    Confucianism, **I**:282
    dharmic, **I**:54–55
    Hinduism, **I**:318–319
    sacral, **I**:476
    Swaziland, **3**:396, 397, 398, 400,
      401
    See also Monarchs

Kinjikitile Ngwale, **3**:439

Kippah, **I**:434

Kirdīr, **I**:557

Kiribati, **2**:*568*, **568–573**

Kiribati Protestant Church, **2**:568, 570–
    572, 573

Kirill, Bishop of Turov, **2**:86

Kirk. *See* Church of Scotland

Kirpan (sword), **I**:517

Kirti Sri Rajasimha, **3**:376

Klein, Isaac, **I**:457

Knight, Alan John, **2**:451

Knopke, Andreas, **2**:594

Ko Hung, **I**:531, 535

Kofuku-ji temple, **I**:479–480

Kogaku, **I**:288, 484–485

Kojiki (Record of Ancient Matters),
    I:476, 478, 484, 485

Kokoro, **I**:483–484

Kokugaku. *See* Nativist movement

Kokugakuin University (Tokyo), **I**:488

Komo, **I**:8

Koné, Idriss Koudouss, **2**:253

Kong, Master, **I**:273, 274, 280, 281,
    287
    disciples of, **I**:285
    holidays and festivals for, **I**:*276*,
      290
    moral code of conduct and, **I**:283,
      285
    sacred places, **I**:290
    temple rites for, **I**:291–292

Kong Anguo, **I**:284

Kong Decheng, **I**:284

Kong Yingda, **I**:284

Konkō-kyō, **I**:486

Kono, **3**:322, 323

Kook, Abraham Isaac, **2**:521–522

Koran, **I**:*352*, 359, 363
    Albania, **2**:9
    Bahai faith and, **I**:32, 35
    Bahrain, **2**:71
    Bangladesh, **2**:77
    Cameroon, **2**:181
    on dietary practices, **I**:372
    Guinea, **2**:436, 437, 438
    Indonesia, **2**:493
    Kazakhstan, **2**:556
    Libya, **2**:618, 619, 621
    on men and women, **I**:377
    Muhammad's revelation in, **I**:353–
      354
    Muslim view of, **I**:358, 359, 395
    Old and New Testaments and,
      I:349, 350
    on preservation of life, **I**:377
    Ramadan and, **I**:362
    recitation of, **I**:363, 378
    on religious tolerance, **I**:373–374
    Saudi Arabia and, **3**:298
    Shiite interpreters of, **I**:384
    Sierra Leone, **3**:319

    on social justice, **I**:360–361, 374–
      375
    Sunnism and, **I**:389, 392, 393, 395,
      396
    Zoroastrianism and, **I**:557

Kordac, F., **2**:275

Korea
    Confucianism, **I**:278, 288, 297
    Methodism, **I**:207
    See also North Korea; South Korea

Korean Christianity, **I**:109

Kornfield, Jack, **I**:89

Kosher, **I**:449
    See also Dietary practices

Kossuth, Lajos, **I**:200

K'ou Ch'ien-chih, **I**:533

Kourouma, Ahmadou, **2**:255

Koyalovich, Michail Osipovich, **2**:86

Kpelle, **2**:615

Kpodzro, Philippe Fanoko Kossi, **3**:451,
    452

Kpojito Hwanjile, **2**:103

K.R. Cama Society, **I**:558

Krama school (Kashmir), **I**:333

Krishna
    Arjuna and, **I**:314–315
    festivals for, **I**:322
    as manifestation of God, **I**:310
    on salvation, **I**:310–311, 315
    Vaishnavism and, **I**:340, 343, 345

Krishna Temple (Guruvayur), **I**:345

Krishnaism. *See* International Society for
    Krishna Consciousness

Krita Yuga (Golden age), **I**:315

Kshatriyas, **I**:48

Kuan, **I**:539–540

Kuan Yin. *See* Avalokiteshvara

Kuharič, Franjo, **2**:260

Kuhn, Paul, **3**:416

Kukai, **2**:545

Kulturkampt (Hungary), **2**:467, 469

Kuman, Yoshitaka, **I**:234

Kumano cults, **I**:482

Kumano Mandala, **I**:482

Kumarajiva, **I**:64

Kumkum, **I**:323

Kundakunda, **I**:411

Kundalini yoga, **I**:311

Kuo Hsiang, **I**:534–535

Kurban Bayram, **2**:61

Kurtaru, Ahmad Muhammad Amin,
    3:420

Kusti (sacred cord), **I**:560

Kuwait, **2**:*574*, **574–580**

Kuyper, Abraham, **I**:223, 232, 234,
    3:128, 129

Kyi, Aung San Suu, **I**:70

Kyrgyzstan, **2**:*581*, **581–584**

L

as reformer, **I**:106–107, 196, 219, 221

on religious art, **I**:135

religious tolerance and, **I**:127

on rituals, **I**:125

salvation and, **I**:113

as theologian and author, **I**:223

Lutheran Orthodoxy, **I**:200

Lutheran World Federation, **I**:110, 200, 201

Lutheranism, **I**:107, **196–203**, *197*, 219, 225

Canada, **2**:191

central doctrines, **I**:113, 198–199

cultural impact, **I**:135, 202

Czech Republic, **2**:278

Denmark, **2**:290, 291–293

dress mode, **I**:123, 201

Estonia, **2**:345, 346, 348

Finland, **2**:366–370, 371

Germany, **2**:396–397

houses of worship and holy places, **I**:121, 201

Hungary, **2**:467

Iceland, **2**:472, 473–475

Jordan, **2**:553

Latvia, **2**:593–596, 597

Liberia, **2**:613

Lithuania, **2**:627, 631

Luxembourg, **2**:635

major theologians and authors, **I**:119, 200, 202

Namibia, **3**:110, 111, 113

Netherlands, **3**:127, 128, 129

Nicaragua, **3**:142

Nigeria, **3**:153

Norway, **3**:167, 168–170

organizational structure, **I**:120, 201

Panama, **3**:196

Papua New Guinea, **3**:198–202

Paraguay, **3**:209

Poland, **3**:223, 228

Republic of the Congo, **3**:242

rituals, **I**:124, 201, 225

saints and, **I**:123

Serbia and Montenegro, **3**:312

Slovakia, **3**:332, 334

South Africa, **3**:351

Spain, **3**:373

Suriname, **3**:392, 393

Swaziland, **3**:397

Sweden, **3**:405 **3**:409

Taiwan, **3**:429

Tajikistan, **3**:433

Tanzania, **3**:435, 436

United States, **3**:520–523

Uzbekistan, **3**:545

Venezuela, **3**:560

Zimbabwe, **3**:586

See also Evangelical Lutheranism

Lutherans for Life (North America), **I**:202

Luwum, Janani, **I**:118, **3**:493

Luxembourg, **2**:*632*, **632–635**, *633*

Luxuriant Dew of the Spring and Autumn Annals, **I**:274–275

Luzius, Saint, **2**:625

Lwa. *See* Deities

Lying

Jainism, **I**:408

Theravada Buddhism, **I**:88

Zoroastrianism, **I**:556

M

Maarouf, Siad Muhammad Al-, **2**:243

Mabuchi, Kamo no, **I**:485

Macauliffe, Max Arthur, **I**:509, 518

Maccabees, Judas, **I**:436

Maccioni, Valerio, **3**:289

Macedo, Edir, **I**:186, **2**:142–143

Macedonia, **3**:*1*, **1–7**

Macedonian Orthodox Church, **3**:1–5, 7

Machel, Samora, **3**:94

Macías Nguema, Francisco, **2**:332, 333, 334

Maciel, Antônio, **2**:139–140

MacKillop, Mary, Blessed, **2**:47, 48

MacLaren, Joseph, **2**:453

Madagascar, **3**:*8*, **8–15**

Madhva, **I**:309, 317, 318, 344

Madhvacarya, **I**:344

Madhyamaka, **I**:64, 76–79

Madjid, Nurcholish, **2**:492

Madrasahs. *See* Education

Magi, **I**:548, 550

Magic and witchcraft

Angola, **2**:23, 25

Cameroon, **2**:174, *175*, 178–179

Dominica, **2**:301, 302

Dominican Republic, **2**:305

Ghana, **2**:411–412

Niger, **3**:148

Portugal, **3**:233

Republic of the Congo, **3**:246

São Tomé and Príncipe, **3**:294

Seychelles, **3**:316

Sierra Leone, **3**:322

South Africa, **3**:355

Sudan, **3**:388

Tanzania, **3**:441

Turkey, **3**:477

witch trials, **I**:127

Magna Carta, **I**:132

Maha Shivaratri, **I**:336

Mahabharata ("Great Epic of India" or the "Great Sons of Bharata"), **I**:312, 314, 333, 340, 344

Mahakaleshwar Temple, **I**:337

Mahakassapa, **I**:62–63

Mahame, Chrysologue, **3**:264

Mahapajapati, **I**:63, 71

The Maharal. *See* Loew, Judah

Mahasanghika (Great Assembly), **I**:53

See also Mahayana Buddhism

Mahavideh, **I**:406

Mahavihara order, **3**:375

Mahavira, Lord, **I**:50, 302, 399–400, 410, 413

Mahavira Jayanti (holiday), **I**:414

Mahayana Buddhism, **I**:47, **74–82**, *75*

Cambodia, **2**:169, 172–173

central doctrines, **I**:57, 58–59, 77–78, 87

China, **2**:224

controversial issues, **I**:71, 82

history, **I**:53, 55, 76–77, 85

holidays and festivals, **I**:66, 80

Japan, **2**:546

Laos, **2**:587, 592

major theologians and authors, **I**:64, 79

Myanmar, **3**:103

Nepal, **3**:122

Papua New Guinea, **3**:202

sacred books and symbols, **I**:62, 65, 78, 80

Singapore, **3**:327

South Korea, **3**:363

Sri Lanka, **3**:376

vs. Theravada Buddhism, **I**:86

vs. Tibetan Buddhism, **I**:95–96

Vietnam, **3**:563–567

Zambia, **3**:583

Mahayugas, **I**:315

Mahdi, Muhammad al-, **I**:385, 388

Mahdiyya order, **3**:384, 387

Mahinda, **I**:55, 63

Maimonides, **I**:428, 431, 433, 441

on charity, **I**:450

opponents of, **I**:442

on religious tolerance, **I**:450

thirteen principles of belief, **I**:467

Mainline churches. *See names of specific churches or denominations*

Maitatsine Kano, **3**:151

Maitreya, **I**:58, 59

Majlisi, Allamah, **I**:384

Makarios III, **2**:271, 272

Makarios III (archbishop), **I**:178

Mal (deity), **I**:340

Mala (rosary), **I**:335

Malankara Orthodox Syrian Church, **I**:166, **2**:580

Worldmark Encyclopedia of Religious Practices

Worldmark Encyclopedia of Religious Practices